D0948959

Ice Age Peoples of North America

Environments, Origins, and Adaptations

edited by
Robson Bonnichsen
Karen L. Turnmire

The Center for the Study of the First Americans

Department of Anthropology, Texas A&M University
4352 TAMU, College Station, TX 77843-4352

The Center for the Study of the First Americans is an affiliate of the Department of Anthropology, Texas A&M University. The CSFA was established in July 1981 by a seed grant from Mr. William Bingham's Trust for Charity (renamed Bingham Trust). The mission of the Center is the promotion of interdisciplinary scholarly dialogue and the stimulation of public interest on the subject of the peopling of the Americas through research, education, and outreach. Toward these goals:

- CSFA designs and implements programs of study and research involving the physical, biological, and, and cultural sciences;
- CSFA provides leadership and coordination to scholars worldwide on the subject of the First Americans;
- CSFA promotes an open dialogue between government, business, avocation archaeologists, and the Native American community on the preservation of cultural resources and other issues relating to the study of the First Americans; and
- CSFA disseminates the product of this synergism through education programs reaching a broad range of groups from school children to the general public and to international scholars.

The Center's publishing program includes *Current Research in the Pleistocene,* presenting note-length articles about current research in the interdisciplinary field of Quaternary Studies as they relate to the peopling of the Americas; and a quarterly newsmagazine, the *Mammoth Trumpet.*

Ice Age Peoples of North America

Environments, Origins, and Adaptations

edited by

Robson Bonnichsen

Karen L. Turnmire

Center for the Study of the First Americans
Department of Anthropology
Texas A&M University

The paper in this book meets the guidelines for permanence and durability of the Committee on Production Guidelines for Book Longevity of the Council on Library Resources and the minimum requirements of the American National Standard for Permanence of Paper for Printed Library Materials Z39.48-1984.

Library of Congress Cataloging-in-Publication Data
Ice Age Peoples of North America / edited by Robson Bonnichsen, Karen L. Turnmire.
— 1st ed.
p. cm.
Includes bibliographical references and index.
ISBN 1-58544-368-9 (alk. paper)
1. Paleo-Indians—North America. 2. Indians of North America—Asian influences. 3. Glacial epoch—North America. 4. Paleoecology—North America—Pleistocene. 5. North America—Antiquities. I. Bonnichsen, Robson. II. Turnmire, Karen L. III. Center for the Study of the First Americans.
E77.9.I34 1999
970.01—dc21 99-23496
CIP

 Second edition 2005
Printed in the United States of America
Distributed by Texas A&M University Press
www.tamu.edu/upress

Ice Age Peoples of North America was originally published in 1999 by Oregon State University Press

Center for the Study of the First Americans
Department of Anthropology
Texas A&M University
4352 TAMU
College Station, TX 77843-4352
979-845-4046 ▪ fax 979-845-4070
csfa@tamu.edu
http://www.centerfirstamericans.com/

Dedication

Edward J. Zeller

This book is dedicated to the memory of one of the major authors of this collection: Dr. Edward J. Zeller, whose long career in geochemistry, geophysics, and geology contributed much to archeology and geoarcheology.

After earning his PhD at the University of Wisconsin in geology, he did active research in both chemistry and geophysics. He was a pioneer in thermoluninescence and in electron spin resonance, developing techniques used throughout the scientific world, especially as applied to archaeology and geoarchaeology.

He contributed his expertise to the Mammoth Meadow project in Montana by applying geophysical techniques to understanding the shape and scale of the quarry pits. Recognizing the need for better maps and photos of the site, he personally planned and flew geophysical and large-scale aerial photo surveys.

In his other work he made significant contributions to studies of the mineral resources of the Antarctic, the paleontology of the Rocky Mountain West, meteor impacts in Nebraska, climatic change, and cyclical changes in sunspots and their effect on the earth.

Contents

An Introduction to the Peopling of the Americas

Robson Bonnichsen[1]
Karen Turnmire[2]

Introduction

The Paradigm Shift

EVEN THOUGH THE PEOPLING of the Americas has been the focus of scientific investigations for more than half a century, there is still no definitive evidence that will allow specialists to say when the first Americans initially arrived or who they were. This, however, in no way diminishes the significance of the many new contributions being made in this field. The goal of this volume is to provide an up-to-date summary of some of the most important new discoveries earlier than 10,000 years old from Northeast Asia and North America that are changing our perceptions about the origin of the First Americans.

An important shift in perspective is reflected in terminology used to characterize America's earliest peoples. Traditionally, the term "Paleoindian" has been used to refer to late Pleistocene and early Holocene populations and archaeological cultural complexes. Shortly after the discovery of the Folsom and Clovis sites in the late 1920s and early 1930s, the assumption was made that modern Native Americans were the descendants of America's first people. Frank H. H. Roberts, Jr. (1935) apparently was the first to use the term Paleoindian. It implies direct biological and cultural continuity between founding populations and modern Native Americans.

Recent research, however, suggests that the origin of America's earliest inhabitants is more complex than originally anticipated. Rather than a single founding population, scholars (Greenberg et al. 1986; Wallace and Torroni 1992; Wallace et al. 1985) now believe that genetic and archaeological evidence support the proposition that the Americas were colonized by multiple founding populations. Some of these early populations could have become extinct, others may have intermarried with later migrants, and other groups may be the direct ancestors of modern-day Native Americans. We suggest that the relationship between modern and ancient human populations represents an important new research frontier. Rather than continuing to use the term Paleoindian, which implies biological and cultural continuity from the time of initial occupation to the present, we propose to use the descriptive term "Paleoamerican" to characterize late Pleistocene and early Holocene populations and archaeological complexes.

Specialists in Paleoamerican prehistory have been embroiled for more than four decades in a controversy regarding the initial timing of human entry into the Americas. Bonnichsen and Schneider (this volume) provide a detailed critique of the Late-Entry and Early-Entry models. One variant of the Late-Entry model known as the Clovis-First model proposes that a small band of human hunters entered the Americas from Siberia about 11,500 years ago (Haynes 1964, 1966, 1977; Martin 1973; Mossiman and Martin 1975). This pioneering population, known as the Clovis people, was equipped with thrusting spears or possibly atlatals tipped with fluted points (specialized flaked-stone points with thinning on both faces of the basal end of the point to facilitate hafting). The Clovis hunters, armed with a new technology, were very successful in their new habitat. Human population levels rapidly increased and descendants of the founding group expanded throughout North America and South America at the expense of Pleistocene fauna. In a matter of approximately 1,000 years, the colonists supposedly exterminated 33 genera in North America and more than 50 genera in South America (Martin 1984).

In contrast to the specialists who adhere to the Late-Entry model, another group of specialists have developed the Early-Entry model to explain the initial peopling of the Americas (Bryan 1978, 1986). The Early-Entry model cannot be reduced to a single scenario that all specialists would agree on. All versions of the Early-Entry model, however, propose that the Americas were peopled well before 11,500 years ago.

---

1. Founder and Director, Center for the Study of the First Americans; deceased December 2004. Address inquiries to CSFA Director Michael R. Waters, Department of Anthropology, Texas A&M University, 4352 TAMU, College Station, TX 77843-4352.
2. Milford, ME 04461

The most common scenario envisions that small groups with a generalized economy and a simple flake-and-core tool technology came to the Americas from Northeast Asia well before the end of the last Ice Age. The proposed timing of this event(s) and route(s) taken remain speculative in the absence of strong empirical data that can be used to support one view over another.

In scientific research, debate should be regarded as a normal part of the process of advancing knowledge. Unfortunately, the debate over the peopling of the Americas has not operated in this manner. Rather than using the debate as a positive forum for testing competing hypotheses about the initial peopling of the Americas, or about site integrity, a very conservative group of Late-Entry advocates has systematically attacked all claims for pre-12,000-year-old occupation in the Americas. The persistent tactic of raising "what if" possibilities, no matter how improbable, has had some very serious consequences. Perhaps the worst consequence of the debate is that it has become next to impossible to raise research funds through competitive grantsmanship to conduct research at archaeological localities that may be greater than 11,500 years old.

After many years of debate, there has been a remarkable turn of events in the First Americans controversy. It is now clear that the Clovis-First version of the Late-Entry model is dead, and the field of First Americans studies is undergoing a significant paradigm shift (Adovasio and Pedler 1997; Meltzer 1997). There are several important factors responsible for this shift. Many individuals and institutions throughout the Americas have contributed to this important change in perspective (Bonnichsen and Steele 1994; Bonnichsen and Turnmire 1991; Bryan 1986: Greenberg et al. 1986; Meltzer 1995; Stanford and Day 1992; Steele and Powell 1992, 1994; Wallace et al. 1985) by developing archaeological, genetic, linguistic, and human skeletal data important to an objective understanding of the peopling of the Americas. Although current press articles attribute the paradigm shift to Tom Dillehay's (1989, 1997b) important work at the Monte Verde site, Chile, our view is that the real situation is somewhat more complex.

The three most important factors responsible for the paradigm shift include:

(1) The occurrence of several pre-11,500-year-old sites in North America and South America that are clearly not part of the Clovis complex and that predate Clovis-age sites (Gruhn 1997);

(2) The identification of a series of distinctive regional co-traditions in North America that are contemporaneous with Clovis; and

(3) The acceptance by skeptics of the 12,500-year-old Monte Verde site, Chile, as evidence for the presence of humans in the Americas prior to the development of Clovis.

In the concluding chapter, Bonnichsen and Schneider (this volume) present a critique of the model-building procedures used by the proponents of the Late-Entry and Early-Entry models. They review important data which suggest that several of the key propositions of the Clovis-First version of the Late-Entry model are not supported by empirical facts from the archaeological record. They argue that the Clovis-First model must be wrong for a number of reasons. Although that model proposes that the Clovis big-game hunters came from Siberia, scientists have failed to find any credible Clovis fluted points in the reputed Siberian homeland. Another issue is that Clovis points from the United States appear to be older than those found in the far north. The Late-Entry model also predicts that Clovis is the first and basal culture from which all other North American cultural patterns developed. Ongoing careful archaeological research has demonstrated that numerous non-fluted projectile points occur in the United States that are as early as Clovis. Some of the most important of these co-traditions include the Nenana complex of Alaska (Goebel et al. 1991), the Chesrow complex of Wisconsin (Overstreet 1993), the Goshen complex of the northern Great Plains (Frison, this volume), and the stemmed lanceolate point complexes found throughout the West (Bryan and Tuohy, this volume). Finally, several North American and South American sites, with an antiquity of greater than 12,000 yr B.P., clearly predate Clovis-age sites (Gruhn 1997). Some of the most important of these localities include Bluefish Caves (Cinq-Mars and Morlan, this volume), Meadowcroft Rockshelter (Adovasio et al., this volume), Pendejo Cave (MacNeish 1996), Rancho la Amopola, El Cedral, Mexico (Lorenzo and Mirambell, this volume), Taima-taima, Venezuela (Ochsenius and Gruhn 1979), Pedra Furada, Brazil (Guidon and Pessis 1996), and Monte Verde, Chile (Dillehay 1989, 1997a, 1997b).

In addition to the above, Dillehay's work at Monte Verde, 41° south latitude near Puerto Montt, Chile, has been instrumental in convincing some critics that the Clovis-First variant of the Late-Entry model is no longer viable. The Monte Verde site, which predates

Clovis by 1,000 years, is a 12,500 yr B.P. settlement along the banks of what is now Chinchihuapi Creek. What is unusual about Monte Verde is that organic archaeological remains were preserved under peat deposits, and that extraordinary care was taken by Dillehay and his research team to investigate this truly significant site. Investigations at Monte Verde have revealed much more than the usual array of bones and possible stone tools. From wood house structures, wooden lances and digging sticks, and wooden mortars with plant residues on their surface, to dozens of medicinal plants, hunks of meat, and human foot prints comes overwhelming evidence demonstrating the presence of humans. The inorganic remains also include some surprises, such as small spherical stones known as "bolas balls," an array of simple flake tools, and a few bifacially flaked stone tools. Three fragmentary projectile points are reminiscent of the El Jobo style that is found far to the north at the Taima-taima site and elsewhere in Venezuela. Collectively, the artifacts and features suggest that Monte Verde was a permanent settlement site located in a cool damp rain forest. More so than any other Paleoamerican site investigated to date, Monte Verde provides more than a glimpse into Ice-Age lifeways. Due to its unique preservation circumstances, it contains an array of perishable organic artifacts that would normally be missing from other pre-11,000 yr B.P. sites. The two-volume Monte Verde site report, which presents research results of 80 scientific collaborators and 20 years of work, is an extraordinary case study (Dillehay 1989, 1997b).

In early January of 1997, several leading specialists, representing both the Late-Entry and Early-Entry models, spent 11 days scrutinizing the Monte Verde project. The review included an examination of artifactual, analytical, and field evidence. The review team examined artifacts at the University of Kentucky and the University of Southern Chile, Valdivia. Site geology and context were examined at the Monte Verde site. At the end of the working conference, the participants reached a consensus that the stratigraphy is good, the radiocarbon record supports the claim that the site is 12,500 yr B.P.; and that Dillehay is indeed correct, Monte Verde is a site and it predates the North American Clovis pattern.

In summary, the paradigm shift and demise of the Clovis-First variant of the Late-Entry model can be attributed to an increasing number of North and South America sites that clearly pre-date Clovis, the occurrence of several co-traditions that are contemporaneous with Clovis, and a definitive case study from Monte Verde that yielded more pre-11,500 yr B.P. evidence for humans than any other American site investigated to date. On the basis of these data, we must conclude that the Clovis-First model is not only dead, but ready for burial! The demise of the Clovis-First model, however, does not nullify the value of the Late-Entry model. At this juncture, the possibility must be kept open that both the Late-Entry and Early-Entry models are correct.

Volume Organization

In developing this volume, we present a detailed compendium of late-Pleistocene Paleoamerican archaeological records that can serve as a foundation of existing knowledge in this field and for creating the next generation of models that seek to explain the peopling of the Americas. Our strategy in constructing this volume has been to invite recognized scholars who have a detailed understanding of regional environmental and archaeological records from Northeast Asia and North America to prepare topical and regional syntheses.

The selection of environmental papers focuses on the environmental history of western Beringia, which is essential for developing an understanding of the events and processes that would have allowed early human populations to move from Northeast Asia to North America. Most, but not all, of the archaeological syntheses were originally presented as papers at the First World Summit that was organized and convened by the CSFA at the University of Maine during May of 1989. Following the conference, it was recognized that there were many gaps in the conference proceedings, and that the original collection of papers did not provide a systematic coverage of Paleoamerican prehistory. Therefore, additional specialists were invited to contribute to the volume; this, in conjunction with a move of the CSFA from the University of Maine to Oregon State University, has made the development of this volume a slow and tedious process. To compensate for these delays, the volume contributors generously agreed to update their manuscripts so that they are now current.

The authors who prepared archaeological syntheses were encouraged to summarize evidence from well-dated stratified archaeological sites. Site reports are the essential building block for developing realistic models for understanding early American prehistory. Sites with ^{14}C dated cultural sequences are regarded as essential to developing a temporal framework for making comparisons within and between regions.

A substantial amount of new information has been synthesized by the volume contributors. Nonetheless, many important topics and sites are not included. Some of the most important new archaeological discoveries important in First Americans studies that are not dealt with by the volume authors are summarized in this chapter. Collectively, the syntheses document that a wide range of cultural diversity was present in North America by Clovis times; and there is suggestive evidence for the presence of pre-11,500-year-old populations throughout the Americas well before the end of the last Ice Age. These new data set the stage for rethinking our strategies for searching and interpreting the origins of the First Americans.

Paradoxes

RECENT RESEARCH, WHILE SERVING to clarify and elucidate certain aspects of the paleoenvironmental and archaeological records from Northeast Asia and North America, is also notable for illuminating the apparent paradoxes and contradictions inherent in the Paleoamerican environmental, archaeological, and biological records. It is important to recognize that there are a number of paradoxes in the orthodox view that the Americas were peopled from Northeast Asia in late glacial times. For example, glaciologists offer sharply contrasting models about the extent of glaciation in western and central Beringia (Grosswald, this volume; Hughes and Hughes 1994; Hughes et al. 1991; West 1996a: Figure 2). The boundary conditions set by the minimum and maximum glacial models of the occurrence of Wisconsinan-age ice in Siberia and North America provide very different limiting conditions on possible marine and overland routes that could have been taken to the Americas during full glacial times.

The smallest ice sheets, or "minimum glacial models," depict Northeast Asia as a wide-open landscape that would have allowed human entry into the Americas at any time, including the last glacial maximum about 18,000 years ago (West 1996a: Figure 2). By contrast, the largest ice sheets, or "maximum glacial models," depict extensive glaciation that covered more of eastern and western Beringia. These large ice sheets would have been a major impediment for populations attempting to move through western Beringia during glacial maximum times (Grosswald, this volume; Hughes and Hughes 1994).

Another enigma of greater Beringia is what is known as the "productivity paradox" (Schweger et al. 1982). On the basis of palynological data, it is proposed that productivity in Beringia was quite low and would not have supported viable human and animal populations in Beringia during full glacial times. Other lines of evidence suggest the occurrence of a mosaic environment, which supported a complex fauna adapted to ice-marginal conditions (Geist, this volume; Guthrie 1968; Turner et al., this volume).

Contradictions and paradoxes are not limited, however, to only the paleoenvironmental record. Ambiguity also exists as to how to interpret the genetic record. Working with modern mtDNA (Torroni et al. 1993) found that that Siberian populations lacked the B mtDNA haplogroup found in Native Americans and East Asian populations. They propose that this lineage either became extinct in Siberia after a split between ancestral Siberian and Native American populations or its presence in Native Americans represented an earlier distinct migration.

Archaeological paradoxes also exist. For example, the Clovis complex appears as a full-blown cultural pattern throughout much of the North American continent about 11,500 yr B.P. Despite years of extensive archaeological investigation, the antecedents of Clovis, whether Old World or New, remain elusive. Other paradoxes and contradictions include:

(1) The wide range of variability in fluted projectile point styles;

(2) The occurrence of non-fluted projectile point industries that seemingly proliferated in North and South America during the late Pleistocene;

(3) The earliest fluted points recovered thus far from the Arctic and the Ice-Free Corridor appear to postdate rather than predate Clovis (Hamilton and Goebel, this volume);

(4) The existence throughout the New World of various sites and industries that appear to predate 11,500 yr B.P. (Dillehay 1997b; Gruhn 1997; MacNeish 1996; Ochsenius and Gruhn 1979); and

(5) The growing awareness that early human skeletal remains greater than 8,000 years old from the Great Plains and the West appear to represent an earlier long-headed population that does not closely resemble more recent Native American or Native Siberian populations (Jantz and Owsley 1997; Steele and Powell 1992, 1994). These and other paradoxes underscore the need

to consider the possibility that the Americas were peopled over a long period of time, including well before the end of the last Ice Age.

The Future of First Americans Studies

NOW THAT THE LONG-STANDING impediment of the Clovis-First model is behind us, and a variety of paradoxes lie before us that have yet to be solved, it is time to refocus our attention on the goals and objectives of First Americans studies. It is time to plan future research efforts, and a time to heal old wounds and gain sight of our common goal of developing a secure and objective knowledge of America's earliest cultural and biological heritage (Adovasio and Pedler 1997; Bonnichsen et al. 1995; Dillehay and Meltzer1991; Meltzer 1997).

As a field of investigation, First Americans studies must seek answers to five questions: Who? When? Where? How? and Why? Although chronology or site age will remain very important, the time has come to broaden our focus, to define new research questions, and to look critically at how we can develop more reliable models that seek to explain the peopling of the Americas.

The advances being made in First Americans studies are directly linked to an understanding held by most specialists that this research must be conducted within an interdisciplinary framework. Specialists who attempt to develop models for explaining the peopling of the Americas must deal with a wide array of environmental, biological, and cultural data. The task of creating synthetic models that will adequately explain the biological, cultural, and environmental events significant to understanding American origins at the local, regional, and global scales is a formidable undertaking with many inherent problems. For example, important data for understanding the peopling of the Americas occur on four continents: North America, South America, Asia, and Europe. Furthermore, the scholarly literature of this field appears in many languages (e.g., Chinese, English, French, Portuguese, Spanish, Russian, Japanese, etc.).

First Americans studies is a relatively immature and highly complex field with a very small number of specialists. Not surprisingly, there are very few pre-11,500-year-old sites that have been carefully investigated by qualified teams of experts. Consequently, the data base of Paleoamerican sites that serves as the foundation for creating models to explain the peopling of the Americas is in many senses woefully inadequate. Indeed, much additional attention must be placed on developing quality site reports as the search for American origins continues and the field matures (Bonnichsen et al. 1995).

Paleoenvironments

QUATERNARY SCIENTISTS HAVE made significant strides in the understanding of global paleoclimates and how these have affected the advances and demise of ice sheets, sea level fluctuations, creation of paleolandforms, and the linkage between paleoclimatic systems and paleoenvironments (Lasca and Donahue 1990; Porter 1988; Ruddiman and Wright 1987; Waters 1992). The temporal framework and events of the Quaternary period provide the essential context for understanding human colonization and the rise and demise of human adaptive patterns. This framework, however, continues to undergo refinement and debate. Mikhail Grosswald (this volume) challenges the orthodox view that the Americas could have been peopled at any time during glacial periods, instead proposing that a continuous systems of ice sheets covered the northern outskirts of Eurasia during the last glacial maximum. Grosswald concludes that an Asian overland route to Alaska during the height of glaciation was improbable. Travelers would have encountered ice sheets, ice-dammed lakes, and a very inhospitable glacial environment. Overland travel would have been possible only during a relatively short and warm late glacial interval near the end of the last Ice Age. Similar constraints imposed by ice sheets and marine transgressions would have inhibited human movement from western to eastern Beringia during earlier periods as well.

Another tenet of the orthodox view of the peopling of the Americas has long assumed that glacial margins would have been barren, cold areas unsuitable for plant, animal, and human life. Turner et al. (this volume) suggest that there is extensive evidence for the occurrence of animal populations, including humans, in ice-marginal zones of continental ice caps in North America, Asia, and Europe.

For most plant species, growth and colonization in recently deglaciated landscapes are limited by three major plant nutrients: potassium, phosphate, and nitrogen. Studies of glacial ice on Antarctica and

Greenland have shown that substantial concentrations of nitrate and lesser amounts of ammonium ions are present in Pleistocene-age ice. This fixed nitrogen is released only through meltwater runoff. Environments along glacial margins are also enriched in potassium and phosphate, especially in areas where glaciers have overridden igneous or metamorphic terrain. Through mechanical grinding at the ice-rock interface, breakage of chemical bonds effectively increases the solubility of the rock potassium and phosphate. The presence of essential plant nutrients in water that saturates unconsolidated glacial deposits may have permitted a kind of natural hydroponic plant growth, accelerating soil formation. Once soils had begun to form, the presence of nutrient-containing solutions would permit an unusually high level of productivity to be maintained in stable ice-marginal regions. The supply of nutrients from glacial ice would have allowed populations of plants, animals, and humans to have lived along ice-sheet margins. These marginal environments would have acted as refugia as the favorable conditions of the Pleistocene deteriorated into the early Holocene.

Geist (this volume) builds on the above ideas by suggesting Pleistocene periglacial environments created young, productive ecosystems, which were favorable for the development of large mammals and humans. From the late Tertiary onward, a set of remarkable mammals exhibiting luxuriant body growth evolved with the increased severity of seasonally cold climates.

Geist proposes that periglacial environments were vital to the appearance and development of human characteristics and that humans, like other mammals, were shaped by hypermorphic speciation. In fact, the periglacial zone was so favorable that two hominid groups flourished during the last glacial period: Neanderthals in the early Würm were followed by Cro-Magnons in the last glacial pulse. Geist concludes that the Upper Paleolithic was a golden age for hominids adapted to periglacial environments. Cultural expression flourished; and it can be seen in the quality of paintings, carvings, and tools, as well as in the excellent health and physical development of individuals.

The importance of Asiatic periglacial steppe is underscored by Dale Guthrie's (1996:172) concept of the Mammoth Steppe biome. Guthrie argues that the special Holarctic biome, the Mammoth Steppe, was the homeland of Mongoloid peoples. The cold dry grassland that developed behind the south face of the Himalayas became the heartland of the Mammoth Steppe.

During Pleistocene cycles of low solar input, this grassy biome spread westward across Europe to the Atlantic, northward to the Arctic Ocean onto the huge exposed continental shelf of North Asia, and eastward to North America via the exposed Beringian land bridge. This combination of cold and aridity led to the elimination of wood plants, and favored certain arid-adapted grasses and forbs.

The Pleistocene steppelands were invaded by a diverse group of mammals, predominantly grazers. Fossils show both large and small mammals were present in the special habitat, including the woolly mammoth (*Mammuthus primigenius*), wooly rhino (*Coelondonta antiquitatis*), steppe bison (*Bison priscus*), caballine horses (*Equus ferus*) hemionids (*Equus hemionus)*, reindeer (*Rangifer tarandus*), muskoxen (*Ovibos moschatus*), saiga antelope (*Saiga tatarica*), and other less numerous species (Guthrie 1996:173). Guthrie notes that many species developed enormous body size to survive the harsh winters. The Mammoth Steppe embraced an enormous area that was not uniform throughout. Animals such as the red deer, wild boar, roe deer, and moose penetrated the southern border of the Mammoth Steppe but never moved out on it.

From the above, it should be clear that paleoecologists interested in the peopling of the Americas have developed environmental parameters that favor an overland terrestrial approach for the peopling of the Americas. Partly, because of the paradigmatic bias of the Clovis-First model, little consideration has been given to the environmental parameters that would have controlled the spread of maritime culture along the Pacific Rim during late Pleistocene times, if not earlier. There is a need to develop an understanding of how the sea/land interface changed between glacial and interglacial periods and how sea currents and temperatures shifted. It seems probable that early maritime peoples would have found reliable food resources such as seaweed, mussels, clams, seals, sea lions, and fish both during glacial and interglacial times.

Asian Origins

Most scholars believe that Beringia is the logical gateway through which the First Americans entered the New World; and that, therefore, a potential colonizing population must first have been in place in Northeast Asia. Recent research from Northeast Asia suggests the presence of Lower Paleolithic human populations. The cultural and biological remains of these early peoples are relatively poorly known. The Upper Paleolithic archaeological record, which is typified by microblade-using peoples, is more abundant and better known (Goebel, this volume). See West (1996b) for a recent overview of the Beringia archaeology.

Many students of prehistory propose that only modern humans (*Homo sapiens sapiens*) had the survival skills to penetrate the far north; and that this could not have occurred until about 40,000 years ago. They reason that fire, shelter, and tailored skin clothing were requirements for surviving the winters in the far north (Fagan 1987). New research reported by Yuri Mochanov (1993) on the Diring Yuriakh site, located at 61° north latitude on the Lena River, is of great importance (Ackerman and Carlson 1991). Mochanov's 26,000 m^2 excavation exposed more than 30 clusters of artifacts that include 4,000 quartz and quartzite cobble cores, unifacial choppers, flake tools, hammerstones, and anvil stones (Waters et al. 1997). Diring is certainly the earliest and most interesting early site in eastern Siberia (see Goebel, this volume). Though critics have suggested that "artifacts" from the site are actually "geofacts" produced by natural processes, there is unanimous agreement among authorities who have visited the site and examined the vast lithic assemblage that the Diring specimens are the product of human behavior.

The age of the site, however, remains a point of contention. On the basis of paleomagnetic and radio-thermoluminesence ages, Mochanov initially proposed that the artifact-bearing level of Diring dated to between 1.8 and 3.1 million years ago. More recent work by Waters et al. (1997) on deposits located stratigraphically below and above artifact level 5 suggest a much later age for this important site. Forman's thermoluminescence method has produced a series of 10 consistent dates that indicate the age of the Diring Yuriakh occupation is about 300,000 years old. If correct, these dates imply that early *Homo* sp. was equipped to withstand the subarctic winters of Siberia far earlier than previously anticipated.

Even though the Diring Yuriakh site appears to be the oldest site found to date in Northeast Asia, Nikolay Drozdov and colleagues (Chlachula et al. 1994) have located another series of early sites on the Krasnoyarsk Reservoir in the vicinity of Kurtak, central Siberia. These sites, situated at 55° north latitude on the Yenisei River, span the last full glacial cycle and are said to yield cobble tools that come from Middle Pleistocene stratigraphic contexts.

In addition to the central and northeastern Siberian Paleolithic sites, the archaeological record from Honshu Island, Japan, is yielding important new data. Along the northeastern coast of Honshu, a series of more than 40 Middle Paleolithic sites have been uncovered in the Sendai area. Tephrachronology indicates that these sites range in age from 150,000 to more than 200,000 years ago (Akazawa, this volume; Hiroshi et al. 1990; Masahito and Hiroyuki 1990; Yoshizaki and Iwasaki 1986), and recent work suggests that the oldest sites in the area may be as much as 400,000 years old (Alan L. Bryan, personal communication 1995). Early peoples could easily have walked from the Asiatic mainland to Japan during a glacial maximum when sea levels were lower and Japan was connected to the mainland. The Honshu archaeological record suggests the presence of humans along the north Pacific Rim for the past 400,000 years and perhaps longer.

From the above, it may be inferred that early *Homo* sp. had spread across Northeast Asia by Lower Paleolithic times. Brace (1996:87), in reviewing the human skeletal data from northeastern Asia, notes two specimens of interest that are transitional between *Homo erectus* and modern populations. The Jinniu Shan specimen is the most complete and was found in 1984 approximately 400 km north of Zhoukoudian at ca. 45° N. latitude. No formal description is yet available on this specimen, although a uranium series age of between 100,000 and 200,000 years has been assigned. A cursory examination of the skull shows that it has the long, low cranial shape, heavy double-arched brow ridges, and large, morphologically complex maxillary incisors common to Neanderthals. Other features, including the shape of the occiput, the lateral margins of the orbits, and the juncture of the nasal bones with the adjacent maxilla, show similarities to the respective anatomical configurations regularly found in the living inhabitants of the area.

Wu (1994), in assessing the chronology and morphology of the human fossil record from China, envisions that *Homo erectus* arrived between one to two million years ago. He infers that Pleistocene humans in China experienced a gradual evolutionary change in morphology. Common skeletal features shared between *Homo erectus* and *Homo sapiens* in China, but not shared by European contemporaries in form or frequency, suggest that human evolution in China has been continuous throughout more than one million years. Morphological evidence, such as Inca bones, indicates gene flow between the human populations of China and those of other parts of the world, especially the western Pacific region and the Americas. Exactly when these early populations moved into the far north is unknown.

In general, the early Asiatic sites strongly imply that by Lower Paleolithic times early human populations had a cold-climate adaptive repertoire (i.e., fire, clothing, shelter, and techniques for processing food) for surviving the rigors of a northern periglacial winter. The periglacial environments of the Asiatic steppe are seen by animal paleoecologists (Geist, this volume; Guthrie 1996) as a Pleistocene evolutionary center that witnessed the development of homorphic mammals adapted to cold, treeless landscapes.

Even though north-central Asia south of Lake Baikal is seen as an evolutionary center for Mongoloid (Guthrie 1996; Turner 1985), Caucasian (Turner 1985), and Mousterian (Geist, this volume) populations, little consideration has been given to the possibility that environmental forcing on the Central Asian steppe may have played an important role in accelerating the evolutionary transition between *Homo erectus* and *Homo sapiens.* The early archaeological discoveries from the Yenisei and Lena river drainages and Japan suggest that humans were early participants in ice marginal environments and co-evolved along with other mammalian hypermorphs. This process did not occur just once, but likely occurred in successive ice ages, accelerating the pace of evolution and giving rise to new biological and cultural adaptations. Through adaptive radiation, new variants of hominids dispersed across the Mammoth Steppe into environments that lay south of the steppe, and possibly into the Americas.

Akazawa (this volume), for example, proposes a model in which the colonization of Japan was accomplished via a wave-like series of human migrations that were linked with the spread of Pleistocene species. A similar event may explain the Upper Paleolithic record from Siberia and Hokkaido. The original colonizing populations followed and developed a specialized subsistence system based on mammoth procurement, which is represented in the archaeological record by microblade/wedge-shaped core assemblages. The relatively late Japanese microblade assemblages (ca. 15,000–10,000 yr B.P.) and those of Alaska (ca. 11,800 yr B.P.) likely are derived from Siberia. Akazawa hypothesizes that the extremely cold climatic conditions of 20,000–18,000 yr B.P. may have been the driving force behind a southward microblade-bearing migration to Asia and the Americas.

Turning north to the Upper Paleolithic and Mesolithic of western Beringia, Goebel (this volume) suggests that the earliest evidence for humans in this region dates to about 14,000 yr B.P. An Upper Paleolithic complex with blade and biface technology is known from the stratified site Ushki-1 (layer VII), in central Kamchatka, and at Berelekh, a campsite in the lower Indigirka Basin. Another important cultural pattern in western Beringia, microblade technology, is widespread but has been dated at Ushki-1 to only about 10,700 yr B.P. Goebel does note, however, that there are many undated late Upper Paleolithic, Diuktai-like industries that have been identified in the Kolyma and Omolon basins of western Beringia, as well as on the Chukotka and Kamchatka peninsulas. These industries suggest a widespread distribution of microlithic industries in the late Pleistocene and early Holocene, and an expansion of the Diuktai-like industries into eastern Beringia at the end of the last glacial maximum.

The American Far North

Hamilton and Goebel (this volume), in their review of the early Alaskan archaeological record, note that the earliest firmly dated assemblages date to 11,800 yr B.P. Four sites ascribed to the Nenana complex (Dry Creek, Walker Road, Moose Creek, and Owl Ridge) are characterized by the occurrence of bifaces and blades, side- and end-scrapers, cores, occasional burins, and the absence of microblades. These sites have a probable age of 11,300-11,000 yr B.P. In the nearby Tanana Valley, the Broken Mammoth, Swan Point, Mead, and Healy Lake (Chindadn assemblage) sites contain occupations ranging in age from 11,800 to 11,000 yr B.P. The Swan Point and Healy Lake sites contain elements of both the Nenana complex and microblades. Hamilton and Goebel (this volume) observe that the relationship of the Nenana and Chindadn assemblages to the Clovis complex of temperate North America is not well understood. They suggest that the Nenana complex could document the appearance of Paleoamericans in Alaska, who are contemporaries with Clovis. The Mesa and other hunting sites in the Brooks Range likely were also occupied by Paleoamericans who spread northward into subarctic Canada and Alaska about 10,500 yr B.P.

There is no indication that fluted points originated in the North. Although about 50 fluted points have been collected in Alaska, most have come from undated surfaces, shallow sites where mixing is likely, or from

Holocene contexts (Hamilton and Goebel, this volume). These points differ typologically from Clovis in that flute removal appears have to been accomplished by pressure rather than percussion, and their younger ages are not surprising. The majority of fluted point finds in Alaska and the Yukon occur within or near the Brooks Range. The apparent absence of sites older than 11,800 yr B.P. in Alaska remains a troubling dilemma for archaeologists, both because of the similar ages of the Nenana and Clovis complexes and because of the lack of potential ancestral sites.

At the Alaskan/Yukon border, there is a cultural and temporal gulf among archaeologists and the archaeological record. Excavations at Bluefish Caves, Yukon Territory, have produced evidence of an early Beringian occupation described by Cinq-Mars and Morlan (this volume). Cave II, Unit B, has yielded a culturally modified mammoth bone flake and core that has been AMS dated to 23,500 yr B.P. The flaked bone, along with microdebitage, underlies a Paleoarctic-Dyuktai assemblage with microblades dated at ca. 15,000 yr B.P.

Cinq-Mars and Morlan also describe a recent program of AMS dating conducted on similar bone specimens from the controversial Old Crow localities. They have found that the humanly modified Old Crow bones are restricted to a time span ranging between 40,000 and 25,000 yr B.P. This grouped age distribution supports the premise that the Old Crow specimens are a deliberately worked bone assemblage, rather than the product of natural taphonomic processes as argued by critics. The Old Crow and lower Bluefish Cave II assemblages suggest an early bone-flaking technology in eastern Beringia before the last glacial maxima.

Pathways

The Coastal Route

If the Americas were peopled by populations coming from Northeast Asia, there are three plausible routes: (1) by boat along the Northwest Coast; (2) by foot through interior British Columbia; and (3) by foot through the Ice-Free Corridor. Gruhn (1994), who has most recently reviewed this topic, has argued that the Pacific Coast route of initial entry of human populations into the New World should be given serious consideration. Although paleoecological and linguistic arguments can be marshaled in support of this view, there is little in the way of substantial archaeological evidence from the Northwest Coast itself. There is, however, indirect evidence from Japan that suggests that human populations along the North Pacific Rim had boats by at least 30,000 years ago (Bonnichsen and Schneider, this volume; Oda 1990). This interpretation can be seen as indirect support for the hypothesis that the Americas could have been colonized by boat-using peoples.

Definitive archaeological data from the West Coast of North America to support the coastal-entry hypothesis has yet to be found. This, however, is not surprising as much of the West Coast was submerged by a rise in sea level that occurred at the end of the Pleistocene. Potentially early sites have been reported from raised coastlines in southern California (Berger 1982; Erlandson and Moss 1996). Although archaeological evidence from these localities has yet to win widespread acceptance from some members of the archaeological community, other sites may be found along uplifted sections of the Pacific Coast that could provide support for the early coastal-entry hypothesis.

The Overland Route

Evidence that could be used to support an overland route through interior British Columbia is totally absent. But absence of evidence does not necessarily mean that evidence is absent. Almost no survey work has been conducted in this mountainous area. Additionally, if humans occupied this area before the onset of the last glaciation, remains from these early occupations likely were either destroyed by glaciation or are deeply buried beneath glacial deposits.

The Ice-Free Corridor

The Ice-Free-Corridor hypothesis, which has long been an important component of the Clovis-first model, has after many years of research failed to yield definitive evidence that relates to human colonization of the Americas. In a recent article on the glacial controls of the Ice-Free Corridor, Jackson and Duk-Rodkin (1996) conclude that Beringia and unglaciated North America were separated by ice from around 20,000 yr B.P. until after 13,000 yr B.P. See Wilson and Burns (this volume) for an overview of the history of the Ice-Free Corridor concept.

Though a number of fluted projectile points have been found in this area, most of these tend to be surface finds. Projectile points that occur in context within the Corridor are infrequent, and the oldest of these have thus far tended to be Charlie Lake points, a triangular, weak, and sometimes multiple-fluted form that appears to be roughly coeval with Folsom. Charlie Lake points have been recorded in context at only two sites: Charlie Lake, British Columbia, which yielded an average date of 10,500 yr B.P. (Fladmark et al. 1988); and Sibbald Creek, Alberta, which produced a questionable date of about a thousand years younger (Ball 1983).

Fluted points finds in western Canada fall within an area that was probably bounded by ice to the east and west between 11,500 and 11,200 yr B.P. (Wilson and Burns, this volume). The distribution of fluted points in an area that was free of ice earlier than the surrounding region does not necessarily support the Clovis-First model. The late age of fluted points in Alaska (Hamilton and Goebel, this volume) and at the Charlie Lake site suggests that Paleoamerican populations were moving northward, rather than southward as predicted by the Clovis-First model. However, as Wilson and Burns (this volume) note, the case is not yet conclusively proven.

An interesting new complexity to the Ice-Free-Corridor hypothesis has been added by recent research at the Varsity Estates and Silver Springs sites, Alberta (A. L. Bryan, personal communication 1997; Chlachula 1996; and Chlachula and LeBlanc 1996). The Varsity Estates and Silver Springs sites were exposed by postglacial downcutting in the Bow River Valley, Calgary. The Varsity Estates site is situated beneath 24 m of glacial lake deposits and above Cordilleran till. The Silver Springs site occurs beneath the Cordilleran till on top of old river deposits. Although absolute ages for the sites have yet to be determined, the Bow Valley was submerged by proglacial Lake Calgary, which was dammed by the advance of Laurentide ice. It has been inferred that since the archaeological remains occur below proglacial lake deposits, occupation at the two sites must have occurred sometime before 20,000 ± 5000 yr B.P., although other interpretations are possible (Gruhn, personal communication 1998).

The discovery of archaeological deposits containing a cobble tool industry with flaked cobbles, hammerstones, anvils, altered flakes, and a biface with refitted flakes, in stratigraphic context, is of considerable importance. If the work now being done by Chlachula and co-workers withstands critical review, these new discoveries will require a rethinking of the Ice-Free-Corridor concept. The occurrence of these sites at the southern end of the Ice-Free Corridor may place humans immediately south of the Ice-Free Corridor before the last glacial maximum. These new data may imply that the Ice-Free Corridor is unimportant to understanding the peopling of the Americas, as humans were here well before closure, and other continental routes may have been possible.

Western North America

Specialists have long believed that the American West is an ideal location to search for pre-12,000 yr B.P. evidence of early human occupation. A substantial number of early stratified sites have been investigated in Western North America. These data are now being used to examine and test implications of competing models that seek to explain the late glacial archaeological record.

The Northwest

At the end of the last Ice Age, a series of extreme environmental events occurred, including volcanism in the Cascades, recession of the glaciers in the Northern Rockies and Cascades, multiple catastrophic flooding events which created the channeled scablands in the Columbia Basin, and extensive deposition of glacial outwash sediments in regional river valleys similar to southern Beringia (Bonnichsen et al. 1994). These events modified the Northwestern landscape and brought about environmental disruption. Yet, the formation of new post-glacial environments presented new opportunities for human adaptation to diverse environments.

There is but a single ice-marginal site in the Pacific Northwest. The Manis Mastodon site, located near Sequim, Washington, is a peat-covered glacial pond basin that has produced butchered mastodon and bison bones. Two radiocarbon dates place the age of this event at about 12,000 yr B.P. (Gustafson et al.1979:158). Although diagnostic projectile points were absent, of interest was the recovery of a bone point embedded in a mastodon rib.

West of the Rocky Mountains, widely scattered Clovis finds suggest the presence of big-game hunting traditions in the Columbia River drainage system. No faunal remains have been found in association with fluted points from this region. Although surface finds of fluted points have been made throughout the region, the East Wenatchee site, located near East Wenatchee, Washington, has the best context for any known fluted point site of the region (Gramly 1993; Mehringer 1988a, 1988b; Mehringer and Foit 1990). During the installation of an irrigation system in Mack Ritchey's apple orchard, a fascinating archaeological assemblage was found 80–100 cm below the surface. Excavations at the site conducted first by P. J. Mehringer, Jr. and later by M. Gramly led to the recovery of 14 exquisitely crafted and very large fluted points, several large bifaces, blades, several scrapers, and bi-beveled bone rods (foreshafts). Glacier Peak volcanic ash found adhering to the lower faces of the artifacts suggests that the site is about 11,200 years old.

Within this region, the Windust phase (Rice 1972) may represent a co-tradition that is coeval with Clovis and continued into post-Clovis times. At the Pilcher Creek site, near Baker, Oregon, D. Brauner (1985, personal communication 1994) found a Windust component with points buried within Glacier Peak tephra in a stratified excavation context. This association appears to be very good and represents the oldest dated occurrence for the Windust phase in the Pacific Northwest.

Post-Clovis human adaptation to this environmentally diverse, but geographically more restricted, setting led to the emergence of several distinct Paleoamerican co-traditions. These local traditions, dating between 11,000 and 9000 yr B.P., include Folsom, Plano, Windust, Hell Gap, and Old Cordilleran point styles.

The most famous recent find from the region, known as Kennewick Man, has yet to be adequately studied. The human remains were found along the banks of the Columbia River by two college students. J. Chatters, who investigated the site and collected the remains for the Kennewick Coroner's Office, initially believed the skeleton to be that of a modern European pioneer. This interpretation was quickly cast aside when CAT scan images of the hip illuminated the presence of what appears to be a broken Cascade point. A ^{14}C date by the UC-Riverside laboratory produced a corrected age of 9300 yr B.P. on bone from the skeleton.

The Kennewick Man skeleton is noteworthy for several reasons. First, it is the most complete early human skeleton found in the Pacific Northwest. Additionally, preliminary observations by three independent observers (J. Chatters, G. Krantz, and K. McMillian) suggest that Kennewick Man differs from modern Native Americans of the region. The Kennewick skeleton is characterized by a long head, a prominent chin, a very large nose, and arms that are long relative to body portions. Additionally, the dental morphology of this individual most closely matches that of the Sundadonty pattern (Turner 1985). On the basis of preliminary evidence, the Kennewick Man remains suggest the presence of an early North American population that was replaced by later peoples with Mongoloid characteristics. Eight scientists have requested the right to study these remains before reburial; but so far, this request has been denied. Five Native American tribes have claimed the Kennewick Man remains, and have asked the Army Corps of Engineers to repatriate the skeleton under the Native Americans Grave Protection and Repatriation Act of 1990 (NAGPRA). As of spring 1999, the Kennewick Man case is still in court.

Great Basin and Snake River Plain

Moving on to the Great Basin and Snake River Plain, Bryan and Tuohy (this volume) offer an argument challenging the Clovis-First model. Research within this region increasingly suggests that a co-tradition characterized by stemmed projectile points existed at the same time as, if not earlier than, Clovis.

Dated fluted-point sites are rare in this region, and the four sites that have thus far produced radiocarbon dates indicate a somewhat anomalous age range for fluted projectiles. Connley Cave #5, Oregon, contained both a fluted point and stemmed points above a level dated at 9540 ± 260 yr B.P.; the Henwood site, California, yielded a fluted point associated with a hearth dated at 8470 ± 370 yr B.P.; and Danger Cave, Utah, produced two fluted points thought to be younger than 10,500 yr B.P. (Bryan and Tuohy, this volume). Finally, the Wasden site, Idaho, has yielded three fluted points (albeit of Folsom-like manufacture) in association with mammoth bone that recently produced a radiocarbon date of 10,910 ± 150, which is considered to be more acceptable than old assays of 12,250 ± 200, and 12,850 ± 150 yr B.P. (Bryan and Tuohy, this volume).

Stemmed points occur throughout this region at sites dated between 11,000 and 8000 yr B.P., and have been found at three sites dated in excess of 11,000 yr B.P. These are: the basal occupation of Fort Rock Cave,

Oregon, which yielded a ^{14}C date of 13,200 ± 720 yr B.P.; Wilson Butte Cave, Idaho, which has produced obsidian hydration dates between 16,000 and 9000 yr B.P.; at Smith Creek Cave, Nevada, where the Mt. Moriah occupation zone yielded eight ^{14}C dates ranging from 9940 ± 160 yr B.P to 11,400 ± 200 yr B.P. (Bryan 1988:65).

Bryan and Tuohy's work calls into question both the assumption that Clovis occurs earlier than the stemmed point tradition and that stemmed forms were derived from Clovis. Instead, it now appears probable that the early stemmed points of the Basin and Range physiographic provinces represent a tradition that evolved independently of, but was coeval with, Clovis. There is some indication that this tradition served as the basal culture for the later Agate Basin and Hell Gap forms of the Plains (Bryan and Tuohy, this volume; Stanford, this volume).

New paleobiological evidence from the Great Basin suggests that late Pleistocene and early Holocene populations from the Great Basin differed from modern-day Native American populations in the region. The discovery that the Spirit Cave male mummy has a radiocarbon age, based on a mean of four dates, of 9410 ± 60 yr B.P. (Tuohy and Dansie 1996:49-50) makes this burial the oldest known mummy from North America. In addition to the mummy, two cremated skeletons were also found at the site. These specimens, in addition to the Wizzard Beach skull from Pyramid Lake, which is dated to 9515 ± 155 (GX-19422G), constitute some of the oldest human skeletal remains from North America (Taylor et al. 1995). Steele (personal communication 1996) indicates these early finds have close affinities with south Asian populations (Jantz and Owsley 1997). They are distinguished by their relatively long and narrow crania and small narrow faces. Later populations tended to be more brachycranic and exhibited larger, broader faces (Steele and Powell 1992, 1994).

The Plains and the Southwest

MORE THAN 60 YEARS of Paleoamerican studies on the Plains and in the Southwest have provided the framework of cultural-environmental history that also has been used to interpret much of the prehistory of the western United States and Canada. Stratified Paleoamerican sites from this region are essential to our understanding of an array of impressive cultural complexes. Before discussing these, a brief review of the environmental history of the region is in order.

On the east side of the Rocky Mountains, the Laurentide ice sheet displaced the Saskatchewan and Missouri rivers to the south. Topographic depression from the weight of the ice sheet led to the creation of glacial Lake Agassiz, which covered part of southern Saskatchewan and most of southern Manitoba. Huge, south-flowing meltwater channels, carrying water and ice from the disintegrating ice sheets, eventually contributed to the damming of the Missouri and Yellowstone rivers (Clayton and Moran 1982). This blockage resulted in the formation of large temporary lakes in northern Montana and the Dakotas. Similarly, breakup and deglaciation of mountain glaciers in the Rockies led to catastrophic flooding of major river systems flowing into the Plains, including the Missouri, the Platte, the Republican, and Canadian drainage systems, as well as the creation of complex terrace sequences and the deposition of immense loess deposits.

Although late Pleistocene catastrophic flooding probably eliminated some deposits of archaeological interest, other deposits were created. The archaeological record from this region is particularly important to our understanding of early Paleoamerican prehistory, as well as many well-stratified sites of late Pleistocene and Holocene age.

New evidence for a pre-12,000 yr B.P. human presence is suggested by Steve Holen's ongoing work on late Pleistocene mammoth sites in southwestern Nebraska and north-central Kansas (Hall 1995a, 1995b; Holen 1994, 1995, 1996; May and Holen 1993). Holen, working with geoarchaeologist David May, has determined that all these discoveries occur in Peorian Loess of late Pleistocene age (20,000 to 14,000 yr B.P.). These sites characteristically contain flaked mammoth bone and lack a stone tool association.

Excavation of the La Sena site on the west side of the Medicine Creek Reservoir, Nebraska, revealed a single Columbian mammoth (*Mammuthus columbi*). Soil dates from the stratigraphic level containing the mammoth remains yielded ages of 18,860 ± 360 yr B.P. (Tx-7006) and 16,730 ± 430 yr B.P. (Tx-6708). Collagen extracted from the mammoth bone was dated to 18,000 ± 190 yr B.P. (Beta 28728) and 18,440 ± 145 (AA-6972). At the La Sena site the bones are disarticulated, and long bones exhibit green bone fractures (broken when fresh). Many of the fractured limb bones exhibit negative bulbs of percussion substantially larger than would be expected if produced by carnivores, but match with expectations for large hammerstones. Unbroken ribs and vertebrae occur among the fractured long bones. Holen suggests that these patterns are identical to flaked bones found at Clovis-age sites such as Lange/Ferguson, South Dakota (Hannus 1989).

Another site currently under investigation by Holen's team is the Shaffert site, located in an arroyo that drains into the Medicine Creek basin. Flaked mammoth bones are exposed in loess deposits approximately 2 m below the surface. Holen (personal communication 1997) reports a 16,500 yr B.P. bone date from the Shaffert mammoth.

Approximately 40 miles away in the Platte River drainage, another mammoth was found on the land of Richard and Harriet Jensen, near Cozad, Nebraska. When the Jensen site, originally investigated as a paleontological salvage project, started to produce flaked bones similar to La Sena, Holen was contacted. Approximately 50–60 percent of the Jensen mammoth has been recovered, and some of the long bone elements exhibit green bone fractures, including impact points and bone flakes. Radiocarbon dates of 13,830 and 14,830 yr B.P. have been obtained on bone collagen and soil humates, respectively, from the Jensen site (Holen, personal communication 1995).

The Lovewell Mammoth site occurs on the Lovewell Reservoir in north-central Kansas. Geomorphic research indicated that the north shoreline of the lake consists of Farmdalian/Woodfordian terrace fill. Test excavation of the site revealed a concentration of mammoth bones and bone fragments, some of which exhibit negative scars suggestive of high-velocity impact points and bone flaking. Of interest is the recovery of the polished end of a bone foreshaft found in the excavation. A radiocarbon date on bone taken from a spirally fractured mammoth bone yielded an age of 18,250 ± 90 yr B.P. (CAMS-1536) (Holen 1996).

Other evidence for a pre-12,000 occupation has been found by R. S. MacNeish's research team (Chrisman et al. 1996; MacNeish 1996) at Pendejo Cave, New Mexico. Pendejo Cave, located near Orogrande, New Mexico, is a stratified site that has produced paleontological, paleobotanical, and possible archaeological remains. More than 55 radiocarbon determinations suggest to MacNeish (1996) that continuous human occupation occurred at Pendejo, dating back to more than 55,000 yr B.P.

The full details of the Pendejo site report have yet to be published, and a book on this project is in press. In an overview, MacNeish (1996) uses the material from Pendejo Cave to address the pre-11,500 yr B.P. debate. MacNeish invited various specialists to the site during excavations. One visiting scholar, C. V. Haynes, Jr., stated at the time of his visit that non-cultural mechanisms could be used to explain many of the discoveries at Pendejo and suggested that multiple working hypotheses that would involve consideration of both naturally and cultural factors should be considered at Pendejo. To date, this suggestion has not been heeded.

MacNeish (1996) has responded by suggesting that there are more lines of evidence indicative of human presence at Pendejo Cave than from any other North American locality, including most Clovis sites. He asserts that in addition to flaked stone artifacts, there are several important independent lines of artifactual evidence found in stratigraphic context that he believes will refute the non-cultural hypothesis. MacNeish argues that diagnostic evidence for the presence of humans includes:

(1) A study of raw material distributions indicating that 186 (54 percent) of 303 lithic artifacts are exotic to the dolomite cave site and must have been transported into the cave by humans;

(2) A total of 23 shaped features dug into lower stratigraphic levels can be attributed to humans;

(3) The occurrence of two logs (15 cm diameter) inside the cave can be attributed to humans;

(4) Thermoluminescence readings of burned cave-floor deposits suggest the fires were internal and did not move into the cave from the outside as would be expected with ground fires;

(5) A *Bison antiquus* humerus with major shaft impact scars (multiple flake scars used to shape one end) thought to be indicative of human behavior;

(6) A shaped-bone projectile point appears to have been driven into a horse phalanx;

(7) 16 friction skin imprints, which match only human prints, found on clay nodules baked at temperatures of over 120°C were recovered from five stratigraphic levels; and

(8) Human hair occurs in pre-12,000-year-old levels.

Certainly an impressive array of data has been recovered from Pendejo, and the final report on this project awaits scrutiny of the profession.

Shortly after 12,000 yr B.P., diagnostic projectile points made their appearance on the Plains, e.g., Clovis and Goshen (cf. Frison 1991). Following the Pleistocene megafaunal extinctions, which occurred about 10,800 years ago, a series of regional co-traditions developed along the flanks of the Rocky

Mountains and on the Northwestern Plains. These included Goshen, Hell Gap, Agate Basin, Folsom, and Cody.

Although questions remain, portions of the Clovis-Folsom-Plainview/Agate Basin-Hell Gap-Cody sequence are a recurring pattern at sites throughout the Plains and Southwest. Recent discoveries continue to refine and elucidate our knowledge of the technologies, settlement patterns, and subsistence and lithic procurement systems of these early Plains traditions. Frison (this volume) and Stanford (this volume) review the phylogenetic and techno-cultural records of the Northern Plains, Central Plains and Southwest, and Southern Plains, respectively.

The Southwest and Plains are characterized by two predominant early projectile point patterns (Stanford, this volume). These traditions, unlike their appearance in the Northwest, are sequential rather than parallel; and include a basally thinned, fluted point pattern, into which Stanford places Clovis, Folsom/Midland, Goshen, and Plainview; and a lanceolate point pattern, which Stanford defines as encompassing the Agate Basin, Hell Gap, and Cody complexes.

Eastern North America

The Ice Margin

FOLLOWING RETREAT of the Laurentide ice sheet, the landscape underwent a rapid evolution characterized by large proglacial lakes and massive meltwater channels. The environment in eastern North America was modified strongly by the retreating ice sheet, which would have had effects on the animals and plants of the ice-marginal zone. Turner et al. (this volume) indicate that the relatively cool, moist marginal zone would have acted as a broad refugium for animals and plants that were adapted to Pleistocene environments. These marginal zone refugia would have persisted as a tundra along the shifting ice front during the late Pleistocene and early Holocene; that was followed by a herb-shrub tundra, which, in turn, was followed by a wide zone of boreal forest (Jacobson et al. 1987). There is an expanding body of evidence that indicates that human populations were in these dynamic ice-marginal zones (Bonnichsen 1980; Bonnichsen et al. 1987; Turner et al., this volume).

D. F. Overstreet (1993), for example, has identified a distinct Paleoamerican complex on the west side of Lake Michigan. On the basis of 35 sites, which occur in a limited geographical area, Overstreet has defined a unique archaeological complex associated with extinct fauna. These sites have a distinct artifact assemblage made of local raw materials, with a wide range of lanceolate points. Overstreet (1993) has named this group of sites the Chesrow complex. In a preliminary settlement/subsistence model, two site types have been identified: well-drained beach ridges of Glacial Lake Chicago, and interior bog-margin sites in swales of lake-borders. Faunal remains associated with this complex include mammoth, mastodon, caribou, and muskox. Artifacts found in direct association with faunal remains are not considered to be parts of the Clovis complex. Artifacts are made from local materials, especially quartzite cobbles. Important tool categories include projectile points, biface preforms and blanks, cores, hammerstones, and utilized flakes. Projectile point forms range from stemmed lanceolate to basally thinned concave-base specimens. The presence of extinct fauna in association with Chesrow-complex sites has led Overstreet to conclude that Chesrow may be related in some way to Clovis; but it should be regarded as an independent co-tradition as early as Clovis, if not ancestral to it. Of particular importance are: Schaefer 10,960 ± yr B.P. (Beta 62822), 12,220 ± 80 yr B.P. (Beta 628323), 12,310 ± yr B.P. (CAMS 30171); 12,480 ± 130 yr B.P. (Beta 62824); Mud Lake 13,440 ± 60 yr B.P. (CAMS 36643); Fenske 13,470 ± 50 yr B.P. (CAMS 36642); and Hebior 12,520 ± 50 yr B.P. (CAMS 25943); 12,520 ± 50 yr B.P. (CAMS 25943) mammoths. Mastodons from the area include the Deerfield Mastodon 1, Deerfield Mastodon 2, and Deerfield Mastodon 3; and these have radiocarbon assays ranging from 10,700 to 11,140 yr B.P. These mammoth and mastodon remains show evidence of human modification, are associated with non-diagnostic stone tools, and are the focus of ongoing research.

Evidence for a human presence along the ice margin in the middle to eastern parts of the continent is not uncommon and supports a focus on big-game hunting. Caribou hunting has been inferred for Paleoamerican sites in south-central and southeastern Ontario (Deller and Ellis 1988), as well as for northern New England and the Maritime provinces (Bonnichsen et al. 1985; Gramly 1982, 1988; MacDonald 1968), and southern New England (Nicholas 1987). Late glacial proboscidean fossils in association with human remains are known from southern Ontario, Michigan, and far western New York (Deller and Ellis 1988; Fisher 1995; Laub 1995).

Mid-Continental North America

LEPPER (THIS VOLUME) provides an overview of the evidence for Pleistocene peoples in Midcontinental North America. He focuses on two primary regions within Midcontinental North America, which he terms the Great Lakes Subarea and the Midcontinental Riverine Subarea. Though fluted points are common to both regions, studies show these subareas exhibit significantly different site and stone-tool distribution patterns.

The early archaeological record of the Great Lakes is characterized by large, single-occupation sites. In contrast, the Midcontinental Subarea has yielded large numbers of isolated fluted points, but few sites. Those rare large sites that have been found in the Midcontinent are generally quarry-related localities with evidence of multiple occupations or occur in settings that are particularly favorable in terms of their environmental situation, such as saline springs. Lepper proposes that these dissimilar regional patterns reflect adaptations that arose as responses to two very diverse environments.

The periglacial environment of the northern boreal forest supported a limited number of faunal species, whereas the warmer and more stable environments of the midcontinental region formed a vegetal mosaic that sustained a diverse faunal and floral assemblage. Lepper suggests that the limited number of game species in the north would have forced humans to concentrate their attention on a few, very productive resources, the procurement of which required a large, cooperative human effort. Quite probably, caribou herds formed the basis of early Great Lakes Paleoindian subsistence patterns, although mastodon and mammoth also may have been hunted, as suggested by the Chesrow complex.

In the more southerly areas, where a number of different and equally desirable game species flourished, there was no such benefit to large human aggregations. On the contrary, although this region contained a diverse faunal assemblage, it was likely a dispersed one. Game species such as deer or elk tend to live as solitary animals or in small groups, unlike the large caribou herds of the north. This dispersed southern resource base easily could have supported a large number of people, but in small bands rather than large settlements.

Reliable radiocarbon-dated sites are presently nonexistent in the midcontinent, and the chronology of the early Paleoindian period in this area is problematic. The Great Lakes Gainey site has yielded two thermoluminescence dates of 12,360 ± 1224 yr B.P. and 11,420 ± 400 yr B.P.; the State Road Ripple site, Pennsylvania, produced a radiocarbon age of 11,385 ± 140 yr B.P. (UGa-878); Cloudsplitter Rockshelter, Kentucky, was dated at 11,278 ± yr B.P (UCLA-2340I); and the fluted point component of the Shriver site, Missouri, was thermoluminescence dated at 10,650 ± 1100 yr B.P. (see Lepper, this volume: Table 3). These few, widely scattered dates suggest the age range of the midcontinental Paleoamerican occupation was similar to that recorded in other parts of the country.

In the Great Lakes region, a Paleoamerican evolutionary sequence encompassing the Gainey, Barnes, and Crowfield point types has been devised on typologic grounds (Storck 1991). The generalized Gainey/Clovis point has been found throughout the Midcontinental Subarea; however, the absence of dates and prevalence of isolated point forms and/or poorly stratified multicomponent sites have precluded the establishment of a projectile point sequence. Barnes and Crowfield points have been recovered only infrequently outside the Great Lakes region; there is some indication that these types reflect a localized adaptation (see Lepper, this volume).

Fluted points disappeared from the Great Lakes region by 10,400 yr B.P. (Deller and Ellis 1988; Lepper, this volume). In the Midcontinent Riverine Subarea, unfluted lanceolate points are present by at least 10,960 ± 240 yr B.P. (Bush 1988; Lepper, this volume), and substantially earlier if the Meadowcroft Miller Lanceolate is not discounted (see Adovasio et al., this volume; Lepper, this volume:Table 4). Dalton projectiles occur in the southern portions of this region by 10,500 yr B.P. (Goodyear 1982; Lepper, this volume:Table 4). The arrival of the lanceolate projectile point tradition (and slightly later notched-point complexes) in the Midcontinent appears to represent a continuation of the broad-based economic strategies characteristic of the Paleoamerican period, rather than an abrupt cultural transition.

Northeastern North America

THE FIRST PEOPLES TO colonize recently deglaciated landscapes in northeastern North America left a record of fluted points and lanceolate forms in their wake. In seeking to determine whether sites in the Northeast are as old as elsewhere in North America, Bonnichsen and Will (this volume) evaluate the ^{14}C record from northeastern North America. They find that various cultural and natural processes—alluvial transport, forest fires, tree throws, and cooking in hearths—are responsible for introducing and mixing carbonized plant remains into archaeological sites. More than 50 percent of the alleged Paleoamerican sites examined yielded ^{14}C ages of Holocene age. This, coupled with the lack of criteria by site investigators to determine whether charcoal is of cultural or natural origin, led the authors to conclude that the radiocarbon record for northeastern Paleoamerican sites is ambiguous. However, the placement of fluted point sites on ancient landforms associated with deglaciation suggest that colonization likely was coincident with regional deglaciation.

Meadowcroft Rockshelter, Pennsylvania

MEADOWCROFT ROCKSHELTER remains the best example of a pre-11,000 yr B.P. occupation yet discovered in eastern North America. Meadowcroft has yielded a long, stratified cultural record, corresponding to a lengthy radiocarbon sequence. Adovasio et al. (this volume) detail the radiocarbon record from the site, addressing assertions that the dates have resulted from particulate or non-particulate contamination.

Thus far, of 104 charcoal samples submitted for radiocarbon dating, 59 dates have been produced, 50 of which are internally consistent. Of these, 39 are younger than about 12,800 yr B.P. and comprise, with the exception of four low-magnitude reversals, an age sequence ranging from the Archaic to the early Historic periods. The younger dates are consistent with artifacts recovered in stratigraphic context from the site, and there is little doubt that they accurately reflect the ages of these materials.

The 13 dates in excess of 12,800 yr B.P. (only six of which have undeniable artifact associations) are internally consistent and in stratigraphic order. As Adovasio et al. (this volume) point out, if the older (pre-12,800 yr B.P.) Meadowcroft dates suffer from contamination or stratigraphic mixing, then there must be an explainable mechanism that would account for the cessation of this process at the beginning of the younger, accepted cultural sequence. Extensive scrutiny of the radiocarbon-dated samples and of the operative site-formation processes show no indication of contamination; and the supposition that some sort of hidden, selective mechanism was effective only during the deposition of the older materials is highly improbable.

Substantial evidence supports the assertion that Meadowcroft Rockshelter represents a pre-11,500 yr B.P. occupation, which would appear to date minimally from 12,000 yr B.P. to perhaps as early as 15,000 yr B.P. (see Lepper, this volume: Table 2). The Stratum IIa lithic assemblage represents a small-core-and-blade industry and is not at variance with what we would expect a pre- or even ancestral Clovis site to look like (Haynes 1987).

Southeastern United States

THE LATE GLACIAL MAXIMUM, circa 20,000–18,000 yr B.P., coincided with a sea-level decrease of around 120 m below present (Bloom 1983). The terminal Pleistocene was a time of rapidly changing landscapes and climates. Deglaciation commenced around 14,000 yr B.P., and sea levels rose slowly from their full glacial minimum stands. Vast areas of the continental shelf, which may have been occupied by humans, were exposed during this period. During the late glacial, a cool temperate "boreal forest" dominated by jack pine (*Pinus banksiana*) and spruce (*Picea*) was replaced by temperate deciduous forest as climate ameliorated in the Southeast (Delcourt and Delcourt 1991; Morse et al. 1996).

Recent archaeological research is enhancing our understanding of pre-Clovis occupation in the Southeast. J. M. McAvoy and D. K. Hazzard, as part of the Nottoway River survey, are investigating the Cactus Hill site (Hall 1996; McAvoy 1992; McAvoy and McAvoy 1997). It is located on a floodplain in the Coastal Plain area. What is notable about this stratified sand-dune site is an occupation found stratigraphically below Clovis that is producing artifacts. A hearth from the Clovis level included a scatter of southern pine charcoal that ^{14}C dated to 10,920 yr B.P. (Beta 81589). Eight to 10 cm below and capped by the Clovis surface, a scatter of white pine charcoal produced an AMS ^{14}C age of 15,070 ± 70 yr B.P. (Beta 81590). Associated with this feature are seven quartzite flakes and three quartz core blades. McAvoy notes that the site's sandy deposits pose questions of integrity. Additional work in another area of the site has produced more blades but no charcoal. Further excavations are in progress with the objectives of locating more charcoal and clarifying the relationship between the Clovis and the pre-15,000-year-old level (Hall 1996). The Clovis level has produced core blades of local quartzite and Clovis-era tools made from chert, including a fluted point.

J. N. MacDonald has been working in the Saltville Valley, Virginia, at the Saltville site (Wisner 1996). During late Pleistocene times, a river flowed through the Saltville Valley until about 13,500 yr ago. Apparently the river was dammed and a lake replaced the valley bottom with muds that preserved a diverse and detailed record of plant and animal life, including evidence of human occupation. Work at the site has exposed the remains of mastodon and muskox (*Bootherium bombifrons*). Many of these bones are broken, some were discolored by fire, and other fragments occur in concentrations and have what appear to be chop marks on their surface, suggesting they were processed for marrow. Although no projectile points are reported, a flaked stone with a serrated edge may be a purposefully shaped stone tool. Another possible artifact is made on a broken muskox tibia with polish on both surfaces of the broken pointed end. What are interpreted as fire-cracked rocks are commingled with the other remains. A single corrected ^{14}C date on twigs has an age of 13,950 yr B.P. (Beta 65209).

The relationship between humans and Pleistocene megafauna in the Southeast is not clear. Arguments advanced vary from favoring generalist adaptations with a minimal emphasis on megafauna (Meltzer 1988) to a big-game hunting focus (Anderson 1995). Ongoing research by J. Dunbar and S. D. Webb has emphasized the investigation of numerous underwater spring localities associated with the Tertiary karst region in northern and central Florida. Direct associations between humans and now-extinct fauna have been found at Little Salt Spring (where a giant land tortoise was recovered with a sharpened wooden stake embedded in its carapace), and at Wacissa River, Florida (Dunbar 1991; Webb et al. 1984). Additional archaeological investigations done in collaboration with a group of divers have yielded numerous other localities with bone and stone tools (Clovis, Suwanee, and Simpson points) in association with extinct fauna (Dunbar 1991; Dunbar, personal communication 1995).

Goodyear (this volume) observes that several thousand fluted and unfluted points have been found throughout the Southeast. The most common fluted point forms are Clovis and Cumberland; unfluted types include Quad, Suwanee, Simpson, and Dalton. Based on radiocarbon and stratigraphic work done outside of the Southeast, these types are thought to span the interval from 11,500 to 10,000 yr B.P. Few sites have been investigated in the Southeast, and Goodyear notes fieldwork is needed at stratified sites to understand fully the cultural and environmental context of early cultures. Toward this end, he provides a detailed overview of the geoarchaeological situation for finding significant sites in the Southeast, as well as summarizing much of the most important research now in progress.

Mexico

Lorenzo and Mirambell (this volume) envision that Mexico was first occupied by humans 40,000 to 35,000 yr B.P. The earliest artifacts are regarded as non-specialized implements and include choppers and chopping tools, scrapers, denticulates, shaped flakes and blades, and utilized flakes. Artifacts tend to be large, rarely less than 5 cm in length. Important sites representing this pattern include Tlapacoya, in the Valley of Mexico, and Rancho La Amapola, El Cedral.

Sometime between 14,000 and 9000 yr B.P., leaf-shaped and fluted points made their appearance. Clovis projectiles and their variants occur throughout Mexico, and Lorenzo and Mirambell (this volume) describe three forms: classic Clovis; a pentagonal variant; and a concave-sided variant. The majority of Mexican fluted points have been recovered from surface contexts, and their chronology is unclear. A Clovis-like point recovered from Los Tapiales, highland Guatemala, has been ^{14}C dated at 10,700 yr B.P. (Gruhn and Bryan 1977).

Mexico demarcates the northward extension of fishtail fluted points, a South American tradition roughly coeval with Clovis. A single Clovis point with a waisted base and two fishtail points occur in association at Los Grifos, Chiapas, where they have been dated between 9700 and 8000 yr B.P. (Lorenzo and Mirambell, this volume; see Ranere and Cook 1991 for alternative dates).

Conclusions

The Clovis-First Model

THE CONCLUDING SECTION is in part a eulogy in acknowledgment of the passing of a paradigm. As noted by Bonnichsen and Schneider (this volume), current archaeological data do not support key propositions of the Clovis-First model. Although the Clovis-first variant of the Late-Entry paradigm no longer can be sustained, it is useful to consider how it has served the development of First Americans studies.

The Clovis-First model has had important implications for the interpretation of regional archaeological records. As will be recalled, the model predicates that the initial Clovis migration represented the first settlement of North America. From an archaeological perspective, this model implies that we should find Clovis-complex artifacts in the basal level of all Clovis-aged archaeological sites. Following a settling-in period, the original colonists are presumed to have adapted to local circumstances. As environmental circumstances of the late Ice Age changed, numerous local traditions evolved, giving rise to a plethora of archaeological complexes.

The Clovis-First model has resulted in the placement of far more emphasis on Clovis than is warranted. Many regional investigators have accepted the key propositions of the model as a matter of faith and have assumed that Clovis is the earliest cultural pattern in their region. Belief in the Clovis-First model has caused some archaeologists to stop their excavations at the Clovis level without further excavation to determine whether older archaeological materials lie in older stratigraphic deposits or to ignore pre-12,000-year-old geological contexts as possibilities for human occupation.

Regional specialists have long been cognizant of the possibility of co-traditions that are of the same age as Clovis. Yet, most have found this proposition unacceptable. Although the reasons for this reluctance are not fully clear, it may be the wide-spread distribution of Clovis-complex sites and artifacts, coupled with secure, narrowly defined chronology based on many ^{14}C dates, that led many to accept the Late-Entry model as a reasonable and valid interpretation. The regional summaries in this volume, however, demonstrate that there is an increasing body of data from stratified, well-dated archaeological sites across North America that supports the propositions that there are a variety of co-traditions that used bifaces and projectile points, and that these complexes are as early as the Clovis. Some of the most important co-traditions discussed by volume contributors include the Nenana complex of Alaska (Hamilton and Goebel, this volume), the Western Stemmed complex from the Great Basin (Bryan and Tuohy, this volume), the Goshen complex from the northern Great Plains (Frison, this volume; Stanford, this volume), and the Great Lakes Chesrow complex (Overstreet 1993). Other co-traditions will surface as specialists develop careful detailed stratigraphic and chronological studies of individual sites. That co-traditions were not only present but proliferated at the same time as Clovis in both North America and South America seems clearly apparent.

The issue of whether Clovis represents a single archaeological culture or a series of new adaptations that spread rapidly across existing populations (Bonnichsen 1991; Bonnichsen et al. 1987) has yet to be adequately resolved. Some scholars propose that Clovis was the first basal culture in North America, and that it originated in Siberia or Beringia. If so, fluted point sites should be older in Alaska and younger in the lower United States. In fact, Hamilton and Goebel (this volume) indicate the reverse to be true. Others propose that Clovis originated in North America, perhaps the Southeast, and spread across North America. Clovis no longer can be characterized as a single big-game hunting society. There are many regional fluted-point varieties, e.g., Cumberland, Gainey, Debert, etc. Regional variants represent differences in point forms and in manufacturing procedures and may be indicative of different socio-cultural groups and in some cases differences in basic adaptive strategies.

Although the details of changes in the archaeological record vary from region to region, the general pattern is clear. In most regions, stratified archaeological sites contain a series of complexes. One archaeological complex is replaced by the next; e.g., on the High Plains, Clovis is followed by Folsom, which is followed by Hell Gap, etc. But just because one pattern follows the next in the stratigraphic record, it does not follow that there is necessarily any close cultural and biological relationship between two complexes juxtaposed in the same site. The causal factors responsible for the development of late Pleistocene and early Holocene archaeological complexes in North America are poorly understood. The comparative study of ancient human DNA and technological analysis of artifact production repertoires have potential for resolving issues concerning biological descent and cultural affiliation. An understanding of mechanisms responsible for change in the Paleoamerican archaeological record is an essential focus for future research.

The traditional Clovis-First model that envisioned all North American projectile points evolving from a basal Clovis pattern is now being reconsidered (Frison and Bonnichsen 1996:304). One version of the Early-Entry model presumes that: (1) humans were in the Americas well before the end of the last Ice Age; (2) global environmental change led to environmental forcing at the end of the Ice Age; and (3) humans responded to their new ecological circumstances in a variety of ways. Some of the most important responses included: (1) utilizing new plant and animal resources; (2) borrowing and innovating new technologies to adapt better to changed circumstances; and (3) reorganizing settlement, subsistence, and trade network patterns to accommodate new circumstances.

The papers presented by the authors of this volume demonstrate that the Paleoamerican archaeological record is characterized by major punctuations or breaks in the cultural record between occupations. The causes of such punctuations are poorly known. In some cases, climate change may be implicated. Rapid climate change in late glacial times likely served as a forcing mechanism that led to changes in the paleoecological systems on which humans were dependent. In other cases, new innovations and population growth may have been catalysts responsible for the changes that can be observed in the archaeological record. Yet in other cases, immigration from Northeast Asia and the arrival of new populations may be the key to explaining changes observed in local sequences.

In contrast to the Clovis-First variant of the Late-Entry model, the Early-Entry model predicts that environmental forcing at the end of the last Ice Age led to the development of a series of cotraditions penecontemporaneous with Clovis. By 11,000 yr B.P., there was cultural diversity, not a single culture, and this diversity is represented in the archaeological record by several archaeological cultures that used bifacially flaked projectile points.

The Early-Entry Model

IN THE PAST, MOST SPECIALISTS interested in the peopling of the Americas have emphasized overland terrestrial colonization models. Current evidence from Japan suggests boats were present in the North Pacific by 30,000 years ago and perhaps much earlier. Archaeological evidence from northern North America that would support a coastal entry route is non-existent. Indeed, this is not surprising, as rising sea levels would have drowned evidence for early coastal sites. Yet, the coastal entry route that proposes boat-using peoples with a maritime life style expanded around the Pacific Rim remains a viable option to overland colonization. It is a model that deserves considerably more attention than it has received in the past.

An increasing amount of new information can be marshaled in support of the Early-Entry terrestrial model. Drozdov's work on the Yenesei, Mochanov's work at the Diring Yuriakh site, and ongoing work at several early sites in northeastern Honshu, support the view that early human populations were both on the coast and in interior Northeast Asia during Lower Paleolithic times. Survival in these environments would have required the development of a sophisticated repertoire for dealing with extremely cold environments at a much earlier time than had previously been anticipated.

The new archaeological evidence from Northeast Asia indicates that cold was not the formidable barrier to human occupation that has long been assumed. Although the empirical record supports human presence in Northeast Asia by Middle Paleolithic times, sites of comparable age have yet to be reported in the Americas. There are, however, stratified sites with multiple radiocarbon dates with flaked stone tools and organic artifacts from the Americas of Upper Paleolithic Age. The most famous are Pendejo Cave, New Mexico, and Pedra Furada, Brazil; the earliest levels at both sites date to about 50,000 years ago. The theoretical possibility remains open that even earlier sites will be found in the Americas. Indeed, if we exclude this possibility, we will never look.

Although the Early-Entry model provides a useful framework, the sparse nature of current knowledge about the earliest peoples who came to the Americas must be emphasized. We do not, for example, know how many discrete populations colonized the Americas, the routes taken, or whether population movement between continents took place by sea or overland. We do not know whether initial colonization occurred by demic expansion or by rapid colonization by skilled boatsmen. And we do not adequately understand the adaptive systems of the early Americans.

What little we do know suggests that variability in regional adaptations occurred prior to 12,000 years ago. There is a possibility that the mammoth steppe adaptation occurred both in the far north and on the Great Plains, as suggested by the emphasis on flaked mammoth bone from Bluefish Caves, Holen's sites from Kansas and Nebraska, and the Dutton, Selby, and Lamb Spring sites (Rancier et al. 1982; Stanford 1979; Stanford and Graham 1985; Stanford et al. 1981). We do not know how these sites relate to Meadowcroft Rockshelter and Pendejo Cave, which have yielded flake tool assemblages. The deeply buried Varsity Estates and Silver Springs sites, Alberta, may represent quarry sites in an ice-marginal environment; but we know next to nothing as to how humans would have survived in this challenging environment.

Yes, there is a pre-11,500-year-old human presence in the Americas; but our knowledge of this period is very thin. The task that lies ahead of us is the development of objective, well-researched knowledge of pre-Clovis archaeological and paleoecological patterns. We will need more quality site reports and paleobiological studies before we can begin to make realistic correlation within regions, let alone between regions.

The most innovative and credible First Americans projects are being guided by specialists who have adopted an interdisciplinary research approach and assembled teams of specialists to assist with their investigations; who adhere to the principles of development of a thorough understanding of site chronology, site stratigraphy, and site formation processes; and who are willing to explore whether or not patterns found are non-cultural or cultural. During the years in which the Clovis-First model was preeminent, grant proposal referees and funding agencies withheld most funding for investigation of pre-11,500 yr B.P. sites; such projects must now be funded.

Many biases are likely to continue to enter into our acceptance of early sites, based largely on our expectations of what a pre- or proto-Clovis assemblage should look like. As Frison points out (this volume), it is important that the distinction between "pre-11,500-yr B.P." and ancestral (proto-) Clovis be kept in mind. While we logically may expect an ancestral Clovis occupation to possess traits resembling Clovis, there should be no such expectation inherent in our assessment of potential "pre-11,500 yr B.P." sites. There is no assurance that "pre-11,500 yr B.P." sites will be characterized by a blade-and-biface technology, nor is there necessarily any reason why they should resemble one another.

Toth (1991), among others, espouses a commonly held view of the criteria that must be present to qualify as a bonafide site. This yardstick includes the presence of unequivocal artifacts, extinct faunal remains, multiple radiocarbon dates in an unambiguous association, and multiple sites in an area that will yield the archaeological sequence. Strict adherence to a yardstick of this nature would not be sensitive to nuances in the Paleoamerican archaeological record. The new research summarized in this volume clearly indicates that there are many valid lines of evidence in addition to the usual litany. For example, at Monte Verde, Dillehay (1997b) reports the presence of wooden artifacts, bolas stones, dozens of medicinal plant remains, house structures, and phosphate and other geochemical signatures documenting the presence of humans. Bonnichsen and Schneider (this volume) report that human and animal remains containing ancient DNA can be found routinely at many sites. Morlan and Cinq-Mars (this volume) and Holen (1996) report flaked mammoth bone. Chrisman et al. (1996) report fingerprints on fired clay nodules as well as numerous other lines of evidence.

First Americans studies traditionally have focused on archaeological data. In recent years, however, this fascinating field has caught the attention of non-archaeologists. Specialists are using human skeletal, linguistic, and genetic data in their search to understand American origins. Even though this expanded focus represents a positive direction, problems remain in respect to how the above lines of information can be integrated with other lines of interdisciplinary data. Bonnichsen and Schneider (this volume) observe that the linguistic evidence and some lines of genetic evidence are based on their own uncalibrated time scales and cannot be related to models based on archaeological and interdisciplinary data sets that use calibrated time scales (e.g., ^{14}C). Nonetheless, at least in the case of genetics, this appears to be a short-term difficulty. By working with ancient DNA extracted from bone, soft tissue, and/or hair from dated archaeological contexts, it is now possible to integrate ancient DNA research with archaeological and other data used to reconstruct the past.

These new approaches and additional lines of evidence underscore the importance of a interdisciplinary framework for conducting Paleoamerican research. The search for American origins requires greater scientific sophistication on the part of project investigators than at any time in the past. It is no longer adequate to just hold a Ph.D.

degree in anthropology. Principal investigators must be able to deal with ambiguity; they must be prepared to develop and implement research designs for separating cultural from natural signatures. And they must be able to work with multiple lines of evidence from many disciplines with the goal of developing valid reconstructions.

An increasing number of specialists are meeting these demands by drawing upon a broad spectrum of Quaternary sciences as well as the disciplines of anthropology, linguistics, paleobiology, genetics, and molecular biology (Bonnichsen and Steele 1994; Bradley 1985; Dillehay and Meltzer 1991; Dillehay 1997b; Greenberg 1987; Holliday 1997; Lascar and Donahue 1990; Porter 1988; Ruddiman and Wright 1987; Schurr et al. 1990; Wallace et al. 1985; Waters 1992; West 1996a, 1996b). In seeking to understand the linkages between natural systems (e.g., climatology, oceanography, geology, pedology, biology), cultural systems (linguistics, archaeology), and paleobiology (genetics, physical anthropology, molecular biology) for a specific project, principal investigators are assembling interdisciplinary research teams. The burden of this approach lies with the principal investigator, who must integrate the results into a coherent and credible picture of the past. It is imperative that young scholars who enter this field receive interdisciplinary training to meet the challenges this exciting arena of research has to offer.

Acknowledgments

Our thanks go to Mila Bonnichsen, Marvin T. Beatty, Bradley Lepper, and Mort D. and Joanne C. Turner for editorial suggestions that led to improvements in the manuscript. We also would like to thank David Overstreet and Steve Holen for making available unpublished radiocarbon dates.

References Cited

Ackerman, R. E., and R. L. Carlson
1991 Diring Yuriakh: An Early Paleolithic Site in Yakutia. *Current Research in the Pleistocene* 8:1–2.

Adovasio, J. M., and D. R. Pedler
1997 Monte Verde and the Antiquity of Humankind in the Americas. *Antiquity* 71:573–580.

Anderson, D.
1995 Recent Advances in Paleoindian and Archaic Period Research in the Southeastern United States. *Archaeology of Eastern North America* 23:145–176.

Ball, B. F.
1983 *Radiocarbon Estimates from the Sibbald Creek Site, EgPr-2. Archaeology in Alberta.* Occasional Paper No. 21. Archaeological Survey of Alberta, Edmonton.

Berger, R.
1982 The Wooley Mammoth Site, Santa Rosa Island, California. In *Peopling of the New World*, edited by J. E. Ericson, R. E. Taylor, and R. Berger, pp. 163–179. Ballena Press, Los Altos.

Bloom, A. L.
1983 Sea Level and Coastal Changes. In *Late Quaternary Environments of the United States*, Volume 2, The Holocene, edited by H. E. Wright, Jr., pp. 42–51. University of Minnesota Press, Minneapolis.

Bonnichsen, R.
1980 *Human Presence in an Ice Marginal Environment in Northern Maine. American Quaternary Association,* Sixth Biennial Meeting Abstracts and program, 18–20. August 1980, p. 45. Institute for Quaternary Studies, University of Maine, Orono, ME.

1985 The Environmental Setting for Human Colonization of Northern New England and Adjacent Canada in Late Pleistocene Time. In *Late Pleistocene History of Northeastern New England and Adjacent Quebec*, edited by H. Borns, Jr., P. LaSalle, and W. B. Thompson, pp. 151–159. Geological Society of America, Special Paper 197, Boulder, CO.

1991 Clovis Origins. In *Clovis: Origins and Adaptations,* edited by K. Turnmire and R. Bonnichsen, pp. 309–329. Center for the Study of the First Americans, Oregon State University, Corvallis, OR.

Bonnichsen, R., G. L. Jacobson, Jr., R. B. Davis, and H. W. Borns, Jr.
1985 The Environmental Setting for Human Colonization of Northern New England and Adjacent Canada in Late Pleistocene Time. In *Late Pleistocene History of Northeastern New England,* edited by H. W. Borns, Jr., P. LaSalle, and W. B. Thompson. Geological Society of America Special Paper 197.

Bonnichsen, R., D. Stanford, and J. L. Fastook.
1987 Environmental Change and Developmental History of Human Adaptive Pattern, the Paleoindian Case. In *North America and Adjacent Oceans During the Last*

Deglaciation: The Geology of North America, vol. K-3, edited by W. F. Ruddiman and H. E. Wright, Jr. pp. 403–424. Geological Society of America, Boulder.

Bonnichsen, R., D. G. Rice, D. Brauner, and G. Curtis
1994 Human Adaptation at the Southern Margin of the Laurentide and Cordilleran Ice Sheets. *Current Research in the Pleistocene* 11:116–118.

Bonnichsen, R. T. D. Dillehay, G. C. Frison, F. Ikawa-Smith, R. Knudson, D. G. Steele, A. R. Taylor, and J. Tomenchuk.
1995 Future Directions in First Americans Research and Management. In *The Public Trust and the First Americans*, edited by R. Knudson and B. C. Keel, pp. 30–71. Oregon State University Press, Corvallis, OR.

Bonnichsen, R., and D. G. Steele (editors)
1994 *Method and Theory for Understanding the Peopling of the Americas.* Center for the Study of the First Americans, Oregon State University, Corvallis, OR.

Bonnichsen, R., and K. Turnmire (editors)
1991 *Clovis: Origins and Adaptations.* Center for the Study of the First Americans, Oregon State University, Corvallis, OR.

Brace, L. C.
1996 Modern Human Origins and the Dynamics of Regional Continuity. In *Prehistoric Mongoloid Dispersals*, edited by T. Akazawa and E. J. E. Szathmary, pp. 81–112. Cambridge University Press, Cambridge.

Bradley, R. S. (editor)
1985 *Quaternary Paleoclimatology: Methods of Paleoclimatic Reconstruction.* Allen & Unwin, Boston.

Brauner, D.
1985 *Early Human Occupation in the Uplands of the Southern Plateau: Archaeological Excavations at the Pilcher Creek Site, Union County Oregon.* Department of Anthropology, Oregon State University and the USDA Soil Conservation Service, Oregon State University, Corvallis, OR.

Bryan, A. L.
1978 *An Overview of Paleo-American Prehistory from a Circum-Pacific Perspective.* Department of Anthropology, University of Alberta, Edmonton, Alberta.

1979 Smith Creek Cave. In *The Archaeology of Smith Creek Canyon, Eastern Nevada*, edited by D. R. Tuohy and D. L .Rendall, pp. 162–251. Nevada State Museum Anthropological Papers No. 17. Nevada State Museum, Carson City.

1986 Paleoamerican Prehistory as Seen from South America. In *New Evidence for the Pleistocene Peopling of the Americas*, edited by A. L. Bryan, pp. 1–14. Center for the Study of Early Man, University of Maine, Orono, ME.

1988 The Relationship of the Stemmed Point and Fluted Point Traditions in the Great Basin. In *Early Human Occupation in Far Western North America: The Clovis-Archaic Interface*, edited by J. A. Willig, C. M. Aikens, and J. L. Fagan, pp. 53–74. Nevada State Museum Anthropological Papers No. 21. Nevada Sate Museum, Carson City.

Bush, D. R.
1988 New Evidence of Paleoindian and Archaic Occupations in Clay and Perry Counties, Kentucky. In *Paleoindian and Archaic Research in Kentucky*, edited by C. D. Hockensmith, D. Pollack, and T. N. Sanders, pp. 47–65. Kentucky Heritage Council, Frankfort.

Chlachula J.
1996 Geology and Quaternary Environments of the First Preglacial Palaeolithic Sites Found in Alberta, Canada. *Quaternary Science Reviews* 15:285–313.

Chlachula, J., N. I. Drozdov, and V. P. Chekha
1994 Early Paleolithic in the Minusinsk Basin, Upper Yenisei River Region, Southern Siberia. *Current Research in the Pleistocene* 11:128–130.

Chlachula, J., and R. Le Blanc
1996 Some Artifact-diagnostic Criteria of Quartzite Cobble-Tool Industries from Alberta. *Canadian Journal of Archaeology* 20:61–74.

Chrisman, D., R. S. MacNeish, J. Mavalwala, and H. Savage
1996 Late Pleistocene Human Friction Skin Prints from Pendejo Cave, New Mexico. *American Antiquity* 61:357–376.

Clayton, L., and S. Moran
1982 Chronology of Late Wisconsin Glaciations in Middle North America. *Quaternary Science Reviews* 1:55–82.

Delcourt, P., and H. Delcourt
1991 *Quaternary Ecology: A Paleoecological Perspective.* Chapman & Hall, New York.

Deller, D. B., and C. J. Ellis
1988 Early Palaeo-Indian Complexes in Southwestern Ontario. In *Late Pleistocene and Early Holocene Paleoecology and Archaeology of the Eastern Great Lakes Region*, edited by R. S. Laub, N. G. Miller, and D. W. Steadman, pp. 251–263. Bulletin of the Buffalo Society of Natural Sciences No. 33. Buffalo.

Dillehay, T. D.
1989 *Monte Verde: A Late Pleistocene Settlement in Chile 1: Paleoenvironment and Site Context.* Smithsonian Institution Press, Washington, D.C.

1997a The Battle of Monte Verde. *The Sciences,* January/ February, pp. 26—33.

1997b *Monte Verde: A Late Pleistocene Settlement in Chile 2: The Archaeological Context.* Smithsonian Press, Washington, D.C.

Dillehay, T. D., and D. J. Meltzer (editors)
1991 *The First Americans: Search and Research*. CRC Press, Boca Raton.

Dunbar, J.
1991 Resource Orientation of Clovis and Suwannee Age Paleoindian Sites in Florida. In *Clovis: Origins and Adaptations*, edited by R. Bonnichsen and K. Turnmire, pp. 185–214. Oregon State University, Corvallis, OR.

Erlandson, J. M., and M. J. Moss
1996 The Pleistocene-Holocene Transition along the Pacific Coast of North America. In *Humans at the End of the Ice Age: The Archaeology of the Pleistocene-Holocene Transition*, edited by L. G. Straus, B. V. Eriksen, J. M. Erlandson, and D. R. Yesner, pp. 207–301. Plenum Press, New York.

Fagan, B. M.
1987 *The Great Journey: The Peopling of Ancient America.* Thames and Hudson, New York.

Fisher, D. C.
1995 Experiments on Subaqueous Meat Caching. *Current Research in the Pleistocene* 12:77–80.

Fladmark, K. R., J. C. Driver, and D. Alexander
1988 The Paleoindian Component at Charlie Lake Cave (HbRf39), British Columbia. *American Antiquity* 53:371–384.

Frison, G. C.
1991 The Goshen Paleoindian Complex: New Data for Paleoindian Research. In *Clovis: Origins and Adaptations*, edited by R. Bonnichsen and K. Turnmire, pp. 133–151. Center for the Study of the First Americans, Oregon State University, Corvallis, OR.

Frison, G. C., and R. Bonnichsen
1996 The Pleistocene-Holocene Transition on the Plains and Rocky Mountains of North America. In *Humans at the End of the Ice-Age: The Archaeology of the Pleistocene-Holocene Transition*, edited by L. G. Straus, B. V. Eriksen, J. M. Erlandson, and D. R. Yesner, pp. 303–318. Plenum Press, New York.

Goebel, T., R. Powers, and N. Bigelow
1991 The Nenana Complex of Alaska and Clovis Origins. In *Clovis: Origins and Adaptations*, edited by R. Bonnichsen and K. Turnmire, pp. 49–79. Center for the Study of the First Americans, Oregon State University, Corvallis, OR.

Goodyear, A. C.
1982 The Chronological Position of the Dalton Horizon in the Southeastern United States. *American Antiquity* 47:382–395.

Gramly, R. M.
1982 The Vail Site: A Palaeo-Indian Encampment in Maine. In *Late Pleistocene and Early Holocene Paleoecology and Archaeology of the Eastern Great Lakes Region*, edited by R. S. Laub, N. G. Miller, and D. W. Steadman, pp. 265–280. Bulletin of the Buffalo Society of Natural Sciences No. 33. Buffalo.

1988 *The Adkins Site: A Paleo-Indian Habitation and Associated Stone Structure.* Persimmon Press, Buffalo.

1993 *The Richey Clovis Cache.* Persimmon Press, Buffalo.

Greenberg, J. H.
1987 *Languages of the Americas.* Stanford University Press, Stanford.

Greenberg, J. H., C. R. Turner II, and S. L. Zegura
1986 The Settlement of the Americas: A Comparison of the Linguistic, Dental, and Genetic Evidence. *Current Anthropology* 27:(5):477–479.

Gruhn, R.
1994 The Pacific Coast Route of Initial Entry: An Overview. In *Method and Theory for Investigating the Peopling of the Americas*, edited by R. Bonnichsen and D. G. Steele, pp. 249–256. Center for the Study of the First Americans, Oregon State University, Corvallis, OR.

1997 The South American Context of the Pedra Pintada Site in Brazil. *Current Research in the Pleistocene* 14:29-32.

Gruhn, R., and A. L. Bryan
1977 *Los Tapiales: A Paleo-Indian Campsite in the Guatemalan Highlands.* Proceedings of the American Philosophical Society 121:235–273. Philadelphia.

Guidon, N., and A. Pessis
1996 Falsehood or Untruth? A Reply to Meltzer, Adovasio & Dillehay. In *Fumdhamentos: Proceedings of the International Meeting on the Peopling of the Americas*, Sao Raimundo Nonato, Piaui, Brazil (1993). Fundacao Museu do Homen Americano, V.1, No. 1, Sao Raimundo Nonato, Piaui, Brasil.

Gustafson, C. E., D. Gilbow, and R. D. Daugherty
1979 The Manis Mastodon Site: Early Man on the Olympic Peninsula. *Canadian Journal of Archaeology* 3:157–164.

Guthrie, R. D.
1968 Paleoecology of the Large-Mammal Community in Interior Alaska during the Late Pleistocene. Amer*ican Midland Naturalist* 99(2):236–268.

1996 The Mammoth Steppe and the Origin of Mongoloids and Their Dispersal. In *Prehistoric Mongolid Dispersals*, edited by T. Akawzwa and E. J. E. Szathmary, pp. 172–186. Oxford University Press, Oxford.

Hall, D. G.
1995a Bones of Nebraska Mammoths Imply Early Human Presence. *Mammoth Trumpet* 10(1):1,4–7.

1995b Ice-Age Wisconsin People Left Unique Cultural Record. *Mammoth Trumpet* 10(2): 5–8.

1996 Simple Tools, Hearth Found Beneath Clovis Horizon. *Mammoth Trumpet* 11(4):1, 14–16.

Hannus, A. L.
1989 Flaked Mammoth Bone from the Lange/Ferguson Site, South Dakota. In *Bone Modification*, edited by R. Bonnichsen and M. H. Sorg, pp. 381–394. Center for the Study of the First Americans, University of Maine, Orono, ME.

Haynes, C. V., Jr.
1964 Fluted Projectile Points; Their Age and Dispersion. *Science* 145:1408–1413.

1966 Elephant-hunting in North America. *Scientific American* 214(6):104–112.

1977 When and From Where Did Man Arrive in Northeastern North America: A Discussion. In *Amerinds and Their Paleoenvironments in Northeastern North America*, edited by W. S. Newman and B. Salwen, pp. 165–166. Annals of the New York Academy of Sciences, 288.

1987 Clovis Origin Update. *The Kiva* 52(2):83–93.

Hiroshi, K., T. Kamata, and A. Yamada
1990 The Early-Middle Paleolithic Period in the Miyagi Prefecture. In *Chronostratigraphy of the Paleolithic in North Central, East Asia, and America*, pp. 79–82. Academy of Sciences of the USSR Institute of History, Philology and Philosophy, Siberian Branch of the Academy of Sciences, Novosibirsk.

Holen, S. R.
1994 Did Someone Eat the La Sena Mammoth? In *Cellars of Time: Paleontology and Archaeology in Nebraska.* Nebraskaland Magazine 72(1):88.

1995 Evidence of the First Humans in Nebraska, pp 1–6. *Museum Notes*, University of Nebraska State Museum, Lincoln.

1996 The Lovewell Mammoth: A Late Wisconsinan Site in North Central Kansas. *Current Research in the Pleistocene* 13: 69–70.

Holliday, V. T.
1997 *Paleoindian Geoarchaeology of the Southern High Plains.* University of Texas Press, Austin.

Hughes, B. A., and T. J. Hughes
1994 Transgressions: Rethinking Beringian Glaciations. *Palaeogeography, Paleoclimatology, and Palaeoecology* 110: 275–294.

Hughes, T. J., R. Bonnichsen, J. L. Fastook, B. Hughes, and M. Grosswald.
1991 Pleistocene Beringia: An Outright Land Bridge or A Glacial Valve Constraining Asian Migrations to North America? In *INQUA 13th International Conference, Abstracts*, Beijing.

Jackson, L. E., and A. Duk-Rodkin
1996 Quaternary Geology of the Ice-free Corridor: Glacial Controls on the Peopling of the New World. In *Prehistoric Mongoloid Dispersals*, edited by T. Akazawa and E. J. Szathmary, pp. 214–227. Oxford University Press, Oxford.

Jacobson, G. L., Jr., T. Webb III, and E. C. Grimm
1987 Patterns and Rates of Vegetation During the Deglaciation of Eastern North America. In *North America and Adjacent Oceans During the Last Deglaciation: The Geology of North America, vol. K-3*, edited by W. F. Ruddiman and H. E. Wright, Jr., pp. 277–288. Geological Society of America, Boulder.

Jantz, R., and D. Owsley
1997 Pathology, Taphonomy, and Cranial Morphometrics of the Spirit Cave Mummy. *Nevada Historical Quarterly* 40: 62–84.

Lasca, N. P., and J. Donahue (editors)
1990 Archaeological Geology of North America. *Geology of North America, DNAG Special Centennial Special Volume 4.* United States Geological Survey, Boulder.

Laub, R. S.
1995 The Site (Western New York): Recent Developments in the Study of the Late Pleistocene Component. *Current Research in the Pleistocene* 12:26–29.

McAvoy, J. M.
1992 Nottoway River Survey Clovis Settlement Patterns Part I. Nottoway River Publications, Sandstron, VA.

McAvoy, J. M., and L. D. McAvoy
1997 *Archaeological Investigations of the Site 44SX202, Cactus Hill, Sussex County Virginia.* Research Report Series No. 8, Commonwealth of Virginia, Department of Historic Resources, Richmond, VA.

MacDonald, G. F.
1968 *Debert: A Palaeo-Indian Site in Central Nova Scotia.* Anthropology Papers of the National Museum of Canada, No. 16, Ottawa.

MacNeish, R. S.
1996 Pendejo Pre-11,500 yr B.P. Proofs and Their Implications. In *Fumdhamentos, Proceedings of the International Meeting on the Peopling of the Americas* São Raimundo Nonato, Piaui, Brasil (1993). Revista da Fundacao Museu do Homenm Americano. V.I, No 1, Sao Raimundo Nonato, Piaui, Brasil.

Martin, P. S.
1973 The Discovery of America. *Science* 179:969–974.

1984 Prehistoric Overkill: The Global Model. In *Quaternary Extinctions: A Prehistoric Revolution*, editors P. S. Martin and R. G. Klein, pp. 354–403, University of Arizona Press, Tucson.

Masahito, A., and S. Hiroyuki,
1990 Transition from Middle to Upper Paleolithic in Japan. In *Chronostratigraphy of the Paleolithic in North Central, East Asia and America*, pp. 97–105. Academy of Sciences of the USSR Institute of History, Philology and Philosophy, Siberian Branch of the Academy of Sciences, Novosibirsk.

May, D. W., and S. R. Holen
1993 Radiocarbon Ages of Soils and Charcoal in Late Wisconsinan Loess, South-Central Nebraska. *Quaternary Research* 39:55–58.

Mehringer, P. J., Jr.
1988a Clovis Cache Find: Weapons of Ancient Americans. *National Geographic* 174: 500–503.

Mehringer, P. J., Jr.
1988b The Richey-Roberts Clovis Cache, East Wenatchee, Washington. *Northwest Science* 62(5):271–272.

Mehringer, P. J., Jr., and F. Foit, Jr.
1990 Volcanic Ash Dating of the Clovis Cache at East Wenatchee, Washington. *National Geographic Research* 6(4):495–503.

Meltzer, D. J.
1988 Late Pleistocene Human Adaptations in Eastern North America. *Journal of World Prehistory* 2: 1–53.

1995 Clocking the First Americans. *Annual Review of Anthropology* 24: 21–45

1997 Monte Verde and the Pleistocene Peopling of the Americas. *Science* 276, 276–755.

Mochanov, Y. A.
1993 The Most Ancient Paleolithic of the Diring and the Problem of a Nontropical Origin for Humanity. *Arctic Anthropology* 30(1): 22–53.

Mosimann, J. E., and P. S. Martin
1975 Simulating Pleistocene Overkill by Palaeo-Indians. *American Scientist* 63:(3)304–313.

Morse, D. F., D. G. Anderson, and A. C. Goodyear
1996 The Pleistocene-Holocene Transition in the Eastern United States. In *Humans at the End of the Ice Age*, edited by L. G. Straus, B. V. Eriksen, J. M. Erlandson, and D. R. Yesner, pp. 319–338. Plenum Press, New York.

Nicholas, G. P.
1987 Redundancy in Early Postglacial Land Use in Robbins Swamp, Southwestern New England. *Current Research in the Pleistocene* 4:21–22

Ochsenius, C., and R. Gruhn (editors)
1979 *Taima-Taima: A Late Pleistocene Paleo-Indian Kill site in Northernmost South America—Final Report of 1976 Excavations.* South American Quaternary Documentation Program. Reprinted by the Center for the Study of the First Americans, Oregon State University, Corvallis.

Oda, S.
1990 A Review of Archaeological Research in the Izu and Ogsawara Islands. *Man and Culture in Oceania* 6:53–79.

Overstreet, D. F.
1993 *Chesrow: A Paleoindian Complex in the Southern Lake Michigan Basin.* Great Lakes Archaeological Press, Milwaukee.

Porter, S. C.
1988 Landscapes of the Last Ice Age in North America. In *Americans before Columbus: Ice-Age Origins*, edited by R. C. Carlisle, pp. 1–24. Ethnology Monographs, No.12, Department of Anthropology, University of Pittsburgh, Pittsburgh.

Rancier, J., G. Haynes, and D. Stanford
1982 Investigation of Lamb Springs. *Southwestern Lore* 48: 1–17.

Ranere, A. J., and R. G. Cooke
1991 Paleoindian Occupation in the Central American Tropics. In *Clovis: Orgins and Adaptations*, edited by R. Bonnichsen and K. Turnmire, pp. 237–254. Oregon State University, Corvallis.

Rice, D.
1972 *The Windust Phase in Lower Snake River Region Prehistory.* Washington State University, Laboratory of Anthropology, Report of Investigations No. 50, Pullman.

Roberts, F. H. H., Jr.
1935 A Folsom Complex: Preliminary Report on Investigations at the Lindenmeier Site in Northern Colorado. *Smithsonian Miscellaneous Collections* 94(4): 1–35.

Ruddiman, W. F., and H. E. Wright, Jr. (editors)
1987 *North America and Adjacent Oceans During the Last Deglaciation, The Geology of North America, DNAG Volume k-3.* Geological Society of America, Boulder.

Schurr, T. G., S. W. Ballinger, Y. Gan, J. A. Hodge, D. A. Merriwether, D. N. Lawrence, W. C. Knowler, W. M. Weiss, and D. C. Wallace
1990 Amerindian Mitochondrial DNAs Have Rare Asian Mutations at High Frequencies, Suggesting They Derived from Four Primary Maternal Lineages. *American Journal of Human Genetics* 46:613–623.

Schweger, C. E., J. V. Matthews, Jr., D. M. Hopkins, and S. B. Young
1982 Paleoecology of Beringia: A Synthesis. In *Paleoecology of Beringia*, edited by D. M. Hopkins, J. V. Matthews, Jr., C. E. Schweger, and S. B. Young, pp. 425–444. Academic Press, New York.

Stanford, D.
1979 The Selby and Dutton Sites; Evidence for a Possible pre-Clovis Occupation of the High Plains. In *Pre-Llano Cultures in the Americas; Paradoxes and Possibilities*, edited by R. L. Humphrey and D. Stanford, pp. 101–125. Anthropological Society of Washington, Washington, D.C.

Stanford, D. J., and J. Day (editors)
1992 *Ice Age Hunters of the Rockies.* Denver Museum of Natural History and University Press of Colorado, Niwot, CO.

Stanford, D., and R. W. Graham
1985 Archaeological Investigations of the Selby and Dutton Mammoth Kill Sites, Yuma, Colorado. *National Geographic Research Reports* 20: 519–541.

Stanford, D., W. R. Wedel, and R. Scott
1981 Archaeological Investigation of the Lamb Spring Site. *Southwestern Lore* 47:14–27.

Steele, D. G., and J. P. Powell
1992 Peopling of the Americas: Paleobiological Evidence. *Human Biology* 64(3):303–316.

1994 Paleobiological Evidence of the Peopling of the Americas: A Morphometric View. In *Method and*

Theory for Investigating the Peopling of the Americas, edited by R. Bonnichsen and D. G. Steele, pp. 141–164. Center for the Study of the First Americans, Oregon State University, Corvallis, OR.

Stork, P. L.
1991 Imperialists Without a State: The Cultural Dynamics of Early Paleoindian Colonization as Seen from the Great Lakes Region. *In Clovis: Origins and Adaptations*, edited by R. Bonnichsen and K. L. Turnmire, pp. 153-162. Center for the Study of the First Americans, Oregon State University, Corvallis, OR.

Taylor, R. E., P. E. Hare, C. A. Prior, D. L. Kirner, L. Wan, and R. B. Burky
1995 Radiocarbon Dating of Biochemically Characterized Hair. *Radiocarbon* 37:1–11.

Torroni, R., I. Sukernik, T. G. Schurr, Y. B. Starikovskaya, M. F. Cabell, M. H. Crawford, A. G. Comuzzie, and D. C. Wallace
1993 mtDNA Variation of Aboriginal Siberians Reveals Distinct Genetic Affinities with Native Americans. *American Journal of Human Genetics* 53:591–608.

Toth, N.
1991 The Material Record. In *The First Americans: Search and Research*, edited by T. Dillehay and D. J. Meltzer, pp. 53–76. CRC Press, Boca Raton.

Tuohy, D., and A. J. Dansie
1996 Radiocarbon Dates from Spirit Cave, Nevada: Early Holocene Occupation of the Western Great Basin. *Current Research in the Pleistocene* 14: 49–50.

Turner, C. G., II
1985 The Dental Search for Native American Origins. In *Out of Asia: Peopling of the Americas and the Pacific*, edited by R. Kirk and E. Szathmary, pp. 31–78. The Journal of Pacific History, Inc., Canberra.

Wallace, D. C., K. Garrison, and W. C. Knowler
1985 Dramatic Founder Effects in Amerindian Mitochondrial DNAs. *American Journal of Physical Anthropology* 68:149–155.

Wallace, D. C., and A. Torroni
1992 American Indian Prehistory as Written in the Mitochondrial DNA: A Review. *Human Biology* 64(3):403–416.

Waters, M. R.
1992 *Principles of Geoarchaeology: A North American Perspective.* University of Arizona Press, Tucson.

Waters, M. R., S. L. Forman, and J. M. Pierson
1997 Diring Yuriakh: A Lower Paleolithic Site in Central Siberia. *Science* 275: 1281–1284.

Webb, S. D., J. T. Milanich, J. T. Alexon, and J. S. Dunbar.
1984 A Bison Antiquus Kill Site: Wacissa River, Jefferson County, Florida. *American Antiquity* 49:384–394.

West, F. H. (editor)
1996a *American Beginnings.* University of Chicago Press, Chicago.

1996b The Study of Beringia. In *American Beginnings*, edited by F. H. West, pp. 1–10. University of Chicago Press, Chicago.

Wisner, G.
1996 Saltville Site Has Evidence of 14,000-year-old Feasts. *Mammoth Trumpet* 11(4):1, 18–20.

Wu Xinzhi
1994 Pleistocene Peoples of China and the Peopling of the Americas. In *Method and Theory for Investigating the Peopling of the Americas*, edited by R. Bonnichsen and D. G. Steele, pp. 73–78. Center for the Study of the First Americans, Oregon State University, Corvallis, OR.

Yoshizaki, Masakazu, and Masami Iwasaki
1986 Babadan Locality A: Recent Discovery of the Middle Pleistocene Occupation of Japan. *Canadian Journal of Anthropology* 5(1):3–9.

Ice Age Environments of Northern Eurasia with Special Reference to the Beringian Margin of Siberia

Mikhail G. Grosswald

Abstract

Geologic evidence—in particular, glacial geomorphology—suggests that a continuous system of ice sheets covered the northern outskirts of Eurasia during the last glacial maximum. A part of the system, the Beringian ice sheet, was centered on the southern Chukchi Sea, spread out to the shallow Beaufort-Sea and Bering-Sea shelves, and continued, as a floating ice shelf, into the deep Bering Sea. This implies that the true image of Ice-Age Beringia was not the conventional scene of a wide, ice-free land bridge with environment favorable for periglacial biotas and prehistoric humans. Rather, it suggests a terrain that was heavily glaciated, partly flooded by ice-dammed lakes, inhospitable, and impenetrable by animals and humans.

Hence, overland Asian migration to North America was improbable during the height of glaciation, when an ice sheet and ice-dammed lakes closed off the migratory paths. It was not probable during Holocene time either, when sea-level rise flooded the Bering Strait. Crossing of Beringia by animals and humans seems possible only during a relatively short and warm late-Glacial interval, most probably—the Bølling-Allerød interstadial. It was during that time that the process of ice-sheet shrinkage went far enough to open ice-free paths, and the process of sea rise had not yet reached the critical level of flooding the strait. One may speculate that earlier Asian migrations to North America were similarly constrained by ice sheets and marine transgressions. This scenario is consistent with available archaeological evidence.

Introduction

What kind of environments prevailed in Arctic Eurasia during the Ice Ages, in particular during the last glacial maximum (LGM)? The answer to this question is of utmost importance to understanding human prehistory and for explaining the distribution of ancient human habitats and migratory paths. Particularly vital is knowledge of the extent and geography of former ice sheets and ice-dammed lakes in the Arctic coastal lowlands and their submarine continuations—the continental shelves.

The extent and type of glaciation on the Barents, Kara, East Siberian, and other continental shelves of Eurasia have been the subject of debate for decades. The competing hypotheses fall into several groups. One of them, still exceptionally influential in Russia, includes a variety of anti-glacialistic, or "diluvialistic," concepts; their adepts deny ice-sheet glaciations of the high-latitude lowlands, let alone the shelves, and believe that recent crustal movements and tectonically induced marine transgressions, not glaciations, played a leading role in past global changes (e.g., Gramberg and Kulakov 1983). Another group adheres to the "concept of restricted glaciation," which admits some, but only minor, polar ice covers. According to this concept, the Ice-Age Arctic was dominated by ice-free environments, while glaciation was represented by small ice caps confined to the western peri-Atlantic region (Biryukov et al. 1988; Pavlidis 1992; Velichko 1994). The third concept, which is the core of our reconstructions, suggests a continuous system of marine ice sheets grounded on the entire Arctic continental margins, with a floating ice shelf over the deep Arctic Basin and a chain of proglacial lakes integrated into a trans-Eurasian meltwater-drainage system (Denton and Hughes 1981; Grosswald 1980, 1988, 1998; Hughes et al. 1977).

Institute of Geography, Russian Academy of Sciences,
29 Staromonetny Street, 109017, Moscow, Russia

The last concept has gained massive support from glaciological and paleoclimate modeling; virtually all the modelings based on reasonable assumptions of climate change suggest a continuous late Pleistocene ice sheet of Arctic Eurasia stretched from the Barents and Kara seas, across most of Northeastern Siberia and the Bering Strait, to Alaska (Fastook and Hughes 1991; Hughes 1995; Huybrechts and T'siobbel 1995; Lindstrom and MacAyeal 1989; Marsiat 1994; Verbitsky and Oglesby 1992).

The model of continuous ice sheets of Arctic Eurasia has been confirmed and substantiated by multidisciplinary studies undertaken in the Barents Sea. In particular, Scandinavian researchers uncovered a wealth of new geological and geophysical evidence for the continuous glaciation of the western part of the Sea (Elverhøi and Solheim 1983; Sættem et al. 1992, Salvigsen 1981; Vorren and Kristoffersen 1986; Vorren et al. 1988; and many others) while Russian geologists did the same in its eastern part (Gataullin et al. 1993).

Later on, the focus of the debate shifted to the eastern Eurasian Arctic, i.e., to the continental shelves and coasts of the Laptev, East Siberian, Chukchi, and Bering Seas. During the LGM, sea-level lowerings had to turn the region into dry land. This would create a link between Siberia and Alaska—a vast lowland up to 1,500 km wide, commonly referred to as the Bering Land Bridge. Unlike the western Eurasian Arctic, that region was, and still is, widely believed to have never been subjected to ice-sheet glaciation. According to published maps and descriptions, its Pleistocene environments were dominated by open, ice-free tundras or grasslands that provided Asian animals and humans with a broad avenue for migration to the Americas (Hoffecker et al. 1993; Laukhin and Drozdov 1991; Morlan 1987; Sher 1976; Turner 1989).

It has been considered self-evident that the Pleistocene climate of the region was too dry to permit glaciation except in major mountain ranges" (Morlan 1987), thus only cirque and small valley glaciers usually are presented on glacial maps of Northeastern Asia (Arkhipov et al. 1986; Baranova and Biske 1964; Biryukov et al. 1988; Glushkova 1984; Velichko 1993). Even in publications by Vaskovsky (1959) and Hopkins (1972), which depict fairly large glaciers in Northeastern Asia and are considered by Yurtsev (1976) as "obviously maximalistic," the adjacent continental shelves are shown to be nearly ice-free. Thus even the "maximalists" believe that the former glaciation of Beringia was largely terrestrial, i.e., restricted to land.

It was this paleogeography that gave birth to the modern concept of Ice-Age Beringia. Based on phytogeographic considerations, Yurtsev (1976) used this term to define an area of ice-free continental shelves and coastal plains, confined between the Kolyma and Mackenzie rivers, with the Bering Land Bridge roughly assuming its center. For archaeological and zoogeographic purposes, the notion of a Mega-Beringia also was introduced to define an even larger region that reached the Lena River delta and Taimyr Peninsula in the west, and Kamchatka Peninsula in the south, and also was basically ice-free. Sher (1976) hypothesizes that, during the height of glaciation, this terrain might have become a vast refugium in which the periglacial floras and faunas, specific to the high-latitude Northern Hemisphere, originated and evolved.

The maximum model of a Eurasian glaciation, with a continuous ice sheet spreading across the Arctic continental shelf of Siberia and Beringia, challenges not only the conventional image of a wide, ice-free Ice-Age land bridge, but also the biogeographic and archaeological reconstructions based upon this concept. The model does not necessarily imply that the reconstructions should be discarded; however, their rethinking and revision are definitely due.

Evidence for Ice-Sheet Glaciation

The Barents-and Kara-Sea Shelves

As was already pointed out, ice-sheet glaciation of the Barents and Kara Seas has been established by geological investigations covering the islands and sea floor. No less convincing evidence for this glaciation was obtained on the adjacent coastal plains. This evidence comprised glacial geomorphic complexes: in particular, end moraines aligned into ice-marginal belts; ice-shoved features; assemblages of drumlins, flutes, glacial striae, grooves, and other ice-motion directional indicators; glacial through valleys breaching mountain ridges; submarine troughs on shelves; traces of ice-dammed lakes and meltwater drainage channels—all attesting to the former landward ice motion from the seas.

These geomorphic complexes were surveyed and mapped by numerous expeditions during decades of research. Their descriptions were published by many researchers (e.g., Andreyeva and Isayeva 1988; Arkhipov et al. 1980, 1986; Arslanov et al. 1987; Kind and Leonov 1982; Lavrov 1977). This author

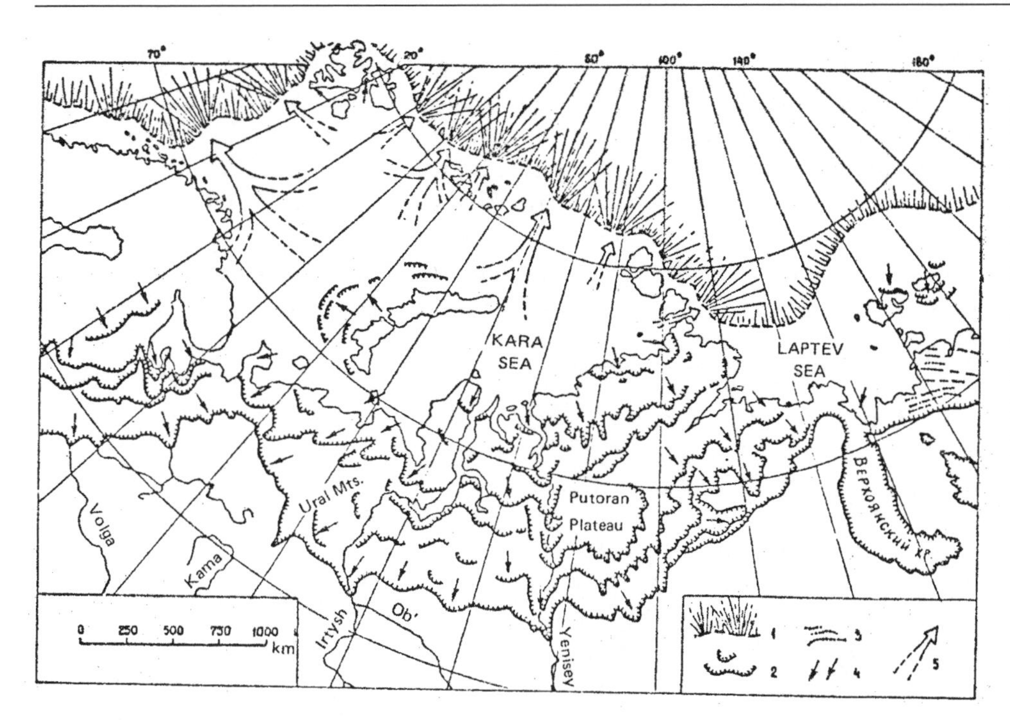

Figure 1. Glacial geomorphology depicting late Weichselian end moraines and traces of ice movement in north-central Eurasia: 1. continental slope; 2. end moraines; 3. yedoma ridges (Grosswald et al. 1994); 4. glacial striae, boulder trains; and 5. major glacial troughs on the continental shelf.

extensively used the above materials. It was from the data presented in these publications, as well as from my own field observations, that the glacial maps in Grosswald (1980, 1988, and 1998) were constructed. Bits and pieces of published information have been put together, in particular, separate segments of moraines integrated into continuous ice-marginal belts. Also, LGM, late-Glacial, and Holocene ages have been assigned to the belts, and my own data and considerations employed to position the former ice-spreading centers and to establish ice-sheet chronologies.

Ice-sheet encroachment upon the northwestern margin of Eurasia also is strongly suggested by evidence for former ice impoundment of the rivers flowing into the Barents and Kara Seas. This evidence—lacustrine terraces and sediments, spillways, and other paleo-lake signatures—was found in the basins of the Severnaya Dvina, Mezen, Pechora, Ob, and Yenisey rivers. In a number of cases, the lacustrine sequences were dated directly to the late Pleistocene (Arkhipov et al. 1980; Arslanov et al. 1987).

The map (Figure 1) presents a pattern of end moraines related to the last glaciation of the west-central Eurasian Arctic. It suggests that a major ice-spreading center of the Kara paleo-ice sheet was situated on the southern Kara Sea floor. The Kara-ice motion radiated from that center in all directions, specifically, southward onto the West Siberian Plain and Mid-Siberian Upland; westward across Novaya Zemlya into the Barents Sea; and northward over the continental shelf edge into the Central Arctic Ocean.

The East Siberian Shelves

UNTIL RECENTLY, EVIDENCE for an ice sheet of the East Siberian shelves and coastal lowlands was sparse, indirect, and inconclusive. The arguments in favor of a New-Siberian ice sheet put forth by Kolosov (1947) and some other researchers have been judged erroneous and been disregarded, and the ice sheet itself considered highly problematic. Indeed, so far, no *prima facie* glacial land forms have been detected on the East Siberian shelves and coasts.

The first convincing geological signatures of a vast East Siberian ice sheet were uncovered during 1987–1990. Initially they were restricted to the glacio-geomorphic complex of the New Siberian Islands and the surrounding shelf. The complex consisted of arcuate asymmetric ridges spaced in such a way that they formed garlands and a fish-scale pattern of outwash plains, tunnel valleys, and lateral meltwater channels (Figure 2a). The arcuate ridges turned out to be obducted heads of glaciotectonic thrust sheets, which were produced and shoved by an ice sheet. Their geometry is indicative of former ice motion from the northeast (Grosswald 1988, 1990). Tusks of *Mammoth primigenius* were found within the ice-deformed beds of the islands, implying a late Weichselian age for the whole complex.

Another complex of ice-shoved features was discovered and mapped in the Tiksi area of North Yakutia. It was found to be represented by well-preserved ice-thrust forms—stacking orders of imbricate rock slices, coupled with glacially excavated basins ("hill-and-hole pairs")—and by parallel rock-drumlin clusters carved from Paleozoic shales (Figure 2b). The rock slices have been displaced to the southwest, the shale plates in drumlins overturned, and the drumlin tails pointed in the same direction. Thus, it is clear that the geomorphology of the Tiksi area also suggests a northeast-to-southwest direction of former ice flow (Grosswald and Spektor 1993).

The Tiksi hill-and-hole pairs were AMS-^{14}C dated. To this end, a Russian-Swedish field party visited the area in the spring of 1990 and drilled several holes into the lake bottoms through the ice. The sediment cores were processed and dated at Uppsala University, Sweden. Their ages suggested that lacustrine sedimentation in the holes did not start before 8500 yr B.P., and that the Tiksi glaciotectonic complex was

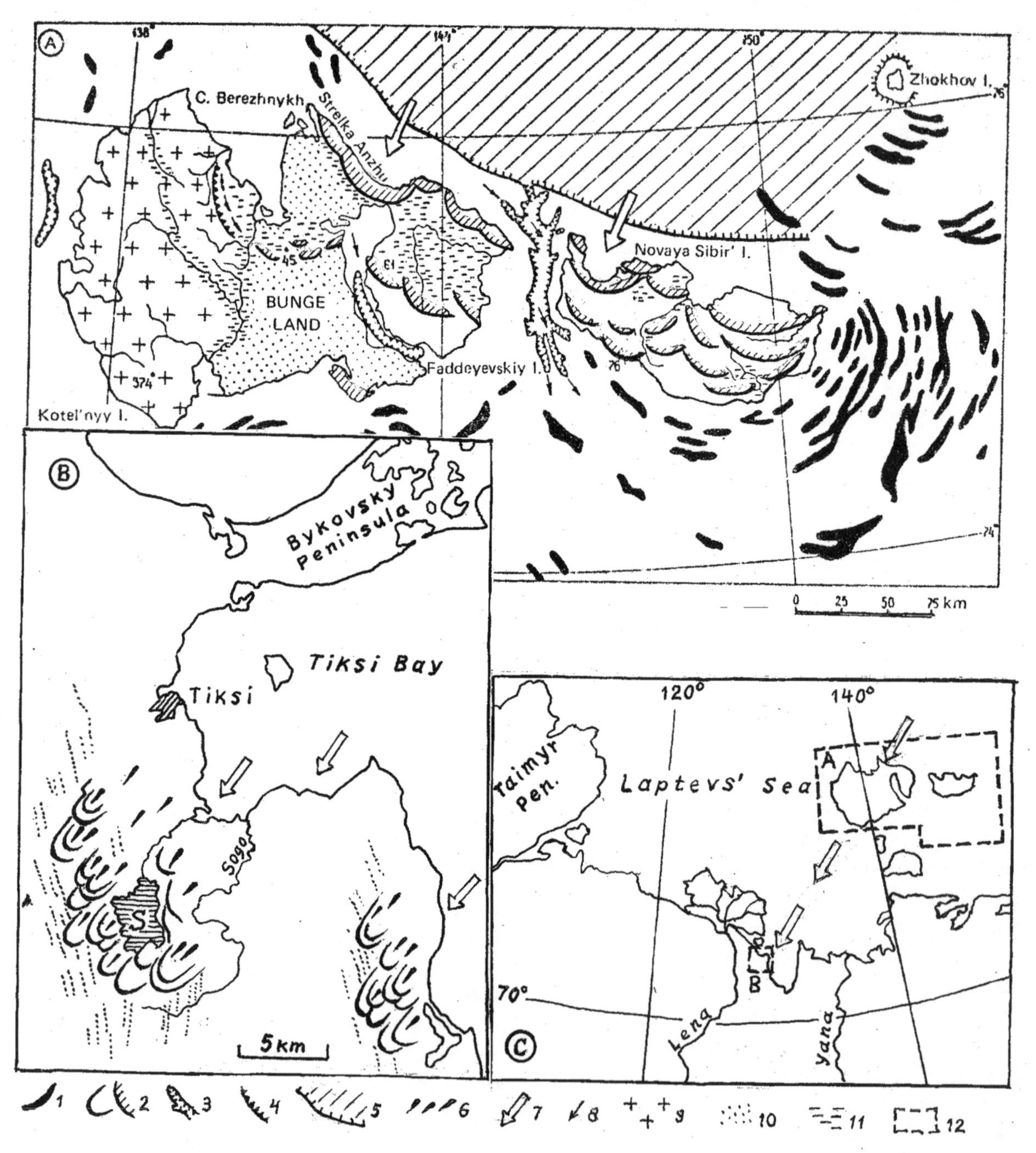

Figure 2. Glacial geomorphology indicating ice flowing over (A) the New Siberian Islands, (B) Tiksi Bay and Tiksi Area and North Yakutua, and (C) the Laptev Sea: 1. submarine push moraines; 2. glaciotectonic (push) moraines on land; 3. tunnel valleys; 4. erosional cliffs; 5. submarine flat-bottom depression (a hole); 6. rock-drumlins; 7. inferred ice-flow directions; 8. meltwater; 9. bedrock outcrops; 10. outwash fans; 11. poorly drained areas; 12. outlines of figures (A) and (B) in (C).

formed during the late Pleistocene (Grosswald et al. 1992). Besides, recorded gravity anomalies over the continental margin of East Siberia—in particular, a negative anomaly of up to -60 milligal centered east of New Siberian Islands—appear to be consistent with ice-sheet glaciation of the region (Tarakanov et al. 1987: Figure 3).

Based on the evidence from the New Siberian Islands and the Tiksi area, a first 400-km long ice flow-band was reconstructed by this author. It extended from the islands southwestward, reaching the foothills of the Verkhoyansky Range. With this accomplished, it became possible to take the following step and outline a tentative margin of the East Siberian ice sheet on the Laptev Sea coast (Grosswald 1988, 1998).

Further progress was made in establishing the ice sheet's southern limits by mapping the oriented tundra meso-forms of the Yana-Indigirka Lowland and the Lena-River delta, including so-called "oriented lakes." Within the entire region, orientation of these forms has proven strikingly consistent with the above flowband and unrelated to directions of summer winds or tectonic structures. Figure 4 shows the geomorphic continuum of the Yana-Indigirka Lowland and adjacent areas, including the oriented forms. The figure shows that the tundra ridges and lakes are clearly aligned along submeridional directions, and that the latter radiate from the New Siberian Islands to form a fan-like pattern, diverging to the south. In addition, the figure displays a second system of parallel ridges and valleys, oriented transversally to the submeridional lake-and-ridge alignments.

Oriented tundra forms of this kind are widespread in Siberia and Alaska. Typically they occur on the Arctic coastal lowlands blanketed by ice-rich silts and sands. The forms have been interpreted commonly as thermokarst features, while their elongation and regular orientation are accounted for by the effects of prevailing summer winds. However, we argued (Grosswald and Hughes 1995; Grosswald and Spector 1993) that this explanation doesn't make sense in Arctic Siberia. Instead, we proposed that the oriented tundra forms had inherited their orientation and alignment from glacial drumlinization and fluting, produced by a marine ice sheet transgressing from the adjacent continental shelf. Among other arguments supporting this hypothesis are drumlin fields occurring on a continuation of the oriented tundra complexes (Grosswald 1996; see Figure 4).

The transverse ridges and valleys appear to have been ice-marginal features, akin to *Urstromtäler* and formed by meltwater streams and pools, marking consecutive positions of a retreating ice margin. These features have been thermo-eroded into a thick blanket of peculiar ice-rich silts and sands, making up a so-called "yedoma." This had accumulated in proglacial environments mainly during late-Glacial and early Holocene times, with an icy dam in the north being a vital prerequisite for their formation. At a number of sites, the yedoma was ^{14}C-dated to the late-Glacial (Kaplina and Lozhkin 1982), and thus provides chronological control for the oriented tundra complexes.

As a result, we suggested (Grosswald 1999) that the forms in question are, in fact, late Weichselian glacial features, and that one can use their orientation for ice-sheet reconstructions. Being carved from deeply frozen and ice-rich sediments, the forms subsequently have been distorted and disfigured by thermokarst,

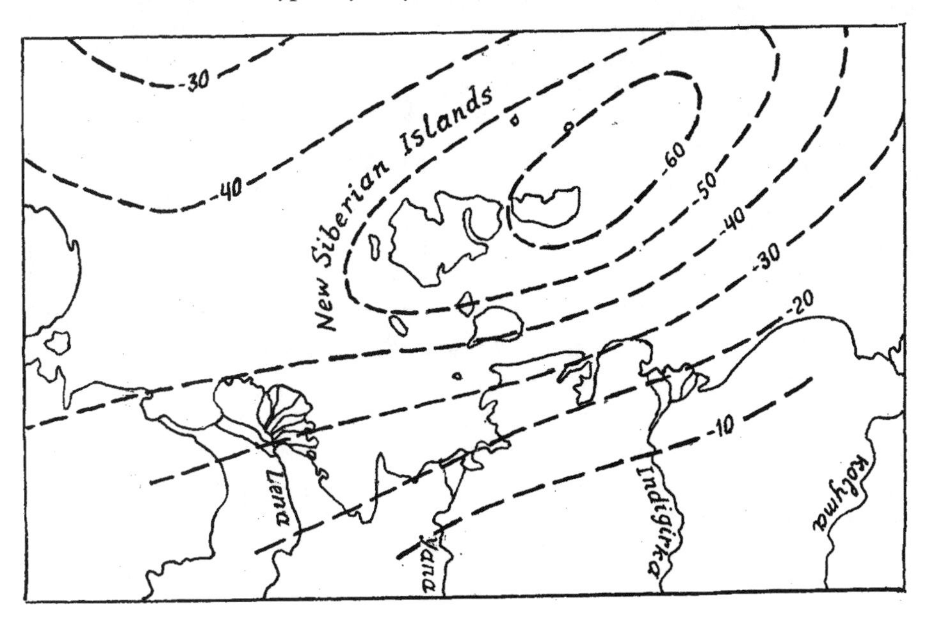

Figure 3. Negative free-air gravity anomalies contoured in 10 milligal isopleths centered northeast of the New Siberian Islands. From Tarakanov et al. (1987).

solifluction, and other periglacial processes, which are gathering speed under current climate warming. This seems to account for their systematic misinterpretation.

Based on the flow lines derived both from the ice-shoved features and oriented tundra forms, an advanced reconstruction of an East Siberian ice sheet was accomplished (Grosswald and Hughes 1995; Hughes 1995). The ice-spreading center of the ice sheet proved to be on the Arctic shelf, in the vicinity of the New Siberian Islands, and its summit reached an altitude of 1,700 m a.s.l. (Figure 5). That ice sheet was coalescent with the Kara ice sheet in the west and with another great ice sheet, the Beringian, in the east. Obviously, this reconstruction of glacial paleo-environments is in conflict with the aforementioned concept of Mega-Beringia as a terrain remaining ice-free throughout the entire glacial hemicycle. The only time imaginable that Mega-Beringia might have stayed both dry and ice-free was some interval of the late-Glacial.

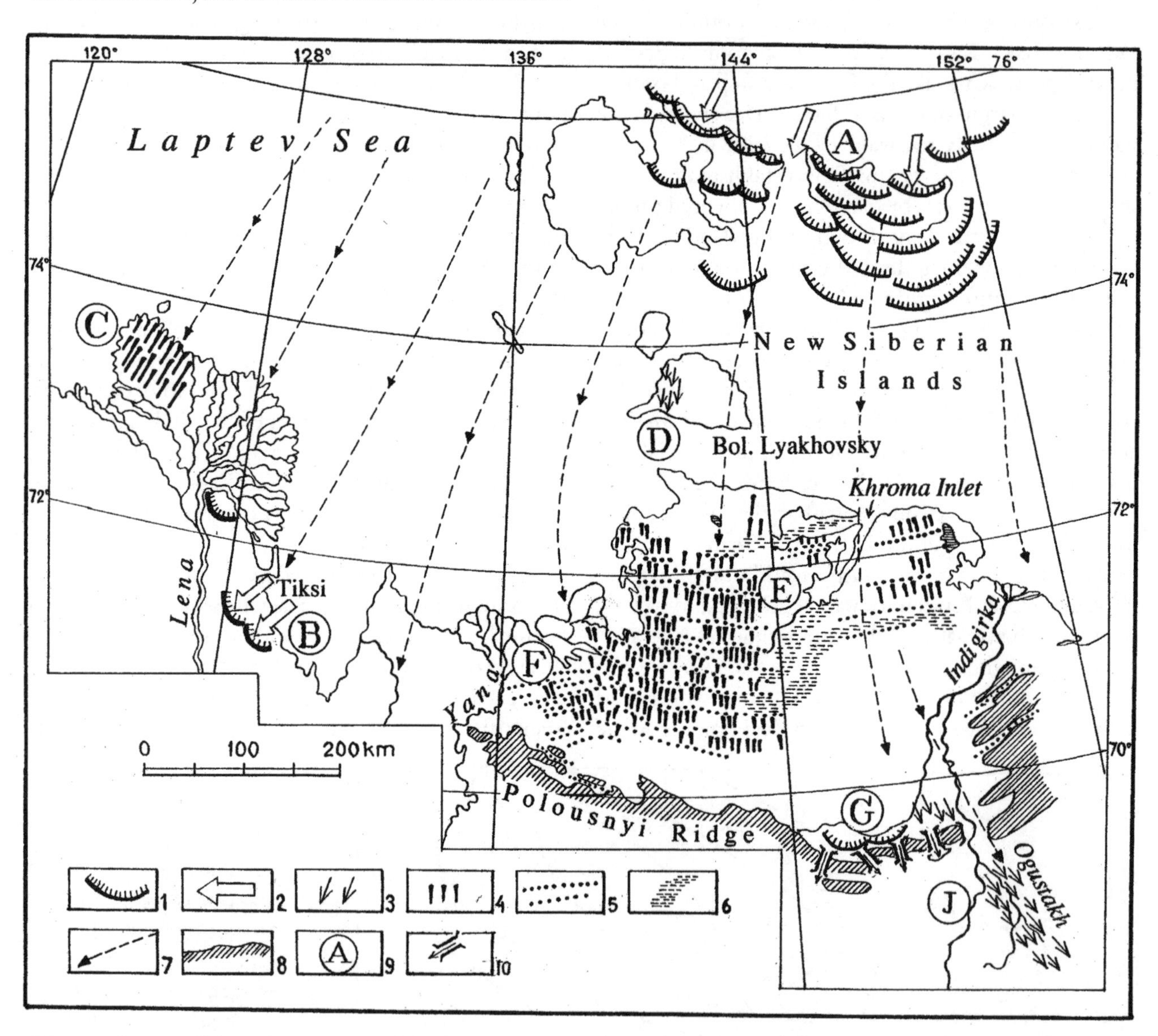

Figure 4. Geomorphological complexes of the Yana-Indigirka Lowland and adjacent areas: 1. large ice-shoved features; 2. direction of horizontal glacial pressure; 3. drumlins; 4. direction of long axes of the tundra oriented forms; 5. transverse tundra ridges; 6. relic valleys of meltwater streams; 7. inferred ice flowlines; 8. mountains and highlands; 9. areas discuused in the text; 10. glacial and meltwater breaches. Areas: A. ice-shoved features, the New Siberian Islands, B. the same, Tiksi area; C. oriented forms, northwestern Lena delta, D. drumlins of the Bol.Lyakhovsky Island, E. field of oriented forms, Yana-Indigirka Lowland, F. site of washboard moraines, G. push-moraine of the Allaikha valley, J. Ogustakh drumlin field.

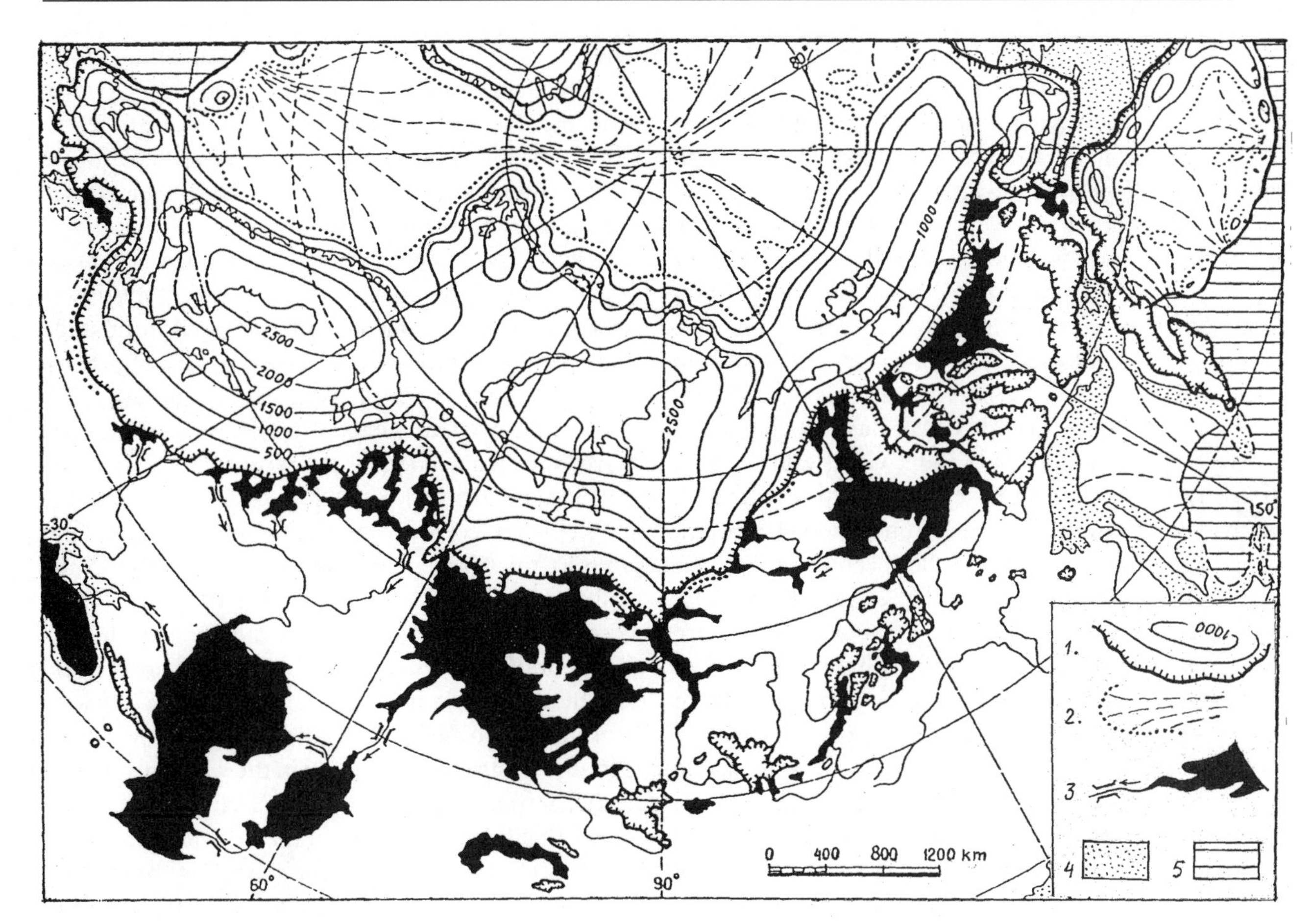

Figure 5. The last East Siberian ice sheet. A 3-D reconstruction of Hughes (1995, Grosswald and Hughes 1995).

The Chukchi-and Bering-Sea Shelves

As pointed out in the introduction, ice-sheet glaciation of the Chukchi Sea-Beringian region is considered improbable. This has been stated repeatedly by Hopkins, Pavlidis, Brigham-Grette, Velichko, and others. The late Weichselian (late Wisconsinan) glaciation of the region is believed to have been particularly small. For instance, according to Brigham-Grette et al. (1992), glaciation throughout central Beringia was restricted and consisted of only rock glaciers and small cirque glaciers, none of which reached even the outer coast. It is only for some earlier glaciations that these authors admit a larger ice extent, and yet, even for them, only terrestrial glaciers centered on Chukchi Peninsula are envisaged. However, considering the earlier glaciations, Hopkins and Brigham-Grette go as far as to conclude that the Chukchi glaciers descended onto a nearby shelf, crossed the northwestern Bering Sea, and encroached onto St. Lawrence Island. This event, characterized by larger ice extent and southward expansion of the Chukchi ice, formerly ascribed to penultimate glaciation (Hopkins 1972), now is considered as post-Sangamon; i.e., taking place after 125 ka B.P. (Heiser et al. 1992). "After 125 ka B.P. but before the LGM" —those are their chronological brackets of the last ice-expansion beyond the shores of Chukchi Peninsula. Thus, for reasons that I fail to comprehend, Hopkins and others keep arguing against a late Weichselian age of the last glaciation of Beringia. Nonetheless, their evolution in "our" direction is obvious: what they used to take for "penultimate" glaciation, now is the "early Weichselian," and what they believed to be one to two million years old, today is dated to 125 ka B.P. (Benson et al. 1994).

Despite these assertions, evidence for a late Weichselian ice-sheet glaciation of Beringia does exist and mounts rapidly. A tentative version of our case for that ice sheet has already been presented (Grosswald 1998; Grosswald and Hughes 1995; Hughes 1995;

Hughes and Hughes 1994; Hughes et al. 1991). The time is ripe to elaborate on the problem.

To begin with, we should address the problem of glaciation within the Chukchi Sea region. Here, though marine geological investigations failed to find glacial forms on the sea floor (Alekseev 1991; Pavlidis 1992), relevant evidence is uncovered on the coasts. Among other things, a strikingly pronounced and large (12,000 km^2) field of push moraines has been found and mapped in the lower Kolyma-River basin, and an oriented tundra complex detected in the Ayon Island area, west of the Chaun-Guba Bay. Having been identified on satellite photos by Grosswald (1996), both geomorphic complexes clearly attest to the ice flow directed southwestward, from the sea landward, and suggest a major ice-spreading center situated on the Arctic shelf, northeast of the Kolyma delta.

There are some additional pieces of corroborative evidence. First is a sequence of five till sheets recovered by drilling on the Vankarem Lowland, Chukchi Peninsula, which belong to the Upper and Middle Pleistocene (Laukhin et al. 1989). Second is the accumulation of glacial erratics—large, faceted and scratched boulders mixed into marine sands and gravels—that this author has observed on Cape Serdtse Kamen. It is noteworthy that both the areas, the Vankarem Lowland and Cape Serdtse Kamen, were believed to be ice-free throughout the Ice Age (Hopkins 1972; Vaskovsky 1959). Third are the glaciated landscapes of Wrangel Island, which also was commonly believed to have remained ice-free. An abundance of faceted and scratched glacial erratics and Lappland-style geomorphology were found to be typical features of the island (observed by the author, 1991–93).

Of particular importance is geomorphic evidence for southward ice flow through the Bering Strait and across the latitudinal Chukchi Range. Cape Dezhnev, bounding the Bering Strait from the west, was found to be a 700-m-high glaciated wall with a truncated spur at its foot and a huge mass of coarse debris on its southern side. In this context, the strait may turn out to be a giant glacial breach. Dozens of other breaches—U-shaped through-valleys—cross the 1,000-km-long mountain barrier formed by the Chukchi Range and Alaska's Seward Peninsula, suggesting a massive southward flow of an extensive ice sheet (Grosswald 1998; Grosswald and Hughes 1995).

Southerly ice flow direction also is implied by large end moraines of the southern Anadyr Lowland. These moraines, first described by Kartashov (1962) and Baranova and Biske (1964), are made up of sandy and gravelly clays; they form arcuate ridges, up to 2 km wide and 30–40 km long, with a relief of 50–70 m. Groups of individual ridges are lined up into lobate rows, or morainic"garlands," all turned by their convex sides to the south and southwest.

Judging from satellite photos, the glaciers suggested by the outermost end moraines crossed the lower Anadyr River and formed a continuous ice front at the southern limit of the Anadyr Lowland (see Figure 6). Note that the ice front extended diagonally, in a northwest-to-southeast direction, and faced southwestward. Generally, the reconstructed ice flow-lines extend from the north—specifically from the Chukchi-Sea continental shelf—to the south, and intersect the whole peninsula and its "backbone," the Chukchi Range. This suggests that the major LGM ice-spreading center of Beringia rested on the Chukchi shelf, not on the highlands of Chukchi Peninsula, and that the peninsula itself was overridden by a marine ice sheet. In other words, the paradigm of marine glaciation, formerly developed in the western Eurasian Arctic, appears applicable also to Beringia.

Another peculiar feature of the flow-lines in Figure 6 is their clear deflection to the west. For instance, on the coasts of the Gulf of Anadyr, the ice, instead of being a "natural" land-to-sea flow, deflected away from the sea. Moreover, the gulf's southwestern coast was transgressed by the ice moving from the sea landward. Resulting from this transgression, large masses of dead glacier ice containing marine microfossils were left behind and buried on the gulf's coasts (B. I. Vtyurin, personal communication, 1996).

Particularly convincing evidence for the westward deflection of ice flow in Beringia comes from the phenomenon of "glacially cut corners." The latter are land promontories jutting out into the sea and intersected by glacial troughs. Judging from the author's observations and satellite photos, this geomorphology is characteristic of Cape Dezhnev, southeastern Chukchi Peninsula, Cape Navarin, Cape Olyutorsky, and other capes and peninsulas of the region. For instance, the southeast-looking "corner" of Chukchi Peninsula, turned into a maze of fjords, displays clear evidence of having been dissected by the Bering-Strait ice stream, deflected westward. Here, ice flow-lines entered the Sinyavino Strait from the northeast, and got out of the Povideniya Fjord, while other adjacent flow-lines had the same NE to SW direction. Thus the ice stream of the Bering Strait, having been strongly deflected to the west, had to

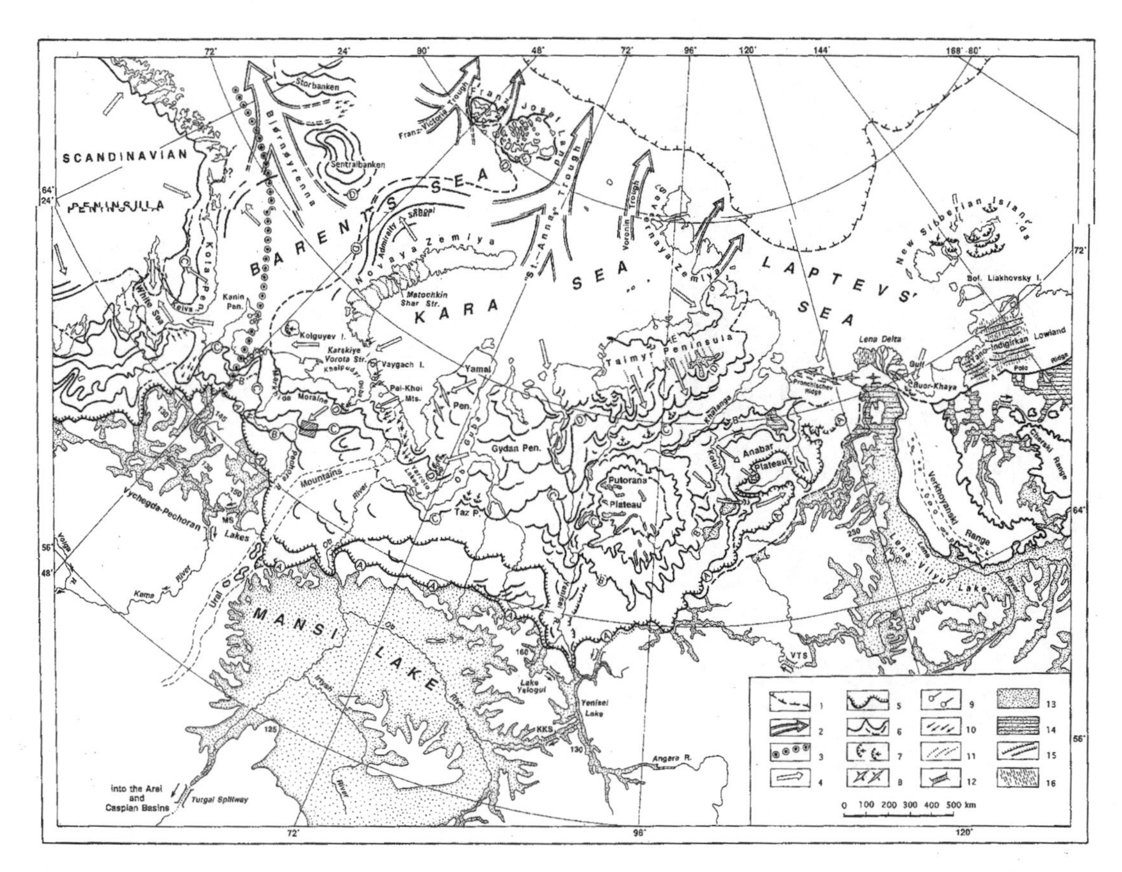

Figure 6. Late Weichselian ice margins, ice flow-lines, and glacial breaches (through valleys) in the eastern Chukchi and Bering Seas. Note the westward deflection of the ice flowlines implying a former ice sheet grounded on the Bering-Sea shelf.

preclude a direct transport of erratics from Chukchi Peninsula to St. Lawrence Island during glacial maxima. This in turn implies that the scenario postulated by Hopkins and colleagues is inconsistent with the reconstructed flow-line pattern and needs reconsideration.

Judging by a multitude of examples, "ice-cut corners" are ubiquitous on the shores bounding the former marine ice sheets (Grosswald 1998). In the case of Beringia, the occurrence of such geomorphic complexes strongly suggests that there was a marine ice sheet confined in the Bering Sea. Having been squeezed between the bounding land masses, the ice sheet exerted back pressure directed landward. The established deflection of the Beringian ice flow-lines clearly resulted from this pressure, while the "glacially cut corners," also suggestive of a pronounced ice flow deflection, are its geomorphic manifestations. It was because of this deflection caused by back pressure of a marine ice sheet that the Beringian ice moved across the bounding headlands and cut them with transverse glacial troughs. Incidentally, one of the headlands, Cape Olyutorsky (Figure 7), lies quite close to a deep basin of the southern Bering Sea, so that the ice, overriding the cape, could only be the edge of an ice shelf floating in this basin.

As it is, the occurrence of "hanging" troughs on Cape Olyutorsky is consistent with the floating Bering ice shelf, which was inferred by Grosswald and Vozovik (1984) from geomorphic and glaciological arguments. An additional piece of evidence for the ice shelf is provided by glaciated troughs crossing the submarine Commander-Aleutian Ridge and its islands (Black 1976). In particular, Bering Island of the ridge is known to have been breached by a few through valleys with U-shaped cross sections and striations on their slopes (Erlich and Melekestsev 1974), and abundant erratic boulders occur on the adjacent sea floor (B. V. Baranov, personal communication, 1997).

Reconstruction of a Beringian ice sheet consisting of a grounded ice dome and a floating ice shelf appears to be consistent with the evidence for a recent, post-Sangamon, episode of ice-overriding St. Lawrence Island (Benson 1993). In addition, it provides a first satisfactory explanation for giant submarine troughs incised into the southern margin of the Bering-Sea continental shelf. So far, these troughs—so-called submarine "canyons" of Bering, Bristol, Pribylov,

Figure 7. Cape Olyutorsky peninsula with intersecting glacial troughs. Drawing from an air photo.

Pervenets, Zhemchug, and others, characterized by U-shaped cross sections and up to 3-km depths—were described by Scholl et al. (1970), but virtually unaccounted for.

Furthermore, the concept of a Beringian ice sheet is in keeping with the results of deep-sea drilling in the high-latitude North Pacific undertaken during Leg 145 of D/V JOIDES *Resolution* (Leg 145..., 1993). Analysis of the core sediments yielded by the drilling has provided compelling evidence for extensive glaciation of the ocean's coasts and shelves between 2.6 million years ago and the end of the Pleistocene. In particular, based on variations in the density of sediments from the top portions of the cores, Kotilainen and Shackleton (1995) inferred that the last 95 ka of the Pleistocene, including isotope stage 2, had been punctuated by a sequence of abrupt paleoceanographic changes similar to and simultaneous with Heinrich events and Dansgaard-Oescher cooling cycles of the North Atlantic (Figure 8). Among other things, signatures of the Bølling-Allerød and Younger Dryas oscillations are readily discernible on the density curves. This discovery puts an end to the speculations, however groundless, as to the "older than the LGM" age of the last Beringian ice-expansion.

Also, it was found that another distinctive event had accompanied the onset and growth of North Pacific glaciation—an order of magnitude increase in the number and volume of volcanic ash beds (Leg 145... 1993). To me, the simultaneity of these two events strongly suggests that the source of ice-rafted debris recovered by the drilling should be looked for in southern Beringia itself, not in remote areas of Arctic Siberia or Alaska. The major volcanic event that "dwarfs any earlier ash eruptions" of the Kamchatka-Aleutian region can be accounted for only by the buildup of a thick local ice sheet, and by its static pressure capable of squeezing out the gases and lavas from deep-set volcanic centers.

The evidence for Beringian glaciation is constantly mounting. By now it has gathered critical mass sufficient to warrant attempts at figuring out the size and shape of the former ice sheet. A tentative reconstruction of a Beringian paleo-ice sheet grounded on the Chukchi and Bering continental shelves is presented in Figure 9. The top of the ice sheet reached an altitude of 2,000 m a.s.l., and its northern margin, buttressed by the Central-Arctic ice shelf, was thick enough to ground on the submarine Chukchi Borderland (i.e., on the Arlis Plateau, Northwind Ridge, and Chukchi Cap) at depths of 300 to 700 or 800 m, probably even deeper.

The southern margin of the ice sheet was fringed by the Bering ice shelf floating in the deep basin of the Bering Sea. The exceptionally great depths of the sea's "canyons" (Sholl et al. 1970) imply the abnormally great thickness of the ice shelf, which in turn suggests that the latter was buttressed by the Commander-Aleutian Ridge. It was across this ridge, through deep straits and shallow saddles, that the Beringian ice was released into the North Pacific Ocean. Another source of North Pacific icebergs seems to have been the Okhtsk-Sea ice sheet (Grosswald and Hughes 1998).

In fact, the Kotilainen-Shackleton density curves suggest that armadas of icebergs were periodically ejected, in synchrony with glacial events of the North Atlantic, into the North Pacific. A scenario of this kind was suggested earlier for the North Atlantic; now there are grounds to apply it to the North Pacific. And if the North Atlantic was partially surrounded by huge ice sheets and ice shelves, isn't it sensible to assume that the North Pacific Ocean was characterized by the same paleo-glacial environment?

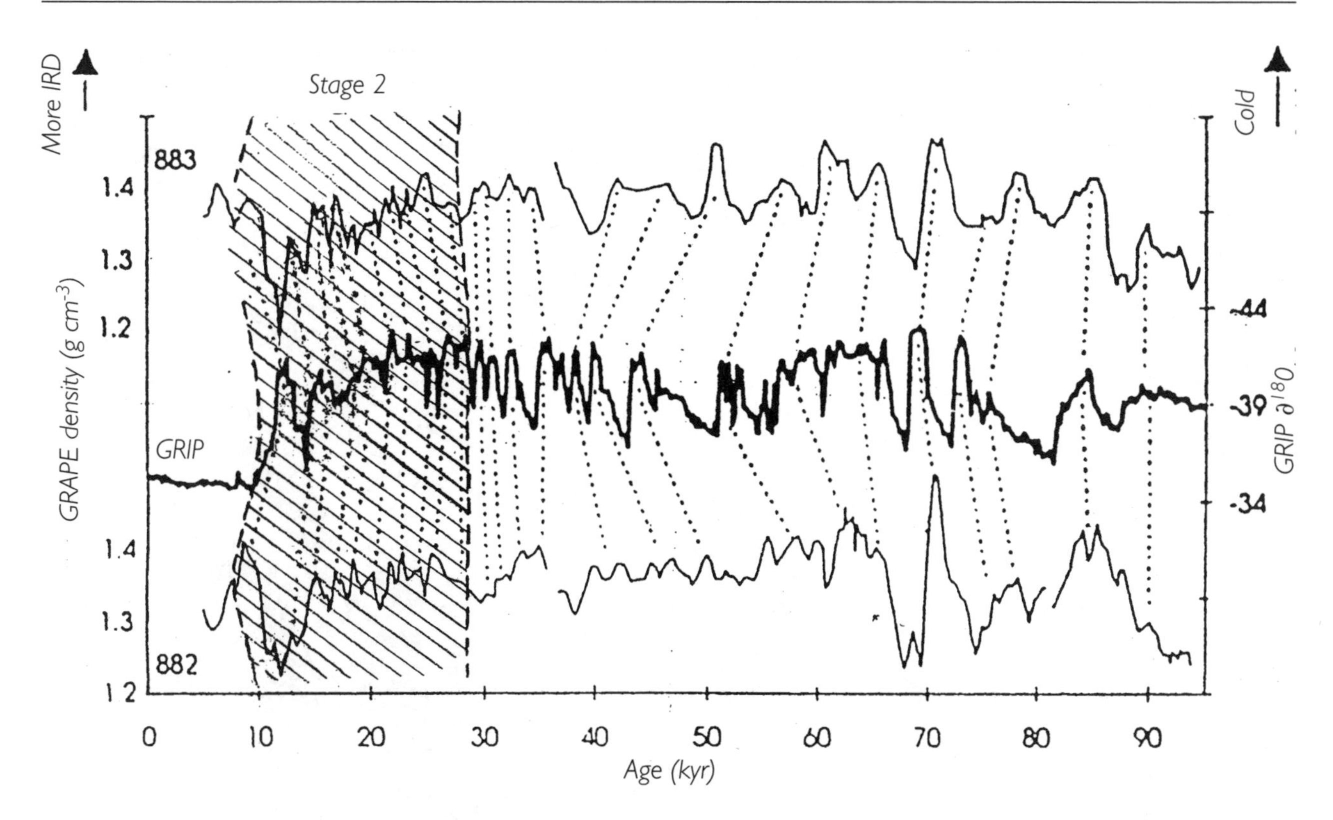

Figure 8. Density variation curves from ODP 145 drilling sites 882 and 883 (thin lines) plotted against oxygen isotope record from the GRIP ice core in Summit, Greenland (thick line). Their possible correlation is shown by dotted lines. After Kotilainen and Shackleton (1995). The isotope Stage 2 zone is added by this author.

Conclusions

GEOLOGICAL EVIDENCE, largely derived from glacial geomorphology, suggests that the Arctic outskirts of Eurasia, including its Beringian shelf, were occupied by a continuous ice sheet during the last glacial maximum. Extensive glacier complexes formed simultaneously in nearby mountain ranges, while ice-dammed lakes inundated the Siberian lowlands and intermontane basins. A part of the system, the Beringian ice sheet, was centered on the southern Chukchi Sea, spread out to the shallow Beaufort-Sea and Bering-Sea shelves, and continued, as floating ice shelves, into the deep Bering Sea and the Central Arctic Ocean. Given this paleogeography of Arctic Eurasia, the true scenery of Ice-Age Beringia differed greatly from its conventional image. Instead of an ice-free steppe or grassland landscape favoring the periglacial biotas and prehistoric humans, there extended, for a few million km^2, a huge polar ice sheet, deadly cold and lifeless. In other words, there was not a wide Bering Land Bridge open for the overland Asian migrations to North America, but an enormous icy highland, inhospitable and impenetrable for plants, animals, and humans. An alternative maritime migration route, the one along the North Pacific Rim, also would have been obstructed by the glacier complexes of the Sea of Okhotsk and adjacent mountains, as well as by the ice shelf and ice domes of southern Beringia.

Hence, overland Asian migration to North America was improbable during the height of glaciation, when an ice sheet closed off the migratory paths. Neither was it probable during Holocene time, when sea-level rise did the same to the paths by flooding the Bering Strait. Only during a relatively short and warm late-Glacial interval—namely, during the Bølling-Allerød interstade—was crossing of Beringia possible for animals and prehistoric humans. Notably, the earliest late Weichselian Stone-Age industries in Alaska, the Clovis and Folsom complexes, were dated to 12,000 and 11,000 yr B.P., respectively (Hoffecker et al. 1993), not to the LGM. It was not before that warm interval that the process of ice-sheet shrinkage went far enough to open ice-free paths, and it was well after that interval that the process of sea rise reached the level of flooding the strait and closed the paths. One may speculate that earlier, during pre-Weichselian glaciations, Asian migrations to North America were similarly constrained by ice sheets and marine transgressions.

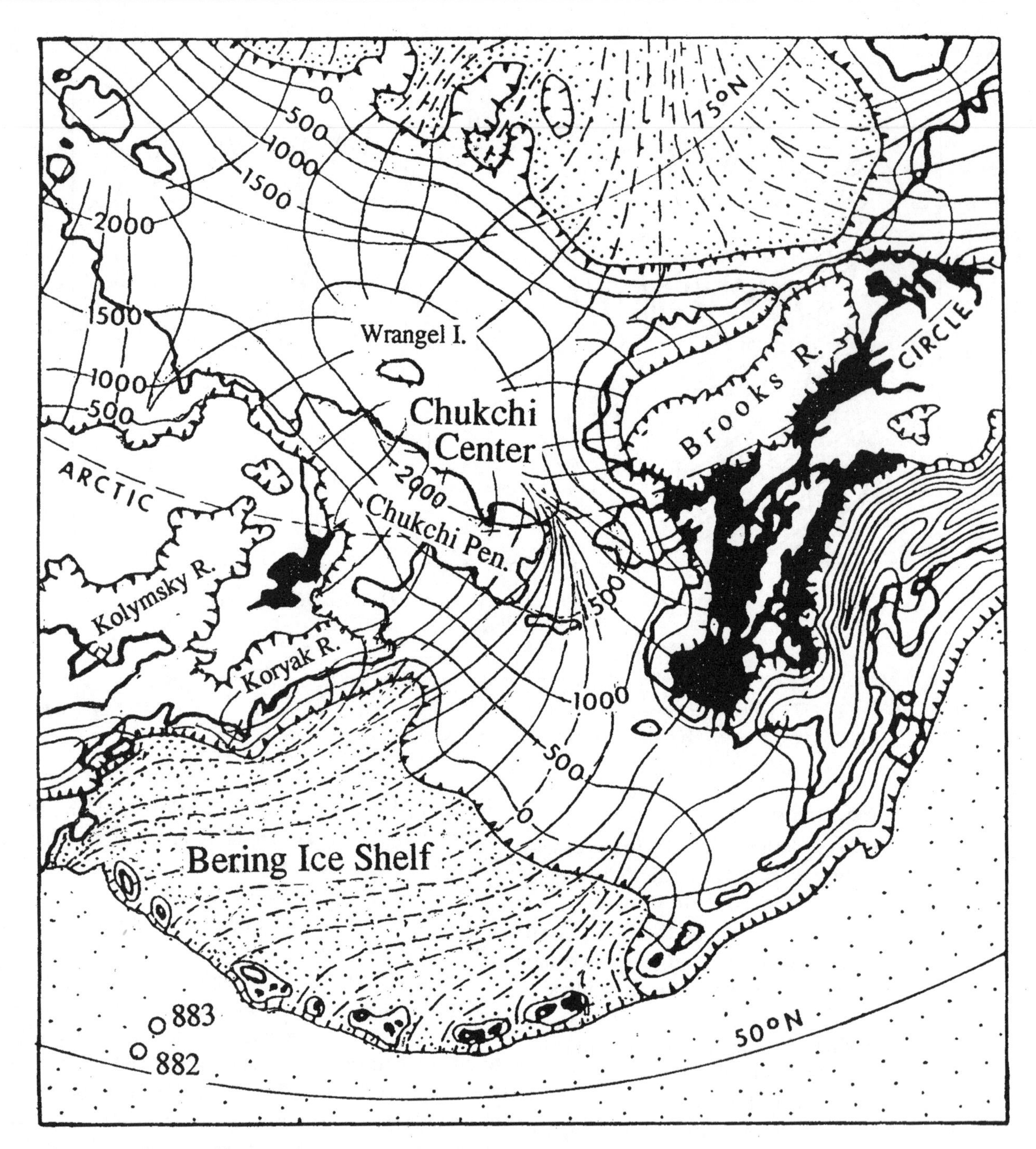

Figure 9. The late Weichselian Beringian ice sheet (a tentative reconstruction). Modified after Hughes and Hughes (1994). The numbered circles show the ODP 145 drilling sites.

Acknowledgments

I thank participants of the seminar at the Center for the Study of the First Americans, and personally Robson Bonnichsen and Terence Hughes, for their encouragement and for the very idea of this paper. My thanks also are due to Susan Simpson for her editing work.

References Cited

Alekseev, M. N. (editor)
1991 *Atlas of the Shelf Regions of Eurasia for the Mesozoic and Cenozoic.* Robertson Group, Llandidno, Gwinedd, U.K.

Andreyeva, S. M., and L. L. Isayeva
1988 The Dynamics of an Ice Sheet on the Northeastern Central Siberian Plateau during the Late Pleistocene. *Polar Geography and Geology* 12: 212–220.

Arkhipov, S. A., V. I. Astakhov, I. A.Volkov, V. S. Volkova, and V. A. Panychev
1980 *Paleogeografiya Zapadno-Sibirskoi ravniny v epokhu pozdnezyryanskogo lednikovogo maksimuma [Paleogeography of the West Siberian Plain during the Late Zyryan glacial maximum].* Nauka, Novosibirsk.

Arkhipov, S. A., L. L. Isayeva, V. G. Bespaly, and O. Glushkova
1986 Glaciation of Siberia and North East USSR. In *Quaternary Glaciations in the Northern Hemisphere,* edited by V. Sibrava, D. Q. Bowen, and G. M. Richmond, pp. 463–474. (*Quaternary Science Reviews* 5) Pergamon, Oxford.

Arslanov, Kh. A., A. S. Lavrov, L. M. Potapenko, T. V. Tertychnaya, and S. B. Chernov
1987 New Data on the Late Pleistocene and Early Holocene Geochronology in the Northern Pechora Lowland. In *Novyye dannyye po geokhronologiy i chetvertichnogo perioda [New data on geochronology of the Quaternary],* edited by Y.-M. K. Punning et al., pp. 101–111. Nauka, Moscow.

Baranova, Y. P., and S. F. Biske
1964 *Severo-Vostok SSSR [The Northeastern USSR].* Nauka, Moscow.

Benson, S. L.
1993 Glacially Deformed Sediments of Lavrentiya Bay, Chukotka Peninsula, Far Eastern Russia, and the North Shore of St. Lawrence Island, Alaska. In *Glaciotectonics and Mapping Glacial Deposits,* edited by J. S. Aber, pp. 1–8. Hignell, Winnipeg.

Benson, S., J. Brigham-Grette, P. Heiser, D. Hopkins, V. Ivanov, and A. Lozhkin
1994 Glaciotectonic and Geochronologic Evidence for Extensive Early Wisconsinan Glaciation in Beringia. *Geological Society of America 1994 Annual Meeting. Abstracts with Programs.* Sesattle, WA, A308.

Biryukov, V. Y., M. A. Faustova, P. A. Kaplin, Y.A. Pavlidis, E. A. Romanova, and A. A. Velichko
1988 The Paleogeography of Arctic Shelf and Coastal Zone of Eurasia at the Time of the Last Glaciation (18,000 yr. B.P.). *Palaeogeography, Palaeoclimatology, Palaeoecology* 68: 117–125

Black, R.
1976 Late Quaternary Glacial Events, Aleutian Islands, Alaska. In *Project 73/1/24 Quaternary Glaciations in the Northern Hemisphere. Report N 3,* edited by V. Sibrava. Bellingham-Prague, pp. 285–301.

Brigham-Grette, J., S. Benson, D. M. Hopkins, P. Heiser, V. F. Ivanov, and A. Basilyan
1992 Middle and Late Pleistocene Russian Glacial Ice Extent in the Bering Strait Region: Results of Recent Field Work. *Geological Society of America 1992 Annual Meeting. Abstracts with Programs.* Cincinnati, Ohio, A346.

Elverhøi, A., and A. Solheim
1983 The Barents Sea Ice Sheet—A Sedimentological Discussion. *Polar Research* 1: 23–42

Erlich, E. N., and I. V. Melekestsev
1974 Commander Islands. In *Kamchatka, Kurilskiye i Komandorskiye ostrova [Kamchatka Peninsula, the Kuril and Commander Islands],* edited by I. V. Luchitsky, pp. 327–337. Nauka, Moscow.

Fastook, J. L., and T. J. Hughes
1991 Changing Ice Loads on the Earth's Surface during the Last Glaciation Cycle. In *Glacial Isostasy, Sea-level and Mantle Rheology,* edited by R. Sabadini, K. Lambeck, and E. Boschi, pp. 165–20. Kluwer Academic Publishers, Dordrecht.

Gataullin V., L. Polyak, O. Epstein, and B. Romanyuk
1993 Glacigenic Deposits of the Central Deep: A Key to the Late Quaternary Evolution of the Eastern Barents Sea. *Boreas* 22: 47–57.

Glushkova, O. Y.
1984 Morphology and Paleogeography of the Late Pleistocene Glaciations in the Northeastern USSR. In *Pleistotsenovyye oledeneniya vostoka Aziyi [Pleistocene glaciations in Eastern Asia*], pp. 28–42, Magadan.

Gramberg, I. S., and Y. N. Kulakov (editors)
1983 *Osnovnyye problemy paleogeografiyi pozdnego kainozoya Arktiki [Basic Problems in Late Cenozoic Paleogeography of the Arctic].* Nedra, Leningrad.

Grosswald, M. G.
1980 Late Weichselian Ice Sheet of Northern Eurasia. *Quaternary Research* 13: 1–32.

1988 Antarctic-style Ice Sheet in the Northern Hemisphere: Toward the New Global Glacial Theory. *Polar Geography and Geology* 12: 239–267.

1990 An Ice Sheet on the East Siberian Shelf in the Late Pleistocene. *Polar Geography and Geology* 14: 294–304.

1996 Evidence for Invading Northeastern Siberia by an Ice Sheet Advancing from the Arctic Shelf. *Doklady Akademii Nauk,* vol. 350, no. 4, 535-540.

1998 Late Weichselian Ice Sheets in Arctic and Pacific Siberia. *Quaternary International,* vol. 45/46, 3-18.

Grosswald, M. G., and T. J. Hughes
1995 Paleoglaciology's Grand Unsolved Problem. *Journal of Glaciology* 41, No 138: 313–332.

Grosswald, M. G., W. Karlén, Z. Shishorina, and A. Bodin
1992 Glacial Landforms and the Age of Deglaciation in the Tiksi Area, East Siberia. *Geografiska Annaler* 74A: 295–304.

Grosswald, M. G., and V. B. Spektor
1993 The Glacial Relief of the Tiksi Region (West Shore of Buor-Khaya Inlet, Northern Yakutia). *Polar Geography and Geology* 17: 154–166.

Grosswald, M. G., and Y. I. Vozovik
1984 A Marine Ice Cap in South Beringia (A Working Hypothesis). *Polar Geography and Geology* 8: 128–146.

Heiser, P. A., D. M. Hopkins, J. Brigham-Grette, S. Benson, V. F. Ivanov, and A. Lozhkin
1992 Pleistocene Glacial Geology of St.Lawrence Island, Alaska. *Geological Society of America 1992 Annual Meeting. Abstracts with Programs.* Cincinnati, Ohio, A345.

Hoffecker, J. F., W. R. Powers, and T. Goebel
1993 The Colonization of Beringia and the Peopling of the New World. *Science* 259: 46–53.

Hopkins, D. M.
1972 The Paleogeography and Climatic history of Beringia during Late Cenozoic Time. *Inter-Nord* 12: 121–150.

Hughes, T.
1995 A Search for Marine Ice Sheets in Pleistocene Beringia. *Tikhookeanskaya Geologiya* 14(4): 37–49

Hughes, T., R. Bonnichsen, J. L. Fastook, B. Hughes, and M. Grosswald
1991 Pleistocene Beringia: An Outright Land Bridge or a Glacial Valve Constraining Asian Migrations to North America? In: *INQUA 13th International Conference, Abstracts,* Beijing, 144.

Hughes, T. J., G. H. Denton, and M. G. Grosswald
1977 Was There a Late-Würm Arctic Ice Sheet? *Nature* 266: 596–602.

Hughes, B. A., and T. J. Hughes
1994 Transgressions: Rethinking Beringian Glaciations. *Palaeogeography, Palaeoclimatology, Palaeoecology* 110: 275–294.

Huybrechts, P., and S. T'siobbel
1995 Thermomechanical Modelling of Northern Hemisphere Ice Sheets with a Two-level Mass-balance Parameterization. *Annals of Glaciology* 21: 111–116.

Kaplina, T. N., and A. V. Lozhkin
1982 On the Aage of the "Icy Complex" of the Arctic Lowlands of Yakutia. *Izvestiya Akademii Nauk, Seriya Geograficheskaya,* N 2: 84–95.

Kartashov, I. P.
1962 Origin of Lake Krasnoye. *Doklady Akademii Nauk* 142, No 1: 156–158.

Kind, N. V., and B. N. Leonov (editors)
1982 *Antropogen Taimyra [The Pleistocene of Taimyr Peninsula].* Moscow, Nauka.

Kolosov, D. M.
1947 *Problemy drevnego oledeneniya Severo-Vostoka SSSR [Problems of former glaciation in the Northeastern USSR)].* Glavsevmorput, Moscow-Leningrad.

Kotilainen, A. T., and N. J. Shackleton
1995 Rapid Climate Variability in the North Pacific Ocean during the past 95,000 years. *Nature* 377: 323–326.

Laukhin, S. A., and N. I. Drozdov
1991 Paleoecological Aspect of Paleolithic Man Settling in Northern Asia and his Migration to North America. In *INQUA Symposium on on stratigraphy and correlation of Quaternary deposits of the Asian and Pacific Regions,* pp. 133–144 (CCOP Proc., v. 22), Bangkok.

Laukhin, S. A., N. I. Drozdov, V. A. Panychev, and S. V. Velichko
1989 The Age of Last Glaciation in Northern East Chukotka. *Izvestiya Akademii Nauk, Seriya Geograficheskaya,* N 3: 136–140.

Lavrov, A. S.
1977 Kola-Mezen, Barents-Pechoran and Novaya Zemlya-Kolvan Paleo-ice Streams. In *Structura i Dinamika Poslednego Evropeiskogo Lednikovogo Pokrova [Structure and Dynamics of the Last European Ice Sheet],* edited by N. S. Chebotariova, pp. 81–100. Moscow, Nauka.

Leg 145 scientific party
1993 Paleoceanographic Record of North Pacific Quantified. *EOS* 74 (36): 406, 411.

Lindstrom, D. R., and D. R. MacAyeal
1989 Scandinavian, Siberian, and Arctic Ocean Glaciation: Effect of Holocene Atmospheric CO_2 Variations. *Science* 245: 628–631.

Marsiat, I.
1994 Simulation of the Northern Hemisphere Continental Ice Sheets over the Last Glacial-interglacial Cycle: Experiments with a Latitude-longitude Vertically Integrated Ice-sheet Model Coupled to a Zonally Averaged Climate Model. *Palaeoclimates—Data and Modelling* 1: 59–98.

Morlan, R. E.
1987 The Pleistocene Archaeology of Beringia. In *The evolution of human hunting,* edited by M. H. Nitecki and D. V. Nitecki, pp. 267–307, Plenum, N.Y.

Pavlidis, Y. A.
1992 *Shelf Mirovogo okeana v pozdnechetvertichnoye vremya [Shelf of the World Ocean during the Late Quaternary]*. Nauka, Moskva.

Salvigsen, O.
1981 Radiocarbon Dated Raised Beaches in Kong Karls Land, Svalbard, and their Consequences for the Glacial History of the Barents Sea Area. *Geografiska Annaler* 63A: 283–291.

Sættem, J., D. A. R. Poole, K. L. Ellingsen, and H. P. Sejrup
1992 Glacial Geology of Outer Bjørnøyrenna, Southwestern Barents Sea. *Marine Geology* 103: 15–51.

Scholl, D. W., E. C. Buffington, D. M. Hopkins, and T. R. Alpha
1970 The Structure and Origin of the Large Submarine Canyons of the Bering Sea. *Marine Geology* 8: 187–210.

Sher, A. V.
1976 Role of Beringia in Formation of the Holarctic Mammal Fauna during the Late Pleistocene. In *Beringiya v kainozoye [Beringia during the Cenozoic]*, pp. 227–241. Far-eastern Branch, USSR Academy of Sciences, Vladivostok.

Tarakanov, Y. A., M. G. Grosswald, N. S. Kambarov, and V. A. Prikhodko
1987 New Data on the Connection between the Figure of Earth and Former Glaciations. *Izvestiya Akademii Nauk, Seriya Geograficheskaya* 295: 1084–1089.

Turner, C. G.
1989 Teeth and Prehistory in Asia. *Scientific American* No 2, 88–96.

Vaskovsky, A.P.
1959 Short Account of Vegetation, Climate and Chronology of the Quaternary in the Upper Reaches of the Kolyma and Indigirka Rivers and on the Northern Coast of the Sea of Okhotsk. In *Lednikovy period na territoriyi Evropeiskoi chasti SSSR i Sibiri [Ice Age in the European USSR and Siberia]*, edited by K. K. Markov and A. I. Popov. Moscow State University, pp. 510–545.

Velichko, A. A. (editor)
1993 *Evolution of Landscapes and Climates of Northern Eurasia. Late Pleistocene–Holocene. 1 -Regional Paleogeography*. Nauka, Moskva.

Vorren, T., M. Hald, and E. Lebesbye
1988 Late Cenozoic Environments in the Barents Sea. *Paleoceanography* 3: 601–612.

Vorren, T. O., and Y. Kristoffersen
1986 Late Quaternary Glaciation in the South-western Barents Sea. *Boreas* 15: 51–59.

Yurtsev, B. A.
1976 Problems in the Late Cenozoic Paleogeography of Beringia (in the Light of Pphytogeographic Data). In *Beringiya v kainozoye [Beringia during the Cenozoic]*. Vladivostok, pp. 101–120.

Impact of Ice-related Plant Nutrients on Glacial Margin Environments

Mort D. Turner[1]
Edward J. Zeller[2,3]
Gisela A. Dreschhoff[3]
Joanne C. Turner[1]

Abstract

A significant number of proboscideans (mammoths, mastodons, and other elephant-like mammals) and proboscidean kill sites have been found along the margins of former ice sheets, especially the southern margins of the Laurentide ice sheet of North America. We postulate that the abundance of large mammals and human predators in these areas is the indirect result of the availability of large quantities of nutrients from the melting ice.

In most plant species, growth is limited by one or more of three essential plant nutrients: potassium (K), phosphate (P), and fixed nitrogen. Glacial-margin environments are enriched in both K and P, particularly in areas where the glaciers have overridden igneous or metamorphic terrains. Mechanical grinding processes along the ice-rock interface result in chemical-bond breakage and increased grain-surface area that effectively increase the solubility of these nutrients, thus enhancing their availability to plants growing in freshly exposed glacial deposits and making K and P in excess supply in the water-saturating fresh glacial deposits along the ice fronts. Therefore, it is the availability of fixed nitrogen that acts as a practical limit to growth for most plant species along the ice fronts.

Substantial concentrations of nitrate (NO_3), as well as small amounts of ammonium ion (NH_4), are present in glacial ice in both Antarctica and Greenland. The nitrate at high latitudes originates in both the stratosphere and the troposphere. A substantial portion of the stratospheric NO_3 is produced by solar-terrestrial interactions. The tropospheric portion of the NO_3 is the result of both solar-terrestrial interactions and strictly terrestrial processes, such as lightning, spray from the ocean, and static discharge from impact of snow and dust particles. Some of the NO_3 and most of the NH_4 are the product of biological processes. Fixed nitrogen from tropospheric and stratospheric sources has accumulated in the Pleistocene and Holocene ice sheets for thousands of years. Sublimation processes, active along the ice margin because of katabatic winds that flow from the interior, increase the concentration of fixed nitrogen in the ice. Fixed nitrogen is released through runoff at the melting margin. This provides a significant addition to the fixed-nitrogen budget for plants growing in soils within the marginal zone. This will, in turn, increase the total biological productivity of the marginal zone. The presence of all the essential plant nutrients in the water that saturates unconsolidated glacial deposits may permit a kind of natural hydroponic plant growth to develop rapidly, thereby accelerating soil formation. Once soils form, the continuing presence of solutions containing complete assemblages of nutrients permits an unusually high level

1. Institute of Arctic and Alpine Research, University of Colorado, Boulder, CO 80309
2. Deceased January 14, 1996
3. Space Technology Center, University of Kansas, Lawrence, KS 66045

of productivity to be maintained. This is especially true where an ice margin remains essentially stable for long periods.

A portion of the fixed nitrogen discharged into the marginal zone of an ice sheet leaves the area by way of the water draining from the marginal zone. Some of this fixed nitrogen becomes incorporated into floodplain silt that is the source of wind-deposited loess. It is in part responsible for the nutrient richness of loess deposits. During the late Pleistocene and early Holocene, at ~30–8 ka B.P. (approximately 30,000 to 8000 yrs B.P.) large ice sheets repeatedly built up and melted back on the continents of the Northern Hemisphere. These ice sheets had volumes of as much as 60 million cubic km at their maximum at ~18 ka B.P., making them act as gigantic reservoirs of NO_3. The NO_3 was released along their edges during melting of the glaciers, and thus large quantities were made available to enhance plant growth in these areas. An abundance of small and large animals flourished in this desirable environment.

Introduction

DURING LATE PLEISTOCENE and early Holocene time (Figure 1), at ~30 ka (approximately 30,000 years) to ~8 ka B.P. (approximately 8000 yrs B.P.), large areas of North America and Eurasia were covered by thick ice sheets (Andrews 1987; Arkhipov et al. 1986; Denton and Hughes 1981; Dyke and Prest 1986; Flint 1963, 1971; Geological Survey of Canada 1984; Grosswald 1980, 1988; Grosswald and Glebova 1992; Richmond and Fullerton 1986; Sibrava et al. 1986; Velichko 1977) (Figures 2, 3, and 4). The southern margins of the major North American ice sheet (the late Pleistocene Laurentide ice sheet) (Figure 4) are shown in some detail on a series of maps by Soller (1992, 1993, 1994, 1997, 1998). The advancing ice sheets (Ives 1974, Love and Love 1974, Nichols 1974) disrupted and displaced plant and animal assemblages southward.

Traditional assumptions have been that the marginal zones of the Pleistocene ice sheets were cold and biologically unproductive. Cwynar and Ritchie, for example, indicate that Alaskan Beringia and periglacial Eurasia were low-productivity Arctic steppe-tundra (Cwynar and Ritchie 1980, Ritchie and Cwynar 1982). Also, Soffer (1985:149–157, 169–211) indicates climatic environments in the central Russian Plain that would have been difficult for life during glacial episodes. However, paleontological and archaeological evidence show that the ice margins and periglacial margins, especially along the southern margins of these ice sheets, were populated by a diverse flora, megafauna, and humans (Bonnichsen 1980; Butzer 1971, 1976; Grichuk 1972; Guthrie 1968, 1982, 1996; Hopkins 1972; Hopkins et al. 1982; Martin 1982; Martin and Klein 1984; Martin and Wright 1967; Schweger 1982; Soffer 1985:169-211; Velichko 1973; Velichko and Morozova 1969; Zeller et al. 1988). As Benedict (1975:73) has pointed out, the human "tendency to exploit the resources of marginal environments whenever climatic conditions permit remains as strong today as at any time during the past 12,000 years."

Selected Abbreviations Used in This Paper

B.P.—before present
O(^{1}D)—Excited oxygen or atomic oxygen
GCR—Galactic Cosmic Rays
H—Holocene
ka—kiloyears or 1,000 years
LGM—last glacial maximum
ng—nanogram (billionth of a gram; 10^{-6} g)
PSC—Polar Stratospheric Clouds
SPE—Solar Proton Events
Tg—Terragrams (unit of 10^{12} grams)

An understanding of the contents of ice sheets leads the authors to the view that the ice sheets themselves were the source of the essential plant and animal nutrients. This included a limited amount of nitrate introduced by direct deposition from the upper atmosphere in the vicinity of the auroral ring (Qin et al. 1992, Zeller and Parker 1981) and by terrestrial nitrates from the troposphere (Delmas et al. 1985, Legrand and Delmas 1988). Nitrate (NO_3) is the terminal oxidation state of nitrogen which can occur in a number of oxidized states of nitrogen/oxygen combinant. Fixed nitrogen is a specific term for the chemically soluble form of nitrogen available to plants. Fixed nitrogen in the atmosphere may occur in reduced form as ammonia (NH_3) or in a number of oxidized states as N_2O, NO_x ($NO + NO_2$), and odd nitrogen NO_y (N_2, NO, NO_2, NO_3, N_2O_5, and HNO_3). Nitrous oxide (N_2O), produced by the biospheric nitrogen cycle, can be transported up from the earth's

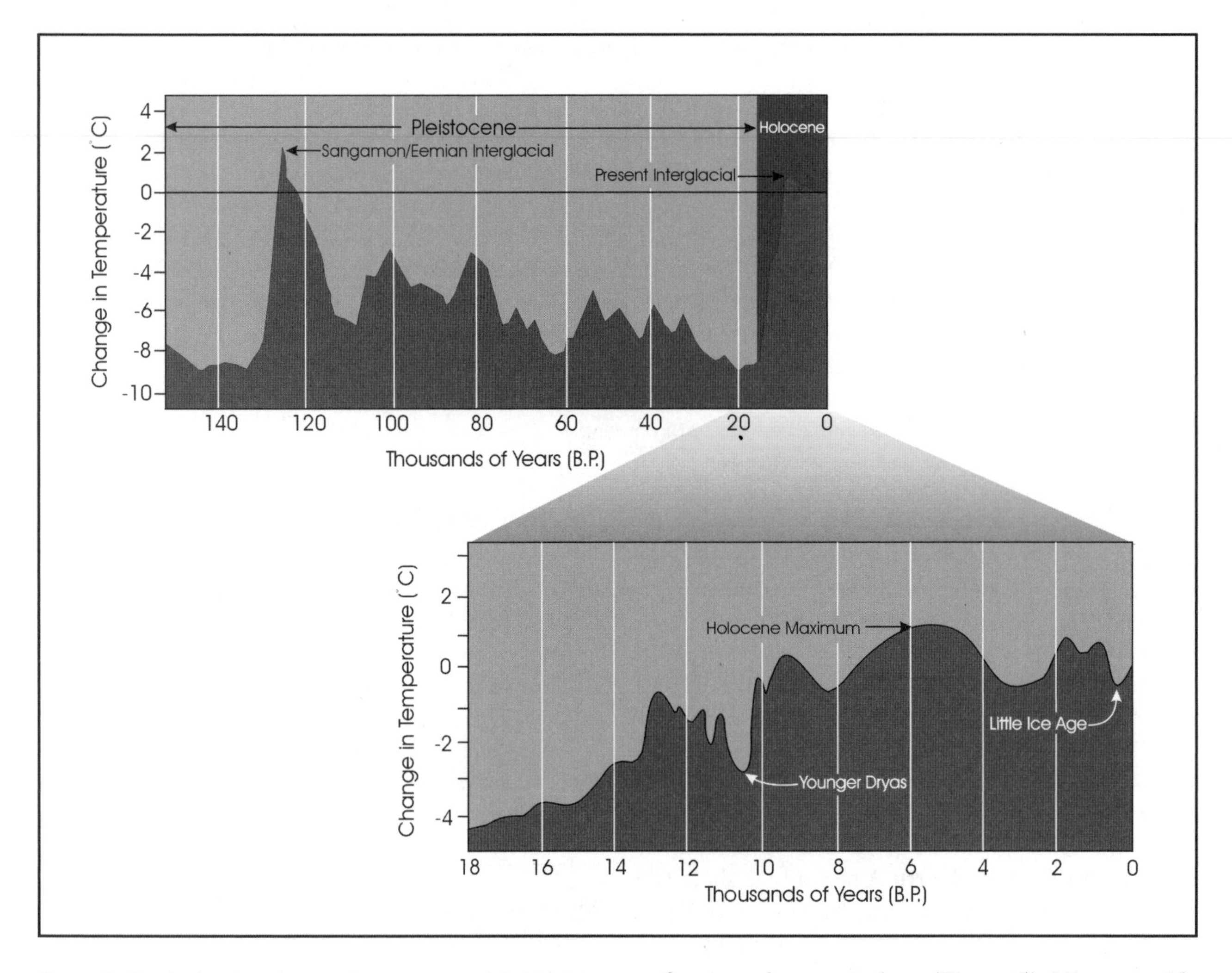

Figure 1. Graph showing changes in temperature during the last 150,000 years, with the expanded curve for the last 18,000 years.

Temperature changes are shown for the last 150 ka. This time period covers the late Pleistocene, including the last interglacial, the Sangamon/Eemian interglacial, several cold episodes (stadials), warmer episodes (interstadials), and the present warm interglacial (the Holocene). During the Sangamon and the Holocene interglacials, the Northern Hemisphere ice sheets were melted away entirely, with the exception of the Greenland ice sheet. During the glacial period between the Sangamon and the Holocene, the Northern Hemisphere ice sheets waxed and waned with the fluctuating climates. The inset, an enlargement of the curve for the last 18,000 years, shows the lesser fluctuations of the climate of the Holocene. [Modified from EarthQuest 1991: insert.]

surface into the stratosphere (Figure 5). Nitrous oxide is an important source of odd nitrogen (NO_y) in the stratosphere, where it can react with an excited oxygen atom $O(^1D)$, which is produced by photolysis of ozone (O_3), to produce NO. Other sources of NO_y include ion chemistry associated with atmospheric ionization. Simple reaction chains ultimately can produce nitrate ion (NO_3^-) or nitric acid (HNO_3) in the presence of moisture in the atmosphere. HNO_3 is transferred from the atmosphere by photolysis in the atmosphere or by removal to the surface in the form of precipitation (Figure 6).

Other trace elements and factors necessary for all plant and animal life were present at the ice-sheet margins in sufficient quantities to allow the high productivity necessary to account for the plants, humans, and other animals that made up the environments indicated by the fossil record.

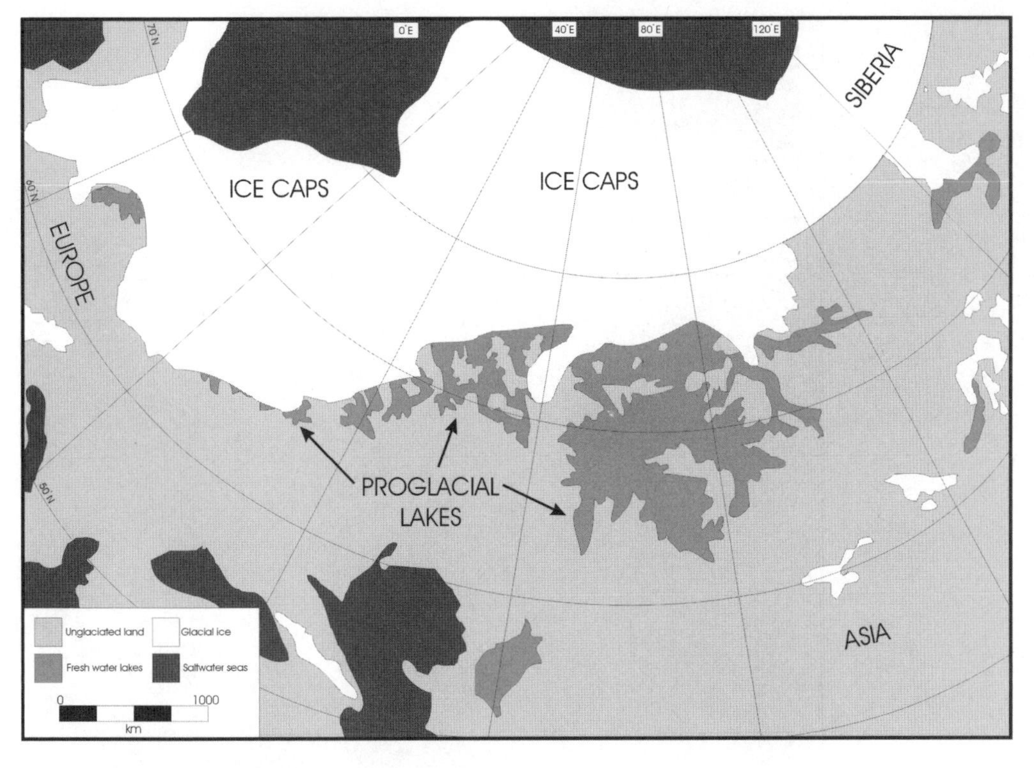

Figure 2. Extent of late Pleistocene ice sheets of Eurasia. At the late Pleistocene glacial maximum, about 18 ka B.P., several ice sheets merged to cover most of Europe north of the Alps, northern Russia, most of northwestern Siberia, and the Arctic Basin continental shelf. Where the land surface sloped downward to the north, glacial meltwater accumulated along the southern edges of the ice sheets. Refugia also existed along the southern front of the ice sheets where large Pleistocene mammals and possibly humans survived the late Pleistocene Ice Age and into the Holocene (Forman et al. 1995:115; Soffer 1985:189–211; see Figure 13, this paper). In some areas the level of the meltwater exceeded the height of the southern divides, and drainage rivers flowed south into the Aral and Caspian Seas. [After Grosswald 1980, 1988, 1992].

Requirements for Plant Growth

Several characteristics of glacial-margin environments have strong positive effects on biological productivity. In general, plant growth is controlled by six major factors, the lack of any one of which can act as the primary limit to growth in a specific environment. These factors are as follows:

(1) Availability of adequate sunlight;

(2) Availability of adequate water;

(3) Sufficient periods of above-freezing temperatures;

(4) Adequate supplies of elements essential for plant growth: carbon (C), hydrogen (H), oxygen (O), phosphorus (P), potassium (K), nitrogen (N), sulfur (S), magnesium (Mg), calcium (C), iron (Fe), manganese (Mn), copper (Cu), zinc (Zn), molybdenum (Mo), and boron (B).

Each of these factors is important to plant productivity and, subsequently, to animal nutrition and productivity.

Availability of light (factor 1) in glacial-margin environments of the late Pleistocene was assured because the retreating ice exposed new terrain that had been free of plant cover for decades or centuries (Birks 1980; Jacobson and Birks 1980; Watson 1980; Whiteside at al. 1980; Wright 1980). Water supply (factor 2) from melting ice was enhanced at times when temperatures were high, so that any plant stress resulting from rising temperatures tended to be

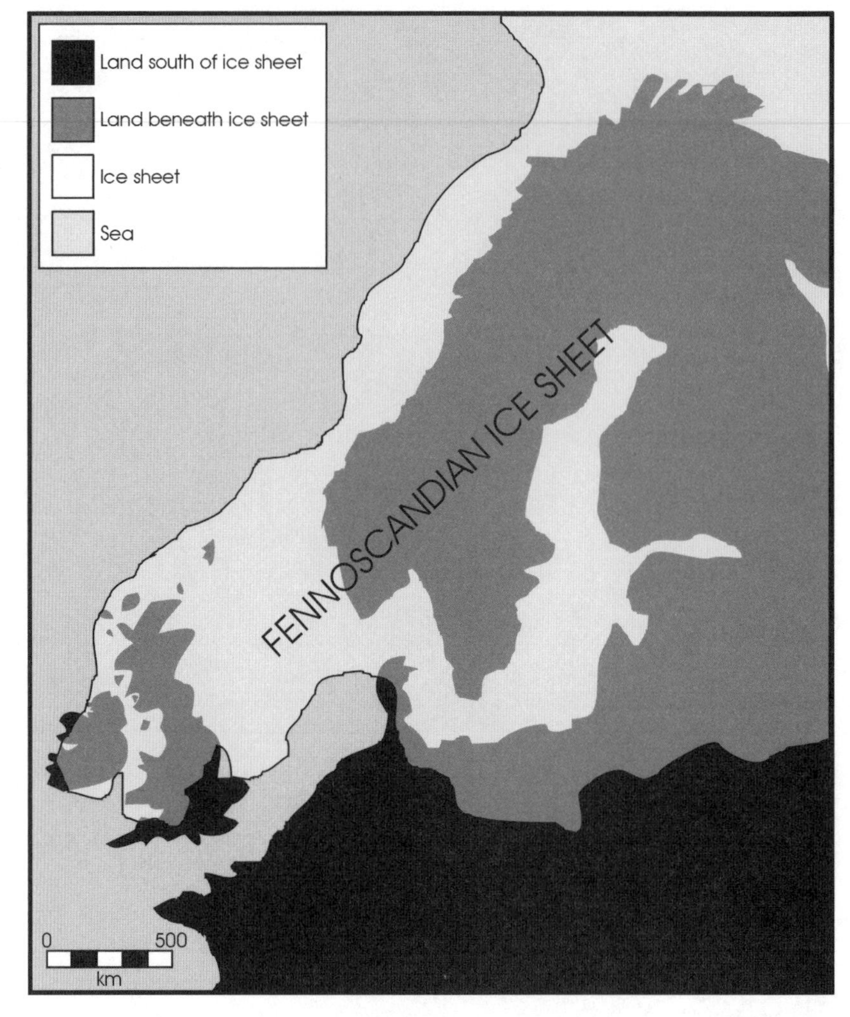

Figure 3. Extent of the Fennoscandian Ice Sheet in northwest Europe. During the late Pleistocene glacial maximum the western part of the Eurasian ice sheets covered all of Scandinavia, most of Great Britain, and most of Ireland. This westward extension is called the Fennoscandian ice sheet. [Modified from Aubrey 1985:85.]

moderated. The presence of numerous proglacial lakes along the southern edges of major ice sheets in the Northern Hemisphere indicates the abundance of meltwater during periods of maximum extent of the ice sheets (Figure 2), as well as during periods of retreat (Figures 7 and 8). The lengths of periods of above-freezing temperatures (factor 3) were dependent upon the latitude of the glacial margin in question and the orbital parameters of earth that existed at the time. It is also important to note that the existence of katabatic wind-flow down the ice sheet (similar to a chinook) tended to increase the average temperature in the marginal zone. The net warming to the margin of the ice sheet by the katabatic wind is limited by cooling of the katabatic air because of sublimation of the snow and ice. The magnitude of the increase depends on the total change in altitude of the air mass from its point of origin over the interior of the glacier to that in the marginal zone. The effect may be small if the ice sheet is thin, but it will always be in the direction of an increase in temperature.

The main objective of this paper is to discuss the ice-related major plant nutrients (N, P, K) that are concentrated along the glacial margin and that cause high levels of productivity in this environment. Amounts of the other elements essential for plant growth can be assumed to be adequate in and around margins of continental glaciers and ice sheets, as most are mineral elements that would have been released in abundant amounts relative to plant needs by the abrasion of glacial ice on rocks.

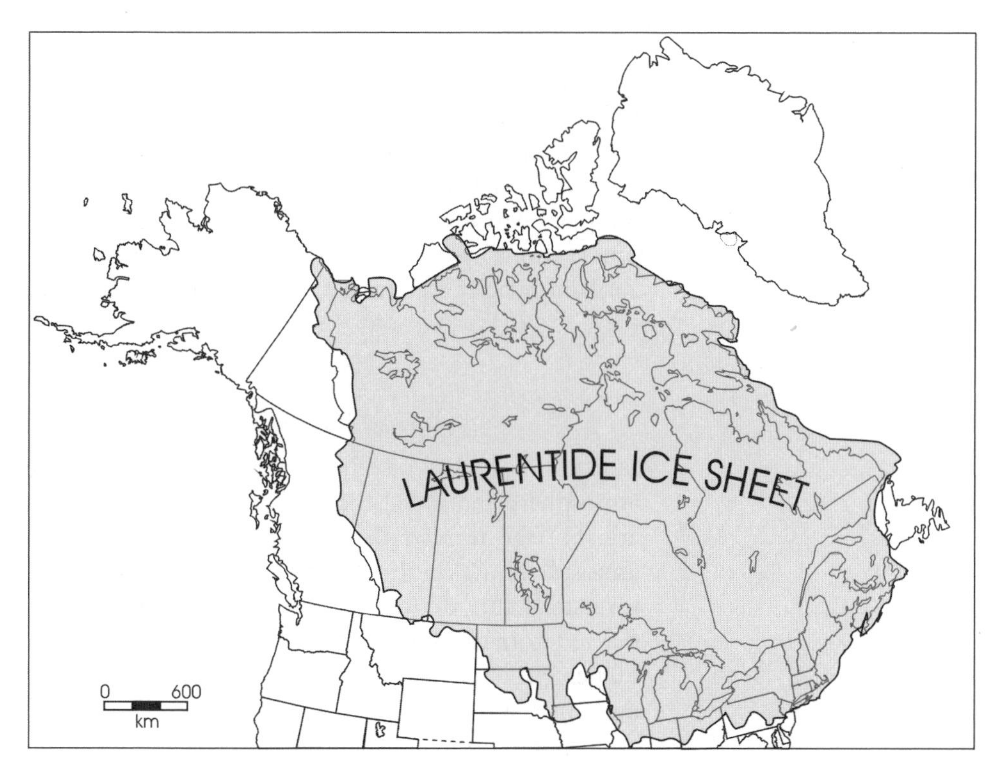

Figure 4. Laurentide Ice Sheet on North America in the Late Pleistocene. North America, showing the extent of the Laurentide ice sheet in late Pleistocene time. The ice sheet spread outward toward the margins from several accumulation centers. Several earlier Laurentide ice sheets developed, some covering larger extents, during the last 2 to 3 million years. [Modified from Andrews 1987:15, 22; Booth 1987:72; Fulton and Prest 1987:182 and Map 1703A.]

Nutrient Sources

Nutrients Derived from Rock

THE NORTH AMERICAN and Eurasian shields are made up largely of crystalline basement rocks. The basement rock mass is present as interlocking mineral aggregates. During Pleistocene time, ice sheets were advancing over the metamorphosed crystalline rock, producing finely ground glacial flour (Fulton and Prest 1987:184). Two of the essential nutrients for plant growth, P and K, were derived directly from this ground-up rock. The primary source of P is as calcium phosphate from the accessory minerals, apatite, $(CaF)Ca_4(PO_4)_3$, and collophane, $Ca_3P_2O_8.H_2O$, that are common in practically all igneous and metamorphic rocks, and many marine sediments. Potassium is widely distributed in both igneous and metamorphic terrains where orthoclase and the other K-containing feldspars and feldspathoids make up a high percentage of the crustal rocks, as they do in the northern part of the North American continent.

Erosion by ice sheets is accomplished mainly by abrasion of the basal rock into extremely fine-grained glacial flour. The nature of the grinding mechanism during glacial advance is such that highly angular grains are produced. Glacial flour, one of the major products of glacial erosion, has many orders of magnitude more surface area than does the parent rock, as shown by electron-microscopy studies (Krinsley and Doornkamp 1973; Krinsley and Newman 1965; Krinsley and Takahashi 1962; Mahaney 1995). The finely ground minerals that result from glacial abrasion have a high surface-to-volume ratio and a high proportion of distorted and dangling chemical bonds on the grain surfaces. The activation energy for ions on the surface of such grains is effectively reduced, and the solubility of the constituent ions is high. The erosion products of ice-sheet movement are incorporated in the glacier and carried along with the basal ice in the direction of the ice movement until they reach the zone in the ice sheet where melting and solution take place. Glacial meltwater flows rapidly down the interior, base, and margins of the ice, picking up a heavy load of glacial erosion products in the process. A major part of the transportation, suspension, and ultimate deposition of the glacial flour containing K and P, two of the essential nutrients, is in an aqueous environment where solution is enhanced.

Nutrients from Glacial Ice

IN VIEW OF THE ABUNDANCE of K and P generated by the grinding effects of glaciers, it is probable that plant growth in glacial-margin environments ultimately is limited by the quantity of fixed nitrogen available in these environments. Of the three necessary plant nutrients—K, P, and NO_3—only fixed nitrogen is not supplied by the rocks that were overridden by the ice.

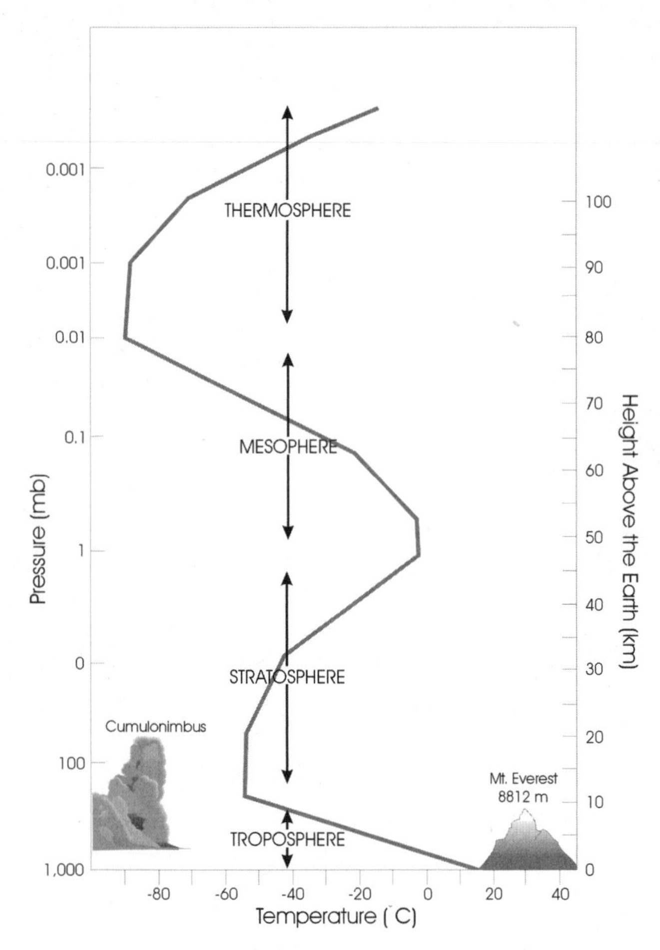

Figure 5. Atmospheric temperature/pressure zones. The Earth's atmosphere, up to about 100 km above the surface, is stratified into a series of zones characterized primarily by their pressure and temperature. Most of the clouds we see and the weather we experience are in the lower 20 km of the atmosphere, however most of the chemical reactions producing the nitrates discussed in this paper take place at higher elevations by reactions between the upper atmosphere and particles from the sun and from cosmic radiation.

The only exception to this might be the occurrence of insignificantly small amounts of ammonium (NH_4) reported in biotite (Tainosho et al. 1991).

Nitrogen fixed by inorganic processes in the atmosphere is known to be deposited on and incorporated into ice sheets, especially in the higher latitudes, as discussed below. As shown above, meltwater flowing from the margin of an ice cap can be expected to contain high enough levels of P, K, and nitrates (NO_3) (Brown et al. 1973, Gorham 1958, Johannessen and Henricksen 1978) to prevent plant stress. Natural hydroponic-type growth can proceed rapidly in such an environment, and plants growing on finely ground glacial till have the additional advantage of direct root contact with nutrient-containing substrates during times when meltwater influx is reduced. Finally, such rapid growth promotes the accumulation of organic residues, accelerating the formation of true soils in the early stages of glacial-margin environments (Wright 1980:16; and personal observations by the authors in the Mount Cook, New Zealand, glacier systems).

Sources of Fixed Nitrogen

Several sources of fixed nitrogen exist in the atmosphere and soil at the surface of the earth. These are: (1) the terrestrial nitrogen cycle in the global atmosphere, (2) high-latitude sources, and (3) solar-terrestrial interactions. All of these ultimately are derived from the nitrogen that makes up approximately 80 percent of the earth's atmosphere, by both organic and inorganic processes in the lower and upper atmosphere. Much of the fixed nitrogen derived from both organic processes and by lightning is produced in, and cycles through, the biosphere, mainly in the low- to mid-latitudes. Significant amounts of inorganic fixed nitrogen in the high northern and high southern latitudes are produced: (1) by ionization in the auroral oval, (2) by ionization from high-energy galactic particles, and (3) from static generation associated with suspended particles of snow and dust. When NO_3 becomes attached to snow crystals and incorporated into glacial ice, it is preserved there until it melts. The fixed nitrogen that becomes part of glaciers or large ice sheets is carried in conveyer-belt fashion to the melting edge of the ice, where it becomes available for incorporation into organic processes.

Global Atmospheric Sources of Fixed Nitrogen and the Nitrogen Cycle

Several types of fixed nitrogen production are active in the troposphere and on the surface of the earth. These include biological activity, biomass burning, lightning, and anthropogenic activities. Nitrogen-fixing bacteria are particularly active in the roots of certain plants and in the guts of plant-eating animals. The rotting of nitrogen-bearing plants and animals releases trapped NO_3 into the atmosphere. These sources of NO_3 dominate in the tropic and temperate zones where the NO_3 cycles from the atmosphere through the biota

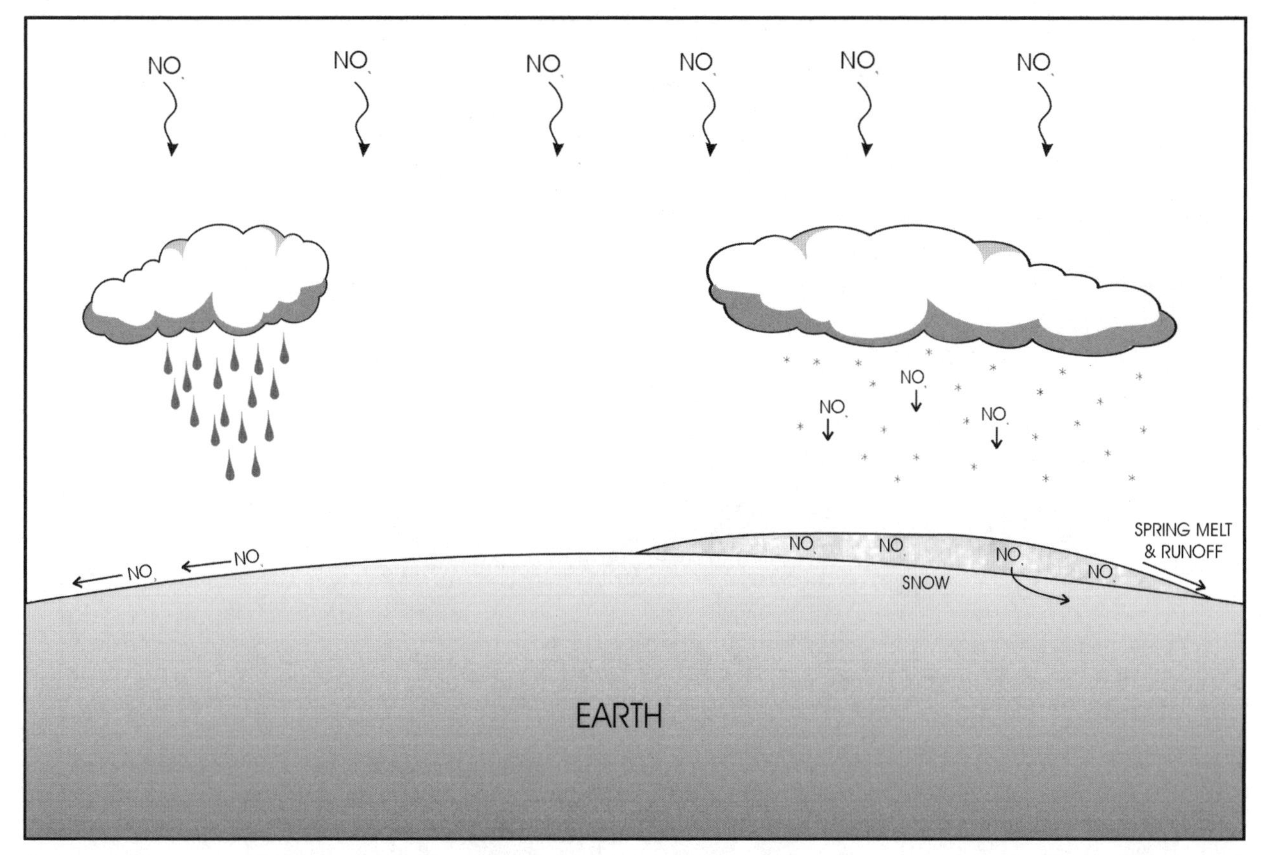

Figure 6. NO_3 in rain and snow. Solar-generated nitrate descends from the upper atmosphere, to be washed out of the lower atmosphere, along with terrestrial nitrate, by rain (left) and snow (right). Nitrate reaching the earth's surface quickly interacts with local plants or runs off into rivers and lakes. Nitrates reaching the surface covered with snow remain in the snow unaltered until spring melt and runoff, when they enrich the runoff water at the time of the spring growth season. If the snow becomes part of a permanent snow and ice mass (glacier or ice sheet), the nitrate remains unaltered in the ice until its eventual release at the melting edge, where it enriches the runoff.

and back into the atmosphere. Another significant source of NO_3 is sea spray thrown by wave action into the atmosphere from marine surfaces at all latitudes.

Other significant sources of nitrates produced at the earth's surface are from biomass burning and lightning strikes. Anthropogenic activities produce very large amounts of nitrates from atmospheric nitrogen through the manufacturing of NO_3 and NH_4, fertilizers for middle-latitude agriculture, and by other manufacturing processes. Lightning produces fixed nitrogen in the lower atmosphere through the direct ionization of atmospheric molecules. These processes can result in ionized N and O, which enhance chemical reactivity to form NO products with the ultimate formation of NO_3.

Atmospheric ionization also may play a major role in the production of NO3. This process is active on a global scale regardless of latitude because of the interaction of galactic cosmic rays (GCRs) throughout the atmosphere. In the polar regions there is additional atmospheric ionization within the middle and upper atmosphere because of the charged particles resulting from solar activity. Changes in solar activity can lead to large variations in the abundance of nitrogen oxides in the thermosphere and mesosphere, particularly through auroral particle precipitation (Baker 1994; Barth 1992; Callis et al. 1991; Garcia et al. 1984).

High-Latitude Sources

RELATIVELY LARGE AMOUNTS of NO_3 are found in the existing ice sheets, and evidence from drilling and sampling of Pleistocene ice shows that NO_3 was being supplied during the Pleistocene, as well. It is this NO_3 in the Pleistocene ice sheets that helped to make the ice-marginal zones suitable to herbivores and carnivores. Most of the NO_3 that reached the ice-marginal zones was from high-latitude sources, deposited on the ice sheets by gravity and carried to

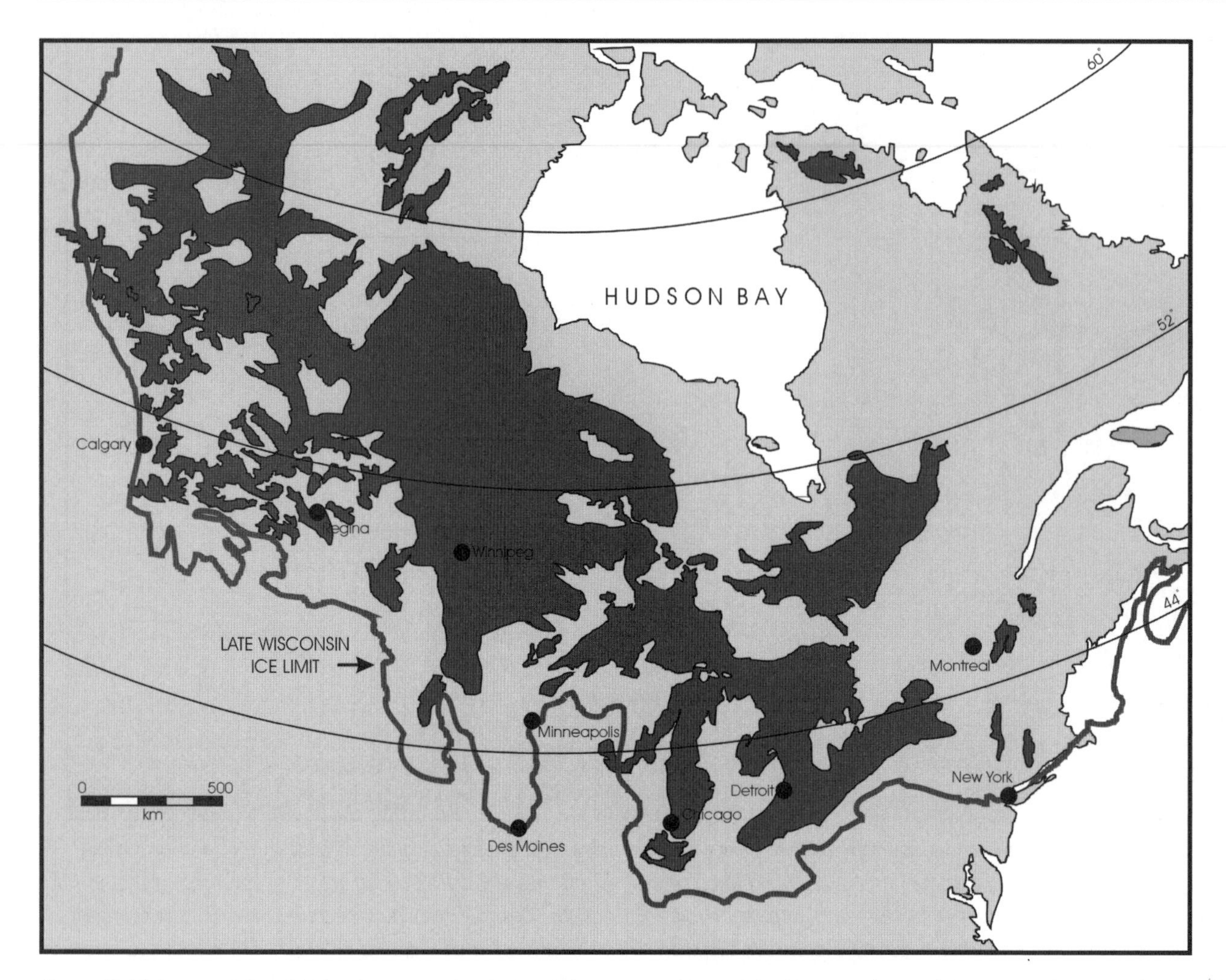

Figure 7. Meltwater lakes left by the retreating Laurentide Ice Sheet. The Laurentide ice sheet of late Wisconsinan time occupied relatively low-relief terrain in northeastern North America. Extensive areas of eastern Canada and large parts of the northeastern United States were covered at the maximum extent of the ice sheet. The land south of the ice sheet generally sloped south and east, causing most of the meltwater to drain down the Mississippi River system or eastward into the Atlantic Ocean. Much of the land under the ice sheet was depressed by the weight of the ice and was slow to rebound after the ice melted. The resulting northward and eastward slope of the land, exposed by melting of the Laurentide ice sheet, caused accumulation of meltwater against the retreating ice margin. Partial rebound of the depressed land eventually drained most of these lakes, although the Great Lakes and Lake Winnipeg still exist as remnants. This figure shows the maximum extent of the proglacial lakes, although they did not all exist at the same time. Much of the nitrate released from the ice sheets by melting was trapped in these lakes. This caused extensive plant and animal production in the areas exposed by the melting of the ice before the water finally found its way to the drainage systems beyond the former edge of the ice sheet. [Modified after Teller 1987:42–43].

the marginal zones by ice movement. This section discusses the origins of the high-latitude NO_3 that became part of the ice sheets and glaciers during Pleistocene and Holocene times.

When we consider the effects on biological productivity at the glacial margins, it is important to look at the relative supply of nutrients in the narrow region of the marginal ice zone. This is in contrast to the large adjacent biogenic reservoirs such as the temperate forests or the Southern Ocean (Biggs 1978). The non-biogenic contribution to the fixed-nitrogen budget in the high latitudes, including the nitrogen budget in glacial ice, is extremely significant, even when compared to the very large biogenic input to the total global nitrate budget. In addition to the normal non-biogenic nitrate infall at high latitudes, there are spike-like additions of non-biogenic NO_3 that add to the nutrient levels (Parker et al. 1978a, 1978b). These higher-level additions of non-biogenic NO_3 become even more significant during the early spring melt,

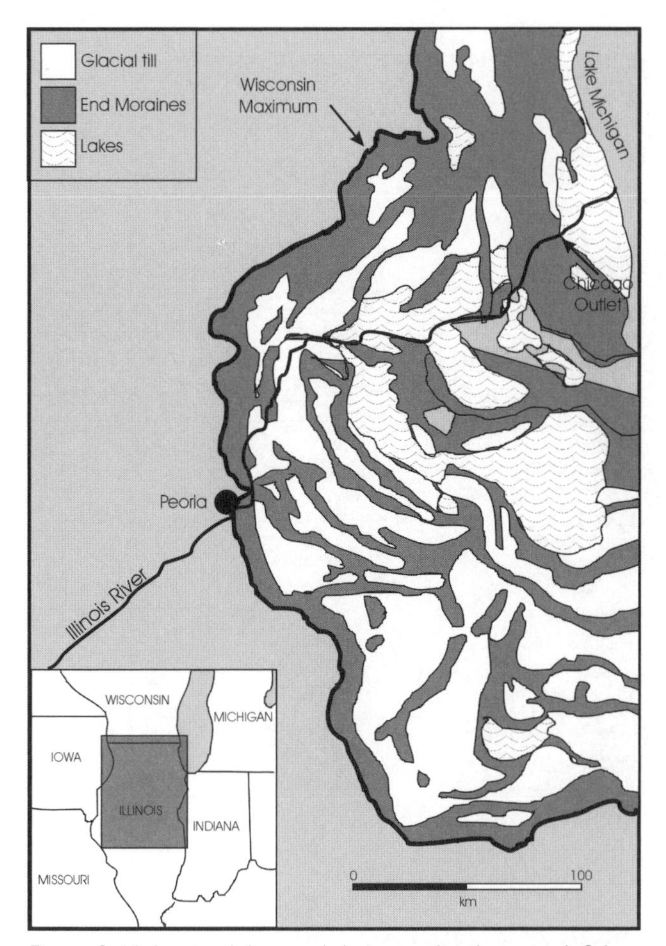

Figure 8. Meltwater lakes and drainage distributaries left by the melting of the Lake Michigan lobe of the Laurentide Ice Sheet in the late Pleistocene. Drainage disrupted by depressions and moraines left by the retreating ice caused the accumulation of meltwater. Nitrate-rich meltwater was very slow to pass through the area before reaching efficient drainage systems, thus contributing to the development of nutrient-rich vegetation in such glacial-margin zones. These regions still contain many areas of standing water and swamps that have not drained or been filled in by sedimentation. [Modified after Teller 1987:47.]

when the most critical growth rate occurs in plants (Brown et al. 1973; Gorham 1958; Johannessen and Henricksen 1978).

The chemical constituents found in polar glacial ice, including the high-latitude NO_3, are vital to the biological productivity of the glacial margins. In order to understand the biological productivity of the glacial-marginal zones, it is necessary, first, to discuss the unusual mechanism that permits high-latitude biogenic and non-biogenic plant nutrients to (a) form and (b) be deposited on the surfaces of both polar regions. Basically, various chemical fluxes to the ice sheets of Greenland (Figure 9) and Antarctica (Figure 10) can be divided into the following groups: crustal (Ca, Mg), sea salt (Na, Cl, K), sulfate (mostly volcanic and marine biogenic sources), and NH_4 and NO_3 (Legrand et al. 1988; Mayewski et al. 1993; Zielinski et al. 1996).

In bulk aerosol samples collected over Antarctica, NH_4 occurs in concentrations that vary by more than 50 percent, with the highest values found in the Antarctic Peninsula (West Antarctica), and the lowest found at Mawson Station (East Antarctica). In contrast, NO_3 values are higher by a factor of two at Mawson Station. Because NH_4 concentrations generally are much lower than NO_3 concentrations in polar ice (Mayewski et al. 1993; Taylor et al. 1993), the origin of NO_3 in high-latitude ice sheets and glaciers is of primary interest.

One source for the NH_4 ions is known from biomass burning on land at lower latitudes, the results of which are then carried to higher latitudes by atmospheric circulation. NH_4 also may occur associated with sulfate as $(NH_4)_2SO_4$ from marine sources (Delmas et al. 1985). Another source of NH_4 may be produced by impacts of extraterrestrial bodies on the atmosphere. Recently, a large spike in ammonium formate that seems to be associated with the Tunguska atmospheric impact event of 1908 has been detected in a Greenland ice core (Peel 1993). Large meteorites may convert atmospheric nitrogen to nitrates, as has been indicated by the coincidence of large quantities of nitric acid on the surface of the earth immediately following the impact of the Cretaceous-Tertiary bolide (Retallack 1996).

All evidence indicates that the Pleistocene ice sheets of the Northern and Southern Hemispheres were great reservoirs of fixed nitrates. A deep core drilled by the Russians at Vostok Station in the central East Antarctic ice sheet has been analyzed for a number of trace species including fixed nitrogen in the form of NO_3, SO_4, and deuterium-hydrogen ratios (delta D). Although these chemical species have been shown to have a very wide range of concentrations (Figure 10), at no time in the last 150 ka B.P. did the quantities of fixed nitrogen in the ice sheet approach zero. This is also true for NO_3 during the last 40 ka measured in ice cores from the Greenland ice sheet (Figure 9).

The natural sources of NO_3 are primarily terrestrial, marine, and atmospheric in origin. The exceptions in the environment are modern anthropogenic NO_3. The global NO_3 sources and their regions of influence within the atmosphere (altitude) are summarized in Table 1, based on summaries in Legrand et al. (1989) and Wolff (1995).

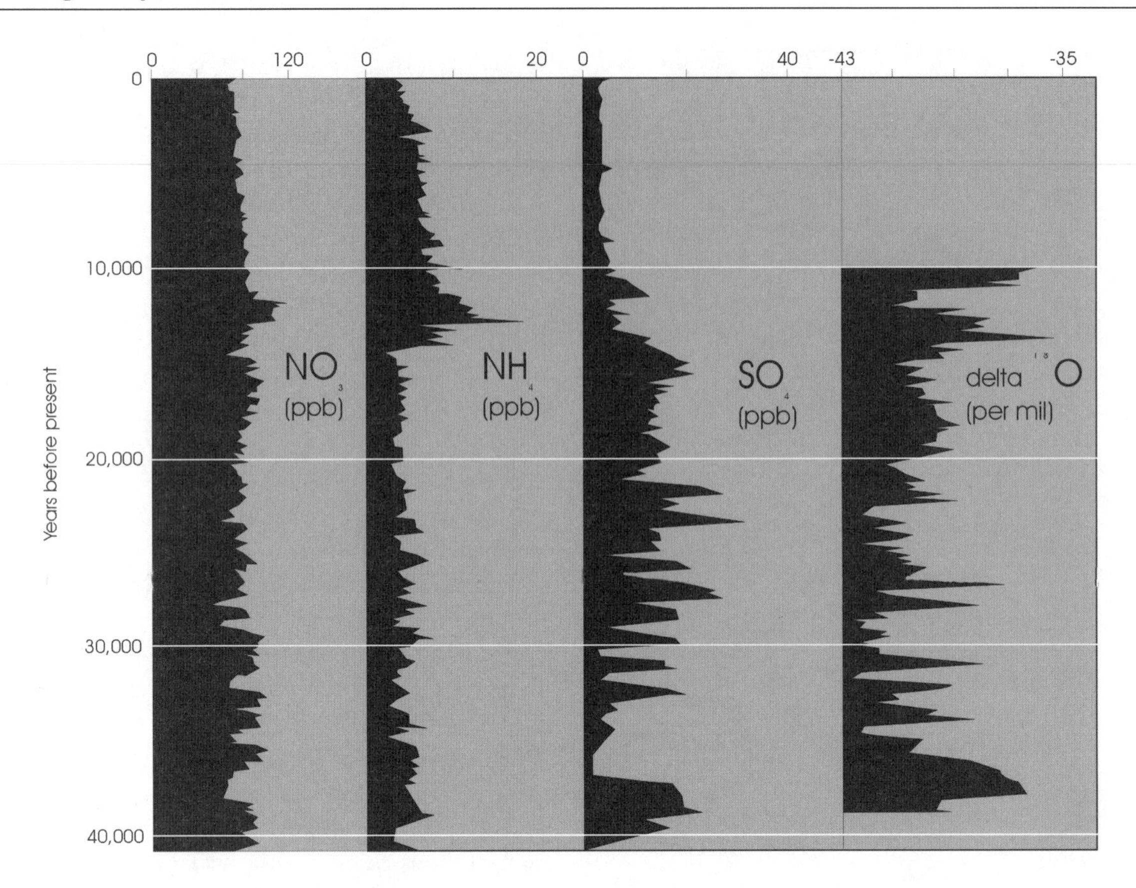

Figure 9. Presence of nitrogen and sulfates and the ratio of oxygen-18 to Oxygen-16 in the Greenland Ice Sheet Project (GISP) ice core during late Pleistocene and Holocene times. The GISP ice core was drilled into the central Greenland ice sheet to reach ice that was deposited as snow over 40,000 years ago (40 ka B.P.). Delta O-18 (d ^{18}O), the ratio of oxygen-18 to oxygen-16, indicates the average temperature at the time of snowfall. Less negative d ^{18}O (to the right on the graph) indicates higher temperatures. Higher sulfate (SO_4) is indicative of greater volcanic activity, especially in the Northern Hemisphere. Nitrogen as ammonia (NH_4) and as nitrate (NO_3) was being deposited on the ice sheet throughout the late Pleistocene and Holocene (40 ka to present), but (NH_4) was highest just prior to the initiation of the Holocene (after Mayewski et al. 1994).

Nitric acid (HNO_3) in gaseous or aerosol form, mostly of tropospheric and stratospheric origin, is incorporated in the snow layers of the ice sheets. Stratospheric nitric acid, whatever its origin, may undergo the process of particulate formation, due to heterogeneous reactions, particularly in winter and spring, in the cold polar atmosphere. Efficient downward transport of NO_3 from the stratosphere to the surface of the polar ice sheet occurs within the isolation of the polar winter atmosphere by formation of Polar Stratospheric Clouds (PSCs). The presence of PSCs suggests the removal of nitric acid from the gas phase by condensation and dehydration to the solid phase, forming relatively large particles of nitric acid trihydrate (McElroy et al. 1988; Woffsy et al. 1990). For the Arctic, it has been shown that denitrification of the atmosphere also can take place without dehydration, by growth and sedimentation of particulates high in nitric acid (Fahey et al. 1990). New insights into the cloud microphysics that lead to the formation of PSCs and downward transport are still evolving; however, there is no doubt that HNO_3 contributes a significant mass fraction to the stratospheric aerosols (Tabazadeh et al. 1994). During the polar night, the low-temperature conditions permit gaseous HNO_3 to be transformed into the solid phase or to liquid-droplet form (Song 1994). The

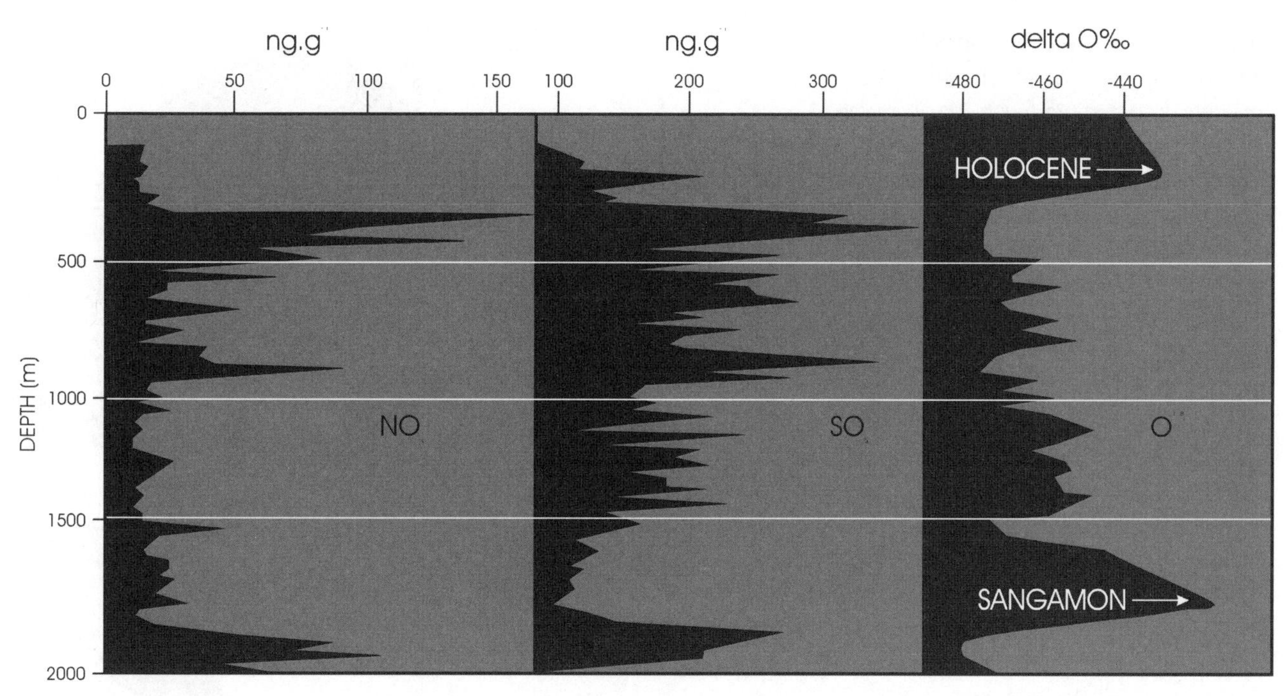

Figure 10. Presence of nitrates, sulfate, and deuterium in the Vostok, Antarctica, ice core during the late Pleistocene. The Vostok core penetrated 2,000 m into the center of the East Antarctic ice sheet, sufficient to reach pre-Sangamon (pre-Eemian) ice. The graph on the right shows the content of deuterium in the ice in relation to hydrogen. Areas of the curve above (to the right of) about $-440^0/_{00}$ indicate precipitation of snow during warm interglacials. The peak at the top of the core is in snow that fell in the Holocene (~10 ka B.P. to present), while the peak at a depth of about 1,700 m is in ice that fell as snow during the last interglacial (Sangamon), about 125 ka B.P. During the late Pleistocene (between about 250 and 1,600 m, 10 ka and 100 ka B.P.), temperatures fluctuated between cool and cold, but at no time were they as warm as during the interglacials. Sulfate (middle graph) and fixed nitrogen (lower graph) show that high quantities were precipitated with snow just before the two interglacials, and lesser amounts during late Pleistocene time. At no time during the last 150 ka did fixed nitrogen in the Vostok ice fall below ~10 ng/g of ice. [Modified from Legrand et al. 1988.]

denitrification of the stratosphere by gravitational sedimentation to the polar ice sheets is clearly not spatially even, e.g., throughout the arctic basin (Notholt 1994). Evidence for efficient downward transport of NO_3 into the upper stratosphere (Kouker et al. 1995) at high latitudes comes from measurements by the Nimbus 7 satellite. In addition, penetration of stratospheric air into the tropopause has been reported by Gruzdev and Sitmov (1992), as well as subsidence in the Arctic winter stratosphere (Toon et al. 1992) and vertical redistribution of HNO_3 aerosols by sedimentation (Arnold et al. 1989).

Solar-Terrestrial Interaction Sources of Nitrates

The sun is the driving force in the environment at the earth's surface. However, when considering solar-terrestrial interactions, the emphasis is not on the large stream of energy that reaches the earth in the form of electromagnetic radiation (which includes the largest source of energy for all processes on earth). Rather, in our discussion of solar-terrestrial reactions, we refer to the variable part of solar radiation that is closely related to the strength of the solar activity, as well as the solar-particle flux intercepted by the earth. This variable solar radiation constitutes only a fraction of the energy that is carried toward the earth by the constant portion (solar constant), but it is extremely significant for the processes we are discussing. We will focus here on the variable radiation and its effect on the upper atmosphere over the magnetic poles of the earth.

Figure 11. Auroral oval. Solar particles approaching the earth interact with the earth's magnetic field and are funneled toward the north and south geomagnetic poles. They produce luminous emissions of atoms and molecules in the polar upper atmosphere in an irregular circle around the geomagnetic poles—the auroral ovals. The position, shape, and strength of the auroral ovals change with the level of activity of the sun and the flux of cosmic radiation reaching the earth. The greatest generation of upper-atmosphere nitrate is associated with the auroral ovals. This illustration shows the usual location of the northern auroral oval during a period of low solar activity. During Pleistocene periods of higher solar activity, the auroral ring expanded to cover a greater extent of the Pleistocene locations of the Northern Hemisphere ice sheets on Eurasia, North America, and Greenland, explaining the high amounts of fixed nitrogen in these ice sheets. [Modified from 1995 Geophysics Institute, University of Alaska.]

The most obvious visible variable on the sun is the change in the number and area of sunspots. Every 11.1 years, on average, they reach a peak that is associated with strong magnetic fields. The sunspots also are subject to a quasi-periodic magnetic cycle, with a duration of about 22.2 years, during which the numbers and areas of the sunspots undergo change. The peaks of sunspot activity usually are not all of the same magnitude, the variation in peak magnitude showing a cyclical pattern of about 80 years, called the Gleisberg cycle. In addition, there are longer-term variations, during which sunspots almost disappear for long periods, such as during the Maunder minimum from 1645 A.D. to 1715 A.D. and the Spoerer minimum from 1450 A.D. to 1550 A.D. (Eddy 1976); or, conversely, periods such as the Medieval maximum from 1100 A.D. to 1250 A.D. (Noyes 1982) in which the sunspot maxima may have been especially high for long periods of time.

The magnetic regions in and around sunspots are called active regions for they are the seat of violent magnetic activity, including the phenomenon of solar flares. Solar flares are the source of large energy releases, including ultraviolet radiation, X-rays, gamma rays, and charged particles. Such eruptions of energetic particles, called solar-proton events (SPEs), may last up to several days. Their travel time to earth ranges from 20 to 40 hours. Often the energy release in a solar flare can produce high-energy particles, which include electrons, protons, and alpha particles. As the charged particles reach the earth's environment, they are guided by the earth's magnetic field lines and thus have almost free access to the polar regions of the earth (Armstrong et al. 1989). These effects produce the auroral ring, illustrated in Figure 11, where many nitrates are formed.

Very large increases in the production of N-O species are known to occur through the ionization process, especially in the polar-winter stratosphere, but mostly at ionospheric altitudes (Barth 1992; Callis et al. 1991). As a result of measurements of NO_3 concentrations across the Antarctic continent, it is believed that the auroral-zone footprint is preserved in Antarctic snow (Dreschhoff et al. 1993; Qin et al. 1992). Larger periods of variation in solar activity (Maunder minimum, Spoerer minimum, Medieval maximum) have been found and identified in two independent ice cores from the high ice sheets of East Antarctica (Zeller and Parker 1981). They reported that modulation by solar activity caused detectable variation in NO_3 concentrations in the 1,200-year sequence from South Pole ice core and in a ~3,200-year sequence from the Geomagnetic South Pole (Vostok Station) ice core on the East Antarctic ice sheet. This variation

Table 1. Global Sources of Nitrates that Contribute to Concentrations Found in Polar Ice Sheets.

Source	*Location*	*Altitude*	*Global Totals Tg(N)/yr*
Soil exhalation	Surface	Troposphere	8-10.8
Biomass burning	Surfaces	Troposphere	12 (70% human control)
Lightning	0-15 km Tropics	Troposphere	2.6-2.8
N_2O oxidation	20-50 km Stratosphere	Stratosphere	0.7
Galactic Cosmic Rays (GCRs)	Stratosphere + Troposphere	Stratosphere + Troposphere	0.06 at solar maximum 0.086 at solar minimum
Downflux from Thermosphere	>85 km Thermosphere	Mesosphere + auroral zone winter Stratosphere	0.003-0.01 at solar maximum ~0 at solar minimum

reveals itself as lower average yearly background values of NO_3 during the two known periods of low sunspot numbers and as higher values during the Medieval maximum from ~850 yr B.P. to 700 yr B.P. (~1100–1250 A.D.)

The Medieval maximum was identified through the study of ^{14}C tree-ring data. This period seems to have been a time of unusually high magnetic activity. The isotope ^{14}C is continuously created by high-energy galactic cosmic ray (GCR) particles entering the global atmosphere. The high-energy particles collide with the nitrogen (^{14}N) atoms in the earth's atmosphere and form ^{14}C. This radioactive isotope of carbon enters living organisms, such as plants, where it can be measured. The GCR flux at the surface of the earth is subject to temporal changes because it can be effectively shielded from the earth by the varying levels of the magnetic fields associated with solar-activity variations. For this reason, ^{14}C tree-ring data are anti-correlated with solar activity. It therefore seems very likely that the ionization of the polar atmosphere by solar particles from the auroral zone down to the stratosphere not only plays a major part in the production of nitrogen oxides, but ultimately contributes to the downward flux of NO_3 (Barth 1992; Garcia et al. 1984). Cloud micro-physics processes in the middle atmosphere make this possible via PSCs (polar stratospheric clouds) and ternary-composition droplets. The conversion of gaseous HNO_3 to the liquid or solid phase results in aerosol particles of nitric acid that can be deposited with the snow on the polar ice sheets.

This concept has been tested further by correlating satellite measurements of solar-particle flux in space with the NO_3-flux measurements on the surface of the polar ice sheets. Very high-resolution sequences from Antarctica (Dreschhoff and Zeller 1990) and recently from Greenland (Dreschhoff and Zeller 1994; Zeller and Dreschhoff 1995) reveal clear evidence that the snow contains a chemical record of ionized chemical species resulting from interaction with charged particles from individual major solar-proton events. Such events represent short pulses (time scales of one to a few weeks) of sharply increased levels of NO_3 concentrations, up to seven standard deviations above the mean of the complete sequence.

In the 415-year NO_3 record from Greenland (Summit site), variation caused by the 11-year solar-activity cycle is less dramatic, but clearly present, as are longer periods of low solar activity, such as the Dalton minimum (1800–1835 A.D.) and the Maunder minimum (1645–1715 A.D.) During these periods, occurrence of anomalous increased values are reduced to about one-third of the average occurrence in the remaining NO_3 (Zeller and Dreschhoff 1995).

Unfortunately, ultra-high-resolution measurements of the NO_3-nutrient levels in ice sheets have been obtained for only the past few hundred years. There is a real need to determine the NO_3 concentrations during the interval near the end of the last glacial period. High levels of NO_3 have been reported in the Vostok ice core from Antarctica in ice deposited through the late Pleistocene/early Holocene time interval (Legrand et al. 1988). These concentrations increase by a factor of about six through this period of several thousand years (see Figure 10). These large increases have been interpreted as being the result of deposition of nitrate salts from terrestrial sources.

Another source of such increases in NO_3 very well could have been the ocean itself. As has been reported (Graneshram et al. 1995), the nutrient inventory of the ocean may have been such that NO_3 levels were much higher during glacial periods than during non-glacial times. An attempt to compare the NO_3 concentrations from two deep ice cores from the ice sheets of both hemispheres shows that major differences exist. For example, the Greenland data between 10 and 30 ka B.P. (Figure 9) fail to show the large increases that characterize the Vostok core (Figure

Table 2. Summary of nitrate concentrations in Pleistocene and Holocene ice from both polar regions. Data from Clausen and Langway (1989); Delmas and Legrand (1989); Legrand et al. (1988); and Mayewski et al. (1994)

Site		*Holocene and Preindustrial Concentrations ng/g(NO_3)*	*Last Glacial Maximum Concentrations ng/g(NO_3)*
Greenland:	Dye 3	52	40
	Crete	60	
	Summit	70	>70 (~15-40 ka B.P.)
	Camp Century	71	20-60
	Average	63	~50
Antarctica:			
	South Pole	74	
	Vostok*	54	
	Vostok**	15	~87 (>150 at ~30 ka B.P.)
	Byrd	40	49
	Average	46	~68

ng/g (NO_3) = nanograms per gram of nitrate

*Clausen and Langway 1989, **Legrand et al. 1988

10) at the same time period. According to Mayewski et al. (1994), pre-Holocene NO_3, as well as NH_4 data, display relatively small variations. The reasons for these differences are not the primary concern of this paper. Rather, we are concerned with the NO_3 variability and accumulation in the polar ice sheets that makes NO_3 available as nutrients at the time the ice sheets melt.

Table 1 presents a summary of global production of NO_3 at different latitudes. Contributions to the high latitudes may vary according to the different source regions. For example, the estimates of contributions from biomass burning and lightning to the high latitudes will have to be reduced considerably below the figures in the summary. In the case of the production of NO_3 formed in the upper atmosphere above the central Greenland ice sheet (Table 1), contributions from large solar-proton events (SPEs) are very small, as compared with total global and yearly production. They range from about 7 percent to 34 percent of the yearly NO_3 value deposited on the central Greenland ice sheet (Zeller and Dreschhoff 1995). However, the component of NO_3 from SPEs can be dominant for a short period of time, on the order of one to two months. Although such increases are short-term, transient, or irregular events, at increased levels of solar activity they may contribute significantly to available nutrient levels when melting in glaciers or ice sheets occurs.

Distribution and Utilization of Plant Nutrients

FIXED NITROGEN IS ABSOLUTELY essential to soil fertility and to the growth and reproduction of both plants and animals. This has been recognized by agriculturalists for thousands of years, as people in central Turkey intentionally have interplanted nitrogen-fixing plants (legumes) with cereal grains to replace the nitrogen depleted from the soil by these grains since at least eight millennia ago (Gimbutas 1991:19). Plants and animals cannot exist without nitrogen (Schreiner and Brown 1938:361). Insufficient NO_3 causes poor color, poor quality, and low production in plants, whereas a sufficient supply of available NO_3 allows early, rapid growth with good color and good health. Plants with sufficient NO_3 also are much better able to utilize P and K in the soil (Schreiner and Brown 1938, p. 370). Nitrogen would have acted as the primary limiter of plant productivity in the Pleistocene, as it did in the Holocene and does in the present.

Distribution of Nitrates

SOME PLANTS, SUCH AS legumes, have the ability to fix N as NO_3 directly, but most plants are dependent upon external sources of this nutrient. For example, in each specific year, atmospheric fallout equivalent ranges from 500 to 800 kg of $NaNO_3/km^2/yr$ in temperate zones (Schreiner and Brown 1938:364). Microorganisms and legume bacteria add an average equivalent of about 12,000 kg of $NaNO_3$/km^2/yr in well-vegetated areas. In another recent estimate, in the absence of human activities the biotic fixation as a primary source of nitrogen is reported to amount to 90–130 Tg (N)/yr on the total continental areas of the world (Galloway et al. 1995). If this amount were to be distributed as fallout over the entire earth, the flux would be 176–255 kg/km^2/yr. This amount is much larger than the NO_3 fixation that occurs from the chemical processes active in both the troposphere and the stratosphere. Actual measurements of NO_3 in polar ice indicate fallout in two of the major ice sheets (see Table 2 for comparison to the estimates above).

The estimate of 7.4 Tg(N) per year for the world atmospheric production may be excessive (Parker et al. 1978a, 1978b). As it is recognized that the stratosphere in the polar regions plays a major role as a source of reactive nitrogen for deposition in the polar ice sheets (Delmas 1994; Wolff 1995), further data are examined and presented which reflect inputs from purely atmospheric processes.

The NO_3 produced in the stratosphere spirals down by general circulation in one-half year or so to the lower atmosphere. General west-to-east circulation of the atmosphere will distribute this NO_3 around the polar areas of the world, and then to the surface by way of rain and snow, largely in the polar regions. Although stratospheric NO_3 is spread by atmospheric circulation, there is still sufficient concentration in the areas of production that most of the NO_3 produced in the auroral ring would precipitate out in the general areas under the auroral ring. The net downward flux of reactive nitrogen from the stratosphere to the troposphere averages 0.45 Tg(N) per year (Murphy and Fahey 1994). This value compares quite well with 0.64 Tg(N) from N_2O oxidation in the stratosphere (Mulvaney and Wolff 1993). If this amount were distributed evenly, the global flux would be about 1.25 kg(N)/km^2/year; however, as discussed above, it is not evenly distributed.

This type of stratospheric fixed nitrogen will contribute, by precipitation and dry deposition, to the background values as they are found in the yearly snow layers of the polar ice sheets. In Table 2 the NO_3 concentrations found in Antarctica (mostly central locations) and Greenland are listed. As shown by Clausen and Langway (1989) and seen in Table 2, the average annual deposition of HNO_3 is clearly higher in Greenland than in Antarctica for periods of time when the anthropogenic contributions in Greenland did not play a role. This is caused in part by the geographical position of Greenland, downwind from major continents (Eurasia and North America), as compared with the isolation of Antarctica. These locational differences lead to major differences in wind circulation and atmospheric-dynamic conditions between the Arctic and Antarctic. If the NO_3 concentrations in Table 2 are converted to flux values (amounts that fall to earth), they are found to range from 18 to 26 kg(NO_3)/km^2/yr (4.1–5.9 kg(N)/km^2/yr) in Greenland and 1–5 kg(NO_3)/km^2/yr (0.29–1.23 kg (N)/km^2/yr) in Antarctica.

Polar ice has been found to contain substantial amounts of the NH_4 ion, which is thought to be from organic sources, because it is not known to be formed by chemical reactions in the atmosphere. Fixed nitrogen from NH_4-ion sources can be shown to make a contribution of up to 70 percent of fixed nitrogen to the NO_3 budget in the ice (Parker et al. 1978a, 1978b). As a matter of fact, a total input of 46,100 metric tons of fixed nitrogen from NO_3^-N and NH_4^-N to the ice sheets per year has been estimated, of which 27,300 metric tons, or more than half, result from NO_3^-N, or an estimated flux of about 2 kg(N)/km^2/yr. This flux value can range substantially, not only across the ice sheet, but also throughout different time periods. On short time scales, such as seasonal variations, ionization in the atmosphere of the polar regions can play a very significant role, particularly during periods of increase in solar cosmic rays. Although N_2O oxidation usually is the largest source of reactive nitrogen in the polar stratosphere, Vitt (1994) has shown that N_2O oxidation is surpassed by a factor of more than 30 during periods of unusually large solar-proton events. Even if only a fraction of this increase reaches the ground (Zeller and Dreschhoff 1995), these events will add relatively large NO_3 values to the NO_3 background in short periods of time.

The spatial distribution of NO_3 flux to the high polar plateau, in association with the auroral oval (Zeller and Parker 1981), is found to be characterized by higher NO_3 values under zones of maximum auroral activity (Qin et al. 1992). This is called the auroral footprint. The difference in flux between the maximum fallout zones and those outside the auroral zone is close to a factor of two, with the highest value being 4.4 kg/km^2/yr. Other mechanisms, such as transport from oceans, seem to be important at some coastal stations on the Antarctic Peninsula, where NO_3 flux values as high as 9 kg/km^2/yr can be reached (Qin et al. 1992). A similar result may be expected in association with

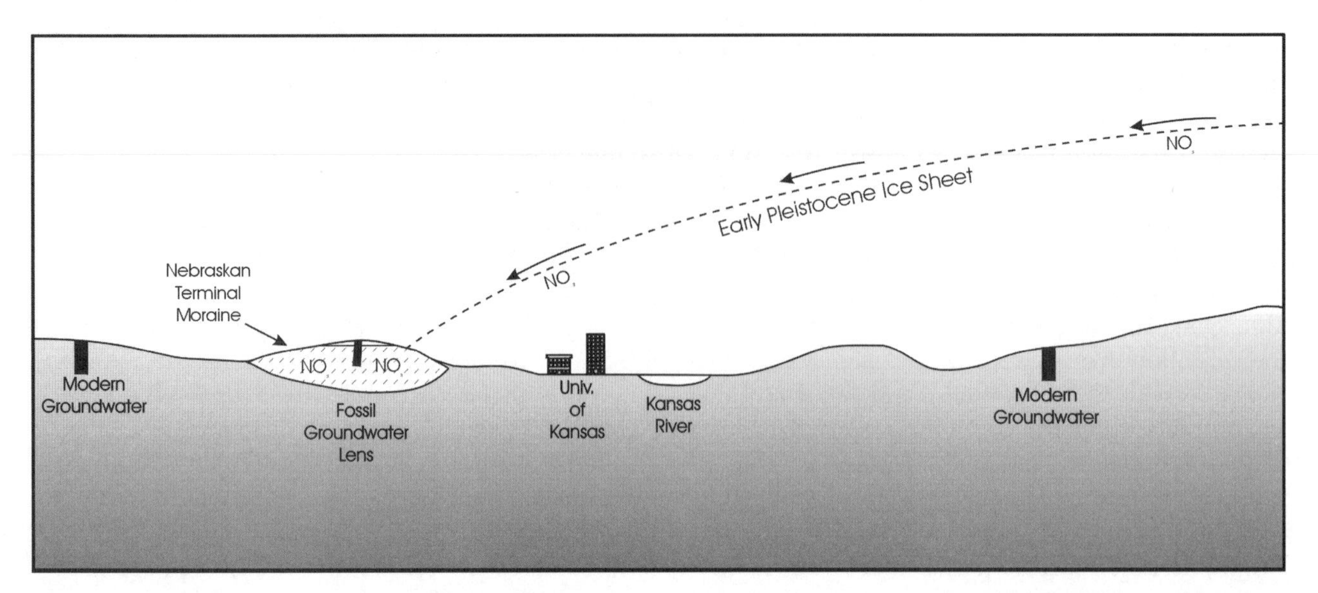

Figure 12. Early Pleistocene-age terminal moraine in Kansas. Diagrammatic cross-section in the vicinity of the University of Kansas, showing the terminal moraine of an early Pleistocene ice sheet, the projected profile of the ice sheet advancing from the north, and the lens of fossil groundwater in the terminal moraine. Vertical black columns below the land surface represent water wells. [Based on personal communication, Dr. Frank Foley, University of Kansas, 1962].

the northern auroral oval in the Northern Hemisphere (Figure 11). However, a series of traverses collecting frequent samples from deep snow pits, equivalent to those in the Antarctic, has not yet been accomplished.

These average values can be considered as a minimum fallout rate for fixed nitrogen compounds, and it is highly unlikely that any of the ice sheets that covered portions of North America during the Pleistocene would have had accumulation rates lower than the accumulation rates during the Holocene. Nitrate accumulations analyzed in ice cores recovered from Pleistocene ice in Greenland and Antarctica show levels as high or higher than NO_3 in Holocene ice in the polar regions (Figures 9 and 10). This is particularly the case for the deep Vostok core (Legrand et al. 1988), where the factor of 5.6 for NO_3 values between the LGM and the H has been reported. This conclusion cannot be applied to other areas in Antarctica, as other locations do not show such large increases during the LGM. The LGM/H ratio for NO_3 is about one in Greenland, and the NH_4 content in Greenland ice for the Holocene is appreciably higher than for the LGM (see Figure 9).

Generally, it can be concluded that NO_3 accumulates in substantial quantities in the polar ice sheets (Zeller and Parker 1981). This means that polar ice sheets acted, and continue to act, as cold traps that accumulate volatile nitrogen compounds by freezing them out of the air as inclusions in snow grains formed in the atmosphere. It is important to remember that once fixed nitrogen is deposited in an ice sheet, it is preserved without significant chemical breakdown until it is released to the environment by melting.

Nutrient Transfer to Glacial Margins

THE NO_3 THAT FALLS OUT on glaciers is not degraded or changed, but is delivered to the glacial snout or margin by normal glacial movement toward the margins and by meltwater flow in the same direction. At the glacier and ice-sheet margins, NO_3 in the meltwater is supplemented by NO_3 in local rain-and snowfalls. The entire mass of fixed nitrogen nutrients is concentrated along the glacial margins, in glacial outwash, in glacial tills, in proglacial lakes, and in runoff water channels (Figures 7 and 8). This concentration of NO_3 is particularly high along stable or retreating ice margins. Glacial tills with very high concentrations of fixed nitrate have been noted in at least two places in North America:

(1) In southern Alberta (Hendry et al. 1984), tills deposited by Pleistocene ice and associated groundwater have been found to contain high levels of fixed nitrogen; and

(2) In Kansas (Dr. Frank Foley, University of Kansas, personal communication 1962), a high concentration of fixed nitrogen was found in an early Pleistocene terminal moraine (Dort 1985) immediately south of the University of Kansas (Figure 12).

Discovery of this occurrence was the result of the investigation of numerous deaths of infants on farms located on the terminal moraine. It was found that artificial fertilizer was not the source of the nitrate. It was determined that high-nitrate water used for making the baby formula was from wells tapping fossil groundwater derived from glacial meltwater from the early Pleistocene ice sheet. The infants being fed liquid formula made with local groundwater died of blue-baby syndrome, a typical reaction to high intake of nitrate, while those that were nursed survived.

Ice sheets during late Pleistocene (Wisconsinan) time, and probably also during prior glacial periods, usually were in dynamic states of advance or retreat, as a result of ongoing climatic changes. Some of these climatic changes are summarized by Mayewski et al. (1981:Figure 2-3, Table 2-1) and by Andersen (1981:Table 1-1).

During periods of ice-sheet stability, when the rate of advance is equal to the rate of meltoff, the fixed-nitrogen contribution to the marginal environment will be proportional to the mass of ice that melts each year, plus the additional atmospheric fallout that occurs during the year on the marginal zone. During periods of actual ice-front retreat, it might be possible to melt in a single year the total amount of ice that would have required many years to accumulate. In this case, the total fixed-nitrogen contribution to the environment would represent the average yearly accumulation, times the number of years mobilized by melting. Therefore, the ice sheet itself can be regarded as a reservoir of fixed nitrogen that releases its supply of this nutrient in direct proportion to the temperature along the ice front. This results in increased fixed-nitrogen release at precisely the time when plant growth is most rapid.

Greenland presently, and as an average for the last 1,000 years, receives about 15–35 kg(NO_3)/km^2/yr of fixed nitrogen from all sources (Clausen and Langway 1989). It is likely that the efficiency of fixed-nitrogen accumulation in the Pleistocene North American ice sheets would have been greater than for the Holocene Greenland ice sheet by about a factor of two because of their locations relative to the North Geomagnetic Pole. The North Geomagnetic Pole is surrounded by a ring of maximum stratospheric ionization that results from incoming charged particles from solar and galactic sources and from electron precipitation from radiation belts surrounding the earth (Figure 11), and are major loci of atmospheric NO_3 production. This auroral ring would have been essentially overhead at the main NO_3 precipitation and accumulation centers of the ice sheets in eastern North America during the Ice Ages, while the Greenland ice sheet was not directly under the auroral ring during the late Holocene.

In a stable ice sheet, the discharge of NO_3 at the margin will be equal to the average annual infall of NO_3 over the entire ice sheet. In an expanding ice sheet, the margin is advancing, and the total volume of ice is increasing and melting is minimal. Thus, during expansion, the fixed nitrogen discharged at the margin will be less than the average infall over the ice sheet. In a shrinking ice sheet, the margin is retreating and the total volume of ice is being reduced, so that, during shrinkage, the fixed nitrogen discharged at the margin will be greater than the average infall.

Fixed-nitrogen discharge will not be even along the ice sheet margins, but will be higher in areas of rapid melting (Denton and Hughes 1981) or in areas of ice streaming (Hughes et al. 1981:Figure 6-6; Mayewski et al. 1981:141–157, Figure 2-2; Monaghan and Larson 1986; Monaghan et al. 1986; Soller 1992, 1993, 1997, 1998; Stuiver et al. 1981:417–431). In areas of ice streaming, larger quantities of ice are delivered per km of the ice margin than in areas between ice streams. The fixed-nitrogen discharge at any specific point along the margin will be in direct ratio to the area of the ice-sheet surface upstream from the margin.

Rates of motion for ice in major existing ice sheets are being measured, but overall average estimates are still preliminary. Ice velocities of 5–10 m/yr have been modeled for interior portions of the West Antarctic ice sheet (Budd et al. 1985). Much higher velocities have been measured for some specific places in Antarctica; for example, the velocity in Ice Stream C in Antarctica is 6.1 m/yr, and ice motion in the Ross ice shelf in Antarctica ranges from 200 to 600 m/yr. (Bindschadler et al. 1987). The effect of these slow velocities is that more time is available for accumulation of nitrates in the ice sheets and quantities of nitrates would be higher than for a faster-moving ice sheet in the same location.

The ice sheets in Antarctica are extremely cold and therefore move much more slowly than is thought to have been the case for the warmer Northern Hemisphere ice sheets in the temperate zone during the Pleistocene. The other presently existing major ice sheet is on Greenland. This ice sheet has surface velocities from near-zero in the center of accumulation to 100 m/year near the major outlet glaciers (Radok et al. 1982:Figure 4/9 following p. 168). For the Laurentide ice sheet of North America at its last maximum (about 18 ka B.P.), the distance from the centers of accumulation to the southern margins in the north-central United States was about 3,000 km (Fulton and Andrews 1987). Ice speed ranged from near zero near the centers of accumulation to estimates of several kms per year near the termini of fast-moving ice streams. Estimates of the total volume of the Laurentide ice sheet (Budd and Smith 1981, 1987) are about 30 x $10^6 km^3$, and the total volume of the Northern Hemisphere ice sheets and ice shelves (Grosswald 1988) was about 60 x $10^6 km^3$. This North American ice sheet of late Pleistocene time, and earlier ice sheets in the same area, served as enormous reservoirs of nitrate.

The Antarctic air mass that nourishes the present Antarctic ice sheets probably is low in fixed nitrogen from non-solar particle sources. The ice sheets are at high average elevations and the trend for prevailing winds over Antarctic coastal regions is primarily offshore; thus marine fixed nitrogen does not transfer easily to ice sheets. Biogenic fixed nitrogen tends to be precipitated out of the atmosphere before reaching the Antarctic from its continents of origin. Another source, atmospheric fixed nitrogen from electrical discharges such as lightning, is very low around Antarctica. Because the northern ice sheets of the late Pleistocene extended to middle latitudes and were largely surrounded by large land masses, they would have had appreciable infall from terrestrial sources, in addition to the solar-terrestrial sources, causing increased total accumulation. Therefore, it is very likely that the northern ice sheets had a higher average NO_3 content than the present Antarctic ice sheet because of the additional contributions from lower atmospheric, terrestrial, and marine sources.

The amount of NO_3 that accumulated on each km^2 of ice surface of the Pleistocene ice sheets each year was relatively small, but significant, because this annual increment remained in the snow and ice and was supplemented by the increment of each subsequent year. Ice moving gradually toward the margin of the ice sheet was up to several kms thick. In the case of the Laurentide ice sheet, it is estimated to have been 4.5 km thick (Budd and Smith 1987:284) at its maximum at approximately 21 to 17 ka B.P. (Mayewski et al. 1981:144–148). This represented some 10,000 years of snowfall (Vincent and Prest 1987:Figure 4). The Antarctic ice sheet, a modern approximate equivalent of the Laurentide ice sheet, is more than 4 km thick (Stuiver et al. 1981:385), and has been calculated to have been at least that thick during the Pleistocene (Hughes et al. 1981:269; Stuiver et al. 1981:376). Thus, each km^2 of the Laurentide ice sheet was the tip of a several-km-tall column of ice containing some 10,000 years of nitrate infall and representing about 400–900 Tg(N) of fixed nitrogen.

The snow and ice from the interior of the ice sheet was carried toward the margin, as if it were on a conveyer belt, in a widening and thinning wedge (Hughes 1981:Figure 5-5). The surface was reduced by ablation of the ice particles (direct transfer from solid to gas phases), causing concentration of the nitrates. In other words, the volume of ice in this hypothetical km-square column was constantly reduced, but continued to contain all its previously acquired nitrate, plus an added annual increment on the top. By the time it reached the melting margin, the entire content of nitrate, representing 10,000+ years of nitrate accumulation, was available for discharge with the meltwater along the front of the ice sheet. Only in periods when the ice sheet was expanding and the ice front advancing would the amount of nitrate discharged be reduced in proportion to the rate of advance.

Nutrient Environment of the Glacial Margins

STUDIES OF THE GEOLOGY of the southern margins of the North American ice sheets and other glacial-margin environments (Monaghan and Larson 1986; Monaghan et al. 1986; Teller 1987, 1989; Watson 1980) show that meltwater discharge at the margin was distributed broadly across ground moraines and outwash plains until channeled by earlier moraines located farther out in the direction of the ice flow. The Vatnajökull in Iceland is a modern ice sheet in the Northern Hemisphere that lies on relatively flat topography, similar to the topography along the southern margins of the Laurentide ice sheet. The Vatnajökull, which is about 2,000 m high in its interior, has surged a number of times at various points along its periphery. The southern margin of Vatnajökull shows a broad, braided outwash plain (Grove 1988:Figure 2.16) that may be similar to that of the southern margins of the Laurentide ice sheet in North America during the Pleistocene. In some areas along the fronts of the Laurentide ice sheet and other continental ice sheets, geological studies show that there have been ice streams that advanced more rapidly and farther than ice in adjacent areas.

The Des Moines lobe of the Laurentide ice sheet advanced several hundred km south of the main ice front, into what is presently Wisconsin and Illinois, during late Wisconsinan time (Frye et al. 1965; Wright 1980:15; Wright and Ruhe 1965). This may represent a mega-surge of the ice sheet. Such extensions of the ice fronts would have channelled ice and related meltwater into restricted zones along the ice-marginal areas. Former drainage patterns beyond the margins of the ice sheet, even in areas that had not been recently directly glaciated, were disrupted and flooded by excess glacial sediments and meltwater that caused glacial discharge to spread across wide areas on outwash plains and outwash valley trains. Nutrient-rich discharge water thus spread widely over a zone bordering the ice sheet. This marginal zone occupied widths of some few kilometers (Wright 1980) to hundreds of kilometers along continental-scale ice sheets (Frye et al. 1965:47, 53–58; Goldthwait et al. 1965; Wayne and Zumberge 1965; Wright and Ruhe 1965). The Lake Michigan ice lobe (Monaghan et al. 1986) that covered the area between present-day Chicago and Peoria, Illinois, during the late Pleistocene (Figure 8) left an extensive and complex system of moraines, glacial outwash, and meltwater lakes that served as distributaries and reservoirs for nitrate-rich water. This, along with other similar ice lobes along the southern front of the Laurentide ice sheet, has been suggested to have been the result of ice sheet surges (Kemmis et al. 1994; Monaghan and Larson 1986).

The discharge waters from the ice sheet were supplying broad areas with NO_3 in amounts many times higher than the NO_3 available to growth areas unaffected by glacial meltwater farther from the ice sheet. As a result of high summer temperatures, ice-sheet melting occurred during the primary growing season of each year.

With essentially unlimited NO_3, P, K, other essential elements, and H_2O, plant growth in this glacial-margin zone would have been very rapid, total production would have been very high, and the growing plants would have been much more nutritious per unit of area. As a probable result, Delcourt and Delcourt (1991:67–69) indicate that reestablishment of vegetation in deglaciated areas of central Minnesota was very rapid, even before the complete melting of ice blocks remaining after regional deglaciation. Thus, the carrying capacity for herbivorous animals, such as mammoths, mastodons, bison, etc., would have been proportionally higher (Schreiner and Brown 1938:370). This effect of NO_3 from the ice may have been significant even during a period of relative stability of an ice sheet, as during the period of maximum development of the North American ice sheets in Wisconsinan time (~21–17 ka B.P.) During a period of major climatic change, as from the late Wisconsinan to the early Holocene (~12–9 ka B.P.), the effect of NO_3 from the melting ice would have been exaggerated. This is because of: (1) greater rate of discharge than rate of accumulation by the ice sheet, therefore higher NO_3 content of the discharge; and (2) despite higher temperatures and higher plant stress over non-glacial North America, there would have been only minimal temperature change along the glacial margin, because the presence of the ice sheet buffered the temperature changes along the glacial margin.

It may be useful to compare the NO_3 yield of melting glaciers with that used in modern farming methods, where maximum coarse-grain production is achieved with a one-time nitrogen application of 20,000 kg NO_3/km^2 (Soil Conservation Service, U.S.D.A., Lawrence, KS, personal communication, April 1992). Efficiency of plant utilization of this NO_3 is lowered by the fact that the applications usually are performed in a single stage and not spaced out over the growing season, as would be the case with glacier meltwater. However, we estimate that the plant density in the ice-margin environment would have been only about one-fifth the density of plants in a modern corn field, because modern farming uses specially bred corn for dense planting, high growth rates, and high yields. Using an estimate of 6 kg$(NO_3)/km^2$/annual ice layer, the melting of an accumulation of about 28 years of ice in a single season would supply a total flux of ~150 kg $(NO_3)/km^2$. However, the spike-like preferential concentration of nutrients during spring melt would increase this amount to ~500 kg $(NO_3)/km^2$ (by assuming 3 x 6 kg $(NO_3)/km^2$ in spring melt). This is comparable to current nitrate fallout in temperate zones. It is important to note that this illustration compares the fixed nitrogen yield from 1 km^2 of ice surface with the biological demand for 1 km^2 of glacial-margin terrain.

In reality, the total area of the melting continental glacier would have been much larger than the total area of the adjacent marginal zone. A 1-km width of ice front represents an average of a 0.5-km wedge of ice between the center of accumulation and the ice margin (Hughes 1981:237). An advance rate of 500 m/yr = 1/4 km(advance)x1/2km(width)/yr = 1/8

$km^2/yr \times 3$ kg (N)/yr/$km^2 \times 10,000$ yrs = 3,750 kg(N)/km-front/yr. The peak contribution during the spring melt could have increased the NO_3 level during the growth period by a factor of ~3 to ~18. If the marginal zone of disrupted drainage were 100 km wide, the average NO_3 introduced to the marginal zone under these conditions would be 37 kg(N)/km^2 (~150 kg NO_3/km^2) of marginal zone. Even this conservative estimate indicates more than adequate NO_3 available to allow immediate production of lush nutrient plant growth at the critical growth time of the year, the spring.

Precipitation of fixed-nitrogen compounds from the troposphere along the glacial-margin zone would have been enhanced because of the added precipitation caused by upslope effects and cooling related directly to the ice front. There also is evidence that nitrogen compounds may serve as nucleation centers for individual ice crystals under the low-temperature conditions that prevailed over continental ice sheets. These influences also would have contributed to a general enrichment of fixed nitrogen in the portion of the ice sheet that was adjacent to the marginal zone. It is important to note that the poor drainage conditions that characterize the terrain left behind by retreating ice masses frequently include kettle holes, marshes, lakes, and ponds that would provide a favorable environment for some types of blue-green algae and legumes capable of fixing nitrogen. These algae and higher nitrogen-fixing plants would contribute heavily to the nitrogen budget in areas where they could grow. The distribution of fixed nitrogen from these sources would be substantially less uniform than that provided by glacial meltwater, but would contribute to the overall biological production of the ice-margin zone. In addition, bacteria in the gut of the animals that feed on the plants would provide an additional source of fixed nitrogen in the form of both nitrate and ammonium compounds. Animals also serve as an efficient distribution mechanism for fixed nitrogen present in the plant residues.

A number of proxies have been used to estimate temperatures in the Pleistocene and early Holocene in the vicinity of the ice sheets. A long series of data have been derived from radiocarbon-dated beetle fossils in North America (Elias et al. 1996) that show that summer temperatures, in general, started to rise by ~13.7 ka B.P., although sites that were near the ice were about 5°C cooler than sites away from the ice. Summer temperatures peaked between 12 and 11 ka B.P., while winter temperatures reached modern values some time after 10 ka B.P.

The close of Pleistocene climatic conditions and the onset of Holocene conditions included severe changes in average temperatures of up to 7°C in as little as three years, as calculated from analyses of the Greenland ice cores (Kerr 1993). These changes would have had drastic modifying effects on the overall environment, but would have had the least effect on the animals and plants of the ice-margin zone as compared with modification to the environment away from the ice. A rapid rise in temperature would have resulted in increased melting of the ice, with a resulting increase in the supply of water, K, P, and NO_3 to the marginal zone. There nutrients would continue to be in excess of the needs for plant growth in the marginal zone. In addition, there would be a modulation of the temperature rise in the marginal zone as a result of the proximity of the ice sheet and the katabatic winds flowing down off the ice and across the marginal zones. The relatively cool, moist, lush marginal zone would act as a long, broad, marginal-zone refugium for animals and plants that had been adapted to the Pleistocene environment of North America. Here, during periods of abrupt warming, they would continue to find a congenial and probably superior environment, in contrast to the rapidly desiccating areas to the south. Models based on plant fossils and geological studies (Hill et al. 1991; Jacobson et al. 1987) indicate that a belt of tundra was present along the southern front of the Laurentide ice sheet, and that south of that was a wide zone of boreal forest, as shown in Figure 13. At ~12 ka yr B.P. in the vicinity of Ottawa, Ontario, the ice front was near the St. Lawrence River, and much of the area to the immediate south was occupied by a proglacial lake and an herb-shrub-tundra environment (Anderson 1989:44–45). These marginal-zone refugia would have been maintained along the shifting ice front during the early Holocene, and the ecological environment, with some of its biota, would have followed the retreat of the ice-sheet margin northward as the ice melted in reaction to the increasingly warmer climate.

Discoveries of remains of large Pleistocene herbivores and carnivores along the ice fronts from late Pleistocene/early Holocene times are not uncommon and demonstrate the existence and occupation of such refugia. Enough sites of early human occupation have been described at or near ice-sheet margins to suggest strongly that there also were significant human populations in these marginal zones (Bonnichsen 1987, 1988; Bonnichsen et al. 1987). Some of these sites include caribou at ~10,000 yr B.P.

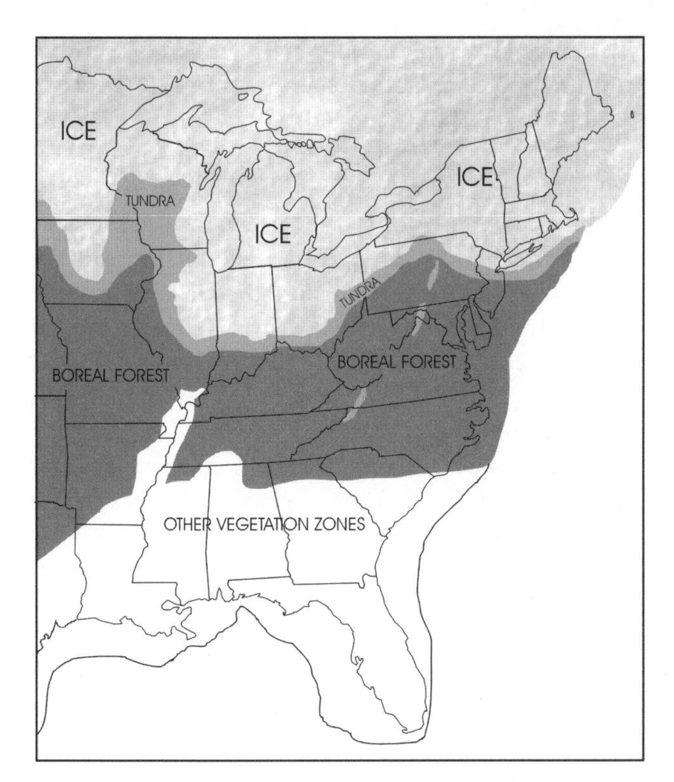

Figure 13. Extent of ice, tundra, and boreal forest along the southern margin of the Laurentide Ice Sheet. Models based on studies of fossil pollen, plants, and geology outline the extent of tundra and boreal forest environments south of the Laurentide ice sheet in the northeastern United States. During the maximum extent of the late Pleistocene glaciation, shown here, these zones were several hundred kms wide, and were habitat for an ice-age flora and fauna. With warming and melting of the margins of the ice sheets, these zones narrowed and moved north with the retreating ice margin, but continued to act as refugia for the cold-adapted plants and animals of the Pleistocene. [Modified after Hill et al. 1991:7.]

(Jackson 1989) and humans at ~10,100 yr B.P. (Jackson 1989; Julig et al. 1987) from northern Ontario; caribou and humans from a late glacial marginal environment in interior south-central Ontario (Jackson and McKillop 1987); an early Paleoindian site in southwestern Ontario (Deller and Ellis 1992); humans in an area of "high resource productivity, biomass, and diversity during the early postglacial period" in southwestern New England (Nicholas 1987:21); evidence of caching of proboscidean meat by humans in late Pleistocene ponds and bogs at the Heisler site in southern Michigan in the Great Lakes region (Fisher 1989, 1995), and about 100 late-glacial proboscidean fossils from a number of sites in southern Ontario (Jackson 1987). At the Arc site, in far-western New York, human artifacts are found in sediments of probable Younger Dryas (~11 ka B.P) age, within an area that had been covered by the Laurentide ice sheet ~2 ka before (Ennis et al. 1995). Nearby, at the Hiscock site, human and mastodon evidence are found that yield dates of ~11 to ~9 ka B.P. (Laub 1995; Smith 1995; Tomenchuk and Laub 1995). A mastodont, with possible human association, has been excavated at Hallsville, Ohio, from a Wisconsinan-age kame complex (Hansen 1993), and human occupation at 12 ka B.P. has been recorded in east-central Ohio at the Eppley Rockshelter (Brush 1993) and in Holmes County, Ohio (Brush and Smith 1994). Overstreet et al. (1993) review many of the known associations of mammoth, mastodons, and humans in the southwestern Lake Michigan basin in late Pleistocene context. Black and Wittry (1959) indicate that excavations at "the Raddatz Rockshelter, Sk 5, beneath the natural bridge in Sauk County, Wisconsin, establish man's presence at the close of the Valders substage and suggest his presence along the front of Cary ice." Uncorrected ^{14}C dating suggests human occupation there at 11,611 yr B.P. Direct association of mastodons and humans is shown by caches of mastodon meat in southern Michigan (Fisher 1989). In Ireland there were giant elk (stag) living in the glacial environment during the period immediately following the glaciation of Ireland by the Scandinavian ice sheet. The giant Irish elk required the high-phosphorus content of willows, which were abundant on glacial outwash deltas and alluvial deposits (Geist 1986). There was also lush growth of willows in glacial environments along lakeshores, along glacial meltwater channels, and on loess plains created downwind of the glacial outwash, indicating the high productivity of this ice-marginal zone. With the disappearance of the glacial environment and its plants with high-phosphorus content, the giant Irish elk became extinct.

However, some glacial-margin areas in the interior of the ice-sheet environment had low productivity, for example, in the narrow, so-called "ice-free corridor" between the Laurentide and the Cordilleran ice sheets. This may have resulted in a biomass for humans to prey upon that would have been too small to allow a socially viable human population, because of the linearly constricted environment of the corridor during the 18–13 ka B.P. time interval. After ~12 ka B.P. the corridor became wide enough to allow a viable environment for prey animals and humans (Mandryk 1992).

Similar nutrient-rich environments also are found in the ocean adjacent to drainage areas of modern glaciers (Apollonio 1973; Iverson et al. 1974), where they promote the growth of Arctic phytoplankton. Such nutrient-rich environments, where glacial meltwater drained into the oceans, probably also existed in the Pleistocene.

Instability of the Glacial Margins

IN NORTH AMERICA, the southern ice margins retreated rapidly northward in late Pleistocene times, probably as a result of rapidly increasing temperatures. Andrews (1987:28–31) suggests that in the St. Lawrence Valley, for example, the ice front was relatively stable from 30–14 ka B.P., but was deglaciated rapidly from 13.4 ka to 12 ka B.P. He reports an ice-retreat rate of the ice on the north shore in Quebec of 160 m/yr. and in the Ottawa Valley of 500 m/yr during this period. Deglaciation rates on the prairies south of the Canadian border were 1,700 m/yr, with retreats of 300 m/yr during the last 2,000 years of the ice sheet history. The rapid fluctuations of the ice fronts resulted in advances and retreats of up to 500 km in a few hundred years. Evidence of such a retreat and readvance is present at Two Creeks in Wisconsin at the time of the Bolling retreat (Twocreekian substage) and at the time of the Younger Dryas advance (Valderan substage) (Frye et al. 1965).

Major glacial lakes, with very complex histories, formed along the same margins during deglaciation. A major series of lakes formed ~14 ka B.P. around the southern Great Lakes; at ~11.7 ka B.P. the southern termination of the ice was in Lake Agazzis, with water of considerable depth and dimensions; at 10 ka B.P. the ice front was on the Precambrian Shield; at 9.9 the ice advanced on a broad front into southern Canada and northern Michigan; and for the next 2 ka the ice retreated 1,000 km (an average of about 500 m/yr).

Rapid Climate Change

RESULTS FROM ICE CORES taken in the Greenland ice sheet indicate temperature changes—both increases and decreases—of as much as 7°C over relatively short time periods (Alley et al. 1993; Kerr 1993). Such changes seem to have affected much of the higher-latitude areas of the Northern Hemisphere. The southern margins of the Laurentide ice sheet were affected profoundly by dramatic changes in climate during the period of 15 ka to 9 ka B.P. (Peteet 1994). Most prominent of these climate changes were an abrupt rise in temperature at ~13 ka B.P. (onset of the Bolling event), a subsequent drop at ~12 ka B.P. (onset of the Younger Dryas event) (Marchitto and Wei 1995), and a sharp rise at 11.5 ka B.P. (the beginning of Holocene time) (Johnsen et al. 1992). Recent work on patterns of dust deposition and on the study of annual layers in the Greenland ice indicate that some of the temperature changes occurred over periods of as little as 20 years and possibly as little as a single year (Alley et al. 1993; Alley, personal communication, March 6, 1996; Mayewski et al. 1996). These changes appear to have occurred across much of the higher and mid-latitudes. Such rapid climate changes would have been especially severe on both terrestrial animals and plants, although the biota of refugia along the ice-sheet fronts would have been much less severely affected.

A temperature rise of ~7°C would have caused extensive melting of the surfaces of the ice sheets near the margins and possible near-surface rises in the temperature of the ice itself. Added warmth in the ice and added meltwater in and under the ice would have contributed to instability in the marginal zones of the ice sheets, with resulting collapse and rapid advance of the ice fronts. The resulting flow of meltwater, released as a result of warming of the ice would also have brought about a rise in sea level. This would have caused buoyant instability in those parts of the ice sheet that were based below sea level. Resulting collapse of ice into the sea would cause further rise of sea level and a positive feedback of more ice-sheet collapse. The result of a comparable series of events during the latter part of the Pleistocene was rapid collapse of major parts of several of the Pleistocene ice sheets (Denton and Hughes 1981). The concurrent effect on the ice sheets was to increase the gradient of the ice surface near the ice margins and to increase the velocity of ice flow to the margins of the ice sheets.

Retreat of Marine-Based Ice Fronts

ANALYSES OF ICE CORES from Greenland suggest that climate oscillations, although of lower magnitude, occurred at intervals of 500 to 1,000 years in the Northern Hemisphere (Kerr 1993). Warmer climates caused ice melting and related sea-level rises, destabilizing ocean-based ice margins. As the ice on ocean margins advanced, it broke off as icebergs. Many of the icebergs carried rock debris that was dropped to the ocean bottom as the bergs melted. Layers of sediments with higher-than-usual proportions of rock fragments, found in Atlantic deep-sea cores, indicate large numbers of icebergs floating across the Atlantic during restricted time periods. Recent studies of sea sediments confirm the climate swings reported from the Greenland ice-core data (Monastersky 1995). Large numbers of icebergs every 2,000 to 3,000 years carried rock debris from the Iceland ice sheet and from the Laurentide ice sheet by way of the Gulf of the St. Lawrence and distributed this debris on the ocean bottom. Very large ice-breakup events from the Laurentide ice sheet, surging into the Hudson Strait and Atlantic Ocean every 7,000 to 10,000 years, also spread rock debris across the North Atlantic Ocean bottom and are known as Heinrich events (Bond and Lotti 1995). Heinrich events are attributed to periods of rapid advance of the ice-sheet margins (Andrews and Tedesco 1992; Andrews et al. 1994; Bond et al. 1992; Dowdeswell et al. 1995). Thus, in the Northern Hemisphere in the late Pleistocene there were periods of climatic equilibrium broken by short periods of disequilibrium.

Periods of change from one climatic equilibrium to another appear to have been periods of unusually high variability in climatic conditions. Such periods of high variability would have been stressful to the biota. Suggestions of such instability appear to be evident during the transition from the glacial period of the Pleistocene to the interglacial of the Holocene. Bonnichsen et al. (1987:418–420), using data derived from Vernekar (1968), show that the "greatest values for seasonality since the Sangamon interglacial (about 80 ka [B.P.]) occurred about 11 ka [B.P.]," at about the time of the transition from glacial to interglacial times. Data from the Greenland ice cores indicate that this transition was extremely rapid, probably in the order of 20 years or less (Dansgaard et al. 1989). Lamb (1977:384) indicates that in earliest postglacial times there was great vigor of the atmospheric circulation, different from now, being especially great in summer. Along some rivers and streams flowing out of the eastern front of the northern Rocky Mountains in the United States, for example, there is geologic evidence of massive floods at about the end of the Pleistocene. These include South Fork Everson Creek, southwestern Montana (Turner et al. 1991:119–122), areas of northeastern Wyoming (Leopold and Miller 1954), and the Hell Gap Site, in eastern Wyoming (Richmond et al. 1965:17–20).

Holocene Climate Changes

WINKLER AND WANG (1993:254–255) discuss rapid and significant changes in the early Holocene of China, an area that evinced increased seasonality despite the absence of a nearby ice cap. Major shifts in the jet streams at the time of the reduction of the size of the ice caps of North America and Siberia may have been, in part, responsible for such instability. Thompson et al. (1993:504) and Webb et al. (1993b:516) suggest shifts in the jet stream and the related prevailing winds, with the glacial anti-cyclone continuing through 9 ka B.P. The anti-cyclone and the ice sheets continually shrank in area during the early Holocene. Similar instability is suggested by the results of pollen-distribution studies near the North American ice sheet (Overpeck et al. 1992; Webb et al. 1993a; Winkler 1992), along with derived plant distributions, mean January temperatures, mean July temperatures, and precipitation. Lamb also discusses periods of major flooding and rainfall variation during periods of transition from warm to cool and cool to warm climates at 3300 to 3100 yr B.P. (Lamb 1977:2:215–217). This time period is approximately that of the Lobben glacial episode of Europe and the beginning of the Temple Lake glacial episode in North America (Denton and Karlen 1973; Grove 1988:300; Heuberger 1974).

Utilization and Significance of Nutrients from the Ice Sheets

PLANT PRODUCTIVITY is the base of support for the total food supply for both herbivores and carnivores. In the high-nitrogen areas along the melting margins of the Pleistocene ice sheets, plant growth would have started more quickly, proceeded more rapidly, and the nutrient value to herbivores would have been high. Because of the ready supply of the necessary components of plant growth, there would have been greater bulk production and a higher nutrient value per unit of plant material consumed. The result would have been a higher carrying capacity of herbivores and their predators, including humans, along the fronts of the ice sheets.

Nitrate falling on normal land surfaces is used immediately by growing plants, with little to none retained for plant growth in subsequent years. Utilization of atmospheric fixed nitrogen by plants and animals is dependent upon total precipitation on a yearly basis. Additional fixed nitrogen is furnished by bacteria in the soil. In other words, substantial storage of this plant nutrient does not occur in normal land surfaces, but it is constantly cycled through the biota and out of the system through water drainage. Environmental stress is enhanced in non-glacial areas because of the lack of constancy in nutrient supply. By comparison, the Pleistocene glacial-margin areas would have been saturated by the plant nutrient supply that would have assured high productivity with less yearly variation.

Loess

A NATURAL BYPRODUCT of continental glaciation, especially during the Pleistocene glacial episodes, is the production of loess (Smalley 1966). Loess is primarily wind-blown, finely divided rock particles (rock flour or glacial flour) that have been carried away from the ice front by glacial meltwater. It is deposited on the wide floodplains of meltwater rivers. As the silt left on the floodplains dries, the NO_3 in the interstitial water attaches to the silt and clay particles. A large proportion of this fine silt and clay is picked up by the katabatic and cyclonic winds sweeping over the floodplains and is deposited downwind as wide-spread sheets of loess. Thick deposits of loess, derived from Pleistocene glacial outwash, are present over large areas of central Asia, Europe, and North America.

Loess deposits have most of the same critical factors for high organic productivity that are to be expected in the immediate glacial-margin environment. The open loess grasslands allow sufficient light to reach growing plants. Water from rain and snow is adequate in most loess regions for plant growth. Summer warmth is generally high. In loess, the mineral fragments are freshly broken by glacial grinding and contain a very high proportion of new fracture faces with broken molecular bonds. Solution on the surfaces of the mineral grains is, therefore, very rapid. Although most loess is composed predominantly of quartz, many other grains of minerals containing K and P are also available in very large quantities.

Loess, with a high content of available K, P, and NO_3, as a result of its origin, produced notably good grazing habitat for megafauna during the Pleistocene and Holocene, as well as excellent farm land during past and present human occupation (Bogucki 1996). Therefore, it is probable that during ice-sheet accumulation, climax, and disintegration, the ice-margin environment would have been highly productive and highly attractive to megafauna in the spring, summer, and fall of the year. The nearby accessible loess areas, with abundant summer growth of grasses for natural winter hay, would have been refugia to which these same megafauna migrated during the winter. Excavated sites containing remains of large herbivores, with evidence of human presence, have been found across the loess areas of the U.S. mid-continent and the grasslands of South America, for example, as reported by Brunswig and Fisher (1993), Hill et al. (1993), and Johnson and Politis (1993).

Ice-margin environments and the nearby loess areas, with their unusually high biological productivity, would have been extraordinarily favorable for hunting and foraging human populations, as shown by the large number of early sites that have been discovered in these environments. It should not be surprising that early peoples exploited these conditions, and it is likely that evidence of extensive human occupation along the ice margins and on the loess plains will continue to be discovered.

The temperature and precipitation shifts that occurred during transition periods from warm to cold or vice versa would have affected living conditions for plants and animals adversely, because adaptations that had developed would no longer have been appropriate to the changed conditions. The greater the magnitude and the more rapid the change, the greater the stress on the biota.

Migration of Fauna

GRADUAL CHANGES IN CLIMATE would modify ice-marginal areas and loess plains in ways that might lead to adaptive changes in the local plants and animals or lead to gradual changes in distribution to more compatible areas. Abrupt changes in climate would change the environment of ice-marginal areas and loess plains in ways that would leave too little time for adaptation, migration, or changes in distribution for some species. Species capable of adapting to the new conditions or of moving to new areas of compatible environments would continue to colonize refugia along the ice-sheet front or on the loess plains (Vrba 1994). Catastrophic changes in the position of the ice margin also would lead to changes in the location and dimensions of the ice-front refugia and loess-plains refugia, and the supply of NO_3 to different areas of the ice-front areas. The paleo-presence of such animals as caribou and musk ox along the southern ice-sheet fronts during the Pleistocene and their presence during current interglacial time in the high Arctic environment suggest that the refugia remained intact during the northward shift of the ice fronts. Some Wisconsinan refugia were in existence over long enough time periods to allow subspecies of larger mammals to evolve, as discussed by Rogers et al. (1991:626–627). Caribou, musk ox, and other high-mobility animals were able to follow the refugia, even during rapid retreat of the ice fronts during the early Holocene (Graham et al. 1996).

Birds that presently migrate to areas of high productivity in the Arctic for summer nesting may have migrated during the Pleistocene to similar environments of high productivity in the ice-front refugia areas. They also had sufficient mobility to follow the refugia northward during the refugia's rapid movement to the north during the early Holocene. Other species of plants and animals were not sufficiently adaptive or mobile to follow the refugia to new areas. They became either totally or locally extinct.

Conclusions

IT HAS BEEN WIDELY BELIEVED that the areas along the fronts of the extensive Pleistocene ice sheets were cold, sterile, inhospitable areas that were largely uninhabited by plants and animals, including humans. Extensive examination of the problem has led the authors to believe the opposite. This paper is primarily an outline of our findings and conclusions on the environment and life along the Pleistocene ice-sheet margins. The evidence points to nutritious and productive marginal zones during the Pleistocene. During the drastic changes of climate that occurred during the late Pleistocene and early Holocene these zones acted as refugia for some of the plants and animals that had adapted to the climates of the Pleistocene.

All essential plant nutrients are available from past and present glacial meltwater and deposits of glacial sediments. Phosphate, K, and other essential mineral elements are derived from the bedrock under the glacier or ice sheet by solution of the freshly ground rock. The authors believe that a large amount of the fixed nitrogen in the upper atmosphere, which descends to the surface in the higher latitudes, is of inorganic origin and complements the abundance of other essential elements. The biological and natural-history literature have emphasized the organic origins of fixed nitrogen and have not indicated awareness of the inorganic origins of a significant portion of the fixed nitrogen produced in the upper and middle atmosphere, especially at higher latitudes. Nitrates are and were deposited on the ice from the atmosphere. During the Pleistocene, when large ice sheets covered major parts of the northern continents and Antarctica, these nutrients were carried along to the glacial front without further alteration. The NO_3 were, in part, from organic and inorganic sources near the base of the atmosphere and from organic processes in soil and surface biota; and, in part, from solar/terrestrial processes that took place, and continue to take place, in the upper atmosphere. The nutrients released from glacial ice at the ice front were available in the marginal zone along the front of the glacier or ice sheet to bring about rapid development of nutritious plant growth in the marginal zone. This early development of vegetation in the marginal zone of glaciers and ice sheets would have promoted early invasion by animals and humans and may explain the frequent discovery of evidence of large mammals and humans near the fronts of past glaciers and ice sheets. In addition, silt carried by glacial meltwater and deposited along floodplains of glacial drainage ways also carried adsorbed NO_3. Upon drying of the floodplains, the NO_3 remained and was attached to silt grains. This NO_3-bearing silt, composed of mineral grains, including apatite and feldspars, was picked up by winds blowing across the floodplains. This wind-blown silt, plus silt from other sources, was deposited as loess. Glacially derived loess is rich in all of the nutrients essential for plant growth, and thus formed areas supporting nutritious and productive plant life.

Many of the loess areas of the world are treeless prairie areas, such as the upper midwest of the United States and the loess steppes of the southern former U.S.S.R. (Ranov 1987:25). During the Pleistocene and Holocene, these loess areas carried heavy populations of plant-eating animals and their predators. At the present time these areas are among the most productive in domestic animals and grain crops. During the Pleistocene, loess areas, with their plant-required nutrients, would have acted as outer extensions of the ice-marginal environment and as winter refugia. The combination of summer refugia along the ice fronts and winter refugia on the loess prairies would have allowed annual migrations of the megafauna and dependent humans to utilize a nutritious, productive, ice-age environment during glacial climates and into the initial stages of a drastic climatic change of the type that occurred at the beginning of the present interglacial (the Holocene). Loess environments supported humans and large numbers of large and small herbivores and predators, such as at the Broken Mammoth site in Alaska at 11.8 ka B.P. (Crossen et al. 1992). Such refugia would have been present during each modification of climate during the Pleistocene. In the New World, the major added factor at the beginning of the current interglacial, in contrast to earlier interglacials, was the presence of big-game hunting humans, including people of the Clovis and Folsom cultures. With the help of such refugia, the megafauna, which were under intense survival pressure from the climatic shifts, had weathered previous interglacials and interstadials. The megafauna during the late Pleistocene and early Holocene, however, suffered an additional toll by the new and efficient carnivore (humans). This may have contributed to the further extinction of many of the megafauna (Martin and Klein 1984; Martin and Neuner 1978; Martin and Wright 1967).

Approximately 90 percent of Pleistocene time had a climate and a related physical environment that was generally cool and moist and included the presence of extensive glacial ice, but was interspersed with rapid, short-term swings of temperature. Much of this time, ice sheets were present over the northern and central parts of the continents of the Northern Hemisphere. The megafauna and microfauna of the Pleistocene were adapted to this colder environment. Biota are more stressed by environmental change than by a steady, harsh climate. Once adapted to what may be considered by us now to have been harsh conditions, plants or animals may have been much more stressed by changes to what we might consider subjectively to be milder conditions, than they were to the maintenance of the original harsh environment. During Wisconsinan time, an environment was developed that was maintained, with modest changes, for about 40 ka. In other words, the present interglacial environment of the last 10 ka is very limited in duration. It is, in effect, extremely harsh and stressful to the biota that were adapted to the average glacial environment of the Pleistocene. Each of the interglacials that have occurred during the Pleistocene have been equally short, harsh, and stressful to the average Pleistocene biota. Evolutionary change is proportional to environmental stress. Evolution of the megafauna would not be sufficiently rapid to adjust to the abrupt climatic shift without the presence of interglacial refugia, such as those along the ice-sheet margins.

The megafauna in North America became extinct relatively quickly during the shift from glacial to interglacial conditions. Present evidence indicates the megafauna in South America became extinct much more gradually, finally dying out completely at about 8 ka B.P. In South America, big-game hunters were present from at least 12 ka B.P. However, in South America there were no continental-size ice sheets, and surges in the existing ice sheets would have been unlikely to have affected the entire periphery of the existing ice sheets (Hollin and Schilling 1981:190). Therefore, ice-margin refugia in South America probably were not destroyed catastrophically and probably existed well into interglacial time.

At about 12 ka B.P. there was a massive and rapid collapse of the Laurentide ice sheet. This collapse has been postulated to have been the result of warming, the Upper Dryas (Boelling) warming of Europe. The massive release of ice into the North Atlantic may have caused the subsequent cold Younger Dryas event that affected Europe and North America. Surges along the southern margins of the Laurentide ice sheet would have carried glacial ice rapidly southward some hundreds of kilometers. The location of the southern margins of the Laurentide ice sheet during this period of general retreat fluctuated rapidly as a result of melting, surging, rebound of the land, and the development of ice-marginal lakes (Teller 1987, 1989). Only animals capable of rapid seasonal migrations, such as birds, or animals capable of surviving the winter stresses of northern ice-marginal zones, such as caribou or musk ox, would have been able to adapt to the rapidly shifting refugia.

Big-game hunting humans were present in both North and South America during the early transition period from the last glacial to the subsequent interglacial, at ~12–11 ka B.P. Why did the extinction of the megafauna take place at different rates in different geographic regions and at different rates for different groups of megafauna? There must have been different factors at work than merely the presence or absence of human big-game hunters.

We postulate that the presence of shifting refugia in the ice-marginal zones and the sudden periodic destruction of such refugia under certain conditions, as well as the development or immigration of big-game hunting cultures at the time of the initiation of the last interglacial, were major contributing factors. Marginal environments would have been destroyed more rapidly than new and similar marginal environments could have developed. Megafauna adapted to the glacial-period environment that had been preserved within the ice-marginal zone would have been displaced into zones with conditions related to the new interglacial climatic environments. These zones would have been dryer and warmer, unsuitable to most of the megafauna adapted to glacial-period environments and to the destroyed ice-marginal environment. The megafauna therefore would have been under intense stress and particularly vulnerable to predators. The added presence of particularly efficient predators—humans—during the glacial-interglacial transition tipped the balance a little further, leading to the extinction of many of the megafauna that were adapted to the glacial environment. We suggest that the migratory birds that make up a major part of the present flourishing Arctic biota adapted during the late Pleistocene or earlier from birds with short migration patterns to the summer ice-margin environments. These, and a limited number of very mobile mammals, were the only animals that were able to maintain their migration patterns, as the migration distances became greater during the development of the Holocene environments. Many of the other animals that shared the Pleistocene ice-margin environments during the summer either became extinct or adapted to a different annual life pattern at the beginning of the Holocene.

Acknowledgments

We wish to thank Dr. Scott Elias, Research Associate, INSTAAR, University of Colorado, for the computer preparation of the illustrations in this paper. Partial funding from the Carl A. Harvis Scholarship Fund for the research on this subject is very much appreciated.

References Cited

Alley, R. B., D. A. Meese, C. A. Shuman, A. J. Gow, K. C. Taylor, P. M. Grootes, M. Ram, E. D. Waddington, J. W. C. White, P. A. Mayewski, and G. A. Zielinski
1993 Abrupt Accumulation Increase at the Younger Dryas Termination in the GISP2 Ice Core. *Nature* 362:527–529.

Andersen, B. G.
1981 Late Weichselian Ice Sheets in Eurasia and Greenland. In *The Last Great Ice Sheets*, edited by G. H. Denton and T. J. Hughes. John Wiley & Sons, New York.

Anderson, T. W.
1989 Vegetation Changes over 12,000 Years. Geos (Energy, Mines, and Resources Canada) 18(3):39–45.

Andrews, J. T.
1987 The Late Wisconsin Glaciation and Deglaciation of the Laurentide Ice Sheet. In *North America and Adjacent Oceans During the Last Deglaciation*, edited by W. F. Ruddiman and H. E. Wright, Jr., pp. 13–37. *The Geology of North America, Special Centennial Volume K-3.* Geological Society of America, Boulder, CO.

Andrews, J. T., H. Erlenkeuser, K. Tedesco, A. E. Aksu, and A. J. T. Jull
1994 Late Quaternary (Stage 2 and 3) Meltwater and Heinrich Events, Northwest Labrador Sea. *Quaternary Research* 41:26–34.

Andrews, J. T., and K. Tedesco
1992 Detrital Carbonate-Rich Sediments, Northwestern Labrador Sea: Implications for Ice-Sheet Dynamics and Iceberg Rafting (Heinrich) Events in the North Atlantic. *Geology* 20:1087–1090.

Apollonio, S.
1973 Glaciers and Nutrients in Arctic Seas. *Science* 180:491–493.

Arkhipov, S. A., M. G. Bespaly, M. A. Faustova, O. Yu. Glushkova, L. L. Isaeva, and A. A.Velichko
1986 Ice-Sheet Reconstructions [in Eurasia]. In *Quaternary Glaciations in the Northern Hemisphere*, edited by V. Sibrava, D. Q. Bowen, and G. M. Richmond, pp. 475–483. Pergamon Press, Oxford.

Armstrong, T. P., C. M. Laird, D. Venkatesan, S. Krishnaswamy, and T. J. Rosenberg
1989 Interplanetary Energetic Ions and Polar Radiowave Absorption. *Journal of Geophysical Research* 94(A4):3543–3554.

Arnold, F., H. Schlager, J. Hoffmann, P. Metzinger, and S. Spreng
1989 Evidence for Stratospheric Nitric Acid Condensation from Balloon and Rocket Measurements in the Arctic. *Nature* 342:493–497.

Aubrey, D. G.
1985 Recent Sea Levels from Tide Gauges: Problems and Prognosis. In *Polar Research Board, Glaciers, Ice Sheets, and Sea Level: Effects of a CO2-Induced Climatic*

Change; Report of a Workshop Held in Seattle, Washington, September 13–15, 1984, pp. 73–91. National Academy Press, National Research Council, Washington, D. C.

Baker, D.
1994 Mission Investigates Radiation Arriving at Earth. *Eos* 75(11):130–131.

Barth, C. A.
1992 Nitric Oxide in the Lower Thermosphere. *Planetary Space Science* 40(2/3):315–336.

Benedict, J. B.
1975 Prehistoric Man and Climate; the View from Timberline. In *Quaternary Studies*, edited by R. P. Suggate and M. M. Cresswell, pp. 67–74. Royal Society of New Zealand, Wellington, N. Z.

Biggs, D. C.
1978 Non-Biogenic Fixed Nitrogen in Antarctic Surface Waters; Comment. *Nature* 276:96–97.

Bindschadler, R. A., D. R. MacAyeal, and S. N. Stephenson
1987 Ice Stream-Ice Shelf Interaction in West Antarctica. In *Dynamics of the West Antarctic Ice Sheet*, edited by C. J. van der Veen and J. Oerlemans, pp. 161–180. D. Reidel Publishing Company, Dordrecht.

Birks, H. J. B.
1980 Modern Pollen Assemblages and Vegetational History of the Moraines of the Klutlan Glacier and Its Surroundings, Yukon Territory, Canada. *Quaternary Research* 14:101–129.

Black, R. F., and W. L. Wittry
1959 Pleistocene Man in South-Central Wisconsin. *Geological Society of America Bulletin* 70:1570–1571.

Bogucki, P.
1996 The Spread of Early Farming in Europe. *American Scientist* 84:242–253.

Bond, G. C., H. Heinrich, W. S. Broecker, L. Labeyrie, J. McManus, J. Andrews, S. Huon, R. Jantschik, S. Clasen, C. Simet, K. Tedesco, M. Klas, G. Bonani, and S. Ivy
1992 Evidence for Massive Discharges of Icebergs Into the North Atlantic Ocean During the Last Glacial Period. *Nature* 360 (6401): 245–249.

Bond, G. C., and R. Lotti
1995 Iceberg Discharges into the North Atlantic on Millennial Time Scales During the Last Glaciation. Science 267:1005–1010.

Bonnichsen, R.
1980 *Human Presence in an Ice Marginal Environment in Northern Maine.* American Quaternary Association, Sixth Biennial Meeting Abstracts and Program, 18–20 August 1980, p. 45. Institute of Quaternary Studies, University of Maine, Orono, Maine.

1987 Human Colonization of Northern New England; What does the Variation of Fluted Points Mean? *International Union for Quaternary Research; XIIth International Congress; Programme and Abstracts*, p. 133. Ottawa, Canada.

1988 Human Adaptation Along the Margins of the Laurentide Ice Sheet from 14,000 to 10,000 Years Ago. *Geological Society of America Abstracts With Programs* 20:8.

Bonnichsen, R., D. Stanford, and J. L. Fastook
1987 Environmental Change and Developmental History of Human Adaptive Pattern; the Paleoindian Case. In *North America and Adjacent Oceans During the Last Deglaciation*, edited by W. F. Ruddiman and H. E. Wright, Jr., pp. 403–424. *The Geology of North America, Special Centennial Volume K-3.* Geological Society of America, Boulder, CO.

Booth, D. B.
1987 Timing and Processes of Deglaciation Along the Southern Margin of the Cordilleran Ice Sheet. In *North America and Adjacent Oceans During the Last Deglaciation*, edited by W. F. Ruddiman and H. E. Wright, Jr., pp. 71–90. *The Geology of North America, Special Centennial Volume K-3.* Geological Society of America, Boulder, CO.

Brown, J. C., C. M. Skau, and W. Howe
1973 Nutrient and Sediment Production from Forested Watersheds. Proc. *ASAE Annual*, University of Kentucky, Lexington.

Brunswig, R. H., Jr., and D. C. Fisher
1993 Research on the Dent Mammoth Site. *Current Research in the Pleistocene* 10:63–64.

Brush, N.
1993 Twelve Thousand Years of Human Occupation at the Eppley Rockshelter. *Current Research in the Pleistocene* 10:5–7.

Brush, N., and F. Smith
1994 The Martins Creek Mastodon: A Paleoindian Butchery Site in Holmes County, Ohio. *Current Research in the Pleistocene* 11:14–15.

Budd, W. F., D. Jenssen, and B. J. McInnes
1985 Numerical Modelling of Ice Stream Flow with Sliding. Anare *Research Notes* 20:130–137.

Budd, W. F., and I. N. Smith
1981 The Growth and Retreat of Ice Sheets in Response to Orbital Radiation Changes, In *Sea Level, Ice and Climate Change.* International Association Hydrological Sciences 131:369–409.

1987 Conditions for Growth and Retreat of the Laurentide Ice Sheet. In *The Laurentide Ice Sheet*, edited by R. J. Fulton and J. T. Andrews. *Geographie physique et Quaternaire* 41(2):279–290.

Butzer, K.
1971 *Environment and Archaeology.* Aldine Chicago.

1976 Pleistocene Climate. In *Ecology of the Pleistocene*, edited by R. C. West and W. G. Haag. *Geoscience and Man* 8:27–44.

Callis, L. B., D. N. Baker, J. B. Blake, J. D. Lambeth, R. E. Boughner, M. Natarajan, R. W. Klebesadel, and D. J. Gorney
1991 Precipitating Relativistic Electrons: Their Long-Term Effect on Stratospheric Odd Nitrogen Levels. *Journal of Geophysical Research* 96:2939–2976.

Clausen, H. B., and C. C. Langway, Jr.
1989 The Ionic Deposits in Polar Ice Cores. In *The Environmental Record in Glaciers and Ice Sheets*, edited by H. Oeschger and C. C. Langway, Jr., pp. 225–247. John Wiley & Sons, Dahlem Konferenzen.

Crossen, K. J., T. R. Dilley, D. R. Yesner, and C. E. Holmes
1992 *Late Quaternary Environmental Change and Human Occupation of the Broken Mammoth Site, Delta Junction, East-Central Alaska*. American Quaternary Association, 12th Biennial Meeting, 24–26 August, 1992, Program and Abstracts, p. 37. University of California, Davis.

Cwynar, L. C., and J. C. Ritchie
1980 Arctic Steppe Tundra: A Yukon Perspective. *Science* 208:1375–1377.

Dansgaard, W., J. W. C. White, and S. J. Johnsen
1989 The Abrupt Termination of the Younger Dryas Climate Event. *Nature* 339(6225):532–534.

Delcourt, H. R., and P. A. Delcourt
1991 *Quaternary Ecology; A Paleoecological Perspective*. Chapman & Hall, London.

Deller, D. B. and C. Ellis
1992 Excavations at the Bolton Site: An Early Paleoindian Crowfield Phase Site in Southwestern Ontario. *Current Research in the Pleistocene* 9:4–7.

Delmas, R. J.
1994 Ice Records of the Past Environments. In *Chemistry for the Protection of the Environment*, edited by R. Kellner and A. Hackl. *The Science of the Total Environment* 143(1):17–30.

Delmas. R. J., and M. Legrand
1989 Long-term Changes in the Concentrations of Major Chemical Compounds (Soluble and Insoluble) along Deep Ice Cores. In *The Environmental Record in Glaciers and Ice Sheets*, edited by H. Oeschger and C. C. Langway, Jr., pp. 319-341. John Wiley and Sons.

Delmas, R. J., M. Legrand, A. J. Aristaraina, and F. Zanolini
1985 Volcanic Deposits in Antarctic Snow and Ice, *Journal of Geophysical Research*; D-Atmospheres 90(7):12,901–912,92.

Denton, G. H., and T. J. Hughes (editors)
1981 *The Last Great Ice Sheets*. John Wiley & Sons, New York.

Denton, G. H., and W. Karlen
1973 Holocene Climatic Variations—Their Pattern and Possible Causes. *Quaternary Research* 3:155–205.

Dort, W., Jr.
1985 Field Evidence of More than Two Early Pleistocene Glaciations of the Central Plains. In *Institute of Tertiary-Quaternary Studies*, edited by W. Dort, Jr. TER-QUA Symposium Series 1:41–51.

Dowdeswell, J. A., M. A. Maslin, J. T. Andrews, and I. N. McCave
1995 Iceberg Production, Debris Rafting, and the Extent and Thickness of Heinrich Layers (H-1, H-2) in North Atlantic Sediments. *Geology* 23:301–304.

Dreschhoff, G., and E. J. Zeller
1990 Evidence of Individual Solar Proton Events in Antarctic Snow. *Solar Physics* 127:33–346.

1994 415-Year Greenland Ice Core Record of Solar Proton Events Dated by Volcanic Eruptive Episodes. *Nebraska Academy of Sciences, Ter-Qua Symposium Series* 2:1–24.

Dreschhoff, G., E. J. Zeller, M. A. Shea, and D. F. Smart
1993 *The Solar Signal from Solar Cycles 14–22 in Nitrate Concentrations in Antarctic Snow*. 23rd ICRC, Calgary, 3:842–845.

Dyke, A. S., and V. K. Prest
1986 *Late Wisconsin and Holocene Retreat of the Laurentide Ice Sheet*. Geological Survey of Canada Map 1702A.

EarthQuest
1991 *Changes in Time in the Temperature of the Earth. EarthQuest Insert*. Office for Interdisciplinary Earth Studies, University Corporation for Atmospheric Research, Boulder, CO.

Eddy, J. A.
1976 The Maunder Minimum. *Science* 192:1189–1202.

Elias, S. A., K. Anderson, and J. T. Andrews
1996 Late Wisconsin Climate in Northeastern North America, Reconstructed from Fossil Beetle Assemblages. *Journal of Quaternary Science* 11:417-421.

Ennis, R., M. Hess, J. D. Holland, V. Honsinger, K. P. Smith, K. B. Tankersley, and S. Vanderlaan
1995 Survey and Test Excavations at the Arc Site, Genesee County, New York. *Current Research in the Pleistocene* 12:9–11.

Fahey, C. W., K. K. Kelly, S. R. Kawa, A. F. Tuck, M. Loewenstein, K. R. Chan, and L. E. Heidt
1990 Observations of Denitrification and Dehydration in the Winter Polar Stratosphere. *Nature* 344:321–324.

Fisher, D. C.
1989 Meat Caches and Clastic Anchors: The Cryptic Record of Paleoindian Subsistence in the Great Lakes Region. *Geological Society of America Abstracts with Program* 21(6):A234.

1995 Experiments on Subaqueous Meat Caching. *Current Research in the Pleistocene* 12:77–80.

Flint, R. F.
1963 *Ledniki i Paleogeografiya Pleistotsena* [*Glaciers and Paleogeography of the Pleistocene*]. Moscow, Map III.

1971 *Glacial and Quaternary Geology*. John Wiley & Sons, New York.

Forman, S. L., D. Lubinski, G. H. Miller, J. Snyder, G. Matishov, S. Korsun, and V. Myslivets
1995 *Geology* 23(2)113–116.

Frye, J. C., H. B. Willman, and R. F. Black
1965 Outline of Glacial Geology of Illinois and Wisconsin. In *The Quaternary of the United States*, edited by H. E. Wright, Jr., and D. G. Frey, pp. 43–61. Princeton University Press, Princeton.

Fulton, R. J., and J. T. Andrews (editors)
1987 The Laurentide Ice Sheet. *Geographie physique et Quaternaire* 41(2):179–318 + map sheets 1–3, & Map 1702A.

Fulton, R. J., and V. K. Prest
1987 The Laurentide Ice Sheet and Its Significance. In *The Laurentide Ice Sheet*, edited by R. J. Fulton and J. T. Andrews. *Geographie physique et Quaternaire* 41(2):181–186.

Galloway, J. N., W. H. Schlesinger, H. Levy II, A. Michaels, and J. L. Schnoor
1995 Nitrogen Fixation: Anthropogenic Enhancement—Environmental Response. *Geophysical Abstracts in Press* 5(3):3, Paper 95GB00158.

Garcia, R. R., S. Solomon, R. G. Roble, and D. W. Rush
1984 A Numerical Response of the Middle Atmosphere to the 11-year Solar Cycle. *Planetary Space Science* 32(4):411–423.

Geist, V.
1986 The Paradox of the Giant Irish Stags. *Natural History* 95(3):54–65.

Geological Survey of Canada
1984 *Late Wisconsin Glacier Complex*. Geological Survey of Canada, Map 1584A.

Gimbutas, M.
1991 *The Civilization of the Goddess:The World of Old Europe*. Harper, San Francisco.

Goldthwait, R. P., A. Dreimanis, J. L. Forsyth, P. F. Karrow, and F. W. White
1965 Pleistocene Deposits of the Erie Lobe. In *The Quaternary of the United States*, edited by H. E. Wright, Jr. and D. G. Frey, pp. 85–97. Princeton University Press, Princeton.

Gorham, E.
1958 Soluble Salts in a Temperate Glacier. *Tellus* 10:496–497.

Graham, R. W., E. L. Lundelius, Jr., M. A. Graham, E. K. Schroeder, R. S. Toomey III, E. Anderson, A. D. Barnosky, J. A. Burns, C. S. Churcher, D. K. Grayson, R. D. Guthrie, C. R. Harington, G. T. Jefferson, L. D. Martin, H. G. McDonald, R. E. Morlan, H. K. Semken jr., S. D. Webb, L. Werdelin, and M. C. Wilson
1996 Spacial Response of Mammals to Late Quaternary Environmental Fluctuations. *Science* 272(5268):1601–1606.

Graneshram, R. S., T. F. Pedersen, S. E. Calvert, and J. W. Murray
1995 Large Changes in Oceanic Nutrient Inventories from Glacial to Interglacial Periods. *Nature* 365:755–757.

Grichuk, L. V.
1972 Osnovniye Etapy Istorii Rastitel'nosti Yugozapada Russkoi Ravnini v Pozdnem Pleistotsene. In *Palinologiya Pleistotsena*, edited by L. V. Grichuk, pp. 9–53. Nauka, Moscow.

Grosswald, M. G.
1980 Late Weichselian Ice Sheet of Northern Eurasia. Quaternary Research 13:1–32. 1988 An Antarctic-Style Ice Sheet in the Northern Hemisphere; Toward New Global Glacial Theory. *Polar Geography and Geology* 12(4):239–267. (From Materialy glyatsiologich eskikh issledovaniy, 1988. 63:3–25).

Grosswald, M. G., and L. N. Glebova
1992 The Ice Sheets of Northern Eurasia and Their Role in the History of the Ocean. *Polar Geography and Geology* 16(1):34–50. (From Materialy glyatsiologich eskikh issledovaniy, 1991, 71:3–15).

Grove, J. M.
1988 *The Little Ice Age*. Methuen, London.

Gruzdev, A. N. and S. A. Sitmov
1992 The Annual Variation of Tropospheric Ozone and Estimates of Tropospheric-Stratospheric Exchange in the Arctic and Antarctica Based on Ozone Sounding Data. Izvestiya, *Atmos. and Oceanic Phys.* 28(9):707–714.

Guthrie, R. D.
1968 Paleoecology of the Large-Mammal Community in Interior Alaska during the Late Pleistocene. *American Midland Naturalist* 79:346–363.

1982 Mammals of the Mammoth Steppe as Paleoenvironmental Indicators. In *Paleoecology of Beringia*, edited by D. M. Hopkins, J. V. Matthews, Jr., C. E. Schweger, and S. B. Young, pp. 307–326. Academic Press, New York.

1996 The Mammoth Steppe and the Origin of Mongoloids and Their Dispersal. In *Prehistoric Mongoloid Dispersals*, edited by T. Akazawa and E. J. Szathmary, pp. 172–186. Oxford University Press, Oxford.

Hansen, M. C.
1993 The Hallsville Mastodont: Evidence for Possible Human Association. *Current Research in the Pleistocene* 10:65–66.

Hendry, M. J., R. G. L. McCready, and W. D. Gould
1984 Distribution, Source and Evolution of Nitrate in a Glacial Till of Southern Alberta, Canada. *Journal of Hydrology* 70:177–198.

Heuberger, H.
1974 Alpine Quaternary Glaciation. In *Arctic and Alpine Environments*, edited by J. D. Ives and R. G. Barry, pp. 318–338. Methuen, London.

Hill, C. L., B. J. Ryan, B. A. McGregor, and M. Rust
1991 *Our Changing Landscape; Indiana Dunes National Lakeshore.* U.S. Geological Survey Circular 1085.

Hill, M. E., Jr., J. L. Hofman, and L. D. Martin
1993 Bone Attritional Processes at the 12 Mile Creek Site, Kansas. *Current Research in the Pleistocene* 10:67–69.

Hollin, J. T., and D. H. Schilling
1981 Late Wisconsin-Weichselian Mountain Glaciers and Small Ice Caps. In *The Last Great Ice Sheets*, edited by G. H. Denton and T. J. Hughes. John Wiley & Sons, New York.

Hopkins, D. M.
1972 The Paleogeography and Climatic History of Beringia During Late Cenozoic Time. *Inter-Nord* 12:121–150.

Hopkins, D. M., J. V. Matthews, Jr., C. E. Schweger, and S. B. Young (editors)
1982 *Paleoecology of Beringia*. Academic Press, New York.

Hughes, T. J.
1981 Numerical Reconstruction of Paleo-Ice Sheets. In *The Last Great Ice Sheets*, edited by G. H. Denton and T. J. Hughes, pp. 221–261. John Wiley & Sons, New York.

Hughes, T. J, G. H. Denton, B. G. Andersen, D. H. Schilling, J. L. Fastook, and C. S. Lingle
1981 The Last Great Ice Sheets; A Global View. In *The Last Great Ice Sheets*, edited by G. H. Denton and T. J. Hughes, pp. 263–317. John Wiley & Sons, New York.

Iverson, R. L., H. C. Curl, and H. B. O'Connors
1974 Summer Phytoplankton Blooms in Auke Bay, Alaska, Driven by Wind Mixing of the Water Column. *Limnology and Oceanography* 19:271–278.

Ives, J. D.
1974 Biological Refugia and the Nunatak Hypothesis. In *Arctic and Alpine Environments*, edited by J. D. Ives and R. G. Barry, pp. 605–636. Methuen & Co., London.

Jackson, L. J.
1987 Ontario Paleoindians and Proboscideans: A Review. *Current Research in the Pleistocene* 4:109–112.

1989 Late Pleistocene Caribou from Northern Ontario. *Current Research in the Pleistocene* 4:72–74.

Jackson, L. J., and H. McKillop
1987 Early Paleoindian Occupation in Interior Southcentral Ontario. *Current Research in the Pleistocene* 4:11–14.

Jacobson, G. L., Jr., and H. J. B. Birks
1980 Soil Development on Recent End Moraines of the Klutlan Glacier, Yukon Territory, Canada. *Quaternary Research* 14:87–100.

Jacobson, G. L, Jr., T. Webb III, and E. C. Grimm
1987 Patterns and Rates of Vegetation Change During the Deglaciation of Eastern North America. In *North America and Adjacent Oceans During the Last Deglaciation*, edited by W. F. Ruddiman and H. E. Wright, Jr., pp. 277–288. *The Geology of North America, Special Centennial Volume K-3.* Geological Society of America, Boulder, CO.

Johannessen, J., and A. Henricksen
1978 Chemistry of Snow Melt-Water; Changes in Concentration During Melting. *Water Resources Research* 14:615–619.

Johnsen, S. J., H. B. Clausen, W. Dansgaard, K. Fuhrer, N. Gunderstrup, C. U. Hammer, P. Iversen, J. Jouzel, B. Stauffer, and J. P. Steffensen
1992 Irregular Glacial Interstadials Recorded in a New Greenland Ice Core. *Nature* 359:311–313.

Johnson, E., and G. G. Politis
1993 New World Grassland Hunter-Gatherers in the Late Pleistocene and Early Holocene. *Current Research in the Pleistocene* 10:24–27.

Julig, P. J., L. A. Pavlish, and R. G. V. Hancock
1987 Instrumental Neutron Activation Analysis of Archaeological Quartzite from Cummins Site Thunder Bay: Determination of Geological Source. *Current Research in the Pleistocene* 4:59–61.

Kemmis, T. J., E. A. Bettis, and D. J. Quade
1994 The Des Moines Lobe in Iowa: A Surging Wisconsinan Glacier. American Quaternary Association Biennial Meeting, 19–22 June 1994, University of Minnesota, *Program and Abstracts:*112.

Kerr, R. A.
1993 How Ice Age Climates Got the Shakes. *Science* 260:890–892.

Kouker, W., A. Beck, H. Fischer, and K. Petzold
1995 Downward Transport in the Upper Stratosphere During the Minor Warming in Feb. 1979. *Journal of Geophysical Research* 100 (D6):11069-11084.

Krinsley, D. H., and J. C. Doornkamp
1973 *Atlas of Quartz Sand Surface Textures.* University of Cambridge Press, England.

Krinsley, D. H., and W. S. Newman
1965 Pleistocene Glaciation: A Criterion for Recognition of its Onset. *Science* 149:442–443.

Krinsley, D. H., and T. Takahashi
1962 Surface Textures of Sand Grains—An Application of Electron Microscopy: Glaciation. *Science* 138:1262–1264.

Lamb, H. H.
1977 *Climate; Present, Past and Future: Vol. II, Climatic History and the Future.* Methuen & Co., London.

Laub, R. S.
1995 The Hiscock Site (Western New York): Recent Developments in the Study of the Late Pleistocene Component. *Current Research in the Pleistocene* 12:26–29.

Legrand, M., and R. Delmas
1988 Soluble Impurities in Four Antarctic Ice Cores Over the Last 30,000 Years. *Annals of Glaciology* 10:116–120.

Legrand, M. R., C. Lorius, N. I Barkov, and V. N. Petrov
1988 Vostok (Antarctica) Ice Core: Atmospheric Chemistry over the Last Climatic Cycle (160,000 Years). *Atmospheric Environment* 22(2):317–331.

Legrand, M. R., F. Stordal, I. A. Isaksen, and B. Rognerud
1989 A Model Study of the Stratospheric Budget of Odd Nitrogen, Including Effects of Solar Cycle Variations. *Tellus* 41B:413–426.

Leopold, L. B., and J. P. Miller
1954 *A Postglacial Chronology for Some Alluvial Valleys in Wyoming.* U.S. Geological Survey Water-Supply Paper 1261.

Love, A., and D. Love
1974 Origin and Evolution of the Arctic and Alpine Floras. In *Arctic and Alpine Environments,* edited by J. D. Ives and R. G. Barr, pp. 571–603. Methuen & Co., London.

Mahaney, W. C.
1995 Pleistocene and Holocene Glacier Thickness, Transport Histories, and Dynamics Inferred from SEM Microtextures on Quartz Particles. *Boreas* 24(4):293–304.

Mandryk, C. S.
1992 Human Viability of the Late Quaternary Ice-Free Corridor. American Quaternary Association, 12th Biennial Meeting, 24–26 August, 1992, *Program and Abstracts,* p. 37. University of California, Davis.

Marchitto, T. M., and Wei, Kuo-Yen
1995 History of Laurentide Meltwater Flow to the Gulf of Mexico During the Last Deglaciation, as Revealed by Reworked Calcareous Nannofossils. *Geology* 23(9):779–782.

Martin, P. S.
1982 The Pattern and Meaning of Holarctic Mammoth Extinction. In *Paleoecology of Beringia,* edited by D. M. Hopkins, J. V. Matthews, Jr., C. E. Schweger, and S. B. Young, pp. 307–326. Academic Press, New York.

Martin, P. S., and R. G. Klein (editors)
1984 *Quaternary Extinctions: A Prehistoric Revolution.* University of Arizona Press, Tucson.

Martin, L. D., and A. M. Neuner
1978 The End of the Pleistocene in North America. *Nebraska Academy Science Transactions* 6:117–126.

Martin, P. S., and H. E. Wright, Jr. (editors)
1967 *Pleistocene Extinctions: A Search for a Cause.* Yale University Press.

Mayewski, P. A., D. H. Denton, and T. J. Hughes
1981 Late Wisconsin Ice Sheets in North America. In *The Last Great Ice Sheets,* edited by G. D. Denton and T. J. Hughes, pp. 67–170. John Wiley & Sons, New York.

Mayewski, P. A., L. D. Meeker, S. Whitlow, M. S. Twickler, M. C. Morrison, R. B. Alley, P. Bloomfield, and K. Taylor
1993 The Atmosphere During the Younger Dryas. *Science* 261:195–197.

Mayewski, P. A., L. D. Meeker, S. Whitlow, M. G. Twickler, M. C. Morrison, P. Bloomfield, G. C., Bond, R. B. Alley, A. J. Gow. P. M. Grootes, D. A. Meese, M. Ram, K. C. Taylor, and W. Wumkes
1994 Changes in Atmospheric Circulation and Ocean Ice Cover over the North Atlantic During the Last 41,000 Years. *Science* 263:1747–1751.

Mayewski, P. A., M. S. Twickler, S. I. Whitlow, L. D. Meeker, Q. Yang, J. Thomas, K. Kreutz, P. M. Grootes, D. L. Morse, E. J. Steig, E. D. Waddington, E. S. Saltzman, P.-Y. Whung, and K. C. Taylor
1996 Climate Change During the Last Deglaciation in Antarctica. *Science* 272(5268):1636–1638.

McElroy, M. B., R. J. Salawitch, and S. C. Wofsy
1988 Chemistry of the Antarctic Stratosphere. *Planetary Space Science* 36:73.

Monaghan, G. W., and G. J. Larson
1986 Late Wisconsinan Drift Stratigraphy of the Saginaw Ice Lobe in South-Central Michigan. *Geological Society Of America Bulletin* 97:324–328.

Monaghan, G. W., G. J. Larson, and G. D. Gephart
1986 Late Wisconsinan Drift Stratigraphy of the Lake Michigan Lobe in Southwestern Michigan. *Geological Society Of America Bulletin* 97:329–334.

Monastersky, R.
1995 New Beat Detected in the Ice Age Rhythm. *Science News* 147:118.

Mulvaney, R., and E. W. Wolff
1993 Evidence for Winter/Spring Denitrification of the Stratosphere in the Nitrate Record of Antarctic Ice Cores. *Journal of Geophysical Research* 98(D3):5213–5220.

Murphy, D. M., and D. W. Fahey
1994 An Estimate of the Flux of the Stratospheric Nitrogen and Ozone into the Troposphere. *Geophysical Abstracts in Press* 4(2):2. Paper 93JD03558.

Nicholas, G. P.
1987 Redundancy in Early Postglacial Land Use in Robbins Swamp, Southwestern New England. *Current Research in the Pleistocene* 4:21–22.

Nichols, H.
1974 Arctic North American Palaeoecology; the Recent History of Vegetation and Climate Deduced from

Pollen Analysis. In *Arctic and Alpine Environments*, edited by J. D. Ives and R. G. Barry, pp. 637–667. Methuen & Co., London.

Notholt, J.
1994 The Moon as a Light Source for FTIR Measurements of Stratospheric Trace Gases During the Polar Night: Application for HNO_3 in the Arctic. *Journal of Geophysical Research* 99(D2):3607–3614.

Noyes, R. W.
1982 *The Sun, Our Star*. Harvard University Press, Cambridge.

Overpeck, J. T., R. S. Webb, and T. Webb III
1992 Mapping Eastern North American Vegetation Change of the Past 18 ka: No-Analogs and the Future. *Geology* 20:1071–1074.

Overstreet, D. F., D. J. Joyce, K. F. Hallin, and D. Wasion
1993 Cultural Contexts of Mammoth and Mastodont in the Southwestern Lake Michigan Basin. *Current Research in the Pleistocene* 10:75–77.

Parker, B. C., L. E. Heiskell, W. J. Thompson, and E. J. Zeller
1978a Non-Biogenic fixed Nitrogen in Antarctica and Some Ecological Implications. *Nature* 271:651–652.

1978b Non-Biogenic Fixed Nitrogen in Antarctic Surface Waters. Reply. *Nature* 276:97.

Peel, D. A.
1993 Cold Answers to Hot Issues. *Nature* 363:403-404.

Peteet, D. M.
1994 North American Evidence for Abrupt Climatic Changes During Deglaciation. American Quaternary Association Biennial Meeting, 19–22 June 1994, University Minnesota, *Program and Abstracts*:35–37.

Qin, D., E. J. Zeller, and G. A. M. Dreschhoff
1992 The Distribution of Nitrate Content on the Antarctic Ice Sheet Along the Route of the 1990 International Trans-Antarctica Expedition. *Journal of Geophysical Research* 97:6277–6284.

Radok, U., R. G. Barry, D. Jenssen, R.A. Keen, G. N. Kiladis, and B. McInnes
1982 *Climatic and Physical Characteristics of the Greenland Ice Sheet*. Cooperative Institute for Research in Environmental Sciences, University of Colorado, Boulder, CO.

Ranov, V. A.
1987 The Loessic Paleolith: A New Term in Paleolithic Terminology. *Current Research in the Pleistocene* 4:25–27.

Retallack, G. J.
1996 Acid Trauma at the Cretaceous-Tertiary Boundary in Eastern Montana. *GSA Today* 6(5):1–7.

Richmond, G. M., R. Fryxell, J. D. L. Montagne, and D. E. Trimble
1965 *Northern and Middle Rocky Mountains, Guidebook for Field Conference E. International Association for Quaternary Research, VIIIth Congress*, Nebraska Academy of Science, Lincoln, NE.

Richmond, G. M., and D. S. Fullerton
1986 Summation of Quaternary Glaciations in the United States of America. In *Quaternary Glaciations in the Northern Hemisphere*, edited by V. Sibrava, D. Q. Bowen, and G. M. Richmond, pp.183–196. Pergamon Press, Oxford.

Ritchie, J. C., and L. C. Cwynar
1982 Late Quaternary Vegetation of the North Yukon. In *Paleoecology of Beringia* edited by D. M. Hopkins, J. V. Matthews, Jr., C. E. Schweger, and S. B. Young, pp. 113–126. Academic Press, New York.

Rogers, R. A., L. A. Rogers, R. S. Hoffman, and L. D. Martin
1991 Native American Biological Diversity and Biogeographic Influences of Ice Age Refugia. *Journal of Biogeography* 18:623–630.

Schreiner, O., and B. E. Brown
1938 Soil Nitrogen. *Soils and Men, Yearbook of Agriculture* 1938, pp. 361–376. U.S. Department of Agriculture, U.S. Government Printing Office, Washington, D. C.

Schweger, C. E.
1982 The Pleistocene Vegetation of Eastern Beringia: Pollen Analysis of Dated Alluvium. In *Paleoecology of Beringia*, edited by D. M. Hopkins, J. V. Matthews, Jr., C. E. Schweger, and S. B. Young, pp. 95–112. Academic Press, New York.

Sibrava,V., D. Q. Bowen, and G. M. Richmond (editors)
1986 *Quaternary Glaciations in the Northern Hemisphere*. Pergamon Press, Oxford.

Smalley, I. J.
1966 The Properties of Glacial Loess and the Formation of Loess Deposits. Sedimentary Petrology 36:669–676.

Smith, K. P.
1995 Paleoindian Manifestations in the Spring Creek Drainage, Genesee County, New York. *Current Research in the Pleistocene* 12:43–45.

Soffer, O.
1985 *The Upper Paleolithic of the Central Russian Plain*. Academic Press, San Diego, CA.

Soller, D. R.
1992 Text and References to Accompany "Map Showing the Thickness and Character of Quaternary Sediments in the Glaciated United States East of the Rocky Mountains." U.S. Geological Survey Bulletin 1921.

1993 *Map Showing the Thickness and Character of Quaternary Sediments in the Glaciated United States East of the Rocky Mountains—Northeastern States, the Great Lakes, and Parts of Southern Ontario and the Atlantic Offshore Area (East of 80o31' West Longitude)*. U.S. Geological Survey Misc. Invest Series Map I-1970-A, scale 1:1,000,000.

1994 *Map Showing the Thickness and Character of Quaternary Sediments in the Glaciated United States East of the Rocky Mountains—Northern Plains (West of 102o West Longitude).* U.S. Geological Survey Misc. Invest. Series Map I-1970-D, scale 1:1,000,000.

1997 *Map Showing the Thickness and Character of Quaternary Sediments in the Glaciated United States East of the Rocky Mountains—Northern and Central Plains (93° to 102° West Longitude).* U.S. Geological Survey Misc. Invest. Series Map I-1970-C, scale 1:1,000,000.

1998 *Map Showing the Thickness and Character of Quaternary Sediments in the Glaciated United States East of the Rocky Mountains—Northern Great Lakes States and Central Mississippi Valley States, the Great Lakes, and Southern Ontario (80°31' to 93° West Longitude).* U.S. Geological Survey Misc. Invest. Series Map I-1970-B, scale 1:1,000,000.

Song, N.
1994 Freezing Temperatures of H2SO4/HNO3/H2O Mixtures: Implications for Polar Stratospheric Clouds. *Geophysics Research Letters* 21(24):2709–2712.

Stuiver, M., D. G. Denton, T. J. Hughes, and J. L. Fastook
1981 History of the Marine Ice Sheet in West Antarctica during the Last Glaciation: A Working Hypothesis. In *The Last Great Ice Sheets,* edited by G. H. Denton and T. J. Hughes, pp. 319–436. John Wiley & Sons, New York.

Tabazadeh, A., A. P. Turco, and M. Z. Jacobson
1994 A Model for Studying the Composition and Chemical Effects of Stratospheric Aerosols. *Journal of Geophysical Research* 99(D6):12897–12914.

Tainosho, Y., Y. Takahashi, Y. Osanai, and N. Tsuchiya
1991 Ammonium Content of Biotites from Granitic and Metamorphic Rocks in the Sor Rondane Mountains, East Antarctica. In *NIPR Symposium on Antarctic Geosciences, Proceedings,* pp. 112–121. No. 5, National Institute of Polar Research, Tokyo.

Taylor, K. C., G. W. Lamorey, G. A. Doyle, R. B. Alley, P. M. Grootes, P. A. Mayewski, J. W. C. White, and L. K. Barlow
1993 The "Flickering Switch" of Late Pleistocene Climate Change. *Nature* 361(6411):432–436.

Teller, J. T.
1987 Proglacial Lakes and the Southern Margin of the Laurentide Ice Sheet. In *North America and Adjacent Oceans during the Last Deglaciation,* edited by W. F. Ruddiman and H. E. Wright, Jr., pp. 39–69. *The Geology of North America, Special Centennial Volume K-3.* Geological Society of America, Boulder, CO.

1989 Importance of the Rossendale Site in Establishing a Deglacial Chronology Along the Southwestern Margin of the Laurentide Ice Sheet. *Quaternary Research* 32:12–23.

Thompson, R. S., C. Whitlock, P. J. Bartlein, S. P. Harrison, and W. G. Spaulding
1993 Climate Changes in the Western United States Since 18,000 Years B. P. In *Global Climates Since the Last Glacial Maximum,* edited by H. E. Wright, J. E. Kutzbach, T. Webb, III, W. F. Ruddiman, F. A. Street-Perrott, and P. J. Bartlein, pp. 468–513. University of Minnesota Press, Minneapolis.

Tomenchuk, J., and R. S. Laub
1995 New Insights into Late-Pleistocene Bone Technology at the Hiscock Site, Western New York State. *Current Research in the Pleistocene* 12:71–74.

Toon, G. C., C. B. Farmer, P. W. Schaper, L. L. Lowes, and R. H. Norton
1992 Evidence for Subsidence in the 1989 Arctic Winter Stratosphere from Airborne Infrared Composition Measurements. *Journal of Geophysical Research* 97(D8):7963–7970.

Turner, M. D., M. T. Beatty, Murray Klages, Paul McDaniel, J. C. Turner, and R. Bonnichsen
1991 Late Pleistocene-Early Holocene Paleoclimates and Environments of Southwestern Montana. *Current Research in the Pleistocene* 8:119–122.

Velichko, A. A.
1973 *The Natural Process in the Pleistocene.* Nauka, Moscow.

Velichko, A. A. (editor)
1977 *Atlas Pleistotsena.* Nauka, Moscow.

Velichko, A. A., and T. D. Morozova
1969 The Loesses of Belgium. USSR Academy of Science. *Izvestiya, Seria Geograficheskaya* 4:69–76.

Vernekar, A. D.
1968 *Long-Period Global Variation of Incoming Solar Radiation. v. II, E.* Final Report to U.S. Department of Commerce; Environmental Science Services Administration, v. III, Contract No. E22-137-67(N). Travelers Research Center Inc., Hartford, CT.

Vincent, J. S., and V. K. Prest
1987 The Early Wisconsinan History of the Laurentide Ice Sheet. In *The Laurentide Ice Sheet,* edited by R. J. Fulton and J. T. Andrews. *Geographie physique et Quaternaire* 41(2):199–213.

Vitt, F. M.
1994 A Comparison of Sources of Odd Nitrogen Production in the Earth's Atmosphere as Calculated Using a Two-Dimensional Model. In *Atmospheric Ionization by Solar Particles Detected by Nitrate Measurements in Antarctic Snow,* edited by G. Dreschhoff, F. Vitt, T. Armstrong, and T. Cravens. Annual Technical Report, AFOSR-F 49620-J-0235DEF.

Vrba, E.
1994 Habitat Theory of How Climate Affects Migration and Evolution. American Quaternary Association Biennial Meeting, 19–22 June 1994, University of Minnesota. *Program and Abstracts*:49–51.

Watson, R. A.
1980 Landform Development on Moraines of the Klutlan Glacier, Yukon Territory, Canada. *Quaternary Research* 14:50–59.

Wayne, W. J., and J. H. Zumberge
1965 Pleistocene Geology of Indiana and Michigan, In *The Quaternary of the United States*, edited by H. R. Wright, Jr. and D. G. Frey, pp. 63–84. Princeton University Press, Princeton.

Webb, T. III, P. J. Bartlein, S. P. Harrison, and K. H. Anderson
1993a Vegetation, Lake Levels, and Climate in Eastern North America for the Last 18,000 Years. In *Global Climates Since the Last Glacial Maximum*, edited by H. E. Wright Jr., J. E. Kutzbach, T. Webb, III, W. F. Ruddiman, F. A. Street-Perrott, and P. J. Bartlein, pp. 415–467. University of Minnesota Press, Minneapolis.

Webb, T., III, W. F. Ruddiman, F. A. Street-Perrott, V. Markgraf, J. E. Kutzbach, P. J. Bartlein, H. E. Wright, Jr., and W. L. Prell
1993b Climatic Changes During the Past 18,000 Years: Regional Syntheses, Mechanisms, and Causes. In *Global Climates Since the Last Glacial Maximum*, edited by H. E. Wright Jr., J. E. Kutzbach, T. Webb, III, W. F. Ruddiman, F. A. Street-Perrott, and P. J. Bartlein, pp. 514–535. University of Minnesota Press, Minneapolis.

Whiteside, M. C., J. P. Bradbury, and S. J. Tarapchak
1980 Limnology of the Klutlan Moraines, Yukon Territory, Canada. *Quaternary Research* 14:130–148.

Winkler, M. G.
1992 Since the Retreat of the Ice Sheet: A Wisconsin Wetland. In *Geographical Snapshots of North America*, edited by D. G. Janelle, pp. 197–203. Guilford Publications Inc., New York.

Winkler, M. G., and P. K. Wang
1993 The Late Quaternary Vegetation and Climate of China. In *Global Climates Since the Last Glacial Maximum*, edited by H. E. Wright, Jr., J. E. Kutzbach, T. Webb III, W. F. Ruddiman, F. A. Street-Perrott and P. J. Bartlein, pp. 221–264. University Of Minnesota Press, Minneapolis.

Woffsy, S. C., R. J. Salawitch, J. H. Yatteu, M. B. McElroy, B. W. Gandrud, J. E. Dye, and D. Baumgardner
1990 Condensation of HNO_3 on the Falling Ice Particles: Mechanism for Denitrification of the Polar Stratosphere. *Geophysics Research Letters* 17:449.

Wolff, E. W.
1995 Nitrate in Polar Ice. In *NATO ASI Series, Vol. I30, Ice Core Studies of Global Biogeochemical Cycles*, edited by R. J. Delmas. Springer Verlag, Berlin.

Wright, H. E., Jr.
1980 Surge Moraines of the Klutlan Glacier, Yukon Territory, Canada: Origin, Wastrage, Vegetation Succession, Lake Development, and Application to the Late-Glacial of Minnesota. *Quaternary Research* 14: 2–18.

Wright, H. E., Jr. and R. V. Ruhe
1965 Glaciation of Minnesota and Iowa. In *The Quaternary of the United States*, edited by H. E. Wright, Jr., and D. G. Frey, pp. 29–41. Princeton University Press, Princeton.

Zeller E. J. and G. A. M. Dreschhoff
1995 Anomalous Nitrate Concentrations in Polar Ice Cores—Do They Result from Solar Particle Injections into the Polar Atmosphere? *Geophysical Research Letters* 22(18):2521–2524.

Zeller, E. J., G. Dreschhoff, and M. D. Turner
1988 Impact of Ice-Related Plant Nutrients on Glacial Margin Environments. *Geological Society of America Abstracts with Programs, N.E. Section, March 10–12, 1988*, p. 80.

Zeller, E. J., and B. C. Parker
1981 Nitrate Ion in Antarctic Firn as a Marker for Solar Activity. *Geophysical Research Letters* 8(8):895–898.

Zielinski, G. A., P. A. Mayewski, L. D. Meeker, S. Whitlow, and M. S. Twickler
1996 A 110,000-Yr Record of Explosive Volcanism from the GISP2 (Greenland) Ice Core. *Quaternary Research* 45(2):109–118.

Periglacial Ecology, Large Mammals, and their Significance to Human Biology

V. Geist

Abstract

The diversity, large size, and luxury organs of large mammals in periglacial environments suggest great resource abundance and long periods of annual body growth. Characteristics of Ice Age mammals are reviewed briefly and compared to human characteristics. Hominids in their late evolution duplicated other mammalian families, evolving ecologically specialized resource defenders in the tropics and hypermorphic forms with large luxury organs in periglacial environments. The terminal Ice Age hominid species, Homo sapiens, is comparable to other terminal periglacial species. Novelty is linked to social selection during explosive colonization; efficiency selection on ecological adaptations generates gradualism. An ecological reconstruction indicates that on the lee side of glaciers, meltwater, loess and silt, katabatic winds, and sunshine produce young, productive, pulse-stabilized ecosystems. Current periglacial ecosystems are more productive than tundra at comparable latitudes. Colonization of cold environments by humans should proceed from periglacial to arctic environments. Large mammals may have been not only an opportunity for early humans, but also a liability in colonizing North America. Such colonization probably took place only after megafauna populations collapsed, accompanied by the extinction of larger carnivores. The exceptional phenotypic development of humans in the Upper Paleolithic suggests deliberate phenotype manipulation, and through this, self-directed evolution.

Introduction

THE EVOLUTION OF ICE AGE mammals and the nature of periglacial environments sheds light on the evolution of humans (Geist 1978). From the late Tertiary onward, a set of remarkable mammals evolved concurrently with the increased severity of seasonally cold climates. They evolved into hypermorphs characterized by luxurious, often morphologically bizarre growth, associated with progressive colonization of tropical, temperate, periglacial, alpine, and arctic landscapes. These species usually differ in structure from their tropical ancestors in increased body size and elaborated social organs, and also in a number of ecological and physiological attributes that are not irrelevant in a consideration of their conservation (Bailey 1980; Geist 1985, 1988). Compared to other mammals, *Homo sapiens* is a classic Ice Age mammal, analogous to other terminal periglacial species within different lineages, such as the Irish elk (*Megaloceros giganteus*), the wooly mammoth (*Mammuthus primigenius*), cave bear (*Ursus spelaeus*); or to living representatives such as *Alces, Ovibos, Thalarctos,* and others. An overview of Ice Age mammals and their characteristics is provided here to address aspects of human evolution, as relevant to the Pleistocene peopling of North America.

Questions regarding Pleistocene paleontological reconstructions may be addressed through the application of testable ecological hypotheses. There is a link between the past and the present in the study of Ice Age mammals: first, if one projects, for instance, the pattern of Cervidae evolution over geologic time, the order of species appearance parallels current biological distributions along latitudinal, altitudinal, and climatic gradients (Figure 1). This distributional pattern, not exclusive to the Cervidae, is repeated by other mammalian families through time. Progressive cooling of global climates is paralleled by the appearance of ever more bizarre large mammals in the paleontological record, and is analogous to modern

Faculty of Environmental Design, University of Calgary, Alberta, Canada

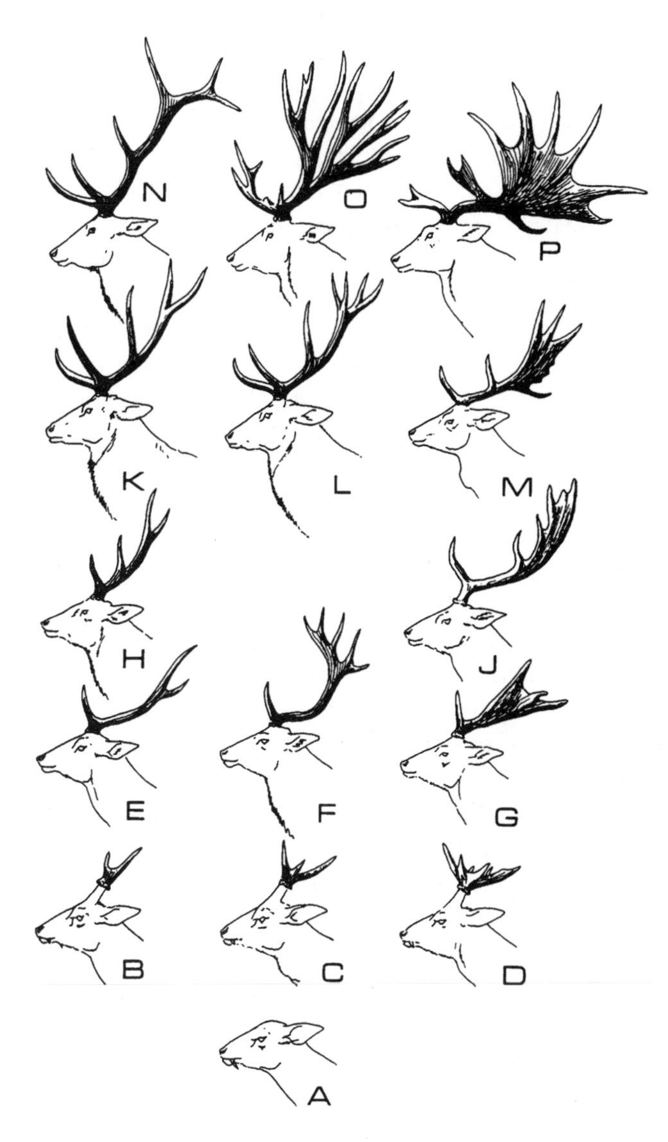

Figure 1. The pattern of evolution typical of Ice Age mammals, illustrated by extant and fossil Old World deer. The evolutionary progression moves from bottom (old forms) to top (latest forms). The evolution of these deer is paced by their antler structure, beginning in row B–D with a two-pronged plan Miocene), and ending in row N–P with a six-pronged plan (late Pleistocene, except for O). Each antler plan is found in simple form (left), with supernumary tines (middle), and with palmation (right). The progression from A through to N–P also is an ecological one from tropical forests to periglacial, subalpine or cold steppe environments. A) an Oligocene tusked deer, hypothetical ancestor; B) Eustylocerus, mid-Miocene; C) Dicrocerus, early Miocene; D) Stephanocemas, mid-Miocene; E) Axis, early Pliocene; F) Rucervus, late Pleistocene–Recent; G) Cervavitus, late Miocene; H) Sika, Villafranchian; J) Anaoglochis, Villafranchian; K) Cervus elaphus acoronatus, early Pleistocene; L) C. e. elaphus, mid-Pleistocene; M) Dama, mid-Pleistocene; N) C. e. canadensis, late Pleistocene–Recent; O) Eucladoceros, Villafranchian; P) Megaloceros gigantheus, late Pleistocene.

zoogeographic mammalian distributions. Second, remnants of periglacial environments analogous to the last Ice Age exist along the great ice fields of the St. Elias Range in the Yukon Territory and Greenland, representing locales where periglacial ecology can be directly studied (Geist 1978:185–210). Other studies shedding significant light on periglacial environments include Guthrie's (1989) treatment of the "mammoth steppe" and Pielou's (1991) popular reconstruction of ecological events following continental deglaciation.

Characteristics of Ice Age Mammals

HYPERMORPHIC ICE AGE mammals differ from Tertiary or xerothermic mammals through the development of hypertrophied or luxurious social organs and behavior including: antler and horn weapons used primarily for wrestling and display and a concomitant reduction in dagger-like weapons (Figure 2); very plastic body growth; relatively larger brains; large, seasonal fat deposits (Geist 1978:116–144, 185–210, 1987a); good insulation (i.e., fur) (Irving 1972); enlarged hair structures used to dissipate social scent (Mueller-Schwarze 1987); a general increase in chromosomes; greater plasticity in food habits; increased adaptation to open, treeless landscapes; and a low resistance to pathogens and parasites transmitted from relatives in more southerly latitudes. Thus far, emphasis has been placed upon the hypermorphs, which change in the aforementioned characteristics with latitude. Brief attention, however, should be given to four additional types of mammalian species, which also underwent evolutionary change during the Pleistocene. These are:

(1) The paedomorphic island dwarfs, which evolved without predators, developed organs that enhanced food acquisition and processing at the expense of anti-predation adaptations (Geist 1987a);

(2) The ecological specialists, usually sympatric, retain physical features developed in adaptation to a specific climatic zone (see Vrba 1980). Note in Figure 3 that the sympatric deer of India are representative of the primitive two- and three-pronged antler varieties. However similar in morphology, the deer occupy several different ecological niches, allowing for the exploitation of diverse food resources, ranging from coarse forage to young shoots and fruit. This pattern also is seen among tropical anthropoids;

(3) The hybrid species, differing from that of both parent forms, is seen in species such as the mule deer, which apparently evolved during post-glacial conditions from crosses of male black-tailed and female white-tailed deer (Carr et al. 1986, Cronin 1986, Geist 1990, Lingle 1989); and

Figure 2. Comparison of (top) an ancient, solitary, tropical forest-dwelling, war-colored, and resource-defending caprid, the serow (Capricornis sumatrensis) of SE Asia with (below) an Ice Age cold-and alpine-adapted, gregarious desert caprid, the Mongolian argali or giant sheep (Ovis ammon darwini) from central Asia. The serow carries dagger-like horns that are used as weapons of offense only. The sheep's horns also serve during parrying as organs of defense and as luxury organs in social life, symbolic of the male's ability to procure forage.

(4) The paedomorphic continental dwarfs that arose by a rare reversed pattern of geographic dispersal, namely from cold to warm climates, and represent the antithesis of hypermorphic evolution (Geist 1987a).

The large social organs of hypermorphic Pleistocene mammals, most notably the cerebral cortex (but not the brain stem) and fat-supported display structures are formed from biologically expensive tissues of low-growth priority (Hammond 1960). Such features develop to their fullest extent only after other tissues are developed. Large quantities of low-growth priority tissue material are developed in response to an abundance of rare material resources. These resources include scarce master nutrients, such as rare amino acids, which are vital to the growth of antlers, horns, and patterns of long hair, utilized for behavioral displays or insulation. Although fat retains twice the calories of protein and carbohydrates (Brody 1945), in proportion it is deposited for energy storage or organ support with great inefficiency; every calorie stored as fat requires the expenditure of at least one calorie during the lipogenesis process (Blaxter 1960). Only when energy and nutrient resources are highly abundant during seasons of growth can the full expression of a species' genetic potential for size be recognized (Waddington 1957), and such traits are subjected to natural selection mechanisms. Ice Age mammals are invariably among the giants in their families, with their biology linked to an abundance in environmental resources. Ice Age body size, although indicative of an effectiveness of resource exploitation, also implies the presence of unusually fertile environments, such as were uncommon otherwise. Since large mammals were larger during glacial periods than during interglacials (Edwards 1967; Guthrie 1984; King and Saunders 1984; Wilson 1980), and since mammals do not simply increase in body size with increasing cold as claimed by Bergmann's Rule (Geist 1987c), it would appear that glaciers are associated with food abundance. This implication is valid; glaciers are indeed sources of fertility, generating nutrient-rich landscapes, as contrasted to the old, leached soils of tropical environments (Geist 1978:199–207).

Luxury Organs

Luxury organs are considered to be those accurately reflecting the availability of scarce resources in the environment. Deer antlers, for example (Figure 4), grow maximally only when required protein, mineral,

Figure 3. Sympatric ecological specialists built on the same pre-Pleistocene body plan, exemplified here by tropical deer from India: A) the muntjac, specialized in feeding on diminutive bits of soft plant food; B) the hog deer, hider, specialized in feeding on grass; C) the spotted deer, gregarious, specialized in collecting short sprouting grasses available in coverless pastures; D) the swamp deer, gregarious, specialized in feeding on tall grasses on swampy ground; E) the sambar, hider, specialized in feeding on tough-fibered vegetation.

and energy resources are freely available (Goss 1983; Vogt 1936, 1948, 1950) and, consequently, are an index of the foraging success of males. As with horns in mountain sheep (Bunnell 1978), antlers reflect annual and regional variations in nutrition (Goss 1983). Antler mass increases with antler complexity from about 1 g (Wtkg)1.35 in small tropical deer with short antlers to 2.5–4.5 g (Wtkg)1.35 in subtropical three-pronged deer, 5.0–7.0 g (Wtkg)1.35 in temperate and cold zone deer, reaching 8.0–15.0 g (Wtkg)1.35 in the largest antlered forms such as reindeer, but also in fallow deer (*Dama*) and probably *Megaloceros gigantheus* (Geist 1987a, 1987b). Current research indicates that, interspecifically, antler size varies with the courtship display of the male to the female, though not with the displays of males toward rivals (Geist 1991a). Antler mass is largest in cursorial deer and tracks the female's ability to produce large young at birth and milk high in solids. This is necessary for runners if their young must outrun swift predators soon after birth (Geist 1986, 1987a, 1987b). Not surprisingly, huge body size and enormous antlers, horns, or tusks are found in prey where there are large, cursorial predators, such as in the Rancholabrean fauna of North America. The between-latitude variation in antler mass also appears to relate to the duration of the productivity pulse of vegetation (Figure 5). That is, the largest luxury organs can exist where there is the longest seasonal freedom from nutritional want. Since the duration of the productivity pulse is curvilinear with latitude, we expect body size in large mammals also to vary curvilinearly with latitude (see Figure 6). It is expected that luxury organs will vary in the same fashion, but no adequate data exist to test this hypothesis. Luxury organs also are represented by horn-like organs other than antlers and include the huge tusks of the extinct cold-adapted elephants and mastodons, the horns of larger-horned bovids and rhinos, and, in humans, the long, ever-growing head hair and fat-supported secondary sexual organs.

Weapons

In a south-to-north direction of dispersal, large mammals lose physical weapons typical of material-resource defense, such as combat canines (cervids, equids, suids, anthropoids), slashing incisors (rhinos), dagger-like horns, ossicones, and antlers (bovids, giraffids, cervids), and instead evolve wrestling-style weapons (Figure 2). This is an indication of an enhanced gregarious existence in open landscapes, in which individuals form coordinated herds for security (Geist 1978:74–80).

Figure 4. Antler evolution in the Alcini (moose): A) small Villafranchian moose adapted to speedy running, probably a dweller of shrub-steppes; B) giant mid-Pleistocene broad- fronted moose, the ancestor of C) the American stag-moose; and D) the recent moose, all of which specialized as trotters over rough, swampy, and snowy terrain. Antler size symbolizes ability to procure resources in excess of need and is apparently the consequence of female choice (sexual selection; Geist 1986, 1987a).

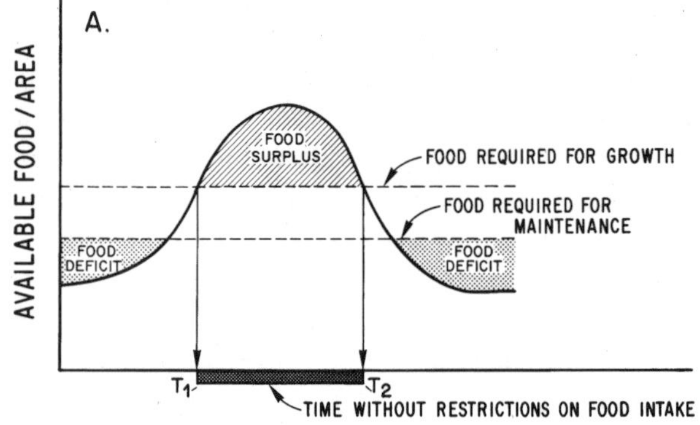

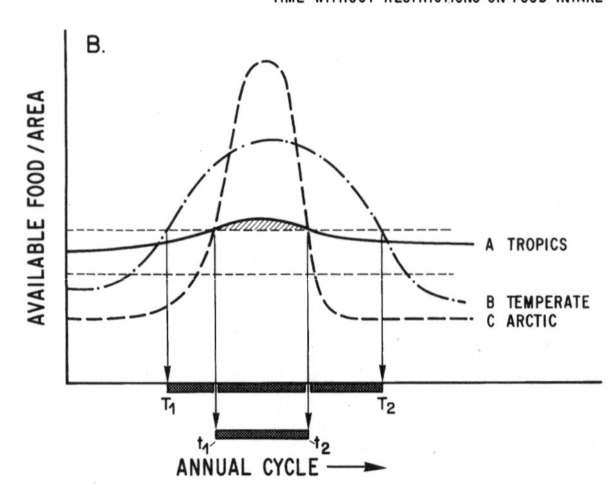

Figure 5. A) Graphic representation of the annual productivity pulse in relation to annual forage needs for maintenance and growth; and B) the productivity pulse, as realized in tropical, temperate, and Arctic environments (Geist 1987a).

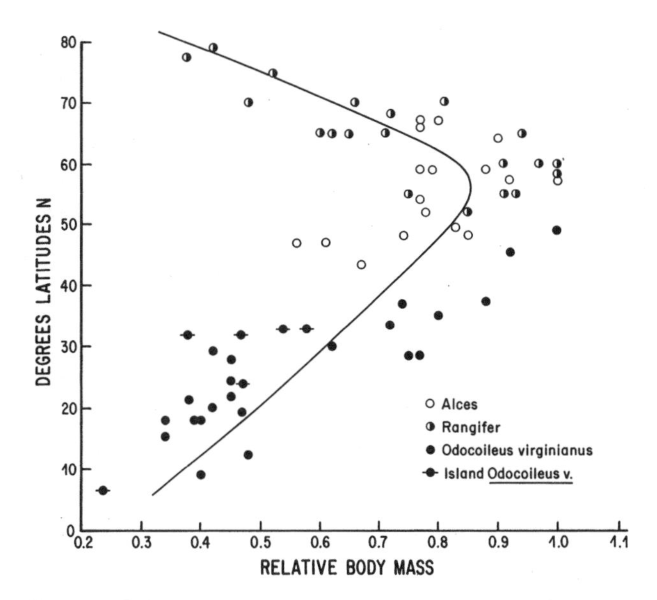

Figure 6. Relative body mass plotted in members of American New World deer. This is based on skull data, where the largest skull I could find was rated 1.0. Maximum size is reached around 60° N latitude and declines thereafter (Geist 1987c).

Fat Storage

LARGE MAMMALS FROM COLD climates tend to seasonally accumulate large amounts of fat to be used by males in rutting, by females in producing young and milk, and by all to subsidize food shortages in winter or to permit hibernation. Seasonal excesses in food are thus stored to subsidize existence in seasons of nutritional shortage. This is in contrast to their tropical and subtropical relatives that deposit very little fat (Graf and Nichols 1967; Ledger and Smith 1964), but utilize food more efficiently, bypassing the lipogenesis process. The inefficiency of much lipogenesis is permissible only where there is a seasonal overproduction of food. In addition to fat storage, there also are seasonal stores of minerals in bones and vitamins in the liver and fat. Seasonal availability of resources generates a seasonal rebuilding of the body and reduces the occurrence of acute demand for scarce nutrients. For example, annual replacement of the hair coat, which occurs at much the same time as antler and body growth, generates a great need for sulfur-based amino acids such as cysteine and methionine. These amino acids can be grown by the digestive microflora of ruminants, provided inorganic sulfur is available. Sulfur is available in many mineral licks (Jones and Hanson 1985), including those found at the margins of glaciers (Geist 1978:200–201).

Karyotype

THE KARYOTYPE OR CHROMOSOMAL architecture of a species varies so that the diploid number increases in relation to climatic severity, being lowest in the tropics. This is illustrated well by Old World and New World deer. The *nombre fondamental* (NF) of chromosomes in the Cervini appears to be 70, a little less than the NF 74 in the New World deer (Baccus et al. 1983; Gustavson and Sundt 1968), but the actual diploid number is a function of fusions. Old World species from cold climates, such as red, sika, and fallow deer, have 2n=68; the cold-adapted white-lipped deer from Tibet has a reduced 2n=66 (Wang et al. 1982). With the exception of the hog deer, which has a diploid number of 2n=68, there is an observed reduction in the diploid chromosome number in tropical deer, associated with an increase in metacentric and submetacentric autosomal chromosomes (in parentheses): the axis deer has 2n=66 (4), the sambar 2n=62–65 (8-5), the Timor deer 2n=60 (10), the Eld's deer 2n=58 (12), and the barasingha 2n=56 (14). The muntjacs are even more extreme in chromosome reductions, from 2n=47 in *Elaphodus* and 2n=46 in *M. reevesi,* the most cold-adapted muntjacs, to 2n=8 in *M. m. muntjak* and 2n=6 in *M. m. vaginalis* in the tropics (see Goss 1983; Groves and Grubb 1987). Similarly in New World deer, the normal diploid number in temperate or cold-adapted ubiquitous species is 2n=70, as seen in white-tailed and black-tailed deer, the American moose (*Alces a. americana*), reindeer, the water deer (*Hydropotes*), and the northernmost and most ubiquitous brocket *Mazama americana*. In the montane Pudu, the diploid value is 2n=69/70, and in the cold-adapted European moose, it is 2n=69. The cold-adapted European roe deer (*Capreolus capreolus*) has a number of 2n=74, while the Siberian roe deer (*C. pygargus*), which is adapted to even colder environments, has a diploid number of 2n=80. However, in tropical species, reduced values are seen: in *Ozetoceros* 2n=68; in *Blastocerus* 2n=66; in *Mazama gouazoubria* 2n=63/64; and in *Mazama americana temama* 2n=50 (see Groves and Grubb 1987). A possible cause of change in chromosomal architecture is found in the process of dispersal evolution (Geist 1987a). The chromosomal structure is rearranged during the dispersal phase of speciation, so that all species involved in a dispersal episode will differ genetically from ancestral populations. That is, we expect parallel changes to occur in chromosomal architecture in relation to the geographical distribution of species. This is indeed found in caprids (Nadler et al. 1973a, 1973b) and in Old World deer. Forms derived from primitive stems appear to have reduced diploid numbers in tropical environments, irrespective of their dispersal. Thus, the gregarious, savannah-dwelling *Rusa timorensis* retains a diploid number of 2n=60 (Neitzel 1982; Wang and Du 1982), compared to the solitary thicket dweller *Rusa unicolor mariannus* with 2n=64/65 (Hsu and Benirschke 1973) or *R. cambojensis* with 2n=62 (Wang and Du 1982). The muntjacs are another example, with the temperate-dwelling species having 2n=46 and the Indian muntjac 2n=6. This also is seen between the chital (2n=66) and the hog deer (2n=68). A case has been made for Odocoileus as the ancestor of all South American cervids (Brokx 1972). If so, derived South American species should have reduced diploid numbers. This has been observed to be true. We also find that in caprids derived forms have reduced diploid numbers, although linked here to dispersal evolution (Geist 1987a, 1987c). While the relationship between speciation and chromosomal architecture was discussed long ago by Goldschmidt (1940), the mechanisms of chromosomal evolution remain uncertain (Groves and Grubb 1987).

Ecology

Ecologically, Ice Age mammals differ from postglacial species by possessing plastic food habits, adaptable to seasonal variations. The large-scale variations in seasonal temperature from winter to summer require mammals to possess a multithermic ecological competence. They are capable of changing the morphology of their digestive systems to suit seasonal needs (Hofmann 1983), and they rarely develop extremely specialized food-related adaptations, such as hypsodont dentition, which is very common in tropical ruminants. As they are specifically adapted to diverse environments, and not to environmental constancy, they are not expected to succeed against their specialist relatives in more southerly latitudes. Therefore, they cannot successfully populate ecosystems with more benign climates, except where ecological specialists are absent. In recent times this was shown by the many unsuccessful attempts to introduce large northern red deer (wapiti) or Siberian roe deer into southern latitudes, where they did compete with southern relatives, or by the fate of North American and Eurasian ungulates introduced into New Zealand (Benide 1937; Stubbe and Passarge 1979; Wodzicki 1950). The success of large mammals of Siberian origin in North America can be attributed only to megafaunal extinction that swept away the ecological specialists, but left behind the specialists in noncompetition. Examples of such specialists include mobile r-strategists, that is, species with high reproductive rates, short, individual life expectancies, and excellent mechanisms of juvenile dispersal, such as white-tailed and black-tailed deer, pronghorn, black bear, peccaries, and coyotes (Geist 1985).

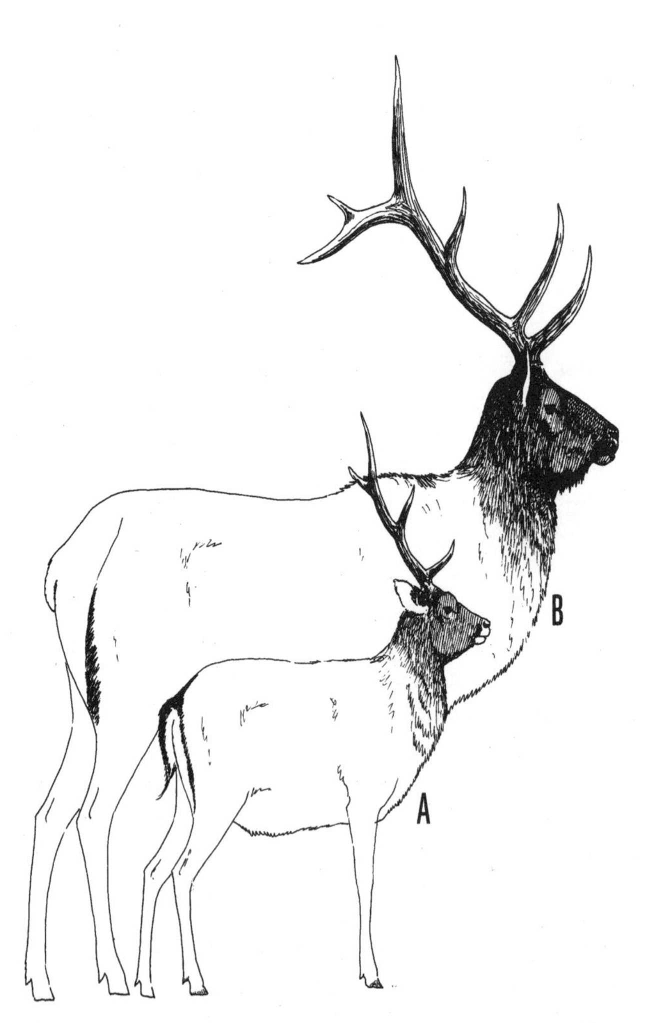

Figure 7. Small forest deer from warm-temperate climates, a sika stag (A), beside a closely related hypermorphic Ice Age giant, the wapiti (B), from the open plains. The sika deer is a "jumper" which runs to hide and has little endurance. The wapiti is the most highly evolved cursor, that is, a speedy, high-endurance runner among Old World deer. The body and limb proportions reveal this difference (Gambaryan 1974).

Security

As to security strategies, Ice Age mammals often are cursors (Gambaryan 1974)—that is, speedy, enduring runners that need space to elude predators (Figure 7). This probably is related to the preponderance of treeless landscapes during stadials. In consideration of the relationship between environment and security strategies, the cursorial adaptations of several species are noted: *Rangifer*—the northernmost New World deer and the most cursorial extant cervid, wapiti—the most cursorial Old World deer, or the Irish Elk (*Megaloceros giganthеus*)—the most cursorial deer ever to evolve (Geist 1986). Other mammalian lineages also possess cursorial open-country adaptations, a security measure that appears to predominate in Ice Age environments.

Phenotype Plasticity

Although currently speculative, it has been suggested that Pleistocene mammals are phenotypically plastic and have the innate ability to readily change their body size through time (see Geist 1978:116–144 and 1989 for review; Ellenberg 1978; Hammond 1960). Great reductions in body size undergone by large mammals since late glacial times have been observed (Edwards 1967; Guthrie 1982, 1984; King and Saunders 1984; Wilson 1980). However, size variation of the same order or greater characterizes current populations of some mammalian species. This is best exemplified by the five-fold difference in mass among populations of European red deer (Figure 8), from 70 kg for stags of the Austrian Weilhart population to 350 kg for Carpathian stags of the same species (Wagenknecht 1981). Experimentally, size differences of 2.2-fold have been demonstrated for red deer and roe deer by Vogt (1948, 1950). However, Vogt began his studies with deer of above-average size. Phenotype plasticity confounds taxonomy, as illustrated by the hapless case of the "wood bison," a "phantom subspecies" based on hair coat characteristics that are environmentally malleable rather than genetically fixed (Geist 1991).

Diseases and Parasites

Investigations of wildlife parasites and diseases (Anderson 1972; Anderson and Lankester 1974; Goodson 1982; Samuel 1979), and also of native American people (Baruzzi et al. 1977; Cook 1973; Dobyns 1983; Joralemon 1982; Neel 1979), indicate that epidemiologically, Ice Age mammals are highly vulnerable. Such species have a long history of life in seasonal environments with long, cold, dry winters that are not conducive to the existence of most parasites and pathogens. Consequently, these animals are not well adapted to handle the diseases and parasites of relatives evolved in milder climates. This causes difficulties for Ice Age or alpine mammals that move into lower latitudes and altitudes. Such migratory events are successful only during an absence of indigenous relatives, as occurred in North America following megafaunal extinctions when Siberian species, previously excluded by the densely packed Rancholabrean fauna, flooded south after the loss of specialists. Today, disease-promoting parasites present

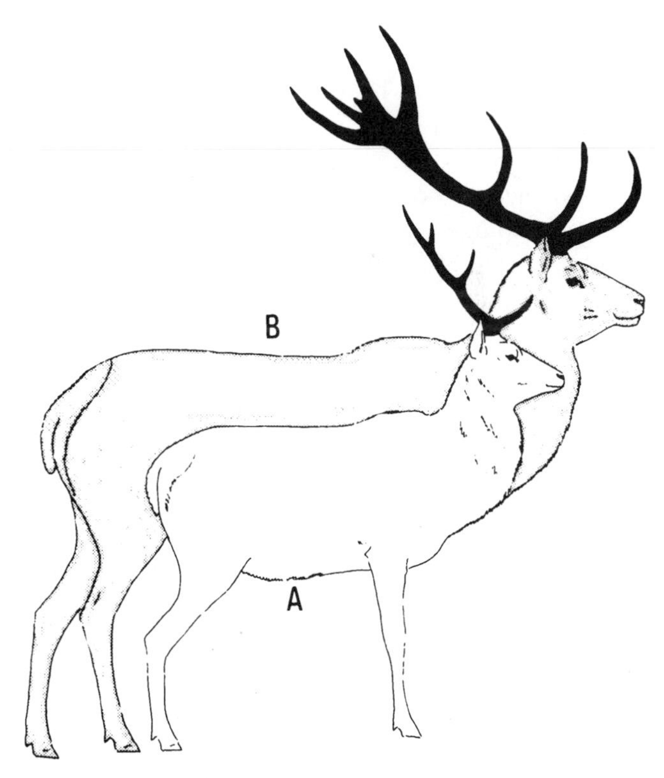

Figure 8. Environmental conditions can grow from similar genomes into vastly different phenotypes. A) This is the efficiency or maintenance phenotype of red deer that lived for generations on poor forage. Stags may at minimum adult size weigh only about one-fifth as much as (B) dispersal phenotypes living under luxurious nutritional conditions.

severe problems in North American wildlife conservation efforts owing to the introduction of non-native big game species for commercial game ranches and hunting enterprises (Geist 1985, 1988). Poor resistance to diseases and parasites and a competitive inferiority caused by a broad-based ecological adaptation indicate that the evolution and dispersion of Ice Age mammals operates most successfully in a unidirectional manner: from climatically benign but biologically demanding environments to climatically demanding but biologically benign regions (Geist 1978).

Homo Sapiens: An Ice Age Mammal?

Homo sapiens FOLLOWED closely the pattern discussed so far for Ice Age mammals, as detailed in Geist (1978):

(1) There was a dispersal of anthropoids from climatically benign to climatically demanding environments as revealed in the fossil record. In tropical environments, ecologically specialized anthropoids, possessing weapons and behavior for classic resource defense, range in size from midget to giant (gibbon, chimpanzee, orangutan, and gorilla). Their body plans, evolved in the mid-Tertiary period, are indicative of adaptation to a subtropical environment. *Australopithecus*, a subtropical form, branched out onto its own divergent evolutionary path in the late Tertiary. Its morphology suggests a dependency upon climbing for security and an adaptation to a savannah environment. It had lost its combat canines and great muscular strength and had increased brain size, characteristics suggesting a gregarious existence within a "selfish herd" and a reduced emphasis upon the defense of material resources. *Australopithecus* was succeeded at the beginning of the major glaciations by *Homo erectus*, which dispersed into temperate climates and was capable of life in the steppe, away from trees, and represents what was most likely the first human species. *H. erectus* was followed in late Pleistocene times by *Homo sapiens*, larger still in body and brain, which successfully occupied periglacial environments as Neanderthal (Geist 1981) and Cro Magnon forms. This basic pattern of geographic evolution, from climatically benign to severe environments, is thus the same as seen in other Ice Age mammals.

(2) Hominids, like cervids, equids, and rhinos, underwent a reduction in size of their combat teeth (canines), which currently remain unchanged in all extant resource-defending tropical anthropoids. The use of teeth and biting were abandoned in favor of other weapons.

(3) *Homo sapiens* remains one of the largest of the extant 160 species of primates as well as fossil forms.

(4) *Homo sapiens* has the largest brain of the anthropoids. (For those delighting in invidious comparisons, it may be pointed out that the allometric increase in hominid brain size is the same as the increase in antler mass in Irish elk).

(5) *Homo sapiens* is a very fat species. Normal males average about 15 percent body fat, while the reproductive ability of females is hindered without a body fat percentage in excess of ca. 25 percent (Frisch 1978, 1988). This percentage is three to five times the amount of fat found in some large tropical mammals (Ledger and Smith 1964)—a fact deserving greater attention.

(6) *Homo sapiens* possesses highly developed luxury organs as compared to other anthropoids. We are endowed with long, ever-growing hair on parts of the head, large breasts and buttocks supported by fatty tissues, eyes with enhanced pupils due to a white sclera, and lips that are large and well marked. Distinct behavior, owing to vocal and visual mimicry abilities, and a sophisticated cultural enhancement of biological displays also defines our species. The economist Thorstein Veblen (1899) long ago recognized that much of the biological display is related to the possession of material resources (a luxury trait); he termed such behavior "conspicuous consumption." The link between biology and culture in human behavior is treated in detail in Geist (1978).

(7) Ecologically, humans are truly generalists lacking an Eltonian niche; as a species, we have no biological profession, and our economic activities are diverse. We could hardly be more unspecialized. Elton's niche defines a species ecological "profession" (i.e., woodpecker niche); Hutchinson's niche describes precisely the outcome of a species profession in space and time. These are complementary conceptions of the ecological niche, with Elton emphasizing process, and Hutchinson the results.

(8) Humans exhibit great variability of body size between populations in both space and time. It has been noted that the physical, mental, and social development of humans is strongly linked to nutrition (see Geist 1978:141; Huber 1968; Steffensen 1958; Tanner 1962; Wercinska 1978). As predicted by the Dispersal Phenotype Model (Geist 1978:116–144), several events occur with improved nutrition: an increase in body size with material wealth is observed;

concurrent changes in personality occur from birth onward (Chauvez and Martinez 1979); an increase in performance of social behavior (Marmot et al. 1984; Young and Willmott 1973); and an increase in health (Stott and Latchford 1976). Contrary to the model, reproduction is not observed to increase, and consequently, longevity is maintained. The reproductive effort of women, as expected, is inversely related to longevity (Kitagawa and Hauser 1973) and is independent of income.

(9) The immune system of humans evolved during late-glacial times, in cold climates, and is thus susceptible to diseases of more southerly relatives (Baruzzi et al. 1977; Cook 1973; Dobyns 1983; Joralemon 1982; Neel 1979). In short, humans appear to be good examples of Ice Age mammals.

Periglacial Ecology

WHILE THE REMAINING periglacial environments vary greatly and are largely unsuitable analogies for modeling processes as they occurred along Pleistocene continental glaciers, some extant periglacial regions are relevant. An understanding of the manner in which Pleistocene glaciers generated fertile environments and increased plant production must be attained, for only such a situation could have led to the evolution of large mammalian hypermorphs. Work in the Ice Field Ranges of the Yukon provides the basis for understanding periglacial ecosystems, (Geist 1978:194–201):

(1) Periglacial environments are seasonally pulse-stabilized ecosystems, characterized by annual production of fertile mineral material in the form of nutrient-rich silt and loess delivered by glaciofluvial processes. This creates a vigorously productive ecosystem with many pioneering plant species and a high proportion of reproductive tissue relative to support tissues. Glacial meltwaters generate expanses of alluvium, creating fens, marshes, and floodplain meadows, while eolian processes generate loess-steppe environments.

(2) The lee side of the glacial system is characterized by winds, frequently katabatic in nature, and abundant sunshine. This down-wind area is of greatest interest because glacial conditions there create environments where mammalian life should be most abundant.

(3) Sharp contrasts in diurnal and seasonal temperatures, coupled with the near unidirectional distribution of loess, produce a mosaic of sharply delineated habitats. Close to and well above the glacier, in areas without loess deposition, tundra environments can be found (probably a very rare ecosystem in glacial times). In areas with loess deposition, the formation of periglacial loess-steppe follows. As a soil constituent, loess introduces important drainage and thermal properties. With the addition of scattered pockets of spruce and lowland flood meadows, a system of habitats in juxtaposition allows for a great diversity of plant and animal species that today are widely separated (Geist 1978:205-207).

(4) The dissolution and evaporation of salts generate mineral licks at the melt-off edge of the glacier. These mineral pans are avidly sought by large mammals (Geist 1978:199–202). Their visits are particularly numerous and lengthy in the spring and early summer, a time that coincides with the maximum availability of young green forage and with a period of intense body and hair growth, late gestation, and lactation. The mineral wealth at the edge or in the vicinity of the glacier is excavated by animals from below its loess covering, following glacial retreat. The sulfur salts gained here are needed for the production of vital amino acids that are essential for the growth of hair, horn, and connective tissues (Jones and Hanson 1985). The acquisition of other minerals, such as sodium and magnesium, also are seasonally important in regulating physiological processes. Magnesium is a vital antidote that counteracts high levels of ingested potassium contained in sprouting spring forage (Jones and Hanson 1985). A preliminary approximation of large mammal biomass derived from a consideration of nine species, including feral horses, in the periglacial region of the St. Elias Range (Geist 1978:195, 204), suggests a carrying capacity of 89 kg/100 ha. This, although a conservative estimate, is about five times greater than tundra environments at comparable latitudes. With Pleistocene megaherbivores and predators in place, the biomass value would have been even higher. The modern species diversity in this area includes 34 species of small mammals and 13 large mammal species. Fifteen additional large mammal species became extinct in the post-glacial period. In perspective, however, predator-prey ratios have remained unchanged. In the modern Yukon, one finds roughly one wolf per 122 large mammals, the same as that observed in the Alaskan fossil record (Guthrie 1968). In essence, glaciers are akin to ocean tides, with the periglacial areas comparable to the intertidal zones wherein the movement of diverse nutrients in concert with energy pulses generates productivity. The annual glacial meltwaters and the concomitant introduction of fertile

Figure 9. Three species that change with distance dispersed. Bottom row is the primitive condition for sheep, goat, and red deer (urial, markhor, and Kashmir stag, respectively). Some distance east, in Turkey, one finds the more highly evolved Anatolian mouflon, the bezoar goat, and the aral stag (middle row). Furthest west, in the western levant, one finds an evolved mouflon, Spanish ibex, and west-European red deer (top row). Note the changes on markings, pelage patterns, and antler branching.

silt create a perpetually young, productive ecosystem. It is only within these rich ecosystems that humans could have advanced along river valleys and subsequently adapted to the arctic (see Geist 1978).

How Ice Age Mammals Evolve

ALTHOUGH OTHER MECHANISMS are involved in the evolutionary process, only the factors involved in the creation of latitudinal hypermorphs through "dispersal evolution" is of concern here (Geist1971a, 1971b, 1978, 1987a). Large mammals form distinctly different phenotypes under the extremes of nutrient and energy availability. Periods of low availability generate *maintenance* phenotypes, specialists in competition for the efficient utilization of scarce material resources. Severe resource shortages generate selection for smaller-sized individuals with increasingly more efficient organs for food acquisition and processing. Efficiency selection should generate a gradualism of physical traits in the fossil record, especially those organs dealing with the defense of resources (teeth) and security (e.g., body form changes, mainly of runners and jumpers). When nutrients and energy are superabundant, which only occurs in the colonization of an uninhabited habitat, a large, luxurious, mobile, strong phenotype develops that, in the process of maximizing reproduction, competes not for material resources, but for mates. This is the *dispersal* phenotype. Thus during dispersal into uncolonized regions, under severe social competition, is novelty and an enhancement of social organs evolved. When a habitat reaches its carrying capacity, individuals are selected for maintenance phenotypes and dispersal evolutionary processes are brought to a halt. Novelty in the external appearance of species evolving during periods of dispersal through intense social selection is followed by a time of gradualism, whereby fine tuning of the new adaptations via efficiency selection occurs. Pulses of dispersal evolution, rapid but brief, serve to "punctuate the equilibrium," while subsequent efficiency selection upon ecological adaptations insures gradual changes with improvement. Dispersal evolution is thus a mechanism that leads to the rapid evolution of novelty, changing social organs with geographic distance and affecting all comparable members of a fauna (Figure 9). A consideration of the dichotomy of phenotype development, that is, dispersal versus maintenance, is vital to an understanding of the characteristics of modern humans.

The Body Size Problem

FOUR HYPOTHESES ARE OFFERED here to account for the large size of Ice Age mammals:

(1) Ice Age mammals experienced a seasonal productivity pulse of extended duration (Geist 1987a, Guthrie 1984). It has been shown by the curvilinear change in body size in relation to latitude (Geist 1987a) that body size varies with the duration, not the height, of the productivity pulse. For extant species to grow to the size of their glacial relatives, an exceedingly long pulse would be required.

(2) The periglacial zones were exceptionally productive and diversely vegetated (Guthrie 1984). Diversity of forage is essential to minimize the effects of toxic secondary plant compounds, and thus maximize the intake of digestible forage. Combined with a long productivity pulse, this generates conditions favorable for maximum body growth.

(3) The productivity of plant matter was high in proportion to area. In a young ecosystem this results in a high percentage of reproductive tissue in proportion to support tissue. That is, there is a great availability of high-energy and protein seeds or flowering parts. In open areas, almost all of the photosynthetic layer is available for grazing, and a large amount of readily obtainable high-quality forage is at hand. Conditions such as these also support maximum growth and lactation.

(4) Attainable body size is dependent upon the size of predators. This hypothesis is presented on the finding that on islands, ungulate species lacking predators shrink in size (Azzaroli 1982). Also, continentally, small, culling predators are associated with small herbivores (e.g., in South America), while large predators are associated with large herbivores (e.g., Africa). In the Rancholabrean period, huge predators and herbivores existed side by side (Kurtén and Anderson 1980). Relevant to this concern are the large horn-like organs of Rancholabrean ruminants, such as those of *Bison latifrons* or *Cervalces*. The size of these features is expected to increase in response to pressure from culling predators (Geist 1986). Why carnivores increase in size remains to be answered. The carnivorous bear *Arctodus*, for example, increased in size along with specialization of its jaws, from the Irvingtonian to the Rancholabrean period (Kurtén and Anderson 1980). That the sizes of wolves also fluctuate in kind with the size of their prey is seen in the curvilinear change in body size in relation to latitude (Geist 1987c).

Were Humans Kept Out of North America by the Rancholabrean Fauna?

APPARENTLY HUMANS APPEARED late in central North America with other Siberian mammals, such as the wolf, grizzly bear, wolverine, wapiti, Siberian bison, and moose (Geist 1989). This Siberian fauna expanded into the vacuum of North America left by the dying megafauna. Evidence for human occupation increases in step with megafaunal die-back over a period of about 6,000 years (Geist 1989). There is no evidence and little reason to believe that humans could have tackled the huge carnivorous bear *Arctodus*. Armed with primitive weapons, people had considerable difficulties dealing with the much smaller brown bear and in California withdrew from areas where brown bears were common. Kurtén (1976) argues that in Eurasia, Upper Paleolithic peoples were capable only of hunting the brown bear; evidence for the successful hunting of the larger cave bear is nonexistent. The overlap between humans and *Arctodus* appears to have been minimal (Johnson and Shipman 1986). It appears that humans colonized the Americas only following the collapse of megafauna populations. The elimination of megaherbivore populations in North America would be needed to trigger a collapse in other faunal groups (see Martin and Klein 1984; Owen-Smith 1987). Thereafter, floristic changes would favor very large, destructive wildfires which would impoverish flora and fauna populations. Pressures introduced by human hunters would have had little impact without a decline in megafauna size and an increase in their vulnerability. Two factors could have produced this situation. First, if areas south of the continental ice sheet experienced cool and snowy winters and dry, cold summers, there would be a time period when snowfalls and cold did not coincide. If an Arctic air mass were to settle over much of the continent during an absence of snow cover, then all surface water would freeze. If the surface water were to stay frozen for a couple of weeks, then a mass mortality of ungulates would be expected. Second, Guthrie (1984) shows that floristic changes would have been detrimental to large caecal digesters (e.g., proboscideans, edentates, and equids) with their conservative K–strategies in reproduction developed at the end of the Pleistocene. The K–strategy must have been pushed by Rancholabrean megaherbivores to extremes in response to pressures from diverse, large-bodied predators. That is, the newborn young had to have been very large and inter-birth intervals must have been extremely long, even under normal conditions. With a drop in plant productivity, reproduction must have been curtailed even more, making the large megaherbivores unusually susceptible to any additional mortality factor. Massive population losses would have been difficult to restore rapidly and the weakened or poorly grown survivors quickly would have fallen prey to predators. If increased aridity of the late Pleistocene forced megaherbivores toward forested areas for water and forage, then the Arctodus threat to human hunters might have been minimized, as hunters could have escaped into the trees. Also, Rancholabrean megaherbivores probably were undaunted by the rather small human predator and therefore would have been relatively easy to hunt. With all things considered, human hunters could have provided the last little push needed to send the struggling megaherbivores into extinction.

Phenotype features

WHAT IS PUZZLING is why Pleistocene hunters retained their large body size for so long a time, changing to the distressingly poor physical development represented by Mesolithic populations only during post-glacial times. Theoretically, after colonizing and reaching an ecological carrying capacity, human populations should have declined from a predominance of dispersal phenotypes to maintenance phenotypes because of resource shortages. Instead, humans behaved, over a span of some 25,000 years, as if resources for ontogenetic development were unlimited. In the absence of colonization, this should occur only if there were conscious attempts at maximizing body size and individual development at the expense of reproduction. This would be, in essence, a culturally enhanced K–strategy of human reproduction. The process of generating maximally developed humans is difficult and depends upon the successful manipulation of the mother's body from a time prior to conception and through lactation. Her physical development must be very good, she must possess adequate fat resources, and her period of lactation must be prolonged. Not only does this demand a diet high in protein, but also an exceptionally supportive family milieu. Here we note the complex Venus cult practiced by the males. I suggest that this is not a coincidence, but an expression of a determined attempt to structure the environment of the female to maximize the physical development, and not the number, of children. Large body size must have been a desirable trait and a prerequisite for the highly athletic performances demanded by the successful use of primitive weapons to kill large mammals. Large brain size also is associated with the diversity of competencies mastered by Pleistocene humans. The high death rate of teenage males suggests a dangerous testing process of adult competence and skills. Consequently, it is likely that we are fixed genetically along the same lines as were successful in the Upper Paleolithic. These successful genes may have been isolated through maximizing physical development, with mechanisms of selection introduced by testing human physical traits against the dangers of the hunt. Only this could have led to the rapid genetic fixation of characteristics essential to survival in that game. If our ancestors consciously structured individual development and severely tested the product against large prey, resulting in high casualty rates, then are we not self-selected in our very own image?

The Importance of Ice Ages to Humans

IT APPEARS THAT THE periglacial environment was not only important, but was vital to the appearance and characteristics of modern humans and continues to exert its importance to this day (see Geist 1978). It is proposed here that we were shaped by hypermorphic speciation. The periglacial environment was so favorable that two types of hominids flourished during the last glacial: the Neanderthal in the long stretch of the early Würm; followed by Cro Magnon in the last glacial pulse. Both groups suffered during deglaciation, with the Neanderthals becoming extinct in the interstadial between Würm I and II, and the Cro Magnon barely surviving deglaciation and suffering severely in the following Mesolithic. In contrast, the Upper Paleolithic was a golden age for hominids, a time of flourishing cultural expression as revealed by the quality of paintings, carvings, and tools, and an age of excellent health and physical development of individuals. It is likely that human populations were not only shaped into permanent dispersal phenotypes, but may have shaped them. To this day, periglacial environments have continued to shape cultures. Many large and important civilizations were built upon glacial loess, taking advantage of fertile environments. Most cultures developed along large, flooding rivers in open plains (Carneiro 1970), with headwaters originating from ice fields and glaciers that released water and fertilizing silt to lands downstream (Geist 1978). We are children of the Ice Ages, relicts of cultures that flourished on the fertility left behind by Pleistocene glaciers.

Acknowledgments

This study was supported by grants from the Natural Sciences and Engineering Research Council of Canada.

References Cited

Anderson, R. C.
1972 The Ecological Relationships of Meningeal Worm and Native Cervids in North America. *Journal of Wildlife Diseases* 8:304–310.

Anderson, R. C., and M. W. Lankester
1974 Infectious and Parasitic Diseases and Arthropod Pests of Moose in North America. *Naturaliste Canadien* 101:25–50.

Azzaroli, A.
1982 Insularity and Its Effects on Terrestrial Vertebrates: Evolutionary and Biogeographic Aspects. In *Paleontology, Essential of Historical Geology*, edited by E. M. Gallitelle, pp. 193–213. S.T.E.M. Mucchi, Modena, Italy.

Baccus, R., N. Ryman, M. H. Smith, C. Reuterwall, and D. Camron
1983 Genetic Variability and Differentiation of Large Grazing Mammals. *Journal of Mammalogy* 64:109–120.

Bailey, J. A.
1980 Desert Bighorn, Forage Competition and Zoogeography. *Wildlife Society Bulletin* 8:208–216.

Baruzzi, R. C., L. F. Marcopito, M. L. C. Serra, F. A. A. Souza, and C. Stabile
1977 The Kren-Akorore: A Recently Contacted Indigenous Tribe. In *Health and Disease in Tribal Society*, edited by P. Hugh-Jones, pp. 179–200. Ciba Foundation Symposium 49 (new series). Elsevier, Amsterdam.

Beninde, J.
1937 Zur Naturgeschichte des Rothirsches. *Monographie der Wildsa Ugetiere*, vol. 4. P. Schoeps, Leipizg.

Blaxter, K. L.

1960 Energy Utilization in Ruminants. In *Digestive Physiology and Nutrition of the Ruminant*, edited by D. Lewis, pp. 183–197. Butterworth, London. Brody, S. 1945 *Bioenergetics and Growth*. Reinhold, New York.

Brokx, P. A.
1972 *A Study of the Biology of Venezuela White-tailed Deer (Odocoileus virginianus gymnotis Wiegmann, 1933), with a Hypothesis on the Origin of South American Cervids.* Ph.D. dissertation, University of Waterloo, Waterloo, ON.

Bunnell, F. L.
1978 Horn Growth and Population Quality in Dall Sheep. *Journal of Wildlife Management* 42:764–775.

Carneiro, R. L.
1970 A Theory of the Origin of State. *Science* 169:733–738.

Carr, S. M., S. W. Ballinger, J. N. Derr, L. H. Blankenship, and J. W. Bickham
1986 Mitochondrial DNA Analysis of Hybridization Between Sympatric White-tailed Deer and Mule Deer in West Texas. *Proceedings National Academy of Sciences USA* 83:9576–9580.

Chauvez, A., and C. Martinez.
1979 Consequences of Insufficient Nutrition on Child Character and Behavior. In *Malnutrition, Environment and Behavior*, edited by D. A. Levitski, pp. 283–255. Cornell University Press, Ithaca.

Cook, S. F.
1973 The Significance of Disease in the Extinction of the New England Indians. *Human Biology* 45:485–508.

Cronin, M.
1986 *Genetic Relationship between White-tailed Deer, Mule Deer and Other Large Mammals Inferred from Mitochondrial DNA Analysis.* Master's thesis, Montana State University, Bozeman.

Dobyns, H. F.
1983 *Their Numbers Become Thinned: Native American Population Dynamics in Eastern North America.* University of Tennessee Press, Knoxville.

Edwards, W. E.
1967 The Late Pleistocene Extinction and Diminution in Size of Many Mammalian Species. In *Pleistocene Extinctions: The Search for a Cause*, edited by P. S. Martin and H. E. Wright, Jr., pp. 141–154. Yale University Press, New Haven.

Ellenberg, H.
1978 Zur Populationsokologie des Rehes (Capreolus capreolus L. Cervidae) in Mitteleuropa. *Spixiana Journal of Zoology* 2:1–211. Staatssammlung Munchen.

Frish, R. E.
1978 Population, Food Intake and Fertility. *Science* 199(4324):22–30.

1988 Fatness and Fertility. *Scientific American* 258(3):8895.

Gambaryan, P. P.
1974 *How Animals Run.* (Translated from Russian.) John Wiley and Sons, New York.

Geist, V.
1971a *Mountain Sheep.* University of Chicago Press, Chicago.

1971b The Relation of Social Evolution and Dispersal in Ungulates During the Pleistocene, with Emphasis on the Old World Deer and the Genus Bison. *Quaternary Research* 285–315.

1978 *Life Strategies, Human Evolution, Environmental Design.* Springer-Verlag, New York.

1981 Neanderthal the Hunter. *Natural History* 90(1):26–36.

1985 On Pleistocene Bighorn Sheep: Some Problems of Adaptation, and Relevance to Today's Megafauna. *Wildlife Society Bulletin* 13:351–359.

1986 The Paradox of the Great Irish Stags. *Natural History* 95(3):54–64.

1987a On Speciation in Ice Age Mammals, with Special Reference to Cervids and Caprids. *Canadian Journal of Zoology* 65:1067–1084.

1987b On the Evolution of Optical Signals in Deer: A Preliminary Analysis. In *Biology and Management of the Cervidae*, edited by C. M. Wemmer, pp. 235–255. Smithsonian Institution Press, Washington, D.C.

1987c Bergmann's Rule is Invalid. *Canadian Journal of Zoology* 65:1035–1038.

1988 How Markets in Wildlife Meat and Parts, and the Sale of Hunting Privileges, Jeopardize Wildlife Conservation. *Conservation Biology* 2(1):1–12.

1989 Did Large Predators Keep Humans Out of North America? In *The Walking Larder: Patterns of Domestication, Pastoralism and Predation*, edited by J. Clutton-Brock, pp. 282–294. George Allen and Unwin Ltd., London.

1990 *Mule Deer Country*, with M. F. Francis (photographer). NorthWord Press, Minoqua, WI.

1991a Bones of Contention Revisited: Did Antlers Enlarge with Sexual Selection as a Consequence of Neonatal Security Strategies? *Applied Animal Behavior Science*19:453–469.

1991b Phantom Subspecies: The Wood Bison Bison bison "athabascae" Rhoads 1987, Is Not a Valid Taxon, but an Ecotype. *Arctic* 44(4):283–300.

Goldschmidt, R.
1940 *The Material Basis for Evolution.* Yale University Press, New Haven.

Goodson, N.
1982 Effects of Domestic Sheep Grazing on Bighorn Sheep Populations: Review. *Biennial Symposium of the North American Wild Sheep and Goat Council* 3:287–313.

Goss, R. J.
1983 *Deer Antlers.* Academic Press, New York.

Graf, W., and L. Nichols, Jr.
1967 The Axis Deer in Hawaii. *Journal of the Bombay Natural History Society* 63:629–734.

Groves, C. P., and P. Grubb
1987 Relationship of Living deer. In *Biology and Management of the Cervidae*, edited by C. Wemmer, pp. 21–59. Smithsonian Institution Press, Washington, D.C.

Gustavsson, J., and C. O. Sundt
1968 Karyotypes in Five Species of Deer (*Alces alces* L., *Capreolus capreolus* L., *Cervus elaphus* L., *Cervus nippon nippon Temm*, and *Dama dama* L.). *Hereditas* 60:233–248.

Guthrie, R. D.
1968 Paleoecology of Large Mammal Community in Interior Alaska During the Late Pleistocene. *American Midland Naturalist* 79:346–363.

1982 Mammals of the Mammoth Steppe as Paleoenvironmental Indicators. In *Paleoecology of Beringia*, edited by D. M. Hopkins, J. V. Matthews, Jr., C. E. Schweger, and S. B. Young, pp. 307–326. Academic Press, New York.

1984 Mosaics, Allochemics and Nutrients. An Ecological Theory of Late Pleistocene Megafaunal Extinctions. In *Quaternary Extinctions: A Prehistoric Revolution*, edited by P. S. Martin and R. G. Klein, pp. 259–298. University of Arizona Press, Tucson.

1989 Frozen Fauna of the Mammoth Steppe. University of Chicago Press, Chicago.

Hammond, J.
1960 *Farm Animals. 4th ed.*, 1971. Arnold, London.

Hofmann, R. R.
1983 Evolutionaere und Saisonbedingte Anpassung des Verdauungsapparates des Gamswildes (Rupicapra rupicapra). In *Wildbiologische Informationen fuer den Jaeger, VI*, pp. 85–93. Jagd and Hege Verlag, St. Gallen.

Hsu, T. C., and K. Benirschke
1973 *An Atlas of Mammalian Chromosomes*. Springer-Verlag, New York.

Huber, N. M.
1968 The Problem of Stature Increase: Looking from the Past to the Present. In *The Skeletal Biology of Earlier Human Populations*, edited by D. R. Brothwell, pp. 67–102. Pergamon, Oxford.

Irving, L.
1972 *Arctic Life of Birds and Mammals*. Springer-Verlag, Berlin.

Johnson, E., and P. Shipman
1986 Scanning Electron Microscope Studies of Bone Modification. *Current Research in the Pleistocene* 3:17–18.

Jones, R. L., and H. C. Hanson
1985 *Mineral Licks, Geophagy, and Biogeochemistry of North American Ungulates*. Iowa State University Press, Ames.

Joralemon, D.
1982 New World Depopulation and the Case of Disease. *Journal of Anthropological Research* 38:108–127.

King, J. E., and J. J. Saunders
1984 Environmental Insularity and the Extinction of the American Mastodont. In *Quaternary Extinctions: A Prehistoric Revolution*, edited by P. S. Martin and R. G. Klein, pp. 315–339. University of Arizona Press, Tucson.

Kitagawa, E. M., and P. M. Hauser
1973 *Differential Mortality in the United States: A Study in Socioeconomic Epidemiology*. Harvard University Press, Cambridge.

Kurtén, B.
1976 *The Cave Bear Story*. Columbia University Press, New York.

Kurtén, B., and E. Anderson
1980 *Pleistocene Mammals of North America*. Columbia University Press, New York.

Ledger, H. P., and N. S. Smith
1964 The Carcass and Body Weight Composition of the Uganda Kob. *Journal of Wildlife Management* 28:827–839.

Lingle, S.
1989 *Kinetic Analysis of White-Tail Mule Deer and Hybrid Gates*. Master's degree project, Faculty of Environmental Design, University of Alberta, Calgary.

Marmot, M. G., G. Rose, and M. J. Shipley
1984 Inequalities in Death ... Specific Explanation of a General Pattern? *The Lancet* May:1003–1006.

Martin, P. S., and R. G. Klein (editors)
1984 *Quaternary Extinctions: A Prehistoric Revolution*. University of Arizona Press, Tucson.

Mueller-Schwarze, D.
1987 Evolution of Cervid Olfactory Communication. In *Biology and Management of the Cervidae*, edited by C. M. Wemmer, pp. 223–234. Smithsonian Institution Press, Washington, D.C.

Nadler, C. F., K. V. Korobitsina, R. S. Hoffman, and N. N. Vorontsov
1973a Cytogenetic Differentiation, Geographic Distribution, and Domestication in Palearctic Sheep (Ovis). *Zeitschrift fuer Saugetierkunde* 38(2):109–125.

Nadler, C. F., R. S. Hoffman, and A. Woolf
1973b G-band Patterns as Chromosomal Markers, and the Interpretation of Chromosomal Evolution in Wild Sheep (Ovis). *Experientia* 29:117–119.

Neel, J. V.
1979 Health and Disease in Unaccultured Amerindian Populations. *Ciba Foundation Symposium* 49 (ns):155–167. Elsevier, Amsterdam.

Neitzel, H.
1979 Chromosomen Evolution in der Familie der Hirsche (Cervidae). *Bongo* 3:27–38.

Owen-Smith, N.
1987 Pleistocene Extinctions: The Pivotal Role of Megaherbivores. *Paleobiology* 13:351–362.

Pielou, E. C.
1991 *After the Ice Age. The Return of Life to Glaciated North America.* University of Chicago Press, Chicago.

Samuel, W. M.
1979 The Winter Tick Dermacentor albipictus (Packard 1869) on Moose, Alces alces (L.) of Central Alberta. *Proceedings of the North American Moose Conference and Workshop* 15: 303–348.

Steffensen, J.
1958 Stature as a Criterion of the Nutritional Level of Viking Age Icelanders. *Third Viking Congress*:39–51.

Stott, D. H., and S. A. Latchford
1976 Prenatal Antecedents of Child Health, Development and Behavior. *Journal of the American Academy of Child Psychiatry* 15:161–191.

Stubbe, C., and H. Passarge
1979 *Rehwild.* Neumann-Neudamm, Berlin.

Tanner, J. M.
1962 *Growth at Adolescence. 2nd ed.* Blackwell Scientific, Oxford.

Vallois, H. V.
1961 The Social Life of Early Man: The Evidence of Skeletons. In *Social Life of Early Man*, edited by S. L. Washburn, pp. 214–235. Aldine, Chicago.

Veblen, T.
1899 *The Theory of the Leisure Class.* Reprinted 1934, Modern Library, New York.

Verba, E. S.
1980 Evolution, Species and Fossils: How Does Life Evolve. *South African Journal of Science* 76:61–84.

Vogt, F.
1936 *Neue Wege der Hege.* Neumann-Neudamm, Berlin. 1948 Das Rotwild. Osterreichischer Jagd und Fischerei Verlag, Vienna.

Vogt, F., and F. Schmid, with an Appendix by H. Kohler
1950 *Das Rehwild. Osterreichischer* Jagd und Fischerei Verlag, Vienna.

Waddington, C. H.
1957 *The Strategy of the Gene.* George Allen and Unwin Ltd., London.

Wagenknecht, E.
1981 *Rotwild.* Neumann-Neudamm, Berlin.

Wang Zongren and Du Ruofu
1982 Evolution of Karyotype of the Genus Cervus. *Acta Genetica Sinica* 9:24–31 (in Chinese).

Wang Zongren, Du Ruofu, Xu Juanhua, and Che Qicheng
1982 Karyotype, C-banding and G-banding Pattern of White-lipped Deer (*Cervus albirostris Przewalski*). *Acta Zoologica Sinica* 28:250–255 (in Chinese).

Wercinska, A.
1978 Postcranial Skeleton and Natural Selection. *Proceedings of the Symposium on Natural Selection*, pp. 337–346. Czechoslovak Academy of Sciences, Liblice, Praha.

Wilson, M.
1980 Morphological Dating of Late Quaternary Bison on the Northern Plains. *Canadian Journal of Anthropology* 1:81–85.

Wodzicki, K. A.
1950 *Introduced Mammals in New Zealand.* Department of Science and Industrial Research Bulletin No. 98, Wellington, N.Z.

Young, M., and P. Willmott
1973 *The Symmetrical Family.* Pantheon Books, Random House, New York.

Pleistocene Peoples of Japan and the Peopling of the Americas

Takeru Akazawa

Abstract

Homo erectus appears to have been the first hominid to leave its African homeland and expand into Eurasia. Whether the first occupation of the Japanese archipelago was part of the expansion of *Homo erectus* during the middle Pleistocene has been discussed in detail, but information pertaining to this subject has not been sufficient and there is still much debate. Recent excavation data, however, show a long series of Paleolithic materials dated from about 200,000 to 30,000 years ago, lithic materials that are definitely human made. Thermoluminescent dates on volcanic materials associated with culture-bearing deposits suggest that the initial colonization of the Japanese archipelago may have begun in the middle Pleistocene. In this study, I present a hypothetical model to explain this new evidence based upon the expansion patterns of Pleistocene mammals in East Asia and also attempt to examine the peopling of the Americas as seen from Northeast Asia.

Japanese Pleistocene Human Remains

IN THE LIGHT OF RECENT research (Endo and Baba 1982; Suzuki 1981, 1982a, 1982b), it has been concluded that human skeletal remains found at Mikkabi and Hamakita in Honshu, and Yamashita and Minatogawa in Okinawa, are most probably those of Japanese Pleistocene humans. The Yamashita specimen was found in a deposit dated to 32,000 ± 1000 yr B.P. (TK-78) and the Minatogawa remains (see Figure 1) were dated to 18,250 ± 650 (TK-99) and 16,600 ± 300 (TK-142) yr B.P. These dates indicate that the first Japanese came from the continent over land bridges during the upper Pleistocene period, around 30,000 years ago.

Suzuki (1981, 1982a), who excavated and analyzed these skeletal remains stated that the earliest Japanese show strong skeletal homogeneity. The most striking feature is their small size, referred to by Suzuki (1981) as pygmy-like. He concluded from his comparative studies of upper Pleistocene humans in Japan and neighboring regions (Figure 2) that:

> *According to the results obtained from the factor analysis on the average values of cranial measurements, which include those from the Pleistocene age to the present day, the morphological position of the Minatogawa man, the Pleistocene man in Okinawa, is located much nearer to the Liukiang man of South China than to the Upper Cave man of North China. . . the Minatogawa man can possibly be regarded morphologically as one of the remote ancestors of the Jomon age man. Therefore, it will be possible to support that the Jomon age man is much closer in general relationship to the Minatogawa man and the Liukiang man than to the Upper Cave man. Consequently, so far as the available skeletal material is concerned, about 32,000 years ago, Pleistocene Homo sapiens on the Chinese continent, represented in the term of generalized proto-Mongoloid people, came to Japan [Suzuki 1981:55–56].*

Yamaguchi (1982:85) concurs, based upon Suzuki's studies, that "such diminutive statures estimated for early inhabitants in the Japanese islands suggest their possible relationship with the small-sized Upper Paleolithic population in the southeastern part of Asia, as represented by Liukiang man from South China and Niah Cave man from Borneo."

Nevertheless, the questions of when, from where, and over which routes these earliest immigrants came

Department of Anthropology and Prehistory , The University Museum, University of Tokyo, Tokyo, Japan

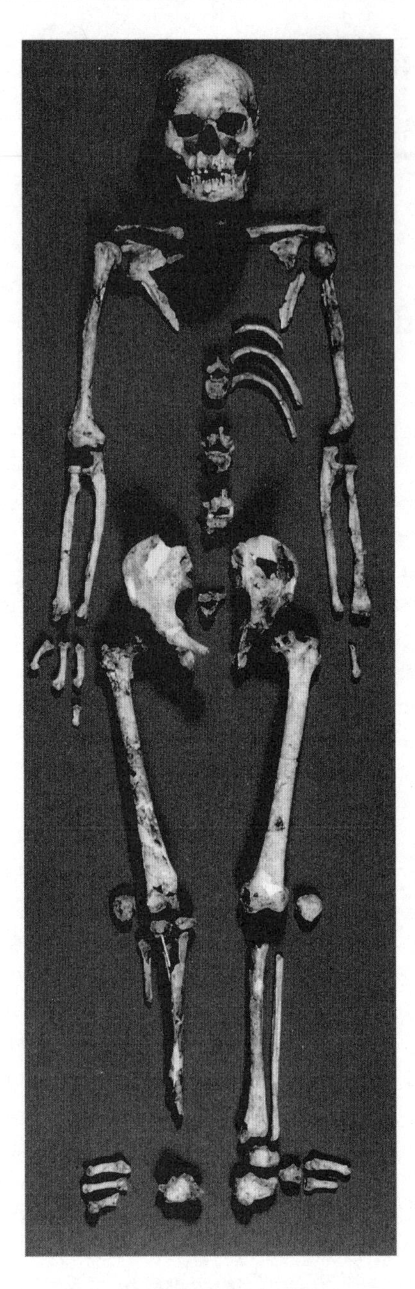

Figure 1. Japanese upper Pleistocene human skeleton found at the Minatogawa site in Okinawa, dated to about 20,000 years ago by the radiocarbon method. This is the best-preserved individual discovered, Minatogawa No. 1, a mostly complete skeleton of a 153-cm-tall male.

remain unanswered. The Pleistocene human remains are of low quantity and quality, and insufficient numbers have been discovered associated with Paleolithic material, although some new finds have been located in southwestern Japan including the Ryukyu Islands (Narasaki 1986). This causes some difficulty in discussing their relationship to lithic industries that already have been ordered chronologically.

Japanese Paleolithic

SINCE THE FIRST DISCOVERY of the Japanese Paleolithic at the Iwajuku site (about 100 km NW of Tokyo) in 1949, hundreds of excavations have contributed to our understanding of the Japanese Paleolithic. However, despite the 40 years of work since Iwajuku, the debate over the beginning of the Japanese Paleolithic continues.

The Kanto district, the most intensively investigated and documented area in the Japanese archipelago, has produced much Paleolithic material embedded in the volcanic Kanto Loam formations (e.g., Oda and Keally 1979, 1986). The Kanto Loam is divided into four stratigraphic units; from bottom to top these are the: Tama (more than 130,000 yr B.P.), Shimosueyoshi (ca.130,000–60,000 yr B.P.), Musashino (ca. 60,000–30,000 yr B.P.), and Tachikawa (ca. 30,000–10,000 yr B.P.) loam formations. Paleolithic remains have been obtained from the Tachikawa Loam only (Oda and Keally 1979). Recently, stone implements have been reported in Kanto deposits older than 30,000 years (Tatsuno 1987), but their age has not yet been confirmed.

Paleolithic assemblages recovered from the Kanto deposits so far can be explained with reference to three different traditional tool-making habits (e.g., Akazawa et al. 1980; Oda and Keally 1979, 1986). The first (ca. 30,000–27,000 yr B.P.) chronologically is an assemblage characterized by core-blank production and several types of core tools. This is followed by a second tradition (ca. 27,000–15,000 yr B.P.), which exhibits a high frequency of flake and blade blanks produced from elaborately prepared cores and a wide variety of modified flake and blade tools, called knife-blades. The third tradition (ca. 15,000–10,000 yr B.P.) is characterized by the popularity of microblades and a remarkable decrease of flake and blade tools. This Kanto Paleolithic sequence has been used to construct a framework for the Japanese Paleolithic sequence in other regions.

With respect to human colonization of the Japanese archipelago before 30,000 years ago, interesting excavation data from Miyagi Prefecture in Tohoku have been appearing for several years (Figure 3). These consist of a long series of Paleolithic materials dated from 200,000 to 30,000 years ago (e.g., Okamura 1983, 1985a, 1985b, 1986a, 1986b, 1987; Okamura and Kamata 1980; reviewed by Anderson 1987 and Reynolds 1985). Among them, five different industries were identified in deposits dating from before 30,000 years ago at the Babadan A site. Lithic materials were

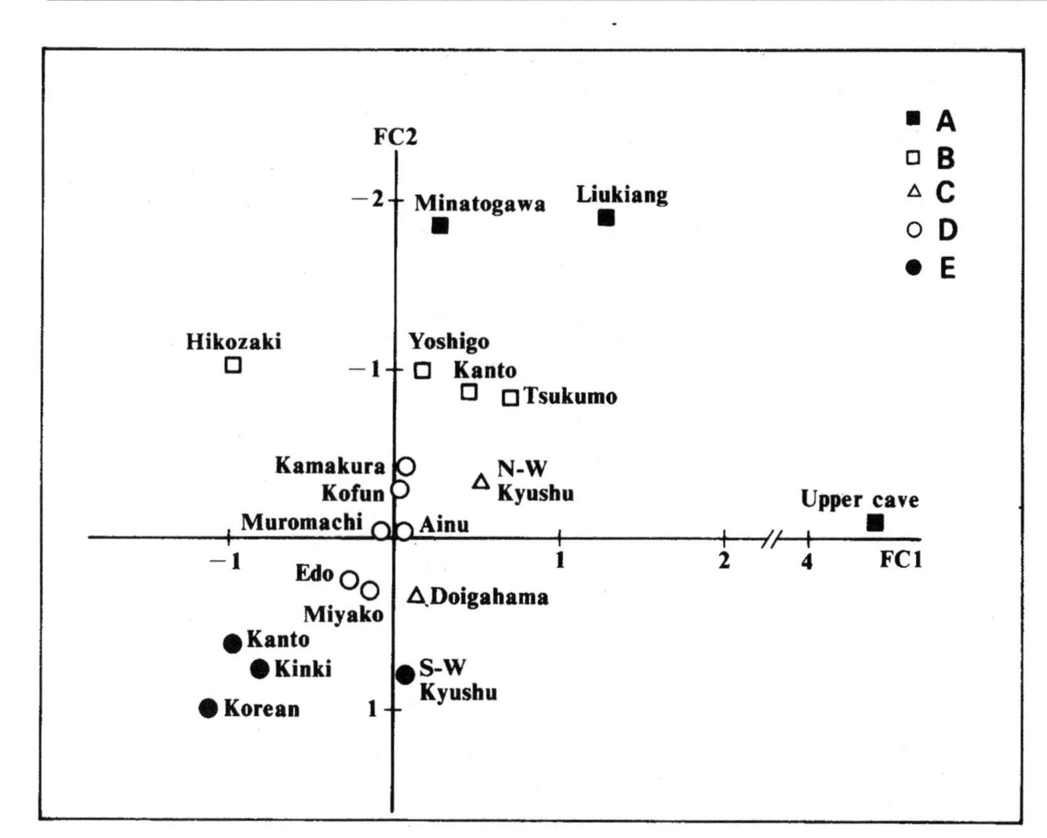

Figure 2. A morphological comparison of East Asian peoples from the upper Pleistocene to the present day (Suzuki 1981). A) Upper Pleistocene; B) Jomon; C) Yayoi; D) Historic; E) Present.

found in deposits between volcanic layers and are definitely human-modified. Dating of the deposits producing the lithics has been obtained by thermoluminescent analysis of volcanic materials.

If these dates are correct, we now have a new possibility in Japanese archaeology that the first colonization of this archipelago began in the middle Pleistocene. Nevertheless, there is much debate over the beginning of the Japanese Paleolithic and the early Paleolithic materials that are considered to be older than 30,000 years. Discussion of this controversial subject centers upon three points: (1) stratigraphic context; (2) antiquity; and (3) the morphological features and inconclusive form of the material. Although debate continues as to whether the objects from Babadan A and other related sites in northern Japan were found in stratified deposits dating to 200,000 and 30,000 years ago (Oda and Keally 1986), there is no doubt that these materials were produced by humans.

In this study, I would like to discuss a hypothetical model that examines the recent finds of Japanese early Paleolithic material based upon the expansion patterns of three species of Pleistocene mammalian fauna in East Asia. As noted by Aikens and Higuchi (1982) and Shutler (1988), human migration to Japan from the Asian mainland seems to have followed Pleistocene megafauna migrations.

Japanese Pleistocene Mammalian Fauna

THIS PAPER DEALS with the three key species of mammalian fauna that are most common in the Pleistocene deposits of the Japanese archipelago and neighboring regions in continental Asia: *Palaeoloxodon naumanni*, *Sinomegaceros yabei*, and *Mammuthus primigenius*. As shown in Figure 4, the Japanese Pleistocene mammalian fauna can be divided into two major types comprising temperate and boreal elements.

Palaeoloxodon naumanni

Palaeoloxodon naumanni, also known as Naumann's elephant, is the most common and well-documented species of the Japanese Pleistocene fauna and is distributed throughout the Japanese archipelago (e.g., Hasegawa 1972, 1977; Kamei et al. 1988; Otsuka 1987). Nevertheless, evidence to date suggests its distribution pattern shows regional differences in density. Locations producing Naumann's elephant remains are more concentrated in southwestern Japan, whereas finds are scarcer in northeastern Japan, especially Hokkaido.

The origins of Naumann's elephant are still in question, since its existence on the Asian continent

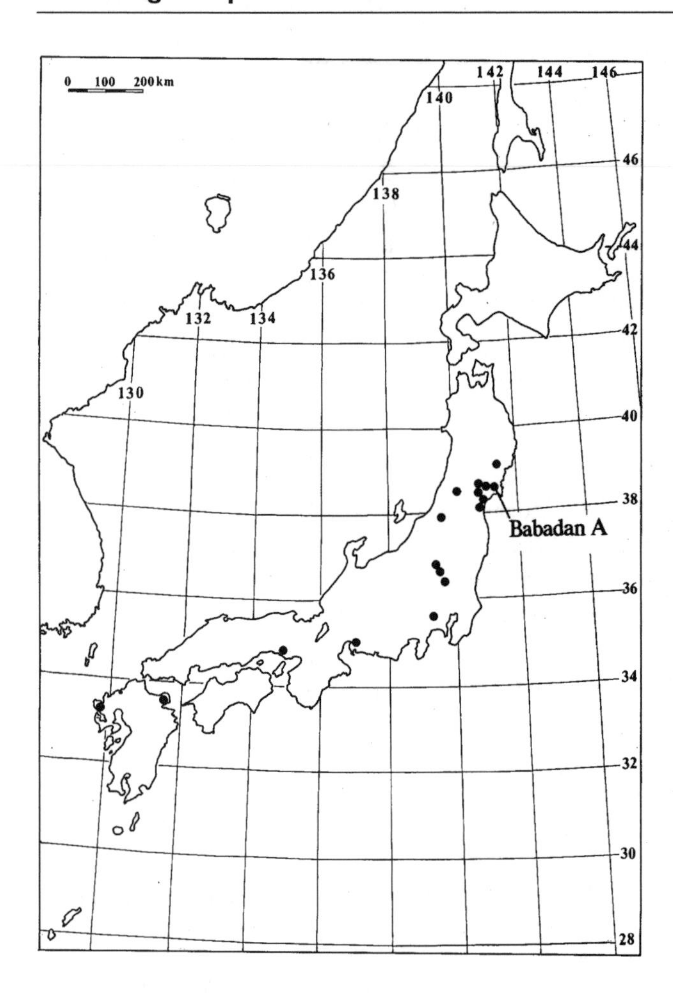

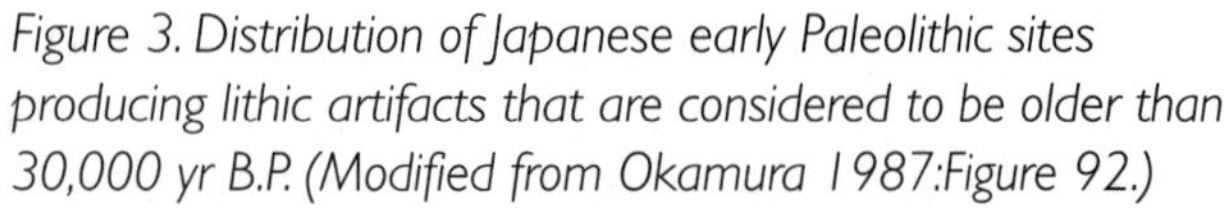
Figure 3. Distribution of Japanese early Paleolithic sites producing lithic artifacts that are considered to be older than 30,000 yr B.P. (Modified from Okamura 1987:Figure 92.)

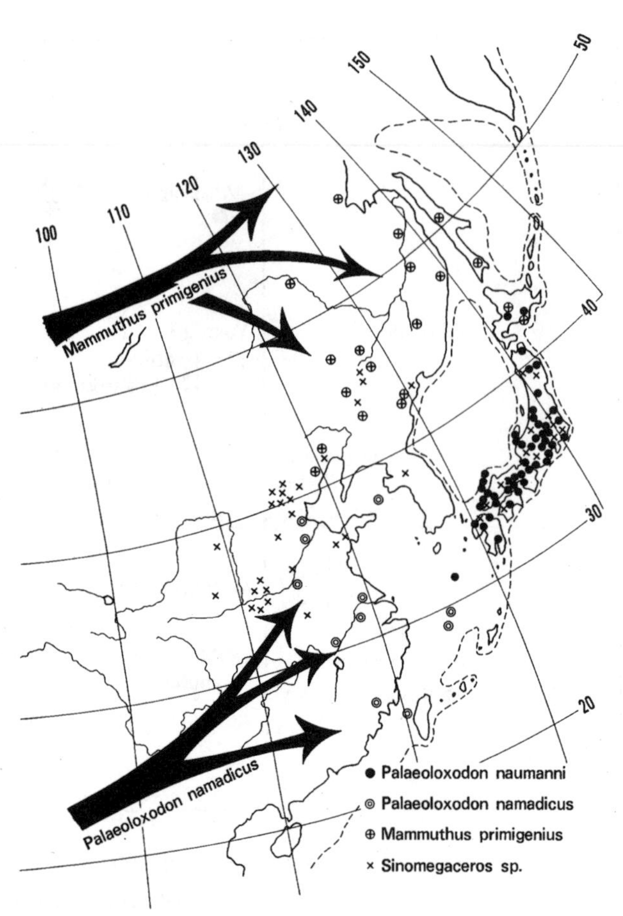

Figure 4. Site distribution of the four key species of Pleistocene mammalian fauna, divided into temperate (Palaeoloxodon naumanni, Palaeoloxodon namadicus, and Sinomegaceros sp.) and boreal (Mammuthus primigenius) elements. (Modified from Hasegawa 1977, Kamei et al. 1988, and Otsuka 1987.)

has not yet been documented. In this connection, we are able to propose three different hypothetical models to explain Naumann's elephant and its taxonomic relation to *Palaeoloxodon namadicus* on the continent (Figure 4):

(1) *Palaeoloxodon namadicus* and *Palaeoloxodon naumanni* originated from a different ancestry. In this model, the problem of when and from where Naumann's elephant came to the Japanese archipelago remains unanswered, as does the question of why Namadicus' elephant is absent; these questions must be explained.

(2) Naumann's and Namadicus' elephants might be classifiable as the same species. Using molars, which are the most common fossilized sample to be analyzed, morphological differences are too small to distinguish between these two species (Inuzuka, personal communication 1988). That is to say, these two groups were originally the same species, but they have been wrongly divided into two different groups: *naumanni* and *namadicus*.

(3) The final model is linked to the preceding hypothesis. The genus *Palaeoloxodon*, which was widely distributed in East Asia, radiated under different environmental conditions. Groups of *Palaeoloxodon* that came to Japan became progressively insular-adapted in the archipelago, isolated from the continent after the disappearance of the land bridges. As a result, two different individual species evolved—*Palaeoloxodon namadicus* and *Palaeoloxodon naumanni*.

If the second and/or third models are acceptable, Naumann's elephant can be explained as one of the temperate elephants found in the Japanese Pleistocene fauna. This idea is supported, in addition to the regional distribution differences in Japan mentioned earlier, by samples of both *Palaeoloxodon namadicus* and *Palaeoloxodon naumanni* that were dredged from the bottom of the continental shelf of the East China Sea (Figure 4).

The next point to be examined here concerns the time of the expansion of Naumann's elephant into the Japanese archipelago. A number of Naumann's elephant fossil remains have been found in stratified deposits dating from the middle and upper Pleistocene at different locations in Japan. From the geological context of the deposits, we can postulate that Naumann's elephant dates back to the middle Pleistocene and that around 300,000 years ago, it came from the continent over the southern land bridge, persisting into the upper Pleistocene, ca. 10,000 years ago (Kamei et al. 1988; Otsuka 1987). Also, other temperate fauna such as the genera *Bubalus, Bison,* and *Cervus* diffused to Japan (Hasegawa 1977; Kamei et al. 1988), although well-documented data on these types are not yet available.

Sinomegaceros Yabei

Sinomegaceros yabei is a well-known Japanese Pleistocene mammal that was widely distributed throughout the archipelago, with the exception of Hokkaido. Thus, its distribution pattern is closely related to that of Naumann's elephant (Figure 4). Based upon this fact, this species also may be a southern temperate form like Naumann's elephant, although it generally is said to be a boreal element arriving in Japan via northern routes (e.g., Hasegawa 1977).

Based upon the distribution pattern of the genus *Sinomegaceros* in continental Asia, the Japanese species *Sinomegaceros yabei* is said to be a boreal element associated with *Mammuthus primigenius* (e.g., Hasegawa 1977). Although its distribution partly overlaps that of *Mammuthus*, the continental species are more concentrated in the temperate zone between 30° and 40° N latitude, mostly parallel to the Japanese archipelago, excluding the Ryukyu Islands.

From the geological context of the deposits yielding the fossil samples (Kamei et al. 1988), the first appearance of *Sinomegaceros yabei* dates back to the middle Pleistocene, and they are known to have lived from 300,000 to 10,000 years ago in the Japanese archipelago.

Mammuthus primigenius

THE BOREAL ELEMENT is typified by the existence of *Mammuthus primigenius* from two locations in Hokkaido, the northern extremity of the Japanese archipelago. The *Mammuthus* groups, originating in sub-Saharan Africa with a rapid northward expansion, became progressively cold-adapted in Europe and northern Asia, and the woolly mammoth survived into the latest Pleistocene of both Europe and Asia (Maglio 1973).

There can be no doubt that *Mammuthus primigenius* travelled to Hokkaido from northeastern continental Asia via the Sakhalin land bridge. The problem of when *Mammuthus* came to Hokkaido is still controversial. However, in light of recent research, it has been suggested that *Mammuthus* spread into Hokkaido during the latest stage of the Pleistocene, based upon the geological context of deposits associated with mammoth remains (Kamei et al. 1988). This is strengthened by accelerator radiocarbon dates obtained from *Mammuthus* remains (Akiyama and Nakai 1988; Akiyama et al. 1988; Nakai and Nakamura 1988): 20,243 ± 670 yr B.P. for a sample in Hokkaido, and 23,816 ± 884 yr B.P. for a sample dredged from the Japan Sea.

Although not well documented, boreal elements such as *Ursus arctos, Canis lupus, Bison* sp., *Alces* sp., and others may have diffused to the Japanese archipelago together with *Mammuthus* (Kamei et al. 1988).

Discussion

BECAUSE PLEISTOCENE MAMMAL remains are still low in quantity and quality, and because so few have been discovered associated with Paleolithic materials, it remains difficult to discuss their relationship to the human colonization of the Japanese archipelago. The final conclusions proposed here are derived from the chronological context of Pleistocene fauna and their relation to geological and radiocarbon data obtained to date.

(1) During the middle Pleistocene, the first emigration from the Asian continent to the Japanese archipelago by southern routes seems to best account for the distribution of *Palaeoloxodon naumanni.* Although the geographic origins of this species are unknown, it crossed over land bridges into the Japanese archipelago. *Palaeoloxodon naumanni* spread into Japan, where it is well documented in middle

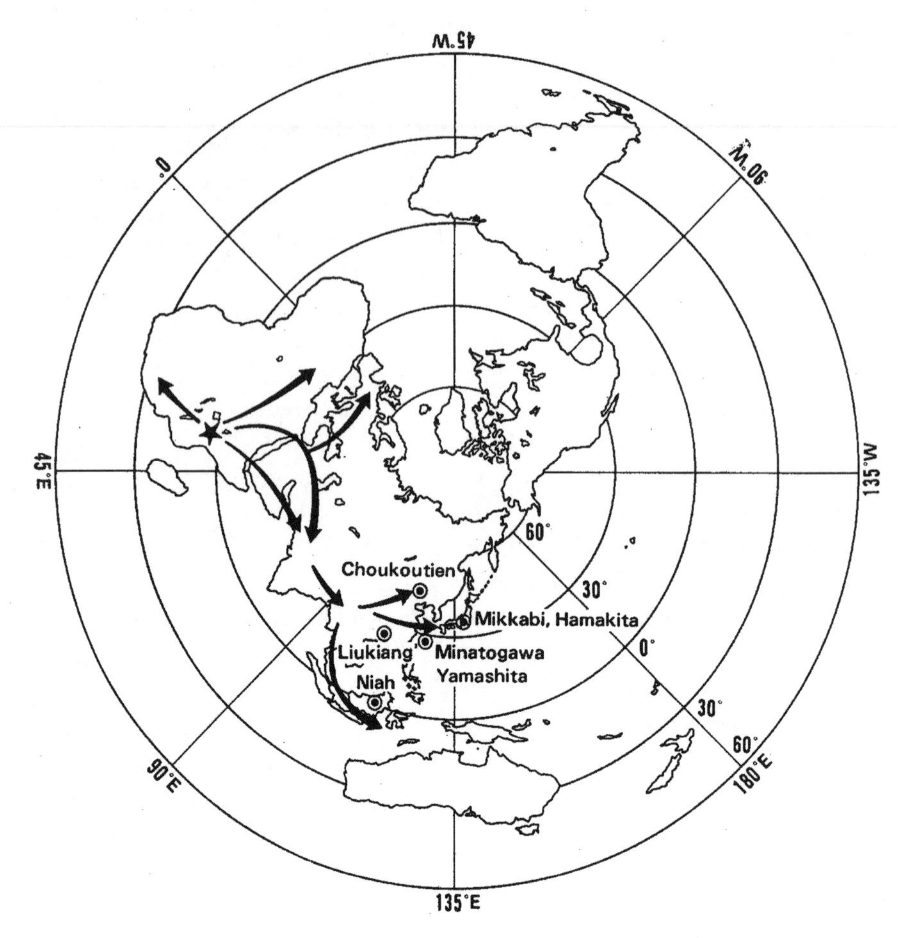

Figure 5. Proposed geographic expansion of the genus Palaeoloxodon from Africa to Asia (Maglio 1973), showing the distribution of upper Pleistocene human skeletal remains in the Japanese archipelago and other neighboring regions referred to in the text.

Pleistocene deposits of Honshu Island. The species expanded to become the dominant large mammal of Japan, persisting into the upper Pleistocene.

(2) At about the same time, the genus *Sinomegaceros* expanded in East Asia, especially southward, crossing into the Japanese archipelago over land bridges covering the East China Sea. From this land bridge, the species spread farther east and northward over most of the Japanese archipelago, with the exception of Hokkaido.

(3) During the late Quaternary, possibly in the maximum cold stage of the upper Pleistocene, *Mammuthus primigenius* spread throughout northern Asia and into North America. One branch of this species advanced southward into Hokkaido across land bridges, which seemed to have been widely formed around Sakhalin Island.

From these various lines of discussion, we can propose a hypothetical model to explain the link between the geographic expansion of some Pleistocene mammalian species and the human colonization of the Japanese archipelago.

Homo erectus appears to have been the first hominid to leave its African homeland and expand into East Asia. The distribution of *Homo erectus* sites in East Asia indicates there can be no doubt that *Homo erectus* penetrated as far as latitude 40° N around the Choukoutien (Zhoukoudian) site. *Homo erectus* could have migrated to Japan during the middle Pleistocene, since its continental distribution was mostly parallel to the Japanese archipelago. Quite possibly, this migration was linked with the presence of Naumann's elephant throughout the Japanese archipelago during the middle Pleistocene, which indicates land connections with the Asian mainland.

In Asia, Neanderthaloid-type hominids evolved from *Homo erectus* populations, and their remains have been found at several locations in China. The migration of Neanderthaloid-type hominids to the Japanese archipelago can be understood by the distribution of Pleistocene mammalian species, as in the case of Naumann's elephant and *Homo erectus*. *Sinomegaceros yabei* occurred throughout the Japanese islands. This species came to Japan later than Naumann's elephant, during the upper Pleistocene (Kamei et al. 1988). In the same way as *Homo erectus*, Neanderthal-type people could have migrated to Japan over the land bridge formed in the East China Sea during the upper Pleistocene (Figure 5).

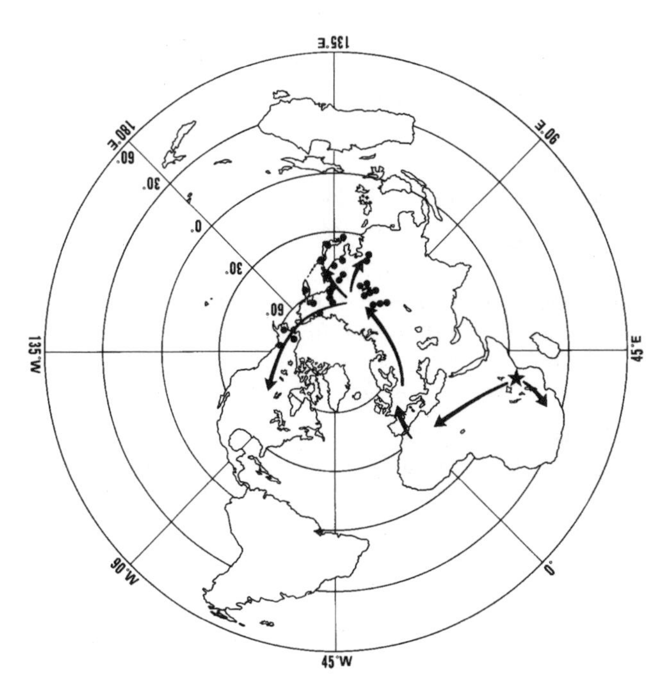

Figure 6. Proposed geographic expansion of the genus Mammuthus from Africa to Asia (Maglio 1973) and its relation to the distribution of microblade culture sites with wedge-shaped cores in Northeast Asia.

Until now, we have not obtained direct evidence to support this hypothetical model. Recent discoveries of Japanese early Paleolithic material, however, make it possible to reconsider that the first human colonization of Japan may have taken place during the middle Pleistocene. Thus, I propose that the initial human colonization of Japan occurred by southern routes associated with temperate-zone animal species, which were dominated by *Palaeoloxodon naumanni* and *Sinomegaceros yabei* during the middle and upper Pleistocene.

The Neanderthal-type people expanded further north than the preceding *Homo erectus* (Praslov 1984). Although the exact taxonomic status of these groups is still unclear, they seem to have possessed the technology to penetrate further north than their predecessors. Lithic assemblages morphologically similar to Mousterian assemblages have been found at several sites in Siberia north of latitude 50° N (Praslov 1984). Nevertheless, it has not yet been confirmed that they penetrated into the cold areas above latitude 60° N, the latitude of the Siberian-Alaskan land bridge. Although Paleolithic peoples expanded into northern Asia in the early and middle Pleistocene, at present, there is no evidence that they penetrated farther north than latitude 50° N in Siberia (Praslov 1984).

It was only with the evolution of *Homo sapiens sapiens* that human beings began to move into far northern Eurasia. It was here, in northeastern Siberia in the upper Pleistocene, that a distinctive microblade culture with wedge-shaped cores was developed (e.g., Ikawa-Smith 1982; Mochanov 1977, 1980; Praslov 1984). The earliest such microblade sites, dating 35,000 to 25,000 years ago, were distributed in far northern Siberia, between latitude 60° to 70° N (Martin 1984, Praslov 1982). Evidence of human occupation as early as 30,000 years ago has been located at Ikhine and Ust-Mil in the Aldan River region at latitude 64° N (Mochanov 1980; see Figure 6).

Most sites of the same microblade culture, located in northern China, the Korean Peninsula, Japan, and Alaska, date to less than 20,000 years ago (Ikawa-Smith 1982; Yi and Clark 1985). For instance, the wedge-shaped core tradition was developed in Japan around 15,000 years ago and in Alaska about 12,000 years ago.

Evaluating the recent Siberian geoarchaeological and chronometric data, Yi and Clark (1985) are dubious that the human occupation of northeastern Siberia around the Aldan region (above latitude 60° N) dates back to the Kargin interglacial age (35,000–25,000 yr B.P.). They conclude that the Dyuktai culture, characterized by Siberian microblade assemblages, appeared after about 18,000 years ago—that is, during the early Saltan glacial age.

Martin (1982), however, has suggested that occupation of northeastern Siberia would have been easier during the interstadial, when woodland was more widespread, than during later glacial conditions when woodland was more restricted. If this is true, it is probable that migration of some human groups to above latitude 60° N occurred during the last interstadial, more than 25,000 years ago. The age of the related prehistoric assemblages has still to be confirmed, however. Based upon these data, three points become clear:

(1) *Home sapiens sapiens* penetrated into far northern Siberia above latitude 60° N possibly during the last interstadial, more than 25,000 years ago. Occupation would have been easier during this interstadial, when woodland was more widespread, than later, during glacial conditions, when woodland was more restricted, as noted by Martin (1982:404).

(2) Under these circumstances, the initial immigrant groups developed a specialized subsistence system,

heavily dependent upon megafauna such as *Mammuthus* and equipped with distinctive tool kits dominated by microblade assemblages.

(3) The extremely cold climatic conditions that occurred during the last glacial maximum around 20,000 to 18,000 years ago seem to have forced certain groups to migrate south to China, the Korean Peninsula, and the Japanese archipelago, and northeast into Alaska.

(4) For some reason which we do not yet understand, certain groups seem not to have migrated from Siberia at this time. These groups appear to have evolved cold-adapted Mongoloid characteristics during this stage.

Conclusion

THE EAST ASIAN POPULATION does not seem to have been able to penetrate into the cold areas above about latitude 60° N before the evolution of *Homo sapiens sapiens*. It thus seems highly unlikely that the Beringian land bridge, which formed between latitude 60° and 70° N, could have been crossed before approximately 40,000 to 30,000 years ago. In fact, the actual movement into Alaska and also into the Japanese archipelago appears to have been a part of the expansion of microblade-culture people from Siberia, associated with boreal-zone species dominated by *Mammuthus*, during the last glacial maximum. Thus, drastic climatic change at the end of the last interstadial seems to have been responsible for the final human expansion and dispersals that occurred in the arctic region.

Acknowledgments

I would like to thank particularly Robson Bonnichsen, who read this study and presented thoughtful and careful comments. I am also grateful for the cooperation of Mark Hudson, Visiting Research Associate for the Tokyo University Museum.

References Cited

Aikens, C. M., and T. Higuchi
1982 *Prehistory of Japan*. Academic Press, New York.

Akazawa, T., S. Oda, and I. Yamanaka
1980 The Japanese Palaeolithics: A Techno-Typological Study. Rippu Shobo, Tokyo.

Akiyama, M., T. Kamei, and N. Nakai
1988 ^{14}C Ages of Naumann's Elephant *Palaeoloxodon naumanni* (Makiyama) from the Sea Bottom off the San'in District in the Sea of Japan by Accelerator Mass Spectrometry. *Earth Science* 421:29–31.

Akiyama, M., and N. Nakai
1988 ^{14}C Ages of Naumann's Elephants in Japan. *Summaries of Researchers Using AMS at Nagoya University* 1:67–71. Radioisotopic Center, Nagoya University.

Anderson, A.
1987 Recent Developments in Japanese Prehistory: A Review. *Antiquity* 61:270–281.

Endo, B., and H. Baba
1982 Morphological Investigation of Innominate Bones from Pleistocene in Japan with Special Reference to the Akashi Man. *Journal of the Anthropological Society of Nippon*. 90(supplement):27–54.

Hasegawa, Y.
1972 The Naumann's Elephant, *Palaeoloxodon naumanni* (Makiyama) from the Late Pleistocene of Shakagahara Shodoshima Island in Seto Inland Sea, Japan. *Bulletin of the National Science Museum* 15:513–591.

1977 Vertebrates. In *The Japanese Quaternary Research*, edited by The Association for Quaternary Research, pp. 227–243. University of Tokyo Press, Tokyo.

Ikawa-Smith, F.
1982 The Early Prehistory of the Americans as seen from Northeast Asia. In *Peopling of the New World*, edited by J. E. Ericson, R. E. Taylor, and R. Berger, pp. 15–33. Ballena Press, Los Altos.

Kamei, T., Y. Kawamura, and H. Taruno
1988 Mammalian Stratigraphy of the Late Neogene and Quaternary in the Japanese Islands. *The Memoirs of the Geological Society of Japan* 30:181–204.

Maglio, V. J.
1973 Origin and Evolution of the Elephantidae. *Transactions of the American Philosophical Society* (n. s.) 63(3):5–145.

Martin, P. S.
1982 The Pattern and Meaning of Holarctic Mammoth Extinction. In *Paleoecology of Beringia*, edited by D. H. Hopkins, J. V. Matthews, Jr., C. E. Schweger, and S. B. Young, pp. 399–408. Academic Press, New York.

Mochanov, Y.
1977 *The Most Ancient Stages of Settlement of Northeast Asia by Man*. Nauka, Novosibirsk.

1980 Early Migrations to America in the Light of a Study of the Dyuktai Paleolithic Culture in Northeast Asia. In *Early Native Americans*, edited by D. Browman, pp. 119–131. The Hague, Mouton.

Nakai, N., and T. Nakamura
1988 Radiocarbon Dating. *Memoirs of Geological Society in Japan* 29:235–252.

Narasaki, S.
1986 *Catalogue of Fossil Hominids in Japan.* B.A. Thesis, Department of Anthropology, University of Oregon, Eugene.

Oda, S., and C. T. Keally
1979 Japanese Palaeolithic Cultural Chronology. Paper presented at the XIV Pacific Science Congress, Khabarovsk, USSR.

1986 A Critical Look at the Paleolithic and "Lower Paleolithic" Research in Miyagi Prefecture, Japan. *Journal of the Anthropological Society of Nippon* 94(3): 325–361.

Okamura, M.
1983 The Oldest Assemblages of Stone Artifacts in Japan and the Palaeolithic of Northern Miyagi Prefecture. In *Panel Discussion on the Natural Scientific Approach to the Zazaragi Site,* edited by Sekki-Bunka-Danwakai, pp. 2–3. Tohoku Rekishi Shiryokan, Tagajo City.

1985a Geomorphology and Geological Stratification along the Eai River. In *The Palaeolithic along the Eai River,* edited by T. R. Shiryokan, pp. 7–15. Tohoku Museum of History, Tagajo City.

1985b The "Lower Palaeolithic" in Miyagi Prefecture and the Chinese Middle Paleolithic. In *Resumes of Papers Presented at the Autumn Meeting of the Japanese Archaeologists Association* , pp. 2–3.

1986a Relationships of the Oldest Human Cultures in the Archipelago. *Rekishi Techo* 14(4):12–18.

1986b The Babadan A Site in Miyagi Prefecture. In *Resumes of Papers Presented at the Annual Meeting of the Japanese Association for Cultural Resources Sciences,* pp. 12–13.

1987 Overview of Studies on the Japanese Early Palaeolithic Period. *Bulletin of the National Museum of Japanese History* 13:233–246.

Okamura, M., and T. Kamata
1980 A Chronological Study of the Paleolithic in the Northern Part of the Miyagi Prefecture. *Bulletin of the Tohoku Museum of History* 6:1–28.

Otsuka, H.
1987 Middle and Late Pleistocene Mammalian Faunae in the Japanese Islands with Special Reference to the Mammalian Fauna of the Nishiyagi Formation in Akashi District. *Bulletin of the National Museum of Japanese History* 13:275–287.

Praslov, N. D.
1984 Paleolithic Cultures in the Late Pleistocene. In *Late Quaternary Environments of the Soviet Union*, edited by A. A. Velichko, pp. 313–318. University of Minnesota Press, Minneapolis.

Reynolds, T.
1985 The Early Palaeolithic of Japan. *Antiquity* 59: 93–96.

Shutler, R., Jr.
1988 *Current Status of the Japanese Early Paleolithic and Possible Asian Mainland Relationships.* Proceedings of the 10th International Symposium on Asian Studies, pp. 649–676. Asian Research Service, Hong Kong.

Suzuki, H.
1981 Racial History of the Japanese. In *Rassengeschichte der Memschheit*, edited by J. Schwidetzley, pp. 7–69. 8 Lieferung.

1982a Skulls of the Minatogawa Man. In *The Minatogawa Man*, edited by H. Suzuki and K. Hanihara, pp. 7–80. Bulletin No.19. The University Museum, The University of Tokyo.

1982b Pleistocene Man in Japan. *Journal of the Anthropological Society of Nippon* 90 (supplement):11–26.

Tatsuno, T.
1987 Progress Excavation Report of No. 471-B site, RTRama, Tokyo. *Monthly Kobunkazai* 291:17–23.

Yamaguchi, B.
1982 A Review of the Osteological Characteristics of the Jomon Population in Prehistoric Japan. *Journal of the Anthropological Society of Nippon* 90 (supplement):77–90.

Yi, S., and G. Clark
1985 The "Dyuktai Culture" and New World Origins. *Current Anthropology* 26(1):1–20.

The Colonization of Western Beringia
Technology, Ecology, and Adaptations

Ted Goebel[1]
Sergei B. Slobodin[2]

Abstract

Currently in western Beringia there are 35 archaeological occupations that are considered to date to the late Pleistocene or early Holocene. Only 15 of these, however, have been chronometrically dated to before 7000 radiocarbon years ago (yr B.P.), while the rest are dated solely on typological or stratigraphic grounds. Of the radiocarbon dated occupations, three are assigned to the Paleolithic (>10,000 yr B.P.) and 12 to the Mesolithic (9000–7000 yr B.P.). The majority are located in the upper Kolyma basin in southwestern Beringia and in the Chukotka Peninsula opposite Alaska. This paper reviews each of these sites in detail, providing updates on old sites and introductions to new sites not previously described in English-language publications.

The earliest evidence for humans in western Beringia dates to about 14,000 yr B.P., as documented by the blade-and-biface assemblage (layer VII) at the stratified Ushki-1 site, central Kamchatka. Similar assemblages have been identified at Berelekh, an Upper Paleolithic campsite in the lower Indigirka Basin radiocarbon dated to about 12,200 yr B.P., and El'gakhchan, a site that occurs in a stratified context but has not yet been dated. The Uptar-1 site also contains a bifacial industry that may be latest Pleistocene in age, but this site has only an upper-limiting date of 8260 yr B.P. Together these sites suggest the presence in western Beringia of a pre-11,000-yr-B.P. Upper Paleolithic complex characterized by blade and biface technologies, which may be related to similar industries (e.g., the Nenana complex) in central Alaska.

The earliest clear evidence for microblade technologies in western Beringia, again found at Ushki-1, dates to about 10,700 yr B.P. No other wedge-shaped core and microblade sites have been directly dated, and only one, Kheta, located in the upper Kolyma basin, occurs in a datable context. Nonetheless, many undated wedge-shaped core and microblade sites have been identified in the Kolyma and Omolon basins of southwestern Beringia, as well as on the Chukotka and Kamchatka peninsulas, suggesting a widespread distribution of a "Diuktai-like" complex very late in the Pleistocene or early in the Holocene.

The Mesolithic of western Beringia has a probable age of 9000–7000 yr B.P. During this interval, conical core and blade/microblade industries lacking ceramics and polished stone tools dominate the archaeological record. Most of the known Mesolithic sites occur in the upper Kolyma region, but they also have been identified on Zhokhov Island, located far to the north in the East Siberian Sea, and possibly at Lake Tytyl' (interior Chukotka) and Puturak Pass (Chukotka Peninsula). These industries may be tied to the Sumnagin Mesolithic complex of the Lena River basin west of Beringia.

1. Department of Anthropology, University of Nevada, Las Vegas, 4505 Maryland Parkway, Las Vegas NV 89154-5003
2. Northeast Interdisciplinary Scientific Research Institute, Russian Academy of Sciences, Magadan, Russia

Introduction

THE LATE PLEISTOCENE-early Holocene archaeological record of western Beringia offers a unique perspective on the peopling of the Americas problem; however, the Paleolithic and Mesolithic sites of this area often are not considered when peopling models are proposed and the timing of migrations is discussed. This is due not only to past language and political barriers separating the two sides of the Bering Strait, but also to the lack of reported late Pleistocene-early Holocene sites in far northeast Asia. Even today the sample of Paleolithic and Mesolithic sites in western Beringia is exceedingly small when compared to neighboring Alaska, Yakutia, and Japan.

We follow Hoffecker et al. (1993) and Yurtsev (1984) in drawing the boundaries of Beringia along the Verkhoiansk Range in the west and the maximum northwestern limit of the Laurentide ice sheet in the east. By this definition, western Beringia includes northeastern Yakutia, Magadan Oblast', Chukotka Autonomous Okrug, Kamchatka Oblast', and northernmost Khabarovsk Krai[1] (Figure 1). During the last glacial maximum (22,000–18,000 years ago [yr B.P.]),[2] these regions would have been closely tied

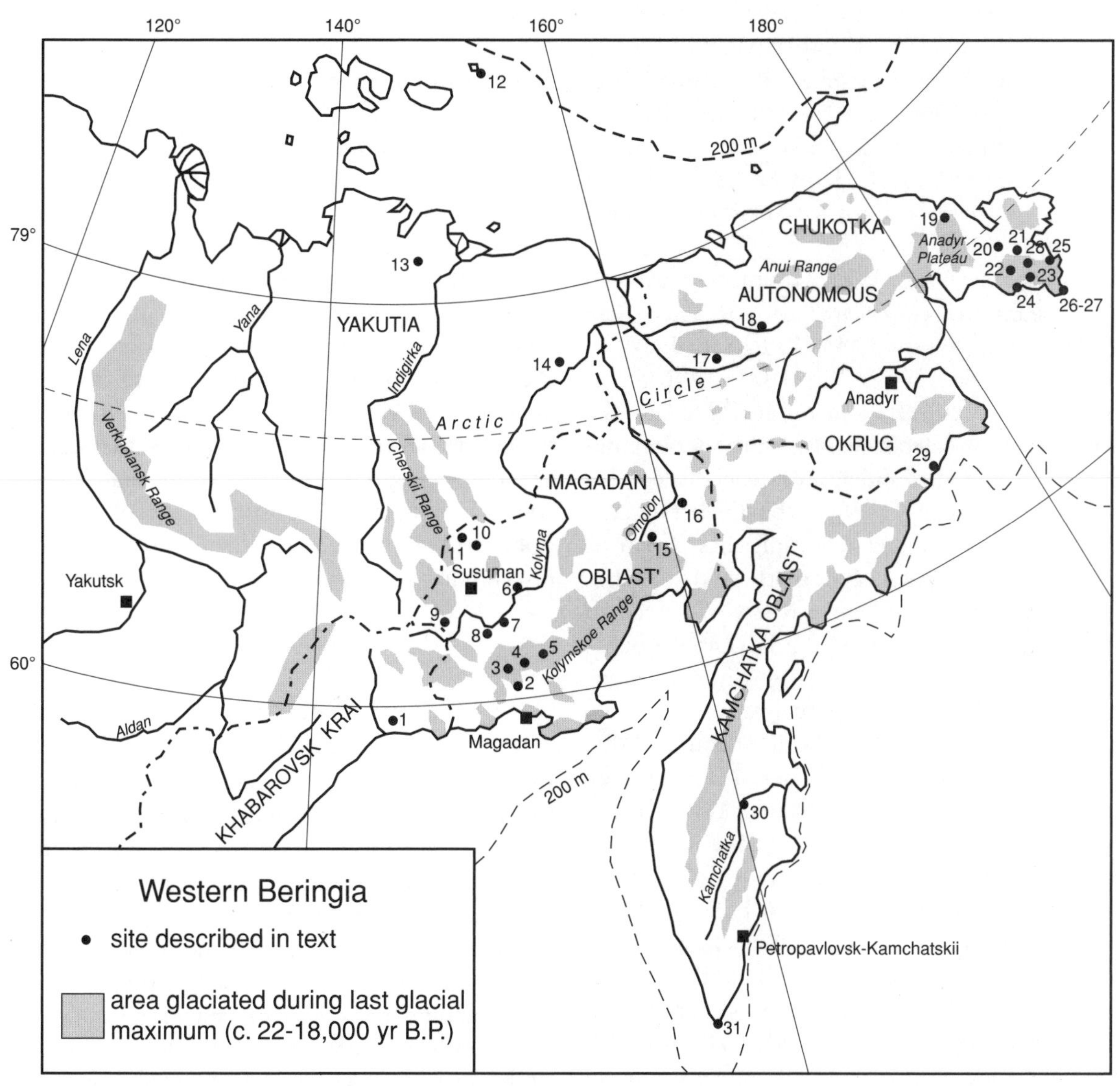

Figure 1. Map of western Beringia, showing late Pleistocene geography and locations of archaeological sites described in text: (1) Kukhtui-3, (2) Uptar-1, (3) Maltan, (4) Kheta, (5) Buiunda-3, (6) Maiorych, (7) Kongo, (8) Siberdik, (9) Shilo, (10) Zima, (11) Ui-1, (12) Zhokhov Island, (13) Berelekh, (14) Bochanut, (15) Druchak-V, (16) El'gakhchan-1, (17) Orlovka-2, (18) Tytyl'-1, (19) Kymyneikei, (20) Kym'ynanonvyvaam, (21) Ioni-10, (22) Chel'kun, (23) Chaatam'e-1, (24) Kurupka-1, (25) Marich-2, (26) Puturak Pass, (27) Ul'khum-1, (28) Ananaiveem-1, (29) Inas'kvaam and Taliain, (30) Ushki, (31) Lopatka-4.

to Alaska in terms of vegetation and faunal communities. Glaciers were restricted to mountainous areas like the Verkhoiansk, Cherskii, and Kolyma ranges in the southwest, the Anui range in interior Chukotka, and the Koriak and Sredinnyi ranges in Kamchatka, while much of the lowlands of western Beringia remained ice-free and were suitable for human habitation in the late Pleistocene (Braitseva et al. 1968; Isayeva 1984; Ivanov 1986). Palynological and paleontological evidence from the Kolyma basin suggests that full glacial vegetation in many places was dominated by wormwood (*Artemisia*), various grasses, and tundra plants (Grichuk 1984; Lozhkin et al. 1993; Ukraintseva 1993). As the last glacial came to a close, the open landscapes of Beringia were gradually transformed into the vegetation zones existing in the region today—boreal forest in the south grading into forest-tundra and tundra in the north, and alpine tundra in high mountain landscapes. Regional differences between western and eastern Beringia emerged at this time.

Others have used a broader definition of western Beringia, referring to an area of northeast Asia including Yakutia and the Lena River basin almost to Lake Baikal (Morlan 1987; West 1981, 1996). This idea of a "Megaberingia" can be attributed to the relative scarcity of Paleolithic sites in the region and the need to include surrounding areas where Paleolithic sites are more abundant. Largely within the last decade, however, Beringia (by our definition) has begun to emerge with its own Paleolithic-Mesolithic archaeological record, and there is less of a need to look further south and west in Yakutia, central Siberia, or Japan for evidence indicating when humans colonized the Bering Land Bridge area.

The presently known Paleolithic and Mesolithic archaeological record of western Beringia is, in large part, the product of one man, Nikolai Dikov. From 1956 to 1976, Dikov and his crews discovered and studied over 400 prehistoric sites, ranging from the early Russian historic period to as far back as 14,000 yr B.P., from the southern tip of Kamchatka (Cape Lopatka) to the northeastern tip of Chukotka (Uelen) (Dikov 1977, 1979a). Today a new generation of Russian archaeologists has succeeded Dikov in his lifelong quest for evidence of early Beringians. Among the region's currently active archaeologists are A. Lebedintsev (Sea of Okhotsk coast), I. Vorobei (Omolon basin), M. Kir'iak (Anui and Omolon basins), A. Orekhov (Bering Sea coast south of Anadyr), V. Pitul'ko (East Siberian Sea coast), T. Tein (Wrangell Island), A. Ptashinskii (north coast of Kamchatka), and S. Slobodin (Upper Kolyma basin). By American standards this is a relatively small cadre (8) of archaeologists, considering that the total area studied is larger than the State of Alaska. Nonetheless, archaeological work in western Beringia continues at a record pace, and as results of this research become available, our understanding of the late Pleistocene-early Holocene record of the area grows and changes.

In this paper we review the archaeological records of 35 sites (Figure 1) and present a complete list of radiocarbon (^{14}C) determinations (Table 1). We divide western Beringia physiographically into the following provinces: (1) Sea of Okhotsk Coast, (2) Upper Kolyma Mountains, (3) Indigirka-Kolyma Lowlands, (4) Western Interior Chukotka, (5) Chukotka Peninsula and Bering Sea Coast, and (6) Kamchatka Peninsula. The following broad questions are addressed: When did the first humans appear in western Beringia? Is there evidence for a "pre-microblade" Upper Paleolithic complex, as described for the early Alaskan record (Hoffecker et al. 1993)? When do late Upper Paleolithic wedge-shaped core and microblade technologies appear? How can we characterize late Pleistocene human adaptations? And how can we characterize Mesolithic (i.e., 9000–7000 yr B.P.) technology and subsistence in western Beringia? While acknowledging that western Beringian archaeology is still in its infancy, the existing archaeological record does permit us to formulate hypotheses that will guide research in the region into the next century.

Northern Sea of Okhotsk Coast

The northern Sea of Okhotsk Coast is the maritime region of southwestern Beringia, stretching from Okhotsk (Khabarovsk Krai) to Kamenskoe (Kamchatka Oblast'). This area is dominated by the southern flank of the Kolymskoe Range, with peaks rising to about 2,000 m. Many small rivers with narrow, steep-sided valleys flow south out of these mountains into the Sea of Okhotsk (Figure 2). Lebedintsev (1990) has reported numerous late Holocene sites from along the coast, but earlier Paleolithic-Mesolithic sites are rare. At the time of this writing, only two such sites, Kukhtui-3 and Uptar-1, have been discovered and described.

Kukhtui-3

Kukhtui-3 (*1*, Figure 1) is located along the left bank of the Kukhtui River, 1.5 km from the Sea of Okhotsk, near the town of Okhotsk, Khabarovskii Krai (59° 26'N, 143° 13'E). Mochanov (1972, 1977) discovered and excavated the site in 1970; brief English-language descriptions can be found in Kozlowski and Bandi (1984), West (1981), Michael (1984:20–21), Morlan (1987), and Mochanov and Fedoseeva (1996b). Although initially assigned to the Paleolithic by Mochanov (1977), more recent analyses suggest a late Holocene age.

Kukhtui-3 is a multi-component site situated upon the 25-m terrace of the Kukhtui River. Lithic artifacts assigned by Mochanov (1977:87) to the Paleolithic occur at a depth of about 90 cm below the modern surface. Sediments are heavily disturbed by ice wedge pseudomorphs penetrating to a depth of over 1 m (Mochanov 1977:87–88). The site's single radiocarbon determination, 4700 ± 100 (LE-995) yr B.P., reportedly was associated with a Neolithic component situated about 50 cm above the Paleolithic component (Mochanov 1977:87).

Artifacts assigned to the Paleolithic by Mochanov (1977:88) make up a "heterogeneous" assemblage. Raw materials include black chert, silicified slate, and silicified limestone. Artifacts include 19 flakes, one discoidal core, one side scraper, two flake knives, two oval bifaces, one biface fragment, two biface preforms, one bifacial point, and one wedge (or bipolar core). Wedge-shaped cores, microblades, and burins are absent. Based on the presence of oval bifaces, however, Mochanov (1977:90) assigns the industry to the late Paleolithic Diuktai culture.

Others have questioned the assignment of Kukhtui-3 to the Paleolithic. Dikov (1979a:30, 103–104) argues that the assemblage is more similar to mid-Holocene industries on the upper Kolyma (e.g., the Maltan culture), and Lebedintsev (1990:24–27) points to similarities with the Tokarev culture, a late Holocene maritime complex found along the northern Sea of Okhotsk shore. According to Lebedintsev (1990:25–26, 179), Mochanov's Paleolithic artifacts (scrapers, flake-knives, oval bifaces) are common in Tokarev sites dating to less than 3000 yr B.P. Given the problems with stratigraphy and assemblage interpretation, the assignment of Kukhtui-3 to the late Pleistocene or even early Holocene remains equivocal.

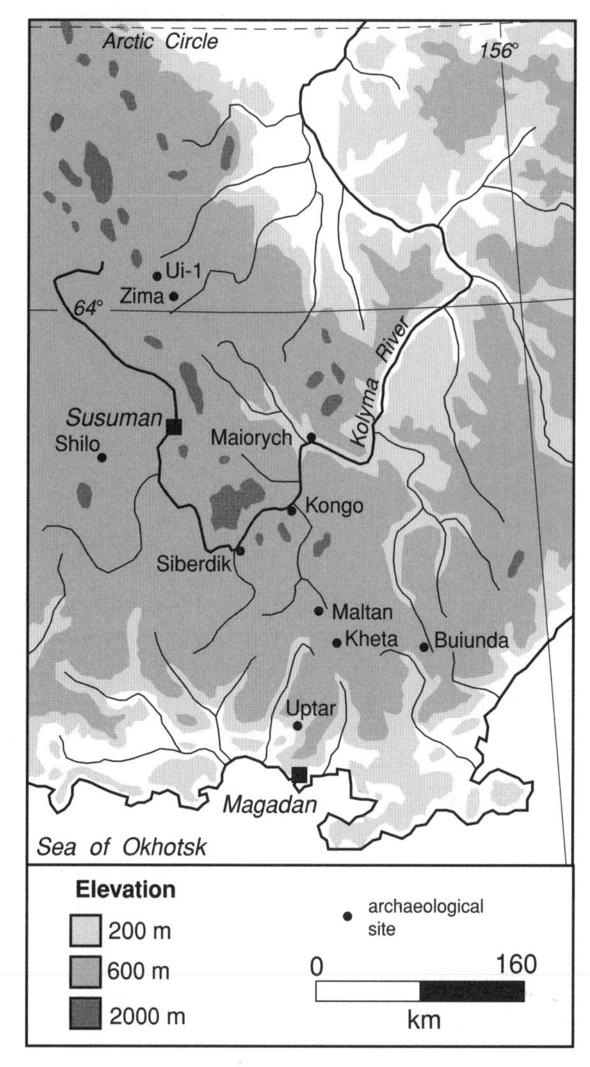

Figure 2. Map of upper Kolyma-Sea of Okhotsk region, showing locations of sites described in text.

Uptar-1

Uptar-1 (*2*, Figures 1 and 2) is located about 50 km north of Magadan, along the right bank of the Uptar River, a tributary of the Khasyn River, near the town of Sokol, Magadan Oblast' (59° 54'N, 150° 42'E). Slobodin (1990) discovered the site in 1985 and conducted limited excavations through 1988. In 1990, Slobodin and Goebel excavated an additional 1-m^2 area to collect radiocarbon and tephra samples. To date, approximately 35 m^2 have been excavated (Slobodin 1990:65–66, Slobodin and King 1996).

Uptar-1 is situated on the third terrace of the Uptar River, 4–5 m above the modern river floodplain. The site's single cultural component occurs in an orange-colored sand 10–35 cm below the modern surface. The component is stratigraphically sealed by the Elikchan tephra (Slobodin 1990; J. Begét, personal

Table 1. Radiocarbon Ages from Western Beringia Archaeological Sites Discussed in Text.

Site	*Material*	*Lab No.*	*Date*	*Ref.*
Kukhtui-3	charcoal	LE-995	4700 ± 100	1
Uptar-1	charcoal	MAG-1262	8260 ± 330	2
Maltan, upper	charcoal	KRIL-247	4450 ± 50	3
Maltan, upper	not reported	MAG-361	3800 ± 100	4
Maltan, upper	charcoal	KRIL-246	3690 ± 50	3
Maltan, upper	charcoal	KRIL-316	3640 ± 45	3
Maltan, upper	not reported	MAG-915	2770 ± 50	5
Maltan, upper	not reported	MAG-914	2720 ± 50	5
Maltan, upper	charcoal	MAG-605	2150 ± 50	5
Maltan, upper	charcoal	MAG-607	2120 ± 50	5
Maltan, upper	hearth charcoal	MAG-195	1790 ± 25	6
Maltan, upper	not reported	MAG-767	1300 ± 200	5
Maltan, lower	charcoal	MAG-183	7490 ± 70	7
Maltan, lower	not reported	not reported	6950 ± 250	8
Buiunda-3	charcoal	GX-17064	8135 ± 220	9
Buiunda-3	charcoal	LE-3991	7790 ± 190	9
Buiunda-3	charcoal	GX-17065	7510 ± 205	9
Buiunda-3	charcoal	LE-3898	5610 ± 110*	9
Kongo, layer 2	charcoal	MAG-196	8655 ± 220[2]	10
Kongo, layer 2	charcoal	MAG-406[3]	8080 ± 500	10
Kongo, layer 3	charcoal	KRIL-314	9470 ± 530	3
Kongo, layer 3	charcoal	KRIL-313	9020 ± 510	3
Kongo, layer 3	charcoal	KRIL-315	8850 ± 500	3
Kongo, layer 3	charcoal	MAG-595	8700 ± 400	5
Siberdik, layer 1	not reported	MAG-363	640 ± 40	4
Siberdik, layer 1	not reported	MAG-385	640 ± 40	4
Siberdik, layer 2	charcoal	MAG-408	6590 ± 250	10
Siberdik, layer 2	charcoal	KRIL-248	6030 ± 170[4]	3
Siberdik, layer 2	charcoal	KRIL-253	5530 ± 170	3
Siberdik, layer 2	hearth charcoal	MAG-1021	4420 ± 60	5
Siberdik, layer 2	hearth charcoal	MAG-1022	4720 ± 100	5
Siberdik, layer 3	not reported	MAG-916	13225 ± 230*	5
Siberdik, layer 3	hearth charcoal	MAG-1019	9700 ± 500	5
Siberdik, layer 3	charcoal	KRIL-249	8480 ± 200	3
Siberdik, layer 3	charcoal	MAG-606	8130 ± 100	5
Siberdik, layer 3	charcoal	KRIL-250	8020 ± 280	3
Siberdik, layer 3	charcoal	MAG-184	7865 ± 310	11
Siberdik, layer 3	charcoal	KRIL-251	7080 ± 600	3
Siberdik, layer 3	charcoal	MAG-130	4570 ± 370	12
Zima	charcoal	MAG-1260	7070 ± 60	13
Ui-1	charcoal	GX-17067	8810 ± 235	9
Ui-1	charcoal	GX-17066	8695 ± 100	9
Ui-1	charcoal	LE-3990	8370 ± 190	9
Ui-1	charcoal	LE-3900	5950 ± 90*	9

Zhokov Island	wood	GIN-6399	8200 ± 40	14
Zhokov Island	bone	GIN-6400	7930 ± 40	14
Zhokov Island	charcoal	LE-3527	8560 ± 180	14
Zhokov Island	wood	LE-4048a	7880 ± 160	15
Zhokov Island	wood	LE-4048b	8930 ± 180	15
Zhokov Island	bone	LE-4533a	10810 ± 390	15
Zhokov Island	bone	LE-4533b	7940 ± 170	15
Zhokov Island	wood	LE-4534a	7450 ± 200	15[5]
Zhokov Island	wood	LE-4534b	7890 ± 150	15
Zhokov Island	wood	LU-2432	7870 ± 60	14
Zhokov Island	wood	LU-2433	7850 ± 40	14
Zhokov Island	wood	LU-2499	8020 ± 50	14
Zhokov Island	wood below layer	LU-2502	8790 ± 90	14
Berelekh cemetery	soft tissue	MAG-114	13700 ± 80	16
Berelekh cemetery	mammoth tusk	LU-149	12240 ± 160	17
Berelekh cemetery[6]	wood	MAG-117	11870 ± 60	12
Berelekh cemetery[6]	wood	LU-147	11830 ± 110	1
Berelekh cemetery[6]	wood	MAG-119	10440 ± 100	12
Berelekh cemetery[6]	wood	MAG-118	10260 ± 155	12
Berelekh	wood	IM-152	13420 ± 200	1
Berelekh	wood	GIN-1021	12930 ± 80	1
Berelekh	wood	LE-998	10600 ± 90	1
Berelekh[7]	soil detritus	LE-1112	>42,000	1
Chel'kun-4	hearth charcoal	MAG-719	8150 ± 450	18
Ananaiveem-1	not reported	LE-2791	8410 ± 80	23
Ushki-1, layer 7	charcoal	GIN-168	14300 ± 200	14
Ushki-1, layer 7	not reported	MAG-550	14200 ± 700	19[8]
Ushki-1, layer 7	not reported	MAG-522	13800 ± 500	19
Ushki-1, layer 7	charcoal	GIN-167	13600 ± 250	20[9]
Ushki-1, layer 7	charcoal	MAG-637	9750 ± 100*	21
Ushki-1, layer 6 (?)	charcoal	GIN-186	21000 ± 100*	14
Ushki-1, layer 6b	charcoal	MAG-400	10860 ± 400	10[10]
Ushki-1, layer 6	not reported	MAG-518	10790 ± 100	19
Ushki-1, layer 6	carbonized clay	MAG-219	10760 ± 110	6
Ushki-1, layer 6a	charcoal	MAG-401	10360 ± 220	10
Ushki-1, layer 6	charcoal	MO-345	10360 ± 350	10
Ushki-1, layer 4	hearth charcoal	MAG-132	4200 ± 100	11
Ushki-1, layer 2	not reported	RKHL-607	2440 ± 80	19
Ushki-1, layer 2	not reported	MAG-5	2160 ± 290	19
Ushki-1, layer 2	not reported	MAG-32	1052 ± 25	22
Ushki-1, layer 1	not reported	LE-70	675 ± 80	19
Ushki-1, layer 1a	not reported	MO-353	235 ± 145	19
Ushki-5, layer 2	charcoal	MAG-220	770 ± 30	6
Ushki-5, layer 5	not reported	MAG-321	8790 ± 150	19

Notes and references on following page

Notes to Table 1
*Aberrant date.
[1]Method of averaging described in Long and Rippeteau (1974).
[2]Date reported by Lozhkin et al. (1980) as 8600 ± 220.
[3]Dikov (1985) assigns this date to Siberdik, not Kongo.
[4]Reported in Dikov (1977), Dikov et al. (1983:25), and Krushanov (1989:34) as 6,300 ± 1700 (KRIL-248).
[5]LE-4534a reported by Kuzmin (1994) as wood, not bone.
[6]Sample collected 20 cm above bone-bearing deposit.
[7]Sample collected from base of profile, far below artifact-bearing deposit.
[8]MAG-550 is reported by Dikov (1985) as 14300 ± 200.
[9]GIN-167 is reported by Dikov and Titov (1984) as 14300 ± 200, but by Dikov (1986) and Cherdintsev et al. (1969) as 13600 ± 250 (GIN-167).
[10]Michael (1984:51) questions whether this date is from layer 6 at Ushki-1 or Ushki-5.

References to Table 1
(1) Mochanov 1977.
(2) Slobodin 1990.
(3) Starikov and Zhidovlenko 1987.
(4) Shilo et al. 1977.
(5) Lozhkin and Trumpe 1990.
(6) Lozhkin et al. 1980.
(7) Dikov 1977.
(8) Dikov 1983:25.
(9) This study.
(10) Shilo et al. 1979.
(11) Lozhkin et al. 1977.
(12) Lozhkin and Parii 1976.
(13) Slobodin 1991b.
(14) Kuzmin 1994.
(15) Pitul'ko et al. 1990.
(16) Lozhkin 1987.
(17) Vereshchagin and Ukraintseva 1985.
(18) Lozhkin 1985.
(19) Dikov and Titov 1984.
(20) Cherdyntsevet al. 1969.
(21) Lozhkin and Parii 1985.
(22) Titov 1980.
(23) Dikov 1993.

communication 1996), a volcanic ash dated elsewhere in the Okhotsk region to 8800 ± 100 (MAG-978) and 8500 ± 100 (MAG-976) yr B.P. (Begét et al. 1991, Lozhkin 1987:153). A wood charcoal bulk sample recovered from the lower contact of the tephra yielded a conventional radiocarbon determination of 8260 ± 330 (MAG-1262) yr B.P. (Slobodin 1990, 1991a). Lithic artifacts were found at and below this contact, indicating that this date serves as an upper-limiting age for the Uptar-1 cultural occupation. Some artifacts also were collected from sediments disturbed by bulldozer activity.

The Uptar lithic assemblage is made up of more than 2,000 pieces; most are flakes and tiny retouching chips. The industry is characterized by flake and blade primary reduction technologies[3] (only five microblades have been found), unifacial and bifacial secondary reduction technologies, and a tool assemblage (n = 45) of bifacial points, miscellaneous bifaces, side scrapers, end scrapers, cobble tools, and a possible burin (Figure 3a-f) (Slobodin 1990, 1991a). Most of the projectile points have pointed to sharply convex bases (Figure 3b-c), and one appears to be fluted (King and Slobodin 1996). The "flute" on this point appears to be a deep basal thinning flake that was removed relatively early in the reduction sequence. Two small, abraded pendants also have been recovered (Slobodin and King 1996). Neither faunal remains nor features were discovered during excavations. The Uptar industry appears to be early Holocene to late Pleistocene in age, based on its stratigraphic position below the Elikchan tephra and similarities in bifacial point styles with the Siberdik sites (Slobodin and King 1996) and possibly the Osipovka site on the Amur River in the Russian Far East (Slobodin 1995).

Figure 3 (facing page). Lithic artifacts from Uptar-1 (a–f), Kheta (g–l), and Buiunda-3 (m–r) [a,d: side scrapers; b–c, e, i–j: bifaces; f, m–n: bladelets; g: wedge-shaped core; h: stone pendant; k, end scraper; l: transverse burin; o: crested blade; p–r: prismatic, pencil-shaped cores].

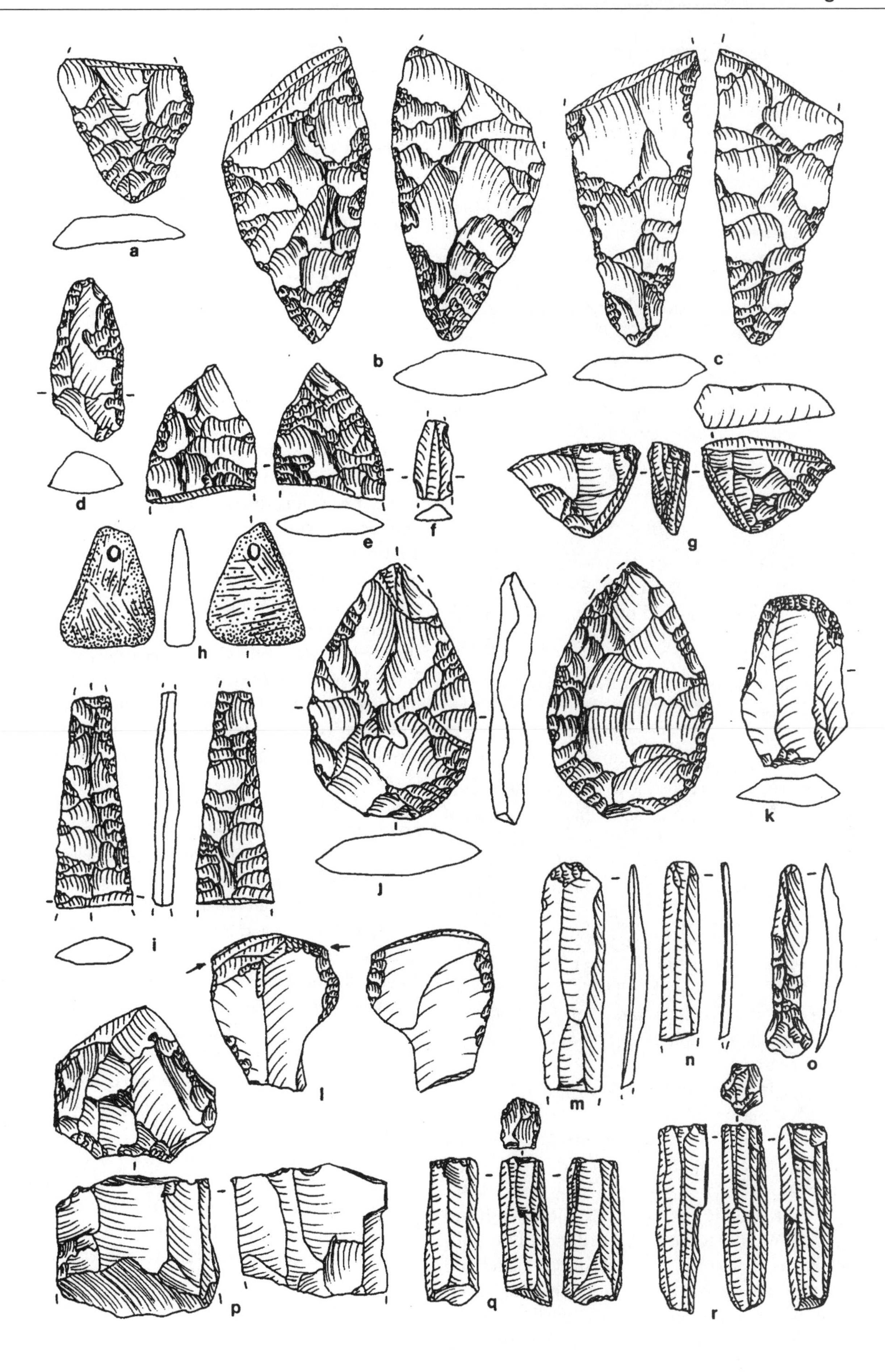
a
b
c
d
e
f
g
h
i
j
k
l
m
n
o
p
q
r

Upper Kolyma Mountains

THE UPPER KOLYMA REGION (Figure 2) includes the vast watershed of the upper Kolyma River, including its major tributaries. These rivers drain the north slopes of the Kolymskoe and Cherskii mountain ranges. Mountain peaks in the Cherskii range reach 2,500 m; mountain valleys are narrow and steep-sided. Much archaeological research has been accomplished in the valleys and uplands of the Upper Kolyma basin, initially by N. Dikov, and more recently by S. Slobodin. Their efforts have brought to light at least eight sites thought to date to before 7,000 yr B.P.: Maltan, Kheta, Buiunda-3, Kongo, Siberdik, Zima, and Ui-1. Two other sites, Maiorych and Shilo, were originally proposed by their excavators to date to the Paleolithic, but these age assignments are tenuous.

Maltan

MALTAN (*3*, FIGURES 1 AND 2) is located along the Maltan River, Magadan Oblast' (60° 55'N, 151° 25'E). Dikov (1977:223) excavated the site in 1974–1975, exposing more than 100 m^2 and identifying two cultural layers.

The site is situated upon a protruding ledge of the 8-m terrace of the Maltan River (Dikov 1977:223, 1995a). Site stratigraphy is characterized by a 20–50-cm thick mantle of yellow to grey-yellow sandy loam overlain by the modern soil. The lower cultural layer occurs in the unweathered sandy loam; a sample of wood charcoal from a hearth feature yielded a conventional ^{14}C determination of 7490 ± 70 (MAG-183) yr B.P. (Dikov 1977:225). The upper cultural layer occurs within the modern soil. Ten conventional ^{14}C determinations from the upper layer range from about 4500 ± 50 to 1300 ± 200 yr B.P. (Table 1) (Dikov 1977:223; Lozhkin 1985; Lozhkin and Prokhorova 1980; Lozhkin and Trumpe 1990:177) and may indicate multiple occupations or the dating of natural charcoal.

The lithic industry for the lower cultural layer has been briefly described by Dikov (1979a:100). Primary reduction technologies are dominated by the production of bladelets and microblades from conical and prismatic bidirectional cores (Dikov 1979a:100). Raw materials include grey and black silicified tuff and slate, yellow chert, and chalcedony. The tool assemblage is characterized by retouched blades and microblades, end scrapers, side scrapers, backed knives, dihedral burins, leaf-shaped bifaces, small triangular projectile points (found on the surface along the edge of the terrace), and large coarsely ground and flaked "scraper-like adzes" (Dikov 1979a:100). Also identified in the lower cultural layer are three possible storage pits and eight hearth stains with associated lithic debris (Dikov 1977:224). Dikov (1979a:100) assigns this occupation to an early phase of the "Kolyma Preceramic Neolithic," but the principal characteristics of the Maltan lower cultural layer can also be seen in late Holocene complexes from the Upper Kolyma (Slobodin 1995).

Kheta

KHETA (*4*, FIGURES 1 AND 2) is located at the confluence of the right and left Kheta rivers, near the village of Atka, Magadan Oblast' (60° 58'N, 151° 48'E). The site, situated on the third (15–20-m) terrace of the Kheta River, was discovered by S. Slobodin in 1990 (Slobodin and Glushkova 1992). Excavations continued through 1992 (King and Slobodin 1994; Slobodin and King 1996).

Artifacts occur beneath volcanic ash and red sand in a gravel lag deposit about 20 cm below the modern surface (Slobodin and Glushkova 1992; Slobodin and King 1996). Upper deposits have been removed by bulldozer activity. The ash is thought to represent the Elikchan Tephra (Slobodin and Glushkova 1992), absolutely dated elsewhere to about 8500 yr B.P. (Lozhkin 1987). The sand is considered a reworked-eolian deposit and is masked by a possible paleosol horizon (King and Slobodin 1994). Slobodin and King (1996) assign the sand to the terminal Pleistocene.

The lithic assemblage (around 500 pieces) includes a wedge-shaped microblade core, microblades, end scrapers, bifaces, a transverse burin, and numerous flakes (Figure 3g-l) (Slobodin and Glushkova 1992; King and Slobodin 1994). The wedge-shaped core is bifacially worked, has a beveled platform, and appears exhausted. Bifacial artifacts include a large oval biface and two leaf-shaped point fragments. Also present are a polished stone bead and a polished stone pendant; each has a biconically drilled hole (Slobodin and King 1996).

Slobodin and Glushkova (1992) compare the assemblage to those from Diuktai Cave, Yakutia, and Ushki-1 (layer VI), Kamchatka, and assign a late Pleistocene (>10,000 yr B.P.) age, although chronometric age estimates are needed to confirm this. Given its occurrence below the presumed Elikchan tephra, however, the Kheta occupation almost certainly dates to before 8500 yr B.P.

Buiunda-3

BUIUNDA-3 (*5*, FIGURES 1 AND 2) is located along the Okhotsk-Kolyma divide, at the headwaters of the Buiunda River (60° 51'N, 153° 24'E). The site was discovered and tested by Slobodin in 1990. In 1993, test excavations were conducted by Slobodin and M. L. King. To date, an area of 5 m^2 has been excavated.

This buried site contains lithic artifacts and a stone-lined hearth pit 40–80 cm below the modern surface. The artifacts occur within and around a concentration of charcoal from the hearth (Slobodin 1995, 1997). Samples of this charcoal yielded four conventional radiocarbon determinations of 8135 ± 220 (GX-17064), 7790 ± 190 (LE-3991), 7510 ± 205 (GX-17065), and 5610 ± 110 (LE-3898) yr B.P. The latter date is discordantly young and probably aberrant. Assuming the charcoal samples dated are associated primarily with the lithic artifacts, this industry can be assigned to the early Holocene (8300–7500 yr B.P.).

A lithic assemblage of more than 2,000 pieces has been recovered. Primary reduction technologies are represented by conical blade and microblade cores, some with circumferential blade detachments giving them a pencil-like appearance, core tablets, crested blades, numerous narrow blades and microblades, and associated debitage (Figure 3m-r). Tools are limited to a handful of utilized or marginally retouched blades, angle burins, end scrapers on blades, and a bifacial adze. Slobodin (1995) assigns the industry to the Sumnagin Mesolithic complex.

Maiorych

MAIORYCH (*6*, FIGURES 1 AND 2) was discovered by Iu. A. Mochanov in 1970. The site is located near the village of Debin, along the left bank of the Kolyma River, Magadan Oblast' (64° 42'N, 150° 55'E). It is situated on the 14-m, first (lowest) terrace of the Kolyma River, on a bluff overlooking the confluence of the Kolyma River and Maiorych Creek. Mochanov (1977) collected a possible core and several retouched pieces from surface blowouts along the edge of the terrace. The core is described as being manufactured on a chert plate and having a wedge-shaped cross-section and steeply beveled platform (Mochanov 1977). Tools include a combination knife/end scraper on a blade and a utilized flake. English-language descriptions of the site can be found in Michael (1984:21) and Mochanov and Fedoseeva (1996c).

Mochanov (1977) compares the Maiorych finds typologically to artifacts found at Verkhne-Troitskaia on the Aldan River, Yakutia. Based on typological similarities, he assigns them to the Diuktai culture and suggests an age of between 30,000 and 12,000 yr B.P. for the site. Kashin (1983a), however, argues that the core is not a clear wedge-shaped core, that its "platform" is too beveled to be considered a platform, and that its front does not display any obvious microblade removals. Thus, it may better be described as a biface fragment or perhaps a core preform. In Kashin's (1983a) opinion, the undated Maiorych site should not be considered Paleolithic, let alone Diuktai, because biface fragments and blades like those from Maiorych occur throughout the region's Mesolithic and Neolithic periods.

Kongo

THE KONGO SITE (*7*, FIGURES 1 AND 2) is located along the upper Kolyma River near the mouth of Kongo Creek, in the flooded zone of the Kolyma Reservoir, Magadan Oblast' (61° 57'N, 149° 54'E). Dikov (1977:221–222; 1995c) discovered Kongo in 1971; test excavations in 1973 revealed archaeological materials in a buried, stratified context, and excavations in 1973–1975 uncovered two early Holocene cultural components across an area of more than 275 m^2.

The Kongo site is situated upon the 14-m terrace of the Kolyma River. Terrace-mantling sediments reach 1.5 m in depth and consist of alternating loams, sandy loams, and sands (Figure 4). The lowermost component, cultural layer 3, occurs in the lowest band of a humified red-brown loam (Dikov 1977:222), presumably a paleosol. Four wood charcoal samples yielded conventional ^{14}C determinations which range from 9470 ± 530 to 8700 ± 400 yr B.P. (Table 1) (Dikov 1977:222; Kuzmin 1989). Above this is cultural layer 2, situated in unweathered rose and grey sand bands. Wood charcoal samples collected from hearth features yielded conventional ^{14}C determinations of 8655 ± 220 (MAG-196) (Dikov 1977:222; Lozhkin et al. 1980:204) and 8080 ± 500 (MAG-406) yr B.P. (Shilo et al. 1979:10; Lozhkin and Trumpe 1990:177). Cultural layer 1 is undescribed but determined stratigraphically to date to the late Holocene.

Only cursory descriptions of archaeological finds from Kongo are available (Dikov 1977, 1979a; Dikov et al. 1983). For cultural layer 3, Dikov et al. (1983:23) describe a single conical microblade core and a tool

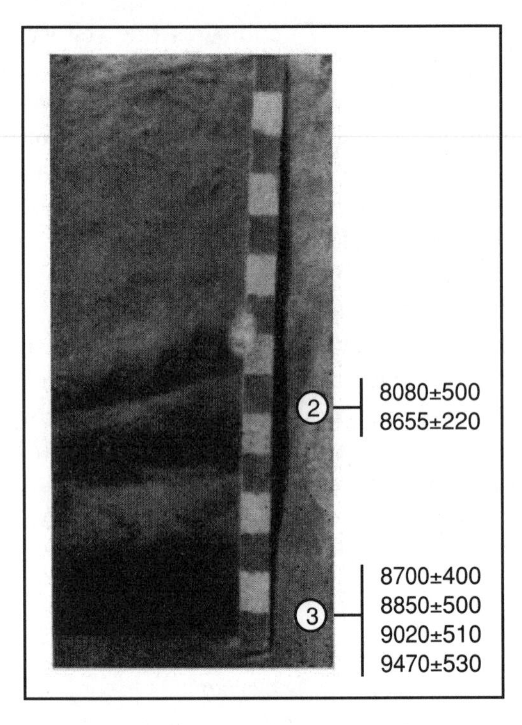

Figure 4. Stratigraphic profile of Kongo site, showing provenience of cultural layers and radiocarbon dates (after Dikov 1977).

assemblage characterized by "primitive" cobble choppers (retouched unifacially), retouched bladelets and microblades, and angle burins made on large blade-like flakes (Figure 5b, e-f, h-i). The lithic assemblage from cultural layer 2 also has cobble choppers, bifacial leaf-shaped points, and bladelets and microblades (some retouched) (Figure 5a, c-d, g), but no burins (Dikov 1977:222). Dikov (1977:222) also notes the occurrence of small spalls of burnt bone, several hearth stains, and discernible activity areas in both cultural layers, and a possible storage pit in cultural layer 2. Dikov assigns cultural layers 3 and 2 to the "Siberdik Relict Paleolithic culture," a local early Holocene complex.

Siberdik

SIBERDIK (*8*, FIGURES 1 AND 2) is located at the confluence of Malyi Siberdik Creek and the Detrin River, in the flooded zone of the Kolyma Reservoir, Magadan Oblast' (61° 36'N, 149° 44'E). The site was discovered in 1971 (Dikov and Dikova 1972:252) and excavated by Dikov (1977, 1979a, 1985a; 1995d) in 1971–1974. Excavations uncovered 800 m^2 and revealed three stratigraphically distinct cultural components spanning the Holocene.

Siberdik is situated on a protruding knob of the 14-m terrace of the Detrin River (Dikov 1977:213). Bedrock is mantled by a 1-m thick bed of cobble alluvium, in turn overlain by a 2-m thick mantle of alternating sand, sandy loam, and loam (Figure 6). These mantling sediments contain three separate cultural components. Cultural layer 3 occurs in a "peaty horizon" mixed with sandy loam about 1 m below the surface (Dikov 1977:218). Eight radiocarbon determinations range from 13,500 to 4570 yr B.P. (Table 1) (Lozhkin and Prokhorova 1980; Lozhkin and Trumpe 1990; Lozhkin et al. 1977; Shilo et al. 1976). The oldest (13,225 ± 230) and youngest dates (4570 ± 370) are discordant; the remaining six determinations range from 9700 to 7080 yr B.P. and indicate an early Holocene age.[4] Cultural layer 2 is situated within a white loam 50–80 cm below the surface (Dikov 1977:214–215). This component has five radiocarbon determinations which range from about 6590 to 4420 yr B.P. (Table 1). Cultural layer 1, the uppermost component, occurs in the modern soil and has been radiocarbon dated to about 600 yr B.P. (Table 1) (Lozhkin and Prokhorova 1980). Dikov (1977:213) assigns it to the late Neolithic.

Only the assemblage from cultural layer 3 is discussed here. Primary reduction technology is characterized by the manufacture of flakes, blades, and microblades for use as tools. One wedge-shaped microblade core was found in a dense scatter of lithic debris (Dikov 1977:220). Unifacial, bifacial, and burin secondary reduction technologies also are present. The tool assemblage is made up of anvilstones, hammerstones, cobble choppers and picks, side scrapers, end scrapers (many on massive blades), "flake-points," knives, a burin hafted in a bone handle, and bifacial leaf-shaped points (Figure 5j-r) (Dikov 1977, 1979a). Faunal remains were recovered, but detailed identifications have not been published. Dikov (1977:218–221) describes only a horse tooth, deer antler, and herbivore scapula.

Although much of the area has been deformed by frost cracks and ice-wedge polygons, several features are present in cultural layer 3. Dikov (1977:218–220) describes hearths consisting of charred stones, calcined bones, and heated lithics. Several stone-working areas or "workshops" also were identified, and a stain of red ochre may represent the poorly preserved remains of a human burial (Dikov 1977:218).

Dikov (1977:96, 1985a:176) assigns cultural layer 3 to the late Siberdik Relict Paleolithic culture, based on the apparent early Holocene age of the component

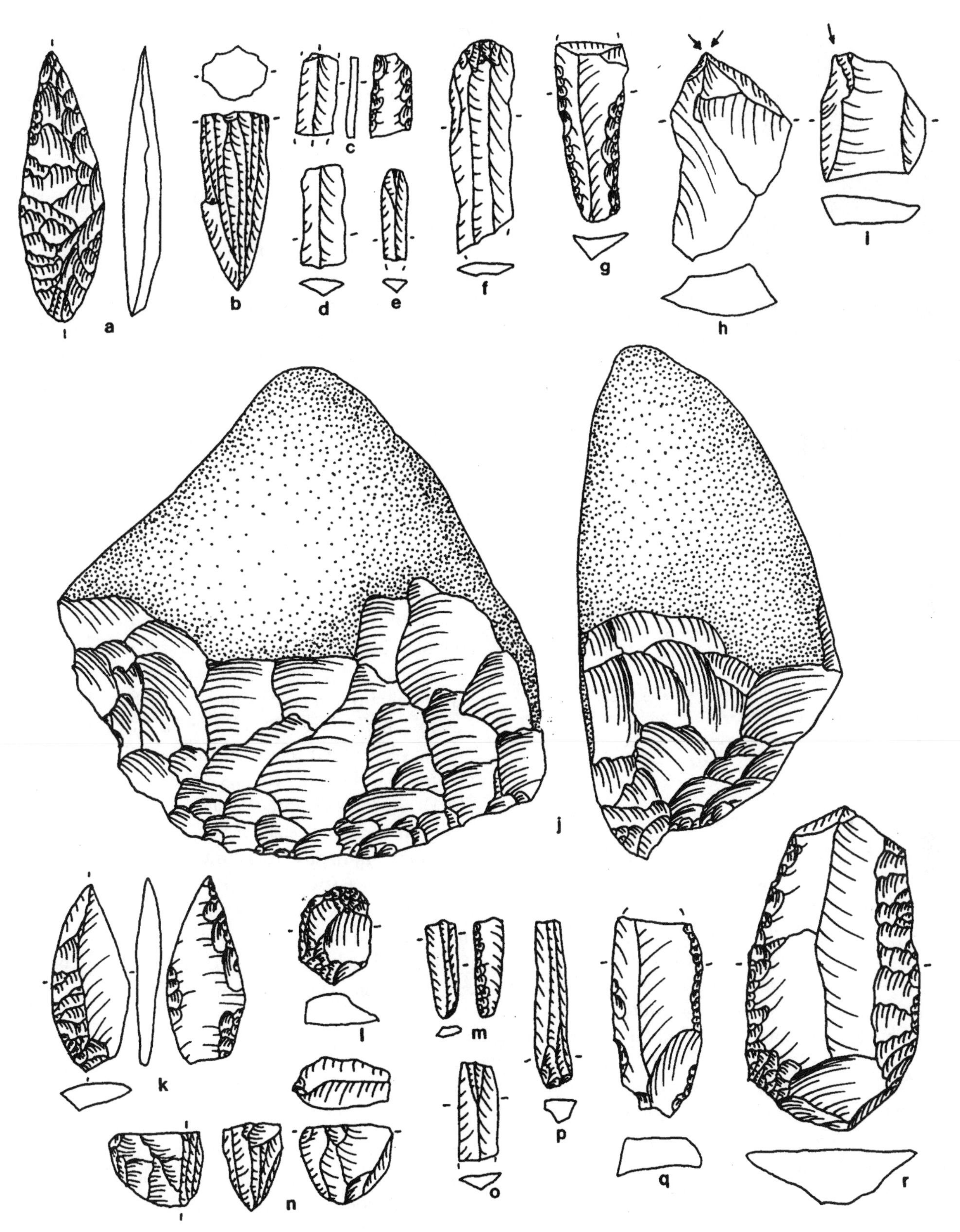

Figure 5. Lithic artifacts from Kongo (cultural layers 3 [b, e–f, h–i] and 2 [a, c–d, g]) and Siberdik (j–r) (after Dikov 1977) [a, k: bifaces; b: conical core; c–e, m–p: bladelets; f: blade; g, q: retouched blades; h–i: burins; j: cobble tools; l: end scraper; n: microblade core; r: side scraper].

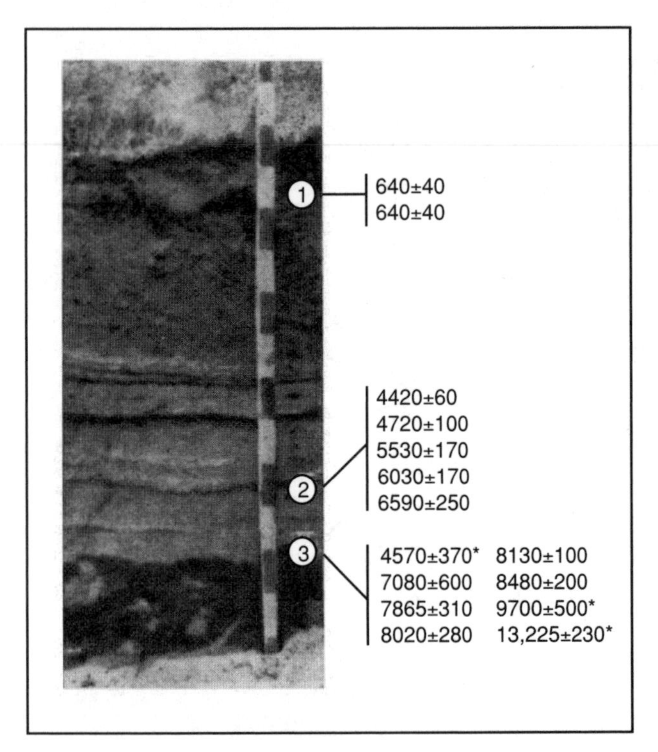

Figure 6. Stratigraphic profile of Siberdik site, showing provenience of cultural layers and radiocarbon dates (after Dikov 1977) [asterisks denote aberrant dates].

and the presence of bifacial leaf-shaped points and a wedge-shaped core.

Shilo

SHILO (*9*, FIGURES 1 AND 2) is located near the source of Shilo Creek, a tributary of the upper Kolyma River, about 80 km southwest of Susuman, Magadan Oblast' (62° 11'N, 146° 42'E). The site was discovered in 1970 by V. I. Gerasimchuk, who surface-collected an end scraper made on a blade (Dikov and Gerasimchuk 1971). No excavations were carried out, but the scraper is heavily patinized and considered Upper Paleolithic in appearance (Dikov and Gerasimchuk 1971). Mochanov (1977:94), however, argues that "intensive patina" is not a good indicator of great antiquity, and that end scrapers like that from Shilo are common in the region's Neolithic and early Iron Age. Without further information, the site should not be considered part of the early prehistoric record of southwestern Beringia.

Zima

ZIMA (*10*, FIGURES 1 AND 2) is located along the left bank of the Zima River, a small tributary of the Momontai River, 6 km downstream of Lake Momontai, Magadan Oblast' (63° 43'N, 148° 10'E). Slobodin discovered the site in 1986; he conducted excavations there in 1987 and 1988 (Slobodin 1991b, 1995).

Zima is a small, shallowly buried site with some discernible stratigraphy. It is situated upon a low (20 x 30 m) knob of the first (lowest), 2-m terrace of the Zima River. The surface of the site is devoid of vegetation; more than 100 lithic artifacts were collected from the surface. Excavations recovered additional artifacts in a shallow (<25 cm) context. The site's single cultural layer occurs beneath the modern soil in a band of grey sandy loam 7–13 cm thick. Wood charcoal collected from this grey sandy loam in association with lithic artifacts yielded a conventional radiocarbon determination of 7070 ± 60 (MAG-1260) yr B.P. (Slobodin 1991b).

The lithic assemblage (collected from the surface and *in situ*) is characterized by conical cores, blades and microblades, and a tool assemblage of end scrapers (some on large blades), retouched blades and bladelets, a dihedral burin, bifacial projectile point fragment, and possible hammerstone (Figure 7a-h). Excavations revealed a 100-cm diameter ring of 10 stones. This feature may be the remains of a hearth (Slobodin 1991b) but was devoid of charcoal.

Given the small size of the assemblage and the uncertainty in dating, it is difficult to assign the Zima industry to a specific early Holocene Beringian complex; however, there are some similarities with the undated Tytyl' complex of interior western Chukotka (Kiriak 1988) (discussed below) and the Sumnagin culture of Yakutia (Mochanov 1977).

Ui-1

UI-1 (*11*, FIGURES 1 AND 2) is located along the north side of Lake Ui, a small lake that empties into the Ozernaia River, a tributary of the Momontai River, Magadan Oblast' (63° 45'N, 147° 55'E). Slobodin discovered the site in 1987, and excavations took place from 1989 through 1991. To date, at least 60 m^2 have been excavated (Slobodin 1995, 1996).

Ui-1 is situated upon a 3-m lake terrace about 50 m from the water's edge. Lithic artifacts occur in a grey-brown soil horizon at a depth of 1 to 14 cm below the

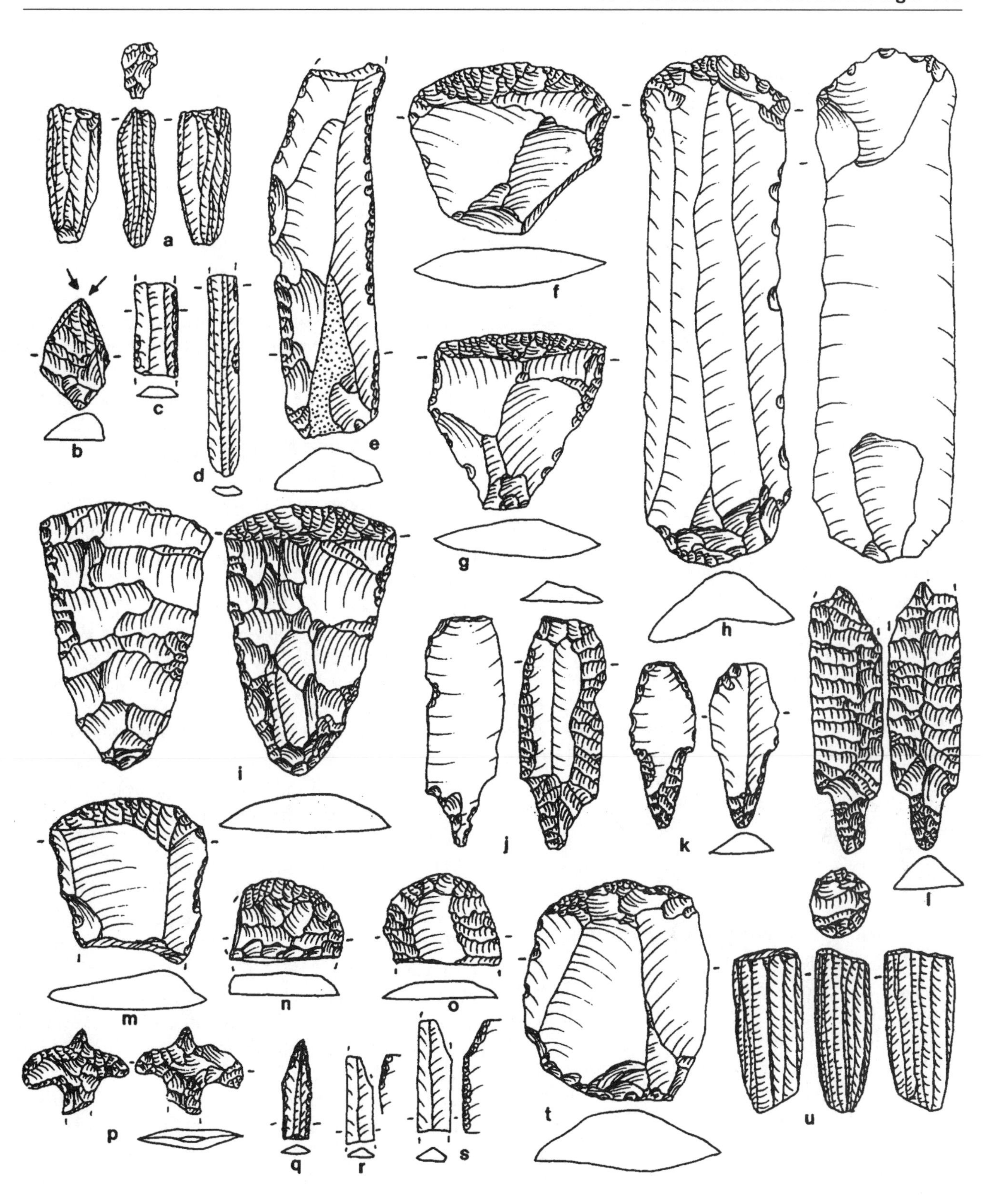

Figure 7. Lithic artifacts from Zima (a–h) and Ui-1 (i–u) [a, u: pencil-shaped, conical cores; b: burin; c–d, q–s: microblades-bladelets; e: retouched blade; f–h, m–o, t: end scrapers; i: bifacial end scraper; j–l: stemmed points on blades; p: bird ornament].

modern surface. Associated with the artifacts are numerous lenses of charcoal and ash; samples of this charcoal yielded conventional radiocarbon determinations of 8810 ± 235 (GX-17067), 8695 ± 100 (GX-17066), 8370 ± 190 (LE-3990), and 5950 ± 90 (LE-3900) yr B.P. The youngest determination (LE-3900) seems discordant; the remaining three average 8644 ± 83 yr B.P.

The lithic assemblage recovered from Ui-1 through 1990 consists of 3,071 flakes, 1,572 small blades and microblades, and 120 diagnostic artifacts. Primary reduction technologies are represented by conical cores in various stages of reduction, core tablets, and crested blades (Figure 7u). Raw materials include cherts, basalt, and rhyolite. The tool assemblage is made up of end scrapers (one bifacially worked), small side scrapers, unifacial knives, retouched blades and microblades, angle burins, cobble tools, biface fragments, and bifacial points (Figure 7i-t). Points are made on blades, often only marginally retouched, and have basal stems and shoulders (Figure 7j-l). The one exception is invasively retouched and lanceolate-shaped. Other items include a bifacially worked bird-like ornament (Figure 7p) (Slobodin 1995, 1996).

Although stemmed points like those found at Ui-1 have been found at other sites in Northeast Asia (Kashin 1983b; Mochanov 1977:247), none have been dated absolutely. Kashin (1983b) originally suggested an early Holocene age for these sites, and the tight cluster of radiocarbon determinations from Ui-1 corroborates this interpretation.

Indigirka-Kolyma Lowlands

THE INDIGIRKA-KOLYMA LOWLANDS of northwestern Beringia consist of a broad plain stretching from the mouth of the Lena River east to the mouth of the Kolyma River. It is characterized by lakes and bogs and tundra vegetation. During glacial periods of the Upper Pleistocene, this plain extended northward across the East Siberian Sea platform, connecting Wrangell Island and the Novosibirsk Islands to the mainland. This region is almost entirely within Yakutia. Archaeological research has been undertaken by Iu. Mochanov and more recently by S. Kistenev (1988). However, only two unequivocal archaeological sites predating 7000 yr B.P. have been found in this region: Berelekh and Zhokhov Island. A third site, Bochanut, is an accumulation of large mammal bones which probably was not the product of human hunters.

Zhokhov Island

THE EARLY HOLOCENE Zhokhov Island site (*12*, Figure 1) is located in the southwestern part of Zhokhov Island, approximately 120 km northeast of New Siberian Island and 500 km north of the mouth of the Indigirka River (76° 14'N, 152° 40'E). The site was discovered during the 1960s (Giria and Pitul'ko 1994:31), but was not investigated thoroughly until 1989–1990 (Giria and Pitul'ko 1994; Pitul'ko 1993; Pitul'ko et al. 1990).

The Zhokhov Island site is situated upon a 10–15-m terrace along the edge of a small creek valley, not far from the sea shore (Pitul'ko et al. 1990:259–260). The well-drained terrace edge is adjacent to a high hill that formed a barrier against strong northern winds (Giria and Pitul'ko 1994:31; Pitul'ko et al. 1990:260). Cultural remains were collected from the surface and during the excavation of a buried cultural layer (Pitul'ko et al. 1990:260). Site stratigraphy has not been presented in detail. A series of 12 radiocarbon determinations on wood, bone, and charcoal apparently collected from the buried cultural layer range from 10,810 ± 390 to 7450 ± 200 yr B.P., but the majority (eight) cluster between 8200 ± 40 and 7850 ± 40 yr B.P. (Table 1). A thirteenth date of 8790 was produced on wood immediately below the cultural layer. According to palynological data from nearby Kotel'nyi Island, vegetation at this time was dominated by shrub vegetation and heaths (Ericaceae), suggesting a landscape similar to the modern southern tundra zone (Pitul'ko et al. 1990:261).

The artifact assemblage from the Zhokhov Island site has been described in detail by Giria and Pitul'ko (1994). More than 1,200 lithic pieces have been collected from the surface of the site and excavations (Giria and Pitul'ko 1994:32), and these are treated as a single industry. Locally procured raw materials include a variety of cherts, silicified tuffs, sandstones, and chalcedonies; four obsidian microblade segments are from an unknown, presumed exotic, source (Pitul'ko et al. 1990:260). Primary reduction technology is based on the production of bladelets and microblades (Figure 8f-g) from polyhedral cores with wide and flat faces, or from "end" [*tortsovyi*] cores with bladelets/microblades removed from an edge rather than a face (Figure 8c-e). Many microblades are segmented, intentionally shaped through backing, and inset into laterally grooved bone, antler, or ivory points (Giria and Pitul'ko 1994:32–37) (Figure 8a-b). Edge damage is apparent on seven isolated segments (Figure 8h-k) and on many of the segments still inset in the preserved

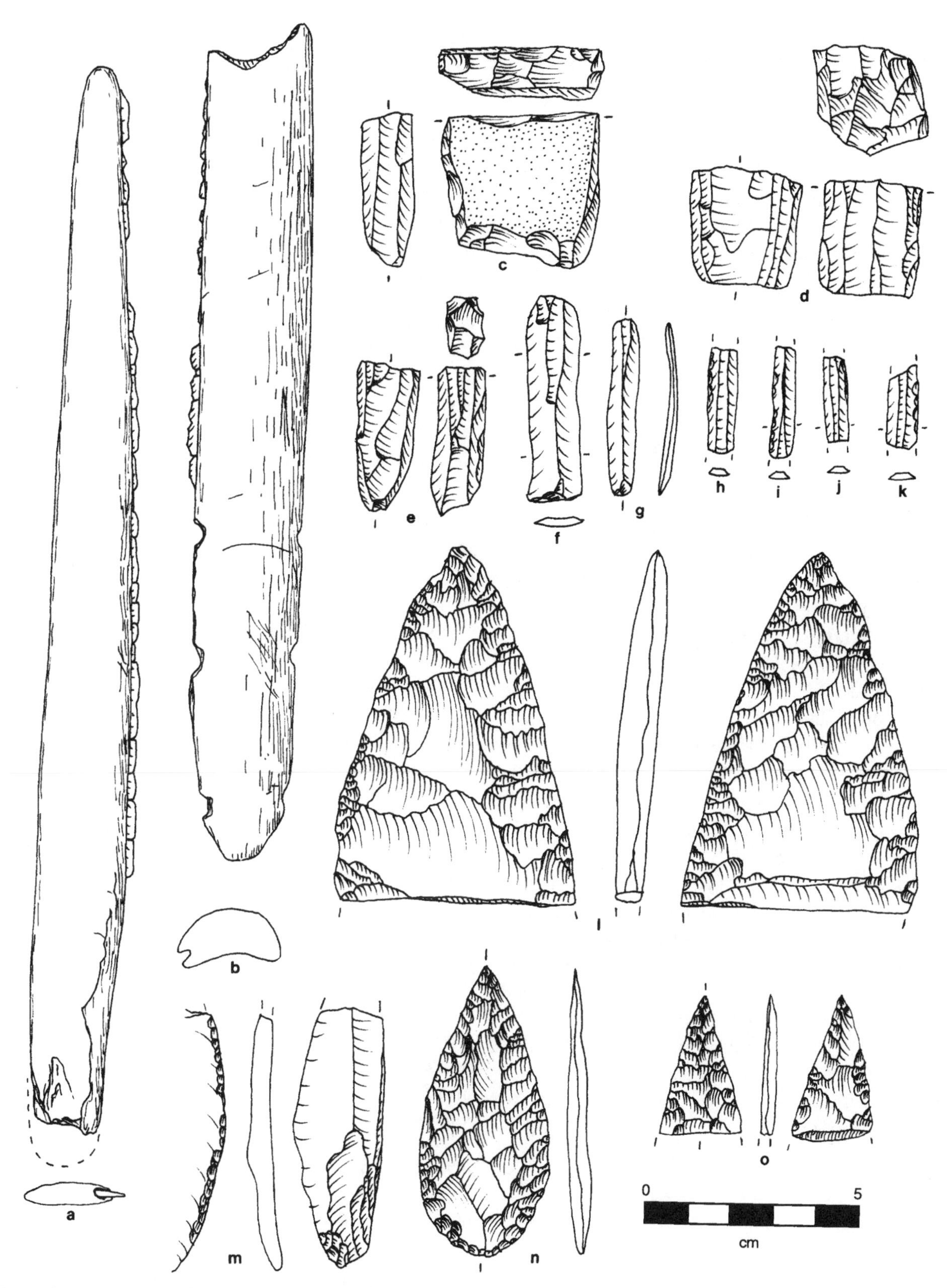

Figure 8. Artifacts from Zhokhov Island (a–k) after Giria and Pitul'ko (1994) and Berelekh (l–o) after Mochanov (1977) and Vereshchagin and Ukraintseva (1985) [a–b: slotted bone points with insets; c–e: prismatic cores; f–k: bladelets-microblades; l, n–o: bifaces; m: retouched blade].

grooved points. Their lengths range from 11 to 25 mm. Interestingly, 20 other segments without wear range from 5.3 to 8.3 mm, suggesting that longer microblade segments were selected over shorter ones for use as insets (Giria and Pitul'ko 1994:37). Other retouched lithic artifacts include two large chipped and ground axe-like implements found on the surface of the site (Pitul'ko et al. 1990:260).

The Zhokhov Island site also has yielded a number of well-preserved bone, antler, and ivory (fossil mammoth and walrus) implements, including 13 unilaterally slotted points, 12 bilaterally slotted points, and two massive "hoe-like tools" (Giria and Pitul'ko 1994:32–34; Pitul'ko et al. 1990:260). All of the bilaterally slotted points are symmetrical and have concavo-convex cross-sections, while the unilaterally slotted points are much more heterogeneous, with symmetrical and asymmetrical shapes and concavo-convex, plano-convex, or lenticular cross-sections (Giria and Pitul'ko 1994:32–34) (Figure 8a-b). Almost all of the points have grooves that extend along a portion of their lateral margins.

The site's faunal assemblage of 906 specimens includes reindeer (49.7 percent), polar bear (43.8 percent), and isolated bones (6.5 percent) of sea mammals, birds, and wolf (Giria and Pitul'ko 1994:32; Pitul'ko et al. 1990:261). Reindeer teeth suggest an autumn occupation of the site, while associated antler (if not collected after being shed) suggests a winter occupation (Pitul'ko et al. 1990:261). Further details have not been reported.

Pitul'ko et al. (1990:261) also describe 13 natural thermokarst depressions that appear to have been transformed by humans into circular house pits 3–4 m in diameter. The available evidence indicates that the Zhokhov Island site was a fall-winter village occupied by early Holocene hunters of terrestrial mammals, particularly reindeer and polar bear (Giria and Pitul'ko 1994:32). The Mesolithic quality of the site's lithic and organic artifact assemblages suggests ties with the Yakutian Sumnagin complex (Giria and Pitul'ko 1994:44).

Berelekh

THE BERELEKH MAMMOTH cemetery and archaeological site (*13*, Figure 1) are located along the Berelekh River, a tributary of the Indigirka River, Yakutia (70° 50'N, 145° 30'E). Both localities have been the subject of much interest among paleontologists and archaeologists; English-language descriptions can be found in Hopkins et al. (1982:440), Kozlowski and Bandi (1984:367–368), Larichev et al. (1992), Michael (1984:18–20), Morlan (1987:280), and Soffer (1985:304–308).

The Berelekh Mammoth Cemetery. The mammoth cemetery was discovered by Grigor'ev in 1947 and excavated by Vereshchagin in 1970, 1971, and 1980 (Vereshchagin 1974, 1977; Vereshchagin and Ukraintseva 1985). Excavations resulted in an extensive faunal assemblage from a distinct horizon 3.5 m below the modern surface extending along the bank of the river for about 150 m (Vereshchagin and Mochanov 1972; Vereshchagin and Ukraintseva 1985). Bone and soft tissue samples yielded conventional radiocarbon determinations of 13,700 ± 80 (MAG-114) and 12,240 ± 160 (LU-149) yr B.P. (Vereshchagin and Ukraintseva 1985; Lozhkin 1987), respectively, and wood samples from sediments immediately overlying the bone bed led to conventional radiocarbon determinations of 11,870 ± 60 (NII DVNTS AN SSSR), 11,830 ± 110 (LU-147), 10,440 ± 100 (MAG-119), and 10,260±155 (MAG-118) yr B.P. (Vereshchagin and Ukraintseva 1985).

The agents responsible for the accumulation of the mammoth cemetery are not well understood. Mochanov (1977) and Hopkins et al. (1982:440) suggest that the dense concentration of mammoth tusk and bone is a cultural feature comparable to the collapsed mammoth-bone dwellings of the Russian Plain Upper Paleolithic (Soffer 1985). No artifacts, however, have been found, leading Vereshchagin (1974:7) and Vereshchagin and Ukraintseva (1985) to suggest that the bones accumulated through some natural phenomenon. Perhaps the bone accumulation is the result of long-term fluvial activity (Vereshchagin 1974:7), but mammoth mortality profiles appear to represent a catastrophic event, perhaps the simultaneous death of an entire herd while crossing thin ice on a newly frozen river (Vereshchagin 1977).

Berelekh Archaeological Site. The archaeological site at Berelekh is located 130 m downriver from the principal area of the mammoth cemetery (Vereshchagin and Ukraintseva 1985). It too is situated 12 m above the modern river floodplain. The site was discovered by Vereshchagin in 1970, and excavations were conducted in 1971–1973 by Mochanov (1977), and again in 1981 (Mochanov and Fedoseeva 1996a). Archaeological materials include stone tools and debitage and abundant faunal remains.

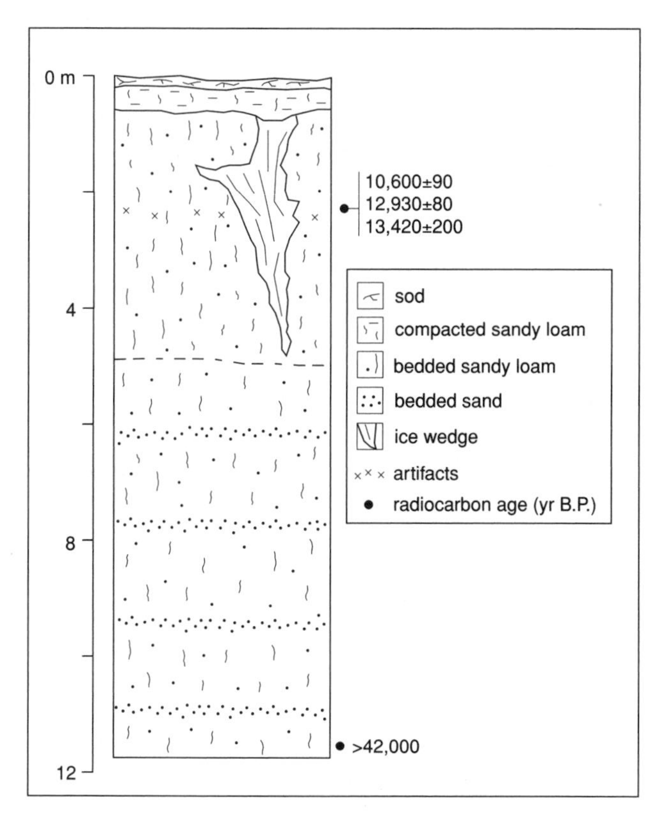

Figure 9. Stratigraphic profile from Berelekh archaeological site, showing provenience of cultural layer and radiocarbon dates (after Mochanov 1977).

Geologic stratigraphy consists of interbedded loams and sandy loams up to 12 m thick (Figure 9). The top of the profile consists of the modern soil (layer 1) and an unweathered yellow-brown sandy loam (layer 2). Underlying this is a series of grey sands interbedded with grey-brown sandy loams together up to 400–450 cm thick (layer 3), followed by a series of yellow sands interbedded with grey-blue sandy loams up to 700–750 cm thick (layer 4). Layers 1 and 2 appear to be eolian in origin and Holocene in age, while layers 3 and 4 are alluvial and late to mid-Upper Pleistocene (Mochanov 1977). D. M. Hopkins (personal communication 1996) suggests that the stratigraphic profile represents a thaw lake sequence. The cultural occupation at Berelekh has been deformed by a polygonal network of ice wedges spanning the site and penetrating up to 4 m below the modern surface.

Paleolithic artifacts occur in the upper 1 m of layer 3. Three conventional radiocarbon determinations on wood in apparent association with lithic artifacts range from 13,420 ± 200 to 10,600 ± 90 yr B.P. (Table 1) (Mochanov 1977; Vereshchagin and Ukraintseva 1985). Mochanov (1977:77) also reports an infinite radiocarbon determination of >42,000 (LE-1112) yr B.P. from near the base of the profile.

The excavated lithic assemblage includes 64 flakes, 44 tiny retouching chips, four blades, one core, 10 tools, and four stone pendants (with biconically drilled holes) (Mochanov 1977:79; Vereshchagin and Mochanov 1972) (Figure 8l-o). Raw materials include cherts, silicified slate, and silicified limestone. Mochanov (1977:79) describes the core as a microblade core made on a flake, but also suggests it could be a multifaceted angle burin. It also could be a bipolar core. [Mochanov (1977:79) describes a second core found along the terrace edge, but Kozlowski and Bandi (1984:368) identify it as a "scaled piece" (bipolar core).] The four blades may be microblades, but, contrary to Morlan (1987:280), Mochanov (1977:79) does not call them such. One is 0.7 cm wide and has a partially cortical dorsal surface, while the other three are >1 cm wide. Secondary reduction technologies include unifacial and bifacial retouch. The tool assemblage includes the tip fragment of a bifacial point, two biface fragments, and seven retouched blade-like flakes and flakes. Mochanov (1977:79) also reports the discovery of 49 worked pieces of mammoth bone and ivory.

More recently, Vereshchagin and Ukraintseva (1985) discovered a bifacial teardrop-shaped point from along the bluff edge near Mochanov's excavations (Figure 8n). Other "new" finds from Berelekh are illustrated by Mochanov et al. (1991:214–216), but with no corresponding descriptions or details of provenience. These include what appear to be a wedge-shaped core, tanged biface, and stone pendant.

Faunal remains recovered from the cultural component at Berelekh include 78 bones of mammoth, three of bison or horse, one of reindeer, 827 of hare, 92 of ptarmigan, and two of fish. Some of these are charred and associated with hearth features. Possibly some of the mammoth remains were scavenged from the nearby mammoth cemetery (Abramova 1989:232; Vereshchagin 1974:10).

Mochanov (1977) and others (Kuzmin and Tankersley 1997; Powers 1996) assign the Berelekh lithic industry to the Diuktai culture, based on its age and the presence of bifaces and a putative microblade core. However, microblades are absent, the microblade core recovered during Mochanov's excavation may not be a microblade core, and the one unequivocal wedge-shaped microblade core was not found *in situ*. The other recent finds, especially the teardrop-shaped point and tanged biface, although not recovered *in situ*, are intriguing. Tanged bifaces have been found in the "pre-microblade" industry from Ushki-1 (layer VII),

Kamchatka, and teardrop-shaped, "Chindadn" points are common in central Alaska's Nenana complex. Could there be two separate cultural occupations at Berelekh—one nonmicroblade and 13,000 yr B.P., and the other microblade and 10,000 yr B.P.? Additional fieldwork is necessary to clear up this issue.

Bochanut

THE BOCHANUT SITE (*14*, Figure 1) is located on Lake Bochanut in the lower Kolyma basin, 80 km northeast of the village of Srednekolymsk, Yakutia (68° 24'N, 156° 10'E). In 1972, geologist A. Miziskii discovered a 15-m-high exposure containing bones of woolly mammoth, woolly rhinoceros, bison, horse, musk-ox, reindeer, and moose (Mochanov 1977:93). Their stratigraphic context has not been reported. A brief English-language description of Bochanut can be found in Michael (1984:21).

On several of the Bochanut bones, S. Semenov identified traces of wear presumed to represent human activity (Mochanov 1977). No lithic artifacts nor unequivocal bone artifacts were recovered. Until proven otherwise, the Bochanut faunal assemblage should be viewed as a natural accumulation of bones, not a Paleolithic site (Mochanov 1977:93).

Western Interior Chukotka

THE AREA REFERRED TO HERE as Western Interior Chukotka includes the Omolon, Bol'shoi Anui, and Malyi Anui rivers, three major rivers that flow into the Kolyma River near where it empties into the East Siberian Sea (Figure 1). The Omolon River drains the northern slope of the eastern Kolyma mountains, while the Anui rivers empty the Anui range and the western slope of the Anadyr Plateau. I. Vorobei and M. Kir'iak recently conducted archaeological research in the Omolon and Anui basins, respectively. Four sites, including Druchak-V, El'gakhchan-1, Orlovka-2, and Tytyl'-1, have been assigned to the early, pre-7000-yr B.P. period. Unfortunately, none of these sites has been radiocarbon dated.

Druchak-V

DRUCHAK-V (*15*, Figure 1), discovered and studied by Vorobei (1992), is located along the upper Druchak River, 140 km north of the Sea of Okhotsk coast, Magadan Oblast' (63° 19'N, 159° 8'E). Druchak-V is situated upon the 23-m terrace of the Druchak River, and lithic artifacts occur in a buried context, within a sandy loam varying from 0.15 to 1.3 m thick (Vorobei 1992). The cultural component has been heavily deformed by cryogenic activity. Although dating is problematic, pollen data suggest an age of 10,000-8000 yr B.P. (Vorobei 1992).

The Druchak lithic assemblage is characterized by blade and microblade primary reduction technologies. Blades are detached from unidirectional and bidirectional monofrontal subprismatic cores, while microblades are detached from small wedge-shaped cores (Figure 10h, k). Unifacial, bifacial, and burin secondary reduction technologies also are represented. The tool assemblage consists of bifacial point fragments, miscellaneous bifaces, retouched blades and flakes, side scrapers, end scrapers, transverse, dihedral and angle burins, cobble tools, notches, and gravers (Figure 10e-g). According to Vorobei (1992), the "triad" of wedge-shaped cores, transverse burins, and bifacial points indicates affinities with the Alaskan Paleoarctic tradition, the Kamchatkan Ushki layer VI complex, and the Yakutian Diuktai culture.

El'gakhchan-1

EL'GAKHCHAN-1 (*16*, Figure 1), discovered in 1980, is located at the confluence of the Bol'shoi El'gakhchan and Omolon rivers, approximately 600 km northeast of Magadan (64° 3'N, 160° 58'E). To date, an area of 97 m^2 has been excavated (Kir'iak 1990, 1992, 1993).

El'gakhchan-1 is situated upon a high bluff overlooking the Omolon River floodplain. It is a multicomponent site with Neolithic and possible Paleolithic cultural layers buried within a mantle of loose sediments reaching a thickness of 1 m. The stratigraphic profile is characterized by a series of sandy loams of varying colors (Kir'iak 1990). Neolithic artifacts occur in the soil profile 4–14 cm below the surface; presumed Paleolithic artifacts occur in unweathered sandy loam approximately 40 cm below the surface (Kir'iak 1990). There are no radiocarbon dates from the site, but the presence of a charcoal-rich sandy loam deposit immediately below the Paleolithic component may in the future provide a lower-limiting determination for the occupation.

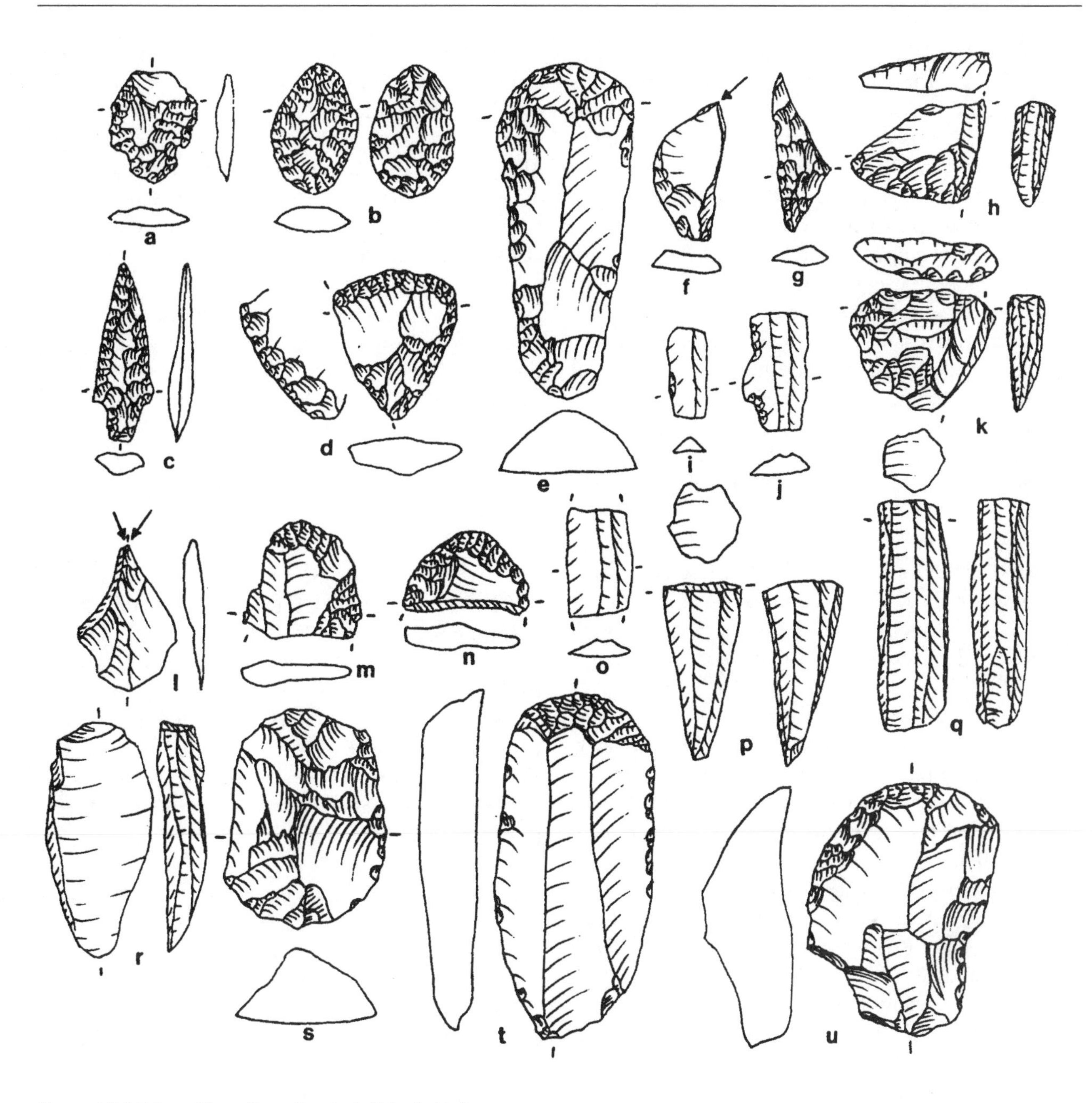

Figure 10. Lithic artifacts from Druchak-V (e–h, k) (not drawn to scale), El'gakhchan-1 (b–d, l–n), El'gakhchan-2 (a), Tytyl'-1 (i–j, o–u) (after Kir'iak 1988, 1990; Vorobei 1992) [a, c: stemmed bifacial points; b, g: bifaces; d–e, m–n, t: end scrapers; f, l: burins; h, k: wedge-shaped cores; i–j, o: bladelets; p–q: pencil-shaped, conical cores; r: end core; s, u: scrapers].

The lower El'gakhchan lithic industry includes 1,338 items (Kir'iak 1990, 1996). Raw materials include silicified slate, basalt, argillite, obsidian, chalcedony, and cherts. Primary reduction technologies are characterized by subprismatic blade cores and prepared flake cores. Blades and flake-blades are the most prevalent tool blanks, while tools made on flakes and cobbles are uncommon. Microblade cores are absent, although several microblades (0.5–1 cm wide) occur in the assemblage. However, Kir'iak (1990) notes that these microblades were found concentrated near the bluff edge where sediments thin considerably, and she suggests that their presence is a product of mixing between the two otherwise stratigraphically separate cultural layers (Kir'iak 1990). Secondary reduction technologies include unifacial, bifacial, and burin retouch. Burins, however, are "atypical" (Kir'iak 1990). The tool assemblage includes side scrapers, end scrapers, an end scraper/burin, leaf-shaped bifacial knives, and bifacial points (Figure 10a-d, l-n). Four of the points are stemmed and one is leaf-shaped. Kir'iak (1990) also reports a single bone tool. Faunal remains and features have not been reported.

Kir'iak considers the El'gakhchan industry to be closely related to the Ushki-1 layer VII industry, pointing to similarities in stemmed points and the supposed absence of microblades. Further, Kir'iak (1990:51) writes, "the stone inventory of Bol'shoi El'gakhchan-1 bears striking similarities with the Walker Road assemblage from the Nenana Valley, Alaska." Stemmed points, however, have not been found at Walker Road (Goebel et al. 1991). Lacking radiocarbon dates and a clearly described stratigraphic context, such conclusions are tentative.

Kir'iak (1990;1996) also reports the discovery of two additional Paleolithic sites in the El'gakhchan vicinity. At one of these (El'gakhchan-2), wedge-shaped cores, microblades, and stemmed points were collected from a deflated surface.

Orlovka-2

ORLOVKA-2 (*17*, FIGURE 1) is located along the Orlovka River, a small tributary of the Bol'shoi Anui River, Chukotka Autonomous Okrug (66° 55'N, 165° 5'E). The site was discovered and tested in 1980 (Kir'iak 1985). Orlovka-2 is situated upon a 120-m-high terrace about 2 km from the left bank of the Orlovka River. Lithic artifacts occur in a buried context 7–10 cm from the modern surface; however, many were collected from the surface (Kir'iak 1985).

The lithic assemblage includes two subprismatic blade cores on cobbles, four large blade fragments, two large flake-blades, two end scrapers, one side scraper, one chopper, and three burins (Kir'iak 1985). All of these are manufactured on coarse chert or diabase, and many are polished from sandblasting. Faunal remains have not been preserved. Kir'iak (1985:22) suggests that the Orlovka-2 industry is technologically and typologically close to the Middle Paleolithic of southern Siberia; however, due to the uncertainties surrounding the stratigraphic and chronometric age of this site, as well as the lack of diagnostic artifacts, assignment to the Paleolithic seems unwarranted at this time.

Tytyl'-1

TYTYL'-1 (*18*, FIGURE 1) is located along the southwestern shore of Lake Tytyl', Chukotka Autonomous Okrug (67° 6'N, 169° 10'E). The site was discovered and excavated in 1973 (Kir'iak 1979:39). The site is situated upon an 18–20-m-high knob of glacial drift overlooking Lake Tytyl' (Kir'iak 1989:6). Some artifacts were collected from surface blowouts while others were encountered beneath a thin soil mantle less than 10 cm from the surface (Kir'iak 1979:42).

The Tytyl'-1 lithic debitage assemblage consists of 103 large flakes and several hundred small flakes and other debitage pieces (Kir'iak 1979:42). Primary reduction technologies are represented by two conical microblade cores and 14 bladelets and microblades (Kir'iak 1979:42) (Figure 10o-q). Raw materials include grey tuffite, obsidian, and chalcedony (Kir'iak 1989:6). The tool assemblage includes several large end scrapers on blades (one is notched), "notched knives," and a burin (Kir'iak 1989:6) (Figure 10i-j, r-u). No bifacial tools have been found. An interesting feature at Tytyl'-1 is the presence of a number of circular stone rings, which Kir'iak (1988) interprets as dwelling features. No subsurface structural elements, however, have been identified. These features are undated.

Kir'iak (1979:43) compares the Tytyl'-1 industry to the Yakutian Sumnagin culture, but also points out that many diagnostic Sumnagin tool types including truncated bladelets, end scrapers on bladelets, prismatic burins, and engravers (*rezchiki*) are absent at Tytyl'-1 (Kir'iak 1989:7). She nonetheless assigns the site to the Mesolithic on typological grounds, and assigns it to the period of 11,000–7000 yr B.P. (Kir'iak 1989, 1993).

Chukotka Peninsula and Bering Sea Coast

THE CHUKOTKA PENINSULA is the northeasternmost point of Asia, a mountainous area with peaks reaching 1,800 m in the west and 1,000 m in the east. Tundra vegetation dominates the landscape. Owing primarily to the work of N. Dikov, we can identify at least 14 archaeological localities on the Chukotka Peninsula that are possibly Paleolithic in age: Kymyneikei, Kym'ynanonvyvaam, Kus'iuveem, Ioni-10, Chel'kun-2, Chel'kun-3, Chel'kun-4, Chaatam'e-1, Kurupka-1, Marich-2, Puturak Pass, Ul'khum-1, Inas'kvaam, and Taliain (Figures 1 and 11). None of these sites, however, has been directly radiocarbon dated, and only one, Kymyneikei, occurs in a stratified datable context. Kymyneikei, though, may not be an archaeological site at all. Assignment of the rest of the sites to the Paleolithic is based solely on typological grounds.

Kymyneikei

KYMYNEIKEI (*19*, Figures 1 and 11) is located along the Kymyneiveem River, about 75 km south of the village of Vankarem, Chukotka Autonomous Okrug (67° 27'N, 177° 41'W). The site was recently discovered by S. A. Laukhin, during geologic coring of Upper Pleistocene morainal deposits west of the bay (Laukhin et al. 1989). Seven artifacts were discovered in a buried, stratified context at a depth of about 33 m from the surface.

Laukhin extracted the flakes from core spoils. They were found to occur in moraine sediments overlying a peat deposit radiocarbon dated to 40,170 ± 620 and 39,300 ± 1130 yr B.P. (lab numbers not reported). According to Laukhin et al. (1989), these dates indicate an early Sartan age (around 25,000 to 20,000 yr B.P.) for the moraine.

Laukhin et al. (1989) describe the seven artifacts as a wedge-shaped core and six flakes. In a later report, Laukhin and Drozdov (1990) refer to the core as a "wedge-shaped artifact." They link the site to the proto-Diuktai complex of Yakutia, pointing to similarities with the lithic assemblage from Ezhantsy, which is thought by Mochanov (1977) to date to the early Sartan as well.

According to R. Powers (personal communication 1991), the artifacts from Kymyneikei may not be flakes, but merely broken cobbles with sharp edges. Their geologic context, from within a glacial moraine, also calls into question the validity of the finds. Clearly, these specimens should not be considered as evidence of an early Sartan human presence in western Beringia.

Kym'ynanonvyvaam and Kus'iuveem

The Kym'ynanonvyvaam sites (*20*, Figures 1 and 11) are located along the Uliuveem River south of Koliuchinskii Bay, Chukotka Autonomous Okrug (66° 00'N, 175° 73'W). Dikov (1990b) describes two sets of sites, which he assigns to the Paleolithic. The first includes Kym'ynanonvyvaam-9, Kym'ynanonvyvaam-12 and Kym'ynanonvyvaam-13. These sites are located on a high terrace of the Kym'ynanonvyvaam River. Surface-collected assemblages are characterized by large "axe-like tools" manufactured on "jasper-chert" procured at a nearby outcrop (Dikov 1990b:26). Similar cobble tools were also found at two other localities in the Uliuveemskii lowland, Kus'iuveem-4 and Kus'iuveem-6. Dikov (1990a:25, 1990b:26) assigns these sites to an ancient stage of the Paleolithic and identifies Calico Hills as a possible North American analog. Some of these probably are not artifacts at all; others probably are roughed-out bifaces that could be any age.

The second Kym'ynanonvyvaam complex includes the localities Kym'ynanonvyvaam-8 and Kym'ynanonvyvaam-14 (Dikov 1990b:26). Surface-collected lithic assemblages are characterized by wedge-shaped microblade cores, end microblade cores, slender blades and microblades, bifaces, scrapers, and burins. Typologically they appear to be late Pleistocene-early Holocene in age.

Ioni-10

IONI-10 (*21*, Figures 1 and 11) is located along the north shore of Ioni Lake, Chukotka Autonomous Okrug (65° 49'N, 174° 43'W). Dikov (1990b:17) discovered the site in 1981. Artifacts collected from the surface of the lake's 25–30 m terrace include an end microblade core on a flake, microblades, burins, scrapers, and several biface fragments manufactured on chert or grey slate. The age of these artifacts is unknown but presumed to be late Pleistocene (Dikov 1990b).

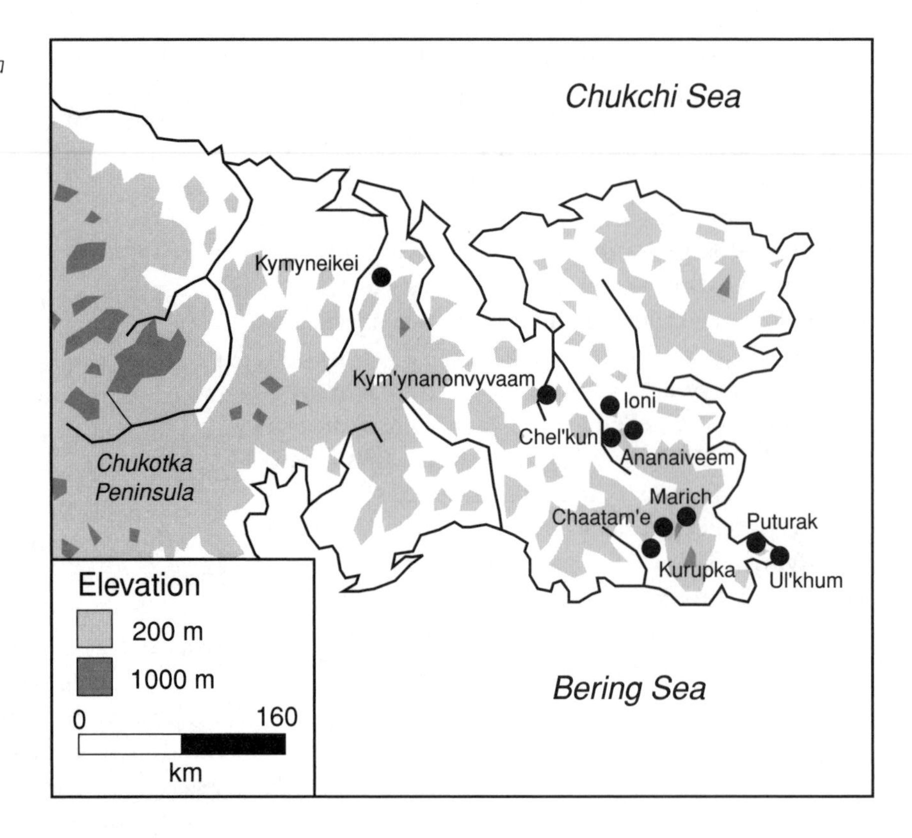

Figure 11. Map of Chukotka Peninsula showing locations of archaeological sites described in text.

Chel'kun

THE CHEL'KUN LOCALITIES (*22*, Figures 1 and 11) are located near the confluence of the Chel'kun and Ioniveem rivers, Chukotka Autonomous Okrug (65° 31'N, 173° 57'W). At least three of these sites, Chel'kun-2, Chel'kun-3, and Chel'kun-4, have been assigned to the late Paleolithic or Mesolithic by Dikov (1980, 1985a, 1990b).

Chel'kun-2 lies upon the 12-m terrace of the Ioniveem River. The site was discovered in 1979 (Dikov 1980:6) and further investigated in 1982 (Dikov 1985a:10). Artifacts collected from the surface of the terrace include a subprismatic blade core fragment, an end scraper, and several "stemmed and pointed" flakes (Dikov 1980:7–8, 1985a:10, 1990b:22).

Discovered in 1979, Chel'kun-3 is situated immediately above the mouth of the Chel'kun River on an isolated spur of the 8-m terrace (Dikov 1980:6). Lithic artifacts collected from the surface include a number of flake-blades and flakes, several side scrapers and possible burins, a leaf-shaped biface fragment, and a "stemmed and pointed" flake (Dikov 1980:6–7) (Figure 12a-b).

Chel'kun-4 is situated upon the 8-m terrace of the Ioniveem River. Dikov (1980:5, 1985b:10, 1990b:10) discovered the site in 1979 and conducted test excavations there in 1982. A small number of lithic artifacts were encountered within the modern soil less than 20 cm below the surface. Artifacts include two prismatic blade cores and a number of narrow blades and microblades, all manufactured on a yellow-grey chert (Dikov 1980:6). Dikov (1993:54) links these artifacts to charcoal from a hearth radiocarbon dated to 8150 ± 450 yr B.P. (MAG-719).

Chaatam'e-1

CHAATAM'E-1 (*23*, Figures 1 and 11), discovered by Dikov (1985b:9) in 1982, is located along the Chaatam'e River, a small tributary of the Kurupka River, Chukotka Autonomous Okrug (64° 57'N, 174° 00'W). The site is situated upon the 50-m terrace of the Chaatam'e River, and lithic artifacts occur on the surface. Collected artifacts include an end microblade core (on a flake) and preforms, two small side scrapers, and a bifacial point fragment (Dikov 1985b:9–10, 1990b:20) (Figure 12c-d).

Kurupka-1

KURUPKA-1 (*24*, Figures 1 and 11) is located near the confluence of the Chaatam'e and Kurupka rivers, 5 km southwest of Chaatam'e-1, Chukotka Autonomous Okrug (64° 56'N, 174° 7'W). The site was discovered

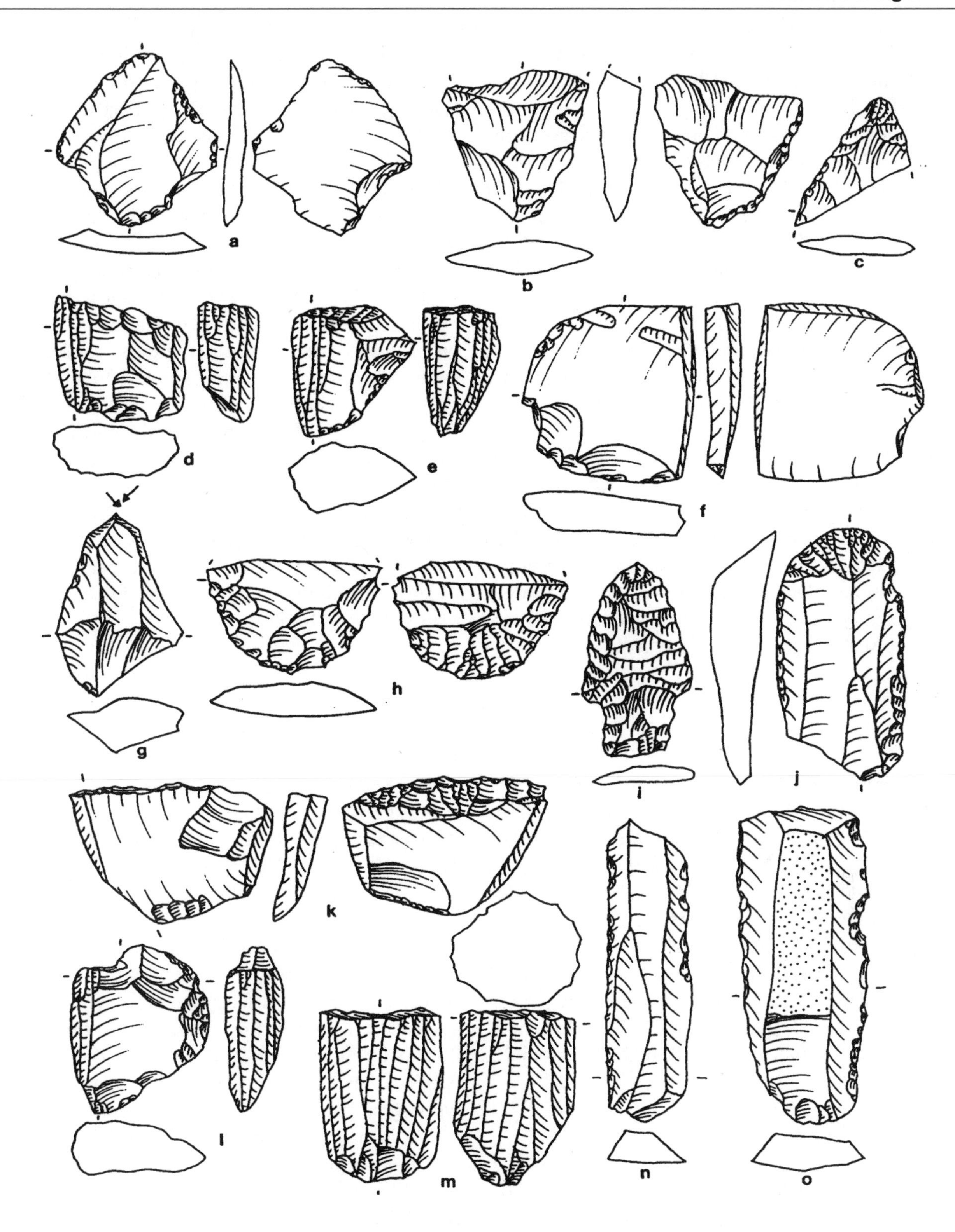

Figure 12. Lithic artifacts from Ul'khum-1 (i–k), Chel'kun-3 (a–b), Chaatam'e-1 (c–d), Kurupka-1 (e–h), Puturak Pass (m–o), and Taliain (l) (after Dikov 1990b, Dikov et al. 1983) [a: "stemmed flake;" b–c, h: bifaces; d–e, l: wedge-shaped microblade cores; f, k: end microblade cores; g: burin; i: stemmed bifacial point; j: end scraper; m: pencil-shaped microblade core; n–o: retouched blades].

by Kazinskaia in 1978 and investigated by Dikov in 1980 and 1982 (Dikov 1990b:12,21; Dikov and Kazinskaia 1980).

Kurupka-1 is situated upon the 20-m terrace of the Kurupka River (Dikov 1990b:12). Most lithic artifacts were collected from the surface of the terrace, but some were encountered during the excavation of several small test pits (Dikov 1990b:12). Two horizontally defined artifact clusters occur. The first is characterized by Neolithic artifacts including conical cores and several sherds of coarse black ceramic (Dikov 1990b:15). The second cluster of artifacts is more extensive and thought to date to the Paleolithic (Dikov and Kazinskaia 1980). Lithic artifacts include three wedge-shaped microblade cores, numerous microblades and associated debitage, dihedral and angle burins, side scrapers, end scrapers, and bifacial knives (Figure 12e-h). Raw materials include light-grey silicified slate, yellow or red chert, pink chalcedony, and white tufa (Dikov and Kazinskaia 1980:25). Also reported are several fragmented reindeer bones (Dikov and Kazinskaia 1980:25) and a possible charcoal hearth stain (the latter associated with a wedge-shaped core) (Dikov 1990b:15).

Marich-2

The Marich-2 site (*25*, Figures 1 and 11) is located along the Marich River, Chukotka Autonomous Okrug (65° 00'N, 173° 09'W). The site was discovered in 1983 during a reconnaissance survey conducted by Dikov (1990b:22). Artifacts collected from the surface of the 25-m terrace of the Marich River include numerous flakes, leaf-shaped bifaces, and a possible ski-spall from a wedge-shaped core. Dikov (1990b:22) describes similar surface scatters at the nearby terrace-edge localities of Igel'khveem-5, Igel'khveem-9, Igel'khveem-15, Igel'khveem-20 and Igel'khveem-22.

Puturak Pass

Puturak Pass (*26*, Figures 1 and 11) is located at the divide separating the Tkachen and Itkhat River valleys, about 20 km west of Cape Chaplina, Chukotka Autonomous Okrug (64° 49'N, 172° 27'W). Dikov (1990b) discovered the site in 1985 and excavated a total of 10 m^2 in 1985 and 1986.

The Puturak Pass site is situated on a flat knoll (about 100 m in diameter) elevated almost 20 m above the sources of the adjoining rivers. Lithic artifacts were collected from the exposed surface of the knoll as well as from a buried context in a sandy loam deposit reaching a depth of 60 cm (Dikov 1990a, 1990b:30, 1995b). Besides numerous lithic artifacts, Dikov (1990b:30) reports the possible remains of a dwelling, consisting of a circular charred area and a ring of stones forming a hearth, and five other small charred hearth stains.

Nearly all artifacts were manufactured on a "fragile" light-grey silicified slate. The assemblage is dominated by blades, blade-like flakes, bladelets, and tools made on blades: scrapers, knives, engravers (*rezchiki*), and marginally retouched blades (Figure 12n-o). Most of these were removed from large monofrontal "cylindrical" and "subcylindrical" cores or small subconical cores (Dikov 1990a) (Figure 12m). According to Dikov (1990a, 1990b:31), Puturak Pass has no analog in Asian Beringia, but does display similarities with the lithic industries from Gallagher Flint Station in northern Alaska and Anangula in the Aleutian Islands. Based on these similarities, he assigns the site to the Mesolithic.

Ul'khum-1

Ul'khum-1 (*27*, Figures 1 and 11) is located along the lower Ul'khum River, the major tributary draining into Lake Naivan, 10 km inland from Cape Chaplin, Chukotka Autonomous Okrug (64° 48'N, 172° 25'W). Dikov (1985b, 1990b:17, 21–27, 1995e) discovered the site in 1981. Surface collections and test excavations were conducted in 1982 and 1985.

Ul'khum-1 lies upon the 12-m terrace of the Ul'khum River (Dikov 1985b:3). Most artifacts were collected from the surface of the terrace, but some also were encountered in a thin soil mantle down to 20 cm below the surface (Dikov 1990b:17,21). Artifacts have been recovered that are assigned on typological grounds to the late Paleolithic, Neolithic, and a "later maritime culture" (Dikov 1990b:30).

The Paleolithic assemblage includes wedge-shaped microblade cores, end microblade cores, microblades, small blades, flakes, bifacial knifes, bifacial stemmed points, burins, scrapers, and a small cobble-chopping tool (Figure 12i-k). Most of these are made on a grey siliceous slate (Dikov 1985b:3). Also collected were several small triangular-shaped flakes with stems. Dikov (1985b, 1990b) assigns this assemblage to two phases of the late Paleolithic, with the stemmed points and flakes corresponding to the Ushki-1 layer VII industry, and the microblade cores, microblades, and associated debitage corresponding to the Ushki-1 layer VI industry.

Ananaiveem-1

ANANAIVEEM-1 (*28*, Figures 1 and 11) is located along the left bank of the Ananaiveem River, upon a south-facing bluff 8 m above the modern river floodplain (65° 21'N, 173° 45'W). Dikov (1993:16) discovered the site in 1984. Excavations reaching an area of 14 m^2 uncovered a stone-lined hearth, small convex scraper, and bone fragments, some identified as reindeer (Dikov 1993:56). Dikov (1993:149) reports a single radiocarbon determination of 8410 ± 80 (LE-2791) for the site, but does not describe the material dated or provenience of the sample. He tentatively assigns Ananaiveem-1 to the Mesolithic (Dikov et al. 1983:57,149).

Inas'kvaam and Taliain

ALONG THE BERING SEA coast south of the town of Anadyr', two possible Paleolithic sites have been investigated. At Inas'kvaam (*29*, Figure 1) (62° 16'N, 172° 55'E), Dikov collected an obsidian wedge-shaped core, a lanceolate projectile point base, and a retouched blade from the surface of a high terrace (Dikov 1990b). At nearby Taliain, also a surface site, an obsidian wedge-shaped core and bimarginally flaked end core were collected (Figure 12l).

Kamchatka Peninsula

DURING THE LATE PLEISTOCENE, glacial ice covered nearly all of the central chain of mountain volcanoes (Braitseva et al. 1968) forming the backbone of the Kamchatka Peninsula, the southernmost area of western Beringia. Archaeological sites thought to date to the late Pleistocene-early Holocene have been found along the Kamchatka River in the vicinity of Ushki Lake, as well as at Cape Lopatka, the southern tip of the Kamchatka Peninsula.

Ushki Lake Sites

THE SOUTHERN SHORE of Ushki Lake in the Kamchatka River valley, located about 18 km north of Kozyrevsk, Kamchatka Oblast' (56° 06'N, 159° 54'E), contains four late Pleistocene-early Holocene archaeological sites: Ushki-1, Ushki-2, Ushki-4, and Ushki-5 (*30*, Figure 1). The most complete stratigraphic and cultural sequence is found at Ushki-1, which serves as a reference profile for the other Ushki sites. Geological and archaeological layers at the sites can be correlated based on a series of well-defined tephras (Dikov and Titov 1984; Ivanov 1990). The Ushki-1 late Pleistocene-early Holocene sequence is described in detail below, and the other Ushki sites are described briefly with reference to the Ushki-1 sequence.

Geomorphology of the Ushki Lake area has been presented by Titov (1980), Dikov and Titov (1984), and Ivanov (1990). The lake itself appears to be a remnant oxbow lake cut off from the Kamchatka River by the second alluvial terrace, thought to have formed during the late Middle Pleniglacial (oxygen-isotope stage 3), around 25,000 yr B.P. (Ivanov 1990:166) (Figure 13). At that time, the lake probably was larger than it is today (Ivanov 1990:167). During the last glacial period, between 22,000 and 17,000 yr B.P., expanding glaciers did not reach beyond the high mountain valleys of the Kliuchevskii mountains far to the east (Ivanov 1990). Contrary to Titov (1980), Ivanov (1990:167) argues that there is no evidence that the alluvial sediments surrounding the lake were reworked at this time by fluvioglacial or frozen-ground processes. Late Pleistocene sediments show no cryogenic features like frost cracks or ice-wedge pseudomorphs. The lake persisted through the last glacial into the early Holocene, but by 8000 yr B.P. the Kamchatka River had cut through the second terrace, made the lake its active channel, and flowed up to the southern margin of the former lake (Ivanov 1990:168). Soon thereafter the river channel shifted to the north, and the first alluvial terrace of the Kamchatka River was deposited, forming the present Ushki Lake (Ivanov 1990:168). Through all this, the Ushki-1 site and its late Pleistocene cultural occupations were spared from the extensive cutting and filling of the river.

Ushki-1

Ushki-1 is situated upon Cape Kamennyi, a 4-m high bedrock knob jutting into Ushki Lake. Dikov (1977:43) discovered the site in 1961; excavations have been conducted periodically from 1962 into the 1990s (Dikov 1977, 1990a).

The geologic and cultural stratigraphy of the Ushki-1 site has been described by Dikov (1977) and Dikov and Titov (1984). The site lies on volcanic bedrock that is mantled by a 3-m-thick set of alternating bands of sandy loam, loam, and tephra (Figure 14). Cryogenic disturbances are absent from the entire profile, and seven stratigraphically distinct cultural layers have been identified (Dikov 1977) (Figure 14). The lower three cultural layers (VII, VI, and V) predate 7000 yr B.P. and are discussed below.

Cultural layer VII is the lowermost cultural layer identified at Ushki-1. Four conventional ^{14}C determinations average 13,980 ± 146 yr B.P. (Table 1). Artifacts occur within a set of loam, sandy loam, and sand deposits 210–220 cm below the modern surface (Dikov 1977:48) (Figure 14). In places, cultural layer VII appears as a thin floor of red ochre, especially in and around the remains of a human burial and several dwelling structures. At the time of the layer VII occupation, Ushki-1 was situated along the margin of late Pleistocene Ushki Lake (Ivanov 1990). Palynological analysis suggests that during this time local vegetation was dominated by birch and alder forest, stands of willow, and pockets of ferns and grasses (Ivanov 1990:168).

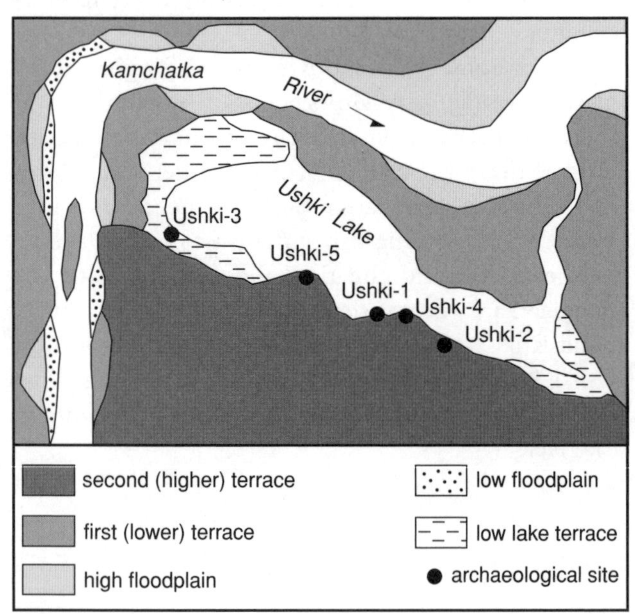

Figure 13. Ushki Lake geomorphology (after Ivanov 1990).

The lithic assemblage from cultural layer VII has been described cursorily by Dikov (1977:50–51, 1979a:33–38, 1985a:174, 1990a). It is characterized by blade and flake primary reduction technologies, and unifacial, bifacial, and burin secondary reduction technologies. Microblade cores and microblades are absent (Dikov 1979a:33). Blades were detached from subprismatic blade cores, while flakes were detached from minimally prepared flake cores (Dikov 1979a:33). Among the tools are more than 50 bifacially worked stemmed points and numerous leaf-shaped and teardrop-shaped points and bifaces (Dikov 1979a:34, 1990a) (Figure 15a-f, h). Most of the stemmed points are less than 5 cm long and appear to have been made on flakes. Teardrop-shaped points also are small and made on flakes. Two "stemmed flakes" also have been described (Figure 15i); these are thought by Dikov et al. (1983:11) to be "prototypes" or possibly preforms of the finished Ushki stemmed points. End scrapers and side scrapers are found in high frequencies (Figure 15j-l), as are retouched blades, flake-blades, and flakes (Dikov 1979a:34). Angle burins also occur, but less frequently (Dikov 1979a:34). Other finds from cultural layer VII include numerous stone beads and pendants, as well as chalcedony gravers apparently used to incise holes into the beads and pendants (Dikov 1979a:34–35).

Faunal remains from cultural layer VII have not been studied thoroughly. The only taxon reported is moose (Alces sp.) (Dikov 1977:50). Twelve archaeological features, however, have been described (Dikov 1968, 1977, 1990a), including one human burial pit and 11 dwelling structures (Figure 16, Table 2). The burial pit was circular, 1.8 m in diameter, and filled with stones, red ochre, and more than 800 tiny stone beads (Dikov 1968:197–199). Traces of human bones interred in the grave were barely perceptible (Dikov 1968:199). The remains of 11 structures ranged from 8 to 10 m^2 in area. The largest structure (Feature 9) appears to have been a double-roomed semi-subterranean dwelling with six separate hearths. Its floor was stained by charcoal and red ochre, and littered with stone tools, cores, debitage, pendants, grinding plates, a moose antler, and bones of unidentified fauna (Table 2). A second two-chambered structure also was excavated (Feature 7). The remaining nine structures were oval-shaped and had at least one central unlined hearth. Several hearths contained multiple layers of ash and burned bone, suggesting long-term, repeated use of the site (Dikov 1990a).

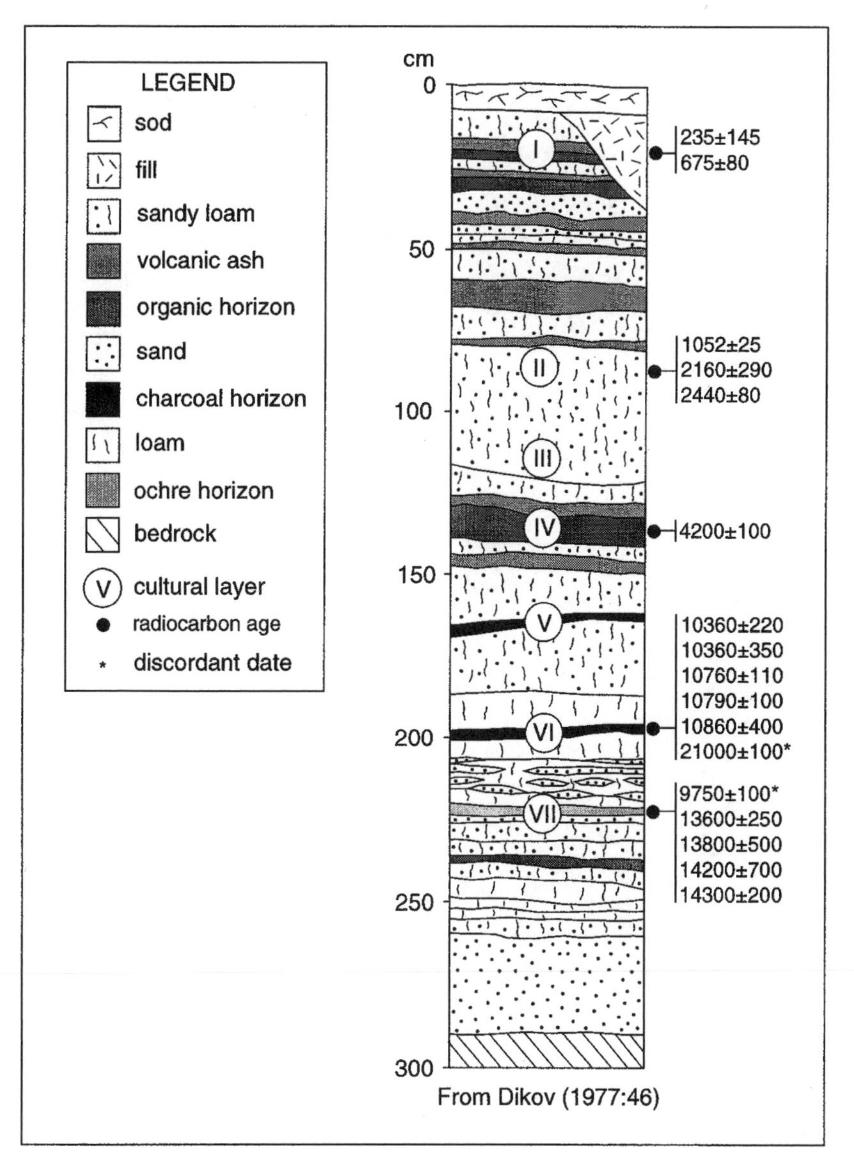

Figure 14. Stratigraphic profile from Ushki-1 site, showing provenience of cultural layers and radiocarbon dates (after Dikov 1977).

Cultural layer VI lies about 190–180 cm below the modern surface (Dikov 1977:52) (Figure 14). It is stratigraphically separated from lower-lying cultural layer VII by about 35 cm of interbedded sands and sandy loams. There is no indication that the two cultural layers have been mixed, redeposited, or disturbed by postdepositional processes (Dikov 1977, 1990a). Five conventional ^{14}C determinations for layer VI average 10,643 ± 68 yr B.P. (Table 1). At that time, the site was situated along the shore of late Pleistocene Ushki Lake. Local vegetation consisted of a mosaic of birch-alder forest, with grassy meadows surrounding the site (Dikov 1979a:54; Ivanov 1990).

The layer VI lithic industry is characterized by both wedge-shaped core/microblade and prismatic core/blade primary reduction technologies (Dikov 1979a:57, Dikov and Kononenko 1990) (Figure 17c, g), as well as burin, bifacial, and unifacial secondary technologies. The tool assemblage consists of lanceolate and leaf-shaped bifacial points, bifaces of various shapes, transverse, angle, and dihedral burins, end scrapers, side scrapers, grooved pumice shaft straighteners, large chopping tools, hammerstones, anvil stones, and retouched blades, blade-like flakes, and flakes (Figure 17a-b, d-f, h-k) (Dikov 1977:56, 1979a:57,60). Stone pendants also have been recovered, as have three sandstone plates—one with incised pits thought to represent a lunar calendar, and two with incised lines, one of which is interpreted to be a conical hut (Dikov 1979a:60). Dikov (1979a:63) also describes a 32-cm-long shovel-like object made on the bone of a bison, an ochre fish profile on a stone, and several steatite labrets.

Faunal remains have not been studied thoroughly, but Vereshchagin (1979) notes the occurrence of domesticated dog (*Canis familiaris*), steppe bison

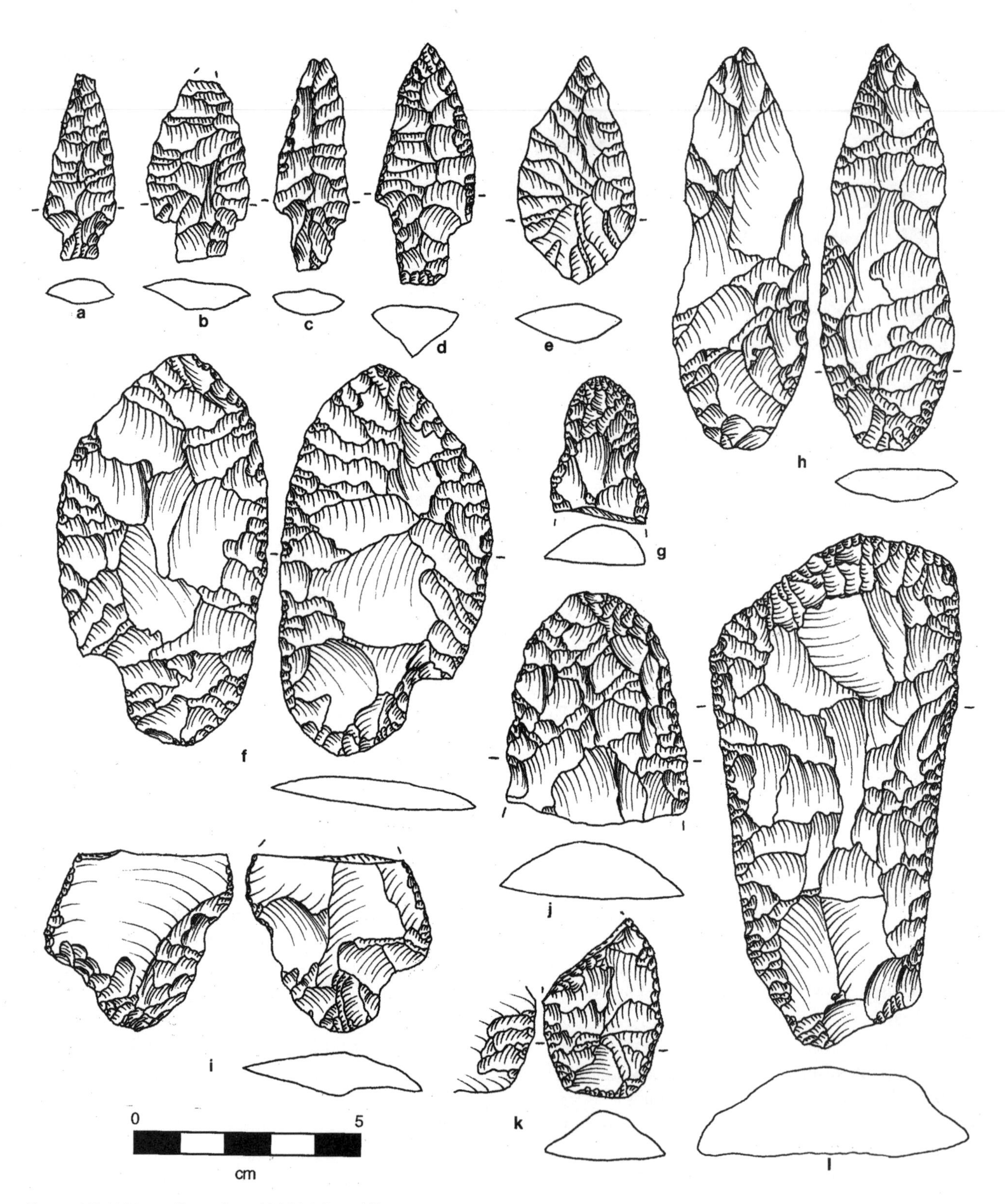

Figure 15. Lithic artifacts from Ushki-1 layer VII [a–d: stemmed bifacial points; e: teardrop-shaped point; f, h: bifaces; g: end scraper; i: "stemmed flake"; j–l: scrapers].

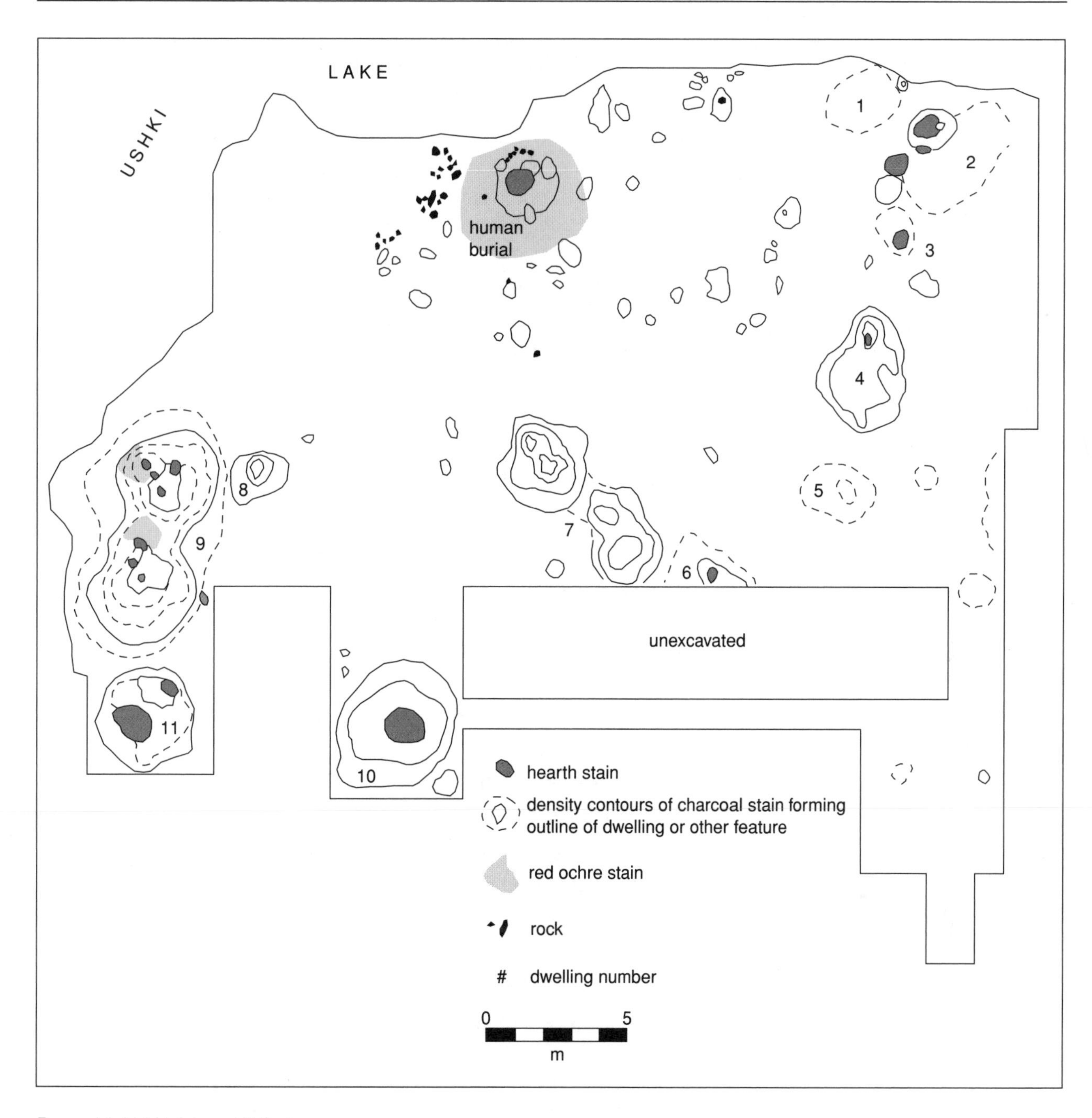

Figure 16. Ushki-1 layer VII feature map.

(*Bison priscus*), mountain sheep (*Ovis nivicola*), lemming (*Lemmus* or *Dicrostonyx* sp.), and horse (*Equus caballus*). Dikov (1977:55–56) also describes bones of birds (for the most part duck [Dikov 1990a]) and fish, presumably salmon.

Remains of 41 dwelling structures have been uncovered (Figure 18, Table 3). Interpretations of these dwellings fall into three categories. Type 1 structures (features 1–12) are described as round semi-subterranean dwellings with narrow entrance corridors. These ranged in size from 9 to 44 m^2, and apparently were supported by wooden posts. Dikov (1977, 1990a) reports the discovery of charred remains of several posts in structures 5 and 6, and posthole molds in the floors of structures 1, 5, 6, 7, and 8. All of the type 1 structures had centrally located stone-lined hearths. One of these also contained the remains of a dog burial pit (Dikov 1979b). Type 2 structures (features 14–27) were circular or irregularly shaped surface dwellings from 3 to 27 m^2 in size. They did not have entrance corridors but their centrally located hearths were usually stone-lined. Type 3 structures (features I–XIV)

Table 2. Description of Features from Ushki-1 Layer VII.

Feature Number	*Year Excavated*	*Grid Location*	*Size (m^2)*	*Description*	*Reference*
Burial	1964	11Z	80	Round burial pit 1.8 m in diameter, .7 m deep, filled with stones, red ochre, human bones poorly preserved, 800 stone beads, burin-like awls, 2 stemmed points on edge of pit; burial surrounded by ochre-stained ground; dates of 13600 ± 250 and 14300 ± 200 run on charcoal from fill of burial pit.	1,2,4
1	1964	24L	18	Small oval-shaped surface structure marked by charcoal stain.	2,4
2	1964	27K	50	Elongate oval-shaped surface structure with large (4 x 3 m) hearth pit; stone tools, stone beads and pendants, chalcedony burin-awls, leaf-shaped points and bifaces, stemmed points, scrapers, flakes, and blades.	2
3	1964	26Zh	8	Small oval-shaped surface structure with large hearth pit.	2,4
4	1978	24B	47	Irregular oval-shaped surface structure with large hearth pit; charred bird and animal bones, ochre, leaf-shaped bifaces, stemmed point, end scrapers.	4
5	1978-79?	24b	20	Small oval-shaped surface structure with possible central hearth marked by dense charcoal concentration.	4
6	1979	19e	18	Partially excavated surface structure with multilayered hearth and pit 5 cm deep and15 cm in diameter; charred bones, hematite, ochre, flint knife, flake.	4
7	1979	13b	75	2-chambered surface structure with 2 hearths; ochre, hematite, 3 stemmed points, grinding stone, chopping tools, flakes, charred clay, animal bones, gizzard stones.	4
8	after 1977	2b	16	Small oval-shaped surface structure with possible hearth marked by dense charcoal stain.	4
9	1974	-3d	100	2-chambered semi-subterranean structure (c. 20 cm deep); each chamber with 2-3 hearths; floor charcoal-stained; ochre, hematite, 23 stemmed points, 17 leaf-shaped bifaces, end scrapers, side scrapers, cores, preforms, 3 stone pendants, grinding plates, moose antler animal bones.	2,3
10	1989	7m	75	Oval-shaped surface structure with central hearth 1.7 x 1.2 m in size; tools, stemmed point, flakes.	4
11	1989	-3m	42	Oval-shaped surface structure with 2 large hearth pits; charred bones, 8 stemmed points, debitage.	4

References:
(1) Dikov 1968; (2) Dikov 1977; (3) Dikov 1979a; (4) Dikov 1990a.

were large irregularly shaped smears of charcoal ranging from 30 to 152 m^2 in size.

During the time of the layer VI occupation, the Ushki-1 site appears to have served as a semi-permanent village where hunting, gathering, and fishing took place. Type 1 and type 2 structures probably are contemporaneous, but Dikov (1990a) notes that type 3 structures are positioned stratigraphically below all of the type 1 and type 2 structures, so that they may represent an earlier occupation. The presence of multiple-layered floors and hearths in many of the type 1 and 2 dwellings indicates that they were repeatedly occupied. Using contemporary Siberian and North American arctic and subarctic hunter-gatherers as analogs, the large (averaging 22 m^2 in size) semi-subterranean dwellings (type 1) may represent winter huts, while the less substantial (averaging 13.5 m^2) surface dwellings (type 2) may represent summer huts. This hypothesis requires verification through other indicators of seasonality.

Cultural layer V is situated in the lower part of a sandy loam deposit c. 130–150 cm below the modern surface (Dikov 1977:58) (Figure 14). It is separated from lower-lying cultural layer VI by 40–50 cm of horizontally bedded sandy loam (Dikov 1990a) and is sealed by a tephra band (Dikov 1977). The layer V occupation has not been radiocarbon dated at Ushki-1, but at nearby Ushki-5, Dikov and Titov (1984) report a date of about 8800 yr B.P. from a similar industry in the same stratigraphic context (discussed below).

At the time of this occupation, late Pleistocene Ushki Lake had been replaced by a channel of the Kamchatka River which flowed along the northern margin of the site (Ivanov 1990). Palynological studies indicate that climatic conditions were somewhat milder than during previous occupations at the site, with coniferous forests dominating the landscape (Ivanov 1990).

The cultural layer V lithic assemblage is relatively small, but similar to that of layer VI. Primary reduction technologies involve the production of microblades from relatively wide wedge-shaped cores, and blades from "crudely" fashioned prismatic cores (Dikov 1990a). Secondary reduction technologies include unifacial, bifacial, and burin techniques. The tool assemblage consists of leaf-shaped bifacial points, bifaces, end scrapers, side scrapers, sandstone shaft straighteners, and burins (Dikov 1977:58-60). Faunal remains (fish and mammal) have been recovered, but taxonomic identifications have not been reported (Dikov 1977). Excavations through 1977 uncovered the remains of four surface dwelling structures with circular outlines and stone-lined hearths (Dikov 1977:58–60).

Ushki-2

Ushki-2 is located about 500 m east of Ushki-1 (Figure 13). In 1962 and 1964, a total area of 260 m^2 was excavated (Dikov 1977:65), revealing the presence of cultural layer V, situated within a grey loam about 170 cm below the surface and sealed by a 2–4-cm thick tephra. No radiocarbon dates have been reported, but the stratigraphic position of this cultural layer suggests to Dikov (1977) an age of about 8000 yr B.P. Lithic artifacts include wedge-shaped cores and microblades, minimally worked flake cores, blade-like flakes and flakes, and a few retouched pieces including narrow leaf-shaped bifacial points, end scrapers, and a large side scraper made on a flat cobble (Dikov 1977:68). These artifacts were concentrated around a hearth (Dikov 1977:68).

Ushki-4

The Ushki-4 site is located on "Pervyi Cape," about halfway between Ushki-1 and Ushki-2 (Figure 13). Excavations in the 1960s revealed two areas of late Pleistocene-early Holocene cultural remains, known as the East Locus and West Locus (Dikov 1970, 1977:75–79). Occupations stratigraphically assigned to cultural layer VI occur at both loci. Neither, however, has been radiocarbon dated.

At the East Locus, cultural layer VI (dated to about 10,000 yr B.P.) occurs at the base of a grey loam that is situated about 150 cm below the modern surface and sealed by a tephra (Dikov 1977:76). Lithic artifacts recovered from a 64-m^2 excavation include wedge-shaped cores, microblades, flakes, leaf-shaped bifacial points, bifaces, end scrapers, side scrapers, coarse-grained shaft-smoothers, cobble tools, and ochre bits (Dikov 1977:76–78). Poorly preserved faunal remains were not retrievable (Dikov 1977:77). Features uncovered include a small pit and hearth (each about 50 cm in diameter), and a large (20-m^2) round charcoal stain, interpreted to be the floor of a surface dwelling structure, with a 70-cm^2 hearth stain in its northern section (Dikov 1977:76).

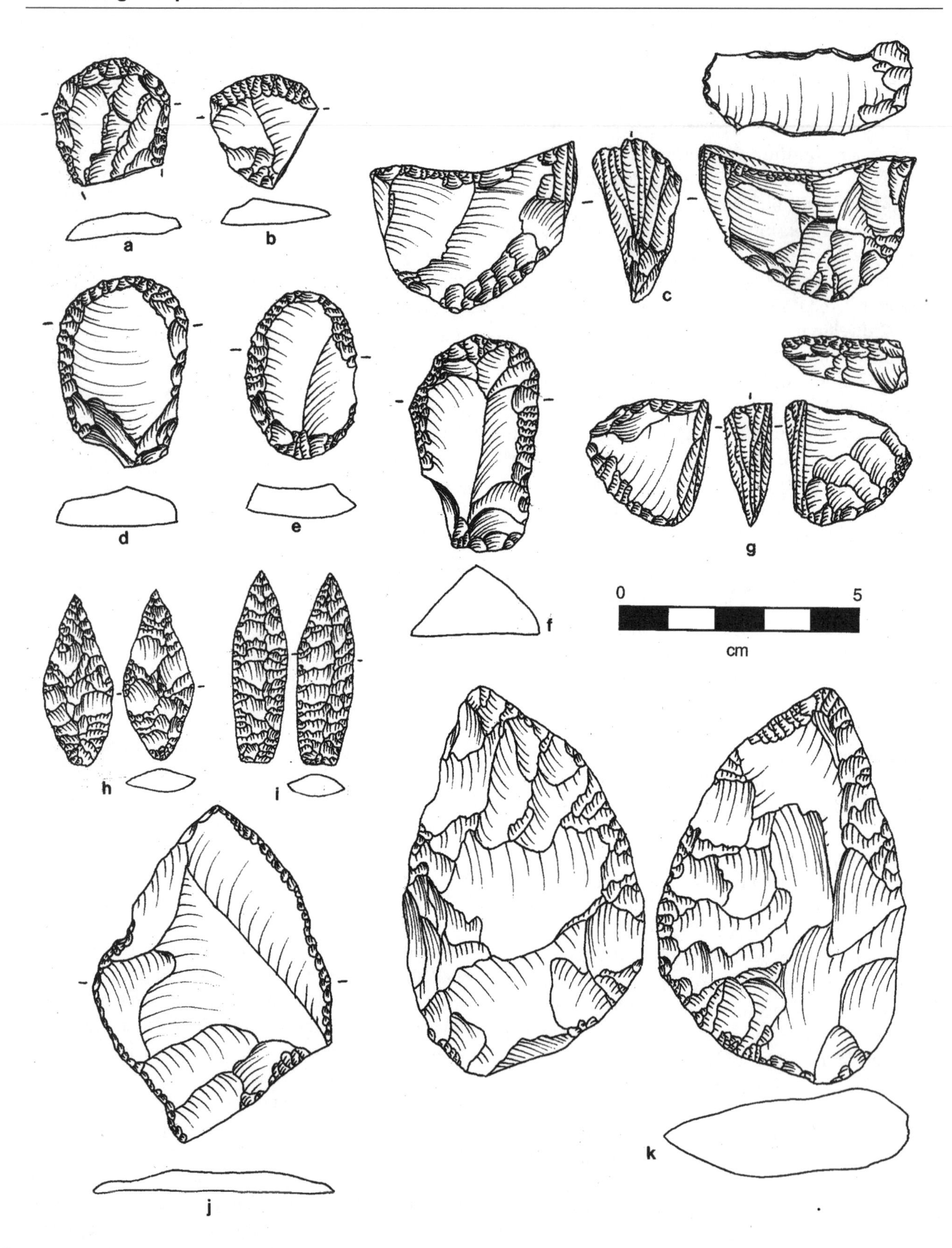

Figure 17. Lithic artifacts from Ushki-1 layer VI [a–b, d–f: end scrapers; c, g: wedge-shaped microblade cores; h–i: lanceolate bifacial points; j: retouched flake; k: biface].

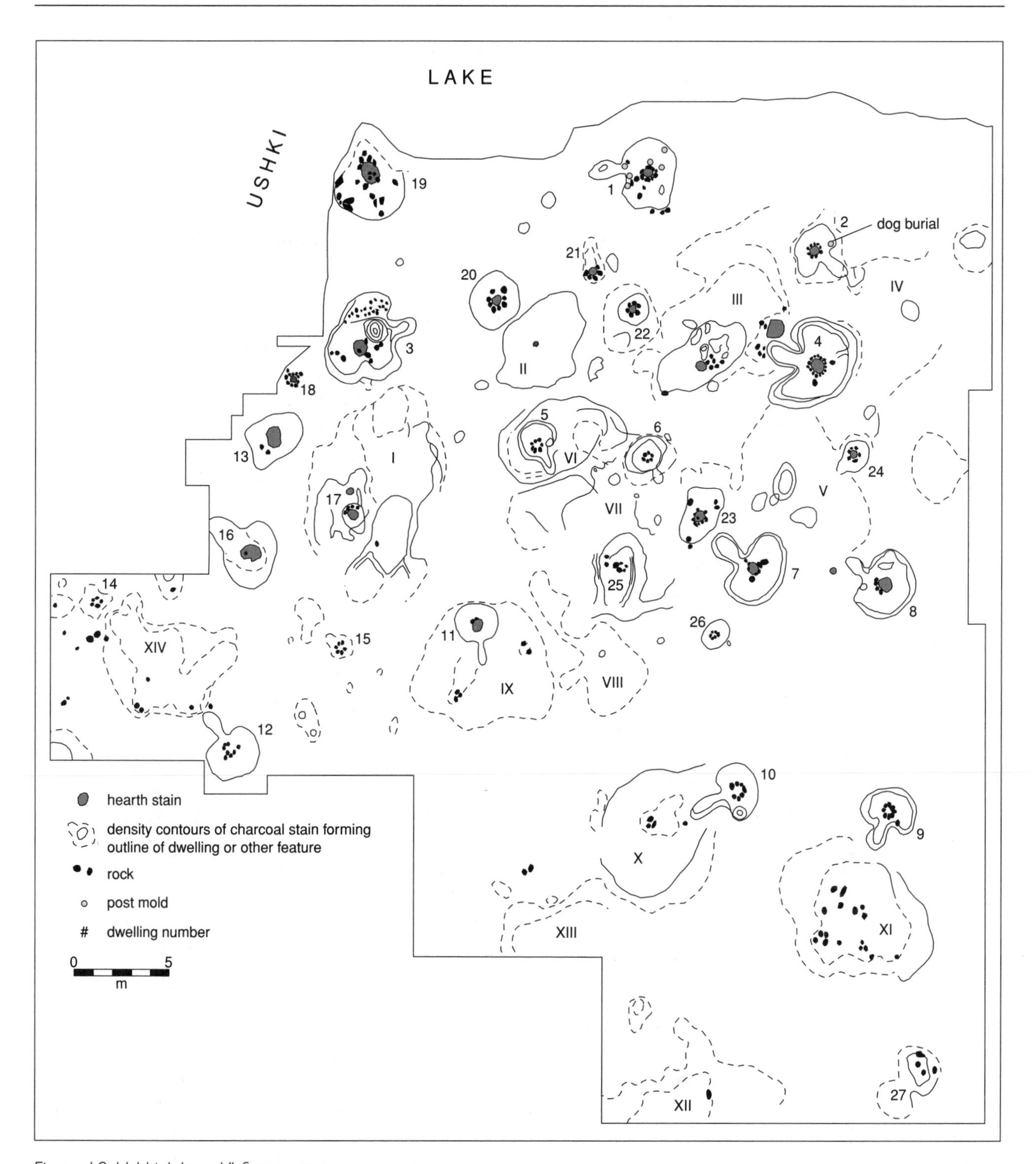

Figure 18. Ushki-1 layer VI feature map.

At the West Locus, Dikov (1970, 1977:79) discovered charred cobbles and charcoal eroding from the bluff edge along the lake. Excavations in 1966 revealed that these came from a set of banded loam and sand layers similar to that containing cultural layer VI at Ushki-1. An excavation of 12 m^2 yielded a two-layered circular surface structure with two stone-lined hearths superimposed one on the other (Dikov 1970). This structure is comparable to the Type 2 dwellings from cultural layer VI at Ushki-1 (Dikov 1977:79). Lithic artifacts recovered from both floors of the dwelling include wedge-shaped cores, microblades, narrow leaf-shaped bifacial points, bifaces, scrapers, coarse shaft-smoothers, ochre bits, and plates for grinding ochre (Dikov 1970, 1979b:79).

Ushki-5

Ushki-5 is located about 250 m west of Ushki-1 (Figure 13). Dikov (1977:79) discovered the site in 1964, but did not begin excavations there until 1974. At this locality, materials assigned to cultural layers V and VII have been identified, while layer VI materials are absent. Here, cultural layer V has been radiocarbon dated to 8790 ± 150 yr B.P. (MAG-321) (Dikov and Titov 1984) (Table 1). The assemblages from Ushki-5 include only chert and obsidian flakes from layer V (Dikov 1977:81–82), and a platform rejuvenation spall from a small prismatic blade core and a stemmed point from layer VII (Dikov 1977:82, 281).

Lopatka-4

Cape Lopatka (*31*, Figure 1) is located at the southern tip of the Kamchatka Peninsula, Kamchatka Oblast' (51° 00'N, 158° 45'E). The area was first investigated in 1972 by Dikova (1979, 1983), who discovered four archaeological localities. She assigns one of the localities, Lopatka-4 (locus 3), to the Paleolithic (Dikova 1983:16). Excavations were conducted there in 1973 and 1975.

Lopatka-4 is situated in the high tidal and tsunami zone of the cape. Most of the lithic artifacts were recovered from a wind-deflated surface. Some artifacts and charcoal were recovered from beneath the exposed surface during excavations, but charcoal samples were not large enough to permit radiocarbon dating (Dikova 1983:17–18).

Dikova (1979, 1983:18–25) characterizes the assemblage as "Paleolithic" in appearance. Raw materials include andesitic basalt, quartzite, and a low-grade chert. These were procured locally from beaches in the form of highly rounded cobbles (Dikova 1983:21). Cores are simply prepared, typically with single platforms and fronts. Tools described include chopping tools, choppers, scraper-like unifaces, triangular picks, retouched flakes, and "leaf-shaped" bifacial points. Dikova (1983:24) suggests that the bifacial points are intrusive and represent a later occupation of the site. The remaining artifacts, she argues, have a decided "primitive" appearance and are analogous to ancient Paleolithic artifacts from Japan, Mongolia, and Vietnam, or to the cobble tools from Siberdik (Dikova 1983:24). This interpretation is tenuous given the lack of chronometric dates from the site.

Discussion

Western Beringia's First Human Inhabitants

Current archaeological evidence indicates that the first inhabitants of western Beringia were late Upper Paleolithic peoples. The oldest firmly dated occupation in western Beringia is Ushki-1 layer VII, dating to about 14,000 yr B.P. In northern Beringia, the oldest site, Berelekh, dates to about 12,200 yr B.P. Claims for an earlier Paleolithic occupation of Beringia have not been substantiated: the archaic-looking assemblages from Orlovka-2, Kym'ynanonvyvaam, Kus'iuveem, and Lopatka-4 have not been (and probably never will be) chronometrically or stratigraphically dated, and the putative "proto-Diuktai" artifacts from Kymyneikei probably are not artifacts at all.

Colonization of western Beringia after the last glacial maximum (about 22,000–18,000 yr B.P.) is supported further by archaeological evidence in the Lena River basin, west of Beringia, where the earliest unequivocal sites date to around 18,000–17,000 yr B.P. Upper Paleolithic humans were camping at Verkhne-Troitskaia by perhaps 18,000 yr B.P. (Mochanov 1977, 1978), and at nearby Ezhantsy by 17,000 yr B.P. (Kuzmin 1990).[5] The earlier "Proto-Diuktai" sites, Ust'-Mil'-II and Ikhine-II, considered by Mochanov (1977) to date to between 35,000 and 20,000 yr B.P., remain problematic. Stratigraphic profiles at these sites are complex and display obvious deformation features, rendering the proposed age of the assemblages questionable (Hopkins et al. 1982:438; Tseitlin 1979; Yi and Clark 1985).

Mochanov (1988, 1992, 1993) recently has reported the discovery and excavation of Diring Iuriakh, a possible Lower Paleolithic site located on an ancient terrace of the Lena River 140 km south of Yakutsk. Lithic artifacts originally were reported to date to between 3.2 and 1.8 million years ago (Mochanov 1988), but others who have investigated the geology of the site are more conservative in their estimates of its antiquity. Based on geomorphological and sedimentological evidence, Ranov and Tseitlin (1991:86) suggest that the site more likely dates to between 300,000 and 200,000 yr B.P., while Kuzmin and Krivonogov (1994) argue that the site could even be as young as the late Pleistocene. A pair of sediment samples collected from above and below the archaeological component yielded thermoluminescence (TL) age estimates of about 260,000 and 370,000 yr B.P., respectively (Waters 1995; Waters et al. 1997). These dates press the limit of TL dating and indicate that the finds from Diring date to 260,000 yr B.P. or earlier (M. R. Waters, personal communication 1996). The lithic industry on the site is characterized by cores and flakes (Ackerman and Carlson 1991) manufactured through an anvil technique (R. E. Ackerman, personal communication 1996). Mochanov (1992) reports that some of the clusters of broken cobbles and spalls, however, may have formed naturally through the cryogenic process of "desquamation," the peeling and exfoliation of rock under the influence of extreme temperatures. Further, many of the artifacts are heavily polished from sandblasting (Ackerman and Carlson 1991), indicating that they are not necessarily in a primary context. Some of the items from Diring clearly are artifactual (Waters, personal communication 1997), but given the issues surrounding their origin and context, recognition of Diring as a Middle Pleistocene hominid site should remain provisional until more detailed site formation studies and technological analyses are presented.

Pre-Microblade Industries

ARCHAEOLOGISTS HAVE LONG recognized the existence of a late Paleolithic non-microblade complex in Kamchatka (Dikov 1977, 1979a). At Ushki-1, cultural layer VII yielded a 14,000-yr-B.P. lithic industry of small stemmed and leaf-shaped bifacial points, bifaces, angle burins, end scrapers, side scrapers, backed knives, and retouched blades and flakes. Absent from this living floor are wedge-shaped cores, microblades, transverse burins, and large lanceolate points. A second occupation assigned to layer VII (although undated) was uncovered at Ushki-5. Here, too, microblades are absent.

Elsewhere in western Beringia the presence of a pre-microblade complex is less certain. The Berelekh site contains a bifacial point and blade assemblage that may lack wedge-shaped cores and microblades, but, as described earlier, reports have been conflicting. Besides blade and biface technologies, the recent discoveries at Berelekh of a leaf-shaped (Chindadn) point and tanged biface indicate possible affinities with the non-microblade Ushki-1 layer VII assemblage. Interestingly, of the three radiocarbon dates from Berelekh, two are around 13,000 yr B.P. and a third around 10,600 yr B.P. (Figure 19). Perhaps these dates reflect two different, as yet unrecognized, occupations, one associated with the blade and biface industry (13,000 yr B.P.) and the other with the recently discovered wedge-shaped microblade core (10,600 yr B.P.).

The El'gakhchan site located along the upper Omolon River also may be a pre-microblade site. The lithic assemblage contains many of the same elements as the layer VII assemblage at Ushki-1, including stemmed bifacial points and end scrapers. Further, it lacks wedge-shaped cores and associated debitage, and the few microblades in the assemblage may be intrusive. Radiocarbon dates are needed, however, to determine the age of this occupation. The bifacial point industry at Uptar-1, which contains a possible fluted point preform, is dated to before 8250 yr B.P. and may be another premicroblade site, but unfortunately we may never know its precise age.

Assemblages that fit the technological/typological pattern of layer VII at Ushki-1 also have been identified in central Alaska, where they are ascribed to the Nenana complex. The Nenana assemblages, while nearly 3,000 years younger than Ushki layer VII, contain small bifacial points, bifaces, unifacially retouched pieces (i.e., end scrapers, side scrapers, gravers, retouched blades, and flakes), and cobble tools (Goebel et al. 1991; Hamilton and Goebel, this volume; Hoffecker et al. 1993; Powers and Hoffecker 1989). While lacking stemmed points, the Nenana complex exhibits the same broad technological pattern found in the 14,000-yr-B.P. occupation at Ushki-1.

Text continues on page 142

Table 3. Description of Features from Ushki-I Layer VI.

Feature Number	*Grid Location*	*Size (m^2)*	*Description*	*Reference*
1	15l	30	Round semi-subterranean dwelling with entrance corridor on west side of structure; stone-lined centrally located hearth with 3 successive layers of ash and bone; 7 thin layers of charcoal interdigitated with sterile loam layers in area immediately surrounding hearth; 8 posthole molds (10-15 cm in diameter) (4 along perimeter, 2 near hearth, and 2 near entrance propped up by stones); 5 small pits (5 cm in diameter) near hearth; stone anvil, hammerstones, scrapers, wedge-shaped core, microblades, leaf-shaped points, shaft smoother, red ochre bits, faunal remains.	1,3
2	23Zh	17	"The Sorcerer's Dwelling"; round semi-subterranean dwelling with entrance corridor on east side of structure; stone-lined centrally located hearth; 3-layered charcoal floor around hearth; several small posthole molds around hearth; burial pit with remains of domesticated dog in "flexed" position; biface, scraper, red ochre, possible human burial pit, charred mat of dried grass, bison scapula for "fortune telling."	1,2,3
3	2V	40	Round semi-subterranean dwelling with entrance corridor on east side of structure; stone-lined hearth located in southcentral area of structure, burial pit of human child (remains not intact) in flexed position; under the remains was a mat of >100 lemming incisors; pit filled with ochre, along with broken pendant, wedge-shaped cores, microblades, ground-stone plates.	1,3
4	23B	44	Round semi-subterranean dwelling with entrance corridor on west side of structure; stone-lined centrally located hearth; bones of fish, presumably salmon.	1,3
5	10v	13	Round semi-subterranean dwelling with entrance corridor on south side of structure; stone-lined centrally located hearth; posthole molds in floor; remains of several charred wooden poles; possible cache pit (35 cm deep, 40 cm in diameter) with grinding stones, slate knife, burin.	3
6	15g	9	Round semi-subterranean structure with entrance corridor on south side of structure; stone-lined centrally located hearth; posthole molds in floor; remains of several charred wooden poles.	3
7	20z	24	Round semi-subterranean structure with entrance corridor on west side of structure; stone-lined centrally located hearth; posthole molds in floor.	3
8	26i	24	Round semi-subterranean structure with entrance corridor on west side of structure; stone-lined centrally located hearth; posthole molds in floor.	3
9	26t	14	Round semi-subterranean structure with entrance corridor on south side of structure; stone-lined centrally located hearth; several small posthole molds in floor around hearth; cache pit with 10 bifacially prepared wedge-shaped core preforms.	3
10	19t	16	Round semi-subterranean structure with entrance corridor on west side of structure; stone-lined centrally located hearth; several small posthole molds in floor around hearth; undescribed human burial pit like that found in Feature 3.	3

Feature Number	Grid Location	Size (m^2)	Description	Reference
11	8k	13	Round semi-subterranean structure with entrance corridor on south side of structure; stone-lined centrally located hearth.	3
12	-3r	17	Round semi-subterranean structure with entrance corridor on northwest side of structure; stone-lined centrally located hearth.	3
13	—	—	Undescribed.	—
14	-11k	7	Irregularly shaped surface structure with stone-lined hearth.	3
15	1l	5	Irregularly shaped surface structure with stone-lined hearth.	3
16	-4zh	27	Irregularly shaped surface structure with centrally located hearth.	3
17	2z	25	Irregularly shaped surface structure with centrally located hearth.	3
18	-2A	3	Irregularly shaped surface structure with centrally located hearth and dispersed cluster of stones.	1,3
19	2l	25	Partially excavated circular, surface structure with numerous rocks around perimeter; centrally located stone-lined hearth.	1,3
20	8D	19	Circular surface structure with stone-lined centrally located hearth.	1,3
21	12Z	7	Irregularly shaped surface structure with stone-lined hearth.	1,3
22	14G	7	Circular surface structure with stone-lined centrally located hearth.	3
23	17z	15	Irregularly shaped surface structure with stone-lined centrally located hearth.	3
24	24g	7	Irregularly shaped surface structure with stone-lined centrally located hearth.	3
25	14z	17	Irregularly shaped surface structure with stone-lined hearth and sandstone plate depicting conical tents.	3
26	18l	6	Circular surface structure with stone-lined centrally located hearth.	3
27	27a'	20	Irregularly shaped surface structure with stone-lined hearth.	3
I	4v	152	Irregularly shaped charcoal stain interpreted to be surface structure.	1,3
II	10V	46	Irregularly shaped charcoal stain interpreted to be surface structure, with anvil stone near center.	1,3
III	18B	30	Irregularly shaped charcoal stain with stone-lined hearth interpreted to be surface structure.	1,3
IV	27G	70	Irregularly shaped charcoal stain interpreted to be surface structure, with patch of red ochre, unlined hearth stain, wedge-shaped core, biface, blades, flakes, and some isolated frost cracks.	1,3
V	21d	143	Irregularly shaped charcoal stain interpreted to be surface structure, with three dense concentrations of charcoal interpreted to be hearths.	3
VI	11b	57	Oval-shaped charcoal stain interpreted to be surface structure.	3
VII	14d	133	Irregularly shaped charcoal stain interpreted to be surface structure, with several small hearth stains.	3
VIII	14m	47	Irregularly shaped charcoal stain interpreted to be surface structure.	3
IX	8m	105	Oval-shaped charcoal stain interpreted to be surface structure, with two stone-lined hearths.	3

Feature Number	Grid Location	Size (m^2)	Description	Reference
X	16u	102	Oval-shaped charcoal stain interpreted to be surface structure, with stone-lined centrally located hearth.	3
XI	24ch	116	Oval-shaped charcoal stain interpreted to be surface structure, with isolated rocks.	3
XII	18v'	70	Partially excavated irregular-shaped charcoal stain interpreted to be surface structure.	3
XIII	12ch	53	Partially excavated irregular-shaped charcoal stain interpreted to be surface structure.	3
XIV	-7m	83	Irregularly shaped charcoal stain interpreted to be surface structure.	3
A	10z	—	Hearth stain.	1
B	111	—	Hearth stain.	1
C	8A	—	Hearth stain.	1
D	1A	—	Pit.	1
E	18A	—	Pit.	1
F	13E	—	Pit.	1
G	4E	—	Pit with cache of leaf-shaped bifacial points.	1

References
(1) Dikov 1977; (2) Dikov 1979b; (3) Dikov 1990a.

The origin of the Beringian pre-microblade assemblages is unknown. Two possible areas of origin, though, can be singled out: subarctic central Siberia to the west and the Japanese Archipelago to the south. The central Siberian subarctic is a vast interior region stretching from the Yenisei River in the west to the Lena River in the east. During the late Pleistocene, this area made up a major portion of the flat, featureless mammoth steppe that also encompassed part of western Beringia. Paleolithic sites in this region are scarce, probably because so little archaeological survey has taken place. Recent studies along the Nizhnaia Tunguska River have led to the discovery of several Upper Paleolithic sites thought to date to between 30,000 and 20,000 yr B.P.; lithic industries include blades and bifaces but no wedge-shaped cores or microblades (Goebel 1995). Late Upper Paleolithic sites post-dating 18,000 yr B.P. have not been identified in this region, but further south in the upper Yenisei and Lena River basins, as well as to the east in the Aldan basin, wedge-shaped core and microblade industries appear as early as 18,000 yr B.P.—4,000 years earlier than the earliest known non-microblade inhabitants of western Beringia (Goebel 1995). Only continued work in the central Siberian subarctic will demonstrate whether microblades were common across the mammoth steppe soon after the late glacial maximum, or whether blade and biface industries without microblades persisted until late in the Pleistocene as they may have in Beringia.

In Japan, the archaeological sequence parallels that of western Beringia. From about 20,000 to 14,000 yr B.P. the Japanese record is dominated by Upper Paleolithic blade and biface assemblages, with wedge-shaped core and microblade technologies appearing after 14,000 yr B.P. (Aikens 1990:5–6; Aikens and Higuchi 1982:91; Reynolds and Kaner 1990:300). This parallel with the Beringian record is intriguing, and hints at the possibility that the pre-microblade industry at Ushki-1 was the result of a dispersal event northward from Hokkaido via the Kuril Islands (Powers 1990, 1996). This hypothesis, however, will remain tenuous until the Japanese Paleolithic record is more firmly dated and detailed lithic technological comparisons are made between the Beringian and Japanese assemblages.

Wedge-shaped Core and Microblade Industries

THE EARLIEST MICROBLADES in western Beringia occur in the layer VI assemblage at Ushki-1, central Kamchatka. Five radiocarbon dates on this layer average 10,643 ± 68 yr B.P. The industry is characterized by wedge-shaped microblade cores produced through the Yubetsu bifacial technique, as well as smaller end microblade cores made on thin flakes. Bifacial points typically are small and leaf-shaped or lanceolate in design. Other lithic implements include burins, bifaces, end scrapers, side scrapers, grooved stones (shaft smoothers) and other cobble tools, and retouched blades and flakes. Associated with these are the remains of more than 40 dwelling structures, as well as storage pits, a human burial, and a dog burial. Faunal remains include large terrestrial mammals, waterfowl, and fish (possibly salmon). The diversity and richness of the site indicate a long-term, perhaps year-round, occupation of Ushki-1 by a relatively large band of hunter-gatherer-fishers.

Elsewhere in western Beringia, no other unequivocal wedge-shaped microblade core assemblage has been precisely dated, and only one, Kheta, has been determined on stratigraphic grounds to predate 8000 yr B.P. The remaining handful of late Paleolithic microblade industries, including Druchak-V (upper Omolon River), Ioni-10, Kurupka-1, Ul'khum-1, Inas'kvaam, and Taliain (Chukotka Peninsula), have not been dated and occur in surface or near-surface contexts. Nevertheless, taken together, these sites suggest the widespread distribution of wedge-shaped core and microblade technologies early in the Holocene (Dikov 1990b).

In Alaska, securely dated wedge-shaped core and microblade industries are more common. Sites like Dry Creek (component II), Akmak, and Mt. Hayes 111 document the emergence of these technologies

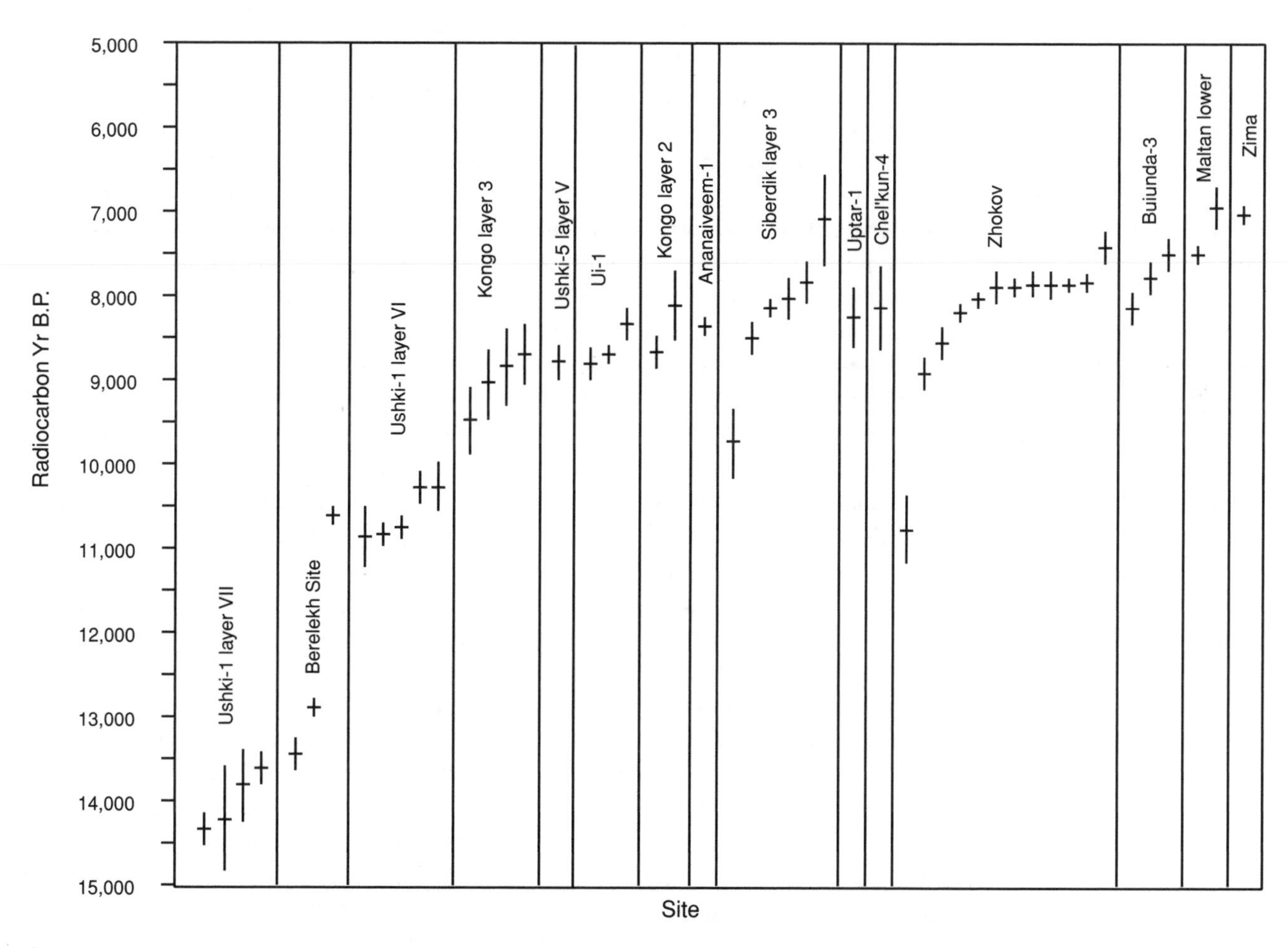

Figure 19. Radiocarbon chronology of the early Holocene Mesolithic sites of western Beringia (all are average dates with the exception Ushki-5 layer V, Uptar, Chel'kun-4, and Zima).

sometime after 11,000 yr B.P. (Anderson 1970, 1988; Hamilton and Goebel this volume; Powers and Hoffecker 1989; West 1981). At Dry Creek and other well-stratified, multi-component sites in central Alaska, microblades are absent in the pre-11,000 yr B.P. cultural horizons, while they are abundant throughout the early Holocene cultural horizons, mirroring the sequence in central Kamchatka. Contradicting this pattern, however, are two sites, Bluefish Caves and Swan Point, which may contain microblades older than 11,000 yr B.P. The dating of both sites is open to question, however. At Bluefish Caves, microblades were recovered from heavily bioturbated and cryoturbated cave sediments (Ackerman 1996; Cinq-Mars 1979), and microblades may have been displaced downward through the profile (D. M. Hopkins, personal communication 1996). The microblades from Swan Point were collected from colluvial sediments (Holmes et al. 1996), and associated charcoal samples yielding dates of about 11,600 yr B.P. could be redeposited detritus from an earlier fire of natural or human origin (Hamilton and Goebel, this volume). But if the continuing excavations at Swan Point confirm the early existence of microblades, we must accept that the late Pleistocene archaeological record of Beringia is more complicated than currently thought.

The bulk of the present evidence, then, indicates that microblade technologies emerged in western Beringia sometime after 11,000 yr B.P. The proximate origin of these technologies, however, is unclear. In neighboring Yakutia, microblade industries, labeled Diuktai, probably appeared by 17,000 yr B.P. (Aikens and Dumond 1986; Goebel et al. 1991:76; Yi and Clark 1985), but disappeared by 10,500 yr B.P. (Mochanov 1977). In Japan, insularly connected to southern Kamchatka by the Kuril Islands, the microblade phase of the late Upper Paleolithic probably began sometime after 14,000 yr B.P. and continued until about 10,000 yr B.P. (Aikens and Dumond 1986; Aikens and Higuchi 1982; Ikawa-Smith 1980; Reynolds and Kaner 1990). Both regions are potential sources of the early Beringian microblade industries.

Late Paleolithic Adaptations

Information on western Beringian late Paleolithic adaptations can be gleaned from analysis of faunal remains, site distribution and size, and site features. While the evidence is limited, we can begin to discern some patterns.

Well-preserved faunal remains are found only at Berlekh and the Ushki sites. Berelekh is commonly considered a "mammoth-hunter" site, but mammoth remains at the archaeological locality do not dominate the assemblage. Instead, bones of hare and ptarmigan outnumber those of mammoth, suggesting that the late Paleolithic inhabitants of Berelekh did not concentrate specifically on the hunting of large mammals. Some researchers (Abramova 1989; Vereshchagin 1974) have even suggested that the mammoth remains at the archaeological locality were scavenged from the nearby mammoth cemetery. Other large mammal bones at the Berelekh archaeological site include three specimens of bison or horse and one specimen of reindeer. At Ushki-1, mammal remains are relatively scarce but include moose from layer VII and steppe bison, mountain sheep, lemming, and horse from layer VI. As at Berelekh, remains of birds and fish occur in layer VI. The present evidence, then, suggests that late Paleolithic hunter-gatherers of western Beringia procured a variety of resources, including large mammals, small mammals, birds, and fish. There is little evidence to suggest they were specialized big game hunters or "mammoth predators," as others have speculated (Martin 1982).

Analysis of site distribution and site features indicates late Paleolithic western Beringians inhabited two types of camps. Layers VII and VI at Ushki-1 have a large number of dwelling features that are unquestionably the remains of long-term villages. The two distinctive types of dwellings (semi-subterranean and surface) in layer VI resemble the winter and summer dwellings of ethnographically known arctic populations, and may indicate year-round occupation. During the late Pleistocene, this village would have been situated along the margin of a lake, and remains of lacustrine/riverine faunal resources are present in some of the dwellings. Other western Beringian late Paleolithic sites may represent small camps where more specific resource procurement activities took place over a short time. These include Berelekh, El'gakhchan, Kheta, and Chel'kun-4. These sites are situated along terrace edges or other promontories and have relatively small scatters of lithic debris and limited sets of tools, suggesting they served primarily as short-term hunting overlooks. Interestingly, at Berelekh, presumably a short-term camp, faunal remains indicate a winter occupation (Hopkins et al. 1982:440). While our evidence is limited, it appears that late Paleolithic settlement patterns were characterized by a relatively stable village or base camp that was connected to numerous outlying

Table 4. Characteristics of Early Holocene, Mesolithic Occupations in Western Beringia.

Characteristic	*Site*												
	Uptar I	*Maltan, lower*	*Buiunda-3*	*Kongo, layer 3*	*Kongo, layer 2*	*Siberdik, layer 3*	*Zima*	*Ui-I*	*Zhokhov Island*	*Tytyl'-I*	*Chel'kun-4*	*Puturak Pass*	*Ushki-5, layer V*
Primary Reduction Technology													
Prismatic blade cores		X							X		X	X	X
Wedge-shaped microblade cores						X							X
Conical microblade cores		X	X	X			X	X		X		X	
End microblade cores									X				
Blades	X	X	X	X	X	X	X	X	X	X	X	X	X
Microblades	X	X	X	X	X	X	X	X	X	X	X		X
Flakes	X	X	X	X	X	X	X	X	X	X	X	X	X
Secondary Reduction Technology													
Unifacial	X	X	X	X	X	X	X	X	X	X		X	X
Bifacial	X	X			X	X	X	X					X
Burin	X	X		X		X	X	X		X			X
Backing		X											
Blade/microblade segmentation									X				
Retouched pieces													
Retouched blades		X	X	X		X	X	X				X	
Retouched microblades		X		X			X	X	X				
Leaf-shaped bifacial points	X	X			X	X		X					X
Triangular bifacial points		X											
Pointed, stemmed, shouldered blades								X					
Bifaces	X						X	X					X
Side scrapers	X	X						X				X	X
End scrapers	X	X				X	X	X		X		X	X
Cobble choppers	X			X	X	X							
Burins	X	X		X		X	X	X		X			X
Backed knives		X											
Scraper-like adzes		X							X				
Bone/antler artifacts									X				
Ceramic								X					

"spike camps" where specific activities related to the procurement of resources took place. Such a "base camp-spike camp" pattern has been suggested for Paleoindians in Alaska (Guthrie 1983, Yesner 1996) and North America south of the Laurentide ice sheet (Kelly and Todd 1988).

Mesolithic Adaptations

The Mesolithic of western Beringia is even more poorly defined than the region's late Paleolithic. Kir'iak (1988) defines the Mesolithic as the period of prehistory from 11,000 to 7000 yr B.P. We use the term "Mesolithic" to define the group of archaeological sites dating to the early Holocene, between about 9000 and 7000 yr B.P. (Figure 19) that contain conical, pencil-shaped core and blade/microblade technologies. They also lack elements common in the region's Neolithic, namely ceramics, polyhedral burins, and polished stone tools.

At least 12 cultural occupations have radiocarbon dates falling within the interval of 9000-7000 yr B.P. (Figure 19); eight of these are in the Kolyma area. Unfortunately, many of these sites are in shallow stratigraphic contexts, and charcoal samples dated are not always of clear cultural origin, so some of these sites may not be accurately dated. Chronological, technological, and other characteristics of the western Beringian Mesolithic are discussed below and summarized in Table 4.

The technological information in Table 4 reveals that wedge-shaped core and microblade technologies, so common in the latest Paleolithic of western Beringia, are rare in the Mesolithic. Siberdik (layer 3) has a possible wedge-shaped core, but some disagreement exists about whether it really is wedge-shaped in design (Slobodin 1995). Only the layer V assemblage at Ushki appears to be a true wedge-shaped core industry, perhaps indicating the persistence of late Paleolithic technologies in the Kamchatka region. At other sites like Maltan (lower), Buiunda-3, Kongo (layers 3 and 2), Zima, Ui-1, Tytyl'-1, and Puturak Pass, primary reduction technologies are directed toward the production of slender blades and microblades from prismatic cores reduced in the process of blade/microblade removal to small conical, pencil-shaped cores. At Zhokhov Island, conical cores are absent, and blades and microblades were detached from small, more simply prepared prismatic cores. Secondary reduction technologies represented at most of the western Beringian Mesolithic sites include unifacial, bifacial, and burin techniques. Segmenting and backing of blades have been noted at Zhokhov Island, Ui-1, and Maltan (lower cultural layer). Tool assemblages vary in terms of the forms and frequencies of retouched pieces, but normally include leaf-shaped bifacial points, bifaces, end scrapers (often on massive blades), burins, cobble choppers, and other cobble tools. There also are isolated occurrences of triangular bifacial points and backed knives at Maltan (lower), stemmed and shouldered unifacial points on blades at Ui-1, scraper-like adzes at Maltan (lower) and Zhokhov Island, and a bird-like ornament at Ui-1.

The Mesolithic sites occur in a variety of environments and topographic settings. Maltan, Kongo, Siberdik, and Zima are situated upon low terraces (2–14 m high) overlooking river floodplains, but archaeological features at these sites suggest different lengths of occupation. Zima, Buiunda, and Maltan contain the remains of hearths, and Kongo, Siberdik, and Maltan contain the remains of storage pits, workshop areas, and a possible human burial (at Siberdik). Buiunda-3 is located near the divide of two river drainages on a fossil bar of a braided stream. Ui-1, Tytyl'-1, and Ushki-5 are situated alongside lakes, while Zhokhov Island is clearly in a maritime setting. Remains of fairly substantial dwellings were recovered at the latter three. Preserved faunal remains have not been examined thoroughly and reported, but there are indications of large mammal hunting at Siberdik and Zhokhov Island, and fishing at Ushki-1 (layer V).

The relationship of the western Beringian Mesolithic to similarly aged industries in Yakutia to the west is unclear. In the Lena River basin, the Mesolithic period is represented by the Sumnagin complex. Sumnagin occupations have been identified at a series of multilayered sites in the Aldan (i.e., Ust'-Timpton-1, Bel'kachi-1) and other valleys where they range in age from about 10,500-6,000 yr B.P. (Alekseev 1987; Alekseev and Cherosov 1990:64; Argunov 1990; Mochanov 1977; Powers 1990, 1996). Sumnagin lithic assemblages are dominated by blades and microblades struck from prismatic, conical cores (Alekseev and Cherosov 1990:67; Mochanov 1977:242). Bifacial techniques are rare, except in the flaking of large cobble tools and some cores (Alekseev and Cherosov 1990:67; Mochanov 1977). Several Mesolithic-aged sites in northern Yakutia have long and slender stemmed points, although these are not commonly assigned to the Sumnagin complex by their excavators (Argunov 1990:86,97,151; Kashin 1983b; Kol'tsov 1989:192;

Mochanov et al. 1991:25). These points typically are made on blades and only partially bifacially retouched—on the distal end to form a point and on the proximal end to form shoulders and a stem (Kol'tsov 1989:191). Sumnagin tool assemblages include burins, end scrapers (many on large blades), backed blades, small perforators and engravers (*rezchiki*), wedges (or bipolar cores), axes, adzes, and other cobble tools (Mochanov 1977). Bone needles, awls, and points (some slotted) also occur (Mochanov 1977). Faunal remains indicate a reliance on large mammals and birds (Alekseev and Cherosov 1990:69-70; Powers 1990). The role of fishing is less clear, but Mochanov (1977:248) notes fish bones at Bel'kachi-1.

Nearly 20 years ago, Mochanov (1977:250–253) concluded that the western Beringian Mesolithic documented the spread of Sumnagin populations from the Lena River basin across northeast Asia as far east as the Sea of Okhotsk coast and perhaps even the Bering Strait and Alaska. This scenario was based on information from only three western Beringian sites (Kongo, Siberdik, and Ushki) and two sites in Alaska (Gallagher Flint Station and Anangula). Dikov (1977), on the other hand, concluded at the same time that the western Beringian sites had nothing in common with Sumnagin, and instead constituted a local "Relict Paleolithic" complex.

Today, with more sites and more data, what can we say about the supposed distribution of the Sumnagin complex in western Beringia? Despite the fact that bifacial points appear to be more common in the western Beringian Mesolithic industries than they are in Yakutian Sumnagin industries, the western Beringian assemblages share many technological and typological characteristics with the Yakutian Sumnagin, including blades and microblades detached from conical cores and inset into slotted bone/antler points, long and slender bifacial stemmed points on blades, angle and dihedral burins, end scrapers on blades, and large cobble choppers or adzes. In terms of subsistence strategies, the western Beringian Mesolithic occupations, like those from Yakutia, occur in a variety of topographic situations (e.g., on terrace edges near the mouths of rivers, along the shores of lakes, in high upland passes) and contain evidence of large mammal hunting and possibly fishing. The present evidence, then, does point to the widespread distribution of Sumnagin-like industries throughout northeast Asia during the early Holocene, as Mochanov (1977) suggested nearly two decades ago. Whether these populations spread further across the Bering Sea to Anangula and Koggiung in southwest Alaska is still debatable (Ackerman 1992; Dumond 1984; Powers 1990).

Conclusions

(1) *The earliest unequivocal archaeological traces of humans in western Beringia date to about 14,000 yr B.P.* Layer VII at Ushki-1, central Kamchatka, dates to 14,000 yr B.P. Further north, in the arctic of western Beringia, the oldest known site is Berelekh, radiocarbon dated to about 12,200 yr B.P. Claims for an occupation predating 14,000 yr B.P. have not been substantiated.

(2) *An Upper Paleolithic pre-microblade complex dating between approximately 14,000 and 11,000 yr B.P. exists in western Beringia.* The best documented pre-microblade assemblages come from the cultural layer VII occupations at Ushki-1 and possibly Ushki-5, central Kamchatka, thought to date to 14,000 yr B.P. These assemblages are blade- and biface-based and lack wedge-shaped cores and microblades. Similar industries may occur at the Berelekh, El'gakhchan, and Uptar-1 sites, but additional excavations and chronometric dates are needed to confirm this.

(3) *The earliest occurrence of late Upper Paleolithic microblade-producing technologies in western Beringia postdates 10,700 yr B.P.* However, the only directly dated wedge-shaped core assemblage in the region is Ushki-1 layer VI. All other wedge-shaped core sites remain undated, and only one, Kheta, appears to be in a datable context.

(4) *Late Upper Paleolithic hunter-gatherer adaptations appear to have been based on broad-based subsistence strategies and a "base camp-spike camp" settlement strategy.* Subsistence economies were diversified, with large terrestrial mammal hunting being coupled with the procurement of small mammals, birds, and possibly fish.

(5) *The emerging early Holocene record of western Beringia indicates that the area was occupied by Mesolithic hunter-gatherers with new lithic technologies and land use strategies.* The Mesolithic transformation in technologies may represent a response to dramatic climatic and environmental changes; however, similarities with the Sumnagin Mesolithic complex of Yakutia may indicate that these new technologies spread from Yakutia into western Beringia around 9000 yr B.P. Although evidence of subsistence pursuits is rare, data on site locations suggest more intensive and diversified land use patterns than in the Upper Paleolithic.

The late Pleistocene archaeological record of western Beringia, then, follows some of the same patterns seen in neighboring Alaska. Both regions appear to have been occupied by modern humans very late in the Upper Pleistocene, by 14,000 yr B.P. in the west and 11,700 yr B.P. in the east (Hamilton and Goebel, this volume). These earliest inhabitants carried a lithic tool kit based for the most part on blade and biface technologies; they do not appear to have manufactured or used microblades. They hunted large mammals such as bison, small mammals such as hare, and birds such as ptarmigan. They also may have fished. In western Beringia and Alaska, microblade-producing technologies appear in the archaeological record around 10,700 yr B.P. These new technologies may signal the migration of a second late Upper Paleolithic population from Siberia or Japan into Beringia. After 10,000 yr B.P. the similarities between the western and eastern Beringian records end. A new Mesolithic complex emerges across most of the region. The western Beringian Mesolithic complex of sites dates to between 9000 and 7000 yr B.P. and is characterized by conical core and blade/microblade technologies that may have originated from the Sumnagin complex of Yakutia. Sites assigned to this western Beringian Mesolithic complex have been identified primarily in the upper Kolyma basin, but also have been found on Zhokhov Island in the High Arctic, in the Anui basin of western Chukotka, and even on the Chukotka Peninsula within sight of St. Lawrence Island and Alaska. In Alaska, on the other hand, wedge-shaped core and microblade industries continue through the early Holocene, and only in southwest Alaska is there a suggestion that Sumnagin populations or technologies ever crossed the Bering Strait.

Major shortcomings still exist in the western Beringian Paleolithic and Mesolithic record. Dated Paleolithic sites are rare. Besides Ushki and Berelekh, no sites have been radiocarbon dated to before 9000 yr B.P. Additionally, the region's Mesolithic complex needs to be examined more closely, in order to understand some of the variation that has been noted among its assemblages and to better define their relation to the Sumnagin complex of Yakutia. Clearly, many more sites and more in-depth analyses are needed to test and refine the scenarios presented here. As the early archaeological record of western Beringia continues to unfold, we will be able to turn our attention to other aspects of the record, including subsistence, settlement, and social organization. Future discoveries undoubtedly will change our interpretations, and we look forward to the exciting discoveries that will be made in western Beringia in the years to come.

Acknowledgments

Funding support for this research was provided by the University of Alaska Museum Geist Fund and the Dean of the College of Liberal Arts, University of Alaska Fairbanks. We are indebted to Nikolai Dikov, Magarita Kir'iak, and Aleksander Lebedintsev for allowing us to study some of the western Beringian artifact assemblages described in this paper. John Cook was invaluable in providing support for radiocarbon dating. Finally, we thank Robert Ackerman, Melvin Aikens, Thomas Hamilton, David Hopkins, Maureen King, and Roger Powers for their helpful comments on earlier drafts of this work. We dedicate this paper to the memory of Nikolai Dikov, who recently passed away in Magadan.

References Cited

Abramova, Z. A.
1989 Paleolit Severnoi Azii. In *Paleolit Kavkaza i Severnoi Azii*, pp. 143–243. Nauka, Leningrad.

Ackerman, R. E.
1992 Earliest Stone Industries on the North Pacific Coast of North America. In *Maritime Cultures of Southern Alaska: Papers in Honor of Richard H. Jordan, Arctic Anthropology* 29(2):18–27.

1996 Bluefish Caves. In *American Beginnings: The Prehistory and Palaeoecology of Beringia*, edited by F. H. West, pp. 511–513. The University of Chicago Press, Chicago.

Ackerman, R. E., and R. L. Carlson
1991 Diring Yuriak: An Early Paleolithic Site in Yakutia. *Current Research in the Pleistocene* 8:1–2.

Aikens, C. M.
1990 From Asia to America: The First Peopling of the New World. *Prehistoric Mongoloid Dispersals* 7:1–34.

Aikens, C. M., and D. E. Dumond
1986 Convergence and Common Heritage: Some Parallels in the Archaeology of Japan and Western North America. In *Windows on the Japanese Past: Studies in Archaeology and Prehistory*, edited by R. J. Pearson, pp. 163–178. Center for Japanese Studies, University of Michigan, Ann Arbor.

Aikens, C. M., and T. Higuchi
1982 *Prehistory of Japan*. Academic Press, San Diego.

Alekseev, A. N.
1987 *Kamennyi Vek Olekmy*. Izdatel'stvo Irkutskogo Universiteta, Irkutsk.

Alekseev, A. N., and N. M. Cherosov
1990 *Arkheologiia Iakutii*. Iakutskii Gosudarstvennyi Universitet, Iakutsk.

Anderson, D. D.
1970 *Akmak: An Early Archaeological Assemblage from Onion Portage, Northwest Alaska. Acta Arctica*, Vol. 16. Copenhagen.

1988 *Onion Portage: The Archaeology of a Stratified Site from the Kobuk River, Northwest Alaska. Anthropological Papers of the University of Alaska* 22(1–2).

Argunov, V. G.
1990 *Kamennyi Vek Severo-Zapadnoi Iakutii*. Nauka, Novosibirsk.

Bar-Yosef, O., and L. Meignen
1992 Insights into Levantine Middle Paleolithic Cultural Variability. In *The Middle Paleolithic: Adaptation, Behavior, and Variability*, edited by H. L. Dibble and P. Mellars, pp. 163–182. The University Museum, University of Pennsylvania, Philadelphia.

Bejét, J. E., D. M. Hopkins, A. V. Lozhkin, P. M. Anderson, and W. R. Eisner
1991 The Newly Discovered Elikchan Tephra on the Mainland of Soviet Asia. *Geological Society of America Abstracts with Programs 1991* A62.

Boëda, E.
1988 Le Concept Levallois et Évaluation de son Champ d'Application. In: Otte, M. (ed.), *L'Homme de Néandertal*, Vol. 4, Binford, L., and Rigaud, J.-P. (eds.) *La Technique*. Université de Liège, Liège.

Braitseva, O. A., I. V. Melekestsev, I. S. Evteeva, and E. G. Lupikina
1968 *Stratigrafiia Chetvertichnykh Otlozhenii i Oledeneniia Kamchatki*. Nauka, Moscow.

Cherdyntsev, V. V., F. S. Zavel'skii, N. V. Kind, L. D. Sulerzhintskii, and V. S. Forova
1969 Radiouglerodnye Daty GIN AN SSSR: Soobshchenie IV. *Biulleten' Komissii po Izucheniiu Chetvertichnogo Perioda* 36:172–193.

Cinq-Mars, J.
1979 Bluefish Cave I: A Late Pleistocene Eastern Beringian Cave Site in the Northern Yukon. *Canadian Journal of Archaeology* 3:1–32.

Dikov, N. N.
1968 The Discovery of the Palaeolithic in Kamchatka and the Problem of the Initial Occupation of America. *Arctic Anthropology* 5(1):191–203.

1970 Paleoliticheskoe Zhilishche na Kamchatskoi Stoianke Ushki IV. In *Sibir' i Eë Sosedi v Drevnosti*, pp. 34–42. Nauka, Novosibirsk.

1977 *Arkheologicheskie Pamiatniki Kamchatki, Chukotki i Verkhnei Kolymy*. Nauka, Moscow.

1979a *Drevnie Kul'tury Severo-Vostochnoi Azii*. Nauka, Moscow.

1979b Zakhoronenie Domashnei Sobaki v Zhilishche Pozdnepaleoliticheskoi Stoianki Ushki-1 na Kamchatke. In *Novye Arkheologicheskie Pamiatniki Severa Dal'nego Vostoka (po Dannym Severo-Vostochno-Aziatskoi Kompleksnoi Arkheologicheskoi Ekspeditsii)*, pp. 12–17. Severo-Vostochnyi Kompleksnyi Nauchno-Issledovatel'skii Institut, Dal'nevostochnyi Nauchnyi Tsentr, Akademiia Nauk SSSR, Magadan.

1980 Pervye Paleoliticheskie Pamiatniki na Chukotskom Poluostrove (Stoianki na Rr. Chel'kun i Kurupke). In *Noveishie Dannye po Arkheologii Severa Dal'nego Vostoka*, pp. 5–23. Severo-Vostochnyi Kompleksnyi Nauchno-Issledovatel'skii Institut, Dal'nevostochnyi Nauchnyi Tsentr, Akademiia Nauk SSSR, Magadan.

1985a The Paleolithic of Northeastern Asia and Its Relations with the Paleolithic of America. *Inter-Nord* 17:173–177.

1985b Ul'khum i Chaatam'e I—Novye Paleoliticheskie Mestonakhozhdeniia na Iugo-Vostoke Chukotskogo Poluostrova. In *Novoe v Arkheologii Severa Dal'nego*

Vostoka (Materialy Severo-Vostochno-Aziatskoi Kompleksnoi Arkheologicheskoi Ekspeditsii): Sbornik Nauchnykh Trudov, pp. 3–11. Akademiia Nauk SSSR, Magadan.

1990a Population Migration from Asia to Pre-Columbian America. Paper presented at the 17th International Congress of Historical Sciences, Madrid.

1990b Osnovnye Rezul'taty Arkheologicheskikh Razvedok na Vostoke Chukotskogo Poluostrova v 1979–1986 gg. In *Drevnie Pamiatniki Severa Dal'nego Vostoka (Novye Materialy i Issledovaniia Severo-Vostochno-Aziatskoi Kompleksnoi Arkheologicheskoi Ekspeditsii)*, pp. 7–35. Akademiia Nauk SSSR, Magadan.

1993 *Aziia na Styke s Amerikoi v Drevnosti: Kamennyi Vek Chukotskogo Poluostrova*. Nauka, Sankt-Peterburg.

1995a Drevniaia Stoianka Maltan I. In *Pamiatniki, Pamiatnyi Mesta Istorii I Kul'tury Severo-Vostoka Rossii (Magadanskaia Oblast' I Chukotka)*, pp. 19–22. Magadanskoe Knizhnoe Izdatel'stvo, Magadan.

1995b Puturak—Pamiatnik Kul'tury Pozdnego Paleolita na Chukotke. In *Pamiatniki, Pamiatnyi Mesta Istorii i Kul'tury Severo-Vostoka Rossii (Magadanskaia Oblast' i Chukotka)*, pp. 11–13. Magadanskoe Knizhnoe Izdatel'stvo, Magadan.

1995c Ranniaia Poslepaleoliticheskaia Stoianka u Ruch. Kongo. In *Pamiatniki, Pamiatnyi Mesta Istorii i Kul'tury Severo-Vostoka Rossii (Magadanskaia Oblast' i Chukotka)*, pp. 18–19. Magadanskoe Knizhnoe Izdatel'stvo, Magadan.

1995d Siberdikovskaia Pozdnepaleoliticheskaia Stoianka na Kolyme. In *Pamiatniki, Pamiatnyi Mesta Istorii i Kul'tury Severo-Vostoka Rossii (Magadanskaia Oblast' i Chukotka)*, pp. 13–17. Magadanskoe Knizhnoe Izdatel'stvo, Magadan.

1995e Stoianka Ul'khum—Drevneishii Pamiatnik Paleolita na Chukotskom P-ove. In *Pamiatniki, Pamiatnyi Mesta Istorii i Kul'tury Severo-Vostoka Rossii (Magadanskaia Oblast' i Chukotka)*, pp. 10–11. Magadanskoe Knizhnoe Izdatel'stvo, Magadan.

Dikov, N. N., and T. M. Dikova
1972 Issledovaniia na Kolyme i Kamchatke. *Arkheologicheskie Otkrytiia 1971 Goda*, p. 252. Moscow.

Dikov, N. N., and V. I. Gerasimchuk
1971 Sledy Verkhnego Paleolita u Ruch'ia Shilo v Basseine Kolymy. *Arkheologicheskie Otkrytiia 1970 Goda*, p. 186. Moscow.

Dikov, N. N., and G. I. Kazinskaia
1980 Sledy Kamennogo Veka na r. Kurupke (Chukotskii Poluostrov). In *Noveishie Dannye po Arkheologii Severa Dal'nego Vostoka*. Akademiia Nauk SSSR, Magadan.

Dikov, N. N., and N. A. Kononenko
1990 Rezul'taty Trasologicheskogo Issledovaniia Klinovidnykh Nukleusov iz Shestogo Sloia Stoianok Ushki I-V na Kamchatke. In *Drevnie Pamiatniki Severa Dal'nego Vostoka (Novye Materialy i Issledovaniia Severo-Vostochno-Aziatskoi Kompleksnoi Arkheologicheskoi Ekspeditsii)*, pp. 170–175. Akademiia Nauk SSSR, Magadan.

Dikov, N. N., and E. E. Titov
1984 Problems of the Stratification and Periodization of the Ushki Sites. *Arctic Anthropology* 21(2):69–80.

Dikov, N. N., D. L. Brodianskii, and V. I. D'iakov
1983 *Drevnie Kul'tury Tikhookeanskogo Poberezh'ia SSSR: Uchebnoe Posobie*. Izdatel'stvo Dal'nevostochnogo Universiteta, Vladivostok.

Dikova, T. M.
1979 Pervye Nakhodki Paleolita na Iuge Kamchatki (M. Lopatka). In *Novye Arkheologicheskie Pamiatniki Severa Dal'nego Vostoka*, pp. 29-38. Akademiia Nauk SSSR, Dal'nevostochnyi Nauchnyi Tsentr, Severo-Vostochnyi Kompleksnyi Nauchno-Issledovatel'skii Institut, Magadan.

1983 *Arkheologiia Iuzhnoi Kamchatki v Sviazi c Problemoi Rasseleniia Ainov*. Nauka, Moscow.

Dumond, D. E.
1984 Prehistory of the Bering Sea Region. In *Handbook of North American Indians, Volume 5: Arctic*, edited by D. Damas, pp. 94–105. Smithsonian Institution, Washington.

Giria, E. Yu., and V. V. Pitul'ko
1994 A High Arctic Mesolithic Industry on Zhokov Island: Inset Tools and Knapping Technology. *Arctic Anthropology* 31(2):31–-44.

Goebel, T.
1995 The Record of Human Occupation of the Russian Subarctic and Arctic. In *Workshop to Define Research Priorities for Russian Arctic Land-Shelf Systems*, edited by S. L. Forman and L. R. Tipton-Everett, pp. 41–46. Byrd Polar Research Center Miscellaneous Series M-335, Columbus, Ohio.

Goebel, T., R. Powers, and N. Bigelow
1991 The Nenana Complex of Alaska and Clovis Origins. In *Clovis Origins and Adaptations*, edited by R. Bonnichsen and K. L. Turnmire, pp. 49–79. Center for the Study of the First Americans, Oregon State University, Corvallis.

Grichuk, V. P.
1984 Late Pleistocene Vegetation History. In *Late Quaternary Environments of the Soviet Union*, edited by A. A. Velichko, pp. 155–178. University of Minnesota Press, Minneapolis.

Guthrie, R. D.
1983 Paleoecology of the Site and Its Implications for Early Hunters. In *Dry Creek*, edited by W. R. Powers, R. D. Guthrie, and J. F. Hoffecker, pp. 209–287. National Park Service, Washington, D.C.

Hoffecker, J., W. R. Powers, and T. Goebel
1993 The Colonization of Beringia and the Peopling of the New World. *Science* 259:46–53.

Holmes, C. E., R. VanderHoek, and T. E. Dilley
1996 Swan Point. In *American Beginnings: The Prehistory and Palaeoecology of Beringia*, edited by F. H. West, pp. 319–323. The University of Chicago Press, Chicago.

Hopkins, D. M., J. V. Matthews, C. E. Schweger, and S. B. Young (editors)
1982 *Paleoecology of Beringia*. Academic Press, New York.

Ikawa-Smith, F.
1980 Current Issues in Japanese Archaeology. *American Scientist* 68(2):134–145.

Isayeva, L. L.
1984 Late Pleistocene Glaciation of North-Central Siberia. In *Late Quaternary Environments of the Soviet Union*, edited by A. A. Velichko, pp. 21–30. University of Minnesota Press, Minneapolis.

Ivanov, V. F.
1986 *Chetvertichnye Otlozheniia Poberezh'ia Vostochnyi Chukotki*. Akademiia Nauk SSSR, Dal'nevostochnyi Nauchnyi Tsentr, Vladivostok.

1990 Problemy Geomorfologii i Chetvertichnoi Geologii v Raione Stoianki Ushki (Dolina Reki Kamchatki). In *Drevnie Pamiatniki Severa Dal'nego Vostoka*, pp. 161–170. Akademiia Nauk SSSR, Dal'nevostochnoe Otdelenie, Severo-Vostochnyi Kompleksnyi Nauchno-Issledovatel'skii Institut, Magadan.

Kashin, V. A.
1983a Istoriia i Nekotorye Itogi Izucheniia Geologii Paleolita Iakutii. *Paleolit Sibiri*, pp. 111–123. Nauka, Novosibirsk.

1983b Stoianka Iubileinyi i ee Mesto v Kul'ture Kamennogo Veka Iakutii. In *Pozdnepleistotsenovye i Rannegolotsenovye Kul'turnye Sviazi Azii i Ameriki*, pp. 93–101. Nauka, Novosibirsk.

Kelly, R., and L. Todd
1988 Coming into the Country: Early Paleoindian Hunting and Mobility. *American Antiquity* 53:231–244.

King, M. L., and S. B. Slobodin
1994 Terminal Pleistocene Occupation of the Kheta Site, Upper Kolyma Region, Northeastern Russia. *Current Research in the Pleistocene* 11:138–140.

1996 A Fluted Point from the Uptar Site, Northeastern Siberia. *Science* 273:634–636.

Kir'iak, M. A.
1979 Pervye Mezoliticheskie i Neoliticheskie Stoianki Zapadnoi Chukotki (Oz. Tytyl' v Verkhov'iakh M. Aniuia). In *Novye Arkheologicheskie Pamiatniki Severa Dal'nego Vostoka*, pp. 39–52. Akademiia Nauk SSSR, Magadan.

1985 Orlovka II—Pervaia Paleoliticheskaia Stoianka Zapadnoi Chukotki. In *Novoe v Arkheologii Severa Dal'nego Vostoka*. Akademiia Nauk SSSR, Magadan.

1988 Mezoliticheskaia Stoianka na Ozere Tytyl' (Tytyl' I). *Kraevedcheskie Zapiski* 15:138–150.

1989 *Arkheologiia Zapadnoi Chukotki, Kolymy, i Etnogenesis Iukagiri*. Abstract of Dissertation for Degree of Kandidat of Historical Sciences, Akademiia Nauk, Leningrad.

1990 Stoianka Bol'shoi El'gakhchan I (Bassein Reki Omolon)—Analog Paleoliticheskogo Kompleksa VII Sloia Stoianki Ushki I na Kamchatke. In *Drevnie Pamiatniki Severa Dal'nego Vostoka (Novye Materialy i Issledovaniia Severo-Vostochno-Aziatskoi Kompleksnoi Arkheologicheskoi Ekspeditsii)*, pp. 35–52. Akademiia Nauk SSSR, Magadan.

1992 Verkhnepaleoliticheskaia Stoianka Bol'shoi El'gakhchan I v Verkhov'iakh R. Omolon. In *Paleoekologiia i Rasselenie Drevnego Cheloveka v Severnoi Azii i Amerike*, pp. 114–119. Nauka, Krasnoyarsk.

1993 *Arkheologiia Zapadnoi Chukotki v Sviazi s Iukagirskoi Problemoi*. Nauka, Moscow.

1996 Bolshoi El'gakhchan 1 and 2, Omolon River Basin, Magadan District. In: *American Beginnings: The Prehistory and Palaeoecology of Beringia*, edited by F. H. West, pp. 228–236. The University of Chicago Press, Chicago.

Kistenev, S. P.
1988 Drevnie Stoianki Levoberezh'ia Nizhnei Kolymy (Khallerchinskaia Tundra). In *Arkheologiia Iakutii*, pp. 98–104. Iakutskii Gosudarstvennyi Universitet, Yakutsk.

Kol'tsov, L. V.
1989 Mezolit Severa Sibiri i Dal'nego Vostoka. In *Mezolit SSSR*, edited by L. V. Kol'tsov, pp. 187–194. Nauka, Moskva.

Kozlowski, J. and H.-G. Bandi
1984 The Paleohistory of Circumpolar Arctic Colonization. *Arctic* 37(4):359–372.

Krushanov, A. I.
1989 *Istoriia Dal'nego Vostoka SSSR: c Drevneishikh Vremen do XVII Veka*. Nauka, Moscow.

Kuzmin, Y. V.
1989 *Radiouglerodnaia Khronologiia Drevnikh Kul'tur Dal'nego Vostoka SSSR: Katalog Datirovok*. Preprint, Nauka, Vladivostok.

1990 Radiouglerodnaia Khronologiia Arkheologicheskikh Pamiatnikov Iuga Dal'nego Vostoka SSSR. In *Khronostratigrafiia Paleolita Severnoi, Tsentral'noi, i Vostochnoi Azii i Ameriki (Doklady Mezhdunarodnogo Simposiuma)*, pp. 204–209. Nauka, Novosibirsk.

1994 Prehistoric Colonization of Northeastern Siberia and Migration to America: Radiocarbon Evidence. *Radiocarbon* 36(3):367–376.

Kuzmin, Y. V., and S. K. Krivonogov
1994 The Diring Paleolithic Site, Eastern Siberia: Review of Geoarchaeological Studies. *Geoarchaeology: An International Journal* 9(4):287–300.

Kuzmin, Y. V., and K. B. Tankersley
1996 The Colonization of Eastern Siberia: An Evaluation of the Paleolithic Age Radiocarbon Dates. *Journal of Archaeological Science* 23:577–585.

1997 Late Pleistocene/Early Holocene Culture Change in Eastern Siberia. Paper presented at the 62nd Annual Meeting of the Society for American Archaeology, Nashville.

Larichev, V., U. Khol'ushkin, and I. Laricheva
1992 The Upper Paleolithic of Northern Asia: Achievements, Problems, and Perspectives. III. Northeastern Siberia and Russian Far East. *Journal of World Prehistory* 6(4):441–476.

Laukhin, S. A., and N. I. Drozdov
1990 Nakhodka Paleoliticheskikh Artefaktov na Severe Vostochnoi Chukotki i Problema Migratsii Paleoliticheskogo Cheloveka iz Azii v Severnuiu Ameriku. Unpublished manuscript.

Laukhin, S. A., N. I. Drozdov, V. A. Panychev, and S. V. Belichko
1989 Vosrast Poslednego Oledeneniia na Severe Vostochnoi Chukotki. *Izvestiia Akademii Nauk SSSR: Seriia Geologicheskaia* 3:136-140.

Lebedintsev, A. I.
1990 *Drevnie Primorskie Kul'tury Severo-Zapadnogo Priokhot'ia.* Nauka, Leningrad.

Long, A., and B. Rippeteau
1974 Testing Contemporaneity and Averaging Radiocarbon Dates. *American Antiquity* 39:205–215.

Lozhkin, A. V.
1985 Radiouglerodnye Datirovki Arkheologicheskikh Pamiatnikov Severo-Vostoka Azii. *Novoe v Arkheologii Severa dal'nego Vostoka*, pp. 66–70. Severo-Vostochnyi Kompleksnyi Nauchno-Issledovatel'skii Institut, Dal'nevostochnyi Nauchnyi Tsentr, Akademiia Nauk SSSR, Magadan.

1987 Radiouglerodnoe Datirovanie v Geokhronologicheskikh i Paleogeograficheskikh Issledovaniiakh na Severo-Vostoke SSSR. In *Regional'naia Geokhronologiia Sibiri i Dal'nego Vostoka*, pp. 150–154. Nauka, Novosibirsk.

Lozhkin, A. V., and V. P. Parii
1976 Radiouglerodnye Datirovki Laboratorii Severo-Vostochnogo Kompleksnogo NII DVNTs AN SSSR. *Biulleten' Komissii po Izucheniiu Chetvertichnogo Perioda* 45:152–154.

1985 Opyt Radiouglerodnogo Datirovaniia Verkhnechetvertichnykh Otlozhenii. Preprint. DVNTs AN SSSR, Magadan, 43 p.

Lozhkin, A. V., and T. P. Prokhorova
1980 Rezul'taty Palinologicheskogo Izucheniia Arkheologicheskikh Pamiatnikov Kolymy. In *Noveishie Dannye po Arkheologii Severa Dal'nego Vostoka.* Severo-Vostochnyi Kompleksnyi Nauchno-Issledovatel'skii Institut, Dal'nevostochnyi Nauchnyi Tsentr, Akademiia Nauk SSSR, Magadan.

Lozhkin, A. V., and M. A. Trumpe
1990 Sistematizatsiia Radiouglerodnykh Datirovok Arkheologicheskikh Pamiatnikov Magadanskoi Oblasti. In *Drevnie Pamiatniki Severa Dal'nego Vostoka (Novye Materialy i Issledovaniia Severo-Vostochno-Aziatskoi Kompleksnoi Arkheologicheskoi Ekspeditsii)*, pp. 176–179. Akademiia Nauk SSSR, Dal'nevostochnoe Otdelenie, Severo-Vostochnyi Kompleksnyi Nauchno-Issledovatel'skii Institut, Magadan.

Lozhkin, A. V., P. M. Anderson, W. R. Eisner, L. G. Ravako, D. M. Hopkins, L. B. Brubaker, P. A. Colinvaux, and M. C. Miller
1993 Late Quaternary Lacustrine Pollen Records from Southwestern Beringia. *Quaternary Research* 39:314–324.

Lozhkin, A. V., V. P. Parii, E. D. Takmazian, and L. N. Kotova
1977 Radiouglerodnye Datirovki Laboratorii Severo-Vostochnogo Kompleksnogo Nauchno-Issledovatel'skogo Instituta DVNTs AN SSSR: Soobshchenie II. *Biulleten' Kommissii po Izucheniiu Chetvertichnogo Perioda* 47:156–160.

Lozhkin, A. V., V. P. Parii, L. N. Kotova, and E. D. Takmazian
1980 Radiouglerodnye Datirovki Laboratorii Severo-Vostochnogo Kompleksnogo NIIDVNTs AN SSSR. *Biulleten' Komissii po Izucheniiu Chetvertichnogo Perioda* 50:202–206.

Martin, P. S.
1982 The Pattern and Meaning of Holarctic Mammoth Extinction. In *Paleoecology of Beringia*, edited by D. M. Hopkins, J. V. Matthews, Jr., C. E. Schweger, and S. B. Young, pp. 399–408. Academic Press, New York.

Michael, H. N.
1984 Absolute Chronologies of Late Pleistocene and Early Holocene Cultures of Northeastern Asia. *Arctic Anthropology* 21(2):1–68.

Mochanov, Iu. A.
1972 Issledovanie Paleolita na Indigirke, Kolyme i Zapadnom Poberezh'e Okhotskogo Moria. *Arkheologicheskie Otkrytiia 1971 g.* Nauka, Moscow, p. 251.

1977 *Drevneishie Etapy Zaseleniia Chelovekom Severo-Vostochnoi Azii.* Nauka, Novosibirsk.

1978 Stratigraphy and Absolute Chronology of the Paleolithic of Northeast Asia, According to the Work of 1963–1973. In *Early Man in America from a Circum-Pacific Perspective*, edited by A. L. Bryan, pp. 54–67. Occasional Papers No. 1, Department of Anthropology, University of Alberta, Edmonton.

1988 Drevneishii Paleolit Diringa i Problema Vnetropicheskoi Prarodiny Chelovechestva. In *Arkheologiia Iakutii*, pp. 15-54. Iakutskii Gosudarstvennyi Universitet, Yakustk.

1992 The Earliest Palaeolithic of Northeastern Asia and the Problem of an Extratropical Cradle of Man. Paper presented at the 45th Annual Northwest Anthropological Conference, Simon Fraser University, British Columbia, April 16–18, 1992.

1993 The Most Ancient Paleolithic of the Diring Site and the Problem of a Nontropical Origin for Humanity. *Arctic Anthropology* 30(1):22–53.

Mochanov, Y. A., and S. A. Fedoseeva

1996a Berelekh, Allakhovsk Region. In: *American Beginnings: The Prehistory and Palaeoecology of Beringia*, edited by F. H. West, pp. 218–222. The University of Chicago Press, Chicago.

1996b Kukhtuy 3. In: *American Beginnings: The Prehistory and Palaeoecology of Beringia*, edited by F. H. West, pp. 224–227. The University of Chicago Press, Chicago.

1996c Mayorych, Yagodinskiy Region, Magadan District. In: *American Beginnings: The Prehistory and Palaeoecology of Beringia*, edited by F. H. West, p. 223. The University of Chicago Press, Chicago.

Mochanov, Iu. A., S. A. Fedoseeva, I. V. Konstantinov, N. V. Antipina, and V. G. Argunov

1991 *Arkheologicheskie Pamiatniki Iakutii: Basseiny Viliuia, Anabara, i Oleneka*. Nauka, Moscow.

Morlan, R. E.

1987 The Pleistocene Archaeology of Beringia. In *The Evolution of Human Hunting*, edited by M. H. Nitecki and D. V. Nitecki, pp. 267–307. Plenum Press, New York.

Pitul'ko, V. V.

1993 An Early Holocene Site in the Siberian High Arctic. *Arctic Anthropology* 30(1):13–21.

Pitul'ko, V. V., V. M. Makeev, and M. B. Samarskii

1990 Drevneishaia Stoianka v Vycokoshirotnoi Arktike. In *Khronostratigrafiia Paleolita Severnoi, Tsentral'noi, i Vostochnoi Azii i Ameriki (Doklady Mezhdunarodnogo Simposiuma)*, pp. 259–261. Akademiia Nauk SSSR, Institut Istorii, Filologii i Filosofii SO AN SSSR, Novosibirsk.

Powers, W. R.

1990 The Peoples of Eastern Beringia. *Prehistoric Mongoloid Dispersals* 7:53–74.

1996 Siberia in the Late Glacial and Early Postglacial. In *Humans at the End of the Ice Age: The Archaeology of the Pleistocene-Holocene Transition*, edited by L. G. Straus, B. V. Eriksen, J. M. Erlandson, and D. R. Yesner, pp. 229–242. Plenum Press, New York.

Powers, W. R., and J. F. Hoffecker

1989 Late Pleistocene Settlement in the Nenana Valley, Central Alaska. *American Antiquity* 54(2):263–287.

Ranov, V. A., and S. M. Tseitlin

1991 Paleoliticheskaia Stoianka Diring Glazami Geologa i Arkheologa. *Biulleten' Komissii po Izucheniiu Chetvertichnogo Perioda* 60:79–87.

Reynolds, T. E. G., and S. C. Kaner

1990 Japan and Korea at 18 000 BP. In *The World at 18 000 BP: Volume 1, High Latitudes*, edited by O. Soffer and C. Gamble, pp. 296–311. Unwin Hyman, London.

Shilo, N. A., N. N. Dikov, and A. V. Lozhkin

1976 Radiouglerodnye Datirovki Drevnikh Kul'tur v Verkhnechetvertichnykh Otlozheniiakh Severo-Vostoka SSSR. *Doklady AN SSSR* 231(5):1204–1205.

Shilo, N. A., N. N. Dikov, A. V. Lozhkin, and A. V. Starikov

1977 Novye Radiouglerodnye Datirovki Arkheologicheskikh Pamiatnikov iz Verkhnechetvertichnykh Otlozhenii Severa Dal'nego Vostoka. *Doklady Akademiia Nauk* SSSR 237 (3).

Shilo, N. A., N. N. Dikov, A. V. Lozhkin, A. A. Orekhov, and T. S. Tein

1979 Novye Radiouglerodnye Datirovki Arkheologicheskikh Pamiatnikov Severo-Vostochnoi Azii. In *Novye Arkheologicheskie Pamiatniki Severa Dal'nego Vostoka*. Severo-Vostochnyi Kompleksnyi Nauchno-Issledovatel'skii Institut, Dal'nevostochnyi Nauchnyi Tsentr, Akademiia Nauk SSSR, Magadan.

Slobodin, S. B.

1990 Issledovanie Kontinental'noi Stoianki Uptar I v Severnom Priokhot'e. In *Drevnie Pamiatniki Severa Dal'nego Vostoka*, pp. 65–74. Academiia Nauk SSSR, Dal'nevostochnoe Otdelenie, Severo-Vostochnyi Kompleksnyi Nauchno-Issledovatel'skii Institut, Magadan.

1991a Kamennyi Vek Verkhnei Kolymy i Kontinental'nogo Priokhot'ia. In *Problemy Arkheologii i Etnografii Sibiri i Dal'nego Vostoka: Posviashchaetsia 100-letiiu N. K. Auerbakha*, Vol. I. Ministerstvo Narodnogo Obrazovaniia RSFSR, Krasnoyarsk.

1991b Stoianka Zima—Pervyi Pamiatnik Kamennogo Veka v Susumanskom Raione. *Kraevedcheskie Zapiski* 17:111–116.

1995 *Kamennyi Vek Verkhnei Kolymy i Kontinentalnogo Priokhot'ia*. Abstract of Dissertation for Degree of Kandidat of Historical Sciences. Institute of Archaeology, Siberian Branch, Russian Academy of Sciences, Novosibirsk.

1996 Stoianki Kamennogo Veka Okhandgiiskogo Arkheologicheskogo Raiona (Verkhnaia Kolyma). In: *Arkheologicheskie Issledovaniia na Severe Dal'nego Vostoka*, pp. 77–115. Academiia Nauk, Dal'nevostochnoe Otdelenie, Severo-Vostochnyi Kompleksnyi Nauchno-Issledovatel'skii Institut, Magadan.

1997 Arkheologicheskie Kompleksy Okhotsko-Kolymskogo Nagoria. In: *Materialy i Issledovanniia po Arkheologii Severa Dal'nego Vostoka i Sopredel'nykh Territorii*, pp. 18–67. Academiia Nauk, Dal'nevostochnoe Otdelenie, Severo-Vostochnyi Kompleksnyi Nauchno-Issledovatel'skii Institut, Magadan.

Slobodin, S. B., and O. Iu. Glushkova
1992 Stoianka Kheta—Pervyi Stratifitsirovannyi Verkhnepaleoliticheskii Kompleks na Kolyme. In *Paleoekologiia i Rasselenie Drevnego Cheloveka v Severnoi Azii i Amerike*, pp. 225–228. Nauka, Krasnoyarsk.

Slobodin, S. B., and M. L. King
1996 Uptar and Kheta: Upper Palaeolithic Sites of the Upper Kolyma Region. In: *American Beginnings: The Prehistory and Palaeoecology of Beringia*, edited by F. H. West, pp. 236–244. The University of Chicago Press, Chicago.

Soffer, O.
1985 *The Upper Paleolithic of the Central Russian Plain.* Academic Press, New York.

Starikov, E. V. and V. A. Zhidovlenko
1987 Radiouglerodnye Datirovki Instituta Lesa i Drevesiny im. V. N. Sukacheva SO AN SSSR: Soobshchenie III. *Biulleten' Komissii po Izucheniiu Chetvertichnogo Perioda* 56:161–164.

Titov, E. E.
1980 Geomorfologiia i Usloviia Nakopleniia Osadkov v Raione Ushkovskikh Stoianok. In *Noveishie Dannye po Arkheologii Severa Dal'nego Vostoka*, pp. 134–156. Akademiia Nauk SSSR, Dal'nevostochnoe Nauchnyi Tsentr, Severo-Vostochnyi Kompleksnyi Nauchno-Issledovatel'skii Institut.

Tseitlin, S. M.
1979 *Geologiia Paleolita Severnoi Azii.* Nauka, Moscow.

Ukraintseva, V. V.
1993 *Vegetation Cover and Environment of the "Mammoth Epoch" in Siberia.* Mammoth Site of Hot Springs, Hot Springs, South Dakota.

Van Peer, P.
1992 *The Levallois Reduction Strategy.* Prehistory Press, Madison, Wisconsin.

Vereshchagin, N. K.
1974 The Mammoth "Cemeteries" of North-East Siberia. *Polar Record* 17(106):3–12.

1977 Berelekhskoe "Kladbishche" Mamontov. *Trudy Zoologicheskogo Instituta AN SSSR* 72:5–50.

1979 Ostatki Mlekopitaiushchikh iz Paleoliticheskogo Sloia VI Stoianki Ushki-1. In *Novye Arkheologicheskie Pamiatniki Severa Dal'nego Vostoka (po Dannym Severo-Vostochno-Aziatskoi Kompleksnoi Arkheologicheskoi Ekspeditsii)*, pp. 18–19. Severo-Vostochnyi Kompleksnyi Nauchno-Issledovatel'skii Institut, Dal'nevostochnyi Nauchnyi Tsentr, Akademiia Nauk SSSR, Magadan.

Vereshchagin, N. K., and Iu. A. Mochanov
1972 Samye Severnye v Mire Sledy Verkhnego Paleolita (Berelekhskoe Mestonakhozhdenie v Nizov'iakh R. Indigirka). *Sovetskaia Arkheologiia* 3:332–336.

Vereshchagin, N. K., and V. V. Ukraintseva
1985 Proiskhozhdenie i Stratigrafiia Berelekhskogo "Kladbishcha" Mamontov. *Trudy Zoologicheskogo Instituta AN SSSR* 131:104–113.

Vorobei, I. E.
1992 Druchak-V—Novaia Dokeramicheskaia Stoianka v Severnom Priokhot'e. In *Paleoekologiia i Rasselenie Drevnego Cheloveka v Severnoi Azii i Amerike*, pp. 43–45. Nauka, Krasnoyarsk.

Waters, M. R.
1995 Archaeological Research in Northeastern Siberia. In *Workshop to Define Research Priorities for Russian Arctic Land-Shelf Systems (Abstracts), January 10–12, 1995*, edited by S. L. Forman and L. R. Tipton-Everett, pp. 121–123. *Byrd Polar Research Center Miscellaneous Series M-335.* Byrd Polar Research Center, The Ohio State University, Columbus.

Waters, M. R., S. L. Forman, and J. M. Pierson
1997 Diring Yuriakh: A Lower Paleolithic Site in Central Siberia. *Science* 275:1281–1284.

West, F. H.
1981 *Archaeology of Beringia.* Columbia University Press, New York.

1996 The Study of Beringia. In *American Beginnings: The Prehistory and Palaeoecology of Beringia*, edited by F. H. West, pp. 1-10. The University of Chicago Press, Chicago.

Yesner, D. R.
1996 Human Adaptation at the Pleistocene-Holocene Boundary (Circa 13,000-8,000 BP) in Eastern Beringia. In *Humans at the End of the Ice Age: The Archaeology of the Pleistocene-Holocene Transition*, edited by L. G. Straus, B. V. Eriksen, J. M. Erlandson, and D. R. Yesner, pp. 255–276. Plenum Press, New York.

Yi, S., and G. Clark
1985 The "Dyuktai Culture" and New World Origins. *Current Anthropology* 26(1):1–20.

Yurtsev, V. A.
1984 Problems of the Late Cenozoic Paleogeography of Beringia in Light of Phytogeographic Evidence. In *Beringia in the Cenozoic Era*, edited by V. L. Kontrimavichus, pp. 129–153. Amerind Publishing Co., New Delhi.

Notes

1. The Russian terms *Oblast'*, *Okrug*, and *Krai* are regional administrative units that translate as province, region, and territory, respectively.
2. All dates are presented in uncalibrated radiocarbon years before present (yr B.P.). For the most part, contextual and analytical information on dates is lacking, making it difficult to judge which dates are most accurate. In a few cases where dates from an occupation can be evaluated, they are averaged according to the method described by Long and Rippeteau (1994).
3. Primary reduction technology here refers to the techniques used to select raw material, prepare cores, and detach blanks from those cores; secondary reduction technology refers to the techniques used to choose, shape, and resharpen/rejuvenate blanks. These are considered to be identifiable stages in the reduction stream of stone tool mproduction (Bar Yosef and Meignen 1992; Boëda 1988; Van Peer 1992).
4. Kuzmin and Tankersley (1996:585) cite the earliest Siberdik date as evidence that humans were in the Kolyma basin between 12,000 and 14,000 yr B.P., perhaps not realizing that this date comes from the same cultural layer as the suite of early-mid Holocene dates for cultural layer 3.
5. Kuzmin (1990) reports a radiocarbon date of 17,150 ± 135 yr B.P. (IM-459) from Ezhantsy.

Late Pleistocene Peopling of Alaska

Thomas D. Hamilton[1]
Ted Goebel[2]

Abstract

The earliest firm evidence for humans in central Alaska dates to about 11,800 radiocarbon yr B.P. Four stratified archaeological sites in the Nenana valley region (Dry Creek, Walker Road, Moose Creek, and Owl Ridge) contain artifacts ascribed to the Nenana complex, a blade-and-biface industry with a probable age of 11,300–11,000 yr B.P. Microblade technologies are absent from these assemblages. In the nearby upper Tanana valley, three well-stratified sites (Broken Mammoth, Swan Point, and Mead) and a shallower site with greater vertical mixture (Healy Lake; type locality for the Chindadn complex) contain cultural occupations ranging from 11,800 to 11,000 yr B.P. The Broken Mammoth and Mead sites contain elements of the Nenana complex, but at Swan Point and Healy Lake, microblades may be associated with dated charcoal as old as 11,700 yr B.P. The relationship of the Nenana and Chindadn assemblages to the Clovis tradition of temperate North America is not well understood, but the Nenana complex could document Paleoindians in central Alaska slightly before the appearance of Clovis farther south.

The earliest clear evidence for microblade technologies in western Beringia and Alaska has been dated to around 10,600 yr B.P., but recent discoveries at Swan Point might increase their antiquity by as much as 1,000 years. Microblade technologies persisted in central Alaska through middle Holocene time, probably reflecting environmental stability that contrasts markedly with the more extreme fluctuations of the latest Pleistocene.

The Mesa site and other hunting lookouts north of the Brooks Range were occupied by Paleoindians that probably spread northward into subarctic Canada and Alaska about 10,500 yr B.P. Fluted points throughout northern Alaska evidently also diffused northward, because they appear to be significantly younger than in temperate North America. In contrast, the probably contemporaneous Akmak tradition shows clear typological affinities with western Beringia.

Recent field studies and radiocarbon dating have shown that several "Pleistocene" archaeological sites or localities first reported from northern and central Alaska (e.g., Putu and Campus sites; Trail Creek Caves and Tangle Lakes) are significantly younger than previously claimed.

Ongoing excavations in southeastern Alaska have uncovered human skeletal remains dating to about 9800 yr B.P. and an isolated bone tool that may be about 500 years older. Maritime adaptations of early Holocene inhabitants of southeastern Alaska seem well established, but evidence for late Pleistocene arrival via a coastal route remains elusive.

1. U.S. Geological Survey, 4200 University Drive, Anchorage, AK 99508-4667.
2. Department of Anthropology, University of Nevada, Las Vegas, 4505 Maryland Parkway, Las Vegas NV 89154-5003

Introduction

DURING LATE PLEISTOCENE glacial maxima, about two-thirds of the present land area of Alaska remained free of glacier ice (Figure 1). Although some localities were covered by glacier-dammed lakes and active sand sheets or dunes, most unglaciated areas were vegetated and suitable for habitation (e.g., Anderson and Brubaker 1994; Hamilton et al. 1993; Péwé 1975). The position of Alaska at the eastern end of the Bering platform should cause it to be the initial point of arrival for people entering the Americas, and apparent human occupation of the northern Yukon spanning about 25,000 to 10,000 yr B.P. (Cinq-Mars and Morlan, this volume) would seem to support a time depth at least this great for habitation of Alaska as well.

In this paper, we review 22 Alaskan archaeological sites of known or alleged late Pleistocene age (Figure 1). Some of these sites are now known to be significantly younger than originally assumed; others are in shallow, frost-churned silt, where radiocarbon ages commonly are discordant and mixing of cultural remains is highly likely. Fortunately, several recently discovered sites are deeply buried in thick loess that contains undisturbed paleosol and cultural horizons. However, none of these sites have radiocarbon ages older than about 11,800 yr B.P. that are clearly associated with archaeological artifacts. The apparent absence of older sites in Alaska poses a troubling dilemma for advocates of a pre-Clovis peopling of the Americas.

The development of accelerator mass spectrometry (AMS) radiocarbon dating, which requires only very small quantities of organic material, has led to major recent breakthroughs in Alaskan Pleistocene archaeology. AMS dating has provided sets of concordant, replicable radiocarbon ages on recently excavated sites, and redating of older sites by the AMS method commonly has clarified their occupational histories. In this paper we report all radiocarbon ages, both conventional and AMS, as radiocarbon years rather than converting them to calendar years. Use of "radiocarbon years" allows direct comparisons with the site reports on which our review is based, as well as with other radiocarbon dates and date lists elsewhere in this volume.

This paper was written in 1989 and updated in 1995, but unfortunately has been still further delayed in publication. We have attempted to update all sections through 1997, but could not do as thorough a job of research as for the initial version and revision. We apologize to those workers whose recent sites or studies may have been neglected in this revision.

Nenana Valley Region: The Nenana and Denali Complexes

THE NENANA RIVER FLOWS north from the Alaska Range and crosses a 30-km-wide belt of foothills, whose parallel ridges bear vegetation transitional between the spruce-hardwood forest of the Tanana River valley and herbaceous tundra of the Alaska Range (Hoffecker 1988a). Along its course through the foothills, the Nenana River is bordered by spectacular flights of alluvial terraces—some constructed of outwash from late Pleistocene glaciers and others formed when streams downcut following glacial recession (Ritter 1982; Ritter and Ten Brink 1986). The oldest dated archaeological sites in the foothills sectors of the Nenana valley (Dry Creek, Walker Road, Moose Creek, and Panguingue Creek; Figure 2) and the neighboring Teklanika valley (Owl Ridge) occur in loess and eolian sand which cap alluvial terraces (Hoffecker et al. 1988). All five sites are situated on outer terrace margins adjacent to side-valley ravines (Powers and Hoffecker 1989). They are deeply stratified and contain apparently unmixed artifact assemblages assignable to two separate late Pleistocene complexes—Nenana and Denali (Powers and Hoffecker 1989). The Nenana complex, which occurs stratigraphically below the Denali, is one of the oldest well-documented cultural horizons in Alaska.

Dry Creek

THE DRY CREEK ARCHAEOLOGICAL site was discovered in 1973 by C. E. Holmes and was excavated during 1973–1977 by W. R. Powers. A 2-m section of loess and eolian sand (Figure 3a) overlies outwash gravel on a 25-m bluff along the north side of Dry Creek (Powers and Hamilton 1978; Thorson and Hamilton 1977). The outwash surface was weathered prior to loess deposition—clasts were abraded and polished by wind and fractured by frost action. Loess deposition began about 12,000 yr B.P., probably as strong katabatic winds from glaciers in the Alaska Range weakened following rapid recession of the glaciers (Thorson and Bender 1985).

Loess deposition at Dry Creek alternated with deposition of eolian sand and formation of thin soil horizons. The lowest sand unit may be a regional feature that formed during an interval of increased wind velocity (Bigelow et al. 1990). The overlying sand units probably formed by strong winds scouring the bluff face at times when Dry Creek was eroding laterally into the bluff, causing it to be unstable and unvegetated

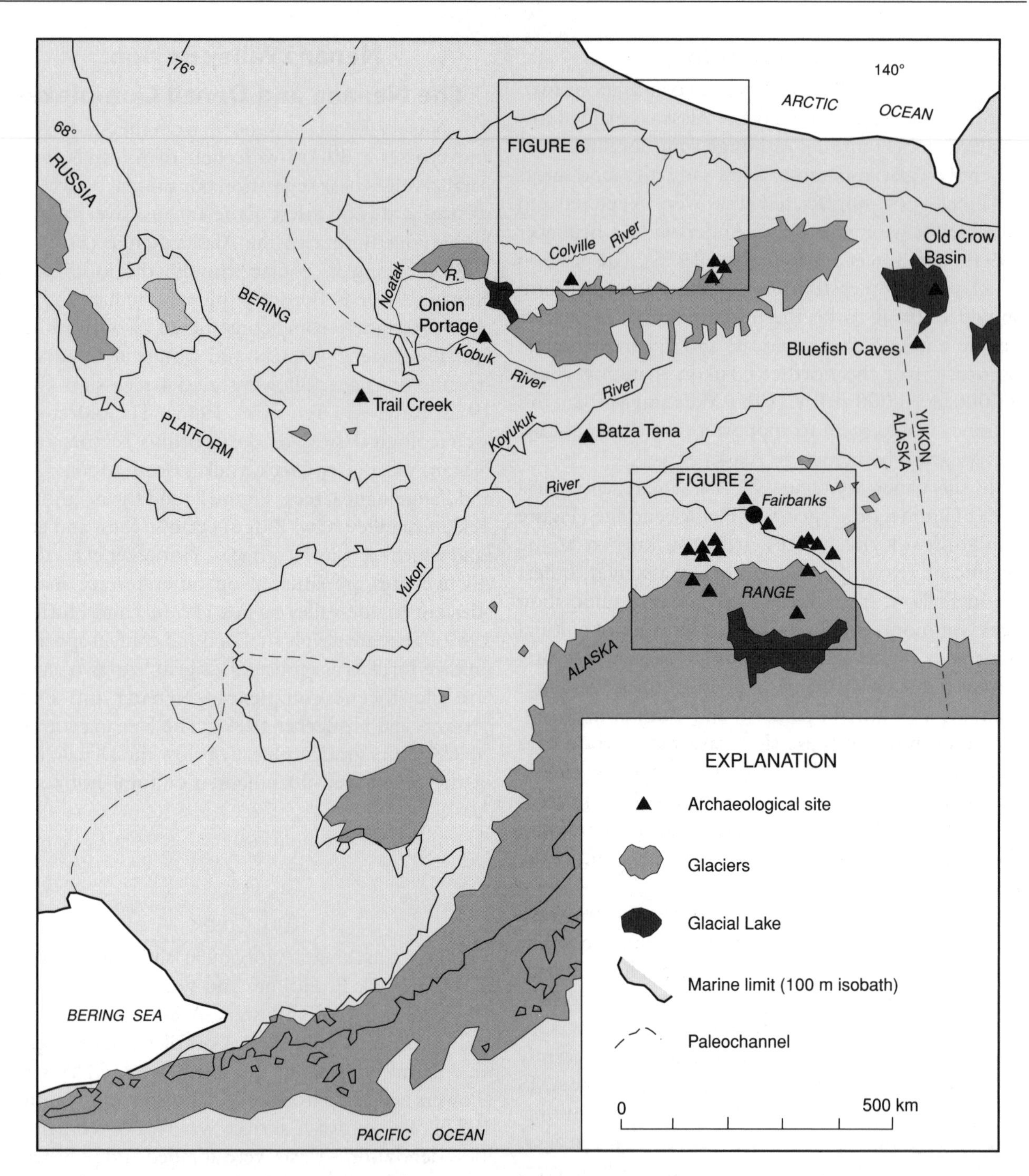

Figure 1. Eastern Beringia at height of late Wisconsin glaciation, showing marine and glacial limits, principal drainages, and archaeological sites reviewed in this paper (after Hamilton 1994, Mann and Hamilton 1995, Péwé 1975).

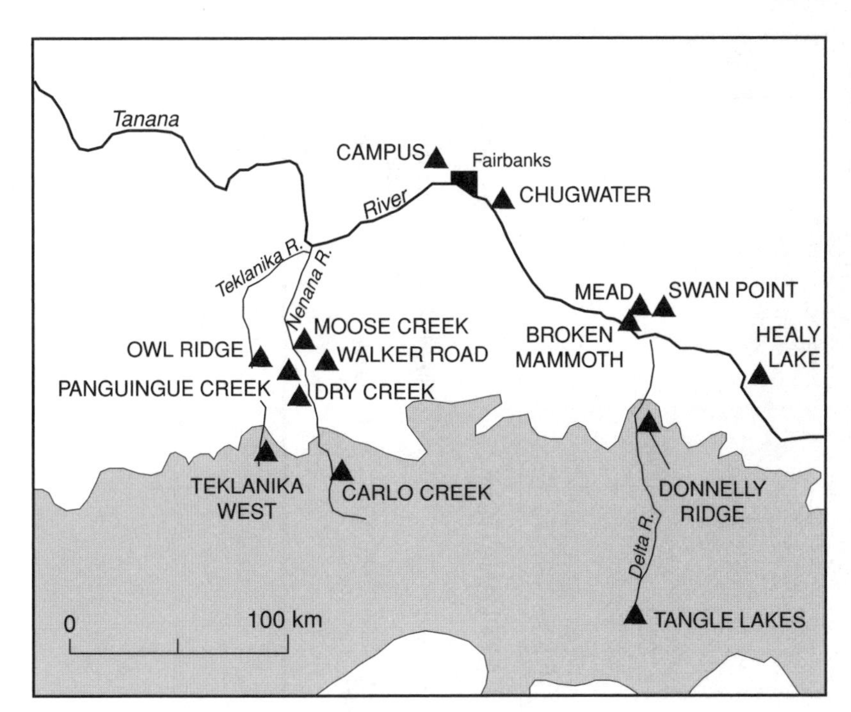

Figure 2. Detail map showing archaeological sites in central Alaska in relation to last major (late Wisconsin) glaciation of Alaska Range (shaded).

(Thorson and Hamilton 1977). The three oldest paleosols are immature tundra soils of a type that does not form in the Dry Creek area today; they typically consist of dark organic A horizons overlying mottled loess. The two uppermost soils are typical of the Subarctic Brown Forest soils that presently are forming in the boreal forest of interior Alaska. These are relatively thick and continuous, with prominent reddish-brown oxidized horizons. Twelve conventional radiocarbon dates on charcoal from the Dry Creek site are mutually concordant, but five other dates with large counting errors (450 years or more) are older than expected from their stratigraphic positions (Figure 3a and Appendix, A). These samples yielded very small amounts of datable carbon after pretreatment and possibly had proportionally large volumes of recycled ancient carbon from the Tertiary coal-and lignite-bearing formations of the Nenana valley (Thorson and Hamilton 1977). The basal loess unit has a preliminary thermoluminescence age between 11,000 and 13,000 years ago (Powers and Hoffecker 1989).

Six AMS radiocarbon ages recently were obtained from the lowest paleosol horizons at the Dry Creek site by N. H. Bigelow and W. R. Powers (1994). The age determinations were on plant remains or charcoal from natural wildfires that were recovered from the suites of thin organic horizons that comprise Paleosols 1 and 2 (Figure 3a). Three dates from the lowest set of recognizable buried soils (Paleosol 1) are about 8915, 10,060, and 10,615 yr B.P.; ages from Paleosol 2 are about 9340, 9690, and 10,540 yr B.P. The dates show troubling internal discordances within each paleosol set and virtually total overlap between the two paleosols. However, the AMS ages seem to confirm the original conventional radiocarbon age determinations of about 10,690 and 9340 yr B.P. for Paleosols 1 and 2, respectively (Thorson and Hamilton 1977), and they indicate that the two paleosols probably represent elements of a single soil complex (Bigelow and Powers 1994). The AMS ages also confirm that the original age assignment of about 10,700 to 9300 yr B.P. for the Denali complex at Dry Creek (Powers et al. 1983) probably is correct and that the site has intractable dating problems (Thorson and Hamilton 1977).

Archaeological component I at Dry Creek contains a poorly preserved fauna that is represented primarily by dentition of Dall sheep and wapiti. The associated lithic assemblage consists of 4,468 debitage pieces and 56 retouched pieces (i.e., tools) (Table 1). Primary reduction technology was directed toward the manufacture of blades and flakes from small cobbles of cryptocrystalline silicates and coarse-grained quartzites. A single bipolar core was found indicating the infrequent use of the block-on-block (bipolar) technique. Most tools were retouched unifacially (86 percent), but seven bifacially worked pieces and one burinated end scraper also occur. End scrapers, marginally retouched blades and flakes, cobble tools (choppers and quadrilateral plane), side scrapers, bifaces, projectile points, gravers, and notches make up the tool assemblage (Goebel et al. 1991). The

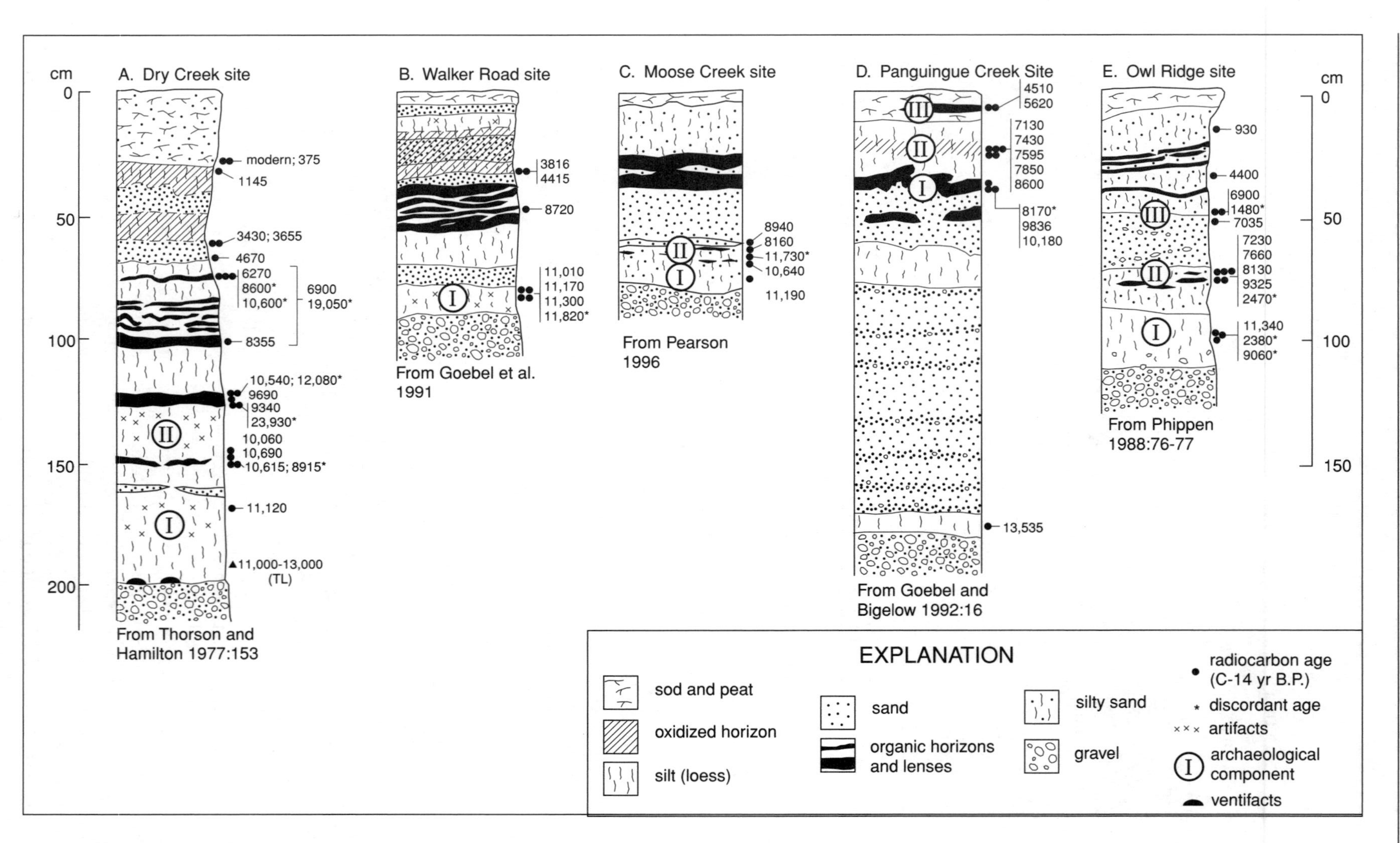

Figure 3. Stratigraphy and radiocarbon ages, late Pleistocene archaeological sites in the Nenana valley region. Weathered faces are not shown for Moose Creek and Panguingue Creek because they lack natural exposures. See Appendices A–E for additional data on radiocarbon ages.

Table 1. Artifacts reported from Alaskan archaeological sites discussed in this paper.

SITE / ARTIFACTS	NENANA VALLEY								TANANA VALLEY										AK RANGE		NORTHERN ALASKA				NW ALASKA			
	Dry Creek C-I	Dry Creek C-II	Walker Road	Moose Creek	Panguingue Creek-I	Panguingue Creek-II	Owl Ridge-I	Owl Ridge-II	Broken Mammoth-4	Broken Mammoth-3	Swan Point-7	Swan Point-6	Mead-4	Mead-3	Healy Lake-Chindadn	Chugwater-I	Chugwater-II	Campus	Tangle Lakes	Carlo Creek	Mesa	Putu	Hilltop	Gallagher-1	Onion Portage-Band 8	Onion Portage-Akmak	Batza Tena*	Trail Creek Caves
Blades and cores																												
Microblade cores																												
wedge-shaped	—	●	—	—	—	◍	—	—	—	—	—	—	—	—	○	—	—	●	●	—	—	—	—	◍	○	○	○	—
other	—	●	—	—	—	◍	—	—	—	—	—	—	—	—	—	—	—	●	●	—	—	—	—	◍	—	○	○	—
Core tablets	—	●	—	—	—	◍	—	—	—	—	+	—	—	—	—	—	—	◍	◍	—	—	—	—	◍	—	—	—	—
Microblades	—	●	—	—	—	●	—	—	—	—	+	+	—	—	◍	—	+	●	●	—	—	—	—	◍	●	○	—	+
Blade cores	○	○	○	—	+	◍	—	—	—	—	—	—	—	—	—	—	—	◍	◍	—	—	●	—	◍	○	◍	○	—
Blades or blade-like flakes	◍	◍	◍	—	+	◍	+	+	—	—	+	—	—	—	◍	—	—	◍	◍	○	—	●	—	●	○	●	◍	—
Tools on blades	◍	◍	●	—	—	◍	—	—	—	—	+	—	—	—	◍	—	+	◍	◍	—	○	◍	—	●	◍	◍	○	—
Burins and burin spalls	—	●	—	—	+	●	—	—	—	—	+	—	—	—	◍	—	—	◍	◍	—	—	●	—	—	○	●	—	—
Bifaces	○	●	○	○	+	◍	+		○[1]	◍	○[1]	+	+	—	◍	+	+	◍	◍	◍	●	●	+	—	—	●	●	—
Bifacial points																												
Chindadn	—	—	○	○	—	—	—	—	—	—	—	—	—	—	◍	+	—	—	—	—	—	—	—	—	—	—	—	—
Triangular	○	—	—	○	—	—	—	—	—	○	—	◍	—	—	◍	—	—	—	—	—	—	○	—	—	—	—	—	—
Lanceolate	◍	—	—	○	+	◍	—	—	—	—	—	—	—	—	○	—	—	◍	◍	—	●[2]	◍	+	—	—	—	○	—
Concave-based	—	—	—	—	—	—	—	—	—	○	—	+	—	—	—	—	—	—	—	—	—	—	—	—	—	—	○	—
Fluted	—	—	—	—	—	—	—	—	—	—	—	—	—	—	—	—	—	—	—	—	—	◍	—	—	—	—	●	—
Other	—	—	—	—	+	—	—	—	—	—	—	+	—	—	—	+	—	◍	—	—	—	—	—	—	—	—	●	—
Scrapers																												
End scrapers	●	○	●	—	—	◍	—	—	○	—	—	—	+	—	●	+	—	◍	○	—	○	○	—	—	—	○	●	—
Side scrapers	◍	●	●	○	+	◍	—	—	○	—	—	—	—	—	◍	+	+	◍	◍	—	—	○	—	—	○	○	—	—
Other Lithics																												
Drills or gravers	○	○	◍	—	—	—	—	—	—	—	—	+	—	—	○	—	+	○	—	—	●	◍	+	—	○	—	○	—
Hammerstones	—	○	○	—	—	○	+	—	—	—	+	—	—	—	—	—	—	○	—	—	◍	○	—	—	—	—	—	—
Grooved stones	—	—	—	—	—	—	—	—	—	—	—	—	—	—	—	—	—	—	—	—	—	—	—	—	—	○	—	—
Other cobble tools	◍	●	◍	—	—	○	+	+	○	—	+	+	—	—	—	—	—	—	—	—	○	—	—	—	○	—	○	—
Wedge-like tools	○	—	◍	—	—	—	—	—	—	—	—	—	—	—	○	—	—	—	—	—	—	—	—	—	—	—	—	—
Retouched flakes	◍	●	●	○	—	●	+	+	○	◍	+	+	—	—	◍	—	+	◍	◍	◍	●	●	—	◍	○	◍	●	—
Unaltered flakes	●	●	●	●	+	●	+	+	●	●	+	+	+	+	●	—	+	●	●	●	●	●	—	●	◍	◍	●	—
Bone/antler/ivory artifacts	—	—	—	—	—	—	—	—	◍	◍	+	—	+	—	—	—	—	—	—	—	—	—	—	—	—	—	—	+

● abundant ◍ common ○ rare — absent + present, from small sample *fluted point localities

[1] bifacial thinning flakes present, but bifaces absent
[2] lanceolate but with concave bases

complete and fragmented projectile points are small, straight-based, and triangular. This occupation, radiocarbon dated to about 11,100 yr B.P., appears to represent a temporary hunter–gatherer camp where lithic implements were manufactured and curated, and perhaps animal carcasses were butchered and processed (Hoffecker 1988b). It has been assigned to the Nenana complex (Powers and Hoffecker 1989).

Component II at Dry Creek contains teeth of Dall sheep and steppe bison (*Bison priscus*). The associated lithic assemblage (over 28,000 debitage and 330 retouched pieces) principally represents a microblade industry based on wedge-shaped cores (Table 1). Other primary reduction technologies include the simple preparation of blade and flake cores on small nodules of cryptocrystalline silicates, quartzites, and obsidian. Most retouched pieces are bifacially worked or burinated; however, unifacial retouching also is common. Tools include burins and burin spalls, bifaces, projectile points, marginally retouched flakes, microblades and blades, side scrapers, cobble tools (chopping tools, choppers, hammerstones, and a retoucher), gravers, notches, denticulates, and an end scraper. Projectile points typically are lanceolate or bipointed. During this time, the Dry Creek site appears to have been used repeatedly as a hunting camp where lithic implements were manufactured, utilized, and curated. Whether animal carcasses were butchered and processed here as well is difficult to tell, given the poor preservation of faunal remains (Hoffecker 1988b). This occupation is radiocarbon dated to 10,700–9300 yr B.P. and ascribed to the Denali complex.

Walker Road

THE WALKER ROAD SITE was discovered in 1980 by J. F. Hoffecker and excavated from 1985 to 1989 by W. R. Powers. Site stratigraphy consists of about 0.9 m of loess and eolian sand above fluvial gravel (Figure 3b). The basal 50 cm of eolian sediment shows little weathering, but its upper part contains a tundra-soil complex that records multiple episodes of soil formation about 8700 yr B.P. (Goebel et al. 1991). Overlying loess and eolian sand bear strongly oxidized soils that formed under boreal-forest vegetation. Deformed loess and paleosols indicate mass movement of the eolian mantle toward the face of the bluff (Bigelow 1991; Waythomas 1989). Two cultural components have been identified at the base and top of the loess mantle. Four radiocarbon dates on cultural charcoal from two hearths in component I (the lower component) average 11,330 ± 80 yr B.P. (Goebel et al. 1991). Three accelerator ages cluster between about 11,300 and 11,000 yr B.P., but a conventional radiocarbon age is slightly discordant at 11,820 ± 120 yr B.P. (Appendix, B). The discordant age could indicate contamination by recycled ancient carbon.

Two circular clusters of cultural debris, each roughly 5 m in diameter, contain hearths, abundant stone tools, and possible red ocher; these circular features may represent former dwellings (Goebel et al. 1996, Powers et al. 1990). The lithic assemblage includes 4,762 debitage and 209 retouched pieces (Table 1). Flakes and blades were detached from simply prepared cores of cryptocrystalline silicates, basalt, quartzite, and obsidian, as well as from eight chalcedony bipolar cores through the block-on-block technique. Most tools are retouched unifacially, although bifacial tools are present. The tool assemblage consists of marginally retouched flakes and blades, end scrapers, side scrapers, cobble tools, projectile points, bifaces, gravers, notches, denticulates, and a knife. This industry has been ascribed to the Nenana complex, due to its age and its technological and typological similarities with the Dry Creek component I assemblage (Goebel et al. 1991). The site appears to have functioned as a short-term camp where stone tools were manufactured, used, and recycled. The discrete clusters of artifacts and accompanying hearths suggest the site was occupied only once.

Moose Creek

THE MOOSE CREEK SITE was discovered in 1978 by J. F. Hoffecker and C. F. Waythomas, tested by Hoffecker in 1979 and 1984, and excavated by G. Pearson in 1996. This site is situated on a stream-cut remnant of an ancient glaciated surface 210 m above Moose Creek near its confluence with the Nenana River. It commands an excellent view south and west across the Nenana valley and probably was a lookout site (Hoffecker 1985). The stratigraphic section consists of 1.8 m of loess and sand above alluvial gravel (Figure 3c). The basal loess is a grayish-brown mottled silt that contains some pebbles that were elevated from the gravel surface by frost activity. The loess is capped by three or more buried organic soils, 1 to 3 cm thick, which formed as loess deposition waned. Four conventional radiocarbon dates on unidentifiable organic material from the buried soils range from about 11,700 to 8200 yr B.P. (Hoffecker 1985) and exhibit some stratigraphic inconsistencies (Figure 3c and Appendix, C). Pearson (personal communication 1996; Hall 1997) reports a new AMS date of 11,190 ± 60 yr B.P. (Beta-96627) on hearth charcoal found in the lowest buried soil. The basal loess is overlain by a thick layer of yellowish-brown fine to medium sand that contains a single discontinuous reddish-brown paleosol at about 70-cm depth. The upper loess, which also contains paleosols, coarsens upward into a silty sand, then fines to organic-rich silt that underlies the modern sod cap.

Artifacts from component I at Moose Creek are concentrated near the base of the lower silt (W. R. Powers, personal communication 1989), but most of the cultural remains cluster near the bluff edge, where the loess mantle thins to less than 1 m. More than 2,200 debitage pieces were recovered from Hoffecker's early excavations; however, the only retouched pieces are four biface fragments, two lanceolate point fragments, one side scraper, and several retouched flakes (Table 1). A possible microblade fragment also has been reported (Powers and Hoffecker 1989). Due to its stratigraphic position in the basal loess and the lack of microblades in the assemblage, Powers and Hoffecker (1989) initially assigned the assemblage to the Nenana complex. This assignment was later questioned (Hoffecker et al. 1993a, 1993b), because lanceolate points have not been found in other Nenana complex assemblages (Goebel et al. 1991; Hoffecker et al. 1993b).

Pearson's recent excavations have cleared up the earlier uncertainties of Moose Creek's early archaeological record. Two stratigraphically separate cultural components are clearly present in the basal loess (Pearson 1996). The lower component contained a hearth surrounded by lithic debitage and a small set of tools including a Chindadn point, sub-triangular point, and several side scrapers. Microblades were not found. Charcoal from the hearth was AMS dated to 11,200 yr B.P. The artifact assemblage, stratigraphic position, and age of this lowest component has led Pearson (1996; Hall 1997) to assign it to the Nenana complex. The second component found in the basal loess occurs 15 cm above the Nenana complex occupation. Lithic artifacts recovered in 1996 include a cluster of microblades and a transverse burin. Although undated, these materials are clearly assignable to the Denali complex (Pearson 1996). Two later components also were identified higher in the profile; these are thought to date to the middle and late Holocene. The new record for Moose Creek replicates the pattern seen at Dry Creek: clear stratigraphic separation between Nenana and Denali complex occupations, with the former dating to shortly before 11,000 yr B.P.

Panguingue Creek

The Panguingue Creek site was discovered by T. Smith and J. Hoffecker in 1976, tested in 1977 by T. Smith and in 1985 by H. E. Maxwell (Powers and Maxwell 1986), and extensively excavated in 1991 by W. R. Powers and T. Goebel (Goebel and Bigelow 1992). The site is located on the west side of the Nenana Valley, 5 km northwest of the Dry Creek site. It is situated on a south-facing promontory of the Healy terrace, 200 m above Panguingue Creek near its confluence with the Nenana River. The stratigraphic section consists of 1.8–2.0 m of sand and loess above alluvial gravel (Figure 3d). The base of the sand/loess mantle is a gleyed silt loam; a conventional radiocarbon date of about 13,500 yr B.P. was obtained on soil organics extracted from this unit (C. L. Ping, personal communication 1993). The basal loess is capped by a 1-m-thick bed of medium sand intercalated with 2-cm-thick bands of coarse sand, pebbles, and granules. Overlying this are alternating layers of silt loam and loam containing four separate paleosols. Paleosol 1 is a discontinuous set of organic stringers and has not been dated. Paleosol 2 is a nearly continuous but contorted organic horizon reaching 10 cm thick. Radiocarbon dates on natural wood charcoal from this paleosol range from about 10,200 to 8200 yr B.P. Paleosols 3 and 4 occur within the top 30 cm of the profile and have been radiocarbon dated to about 8000 and 5000 yr B.P., respectively (Figure 3d and Appendix, D).

Artifacts from Panguingue Creek occur in three cultural components, the two lowest of which are associated with the site's early Holocene paleosols. Component I, the lowermost component and associated with Paleosol 1, consists of about 60 debitage pieces, one subprismatic blade core, and six retouched pieces (Table 1). Tools include transverse scrapers on short, wide flakes, lanceolate bifacial points, and a *chi-tho* (boulder-spall scraper/knife). No faunal remains or features were recovered from this component. Component II, associated with Paleosol 2, is the site's major occupation. Two separate activity areas, each 8–10 m in diameter (one with a hearth feature of wood charcoal and calcined/burned bone), contain a lithic assemblage of more than 5,000 debitage pieces and 60 retouched pieces. Artifacts include more than 150 microblades, seven wedge-shaped and subconical microblade cores, lanceolate and ovate bifaces, side scrapers, end scrapers, cobble tools, and retouched flakes and microblades (Table 1). Goebel and Bigelow (1992) assign components I and II to the Denali complex.

Owl Ridge

The Owl Ridge site is situated on an 80-m terrace on the east side of the Teklanika River, about 28 km north of the Alaska Range (Phippen 1988). Nine concordant radiocarbon dates span the interval of about 11,340 to 930 yr B.P. (Figure 3e and Appendix, E); four other ages are too young for their stratigraphic position, perhaps because of contamination by roots or rootlets (Phippen 1988). Eolian silt and sand at Owl Ridge form a cap about 1.2 m thick above alluvial terrace gravel (Figure 3e). Loess that directly overlies the gravel has an accelerator age on charcoal of 11,300 yr B. P. and contains archaeological component I, which includes bifaces and biface fragments, utilized flakes, and blade-like flakes (Table 1). The loess is overlain by sand and silty sand that was largely redeposited from terrace alluvium by strong winds sweeping up the bluff face. Component II is present near the top of a subunit of the sand that accumulated slowly over the interval of about 9500 to 7000 yr B.P. It includes a possible tent ring composed of flat-based cobbles that rest on peat dated at about 9325 to 8130 yr B.P. (Phippen 1988) and a sparse assemblage of bifaces, flakes, and a medial blade fragment (Table 1).

Discussion

ALTHOUGH THE OLDEST documented human occupation of the Nenana River valley commonly has been assumed to date from about 11,700–11,800 yr B.P. (Powers and Hoffecker 1989), we believe that it is actually about 500 years younger. The oldest valid archaeological date at Dry Creek is about 11,100 yr B.P., and this age seems concordant with AMS radiocarbon determinations at slightly shallower levels. A conventional radiocarbon age of 11,800 yr B.P. near the base of the Walker Road site appears to be contradicted by three concordant AMS ages of about 11,000–11,300 yr B.P. at the same stratigraphic level. An age of about 11,300 yr B.P. also is associated with the oldest occupation of the Owl Ridge site. The new AMS age of 11,190 yr B.P. on hearth charcoal at the Moose Creek site finally provides clear evidence that the basal occupation there is contemporaneous with the basal occupations at Dry Creek, Walker Road, and Owl Ridge.

The basal archaeological industries at Dry Creek, Walker Road, Owl Ridge, and Moose Creek, consistently dated at about 11,300 to 11,000 yr B.P., have been assigned to the Nenana complex (Powers and Hoffecker 1989). This complex contains abundant bifacial implements, retouched flakes and blades, end scrapers, and side scrapers. Projectile points include small triangular-shaped forms and small teardrop-shaped "Chindadn" points like those that Cook (1969) described at Healy Lake. Microblades are absent, and burins are rare (Table 1). This assemblage, the Nenana complex of Powers and Hoffecker (1989), represents the earliest known occupation of the northern foothills of the Alaska Range. Clovis-like characteristics (i.e., blades, bifaces, scrapers, and gravers) described by Goebel et al. (1991) suggest that the Nenana complex could represent a regional manifestation of the Paleoindian tradition.

A younger set of industries is dated at about 10,700 to 9300 yr B.P. at Dry Creek; about 8500 to 7500 yr B.P. at Owl Ridge; and 10,000 to 9500 yr B.P. and 8600 to 7000 yr B.P. at Panguingue Creek. These industries are characterized by abundant wedge-shaped microblade cores, core tablets, microblades, and burins, and also by lanceolate bifacial points, bifaces, and boulder-chip scrapers (Table 1). Powers and Hoffecker (1989) assign all of these industries to the Denali complex, despite some temporal variability in microblade core preparation and bifacial point morphology. The Moose Creek site also contains a Denali complex microblade industry that is stratigraphically younger than the site's Nenana complex component, but radiocarbon ages for this industry have not yet been reported.

Despite intensive archaeological survey and testing, no sites unambiguously older than about 11,300 yr B.P. have been located in the Nenana Valley region. The northern foothills of the Alaska Range may have been a poor locality for human habitation prior to that time, owing to latest Pleistocene glacial readvances in nearby mountain valleys (Child 1995a, 1995b; Ten Brink and Waythomas 1985). Scouring by strong katabatic winds from the glaciers would have inhibited soils and vegetation (Thorson and Bender 1985). Loess later began to accrete as the glaciers receded; the foothills belt could then have become a refugium for large grazing mammals and their human predators during general deterioration of the late Wisconsin steppe-tundra biome (Ager 1975:85–86).

The Tanana Valley: Mammoth-Hunters or -Scavengers?

THE OLDEST KNOWN archaeological sites in the Tanana River Valley are the Broken Mammoth, Swan Point, and Mead sites, about 100 km upvalley (southeast) from Fairbanks, and the Village site at Healy Lake, which lies about 75 km farther upvalley (Figure 2). All four sites have generally similar histories of eolian sand and loess accumulation, and all have basal cultural components that date between about 11,600 and 10,000 yr B.P. Closer to Fairbanks, the Chugwater site, although in a shallower context, shows good correlations with lower cultural horizons at the other sites. One additional locality, the Campus site, was formerly assumed to be of late Pleistocene age. However, this site now appears to be a severely mixed assemblage that is no older than middle Holocene.

Broken Mammoth

THE BROKEN MAMMOTH SITE is situated on a prominent bluff on the north side of the Tanana River. The bluff overlooks a broad sector of the Tanana River valley as well as the lower part of the Shaw Creek Flats, an extensive marshland along the lower course of a major northern tributary of the Tanana. The site was discovered and tested in 1989 by C. E. Holmes and D. McAllister, and excavated during 1990–1993 by field crews directed by Holmes and D. R. Yesner (Holmes 1996; Yesner and Crossen 1994; Yesner et al. 1992b).

A blanket of eolian sand and silt about 2 m thick overlies frost-shattered and weathered bedrock that has wind-polished ventifacts dispersed across its surface (Figure 4a). Interbedded fine sand and silty sand at the base of the eolian section is overlain by a thick sheet of nonbedded silt (loess) that contains buried soils, cultural horizons, and faunal remains (Holmes 1996; Yesner 1994). Upper and lower units of loess are separated by a thin (1–5 cm) sheet of fine sand. The upper loess contains three cultural horizons that formed within the last 7700 years (Holmes 1996; Holmes and Yesner 1992a). The lower loess contains three paleosol complexes—closely spaced clusters of continuous to discontinuous, generally undulating, organic-rich layers. The upper paleosol complex lacks evidence for human occupation, but the lower two complexes contain charcoal, bone fragments, artifacts, and lithic debris indicative of substantial human usage. Each of the two lowest paleosols consists of two to three individual soils clustered together in complexes 3–10 cm thick (T. Dilley, cited in Holmes 1996). Six radiocarbon ages on the lower paleosol are about 11,280 to 11,770 yr B.P. (Appendix, F; Figure 4a), and show good internal concordance. Several hearths in the middle part of the lower paleosol evidently were used about 11,500 yr B.P., and the lower part of that paleosol was occupied about 11,800 yr B.P. Hearths in the middle paleosol are dated at about 10,300 yr B.P., but a radiocarbon age of about 9310 yr B.P. higher in the complex and the remains of red squirrel and porcupine suggest that development of this paleosol may have continued into earliest Holocene time. Two bones in the culturally sterile loess between the two paleosols have ages of about 11,000 and 11,100 yr B.P., providing further evidence that the stratigraphy at Broken Mammoth is undisturbed and that the sequence of radiocarbon age determinations is valid.

Cultural zone 4, the lowermost occupation, is associated with the lower paleosol complex. The lithic artifact assemblage has not yet been fully described, but consists of numerous debitage pieces and a few finished tools (Holmes 1996). Although bifaces have not been found, bifacial thinning flakes are present. Retouched pieces include marginally retouched flakes, scrapers, and a large quartz cobble tool (Table 1). In addition, two ivory points, a possible ivory handle, and several proboscidean (probably mammoth) tusk fragments with scratches produced by stone tools have been recovered (Holmes 1996). Associated faunal remains are predominantly birds, mostly swans (Yesner 1996). Other taxa include bison, elk, arctic fox, river otter, hare, marmot, ground squirrel, goose, duck, and ptarmigan; also scales of a salmonid, perhaps grayling, have been found (Holmes and Yesner 1992b; Yesner 1996). Many of these remains were associated with two large charcoal concentrations ("hearth smears").

Cultural zone 3, associated with the middle paleosol, contains a larger assemblage of diagnostic lithic artifacts (Table 1). Technological aspects of this assemblage have not been reported, but tools include retouched flakes, biface fragments, bifacial point fragments, hammerstones, and anvilstones (Holmes 1996). Three of the four bifacial point fragments have discernible shapes; two are concave-based and a third is triangular. The non-lithic artifact assemblage includes an eyed bone needle (Holmes 1996). Faunal remains are dominated by large ungulates, mostly bison and elk (Yesner 1996). Proboscidean ivory, and the remains of sheep, canid, river otter, porcupine, marmot, ground squirrel, red squirrel, swan, goose, duck, ptarmigan, and fish (perhaps arctic grayling) also are present (Holmes and Yesner 1992b; Yesner 1996). The remains of three different hearth features were identified in cultural zone 3.

Worked pieces of tusk are present in both of the late Pleistocene–early Holocene cultural layers, but a date of 15,830 ± 70 yr B.P. from one of the ivory points from cultural zone 4 indicates probable scavenging of old proboscidean tusks as raw materials for tool-making (Holmes 1996).

Swan Point

THE SWAN POINT SITE is situated near the north edge of Shaw Creek Flats about 7 km north-northeast of Broken Mammoth (Holmes et al. 1994). The site occupies a prominent rock-cored knoll that rises about 25 m above a broad complex of stabilized sand dunes, thaw ponds, and marshlands along the lower course of

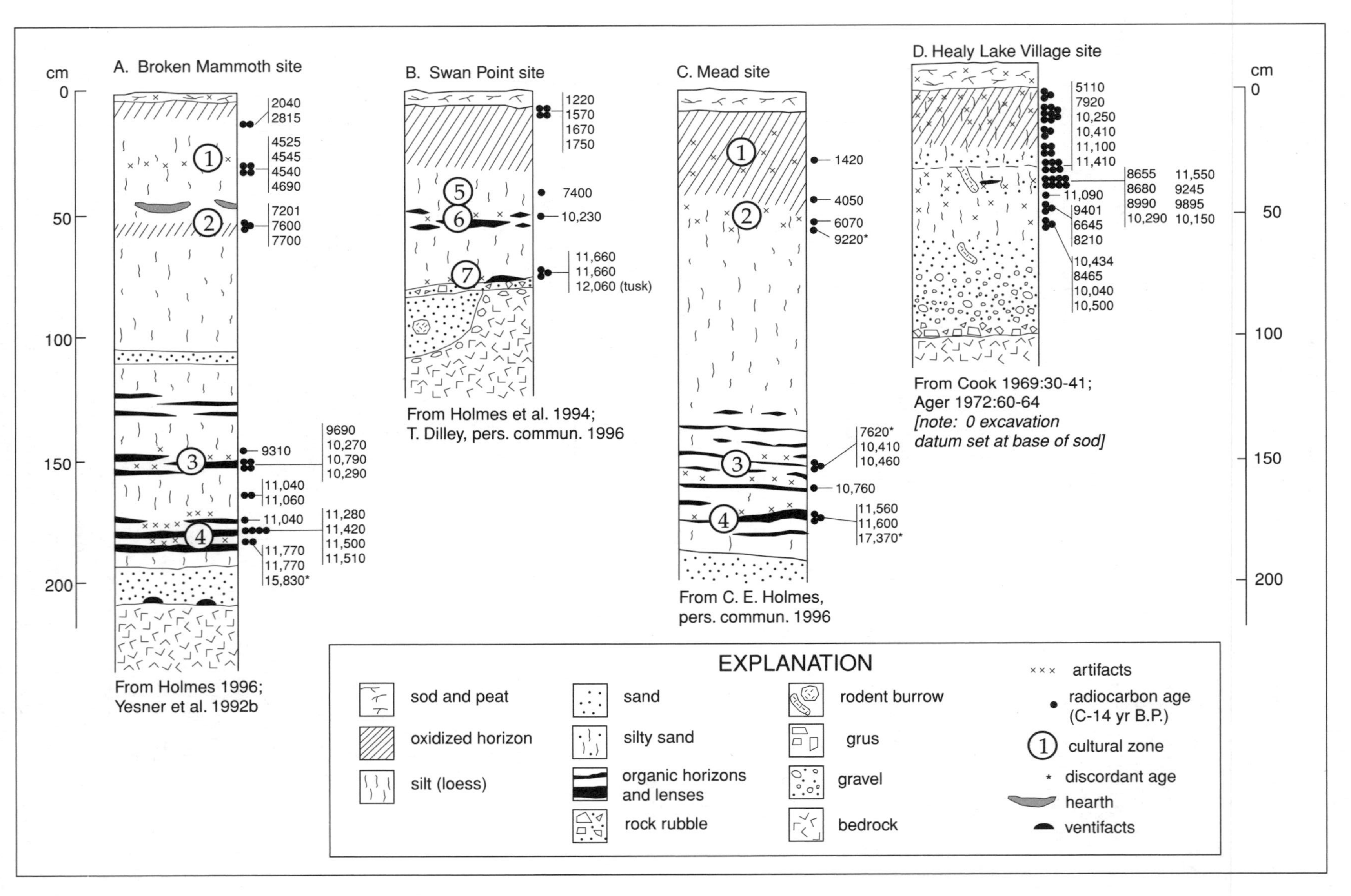

Figure 4. Stratigraphy and radiocarbon ages, late Pleistocene archaeological sites in the upper Tanana valley region. See Appendix (F–I) for additional data on radiocarbon ages.

Shaw Creek. The site was discovered by R. VanderHoek and T. Dilley in 1991, and excavated during 1992, 1993, and 1995. An area of less than 10 m^2 has been excavated to date (T. Dilley, personal communication 1995; Holmes et al. 1996).

Site stratigraphy (Figure 4b) generally is similar to that of Broken Mammoth, but the eolian sediment cover above bedrock is about half as thick because Swan Point is more distant from sources of windblown sediments along the Tanana River and its glacier-fed southern tributaries. Gneissic bedrock similar to that at Broken Mammoth bears scattered slightly ventifacted and wind-polished pebbles on its frost-battered surface (Holmes et al. 1994, 1996). Depressions on the irregular bedrock surface are filled with up to 40 cm of eolian sand that contains rodent burrows (Figure 4b). A layer about 3–5 cm thick of small, angular gneiss fragments in a matrix of sandy silt covers the slightly irregular surface of bedrock and sand. This rubble unit has sharp upper and lower contacts, and must have formed as colluvium transported by frost creep, sheetwash, or other slope processes from bedrock irregularities on the knoll (Holmes et al. 1994). The uppermost sediment is a massive, nonbedded loess that bears a modern forest soil at its surface and contains numerous buried cultural layers and paleosols (Holmes et al. 1994). The paleosols, like those at Broken Mammoth, are thin organic lenses and stringers that formed by a combination of natural soil processes and accumulation of anthropogenic detritus (Yesner 1994).

Within 35 cm of its surface, Swan Point contains four archaeological components of middle to late Holocene age (Holmes et al. 1994). Two lower cultural components, dating to latest Pleistocene time, formed at approximately the same times as the lower two components at Broken Mammoth. The basal component occurs on and within the colluvial layer at the base of the loess (Holmes et al. 1994, 1996; T. Dilley, personal communication 1996). Virtually identical radiocarbon ages of about 11,600 yr B.P. were obtained on two charcoal fragments from this layer, and a slightly older date of 12,060 yr B.P. was obtained on proboscidean ivory (Appendix, G). The overlying component, associated with discontinuous hearth-like (lenticular) charcoal smears at a depth of about 55 cm (T. Dilley, personal communication 1996), has a single radiocarbon age of about 10,230 yr B.P. (Holmes et al. 1994).

Faunal remains from Swan Point are not as well-preserved as at the nearby Broken Mammoth site, but the lowest cultural component has yielded remains of goose and large cervid, as well as chopped, battered, and splintered ivory tusk fragments, one of which is more than 50 cm long (Holmes and VanderHoek 1994; C. E. Holmes, personal communication 1996). Lithic artifacts from the lowest Swan Point component include a small assemblage of microblades, blades, microblade core preparation flakes, dihedral burins, hammerstones, and split quartz cobble tools called choppers or planes (Holmes and VanderHoek 1994; Holmes et al. 1996; Table 1). One microblade was found directly underneath the large section of mammoth tusk dated to about 12,000 yr B.P. (Hall 1995; Holmes et al. 1994).

The overlying cultural component at Swan Point is radiocarbon dated to about 10,200 yr B.P. This component includes a lithic assemblage of small bifacial points with convex, straight, and concave bases, spurred gravers made on broken bifacial points, and quartz cobble choppers or hammerstones (Holmes and VanderHoek 1994; Table 1). Faunal remains are present but for the most part unidentifiable (C. E. Holmes, personal communication 1996).

The Mead Site

THE MEAD SITE is located about 1 km north of Broken Mammoth on the bluffs overlooking the west side of Shaw Creek Flats. The site initially was a borrow-pit exposure about 50 m long that had been mapped by T. L. Péwé in 1964 (Péwé 1965:48–49; Péwé and Reger 1983:33–39). That section exhibits fractured bedrock and solifluction debris overlain by cross-bedded sand that is capped by about 2 m of loess. A stratigraphic profile of the exposure shows a proboscidean tusk fragment at the contact between the sand and the overlying loess mantle (Péwé and Reger 1983:38).

Archaeological testing at the Mead site during the early 1990s (C. E. Holmes, personal communication 1996) exposed an undisturbed stratigraphic profile analogous to that from Broken Mammoth. Two stratigraphically separate paleosols—organic horizons similar to those at Broken Mammoth and Swan Point—occur in the basal 0.5 m of the loess (Figure 4c). The lowest paleosol is dated to about 11,600 yr B.P. by two concordant AMS radiocarbon ages (Appendix, H). Archaeological materials from this paleosol include a small point presumably made from the tip fragment of a proboscidean tusk (Yesner et al. 1992a), stone flakes, and fragments of a biface and scraper (Holmes, personal communication 1996; Table 1). Other presumably scavenged fragments of ivory also occur at this level, one of them dating about 17,370 yr B.P. The overlying paleosol, a complex of mostly discontinuous organic layers and lenses, has two concordant AMS radiocarbon ages of about 10,400 yr B.P. near its center and a conventional radiocarbon age of about 10,760 yr B.P. near its base (Figure 4c and Appendix, H). Younger cultural components, dating within the last 6,100 years, are found within and near the base of a forest-soil profile near the top of the section.

Two conventional radiocarbon ages on the Mead site are discordant and appear to be spurious (C. E. Holmes, personal communication 1996). Dispersed charcoal fragments collected from the initial test pit at the site had an age of about 7600 yr B.P., and a very small charcoal sample near the base of the upper forest soil dates about 9200 yr B.P. with a very large counting error.

The Healy Lake Village Site

HEALY LAKE WAS FORMED when the lower course of the Healy River, a tributary of the Tanana River, was dammed by alluviation of the Tanana (Ager 1972). The age of this event is uncertain, but an ancestral lake may have existed during late Wisconsin time, owing to alluviation of the Tanana River by outwash from the Alaska Range. Although the lake occupies a forested lowland, alpine tundra occurs in uplands only 10 km to the northeast. The Village site is located at an abandoned Athabaskan village situated on the tip of a bedrock ridge spur that projects into the lake near its outlet (Cook 1969, 1989). The site was tested in 1966 by J. P. Cook, R. A. McKennan, and others, and was excavated by Cook during 1968–1972 (Cook 1996).

Shallow unconsolidated deposits above bedrock at the Village site are only 0.5 to 1 m thick, but they commonly are divisible into four units (Figure 4d) (Ager 1972:60–64). The basal unit consists of 20 cm or more of angular rock particles (grus) that formed from the weathering of underlying bedrock. Many of the rock fragments at the upper contact of this unit have been polished and abraded by wind to form ventifacts. The grus is overlain by a discontinuous probable beach deposit of pebbly sand as much as 15 cm thick that contains unidentifiable bone fragments. The two gravelly units are buried by eolian fine sand that fines upward into sandy loess and then into silty loess, forming an unstratified deposit as much as 75 cm thick that contains soil horizons, frost cracks, animal burrows, and clay bands. The basal sandy part of the eolian unit is culturally sterile, but it contains filled burrows that do not occur higher in the eolian unit. The upper 60 cm of the deposit contains charcoal, thin organic horizons, and artifacts. A buried podzolic soil is widely present at the site. The B horizon of this paleosol, a zone of oxide and clay accumulation 15–20 cm thick, extends downward from a thin leached horizon 25–30 cm below the top of the loess (J. P. Cook, personal communication 1996). The organic mat that caps the section averages 10 cm thick and consists of plant fragments, roots, and recent Athabaskan cultural debris. Because of the generally nonstratified nature of the loess, the Village site was excavated in 5-cm levels beginning at the base of the surface sod.

Thirty-two radiocarbon ages initially were obtained at the Village site (Erlandson et al. 1991), and 12 AMS ages have subsequently been added to the radiocarbon record (J. P. Cook, personal communication 1996; see Appendix, I). Most of the dates were on charcoal, which generally was collected from hearths or hearth-like accumulations. The conventional radiocarbon ages showed a general increase with depth, but indicated severe mixing at all levels (Figure 4d). The AMS ages also show significant mixing, but are more clearly separated into different age populations above and below the top of the buried podzol. If the AMS ages are correct, they indicate that the loess cover at Healy Lake began to accumulate shortly before 11,500 yr B.P., and that windblown silt continued to accrete until 10,000 or 9000 yr B.P. A subsequent hiatus, marked by the buried podzolic soil, lasted until 4500 to 3500 yr B.P., when renewed loess accretion must have accompanied intensified glaciation (Neoglaciation) in the Alaska Range (Calkin 1988). Healy Lake may have been reborn at this time, as suggested by Ager (1972:83–89), because of renewed alluviation by the glacier-fed Tanana River.

The Healy Lake Village site contains three recognized cultural components, the earliest of which includes artifacts recovered from excavation levels greater than 25 cm below the organic mat (Cook 1969). This early component subsequently was termed the "Chindadn complex" (Cook 1975, 1996; Cook and McKennan 1970; Dixon 1985; Morlan and Cinq-Mars 1982). In 1990 Goebel conducted an analysis of the retouched pieces and a sample of the debitage. In the sample studied, he found that more than a third of the tools are made on blades, although there are no blade cores in the assemblage. A simply prepared flake core, wedge-shaped microblade core, and several bipolar cores (*pièces ésquillées*), however, do occur. Microblades are common throughout the Chindadn levels. Secondary reduction techniques are unifacial, bifacial, and burin. The tool assemblage (n=165) also consists of marginally retouched blades and flakes, end scrapers, side scrapers, bifaces, bifacial points, burins (angle, dihedral, and transverse), gravers, and a notched tool (Table 1). Most bifaces are broken, but complete ones are oval, lanceolate, and triangular in shape. Projectile points are for the most part tear-drop shaped or triangular, but several lanceolate points also occur.

Hearth-like concentrations of fire-reddened earth, with charcoal and calcined bone, are common in the Chindadn levels (Cook 1969:240–242; personal communication 1996), as are flake clusters and concentrations of firecracked rock. The hearth-like features are about 1 m in diameter by 10 cm deep; their boundaries are diffuse but not contorted or intermixed with adjoining sediments (J. P. Cook, personal communication 1996). Most of the bones are of small mammals and birds, presumably waterfowl taken along the shore of ancestral Healy Lake. Some ruminant (caribou or sheep) remains also are present (J. P. Cook, personal communication 1996).

The radiocarbon-dated time span of the Chindadn complex at Healy Lake is equivalent to the range of Nenana and Denali complex occupations identified elsewhere in central Alaska. The Chindadn assemblage also shows many affinities with both of these complexes. The association of Chindadn points and small triangular points with microblades and burins, which does not occur in the more deeply stratified sites in the Nenana Valley, suggests that some postdepositional mixing of artifacts may have occurred at the Village site. More detailed studies of the Chindadn artifacts and their recorded proveniences, as well as renewed test excavations, are needed to clarify this issue.

The Chugwater Site

The Chugwater site is situated along the crest of Moose Creek bluff, an isolated bedrock ridge that rises 67 m above the Tanana River floodplain, 35 km east-southeast of Fairbanks. The south-facing edge of the bluff overlooks the Tanana River valley and the floodplain of Moose Creek, a clearwater stream that flows into the silt-laden Tanana. Artifacts are present in thin (15–40 cm) loess that overlies weathered bedrock and discontinuous bodies of eolian sand and colluvium. The loess locally contains a convoluted, dark "marker line" that is enriched in oxides of iron, manganese, magnesium, and aluminum that may have been deposited from percolating soil water at a former frost table or water table (Lively 1988). Twenty radiocarbon dates from the site range from modern to 9460 ± 130 yr B.P., but only four dates are older than about 2500 yr B.P. (Appendix, J). The dates show poor correlation with depth below surface. Some samples may be from burned roots, which commonly can be traced downward from the surface to weathered bedrock that underlies the site. Two charcoal samples 3 cm below the "marker line" have AMS radiocarbon ages of about 8960 and 9460 yr B.P. Artifacts of component I, which underlie the oldest dated charcoal, include small teardrop-shaped and triangular points and end scrapers (Table 1) that are correlated with artifacts of the Chindadn complex at Healy Lake and the Nenana complex in the Nenana valley. Component II artifacts, which are associated with the dated (8960 to 9460 yr B.P.) horizon, include microblades, bifacial points or knives, and crested scrapers (Table 1) that are correlated with the Denali complex.

The Campus Site

Located on the University of Alaska campus near Fairbanks, the Campus site occupies the edge of a southeast-facing bluff that rises 20 m above the broad floor of the Tanana River valley. The site was discovered in 1933 and excavated intermittently from 1934 until 1971 (Mobley 1990), with further excavation in 1996 by Pearson and Powers (1996). For several decades after its discovery, the Campus site was believed to be the oldest known archaeological site in Alaska.

Artifacts are present within thin (45 cm or less) loess and colluvium that overlies bedrock and is capped by Subarctic Brown Forest soil. Bandi (1969:52) estimated an age of 8400 yr B.P. based on obsidian hydration measurements, but more recent age estimates utilizing this technique are between 4500 and 1000 yr B.P. (Mobley 1990). Three radiocarbon dates on charcoal from 15- to 30-cm depth cluster between 3500 and 2700 yr B.P., but two other dates on charcoal from 20- to 30-cm depth are modern (Appendix, K). These dates show that recent disturbance has penetrated 25 cm or more into at least the central part of the site (Mobley 1990) and that none of the occupation is demonstrably older than about 3500 yr B.P. Pearson and Powers' (1996) work corroborates Mobley's conclusion that the Campus site dates to the late Holocene.

Artifacts from the Campus site have been dispersed internationally into at least four (and possibly six) museum collections, but a nearly complete inventory has been compiled by Mobley (1990). Tool types include microblades and microblade cores, large blades, burins, lanceolate and side-notched projectile points, and oval and triangular bifaces (Table 1).

Discussion

THE BROKEN MAMMOTH and Swan Point sites have provided the earliest direct evidence for late Pleistocene human subsistence activities in Alaska. Rather than an exclusively big-game hunting culture, the emerging record points to a subsistence strategy directed toward a wide range of resources including small mammals, waterfowl, ptarmigan, and fish, in addition to large mammals such as bison and elk. The site occupants also were procuring fur-bearing mammals such as arctic fox and river otter, and were collecting fossil ivory from nearby exposures.

Microblades are absent from the lithic assemblages of cultural zones 4 and 3 at Broken Mammoth, perhaps strengthening the case that a Nenana–Chindadn-like industry characterized by small bifacial points, unifacial scrapers, and cobble tools existed in central Alaska prior to 11,000 yr B.P. Although diagnostic artifacts are uncommon in the earliest cultural zone, a bifacial industry is present, as are a few unifacially worked scrapers. The concave-based points from cultural zone 3, though, are distinct, and may represent a previously unrecognized bifacial point complex dating to around 10,300 yr B.P.

However, at Swan Point the microblade assemblage in the cultural layer dated about 11,600 yr B.P. is inconsistent with cultural inventories from all other deeply buried sites of this age in the Nenana and Tanana valleys. It also would predate all known microblade industries in western Beringia (east of the Verkhoiansk Range). Perhaps the microblades and related flakes were mixed with older charcoal and other cultural materials during and immediately after deposition of the thin sheet of colluvial detritus and before loess accumulation began at the site. Although a tusk fragment was found directly above a microblade, clear evidence for scavenging of old ivory at the Broken Mammoth and Mead sites demonstrates that this association cannot provide any direct age or age limit on the microblades at Swan Point. On the other hand, the 20–25 cm of loess that separates the two lowest cultural horizons at Swan Point lacks any evidence of cryoturbation, animal burrowing, or other disturbance (Holmes et al. 1994). Soil chemistry shows no evidence for mixing, and artifacts have not been mixed into this "sterile" zone from either of the cultural horizons that bound it (T. Dilley, personal communication 1996). Based on rates of regional loess accumulation, T. Dilley (personal communication 1996) believes that the sterile loess beneath the 10,200-year-old hearth may have required 1,000–1,500 years to accumulate. If this estimate proves to be correct, microblade industries in Alaska would be significantly older than presently believed.

The Alaska Range: Denali Complex Sites

FOUR LOCALITIES WITHIN and at the flanks of the Alaska Range have yielded artifacts assignable to the Denali complex. The Tangle Lakes, Donnelly Ridge, and Teklanika West localities are near-surface or surface sites; Carlo Creek is a deeply buried site. All four localities occur within the limits of late Wisconsin glaciers (Figure 2), and human occupation was dominantly of Holocene age.

We shall discuss the geologic setting and geochronology of the Tangle Lakes area in some detail because of the great antiquity formerly claimed for some of its archaeological assemblages. The three other localities are summarized only briefly and representative stratigraphic sections are not illustrated.

The Tangle Lakes

NUMEROUS ARCHAEOLOGICAL sites with Denali complex artifacts occur at the Tangle Lakes, where irregular knobs and ridges of sand and gravel interspersed with kettle lakes mark the position of stagnating glacier ice during late Wisconsin deglaciation at the south flank of the Alaska Range (Figure 2). The glacial deposits probably were exposed and became stabilized sometime after 13,500 yr B.P., when rapid glacier recession began in the central Alaska Range (Ten Brink and Waythomas 1985). A high-level phase of the lake complex, 30 m

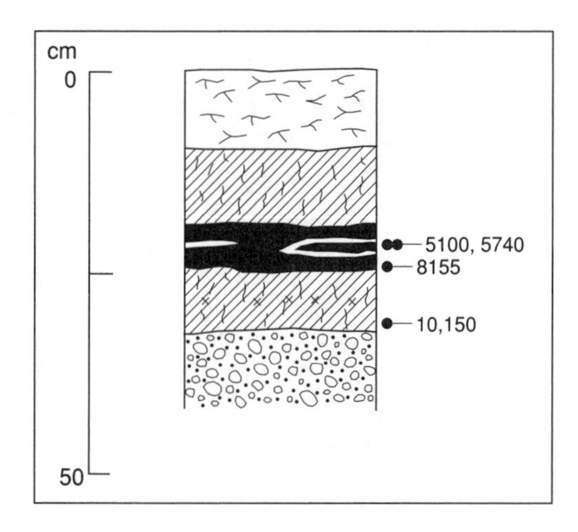

Figure 5. Stratigraphy and radiocarbon ages for the Mt. Hayes-111 site, Tangle Lakes (symbols as in Figure 4). See Appendix (L) for additional data on radiocarbon ages.

above the surface of the present-day lakes, developed about 11,800 yr B.P. (Schweger 1981) and persisted until at least 7700 yr B.P. (Campbell and Begét 1989). Tundra vegetation covered the area until about 11,000 yr B.P., then was replaced by shrub tundra with abundant dwarf willow and birch. *Populus* arrived at the Tangle Lakes about 9500 yr B.P. and *Picea* about 9100 yr B.P. (Ager and Sims 1981; Schweger 1981).

All of the known Denali complex sites occur on the well-drained crests of knobs and ridges just above the limits of the +30-m stand of the ancestral Tangle Lakes; none occur below that former surface (West 1981:113–135). Initial site discovery was in 1957; additional sites were discovered and excavated by F. H. West between 1964 and 1974 (West et al. 1996a, 1996b, 1996c). Subsequent surveys have shown that at least 20 sites containing Denali complex artifacts occur in the Tangle Lakes area (P. M. Bowers, personal communication 1989). Lithic assemblages include wedge-shaped and conical microcores, subprismatic blade cores, microblades and large blades, burins, bifaces, and boulder-chip scrapers (Table 1). Two sites in particular, Phipps and Whitmore Ridge, contain Denali complex occupations that may date to about 10,000 yr B.P. (West et al. 1996a, 1996c). An assemblage with large and roughly formed bifaces was termed the Amphitheater Mountain complex by West (1976), who believed that it predated the Denali complex. However, recent studies by Mobley (1982) have shown that similar generalized tools and debris are characteristic of quarry and workshop sites as young as middle Holocene age (4300 yr B.P.) in the Tangle Lakes area.

Denali complex sites at the Tangle Lakes range from surface scatters to shallow loess above glacial gravel (West et al. 1996a, 1996b, 1996c). In the comparatively scarce buried sites, Denali complex artifacts occur near the base of a paleosol that was buried by renewed loess deposition between about 7000 and 5000 yr B.P. (Figure 5), presumably when the +30-m lake drained abruptly and silt was redeposited from newly exposed lake beds (West 1975, 1981:133–135). On the basis of a limited number of radiocarbon ages (Appendix, L), the Denali complex occupation of the area is dated from 10,200 to at least 9100 yr B.P. by West (1981:129), between 10,500 and 8200 yr B.P. by Schweger (1981), and between 10,200 and 8200 yr B.P. by Dixon (1985).

Other Sites

WITHIN THE ALASKA RANGE, the Denali complex probably is represented at the Carlo Creek site, and possibly at the Donnelly Ridge and Teklanika West sites as well (Figure 2). The deeply buried Carlo Creek site, located close to a perennial spring near the head of the Nenana River, contained well-preserved remains of butchered caribou, sheep, and ground squirrels (Bowers 1980). The site was first occupied about 8700 to 8400 yr B.P. if two discordant radiocarbon ages (Appendix, M) can safely be ignored.[1] The oldest component contains a sparse assemblage of bifaces and biface fragments, retouched flakes, and possible bone tools (Table 1).

The Donnelly Ridge site occurs on end moraines of late Wisconsin age at the north flank of the Alaska Range, about 140 km southeast of Fairbanks (West 1967). The area today is situated at the ecotone where boreal forest interfingers with alpine tundra. Some artifacts were found scattered across the surfaces of blowouts; others were buried in thin (<25 cm) loess that overlies the glacial deposits. According to West (1967), the archaeological assemblage is dominated by bifacial knives, wedge-shaped microblade cores, both large blades and microblades, and burins. The site lacks stratigraphy, and no hearths were found. Two radiocarbon ages of about 1800 yr B.P. are interpreted by the site's excavator to date a later tundra fire and not the cultural materials (West 1967). However, some wedge-shaped core and microblade assemblages elsewhere in central Alaska have been radiocarbon dated to the late Holocene (i.e., the "late Denali complex" represented at Little Panguingue Creek in the Nenana Valley and the Campus site near Fairbanks) (Mobley 1990; Powers and Hoffecker 1989).

Therefore, a late Holocene age for the Donnelly Ridge site should not be ruled out.

The Teklanika West site was originally described as shallow and nonstratified (West 1967), and later described as stratified and containing two cultural components (West 1996). The site lacks any hearths or other archaeological features. More recent geoarchaeological research at Teklanika West has indicated that up to three cultural components can be delineated in a stratigraphic profile reaching 1 m in thickness (Goebel 1996). Component I occurs at the base of the section in a loess-like sediment that also contains a discontinuous, reworked paleosol. An associated charcoal fragment produced an AMS date of 7100 yr B.P. (Appendix, N). Component II materials were found immediately underneath an unidentified tephra band; two charcoal samples associated with lithic artifacts yielded radiocarbon ages of 5300 and 3300 yr B.P. Component III occurs at the very top of the profile in the modern soil and has not been dated. In all likelihood, then, the Teklanika West assemblage of West (1967, 1996) is made up of artifacts from three different-aged occupations spanning a period of more than 5,000 years.

Discussion

The known archaeological sites from the Alaska Range record later human occupation than in the foothills region of the Nenana Valley or in the Tanana River valley. The oldest known sites, Tangle Lakes and Carlo Creek, contain Denali complex industries and fit within the age range for Denali within the Nenana and Tanana valleys. Although the Teklanika West and Donnelly Ridge sites are probably of middle to late Holocene age, they contain Denali elements such as wedge-shaped cores, transverse burins, and lanceolate bifaces. The apparent persistence of these elements suggests continuity in the prehistoric populations of central Alaska from the earliest Holocene until about 2000 yr B.P.

Northern Alaska: Paleoindians of the Arctic Foothills

The Arctic Foothills comprise an east-west-trending belt of rock-cored ridges along the north flank of the Brooks Range (Wahrhaftig 1965:20). The region is underlain by continuous permafrost (Ferrians 1965); it supports treeless tundra, with riparian willow shrubs along the larger drainages. Four radiocarbon-dated archaeological sites in this region have yielded ages of about 11,700 to 9000 yr B.P. (Figure 1). Three of the sites—Mesa, Putu–Bedwell, and Hilltop—contain lanceolate points and other diagnostic Paleoindian artifacts. The remaining site, Gallagher Flint Station, is a quarry and lookout site with multiple occupations of late Holocene age that may have largely obliterated older archaeological records.

The Mesa Site

The Mesa site, on a prominent ridge of resistant igneous rock that rises 60 m above Iteriak Creek (Figure 6), offers a commanding view of Iteriak valley and adjoining hills. Surface and near-surface artifacts and shallow hearths along the ridge crest were discovered during an archaeological survey in 1978 (Kunz 1982); the site was tested in 1979 and 1980, and excavated during 1989 and 1991–1997 (Kunz and Mann 1997; Kunz and Reanier 1994, 1995).

More than 20 buried hearths with artifact concentrations were found at and near the base of a thin (30 cm or less) layer of frost-mixed stony silt that overlies frost-shattered bedrock (Figure 7a). The charcoal-rich hearths generally are lenticular in cross-section, and up to 12 cm thick and 20 cm in diameter; they are surrounded by halos 7–15 cm wide of oxidized reddish soil with charcoal flecks (Kunz and Reanier 1995). Artifacts include edge-ground lanceolate projectile points, large bifaces, gravers, and scrapers that resemble Paleoindian implements from midcontinental North America (Table 1). They are reported to be "Technologically … closely related to the Agate Basin Complex of the North American High Plains" (Kunz and Reanier 1995:22). The site is considered to be essentially a single-component Paleoindian occupation, with additional use evident only as a single small microblade locality.

Twenty-seven radiocarbon ages have been determined from charcoal that is associated directly with 19 individual hearths (Appendix, O). All but two of the ages are AMS radiocarbon determinations with

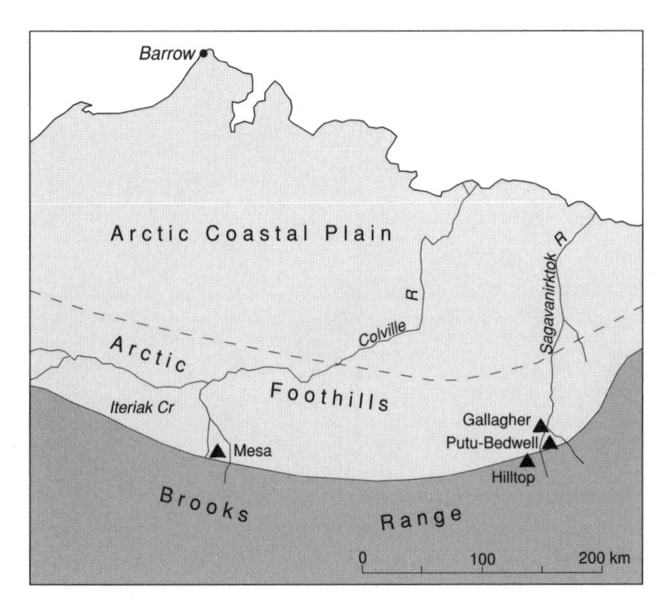

Figure 6. Detail map showing archaeological sites in the arctic foothills of northern Alaska.

closely constrained counting errors; the others are conventional radiocarbon ages. One of the conventional ages, 7620 ± 95 yr B.P., is dismissed by the excavators as "incorrect due to laboratory error" (Kunz and Reanier 1995:17). An archived duplicate sample was redated as 10,060 ± 70 yr B.P. (Kunz and Reanier 1995). The other conventional age, 10,980 ± 280 yr B.P., is from a very small sample that could be dated only with difficulty by using an extended count (M. Kunz, personal communication 1995). It was split from a sample from which an AMS date of 9945 ± 75 yr B.P. was obtained, and the AMS age is considered by Kunz to be the more reliable of the pair. Eighteen of the AMS ages cluster tightly within a 300-year interval, 10,200–9900 yr B.P. (Figure 8). Five others are slightly younger and older, but four of these are statistically indistinguishable from the 10,200-9900 yr B.P. age group. The remaining two AMS ages, 11,190 ± 70 and 11,660 ± 80 yr B.P., are separated from the younger cluster by surprisingly large time gaps of nearly 1,200 and 1,700 years. Both of these older ages are on charcoal from a single hearth in the central part of the site that is identical to all of the others in depth, size, configuration, and associated artifact types. Implements and waste flakes are much more abundant around this hearth than they are around the others (Kunz and Reanier 1995). Kunz and Reanier (1994) believe that Paleoindian occupation of the Mesa site occurred in two separate episodes, with an intervening hiatus between 11,000 and 10,300 yr B.P. that corresponds to climatic deterioration of the Younger Dryas interval.

Putu–Bedwell

The Putu site is located along the east flank of the Sagavanirktok River valley near the north flank of the Brooks Range (Figure 6). It is situated on a level bench about 215 m above the valley floor near the base of a prominent rock knob that provides an unrestricted view across the valley and its margins. The bench is at or just above the margin of glacial deposits that were laid down during a short-lived readvance about 13,000 to 11,500 yr B.P. (Hamilton 1978, 1986).

The site was discovered in 1970 and excavated in 1970 and 1973 by H. L. Alexander (Alexander 1987). Artifacts were recovered from unstratified stony loess that overlies shale bedrock and is capped by a loose-textured dark organic soil with abundant rootlets (Figure 7b). Mapped profiles of the site (Alexander 1987:6) show rounded glacial pebbles, cobbles, and small boulders dispersed within the loess and concentrated at its base, where some clasts are embedded deeply in the underlying "bedrock." Artifacts were concentrated about 2 to 8 cm above the base of the loess, but they also were dispersed higher in the site. In several separate areas, fragments of an individual artifact were found near the base of the loess and near the ground surface, where they probably had been displaced by burrowing ground squirrels.

Radiocarbon ages within the lower half of the loess range from about 8450 to 6100 yr B.P., and charcoal flakes from an oval hearth-like feature 5 cm above the base of the loess have an age of 11,470 ± 500 yr B.P. (Appendix, P). The 11,500 yr B.P. radiocarbon age on an apparent hearth has been puzzling because the Putu site at that time probably would have been at or just above the flank of a disintegrating glacier. The erratic radiocarbon ages and diverse tool assemblage [see below] reported by Alexander (1987), as well as dispersed glacial stones and vertical and horizontal displacement of artifact fragments, seem to indicate severe mixing at the site, probably by frost action and burrowing animals. Mixture of glacial stones into weathered bedrock fragments may indicate deep-seated disturbance by solifluction or other slope processes, perhaps when the margin of the reactivated glacier was adjacent to the Putu locality.

As reported by Alexander (1987:25–33), the lithic assemblage from Putu contains abundant blades and blade-like flakes which were produced from polyhedral, subprismatic blade cores on locally procured cherts. Blades are slightly larger than the maximum size defined for microblades, and none of the cores appear to be microcores. Unifacial, bifacial, and burin

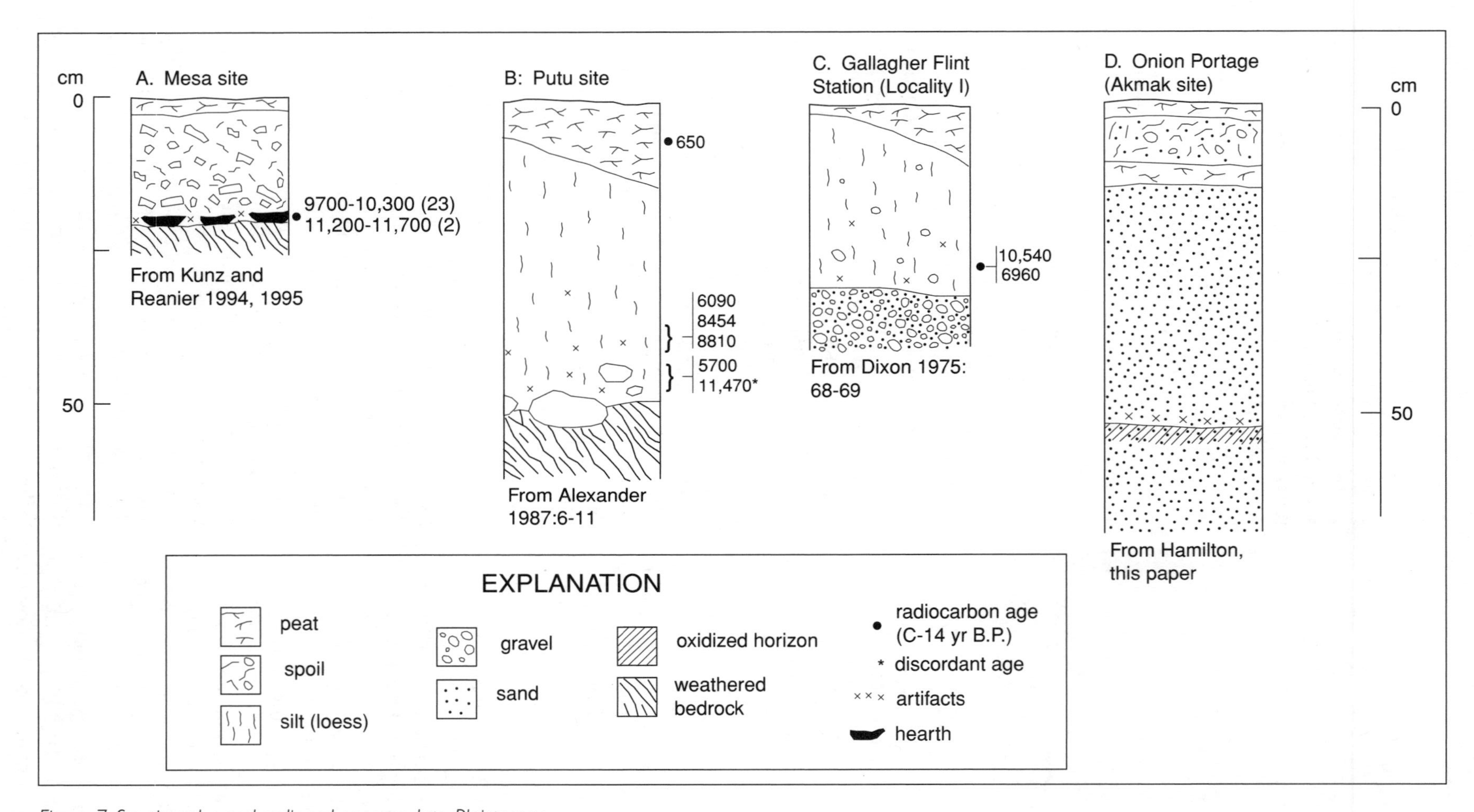

Figure 7. Stratigraphy and radiocarbon ages, late Pleistocene archaeological sites in northern and northwestern Alaska. See Appendix (O–T) for additional data on radiocarbon ages.

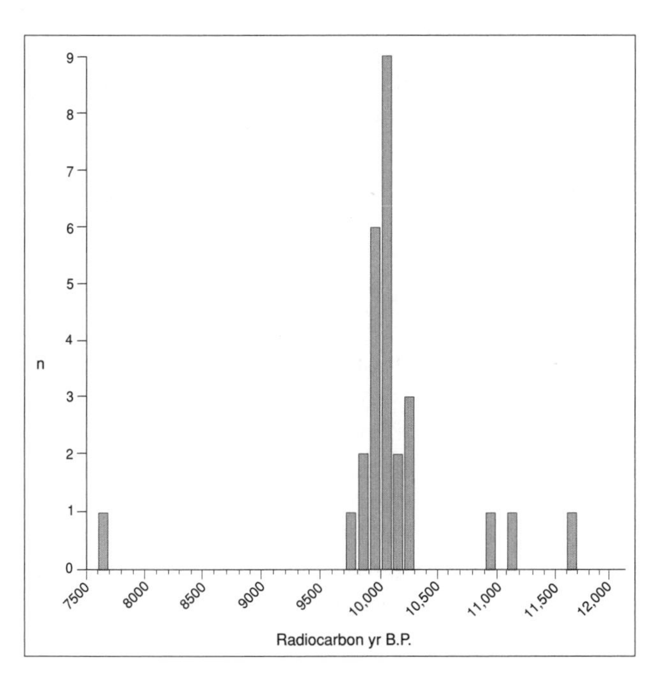

Figure 8. Age distribution of dated charcoal samples from the Mesa site.

techniques were used to secondarily shape and resharpen tools. Unifacially retouched pieces include marginally retouched flakes and blades, single-and multi-spurred gravers, several end scrapers, and one side scraper. Burins are commonly angle or dihedral types. Bifaces are large and leaf-shaped, while projectile points are chiefly lanceolate or fluted (Table 1) (Alexander 1987:12–20).

R. E. Reanier (1995) recently has reexamined the Putu site, studied the original investigators' field notes, and obtained an additional AMS radiocarbon age from an archived charcoal sample. Reanier's new AMS date (Appendix, P) confirms an original determination of 8450 ± 130 yr B.P. on a buried hearth and appears to date an associated edge-ground lanceolate point base. Careful examination of original field notes led Reanier (1995) to conclude that the suspect 11,470-year-old radiocarbon age may have come from culturally sterile gravel at the base of the stony loess. It may date surface vegetation buried by loess or colluvium at the time of glacier retreat from the site area.

Reanier (1995) also examined the "Bedwell site," a prominent rock knob about 100 m north of Putu, where Alexander had found lanceolate projectile points. Reanier obtained an AMS radiocarbon age of 10,490 ± 70 yr B.P. on an archived charcoal sample that appeared to be associated with one of the lanceolate points.

The Hilltop Site

A BEDROCK KNOLL 17 km southwest of Putu has yielded edge-ground lanceolate points similar to those from the Mesa site, in addition to multi-spurred gravers and bifaces (Reanier 1995; Table 1). A conventional radiocarbon age of 6160 ± 130 yr B.P. was obtained on mixed charcoal and "black soil," but later AMS dating of uncontaminated charcoal yielded an age of 10,360 ± 60 yr B.P. (Reanier 1995; Appendix, Q).

Gallagher Flint Station

THE GALLAGHER FLINT STATION is located on the floor of the Sagavanirktok River valley 16 km north of the Putu site. The Gallagher site is on the crest of a large kame, close to the limit of late Wisconsin glaciation in the Sagavanirktok valley (Hamilton 1978, 1979), that provides a clear view of the surrounding valley floor (Bowers 1983). Although it began to form during glacial stagnation, probably sometime after 17,000 yr B.P., the kame must have remained ice-cored and unstable for thousands of years thereafter. However, abundant willow wood and peat in this sector of the Sagavanirktok valley is dated by radiocarbon at 11,800 to 12,800 yr B.P. (Hamilton 1979), indicating that at least parts of the valley floor had stabilized and become vegetated by that time.

The Gallagher site, a quarry and lookout site with multiple occupations, was excavated in 1970, 1971, and 1974 by E. J. Dixon, Jr. (Bowers 1983; Dixon 1975). Artifacts occur in frost-churned stony brown loess 20 to 28 cm thick that is capped by a discontinuous organic soil up to 5 cm thick (Figure 7c). At least 13 separate artifact concentrations spaced 1 to 50 m apart occur on the crest and upper slopes of the kame and on a bench along its southern flank (Bowers 1983). Eleven of the concentrations contain either undiagnostic quarry detritus or tool assemblages of middle to late Holocene age. Six of these localities yielded a total of 12 radiocarbon ages, all of which are between about 3200 and 1000 yr B.P. (Bowers 1983). Another locality contains a mixed artifact assemblage that may include latest Pleistocene or early Holocene material, but four dates from this concentration are all between 2500 and 1100 yr B.P. The remaining locality (Locality 1) is dated at 10,540 ± 150 yr B.P. (Appendix, R) from charcoal directly associated with artifacts at 20-25 cm depth within loess (Dixon 1975).

The occupation at Locality 1 is a generalized core and blade industry that includes cores, blades, microblades, platform flakes, and retouched flakes, but lacks burins, bifaces, and scrapers (Table 1). The cores are of diverse types—tabular, conical, and wedge-shaped—and blades and microblades have in some cases been struck from the same core. This assemblage largely reflects quarry activity in which cores and microcores were roughed out from glacial gravels (E. J. Dixon, personal communication 1989).

Following renewed excavations at the Gallagher site in 1995, D. E. Ferguson (1997a, 1997b) has questioned Dixon's age assignment of the Locality 1 core and blade industry. Ferguson maintains that most of the core and blade material occurs stratigraphically higher than the charcoal dated by Dixon, and that the few artifacts recovered from lower levels of Locality 1 were displaced downward by post-depositional processes. According to Ferguson, artifacts identical to those at Locality 1 are directly associated with charcoal dated at 6960 + 90 yr B.P. in a nearby test pit. Ferguson believes that the artifacts at Locality 1 are typologically related to Mesolithic industries of northeast Asia, and his mid-Holocene radiocarbon date appears to support this temporal assignment.

Discussion

THE TIGHTLY CLUSTERED AMS ages at the Mesa site and the slightly older ages at the Bedwell and Hilltop sites are very similar to the accepted age range of 10,500 to 10,000 yr B.P. for the Agate Basin component of the Paleoindian tradition in the Great Plains region.[2] The two older radiocarbon determinations for the Mesa site, 11,190 and 11,660 yr B.P., are more difficult to accept, although Kunz and Reanier (1994, 1995) and Reanier (1995) believe that they are valid.

If correct, the two older dates from the Mesa site would imply that:

(1) The site was occupied intermittently with no detectable cultural change over an interval of nearly 2,000 years;

(2) A hearth was reused after a 500-year interval, showing no detectable unconformity between the two occupations;

(3) A time gap of nearly 1,000 years separates the oldest occupation from all other dated Paleoindian occupations at the Mesa site and elsewhere on the Alaskan North Slope; and

(4) Non-fluted lanceolate points and other cultural elements of the Paleoindian tradition, which have no known Siberian antecedents, originated on the Alaskan North Slope.

In addition, the apparently older hearth shows no evidence of unusually severe frost disruption, wind scour, or other periglacial disturbance despite the 1,000–1,500 years of harsh "Younger Dryas" conditions that Kunz and Reanier (1994) believe must have separated the two episodes of Paleoindian occupation at the site.

The 2,000-year cultural continuity implied by the two older AMS ages at the Mesa site is difficult to accept because of the dramatic cultural changes that occurred at intervals of 500 years or less during the time span of the Paleoindian tradition elsewhere in North America (Kunz and Reanier 1995) and the similarly dramatic environmental changes that took place about 12,000–10,000 yr B.P. in northern Alaska. For example, passes across the Brooks Range may have become ice-free at or shortly after 11,500 yr B.P. (Hamilton 1982, 1986), and stands of poplars and large willows dating about 12,000–11,000 yr B.P. were widespread across the Alaskan North Slope from the Sagavanirktok valley westward to the Etivluk valley (Hamilton 1979; Hopkins et al. 1981). During the following millennium, however, vegetation cover decreased as eolian sand became reactivated on at least parts of the North Slope (Carter 1993).

Although Kunz and Reanier (1995:15) reject this scenario, we believe that burning of "recycled" wood is a plausible explanation for the two disparate AMS ages at the Mesa site. Because only sparse small shrubs occur in the area today, shrubs also may have been limited in size and abundance during the site's main occupation around 10,000 yr B.P. Larger pieces of older wood, perhaps dating from the 12,000–11,000 yr B.P. growth episode, may have been collected by the site's occupants from exposures along eroding stream banks. These may have been carried to the Mesa site occasionally for use as firewood or as poles for dwellings or other structures. After a period of surface exposure or structural use, the wood would become well dried and suitable for burning. It may be significant that the hearth with the most intensive human use yielded the oldest dates. Could depletion of the usual sources of nearby firewood perhaps have led to exploitation of unconventional sources? Although the Mesa site is a demonstrably Paleoindian site that was occupied during at least 10,100 to 9900 yr B.P., we conclude that significantly older occupation of the site is unlikely.

Northwest Alaska: Three Diverse Sites

THREE ARCHAEOLOGICAL SITES that extend back in age to the early Holocene or the latest Pleistocene are widely dispersed across northwest Alaska (Figure 1). Onion Portage, a deeply stratified site, is situated on the Kobuk River near the southwestern corner of the Brooks Range. Batza Téna consists of numerous individual shallow to surface sites associated with an obsidian source near the Koyukuk River. The Trail Creek Caves occur in hilly terrain on the Seward Peninsula.

Onion Portage

THE ONION PORTAGE site is located at the south flank of the Brooks Range, close to major mountain passes. The site area was not glaciated during late Pleistocene time, but extensive sand dunes were active during cold, arid episodes and caused alluviation of the Kobuk River (Hamilton 1984; Hamilton and Ashley 1993; Hamilton et al. 1988). Spruce-covered river floodplains around Onion Portage give way to forest-tundra mosaics on higher parts of the valley floor and to alpine tundra on the uplands.

Human occupation at Onion Portage occurred at the base and crest of a south-facing river bluff 30 m high that provides a clear overlook across the Kobuk valley. Although the Kobuk River meanders freely across a wide (4–5 km) floodplain in highly erodible sand, the site lies at the downstream end of a resistant outcrop of bouldery glacial till that provides local defense against river erosion. Late prehistoric components of the site were discovered in 1941 by J. L. Giddings, and deeper occupation levels were found by Giddings during further testing in 1961 and 1963. The major excavation of the site was carried out by J. L. Giddings and later by D. D. Anderson and R. W. Giddings during 1965 through 1967 (Anderson 1988).

The site contains two principal elements: (1) eight cultural strata ("bands") in fans of stratified sand that were deposited at the mouths of gullies that incise the bluff face (Anderson 1988:30–47); and (2) the Akmak occupation on a bench cut into the bluff face 14 m above river level (Anderson 1970; Hamilton 1970). The fans of sand are as much as 3.5 m thick and contain stacked occupation surfaces. These cultural "bands" are securely dated back to about 8200 yr B.P. by 45 generally concordant radiocarbon age determinations (Anderson 1988:48). In contrast, the Akmak site is a shallow occupation floor that lacks datable organic material.

The Kobuk complex (Band 8) is dated between about 8200 and 7900 yr B.P. (Appendix, S).[3] Occupation was on moist silty alluvium at the edge of the Kobuk River, and unlined hearths interpreted as single-use features are those of temporary hunters' camps rather than more permanent habitation. All identified charcoal is of willow (Anderson 1988:70), and paleosol horizons are those of poorly drained tundra soils with shallow permafrost (Schweger 1985). The Kobuk complex artifacts are dominantly microblades (60 percent), with flakes, utilized flakes, blades, and burin spalls also common (Table 1). Most tools are of black or gray chert; a few are of obsidian.

The Akmak locality, which has been partly destroyed by subsequent gully erosion and excavation of a house pit, occupies a remnant of the 14-m bench that is about 20 m^2 in area (Hamilton 1970). The site is buried beneath 30 to 40 cm of structureless fine sand, which probably was scoured from the bluff face by strong winds and redeposited on the bench. The sand is capped by sod and sandy peat 15 to 20 cm thick, and locally by a thicker lens of spoil from a late prehistoric house pit (Figure 7d). It bears a well-developed podzolic soil profile in which an intensely leached horizon 10 to 15 cm thick overlies a strongly oxidized horizon (T. D. Hamilton, unpublished field notes, 1966). Akmak artifacts, which occur at the base of the eolian sand, are of a high-quality black to gray chert with a fine-grained glassy texture—a distinctive lithology whose source is unknown (Anderson 1988:60). Primary reduction technologies include the manufacture of blades from large "core-bifaces" and flat-faced blade cores, and microblades from small wedge-shaped cores. Unifacial, bifacial, and burin secondary technologies are present, and the tool assemblage consists of retouched blades, blade-like flakes, microblades, and flakes, side scrapers, end scrapers, burins (angle, transverse, and dihedral forms), leaf-shaped bifaces, longitudinally grooved stones (i.e., "shaft smoothers"), and backed knives (Anderson 1970) (Table 1). Many artifacts are unusually large: core-bifaces and blades are as much as 11 cm long, and lengths of scrapers and bifaces are as much as 15 cm. According to Anderson (1970:60), the Akmak occupation probably was relatively permanent, with varied activities such as hide preparation, butchering, woodworking, and weapons manufacture carried out at the site.

The generally accepted age for the Akmak site of 9570 ± 150 yr B.P. (Anderson 1988:55–57) was obtained on caribou bone that was deposited or redeposited in the same deeply buried gully system that yielded redeposited Akmak artifacts (Anderson 1970:70; Hamilton 1970). This age estimate was on bone apatite (Appendix, S) and may be spurious, but even a valid age estimate would not necessarily date any primary association with humans.

Batza Téna

MOST OF THE ARCHAEOLOGICAL obsidian in northern Alaska, including that from the Onion Portage and Mesa sites, is derived from the Batza Téna area. Batza Téna is located about 30 km south of Hughes at the east margin of the forested floodplain of the Koyukuk River (Figure 1). This obsidian source, although known to local natives, was first reported in the scientific literature by Patton and Miller (1970).

Investigations by D. W. Clark and A. M. Clark during 1969–1971 documented 89 individual archaeological sites in the Batza Téna area (Clark and Clark 1975, 1993). Most of these sites were flake clusters surrounded by wider scatters of lithic detritus, and were primarily flaking stations with surface assemblages only (Clark and Clark 1993:35–39). The Clarks found that obsidian was obtained from bedrock sources, from gravel bars along local rivers, from colluvium, and from gravel along the shore of at least one lake. Fluted points were found at 10 localities (we discuss these in detail later in the paper). Lithic artifacts identified in association with fluted points include sparse side-notched and lanceolate bifacial points, as well as numerous bifaces, end scrapers, and retouched flakes (Table 1). No deeply buried sites were located, and the eight radiocarbon determinations from the Batza Téna area are all 1500 yr B.P. or younger (Clark and Clark 1993:25).

Other approaches to dating human use of obsidian from Batza Téna have included obsidian hydration analysis, typological cross-dating of obsidian artifacts, and dating other archaeological sites at which the obsidian has been found. Attempts to directly date obsidian flakes and artifacts by hydration analysis have been inconclusive (Clark and Clark 1993:23–24; Reanier 1995). Although the Clarks (1993:59) found an age cluster of about 9000 yr B.P. on one group of fluted points, both they and Reanier generally found highly variable rind thicknesses attributable to forest fires, local microclimates, measurement problems, and other variables. Some fluted points, which are widely distributed through northern Alaska (Clark 1991; Reanier 1995), were fabricated from Batza Téna obsidian. However, attempts at dating the fluted points have so far been unsuccessful (Clark 1991; Clark and Clark 1993:81–82; Reanier 1995). The strongest evidence for antiquity of humans at Batza Téna currently is provided by the Broken Mammoth site in the Tanana River valley, where obsidian that is identified geochemically as Batza Téna in origin is closely associated with charcoal dated about 11,800 yr B.P. (C. E. Holmes, personal communication 1996). Batza Téna obsidian has also been tentatively identified at the Mesa site (J. Cook, personal communication 1996; Kunz and Reanier 1995), indicating that passes through the Brooks Range may have been open to humans by at least 10,000 yr B.P.

The Trail Creek Caves

THE TRAIL CREEK CAVES occur along the steep southeast-facing flank of a limestone ridge in northeastern Seward Peninsula (Larsen 1968). The rugged and unvegetated ridge face has numerous solution cavities, and at least 13 of these are large enough to potentially shelter humans (Schaaf 1988). Vertebrate remains are present in about half of the caves (Schaaf 1988), and nine caves show evidence of use by humans (Larsen 1968). The caves were first tested by D. M. Hopkins in 1948, and two of them were excavated by H. Larsen in 1949 and 1950 (Larsen 1968). The National Park Service tested five of the other 11 caves in 1985 (Schaaf 1988).

The caves contain poorly sorted breccia that has accumulated by weathering of their walls and roofs. Stratigraphy of these deposits is complex, owing to disturbance by frost action, digging by animals, rock falls from roof and walls, gravitational movements down sloping cave floors, activities of humans, and downward movement of fine detritus through coarse angular rubble. Basal clayey sediments have deformed plastically where compressed beneath fallen rocks or where subject to flow down sloping surfaces.

Larsen (1968:22–27) defined four principal stratigraphic units in Cave 2 (Figure 9). Units I and II, which merge into a single unit about 6 m inside the cave entrance and wedge out entirely beyond 11 m, contain artifacts of Historic through Denbigh age (Larsen 1968:66–71). They probably span about the last 4,100 years (see Giddings and Anderson 1986). Units III and IV interpenetrate, owing to plastic deformation of the clayey unit IV. Unit III, which wedges out about 12.5 m into Cave 2, contains microblades and slotted antler spearheads (Table 1); a nearby caribou bone is dated at 9070 ± 150 yr B.P. (Appendix, T). Unit IV, which probably is insoluble residue derived from solution of the limestone, is the only sediment that persists throughout the deepest parts of both caves. Bones of sheep, elk, horse, and bison were recovered from this layer (Larsen 1968:57–63). Sheep live today only in the Bendeleben Mountains, 50 km south of the Trail Creek Caves. Elk possibly ranged widely through eastern Beringia during the early and middle Holocene but are no longer present in this region. Horse and bison, which were found outside the entrance to Cave 9, are diagnostic elements of the late Pleistocene megafauna. A fragment of bison calcaneus (heel bone) that Larsen (1968:61–63) believed was broken by humans has a collagen age of 13,070 ± 280 yr B.P., and a broken horse scapula that showed no sign of human alteration is dated at 15,750 ± 350 yr B.P. During the National Park Service study in 1985, horse and bison bones were found in two additional caves, and one of those caves also yielded remains of sheep and a proboscidean (probably mammoth). None of the bones showed any evidence of butchering (Vinson 1988, 1993). Larsen also reported "dog" teeth in all levels of both of the caves that he excavated, but subsequent studies have shown that these are deciduous bear teeth that were lost naturally during denning (Dixon and Smith 1986; Vinson 1988).

Larsen's arguments for human modification of the bison calcaneus were initially accepted by archaeologists, but recent observations have shown that this form of breakage is a common result of gnawing by canids (including dogs, wolves, and foxes) during dismemberment of the hind limbs of a carcass (S. C. Gerlach, personal communication 1989). For this reason, human occupation of the Trail Creek Caves is no longer considered demonstrably older than about 9100 yr B.P.

Discussion

Maximum ages of at least 11,800 yr B.P. for Batza Téna and about 9100 yr B.P. for the Trail Creek Caves seem well documented, but the Akmak component at Onion Portage remains undated. The Akmak assemblage is significant because of its unusually large artifacts fabricated from high-quality chert from an unknown distant source, and because of its probable western Beringian affinities.

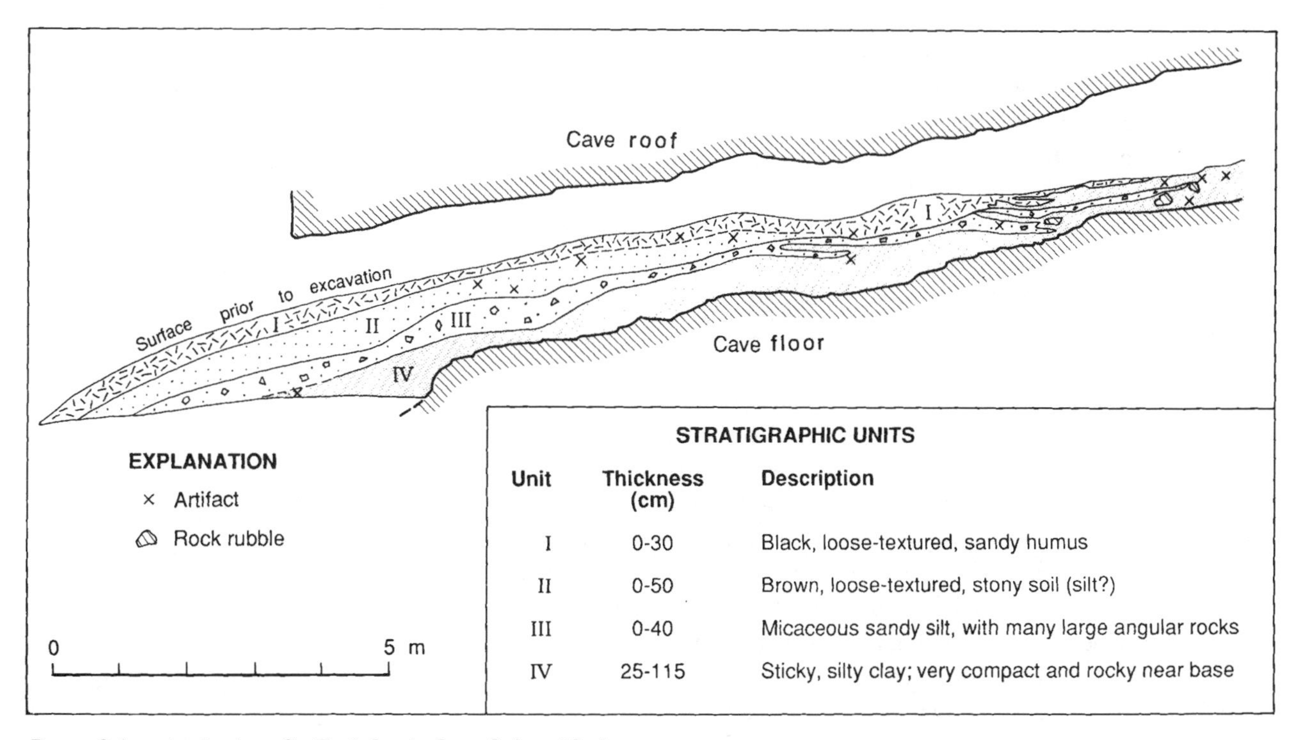

Figure 9. Longitudinal profile, Trail Creek Cave 2 (modified from Larsen 1968:Plate IX).

Although the Akmak site cannot be dated directly, an age estimate can be derived from (1) its presence on the 14-m bench, (2) stratigraphic relations to Band 8, (3) typological relations to Band 8 artifacts, and (4) typological affinities to dated occupations in northeastern Siberia. Radiocarbon ages from Epiguruk Bluff, 6 km upvalley from Onion Portage, show that the Kobuk River alluviated to a height about 14 m above its modern surface during the late Wisconsin glaciation, but that it downcut abruptly from that level about 18,500 yr B.P. (Hamilton et al. 1993). The river remained 6 to 7 m above its present level until sometime after 15,000 years ago, meandering north across the valley floor toward Onion Portage. The Kobuk River then cut down to its present level, which it reached about 8500 yr B.P. (see Schweger 1982:Figure 2). The Akmak site could have been occupied after 18,500 yr B.P., but it probably would not have been used by humans until approached by the meandering Kobuk River after about 15,000 years ago; the firm occupation floor also suggests that habitation was on a mature surface rather than freshly deposited soft alluvium. Akmak artifacts are dispersed throughout the gully system to its mouth, where they occupy a channel floor directly beneath Band 8 (Hamilton 1970:Figure 64). The absence of diagnostic Akmak artifacts or lithologies from Band 8 and overlying cultural levels supports the stratigraphic evidence that the Akmak occupation preceded that of Band 8. Typological comparisons between Akmak and Band 8 suggest to Anderson (1970:70, 1988:55–72) that the two assemblages may be closely related in time and that they belong together as components of the American Paleoarctic tradition. However, comparison with northeast Siberian sites suggests that those most closely related to Akmak are no younger than 10,500 yr B.P. (Anderson 1988:57). Specifically, the most comparable assemblage to Akmak appears to be Ushki-1, layer VI, a late Pleistocene occupation in central Kamchatka dated to about 10,600 yr B.P. Layer VI has a vast inventory of wedge-shaped microblade cores and their preforms (similar in size and shape to some of the Akmak core-bifaces), flat-faced blade cores (similar to the Akmak "polyhedral blade cores"), burins, leaf-shaped points and bifaces, end scrapers, side scrapers, and longitudinally grooved stones (Dikov 1977, 1979; Goebel and Slobodin, this volume). When compared to this assemblage, the distinctiveness of Akmak lessens, suggesting that it is more likely the result of raw material availability than cultural-historical differences with other Beringian microblade-producing industries. Based on stratigraphy and geologic history, the Akmak site must have been occupied sometime between 15,000 and 8200 yr B.P.; typological comparisons suggest a probable age span between about 11,000 and 10,000 yr B.P.

Artifacts that may be related to the Akmak assemblage in size, typology, and lithic material have been found by D. J. Stanford at two other localities in northwest Alaska. At Walakpa Bay, on the Chukchi Sea coast about 18 km southwest of Barrow, D. J. Stanford (personal communication 1989) found Akmak-like implements at the base of a thin (1–2 cm) organic mat on the crest of a low rise on the northeast side of the bay. The second possible Akmak locality, discovered in 1989 and collected in 1992 by Stanford and others, is near the margin of the Kobuk Dunes, an active dune field south of the Kobuk River near Onion Portage. Implements of high-quality chert, which occur on the surface in recent sand "blowouts," include blades, microblades, large bifaces, end scrapers, side scrapers, two transverse flake burins, and a possible core tablet (Stanford et al. 1990; R. Gal, written communication 1996). Many of the implements from the Kobuk Dunes may be related to the Kobuk complex rather than Akmak, however, and the burins resemble those reported from Denali complex assemblages in central Alaska (R. Gal, personal communication 1996).

Other Considerations

In addition to the question of antiquity, other significant issues in the peopling of the Americas include (1) origins of fluted points and other aspects of Clovis technology and (2) feasibility of early entry via coastal routes. Because of their location at the entrance to the Americas, Alaskan archaeological sites might provide information relevant to both of these issues.

Fluted Points and Clovis Affinities

About 50 fluted points have been recovered from northern Alaska (Clark 1984, 1987, 1991), but their antiquity is still uncertain. Most of the points have been recovered from surface sites that lack stratigraphy and datable organic material (Clark 1984); the others are from shallow sites where vertical movements of artifacts are likely (Table 2). Some reported points with basal thinning, as at the Dry Creek, Healy Lake Village, and

Table 2. Fluted point sites in Alaska. See Clark (1984; 1991) for additional surface or near-surface sites for which ages are unavailable.

Locality	*Number of points*	*Age estimates (yr B.P.)*	*Setting*	*Reference*
Girls Hill	4	4440 ± 90 (radiocarbon)	In shallow (<0.5 m) loess above rock rubble; date is minimum limit.	1
Putu	4	5700-11,470 (radiocarbon)*	Shallow site in frost-mixed loess.	2
Bonanza Creek	3	700-1800 (obsidian)	Site K-8, localities A and C; at base of sod.	3
Batza Téna	18	1800-21,600 (obsidian)	Surface sites near ridge top.	4
North Fork, Koyukuk River	1	12,300 ± 1700 (obsidian)	Surface site on hilltop.	5

* See Appendix (N)

References: 1. R. Gal, personal communication; Reanier 1995. 2. Alexander 1987; Reanier 1995. 3. Holmes 1971; C. E. Holmes, personal communication 1989. 4. Clark and Clark 1993. 5. M. Kunz, personal communication 1989.

Mesa sites (Clark 1984, 1991; Kunz and Reanier 1995), are not considered to be true fluted points by many investigators. If the basally thinned points from Dry Creek and Healy Lake are disregarded, then virtually all known fluted-point occurrences in Alaska and the Yukon occur at and north of about 66° N latitude, and most are distributed within or near the flanks of the Brooks Range (Clark 1991:36).

Radiocarbon ages on charcoal in apparent association with fluted points range from about 11,500 yr B.P. at the Putu site to mid-Holocene age at Girls Hill and Putu (Table 2; see also Clark 1991), and a point with a flute-like base has even been reported in a late Holocene Paleoeskimo site (Giddings 1964:233–235). Except for the discredited age estimate of about 11,500 yr B.P. from the Putu site (discussed previously), all radiocarbon ages are younger than the accepted age range of 11,300 to 10,900 yr B.P. (Haynes 1992) for the Clovis horizon in the western United States. The points also differ technologically from early Clovis projectile points in that they have triple flutes of equal length on both faces and concave bases forming distinct corner "ears" (Figure 10), so the age discrepancy with the Clovis horizon is not surprising.

The obsidian hydration method has been used by several investigators to provide age estimates on fluted points found at or just below the ground surface. Ages on fluted points at the Batza Téna locality tend to cluster between about 8000 and 10,000 yr B.P. (Table 2), but they range from 1800 to 21,600 yr B.P. (Clark 1984, Clark and Clark 1993). Other hydration age estimates are as young as 700 to 1,800 yr B.P. at the Bonanza Creek locality, about 250 km northeast of Batza Téna, where forest fires may have caused spalling of hydration rinds (Clark 1984). Clark concludes that obsidian hydration is affected by too many variables to be a reliable technique for dating individual artifacts, but that date clusters such as that at Batza Téna may be significant. A more recent approach to obsidian-hydration age estimates utilizes buried thermal cells to determine effective hydration temperatures over time spans of a year or more (M. A. Kunz, personal communication 1989). This approach was utilized to derive an age estimate of about 12,200 ± 1700 yr B.P. for a fluted point from the Koyukuk valley (Table 2), but this single age assessment could not be confirmed by additional dating at the site. Blood residue found on several Alaskan fluted points has been tentatively identified as mammoth (Dixon 1993:107). If corroborated, this information may indicate that some Alaskan fluted points are of late Pleistocene age.

There is increasing evidence that Paleoindian fluting technologies spread into Canada from the south soon after 10,500 yr B.P. as the Laurentide ice sheet melted and a zone of habitable land emerged. Multiply-fluted and eared points similar to those from north Alaska have been found at sites like Charlie Lake Cave in British Columbia (10,500 yr B.P.) and Sibbald Creek in Alberta (9500 yr B.P.) (Carlson 1991; Clark 1991; Fladmark et al. 1988; Gryba 1983). This information supports hypotheses that fluted point technologies in north Alaska postdate 10,500 yr B.P. and originated in the south.

Also important to this discussion is the absence of fluted point technologies in the lithic assemblages of central Alaska that have been shown to be contemporaneous to the Clovis horizon. Goebel et al. (1991) recognize many Clovis-like characteristics in the component I (Nenana complex) assemblages from

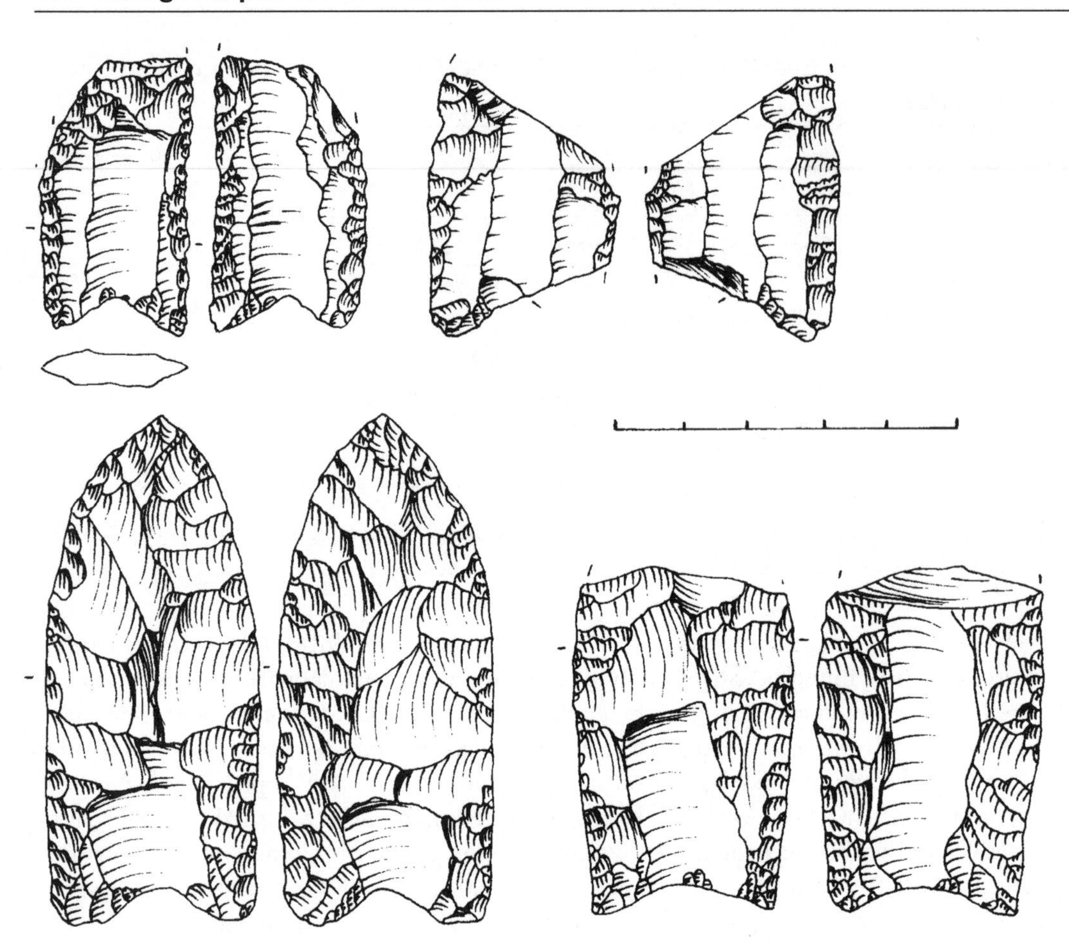

Figure 10. Fluted points from Batza Téna, northern Alaska (a, b; after Clark 1991) and Blackwater Draw, New Mexico, the type-site for the Clovis tradition (c, d; after Goebel et al. 1991).

the Dry Creek and Walker Road sites, and they conclude that, except for projectile point forms, the two stone industries are virtually identical. However, fluted points are absent from the Nenana complex, again suggesting that fluted point technologies developed south of the Laurentide ice sheet and from there spread north into Alaska sometime after 11,500–11,000 yr B.P. A fluted biface reportedly has been found at Uptar-1 near Magadan, Russia (King and Slobodin 1996), but this site is not clearly dated to the late Pleistocene and the "flute" may be just an unusually deep basal thinning scar (Goebel and Slobodin, this volume).

Maritime Adaptations

Some workers have speculated that the south coast of the Bering land bridge was rich in food resources (e.g., Laughlin 1967) and that marine-adapted humans may have occupied parts of the Northwest Coast during the late Wisconsin glaciation (Ackerman et al. 1979; Fladmark 1978; Josenhans et al. 1997). Other studies seem to provide little encouragement for these ideas; they show instead that (1) the south shore of the Bering land bridge and the north margin of the Gulf of Alaska probably had inhospitable environments during much of the late Pleistocene; (2) the oldest known archaeological sites in coastal southern and southeast Alaska are of early Holocene age; (3) coastal sites of this antiquity occur to the south in British Columbia, but are not known northward toward the Bering platform; and (4) human adaptations to a severe sea-ice environment may not have taken place until late Holocene time.

Sancetta (1983) and Sancetta and Robinson (1983) believe that the Bering Sea had long-lasting sea ice and short, cold summers during late Pleistocene glacial intervals; and pollen studies by Colinvaux (1981) and Sancetta et al. (1985) also have demonstrated that the climate of the adjoining south coast of the Bering land bridge could not have been appreciably tempered by maritime influences. Reconstructions by D. H. Mann (Mann and Hamilton 1995; Mann and Peteet 1994) show unbroken glacier ice along the northern margin of the Gulf of Alaska during the last glacial maximum (about 22,000–18,000 yr B.P.). This continuous ice mass would have disintegrated as sea level subsequently rose, but major glacial readvances in the region took place as recently as 11,700 yr B.P. (Mann and Hamilton 1995) and must have severely impacted large sectors of the coast. Vegetation also remained in a late-glacial mode until 11,000–10,000 yr B.P., as summarized by Ager and Brubaker (1985), Heusser (1985), and Hu et al. (1995). Cave deposits on Prince of Wales Island, southeast Alaska, have yielded remains of terrestrial fauna dating to about 44,000–24,000 and 12,000–7000 yr B.P., but only seal bones have been dated to the intervening time span that represents the last glacial maximum (Dixon et al. 1997; Heaton and Grady 1997; Heaton et al. 1996).

Despite intensive site surveys along the southern Alaska coast, no archaeological sites have yet been discovered that predate 10,000 yr B.P., although an isolated bone tool may be slightly older. Hidden Falls and Ground Hog Bay were first occupied about 9500–9000 yr B.P. (Ackerman 1988a, 1988b, 1996a, 1996b; Davis 1989, 1996). Ongoing excavations at PET-408, a cave on Prince of Wales Island, have uncovered human skeletal remains dated at about 9800 yr B.P. by two concordant radiocarbon ages (Dixon et al. 1997; Dixon 1998). Two isolated bone tools in separate chambers of the cave are dated to about 10,300 and 5800 yr B.P. (Dixon 1998). Pollen records show that spruce-hemlock coastal forest developed about the time that Hidden Falls and Ground Hog Bay were occupied (Heusser 1985), indicating that habitation probably was associated with Holocene forests much like those of today. Cultural inventories at these two sites include wedge-shaped cores, microblades, and bifacial tools, assemblages similar to that of the Denali complex of central Alaska (Ackerman 1996b). This relationship indicates good communication with the interior, and perhaps derivation from an inland, rather than a maritime, population. However, occupation of both sites required use of boats and marine resources, and obsidian obtained from northern British Columbia indicates long-distance (as much as 550 km) and presumably well-established coastal trade connections (Ackerman 1996a). In addition, a stable isotope ($\delta^{13}C$) value on a human bone from PET-408 suggests a primarily marine diet (Dixon 1998; Dixon et al. 1997). These relations suggest some time depth to the marine adaptation.[4]

The skeletal remains from PET-408 represent the earliest human remains yet found in Alaska, and their study will be integral to understanding relationships of these early southeast Alaskans with later northwest coast human populations.

Coastal sites as old as the southeast Alaska sites have been reported from the Queen Charlotte Islands and central coast of British Columbia (Ackerman 1996a; Erlandson and Moss 1996; Fladmark 1982; Josenhans et al. 1997), but the earliest known coastal occupation within the Bering Sea region is the 8,400-year-old Blade site on Anangula Island, one of the Aleutian Islands (Ackerman 1988b; Laughlin 1975). These age relations suggest that early human populations in southeast Alaska might have been more closely related to maritime populations to the south along the Northwest Coast, than to the north in the south-central Alaska or Bering Sea regions.

Anderson (1984) has shown that intensive year-round occupation of the northern Bering Sea coast dates only from the beginning of Choris time (about 3600 yr B.P.). This event may mark the initial development in the Bering Sea region of an economy partly dependent on sea-ice hunting, and it would severely constrain peopling of eastern Beringia by much earlier maritime groups during intervals of severe sea-ice conditions in the late Pleistocene.

If the Americas were initially peopled during middle Wisconsin time, movement of maritime populations through southern parts of Beringia would be more feasible during that interval (Gruhn 1994). Cave deposits on Prince of Wales Island have produced a diverse fauna of middle Wisconsin age that includes brown and black bears, caribou, marmot, lemming, heather vole, and possibly wolverine (Heaton and Grady 1997). However, in some places middle Wisconsin glaciers probably would have blocked extensive stretches of coastline, and rugged fjords and headlands also would have impeded passage by populations lacking sturdy and seaworthy boats. If glaciers remained extensive throughout southern Alaska during the middle Wisconsin, coastal routes almost certainly would have been less favorable for travel than routes farther inland.

Synthesis

THE DEEPLY STRATIFIED and well-dated archaeological sites from the Nenana valley region provide an extremely important perspective on early human occupation of central Alaska. The two basal components, the Nenana complex (about 11,300 to 11,000 yr B.P.) and the Denali complex (about 10,700 to 7000 yr B.P.), are clearly separated, and their artifacts seem to be unmixed. The record appears to show that several types of unfluted bifacial points were early arrivals in central Alaska and that extensive use of microblades and burins came later. Despite deep burial and little soil mixture, six radiocarbon dates at Dry Creek, four at Owl Ridge, and probably one each at Walker Road, Moose Creek, and Panguingue Creek are aberrant. The suspect Dry Creek ages become systematically older with decreasing sample size, suggesting contamination by older carbon, but the anomalously young ages at Owl Ridge and the oldest ages at the Walker Road and Moose Creek sites are distinguished mainly by deviation from an otherwise concordant suite of ages. It is clear that no archaeological site or cultural component should be considered to be "dated" on the basis of a single radiocarbon-age estimate.

Within the Tanana River valley, the Broken Mammoth site and the neighboring Swan Point and Mead sites show virtually synchronous late Pleistocene occupations—the oldest between about 11,800 and 11,000 yr B.P. and the younger about 10,800–9300 yr B.P. The older occupation overlaps the Nenana complex, but it evidently began about 500 years earlier. The younger occupation is generally contemporaneous with the older part of the Denali complex in the Nenana Valley and Alaska Range. The compressed record in the thinner loess at Healy Lake shows a broadly similar sequence—the Chindadn complex (from about 11,500 to between 10,000 and 9000 yr B.P.) being broadly equivalent to the two oldest cultural horizons at the other sites.

The presently known late Pleistocene cultural sequence from the upper Tanana valley shows significant differences from that in the Nenana valley. Given the record provided by Dry Creek, Walker Road, and the other multi-layered sites in the Nenana valley, we would expect to find bifacial point industries without microblades predating 11,000 yr B.P., followed by wedge-shaped core, microblade, and burin industries after about 10,500 yr B.P. Although the lowest cultural horizon at Broken Mammoth follows this pattern (it contains a non-microblade, bifacial point industry and has an age of 11,800–11,000 yr B.P.), the next higher horizon does not (it also contains a non-microblade, bifacial point industry but has an age 10,300–9300 yr B.P.). Furthermore, the lowest cultural horizon at Swan Point, dated to about 11,700 yr B.P., includes microblades, whereas the next higher cultural horizon (about 10,200 yr B.P.) has bifacial points apparently with few or no microblades. Clearly there is much more variation in the lithic record of late Pleistocene central Alaska than the Nenana valley model accounts for, and the dichotomy between non-microblade and microblade complexes is not well understood.

The faunal remains from Broken Mammoth and Swan Point also disprove the common supposition that late Pleistocene humans in Alaska were dominantly big-game hunters (West 1983). For example, the remains of wapiti, steppe bison, and Dall sheep at the Dry Creek site led to the supposition that human food quest in the Nenana valley centered on the seasonal hunting of large mammals (Powers and Hoffecker 1989). In contrast, bones recovered from the Broken Mammoth site show that this is just one facet of late Pleistocene subsistence, and that small mammals, waterfowl, ptarmigan, and fish also were important diet items. A broad faunal spectrum also is represented at the Ushki and Berelekh sites in western Beringia, which also predate 11,000 yr B.P. At Ushki (layer VI) faunal remains include steppe bison, horse, mountain sheep, lemming, domesticated dog, waterfowl, and fish; at Berelekh, the remains of hare, ptarmigan, and mammoth are prevalent, while reindeer, bison or horse, and fish occur in lower frequencies (Goebel and Slobodin, this volume). Vereshchagin (1974:10), Vereshchagin and Ukraintseva (1985:105), and Abramova (1989:232) have suggested that some of the Berelekh proboscidean remains were scavenged from nearby mammoth bone accumulations, an activity that also took place in central Alaska.

Most late Pleistocene sites in the Nenana and Tanana river valleys occupy river-cut bluffs that provide sweeping views across adjoining valley floors and the nearby northern foothills of the Alaska Range. Most of the sites are in loess that overlies wind-scoured bedrock and rock rubble capped by wind-deposited sand. Loess began to accumulate in parts of the Tanana Valley at or shortly before 11,800-11,700 yr B.P. and in the Nenana Valley by 11,200 yr B.P., probably as glaciers retreated and strong katabatic winds from the Alaska Range diminished in intensity. The Batza Téna obsidian locality in northwest Alaska was utilized at least as early as 11,700 yr B.P., with obsidian distributed at least as far as the Tanana Valley at that time. Obsidian from the Wrangell Mountains also occurs in the lowest cultural layers at Broken Mammoth as well as in component I at Walker Road (J. P. Cook, personal communication 1996), indicating a widespread distribution network through all of central Alaska between the Brooks Range and the Alaska Range by 11,700 yr B.P. These observations imply that older archaeological sites must be present, at least in central Alaska, but have yet to be discovered. Perhaps those sites were in wind-sheltered locations on the valley floors or farther north in uplands more remote from the Alaska Range.

In contrast, the foothills and coastal plain north of the Brooks Range show no unassailable evidence for human occupation older than about 10,500 yr B.P. The Mesa site and other hunting lookouts in the Arctic Foothills were occupied by Paleoindians about 10,500–10,000 yr B.P., but probably not earlier. Lanceolate points at these hunting stations resemble those of the Agate Basin complex of the Great Plains, and we believe it most likely that late Paleoindian cultures spread northward into subarctic Canada and Alaska sometime after 10,500 yr B.P. The presence of Batza Téna obsidian at the Mesa site, if verified, would indicate that passes through the Brooks Range must have been open by at least 10,000 yr B.P., which is in accord with the known record of late Pleistocene glaciation. The Mesa complex reflects little cultural legacy from the earlier Nenana–Chindadn complex of central Alaska. For example, the lanceolate-shaped, concave-based, and edge-ground bifacial points of Mesa have not been identified in the central Alaskan assemblages predating 11,000 yr B.P. Furthermore, bifacial points characteristic of the Nenana complex in central Alaska (i.e., small Chindadn and triangular points) have not been found north of the Tanana basin. This may be an indication that humans in central Alaska were physically confined by the glaciated Brooks Range to the north as well as the Alaska Range to the south until about 10,500–10,000 yr B.P.

Fluted point technology also appears to postdate 10,500 yr B.P. in Alaska, and therefore is significantly younger than in temperate North America. As with the lanceolate points, fluted points evidently spread northward through Canada into Alaska. Whether they represent the same or a separate diffusion or migration event is not presently known. Clearly, though, the multiply fluted and "eared" bases of the Alaskan fluted points are distinct from early Clovis points on the High Plains and are more closely related to late Paleoindian fluted points found in western Canada after 10,500 yr B.P.

No dates are available on the enigmatic Akmak artifacts, which are known from Onion Portage and possibly two other localities in northwest Alaska. The uniqueness of the assemblage may be due to the exceptional raw materials that were utilized; correlations with Kamchatkan sites suggest a probable age span between 11,000 and 10,000 yr B.P., and therefore probable contemporaneity with the Mesa Paleoindians to the north and the Denali complex to the south. Although the Akmak assemblage is entirely distinct from Mesa, the presence of a wedge-shaped core, microblades, and burins suggest some affinities between Akmak and the Denali complex.

In addition to providing an age estimate for the Akmak artifacts, the late Pleistocene human record from western Beringia provides other significant insights into the peopling of Alaska. For example, the earliest evidence of humans in western Beringia dates to about 14,000 yr B.P., suggesting that Alaska could also have been occupied by this time. The blade-and-biface pattern documented in the Nenana valley sites predating 11,000 yr B.P. has been replicated at the Ushki-1 site in Kamchatka, and possibly at the Berelekh site in arctic northwestern Beringia. At these sites, bifaces and small bifacial points, retouched blades, end scrapers, and side scrapers are common, while microblades are absent (Goebel and Slobodin, this volume). On the other hand, fluted points and edge-ground lanceolate Paleoindian points like those from Mesa have not been found anywhere in western Beringia, implying that they were more likely derived from continental North America than from northeast Asia. Instead, as in central Alaska, the post-11,000-yr-B.P. record of late Pleistocene western Beringia is dominated by wedge-shaped core and microblade technologies.

Acknowledgments

We are pleased to acknowledge the following individuals for helpful discussions and patient answers to our numerous questions: R. E. Ackerman, D. D. Anderson, N. H. Bigelow, P. M. Bowers, J. P. Cook, T. Dilley, E. J. Dixon, R. Gal, S. C. Gerlach, R. D. Guthrie, J. F. Hoffecker, C. E. Holmes, D. M. Hopkins, M. L. Kunz, R. D. Lively, C. M. Mobley, G. A. Pearson, W. R. Powers, R. Reanier, J. Schaaf, D. Stanford, R. M. Thorson, R. VanderHoek, and D. Vinson. Many of the contributions of these individuals are acknowledged as "personal communications" in the text, but this reflects only a small part of their very generous assistance.

Earlier versions of this report were reviewed by P. M. Bowers, L. D. Carter, J. P. Galloway, S. C. Gerlach, T. H. Heaton, J. F. Hoffecker, C. E. Holmes, D. M. Hopkins, M. L. Kunz, R. M. Thorson, and W. B. Workman. Their criticisms and suggestions helped greatly to improve the final paper.

Appendix

Radiocarbon ages from Alaskan archaeological sites discussed in text. Symbols, references, and laboratories are listed at end of appendix.

Radiocarbon Years B.P.	*Laboratory No.*	*Material (c = charcoal)*	*Provenience (co = component; cz = cultural zone; ps = paleosol)*	*Reference*
A. Dry Creek				
modern	SI-1933A	c	ps 4b	1
375±40	SI-1933B	peat and roots	ps 4b	1
1145±60	SI-2333	c	ps 4b	1
3430±75	SI-2332	c	ps 4a	1
3655±60	SI-1934	c	ps 4a	1
4670±95	SI-1937	c	ps 4a	1
6270±110	SI-2331	c	ps 3	1
6900±95	SI-1935C	c	ps 3	1
8355±190	SI-1935B	c	ps 3	1
8600±460	SI-2115	c	ps 3	1
10,600±500*	SI-1935A	c	ps 3	1
19,050±1500*	SI-1544	c	ps 3	1
10,540±70††	AA-11731	c	upper member, ps 2	2
9340±190	SI-2329	c	ps 2; co II	1
9690±75††	AA-11732	c	middle, ps 2	2
12,080±1025*	SI-1936	c	ps 2	1
23,930±9300*	SI-1938	c	ps 2	1
9340±95††	AA-11733	c	lower member, ps 2	2
10,060±75††	AA-11727	c	upper member, ps 1	2
10,615±100††	AA-11728	c	lower member, ps 1	2
10,690±250	SI-1561	c	ps 1; co II	1
8915±70††	AA-11730	c	lower member, ps 1	2
11,120±85	SI-2880	c	co I	1
B. Walker Road				
3816±79††	AA-1693	c	ps, ~ 40 cm depth	3
4415±95	GX-12875	soil organics	ps, ~ 40 cm depth	3
8720±250††	AA-1692	c	ps, ~ 50-60 cm depth	3
11,010±230††	AA-1683	c	co I	3
11,170±180††	AA-1681	c	co I	3
11,300±120††	AA-2264	c	co I	3
11,820±200	Beta-11254	c	co I	3
C. Moose Creek				
8160±260	A-2168	soil organics	lower ps complex	3
8940±270	A-2144	soil organics	lower ps complex	3
10,640±280	I-11227	soil organics	lower ps complex	3
11,190±60††	Beta-96627	c	co I; hearth	4
11,730±250	GX-6281	soil organics	lower ps complex	3
D. Panguingue Creek				
4510±95	GX-13011	c	co III	5
5620±65	SI-3237	c	co III	5

Radiocarbon Years B.P.	*Laboratory No.*	*Material (c = charcoal)*	*Provenience (co = component; cz = cultural zone; ps = paleosol)*	*Reference*
7130± 180	Beta-15094	c	co II	5
7430±270††	AA-1688	c	co II	5
7595±405	GX-13012	c	co II	5
7850± 180	Beta-15093	c	co II	5
8600±200††	AA-1689	c	co II	5
8170± 120*††	AA-1687	carbonized sediment (?)	co I	5
9836±62††	GX-17457	c	co I	5
10,180± 130††	AA-1686	c	co I	5
13,535+400/-380	A-6744	soil organics	basal loess	6
E. Owl Ridge				
930±50	D-3071	c	upper sand	7
4400±70	Beta-11080	c	upper sand	7
1480± 180*	Beta-11082	c	co III	7
6900±265	D-3070	c	co III	7
7035±380	GX-13009	c	co III	7
2470± 120*	Beta-11081	c?	co II	7
7230± 100	Beta-11437	soil organics	co II	7
7660± 100	Beta-11436	soil organics	co II	7
8130± 140	Beta-5418	soil organics	co II	7
9325±305	GX-6283	soil organics	co II	7
2380±90*	Beta-11079	c?	co I	7
9060±410*	Beta-5416	c	co I	7
11,340± 150	Beta-11209	c	co I	7
F. Broken Mammoth				
2040±65	WSU-4267	c	cz 1 (upper)	8
2815± 180	UGA-6255D	c	cz 1 (upper)	8
4525±90	WSU-4458	c	cz 1 (lower)	8
4545±90	WSU-4457	c	cz 1 (lower)	8
4540±90	WSU-4456	c	cz 1(lower)	8
4690± 110	WSU-4350	c	cz 1 (lower)	8
7201±205	UGA-6281D	c	cz 2	8
7600± 140	WSU-4264	c	cz 2	8
7700±80	WSU-4508	c	cz 2	8
9310± 165	WSU-4266	c	cz 3 (upper)	8
9690±960	UGA-6256Da	c	cz 3	8
10,270± 110	WSU-4263a	c	cz 3	8
10,790±230	WSU-4019	c	cz 3	8
10,290±70††	CAMS-5358	c	cz 3	8
11,040±80††	CAMS-7203	large mammal bone	cz 3/4?	8
11,060±90††	CAMS-7204	wapiti bone	cz 3/4?	8
11,040±260	UGA-6257D	c	cz 4 (upper?)	8
11,280± 190	WSU-4265	c	cz 4 (middle)	8
11,420±70††	CAMS-5358	c	cz 4 (middle)	8
11,500±80††	CAMS-8261	swan bone	cz 4 (middle)	8

Radiocarbon Years B.P.	*Laboratory No.*	*Material (c = charcoal)*	*Provenience (co = component; cz = cultural zone; ps = paleosol)*	*Reference*
11,510±120	WSU-4262	c	cz 4 (middle)	8
11,770±210	WSU-4351	c	cz 4 (lower)	8
11,770±220	WSU-4364	c	cz 4 (lower)	8
15,830±70††	CAMS-9898	ivory artifact	cz 4 (lower?)	8
G. Swan Point				
1220±70	WSU-4523	c	co 2	9
1570±70	WSU-4524	c	co 2	9
1670±60	WSU-4522	c	co 2	9
1750±80	WSU-4521	c/resin?	co 2	9
7400±80	WSU-4426	c	co 5	9
10,230±80††	CAMS-4251	c	co 6	9
11,660±70††	CAMS-4252	c	co 7	9
11,660±60††	CAMS-12389	c	co 7	9
12,060±70††	CAMS-17405	collagen (from ivory)	co 7	9
H. Mead				
1430±60	WSU-4348	c	upper forest soil; cz 1	10
4050±140	WSU-4349	c	middle forest soil	10
6070±170	Beta-59115	c	lower forest soil; cz 2	10
9220±370*	Beta-59117	c	base, forest soil; cz 2	10
7620±100*	WSU-4261	c	ps; bulk sample from test pit	10
10,410±80††	CAMS-5197	c	middle ps; cz 3	10
10,460±110††	CAMS-4876	c	middle ps; cz 3	10
10,760±170	WSU-4425	c	lower-middle ps; cz 3	10
11,560±80††	CAMS-5198	c	lower ps; cz 4	10
11,600±80††	CAMS-4877	c	lower ps; cz 4	10
17,370±90††	CAMS-17408	collagen (from ivory)	cz 4	10
I. Healy Lake				
455±130	GX-2166	c	level 1 (0-5 cm)	11
900±90	GaK-1886	c	level 1	11
modern	GX-1945	c	level 1	11
380±50††	CAMS-16521	plant material	level 2 (5-10 cm)	12
905±90	GX-2160	c	level 2	11
1360±80	GaK-1887	c	level 2	11
1655±180	GX-2168	c	level 2	11
2875±140	GX-2169	c	level 2	11
3850±140	GX-2165	c	level 2	11
3655±426	AU-4	c	level 2	11
4460±60††	CAMS-16524	plant material	level 2	12
1790±50††	CAMS-16522	plant material	level 3 (10-15 cm)	12
2660±100	GX-2176	c	level 3	11
3350±50††	CAMS-15915	c	level 3	12
2150±180	GX-2161	c	level 4 (15-20 cm)	11
3020±50††	CAMS-15916	c	level 4	12

Radiocarbon Years B.P.	*Laboratory No.*	*Material (c = charcoal)*	*Provenience (co = component; cz = cultural zone; ps = paleosol)*	*Reference*
4010± 110	GX-2163	c	level 4	11
8960± 150	GX-1340	bone	level 4	11
modern	GX-2162	c	level 5 (20-25 cm)	11
5000± 60††	CAMS-16525	plant material	level 5	12
5110±90	Beta-76064	c	level 6 (25-31 cm)	11
7920±90	Beta-76062	soil	level 6	11
10,250± 380	GX-2173	c	level 6	11
10,410± 60††	CAMS-15920	c	level 6	12
11,100± 60††	CAMS-15918	c	level 6	12
11,410± 60††	CAMS-15914	c	level 6	12
8655± 280	GX-2171	c	level 7 (31-36cm)	11
8680± 240	GX-2170	c	level 7	11
8990± 60††	CAMS-15919	c	level 7	12
10,290± 60††	CAMS-15917	c	level 7	12
11,550± 50††	CAMS-16523	plant material	level 7	12
9245± 213b	AU-1	c	level 7	11
9895± 210b	GX-2174	c	level 7	11
10,150± 210b	SI-737	c	level 7	11
11,090± 170	GX-1341	bone	level 8 (36-41 cm)	11
9401± 528c	AU-2	c	level 9 (41-46 cm)	11
6645± 280c	GX-2159	c	level 9	11
8210± 155c	SI-738	c	level 9	11
10,434± 279d	AU-3	c	level 10 (46-51 cm)	11
8465± 360d	GX-2175	c	level 10	11
10,040± 210d	SI-739	c	level 10	11
10,500± 280	GX-1944	c	level 10	11
J. Chugwater				
6260± 390	Beta-7570	c	uncertain	13
7760± 130	Beta-7569	c	uncertain	13
8960± 130††	Beta-18509	c	3 cm below "marker line"	13
9460± 130††	Beta-19496	c	3 cm below "marker line"	13
K. Campus				
modern	DIC-2793	c	5-10 cm depth	14
650± 200††	Beta-10879	bone collagen	10-15 cm depth	14
2860± 180	Beta-4260	c	15-20 cm depth	14
modern††	Beta-10878	c	20-25 cm depth	14
2725± 125	Beta-7075	c	20-25 cm depth	14
240± 120	Beta-7224	c	20-30 cm depth	14
3500± 140	Beta-6829	c	20-30 cm depth	14
L. Tangle Lakes				
5100± 60	SI-2171B-2	organic soil (humic acid)	overlying cz, Phipps (Mt. Hayes 111)	15
5740± 110	SI-2171B-1	organic soil (humic acid)	overlying cz, Phipps (Mt. Hayes 111)	15

Radiocarbon Years B.P.	Laboratory No.	Material (c = charcoal)	Provenience (co = component; cz = cultural zone; ps = paleosol)	Reference
8155±265	UGa-927	c	overlying cz, Phipps (Mt. Hayes 111)	15
9060±265	UGa-941	c?	cz, Sparks Point (Mt. Hayes 149)	15
9110±80††	Beta-64577	c?	cz, (Mt. Hayes 149)	17
9200±60††	Beta-62773	c?	cz, (Mt. Hayes 149)	17
9600±140††	Beta-64578	c	cz, Whitmore Ridge (Mt. Hayes 72)	18
9830±60††	Beta-70240	c	cz, Whitmore Ridge (Mt. Hayes 72)	18
9890±70††	Beta-62222	c	cz, Whitmore Ridge (Mt. Hayes 72)	18
10,150±280	UGa-572	c	3 cm below cz, Phipps (Mt. Hayes 111)	15
10,230±70††	Beta-63672	c	cz, Phipps (Mt. Hayes 111)	16
10,270±70††	Beta-77286	c	cz, Whitmore Ridge (Mt. Hayes 72)	18
M. Carlo Creek				
5120±265*	WSU-1727	soil humic acid	co I; lower ps	19
8400±200	WSU-1700	c	co I; hearth 1	19
8690±330	GX-5132	c	co I; hearth 2	19
10,040±435*	GX-5131	c	co I; hearth 1	19
N. Teklanika West				
1770±70††	Beta-59592	c	above co II	20
3310±100	Beta-59591	c	co II	20
5340±90††	GX-18517	c	co II	20
7130±98††	GX-18518	c	co I	20
O. Mesa				
7620±95	DIC-1589	c	combined from 3 hearths	21
9730±80††	ETH-6570	c	N117-121/E96-100; soil charcoal	23
9810±110††	Beta-96065	c	S1-N1/E34-36A; hearth	24
9850±150††	Beta-96067	c	S1-N1/E34-36C; hearth	24
9900±70††	CAMS-4146	c	N209-211/E176-178; hearth	23
9900±80††	CAMS-11036	c	N211-215/E174-178; hearth	22
9930±80††	CAMS-3570	c	N213-215/E180-182; hearth	23
9945±75††	ETH-9087	c	N103-107/E94-98; hearth	23
9980±60††	Beta-84649	c	N230-231/E178-179; hearth	24
9990±80††	CAMS-3568	c	N109-111/E88-90; hearth	23
10,000±80††	CAMS-3571	c	N217-219/E176-178; hearth	23
10,050±90††	CAMS-11037	c	N211-215/E182-186; hearth	23
10,060±70††	CAMS-2688	c	N179-183/E146-150; hearth	23
10,070±60††	CAMS-11035	c	N111-115/E98-102; hearth	22
10,080±50††	Beta-84650	c	S23-24/W21-22; hearth	24
10,080±60††	Beta-95913	c	S27-29/W56-58; hearth	24
10,080±120††	Beta-96068	c	S1-N1/E34-36D; hearth	24
10,090±85††	ETH-9086	c	S1-5/E16-20; hearth	23
10,090±110††	Beta-96066	c	S1-N1/E34-36B; hearth	24
10,130±60††	Beta-95914	c	S31-33/W86-88; hearth	24
10,150±120††	Beta-96069	c	S1-N1/E34-36E; hearth	24
10,230±60††	Beta-95600	c	N1-3/S34-36; hearth	24
10,240±80††	CAMS-3569	c	N209-211/E184-186; hearth	23

Radiocarbon Years B.P.	*Laboratory No.*	*Material (c = charcoal)*	*Provenience (co = component; cz = cultural zone; ps = paleosol)*	*Reference*
10,260±110††	Beta-96070	c	N1-3/S34-36A; hearth	24
10,980±280*	Beta-50429	c	N103-107/E94-98; hearth	22
11,190±70††	CAMS-4147	c	N217-219/E180-182; hearth	23
11,660±80††	CAMS-3572	c	N217-219/E180-182; hearth	23
P. Putu-Bedwell				
650±100	Gak-4940	c	upper soil; hearth	25
5700±190	Gak-4941	c	cz; combined samples	25
6090±430	Gak-4939	soil organics	lower half of loess	25
8454±130	WSU-1318	soil organics	lower half of loess	25
8810±60††	Beta-69901	c	hearth (feature 9)	26
11,470±500*	SI-2382	c	hearth (feature 3)	25
10,490±70††	CAMS-11032	c	Bedwell site	26
Q. Hilltop				
6160±130	GaK-4924	soil organics and c	1970 excavation	26
10,360±60††	CAMS-11034	c	1993 test pit	26
R. Gallagher (locality 1 only)				
6960±90††	Beta-97211	c	loess, 14 cm depth; test pit near Locality 1	27
10,540±150	SI-974	c	loess, 20-25 cm depth	28
S. Onion Portage (band 8 and Akmak only)				
7180±90*	P-1111	c	level 1, Kobuk complex	29
7320±100*	P-1111A	c	level 1, Kobuk complex	29
7900±100	P-1076	c	level 1, Kobuk complex	29
7920±100	P-984A	c	level 1, Kobuk complex	29
8100±100	P-985	c	level 1, Kobuk complex	29
8195±280	P-985	c	level 1, Kobuk complex	29
9570±150*	K-1583	bone (apatite)	redeposited in gully with Akmak artifacts	30
T. Trail Creek Caves				
9070±150	K-980	caribou bone (collagen?)	associated with microblade and slotted spearpoint; unit III of cave 2	31,32
11,360±280	K-1327	mammoth scapula (collagen)	floor, cave B	31
14,270±950	Beta-20027	mammoth vertebra (collagen)	just above floor, cave B	32
13,070±280	K-1327	bison calcaneus (collagen)	unit IV, cave 9	31
15,750±350	K-1210	horse scapula (collagen?)	unit IV, cave 9	31

Notes to Appendix on next page.

Notes to Appendix:
* Problem date considered discordant by primary researchers
†† AMS date
a. Split sample, cultural zone 3, Broken Mammoth
b. Split sample, level 7, Healy Lake
c. Split sample, level 9, Healy Lake
d. Split sample, level 10, Healy Lake

References:
(1) Thorson and Hamilton 1977
(2) Bigelow and Powers 1994
(3) Powers and Hoffecker 1989
(4) Pearson 1997
(5) Goebel and Bigelow 1992
(6) C. L. Ping, pers. commun., 1993
(7) Phippen 1988
8) Holmes 1996
(9) Holmes et al. 1996
(10) C. E. Holmes, personal communication 1996
(11) Erlandson et al. 1991
(12) Cook 1996
(13) Lively 1988
(14) Mobley 1990
(15) West 1975; 1981
(16) West et al. 1996a
(17) West et al. 1997b
(18) West et al. 1996c
(19) Bowers 1980
(20) Goebel 1996
(21) Kunz 1982
(22) Kunz and Reanier 1995
(23) Kunz and Reanier 1994
(24) M. L. Kunz, pers. commun., 1998
(25) Alexander 1987
(26) Reanier 1995
(27) Ferguson 1997a
(28) Dixon 1975
(29) Anderson 1988
(30) Anderson 1970; Hamilton 1970
(31) Larsen 1968
(32) Vinson 1988

Laboratories:

A	University of Arizona
AA	University of Arizona Accelerator
AU	University of Alaska
B	Bern, Switzerland
Beta	Beta Analytic
CAMS	Lawrence Livermore National Laboratory
D	Dicarb Radioisotope Company (?)
DIC	Dicarb Radioisotope Company
ETH	Eidgenössiche Technische Hochschule
GaK	Gakushuin University, Japan
GX	Geochron
K	Copenhagen, Denmark
I	Teledyne Isotopes
P	University of Pennsylvania
SI	Smithsonian Institution
UGa	University of Georgia
WSU	Washington State University

References Cited

Abramova, Z. A.
1989 Paleolit Severnoi Azii [Paleolithic of Northern Asia]. In *Paleolit Kavkaza i Severnoi Azii [Paleolithic of the Caucasus and Northern Asia]*, pp. 143–243. Nauka, Leningrad [in Russian].

Ackerman, R. E.
1988a Early Subsistence Patterns in Southeast Alaska. In *Diet and Subsistence: Current Archaeological Perspectives*, edited by B. V. Kennedy and G. M. LeMoine, pp. 175–189. University of Calgary Archaeological Association, Calgary.

1988b Settlements and Sea-Mammal Hunting in the Bering Chukchi Sea Region. *Arctic Anthropology* 25:52–79.

1996a Early Maritime Culture Complexes of the Northern Northwest Coast. In *Early Human Occupation of British Columbia*, edited by R. L. Carlson and L. Dalla-Bona, pp. 123–132. University of British Columbia Press, Vancouver.

1996b Ground Hog Bay, Site 2. In *American Beginnings: The Prehistory and Palaeoecology of Beringia*, edited by F. H. West, pp. 424–430. University of Chicago Press, Chicago.

Ackerman, R. E., and T. K. Bundtzen
1994 Late Pleistocene/Early Holocene Sites in Southwestern Alaska. Paper presented at the 21st Annual Meeting of the Alaska Anthropological Association, Juneau.

Ackerman, R. E., T. D. Hamilton, and R. Stuckenrath
1979 Early Culture Complexes on the Northern Northwest Coast. *Canadian Journal of Archaeology* 3:195–209.

Ager, T. A.
1972 *Surficial Geology and Quaternary History of the Healy Lake Area, Alaska.* Master's thesis, Department of Geology, University of Alaska, College.

1975 *Late Quaternary Environmental History of the Tanana Valley, Alaska.* Ohio State University Institute of Polar Studies Report No. 54. Columbus.

Ager, T. A., and L. Brubaker
1985 Quaternary Palynology and Vegetational History of Alaska. In *Pollen Records of Late-Quaternary North American Sediments*, edited by V. Bryant, Jr. and R. Holloway, pp. 353–384. American Association of Stratigraphic Palynologists Foundation, Dallas.

Ager, T. A., and J. D. Sims
1981 Holocene Pollen and Sediment Record from the Tangle Lakes Area, Central Alaska. *Palynology* 5:85–98.

Alexander, H. L.
1987 *Putu: A Fluted Point Site in Alaska.* Simon Fraser University Publication No. 17. Archaeology Press, Simon Fraser University, Burnaby.

Anderson, D. D.
1970 *Akmak: An Early Archaeological Assemblage from Onion Portage, Northwest Alaska. Acta Arctica*, vol 16. Copenhagen.

1984 Prehistory of North Alaska. In *Arctic*, edited by D. Dumas, pp. 80–93. *Handbook of North American Indians*, vol. 5, W. C. Sturtevant, general editor. Smithsonian Institution, Washington, D.C.

1988 *Onion Portage: The Archaeology of a Stratified Site from the Kobuk River, Northwest Alaska. Anthropological Papers of the University of Alaska* 22(1–2).

Anderson, P. M., and L. B. Brubaker
1994 Vegetation History of Northcentral Alaska—A Mapped Summary of Late-Quaternary Pollen Data. *Quaternary Science Reviews* 13:71–92.

Bandi, H.-G.
1969 *Eskimo Prehistory*. University of Alaska Press, College.

Bigelow, N. H.
1991 *Analysis of Late Pleistocene Soils and Sediments in the Nenana Valley, Central Alaska*. M.A. thesis, Department of Anthropology, University of Alaska Fairbanks.

Bigelow, N., J. Begét, and W. R. Powers
1990 Latest Pleistocene Increase in Wind Intensity Recorded in Eolian Sediments from Central Alaska. *Quaternary Research* 34:160–168.

Bigelow, N. H., and W. R. Powers
1994 New AMS Dates from the Dry Creek Paleoindian Site, Central Alaska. *Current Research in the Pleistocene* 11:114–115.

Bowers, P. M.
1980 *The Carlo Creek Site: Geology and Archeology of an Early Holocene Site in the Central Alaska Range*. Occasional Paper No. 27. University of Alaska Cooperative Park Studies Unit, Fairbanks.

1983 *A Status Report On the Gallagher Flint Station National Historic Landmark*. Bureau of Land Management, Arctic Resource Area, Fairbanks.

Calkin, P. E.
1988 Holocene Glaciation of Alaska (and Adjoining Yukon Territory, Canada). *Quaternary Science Reviews* 7:159–184.

Campbell, K., and J. Begét
1989 Moraine Dam Failure and Flood at Tangle Lakes, Alaska, Circa 8,000 Years B.P. *Geological Society of America Abstracts With Programs* 21(5):63.

Carlson, R. L.
1991 Clovis from the Perspective of the Ice-Free Corridor. In *Clovis: Origins and Adaptations*, edited by R. Bonnichsen and K. L. Turnmire, pp. 81–90. Center for the Study of the First Americans, Oregon State University, Corvallis.

Carter, L. D.
1993 Late Pleistocene Stabilization and Reactivation of Eolian Sand in Northern Alaska—Implications for the Effects of Future Climatic Change on an Eolian Landscape in Continuous Permafrost. In *Proceedings, 6th International Conferences on Permafrost, Beijing, China, July 1993*, pp. 78–83. South China University of Technology Press, Guangzhou, China.

Child, J.
1995a *A Late Quaternary Lacustrine Record of Environmental Change in the Wonder Lake Area, Denali National Park and Preserve, Alaska*. M.S. thesis, University of Massachusetts, Amherst.

1995b A Late Wisconsinan Lacustrine Record of Environmental Change in the Wonder Lake Area, Denali National Park and Preserve, Alaska. *Geological Society of America Abstracts with Programs* 27(6):A-210.

Clark, D. W.
1984 Some Practical Applications of Obsidian Hydration Dating in the Subarctic. *Arctic* 37:91–109.

1987 Northern (Alaska-Yukon) Fluted Points. In *Programme with Abstracts*, pp. 144. XII International Congress, International Union for Quaternary Research, Ottawa.

1991 The Northern (Alaska-Yukon) Fluted Points. In *Clovis: Origins and Adaptations*, edited by R. Bonnichsen and K. L. Turnmire, pp. 35–48. Center for the Study of the First Americans, Oregon State University, Corvallis.

Clark, D.W., and A. M. Clark
1975 Fluted Points from the Batza Tena Obsidian Source of the Koyukuk River Region, Alaska. *Anthropological Papers of the University of Alaska* 17:31–38.

1993 *Batza Téna: Trail to Obsidian (Archaeology at an Alaskan Obsidian Source)*. Archaeological Survey of Canada, Mercury Series Paper 147, Canadian Museum of Civilization.

Colinvaux, P.
1981 Historical Ecology in Beringia: The South Land Bridge Coast at St. Paul Island. *Quaternary Research* 22:189–200.

Cook, J. P.
1969 *The Early Prehistory of Healy Lake, Alaska*. Ph.D. dissertation, Department of Anthropology, University of Wisconsin, Madison.

1975 Archaeology of Interior Alaska. *Western Canadian Journal of Anthropology* 5:125–133.

1989 Historic Archaeology and Ethnohistory at Healy Lake, Alaska. *Arctic* 42:109–118.

1996 Healy Lake. In *American Beginnings: The Prehistory and Palaeoecology of Beringia*, edited by F. H. West, pp. 323–327. University of Chicago Press, Chicago.

Cook, J. P., and R. McKennan
1970 The Village Site at Healy Lake, Alaska: An Interim Report. Paper presented at the 35th Annual Meeting of the Society for American Archaeology, Mexico City.

Davis, S. D. (ed.)
1989 The Hidden Falls Site, Baranof Island, Alaska. *Alaska Anthropological Association, Aurora Monograph Series* 5.

1996 Hidden Falls. In *American Beginnings: The Prehistory and Palaeoecology of Beringia*, edited by F. H. West, pp. 413–424. University of Chicago Press, Chicago.

Dikov, N. N.
1977 *Arkheologicheskie Pamiatniki Kamchatki, Chukotki, i Verkhnei Kolymy [Archaeological Monuments of Kamchatka, Chukotka, and the Upper Kolyma].* Nauka, Moscow.

1979 *Drevnie Kul'tury Severo-Vostochnoi Azii [Ancient Cultures of North-Eastern Asia].* Nauka, Moscow.

Dixon, E. J., Jr.
1975 The Gallagher Flint Station, An Early Man Site on the North Slope, Arctic Alaska, and Its Role in Relation to the Bering Land Bridge. *Arctic Anthropology* 7:68–75.

1985 Cultural Chronology of Central Interior Alaska. *Arctic Anthropology* 22:47–66.

1993 *Quest for the Origins of the First Americans.* University of New Mexico Press, Albuquerque.

1998 Excavations at PET-408, Prince of Wales Island, Southeast Alaska: A Progress Report. Paper presented at 26th Annual Meeting of the Alaska Anthropological Association, Anchorage.

Dixon, E. J., Jr., and G. S. Smith
1986 Broken Canines from Alaskan Cave Deposits: Reevaluating Evidence for Domesticated Dog and Early Humans in Alaska. *American Antiquity* 51:341–351.

Dixon, E. J., T. H. Heaton, T. E. Fifield, T. D. Hamilton, D. E. Putnam, and F. Grady
1997 Late Quaternary Regional Geoarchaeology of Southeast Alaska Karst: a Progress Report. *Geoarchaeology* 12(6):689–712.

Erlandson, J. M., and M. L. Moss
1996 The Pleistocene-Holocene Transition along the Pacific Coast of North America. In *Humans at the End of the Ice Age: The Archaeology of the Pleistocene-Holocene Transition*, edited by L. G. Straus, B. V. Eriksen, J. M. Erlandson, and D. R. Yesner, pp. 277–302. Plenum Press, New York.

Erlandson, J., R. Walser, H. Maxwell, N. Bigelow, J. Cook, R. Lively, C. Adkins, D. Dodson, A. Higgs, and J. Wilber
1991 Two Early Sites of Eastern Beringia: Context and Chronology in Alaskan Interior Archaeology. *Radiocarbon* 33(1):35–50.

Ferguson, D. E.
1997a *Gallagher Flint Station, Locality 1: A Reappraisal of a Proposed Late Pleistocene Site in the Sagavanirktok River Valley, Arctic Alaska.* M.A. thesis, University of Alaska Fairbanks, Fairbanks.

1997b Revised Temporal Assessment of a Proposed Paleoarctic Site in the Sagavanirktok Valley, Northern Alaska. *Current Research in the Pleistocene* 14:24–26.

Ferrians, O. J.
1965 *Permafrost Map of Alaska.* U.S. Geological Survey Miscellaneous Geological Investigations Map I-445, scale 1:2,500,000.

Fladmark, K. R.
1978 The Feasibility of the Northwest Coast as a Migration Route for Early Man. In *Early Man in America from a Circum-Pacific Perspective*, edited by A. L. Bryan, pp. 119–128. Occasional Papers No. 1. Department of Anthropology, University of Alberta, Edmonton.

1982 An Introduction to the Prehistory of British Columbia. *Canadian Journal of Archaeology* 6:95–156.

Fladmark, K. R., J. C. Driver, and D. Alexander
1988 The Paleoindian Component at Charlie Lake Cave (HbRf39). *American Antiquity* 53:371–384.

Giddings, J. L.
1964 *The Archaeology of Cape Denbigh.* Brown University Press, Providence.

Giddings, J. L. and D. D. Anderson
1986 *Beach Ridge Archeology of Cape Krusenstern.* Publications in Archeology No. 20. National Park Service, Washington, D.C.

Goebel, T.
1996 Recent Research at Teklanika West: Site Stratigraphy and Dating. In *American Beginnings: The Prehistory and Palaeoecology of Beringia*, edited by F. H. West, pp. 341–343. University of Chicago Press, Chicago.

Goebel, T., and N. Bigelow
1992 The Denali Complex at Panguingue Creek, Central Alaska. *Current Research in the Pleistocene* 9:15–18.

Goebel, T., W. R. Powers, and N. H. Bigelow
1991 The Nenana Complex of Alaska and Clovis Origins. In *Clovis: Origins and Adaptations*, edited by R. Bonnichsen and K. L. Turnmire, pp. 49–79. Center for the Study of the First Americans, Oregon State University, Corvallis.

Goebel, T., W. R. Powers, N. H. Bigelow, and A. S. Higgs
1996 Walker Road. In *American Beginnings: The Prehistory and Palaeoecology of Beringia*, edited by F. H. West, pp. 356–363. University of Chicago Press, Chicago.

Gruhn, R.
1994 The Pacific Coast Route of Initial Entry: An Overview. In *Method and Theory for Investigating the Peopling of the Americas*, edited by R. Bonnichsen and D. G. Steele, pp. 249–256. Center for the Study of the First Americans, Oregon State University, Corvallis.

Gryba, E. M.
1983 *Sibbald Creek: 11,000 Years of Human Use of the Alberta Foothills.* Archaeological Survey of Alberta Occasional Paper No. 22, Edmonton.

Hall, D. A.
1995 Tanana Sites Connect Alaska with Eurasia (Commentary). *Mammoth Trumpet* 10(4):1, 12–13.

1997 Expedition Affirms Significance of Moose Creek Site. *Mammoth Trumpet* 12(4):13–18.

Hamilton, T. D.
1970 Geologic Relations of the Akmak Assemblage, Onion Portage Area. In *Akmak: An Early Archeological Assemblage from Onion Portage, Northwest Alaska,* edited by D. D. Anderson, pp. 71–80. *Acta Arctica,* Vol 16. Copenhagen.

1978 *Surficial Geologic Map of the Philip Smith Mountains Quadrangle, Alaska.* U.S. Geological Survey Miscellaneous Field Studies Map MF-879-A, 1:250,000.

1979 *Radiocarbon Dates and Quaternary Stratigraphic Sections, Philip Smith Mountains Quadrangle, Alaska.* U.S. Geological Survey Open-File Report 79-866.

1982 A Late Pleistocene Glacial Chronology for the Southern Brooks Range—Stratigraphic Record and Regional Significance. *Geological Society of America Bulletin* 93:700–716.

1984 *Surficial Geologic Map of the Ambler River Quadrangle, Alaska.* U.S. Geological Survey Miscellaneous Field Studies Map MF-1678, scale 1:250,000.

1986 Late Cenozoic Glaciation of the Central Brooks Range. In *Glaciation in Alaska: The Geologic Record,* edited by T. D. Hamilton, K. M. Reed, and R. M. Thorson, pp. 9–49. Alaska Geological Society, Anchorage.

1994 Late Cenozoic Glaciation of Alaska. In *The Geology of Alaska,* edited by G. Plafker and H. C. Berg, pp. 813–844. *The Geology of North America,* Vol G-1. Geological Society of America, Boulder, CO.

Hamilton, T. D., and G. M. Ashley
1993 Epiguruk—A Late Quaternary Environmental Record from Northwestern Alaska. *Geological Society of America Bulletin* 105:583–602.

Hamilton, T. D., G. M. Ashley, K. M. Reed, and C. E. Schweger
1993 Late Pleistocene Vertebrates and Other Fossils from Epiguruk, Northwestern Alaska. *Quaternary Research* 39:381–389.

Hamilton, T. D., J. P. Galloway, and E. A. Koster
1988 Late Wisconsin Eolian Activity and Related Alluviation, Central Kobuk River Valley. In *Geologic Studies in Alaska by the U.S. Geological Survey During 1987,* edited by J. P. Galloway and T. D. Hamilton, pp. 39–43. U.S. Geological Survey Circular No. 1016.

Haynes, C. V., Jr.
1992 Contributions of Radiocarbon Dating to the Geochronology of the Peopling of the New World. In *Radiocarbon After Four Decades,* edited by R. E. Taylor, A. Long, and R. S. Kra, pp. 355–374. Springer-Verlag, New York.

Heaton, T. H., and F. Grady
1997 The Preliminary Late Wisconsin Mammalian Biochronology of Prince of Wales Island, Southeastern Alaska. *Journal of Vertebrate Paleontology* 17(3):52A.

Heaton, T. H., S. L. Talbot, and G. F. Shields
1996 An Ice Age Refugium for Large Mammals in the Alexander Archipelago, Southeastern Alaska. *Quaternary Research* 46(2):186–192.

Heusser, C. J.
1985 Quaternary Pollen Records from the Pacific Northwest Coast—Aleutians to the Oregon–California Boundary. In *Pollen Records of Late-Quaternary North American Sediments,* edited by V. M. Bryant, Jr. and R. G. Holloway, pp. 141–165. American Association of Stratigraphic Palynologists, Dallas.

Hoffecker, J. F.
1985 The Moose Creek Site. In *North Alaska Range Early Man Project,* edited by W. R. Powers and others, pp. 38–48. *National Geographic Society Research Reports* 19.

1988a Applied Geomorphology and Archaeological Survey Strategy for Sites of Pleistocene Age: An Example from Central Alaska. *Journal of Archaeological Science* 15:683–713.

1988b A Preliminary Analysis of Occupation Floors at the Dry Creek Site. Unpublished manuscript.

Hoffecker, J. F., C. F. Waythomas, and W. R. Powers
1988 Late Glacial Loess Stratigraphy and Archaeology in the Nenana Valley, Central Alaska. *Current Research in the Pleistocene* 5:83–86.

Hoffecker, J. F., W. R. Powers, and T. Goebel
1993a The Colonization of Beringia and the Peopling of the New World. *Science* 259:46–53.

Hoffecker, J. F., W. R. Powers, T. Goebel, and N. Bigelow.
1993b The Nenana Complex and the Peopling of the New World. Paper presented at the 58th Annual Meeting of the Society for American Archaeology, St. Louis.

Holmes, C. E.
1971 The Prehistory of the Upper Koyukuk River Region in North-Central Alaska. In *Final Report of the Archeological Survey and Excavations along the Alyeska Pipeline Route,* edited by J. P. Cook, pp. 326–400. Department of Anthropology, University of Alaska, College.

1996 Broken Mammoth. In *American Beginnings: The Prehistory and Palaeoecology of Beringia,* edited by F. H. West, pp. 312–318. University of Chicago Press, Chicago.

Holmes, C. E., and R. VanderHoek
1994 Swan Point: A Multi-Component, Late Pleistocene/Holocene Site in the Tanana Valley, Central Alaska. Paper presented at 59th Annual Meeting of the Society for American Archaeology, Anaheim.

Holmes, C. E., and D. R. Yesner
1992a Investigating the Earliest Americans: The Broken Mammoth Archaeological Project. *Arctic Research of the United States* 6:6–9.

1992b The Broken Mammoth Archaeological Project, Central Tanana Valley, Interior Alaska: Progress Update. Paper presented at 57th Annual Meeting of the Society for American Archaeology.

Holmes, C. E., R. VanderHoek, and T. Dilley
1994 Old Microblades in the Tanana Valley: The View from Swan Point. Paper presented at 21st Annual Meeting of Alaska Anthropological Association, Juneau, Alaska, March–April.

1996 Swan Point. In *American Beginnings: The Prehistory and Palaeoecology of Beringia*, edited by F. H. West, pp. 319–323. University of Chicago Press, Chicago.

Hopkins, D. M., P. A. Smith, and J. V. Matthews, Jr.
1981 Dated Wood from Alaska and the Yukon—Implications for Forest Refugia in Beringia. *Quaternary Research* 15:217–249.

Hu, F. S., L. B. Brubaker, and P. M. Anderson
1995 Postglacial Vegetation and Climate Change in the Northern Bristol Bay Region, Southwestern Alaska. *Quaternary Research* 43:382–392.

Josenhans, H., D. Fedje, R. Pienitz, and J. Souton
1997 Early Humans and Rapidly Changing Holocene Sea Levels in the Queen Charlotte Islands-Hecate Strait, British Columbia. *Science* 277:71–74.

King, M. L., and S. B. Slobodin
1996 A Fluted Point from the Uptar Site, Northeastern Siberia. *Science* 273:634-636.

Kunz, M. L.
1982 The Mesa Site: An Early Holocene Hunting Stand in the Iteriak Valley, Northern Alaska. In *Archaeological Investigations by the U.S. Geological Survey and the Bureau of Land Management in the National Petroleum Reserve in Alaska*, edited by E. S. Hall, Jr. and R. Gal, pp. 113–122. *Anthropological Papers of the University of Alaska* 20(1–2).

Kunz, M. L., and D. H. Mann
1997 The Mesa Project: Interactions between Early Prehistoric Humans and Environmental Change in Arctic Alaska. *Arctic Research of the United States* 11:55–62.

Kunz, M. L., and R. E. Reanier
1994 Paleoindians in Beringia: Evidence from Arctic Alaska. *Science* 263:660–662.

1995 The Mesa Site: A Paleoindian Hunting Lookout in Arctic Alaska. *Arctic Anthropology* 32:5–30.

Larsen, H.
1968 *Trail Creek: Final Report on the Excavation of Two Caves on Seward Peninsula, Alaska. Acta Arctica*, Vol. 15. Copenhagen.

Laughlin, W. S.
1967 Human Migration and Permanent Occupation in the Bering Sea area. In *The Bering Land Bridge*, edited by D. M. Hopkins, pp. 409–450. Stanford University Press, Stanford.

1975 Aleuts: Ecosystem, Holocene History, and Siberian Origin. *Science* 189:507–515.

Lively, R. D.
1988 *Chugwater (FAI-035): A Study of the Effectiveness of a Small Scale Probabilistic Sampling Design at an Interior Alaskan Site.* Chena River Lakes Flood Control Project, U.S. Army Corps of Engineers, Alaska District.

Mann, D. H., and T. D. Hamilton
1995 Late Pleistocene and Holocene Paleoenvironments of the North Pacific Coast. *Quaternary Science Reviews* 14:449–471.

Mann, D. H., and D. M. Peteet
1994 Extent and Timing of the Last Glacial Maximum in Southwest Alaska. *Quaternary Research* 42:136–148.

Mobley, C. M.
1982 The Landmark Gap Trail Site, Tangle Lakes, Alaska: Another Perspective on the Amphitheater Mountain Complex. *Arctic Anthropology* 19:81–102.

1990 *The Campus Site: A Prehistoric Camp at Fairbanks, Alaska.* University of Alaska Press, Fairbanks.

Morlan, R. E., and J. Cinq-Mars
1982 Ancient Beringians: Human Occupation in the Late Pleistocene of Alaska and the Yukon Territory. In *Paleoecology of Beringia*, edited by D. M. Hopkins, J. V. Matthews, Jr., C. E. Schweger, and S. B. Young, pp. 353–381. Academic Press, New York.

Patton, W. W., and T. P. Miller
1970 A Possible Bedrock Source for Obsidian Found in Archaeological Sites in Northwestern Alaska. *Science* 169:760–761.

Pearson, G. A.
1996 Paleoindians in the Alaskan Interior: Results of the 1996 Moose Creek Expedition. Paper presented at the 62nd Annual Meeting of the Society for American Archaeology.

Pearson, G. A., and W. R. Powers
1996 The Campus Site Re-Revisited: Preliminary Results of the 1995 Excavations. Paper presented at the 23rd Annual Meeting of the Alaska Anthropological Association.

Péwé, T. L.
1965 Middle Tanana River Valley. In *Guidebook for Field Conference F, Central and South-Central Alaska, International Association for Quaternary Research, 7th*

Congress, Fairbanks, edited by T. L. Péwé, O. J. Ferrians, T. N. V. Karlstrom, and D. R. Nichols, pp. 36–54. Nebraska Academy of Science, Lincoln.

1975 *Quaternary Geology of Alaska*. U.S. Geological Survey Professional Paper 835.

Péwé, T. L., and R. D. Reger
1983 Middle Tanana River Valley. In *Guidebook to Permafrost and Quaternary Geology along the Richardson and Glenn Highways between Fairbanks and Anchorage, Alaska*, edited by T. L. Péwé and R. D. Reger, pp. 5–45. Division of Geological and Geophysical Surveys, Department of Natural Resources, State of Alaska, Fairbanks.

Phippen, P. G.
1988 *Archaeology At Owl Ridge: A Pleistocene–Holocene Boundary Age Site in Central Alaska*. Master's thesis, Department of Anthropology, University of Alaska, Fairbanks.

Powers, W.R., T. Goebel, and N. H. Bigelow
1990 Late Pleistocene Occupation at Walker Road: New Data on the Central Alaskan Nenana Complex. *Current Research in the Pleistocene* 7:40–43.

Powers, W.R., and T. D. Hamilton
1978 Dry Creek: A Late Pleistocene Human Occupation in Central Alaska. In *Early Man in America from a Circum-Pacific Perspective*, edited by A. L. Bryan, pp.72–77. Occasional Papers No. 1. Department of Anthropology, University of Alberta, Edmonton.

Powers, W. R., and J. F. Hoffecker
1989 Late Pleistocene Settlement in the Nenana Valley, Central Alaska. *American Antiquity* 54:263–278.

Powers, W. R., and H. E. Maxwell
1986 *Lithic Remains from Panguingue Creek: An Early Holocene Site in the Northern Foothills of the Alaska Range*. Alaska Historical Commission Studies in History No. 189.

Powers, W. R., R. D. Guthrie, and J. F. Hoffecker
1983 *Dry Creek: Archeology and Paleoecology of a Late Pleistocene Alaskan Hunting Camp*. Report submitted to the National Park Service, Contract No. CX-9000-7-0047.

Reanier, R. E.
1995 The Antiquity of Paleoindian Materials in Northern Alaska. *Arctic Anthropology* 32:31–50.

Ritter, D. F.
1982 Complex River Terrace Development in the Nenana Valley near Healy, Alaska. *Geological Society of America Bulletin* 93:346–356.

Ritter, D. F. and N. W. Ten Brink
1986 Alluvial Fan Development and the Glacial-Glaciofluvial Cycle, Nenana Valley, Alaska. *Journal of Geology* 94:613–625.

Sancetta, C.
1983 Effect of Pleistocene Glaciation Upon Oceanographic Characteristics of the North Pacific Ocean and Bering Sea. *Deep-Sea Research* 30:851–869.

Sancetta, C., and W. W. Robinson
1983 Diatom Evidence on Wisconsin and Holocene Events in the Bering Sea. *Quaternary Research* 20:232–245.

Sancetta, C., L. Heusser, L. Labeyrie, A. S. Naidu, and S. W. Robinson
1985 Wisconsin–Holocene Paleoenvironment of the Bering Sea: Evidence from Diatoms, Pollen, Oxygen Isotopes, and Clay Minerals. *Marine Geology* 62:55–68.

Schaaf, J.
1988 *The Bering Land Bridge National Preserve: An Archaeological Survey*. National Park Service Research/Resources Management Report AR-14. Anchorage.

Schweger, C. E.
1981 Chronology of Late Glacial Events from the Tangle Lakes, Alaska Range, Alaska. *Arctic Anthropology* 18:97–101.

1982 Late Pleistocene Vegetation of Eastern Beringia: Pollen Analysis of Dated Alluvium. In *Paleoecology of Beringia*, edited by D. M. Hopkins, J. V. Matthews, Jr., C. E. Schweger, and S. B. Young, pp. 95–112. Academic Press, New York.

1985 Geoarcheology of Northern Regions: Lessons from Cryoturbation at Onion Portage, Alaska. In *Archaeological Sediments in Context*, edited by J. K. Stein and W. R. Farrand, pp. 127–141. Center for The Study of Early Man, University of Maine, Orono.

Stanford, D. J., J. W. Jordan, E. J. Dixon, and M. A. Jodry
1990 Archaeological Reconnaissance in the Great Kobuk Sand Dunes, Northwest Alaska. *Current Research in the Pleistocene* 7:44–47.

Ten Brink, N. W., and C. F. Waythomas
1985 Late Wisconsin Glacial Chronology of the North-Central Alaska Range: A Regional Synthesis and Its Implications for Early Human Settlements. In *North Alaska Range Early Man Project*, edited by W.R. Powers and others, pp. 15–32. *National Geographic Society Research Reports* 19.

Thorson, R. M., and G. Bender
1985 Eolian Deflation by Ancient Katabatic Winds: A Late Quaternary Example from the North Alaska Range. *Geological Society of America Bulletin* 96:702–709.

Thorson, R. M., and T. D. Hamilton
1977 Geology of the Dry Creek Site: A Stratified Early Man Site in Interior Alaska. *Quaternary Research* 7:149–176.

Vereshchagin, N. K.
1974 The Mammoth "Cemeteries" of North-East Siberia. *Polar Record* 17(106):3–12.

Vereshchagin, N. K. and V. V. Ukraintseva
1985 Proiskhozhdenie i Stratigrafiia Berelekhskogo "Kladbishcha" Mamontov [Origin and Stratigraphy of the Berelekh "Cemetery" of Mammoths]. *Trudy Zoologicheskogo Instituta AN SSSR [Works of the Zoological Institute of the Academy of Sciences, USSR]* 131:104–113.

Vinson, D.
1988 Preliminary Report on Faunal Identifications from Trail Creek Caves. In *The Bering Land Bridge National Preserve: An Archeological Survey*, edited by J. Schaaf, pp. 410–438. National Park Service Research/Resources Management Report AR-14. Anchorage.

1993 *Taphonomic Analysis of Faunal Remains from Trail Creek Caves, Seward Peninsula, Alaska.* Unpublished Masters thesis, Department of Anthropology, University of Alaska Fairbanks.

Wahrhaftig, C.
1965 *Physiographic Provinces of Alaska.* U.S. Geological Survey Professional Paper 482.

Waythomas, C. F.
1989 Stratigraphic Setting, Correlation and Geoarchaeological Significance of Loess and Buried Soils of the Walker Road Early Man Site, Nenana Valley, Central Alaska. *Geological Society of America Abstracts with Programs* 21:A283.

West, F. H.
1967 The Donnelly Ridge Site and the Definition of an Early Core and Blade Complex in Central Alaska. *American Antiquity* 32:360–382.

1975 Dating The Denali Complex. *Arctic Anthropology* 12:76–81.

1976 Old World Affinities Of Archaeological Complexes from Tangle Lakes Central Alaska. In *Beringia in the Cenozoic Era*, edited by V. L. Kontrimavichus, pp. 571–596. U.S.S.R. Academy of Sciences, Vladivostok. (Reprinted 1984 as U.S. Department of Interior TT 78-52016).

1981 *The Archaeology of Beringia.* Columbia University Press, New York.

1983 The Antiquity of Man in America. In *Late-Quaternary Environments of the United States*, edited by H. E. Wright, Jr., pp. 364–382. University of Minnesota Press, Minneapolis.

1996 Teklanika West. In *American Beginnings: The Prehistory and Palaeoecology of Beringia*, edited by F. H. West, pp. 332–341. University of Chicago Press, Chicago.

West, F. H., B. S. Robinson, and M. L. Curran
1996a Phipps Site. In *American Beginnings: The Prehistory and Palaeoecology of Beringia*, edited by F. H. West, pp. 381–386. University of Chicago Press, Chicago.

West, F. H., B. S. Robinson, and R. G. Dixon
1996b Sparks Point. In *American Beginnings: The Prehistory and Palaeoecology of Beringia*, edited by F. H. West, pp. 394–398. University of Chicago Press, Chicago.

West, F. H., B. S. Robinson, and C. F. West
1996c Whitmore Ridge. In *American Beginnings: The Prehistory and Palaeoecology of Beringia*, edited by F. H. West, pp. 386-394. University of Chicago Press, Chicago.

Yesner, D. R.
1994 Subsistence Diversity and Hunter-Gatherer Strategies in Late Pleistocene/Early Holocene Beringia: Evidence from the Broken Mammoth Site, Big Delta, Alaska. *Current Research in the Pleistocene* 11:154–156.

1996 Human Adaptation at the Pleistocene-Holocene Boundary (Circa 13,000 to 8,000 BP) in Eastern Beringia. In *Humans at the End of the Ice Age: The Archaeology of the Pleistocene-Holocene Transition*, edited by L. G. Straus, B. V. Eriksen, J. M. Erlandson, and D. R. Yesner, pp. 255–276. Plenum Press, New York.

Yesner, D. R., and K. J. Crossen
1994 Prehistoric People of Alaska's Interior. *Alaska Geographic* 21(4):90–93.

Yesner, D. R., K. J. Crossen, and C. E. Holmes
1992a Arkheologiia i Paleoekologiia Stoianki Broken Memot [Archaeology and Paleoecology of the Broken Mammoth site]. In *Paleoekologiia i Rasselenie Drevnego Cheloveka v Severnoi Azii i Amerike* [Paleoecology and Settlement of Ancient Humans in Northern Asia and America] [In Russian], pp. 109–114. Krasnoyarsk.

Yesner, D. R., C. E. Holmes, and K. J. Crossen
1992b Archaeology and Paleoecology of the Broken Mammoth Site, Central Tanana Valley, Interior Alaska. *Current Research in the Pleistocene* 9:53–57.

Notes

1. Soil organic matter dating about 5120 ± 265 yr B.P. from Carlo Creek may be contaminated by percolating ground water; a very small charcoal sample with apparent age of about 10,000 yr B.P. may be contaminated by small amounts of reworked coal or lignite (Bowers 1980:97).
2. Lanceolate projectile points similar to those from the Mesa site (M.L. Kunz, personal communication 1996) have also been reported from the Spein Mountain site in southwestern Alaska (Ackerman and Bundtzen 1994). Charcoal from a pit feature associated with the points has been dated to 10,050 ± 70 yr B.P. (CAMS-8281; R. E. Ackerman, personal communication 1996).
3. Anderson (1988) variously dates Band 8 at 8500 to 8000 yr B.P. (p. 70) and 8200 to 8000 yr B.P. (p. 48), but these ages are based on his former use of a 5730-year radiocarbon half life rather than the conventional Libby value.
4. Because of this predominantly maritime diet, the radiocarbon age of the human remains at PET-408 probably should be corrected for the maritime reservoir effect, which is about 600 years along this sector of the Pacific coast (E. J. Dixon, personal communication 1998). This correlation would decrease the apparent age of the skeletal remains to about 9200 ^{14}C yr B.P., making them about the same age as three concordant ^{14}C determinations reported by Dixon on a cultural horizon at the mouth of the cave.

Bluefish Caves and Old Crow Basin: A New Rapport

Jacques Cinq-Mars[1]
Richard E. Morlan[2]

Abstract

Located in northeastern Beringia (northern Yukon Territory), the Bluefish Caves have yielded evidence of episodic human activity spanning the last 15 millennia of the late Pleistocene (25,000 to 10,000 yr B.P.). One such piece of evidence consists of a mammoth bone flake and its parent core, radiocarbon dated by accelerator mass spectrometry (AMS) to 23,500 yr B.P. The context of the Bluefish Caves site places constraints on the range of taphonomic processes that could account for the breaking and flaking of a large mammoth bone, and we conclude that the flake and core represent the results of a culturally modulated bone-reduction strategy.

The core and flake are reminiscent of some fresh-fractured mammoth bones collected from a number of localities in Old Crow Basin, located about 60 km farther northeast in the Yukon. Lack of relevant site context at the Old Crow localities renders interpretation much more difficult, but many of the mammoth bones have been AMS-dated to between 25,000 and 40,000 yr B.P. A larger range of taphonomic processes may be responsible for the Old Crow Basin specimens, but we argue that at least some of them comprise evidence of human presence during the dated interval. We also consider the implications of this conclusion for the larger picture of Beringian and New World archaeology.

Introduction

A COLD, ARID REGION known as Beringia played an unusually important role in the peopling of the Americas. Stretching from eastern Siberia across Alaska to the Yukon Territory of Canada, Beringia represented the gateway to the New World. During glacial advances, this region served as a refugium for plants and animals, and recent evidence indicates that it was always available as a rich habitat for human societies adapted to survive and prosper there. Beringia has played a pivotal role in the evolution and dispersal of many organisms, and it is not surprising that it has been the subject of special study by scientists in many disciplines and nations (e.g., Hopkins et al. 1982; Kontrimavichus 1984). Yet in many respects, Beringia remains little known and poorly understood, and the archaeology of the region is one aspect that is still in its infancy.

This paper presents some of the principal conclusions of Pleistocene archaeological research in the northeastern corner of Beringia—the northern Yukon interior. This is an extensive area of plateaus, uplands, and ranges bordering several large lowland basins (Hughes 1972; Hughes et al. 1981). During the past three decades, the authors of this paper have conducted research in the Yukon. One has focused his attention primarily on the uplands (Cinq-Mars 1978, 1990), while the other has concentrated on the lowlands (Morlan 1980, 1984, 1986). At present, neither of these areas provides a complete picture of late Pleistocene developments, but a provisional outline can be glimpsed by integrating results of studies in both settings.

The paper begins with a consideration of paleoecological and archaeological findings at an upland site known as the Bluefish Caves. The record at this site spans approximately 25,000 years, including a lengthy period during which the lowland record appears to be muted by events marking the final stages of a prolonged, late Wisconsinan glaciolacustrine

1. Curator, Quebec Archaeology, Archaeological Survey of Canada, Canadian Museum of Civilization, Hull, Quebec, Canada J8X 4H2.
2. Curator, Palaeoenvironmental Studies, Archaeological Survey of Canada, Canadian Museum of Civilization, Hull, Quebec, Canada J8X 4H2.

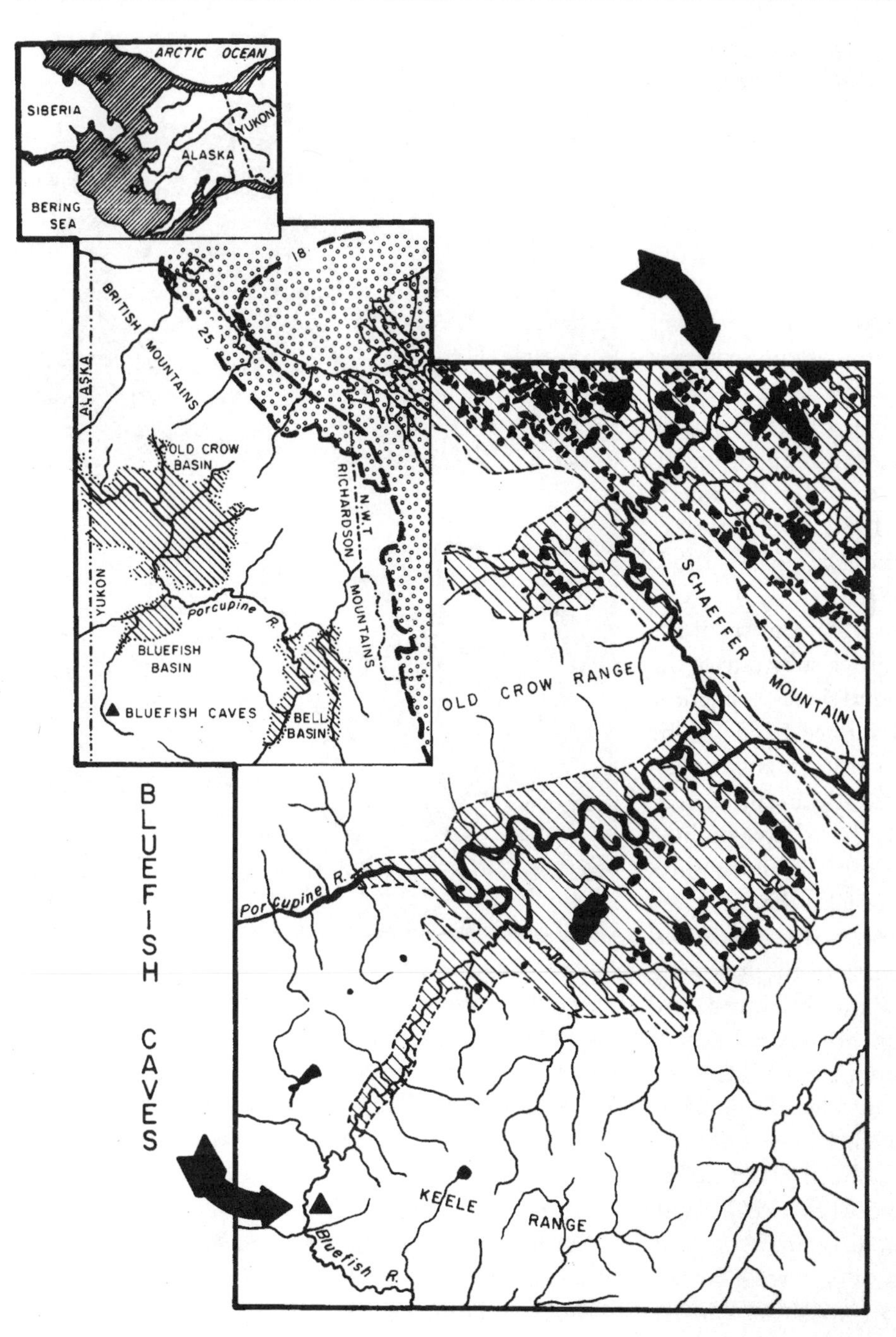

Figure 1. Map showing: (upper box) the position of the northern Yukon or easternmost Beringia relative to Alaska, the Bering land bridge (hatched area), and eastern Siberia; (middle box) the location of the northern Yukon interior glacial lake basins, relative to the approximate eastern boundaries of Beringia delineated by the continental glacial ice limits of 25,000 and 18,000 years ago; and (lower box) the location of the Bluefish Caves and Old Crow River localities relative to one another and to the Bluefish and Old Crow glacial lakes (hatched areas).

inundation. More importantly, the archaeological evidence at the Bluefish Caves has been derived from a primary depositional context that provides a degree of chronostratigraphic and taphonomic control not yet available in the lowland region. The Bluefish Caves evidence enables us to demonstrate human occupation in eastern Beringia during the height and decline of the last glaciation. The implications of that evidence form a basis for reconsidering older materials from the lowlands for which fewer controls are available. In this process of reevaluating the evidence from both the uplands and the lowlands, we are aided by new data from accelerator mass spectrometry (AMS) measurements on bone collagen.

The Bluefish Caves: Context and Content

The Bluefish Caves are located 54 km southwest of the village of Old Crow, at an altitude of 250 m, overlooking the middle course of Bluefish River, which flows north out of the Keele Range (Cinq-Mars 1979). During the late Wisconsin, the nearby valley was, for a time, occupied by the apex of a long, narrow deltaic estuary that formed where Bluefish River reached a glacial lake occupying the Bluefish Basin (Figure 1).

The caves are situated at the foot of a Devonian limestone outcrop forming part of an extensive tract of limestone plateaus and ranges that exhibit a broad range of both ancient and recent karst features (Cinq-Mars and Lauriol 1985; Lauriol et al. 1991). The Bluefish Caves consist of three small, cryoclastically altered cavities that represent vestigial conduits of such karstic development (Figure 2) (Cinq-Mars 1990). Ranging in volume from about 10 m^3 to 30 m^3, the cavities contain sediments varying in thickness from about 30 cm to 2 m.

Excavations have been conducted inside the caves as well as immediately outside, downslope from the driplines. They have revealed a depositional sequence that is summarized below on the basis of a combination of stratigraphic, pedological, sedimentological, paleontological, palynological, and radiometric information (Cinq-Mars 1979, 1982, 1990; Morlan 1983a, 1984, 1989; Morlan and Cinq-Mars 1982; Ritchie 1984; Ritchie et al. 1982).

The floor of the sequence (Unit A) consists of the frost-spalled and lag-covered bedrock substrate of the caves and adjacent outside ledges and slopes. Sometime around 25,000 years ago, this surface began to be covered by a series of three faintly differentiated eolian silt or loess mantles (Unit B; C. Tarnocai, written communication to J. Cinq-Mars). The source of these sediments is thought to have been the expanding margins of the then receding glacial lakes that occupied Old Crow and Bluefish Basins to the north and northeast (Figure 1). In the course of the following millennia, Unit B sediments incorporated and preserved a wealth of vertebrate remains that collectively represent the "Mammoth fauna" (Guthrie 1982). At Bluefish Caves, this late Pleistocene fauna includes mammoth (*Mammuthus* sp.); bison (*Bison* cf. *priscus*); horse (*Equus lambei*); sheep (*Ovis dalli*); caribou (*Rangifer tarandus*); moose (cf. Alces); wapiti (*Cervus elaphus*); saiga (*Saiga tatarica*); muskox (*Ovibos moschatus*); lion (*Panthera leo* atrox); cougar (*Felis concolor*); bear (*Ursus arctos*); wolf (*Canis lupus*); and a large variety of smaller mammals, birds, and fish (Cinq-Mars 1990:Table 1; Harington and Cinq-Mars 1995; Morlan 1983a, 1984, 1989).

Unit B formed over a period of about 15,000 years, spanning most of the Duvanny Yar interval, which represents full-glacial time, as well as the subsequent late-glacial Birch interval (Hopkins 1982). The beginning of the Birch interval, around 13,500 years ago, marks a vegetation shift from xeric herbaceous tundra to mesic shrub tundra. The end of this time is characterized by the invasion of boreal forest around 10,000 years ago. The latter date corresponds to both the end of aeolian deposition and a conspicuous change in faunal composition. The diverse late Pleistocene fauna was replaced, through processes of extinction and extirpation, by the relatively impoverished Holocene fauna of the northwestern Cordilleran interior (Youngman 1975). These more recent faunal remains are contained in Unit C, a thick, humus-rich cryoclastic rubble indicative of wetter boreal conditions. Unit C is overlain by Unit D, corresponding to modern humus, litter, and vegetation. Together, Units C and D accumulated during the past 10,000 years under the climatic regime that has characterized the boreal forest environment of northwestern North America during the Holocene (Figure 3) (Ritchie 1984).

Figure 2. (A) Aerial photograph of Bluefish Cave I, taken from the north-northwest and showing a portion of the limestone ridge complex together with a view of the surrounding upland settings. (B) Aerial photograph of Bluefish Cave II, which is located just behind Cave I; the view is from the south and shows the forest-covered Bluefish River valley. (Photo: J. C.-M.)

Particularly important here is the fact that Unit B, in Caves I and II and, to a lesser degree, Cave III, have yielded a variety of cultural indicators. These

Figure 3. A 3.5-m-long profile of the deposit found downslope from the mouth of Cave II. (See text for unit descriptions.) The large limestone block can be seen, from the opposite direction, in the right foreground of Figure 2A. (Photo: J. C.-M.)

include (1) a small series of lithic artifacts, (2) bone alterations representing butchering activities, (3) a few examples of bone tool making and use, and (4) examples of bone reduction by flaking techniques. Each of these is briefly described below.

The lithic artifacts are presented in three classes. First, there are a few culturally diagnostic elements: microblade cores, microblades, core tablets, burins, burin spalls, and their byproducts (Figure 4). All of these are made of high-quality cherts that—based on ongoing explorations of these limestone uplands—are believed to be exotic to the region. Most of the artifacts were found in Cave II, but a few (a burin spall and a few microblade fragments) were recovered from Cave I. All but two were found in the Unit B loess in levels that also contained the remains of the late Pleistocene vertebrate fauna. The two exceptions are thought to have been redeposited locally. These artifacts represent the American Paleoarctic-Diuktai technological complex, which has been dated in neighboring Alaska to around 10,500 years ago and in Siberia to at least 18,000 yr B.P. (Cinq-Mars 1990; Morlan 1987; Powers 1990). Unfortunately, at the present time, these diagnostic Bluefish Caves specimens cannot be dated with precision. Various lines of evidence, however, suggest that they are certainly as old, if not older, than their Alaskan counterparts (Cinq-Mars 1990).

The second class of lithics consists of microflakes, which measure about 1–3 mm in their greatest dimension. They are the characteristic residue of flintknapping, retouching, and stone tool use (Cinq-Mars 1979; Fladmark 1982). They were recovered in the laboratory from both sieved and bulk sediment samples taken from all three caves. Those recovered from the main stratigraphic control column in Cave I represent a much broader range of raw materials than is represented among the more formal artifacts. The microflakes are present in various frequencies throughout the thickness of Unit B and therefore appear to span much of the 25,000- to 10,000-years-ago interval. The largest observed concentration straddles the stratigraphic position, which is palynologically associated with the transition from herbaceous tundra to shrub tundra. As noted earlier, this transition is dated to around 13,500 yr B.P. in this area of eastern Beringia (Ritchie 1984; Ritchie and Cwynar 1982; Ritchie et al. 1982).

The third class of lithic specimens consists of small cobbles and even more numerous pebbles. These previously have been described as indicators of human presence at the caves (Cinq-Mars 1979; Morlan and Cinq-Mars 1982), but subsequent investigation has shown that their presence in the basal late Pleistocene sediments might be explained by paleokarstic stream transport (Cinq-Mars 1990). Although some of the largest ones (small cobbles) may have been used as tools (Morlan and Cinq-Mars 1982:Figure 9), the vast majority (pebbles) is likely to consist of noncultural lag.

The second category of cultural indicators is comprised of cut marks or butchering marks on various large mammal bones from Unit B (Morlan and Cinq-Mars 1982:Figure 10) (see description of bone core and flake below and Figure 5). Thus far, the cut marks

Figure 4. Selected lithics from Bluefish Cave II: (a) microblade; (b) microblade; (c) burin spall; (d) core tablet; (e) wedge-shaped microblade core; (f) multiple angle burin on a truncated flake; (g) multiple angle burin on a flake fragment truncated at both ends; (h) angle burin on a small truncated blade. (Photo: J. C.-M.)

have been examined only by binocular light microscopy, but plans are underway to examine a sample of them with a scanning electron microscope to document them in greater detail (e.g., Shipman 1981; Shipman and Rose 1983). Some of the cut-marked specimens have been radiocarbon dated by AMS, and the results are concordant with the distribution of microflakes in suggesting that human activity took place sporadically at the caves throughout the interval from 25,000 to 10,000 years ago.

A third type of cultural manifestation consists of a few bones that appear to have been shaped and used as tools. Mostly, these are split long bones, which show traces of whittling or shaving, together with abraded and/or polished areas that may have resulted from use wear. One such specimen is made from a split caribou tibia that has all the attributes of a broken fleshing tool (see Morlan and Cinq-Mars 1982:Figure 9). It has been radiocarbon dated by AMS to 24,800 yr B.P. (Erle Nelson, written communication to J. Cinq-Mars), making it the earliest dated artifact from a documented stratigraphic context in eastern Beringia.

The fourth category of cultural manifestation is represented by a mammoth bone flake and its parent core (Cinq-Mars 1990). These two specimens (Figure 5) were found in an area of the Cave II deposit that yielded a relatively high concentration of megafaunal remains, including many mammoth bones. All were found lying on or near bedrock in the lowest levels of Unit B. The flake has been detached longitudinally from the outer compact bone of a fresh proboscidean long bone. Its distal end is hinged, and its proximal

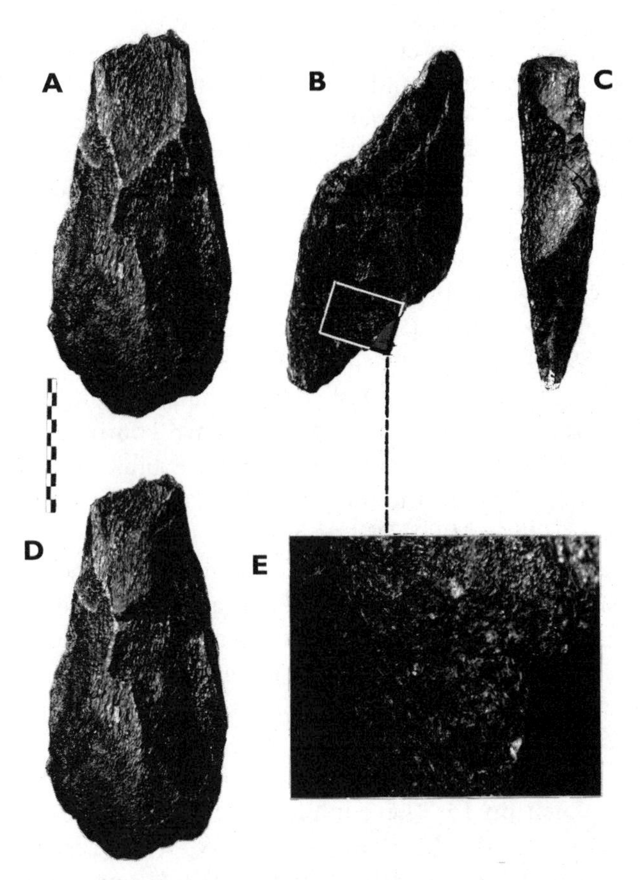

Figure 5. Composite plate showing various aspects of the Bluefish Cave II mammoth bone flake and parent core: (a) a front view of the core exhibiting three flake facets; (b) the same view of the core with the flake refitted on the main central facet; (c) the flake exhibiting the dorsal aspect of the proximal (upper), bifacially worked edge; (d) a rotated (left lateral) view of the flake showing the other side of the bifacial modification; (e) macrophotography of one of the cutmarks. (Scale/core: 10 cm; length of cutmark: approximately 1.3 cm.) (Photo: J. C.-M.)

end bears traces of extensive bifacial trimming or platform preparation. Cut marks also can be seen on the dorsal face, near the bifacially retouched proximal area, and near the hinged extremity. The flake is well preserved and shows no traces of carnivore gnawing. The proboscidean long bone that was used to fashion the parent core is so heavily reduced as to preclude precise anatomical positioning. The core exhibits three clear flake-removal facets originating from the mid-shaft region. The latter, corresponding to the core platform area, is somewhat amorphous, its features having been possibly obscured in part by post-burial taphonomic processes. Post-burial damage also occurs at the base of the core, which corresponds to the epiphysis of a somewhat immature animal. Like the flake, the core exhibits no evidence of carnivore gnawing. The flake can be refitted to the central flake scar on the core (Figures 5 and 6). Refitting shows that following its detachment, the flake was reduced bifacially and diagonally by slightly more than a third of its original size. Both the flake and the core have been radiocarbon dated by AMS (Erle Nelson, written communication to J. Cinq-Mars); the dates overlap at one sigma and provide an average age of 23,500 yr B.P.

The bone flake and core closely resemble some of the mammoth bone specimens that have been recovered from the Old Crow Basin, about 100 km north of the Bluefish Caves (Bonnichsen 1979; Irving et al. 1989; Morlan 1980). The Old Crow specimens have prompted extensive discussions on bone taphonomy (see below), raising the problem of equifinality in the actions of many bone-altering agencies. It is difficult to address this problem in the Old Crow Basin, because redeposition has divorced the altered bones from their original stratigraphic contexts. The relatively undisturbed context of the Bluefish Caves specimens encourages us to reexamine some of the most pertinent arguments that have been put forth to explain flaked mammoth bones.

One such argument is that fluvial transport, and particularly the movement of river ice at break-up, can account for these bone alterations (e.g., Thorson and Guthrie 1984). Obviously, such processes have never occurred at the Bluefish Caves within the time span under consideration, thus indicating that the Bluefish mammoth bone core and flake have been produced by other means. More generally, it has not been demonstrated that fluvial processes can actually mimic complex bone-reduction sequences, such as those described above. We believe that fluvial entrainment, especially in the presence of ice, is likely to produce a variety of bone alterations, including polishing, abrasions, striations (including some cut-mark mimics), battering, crushing, and some spiral fracturing on some bones; it also will lead to the total destruction of many faunal elements. However, the massive forces released by fluvial and ice transport are very unlikely to duplicate the complex sequence of actions that can be inferred from the Bluefish mammoth bone core and flake, as well as from analogous specimens found in the Old Crow Basin.

Another proposed explanation for proboscidean bone fracture is the trampling or tossing of bones by living animals (Agenbroad 1989; Binford 1981; Haynes 1988; Myers et al. 1980). This may be an appropriate explanation where limited space or

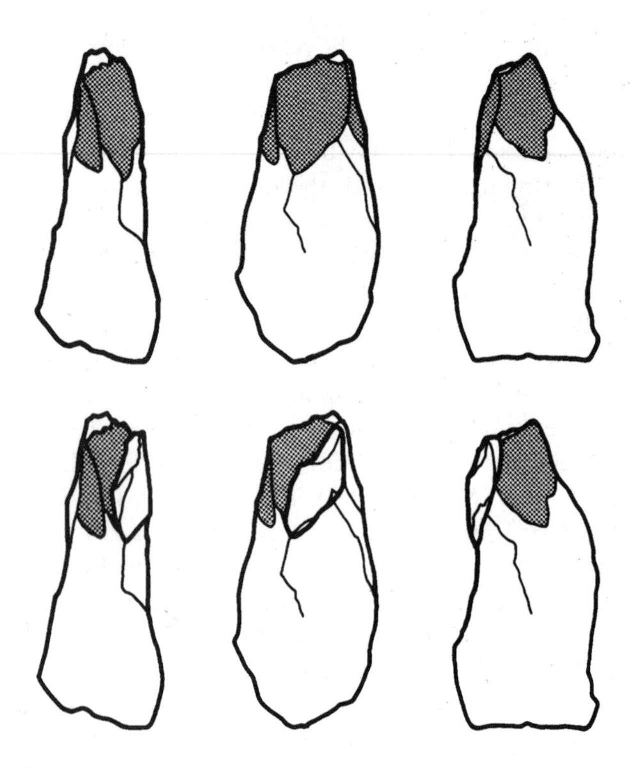

Figure 6. Schematic illustration showing (upper row) three views of the bone core and its flake facets, and (lower row) the same views with the refitted flake.

restricted access to a waterhole causes crowding of perishing animals, but such an environmental or behavioral context hardly can be found either now or in the past at the Bluefish Caves. Furthermore, neither field observations nor experiments have demonstrated that tossing or trampling ever produces such a complex series of reduction stages as seen in the Cave II specimens. Drought-induced crowding around African waterholes is known to cause extensive bone fragmentation from elephant trampling (Haynes 1988), but none of the examples seen thus far approaches the complexity of the mammoth bone core and flake recovered from the Bluefish Caves or some of those from the Old Crow Basin (G. Haynes, personal communication to R. E. Morlan).

A third hypothesis has identified rockfall as an agency capable, under certain circumstances, of fracturing fresh proboscidean bones (Agenbroad 1988, 1989:143). Rockfall undoubtedly has occurred at the Bluefish Caves, and this process has altered some of the bones, especially by crushing and splintering bones already in the burial environment. Very few of the mammoth bones exhibit fresh-state fracture, and none of them was found in a position where rockfall could clearly be implicated as the fracturing agency. Furthermore, there is an enormous conceptual and operational difference between random events that cause simple alterations, such as fractures, and the implementation of a step-by-step, ordered sequence of bone reduction such as we have described. With each passing step, the probability declines that random events could be responsible for the cumulative alterations.

A fourth bone-breaking hypothesis concerns accidental falls by living animals, which might fracture their own bones ("torsion/falling" [Agenbroad 1989:143]). In some circumstances, the broken bone may even become polished and chipped along the fracture surfaces as the injured animal continues to move; however, such bones also may exhibit signs of healing through the formation of periosteal reactive bone (Oliver 1989). No examples of such healing have been seen on the Bluefish Caves mammoth bones. More importantly, accidental falls are no more likely than other random events to produce an ordered sequence of bone reduction leading to the detachment of large flakes from cores and further reduction of the flakes.

Carnivore gnawing represents a more interesting explanation for the complex fracturing of bones, because, like human technology, it represents purposeful behavior (see Guthrie 1988; Haynes 1988; Voorhies and Corner 1986). Both large and small carnivores have played important roles in the accumulation and postmortem alteration of bones at the Bluefish Caves. In particular, many of the mammoth bones exhibit massive epiphyseal reduction by gnawing, gouging, and scooping—features obviously inflicted by large carnivores. Of the approximately 15 mammoth long bones recovered from Caves I and II, only three specimens fail to exhibit carnivore alterations: the bone flake; its parent core; and a third specimen that exhibits the same color and surface texture attributes of the first two, and that also may be culturally altered. Of the carnivore-gnawed bones, including juvenile specimens, none of the residual shaft segments has been spirally fractured, and only a few bear random traces of very small bone chips having been pulled or levered back.

Overall, the mammoth bone alterations can be divided into two classes that exhibit no overlap whatsoever. The first class consists of those specimens showing the pattern and range of surface marks attributable to carnivore activity (Haynes 1983a, 1983b; Hill 1989; Marshall 1989). The other class consists primarily of the core and flake. This class exhibits a completely different set and range of modifications, with patterning that clearly is a result of nonrandom events. Moreover, this patterning achieves a degree of resolution, of sharpness, which is presumably indicative of clarity of purpose that is never found in carnivore-altered specimens. We attribute this to human behavior, in accordance with the associated evidence represented by the butchering marks seen on the flake. To attribute these types of mammoth bone alterations to two different causes is neither arbitrary nor deceiving. The attributions reflect the different purposes of carnivore and human behavior, while the recognition of purpose removes both classes of altered bones from explanation by random events.

Old Crow Basin as Seen from the Bluefish Caves

As alluded to earlier, the observations derived from the Bluefish Caves context have several implications for the interpretation of some of the redeposited bones from Old Crow Basin. First, we can apply some of our arguments concerning random versus patterned bone alterations to the circumstances that must have altered mammoth bones in the Old Crow Basin. Second, spiral fractures are not seen on the heavily gnawed mammoth bones from the Bluefish Caves; their absence supports the hypothesis that Beringian carnivores were unable to fracture fresh proboscidean bones in mid-shaft (Morlan 1980). Third, the bone flake and core from Bluefish Cave II are only slightly younger than some of the Old Crow Basin specimens, and the latter can be construed as technological antecedents to the former.

We already have expressed our doubts that fluvial entrainment, river ice, trampling, tossing, and accidental falls represent adequate explanations for patterned bone flaking. We have argued that the patterning inferred to account for complex altered bone morphology cannot be explained by such random events. A sequence of actions is required to produce a bone fragment that we would classify as a core or flake. Each step in the sequence entails dynamic loading that must be delivered within certain geometric limits. Such limits govern the size of the contact area, as well as the angle of delivery. The bone or fragment must be held securely to receive the loading, and it must be rotated precisely from one holding position to another. We believe that sequential random events are unlikely to follow such a course of actions; in fact, at each step in the sequence the probability of the next step occurring declines in random action.

We regard both carnivore gnawing and human technology as processes of nonrandom action on bones. The action is nonrandom by definition because it is purposeful. The processes differ, however, in clarity of purpose and therefore in result. Carnivores are interested in bones as sources of fat and protein. They attack the ends of bones where fat is most concentrated (see Brink and Dawe 1989:124 ff.), cortical layers are thin, and bone geometry is conducive to forceful mastication. Humans are interested in bones as sources of food and raw material. They are able to "attack" even the largest bones in mid-shaft to retrieve fat-rich marrow and thick cortical fragments for use as tools, and some cultures pulverize the fat-rich ends of bones to make bone grease (Binford 1978; Brink and Dawe 1989). As mentioned earlier and argued elsewhere (Morlan 1983b), we believe there is an upper limit to the size of bone that can be broken in mid-shaft by a given species of carnivore. The Bluefish Caves bones support the view that Beringian carnivores were unable to fracture mammoth bones in mid-shaft even though they extensively altered the ends of such bones.

One study of Old Crow Basin bones (Friesen 1989) finds a significant association between signs of carnivore gnawing on mammoth bones and fragmentation patterns, which are classified as bone cores. We find this study difficult to evaluate for three reasons: (1) it is at variance with our own observations on bones from the Old Crow Basin; (2) it does not specify the morphological criteria that are diagnostic of carnivore gnawing; and (3) it does not indicate the placement of gnawing marks in relation to the flake scars, which guide classification of cores. Thus, gnawing and core production are said to be associated, but no functional association is demonstrated.

Dates obtained on bones from the Old Crow Basin provide an additional perspective on these arguments. Both carnivore gnawing and random processes can be assumed to have been operating on bones throughout the time period represented in the fossiliferous bluffs along the Old Crow River—more than one million years (Schweger 1989). Therefore, these deposits should yield bone cores and flakes older than the measurement limits of radiocarbon dating if any of these processes are capable of their production.

A program of AMS dating was undertaken on bone cores and flakes to determine whether the distribution of ages would be random or grouped in time. A random distribution, including ages beyond the limits of radiocarbon measurement, could be explained by the action of one or more long-term natural processes of bone alteration, whereas a restricted distribution younger than the limits of measurement would require the onset of a new process of bone alteration (Morlan et al. 1990:75).

The resulting ages were found to be restricted to a 15,000-year time span, beginning around 40,000 B.P. and ending around 25,000 B.P. Since we believe that our measurement methods would have allowed us to measure samples 10,000 years older than those encountered here, this implies that a new agency or process enters into the taphonomic histories of large vertebrates in the Old Crow Basin around 40,000 B.P. (Morlan et al. 1990:86).

As in the AMS study (Morlan et al. 1990), and with support from the Bluefish Caves evidence presented above, we hypothesize that the new agency is *Homo sapiens*, whose bone-flaking technology represented part of a cultural adaptation to northern habitats. This view has precedent in other technological examples known from sites scattered across Eurasia, from Europe (Absolon and Klima 1977; Valoch 1982; Villa 1991) to Siberia (Mochanov 1977; Morlan 1987; N. Drozdov, personal communication to J. Cinq-Mars 1990). Additional examples are known from younger localities in the New World (e.g., Hannus 1989; Miller 1989).

Discussion

In addition to their archaeological importance, the dated mammoth bones from the Old Crow Basin demonstrate a degree of biological productivity in northeastern Beringia throughout mid-Wisconsinan time (Morlan et al. 1990). Although this lowland record is curtailed by a long cycle of complex glaciolacustrine inundation beginning around 30,000 yr B.P. (Lemmen et al. 1994), the complementary upland record, as seen at Bluefish Caves, shows ongoing productivity throughout the height and decline of the late Wisconsinan glaciation (Cinq-Mars 1990). It follows that eastern Beringia offered no known ecological obstacle to colonization by humans adapted to northern latitudes. Our interpretation of altered mammoth bones indicates that such a level of adaptation had been achieved by at least 40,000 years ago. We presume that humans had spread across Beringia by that time.

If this presumption is correct, there should have been no impediment to the movement of humans from the Beringian interior southward through much of the northwestern Cordilleran to the rest of the North American continent. Ancient Beringians would have had no need to search for corridors to the south (see Bobrowsky and Rutter 1990; Dredge and Thorleifson 1987; Fulton et al. 1984:76–77), be they interior (Beaudoin 1989; Ives et al. 1989) or coastal (Fladmark 1979; Gruhn 1988). Beginning as early as 40,000 yr B.P., it is not difficult to imagine a southward dispersal rapid enough to account for some of the earliest purported evidence in midcontinental North America (e.g., Adovasio et al. 1990) and in South America (e.g., Dillehay 1989; Guidon and Delibrias 1986). Whether or not such a dispersion actually took place is another matter altogether (Aikens 1990; Cinq-Mars 1990; Morlan 1988).

People utilized the Bluefish Caves beginning around 25,000 years ago and sporadically throughout the late Wisconsinan glaciation. They may or may not have represented a single cultural tradition throughout this period. Our only clues are elements of a bone-flaking technology, with likely ties to the Old Crow Basin and a few Eurasian sites, and the microblade and burin technology, with clearer ties to Alaska and Siberia. These technological manifestations may or may not be related historically.

The late Pleistocene archaeological record of the Old Crow Basin and the Bluefish Caves allows us to catch a glimpse of more than 25,000 years of prehistory. It shows that the existing archaeological picture farther west, in Siberia and Alaska, is woefully incomplete. For example, the Chukotsk Peninsula of Siberia remains blank on the archaeological map of late Pleistocene Beringia. The same would hold true for interior Alaska were it not for the growing number of sites that can now be ascribed to the 11,600-year-old Nenana complex (Powers and Hoffecker 1989; Yesner et al. 1992). The latter, and its likely antecedents, may provide us with a better appreciation of the technological trajectories, which must have been present in eastern Beringia over the longer term (Cinq-Mars 1990:26, note 13; Powers 1990).

We reiterate that Beringian archaeology is in its infancy. Beringia is an imposingly vast, subcontinental landmass whose expanses barely have been explored for paleontological and archaeological remains. A careful investigation in one small portion of its northeastern corner has revealed the Bluefish Caves with a record that provides us with, among other things, a better appreciation of some of the older lowland evidence. While some eastern Beringian cave sites are not highly informative with respect to late Pleistocene archaeology (e.g., Dixon 1984; Vinson 1988), we believe that all of them can serve as windows into the distant past. Through them, we will continue to decipher the complex environmental and cultural processes that led to the peopling of a truly New World.

Acknowledgments

This report is based on research carried out with the financial and logistic support of the Archaeological Survey of Canada, Canadian Museum of Civilization, and the Polar Continental Shelf Project, Energy, Mines and Resources Canada. The discovery and earliest investigations at the Bluefish Caves were made possible by assistance from the Social Sciences and Humanities Research Council (Canada). We are especially grateful to Erle Nelson and his RIDDL laboratory colleagues for providing J. Cinq-Mars with the Bluefish Caves AMS C-14 determinations. Finally, we want to acknowledge the help provided by numerous colleagues and field assistants during the course of these interdisciplinary investigations, as well as that of numerous Vuntut Gwichin residents of Old Crow, who greatly facilitated our field research. Ian Dyck and J. V. Wright made helpful comments on an earlier draft of this manuscript. This paper was last revised in 1994.

References Cited

Absolon, K., and B. Klima
1977 Predmosti: Ein Mammut-Jägerplatz in *Mähren. Fontes Archaeologiae Moraviae*, vol. 8. Academia, Prague.

Adovasio, J. M., J. Donahue, and R. Stuckenrath
1990 The Meadowcroft Rockshelter Radiocarbon Chronology 1975–1990. *American Antiquity* 55:348–354.

Agenbroad, L. D.
1988 Clovis People: The Human Factor in the Extinction Equation. In *Americans Before Columbus: Ice-Age Origins*, edited by R. C. Carlisle, pp. 63–74. Ethnology Monographs 12, Department of Anthropology, University of Pittsburgh, Pittsburgh.

1989 Spiral Fractured Mammoth Bone from Nonhuman Taphonomic Processes at Hot Springs Mammoth Site. In *Bone Modification*, edited by R. Bonnichsen and M. A. Sorg, pp. 139–147. Center for the Study of the First Americans, University of Maine, Orono.

Aikens, C. M.
1990 From Asia to America: The First Peopling of the New World. In *Prehistoric Mongoloid Dispersals*, pp. 1–34. Newsletter of the "Prehistoric Mongoloid Dispersals" Project, No. 7, University of Tokyo, Tokyo.

Beaudoin, A. B.
1989 *Annotated Bibliography: Late Quaternary Studies in Alberta's Western Corridor, 1950–1988.* Archaeological Survey of Alberta Manuscript Series No. 15, Edmonton.

Binford, L. R.
1978 *Nunamiut Ethnoarchaeology.* Academic Press, New York.

1981 *Bones: Ancient Men and Modern Myths.* Academic Press, New York.

Bobrowsky, P. T. and N. Rutter
1990 *Geological Evidence for an Ice-free Corridor in Northeastern British Columbia, Canada.* Current Research in the Pleistocene 7:133–135.

Bonnichsen, R.
1979 *Pleistocene Bone Technology in the Beringian Refugium.* Archaeological Survey of Canada Paper No. 89, Mercury Series. National Museum of Man, Ottawa.

Brink, J., and B. Dawe
1989 *Final Report of the 1985 and 1986 Field Season at Head-Smashed-In Buffalo Jump, Alberta.* Archaeological Survey of Alberta Manuscript Series No. 16, Edmonton.

Cinq-Mars, J.
1978 Northern Yukon Research Programme: Survey and Excavations. *Fifth AMQUA Abstracts*, pp. 160–161. Edmonton.

1979 Bluefish Cave I: A Late Pleistocene Eastern Beringian Cave Deposit in the Northern Yukon. *Canadian Journal of Archaeology* 3:1–32.

1982 Les Grottes du Poisson-Bleu. *GEOS* 11(l):19–21.

1990 La Place des Grottes du Poisson-Bleu dans la Préhistoire Béringienne. *Revista de Arqueologia Americana* 1:9–32.

Cinq-Mars, J., and B. Lauriol
1985 Le Karst de Tsi-it-toh-choh: Notes Préliminaires sur Quelques Phénomènes Karstiques du Yukon Septentrional, Canada. *Annales de la Société Géologique de Belgique* 108:185–195.

Dillehay, T. D.
1989 *Monte Verde: A Late Pleistocene Settlement in Chile, Volume 1, Palaeoenvironment and Site Context.* Smithsonian Institution Press, Washington, D.C.

Dixon, E. J.
1984 Context and Environment in Taphonomic Analysis: Examples from Alaska's Porcupine River Caves. *Quaternary Research* 22:201–215.

Dredge, L. A., and L. H. Thorleifson
1987 The Middle Wisconsinan History of the Laurentide Ice Sheet. *Géographie physique et Quaternaire* 41:215–235.

Fladmark, K.
1979 Routes: Alternative Migration Corridors for Early Man in North America. *American Antiquity* 44:55–69.

1982 Microdebitage Analysis: Initial Considerations. *Journal of Archaeological Science* 9:205–220.

Friesen, T. M.
1989 *Analysis of Fracture Patterns on Proboscidean Bones from Locality 11A, Old Crow, Northern Yukon Territory.* Unpublished M.A. thesis, University of Toronto, Toronto.

Fulton, R. J., M. M. Fenton, and N. W. Rutter
1984 *Summary of Quaternary Stratigraphy and History, Western Canada*. Geological Survey of Canada Paper 84-10:69–83. Ottawa.

Gruhn, R.
1988 Linguistic Evidence in Support of the Coastal Route of Earliest Entry in the New World. Man (N.S.) 23:77–100.

Guidon, N., and G. Delibrias
1986 Carbon-14 Dates Point to Man in the Americas 32,000 Years Ago. *Nature* 321:769–771.

Guthrie, R. D.
1982 Mammals of the Mammoth Steppe as Paleoenvironmental Indicators. In *Paleoecology of Beringia*, edited by D. M. Hopkins, J. V. Matthews, Jr., C. E. Schweger, and S. B. Young, pp. 307–326. Academic Press, New York.

1988 Bone Litter from an Alaskan Pleistocene Carnivore Den. *Current Research in the Pleistocene* 5:69–71.

Hannus, L. A.
1989 Flaked mammoth bone from the Lange/Ferguson site, White River Badlands area, South Dakota. In *Bone Modification*, edited by R. Bonnichsen and M. A. Sorg, pp. 395–412. Center for the Study of the First Americans, University of Maine, Orono.

Harington, C. R., and J. Cinq-Mars
1995 Radiocarbon Dates on Saiga Antelope (*Saiga tatarica*) Fossils from Yukon and the Northwest Territories. *Arctic* 48(1):1–7.

Haynes, G.
1983a Frequencies of Spiral and Green-bone Fractures on Ungulate Limb Bones in Modern Surface Assemblages. *American Antiquity* 48:102–114.

1983b A Guide for Differentiating Mammalian Carnivore Taxa Responsible for Gnaw Damage to Herbivore Limb Bones. *Paleobiology* 9:164–172.

1988 Longitudinal Studies of African Elephant Death and Bone Deposits. *Journal of Archaeological Science* 15:131–157.

Hill, A.
1989 Bone Modification by Modern Spotted Hyenas. In *Bone Modification*, edited by R. Bonnichsen and M. A. Sorg, pp. 169–178. Center for the Study of the First Americans, University of Maine, Orono.

Hopkins, D. M.
1982 Aspects of the Paleogeography of Beringia during the Late Pleistocene. In *Paleoecology of Beringia*, edited by D. M. Hopkins, J. V. Matthews, Jr., C. E. Schweger, and S. B. Young, pp. 3–28. Academic Press, New York.

Hopkins, D. M., J. V. Matthews, Jr., C. E. Schweger, and S. B. Young (editors)
1982 *Paleoecology of Beringia*. Academic Press, New York.

Hughes, O. L.
1972 *Surficial Geology of Northern Yukon Territory and Northwestern District of Mackenzie, Northwest Territories.* Geological Survey of Canada Paper 69-36. Ottawa.

Hughes, O. L., C. R. Harington, J. A. Janssens, J. V. Matthews, Jr., R. E. Morlan, N. W. Rutter, and C. E. Schweger
1981 Upper Pleistocene Stratigraphy, Paleoecology, and Archaeology of the Northern Yukon Interior, Eastern Beringia. *Arctic* 34:329–365.

Irving, W. N., A. V. Jopling, and I. Kritsch-Armstrong
1989 Studies of Bone Technology and Taphonomy, Old Crow Basin, Yukon Territory. In *Bone Modification*, edited by R. Bonnichsen and M. A. Sorg, pp. 347–379. Center for the Study of the First Americans, University of Maine, Orono.

Ives, J. W., A. B. Beaudoin, and M. Magne
1989 *Evaluating the Role of a Western Corridor in the Peopling of the Americas.* Paper presented at the

Circum-Pacific Prehistory Conference, Seattle, Washington.

Kontrimavichus, V. L. (editor)
1984 *Beringia in the Cenozoic Era.* Amerind Publishing Co., New Delhi.

Lauriol, B., D. C. Ford, and J. Cinq-Mars
1991 *Landscape Development from Caves and Speleothem Data.* Evidence from Northern Yukon, Canada. (Article submitted for publication).

Lemmen, D. S., A. Duk-Rodkin, and J. M. Bednarski
1994 Late Glacial Drainage Systems along the Northwestern Margin of the Laurentide Ice Sheet. *Quaternary Science Reviews* 13:805–828.

Marshall, L.
1989 Bone Modification and "The Laws of Burial." In *Bone Modification*, edited by R. Bonnichsen and M. A. Sorg, pp. 7–24. Center for the Study of the First Americans, University of Maine, Orono.

Miller, S. J.
1989 Characteristics of Mammoth Bone Reduction at Owl Cave, the Wasden Site, Idaho. In *Bone Modification*, edited by R. Bonnichsen and M. A. Sorg, pp. 381–393. Center for the Study of the First Americans, University of Maine, Orono.

Mochanov, Y. A.
1977 *Drevneishie Etapy Zaseleniia Chelovekom Severo-Vostochnoi Azii* (The Earliest Stages of Human Occupation of Northeastern Asia). Nauka, Novosibirsk.

Morlan, R. E.
1980 *Taphonomy and Archaeology in the Upper Pleistocene of the Northern Yukon Territory: A Glimpse of the Peopling of the New World.* Archaeological Survey of Canada Paper No. 94, Mercury Series, National Museum of Man, Ottawa.

1983a Counts and Estimates of Taxonomic Abundance in Faunal Remains: Microtine Rodents from Bluefish Cave I. *Canadian Journal of Archaeology* 7:61–76.

1983b Spiral Fractures on Limb Bones: Which Ones are Artificial? In *Carnivores, Human Scavengers, and Predators: A Question of Bone Technology*, edited by G. M. LeMoine and A. S. MacEachern, pp. 241–269. University of Calgary Archaeological Association, Calgary.

1984 Biostratigraphy and Biogeography of Quaternary Microtine Rodents from Northern Yukon Territory, Eastern Beringia. In *Contributions in Quaternary Vertebrate Paleontology: A Volume in Memorial to John E.Guilday*, edited by H. H. Genoways and M. R. Dawson, pp. 184–199. Carnegie Museum of Natural History Special Publication No. 8, Pittsburgh.

1986 Pleistocene Archaeology in Old Crow Basin: A Critical Reappraisal. In *New Evidence for the Pleistocene Peopling of the Americas*, edited by A. L. Bryan, pp. 27–48. Center for the Study of Early Man, University of Maine, Orono.

1987 The Pleistocene Archaeology of Beringia. In *The Evolution of Human Hunting*, edited by M. H. Nitecki and D. V. Nitecki, pp. 267–307. Plenum Press, New York.

1988 Pre-Clovis People: Early Discoveries of America? In *Americans Before Columbus: Ice-Age Origins*, edited by R. C. Carlisle, pp. 31–43. *Ethnology Monographs* No. 12, Department of Anthropology, University of Pittsburgh, Pittsburgh.

1989 Paleoecological Implications of Late Pleistocene and Holocene Microtine Rodents from the Bluefish Caves, Northern Yukon Territory. *Canadian Journal of Earth Sciences* 26:149–156.

Morlan, R. E., and J. Cinq-Mars
1982 Ancient Beringians: Human Occupation in the Late Pleistocene of Alaska and the Yukon Territory. In *Paleoecology of Beringia*, edited by D. M. Hopkins, J. V. Matthews, Jr., C. E. Schweger, and S. B. Young, pp. 353–381. Academic Press, New York.

Morlan, R. E., D. E. Nelson, T. A. Brown, J. S. Vogel, and J. R. Southon
1990 Accelerator Mass Spectrometry Dates on Bones from Old Crow Basin, Northern Yukon Territory. *Canadian Journal of Archaeology* 14:75–92.

Myers, T. P., M. R. Voorhies, and R. G. Corner
1980 Spiral Fractures and Bone Pseudotools at Paleontological Sites. *American Antiquity* 45:483–490.

Oliver, J. S.
1989 Analogues and Site Context: Bone Damages from Shield Trap Cave (24CB91), Carbon County, Montana, U.S.A. In *Bone Modification*, edited by R. Bonnichsen and M. H. Sorg, pp. 73–98. Center for the Study of the First Americans, University of Maine, Orono.

Powers, W. R.
1990 The Peoples of Eastern Beringia. In *Prehistoric Mongoloid Dispersals*, pp. 53–74. Newsletter of the "Prehistoric Mongoloid Dispersals" Project, No. 7, University of Tokyo, Tokyo.

Powers, W. R., and J. F. Hoffecker
1989 Late Pleistocene Settlement in the Nenana Valley, Central Alaska. *American Antiquity* 54:263–287.

Ritchie, J. C.
1984 *Past and Present Vegetation of the Far Northwest of Canada.* University of Toronto Press, Toronto.

Ritchie, J. C., J. Cinq-Mars, and L. C. Cwynar
1982 L'environnement Tardiglaciaire du Yukon Septentrional, Canada. *Géographie physique et Quaternaire* 36:241–250.

Ritchie, J. C., and L. Cwynar
1982 The Late Quaternary Vegetation of the Northern Yukon. In *Paleoecology of Beringia*, edited by D. M. Hopkins, J. V. Matthews, Jr., C. E. Schweger, and S. B. Young, pp. 113–126. Academic Press, New York.

Schweger, C. E.
1989 The Old Crow and Bluefish Basins, Northern Yukon: Development of the Quaternary History. In *Late Cenozoic History of the Interior Basins of Alaska and the Yukon*, edited by L. D. Carter, T. D. Hamilton, and J. P. Galloway, pp. 30–33. U.S. Geological Survey Circular No. 1026.

Shipman, P.
1981 Applications of Scanning Electron Microscopy to Taphonomic Problems. *Annals of the New York Academy of Sciences* 376: 357-386.

Shipman, P., and J. J. Rose
1983 Early Hominid Hunting, Butchering and Carcass Processing Behaviors: Approaches to the Fossil Record. *Journal of Anthropological Archaeology* 2:57–98.

Thorson, R. M., and R. D. Guthrie
1984 River Ice as a Taphonomic Agent: Alternative Hypothesis for Bone Artifacts. *Quaternary Research* 22:172–188.

Valoch, K.
1982 Die Beingerate von Predmosti in Mähren (Tschechoslowakei). *Anthropologie* 20:57–69.

Villa, P.
1991 Middle Pleistocene Prehistory in Southwestern Europe: The State of Our Knowledge and Ignorance. *Journal of Anthropological Research* 47:193–217.

Vinson, D.
1988 Preliminary Report on Faunal Identifications from Trail Creek Caves. In *The Bering Land Bridge National Preserve: An Archaeological Survey*, edited by H. Schaaf, pp. 410–438. National Park Service Research/ Resources Management Report AR-14, Anchorage.

Voorhies, M. R., and R. G. Corner
1986 The Giant Bear *Arctodus* as a Potential Breaker and Flaker of Late Pleistocene Megafaunal Remains. *Current Research in the Pleistocene* 3:49–51.

Yesner, D. R., C. E. Holmes, and K. J. Crossen
1992 Archaeology and Paleoecology of the Broken

Searching for the Earliest Canadians: Wide Corridors, Narrow Doorways, Small Windows

Michael Clayton Wilson[1]
James A. Burns[2]

Abstract

Despite claims for archaeological sites in Canada that predate the last glaciation, all of these occurrences have been rejected or are unconvincing. Bluefish Caves remain a weak possibility for such antiquity but, being in Beringia, do little to resolve the question of southward movement of people. The Ice-Free Corridor was open for southward movement of human and megafaunal populations perhaps as early as 14,000 yr B.P. but finds of that antiquity are almost nonexistent. Physical opening of a corridor did not necessarily constitute its "biotic opening" for migratory populations. The established archaeological record begins with fluted points in eastern and western Canada and follows a sequence of horizon styles much as in areas to the south. There is little direct evidence to support a northward "lag" in dates for these specific horizon styles, despite past suggestions of such an effect. Glacial lake shorelines hold potential for surveys in search of older sites, and the 12,000-year-old Kyle mammoth site remains incompletely studied for evidence of human activity. The distribution of fluted points in western Canada fits within the postulated corridor between eastern and western ice margins ca. 11,500 yr B.P., as do dated postglacial mammoth occurrences; similar relationships are noted between eastern fluted point occurrences and mapped ice fronts. Late glacial landscapes on the Canadian plains and in the Great Lakes area repeatedly were swept and scoured by outburst floods from ephemeral proglacial meltwater lakes as the Laurentide ice sheet retreated; such floods could have devastated human and megafaunal populations but also could have led to erosional loss of early archaeological sites if not deep burial of others in depositional areas downstream. The Canadian Plains area during the Holocene was less erosional than areas to the south, so that exposures are less frequent and the record less accessible. Deep-testing strategies are imperative in surveys for early sites in the Ice-Free Corridor and have become common practice in the area; their use in the past two decades has led to discovery of several Paleoindian sites. Nevertheless, a coastal migration route remains a strong possibility.

Introduction

Canada constitutes about 40 percent of the North American landmass and includes a substantial portion of the route by which the first people arrived in the midcontinent. There is a rich archaeological heritage in Canada, one that is admittedly less well understood for the Paleoindian period than is its United States counterpart. Although avocational archaeologists were widespread by the turn of the twentieth century, in some of the western Canadian provinces formal archaeological studies did not get under way until as recently as the late 1950s. The literature is nevertheless extensive and it is beyond the scope of this paper to summarize it all.

What follows is an attempt to isolate several major issues pertaining to Canadian Paleoindian studies and to place them into an historical context. The authors draw upon the technical literature and also upon the first volume of the *Historical Atlas of Canada* (R. C. Harris 1987), which includes important archaeological summaries produced under the general coordination of J. V. Wright. Some of the ideas in the present report,

1. Geology Department, Douglas College, P.O. Box 2503, New Westminster, BC V3L 5B2, Canada.
2. Provincial Museum of Alberta, Edmonton, AB T5N 0M6, Canada.

along with more extensive discussions of related geological and paleontological matters, have appeared in Burns (1990, 1996) and Wilson (1990a, 1993a, 1996). This paper was written largely in 1990–91 and has been updated as best possible; however, its overall structure and emphases remain much as originally set out. Our emphasis is upon the earliest cultural complexes from Canadian localities, and references to later Paleoindian assemblages are made only to illustrate specific lines of reasoning. Given that a major focus of this symposium is the evidence for initial peopling of the midcontinental area, we devote special attention to the "Ice-free Corridor" issue with the full knowledge that this will make our coverage of other areas appear, by comparison, to be cursory. No slight is intended to workers in other areas.

Many aspects of the Paleoindian peopling of Canada remain frustratingly obscure, despite the dedicated efforts of archaeologists. In a strict sense it will never be possible to identify the precise instant in time when the first person set foot in what is now Canada (or, for that matter, North America), but one can be forgiven for a growing impatience over an answer to the question of whether the event was glacial or interglacial. Such a question is not simply a matter of chronology; arguably, the precise dating of the first footstep on the continent is among the less interesting issues involved. Of greater interest is an understanding of the processes involved, of the means by which people arrived in the New World, and of the cultural and ecological setting and consequences of their arrival. Given the possibility of a relatively late Pleistocene first arrival, there is the tangible possibility to examine in detail the cultural implications of dispersal into unoccupied territory and to search for a cultural counterpart to the dispersal theory implicated in mammalian evolution (Geist 1971; Wilson 1993b). Despite suggestions of earlier sites, for the most part the sample in more southerly areas of Canada is consistent with an arrival of ca. 14,000 to 11,500 yr B.P. This is not entirely for want of searching, though the amount of person-days spent in the search definitely is a factor.

The history of Paleoindian studies in Canada, as in the United States, has seen wholesale swings back and forth from enthusiastic acceptance of purported interglacial sites to rejection of such claims. There have been suggestions of great antiquity for human presence at Sheguiandah, Ontario (Lee 1957); the Taber Child site, Alberta (Stalker 1969, 1977a, 1983; Wilson 1983a); Medicine Hat sites, Alberta (Stalker 1977a); the Saskatoon site, Saskatchewan (Pohorecky 1988; Pohorecky and Wilson 1968); Old Crow, Yukon Territory (Irving and Harington 1973); Bonnet Plume Basin, Y. T. (Hughes et al. 1981); Bluefish Caves, Y. T. (Cinq-Mars 1979; Morlan 1987; Morlan and Cinq-Mars 1982); and, most recently, sites at Calgary, Alberta (Chlachula 1996a, 1996b; Chlachula and LeBlanc 1996). None of these claims has been in any way frivolous, all having arisen from extensive scientific studies. Yet all have faced skepticism or rejection by the scientific community for equally well-stated reasons, and it may be that Clovis and related fluted-point types still will emerge as representative of the earliest wave of immigration.

The present authors take a relatively conservative stance on the antiquity of humans in Canada, although this admittedly is in contrast to the senior author's earlier euphoric claims about the antiquity of human occupation in Alberta (e.g., Wilson 1983a:327). Both authors have heard colleagues decrying the critics of early sites as "closed-minded" to the possibility of an early peopling event, and such complaints also have been published (e.g. Lee 1986; Pohorecky 1988). Here, however, we couple our conservative stance with the fervent hope that such early sites will be found. The conclusion to reject most, if not all, of the sites listed above is a source of frustration, not triumph, and only strengthens our resolve to keep looking for better candidates.

Apparently, if the first colonists used the Ice-free Corridor at all, they moved swiftly southward through it, between the Laurentide and Cordilleran ice sheets, the corridor being widely open (and therefore hardly deserving of the name any more) by about 11,000 years ago. The tool kits of these early travellers included well-made bifacially flaked knives and points as well as blades, all of which offered resemblances to Old World counterparts (Hoffecker et al. 1993; Morlan 1987; Müller-Beck 1967). Old World ties also are suggested by the use of red ocher and the presence of bone-and-ivory tool technology, including foreshafts and (in more southerly Clovis, at least) "shaft wrenches" (*batons de commandement*) (Haynes 1980). Later immigrants soon added microblade technologies to the repertoire. Archaeologists in Canada appear thus far to have been stymied in the search for anything convincing that is older than Clovis, even in the late-glacial record. Possible reasons for this follow.

This being a summary article, we agree with an anonymous reviewer as to the need for more detailed and critical evaluation of radiocarbon dates, particularly as they bear upon questions of chronoclinal trends.

We are pleased to report that such a review in relation to Ice-free Corridor dates is under way by Thomas G. Arnold as a Ph.D. project at Simon Fraser University. In the present setting, we can only acknowledge that dates as cited are not necessarily comparable at face value, for a variety of taphonomic reasons (see Clayton and Moran 1982, Wilson 1993a). Nevertheless, they do allow us to formulate hypotheses for further testing, which is our primary goal. If one insists upon dating only wood charcoal, as Clayton and Moran (1982) and Kuzmin and Tankersley (1996) have suggested, there is a logical fallacy if the earliest sites were in tundra without trees. By definition, all dates from areas without trees would be rejected and the earliest dates chosen would mark the arrival of trees rather than people. At this stage in review of the evidence, we choose not to invoke such paradoxes.

Historical Perspectives

THE POSSIBILITY OF AN origin in Asia for American Indians was widely discussed by the late nineteenth century (e.g., Bancroft 1882), even though a wide variety of other hypotheses, ranging from itinerant Welshmen to the Lost Tribes of Israel, were persistently popular. The main problem was one of chronology, because a limited time depth to the occupation of the Americas would allow for colonization by technologically advanced groups using ocean-going craft. A great time depth, with arrival in the Tertiary, would allow for long, independent development of humans and their cultures, but would mean an arrival in North America of humans who were not technologically advanced and who, therefore, most likely came by land. The 19th-century anthropological and geological literature offered many claims for the extreme antiquity of humans in the New World. Human skeletal material and apparent artifacts from the auriferous gravels of California were assigned to the Tertiary period as late as the turn of the century (Holmes 1899, Whitney 1879). Were this to have been true, the first peopling would have been a preglacial event and most early sites in Canada would have been overridden by subsequent ice advances. A cautious summary by Wright (1893), despite lengthy consideration of the New World evidence for early human occupation, dismissed the California evidence but otherwise simply avoided discussion of the mechanisms and timing of the first peopling event. For Canadian scientists, this uncertainty was of great significance, for the territory was extensive and it was not at all clear where one should search for early sites.

Geological findings and hypotheses played an important role in the development and testing of early models of the peopling of the New World. Fieldwork by Dawson (1875, 1885), Hector (1861), and Hind (1859, 1864) revealed that a major glaciation had indeed affected western Canada; but interpretations varied widely. Both Dawson and Hector believed that the widespread drift on the Canadian Plains was of subaqueous origin, its boulders having been carried across a shallow sea by icebergs that calved from glaciers to the west (in the Rockies) and the east (Canadian Shield). It was thought that the weight of the ice had caused enough depression of the intervening landmass that there had been a southward transgression of Arctic Ocean waters. Such a view, which would have ruled out a land "corridor" between ice masses at their maximum, was challenged by Bell (1890), Tyrrell (1890), and Upham (1891, 1895), who all believed that widespread continental glaciers were the direct agency of till deposition. Dawson, the influential director of the Geological Survey of Canada, clung to the "glacionatant" (iceberg) hypothesis until the end of the century (Dawson 1891a, 1897).

Recognition of evidence for multiple glaciations (Dawson 1891b, 1895; Dawson and McConnell 1895; Tyrrell 1898) meant that there had been an interglacial period and that even if a sea had been present, presumably there had been times when its regression allowed a land corridor to link Beringia with the midcontinent. Such a corridor was illustrated as early as 1894 in the form of T. C. Chamberlin's "Ideal Map of North America During the Ice Age," published as Plate XIV in Geikie (1894). With the recognition of ice-push and ice-scoured features on the open plains, the "glacionatant" hypothesis was laid to rest, and work began to concentrate upon details of the Plains glacial sequence (e.g., Coleman 1910). The former existence of freshwater glacial lakes, long advocated by authors such as Agassiz and Upham, was acknowledged widely and a sequence of retreatal ice-marginal lakes was documented (e.g., Johnston and Wickenden 1931).

The ice-free "corridor" between the Cordilleran and Laurentide ice masses soon was hypothesized by Johnston (1933) to have played a direct role in the peopling of the North American midcontinent (see also Antevs 1935, 1937; K. Bryan 1941). Bryan, suggesting only that humans "filter[ed] south as the ice dam in the Plains disappeared about 10,000 years after the glacial maximum," acknowledged the absence of concrete evidence. "In the absence of archaeological data such an idea is intriguing, but perhaps fanciful," he lamented.

Rejection of the California claims for great antiquity (e.g., Lindgren 1911:52–53; Wright 1893:294–301, 372–374) arose from critical reanalysis that reflected a changing analytical "climate" for other sites as well. Although these trends were most apparent in United States research, the role of Canadian territory (western or otherwise) as a conduit for migration was widely acknowledged. Hrdlièka (1907, 1918) debunked claims of the early Quaternary or even Tertiary peopling of North America and advocated a late Pleistocene arrival via the Bering Strait, possibly in waves of colonization. Differences in morphology, ethnographic characteristics, and linguistics were seen as possibly supporting a migratory wave hypothesis, new versions of which are again waxing and waning (Greenberg 1987; Greenberg et al. 1986). Rivet (1943) and others argued for additional migratory waves across the Pacific but agreed that the Bering route was of great importance. White admixture (Cro-Magnon) was envisaged by others, with humans island-hopping from Europe via Greenland to Labrador on the Canadian mainland. Physical and ethnographic parallels, especially with the Magdalenian, were cited in support of this view (Cotteville-Giraudet 1928; for a more recent view, see Greenman 1962). Imbelloni (1938), while not accepting the eastern route, discerned seven physical types in the New World and hypothesized seven distinct migrations, ranging from Eskimo to Tasmanians! To this day, authors differ in views as to whether concrete evidence exists among modern American Indian groups, either in physical or cultural attributes, to allow postulation of direct linkages with any particular subarea of Asia or particular ethnic groupings (e.g., papers in Laughlin and Harper 1979). Recent efforts have centered upon the possibility of three distinct groupings (Paleoamerican, Na-Dene, and Eskimo-Aleut), but these distinctions appear again on the verge of breaking down (Greenberg 1987; Greenberg et al. 1986; see also discussions by Gibbons 1993, 1996; Morell 1990). The archaeological arguments remain in a similar state, though an origin in Asia for most, if not all, native North American groups is no longer seriously questioned. An origin in Asia does not, however, mandate a Mongoloid origin, given the diversity of Asiatic groups including central Asiatic Caucasoid groups of long standing.

Once identified, the Ice-Free Corridor became the subject of archaeological surveys in the late 1930s. Early exploratory surveys of the Corridor area by Bird (1939) and Bliss (1937, 1939a, 1939b) were tantalizing but provided few specific leads for immediate investigation. Parks (1925) had reported the association of artifacts in Saskatchewan with the new extinct antilocaprid, *Neomeryx finni*, but the latter proved to be nothing more than a variant form of the modern pronghorn antelope, and of no great antiquity. Clear evidence of ancient sites was not found, but at least the archaeological potential of the area was confirmed. Follow-up work was interrupted by World War II and surveys did not resume until the late 1940s and the 1950s (Johnson 1946; Johnson and Raup 1964; MacNeish 1951, 1953, 1954, 1956a, 1956b, 1963, 1964). Surface finds from Alberta included "classic" examples of virtually all the major Paleoindian projectile point types known from the Plains to the south, and fluted points were widespread (Kehoe 1966; Wormington and Forbis 1965). Despite claims of substantial antiquity for the British Mountain complex of the northern Yukon (MacNeish 1959), based upon technological considerations, confirmation was not forthcoming and the assemblage is now interpreted as Holocene lithic workshop debris (Greer 1991).

Claims for the Earliest (Preglacial) Sites

During the 1970s and early 1980s, the outlook for discoveries of pre-Wisconsinan human remains in western Canada looked extremely promising. Discoveries at Old Crow, Yukon Territory, included a caribou tibia flesher dated by radiocarbon in excess of 27,000 yr B.P., an antler wedge, an antler billet, spirally fractured and flaked mammoth bones, and even a human mandible. Most of these were from point-bar placer deposits (Bonnichsen 1978; Harington et al. 1975; Irving 1978; Irving and Harington 1973; Irving et al. 1977; Morlan 1978). Major expeditions were organized by the National Museum of Man (Ottawa; now the Canadian Museum of Civilization) and the University of Toronto in pursuit of in-place material (Irving 1986; Jopling et al. 1981; Morlan 1979, 1980).

In southern Alberta, the "Taber Child," from what came to be known as the Stalker site, seemed to be an in-place Pleistocene human skeleton, age estimates for which ranged as far back as 60,000 to 90,000 yr B.P. (Stalker 1969, 1977a). The remains were of an infant, the morphological characters of which defied detailed comparisons (Sundick 1980). Enigmatic flaked-chert

objects from Sangamonian or mid-Wisconsinan deposits near Medicine Hat, Alberta, prompted naming of the "Artifact Band" and seemed, along with broken large-mammal bones, to indicate human activity (Stalker and Churcher 1970; Szabo et al. 1973). Similar flaked objects and spirally fractured large-mammal bones recovered from Sangamonian alluvium at Saskatoon, Saskatchewan, also were interpreted as archaeological in origin (Pohorecky and Wilson 1968).

Regrettably, none of this evidence has fully withstood scientific scrutiny. Three Old Crow specimens—the flesher, antler wedge, and antler billet—have been redated by accelerator mass spectrometry to the late Holocene (Morlan et al. 1990; Nelson et al. 1986). Fractured mammoth-bone remains from Old Crow and particularly from Bluefish Caves may be witness to human activity (Morlan 1986, Morlan et al. 1990). Nevertheless, in the case of these finds, serious concerns still exist about natural mechanisms of bone breakage, including carnivore activity and physical processes. For example, fresh-frozen bones thawing from permafrost might be subjected to apparent green-bone fracture during active-zone detachment of sediments (gelifluction), much as conchoidal fracture of cobbles can occur in

Figure 1. Glacially flaked cobbles at Athabasca Glacier, Columbia Icefields, Jasper National Park, Alberta; and cobbles in the immediate area of the glacier terminus. (a) View of rapidly retreating terminus of Athabasca Glacier, with recessional moraine to right (east) and lateral moraine in distance. Cobbles in (b), (c), and (d) were photographed in situ at this location and lay within 2 m of one another, about 3 m from the glacier in an area exposed at most a few decades ago. (b) Angular quartzite cobble with multiple conchoidal flake scars, two of which (black and white arrows) are deep and show hinged terminations. (c) Fine-grained quartzite to metasiltstone cobble spall with multiple conchoidal flake scars, one of which (arrow) displays "a point of percussion," likely in fact from pressure flaking within the ice. (d) Striated metacarbonate cobble with multiple cycles of flaking, followed by abrasion and fresh overlapping hinged "retouch" scars along much of the lower margin. Note, in (b) - (d), the angularity of most other cobbles and pebbles, others of which (regardless of size) also display crescentic flake scars. Such cobbles were found in abundance throughout the terminal moraine area.

moving ice. River ice pushing against exposed bones in such deposits also can cause breakage and abrasion (Thorson and Guthrie 1984). No natural breakage mechanism seems to explain *all* of the patterns noted at Old Crow, leaving a cultural origin possible for some specimens (Morlan 1986, 1987). Nevertheless, taphonomic considerations leave no clear case for cultural agency, either, and make interstadial occupation of Beringia doubtful (Guthrie 1984).

The sample from Bluefish Caves included microdebitage (Cinq-Mars 1979) that has, at other sites, been linked with cultural activity (Fladmark 1982; Hull 1983; Nicholson 1983). Similar tiny flakes of cryptocrystalline silica were recovered from Pleistocene sediments in the Bonnet Plume Basin, Yukon, and were hypothesized (with appropriate caution) to be of cultural origin (Hughes et al. 1981; Morlan 1983). The weakness in this case rests with the likelihood of equifinality; that is, microdebitage can result from both cultural and natural processes.

Conchoidal fracturing of sediment grains is widespread in natural environments and is particularly prevalent in sediments of glacial origin (Julig et al. 1990; Mahaney et al. 1988; Margolis and Krinsley 1974; Rogerson and Hudson 1983), as a result of pressure-contact of clasts during ice-flow. Thus, glacial deposits are full of "microdebitage," as well as macroscopically flaked specimens. The first author examined recently exposed cobbles at the snout of the Athabasca Glacier in the Columbia Icefield, Alberta, and found that macroscopic conchoidal fracturing was represented abundantly (Figure 1). Interpretive signs at the glacier mark recessional margins of the past century, and these cobbles had been exposed no more than a few decades—most likely, less than 20 years. Such cobbles also are abundant in tills; the largest observed by Wilson at Kipp, in the Lethbridge area of southern Alberta, was a 1-m-long boulder with conchoidal scars up to 30 cm across, the scars displaying clear "impact points," likely points where intense pressure was applied. While further studies are required, it is clear that conchoidal fracturing, as represented by cores or flakes in any size category, cannot be taken by itself as culturally diagnostic in formerly glaciated terrain. Many pebble fragments in till show multiple and even overlapping flakes. Wilson's observations, which are part of a continuing study, suggest that once a cobble has been split (e.g., by point-loading against another cobble in ice), subsequent removal of multiple flakes from pressure against the platform is facilitated because the new platform angle eases detachment. Multiple and even overlapping flaking therefore can be seen as a mechanical cascade of interdependent events that can speed up under natural circumstances (through deviation-amplifying feedback as a result of platform development), and not as necessarily cultural. Secondary flakes also can be detached from a platform at the same time as primary flake removal, and this can be accomplished by natural means (Jelinek et al. 1971). Furthermore, although most geological descriptions have talked of conchoidally fractured grains as markers of glacial environments, the flakes removed in natural primary comminution cannot simply vanish. The undisputed observation that microdebitage can be produced culturally does not, therefore, necessarily work in the other direction.

As far as the more southerly evidence is concerned, detailed excavation and restudy of the Taber Child (Stalker) site shows that the skeleton likely was emplaced or redeposited in a Holocene sandy mudflow, deposits of which form a dendritic pattern inset into Pleistocene sands in the face of the river bluff (Wilson 1984; Wilson et al. 1983). AMS dating and protein content analysis indicate a Holocene age (Brown et al. 1983; Gowlett 1987; Moffat and Wainwright 1983). Although Stalker (1983) has restated the case for a Pleistocene age, we no longer can accept such a view. Even the Taber Child's unusual reddish coloration, similar to that of many Pleistocene bones from the region, need not support great antiquity. The specimen appears to date between 5000 and 4000 yr B.P., a time when red ocher was being lavished upon other burials in nearby Saskatchewan (Walker 1984).

The flaked-chert specimens from the "Artifact Band" at Medicine Hat were restudied by Reeves (1980), who concluded on the basis of edge-angle comparisons that they were not of cultural origin. Instead, they appear to more closely resemble naturally flaked specimens (in effect, "eoliths") encountered in glacial and other deposits (see discussion above). The "Artifact Band" likely includes clasts reworked from tills. An important factor in their creation was the fact that many specimens were good-quality chert (which occurs as nodules in Paleozoic dolomites and limestones carried from Manitoba or northeastern Saskatchewan), irregular in shape and particularly vulnerable to flaking by natural means. Examination of the Medicine Hat broken bones yielded equivocal results, there also being natural processes that could account for their breakage (Reeves 1980).

These same arguments can be applied to the lithic and fractured bone sample from the Saskatoon site, which, like the "Artifact Band," represents an alluvial deposit. Pohorecky (1988) restated the case for their acceptance as cultural but made no reference of Reeves' obviously relevant study. Pohorecky instead railed against the "politics of science" and prejudgment of the Saskatoon site by uncharitable colleagues bent on disproof of the early peopling of North America (1988:63). Similar accusations often have been made on behalf of other sites and their champions. Yet the period from the late 1960s to the early 1980s in western Canada was a time of acceptance, not rejection, of the early peopling hypothesis. Most of the examples of potentially early finds were examined, and reluctantly dismissed, by archaeologists vigorously *seeking* evidence of pre-Clovis human occupation in the New World—a fact that is too easily forgotten. Groups involved in reanalysis or dating of the Old Crow and Taber specimens, for example, were seeking to secure, not reject, these respective cases. At the time Reeves was rejecting the Medicine Hat material, he also was making arguments in favor of even greater antiquity for sites in the San Diego area of California, and lamenting to the *Calgary Herald* that some of his colleagues considered him "a kook" for making such extravagant claims (Bragg 1977). This hardly sounds like the forces of evil conjured up by Pohorecky.

The Sheguiandah site, on Manitoulin Island in Lake Huron, Ontario (T. E. Lee 1957, 1972), until recently was regarded as equivocal in nature, with arguments centering upon the interpretation of overlying sediments as till. Recent arguments by R. E. Lee (1986) attempting to reassert the site's claim to great antiquity were directed more at securing the reputation of past workers (especially his father, T. E. Lee) whose views had been discarded. R. E. Lee sought to demonstrate the arbitrariness of skeptics rather than to provide new information. According to him, the till was identified by a competent geologist (Sanford 1957, 1971); therefore, its nature cannot be questioned by archaeologists. What should have been made clear was that the overlying sediment was observably a *diamict* (in Sanford's usage, a "mictolite"); identification of the diamict as a *till* required an extra interpretive step that depended both upon experience and detailed comparison (Karrow 1987). Lee (1986:404) blasted critics for their collective view that, as he paraphrased it, "if there are artifacts, then those deposits cannot be till." Although artifacts could, in theory, be found in till, one would expect their dispersion, not their concentration at a particular site; so there is reason behind such a view.

This caution indeed would appear to have been justified; recent discovery of evidence for glacial outburst floods that probably ripped through the Great Lakes in earliest Holocene times provides a testable non-till alternative for the diamict at Sheguiandah (Julig 1990:21; Julig et al. 1990). This hypothesis also easily allows for a latest Pleistocene or even earliest Holocene age for the site. "At Sheguiandah ... water worn artifacts in the lower levels of a stratified sequence suggests ... continued site use before and after the early Mattawa flood event" (Julig 1990:21), which occurred ca. 9,600 yr B.P. Obviously, restudy of the geologic settings of such sites and the development of new understandings are preferable to sterile arguments about the credentials of past workers who "laid hands" upon them.

Recent publications concerning flaked stones from two localities in the Calgary area, Varsity Estates and Silver Springs (Chlachula 1996a, 1996b; Chlachula and LeBlanc 1996), are subject to similar concerns. Flaked stones, *per se*, are not automatically diagnostic of human behavior, but some of the pieces recovered may be of cultural origin. The material recovered by Chlachula comes from test pits on a retreating slope; upslope from the occurrence are glacial lake silts that Chlachula projects forward over the site to demonstrate an age older than the late Wisconsinan glaciation (>20,000 yr B.P.). As described by Chlachula, the purported artifacts are derived from multiple contexts; some of the stones come from within the uppermost part of the underlying till, while others are from gravels atop the till. These deposits do not represent in-place living floors. The published descriptions do not preclude the possibility that some specimens could even be derived from cliff-face colluvium or slope diamicts.

A date for the sites of before the last Wisconsinan glaciation is based upon regional correlations rooted in a multiple glaciation model. If, as evidence now suggests, the coalescence of ice in western Alberta occurred only once and was during the late Wisconsinan, then the till upon which the sites rest (if the sites are truly even of the same age) would be of this age, and the glacial lake silts would mark a brief lacustrine phase in the early recession of the ice. It has now been determined that the underlying till contains clasts derived from the Canadian Shield (i.e., that it was influenced by proximity to eastern ice), which indicates it to be of late Wisconsinan age (L. E. Jackson Jr., personal communication, 1998). These considerations suggest that the site, if the artifacts are truly cultural, is of late glacial age, possibly pre-Clovis but not of the antiquity claimed by Chlachula.

The Calgary artifacts (illustrated by Chlachula 1996b) could be a mixed bag of cultural and non-cultural flaked specimens, and additional study is needed to clarify the basis for cultural assignment. A biface that was found on the surface of the slope at the level of the till-to-glacial lake silt contact remains the single most convincing specimen. Flakes that could be refit to it were recovered from distances up to 1 m into the slope. This, however, is still close to the surface in the instance of a slope subject to creep and colluviation. Chlachula (1996b) argues that the specimens resemble things that are called artifacts in Europe; therefore, they are artifacts. Indeed, in Chlachula and LeBlanc (1996:72), a footnote larded with a degree of sarcasm indicates that visitors were invited to the site, and the Europeans had no trouble identifying the materials as artifacts, whereas the North Americans were not as ready to accept them. The assumption that European scholars must, by definition, be more insightful is inappropriate, for one of the fundamental tenets of the processualist movement in archaeology was denial of the "rule of authority" in favor of direct experimentation and proper scientific establishment of criteria and tests. To appeal to the diffuse authority of unnamed European scholars (not all of whom necessarily have worked in formerly glaciated landscapes) is specious and calls to mind the attempt to use Louis Leakey's opinions to "establish" the truth of the Calico Mountains "artifacts."

Since Chlachula conducted such a poll, the first author did too. One concern repeatedly expressed was that the line drawings of the lithic specimens are more convincing than the photographs, because of the line-shading technique used; although the flake surfaces on the quartzite artifacts are rough, the artist has indeed shaded them as for high-quality cryptocrystalline materials and has shown the surfaces as smooth and arcuate (e.g., Chlachula 1996b, Figs. 13 and 25; see Addington 1986:18 and her Figs. 50–51 for proper procedures). Thus the drawings seem to idealize rather than to portray the artifacts. Another more serious matter was that many Canadian archaeologists have had the opportunity to become acquainted with the matter of till stones exhibiting flaking; therefore, they in turn and with justice had strong concerns about the possibility of a natural agency accounting for much of the Calgary material.

Chlachula and LeBlanc (1996) compare the Calgary materials with cobble artifacts from a middle to late Prehistoric site (the Slump site) near Lesser Slave Lake, northern Alberta, and find favorable similarities. They derive, on this basis, 12 criteria for the recognition of flaked artifacts as cultural. These include

> *(1) effective edge modification complying with an appropriate hand-manipulation of the particular lithic specimen; (2) point of percussion at the base of negative scars; (3) concave and smooth negative flake scars; (4) unidirectional flaking; (5) long and parallel or concentric flake-scar orientation; (6) non-cortical flat striking platform preparation; (7) restricted (distal/lateral) location of edge modification; (8) regular unifacial retouching on the dorsal flake faces; (9) low-angle, alternately flaked bifacial edges; (10) organized overlapping retouch; (11) size and angle uniformity of small edge-flake scars; and (12) deep negative flake-scar terminations. (1996:72)*

Chlachula and LeBlanc feel that these attributes are "diagnostic of cultural flaking for quartzite lithic assemblages, especially if they occur in combinations and with recurrent patterning" (ibid.). Yet their article does not provide any distributional data to show which occur in combinations (and how often) in the Calgary samples.

This listing of criteria developed (but not tested) by Chlachula and LeBlanc merely sidesteps the question of evaluating a cultural versus a natural origin for lithics, for there is a considerable literature already established on the subject, none of which they cite (e.g., Ascher and Ascher 1965; Grayson 1986; Patterson 1983; and including Reeves 1980, again not cited despite being in the same department as was Chlachula). Such arguments have long been debated (as, for example, with the Calico Site "artifacts"; see Duvall and Venner 1979; Simpson 1980). In fact, similar controversies exist in Europe, some of very long standing, about the cultural versus natural origin of the earliest hypothesized industries (for example, at Saint-Elbe; see Ackerman 1989; also regarding eoliths see Oakley 1967 and Grayson 1986). Chlachula (1996b) simply argues that the specimens are cultural because they exhibit "patterned" as opposed to "random" flaking. However, as noted above, the splitting of a cobble by natural point-loading provides a platform that is much more vulnerable to repeated, even overlapping flaking; in fact, natural flaking is patterned too. Labelling of secondary flaking as "edge utilization" (Chlachula and LeBlanc 1996:68) is interpretive, not descriptive, and presumes a cultural context. Chlachula and LeBlanc (1996:72) find their criteria to exclude the possibility of natural production by "high-energy glacial and glaciofluvial processes" but focus upon the possibility for natural percussion; what is needed is a careful consideration of the possibility within flowing ice for high-intensity pressure flaking. Ice moves by microthrusting, with considerable internal deformation during flow; this means that pebbles encased in ice can be pressed against one another and dragged past one another within the ice. This in turn means that splitting followed by a cascade of directional, repetitive flaking indeed can occur, and the great abundance of flaked specimens at the snout of the Athabaska Glacier (first author's observations; see Figure 1) is testimony to it. Large flake scars with hinged terminations abound and may well be the product of high-intensity pressure rather than of percussion, despite the contention that such scars are "especially indicative of heavy percussion flaking" (Chlachula and LeBlanc 1996:69). Many of the concave and smooth negative flake scars (with "points of percussion"—more likely points of contact involving pressure) in cobbles or even boulders from tills in southern Alberta are much too large to be accounted for by human agency, but the glacial context of conchoidal fracturing has been known to geologists for many decades. British archaeologist Kenneth Oakley (1967:7,8) illustrated a retouched conchoidal flake from Permian glacial deposits of Africa (250 million years old), along with pre-Eocene flint flakes from England showing extensive series of overlapping retouch scars. Oakley noted (1967:12) that "stones flaked by glacial action into forms showing a remarkable resemblance to artifacts have been found in Pleistocene boulder clays, and in the Permian glacial beds of South Africa... Thus geologists are inclined to adopt a cautious attitude with regard to crudely chipped stones resembling artifacts, particularly if they occur in situations where natural flaking cannot be ruled out." Thorson and Guthrie (1984:173) show, furthermore, that river ice can facet and flake boulders and cobbles as well as bones; so the possibilities for natural flaking extend beyond glacial ice.

Arguments for cultural agency based solely upon typological comparison with simply flaked assemblages in Eurasia (and especially appeals to European authority) are circumstantial and verge on tautology; much better evidence will be needed to resolve this question. Chlachula and LeBlanc lament that rejection of the Calgary material also would necessitate rejection of much of the later cobble tool industries from the middle and late Prehistoric of the Northwestern Plains as non-cultural, or redefine what we mean by "artifact." These outcomes do not logically follow, because the flaked-cobble problem set simply exhibits equifinality from multiple pathways (cultural and non-cultural). There are specimens in the late Prehistoric record of Alberta that fully resemble Oldowan choppers, but we do not call them Oldowan, either; nor do they necessarily reflect the same sequence of thought processes or the same technological environment of production.

Early occupation of Bluefish Caves in the northern Yukon has not yet been demonstrated despite the presence of an impressive bone bed (Cinq-Mars 1979; Morlan 1987; Morlan and Cinq-Mars 1982). Acceptability of this site would have to rest with a close stratigraphic association of stone artifacts (not microdebitage) with datable Pleistocene fauna. At present it seems equally likely, if not more so, that the bone bed represents a natural trap accumulation. Yet despite the weakness of the Bluefish Caves case and the demise of the famous Old Crow caribou tibia flesher as a Pleistocene artifact, we remain optimistic that evidence will be found for early human occupation of eastern Beringia. Of course, Beringia could have been occupied at a considerably earlier date than the midcontinent, so the case for early southward movement remains more problematic. Survey for such sites is very much a geological matter, involving stratigraphic studies of sites in deeply buried contexts, reconstruction of dramatically altered geomorphic settings, and use of varied dating methods.

The Ice-Free Corridor and Southward Movement of Early Human Groups

The Corridor

THE "ICE-FREE CORRIDOR" of the western Canadian Plains for decades has been considered a phenomenon of at least late glacial times, if not a feature of the entire late Wisconsinan glaciation, separating Cordilleran and Laurentide ice sheets. Evidence is accruing, both from glacial sequences in neighboring areas and from radiocarbon dates on paleontological remains, that the last major glacial advance on the Canadian Plains began somewhere between about 22,000 and 18,000 years ago (Burns 1990:63–64, 1996; Jackson et al. 1997;

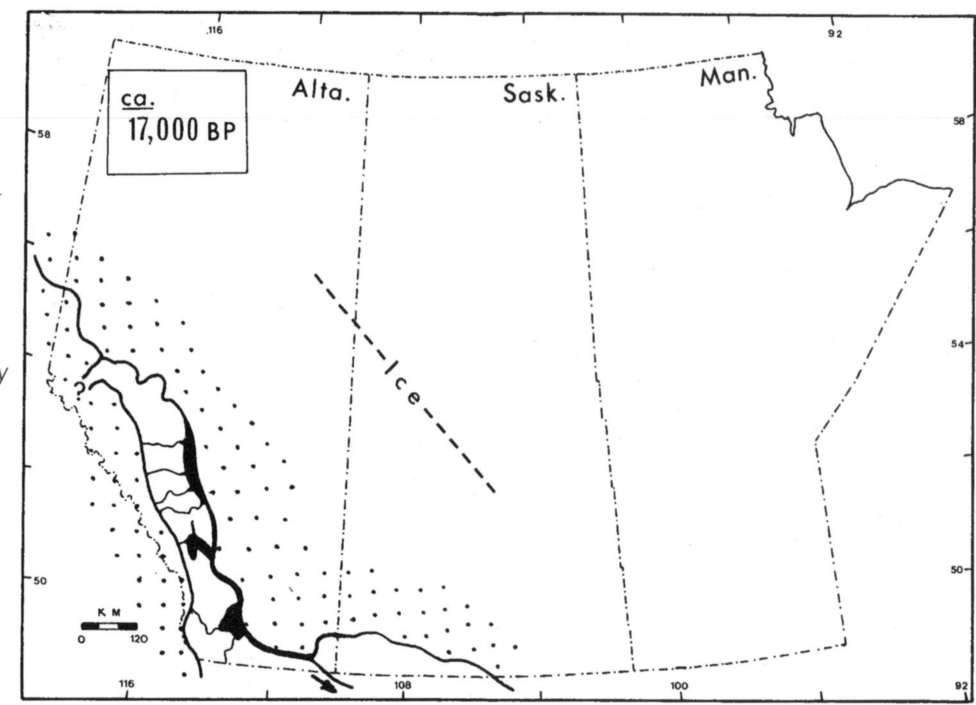

Figure 2. Map of the Canadian prairie provinces showing near-maximum ice position and early stage of opening of the "Ice-Free Corridor." There is increasing evidence that ice extended farther south in the late Wisconsinan, in which case the date for the stage illustrated here is more likely about 15,000 years ago. This map shows the origin of the Saskatchewan River system in meltwater channels and interconnected proglacial lakes (solid black) that drained southward into the Missouri/Mississippi system. After Wilson (1990).

Wilson 1983a:286–295; Young et al. 1994). Prevailing opinion at the time of this writing seems to be against the presence of an open, passable corridor during the maximum extent of ice, a position with which we must agree. In addition to references cited above, various positions as to the timing of closure of the Corridor have been outlined by Beaudoin (1989), Bobrowsky et al. (1990), A. Bryan (1969), Burns (1990, 1996), Catto and Mandryk (1990), Clayton and Moran (1982), Fullerton and Colton (1986), Jackson (1979), MacDonald et al. (1987), Mandryk and Rutter (1996), Mathews (1980), Moran (1986), Reeves (1973), Rutter (1984), Rutter and Schweger (1980), Stalker (1977b), and Wilson (1990a), and and the reader is referred to these sources for detailed discussions of the many viewpoints.

Despite differences of opinion, the role of this corridor in the first peopling of the North American midcontinent arguably is the most dominant and long-lived environmental archaeological paradigm in Canada, rivaling in acceptance the proposition that people hunted bison on the Plains. Nevertheless, searches for the Holy Grail of "first footsteps" have proved frustrating; few paleontological sites in excess of 12,000 years old have been found within the corridor, and no archaeological sites are clearly older than about 11,000 yr B.P. (Driver 1995). Reasons for the apparent paucity of sites are beginning to emerge and constitute a mixed bag. They include (1) the relatively limited extent of archaeological surveys to date; (2) the paucity of excavations that have gone beyond the test-pit or test-trench stage; (3) the deep burial of sites in certain geomorphic settings, partly as a result of periglacial and paraglacial activity (see below for definition and discussion of "paraglacial") and partly because of Hypsithermal landscape remodelling; (4) the loss of sites because of the erosive effects of outburst floods and Hypsithermal deflation; and (5) the possibility that another route was used for human migrations. The first two require little additional comment; archaeological studies require time, people, and money, and none of these has been in good supply in the area until the past two or three decades. Funding is again being cut dramatically as a result of government budget-cutting and the recent recession. Much of the effort directed toward environmental-impact studies and salvage archaeology has dealt with more readily visible sites of the middle and late Prehistoric periods, and fewer programs of deep testing have been undertaken to locate deeply buried resources, needles in the proverbial haystack.

The "Ice-Free Corridor" has been an evocative model, one that conjures up visions of a narrow tundra band between towering ice barriers to the east and west. Anything resembling this, if it existed at all, would have been of extremely short duration; much of the north-south faunal interchange occurred under much more open conditions, or was restrained by a "corridor" of vegetation rather than ice (MacDonald and McLeod 1996; M. C. Wilson 1996). It can be

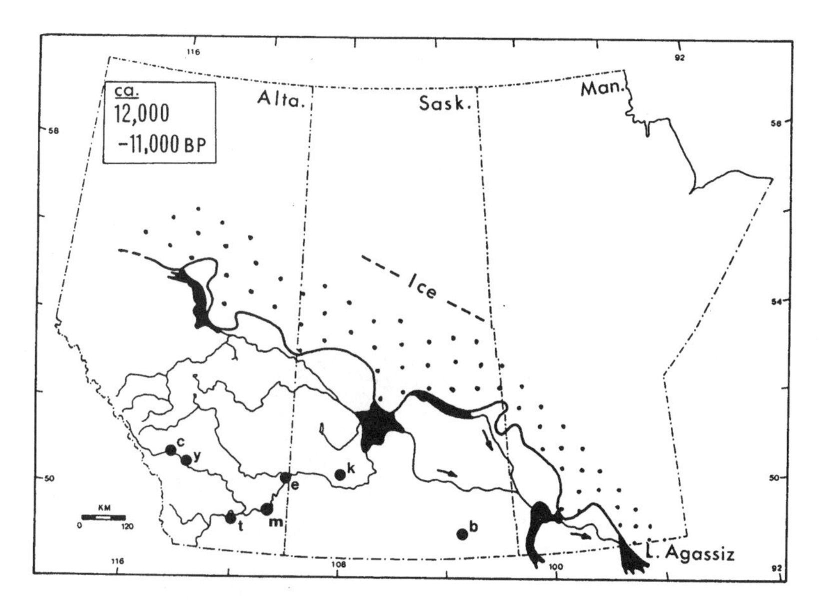

Figure 3. Generalized map of Canadian prairie provinces showing ice position during mid-retreat, by which time the "Ice-Free Corridor" was widely open for faunal interchange between Beringia and the midcontinent. The map is designed to illustrate a stage in the evolution of the Saskatchewan River system and hence should not be over-interpreted as a "point-in-time" representation. By 11,000 years ago, Lake Agassiz had extended northwestward into Saskatchewan (far beyond the limits shown here) in Christensen's (1979) reconstruction. The expansion may have been slightly later, however (Fenton et al. 1983). Map modified after Wilson (1990). Indicated sites have yielded vertebrate paleontological material dating before 11,000 yr B.P. or associated with Clovis culture:

b. Clovis bone "foreshaft" (projectile point?); isolated find (Wilmeth 1968). Specimen not dated.

c. Cochrane, Alberta, gravel pits, with two dates in excess of 11,000 yr B.P. and bones of caribou, mountain sheep, wapiti, bison, and horse (Stalker 1968; Churcher 1968, 1975; Wilson and Churcher 1984).

e. Empress, Alberta, gravel pits, dated 14,200± 1120 yr B.P. (GSC-1199; Lowdon and Blake 1975), yielding bones of mammoth and horse.

k. Kyle Mammoth Site, Saskatchewan, dated 12,000 yr B.P. (see text).

m. Medicine Hat sites, richly fossiliferous gravels of Sangamonian, mid-Wisconsinan, and early post-glacial age, including Lindoe Bluff with bison and extinct horse dated to 11,200±200 yr B.P. (GSC-220; Lowdon and Blake 1968).

t. Bayrock Site, Taber, Alberta, with bison skeleton and wood, the latter dated to 11,000±250 (S-68) and 10,500±200 yr B.P. (GSC-3) (Trylich and Bayrock 1966).

y. Calgary, Alberta, gravel pits, with date of 11,300±290 yr B.P. (RL-757; Wilson 1983a; Wilson and Churcher 1984) and bones of bison (dated), horse, camel, and possibly mammoth.

Numerous isolated finds of mammoth teeth, tusks, and bones from all three provinces likely date from this interval, but are not shown because of the possibility they may be older.

argued, therefore, that the name is misleading and analytically anachronistic (Beaudoin 1989; Burns 1996). Nevertheless, the term is deeply rooted and no doubt will persist far beyond its usefulness. Beaudoin's suggested alternative, "Western Corridor," seemingly preempts anything further west and implies an eastern counterpart; it has not seen acceptance.

Evidence is increasing that central and southwestern Alberta saw only one glaciation—that of the late Wisconsinan (Burns 1996; Jackson and Duk-Rodkin 1996; Little 1995; Young et al. 1994). Direct dating of glacial erratics on the basis of cosmogenic ^{36}Cl exposure supports a growing view that the Foothills Erratics Train, marking the coalescence of Laurentide and Cordilleran ice, was emplaced during the late Wisconsinan (Jackson et al. 1997). Efforts to establish the presence or absence of an Ice-Free Corridor at the time of the late Wisconsinan maximum some 18,000 to 16,000 years ago have been many, based largely upon dates from bogs and alluvial deposits (e.g., Burns 1996; Catto and Mandryk 1990; Clayton and Moran 1982; Jackson 1979; MacDonald et al. 1987; Mandryk 1996a; Reeves 1973; M. C. Wilson 1996). Limiting dates from bogs require an assumption that bog formation began immediately upon deglaciation, ignoring some unspecified lag time. However, studies of western Canadian peatlands show that peat deposition did not begin in many areas until thousands of years after ice retreat, responding instead to fluctuations in regional ground-water tables (Zoltai and Vitt 1990). Furthermore, the patchiness of permafrost influenced subsequent development of forests and must have influenced bog formation dramatically (Pielou 1991). Bones and wood from alluvium in river systems

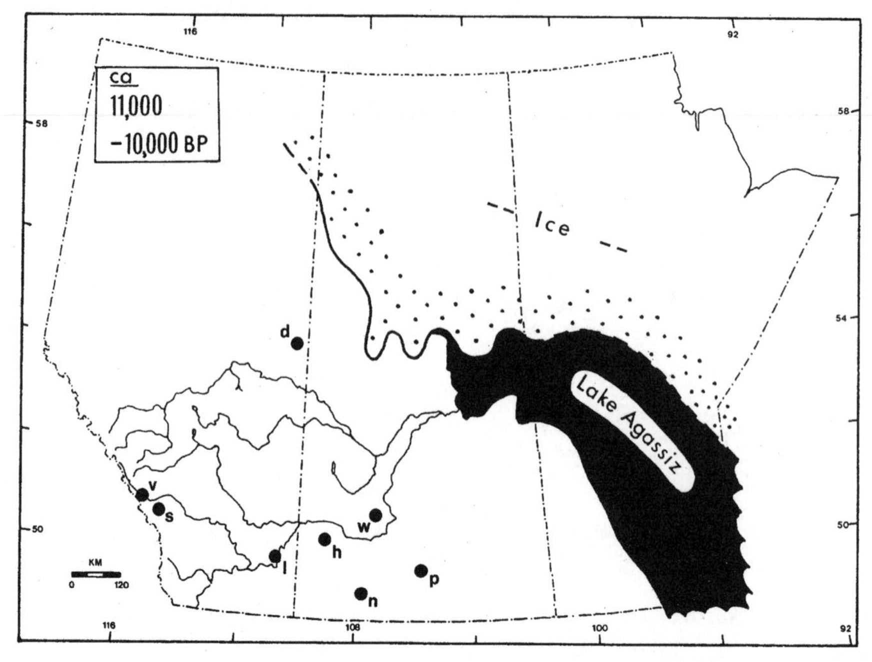

Figure 4. Generalized map of Canadian prairie provinces showing ice position well into retreat and Saskatchewan River system nearly complete at a time when Glacial Lake Agassiz was near its greatest extent. Lake Agassiz at various times drained either southward or eastward; later it empted northward into Hudson Bay. Map modified after Wilson (1990); sites are discussed in text. Indicated sites have yielded archaeological or paleontological material dating to or probably referable to the indicated interval. Many more surface archaeological sites and in situ paleontological sites are known from the area.

d. Duckett Site, near Cold Lake, Alberta, with triangular fluted point on surface and other Paleoindian points in situ; not dated.

h. Heron Eden Site, Great Sand Hills, Saskatchewan, with Cody component and underlying materials; Agate Basin point may be associated with date of 10,210 yr B.P.

l. Lindoe Site, near Medicine Hat, Alberta, with in situ bone bed dated to 9900 yr B.P. and Hell Gap point on surface.

n. Niska Site, Saskatchewan, with Cody component and underlying material dated to 10,880 yr B.P. (cultural affinities not known).

p. Parkhill Site, Saskatchewan, with large surface sample of Agate Basin projectile points.

s. Sibbald Creek Site, Alberta, with extensive stratified record including triangular fluted points.

v. Vermilion Lakes Site, near Banff, Alberta; lanceolate (Agate Basin-like) points are in a component dated to about 10,500 yr B.P.

w. Wiseton Mammoth, Saskatchewan, a limb bone from lacustrine deposits, dated (collagen) to 10,600 yr B.P.

that traverse the putative corridor provide limiting dates also, but few dates in excess of 12,000 yr B.P. are available—and those that are available are either hotly debated or quietly ignored (Clayton and Moran 1982; Jackson 1983; Klassen 1972, 1983; Wilson and Churcher 1984). If one insists upon dating only wood charcoal (Clayton and Moran 1982; Kuzmin and Tankersley 1996), the dates are even more constrained and the earlier ones tend to be rejected; however, as noted earlier, this could contain a logical fallacy if the earliest sites were in tundra and there is no wood charcoal to date. Early dates "inconsistent" with wood dates simply would be rejected rather than being taken as evidence of a pre-forest period, even though regional pollen records suggest such a period to have existed.

A second, related debate concerns the maximum extent of Laurentide ice in late Wisconsinan times: whether it reached just to southern Alberta (Stalker 1977b, 1980) or moved farther south to Montana and North Dakota (Christiansen 1979; Clayton and Moran 1982; Fullerton and Colton 1986). It is a sobering realization that none of the ice margin fluctuations from the late Wisconsinan ice retreat in Alberta, a key "corridor" area, are as yet securely dated (Catto and Mandryk 1990). However, views are crystallizing around the belief that the late Wisconsinan event was the most extensive glaciation to have affected western Canada and the northern U.S. plains (Jackson et al. 1997).

Generalized ice-retreat stages for the prairie provinces are illustrated here, after Wilson (1990a) (Figures 2, 3, 4). These maps are for general discussion

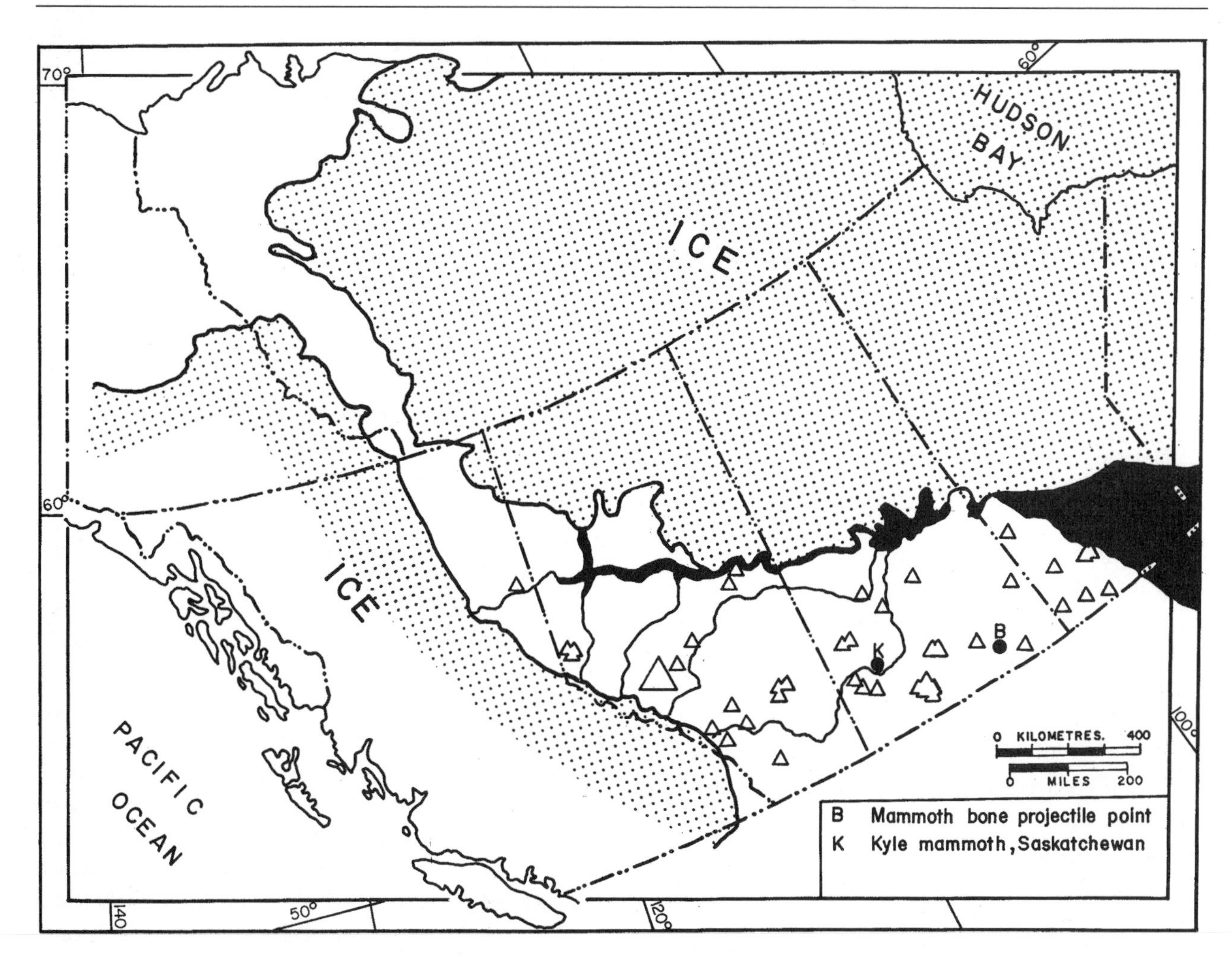

Figure 5. Map of western Canada showing ice front positions approximately 11,500 yr B.P. (i.e., intermediate between Figures 2 and 3) and location of fluted point finds and related discoveries (after Wormington and Forbis 1965; Kehoe 1966; Wilson 1983a, 1990). Finds made since 1983 have added substantially to the filling of spaces on the map but have not extended the distribution beyond the ice boundaries; thus the "fit" is a significant one. The largest triangle represents several finds in the same small area. See Roberts and others (1987) for an updated version that also maps the Beringian finds of fluted points.

only and acknowledge the indefinite state of the chronology. Their primary purpose is to illustrate how the river systems evolved from chains of ice-marginal meltwater lakes, many of which probably drained in large-discharge events. It seems safe to conclude that the Canadian Plains were free of active ice by about 11,000 yr B.P., if not earlier (Christiansen 1979; Clayton and Moran 1982; Teller et al. 1980), though stagnant ice masses may have persisted in some areas for a millennium or more (cf. S.A. Harris 1987). The onset of recession in the mountains to the west seems to have been comparably early (Jackson et al. 1982; Kearney and Luckman 1983; Roberts 1991). However, human occupation in coastal British Columbia seems to have begun several hundred years later than in the Corridor area to the east (Carlson 1996).

Possible Southward Movements

FLUTED-POINT FINDS in western Canada, as mapped by Driver (1995), Gryba (1985, 1988), Roberts et al. (1987), and Wilson (1983a, 1990a), all fall within the area between hypothesized ice boundaries for the period 11,500 to 11,200 yr B.P. (Dyke and Prest 1987; Prest 1969) (Figure 5). Because these ice margins are based upon other sources of chronological data, the correspondence is both striking and informative. The forms of the fluted points vary, but among them are classic Clovis and Folsom examples (Fedje 1996; Forbis 1970; Kehoe 1966; Wormington and Forbis 1965). Assuming that fluted points were used until about 10,500 years ago, ice retreat no doubt widened the Corridor somewhat from the stage depicted, so users of the points may not have spent much time in close

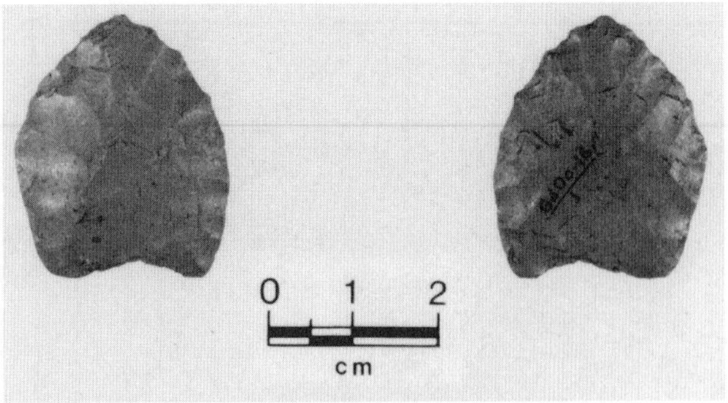

Figure 6. Triangular fluted point ("Charlie Lake" point) from the Duckett Site, near Cold Lake, Alberta (see Figure 3, site d). Its pentagonal shape suggests reworking after breakage of a longer point. Photograph courtesy of G. Fedirchuk and E. J. McCullough.

proximity to the ice front itself. Areas immediately next to the eastern ice front supported ephemeral glacial lakes subject to rapid outburst floods, making the corridor both dangerous for occupation and a poor environment for site preservation (Morlan 1977; Mandryk 1996b; Wilson 1990a). A typical Clovis point has been recovered from the Minnewanka Site near Banff, in the Rocky Mountain Front Ranges (Fedje 1996). The presence of small numbers of fluted points in Alaska brought hope that a Clovis ancestor could be found there (Morlan 1977, 1983), but this has yet to be supported by absolute dating (Reanier 1995).

If there is meaningful typological variation within the Canadian Plains sample, fluted points in a zone west of the central axis of this area may emerge as including the oldest varieties, whereas those on the peripheries east and west should be restricted to the younger varieties. This notion is supported by the variety in styles of Clovis-like fluted points in the Corridor (Carlson 1991) and the occurrence in the peripheries of so-called "Charlie Lake" points (small, triangular, variably fluted points) (1) at Charlie Lake and Pink Mountain, British Columbia (Driver et al. 1996; Fladmark 1996; Fladmark et al. 1988; I. Wilson 1989, 1996); (2) in northwestern Alberta (Gryba 1988; Haynes 1980); (3) possibly at the Duckett site, near Cold Lake, in east-central Alberta (Dingle 1987; McCullough et al. 1981); and (4) at Sibbald Creek in the Alberta foothills (Beaudoin et al. 1996; Gryba 1983) (see Figures 4 and 6). The occupation at Charlie Lake has three bone radiocarbon dates averaging about 10,500 yr B.P. A charcoal date from the Sibbald Creek site is a thousand years younger (Ball 1983), but the nature of this sample (scattered flecks of charcoal from a 10-cm interval in a site with multiple, closely superimposed components spanning the late Pleistocene and Holocene) and possible laboratory counter malfunction render it meaningless and unsuitable for continued citation.

The triangular points seem to represent a relatively late northern variant roughly coeval with Folsom, though technologically reminiscent of Clovis. Of particular interest is the presence of multiple fluting (Gryba 1988), something also seen in the Alaskan points, as at Batza Téna (Clark and Clark 1980). Driver (1993:124) and Driver et al. (1996:271) noted similarities of the Charlie Lake specimen with points from Indian Creek and Mill Iron, Montana (Davis and Greiser 1992; Frison 1991). Davis and Greiser had noted only that their Folsom-aged point fragment from Indian Creek showed Clovis-like characteristics, without discussing possible northern linkages. A hearth at the Niska site, on the Old Wives glacial lake plain in southwestern Saskatchewan, has yielded a distinctive flaked drill and has been dated to 10,880±70 yr B.P. (TO-956, Meyer and Liboiron 1990). This component of the Niska Site ultimately may prove to be of Folsom or Charlie Lake affinity. Comparably early human occupation has been documented at the Vermilion Lakes Site, near Banff in the Alberta Rocky Mountains. Two dates from the earliest component at the site average 10,770±175 yr B.P. (Fedje et al. 1995:90). Unfortunately, again no diagnostic projectile points were recovered from this occupation. Later levels, dating to about 9900 yr B.P., yielded stemmed lanceolate points reminiscent of the Agate Basin and Hell Gap types as well as of Intermontane Stemmed tradition points (Fedje 1996; Fedje et al. 1995:93–94).

Excavations at James Pass, in the Alberta Front Ranges, were conducted to follow up on a fluted point find (distal half of blade). No fluted points were excavated, but a lithic-bearing horizon was revealed, dating to 10,120±80 yr B.P. (TO-3000) on AMS dating of bone. An even earlier, undated occupation is indicated by scattered debitage; an overlying occupation is dated to 9750±80 yr B.P. (TO-2999), again by AMS on bone (Beaudoin et al. 1996; Ronaghan 1993:89).

Clearly, more sites and more dates are needed from the Corridor before a convincing case can be built for the long-supposed peopling event. Nothing from the corridor area predates finds from the Plains to the south; no gradient in dates yet can be demonstrated in direct support of a southward movement. Fluted point finds from Beringia still are not securely dated, and the Putu site date of 11,470±500 yr B.P. (SI-2382) is rejected as not cultural (Reanier 1995:40, 44). North-south linkages at this time level remain elusive, at least in terms of chronology. Late glacial and early postglacial landscape change was dramatic (Beaudoin et al. 1996; Church and Ryder 1972; Jackson et al. 1982; Mandryk 1996a, 1996b; Wilson 1983a, 1986, 1990a; see below, "Landscape Evolution"). The percentage of sites either destroyed outright or buried deeply must have been high during the early stages of ice retreat. Because postburial taphonomic and diagenetic processes are a function of elapsed time, again the earliest sites would have been subject to the greatest disturbance from processes such as weathering and erosion. Pronounced aeolian activity, including deflation as well as loess deposition, occurred during the Hypsithermal, reducing many archaeological assemblages to lag horizons, some of which were reburied.

Glacial lake shorelines should prove to be profitable places to search for Paleoindian sites, both on the Plains and in the boreal forest. Strings of interconnected lakes have been mapped for ice-recessional stages in Alberta, Saskatchewan, and Manitoba (Christiansen 1979; Dyke and Prest 1987; St-Onge 1972; Teller and Clayton 1983). Because of the short-lived nature of most lakes in the western part of this region, beaches are difficult to discern. Archaeological surveys have been limited (e.g., Anderson 1969; Buchner and Pettipas 1990; Pettipas and Buchner 1983; Pohorecky and Anderson 1968; Roberts 1984b; Wilson 1983a), though associations of mammoth bones or specific Paleoindian complexes with beaches appear to exist. For example, in the case of the relatively well-dated Lake Agassiz beaches, (Fenton et al. 1983), the distribution of stemmed Plano (Horner-like) projectile points is outside the western Campbell shoreline (ca. 10,000 yr B.P.), while leaf-shaped Plano (Hell Gap/Agate Basin-like) points are found both inside and outside the shoreline (Buchner and Pettipas 1990; Nielsen et al. 1984; Pettipas 1967, 1970, 1983, 1985). As will be discussed below, the leaf-shaped group likely includes both early and late material.

Few lakes and beaches on the open plains to the west have been dated as securely, and distributional patterns remain to be discerned. Of considerable interest is the Kyle mammoth, a partial skeleton found in southwestern Saskatchewan in association with glacial lake silts (Kehoe 1964; Kehoe and Kehoe 1968; Saskatchewan Museum of Natural History 1965). The specimen was radiocarbon dated (by the whole-bone method rather than collagen) to 12,000±200 yr B.P. (S-246; McCallum and Wittenberg 1968:369). The date can be taken only as a "ball-park estimate" in the absence of a collagen or collagen fraction date. The site never was completely excavated and the Kehoes felt that the bones may have been disturbed by human agency. E. A. Christiansen (commenting in the date report cited above) concluded that the bones "were disturbed during the melting of stagnant ice after mammoth died." This partially articulated specimen is among the earliest dated, late-glacial mammoths from the Canadian Plains; if its context is archaeological, further excavations at the locality could provide evidence bearing upon Clovis or even earlier colonists. Another mammoth limb bone from Wiseton, Saskatchewan was found in lacustrine sediments and gave a date (on whole bone) of 10,600±140 yr B.P. (S-232; Rutherford et al. 1973:193).

The Fluted Point tradition in British Columbia is restricted to the former Corridor area, where it was replaced by the Plano Tradition (Carlson 1991). In intermontane areas to the west, the Intermontane Stemmed Point tradition probably was comparable in date with the Plano tradition. Suggestions of an early Pebble Tool tradition without projectile points have been discarded (Haley 1996); early tools of this tradition are associated with foliate projectile points. The earliest cultural date thus far available from intermontane British Columbia is 9700 yr B.P., again comparable with the Plano tradition (Carlson 1996:8–9). There is no evidence of human occupation of the intermontane British Columbia Interior during Clovis times; nevertheless, interest still exists in the possibility of early coastal migrations.

An alternative route for the earliest human migrants to the midcontinent via the western fjordlands had been considered by K. Bryan (1941), who argued that it would have required a specialized fishing culture and boats, and who preferred a route through the Plains. The possibility that this west coastal route was used, and that the "Ice-Free Corridor" was largely impassable to early migrants, was again advanced by Fladmark (1978, 1979, 1983) in a series of superbly crafted papers. Ruth Gruhn, at the Summit Conference, similarly discussed the west coast as an alternative route, building upon Fladmark's hypothesis. She argued, however, against a theory of late arrival via the coastal route, advocating an earlier (pre-Wisconsinan) peopling event. Fladmark's papers appropriately have put the brakes on those who have almost dogmatically accepted the Ice-Free Corridor as the only viable route, but dated evidence for early coastal movements has been elusive. Discoveries in southern Alaska provide cultural materials of comparable antiquity to the oldest British Columbia materials and faunal remains that likely predate them, leaving open a strong possibility for the discovery of older coastal cultural traditions (Fifield 1996; Heaton 1995). Although postglacial sea-level rise surely has inundated many such sites (if they exist), islands such as the Queen Charlottes have yielded sites in raised beach and intertidal settings suggesting an age older than 10,000 yr B.P., based on the sea level curve (Ackerman 1996:125–126; Fladmark 1979, 1990) and older sites could well lie just below sea level.

Clearly at present, in the absence of hard evidence, acceptance of the primacy of one route over the other remains little more than an act of faith as we await the test of further field survey. Arguments for a western (coastal) route, for example, cannot depend solely upon the absence of good sites in the Ice-Free Corridor or elsewhere, or they risk sounding like a search (by elimination) for the location of the West Pole. In searching for the route south, we all are seeking something that we assume, on the basis of indirect evidence, existed. The indirect evidence may seem compelling, but *caveat emptor*. Fladmark chose to avoid such logic and to concentrate upon the positive contextual evidence from paleogeography and paleoenvironmental studies, but others have employed the argument-by-elimination, and the case remains unresolved (Easton 1992; Gruhn 1994). Whatever the case may be, new generations of archaeologists continue to rediscover the Ice-Free Corridor and to restate relationships that were discussed long ago by W. A. Johnston and Ernst Antevs. Aside from firming up the chronology, we may not have progressed far on the Corridor issue in half a century, and Fladmark's powerful enunciation of an alternative coastal hypothesis ironically emerges as one of the greatest advances. In this light, it is not at all unreasonable to consider that the fluted-point users of the Canadian Plains were "southerners" accompanying a southern fauna of mammoths, camels, and bison (*Bison bison antiquus* rather than the northern *B. b. occidentalis*) in the late glacial move northward, rather than meeting these animals "on the way through" (Fladmark 1996; M. C. Wilson 1996).

Was There a Northward Drift?

In the 1960s it appeared, based on scanty absolute-dating evidence and generalized similarities of projectile-point types, that there may have been a northward movement of Paleoindian peoples after the retreating ice sheet. Given the virtual absence of dates for the ice retreat itself, it seemed reasonable that "cultures" such as Agate Basin moved northward over time. This would be reflected in a south-to-north gradient in dates and late "survival" in the north. Such a view, for example, was presented by MacNeish (1962) and persisted in subsequent work (e.g., Bryan 1968; Ebell 1980:72–75; Roberts and Wright 1987). This persistence depends largely upon a linkage of "Northern Plano" points from several Northwest Territories sites with Agate Basin. Underscoring the frailty of this view is the fact that unstemmed, leaf-shaped points are the simplest form to make and the easiest to reinvent; unlike biological species, projectile-point types can recur without necessary historical linkages. It also must be remembered that the location of the "type site" by no means signals an area of origin for Agate Basin; it was merely the site at which the point type was defined. But the question remains: was there a northward drift?

Dates for Agate Basin in the midcontinent range from about 10,500 to 9700 yr B.P. (e.g., Frison 1978; Frison and Stanford 1982; Wyckoff 1989) and apparently overlap with Hell Gap dates. Dates for Northern Plano extend from about 9000 to as late as 6000 yr B.P., and leaf-shaped forms persist into the Shield Archaic in the east and through Acasta into Taltheilei in the western Northwest Territories (Stewart 1991). Northern Plano points are difficult to discriminate from those of the Taltheilei tradition, which persisted until much later dates. At present, these occurrences are separated by a considerable distance and time from Plains occurrences, and postulation of a direct linkage with Agate Basin "stretches the point," so to speak (see also Frison and Stanford 1982:366). In Manitoba, as noted above, stemmed Plano points occur only outside the western Campbell shoreline (ca. 10,000 yr B.P.), whereas leaf-shaped points are found both inside and outside (Buchner and Pettipas 1990). Given the relationship of beaches to the recession of Lake Agassiz, this would imply either that the leaf-shaped forms (including Agate Basin and Hell Gap) are younger than the stemmed forms (the opposite of the case in Wyoming and other Plains areas; see Frison 1978), or that more than one unstemmed horizon is present. Wyoming dates presented not only by Frison

(1978) but also by Ebell (1980:73) in discussion of the Parkhill site, Saskatchewan, clearly indicate that a second leaf-shaped point horizon occurs in the south at the same time as late occurrences in the north. Why, then, can one prefer a linkage of the northern material with a southern culture up to 3,000 years older, over a linkage with material of the same age?

Paleoindian site distribution in relation to the glacial Lake Agassiz shorelines agrees, in our view, with evidence from elsewhere on the Plains that a young "Agate Basin-like" horizon (including Lusk) follows stemmed-point horizons and is fully distinct from classic Agate Basin and Hell Gap (see Frison 1978:34–39). Now that the Agate Basin type-site collection has been described in detail and illustrated (Frison and Stanford 1982), it is clear that many of the "Agate Basin-like" lanceolate forms excavated or picked up in surface surveys in Canada are differentiable from the Agate Basin type in pattern and quality of flaking. We would, in fact, exclude most of the dated examples cited as Agate Basin by Ebell, even those in the United States (e.g., Mangus), from a formal relationship with type Agate Basin, though the Parkhill site, Saskatchewan, is apparently true Agate Basin. The presence of such late Paleoindian "Agate Basin-like" points (ca. 8500–7500 yr B.P.), with a variety of type names but shared lanceolate form, at several sites in the Northwestern Plains, including the Hawkwood site, Calgary (Van Dyke and Stewart 1985), counters suggestions of a northward gradient in the age of Agate Basin-like points. This, in turn, invalidates the hypothesis that the points were used by a single migrating cultural group over time (see also Meyer 1989). The late points, which appear to comprise several distinct but related local types, are desperately in need of regional systematization. With more extensive description, they should emerge more clearly as a distinct horizon.

There are as yet few indications for an early lanceolate-point horizon on the open Canadian Plains fully comparable in antiquity with Agate Basin, though surface finds such as the Parkhill material indicate its likely presence. At the Vermilion Lakes site, in the Front Ranges near Banff, Alberta, lanceolate points were associated with components dating to about 9900 yr B.P. on the basis of a lengthy series of dates (both conventional and AMS) on varied materials (Fedje 1986; Fedje et al. 1995). One of the illustrated points resembles the Agate Basin type, while another is more reminiscent of Hell Gap. At the Heron Eden site in the Great Sand Hills of southwestern Saskatchewan, new discoveries below the Cody component include the base of an Agate Basin point and a feature dated to 10,210 yr B.P. (Linnamae 1990; lab no. and sigma not given). The point and the date may be associated, but this remains to be demonstrated by further excavations. Evaluation and comparison of dates in the interval assigned to Agate Basin also must take into account the two radiocarbon "plateaux" now documented from 10,000 and 9600 ^{14}C years B.P. (Becker and Kromer 1993:69).

Finds at the Mesa site, Alaska, have a clear bearing here. Mesa has yielded a large sample of lanceolate points with slightly concave bases; some exhibit well-controlled parallel flaking. Overall they are strongly reminiscent of points from the midcontinent, and Kunz and Reanier (1995:22) see them as closely related to (and ancestral to) Agate Basin. Dates on 13 Mesa site hearths range from 11,700 to 9700 yr B.P., spanning a time period longer than that for Agate Basin. The oldest dates, 11,660±80 (Beta-55286, CAMS-3572) and 11,190±70 (Beta-57430, CAMS-3572) came from the same split sample and do not overlap at two sigma, suggesting a problem. Kunz and Reanier (1995:19) consider the possibility that they signal the burning of old wood, but reject that because frozen wood is wet and good wood is locally available today. They doubt that the true age is more than 1,000 years younger, but persist in assigning the complex a timespan of fully 2,000 years anyway, with no apparent cultural changes in that time. Such cultural longevity is, according to them, not unusual in the Arctic because of the harsh environment, "with little pressure exerted between neighboring cultural groups and thus little impetus for change or territorial shifts" (1995:25). Yet we are told in the same article that "chaotic climatic events" in fact forced them to move southward at the close of the Pleistocene, encroaching upon Folsom people by 10,500 yr B.P. and founding Agate Basin (1995:24). Despite all of this movement, they were unaffected by the apparently coeval American Paleoarctic and Nenana Complex peoples who also inhabited portions of Alaska. We take the cautious view here that Mesa represents the shorter timespan that they offer, from 11,000 (or later) to 9700 yr B.P., in which case the lack of evidence for cultural contact is somewhat more plausible.

As Kunz and Reanier point out, Agate Basin assemblages exhibit a small number of Mesa-like concave based points, while Mesa exhibits a few Agate Basin-like convex based points. The complexes also differ in terms of the reduction sequences used to make the points (ascribed to differences in availability of raw materials) and the method of basal flaking (1995:22). It should be cautioned that Paleoindian assemblages in the midcontinent have been split (and perhaps over-split) in the past on the basis of criteria no more compelling than this, and that to link Mesa specifically with Agate Basin may be premature. Nevertheless, it remains a plausible hypothesis that Mesa peoples moved southward through the Ice-free Corridor area to become Agate Basin. This hypothesis should be testable through continued sampling in Alberta and careful comparative studies between Mesa and the material from the Vermilion Lakes site and related assemblages (Fedje 1986, 1996; Fedje et al. 1995).

Despite these discoveries, the feeling has persisted until recently (if not to the present) among researchers that radiocarbon dates for most Paleoindian complexes may, or even should, be younger on the Canadian Plains than on the Plains to the south. As Wilson has already discussed elsewhere (1993b), an exchange between Meyer (1985, 1986) and Pettipas (1986) clearly illustrates this controversy. Meyer (1985) described the Niska site, a Cody complex site in southwestern Saskatchewan. Cultural materials, including bison bones, were associated with a dark paleosol but in fact lay within the lower part of the thick, buried A horizon. Thus, if the occupation was not overprinted by downward movement of organic matter from a later soil, it should date from the initial stabilization of the surface by sod (Meyer 1985:10).

Two dates were obtained from the paleosol itself: 7000±185 yr B.P. (S-2353) and 5910±270 yr B.P. (S-2235). The second sample was taken where the paleosol was near the modern surface, which supported a grain crop. Given that soils are dynamic with a definable mean-residence time of organic material, a soil date represents some sort of "average" from within the time period represented by the soil and likely will mark a time close to the end of the soil-forming period (Turchenek et al. 1974:914). The Niska dates, therefore, confirm only that the occupation is older than 7000 yr B.P. A collagen date of 7165±320 yr B.P. (S-2453; Meyer 1985:28) was obtained for bone that was "very poor ... with eroded, disintegrating surfaces ... [and in water] a tendency to disintegrate, forming a slurry" (Meyer 1985:15). Given the condition of the bone, the chance of contamination by soil organics was very high (see, for example, Stafford 1984), in which case one would expect a sample to approximate the age of the paleosol rather than its own true age. Meyer (1985:33) chose, appropriately, to be cautious about the dates, suggesting that the site probably was older. He was chided sternly for this by Pettipas, who suggested as an alternative that this was a late northern facies of Cody. Pettipas despaired,

> *I get the distinct impression that these reasons for questioning the dates were marshalled after the results came in and were found, for other reasons, to be unacceptable ... it was only after they did not produce the expected results that problems with the samples were sought ... I suggest that had the results of the analysis been as expected, such questions would never have been raised.* (1986:167)

Pettipas scored a direct hit in terms of Plains archaeology. All too often, archaeologists send in what amount to "Hail Mary" samples, in the hope that they will produce an "acceptable" result. All too often, the results fall short of expectations, for reasons that should be both familiar and anticipated. The charcoal date for the Sibbald Creek site, mentioned above, is just such an example. Regrettably, however, one of the best tests for contamination, aside from circumstantial arguments, is to date the sample—which blunts Pettipas' criticism.

This accepted, Pettipas' discussion revealed his clear preference for the late dates and for the idea of late persistence of a Cody facies. This viewpoint, interestingly, required him to accept the dates as valid despite the descriptions of possible contaminants and despite his arguments that these reasons for questioning the dates should have been thought about before the samples were submitted. His preferred hypothesis is challenged by a new radiocarbon date of 8475±650 yr B.P. from the site (Meyer and Liboiron 1990:299), which supports the view that Cody in the north is similar in age to its southern counterpart and underscores previously stated concerns about the paleosol and bone dates. In addition, the Heron Eden site, another Cody complex site in the Great Sand Hills of southwestern Saskatchewan, has yielded a date of 8,930 yr B.P. for the Cody component (Jones 1989:128; lab no. and sigma not given). Both Pettipas and Meyer have scored qualified victories, therefore: the former for having called attention to certain attitudes regarding radiocarbon dates, and the latter for having been correct after all about the date of the site.

Other dates from the Canadian Plains similarly parallel those from comparable assemblages in areas to the south. At the Lindoe site, near Medicine Hat in southeastern Alberta, an in situ bone bed was dated to 9900±120 yr B.P. (S-230). A stemmed projectile point closely resembling the Hell Gap type was found on the surface of the slope immediately below the cutbank exposure of the bone bed (Bryan 1966). An occupation yielding an Alberta point at the J Crossing Site, in the southwestern Alberta foothills, gave conflicting dates of 9600±310 yr B.P. (AECV-746C) and 8580±160 yr B.P. (AECV-1198C) (Wilson 1990b). A limiting date obtained for the Alberta/Scottsbluff Fletcher site in southern Alberta indicates that it is slightly younger than 9380±110 yr B.P. (TO-1097, Vickers and Beaudoin 1989) and therefore consistent in age with occurrences to the south. As discussed in the present paper, the fit of fluted point occurrences with the postulated 11,500 yr B.P. ice-frontal position similarly indicates that there is no environmental evidence that mandates a significant northward time lag of cultural migrations. The evidence obtained thus far is fully consistent with a "horizon style" model. Based upon available dates, the Canadian occurrences suggest this extremely tentative chronology: northern fluted (ca. 11,000–10,500 yr B.P.), Agate Basin (ca. 10,500–9900 yr B.P.), Hell Gap (ca. 10,000–9500 yr B.P.), Alberta (ca. 9500–9000 yr B.P.), Scottsbluff (ca. 9300–8500 yr B.P.), late lanceolate (Lusk, etc.; ca. 8500–7500 yr B.P.) (late Paleoindian dates not summarized here; see also Vickers 1986).

Walking the Mason-Quimby Line

Points and Proboscideans

Paul Martin (1967) presented evidence from the Great Lakes region for the spatial association of fluted points and proboscidean sites and for their restriction south of what he called the "Mason-Quimby line," in deference to two of the scientists who had amassed much of the information. Given the correspondence between fluted-point distribution and a postulated ice-frontal position for about 11,500 yr B.P. in western Canada (Figure 5), it is obvious that we simply are providing a westward extension of the Mason-Quimby line. Clearly dated, late-glacial/postglacial mammoth finds with cultural associations are almost nonexistent and there are many earlier Pleistocene occurrences, so the map cites only the Kyle Mammoth and the location of a bone or ivory foreshaft (Wilmeth 1968). An additional "elephant bone" artifact was described by Leechman (1950) from a site on the Lake Agassiz plain in Manitoba, a context that suggested a relatively late (post-Lake Agassiz) date. The specimen, supposedly a hewn limb bone, was examined at the Manitoba Museum of Man and Nature by the first author in 1986 and clearly displayed a suture line. It has turned out, in fact, to be a fragment of moose skull with the artificially shaped base of the antler still attached (G. Lammers, personal communication), and has been dated by AMS to less than 1000 yr B.P. (Buchner and Pettipas 1990:53).

The situation with regard to the lack of direct cultural associations (kill sites) is the same in eastern Canada, but the distribution of fluted points again is similar to that of proboscideans in southern Ontario. Coincident paleogeography suggests that a predator-prey relationship could have existed between humans and proboscideans but of course is not proof of such a link. Both fluted points and proboscidean finds are abundant in southern Ontario (Deller and Ellis 1988; Dreimanis 1967; Jackson 1987; McAndrews and Jackson 1988; Roberts and McAndrews 1987; Storck 1988). However, it seems equally possible that these cultural groups were not specialized hunters of proboscideans but rather hunters of various megafaunal species, particularly caribou, whose late-glacial distribution extended well southward into the United States (Julig 1991).

Eastern Canadian Fluted Point Complexes

Laurentide ice persisted longer in eastern Canada than in the west, lasting until about 10,000 years ago in much of Ontario and Quebec. However, more southerly areas were available for occupation by 11,000 yr B.P., and the close resemblance of some fluted-point finds to classic Clovis suggests comparable antiquity (Deller and Ellis 1988; Julig 1991; Storck 1984, 1988). Exotic lithic materials (e.g., North Dakota cherts) with Clovis points in Maine suggest a true colonizing population, ranging widely over the midcontinent (Gramly and Funk 1990:6). Fluted points also occur in New Brunswick (Kingsclear and Quaco Head), Prince Edward Island (North Tryon), and Nova Scotia at the Debert site and Amherst Shore (Davis and Chistianson 1988; Keenlyside 1985; MacDonald 1968; Turnbull 1974; Turnbull and Allen 1978). The sites are ice-marginal and it is apparent that, by about 11,000 years ago, the ice sheet in the Maritime Provinces and the Gaspé Peninsula of Quebec had broken up into scattered remnants (LaSalle and Chapdelaine 1990; Parent et al. 1985:25–26). The Champlain Sea still inundated low-lying areas along the St. Lawrence valley. At this time, much of the open area was herbaceous tundra, with forests of varied character to the south in the New England states (Richard 1985:49). The fluted points seem to indicate a succession of assemblages after colonization and may have persisted for many hundreds of years in the area (Gramly and Funk 1990). The makers of the earliest assemblages probably represented no more than a few bands of humans, widely ranging and exploiting migratory caribou on the tundra.

The Gainey and Debert point types are Clovis-like while the younger Parkhill [not the same as the Parkhill site discussed above] and Crowfield types from southern Ontario are more reminiscent of Folsom (Deller 1988; Deller and Ellis 1988; Roosa and Deller 1982; Storck 1988). Thermoluminescence dating of the type Gainey Site, Michigan, specimens indicates broad contemporaneity with Clovis (Simons et al. 1987). Debert points, with deep basal concavities, are restricted to the Maritime provinces in Canada, and apparently date between about 10,700 and 10,600 yr B.P., slightly later than true Clovis (Levine 1990:59). Gainey points, with shallow basal concavities and multiple fluting, occur in southern Ontario as well as in the Great Lakes states and appear on circumstantial grounds (distribution) to predate Parkhill and Crowfield in Ontario (Deller and Ellis 1988:255; Gramly and Funk 1990). Although technological variation suggests regional differentiation comparable to that already documented from the United States (Howard 1990), it therefore could also reflect chronological differences. The deeply basally indented unfluted points from the Jones site, Prince Edward Island, may represent a descendant form derived from Clovis/Debert and could predate 9000 yr B.P. (Keenlyside 1985:121).

Storck (1988) argues that the Ontario group represented by the Parkhill Complex possesses so many fundamental similarities with other early Paleoindian complexes from the midcontinent that it is best viewed as a colonizing group, and not as a group that had received the technology through diffusion (see also Gramly and Funk 1990; Tankersley 1994). This is not in conflict with Deller and Ellis inasmuch as their evolutionary scenario (Gainey to Parkhill) still would accommodate an idea of a colonizing group arriving about 11,000 yr B.P. Correlation of Ontario fluted points with Glacial Lake Algonquin and other shorelines (L. Jackson 1983; Roberts 1984a; Roberts and McAndrews 1987; Storck 1982) shows great potential for shoreline surveys along the ice front in the search for early sites. These associations also provide a basis for preliminary dating: for example, the association of Parkhill materials with Glacial Lake Algonquin is taken to indicate a date between 11,000 and 10,400 yr B.P., the date when the lake drained (Karrow et al. 1975; Storck 1982, 1988:243–244). The absence of fluted point finds below the Lake Algonquin strandline suggests that their use had ceased by the time of lake drainage (Deller and Ellis 1988:250; L. Jackson 1983; Roberts 1984a). Parkhill points are relatively small and are fish-tailed, with pronounced "ears" and with fluting conducted from a Folsom-like basal "nipple."

Archaeological and geoarchaeological studies likewise suggest that the Plano tradition was established in southern Ontario before 9500 yr B.P. and in the Gaspé Peninsula of Quebec by 8500 yr B.P., if not earlier (Balac 1986; Benmouyal 1987; Chapdelaine 1985; LaSalle and Chapdelaine 1990). Plano points from Quebec are parallel-flaked and possibly stemmed; in these respects they resemble Cody Complex points as well as other Plains lanceolate types (Chapdelaine 1994; Chapdelaine and Bourget 1992). It is, however, difficult to discriminate some of this material from Shield Archaic (Martijn 1985). Recognition of a megaflood episode from Lake Agassiz into Lake Superior has provided a geological datum in the form of diamicts and lag gravels that can assist in the cross-dating of early Holocene archaeological assemblages (Julig 1990, 1991; Julig et al. 1990). Nevertheless, dates for eastern Canadian Paleoindian complexes are extremely rare and difficult to obtain given the paucity of associated organic material. As in the west, there seems thus far to be no clear indication of a significant time lag between the midcontinent and southern Canada in dates for Paleoindian assemblages. It remains possible that some traditions will prove to have persisted longer in the north than in the south, but one's immediate impression from the data at hand is that functional and stylistic innovations relating to projectile points were able to travel across much of the continent with surprising rapidity.

Landscape Evolution and Visibility of Early Sites

GEOLOGICAL PROCESSES act to mold the landscape and thus to affect the visibility of archaeological sites. We are presented not with a random sampling of archaeological information from all times and cultural groups, but with a selected, biased assemblage driven in part by landscape processes, present and past (see also Waters and Kuehn 1996; M. C. Wilson 1983a, 1986, 1990a). Any preglacial sites on the Canadian Plains surely would have been overridden by ice (except in small unglaciated patches along the international boundary), suffering the erosive effects of ice-scour in addition to large-scale subglacial floods (Rains et al. 1993). Nevertheless, gravel deposits persisted in buried valleys and have yielded many datable vertebrate remains (Burns 1996). Archaeological remains could yet be found in buried (sub-till) terrace settings, though the Calgary occurrences described by Chlachula (1996) appear not to be of this nature.

Paraglacial processes are a significant landscape process set, long overlooked by researchers and confused with periglacial processes. Whereas periglacial processes reflect lowered temperatures in proximity to an ice mass, paraglacial processes proceed when temperatures rise, so that formerly frozen deposits melt and lose stability on slopes, and formerly ice-supported landforms lose their supporting ice mass. Increased debris-flow activity built large fans and, in hilly or mountainous areas, buried many valley floors under diamicts that often have been mistaken for till (Jackson et al. 1982). Deep excavations under such flows at the Vermilion Lakes site in Banff National Park, Alberta, revealed Paleoindian components dating to 10,500 yr B.P. (Fedje 1986; Fedje et al. 1995). Similarly, thick alluvial units that accumulated along river valleys on the Canadian Plains during the arid Hypsithermal can be implicated along with typological problems in the illusory appearance of a "cultural hiatus" (M. C. Wilson 1983a, 1986, 1990a). To counter these effects, appropriate enhanced recovery methods, tailored to the geologic and geomorphic settings, are required.

Studies on the open plains of Saskatchewan, Manitoba, and North Dakota recently have demonstrated that outburst floods were more important than previously recognized in cutting meltwater channels such as the one now occupied by the Souris River drainage (Lord and Kehew 1987). These channels are recognized as the product of outburst floods on the basis of uniform channel widths, high depth-to-width ratios, and discrete cutbanks (Clayton 1983; Kehew and Lord 1986). The outbursts were highly erosive and, with the exception of large-scale bars composed of poorly sorted, coarse-grained sediment, few deposits were left behind in the channels as bed load. The persisting landforms, many of which are spillways across low divides, conform to the characteristics of channels rather than valleys, and the terrace-like bars are actually in-channel (i.e., underwater) features rather than remnants of former floodplains. These bars on the meltwater channel walls are up to 2 km long and 30 m thick, comprising "homogeneous masses of massive, matrix-supported, very poorly sorted, pebbly cobble gravel, containing boulders as much as 3 m in diameter" (Lord and Kehew 1987:663).

Associated flood-water flows during these outburst floods were high but lasted a matter of days to weeks (Kehew and Lord 1986; Lord and Kehew 1987). Because of the erosive nature of the outburst floods in the Souris drainage example and presumably many others, flood deposits typically are not present in the spillway floor itself. Instead, a fill of Holocene alluvial and lacustrine deposits, up to tens of meters thick, is present in many spillway bottoms (Lord and Kehew 1987, after Boettger 1986). Thick, fine-grained deposits in the floor of Forty Mile Coulee, Alberta, yielded bison bones in the upper few meters that gave only late Holocene dates. Deeper sediments likely were, by extension, early Holocene or even late Pleistocene but were beyond the reach of conventional sampling (Brumley and Dau 1988; Wilson 1983b). Admittedly, it is not yet clear to what extent the meltwater channels of southern Alberta (Chin, Etzikom, Nemiskam, Verdigris, and Forty Mile Coulees, to name a few) were cut or influenced by outburst floods. If they were, it must be admitted that they were cut to their full depth in relatively short periods of time; therefore, a conventional model for archaeological survey based upon the expectation of a chronosequence of terraces would be inappropriate. All terrace-like features, from valley rim to floor, could be of essentially the same age, differing only in weeks rather than in millennia.

Many of the old meltwater channels and spillways, since the time of their abandonment by permanent streams, have been partially filled by slope-derived sediments, both from unchanneled flow of water down valley slopes (sheetwash), building colluvial aprons, and from seasonal flows down tributary coulees, building alluvial fans. Some of the fill in Forty Mile Coulee is certainly of this origin. The fact that material only 3,000 years old is recovered at 3 m depth suggests that material of early Paleoindian age could be expected to lie 10 m or more below the surface, particularly if the rate of sediment movement has declined (as is likely) during the Holocene (Brumley and Dau 1988; Wilson 1983b).

Major sites in the Canadian prairies have come to light through use of deep-sampling strategies (intentional or otherwise). The well-known Fletcher site, an Alberta/Scottsbluff bison kill, lay 3 m below lacustrine and aeolian deposits and was discovered in the excavation of a stock watering dugout (Forbis 1968). The late Paleoindian component at the Mona Lisa site, in the Calgary, Alberta, city core, was discovered in basement excavations 3 m below the surface in a unit of alluvial overbank sediments. Further backhoe testing was used to extend the site limits over an area of two city blocks and to discover additional components dating to the early Middle Prehistoric period (Wilson 1983a). Backhoe testing has become a frequent element of site surveys in Alberta and was used in the discovery (among other examples) of (1) the late Paleoindian Hawkwood site, Calgary; (2) the 9,600-year-old J Crossing site (DjPm-16) on the Oldman River, southwestern Alberta; and (3) the 10,500-year-old and other Paleoindian components at the Vermilion Lakes site, near Banff.

The J Crossing site, now inundated by the Oldman Reservoir, west of Pincher Creek, Alberta, combines several of the themes discussed above. Backhoe testing revealed bison bones below Mazama tephra (ca. 6850 yr B.P.) at a depth between 2 and 3 m below surface. There were no surface indications of an early Holocene component. Excavations revealed a well-defined occupation of early Cody complex (Alberta) affinity, giving conflicting radiocarbon dates of about 9600 and 8600 yr B.P. (see above; Van Dyke et al. 1990). The site was associated with a high terrace-like feature on the south wall of the lower Crowsnest River valley; the component lay within colluvial deposits that carpeted coarse, poorly sorted alluvium. Peak colluvial activity in this area evidently occurred during the Hypsithermal, so that by the time of the Mazama ashfall the surface already had been transformed from a relatively level alluvial filltop to a sloping colluvial apron, and the overall terrace-like feature was progressively being hidden on the valley wall. A nearby boulder field, on both higher and lower terrace-like surfaces, is evidence of a glacial outburst flood that flushed the valley in late Pleistocene times. It is possible that the terrace-like landforms are relict bar forms rather than true terraces. If the flood (or floods) occurred at a time when humans already occupied the area, it could have destroyed any sites in its path (Wilson 1990b).

What about deposits that are beyond the reach of backhoes? It is clear that postglacial fills in certain settings (as in the floors of meltwater channels) can be up to tens of meters thick. Few natural exposures of comparable thickness in appropriate sediments occur on the Canadian prairies, in contrast to the more deeply dissected plains of the Dakotas, Montana, and Wyoming to the south. In valleys where modern rivers occupy former meltwater channels, as in the case of segments of the Bow River valley near Calgary, incision during the Holocene has been on the order of only a few meters (M. C. Wilson 1983a, 1986). Uplift associated with postglacial isostatic rebound has been greater on the eastern plains of Saskatchewan and Manitoba) than in the west, meaning that river gradients have been lowered during the Holocene through raising of the base level. In abandoned meltwater channels, aside from minor aeolian deflation, there has been no significant mechanism of erosion during the Holocene. In fact, the channel floors may have been areas of accumulation of aeolian sediments stripped from nearby uplands, where mid-Holocene (Hypsithermal) erosion was locally severe. The likelihood exists, therefore, of the deep burial of Paleoindian sites on the Canadian Plains at depths beyond our conventional means for testing and recovery.

It is sobering to note that even relatively late Paleolithic sites in eastern Asia often are deeply buried, and not all due to thick loess deposits. In 1988, a team led by the senior author discovered a late Paleolithic site (Cuijiaai) in Gansu Province, China, under 26 m of fine-grained floodplain alluvium and capping loess-like colluvium. The base of the colluvium, 20 m below surface, yielded land snails dated to 12,000 yr B.P. on conchiolin (Wilson 1990c). Do sites exist at comparable depths in many areas of the Canadian Plains? We expect that they do.

What can be done in terms of such sites? Discovery of a deeply buried site might be accomplished though the use of small-diameter coring devices or augers, but there still is the problem of excavation. How could one excavate a late Pleistocene site that lies 15 or 20 m below surface and likely below water table? The strategies would border on fantasy. A modified form of large-diameter auger testing could be employed, with the auger calibrated to allow careful level-by-level recovery. Conventional excavations, if there were no water problems, surely would verge on shaft mining unless it was possible to strip large areas beforehand through use of heavy equipment. In the case of extensive impact by development, it may well be possible to get "open pit" access to deeply buried deposits, much as was the case with the Cherokee excavations in Iowa (Anderson and Semken 1980). Another strategy worthy of suggestion is direct and continuous monitoring of deep pipeline trenching, as an extension of the present emphasis upon pre-impact assessment and mitigation.

Conclusions

THE DECADES CONTINUE to fly by, and the Ice-Free Corridor continues to thwart those who search for indisputable evidence of a Clovis-precursor group that might have moved south in late glacial times, as early as 14,000 years ago. Fluted points have been found, as have mammoths. Significantly, the bison associated with late glacial alluvial deposits comparable in age to Clovis are referable to the southern form, *Bison antiquus* (or *B. bison antiquus*). Fossiliferous gravelly alluvial fills dating between about 11,500 and 10,000 yr B.P. are widespread in southwestern Alberta (Stalker 1968; Wilson and Churcher 1984). At first, bison from these deposits were referred to the northern-derived form, *B. bison occidentalis* (Churcher 1968, 1975). Now that more complete crania are available, it is clear that these bison are referable to *antiquus* (Wilson and Churcher 1984). Another element of the fauna is the camel, *Camelops* sp., cf. *C. hesternus*, and the overall impression is of a fauna with southern affinities (M. C. Wilson 1983a, 1996; Wilson and Churcher 1978, 1984).

The first bison of "northern" phenotype, with narrow frontals, protruding orbits, and backswept horn cores (assigned to *B. bison occidentalis*) appeared in the Ice-Free Corridor area about 10,500 to 10,000 years ago (Trylich and Bayrock 1966; M. C. Wilson 1996). These northern bison may signal not the physical opening of the corridor (for that was likely earlier) but the *biotic* opening of the corridor (MacDonald and McLeod 1996; M. C. Wilson 1996). Southward movement required establishment of vegetation and the draining of any lakes that blocked passage; and these factors would have influenced humans as well as bison, though not necessarily to the extent that they arrived together. With bison, as in the case of mammoth distribution, then, a demonstrable link seems to exist between extinct species and paleogeography. In Manitoba, for example, which was deglaciated later than Alberta and Saskatchewan, only *B. bison occidentalis* has yet been found, though earlier bison of *antiquus* type could remain to be discovered in the extreme southwest of the province.

If the biotic opening of the Corridor did not permit human movement southward until some time after its physical opening, that migration could have been as late as Clovis times, accounting for the sudden appearance of Clovis technology in the absence of a credible precursor. If humans were not able to move southward in the Corridor until the time of the apparent *B. bison occidentalis* migration, we would be forced to conclude that the fluted-point users of the Northwestern Plains were not new arrivals from the north, but instead were an element of the southern fauna, with its mammoths, camels, horses, and southern bison (M. C. Wilson 1996). How these people may have arrived in the south remains in the realm of speculation, for despite much effort there still are no sites in the Ice-Free Corridor area that provide convincing evidence of human occupation prior to the last major glaciation, nor have any yet been found on the British Columbia coast. Where, then, are they? Should archaeologists don hard hats and plumb the depths of plains Quaternary deposits like miners, or should they climb into submersibles and scour the ocean floor for evidence? Or is the story much more simple, and entirely postglacial?

There still are key questions to be asked and answered, and we reiterate our opinion that the precise timing of the "first footstep" may prove to be one of the least interesting of all. We echo Richard Morlan's opinion that whether people reached the midcontinent (and beyond) before or after the last glaciation, "we must still explain the rapid and widespread distribution of fluted points shortly after 12,000 years ago" (1977:96). This is an extremely important question involving lands from Alaska to Central America. Was Clovis, as appears the case in the northeast, a "colonizing population" on virgin ground? It is likely that additional radiocarbon plateaux will be documented, much as had been the case for the 10,000 to 9500 yr B.P. period (Becker and Kromer 1993), and therefore the true timespan for the Clovis dispersal may be longer than has been believed to this point. We wait with great anticipation for the next discovery, for there is so much yet to be learned. Happily, science (and, indeed, knowledge) is open-ended, and therefore it is the solemn duty of scientists to ask more questions than they answer. We are not disappointed, then, to end on these notes of uncertainty. Though the corridors for southward movement may well have been wide, the doorways into them seem to have been much narrower and, from a biotic standpoint, short-lived; and the windows against which we press our analytical noses are small, revealing much less than we have wished. The search continues.

Acknowledgments

We thank Neil A. Mirau (University of Lethbridge) for reviewing an early draft of the manuscript and making many helpful comments. We also thank David Meyer, Robson Bonnichsen, Jonathan Driver and Richard Morlan for suggestions and information. Angélique M. Gillespie drafted Figure 5. The photograph of the Duckett site point was provided by Gloria Fedirchuk and Edward J. McCullough.

We especially would like to thank an anonymous reviewer for insightful and sensitive comments concerning recent discoveries and controversies. The first author's odyssey through positions in China, Japan, the U.S., and Canada since this paper was first written made revisions more difficult than should ever have been the case. In this context, an uncommonly constructive critique was both a pleasant surprise and a vitally important contribution. We are in your debt!

References

Ackerman, R. E.
1996 Early Maritime Culture Complexes of the Northern Northwest Coast. In *Early Human Occupation in British Columbia*, edited by R. L. Carlson and L. Dalla Riva, pp. 123–132. University of British Columbia Press, Vancouver.

Ackerman, S.
1989 European Prehistory gets even Older. When is a rock an artifact? *Science* 246:28–30.

Addington, L. R.
1986 *Lithic Illustration: Drawing Flaked Stone Artifacts for Publication*. University of Chicago Press, Chicago.

Anderson, D. C., and H. A. Semken, Jr.
1980 *The Cherokee Excavations: Holocene Ecology and Human Adaptations in Northwestern Iowa*. Academic Press, New York.

Anderson, D. E.
1969 Lake Agassiz Archaeology in Saskatchewan [abstract]. *Canadian Archaeological Association Bulletin* 1:16–17.

Antevs, E.
1935 The Spread of Aboriginal Man to North America. *Geographical Review* 25:302–312.

1937 Climate and Early Man in North America. In *Early Man*, edited by G. G. MacCurdy, pp. 125–132. Harvard University, Cambridge.

Ascher, R., and M. Ascher
1965 Recognizing the Emergence of Man. *Science* 147(3655):243–250.

Balac, A.
1986 *Archaeology in Québec*. Translated from the French by Alison McGain. Ministère des Affaires culturelles, Gouvernement du Québec, Québec. 48 p.

Ball, B. F.
1983 Radiocarbon Estimates from the Sibbald Creek Site, EgPr-2. In *Archaeology in Alberta*, compiled by D. Burley, pp. 177–185. Occasional Paper No. 21. Archaeological Survey of Alberta, Edmonton.

Bancroft, H. H.
1882 *The Native Races of the Pacific Coast, vol. V. Primitive History*. A. L. Bancroft & Co., San Francisco.

Beaudoin, A. B.
1989 *Annotated Bibliography: Late Quaternary Studies in Alberta's Western Corridor 1950–1988*. Archaeological Survey of Alberta Manuscript Series no. 15. Alberta Culture and Multiculturalism, Edmonton.

Beaudoin, A. B., M. Wright, and B. Ronaghan
1996 Late Quaternary Landscape History and Archaeology in the "Ice-Free Corridor": Some Recent Results from Alberta. *Quaternary International* 32:113–126.

Becker, B., and B. Kromer
1993 The Continental Tree-ring Record—Absolute Chronology, ^{14}C Calibration and Climatic Change at 11 ka. *Palaeogeography, Palaeoclimatology, Palaeoecology* 103:67–71.

Bell, R.
1890 On Glacial Phenomena in Canada. *Bulletin of the Geological Society of America* 1:287–310.

Benmouyal, J.
1987 *Des Paléoindiens aux Iroquoiens en Gaspésie: Six Mille Ans d'Histoire.* Ministère des Affaires Culturelles, Dossiers, no. 63. Québec.

Bird, J. B.
1939 Artifacts in Canadian River Terraces. *Science* 89.

Bliss, W. L.
1937 Preliminary Report on Archaeological Work in Alberta, Canada. *New Mexico Anthropologist* 2(2):46–47.

1939a An Archaeological and Geological Reconnaissance of Alberta, Mackenzie Valley and Upper Yukon. *Yearbook of the American Philosophical Society*, Philadelphia.

1939b Early Man in Western and Northwestern Canada. *Science* 89:365–366.

Bobrowsky, P. T., N. R. Catto, J. W. Brink, B. E. Spurling, T. H. Gibson and N. W. Rutter
1990 Archaeological Geology of Sites in Western and Northwestern Canada. In *Archaeological Geology of North America*, edited by N. P. Lasca and J. Donahue, pp. 87–122. Geological Society of America, Centennial Special Volume 4, Boulder.

Boettger, W. M.
1986 *Origin and Stratigraphy of Holocene Deposits in the Souris and Des Lacs Valleys.* Unpublished Master's thesis, University of North Dakota, Grand Forks.

Bonnichsen, R.
1978 Critical Arguments for Pleistocene Artifacts from the Old Crow Basin, Yukon: A Preliminary Statement. In *Early Man in America from Circum-Pacific Perspective*, edited by A. L. Bryan, pp. 102–118. Occasional Papers No. 1. Department of Anthropology, University of Alberta, Edmonton.

Bragg, R.
1977 Local Scientist Disputes Accepted Early Man Theory. *The Calgary Herald*, 2 June 1977.

Brown, R. M., H. R. Andrews, G. C. Ball, N. Burn, Y. Imahori, and J. C. D. Milton
1983 Accelerator 14C Dating of the Taber Child. *Canadian Journal of Archaeology* 7:233–237.

Brumley, J. H., and B. Dau
1988 *Historical Resource Investigations Within the Forty Mile Coulee Reservoir.* Archaeological Survey of Alberta, Manuscript Series No. 13. Edmonton.

Bryan, A. L.
1966 Preliminary Report on the Lindoe Site. *Archaeological Society of Alberta Newsletter* 10:4–6.

1968 Early Man in Western Canada, a Critical Review. In Early Man in Western North America, edited by C. Irwin-Williams. Eastern New Mexico University, *Contributions in Anthropology*, 1(4):70–77.

1969 Early Man in America and the Late Pleistocene Chronology of Western Canada and Alaska. *Current Anthropology* 10:339–365.

Bryan, K.
1941 Geologic Antiquity of Man in America. *Science* 93:505–514.

Buchner, A. P., and L. F. Pettipas
1990 The Early Occupations of the Glacial Lake Agassiz Basin in Manitoba: 11,500 to 7,700 B.P. In *Archaeological Geology of North America*, edited by N.P. Lasca and J. Donahue, pp. 51–59. Geological Society of America, Centennial Special Volume 4, Boulder.

Burns, J. A.
1990 Paleontological Perspectives on the Ice-Free Corridor. In *Megafauna and Man: Discovery of America's Heartland*, edited by L. D. Agenbroad, J. I. Mead and L. W. Nelson, pp. 61–66. The Mammoth Site of Hot Springs, South Dakota, Inc., Scientific Papers, vol. 1. Hot Springs.

1996 Vertebrate Paleontology and the Alleged Ice-Free Corridor: The Meat of the Matter. *Quaternary International* 32:107–112.

Carlson, R. L.
1991 Clovis from the Perspective of the Ice-Free Corridor. In *Clovis: Origins and Adaptations*, edited by R. Bonnichsen and K. L. Turnmire, pp. 81–90. Center for the Study of the First Americans, Corvallis, OR.

1996 Introduction to Early Human Occupation in British Columbia. In *Early Human Occupation in British Columbia*, edited by R. L. Carlson and L. Dalla Bona, pp. 3–10. University of British Columbia Press, Vancouver.

Catto, N., and C. Mandryk
1990 Geology of the Postulated Ice-Free Corridor. In *Megafauna and Man: Discovery of America's Heartland*, edited by L. D. Agenbroad, J. I. Mead and L. W. Nelson, pp. 80–85. The Mammoth Site of Hot Springs, South Dakota, Inc., Scientific Papers, vol. 1. Hot Springs.

Chapdelaine, C.
1985 Présentation: Sur les Traces des Premiers Québecois. *Recherches Amérindiennes au Québec* 15(1-2):3–6.

Chapdelaine, C., editor
1994 Il y a 8000 Ans: Rimouski. *Paléo-Quebec*, no. 22. *Recherches Amérindiennes au Québec*, Québec.

Chapdelaine, C., and S. Bourget
1992 Premier Regard sur un Site Paléoindien Récent à Rimouski (DcEd-1). *Recherches Amérindiennes au Québec* 22(1):17–32.

Chlachula, J.
1994 *Paleo-American Occupation of the Bow River Valley, Southwestern Alberta, Canada.* Unpublished PhD Dissertation, Department of Archaeology, University of Calgary, Calgary, AB. 234 p.

1996a Geology and Quaternary Environments of the First Preglacial Paleolithic Site Found in Alberta, Canada. *Quaternary Science Reviews* 15:285–315.

1996b Environnements du Pléistocène Final et Occupation Paléo-Américaine du Sud-ouest de l'Alberta, Canada. *L'Anthropologie* (Paris), 100:88–131.

Chlachula, J., and R. LeBlanc
1996 Some Artifact-diagnostic Criteria of Quartzite Cobble-tool Industries from Alberta. *Canadian Journal of Archaeology* 20:61–74.

Christiansen, E. A.
1979 The Wisconsinan Deglaciation of Southern Saskatchewan and Adjacent Areas. *Canadian Journal of Earth Sciences* 6:913–938.

Church, M., and J. M. Ryder
1972 Paraglacial Sedimentation: A Consideration of Fluvial Processes Conditioned by Glaciation. *Geological Society of America Bulletin* 83:3072–3095.

Churcher, C. S.
1968 Pleistocene Ungulates from the Bow River Gravels at Cochrane, Alberta. *Canadian Journal of Earth Sciences* 5:1467–1488.

1975 Additional Evidence of Pleistocene Ungulates from the Bow River Gravels at Cochrane, Alberta. *Canadian Journal of Earth Sciences* 12:68–76.

Cinq-Mars, J.
1979 Bluefish Cave 1: A Late Pleistocene Eastern Beringian Cave Deposit in the Northern Yukon. *Canadian Journal of Archaeology* 3:1–32.

Clark, D. W., and A. McFayden Clark
1980 Fluted points at the Batza Téna obsidian source, northwestern Interior Alaska. In *Early Native Americans: Prehistoric Demography, Economy, and Technology*, ed. By D. L. Browman, pp. 141–159. Mouton, The Hague.

Clayton, L.
1983 Chronology of Lake Agassiz Drainage to Lake Superior. In *Glacial Lake Agassiz*, edited by J. T. Teller and L. Clayton, pp. 291–307. Special Paper No. 26. Geological Association of Canada.

Clayton, L., and S. R. Moran
1982 Chronology of Late Wisconsin Glaciation in Middle North America. *Quaternary Science Reviews* 1:55–82.

Coleman, A. P.
1910 The Drift of Alberta and the Relations of the Cordilleran and Keewatin Ice Sheets. *Transactions of the Royal Society of Canada*, Sec. LV:3–12.

Cotteville-Giraudet, R.
1928 Les Races et la Peuplement du Nouveau Monde. Comment l'Europe y a Participé. *IIIe Session de l'Institut International d'Anthropologie* 3:268.

Davis, L. B., and S. T. Greiser
1992 Indian Creek Paleoindians: Early Occupation of the Elkhorn Mountains' Southeast Flank, West-Central Montana. In *Ice Age Hunters of the Rockies*, ed. by D. A. Stanford and J. S. Day, pp. 225–283. University Press of Colorado, Niwot.

Davis, S. A., and D. Christianson
1988 Three Palaeo-Indian Specimens from Nova Scotia. *Canadian Journal of Archaeology* 12:190–196.

Dawson, G. M.
1875 On the Superficial Geology of the Central Region of North America. *Quarterly Journal of the Geological Society* 31:603–623.

1885 Report on the Region in the Vicinity of Bow and Belly Rivers, North West Territory. *Geological and Natural History Survey of Canada, Report of Progress 1882–1883–1884*: 1C-169C. Ottawa.

1891a Discussion [of a paper by W. Upham]. *Bulletin of the Geological Society of America* 2:275–276.

1891b On the Later Physiographical Geology of the Rocky Mountain Region in Canada, with Special Reference to Changes in Elevation and to the History of the Glacial Period. *Transactions of the Royal Society of Canada* 8:3–74.

1895 Note on the Glacial Deposits of Southwestern Alberta. *Journal of Geology* 3:507–511.

1897 Are the Bowlder Clays of the Great Plains Marine? *Journal of Geology* 5:257–262.

Dawson, G. M., and R. G. McConnell
1895 Glacial Deposits of Southwestern Alberta in the Vicinity of the Rocky Mountains. *Bulletin of the Geological Society of America* 7:31–66.

Deller, D. B.
1988 *The Paleo-Indian Occupations of Southeastern Ontario: Distribution, Technology, and Social Organization.* Ph.D. Dissertation, Department of Anthropology, McGill University, Montreal.

Deller, D. B., and C. J. Ellis
1988 Early Palaeo-Indian Complexes in Southwestern Ontario. In Late Pleistocene and Early Holocene Paleoecology and Archeology of the Eastern Great Lakes Region, edited by R. S. Laub, N. G. Miller, and D. W. Steadman, pp. 251–263. *Bulletin of the Buffalo Society of Natural Sciences* No. 33. Buffalo.

Dingle, J. M.
1987 The Cold Lake Archaeological Program. *Alberta Archaeological Review* 15:3–17.

Dreimanis, A.
1967 Mastodons, Their Geologic Age and Extinction in Ontario, Canada. *Canadian Journal of Earth Sciences* 4:663–675.

Driver, J. C.
1995 Human Adaptation at the Pleistocene/Holocene Boundary in Western Canada, 11,000 to 9,000 B.P. Paper presented at Symposium on the Archaeology of the Pleistocene/Holocene Boundary, Fourteenth INQUA Congress, Berlin, Germany, August 4 and 5, 1995.

Driver, J. C., M. Handly, K. R. Fladmark, D. E. Nelson, G. M. Sullivan, and R. Preston
1996 Stratigraphy, Radiocarbon Dating, and Culture History of Charlie Lake Cave, British Columbia. *Arctic* 49(3):265–277.

Duvall, J. D., and W. T. Venner
1979 A statistical analysis of the lithics from the Calico site (5 BCM 1500A), California. *Journal of Field Archaeology* 6:455–462.

Dyke, A. S., and V. K. Prest
1987 Late Wisconsinan and Holocene History of the Laurentide Ice Sheet. *Géographie physique et Quaternaire* 41:237–263.

Easton, N. A.
1992 Mal de Mer above Terra Incognita, or, "What Ails the Coastal Migration Theory?" *Arctic Anthropology* 29(2):28–42.

Ebell, S. B.
1980 The Parkhill Site: An Agate Basin Surface Collection in South Central Saskatchewan. Saskatchewan Culture and Youth, *Pastlog Manuscript Series in Archaeology and History* No. 4. Regina.

Fedje, D. W.
1986 Banff Archaeology 1983–1985. In *Eastern Slopes Prehistory: Selected Papers*, edited by B. Ronaghan, pp. 25–62. Occasional Paper No. 30. Archaeological Survey of Alberta, Edmonton.

1996 Early Human Presence in Banff National Park. In *Early Human Occupation in British Columbia*, edited by R. L. Carlson and L. Dalla Bona, pp. 35–44. University of British Columbia Press, Vancouver.

Fedje, D. W., J. M. White, M. C. Wilson, D. E. Nelson, J. S. Vogel, and J. E. Southon
1995 Vermilion Lakes Site: Adaptations and Environments in the Canadian Rockies During the Latest Pleistocene and Early Holocene. *American Antiquity* 60(1):81–108.

Fenton, M. M., S. R. Moran, J. T. Teller, and L. Clayton
1983 Quaternary Stratigraphy and History in the Southern Part of the Lake Agassiz Basin. In *Glacial Lake Agassiz*, edited by J. T. Teller and L. Clayton, pp. 49–74. Special Paper No. 26, Geological Association of Canada.

Fladmark, K.R.
1978 The Feasibility of the Northwest Coast as a Migration Route for Early Man. In *Early Man in America from a Circum-Pacific Perspective*, edited by A. L. Bryan, pp. 119–128. Occasional Papers No. 1. Department of Anthropology, University of Alberta, Edmonton.

1979 Routes: Alternative Migration Corridors for Early Man in North America. *American Antiquity* 44:55–69.

1982 Microdebitage Analysis: Initial Considerations. *Journal of Archaeological Science* 9:205–220.

1983 Times and Places: Environmental Correlates of Mid-to-Late Wisconsin Human Population Expansion in North America. In *Early Man in the New World*, edited by R. Shutler, Jr., pp. 13–41. Sage Publications, Beverly Hills.

1990 Possible Early Human Occupation of the Queen Charlotte Islands, British Columbia. *Canadian Journal of Archaeology* 14:183–197.

1996 The Prehistory of Charlie Lake Cave. In *Early Human Occupation in British Columbia*, edited by R. L. Carlson and L. Dalla Bona, pp. 11–20. University of British Columbia Press, Vancouver.

Fladmark, K. R., J. C. Driver, and D. Alexander
1988 The Paleoindian Component at Charlie Lake Cave (HbRf 39), British Columbia. *American Antiquity* 53:371–384.

Forbis, R. G.
1968 Fletcher: A Paleo-Indian Site in Alberta. *American Antiquity* 33:1–10.

1970 *A Review of Alberta Archaeology to 1964.* National Museum of Man, Publications in Archaeology No. 1. Ottawa.

Frison, G. C.
1978 *Prehistoric Hunters of the High Plains.* Academic Press, New York.

1991 The Goshen Paleoindian Complex: New Data for Paleoindian Research. In *Clovis: Origins and Adaptations*, edited by R. Bonnichsen and K. L. Turnmire, pp. 133–151. Center for the Study of the First Americans, Corvallis.

Frison, G. C., and D. J. Stanford
1982 *The Agate Basin Site: A Record of the Paleoindian Occupation of the Northwestern High Plains.* Academic Press, New York.

Fullerton, D. S. and R. B. Colton
1986 Stratigraphy and Correlation of the Glacial Deposits on the Montana Plains. In *Glaciations in the Northern Hemisphere*, edited by V. Šibrava, D. Q. Bowen, and G. M. Richmond. *Quaternary Science Reviews* 5:69–82.

Geikie, J.
1894 *The Great Ice Age*. 3rd Edition. Edward Stanford, London.

Geist, V.
1971 The Relation of Social Evolution and Dispersal in Ungulates During the Pleistocene, with Emphasis on the Old World Deer and the Genus *Bison*. *Quaternary Research* 1:283–315.

Gibbons, A.
1993 Geneticists trace the DNA trail of the First Americans. *Science* 259:312–313.

1996 The Peopling of the Americas. *Science* 274:31–33.

Gowlett, J. A. J.
1987 The Archaeology of Radiocarbon Accelerator Dating. *Journal of World Prehistory* 1:127–170.

Gramly, R. M., and R. E. Funk
1990 What is Known and Not Known about the Human Occupation of the Northeastern United States until 10,000 BP. *Archaeology of Eastern North America* 18:5–31.

Grayson, D. K.
1986 Eoliths, Archaeological Ambiguity, and the Generation of "Middle Range" Research. In *American Archaeology Past and Future*, edited by D. J. Meltzer, D. D. Fowler and J. A. Sabloff, pp. 77–133. Smithsonian Institution Press, Washington.

Greenberg, J. H.
1987 *Language in the Americas*. Stanford University Press, Palo Alto.

Greenberg, J. H., C. G. Turner, and S. L. Zegura
1986 The Settlement of the Americas: a Comparison of the Linguistic, Dental and Genetic Evidence. *Current Anthropology* 27:477–497.

Greenman, E. F.
1962 The Upper Paleolithic and the New World. *Current Anthropology* 4(1):4–91.

Greer, S. C.
1991 The Trout Lake Archaeological Locality and the British Mountain Problem. In *NOGAP Archaeology Project: An Integrated Archaeological Research and Management Approach*, edited by J. Cinq-Mars and J.-L. Pilon, pp. 15–31. Canadian Archaeological Association, Occasional Paper No. 1.

Gruhn, R.
1994 The Pacific Coast Route of Entry: an Overview. In *Method and Theory for Investigating the Peopling of the Americas*, edited by R. Bonnichsen and D. G. Steele, pp. 249–256. Center for the Study of the First Americans, Corvallis, OR.

Gryba, E. M.
1983 *Sibbald Creek: A Record of 11,000 Years of Human Utilization of the Southern Alberta Foothills.* Occasional Paper No. 22. Archaeological Survey of Alberta, Edmonton.

1985 Evidence of the Fluted Point Tradition in Alberta. *Alberta Archaeological Review* 11:3–11.

1988 FhPm-1: An Occurrence of "Charlie Lake" Type Fluted Points Near Thorsby, Alberta. In *Archaeology in Alberta* 1987, compiled by M. Magne, pp. 47–53. Occasional Paper No. 32. Archaeological Survey of Alberta, Edmonton.

Guthrie, R. D.
1984 The Evidence for Middle-Wisconsin Peopling of Beringia: an Evaluation. *Quaternary Research* 22:231–241.

Haley, S.
1996 The Pasika Complex Revisited. In *Early Human Occupation in British Columbia*, edited by R. L. Carlson and L. Dalla Bona, pp. 51–64. University of British Columbia Press, Vancouver.

Harington, C. R., R. Bonnichsen, and R. E. Morlan
1975 Bones Say Man Lived in Yukon 27,000 Years Ago. *Canadian Geographical Journal* 91:42–48.

Harris, R. C. (editor)
1987 *Historical Atlas of Canada, vol. 1. From the Beginning to 1800.* University of Toronto Press, Toronto.

Harris, S. A.
1987 Early Holocene Climate and Paleogeography, High Plains, Alberta. In *Man and the Mid-Holocene Climatic Optimum*, edited by N. A. McKinnon and G. S. L. Stuart, pp. 33–51. Proceedings of the 17th Annual Conference, Chacmool, the Archaeological Association of the University of Calgary, Calgary.

Haynes, C. V., Jr.
1980 The Clovis Culture. In *The Ice-Free Corridor and the Peopling of the New World*, edited by N. W. Rutter and C. E. Schweger. *Canadian Journal of Anthropology* 1:115–121.

1982 Were Clovis progenitors in Beringia? In *Paleoecology of Beringia*, edited by D. M. Hopkins, J. V. Matthews, C. E. Schweger, and S. B. Young, pp. 383–398. Academic Press, New York.

1987 Clovis origin update. *The Kiva* 52:83–93.

Hector, J.
1861 On the Geology of the Country Between Lake Superior and the Pacific Ocean (Between the 48th and 54th Parallels of Latitude), Visited by the Government Exploring Expedition Under the Command of Captain J. Palliser (1857–60). *Proceedings of the Geological Society of London* 17:388–445.

Hind, H. Y.
1859 *Narrative of the Canadian Red River Exploring Expedition of 1857 and of the Assinniboine and Saskatchewan Exploring Expedition of 1858.* 2 vols. Eyre and Spottiswoode, London. Reprinted 1971 in one volume by M. G. Hurtig Publishing, Edmonton.

1864 Observations on Supposed Glacial Drift in the Labrador Peninsula, Western Canada, and on the South Branch of the Saskatchewan. *Journal of the Geological Society of London* 20:122–130.

Hoffecker, J. F., W. R. Powers, and T. Goebel
1993 The Colonization of Beringia and the Peopling of the New World. *Science* 259:46–53.

Holmes, W. H.
1899 Review of the Evidence Relating to Auriferous Gravel Man in California. *Smithsonian Report for 1899*, pp. 419–472. Washington, D.C.

Howard, C. D.
1990 The Clovis Point: Characteristics and Type Description. *Plains Anthropologist* 35(129):255–262.

Hrdliěka, A.
1907 Skeletal Remains Suggesting or Attributed to Early Man in North America. *Bureau of American Ethnology Bulletin* 33:21–28.

1918 Recent Discoveries Attributed to Early Man in America. *Bureau of American Ethnology Bulletin* 66.

Hughes, O. L., C. R. Harington, J. A. Janssens, J. V. Matthews, Jr., R. E. Morlan, N. W. Rutter, and C. E. Schweger
1981 Upper Pleistocene Stratigraphy, Paleoecology, and Archaeology of the Northern Yukon Interior, Eastern Beringia: 1. Bonnet Plume Basin. *Arctic* 34:329–365.

Hull, K.
1983 *Application of Microdebitage Analysis to Examination of Spatial Patterning.* Unpublished Master's thesis. Department of Archaeology, University of Calgary, Calgary.

Imbelloni, J.
1938 Tabla Classificatoria de los Indios, Regiones Biologicas y Grupos Raciales Humanos en America. *Physis* 12:229.

Irving, W. N.
1978 Pleistocene Archaeology in Eastern Beringia. In *Early Man in America from a Circum-Pacific Perspective*, edited by A. L. Bryan, pp. 96–101. Occasional Papers No. 1. Department of Anthropology, University of Alberta, Edmonton.

1986 Indications of Pre-Sangamon Humans near Old Crow, Yukon, Canada. In *New Evidence for the Pleistocene Peopling of the Americas*, edited by A. L. Bryan, pp. 49–63. Center for the Study of Early Man, University of Maine, Orono.

Irving, W. N., and C. R. Harington
1973 Upper Pleistocene Radiocarbon-Dated Artifacts from the Northern Yukon. *Science* 179:335–340.

Irving, W. N., J. T. Mayall, F. J. Melbye, and B. F. Beebe
1977 A Human Mandible in Probable Association with a Pleistocene Faunal Assemblage in Eastern Beringia: A Preliminary Report. *Canadian Journal of Archaeology* 1:81–93.

Jackson, L.
1983 Geochronology and Settlement Disposition in the Early Paleo-Indian Occupation of Southern Ontario, Canada. *Quaternary Research* 19:288–299.

Jackson, L. E., Jr.
1979 New Evidence for the Existence of an Ice-Free Corridor in the Rocky Mountain Foothills near Calgary, Alberta, During Late Wisconsinan Time. *Canadian Journal of Earth Sciences* 17:459–477.

1983 Comments on "Chronology of Late Wisconsinan Glaciation in Middle North America." *Quaternary Science Reviews* 1:vii–xiv.

Jackson, L. E., Jr., and A. Duk-Rodkin
1996 Quaternary Geology of the Ice-free Corridor: Glacial Controls on the Peopling of the New World. In *Prehistoric Mongoloid Dispersals*, ed. By T. Akazawa and E. Szathmary, pp. 214–227. Oxford University Press, Oxford.

Jackson, L. E., Jr., G. M. MacDonald, and M. C. Wilson
1982 Paraglacial Origin for Terraced River Sediments in Bow Valley, Alberta. *Canadian Journal of Earth Sciences* 19:2,219–2,231.

Jackson, L. E., Jr., F. M. Phillips, K. Shimamura, and E. C. Little
1997 Cosmogenic ^{36}Cl Dating of the Foothills Erratics Train, Alberta, Canada. *Geology* 25(3):195–198.

Jackson, L. J.
1987 Ontario Paleoindians and Proboscideans: a Review. *Current Research in the Pleistocene* 4:109–112.

Jelinek, A. J., B. Bradley, and B. Huckell
1971 The Production of Secondary Multiple Flakes. *American Antiquity* 36(2):198–200.

Johnson, F.
1946 An Archaeological Survey Along the Alaskan Highway 1944. *American Antiquity* 11(3):183–186.

Johnson, F., and H. M. Raup
1964 Investigations in the Southwest Yukon, Part I: Geobotanical and Archaeological Reconnaissance. *Papers of the R. S. Peabody Foundation for Archaeology* 6(1). Andover.

Johnston, W. A.
1933 Quaternary Geology of North America in Relation to the Migration of Man. In *The American Aborigines: Their Origin and Antiquity*, edited by D. Jenness, pp. 9–45. University of Toronto Press, Toronto.

Johnston, W. A., and R. T. D. Wickenden
1931 Moraines and Glacial Lakes in Southern Saskatchewan and Southern Alberta, Canada. Transactions of the Royal Society of Canada 25:29–44.

Jones, T.
1989 The Heron Eden Site Makes the News. *Saskatchewan Archaeological Society Newsletter* 10(6):128–129.

Jopling, A. V., W. N. Irving, and B. F. Beebe
1981 Stratigraphic, Sedimentological, and Faunal Evidence for the Occurrence of Pre-Sangamonian Artifacts in Northern Yukon. *Arctic* 34:3–33.

Julig, P. J.
1990 The Effect of Lake Agassiz Flood Events on Northern Great Lakes Paleoindian Sites: Examples from the Superior and Huron Basins [abstract]. In *Programme and Abstracts, Canadian Quaternary Association/American Quaternary Association, First Joint Meeting*, Waterloo, ON.

1991 Late Pleistocene Archaeology in the Great Lakes Region of North America: Current Problems and Prospects. *Revista de Arqueología Americana* 3:7–30.

Julig, P. J., J. H. McAndrews, and W. C. Mahaney
1990 Geoarchaeology of the Cummins Site on the Beach of Proglacial Lake Minong, Lake Superior Basin, Canada. In *Archaeological Geology of North America*, edited by N. P. Lasca and J. Donahue, pp. 21–50. Geological Society of America, Centennial Special Volume 4, Boulder.

Karrow, P. F.
1987 Comments on "Geology of the Sheguiandah Early Man Site: Key Concepts and Issues" by Robert E. Lee. *Géographie physique et Quaternaire* 41:403–406.

Karrow, P. F., T. W. Anderson, A. H. Clarke, L. D. Delorme, and M. R. Sreenivasa
1975 Stratigraphy, Paleontology and Age of Lake Algonquin Sediments in Southwestern Ontario. *Quaternary Research* 5:49–87.

Kearney, S., and B. H. Luckman
1983 Postglacial Vegetational History of Tonquin Pass, British Columbia. *Canadian Journal of Earth Sciences* 20:776–786.

Keenlyside, D. L.
1985 La période Paléoindienne sur l'Île-du-Prince-Edouard. *Recherches Amérindiennes au Québec* 15(1-2):119–126.

Kehew, A. E., and L. Clayton
1983 Late Wisconsinan Catastrophic Floods and Development of the Souris-Pembina Spillway System. In *Glacial Lake Agassiz*, edited by J. T. Teller and L. Clayton, pp. 187–209. Special Paper No. 26. Geological Association of Canada.

Kehoe, T. F.
1964 The Kyle Mammoth. *Saskatchewan Archaeology Newsletter* 8:1–4.

1966 The Distribution and Implications of Fluted Points in Saskatchewan. *American Antiquity* 31:530–539.

Kehoe, T. F., and A. B. Kehoe
1968 Saskatchewan. In *The Northwestern Plains: A Symposium*, edited by W. W. Caldwell, pp. 21–35. Occasional Paper No. 1. Center for Indian Studies, Rocky Mountain College, Billings.

Klassen, R. A.
1972 Wisconsin Events and the Assiniboine and Qu'Appelle Valleys of Manitoba and Saskatchewan. *Canadian Journal of Earth Sciences* 9:544–560.

1983 Assiniboine Delta and the Assiniboine-Qu'Appelle Valley System: Implications Concerning the History of Lake Agassiz in Southwestern Manitoba. In *Glacial Lake Agassiz*, edited by J. T. Teller and L. Clayton, pp. 211–229. Special Paper No. 26. Geological Association of Canada.

Kunz, M., and R. E. Reanier
1995 The Mesa Site: a Paleoindian Hunting Lookout in Arctic Alaska. *Arctic Anthropology* 32(1):5–30.

Kuzmin, Y. V., and K. B. Tankersley
1996 The Colonization of Eastern Siberia: an Evaluation of the Paleolithic Age Radiocarbon Dates. *Journal of Archaeological Science* 23:577–585.

LaSalle, P., and C. Chapdelaine
1990 Review of Late-glacial and Holocene Events in the Champlain and Goldthwait Seas areas and Arrival of Man in Eastern Canada. In *Archaeological Geology of North America*, edited by N. P. Lasca and J. Donahue, pp. 1–19. Geological Society of America, Centennial Special Volume 4, Boulder.

Laughlin, W. S., and A. B. Harper (editors)
1979 *The First Americans: Origins, Affinities, Adaptations.* Gustav Fischer, New York.

Lee, R. E.
1986 Geology of the Sheguiandah Early Man Site: Key Concepts and Issues. *Géographie physique et Quaternaire* 40:325–330.

Lee, T. E.
1957 The Antiquity of the Sheguiandah Site. *Canadian Field-Naturalist* 71:117–137.

1972 Sheguiandah in Retrospect. *Anthropological Journal of Canada* 10:28–30.

Leechman, D.
1950 An Implement of Elephant Bone from Manitoba. *American Antiquity* 16:157–160.

Levine, M. A.
1990 Accommodating Age: Radiocarbon Results and Fluted Point Sites in Northeastern North America. *Archaeology of Eastern North America* 18:33–63.

Lindgren, W.
1911 *The Tertiary Gravels of the Sierra Nevada of California.* United States Geological Survey, Professional Paper No. 73.

Linnamae, U.
1990 The Heron Eden Site: 1990 Update. *Saskatchewan Archaeological Society Newsletter* 11(4):82.

Little, E. C.
1995 *A Single Maximum-Advance Hypothesis of Continental Glaciation Restricted to the Late Wisconsinan, Southwestern Alberta.* Unpublished M.S. Thesis, Department of Earth Sciences, University of Western Ontario, London, ON. 229 p.

Lord, M. L., and A. E. Kehew
1987 Sedimentology and Paleohydrology of Glacial-Lake Outburst Floods in Southeastern Saskatchewan and Northwestern North Dakota. *Geological Society of American Bulletin* 99:663–673.

Lowdon, J. A., and W. Blake, Jr.
1968 Geological Survey of Canada Radiocarbon Dates VII. *Radiocarbon* 10(2): 207-245.

1975 *Geological Survey of Canada Radiocarbon Dates XV.* Geological Survey of Canada Paper No. 75-7. Ottawa.

MacDonald, G. F.
1968 *Debert: A Paleo-Indian Site in Central Nova Scotia.* National Museum of Canada, Anthropological Paper No. 16. Ottawa.

MacDonald, G. M., R. P. Beukens, W. E. Kieser, and D. H. Vitt
1987 Comparative Radiocarbon Dating of Terrestrial Plant Macrofossils and Aquatic Moss from the "Ice-Free Corridor" of Western Canada. *Geology* 15:837–840.

MacDonald, G. M., and T. K. McLeod
1996 The Holocene Closing of the "Ice-Free" Corridor: A Biogeographical Perspective. *Quaternary International* 32:87–95.

MacNeish, R. S.
1951 An Archaeological Reconnaissance in the Northwest Territories. *National Museum of Canada Bulletin* 123:24–41. Ottawa.

1953 Archaeological Reconnaissance in the Mackenzie River Drainage. *National Museum of Canada Bulletin* 128:1–17. Ottawa.

1954 The Pointed Mountain Site near Fort Liard, Northwest Territories, Canada. *American Antiquity* 19(3):234–253.

1956a Two Archaeological Sites on Great Bear Lake, Northwest Territories. *Annual Report of the National Museum of Canada*, Bulletin 136:54–82.

1956b *The Engigstciak Site on the Yukon Arctic Coast.* Anthropological Papers of the University of Alaska 4(2):91–111.

1959 *Men Out of Asia; as Seen from the Southwest Yukon.* Anthropological Papers of the University of Alaska 7(2):41–70.

1962 *The Great Lakes to the Barren Lands.* Arctic Institute of North America, Technical Paper 11:140–142.

1963 *The Peopling of the New World as Seen from the Southwestern Yukon.* Anthropological Papers of the University of Alaska 10(2).

1964 *Investigations in the Southwest Yukon: Archaeological Excavation, Comparisons and Speculations.* Papers of the R. S. Peabody Foundation for Archaeology 6(2). Andover.

Mahaney, W. C., W. B. Vortisch, and P. J. Julig
1988 Relative Difference Between Glacially Crushed Quartz Transported by Mountain and Continental Ice: Some Examples from North America and East Africa. *American Journal of Science* 288:810–826.

Mandryk, C. A. S.
1996a Late Wisconsinan Deglaciation of Alberta: Processes and Paleogeography. *Quaternary International* 32:79–85.

1996b Deglaciation Processes and Paleogeography: Implications for Archaeological Site Formation, Preservation and Discovery in the "Ice-free Corridor." Paper presented at the 61st Annual Meeting of the Society for American Archaeology, New Orleans, LA.

Mandryk, C. A. S., and N. Rutter (editors)
1996 The Ice-Free Corridor Revisited. *Quaternary International* 32.

Margolis, S. V. and D. H. Krinsley
1974 Processes of Formation and Environmental Occurrence of Microfeatures on Detrital Quartz Grains. *American Journal of Science* 274:449–464.

Martijn, C.
1985 Le Complexe Plano de Témiscamie est-il une Illusion? *Recherches Amérindiennes au Québec* 15(1-2):161–164.

Martin, P. S.
1967 Prehistoric Overkill. In *Pleistocene Extinctions: The Search for a Cause*, edited by P. S. Martin and H. E. Wright, Jr., pp. 75–120. Yale University Press, New Haven.

Mathews, W. H.
1980 Retreat of the Last Ice Sheets in Northeastern British Columbia and Adjacent Alberta. *Geological Survey of Canada Bulletin* No. 331. Ottawa.

McAndrews, J. H., and L. J. Jackson
1988 Age and Environment of Late Pleistocene Mastodont and Mammoth in Southern Ontario. In Late Pleistocene and Early Holocene Paleoecology and Archeology of the Eastern Great Lakes Region, edited by R. S. Lamb, N. G. Miller, and D. W. Steadman, pp. 161–172. *Bulletin of the Buffalo Society of Natural Sciences* No. 33.

McCallum, K. J., and J. Wittenberg
1968 University of Saskatchewan Radiocarbon Dates V. *Radiocarbon* 10:365–378.

McCullough, E. J., M. C. Wilson, and G. J. Fedirchuk
1981 *The Duckett Site (GdOo-16), An Evaluative Study.* Report prepared by Fedirchuk, McCullough, and Associates Ltd. for Alberta Culture, Edmonton.

Meyer, D.
1985 A Component in the Scottsbluff Tradition: Excavations at the Niska Site. *Canadian Journal of Archaeology* 9:1–37.

1986 Reply to Pettipas' Comments. Canadian Journal of Archaeology 10:171–172.

1989 [Letter to the Editor Concerning Misidentification of Late Paleoindian Points as "Agate Basin"]. *Saskatchewan Archaeological Society Newsletter* 10(6):126.

Meyer, D., and H. Liboiron
1990 A Paleoindian Drill from the Niska Site in Southern Saskatchewan. *Plains Anthropologist* 35:299–302.

Moffatt, E. A., and I. N. M. Wainwright
1983 Protein Concentrations in the Taber Child Skeleton: Probable Evidence for a Late Chronology. *Canadian Journal of Archaeology* 7:223–231.

Moran, S. R.
1986 *Surficial Geology of the Calgary Urban Area.* Alberta Research Council Bulletin no. 53. Alberta Research Council, Edmonton, AB. 46 p.

Morell, V.
1990 Confusion in Earliest America. *Science* 248:439–441.

Morlan, R. E.
1977 Fluted Point Makers and the Extinction of the Arctic-Steppe Biome in Eastern Beringia. *Canadian Journal of Archaeology* 1:95–108.

1978 Early Man in Northern Yukon Territory: Perspective as of 1977. In *Early Man in America from a Circum-Pacific Perspective*, edited by A. L. Bryan, pp. 78–95. Occasional Papers No. 1. Department of Anthropology, University of Alberta, Edmonton.

1979 A Stratigraphic Framework for Pleistocene Artifacts from Old Crow River, Northern Yukon Territory. In *Pre-Llano Cultures of the Americas: Paradoxes and Possibilities*, edited by R. L. Humphrey and D. Stanford, pp. 128–145. Anthropological Society of Washington, Washington, D.C.

1980 *Taphonomy and Archaeology in the Upper Pleistocene of the Northern Yukon Territory: A Glimpse of the Peopling of the New World.* Archaeological Survey of Canada Paper No. 94. Mercury Series. National Museum of Man, Ottawa.

1983 Pre-Clovis Occupation North of the Ice-Sheets. In *Early Man in the New World*, edited by R. Shutler, Jr., pp. 47–63. Sage Publications, Beverly Hills.

1984 Toward the Definition of Criteria for the Recognition of Artificial Bone Alterations. *Quaternary Research* 22:160–171.

1986 Pleistocene Archaeology in Old Crow Basin: A Critical Reappraisal. In *New Evidence for the Pleistocene Peopling of the Americas*, edited by A. L. Bryan, pp. 27–48. Center for the Study of Early Man, University of Maine, Orono.

1987 The Pleistocene Archaeology of Beringia. In *The Evolution of Human Hunting*, edited by M. H. Nitecki and D. V. Nitecki, pp. 267–307. Plenum Publishing.

Morlan, R. E., and J. Cinq-Mars
1982 Ancient Beringians: Human Occupation in the Late Pleistocene of Alaska and the Yukon Territory. In *Paleoecology of Beringia*, edited by D. M. Hopkins, J. V. Matthews, Jr., C. E. Schewger, and S. B. Young, pp. 353–381. Academic Press, New York.

Morlan, R. E., D. E. Nelson, T. A. Brown, J. S. Vogel, and J. R. Southon
1990 Accelerator Mass Spectrometry Dates on Bones from Old Crow Basin, Northern Yukon Territory. *Canadian Journal of Archaeology* 14:75–92.

Müller-Beck, H-J.
1967 On Migrations of Hunters Across the Bering Land Bridge in the Upper Pleistocene. In *The Bering Land Bridge*, edited by D. M. Hopkins, pp. 373–408. Stanford University Press, Palo Alto, CA.

Nelson, D. E., R. E. Morlan, J. S. Vogel, J. R. Southon, and C. R. Harington
1986 New Dates on Northern Yukon Artifacts: Holocene Not Upper Pleistocene. *Science* 232:749–751.

Nicholson, B. A.
1983 A Comparative Evaluation of Four Sampling Techniques and of the Reliability of Microdebitage as a Cultural Indicator in Regional Surveys. *Plains Anthropologist* 28:273–281.

Nielsen, E., E. M. Gryba, and M. C. Wilson
1984 Bison Remains from Lake Agassiz Context in Swan Valley, Manitoba: Depositional Environment and Paleoecological Implications. *Canadian Journal of Earth Sciences* 21(7):829–842.

Oakley, K. P.
1967 *Man the Tool-Maker.* 5th Edition. Trustees of the British Museum (Natural History), London. 98 p.

Parent, M., J-M. M. Dubois, P. Bail, A. Larocque, and G. Larocque
1985 Paléogeographie du Québec Méridional entre 12 500 et 8000 ans BP. *Recherches Amérindiennes au Québec* 15(1-2):17–37.

Parks, W. A.
1925 Buried Indian Workshop with Remains of an Extinct Mammal. *Bulletin of the Geological Society of America* 36:429–434.

Patterson, L. W.
1988 Criteria for Determining the Attributes of Man-made Lithics. *Journal of Field Archaeology* 10:297–307.

Pettipas, L. F.
1967 *Paleo-Indian Manifestations in Manitoba: Their Spatial and Temporal Relationships with the Campbell Shorelines.* Unpublished Master's thesis. Department of Anthropology, University of Manitoba, Winnipeg.

1970 Early Man in Manitoba. In *Ten Thousand Years: Archaeology in Manitoba*, edited by W. M. Hlady, pp. 5–28. Manitoba Archaeological Society, Altona, MB.

1983 *Manitoba Prehistory.* Papers in Manitoba Archaeology, Popular Series No. 4. Manitoba Department of Cultural Affairs and Historical Resources, Winnipeg.

1985 Recent Developments in Paleo-Indian Archaeology in Manitoba. In *Contributions to Plains Prehistory*, edited by D. Burley, pp. 39–63. Occasional Paper No. 26. Archaeological Survey of Alberta, Edmonton.

1986 Comments on David Meyer's "A Component in the Scottsbluff Tradition: Excavations at the Niska Site." *Canadian Journal of Archaeology* 10:167–169.

Pettipas, L. F., and A. P. Buchner
1983 Paleo-Indian Prehistory of the Glacial Lake Agassiz Region in Southern Manitoba, 11,500 to 6,500 B.P. In *Glacial Lake Agassiz*, edited by J. T. Teller and L. Clayton, pp. 421–451. Special Paper No. 26. Geological Association of Canada.

Pielou, E.C.
1991 *After the Ice Age: The Return of Life to Glaciated North America.* University of Chicago Press, Chicago. 366 p.

Pohorecky, Z. S.
1988 The Saskatoon Site: Palaeontological or Archaeological? In *Out of the Past: Sites, Digs and Artifacts in the Saskatoon Area*, edited by U. Linnamae and T. E. H. Jones, pp. 47–64. Saskatoon Archaeological Society, Saskatoon.

Pohorecky, Z. S., and D. E. Anderson
1968 Agassiz Archaeology in Saskatchewan. *Na'pao, A Saskatchewan Anthropology Journal* 1(2):48–70.

Pohorecky, Z. S., and J. S. Wilson
1968 Preliminary Archaeological Report on the Saskatoon Site. *Na'pao, A Saskatchewan Anthropological Journal* 1:35–70.

Prest, V. K.
1969 *Retreat of Wisconsin and Recent Ice in North America.* Geological Survey of Canada, Map 1257A. Ottawa.

Rains, R. B., J. Shaw, R. Skoye, D. Sjogren, and D. Kvill
1993 Late Wisconsin Subglacial Megaflood Paths in Alberta. *Geology* 21:323–326.

Reanier, R. E.
1995 The Antiquity of Paleoindian Materials in Northern Alaska. *Arctic Anthropology* 32(1):31–50.

Reeves, B. O. K.
1973 The Nature and Age of the Contact Between the Laurentide and Cordilleran Ice Sheets in the Western Interior of North America. *Arctic and Alpine Research* 5:1–16.

1980 Fractured Cherts from Pleistocene Fossiliferous Beds at Medicine Hat, Alberta. In *Early Native Americans: Prehistoric Demography, Economy, and Technology*, edited by D. L. Browman, pp. 83–98. Mouton Publishers, New York.

Richard, P. J. H.
1985 Couvert Végétal et Paléoenvironnements du Québec entre 12 000 et 8000 ans BP: l'Habitabilité dans un Milieu Changeant. *Recherches Amérindiennes au Québec* 15(1-2):39–56.

Rivet, P.
1943 *Los Origenes del Hombre Americano.* Ediciones Cuadernos Americanos, México.

Roberts, A.
1984a Paleo-Indian on the North Shore of Lake Ontario. *Archaeology of Eastern North America* 12:248–265.

1984b Ice Free Corridor Paleoindian survey. *Current Research in the Pleistocene* 1:15-17.

Roberts, A., and J. H. McAndrews
1987 Southern Ontario, 8600 B.C. In *Historical Atlas of Canada, vol 1. From the Beginning to 1800*, edited by R. C. Harris, Plate 3. University of Toronto Press, Toronto.

Roberts, A., J. H. McAndrews, V. K. Prest, and J-S. Vincent
1987 The Fluted Point People, 9500-8200 B.C. In *Historical Atlas of Canada, vol. 1. From the Beginning to 1800*, edited by R. C. Harris, Plate 2. University of Toronto Press, Toronto.

Roberts, A., and J.V. Wright

1987 The Plano People, 8500-6000 B.C. In *Historical Atlas of Canada, vol. 1. From the Beginning to 1800*, edited by R. C. Harris, Plate 5. University of Toronto Press, Toronto.

Roberts, B. L.
1991 Modeling the Cordilleran Ice Sheet. *Géographie physique et Quaternaire* 45(3):287–299.

Rogerson, R. J., and H. M. Hudson
1983 Quartz Surface Textures and Grain-Size Characteristics of Quaternary Sediments in the Porcupine Strand Area of Coastal Labrador, Newfoundland, Canada. *Canadian Journal of Earth Sciences* 20:377–387.

Roosa, W. B., and D. B. Deller
1982 The Parkhill Complex and Eastern Great Lakes Paleo Indian. *Ontario Archaeologist* 37:3–15.

Rutherford, A. A., J. Wittenberg, and K. J. McCallum
1973 University of Saskatchewan Radiocarbon Dates VI. *Radiocarbon* 15:193–211.

Rutter, N. W.
1984 Pleistocene History of the Western Canadian Ice-Free Corridor. In *Quaternary Stratigraphy of Canada*, edited by R. J. Fulton, pp. 49–56. Geological Survey of Canada Paper 84-10.

Rutter, N. W., and C. E. Schweger (editors)
1980 The Ice-Free Corridor and Peopling of the New World. *Canadian Journal of Anthropology* 1.

Sanford, J. T.
1957 Geologic Observations at the Sheguiandah Site. *Canadian Field-Naturalist* 71:138–148.

1971 Sheguiandah Revisited. *Anthropological Journal of Canada* 9:2–15.

Saskatchewan Museum of Natural History
1965 The Kyle Woolly Mammoth. *The Blue Jay* 23:88–89.

Simons, D. L., M. Shott, and H. T. Wright
1987 Paleoindian Research in Michigan: The Gainey and Leavitt Sites. *Current Research in the Pleistocene* 1:21–22.

Simpson, R. D.
1980 The Calico Mountains Site: Pleistocene Archaeology in the Mojave Desert, California. In *Early Native Americans: Prehistoric Demography, Economy, and Technology*, ed. By D. L. Browman, pp. 7–20. Mouton, The Hague.

Stafford, T. W., Jr.
1984 Direct Radiocarbon Dating of Fossil Bones [abstract]. In *Program and Abstracts*, pp. 124. American Quaternary Association, Eighth Biennial Meeting, Boulder.

Stalker, A. MacS.
1968 Geology of the Terraces at Cochrane, Alberta. *Canadian Journal of Earth Sciences* 5:1,455–1,466.

1969 Geology and Age of the Early Man Site at Taber, Alberta. *American Antiquity* 34:425–428.

1977a Indications of Wisconsin and Earlier Man from the Southwest Canadian Prairies. *Annals of the New York Academy of Sciences* 288:119–136.

1977b The Probable Extent of Classical Wisconsin Ice in Southern and Central Alberta. *Canadian Journal of Earth Sciences* 14:2,614–2,619.

1980 The Geology of the Ice-Free Corridor: The Southern Half. In *The Ice-Free Corridor and Peopling of the New World*, edited by N. W. Rutter and C. E. Schweger. *Canadian Journal of Anthropology* 1:11–13.

1983 A Detailed Stratigraphy of the Woodpecker Island Section and Commentary on the Taber Child Bones. *Canadian Journal of Archaeology* 7:209–222.

Stalker, A. MacS., and C. S. Churcher
1970 *Deposits Near Medicine Hat, Alberta, Canada.* Wall Chart. Geological Survey of Canada, Ottawa.

Stewart, A.
1991 Recognition of Northern Plano in the Context of Settlement in the Central Northwest Territories: Developing a Technological Approach. *Canadian Journal of Archaeology* 15:179–191.

St-Onge, D. A.
1972 *Sequence of Glacial Lakes in North-Central Alberta.* Geological Survey of Canada Bulletin No. 213.

Storck, P. L.
1982 Palaeo-Indian Settlement Patterns Associated with the Strandline of Glacial Lake Algonquin in Southcentral Ontario. *Canadian Journal of Archaeology* 6:1–31.

1984 Research into the Paleo-Indian Occupations of Ontario: a Review. *Ontario Archaeologist* 41:3–28.

1988 The Early Palaeo-Indian Occupation of Ontario: Colonization or Diffusion? In *Late Pleistocene and Early Holocene Paleoecology and Archeology of the Eastern Great Lakes Region*, edited by R. S. Laub, N. G. Miller, and D. W. Steadman, pp. 243–250. Bulletin of the Buffalo Society of Natural Sciences No. 33.

Sundick, R. I.
1980 The Skeletal Remains from the Taber Child Site, Taber, Alberta. *Canadian Review of Physical Anthropology* 2:1–6.

Szabo, B. J., A. MacS. Stalker, and C. S. Churcher
1973 Uranium-Series Ages of Some Quaternary Deposits Near Medicine Hat, Alberta, Canada. *Canadian Journal of Earth Sciences* 10:1,464–1,469.

Tankersley, K. B.
1994 Was Clovis a Colonizing Population in Eastern North America? In *The First Discovery of America*, edited by W. S. Dancey, pp. 95–116. The Ohio Archaeological Council, Columbus, OH.

Teller, J. T., and L. Clayton (editors)
1983 *Glacial Lake Agassiz.* Special Paper No. 26, Geological Association of Canada.

Teller, J. T., S. R. Moran, and L. Clayton
1980 The Wisconsinan Deglaciation of Southern Saskatchewan and Adjacent Areas: Discussion. *Canadian Journal of Earth Sciences* 17:539–541.

Thorson, R. M., and R. D. Guthrie
1984 River Ice as a Taphonomic Agent: an Alternative Hypothesis for Bone "Artifacts." *Quaternary Research* 22:172–188.

Trylich, C., and L. A. Bayrock
1966 Bison Occidentalis Lucas Found at Taber, Alberta, Canada. *Canadian Journal of Earth Sciences* 3:987–995.

Turchenek, L. W., R. J. St. Arnaud, and E. A. Christiansen
1974 A Study of Paleosols in the Saskatoon Area of Saskatchewan. *Canadian Journal of Earth Sciences* 11:905–915.

Turnbull, C. J.
1974 The Second Fluted Point in New Brunswick. *Man in the Northeast* 7:109–110.

Turnbull, C. J., and P. Allen
1978 More Paleo-Indian Points from New Brunswick. *Man in the Northeast* 15/16:147–153.

Tyrrell, J. B.
1890 Post-Tertiary Deposits of Manitoba and the Adjoining Territories of Northwestern Canada. *Bulletin of the Geological Society of America* 1:395–410.

1898 The Glaciation of North Central Canada. *Journal of Geology* 6:147–160.

Upham, W.
1891 Glacial Lakes in Canada. *Bulletin of the Geological Society of America* 2:243–276.

1895 *The Glacial Lake Agassiz.* United States Geological Survey Monograph No. 25. Washington, D.C.

Van Dyke, S., S. Hanna, W. Unfreed, and B. Neal
1990 *1989 Oldman River Dam Prehistoric Archaeology Mitigation Program, Campsites Component, Final Report.* A.S.A. Permit 89-25. Report prepared by Bison Historical Services Ltd. for Alberta Public Works, Supply and Services, Edmonton.

Van Dyke, S., and S. Stewart
1985 *Hawkwood Site (EgPm-179): A Multicomponent Prehistoric Campsite on Nose Hill.* Manuscript Series No. 7. Archaeological Survey of Alberta, Edmonton.

Vickers, J. R.
1986 *Alberta Plains Prehistory: A Review.* Archaeological Survey of Alberta, Occasional Paper No. 27. Edmonton.

Vickers, J. R., and A. B. Beaudoin
1989 A Limiting AMS Date for the Cody Complex Occupation at the Fletcher Site, Alberta, Canada. *Plains Anthropologist* 34:261–264.

Walker, E. G.
1984 The Graham Site: A McKean Cremation from Southern Saskatchewan. *Plains Anthropologist* 29(104):139–150.

Waters, M. R., and D. D. Kuehn
1996 The Geoarchaeology of Place: the Effect of Geological Processes on the Preservation and Interpretation of the Archaeological Record. *American Antiquity* 61(3):483–497.

Whitney, J. D.
1879 *The Auriferous Gravels of the Sierra Nevada.* Memoirs of the Museum of Comparative Zoology, Harvard College, Cambridge.

Wilmeth, R.
1968 A Fossilized Bone Artifact from Southern Alberta. *American Antiquity* 33:100–101.

Wilson, I. R.
1986 The Pink Mountain Site (HhRr1): an Early Prehistoric Campsite in Northeastern B.C. *Canadian Journal of Archaeology* 13:51–67.

1996 Paleoinidan Sites in the Vicinity of Pink Mountain. In *Early Human Occupation of British Columbia*, edited by R. L. Carlson and L. Dalla Bona, pp. 29–34. University of British Columbia Press, Vancouver.

Wilson, M. C.
1983a *Once Upon a River: Archaeology and Geology of the Bow River Valley at Calgary, Alberta, Canada.* Archaeological Survey of Canada Paper No. 114. Mercury Series. National Museum of Man, Ottawa.

1983b *Geological Influences on Archaeological Visibility in the Forty Mile Coulee Area, Alberta.* Report prepared for Ethos Consultants, Ltd. and Alberta Environment, Edmonton.

1984 Stalker Site (Taber Child Site) Investigations, Alberta. *Current Research in the Pleistocene* 1:27–29.

1986 Late Quaternary Landscape Modification in the Cochrane-Calgary Area of the Bow Valley and its Influence on Archaeological Visibility. In *Eastern Slopes Prehistory: Selected Papers*, edited by B. Ronaghan, pp. 63–90. Occasional Paper No. 3. Archaeological Survey of Alberta, Edmonton.

1990a Archaeological Geology in Western Canada: Techniques, Approaches, and Integrative Themes. In *Archaeological Geology of North America*, edited by N. P. Lasca and J. Donahue, pp. 61–86. Geological Society of America, Centennial Special vol. 4. Boulder.

1990b Geoarchaeology of DjPm-16, an Alberta/Cody Site in Southwestern Alberta [abstract]. In *Program and Abstracts*, pp. 66. 48th Plains Conference, Oklahoma City.

1990c Geoarchaeological Studies, People's Republic of China: The Cuijiaai Section Near Lanzhou, Gansu Province. *Current Research in the Pleistocene* 7:50–52.

1993a Radiocarbon Dating in the Ice-Free Corridor: Problems and Implications. In *The Palliser Triangle: A Region in Space and Time*, edited by R. W. Barendregt, M. C. Wilson, and F. J. Jankunis, pp. 165–206. Department of Geography, University of Lethbridge, Lethbridge.

1993b How the Pleistocene Extinctions Caused Clovis: An Essay on Event and Process, Cause and Effect. In *Culture and Environment: A Fragile Coexistence*, edited by R. W. Jamieson, S. Abonyi, and N. Mirau, pp. 85–92. Archaeological Association of the University of Calgary, Calgary.

1996 Late Quaternary Vertebrates and the Opening of the Ice-Free Corridor, With Special Reference to the Genus *Bison*. *Quaternary International* 32:97–105.

Wilson, M. C., and C. S. Churcher
1978 Late Pleistocene *Camelops* from the Gallelli Pit, Calgary, Alberta: Morphology and Geologic Setting. *Canadian Journal of Earth Sciences* 15(5):729–740.

1984 The Late Pleistocene Bighill Creek Formation and its Equivalents in Alberta: Correlative Potential and Vertebrate Palaeofauna. In *Correlation of Quaternary Chronologies*, edited by W. C. Mahaney, pp. 159–175. GeoBooks, Norwich, U.K.

Wilson, M. C., D. W. Harvey, and R. G. Forbis
1983 Geoarchaeological Investigations of the Age and Context of the Stalker (Taber Child) Site, DlPa-4, Alberta. *Canadian Journal of Archaeology* 7:179–207.

Wormington, H. M., and R. G. Forbis
1965 *An Introduction to the Archaeology of Alberta, Canada*. Denver Museum of Natural History, Proceedings 11. Denver.

Wright, G. F.
1893 *Man and the Glacial Period*. Kegan Paul, Trench, Trubner & Co., Ltd., London.

Wyckoff, D. G.
1989 Accelerator Dates and Chronology of the Packard Site, Oklahoma. *Current Research in the Pleistocene* 6:24–26.

Young, R. R., J. A. Burns, D. G. Smith, L. D. Arnold, and R. B. Rains
1994 A Single, Late Wisconsin, Laurentide Glaciation, Edmonton Area and Southwestern Alberta. *Geology* 22:683–686.

Zoltai, S. C., and D. H. Vitt
1990 Holocene Climatic Change and the Distribution of Peatlands in Western Interior Canada. *Quaternary Research* 33:231–240.

Prehistory of the Great Basin/Snake River Plain to about 8,500 Years Ago

Alan L. Bryan[1]
Donald R. Tuohy[2]

Abstract

A review of radiocarbon-dated sites in the Great Basin and adjacent regions indicates that there is no sound basis for differentiating Paleoindian from Archaic stages based either on economy or technology. Fluted points, including Clovis, are present in the "Greater" Great Basin between about 11,000 and 8500 yr B.P., but none have been found at mammoth or extinct bison kill sites, as on the Great Plains. Stemmed points are much more abundant in the Great Basin and much better dated, from before 11,000 to about 8000 yr B.P., by which time both earlier hafting traditions (fluted and stemmed) were being superseded by more efficiently hafted side-notched points without any significant changes in economy. Evidently, early humans before about 8500 yr B.P. used different techniques for hafting projectile points during prolonged and overlapping spans of time, so these two distinctive technological traditions cannot be used as horizon markers.

In view of the available dated evidence from the Great Basin, it is unwise to extrapolate a dated projectile point sequence from the Great Plains to the Great Basin in the attempt to establish a standardized pan-continental sequence of stages. The actual sequence for each region must be determined from locally dated evidence.

THE VAST AREA OF INTERNAL drainage aptly termed the Great Basin encompasses California east of the Sierra Nevada Range, all but the northern and southern fringes of Nevada, Utah west of the Wasatch Range, plus southeastern Oregon and portions of southeastern Idaho. Although the environmentally similar Snake River Plain of southern Idaho, as well as portions of northeastern California and most of south-central Oregon east of the Cascade volcanoes, are physiographically outside the Great Basin, cultural-historical similarities and relationships, especially during the critical time (ca. 14,000–8500 yr B.P.) of the Pleistocene/Holocene transition, allow inclusion within an expanded "greater" Great Basin region. These areas later became more differentiated culturally because of local economic adaptations to salmon runs up the Klamath and Snake rivers; but prior to about 8500 years ago, the period of time covered by this paper, the general hunting/gathering way of life apparently was essentially the same throughout the entire region, and occupants of the Great Basin evidently made regular forays farther north to obtain obsidian and ignimbrite (cf. Amick 1993; Jones and Beck 1990), and undoubtedly other goods, as well as spouses.

This overview of the evidence for human occupation of a large part of the Intermontane West south of the Columbia Basin will mention a few relevant sites along the Columbia River, but will exclude northern Idaho and most of the Columbia/Snake Basin because much of that region was either glaciated or scoured by catastrophic floods at the end of the Pleistocene, effectively destroying any evidence of earlier human occupation. However, the possibility of obtaining artifacts deeply buried under Spokane or Bonneville flood deposits should not be ignored. Cressman et al. (1960:65) reported that a basalt slab chopper, two retouched flakes, a small flaked implement with an expanding rounded head and a long shaft ending in a chisel-shaped bit, plus a milling stone fragment were recovered from below flood deposits by a geologist working at The Dalles dam site in Washington State. These artifacts should predate the last flood, which

1. Department of Anthropology, University of Alberta, Edmonton, Alberta, ABT6 G2H4, Canada.
2. Nevada State Museum, Carson City NV 89701

occurred about 13,000 years ago (Mullineaux et al. 1978).

Only in the Mojave Desert of southeastern California is there any indication of human occupation of the "greater" Great Basin region before about 20,000 years ago. The controversial evidence for human occupation of Calico Hills as much as 200,000 years ago (Simpson 1989; Simpson et al. 1986) will remain difficult for archaeologists to assess properly until a detailed descriptive geoarchaeological site report is published, giving exact stratigraphic provenience for definite artifacts described according to their method of manufacture. The evidence from wind-deflated sites like China Lake (Davis 1978) and Manix Lake (Simpson 1958) also is difficult for archaeologists to assess because only surface associations have been reported.

Alsoszatai-Petheo (1975) excavated the East Rim site, located on a ridge at the eastern base of the Yermo fan and above the highest level of Lake Mohave. Most artifacts, including thick bifaces, were embedded in the desert pavement on the wind-deflated surface; however, about 40 percent of the flaked lithics were recovered from a subsurface sandy stratum up to 20 cm thick. Most of the retouched artifacts were small flake tools, with projectile points absent. Datable organic material was lacking; however, pollen was found to be abundant in the sandy loam. Analysis of the pollen revealed an abundance of pine and freshwater marsh plants, which differs significantly from the modern pollen rain, but is nearly identical with the frequencies of taxa recovered from deposits dated 22,000 to 37,000 yr B.P. at the Tule Springs site.

The suggestive evidence from the Mojave Desert sites should stimulate a concerted search for buried sites in datable Pleistocene geological contexts to test the hypothesis that sites predating Clovis (>11,200 yr B.P.) exist in the Great Basin. However, as the data relevant to any claim for really early occupation of the Basin have not yet been thoroughly analyzed or published, this paper will be restricted to the period of time for which detailed published reports on excavated radiocarbon-dated contexts are available for evaluation.

The Problem of Determining a Cultural Sequence in the Great Basin

The problem of what economic adaptations were made to changing ecosystems by early occupants of the Basin (cf. the significant synthesis by Grayson 1993) is more important than the question of dating; however, the two problems are closely interrelated because of certain assumptions held by many archaeologists. Important published evidence of sites between 14,000 and about 10,000 years old, although supported by radiocarbon dates, has not been considered fully by many professional archaeologists. A primary reason for reluctance to consider certain dated evidence is that Basin archaeologists, working before many radiocarbon dates were locally available, had extrapolated a model from the better-dated projectile point sequence of the Great Plains and applied it to the Great Basin. As this model has long seemed reasonable, it has been maintained by most researchers. Extrapolation of the Great Plains sequence, which distinguishes an earlier "Paleoindian" period or stage of economic development characterized by specialized big game hunting, has led to the equation of Paleoindian in the Basin with fluted points, which have been found scattered throughout the region, with concentrations on the edges of now-extinct lakes (Beck and Jones 1997; Grayson 1993:238; Titmus and Woods 1988; Tuohy 1985:15–18, 1986:2–7; Warren and Phagan 1988; Willig 1988, 1990; Willig and Aikens 1988).

It has been recognized tacitly by all archaeologists that there is no actual evidence to support the assumption that specialized big game hunting was ever a dominant economic activity in the Great Basin. Nevertheless, an early Paleoindian period, characterized by fluted points, and a late Paleoindian period (sometimes confusingly referred to as the Initial Archaic), characterized by stemmed points (often identified as Plano varieties, thereby suggesting a Great Plains origin), are assumed to predate the early Archaic period, which was established about 8000 yr B.P. with the appearance of large side-notched points, which presumably came from east of the Rocky Mountains, where they definitely are dated earlier.

It is the position of this paper that all assumptions relevant to the span of time covered by the Paleoindian and early Archaic concepts should be set up as working hypotheses subject to confirmation, refutation, or modification using actual data available within the Great Basin, instead of maintaining a model based on evidence found elsewhere. For instance, consideration of radiocarbon-dated sites containing projectile points earlier than about 8,500 years ago will be used to suggest an alternative model of early Great Basin prehistory which casts doubt on whether Paleoindian and Archaic really are valid concepts, either as economic stages or as time periods, at least in the Great Basin.

Simms' (1988) analytic essay also questions whether it is useful to try to maintain the arbitrary distinction between Paleoindian and Archaic in the Great Basin. He further argues that there were ongoing "frequency shifts" in the use of alternative adaptive strategies that incorporated shifts in use of different technologies and tool types in different time periods and in different ecological settings (Simms 1988:47). Simms' model would explain the evidence for contemporaneous use of various projectile point styles and hafting techniques, as well as lend support to our contention that projectile point hafting traditions should not be used as period markers. We agree with Willig (1988, 1990) that available evidence suggests a general hunting/gathering economic base exploiting a wide variety of habitats was always present in the Basin.

Our alternative model will suggest that because a general hunting/gathering economic base has always been present in the Basin, there is no economic basis for distinguishing Archaic from Paleoindian. Furthermore, as all major projectile point traditions were used in the region during overlapping spans of time (Fluted from about 11,000 to 8500; Stemmed from 12,000 to after 8000; with the ultimately dominant Notched-Point tradition beginning by 8,000 years ago), there is not even a technological basis for distinguishing Archaic from Paleoindian. Many other correlated changes in technology and economy should be present in order to define a new period or stage.

We agree that the term "Paleoarchaic" suggested by Beck and Jones (1997) is a reasonable compromise to use for all cultural entities present during the terminal Pleistocene/early Holocene transition period in the "greater" Great Basin. Actually, this paper, an early version of which was presented several years earlier, should be read as a supplement to Beck and Jones' much more comprehensive survey of the TP/EH period in the Basin. A major difference between the two papers is that Beck and Jones conservatively follow the "Clovis-first" model. They believe that the earliest evidence for human occupation in the Basin is of makers of fluted points that they assume were first used in the Basin about 11,500 yr B. P., and therefore they explain away all dates on stemmed points earlier than 11,200 yr B. P. Our thesis is that available dates indicate that stemmed points were already used in the Basin before fluted points arrived from the east about 11,000 yr B. P. We contend that a dated point sequence on the Great Plains should not be extrapolated to the Basin; also that available dates within the "greater" Great Basin indicate that stemmed points were in use before 11,500 yr B. P. More fundamentally, we contend that archaeologists should not allow any model, no matter how generally accepted it has become, to dictate what data are to be accepted and what are to be rejected.

The following review of available evidence will show that radiocarbon dates indicate that both early hafting traditions were used in the Intermontane West during overlapping spans of time. Clearly, as these broadly defined hafting traditions were both used for prolonged periods of time, they cannot be used as horizon markers to define sequent periods in the Great Basin. Even the innovation of side-notched points about 8000 yr B.P. is inadequate to define the onset of the Archaic simply because a new, more efficient tie-around hafting technique quickly replaced the other two techniques (fluted to fit onto split-stick hafts and stemmed to fit into sockets). We agree with Musil (1988) that innovation of the notching technique, evidently derived from the Eastern Woodlands, made both earlier hafting techniques obsolete; but we disagree with his conclusion that stemmed points had previously replaced fluted points simply because a socketed haft is more efficient than a split-stick haft. Musil does make an important distinction between contracting-sided stemmed points and parallel-sided stemmed points, which are usually shouldered for hafting onto still-efficient split sticks. Shouldered points with parallel-sided stems (e. g., Scottsbluff, Eden, and Alberta on the Plains) appear to have been a somewhat later, more efficient amalgam of the split-stick and socketed hafting techniques. Evidently experimental flintknappers incorporated the advantages of both earlier methods when they created shouldered points with parallel sides and straight bases. Available dates suggest that this innovation first occurred west of the Continental Divide.

What characterizes the Great Basin during the Pleistocene/Holocene transition and sets it aside from the contemporary Paleoindian period on the Great Plains, which has become characterized by mammoth and bison kill sites, is that the many intermontane basins within the Great Basin show extensive signs of utilization and settlement, but little or no evidence of megamammal kills. Though the adjacent mountain range areas also saw some utilization, the lowlands within the basins, the lake terraces and other lake features, show extensive use by prehistoric humans, who left a whole host of lithic artifacts on and near the lakeshores, including many different styles of projectile points. These artifact configurations changed through time in conformance with lake-level changes. Unfortunately, most of these configurations lie on the surface, and rarely have been found in datable stratigraphic contexts. An economic adaptation to the presence of an existing shallow freshwater lake and the bioresources available in and around it clearly was the most important factor to the organization of the annual round followed by early prehistoric occupants of the Great Basin.

Jennings' (1957) concept of a "Desert Archaic" stage, with people adapted to an annual round that allowed them to utilize a wide spectrum of plant and animal resources, was based upon abundant ethnographic and archaeological evidence for effective seasonal hunting/gathering economic adaptations to lakeshore and marsh environments in various parts of the Basin. Available evidence indicates that this flexible adaptation by small groups, who wandered widely wherever the resources were seasonally most abundant, appears to have always been the most effective way to make a living in the Great Basin.

The widely accepted assumption that there was a significant change in basic economic adaptation during the critical Pleistocene/Holocene transition in the Great Basin has never been set up as a testable hypothesis. The available archaeological record does not reveal any major change in economic orientation in the Great Basin until the end of the early Holocene, about 7500 yr B.P., by which time both fluted and stemmed points had given way to the more efficient notched points. Although it is possible, there is as yet no actual evidence that the makers of fluted points actively hunted mammoths in the Great Basin. The reason for this situation may be that the most drastic changes in environment and consequent economic adaptations to those changes previously had occurred when the lakes abruptly began to dry up about 13,000 years ago (Bryan 1988:70; Scott et al. 1983). Freshwater lakes have long existed in all parts of the Great Basin, although most previously fresh lakes now are salty or alkali playas. Mammoth remains have been found on these playas (Tuohy 1968). One, a mammoth excavated in the Black Rock Desert and dated about 11,000 yr B.P., may have died after becoming trapped in a well it had dug for fresh water (Clewlow 1983). Perhaps a more significant change was the reduction of territory occupied by migratory bison herds dependent upon secure and abundant sources of fresh water. As the Pleistocene lakes dried up in the Basin, more abundant water on the Snake River Plain probably forced the larger herds to stay in the north, or to seek higher ground, as they did on the Colorado Plateau (Copeland and Fike 1988:5–28). Humans occupying the Basin during the waning stages of the Pleistocene were forced to adapt their economy to reliable sources of fresh water along streams and especially lakes, which fluctuated greatly in area, depth, and salinity between 13,000 and 9,000 years ago as the region became more desiccated. When at their maximum extent, the larger lakes, Lahontan and Bonneville, with their many inlets and islands, would have hindered long-distance movement by pedestrians. But freshwater lakes of all sizes created productive environments where early humans were able to adapt their economy to utilize locally available land mammals, waterfowl, fish, and edible plants more effectively.

The terminal Pleistocene/early Holocene cultural adaptation to this lacustrine/montane ecosystem has often been referred to as the Western Pluvial Lakes tradition, a term introduced by Bedwell (1973). An easily recognizable part of the technology utilized by the WPLT cultures are willow-leaf-shaped and stemmed points designed for insertion into socketed hafts. For convenience, all of these stemmed point types can be referred to as the Stemmed Point tradition (or the Great Basin or Western Stemmed Point tradition), with the recognition that several point styles belonging to discrete technological traditions were used by contemporary early hunter/gatherers in the "greater" Great Basin. Whether or not these different point styles were used by humans belonging to different cultural traditions remains to be determined. In fact, a strong case has been made that what archaeologists recognize as stemmed projectile points also might have served other purposes (Beck and Jones 1993, 1997). If so, this is another good reason why stemmed points should not be considered as horizon markers.

Another characteristic of the WPLT technological repertoire are crescents. Although found most often along lake shores and on now-dry lake bottoms, stemmed points (but not crescents) also have been excavated from radiocarbon-dated contexts in Fort Rock, Danger, Wilson Butte, Handprint, and Smith Creek caves. Several of these and other sites yielding stemmed points are located in montane settings far above the lake basins, so it no longer seems appropriate to associate the Stemmed Point tradition with an economic adaptation only to lake shores (cf. Grayson 1993:243). Evidently these people already had established an annual round that utilized resources found in several ecosystems, whereas the makers of fluted points seemed to have restricted their economic adaptation to the rich resources found along the edges of shallow lakes. Fluted points, belonging to the technological tradition recognizable as the Fluted Point tradition, frequently have been found in association with former lakes; but the only cave they reportedly have been recovered from is Danger Cave, which is located just above the Bonneville salt flats (Jennings 1957).

Fagan (1988) concluded from a detailed technological analysis of the Dietz site collection from the Alkali Lake basin in southeastern Oregon that the tool kits and manufacturing techniques used to make Western Clovis and stemmed points were strikingly different. His analysis indicates that two quite different groups used the Dietz site at different times, and, at least at Alkali Lake, it refutes an alternative hypothesis that both technological traditions were used by the same cultural group for different purposes. Unfortunately, as all diagnostic artifacts were found on the surface at the Dietz site, there was no direct way to date the two discrete assemblages, either absolutely or relatively. Because the 105 fluted points were found concentrated on the desiccated playa, while the 47 stemmed points were recovered from a higher terrace of an active lake, the possibility was considered that the fluted points were younger. However, it is known that there were several wet periods followed by desiccation; and the authors state that there were other reasons to believe that the fluted points predated the stemmed points at the site. We have no quarrel with the evidence presented that the occupation of Alkali Lake by the makers of fluted points preceded occupations by the makers of stemmed points. Willig (1988) presents detailed justification for concluding that the fluted point assemblage is earlier than the stemmed point assemblages at the Dietz site, although this proposed sequence should be confirmed by radiocarbon dating of stratigraphic contexts at the site itself, as Willig (1990) indicated would be attempted. Our objection is with the attempt to extrapolate relative time for the two hafting traditions (Fluted and Stemmed, each of which includes several point styles) from the Great Plains to the entire Great Basin, and thereby create two sequent "eras" at the Dietz site (Willig 1990).

An early Paleoindian period was extrapolated to the Basin; and the Clovis period at the Dietz site was thereby dated to between about 11,500 and 11,000 yr B.P., which preceded the Stemmed period (Willig 1990; Willig and Aikens 1988). It should be noted that Haynes et al. (1984) previously had redated classic Clovis sites on the Plains and in Arizona to a more limited time horizon between 11,200 and 10,900 yr B.P., so logically this more constricted time frame should be applied to the Great Basin as well. A sequence from early Paleoindian (identified by fluted points) to late Paleoindian, characterized by Plano (stemmed) types, means that all stemmed points in the Great Basin must therefore date to after 10,900 yr B.P.

Such a procedure requires acceptance of certain assumptions, not all of which have been stated by Willig (1988, 1990; Willig and Aikens 1988). These assumptions are:

(1) That Clovis fluted points were the earliest North American projectile points;

(2) That all fluted points therefore can be used as period markers that precede all other point traditions;

(3) That a technological or cultural sequence should be the same in quite different environmental regions, even if economic adaptations to fundamentally different ecosystems might have been quite different;

(4) That Plains Plano point types (many of which, especially Agate Basin and Hell Gap, are quite similar in shape to certain Great Basin stemmed point styles) somehow evolved from Clovis fluted points. It usually is assumed that these developments occurred on the Great Plains, although Carlson (1988) has suggested that the changes might have occurred in the Intermontane West;

(5) That the Stemmed Point cultural tradition rapidly and completely replaced the Fluted Point cultural tradition in the Great Basin about 10,900 years ago;

(6) That the Great Basin stemmed point series, which includes at least eight defined morphological point types (cf. Beck and Jones 1993, 1997), also can be used to define a period marker in the Great Basin. Willig (1990) states that the "Clovis Era" was from about 11,500 to 11,000, while the "Stemmed Era" lasted from 11,000 to 7,000 yr B.P.;

(7) That one cultural group using a similar hunting technology with no proven advantages over that used by others can quickly and completely displace another hunting/gathering culture that had long been well-adapted to its ecosystem. (The only recorded examples of rapid replacement of one culture by another that

we know of involve the introduction of significant major technoeconomic innovations, such as farmers displacing foragers or people with firearms replacing people with spears and arrows); and

(8) That all dated evidence that does not support these untested assumptions, the replacement model based upon these assumptions, or the related "Clovis first" model, which assumes that Clovis hunters were the first Americans, are controversial and for this reason can be ignored or explained away.

Radiocarbon-Dated Evidence for Fluted and Stemmed Points in the Basin

ALTHOUGH FLUTED POINTS have proved to be fairly common surface finds on alluvial fans, at springs, along streams, and especially on lake and marsh shorelines (Tuohy 1985, 1986; Willig 1988), they have been excavated from dated contexts at only five sites in the "greater Great Basin." In our opinion, few of these fluted points are really classic Clovis, although most do fall within the great range of variation found at Clovis sites farther east. Most fluted points found in the Basin therefore have been classified as "Western Clovis" (Willig 1990). They are called Clovis because the flute flakes were removed last in the production sequence (thus excluding Folsom technology, in which long flutes were removed first), and the flute is at least one-fourth the length and one-third the width of the point (cf. Warren and Phagan 1988:121). The Sunshine locality (see Figure 1 for all site locations mentioned in the text) in eastern Nevada yielded a fluted point about 20 cm below charcoal dated 10,320 ± 50 yr B. P. A stemmed point was found in possible association with Camelops in another part of the site that yielded dates between 10,200 and 10,710 yr B.P.

Excavations that produced many stemmed points in Connley Cave #5, near Fort Rock, Oregon, in the extreme northwest corner of the Great Basin, also yielded a fluted point above a level dated 9540 ± 260 yr B.P. (Bedwell 1973:146, Figure 43, Plate 14). The Henwood site in the Mojave Desert near Barstow, California, yielded a fluted point in clear association with two Lake Mohave points and a hearth dated to 8470 ± 370 yr B.P. (Warren and Phagan 1988:123). Two fluted points reportedly were recovered from Danger Cave in deposits that produced many stemmed points (Holmer 1986:94–95; Willig and Aikens 1988:15). David Madsen (personal communication

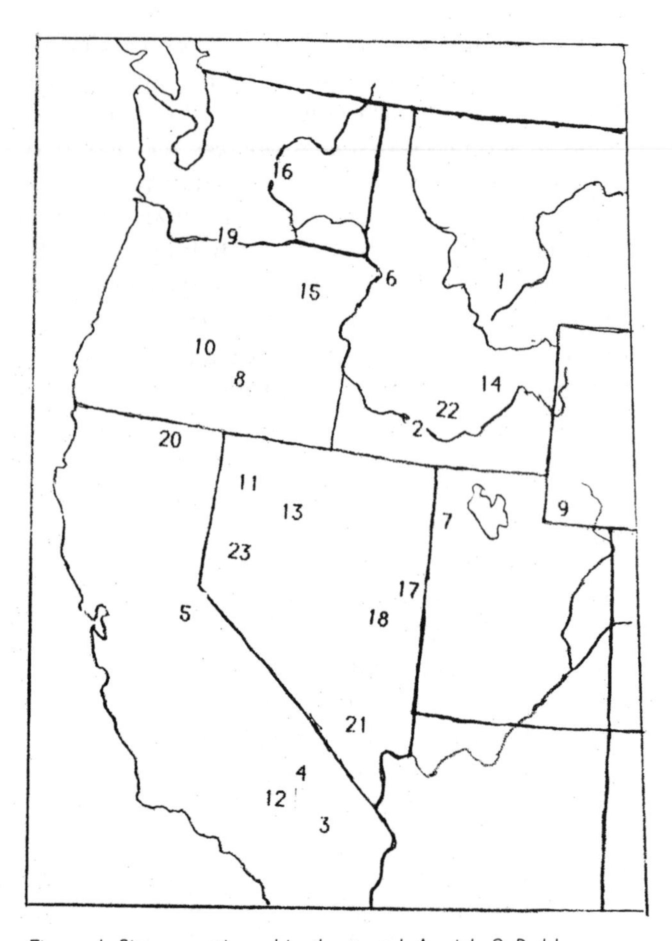

Figure 1. Sites mentioned in the text. 1. Anzick. 2. Buhl. 3. Calico. 4. China Lake. 5. Clark's Flat. 6. Cooper's Ferry. 7. Danger Cave. 8. Dietz. 9. Fenn Clovis Cache. 10. Fort Rock Cave. 11. Handprint Cave. 12. Henwood. 13. Old Humboldt. 14. Owl Cave (Wasden). 15. Pilcher Creek. 16. Richey/Roberts Cache. 17. Smith Creek Cave. 18. Sunshine. 19. The Dalles Damsite. 20. Tule Lake. 21. Tule Springs. 22. Wilson Butte Cave. 23. Wizard's Beach. This map is a duplicate of the map included in Samuel G. Houghton's book A Trace of Desert Waters: The Great Basin Story, published by the Arthur C. Clark Company, Glendale, California, p. 256. It was modified to suit the facts of our paper.

1990, 1991) has concluded from his re-excavations that Danger Cave was not occupied before about 10,500 yr B.P.; the three charcoal dates earlier than 11,000 yr B.P. obtained from the lowest levels were always a puzzle because of the lack of associated extinct fauna (Jennings 1957). At the undated Old Humboldt site in the Lahontan Basin, western Nevada, several stemmed and one fluted point fragment were recovered with remains of modern bison from a 30-cm-thick alluvium that was deposited sometime between 7,000 and 11,000 years ago (Dansie 1984; Davis and Rusco 1987).

The Wasden site (also known as Owl Cave), on the eastern Snake River Plain in Idaho, is the only site where fluted points and associated flute flakes have been recovered from a dated context with extinct fauna (mammoth) anywhere west of the Continental Divide, except in southeastern Arizona. The three broken Owl Cave points are technologically more Folsom-like than Clovis, so the site is an exception to the rule that only Clovis points are associated with mammoths (Miller and Dort 1978). Although the points are too large to be typical Folsom, the technique of manufacture (long and broad single flutes removed before lateral retouch) is recognizably Folsom (Miller and Dort 1978). Soon after discovery of associated mammoth bones, the collagen fraction of those bones yielded two dates—12,250 ± 200 (WSU-1259) and 12,850 ± 150 yr B.P. (WSU-1281)—but several years later another collagen date of 10,920 ± 150 yr B.P. (WSU-1786) was run at the same laboratory with more refined pretreatment. More recently, an AMS date on charcoal from the base of the mammoth layer yielded a date of 10,640 ± 85 yr B.P. (AA-6833) (Susanne Miller, personal communication 1995), which seems to establish the time of occupation at Owl Cave to between 10,900 and 10,600 yr B.P., immediately after the heyday of Clovis mammoth hunters on the Great Plains.

Even farther north, across the Continental Divide in south-central Montana, the Anzick burial, associated with an assemblage of Clovis artifacts (Jones and Bonnichsen 1994), has yielded six AMS dates ranging from 10,240 to 10,940 yr B.P. on specific amino acids extracted from the ocher-stained calvarium (Stafford 1994:Table 4). Only the latter date is within the 10,900–11,200 range of dates for Clovis mammoth kills.

Classic Clovis points have never been recovered from radiocarbon-dated contexts in the Great Basin. In fact, after studying the Dietz points, which are quite similar to Clovis, Willig (1988) suggested that all fluted points are western variants of Clovis; and that they all may be slightly later in time than Clovis on the High Plains. If most western fluted points developed from the earlier classic Clovis form, there is no reason to reject the later radiocarbon dates, as long as these non-Clovis fluted forms are recognized as part of a technological tradition that evidently persisted much later west of the Rockies than on the central High Plains. Certainly, available evidence does not support the hypothesis that fluted points defined as Western Clovis were used in the Basin during the same limited span of time (11,200–10,900 yr B.P.) that mammoth hunters are known to have used Clovis points on the Great Plains and in southeastern Arizona (Haynes 1980, 1984). If so, it is no longer proper to extrapolate a dated temporal range from the Plains and apply them to surface finds in the Basin. Actual dates indicate that fluted points were used in the "greater Great Basin" between about 11,000 and 8500 yr B.P., so they do not make a good period marker. The Fluted Point tradition should not, therefore, be considered a cultural tradition, but rather a technological tradition that spanned a significant amount of time in the Basin.

Nevertheless, when more dates become available, it is possible that truly classic Clovis may yet prove to be a horizon marker, even in the Great Basin and the Pacific Northwest. That this might be so is suggested by the cache of spectacular classic Clovis points and other artifacts excavated from the Richey-Roberts site, near Wenatchee on the Columbia River of eastern Washington. Although undated, one of these artifacts has Glacier Peak volcanic ash adhering to its underside. Glacier Peak last exploded about 11,250 yr B.P., leading Mehringer and Foit (1990) to conclude the artifacts were laid on the ash soon after.

Another association of a projectile point with Glacier Peak ash has been reported from the Pilcher Creek site, northeastern Oregon (Brauner 1985). Though this is a stemmed point, identified as Windust, it was found embedded in redeposited but pure Glacier Peak ash, so it also should date to soon after 11,250 yr B.P. Several other stemmed points were excavated at the Pilcher Creek site.

The Stemmed Point tradition also should be recognized as a technological tradition and not a cultural tradition or a period marker. Stemmed points frequently have been found in contexts radiocarbon dated between 11,000 and 8500 yr B.P., and three sites contain stemmed points in contexts dated earlier than 11,000 yr B.P. Evidence was marshaled by Bryan (1980) to show that stemmed points originated west of the Continental Divide between about 12,000 and 10,500 years ago, and that they began to spread east onto the Great Plains about 10,800 yr B.P., where they are known as Plano points. Plano forms stratigraphically overlie fluted points at several sites on the Plains.

The hypothesis that fluted points were an important part of a discrete "Clovis Culture" (Haynes 1980) has been questioned by Young and Bonnichsen (1985), who concluded from analyses of flaking patterns that Clovis points from Montana (Anzick) and Maine must have been made by different societies utilizing quite different traditional flaking grammars. This interpretation implies that the idea of making fluted points was diffused throughout North America to many already-established societies, rather than distributed by a single, rapidly migrating society. Refutation of the hypothesis of a single continent-wide Clovis culture would make it clear that fluting, stemming, and notching should be considered first of all as functional parts of effective methods for hafting projectile points. Any assumption that such forms can then be used for identifying prehistoric cultures must be set up as working hypotheses subject to testing by analysis of flaking technologies, as Fagan (1988) has done for the Dietz site collection. If the idea of fluting was adopted by many different societies that applied their own traditional flaking techniques to create the fluted form identifiable as Clovis, the generally accepted assumption is weakened that the earliest projectile points in North America were necessarily Clovis.

Setting up this generally accepted basic premise as a hypothesis rather than simply assuming it to be true makes it clear that many archaeologists are troubled by a significant body of available radiocarbon-dated data that does not support the widely held assumption that fluted points were the first throughout North America, and that all stemmed points must be later; plus the correlated assumption that stemmed points somehow evolved from fluted points (Carlson 1988; Willig 1990; Willig and Aikens 1988). In order to extrapolate from the Great Plains record the assumption that early Paleoindians used only fluted points in the Great Basin, it becomes necessary to ignore or explain away all radiocarbon dates from sites in the Great Basin dated earlier than 11,000 yr B.P. because all of those radiocarbon dates pertain to contexts containing only Great Basin Stemmed points.

Although Danger Cave, Utah has yielded two dates earlier than 11,000 yr B.P. for strata yielding stemmed points (Jennings 1957), we await Madsen's report on his re-excavations to clarify the chronological situation at that site. Three other sites yielding stemmed points have been dated earlier than 11,000 yr B.P. The basal occupation of Fort Rock Cave, Oregon, yielded a date of 13,200 ± 720 yr B.P. (GaK-1738), reportedly associated with an assemblage containing a short-stemmed point and a concave-based point, in addition to scrapers and a mano (Bedwell 1973). We agree that this exceptionally early date should be verified. Wilson Butte Cave was re-excavated in 1988–89 by Ruth Gruhn and Alan Bryan, and the report will be ready for publication in 1999. One complete and several stemmed point bases came from the lower part of the gray-brown sand (Stratum C) in apparent association with extinct fauna (horse and camel, plus unidentified bovid [muskox?] and proboscidean [mammoth?]); and radiocarbon dates on charcoal or bone that range between 9000 and 16,000 yr B.P. A piece of ivory (presumably mammoth tusk) yielded an AMS date of 10,700 ± 100 yr B.P. (TO-3330), which correlates well with the Owl Cave dates for mammoth. Obsidian hydration dates on five stemmed point fragments from Stratum C ranged from 8391 ± 326 to 5949 ± 275 yr B.P. Two other stemmed points yielded obsidian hydration dates of 14,600 ± 402 yr B.P. and 13,657 ± 389 yr B.P. (Gruhn 1995). Of course, these dates must be confirmed by radiocarbon, but other obsidian hydration dates on other point typers are as expected, so these dates should not be automatically rejected. The nearby Buhl burial, associated with a stemmed point and an eyed bone needle, yielded an AMS date of 10,675 ± 95 yr B.P. (Beta 43055 and ETH 7729) (Wisner 1992).

The stratigraphy at Smith Creek Cave, eastern Nevada, is very clear, and the associated assemblage of 324 artifacts is exceptionally well dated (Bryan 1979). The earliest Mount Moriah occupation layer has yielded dates of 11,680 ± 160 yr B.P. (Tx-1421) on charcoal and 12,150 ± 120 (Birm-752) on wood, plus AMS dates of 12,060 ± 450 (RIDDL-797) on camelid hair, 10,840 ± 250 (RIDDL-795) on bovid hair, and 10,420 ± 100 (TO-1173) on a piece of cordage. All these materials were associated directly with a lithic assemblage, including stemmed point bases (unbroken Mount Moriah points appear to have been willow-leaf-shaped) and many scrapers and gravers (Bryan 1979, 1988). The archaeological data indicate that the cave was occupied occasionally between 12,000 and 10,000 years ago by sheep hunters who rearmed their broken points and dehaired hides with scrapers. Willig and Aikens (1988:Table 3) list only the six dates ranging from 9940 to 11,140 yr B.P. on intrusive hearths excavated from a later Mount Moriah occupation into the main occupation layer. They simply do not list the above dates from the main occupation layer, as most do not support their contention that all Great Basin Stemmed points must be less than 11,000 years old. Their refusal to accept earlier dates was followed by Beck and Jones (1997:183). Similarly, Mead et al. (1982) and Thompson (1985) had attempted to show that all archaeological dates older than 11,000 yr B.P. from Smith Creek Cave somehow must be wrong because five dates (ranging from 10,450 to 13,340 yr B.P.) had been obtained on the macrofossil contents of woodrat middens located in niches in the cave wall above the area of human occupation. Thompson argued that as all of the woodrat middens contained macrofossils of bristlecone pine, which were not found in the Mount Moriah or any later occupation zone, the biological dates are correct but the archaeological dates must be too old. Bryan (1988) has shown, by reference to his original report (Bryan 1979), that the bristlecone pine remains in the woodrat middens almost certainly had been redeposited from a thin layer of bristlecone remains onto the contemporary surface of the cave. Bristlecone needles and twigs from this stratum, excavated from beneath an interesting sterile layer which underlies the Mount Moriah occupation zone, have produced four consistent dates—12,600 ± 170 (A-1565), 12,610 ± 80 (TO-1176), 12,950 ± 70 (TO-1175), and 13,020 ± 90 (TO-1177)—which overlap with Thompson's woodrat midden dates, but not with the dates from the overlying Mount Moriah occupations. A large portion of the bristlecone layer contained a void created by ground squirrels, which removed this relatively loose material in order to build nests and runways. These removed bristlecone remains were not found on the present surface of the cave, nor in any of the occupation layers. The most likely explanation for the mystery of the missing bristlecone remains is that woodrats incorporated into their "houses" the useful and readily available bristlecone pine twigs and needles that had been redeposited on the surface by ground squirrels.

Thompson (Mead et al. 1982; Thompson 1985; Thompson and Mead 1982) assumed that the woodrats had collected the bristlecone remains from the living ecosystem outside the cave, so he dated identifiable macrofossils extracted from the woodrat middens, including the bristlecone remains, and used them to define the local paleoenvironment during the dated span of time. The discrepancy between the biological and the archaeological sets of data, particularly the radiocarbon dates, is most parsimoniously explained by the hypothesis that relatively recent woodrats had incorporated into their "houses" ancient but perfectly preserved plant macrofossils, thus skewing the apparent age of the woodrat middens and their environmental interpretation. This hypothesis can be refuted readily by dating only what the woodrats actually ate—as represented by their feces, which is the material normally used to date woodrat middens.

Another early, dated stemmed point site is Handprint Cave, overlooking the Black Rock Desert, where a slightly shouldered point (looking like a small Scottsbluff) was found in cave sediments associated with a true blade, bovid hair, and charcoal dated 10,740 ± 70 yr B.P. (Bryan 1988:Figure 1; Gruhn and Bryan 1988). This beautifully pressure-flaked, square-based shouldered point (a form often found on Black Rock playas) evidently was placed beneath a stalagmite decorated with a panel of pictographs of handprints deep within the cave. We hypothesize that this square-based point form may have precipitated development of the later Scottsbluff Planotype on the Plains.

The assumption that the Fluted Point tradition occurred in the Great Basin only during the Clovis occupation of the High Plains (limited to 11,200–10,900 yr B.P.) has never been demonstrated. Available dates indicate that fluted and stemmed points were both present in the Intermontane West by 11,000 yr B.P. and persisted until after 9000 yr B.P., and therefore that the two traditions ran parallel courses. Apparently both stemmed and fluted points and associated hafting techniques (respectively socketed and split-stick or beveled foreshafts) were alternative technological traditions used by contemporary residents of the region for several millennia. Did residents of the Great Basin use both methods of hafting for different purposes, or were there different cultural groups occupying the same region during an overlapping span of time? This question is analogous to the classic Binford–Bordes dialectic regarding the various Mousterian assemblages of southwestern France (v. discussion in Phillips 1980:49–50). The Binfords' hypothesis that the same people used different assemblages of tools for different purposes generally has been favored over Bordes' original hypothesis that different tribes occupied the same region. In the Basin, as was done in France, the two possibilities should be set up as working hypotheses subject to further testing. Available evidence, which suggests that the distribution of fluted points is quite different from the distribution of stemmed points, favors the hypothesis that different cultural groups occupied the Basin during an overlapping span of time; while the evidence from the Dietz site indicates that the two occupations there occurred at different times when lake levels were at different elevations (Fagan 1988; Willig 1988, 1990; however, see Beck and Jones 1997 for alternative arguments).

The possibility that different groups of people co-occupied the region for prolonged spans of time is supported by ethnographic evidence from the Great Basin, which indicates that later people did not occupy specific territories in precontact times. Rather, small groups of people moved without restriction from area to area wherever resources were most abundant, without fear of trespassing. In other words, food sharing actually promoted widespread movement. Several archaeologists have argued that this pattern of cyclic wandering by small family groups exploiting seasonal resources with a simple technology is a very old one in the Intermontane West (cf. discussion in Hanes 1988:7–9). Quite likely this efficient adaptation to a region containing scattered resources and consequently low population density was the most effective adaptive strategy for permanent residents of the region since initial human occupation.

We hold as a basic premise that available radiocarbon dates should not be ignored nor explained away in order to select evidence in support of a deductive model. Working inductively from available data, we have arrived at the working hypothesis that fluted and stemmed points both were present in the Intermontane West before 11,000 yr B.P. and persisted until after 9000 yr B.P., and that different small groups of people co-occupied the Great Basin for prolonged spans of time. We have mentioned two specific instances where excavated evidence indicates that this was true—in the northwestern corner of the Great Basin at Connley Cave #5, and at the Henwood site in the Mojave Desert. We also have presented supporting evidence from Nevada—at Smith Creek Cave (Bryan 1979, 1988) and the Old Humboldt site (Dansie 1984; Davis and Rusco 1987). There is no way to tell whether the stemmed points might have been earlier or later in time than the fluted point at the undated Old Humboldt site; but at Smith Creek Cave, the stemmed points definitely range between 12,000 and 10,000 yr B.P., encompassing the entire span of time that Clovis points are known to have been used by mammoth hunters on the Great Plains and in southeastern Arizona.

We would like to add three other radiocarbon-dated instances from just outside the Great Basin. At the Clark's Flat site, on the western flanks of the Sierra Nevada Range, many stemmed points were recovered from repeatedly dated deposits. Of particular interest is the lowest cultural stratum at the site, a buried paleosol that yielded two dates of 9170 ± 140 (Beta 13192) and 11,720 ± 145 (Beta 14299). The dates are in proper stratigraphic order (Peak et al. 1990:258, 506, Figures 3–4) so there is no inherent reason why both dates are not correct, but only the youngest date was deemed to be acceptable. The older date corroborates the dates on very similar point bases from Smith Creek Cave. An even more conclusive instance in support of the hypothesis that the Stemmed Point tradition was contemporary with Clovis comes from the Cooper's Ferry site on the lower Salmon River, west-central Idaho. The lowest occupation stratum yielded a charcoal date of 11,410 ± 130 yr B. P. A cache pit extending from that stratum contained four stemmed points associated with AMS dates of 11,370 ± 70 and 12,020 ± 170 yr B. P. (L. G. Davis and Sisson 1998; L. G. Davis, personal communication 1998). Just east of the Great Basin, in the area where Wyoming and Utah intersect, the Fenn Clovis cache includes a crescent, an artifact consistently associated with stemmed points on Great Basin playas (Frison 1991:Figure 2.13). Whether traded or picked up on the playa, the crescent originally must have belonged to contemporary or earlier people. The presence of this crescent also suggests the hypothesis that some makers of fluted points may have moved off the High Plains and Colorado Plateau seasonally to occupy productive Great Basin marshlands (or perhaps they were prehistoric "Snowbirds," moving out of the high country to a warmer place in the winter).

From these facts, we hypothesize that there were at least two technological traditions extant in the Great Basin from before 11,000 to after 9,000 years ago. Clovis, with its precise lithic tool kit made from carefully chosen materials, was not the only progenitor of New World cultures; and those archaeologists who have worked in South America are correct that the concept of "fluting" has become a shibboleth or a "password" for the earliest cultures in North and even South America (Mayer-Oakes 1984:231). It is time to replace the outdated "Clovis-first" concept with a less restrictive working hypothesis spawned and nurtured in the Great Basin of North America (cf. E. L. Davis 1978:73 for an earlier version of the co-tradition concept of fluted and stemmed points). Our model hypothesizes that the Stemmed Point tradition had a separate origin west of the Continental Divide, where these points are most common and where they have been dated as early as 12,000 yr B.P. At about the same time, the Fluted Point tradition originated east of the Continental Divide, where fluted points are more abundant (Faught et al. 1994:Figure 2), perhaps in the region of the Gulf of Mexico (Bonnichsen 1990; cf. Bryan 1991). Support for this hypothesis comes from several Clovis sites in the Eastern Woodlands that have provided earlier dates than on the Plains. For example, the deeply buried Johnson site, near Nashville, Tennessee (Wisner 1993), yielded one Clovis point, 25 fluted preforms, and hearths dated between 12,600 and 11,700 yr B.P. The "most acceptable" date of 11,950 ± 110 (Tx-7454) is earlier than western sites. Perhaps the earliest structures in North America were excavated at the Paleo Crossing Clovis site near Akron, Ohio. A charcoal sample from a posthole dated 12,250 ± 100 yr B.P., and an organic sample, said to be possibly noncultural, from the bottom of a cylindrical pit dated 13,100 ± 100 yr B.P. (Brose and Barrish 1992).

The Great Plains has provided evidence for a stratigraphic sequence of fluted points superseded by stemmed Plano points, and ultimately by notched points. This sequence, valid for the central Great Plains, should not be extrapolated either west or east of the Plains. Regional sequences must be determined from dated local sites.

Conclusions and Speculations

The first stemmed points may have been simple willow-leaf forms that fitted into socketed hafts as do ground bone rod projectile points. Our model states that there were multiple technological traditions and probably several cultural traditions at work to produce the earliest generally recognized North American cultures characterized by bifacial projectile points. The probable technological antecedents of these projectile point traditions are dealt with in separate papers (Bryan 1990, 1991, 1994; Bryan and Gruhn 1989).

We must admit that we do not know when people first entered the "greater Great Basin." Certainly it was not precisely 11,000 years ago as the "Clovis-first" model would maintain, although possibly soon afterwards Clovis points were used in the region. Evidence that people were present in the Mojave Desert 20,000 and more years ago should not be rejected out of hand, but rather should be critically examined by open-minded archaeologists, including graduate students pursuing thesis projects. Evidence from the Snake River Plain indicating that humans lived with extinct animals perhaps as early as 14,500 years ago in Wilson Butte Cave (Gruhn 1961, 1965) has received qualified support by re-excavations in the lower undisturbed portions of the cave. Nearby Kelvin's Cave (Meatte et al. 1988) has yielded flakes in association with extinct fauna, so further excavations in that lava tube are necessary. Wherever found, apparent associations between extinct fauna and cultural remains must be excavated with great care. For instance, north of Reno, Nevada, at Wizard's Beach on Pyramid Lake, suggestive evidence was found for the co-occurrence of extinct horse and camel with retouched flakes (Tuohy 1988). Specific amino acids recovered from an apparently associated camel bone yielded a weighted average AMS date of 25,470 ± 230 yr B.P. (Dansie et al. 1988:172–173). However, the authors caution that artifacts and fossils found associated on a modern deflated lake bed surface might possibly be from different periods. It is essential to search for deeply buried datable contexts. One promising area is Tule Lake, which straddles the Oregon/California border in the Klamath River drainage just west of the Great Basin. One of several wave-cut rockshelters on the western shore of this ancient playa yielded a date of 11,450 ± 340 yr B.P. on a hearth found 210 cm below surface (Beatton 1991). A small test pit yielded artifacts, including bifacially flaked fragments and bone tools, in conjunction with fish, bird, and mammal bones, and bone tools to a depth of 240 cm.

Some speculations might be offered as concluding tidbits. One reason why evidence for human occupation of the region earlier than about 12,000 years ago has been found only on the Snake River Plain and in the Mojave Desert may be correlated with restricted access from the Pacific Coast because of mountain glaciation during the Wisconsin maximum. If early humans first expanded down the Pacific Coast, as Gruhn (1988, 1994) has hypothesized, the first break in the glaciated cordilleras may well have been through the Columbia Gap transecting the Cascades, and thence up the Columbia and Snake rivers. The next break in Pleistocene glaciation would have been south of the Sierra Nevada Range over Tehachapi Pass, which leads directly into the Mojave Desert.

With a broader scope stimulated by this first World Conference on the Peopling of the Americas, the suggestion can be made that the appearance of bifacial lithic projectile points between about 18,000 and 11,000 years ago in various parts of temperate Eurasia and both the Americas was due to indigenous technological innovations by experimental flintknappers stimulated by parallel economic adaptations to locally available resources, and not to prolonged forced marches into uncharted territory by specialized big game hunters.

References Cited

Alsoszatai-Petheo, J. A.
1975 *The East Rim Site, California (SBCM 1803): An Early Western Lithic Co-tradition Site.* Unpublished M.A. thesis, Eastern New Mexico University, Portales.

Amick, D. S.
1993 Toolstone Use and Distribution Patterns of Western Pluvial Lakes Points from Southern Nevada. *Current Research in the Pleistocene* 10:49–51.

Beatton, J. M.
1991 Paleoindian Occupation Greater than 11,000 yr B.P. at Tule Lake, Northern California. *Current Research in the Pleistocene* 8:5–7.

Beck, C., and G. T. Jones
1993 The Multipurpose Function of Great Basin Stemmed Series Points. *Current Research in the Pleistocene* 10:52–54.

1997 The Terminal Pleistocene/Early Holocene Archaeology of the Great Basin. Journal of World Prehistory 11(2):161-236.

Bedwell, S. F.
1973 *Fort Rock Basin Prehistory and Environment.* University of Oregon Books, Eugene.

Bonnichsen, J.
1990 Searching for Sites in the Gulf of Mexico. *Mammoth Trumpet* 6(1):1, 4–5.

Brauner, D.
1985 *Early Human Occupation in the Uplands of the Southern Plateau: Archaeological Excavations at the Pilcher Creek Site, Union County, Oregon.* Department of Anthropology, Oregon State University, Corvallis.

Brose, D., and B. Barrish
1992 Investigations at Ohio Site Push Back Dates for Clovis. *Mammoth Trumpet* 7(4):1–3.

Bryan, A. L.
1979 Smith Creek Cave. In *Archaeology of Smith Creek Canyon*, edited by D. R. Tuohy and D. Rendall, pp. 162–251. Nevada State Museum Anthropological Papers, No. 17. Carson City.

1980 The Stemmed Point Tradition: An Early Technological Tradition in Western North America. In *Anthropological Papers in Memory of Earl H. Swanson, Jr.*, edited by L. B. Harten, C. N. Warren, and D. R. Tuohy, pp. 77–107. Special Publication of the Idaho State Museum of Natural History, Pocatello.

1988 The Relationship of the Stemmed and Fluted Point Traditions in the Great Basin. In *Early Human Occupation in Far Western North America: The Clovis–Archaic Interface*, edited by J. A. Willig, C. M. Aikens, and J. L. Fagan, pp. 53–74. Nevada State Museum Anthropological Papers, No. 21. Carson City.

1990 The Pattern of Late Pleistocene Cultural Diversity in Eurasia and the Americas. In *Chronostratigraphy of the Paleolithic in North, Central, East Asia and America*, pp. 3–8. Institute of History, Philology and Philosophy, Siberian Branch of the Academy of Sciences of the USSR. Novosibirsk.

1991 The Fluted Point Tradition in the Americas—One of Several Adaptations to Late Pleistocene American Environments. In *Clovis: Origins and Adaptations*, edited by R. Bonnichsen and K. L. Turnmire, pp. 15–33. Center for the Study of the First Americans, Oregon State University, Corvallis.

1994 Prehistory of North America. In *History of Humanity, Volume 1. Prehistory and the Beginnings of Civilization*, edited by S. J. De Laet, pp. 297–308. UNESCO, Paris; published by Routledge, London.

Bryan, A. L., and R. Gruhn
1989 The Evolutionary Significance of the American Lower Paleolithic. In *Homenaje a Josê Luis Lorenzo*, coordinated by Lorena Mirambell, pp. 88–101. Serie Prehistoria, Instituto Nacional de Antropologia e História, Mexico.

Carlson, R. L.
1988 The View from the North. In *Early Human Occupation in Far Western North America: The Clovis–Archaic Interface*, edited by J. A., Willig, C. M. Aikens, and J. L. Fagan, pp. 319–324. Nevada State Museum Anthropological Papers, No. 21. Carson City.

Clewlow, C. W., Jr.
1983 Report on 1981 and 1982 Archaeological Investig*ations at 26 Hu 8 and 26 Hu 55, Black Rock Desert, Nevada.* Ancient Enterprises, Santa Monica.

Copeland, J. M., and R. B. Fike
1988 Fluted Projectile Points in Utah. *Utah Archaeology* 1(1):5–28.

Cressman, L. S. and collaborators
1960 Cultural Sequences at The Dalles, Oregon. *Transactions of the American Philosophical Society*, n.s. 60(10).

Dansie, A. J.
1984 Archaeofaunas 26 PE 450 and 26 PE 366. In *Studies in Archaeology, Geology and Palaeontology at Rye Patch Reservoir, Pershing County, Nevada*, edited by M. K. Rusco and J. O. Davis, pp. 137–147. Nevada State Museum Anthropological Papers, No. 20. Carson City.

Dansie, A. J., J. O. Davis, and T. W. Stafford, Jr.
1988 The Wizard's Beach Recession: Farmdalian (25,500 yr. B.P.) Vertebrate Fossils Co-occur With Early Holocene Artifacts. In *Early Human Occupation in Far Western North America: The Clovis–Archaic Interface*, edited by J. A. Willig, C. M. Aikens, and J. L. Fagan, pp. 153–200. Nevada State Museum Anthropological Papers, No. 21. Carson City.

Davis, E. L.
1978 *The Ancient Californians. Rancholabrean Hunters of the Mojave Lakes Country.* Natural History Museum of Los Angeles County, Science Series 29. Los Angeles.

Davis, J. O., and J. K. Rusco
1987 The Old Humboldt Site: 26 Pe 670. In *Studies in Archaeology, Geology and Paleontology at Rye Patch Reservoir, Pershing County, Nevada*, edited by M. K. Rusco and J. O. Davis, pp. 41–69. Nevada State Museum Anthropological Papers, No. 20. Carson City.

Davis, L. G., and D. A. Sisson
1998 An Early Stemmed Point Cache from the Lower Salmon River Canyon of West-central Idaho. Current Research in the Pleistocene 15:12-13.

Fagan, J. L.
1988 Clovis and Western Pluvial Lakes Tradition Lithic Technologies at the Dietz Site in South-central Oregon. In *Early Human Occupation in Far Western North America: The Clovis–Archaic Interface*, edited by J. A. Willig, C. M. Aikens, and J. L. Fagan, pp. 389–416. Nevada State Museum Anthropological Papers, No. 21. Carson City.

Faught, M. K., D. G. Anderson, and A. Gisiger
1994 North American Paleoindian Database—An Update. *Current Research in the Pleistocene* 11:32–35.

Frison, G. C.
1991 *Prehistoric Hunters of the High Plains.* 2nd ed. Academic Press, San Diego.

Grayson, D. K.
1993 *The Desert's Past: A Natural Prehistory of the Great Basin.* Smithsonian Institution Press, Washington, D.C.

Gruhn, R.
1961 *The Archaeology of Wilson Butte Cave, South-central Idaho.* Occasional Papers of the Idaho State Museum, No. 6. Pocatello.

1965 Two Early Radiocarbon Dates from the Lower Two Levels of Wilson Butte Cave, South-central Idaho. *Tebiwa* 8(2):57.

1988 Linguistic Evidence in Support of the Coast Route of Earliest Entry into the New World. *Man* 23(1):77–100.

1994 The Pacific Coast Route of Initial Entry: An Overview. In *Method and Theory for Investigating the Peopling of the Americas*, edited by R. Bonnichsen and D. G. Steele, pp. 249–256. Center for the Study of the First Americans, Oregon State University, Corvallis.

1995 Results of New Excavations at Wilson Butte Cave, Idaho. *Current Research in the Pleistocene* 12:16–17.

Gruhn, R., and A. L. Bryan
1988 The 1987 Archaeological Fieldwork at Handprint Cave, Nevada. *Nevada Archaeologist* 6(2):1–13. Reno.

Hanes, R. C.
1988 *Lithic Assemblages of Dirty Shame Rock Shelter: Changing Traditions in the Northern Intermontane.* University of Oregon Anthropological Papers, No. 40. Eugene.

Haynes, C. V., Jr.
1980 The Clovis Culture. *Canadian Journal of Anthropology* 1:115–121.

Haynes, C. V., Jr., D. J. Donahue, A. J. Jull, and T. H. Zabel
1984 Application of Accelerator Dating to Fluted Point Paleo-Indian Sites. *Archaeology of Eastern North America* 12:184–191.

Holmer, R. N.
1986 *Common Projectile Points of the Intermountain West.* University of Utah Anthropological Papers, No. 110, pp. 89–115. Salt Lake City.

Jennings, J. D.
1957 *Danger Cave.* University of Utah Anthropological Papers, No. 27. Salt Lake City.

Jones, G. T., and C. Beck
1990 Chronological Studies of Paleoindian Surface Sites in Eastern Nevada. *Current Research in the Pleistocene* 7:75–77.

Jones, S., and R. Bonnichsen
1994 The Anzick Clovis Burial. *Current Research in the Pleistocene* 11:42–44.

Mayer-Oakes, W. J.
1984 Fluted Projectile Points: A North American Shibboleth Viewed in South American Perspective. *Archaeology of Eastern North America* 12:231–247.

Mead, J. I., R. S. Thompson, and T. R. Van Devender
1982 Late Wisconsinan and Holocene Fauna from Smith Creek Canyon, Snake Range, Nevada. *Transactions of the San Diego Society of Natural History* 20:1–26.

Meatte, D. S., G. L. Titmus, and J. C. Woods
1988 Initial Investigations at Kelvin's Cave (10-LN-93), Lincoln County, Idaho. Paper presented at the 21st Great Basin Anthropological Conference, Park City, Utah.

Mehringer, P. J., Jr., and F. F. Foit, Jr.
1990 Volcanic Ash Dating of the Clovis Cache at East Wenatchee, Washington. *National Geographic Research* 6:495–503.

Miller, S. J.
1989 Characteristics of Mammoth Bone Reduction at Owl Cave, the Wasden Site, Idaho. In *Bone Modification,* edited by R. Bonnichsen and M. H. Sorg, pp. 381–393. Center for the Study of the First Americans, University of Maine, Orono.

Miller, S. J., and W. Dort, Jr.
1978 Early Man at Owl Cave: Current Investigations at the Wasden Site, Eastern Snake River Plain, Idaho. In *Early Man in America From a Circum-Pacific Perspective,* edited by A. L. Bryan, pp. 129–139. Occasional Papers No. l, Department of Anthropology, University of Alberta, Edmonton.

Mullineaux, D. R., R. E. Wilcox, W. F. Ebaugh, R. Fryxell, and M. Rubin
1978 Age of the Last Major Scabland Flood of the Columbia Plateau in Eastern Washington. *Quaternary Research* 10:171–180.

Musil, P. P.
1988 Functional Efficiency and Technological Change: A Hafting Tradition Model for Prehistoric North America. In *Early Human Occupation in Far Western North America,* edited by J. A. Willig, C. M. Aikens, and J. L. Fagan, pp. 373–387. Nevada State Museum Anthropological Papers, No. 21. Carson City.

Peak, A. S., H. L. Crew, D. L. True, D. R. Tuohy, G. J. West, and C. V. Haynes
1990 *An Archaeological Data Recovery Project at CA-CAL-5352, Clark's Flat, Calaveras County, California.* Peak and Associates, Sacramento.

Phillips, P.
1980 *The Prehistory of Europe.* Indiana University Press, Bloomington.

Scott, W. E., W. D. McCoy, R. R. Shroba, and M. Rubin
1983 Reinterpretation of the Exposed Record of the Last Two Cycles of Lake Bonneville, Western United States. *Quaternary Research* 20:261–285.

Simms, S. R.
1988 Conceptualizing the Paleo-Indian and Archaic in the Great Basin. In *Early Human Occupation in Far Western North America: The Clovis–Archaic Interface,* edited by J. A. Willig, C. M. Aikens, and J. L. Fagan, pp. 41–52. Nevada State Museum Anthropological Papers, No. 21. Carson City.

Simpson, R. D.
1958 The Manix Lake Archaeological Survey. *Masterkey* 32(1):4–10.

1989 An Introduction to the Calico Early Man Site Lithic Assemblage. *San Bernardino County Museum Association Quarterly* 36(3):1–91.

Simpson, R. D., L. W. Patterson, and C. A. Singer
1986 Lithic Technology of the Calico Mountains Site, Southern California. In *New Evidence for the Pleistocene Peopling of the Americas,* edited by A. L. Bryan, pp. 89–105. Center for the Study of Early Man, University of Maine at Orono.

Stafford, T. W., Jr.
1994 Accelerator C-14 Dating of Human Fossil Skeletons Assessing Accuracy and Results on New World Specimens. In *Method and Theory in the Peopling of the Americas*, edited by R. Bonnichsen and G. Steele, pp. 45–55. Center for the Study of the First Americans, Oregon State University, Corvallis.

Thompson, R. S.
1985 The Age and Environment of the Mount Moriah (Lake Mohave) Occupation at Smith Creek Cave, Nevada. In *Environments and Extinctions: Man in Late Glacial North America*, edited by J. I. Mead and D. J. Meltzer, pp. 111–119. Center for the Study of Early Man, University of Maine at Orono.

Thompson, R. S., and J. I. Mead
1982 Late Quaternary Environments and Biogeography in the Great Basin. *Quaternary Research* 17:39–55.

Titmus, G., and J. C. Woods
1988 The Evidence of Paleoindian Occupation in Southern Idaho. Paper presented at the 41st Annual Northwest Anthropological Conference, Tacoma, WA.

Tuohy, D. R.
1968 Some Early Lithic Sites in Central Nevada. In *Early Man in Western North America*, edited by C. Irwin-Williams, pp. 27–38. Eastern New Mexico University Contributions in Anthropology 1(4). Portales.

1985 Notes on the Great Basin Distribution of Clovis Fluted and Folsom Projectile Points. *Nevada Archaeological Survey Reporter* 5(1):15–18. Carson City.

1986 Errata and Additional Notes on the Great Basin Distribution of Clovis Fluted and Folsom Projectile Points. *Nevada Archaeologist* 5(2):2–7. Carson City.

1988 Artifacts from the Northwestern Pyramid Lake Shoreline. In *Early Human Occupation in Far Western North America: The Clovis–Archaic Interface*, edited by J. A. Willig, C. M. Aikens, and J. L. Fagan, pp. 210–216. Nevada State Museum Anthropological Papers, No. 21. Carson City.

Warren, C. N., and C. Phagan
1988 Fluted Points in the Mojave Desert: Their Technology and Cultural Context. In *Early Human Occupation in Far Western North America: The Clovis–Archaic Interface*, edited by J. A. Willig, C. M. Aikens, and J. L. Fagan, pp. 121–130. Nevada State Museum Anthropological Papers, No. 21. Carson City.

Willig, J. A.
1988 Paleo-Archaic Adaptations and Lakeside Settlement Patterns at the Dietz Site in the Northern Alkali Basin, Oregon. In *Early Human Occupation in Far Western North America: The Clovis–Archaic Interface*, edited by J. A. Willig, C. M. Aikens, and J. L. Fagan, pp. 417–482. Nevada State Museum Anthropological Papers, No. 21. Carson City.

1990 Western Clovis Occupation at the Dietz Site, Northern Alkali Lake Basin, Oregon. *Current Research in the Pleistocene* 7:52–56.

Willig, J. A., and C. M. Aikens
1988 The Clovis–Archaic Interface in Far Western North America. In *Early Human Occupation in Far Western North America: The Clovis–Archaic Interface*, edited by J. A. Willig, C. M. Aikens, and J. L. Fagan, pp. 1–40. Nevada State Museum Anthropological Papers, No. 21. Carson City.

Wisner, G.
1992 Idaho Burial Suggests Life of Hardships. *Mammoth Trumpet* 7(2):1–2.

1993 Sites in Tennessee Suggest Clovis Originated in the East. *Mammoth Trumpet* 8(2):1, 6.

Young, D. E., and R. Bonnichsen
1985 *Stone Tools as Cultural Indicators.* Center for the Study of Early Man, University of Maine at Orono.

The Late Pleistocene Prehistory of the Northwestern Plains, the Adjacent Mountains, and Intermontane Basins

George C. Frison

Abstract

The late Pleistocene/early Holocene paleoecology of the Northwestern Plains and immediately adjacent areas reveals significant changes in climate and vegetation, along with the disappearance of many faunal species. Evidence for either a pre-Clovis or ancestral Clovis occupation in the area has yet to be provided. Clovis is the only cultural tradition with unequivocal evidence for mammoth procurement. Artifact caches now appear to have been an established part of the Clovis cultural system, although the true function of these caches remains in question.

Renewed interest in the Goshen cultural complex has resulted from the investigations at the Mill Iron site (24CT30) in southeast Montana. Radiocarbon dates and flaked stone technology suggest possible relationships of Goshen with both Clovis and Folsom. There also is a striking similarity between Goshen and Plainview flaked stone technology.

The cultural relationships between plains and foothill/mountain groups changed through time. Both Clovis and Folsom peoples obtained certain high-quality raw lithic materials at the higher elevations of the Rocky Mountains, but apparently were not utilizing local caves and rockshelters. For nearly two millennia following the Folsom occupation, there was an apparent separation between human groups living on the plains and those living in the foothill/mountain areas. The reasons for this may have been the result of ecological differences and mutually exclusive food-procurement systems between the two areas. At the beginning of the early Plains Archaic, at about 8,000 years ago, the cultural distinction between plains and foothill/mountain occupation disappears. These kinds of problems are developing rapidly into a fruitful area for future Paleoindian research.

Introduction

THE ECOLOGICAL SEPARATION between the Great Plains and the Rocky Mountains would appear to be simple and straightforward. However, defining distinct prehistoric ecological and cultural boundaries between the two regions is difficult, if not impossible, in the present geographic area of southern Montana, Wyoming, and the immediately contiguous parts of adjoining states. This is due largely to the physical geography of the region. Enclaves of plains environments are found along major rivers that flow through mountain ranges and in intermontane basins between mountain ranges. Limited areas of plains-like landforms occur at elevations close to timberline, often with open corridors to the plains below. Isolated uplifts are surrounded by the plains but they form islands of high-altitude environments. Rivers flowing from the mountains establish riparian environments in an otherwise strictly plains environment.

Since the area concerned straddles the Continental Divide (Figure 1), rivers drain to both the Pacific Ocean and the Gulf of Mexico. Mountain ranges that trend north to south trap much of the winter snow and summer rain, leaving many areas to the east of the Continental Divide in a rain shadow. For example, annual precipitation at Yellowstone Lake in Yellowstone National Park, at an elevation of 2,356 m, today averages about 45 cm, while in the Bighorn Basin, located 160 km to the east at an elevation of 1,180 m, the annual precipitation averages about 18 cm, as it

Department of Anthropology, University of Wyoming, Laramie, Wyoming 82071

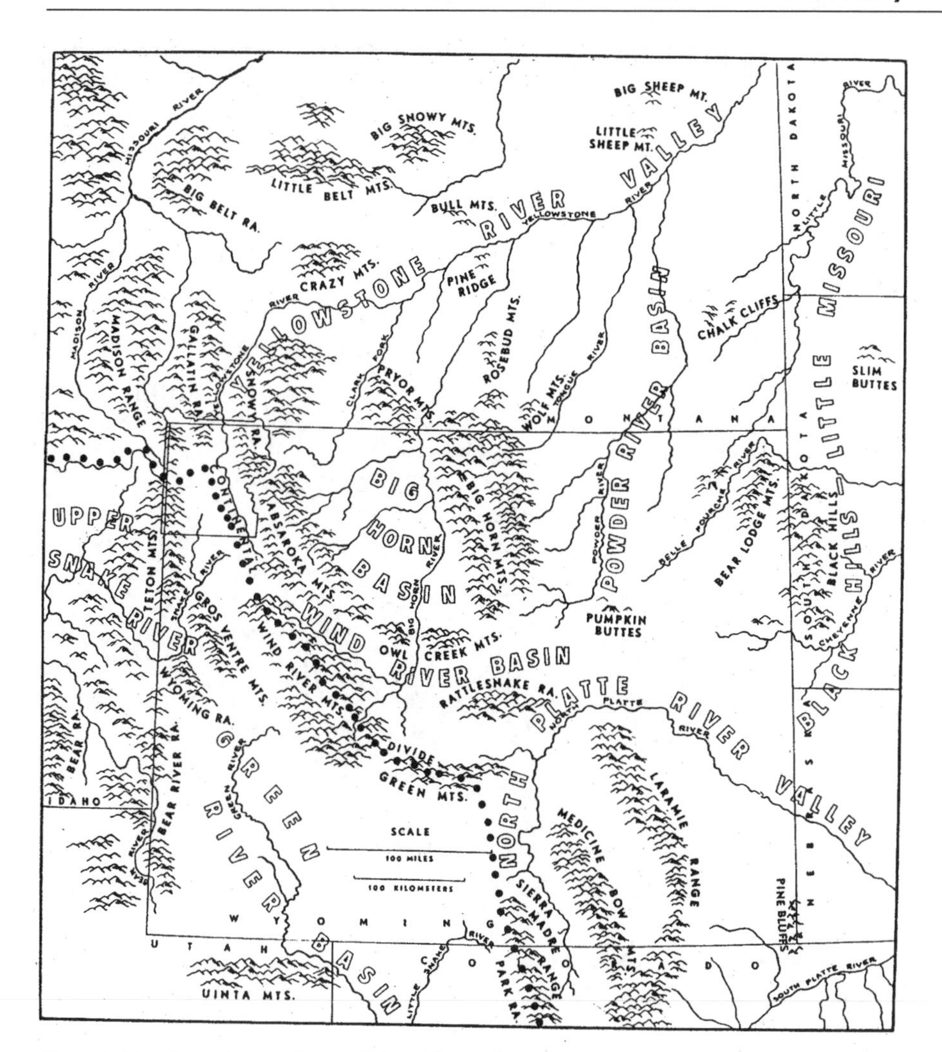

Figure 1. The general area of the Northwestern Plains with the adjacent mountains and intermontane basins.

lies within the rainshadow of the Absaroka Mountains. Another 160 km east, in the central Powder River Basin at an elevation of 1,385 m, but in a location dominated by a different weather pattern, the average annual precipitation is about 33 cm (Becker and Alyea 1964). Small to large increments of change in these amounts of rainfall regularly occur and separate good years from bad in terms of animal carrying capacity. These figures also are critical in that 18 cm of yearly precipitation results in a near-desert environment, while another 15 cm or so of precipitation will support a short-grass plains ecosystem.

Ecological conditions during the late Pleistocene in the area were significantly different than today. Because we can document that present environmental conditions demonstrate significant differences over short distances, we also can use this to argue for changes of similar proportions in the past. Several lines of evidence provide a key to past environmental conditions; however, this evidence comes from a few specific sites in locations determined by accidents of geologic formation and preservation. Without doubt, during the final two millennia of the Pleistocene, cultural factors entered strongly into the accumulation and preservation of data.

An understanding of the paleoecology of the area since the last glacial maximum at about 18,000 years ago is vital to an understanding of its past human occupation. The collection of meaningful data toward this goal requires a broad interdisciplinary approach and a number of specialists. Geology, soils, and taphonomic studies are needed to understand site formation processes so that the investigator will know whether the recovered data have the necessary integrity for reliable interpretations. Geologists, zoologists, paleontologists, botanists, palynologists, paleoclimatologists, radiocarbon dating specialists, and soil scientists are among the specialists needed to properly analyze field data. Many of these specialists will be working on the fringes of their discipline rather than in their primary area of interest and study.

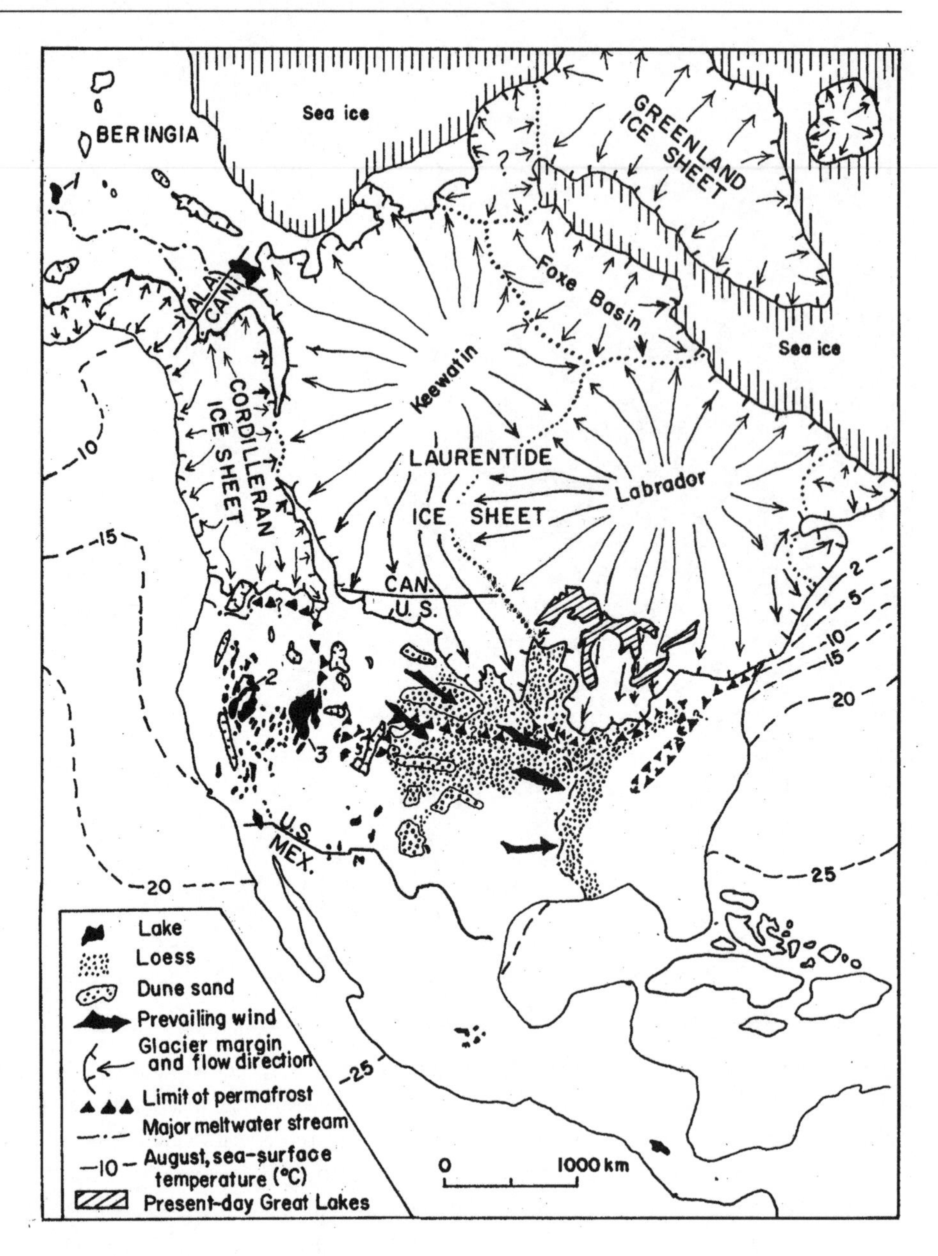

Figure 2. North America at the last glacial maximum about 20,000 years ago. (From Porter 1988).

Late Pleistocene Paleoecology

According to the latest information from paleoecological specialists (Figure 2) (see Porter 1988), the last glacial maximum in North America occurred about 20,000 to 18,000 years ago. The Laurentide ice sheet extended south to the present course of the Missouri River, at the location where it flows from north to east through Montana and across the Dakotas.

South of this, the area was unglaciated except for the higher elevations. The Yellowstone Plateau in Yellowstone National Park (Figure 1) and several contiguous mountain ranges formed the largest single glaciated area south of the continental ice sheets in North America. The headwaters of several major rivers, including the Snake, Missouri, Yellowstone, and the Green, begin in this uplifted area. The North Platte River, another major tributary of the Missouri (Figure 1), has been important in the prehistory of the southern part of the Northwestern Plains. Its major headwaters lie to the south in the Colorado Rockies. Bordering the southern margin of the continental ice sheets was a "tundra-covered periglacial landscape" within which the "vegetation assemblages resembled those existing farther north today" and "both snowline and treeline were depressed about 1,000 m" (Porter 1988:1).

The alpine glaciers reached their maximum advance at about the same time as the continental glaciers. The periglacial zone occupied a "belt up to several hundred kilometers wide along the southern margin of the continental ice sheets" (Porter 1988:4). Ice-wedge casts indicative of past permafrost conditions have been recorded at a number of locations throughout

Wyoming (Mears 1981; Walker 1987:337–340) and are considered late Wisconsin in age.

Analyses of mammalian faunas afford an understanding of changing paleoecological conditions on the Northwestern Plains and adjacent mountains. The Little Mountain area in the northern Bighorn Basin of Wyoming (Figure 1) has produced at least four sites, including natural traps and rockshelters, that have accumulated long-term records of late Pleistocene mammals. Although in a very restricted ecological zone at 1,540 m elevation, the record there provides a basis for understanding late Pleistocene environmental changes. Chomko and Gilbert (1987) postulate that four major faunal horizons can be recognized there during the late Pleistocene.

The first and oldest occurred during a period from about 27,000 to 21,000 years ago. The fauna included *Ovis* sp. (mountain sheep), *Equus* sp. (horse), *Antilocapra americana* (pronghorn), *Sylvilagus* sp. (cottontail), *Gulo gulo* (wolverine), *Vulpes* (fox), and *Lepus arcticus* (arctic hare). At least 17 small mammals were recorded, including several sensitive to small increments of environmental change.

The second and next oldest time period extends from ca. 21,000 yr B.P., or approximately during the last glacial maximum, to ca. 15,500 years ago. By ca. 20,500 yr B.P., *Arctodus* sp. (short faced bear), *Canis dirus* (dire wolf), *Canis lupus* (gray wolf), *Miracinonyx trumani* (American cheetah), *Felis atrox* (American lion), *Camelops* sp. (American camel), and *Bison* sp. (bison) are recorded. At about 18,000 yr B.P., *Bootherium bombifrons* (Harlan's muskox) appeared, along with several small mammals including *Dicrostonyx torquatus*, the collared lemming, a tiny mammal adapted to and unable to survive outside of a periglacial environment.

The third period extends from ca. 15,500 to 12,000 yr B.P., during which the large fauna were reduced in actual numbers. However, *Mammuthus* sp. (Mammoth) appears in the record at ca. 14,000 yr B.P. At ca. 13,500 yr B.P., the small mammal record demonstrates a significant change. *D. torquatus*, *Synaptomys borealis* (northern bog lemming), and *Ochotona princeps* (pika) increased, while *Thomomys* sp. (pocket gopher) decreased.

In the fourth period at ca. 12,000 to 10,000 yr B.P., the large fauna further decreased, with *Equus* sp. remaining up to ca. 11,000 yr B.P. "A steppe community with tundra elements is suggested for this period" (Chomko and Gilbert 1987:405).

Translating this faunal evidence into a late Pleistocene environmental reconstruction of the Little Mountain area suggests a steppe biome with boreal forests restricted to canyons from ca. 27,000 to 15,500 yr B.P. A florescence in the number and variety of species is noted at ca. 21,000 yr B.P., and a reduction of large animals is noted at about 15,500 yr B.P. Around 10,000 yr B.P., alpine and subalpine communities appear with new species. *Bison* sp. show a reduction in size; a process that continued until at least 6000 yr B.P. and possibly several hundred years later. By 5000 yr B.P., bison were present in their modern form (see Wilson 1978). The same trend in size reduction may be true of mountain sheep. Essentially, *Ovis catclawensis* appears to have been a slightly larger counterpart of the modern form, *Ovis canadensis;* however, the point when the modern form demonstrated sufficient contrast with the extinct form for the difference to be detected in the fossil record is not yet known.

Other sites with less complete stratigraphic records than seen in the Little Mountain area of northern Wyoming have been found immediately to the north, in the Pryor Mountains of Montana (Figure 1). This area has produced a partial record of late Pleistocene fauna that is reasonably consistent with the Little Mountain data (Graham et al. 1987). Similar results have also come from the investigation of Little Boxelder Cave at the northern end of the Laramie Range in central Wyoming (Anderson 1968; Long 1971).

Small mammal studies from early Paleoindian sites have expanded our knowledge of environments of the last millennia-and-a-half of the Pleistocene. These studies include the Lange/Ferguson mammoth site in the badlands east of the Black Hills in South Dakota (Hannus 1990; Martin 1987) and the Agate Basin site in extreme eastern Wyoming west of the Black Hills (Walker 1982). At the latter site, large samples of small mammals (noncultural) were recovered in stratified deposits containing cultural material. Of particular significance were the samples taken from the Folsom level, dated at ca. 10,700 yr B.P., and the Hell Gap level, occurring approximately 500 years later. The latter sample reflects significant environmental change from the former, while both are different from the present. The modern area of sympatry for the Folsom micromammal fauna would be the coniferous forest area of northwest Wyoming, whereas the area of sympatry for the Hell Gap micromammal fauna would be several hundred kms further south in a mixed area of coniferous forest stands, sagebrush, and grasslands

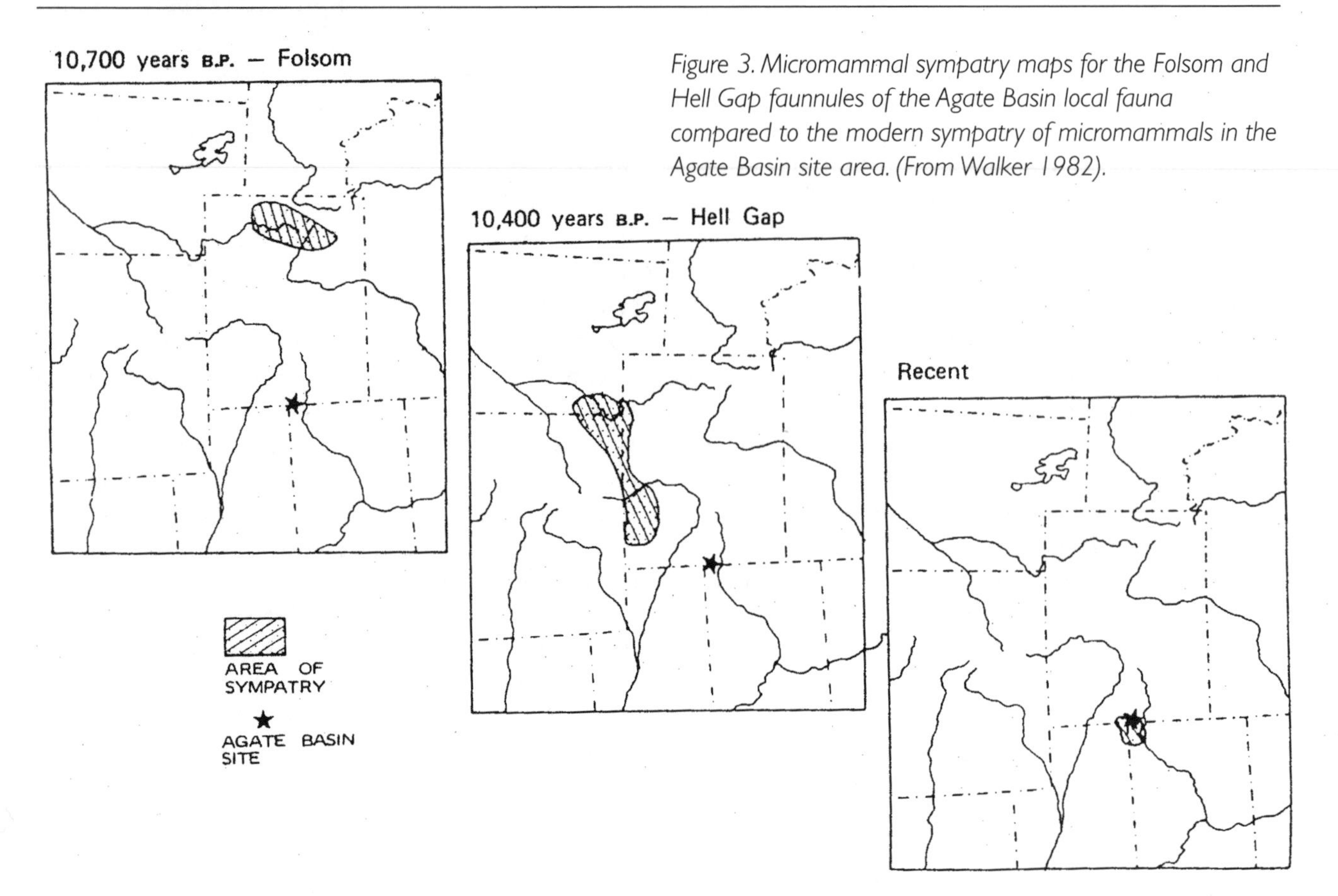

Figure 3. Micromammal sympatry maps for the Folsom and Hell Gap faunnules of the Agate Basin local fauna compared to the modern sympatry of micromammals in the Agate Basin site area. (From Walker 1982).

now found in northwest Colorado and the southern part of the Wyoming Basin (Figure 3).

Other paleoenvironmental studies indicate significant changes during the critical time between ca. 11,000 and 10,000 yr B.P.; however, these individual studies are from specific locations in the Northwestern Plains area. Extreme caution is needed when attempting to generalize from a single site to an entire area, or even over short distances. Results of palynological study from a site in the Powder River Basin (Markgraf and Lennon 1986) in east-central Wyoming and from the Mill Iron site (Goshen–Plainview cultural complex) in southeastern Montana (Figure 4) (Scott-Cummings 1996) suggest that modern grasslands essentially have been in their present form since ca. 13,000 yr B.P. This by no means should be construed as an indication that the same conditions should be generalized to the Wyoming Basin, the Bighorn Basin, the mixed forest–grassland area of southwest Montana, or any other segment of the general area.

Paleoecological data from the Northwestern Plains and adjacent mountains reveal that from the Glacial Maximum (ca. 20,000 yr B.P.) to the end of the Pleistocene (ca. 10,000 yr B.P.), floral and faunal communities changed and shifted as the climate warmed and deglaciation progressed. Even though the area of study was not covered by the Laurentide ice sheet, there were areas of ice (such as that on the Yellowstone Plateau) and valley glaciers in the headwaters of major streams, whose sources were in the higher mountains. During the time between 11,000 and 10,000 yr B.P. significant climatic changes strongly affected cultural groups on the Northwestern Plains. These changes were proposed by Bryson a decade and a half ago (1974:755) based on pollen studies in Minnesota.

The Pre-Clovis/Ancestral Clovis Question

If pre-Clovis or ancestral Clovis occupations were present on the Northwestern Plains and in the adjacent mountains after the glacial maximum, they would have been successfully adapted to the changing environmental conditions described above. To date, there is no evidence of a cultural assemblage in the area that can be accepted as unequivocal or strongly convincing of such an occupation. I strongly feel that a distinction should be made between the concepts of pre-Clovis and ancestral Clovis. A pre-Clovis

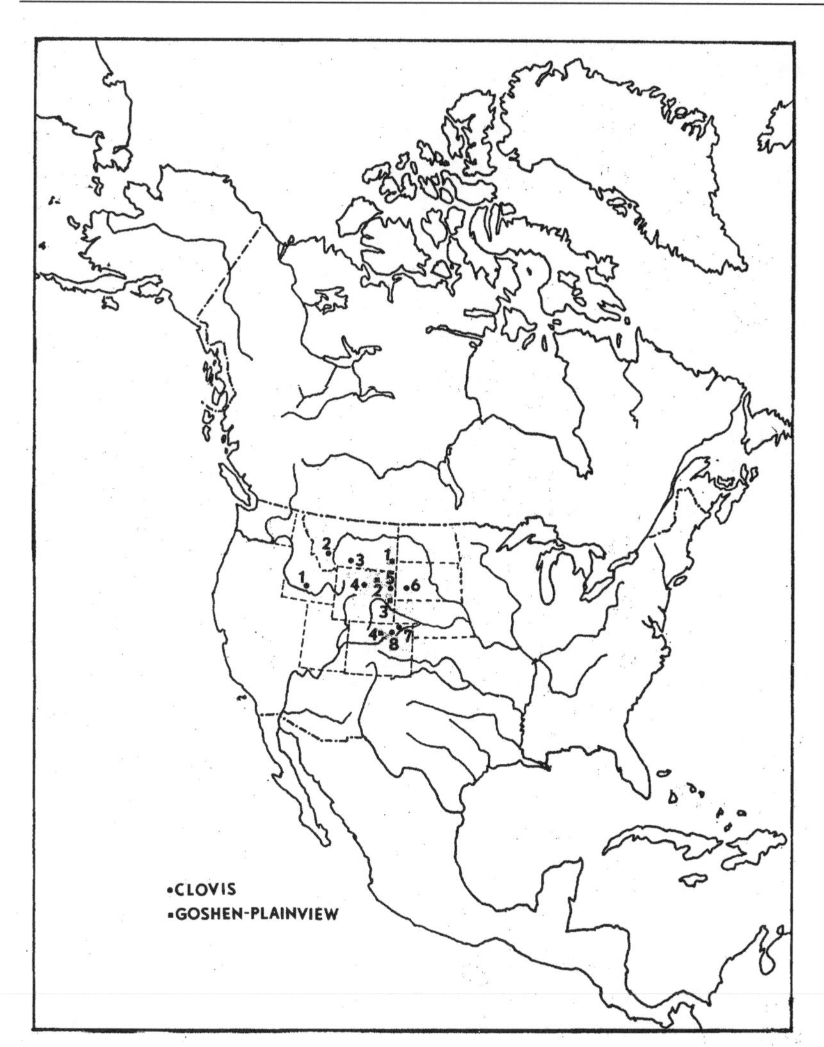

Figure 4. Clovis sites include (1) Simon Cache, (2) Indian Creek, (3) Anzick cache, (4) Colby; (5) Sheaman, (6) Lange-Ferguson, (7) Drake cache, and (8) Dent. Goshen–Plainview sites include (1) Mill Iron, (2) Carter/Kerr-McGee, (3) Hell Gap, and (4) Twin Mountain.

occupation might have been oriented toward scavenging, which would leave the evidence even more difficult to find and confirm. However, we would expect an ancestral Clovis occupation to reflect some of the technology found later in Clovis. Until evidence of either or both is found in the proper geologic context, answers to the pre-Clovis and/or ancestral Clovis question on the Northwestern Plains must remain open and unanswered, with any resolution dependent on future data recovery.

This does not preclude the possibility that such evidence someday may be found. Given the high rates of erosion and deposition resulting from high topographic relief, easily eroded sediments, and low vegetative cover, the probability of preservation of such evidence is relatively low. There are several confirmed Clovis site components in the area (Figure 4), and the preservation of Paleoindian sites in general is largely the result of fortuitous geologic events. Consider for a moment that it took nearly two decades after the first discovery and documentation of the Goshen cultural complex at the Hell Gap site in southwestern Wyoming (Irwin-Williams et al. 1973) to find an *in situ* component of the Goshen complex at the Carter/Kerr-McGee site (Figure 4) in the Powder River Basin of Wyoming (Frison 1984) and the Mill Iron site (24CT30) (Frison 1991a, 1996), located 400 km to the north in southeastern Montana.

Clovis on the Northwestern Plains and in the Mountains

CLOVIS EVIDENCE IS quite visible archaeologically, particularly where it is associated with large animal bones or bone beds, as seen at the Colby site (Frison and Todd 1986). Clovis tools and weaponry, as presently known, reflect an advanced stage of bone, ivory, and flaked stone technology. Clovis has received more than its fair share of attention, largely because of its age, flaked stone technology, and association with extinct fauna. For my discussion of Clovis, I offer some thoughts and ideas gained from studies of paleolandforms and animal behavior, which affected animal procurement strategies. Along with this are the results of experiments on various animals using Clovis tools and weaponry (e.g., Frison 1989). Another line of evidence that may reflect social and ritual aspects of Clovis comes from the recent discovery of three Clovis caches of flaked stone items. Added to earlier data from the Clovis caches at the Simon site (Butler 1963) and the Anzick site (Lahren and Bonnichsen 1974), these features are thought to be burial offerings and reflect some unknown measure of ritual activity.

Clovis Mammoth Hunting

AS THE MAMMOTH IS NO longer around for us to observe, the many thoughts, ideas, and artists' renditions on prehistoric mammoth hunting have surfaced with little chance of arriving at the actual truth. Most are genuine attempts to offer some insights, but are based on limited site data and speculation about prehistoric mammoth hunting as part of a subsistence strategy. Unfortunately, too many of these ideas have become imprinted on students' minds and, lacking alternative interpretations of these data, too often have been accepted as truth. The following discussion on hunting is presented as an alternative, based on a perspective of long-term experience in subsistence hunting of large mammals.

Prehistoric hunting as a means of subsistence has received increasing attention during the past two decades, as cultural process has become accepted as an appropriate way to analyze and interpret the archaeological record. In the process of developing a methodology to handle this new area of research, various forms of innovation and experimentation have resulted. This is especially true of prehistoric hunting models. In this area of interpretation, however, nonhunters have attempted to construct models of hunting. The African Bushmen became the target of much of the research, and one result was a movie entitled "The Hunters," which has had a profound influence on the thinking of a generation of anthropologists. The truth is that if Paleoindian hunters were as inept as those portrayed in this movie, few, if any, would have been able to survive.

Every stage in the hunting sequence, as presented in the movie, was carried out improperly. The initial contact with the animal was botched: the hunters were not careful in stalking the animal (a giraffe), then chanced a desperation shot rather than waiting for a better one. They then pursued the wounded animal too closely, instead of allowing it to become sick and lay down. When the giraffe finally did become sick enough to be cornered (days later), the hunters continued to excite the animal by running up to it and throwing spears. The animal finally had to be dispatched with a rifle to put it out of its misery. The entire episode violated almost every rule of knowledgeable and intelligent hunting.

Too many students of prehistoric hunting apparently feel there is a single hunting strategy, when the truth of the matter is that almost innumerable strategies exist, each dependent on myriad continually changing conditions. Each animal species has a set of behavioral characteristics that sets it apart from other species and that, to varying extents, may make its procurement mutually exclusive of other species. In addition, these behavior patterns change with external conditions, such as time of day, seasonality, weather, terrain, and vegetative cover, and with internal factors, such as the animal's physical condition, sex, and age. The adequately trained and experienced hunter need only open his eyes in the morning, look outside, take all the necessary factors into account, and the strategy for the day's hunt immediately falls into place. If one strategy fails, there is an immediate alternative, with the result that, in the end, game animals are continually at the mercy of man—a superior predator. This predator knows the prey, the territory, and how the animals will behave within it under any and all conditions, at different times of the year.

A modern hunter using Clovis weaponry to experiment with African elephants can, at the least, provide some information on the limitations of Clovis tools and weaponry as they were used on mammoths (Frison 1989). The two species appear physiologically similar, based on comparisons of skeletal elements. Their hides are of similar thickness, although mammoth hide, analyzed from collections in the Zoological Museum in Leningrad, Russia, probably would have been easier to penetrate since it lacks the armor-like quality of African elephant hide. Penetration of the hide has been proven critical to the successful use of chipped stone projectile points on any large mammal. Once the hide has a hole large enough to permit entry of the projectile, very little additional force is needed. One factor that might be considered is the relatively small ears of a mammoth in contrast to the large ears of the African elephant. This variation could have created a significant difference in the effectiveness of head and/or neck shots using Clovis weaponry.

Generalizing African elephant behavior to that of mammoths must be treated with caution in terms of proposing a procurement strategy. A model of mammoth hunting, assuming that these animals operated under a family structure similar to African elephants, should take into account the protection offered the members of a family group under a matriarch. The absence of this kind of protection would allow an altogether different hunting strategy. Either way, modern analogues suggest the Clovis hunter would have been able to devise a successful strategy because the Clovis projectile point, used with either a thrusting spear or with atlatl and dart by a trained person, will easily penetrate the rib cavity of an elephant and result in a lethal wound.

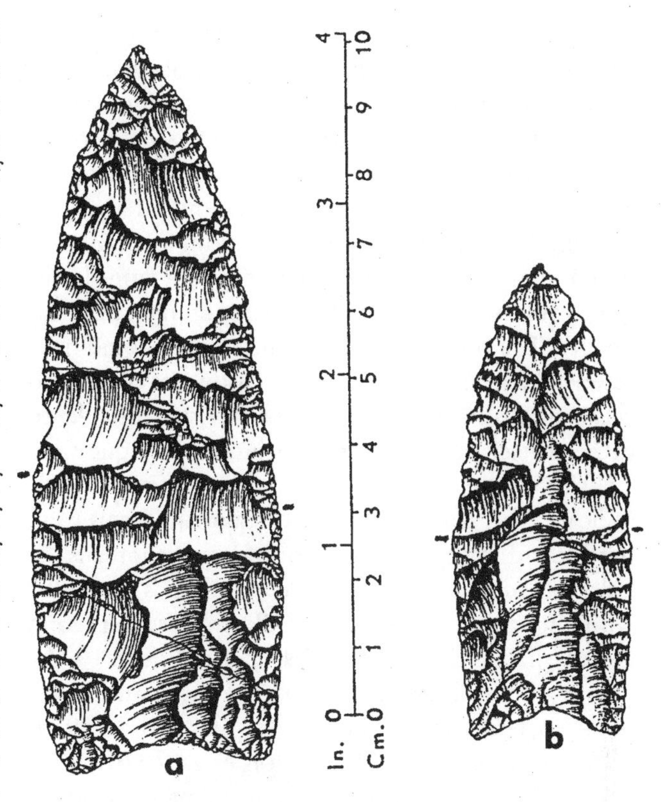

Figure 5. Typical Clovis projectile points: (a) surface find from southeast Wyoming, and (b) surface find at the Casper Hell Gap site.

The typical Clovis projectile point (Figure 5), either accidentally or, more likely, through careful design, may be one of the oldest known manifestations of chipped stone weaponry that allowed a single hunter to go after large mammals, such as mammoth or bison, with enough advantage to ensure a high probability of success. Although it appears simple, it would be difficult to envision a superior projectile point design. The Clovis projectile has a sharp point for initial penetration; blade edges are sharp so as to cut a hole of proper size to allow entry of the hafting element and shaft; the point narrows slightly toward the base to allow a sinew binding that will not impede entry; the flutes provide a basal thinning, which is ideal to fit into the nock of the foreshaft; and the lenticular cross-section provides maximum structural strength. The point is designed to be attached to a wooden foreshaft with sinew and pitch without fear of it loosening during use. The experienced hunter undoubtedly gave each projectile point a careful testing for hidden flaws, such as internal fractures and crystal pockets that could cause failure at critical moments and unnecessarily spoil the hunt and even endanger the hunter. The design also allowed for reworking of broken specimens so that they could be restored quickly and easily to a functional condition and inflict lethal wounds on large mammals.

The ideal approach to killing a mammoth would have been broadside entry, with the projectile point placed in the lung cavity. A less desirable target would have been the stomach cavity. The heart was protected by the anterior ribs, which become relatively flat and wide distally. The heart would have been protected also by the olecranon of the ulna, unless the animal had its front leg in a forward position. Direct frontal attack would have been unwise, since the brain was too well protected and an effective throat shot would have been difficult. A good strategy would have two hunters co-operating closely; one to get the animal's attention, while another maneuvered into the best position for a lethal shot. African elephants have relatively poor eyesight but an excellent sense of smell. If mammoths were similarly endowed, this factor would have been critical to the development of successful procurement strategies.

Somewhere along the way, archaeologists became enamored with the idea that prehistoric hunters were so inept at hunting that they were forced into driving large animals such as mammoths and bison into bogs. In reality, most large mammals—in particular, elephants and bison—spend much of their time in and around bogs and swampy areas. These animals rarely become mired unless they are old, crippled, sick, or afflicted by a combination of these conditions. A mired animal is extremely difficult to remove from a bog, and butchering in a bog is difficult, unpleasant, and almost impossible to perform while maintaining any meat quality. The prospect that human hunters could have removed a healthy mammoth or bison out of a mired position, from which it supposedly was unable to extricate itself before being killed, is out of the question.

On the other hand, there is sufficient evidence to indicate that, to some extent, certain landforms were used to aid in the procurement of large mammals. In Paleoindian times, the best evidence of this is associated with the extinct subspecies of *Bison*. Parabolic sand dunes, such as those at the Casper site (Frison 1974); and head cuts in arroyos, such as at the Agate Basin, Hawken, and Carter/Kerr-McGee sites (Frison 1984; Frison and Stanford 1982; Frison et al. 1976), were used advantageously to hunt these animals. The deep arroyo present at the Colby Mammoth site in northern Wyoming (Figure 4) (Frison and Todd 1986) may have been an important factor in regular and systematic mammoth procurement there.

The use of arroyos as traps has produced special problems in data recovery and in understanding site formation processes. At the Agate Basin site (Frison and Stanford 1982), for example, the arroyo floodplain was used as a campsite during the winter months, presumably to be close to the dead animals. As the weather warmed, the site had to be abandoned because of flooding from snow melt. In some cases, flooding may have deposited materials derived from upstream onto the winter camping surface; in others, it may have scoured materials from the floodplain campsites and moved them downstream to different locations. This is a situation unlike that where sites were located on terraces above normal flood levels and were preserved by the accumulation of colluvial materials.

Clovis Tool and Weaponry Caches

THE SIMON CLOVIS cache (Figure 4) in Idaho evoked considerable interest because of its large Clovis projectile points, projectile point preforms, and exotic materials (e.g., quartz crystal bifaces) (Butler 1963). Later, the discovery of the Anzick Clovis cache in

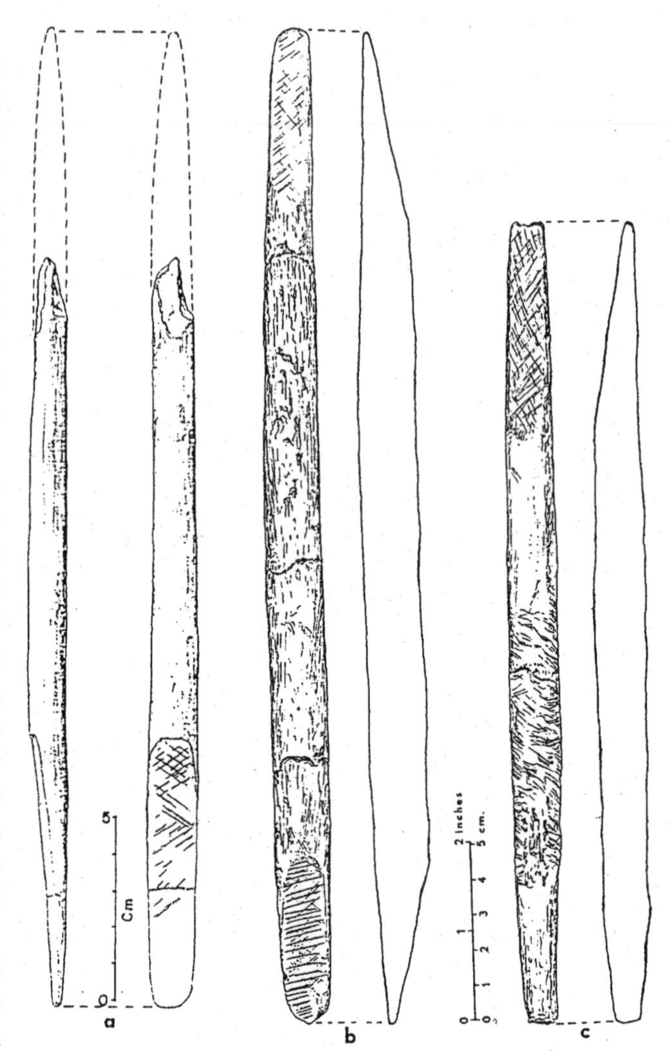

Figure 6. (a) Ivory object from the Sheaman site; and (b, c) bone objects from the Anzick site.

Montana (Figure 4) caused a greater level of interest because of the presence of similar items and, in addition, fragments of human bone, red ocher, and cylindrical bone objects with tapered and cross-hachured ends (Lahren and Bonnichsen 1974) (Figure 6b, c). A similar item made of ivory (Figure 6a) was recovered from the Sheaman Clovis site (Figure 4) in the Agate Basin locality of eastern Wyoming (Frison and Stanford 1982).

In 1988, the Richey Clovis cache in Wenatchee, Washington was partially excavated (Mehringer 1988). In January of the following year, as a result of National Geographic Society coverage of the Richey site, another Clovis cache known as the Fenn cache, discovered many years earlier, came to light (Frison 1991b). The Fenn cache contained 56 ocher-covered lithic items, including projectile points, projectile point preforms, large bifaces, a crescent, and a single blade. The exact location of its discovery is not known, but apparently came from the general area where Wyoming, Idaho, and Utah meet. These four caches, along with the Drake Clovis cache (Figure 4) near Sterling, Colorado, which contained 13 complete Clovis points and fragments of ivory (Dennis Stanford, personal communication 1991), strongly indicate that these sites are not anomalies and instead represent an institutionalized part of the Clovis cultural system.

These five caches are remarkably similar in content and all may be burial offerings, although only the Anzick assemblage contained human bone. Bifaces from them demonstrate an extremely well-developed degree of percussion flaking, using the finest of stone flaking materials available. If the tools from the site were burial offerings, the term "cache" may not be appropriate because these assemblages represent the best raw materials and technological efforts, removed from use, with no intention of recovery. Whatever the answer, these sites will require archaeologists to take a view of Clovis differing from that of small hunting groups pursuing mammoths and bison, concerned only with achieving a basic level of subsistence.

Seasonality

THE DATA PRESENTLY available argue strongly for cold weather bison and mammoth procurement in Paleoindian times on the Northwestern Plains. This argument is based on aging studies conducted on bison remains from communal kill sites (see, for example, Reher 1974; Todd et al. 1996) and on what is believed to have been a cold weather meat cache from the Colby mammoth kill site (Frison and Todd 1986). Catastrophic death situations such as a large bison kill are best for determining the season of death: the assumption can be made that the hunting strategy resulted in mass kills, which contain relatively large samples of bison populations. Tooth eruption among young animals (especially calves and juveniles) is systematic enough to give close approximations of age, expressed in months, that can then be used to establish the time of year of kill events. This does not suggest that warm weather hunting was not also part of the Paleoindian subsistence pattern.

Preservation and Protection of Surplus Meat

COLD-WEATHER COMMUNAL animal procurement required some form of short-term preservation and storage of surplus meat products. The author earlier proposed (Frison 1982) that the mammoth bone piles at the Colby mammoth kill site and the pile of bison carcass units and the associated bone bed in the Agate Basin component at the Agate Basin site were frozen meat caches (Frison and Stanford 1982:363). Meat also may have been dried during the warmer months, but in the situations mentioned above, conditions for drying meat would not have been favorable. At the Colby site, a purposeful method of meat storage is interpreted: the left front quarter of a nearly mature animal was placed on the bank out of the arroyo channel, long bones of other animals were stacked around it, and a small mammoth skull was placed on top. It is proposed that the entire pile was covered with slush and allowed to freeze. This would have preserved the meat and kept out predators. This cache was never opened for use, and the meat simply spoiled with the approach of warm weather (see Frison and Todd 1986:41–56).

Another pile of mammoth bones at the site suggests a similar feature was opened and the contents utilized. These kinds of temporary caches were important to survival in an area with unpredictable winter weather. It was better to have meat products left over to spoil than to have a shortage, which could threaten the livelihood of the human group. A Clovis projectile point found at the bottom of the rib cage of the mammoth quarter in the undisturbed pile leaves little doubt of the human element involved.

The Agate Basin component at the Agate Basin site (Frison and Stanford 1982:77) yielded a pile of bones consisting of several butchered units from bison carcasses. Away from this pile, the carcass units are disarticulated, with individual bones exhibiting tool marks and breakage patterns similar to those commonly observed in butchering and processing activities. In addition, the tool assemblage is one commonly observed in butchering and processing situations. The pile of butchered units is postulated to represent a frozen cache from which units were taken for consumption as needed. The butchered units remaining were ones left over from the winter and spoiled with the arrival of warm weather. Since they were located on the floodplain of a dry arroyo, they were covered and consequently preserved by overbank alluvial deposits. This pattern of bison procurement and freezing of meat is in marked contrast to the

Archaic and late Prehistoric pattern of warm weather communal kills and drying of meat for winter use.

The Goshen Complex

THE GOSHEN COMPLEX first was documented at the Hell Gap site (48GO305) in southeastern Wyoming (Figure 4) nearly a quarter of a century ago (Irwin-Williams et al. 1973). Further evidence to support its existence was not confirmed until the 1984 excavations at the Mill Iron site (24CT30) in southeastern Montana (Frison 1991a, 1996). However, a reanalysis of the data from the Carter/Kerr-McGee site in the Powder River Basin of Wyoming strongly indicates that the oldest component there probably was Goshen rather than Clovis, as described earlier (see Frison 1984). The diagnostic trait of the Goshen complex is a projectile point (Figure 7) with a strong resemblance to Plainview points from the Southern Plains. Radiocarbon dates from the Mill Iron site demonstrated that the Goshen complex was at least as old as the earliest Folsom radiocarbon dates of around 10,900 years ago (see Haynes 1992). Further confirmation of the age of the Goshen complex came recently from the Goshen level at Locality 1 at the Hell Gap site (Figure 4), which produced an AMS date on charcoal of 10,955 ± 135 yr B.P. (AA-14434) (C. Vance Haynes, personal communication 1995).

The Goshen cultural level was found in a stratigraphic context below the Folsom component at the Hell Gap site (Irwin-Williams et al. 1973) and at the Carter/Kerr-McGee site in eastern Wyoming (Frison 1984). At the latter site, a Goshen component was found below a Folsom level dated at 10,400 yr B.P. At that time, the assemblage was regarded as Clovis

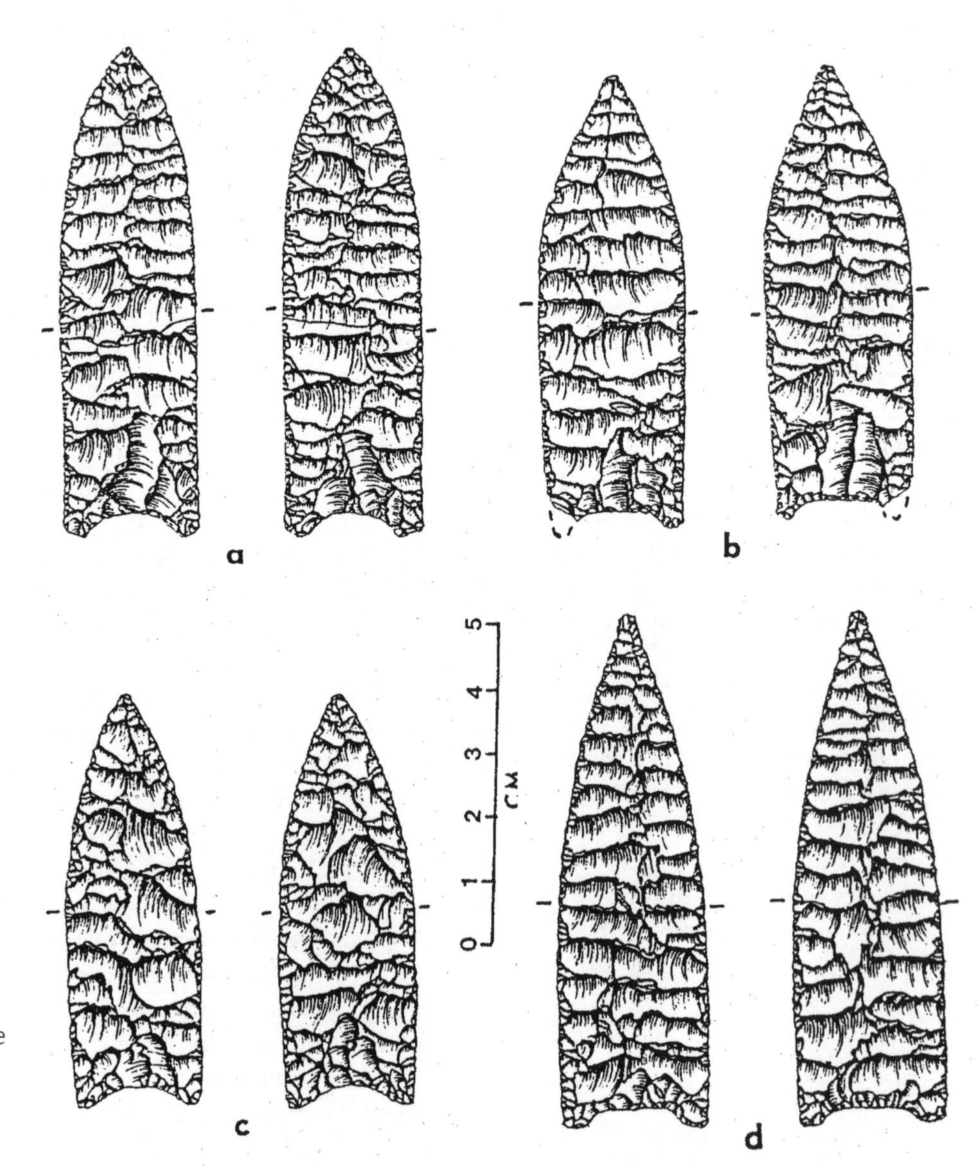

Figure 7. Goshen–Plainview projectile points from (a-c) the Mill Iron campsite area, and (d) the bison bone bed.

because of its stratigraphic position and an association with a projectile point with a resemblance to Clovis (Frison 1984:Figure 13b). I now believe the projectile point in question could be Goshen. No charcoal or datable bone was recovered from the Goshen level.

Goshen peoples developed a pressure-flaking technology on projectile points strongly reminiscent of Folsom. However, instead of fluting, they performed a careful and distinctive basal thinning (Figure 7). Technologically, the difference between Folsom and Goshen points comes down to an absence of fluting on the latter. On the other hand, it can be argued that Goshen tools, at least those from the Mill Iron site, bear a strong resemblance to Clovis, both in the use of tools made on blades and in the strategy of biface reduction. It may have been that Goshen was a variant Clovis group that managed to develop pressure flaking to a high degree. The presence of worked and unworked sections of mammoth rib suggests that Goshen peoples were around during, or shortly after, the disappearance of mammoths. As mentioned above, many Goshen projectile points bear a remarkable resemblance to the Plainview type, as it is known and recognized on the Southern Plains. In fact, when the projectile point assemblages from the Mill Iron site and the Plainview site (Sellards et al. 1947) are combined, subsequent separation on the basis of typology is very difficult (Haynes 1991).

A bone bed at the Mill Iron site indicates that Goshen peoples were aware of the techniques of communal bison procurement. The bone bed is not the location of the actual kill; instead it gives the appearance of being composed of deliberately stacked, butchered units and individual bones. Seasonality, determined from the faunal remains, follows the usual Paleoindian pattern of a late fall or early winter kill. As the bone bed is located in an area of extreme erosion, there are no data on past landforms which might provide clues to the strategy involved in the actual bison procurement.

The Mill Iron site has raised far more questions than it has answered concerning the Goshen cultural complex. This cultural component had been exposed to weathering for some time, as demonstrated by poor preservation of the upper bone surfaces. However, the bones had not been moved, as evidenced by their well-preserved undersides. Two series of radiocarbon dates from the site, one from 11,570 to 11,320 yr B.P. and another from 11,010 to 10,760 yr B.P. (Haynes 1992:361), allow for possibilities of cultural relationships with both Clovis and Folsom. Subsequently, concerns regarding the reliability of these dates have been raised. The possible use of old logs for fuel would yield dates too old, while extended post-occupation exposure of the site raises the possibility of contamination by younger charcoal. At this point, a reinvestigation of the Hell Gap site appears to offer the best future possibility for more reliable information on the Clovis–Goshen–Folsom–Midland problem. Interpretations derived from the Hell Gap site (Irwin-Williams et al. 1973) suggest that Goshen–Folsom–Midland traditions occurred in succession without an overlap in time, although an alternative explanation, based upon presently known radiocarbon dates, is that there may have been a time overlap. At the Hell Gap site, a Folsom level overlies a Goshen level, with a designated Midland level overlying the Folsom level. In terms of projectile point typology, generally speaking, the Midland level looks more like another Goshen component. Other materials at the Hell Gap site that have been classified as Midland could as easily be put into the Goshen category.

The recent discovery and preliminary investigation of a small bison kill in the Middle Park area of Colorado, at an elevation of about 2,620 m, appears at this time to be of Goshen age. Based on evidence of tooth eruption, bison from the site (The Twin Mountain Bison Kill [5GA1315]) (Kornfeld et al. n.d.) probably were killed in October. A strategy of hunting utilizing a distinct landform may explain the site's location. At this time, the similarity of Goshen and Plainview has resulted in a designation of Goshen–Plainview instead of Goshen for these sites, at least until new data can clarify this relationship.

The Folsom Complex

LITTLE, IF ANY, new information has been added recently to our knowledge of Folsom from the Northwestern Plains. The technology of tool and projectile point manufacture, resulting from the analysis of the Hanson site data (Frison and Bradley 1980) remains basically sound. However, the debitage from the site is being analyzed, and the tools are being subjected to an intensive usewear analysis. The results of these studies should be available in the near future.

Bone and antler projectile points were recovered from the Folsom component at the Agate Basin site (Frison and Zeimens 1980). These artifact types are yet unrecorded at other sites, although two items from the Lindenmeier site probably are parts of the same or similar kind of weaponry (Wilmsen and Roberts 1978:131). The function of bone and/or antler projectile points has not yet been demonstrated satisfactorily: these tools will effectively penetrate the hide of deer- or pronghorn-sized mammals, but not the thicker hide of bison. Bone points of this design do not cut a hole but simply expand the hide to allow entry.

The validity of Midland as a separate cultural complex on the Northwestern Plains remains to be explored. Its presence was proposed as a result of the Hell Gap investigations (Irwin-Williams et al. 1973), mainly on the basis of unfluted Folsom projectile points. Folsom components at the Hanson (Frison and Bradley 1980) and Agate Basin sites (Frison and Stanford 1982) have produced both fluted and unfluted projectile points. The question remains open as to whether or not the Folsom–Midland succession is warranted, particularly in the area of the Northwestern Plains.

The Agate Basin Complex

Although the Agate Basin cultural complex immediately follows Folsom in at least three stratified sites (Hell Gap, Agate Basin, and Carter/Kerr-McGee) in Wyoming, it is difficult to see the former developing out of the latter in terms of projectile point typology and technology. By design, the Agate Basin projectile point is possibly the most lethal weaponry seen in any of the Paleoindian complexes. If Agate Basin did develop directly out of Folsom, the concept of weaponry underwent a dramatic and sudden change. Whereas the Folsom projectile point is wide, thin, and fluted, the Agate Basin projectile is relatively thick, but lenticular in transverse cross-section. On the other hand, the potential for an evolutionary shift can be seen: by narrowing some of the earlier-stage Folsom preforms recovered at the Hell Gap site and not preparing the ends for fluting, these implements could be made into acceptable Agate Basin points.

The Hell Gap Complex

There is little reason to doubt that Hell Gap developed directly out of Agate Basin, although it is difficult to understand why the long, thick, lenticular cross-section of the Agate Basin projectile point was abandoned for the wider, shouldered Hell Gap point. Ample evidence, however, demonstrates the efficiency of the latter in bison kills among parabolic sand dune settings, such as seen at the Casper site (Frison 1974), and in arroyo traps, such as the ones observed at the Agate Basin and Carter/Kerr-McGee sites (Frison 1984; Frison and Stanford 1982). These associations show an increased importance upon specific hunting situations; perhaps requiring the Hell Gap technology for its success.

By the introduction of the Hell Gap complex at ca. 10,000 years ago, rapid climatic change at the end of the Pleistocene had resulted in environments not unlike the present. This period marks what most investigators consider the end of the Pleistocene and the beginning of the Holocene. This also was the beginning of the end for Northwestern Plains Paleoindian big-game hunting, although some traditions would linger for another millennium before they were replaced by a more widespread, broad-spectrum hunting-and-gathering pattern.

High-Altitude Adaptations

Evidence of both Clovis and Folsom occur in the higher elevations, particularly in what are now mountain meadows near springs and along permanent water courses (see Frison 1988). Because of heavy surface vegetation, cultural evidence appears where the surface has been disturbed by rodent mounds, road construction, livestock reservoirs, and spring development. Drought years, which reduce grass cover and result in surface erosion and arroyo cutting, reveal diagnostic artifacts. Stratified sites remain to be found and are difficult to locate, mostly because of the nature of past geologic activity. Caves and rockshelters are exceptions, many of which contain stratified deposits but so far have not produced fluted point components. In post-Folsom periods, diagnostic artifact types (projectile points) from the foothill–mountain area and the open plains differ.

The reasons for this are unclear but some possibilities are open for discussion. One suggestion is that as the late Pleistocene extinctions ended, the plains were left with bison and pronghorn primarily, while the foothills and mountains supported mountain sheep and deer. Both Clovis and Folsom groups used the higher elevations; however, after the Folsom period, the bison–pronghorn area required procurement strategies mutually exclusive of those needed to hunt mountain sheep and deer in the foothill–mountain area. Caves and rockshelters became part of the foothill–mountain settlement system, and, along with a subsistence strategy focussed on mountain sheep and deer, post-Folsom peoples became oriented toward an increased dependence upon small mammals and plant foods. The discovery of a late Paleoindian-age net, believed to have been used for mountain sheep procurement, is a strong indicator of a high-altitude procurement strategy (Frison et al. 1986). The oldest stratigraphic evidence of this dichotomy in subsistence strategies appears at ca. 10,000 yr B.P. at the Medicine Lodge Creek site, Little Canyon Creek Cave, and Bush Shelter, all in northern Wyoming (Frison 1976; Miller 1988).

The fact that some of the most desirable raw materials are found at the higher elevations suggests the alternative explanation that Clovis and Folsom groups were in these areas to exploit these lithic sources. At least two high-grade cherts utilized by both groups are exposed only in the higher elevations of the Bighorn Mountains in northern Wyoming. One is found in the Phosphoria Formation (Permian) and the other is in the Madison Formation (Mississippian). Clovis projectile points at the Colby site (Frison and Todd 1986) were made of the Phosphoria material and projectile points, tools, and debitage from both sources were present at the Hanson Folsom site (Frison and Bradley 1980). Both sites are within approximately a day's trek from the quarry sources.

Conclusions

Between the time of the glacial maximum at about 20,000 years ago and the first evidence of Clovis at about 11,500 years ago, there is a lack of acceptable evidence for a pre-Clovis or ancestral Clovis component in the Northwestern Plains and contiguous mountain ranges. Although the area lies well beyond the southern extent of late Wisconsinan continental ice sheets, it straddles an area affected by valley glaciers and persisting periglacial conditions. These conditions gradually changed to warmer regimes following the last glacial maximum. During the period of time between the appearance of Clovis and the glacial maximum, the area apparently supported steppe or steppe tundra environments, with a wide variety of large mammals, including bison, camel, mammoth, horse, pronghorn antelope, mountain sheep, muskox, and many others. Predators included the short-faced bear, grizzly bear, American cheetah, American lion, and wolf.

Clovis appeared on the scene suddenly before 11,000 years ago, and there is evidence these people killed mammoth, bison, and pronghorn, along with an occasional horse, camel, or muskox. Clovis weaponry was well designed and adequate for the purpose of killing large mammals. Clovis caches suggest the performance of burial and possibly other ritual activities, providing a view of relatively sophisticated hunting groups with possible status differentiation. The creation of frozen meat caches was part of the Clovis subsistence strategy, and this practice continued among Paleoindian groups throughout the late Pleistocene and into the early Holocene. Various landforms, such as parabolic sand dunes and head cuts in arroyos, were used throughout the same period as aids in animal procurement. It is argued, however, that bogs were not utilized as traps, as many investigators have postulated. Large mammals such as buffalo and elephant are attracted to bogs, but rarely become trapped unless they are sick or crippled. A good hunter would have first moved the animals out of the bogs and dispatched them on dry land, as skinning, butchering, and retrieving meat products from mired animals was not a practical option.

The Goshen cultural complex is now known to have been a reality, although its relationship to Plainview, Clovis, Folsom, and Midland remains unclear. Goshen groups developed a pressure-flaking technology strongly reminiscent of Folsom, but their tool assemblages retained elements similar to Clovis. Goshen, Folsom, Agate Basin, and Hell Gap appear in stratigraphic sequence in open plains sites such as Hell Gap (Irwin-Williams et al. 1973) and Carter/Kerr-McGee (Frison 1984), but there may have been an overlap in time between the various complexes. More reliable radiocarbon dates, along with the investigation of new sites or reinvestigation of sites such as Hell Gap, constitute the best chances of resolving the evolutionary links between cultural groups.

Clovis and Folsom artifacts appear in mountain meadows at higher elevations, but evidence of their presence is absent from caves and rockshelters. After the decline of Folsom, evidence suggests an apparent dichotomy in subsistence strategies between the plains and the foothill–mountain areas for a millennium or more. This dichotomy is postulated as the result of mutually exclusive subsistence strategies utilized to exploit the different food resources in each area. Other changes in settlement and subsistence appear during this time. Caves and rockshelters, ignored by Clovis and Folsom groups, become part of the settlement system in the foothill–mountain areas and plant foods become increasingly important. At least part of the Clovis–Folsom presence in the higher elevations may have been for the procurement of raw lithic materials.

Between 11,000 and 10,000 years ago, abrupt changes occurred from that of late Pleistocene climates to postglacial conditions similar to the present. This time marks the beginning of the end for the classic Paleoindian big-game hunters of the plains, although some groups, such as those of the Cody complex, maintained a lifestyle strongly oriented toward communal bison hunting for a thousand years or more. Communal mountain sheep hunting in the higher elevations may have survived through the drier conditions, although there is no concrete evidence to support such a hypothesis. We do, however, have evidence for communal mountain sheep hunting in protohistoric times (see Frison et al. 1990).

Acknowledgments

The writer acknowledges the help of the National Science Foundation, the National Geographic Society, the University of Wyoming, the Wyoming Recreation Commission, the Bureau of Land Management, the United States Department of Agriculture, the L.S.B. Leakey Foundation, and the Wyoming Archaeological Foundation for Research funding. I thank Forrest Fenn and Mr. and Mrs. William Simon for study of the Fenn and Simon Clovis caches. In particular, I wish to acknowledge the students and others who aided in the investigations and analyses of archaeological sites that yielded the present database.

References Cited

Anderson, E.
1968 Fauna of the Little Box Elder Cave, Converse County. Wyoming: The Carnivora. *University of Colorado Studies, Series Earth Sciences* 6:1–68.

Becker, C. F., and J. D. Alyea
1964 *Precipitation Probabilities in Wyoming.* Agricultural Experiment Station Bulletin 416. Laramie, University of Wyoming.

Bryson, R. A.
1974 A Perspective on Climatic Change. *Science* 184:753–760.

Butler, B. R.
1963 An Early Man Site at Big Camas Prairie, South-central Idaho. *Tebiwa* 6:22–33.

Chomko, S. A. and B. M. Gilbert
1987 The Late Pleistocene/Holocene Faunal Record in the Northern Bighorn Mountains, Wyoming. In *Late Quaternary Mammalian Biogeography and Environments of the Great Plains and Prairies,* edited by R. W. Graham, H. A. Semken, Jr., and M. A. Graham, pp. 394–408. Illinois State Museum Scientific Papers No. 22. Springfield, IL.

Frison, G. C.
1974 *The Casper Site: A Hell Gap Bison Kill on the High Plains.* Academic Press, New York.

1976 The Chronology of Paleo-Indian and Altithermal Period Groups in the Bighorn Basin, Wyoming. In *Cultural Change and Continuity: Essays in Honor of James Bennet Griffin,* edited by C. E. Cleland, pp. 147–173. Academic Press, New York.

1982 Paleo-Indian Winter Subsistence Strategies on the High Plains. In *Plains Indian Studies: A Collection of Essays in Honor of John C. Ewers and Waldo R. Wedel,* edited by D. H. Ubelaker and H. J. Viola, pp. 193–201. Smithsonian Contributions to Anthropology No. 30. Washington, D.C.

1984 The Carter/Kerr-McGee Paleoindian Site: Cultural Resource Management and Archaeological Research. *American Antiquity* 49:288–314.

1988 Paleoindian Subsistence and Settlement during Post-Clovis Times on the Northwestern Plains, the Adjacent Mountains and Intermontane Basins. In *Americans Before Columbus: Ice-Age Origins,* edited by R. C. Carlisle, pp. 83–106. Ethnology Monographs No. 12. Department of Anthropology, University of Pittsburgh, Pittsburgh.

1989 Experimental Use of Clovis Weaponry and Tools on African Elephants. *American Antiquity* 54:766–784.

1991a The Goshen Cultural Complex: New Data for Paleoindian Research. In *Clovis: Origins and Adaptations,* edited by R. Bonnichsen and K. L. Turnmire, pp. 133–151. Center for the Study of the First Americans, Oregon State University, Corvallis.

1991b The Clovis Cultural Complex: New Data from Caches of Flaked Stone and Worked Bone Artifacts. In *Raw Material Economies among Prehistoric Hunter-Gatherers,* edited by A. Montet-White and S. Holen, pp. 321–333. University of Kansas Publications in Anthropology No. 19. Lawrence, KS.

Frison, G. C. (editor)
1996 *The Mill Iron Site 24CT30 and the Goshen–Plainview Paleoindian Cultural Complex on the Northern High Plains.* University of New Mexico Press, Albuquerque.

Frison, G. C., R. L. Andrews, J. M. Adovasio, R. C. Carlisle, and R. Edgar
1986 A Late Paleoindian Animal Trapping Net from Northern Wyoming. *American Antiquity* 51:352–361.

Frison, G. C., and B. A. Bradley
1980 *Folsom Tools and Technology at the Hanson Site, Wyoming.* University of New Mexico Press, Albuquerque.

Frison, G. C., C. A. Reher, and D. N. Walker
1990 Prehistoric Mountain Sheep Hunting in the Central Rocky Mountains of North America. In *Hunters of the Recent Past,* edited by L. B. Davis and B. O. K. Reeves, pp. 208–240. Unwin-Hyman, London.

Frison, G. C. and D. J. Stanford
1982 *The Agate Basin Site: A Record of the Paleoindian Occupation of the Northwestern High Plains.* Academic Press, New York.

Frison, G. C., and L. C. Todd
1986 *The Colby Mammoth Site: Taphonomy and Archaeology of a Clovis Kill in Northern Wyoming.* University of New Mexico Press, Albuquerque.

Frison, G. C., M. C. Wilson, and D. Wilson
1976 Fossil Bison and Artifacts from an Early Altithermal Period Arroyo Trap in Wyoming. *American Antiquity* 41:28–57.

Frison, G. C., and G. M. Zeimens
1980 Bone Projectile Points: An Addition to the Folsom Cultural Complex. *American Antiquity* 45:231–237.

Graham, M. A., M. C. Wilson, and R. W. Graham
1987 Paleoenvironments and Mammalian Faunas of Montana, Southern Alberta, and Southern Saskatchewan. In *Late Quaternary Mammalian Biogeography of the Great Plains and Prairies,* edited by R. W. Graham, H. A. Semken, Jr., and M. A. Graham, pp. 410-459. Illinois State Museum Scientific Papers No. 22. Springfield, IL.

Hannus, L. A.
1990 Mammoth Hunting in the New World. In *Hunters of the Recent Past,* edited by L. B. Davis and B. O. K. Reeves, pp. 47–67. Unwin-Hyman, London.

Haynes, C. V., Jr.
1991 Clovis–Folsom–Midland–Plainview Geochronology. Paper presented at the 56th Annual Meeting of the Society for American Archaeology, New Orleans.

1992 Contributions of Radiocarbon Dating to the Geochronology of the New World. In *Radiocarbon After Four Decades,* edited by R. E. Taylor, A. Long, and R. S. Kra, pp. 355–374. Springer-Verlag, New York.

Irwin-Williams C., H. Irwin, G. Agogino, and C. V. Haynes, Jr.
1973 Hell Gap: Paleo-Indian Occupation on the High Plains. *Plains Anthropologist* 18:40–53.

Kornfeld, M., J. Saysette, and J. Miller
n.d. Goshen–Plainview Complex at Upper Twin Mountain Sites, Colorado: One Avenue for Future Research. Manuscript on file, Department of Anthropology, University of Wyoming.

Lahren, L. A., and R. Bonnichsen
1974 Bone Foreshafts from a Clovis Burial in Southwestern Montana. *Science* 186(4149):147–150.

Long, C. A.
1971 Significance of the Late Pleistocene Fauna from the Little Boxelder Cave, Wyoming, to Studies of Zoogeography of Recent Mammals. *Great Basin Naturalist* 31:93–105.

Markgraf, V., and T. Lennon
1986 Paleoenvironmental History of the Last 13,000 Years of the Eastern Powder River Basin, Wyoming, and Its Implications for Prehistoric Cultural Patterns. *Plains Anthropologist* 31:1–12.

Martin, J. E.
1987 Paleoenvironment of the Lange/Ferguson Clovis Kill Site in the Badlands of South Dakota. In *Late Quaternary Mammalian Biogeography and Environments of the Great Plains and Prairies,* edited by R. W. Graham, H. A. Semken, Jr., and M. A. Graham, pp. 314–322. Illinois State Museum Scientific Papers No. 22. Springfield, IL.

Mears, B., Jr.
1981 Periglacial Wedges and the Late Pleistocene Environment of Wyoming's Intermontane Basins. *Quaternary Research* 15:171–198.

Mehringer, P. J., Jr.
1988 Weapons of Ancient Americans. *National Geographic* 174:500–503.

Miller, K. G.
1988 *A Comparative Analysis of Cultural Materials from Two Bighorn Mountains Archaeological Sites: A Record of 10,000 Years of Occupation.* Unpublished Master's Thesis, Department of Anthropology, University of Wyoming, Laramie.

Porter, S. C.
1988 Landscapes of the Last Ice Age in North America. In *Americans Before Columbus: Ice-Age Origins,* edited by R. C. Carlisle, pp. 1–24. Ethnology Monographs No. 12. Department of Anthropology, University of Pittsburgh, Pittsburgh.

Reher, C. A.
1974 Population Study of the Casper Site Bison. In *The Casper Site: A Hell Gap Bison Kill on the High Plains*, edited by G. Frison, pp. 113–124. Academic Press, New York.

Scott-Cummings, L.
1996 Paleoenvironmental Interpretations for the Mill Iron Site, Based on Stratigraphic Pollen and Phytolith Analysis. In *The Mill Iron Site 24CT30 and the Goshen–Plainview Paleoindian Cultural Complex on the Northern High Plains*, edited by G. Frison, pp. 177-193. University of New Mexico Press, Albuquerque.

Sellards, E. H., G. L. Evans, and G. E. Meade
1947 Fossil Bison and Associated Artifacts from Plainview, Texas, with Descriptions of Artifacts by A. D. Krieger. *Bulletin of the Geological Society of America* 58:927–954.

Todd, L. C., D. J. Rapson, and J. L. Hofman
1996 Dentition Studies of the Mill Iron and Other Early Paleoindian Bonebed Sites. In *The Mill Iron Site 24CT30 and the Goshen–Plainview Paleoindian Cultural Complex on the Northern High Plains*, edited by G. Frison, pp. 145-175. University of New Mexico Press, Albuquerque.

Walker, D. N.
1982 Early Holocene Vertebrate Fauna. In *The Agate Basin Site: A Record of the Paleoindian Occupation of the Northwestern High Plains*, edited by G. Frison and D. Stanford, pp. 274–308. Academic Press, New York.

1987 Late Pleistocene/Holocene Environmental Changes in Wyoming: The Mammalian Record. In *Late Quaternary Mammalian Biogeography and Environments of the Great Plains and Prairies*, edited by R. W. Graham, H. A. Semken, Jr., and M. A. Graham. Illinois State Museum Scientific Papers No. 22. Springfield, IL.

Wilmsen, E. N., and F. H. H. Roberts Jr.
1978 *Lindenmeier, 1934–1974.* Smithsonian Contributions to Anthropology, No. 24. Washington, D.C.

Wilson, M.
1978 Archaeological Kill Site Populations and the Holocene Evolution of the Genus *Bison*. In *Bison Procurement and Utilization: A Symposium*, edited by L. B. Davis and M. Wilson, pp. 9–22. *Plains Anthropologist Memoir* 14.

Paleoindian Archaeology and Late Pleistocene Environments in the Plains and Southwestern United States

Dennis Stanford

Abstract

Major climatic changes across the late Pleistocene/early Holocene boundary produced significant variability in biotic richness throughout the Paleoindian period. Clovis in the Southwest and Plains was coincident with an interval of decreased effective moisture that contributed to biotic reorganization and Rancholabrean extinctions. Clovis sites appear to have been tied closely to residual wetland habitats where people foraged for a wide array of plant and animal resources. During this interval, bison herd sizes may have been restricted by species competition and a different predator guild than characterized later Paleoindian times.

Shortly thereafter, bison experienced ecological release in response to expanding grassland and wet meadow habitats for which they were ideally suited. Increasing levels of effective moisture led to a greater, if not specialized, focus on this prey animal in the terminal Pleistocene economies of groups using Folsom and Goshen technologies. I suggest that the environment reached a very high carrying capacity at this time, possibly contributing to the higher incidence of Folsom sites noted in the study area relative to any other Paleoindian group, with the possible exception of Cody.

The appearance of hunters using Agate Basin lanceolate projectile points marks the end of Folsom around 10,500 yr B. P. I argue that Agate Basin peoples originated to the west and northwest and moved east to inhabit the foothill ecotones and riverine environments of the Plains. Relatively drier and more seasonal climatic conditions may have resulted in declining bison populations. Agate Basin and later Hell Gap peoples may have augmented a generalized foraging pattern that incorporated smaller animal and plant resources with periodic forays out onto the Plains for seasonal communal bison hunts.

Toward the beginning of the subsequent Cody period, a return to mesic conditions improved plant and animal productivity. Human populations appear to have increased dramatically. By the end of Cody times, significant use of plant processing equipment was established and hunting territories appear to be more constricted, perhaps reflecting a shift to a more generalized Archaic hunting and gathering pattern.

Department of Anthropology, NMNH 304 Smithsonian Institution, Washington, DC 20560

Introduction

THIS PAPER SYNTHESIZES information compiled by scholars since Paleoindian studies began in the western United States 70 years ago. The discussion concentrates primarily on the Paleoindian cultures of the Plains and Southwest, with references and comparisons drawn from other regions, as the early peoples who lived and exploited these areas were not confined therein and did not live in isolation. Thus, to understand the development of Paleoindian cultures, one must consider to a certain extent the surrounding regions.

This presentation discusses the development of Paleoindian studies, reviews the evidence for the earliest human occupation of the area, and briefly summarizes the Plains and Southwest Paleoindian archaeological data. The archaeological data summary is divided into two sections: the fluted point pattern, which includes Clovis, Folsom, and Goshen/Plainview; and the lanceolate point pattern, which includes Agate Basin, Hell Gap, and Cody. These divisions generally follow the system used in Bonnichsen et al. (1987).

The term "pattern," as used here, refers to shared morphological and technological features among projectile point styles, but does not necessarily imply cultural-historical relationships. It is, however, accepted that shared common features of projectile points recovered from a single archaeological horizon signify a consensus among members of that society concerning the desired morphology of their projectile points—that is, a shared mental template (Knudson 1983). Projectile points also may have served, along with a variety of other material items, as symbols that identified specific social groups. Closely related social groups may have shared those symbols to some degree, and temporal changes in projectile point styles may retain elements common to the original pattern of technological knowledge. It is assumed that there is a certain validity in using shared morphological and technological attributes to imply a common social/historic relationship if there is continuity through either time and/or space. It also should be recognized that unrelated groups might adopt for any number of reasons, either wholesale or in part, similar morpho/technic systems. Such an event would be difficult for the archaeologist to discern without preservation of perishable artifacts.

The concluding statements summarize the author's current perspective on Plains and Southwest Paleoindian archaeology.

Summary of the History of Plains and Southwest Paleoindian Studies

IN 1927, EXCAVATIONS under the direction of J. D. Figgens uncovered fluted weapon tips in direct association with the bones of fossil bison near Folsom, New Mexico (Figgins 1927). To counter criticisms raised by skeptics, Figgins left partially exposed artifacts in situ during the following field season. Scientists from several institutions were invited to view the specimens while still in context. Most who viewed the evidence agreed that there was little question as to the association between the artifacts and extinct faunal remains. Subsequent excavations and geological research (Bryan 1937, 1941) established the Pleistocene age of the finds and produced additional fluted points in unquestionable association with more than a dozen bison. These discoveries demonstrated the potential antiquity of human prehistory in the New World. They also opened the door for Paleoindian research at a time when the prevailing scientific dogma considered the New World indigenous populations as relatively recent arrivals in the Western Hemisphere.

In the years following the Folsom discoveries, the North American Plains were afflicted by a severe drought. Productive farmlands were stripped of soil by seemingly unending wind storms. A tremendous number of archaeological sites were exposed by deflation, and artifact collecting became a common pastime. Large private collections were amassed, many containing examples of projectile points which we now know are late Pleistocene/early Holocene in age.

In the absence of chronological data, E. B. Renaud (1931, 1932) proposed an evolutionary scheme for the plethora of projectile point types discovered in the blowouts of eastern Colorado. In his system, the finely crafted unfluted lanceolate projectile points, known as "Yumas," were the oldest, followed in time by large, crudely flaked Folsomoid points, later termed Clovis. Smaller, well-made fluted points, like those from the Folsom site, were considered to be the youngest.

In 1931, Figgins (1931) excavated a deposit near Angus, Nebraska, which contained a crude Folsomoid point, thought to be associated with mammoth bones. The following year near Dent, Colorado, additional Folsomoid points again were found with the remains of mammoths (Figgins 1933). Figgins proposed that the crude "Folsomoid" points simply were large versions of Folsom points used for killing mammoths, while the smaller Folsom points were used for hunting bison.

Within months of the Dent discoveries, Folsomoid points were found with mammoth bones at a gravel quarry on Blackwater Draw, just south of Clovis, New Mexico (Howard 1935a, 1935b). Although the Blackwater Draw site was a stratified, multicomponent archaeological location, early research consisted of salvage efforts while gravel mining uncovered mammoth remains. Most early investigators considered the Folsomoid points to be culturally distinct from the Folsom points (Roberts 1940), thus the larger fluted specimens like those from Blackwater Draw became commonly known as Clovis fluted points (Wormington 1957). Even though it was thought that Clovis points pre-dated Folsom (Cotter 1938a, 1938b), it was not until 1949 that the relative stratigraphic positions of Clovis and Folsom were determined (Sellards 1952).

The association of fluted projectile points with extinct fauna at kill sites demonstrated the relative antiquity of early North Americans and elucidated aspects of their diets, but failed to contribute much information on the general lifeways of these people. The Lindenmeier site in northern Colorado provided the first opportunity to investigate a Paleoindian campsite (Roberts 1935). By excavating a large area of the site in search of living structures, Roberts was able to address many questions concerning the Folsom peoples. A large and diverse array of stone tools was recovered, which provided the first data on lithic reduction sequences and tools other than weaponry. The remains of antelope, deer, and rabbit recovered along with bison suggested to Roberts that the Folsom diet included a variety of animal and plant foods (Roberts 1936).

The Lindenmeier site was a stratified locality, and the upper occupation levels were removed as overburden. However, Roberts observed unfluted lanceolate Yuma-style points in the upper deposits, post-dating Folsom (Roberts 1936).

By the end of the 1940s, the numbers of excavated Paleoindian sites were increasing dramatically. Fluted point sites such as Miami (Sellards 1938) and McLean (Ray and Bryan 1938) cemented the notion that Clovis peoples were specialists in mammoth hunting. The Lipscomb (Schultz 1943), Linger (Hurst 1943), and Lubbock Lake (Sellards 1952) sites added to the Folsom data base. Yuma lanceolate points were found in context at the Ray Long site (Hughes 1949) in South Dakota; the Scottsbluff (Barbour and Shultz 1932) and Lime Creek sites (Davis 1953, Schultz and Frankforter 1948) in Nebraska; the Finley (Howard 1943; Howard et al. 1941), Horner (Jepsen 1953), and Agate Basin (Roberts 1943) sites in Wyoming; the San Jon site (Roberts 1942) in New Mexico; and the Plainview site in Texas (Sellards et al. 1947).

The diverse projectile-point assemblages from these latter sites indicated that Yuma points could be divided into distinct groups based on morphology and flaking technology (Wormington 1948). It also was thought that projectile points were the most diagnostic of the Paleoindian artifacts and could be used for deciphering cultural complexes. In contrast, the other chipped-stone tool categories were considered to be relatively ubiquitous in their occurrence and stylistically similar from site to site. Although it is now known that there is variation in non-projectile point artifacts (see Irwin and Wormington 1970), projectile points continue to be the "*fossile directure*" of Paleoindian cultures.

As the number of distinctive point types proliferated, confusion about their ages and relationships was compounded by the absence of stratified sites and absolute dating methods. Several conferences, one in Philadelphia in 1937 and others in Santa Fe in 1941 and 1951, were convened to sort out nomenclature and establish criteria for identifying meaningful technological attributes (Wormington 1948, 1957).

Excavations at Blackwater Draw in 1949 established the stratigraphic position of the Clovis, Folsom, Agate Basin, and Portales complexes, providing the first chronological ordering of Paleoindian cultures. Sellards (1952) separated the Paleoindian complexes into two categories based on his presumption of their subsistence economies: elephant hunters (known as the Llano complex) and the later bison hunters (Sellards 1952). The non-fluted points eventually became known as the Plano complex (Jennings 1955; Mason 1962).

The discovery of the Hell Gap site, in the chert-rich Hartville uplift of eastern Wyoming (Irwin-Williams et al. 1973) further refined our understanding of Plains Paleoindian chronology. Excavations conducted there during the 1960s and early 1970s examined four localities along an intermittent stream. Locality 1 produced the most complete occupation sequence. This sequence as identified by Irwin (1967) included Goshen, Folsom, Midland, Agate Basin, Hell Gap, Alberta, Cody, and Frederick occupations in ascending order.

The stratigraphy of the Hell Gap and Blackwater Draw sites provided a basic chronological framework for cultural succession on the Plains. However, regional variations in the Plains and the Southwest chronologies still are incompletely understood.

The pioneering geological efforts by Antevs and Bryan (Haynes 1990), and Evans and Meade (1945) established a geological framework and provided remarkably reasonable age estimates before the advent of radiocarbon dating. More recent work by Albanese (1978), Haynes (1975), and Holliday (1985), along with advances in geochronological techniques (Stafford et al. 1991), continue to fine-tune our understanding of the geology of Paleoindian sites and cultural succession on the Plains and in the Southwest.

Interdisciplinary studies have been an important aspect of Paleoindian research since the discovery of the Folsom site. Geologists, paleontologists, and paleoecologists worked hand-in-hand with archaeologists, establishing the environmental parameters that are crucial for any understanding of the cultural adaptations to the changing environments of the Plains and Southwest (see Graham et al. 1987; Ruddiman and Wright 1987; Wendorf and Hester 1975; and Wright 1983).

By the 1960s, the broad chronological order of Paleoindian cultures and ecological parameters were placed in general perspective, and the archaeological database had increased significantly. Scientific attention turned toward the integration of multidisciplinary research with an increasing anthropological orientation. Wendorf and Hester's (1975) Southern High Plains project was the first major regional study that used the interdisciplinary approach to investigate Paleoindian lifeways. The pioneering efforts of Joe Ben Wheat (1972, 1979) and George Frison (1974) on bison kill sites initiated the systematic analysis of animal bones from Paleoindian sites. Wheat (1972) analyzed the Olsen-Chubbock bone bed as an artifact of the occupation, paying close attention to the spatial distribution of skeletal elements as keys to the butchering process. He first fully employed ethnographic analogs to reconstruct activities conducted in a bison kill site. Research also began on bison herd composition and seasonality of site occupation, based on tooth eruptions and wear patterns (Frison and Reher 1970; Reher 1974). Frison's (1978, 1991a) studies of hunting and butchering strategies, based in part on his experience as a rancher and hunting guide, have greatly enhanced our understanding of Paleoindian procurement systems.

Studies of site-formation processes (Frison and Todd 1986, 1987) have contributed to our understanding of natural and cultural factors in the accumulation of bone beds. Detailed analyses of spatial distributions of bison bone, along with refit studies, have provided interpretations of site activities and sequencing of events (Jodry 1992; Jodry and Stanford 1992; Todd and Stanford 1992).

Replicative studies of Paleoindian chipped-stone artifacts begun by Crabtree (1966) and Bradley (1974) have established criteria for discriminating cultural variations in manufacturing and rejuvenation techniques. Likewise, the research of Young and Bonnichsen (1984) used the experimental approach to discern individual behavior in lithic technology. Applications of usewear analysis (Kay 1996; Root and Emerson 1994; Wilmsen and Roberts 1978) have moved functional interpretations from an intuitive art, based on ethnographic analogy and morphology, to more precise identification of tool use.

Analytical techniques for identifying chert sources (Banks 1990; Hofman et al. 1991a) have greatly enhanced our understanding of the distribution of Paleoindian lithic resources. These techniques laid the groundwork for identifying resource areas and, possibly, group social boundaries and exchange systems (Amick 1994a; Hofman 1992). Employment of statistical methods, such as that accomplished by Wilmsen (Wilmsen and Roberts 1978) on the Lindenmeier stone tools and Irwin (1967; Irwin and Wormington 1970) on general Paleoindian assemblages, added a new dimension to artifact analyses in the 1960s and 1970s.

These are a few examples of how Paleoindian studies are centering on anthropological problem orientations. It appears that we are on the threshold of future discoveries that will help to define the past lifeways of the first Americans.

Evidence for Pre-Clovis Cultures

Clovis artifacts (see Figures 7-9) have been found in North America from coast to coast and from Canada to Latin America, making it the most widespread cultural complex in the New World (see Bonnichsen and Turnmire 1991; Haynes 1980). The people who made Clovis points are considered by some scholars to be the earliest Americans (Haynes 1984; Martin 1984). Others believe that Clovis developed in North America from a preexisting population (Bonnichsen and Turnmire 1991). Evidence provided by genetic studies (Szathmary 1985; Williams et al. 1985), tooth morphology (Turner 1985), and language divergence (Greenberg et al. 1986; Nichols 1990) suggests that the ancestors of Native Americans arrived from

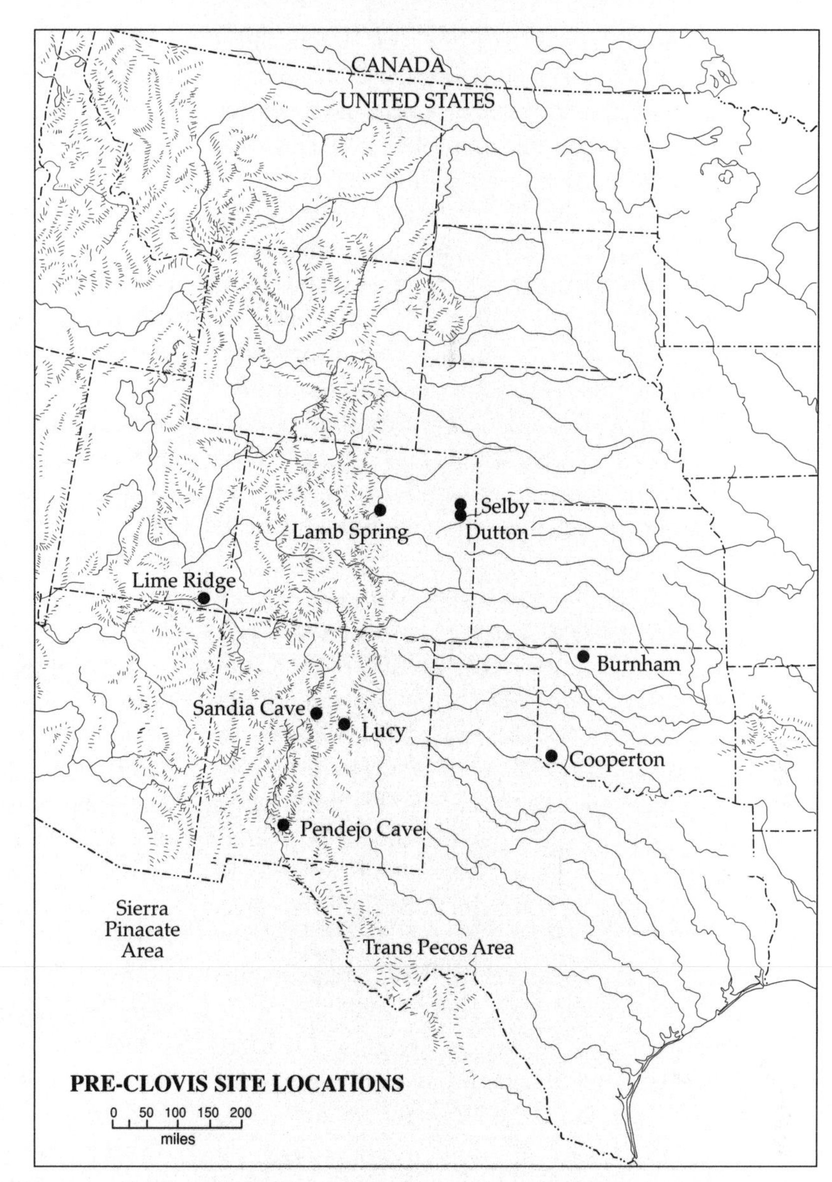

Figure 1. Pre-Clovis site locations.

Table 1. Pre-Clovis Radiocarbon Dates

Site	*Material*	*^{14}C Age Date B.P.*	*Lab. Number*	*Source*
Burnham	charcoal	26,820 ± 350	AA-3838	Wyckoff et al. 1990
	shell	31,150 ± 700	Beta-23045	
	shell	35,890 ± 850	AA-3837	
	charcoal	40,900 ± 1600	AA-3840	
Cooperton	bone	19,100 ± 800	GX-1214	Anderson 1975
	bone	17,575 ± 550	GX-1215	
	bone	20,400 ± 450	GX-1216	
Dutton	bone	11,710 ± 150	SI-2877	Stanford and Graham 1985
	bone	13,600 ± 485	SI-5186	
Lamb Spring	bone	11,735 ± 95	SI-4850	Fisher 1992
	bone	13,140 ± 1000	M-1464	
	organics	12,750 ± 150	SI-6487	
Selby	bone	16,630 ± 320	SI-5185	Stanford and Graham 1985

Northeast Asia. However, Clovis or other fluted projectile points have not been found in archaeological assemblages from Northeast Asia. Therefore, it appears that Clovis technology must have been developed by an indigenous New World population.

The questions of who the first Americans were, what kind of technologies they possessed, how much earlier than Clovis they arrived in the Americas, and when, where, and why fluting originated, have been the subjects of major debates and research efforts since the discovery of the Blackwater Draw site (Bonnichsen 1991). A number of sites that have been involved in these debates occur in our study area (Figure 1; Table 1). However, at present, there are no sites on the Plains or in the Southwest that can be called unequivocally pre-Clovis.

One of the most well known pre-Clovis sites, found during the 1930s, was Sandia Cave, where single-shouldered, unfluted projectile points (Figure 2d–f) occurred in a geologic strata below Folsom artifacts (Hibben 1941). It was suggested that Sandia was ancestral to the fluted-point complexes (Hibben 1955). The discovery of fluted Sandia points (Figure 2a), from a blowout deposit south of Lucy, New Mexico, seemed to verify that assumption (Roosa 1956a, 1956 b). However, 40 years of Paleoindian research has failed to yield additional evidence to substantiate that hypothesis, and the veracity of the finds has been called into question (Stevens and Agogino 1975).

In a recent paper, Haynes and Agogino (1986), re-evaluate the geology of Sandia Cave and suggest that Sandia points may be Clovis knives used for mining ocher deposits found in the cave. Although this explanation may be applicable to the Sandia points from Sandia Cave, it does not account for those from the Lucy site. It appears that the status of Sandia points cannot be resolved unless additional Sandia sites are found and excavated.

Regardless of the controversy surrounding the Sandia points, there was an early human occupation of Sandia Cave. Both Clovis and Folsom artifacts were found in the cave, along with other chipped stone tools estimated to date between 10,900 and 14,000 years old (Haynes and Agogino 1986). Among these artifacts are several unshouldered bifaces (Figure 2b,c), which are technologically similar to specimens that have been recovered from sites dating to ca. 25,000 years old in eastern Siberia (Derevianko 1989); it is intriguing to speculate that these unshouldered Sandia Cave specimens may be pre-Clovis in age.

Another purported pre-Clovis manifestation is known as the Malpais complex. Artifacts of this complex are expediently flaked cobble tools heavily coated with desert varnish (Figure 3). Malpais artifacts are known from several areas, including the Sierra Pinacate of northern Sonora (Hayden 1976), the Trans Pecos area of southwest Texas (Andretta and Hayden, personal communication 1985), Manix Lake, California (Bamforth and Dorn 1988), and Lime Ridge in southeastern Utah (Kearns et al. 1990).

Malpais artifacts have been found on surface localities that are nearly impossible to date. Hayden, however, noted differences in the technology of Malpais artifacts associated with successive strand lines of pluvial lakes in the Sonoran Desert. From this data, he deduced a developmental sequence and a Pleistocene age for the Malpais complex (Hayden 1976).

A recent geochemical analysis, known as the cation-ratio technique, has been used to estimate the relative ages of the microbes responsible for the formation of desert varnish (Dorn 1983, 1989). These ratios suggest that Malpais artifacts may be greater than 20,000 years old, which correlates with the existence of pluvial lakes in the Sonoran Desert (Dolzani 1988; Hayden, personal communication 1988). The accuracy of this dating technique has not yet been determined. However, in a control test of a sample of desert-varnished artifacts including Clovis and Archaic-age surface finds from the Lime Ridge, Utah, localities, the cation ratios fell within the expected range of Clovis and Archaic radiocarbon ages (Kearns et al. 1990). Initial results indicate that the cation-ratio technique might have potential for resolving the Malpais problem. A final determination of the antiquity of these artifacts awaits further research and acceptable chronometric dating.

Sites of pre-Clovis age, such as Dutton and Selby (Stanford and Graham 1985) in Colorado and Cooperton (Anderson 1975) in Oklahoma, contain fractured, flaked, and polished bones that were thought to be the result of human butchery and tool use (Stanford and Graham 1985). The validity of using modified bone as indicators of human activity in the absence of other lines of evidence has since been demonstrated to be ill-advised (see Binford 1981; Bonnichsen and Sorg 1989; G. Haynes 1991). Thus, in light of current analytical techniques for identifying and interpreting bone fracture patterns (Lyman 1994), it is not certain whether these specimens were altered by humans.

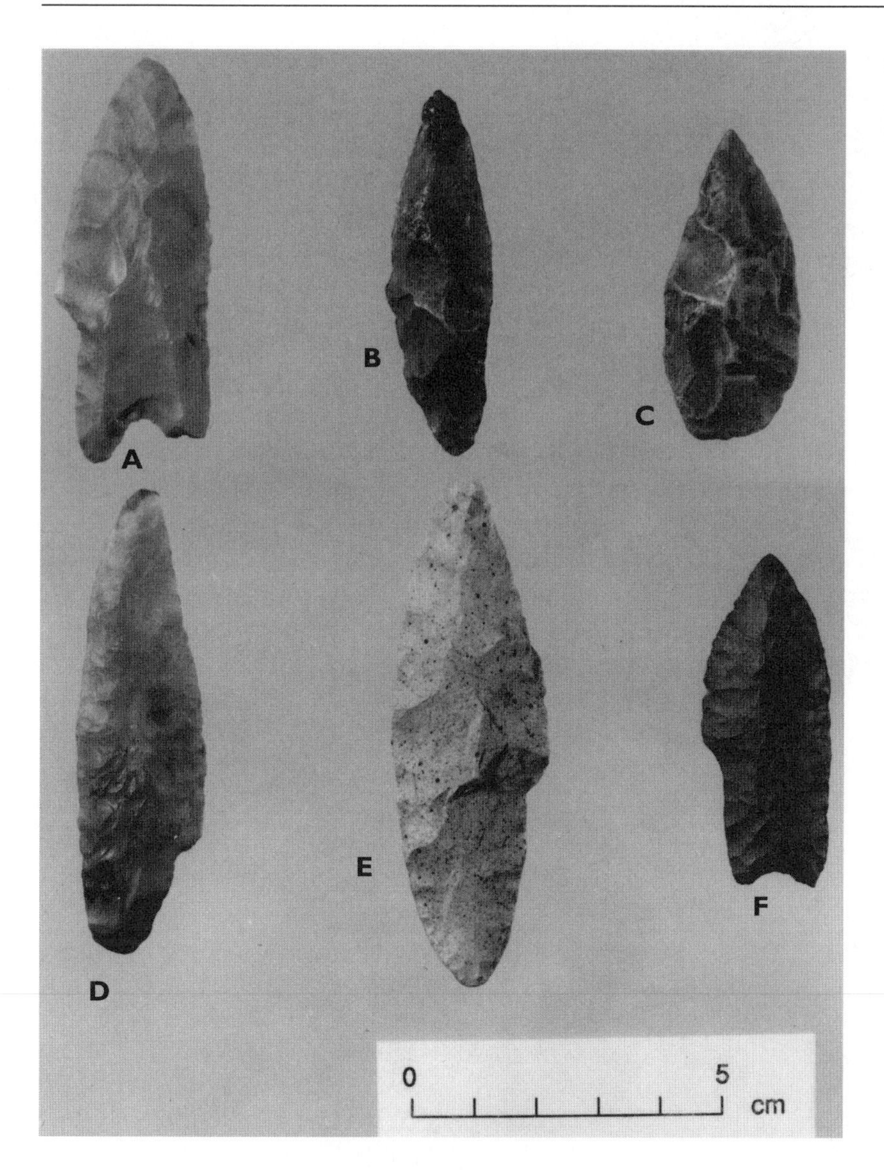

Figure 2. Sandia projectile points—A. Lucy Site, New Mexico; B-F Sandia Cave, New Mexico.

Lamb Spring, a stratified site located near Denver, Colorado, produced mammoth remains concentrated in and around a series of spring seeps (Rancier et al. 1982; Stanford et al. 1981). Although most of the thin-walled bones, such as ribs and scapulae, were intact, the majority of the more durable, thick-walled long bones were green fractured and flaked. Concentrated piles of like elements were found, as well as complete skulls with attached tusks. Two stone artifacts were recovered that are clearly cultural in origin: a 33-pound boulder that is battered along one edge (Figure 4a,b), and a quartzite wedge (Figure 4c). The original radiocarbon determinations suggested that the site was ca. 13,000 years old. A subsequent assay of 11,735±95 yr B.P.(SI-4850) suggests that some of the bone may be early Clovis in age (Rancier et al. 1982).

Several additional sites recently have been reported as pre-Clovis candidates. At the Burnham site, Oklahoma, chipped stone flakes were found with extinct faunal remains dating between 26,820 and 40,900 yr B.P. (Wyckoff et al. 1990). After a careful interdisciplinary excavation and analyses, Wyckoff and Carter (1994) concluded that the artifacts and faunal remains were fortuitously mixed.

Another pre-Clovis candidate is Pendejo Cave. Located in the Tularosa Basin, New Mexico, the cave was investigated by MacNeish from 1990 to 1992, and analyses are still being completed (MacNeish 1992). This site contains well-stratified cave deposits with possible Paleoindian occupations dating as early as 50,000 yr B.P. (MacNeish 1992). Evidence of human occupation from the cave includes clay nodules with putative human skin imprints, possible human hair, and expedient stone tools, some of which were made from stone sources from outside the cave (Chrisman et al. 1996). Further verification of these research results needs to be accomplished before the significance of this site can be adequately assessed.

Figure 3. Sierra Pinacate Malpais cobble tools.

Fluted Point Pattern

PROJECTILE POINTS that are basally thinned by the removal of either channel flakes or well-developed pressure flakes are included within the Fluted Point Pattern. Typically the bases of these specimens are concave, but as a result of rejuvenation of broken points, fluting/basal thinning may be obliterated and the base may become flattened. Included in the Fluted Point Pattern are Clovis, Folsom/Midland, and Goshen/Plainview.

Figure 4. Artifacts from the Mammoth bone level, Lamb Spring Site, Colorado: A. 33 lb. boulder; B. Close-up view of battered surface of boulder; C. Bifacial wedge.

Clovis

CLOVIS IS THE EARLIEST demonstrable cultural complex yet identified in North America. Clovis sites and surface artifacts are distributed throughout the Southwest and Plains (Figure 5), but their numbers are not nearly as great in the eastern United States. Western Clovis sites are now dated between approximately 11,500 and 10,900 yr B.P. (Table 2,; Figure 6).

The Clovis tool kit is reminiscent of the macrocore/blade and biface industries of the upper Paleolithic cultures of Eurasia, but has notable differences (Saunders et al. 1990). The typical lithic tool kit contains bifacial fluted projectile points (Figure 7), large bifaces, blade cores (Figure 8) and blades, cutting and scraping tools made on blades (Figure 9d–g) and flakes (Figure 9c,h), gravers, a variety of end scrapers (Figure 9e), and occasional burins.

Clovis blades are known from many sites, but only recently have blade cores been recognized at sites on the Southern Plains. The first blade cores and core tablets were found at Pavo Real (49BX52), excavated by the Texas Department of Transportation near San Antonio, Texas (Henderson and Goode 1991). These are primarily large polyhedral cores, with well-prepared platforms. Another polyhedral blade core has been reported from the Clovis deposits at Kincaid Rockshelter, Texas (Collins et al. 1989). Evidence for blade manufacture was also recovered at the Aubrey site, located north of Dallas, Texas (Ferring 1990).

Clovis artifact caches have been found on the Central and Southern Plains. The Drake Cache (Stanford and Jodry 1988) in northeastern Colorado consisted of 13 newly completed and resharpened projectile points and a chert hammmerstone. Small ivory fragments suggest that perishable artifacts were once part of the cache. Two presumed Clovis blade caches have been found at Blackwater Draw (Green 1963; Montgomery, personal communication 1991) and another at 41NV659 in east-central Texas (Young and Collins 1989). There is no evidence that these caches were associated with human internments, nor is there any evidence of red ocher.

At the Gault site, located in Central Texas, 10 engraved limestone pebbles and cobbles were recovered with Clovis projectile points (Collins et al. 1991). Designs on these specimens primarily consist of parallel linear incisions, though some have intersecting lines forming rectilinear or diamond-shaped patterns. Two have straight and curving lines, while a possible animal is represented on another specimen.

Among tools made out of perishable raw materials are a bone shaft wrench (Figure 9a) recovered at Murray Springs (Haynes and Hemmings 1968) and a foreshaft or projectile point (Figure 9b) from Blackwater Draw (Hester 1972; Sellards 1952). A possible ivory billet (Saunders et al. 1991), as well as ivory manufacturing technology, has been described from Blackwater Draw (Saunders et al. 1990). Bone-expediency tools and flaked mammoth bones have been reported from the Lubbock Lake site (Johnson 1987), Blackwater Draw (Hester 1972), and the Lange-Ferguson site in South Dakota (Hannus 1989).

Lithic raw materials utilized by Clovis flintknappers tended to be of the best quality, and many artifacts were made from materials imported from distant

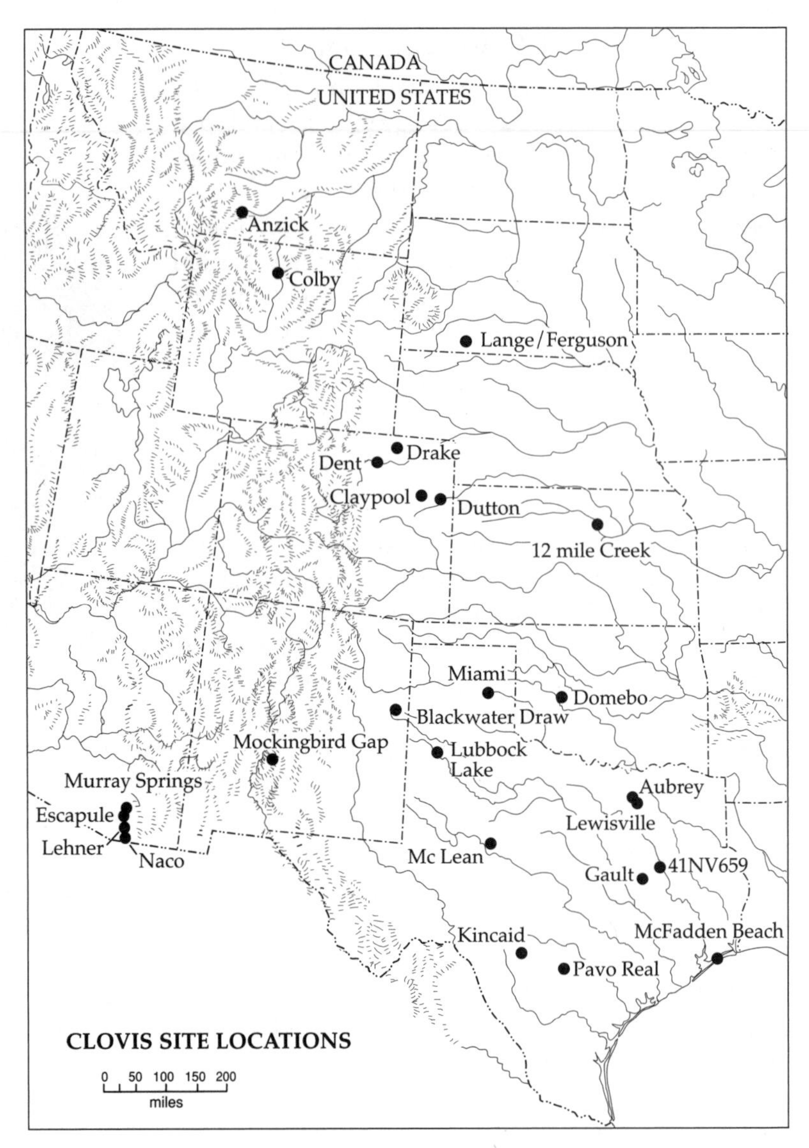

Figure 5. Clovis site locations.

quarries. This suggests exploitation of very large territories or trade distribution of raw materials. Large bifaces and blades were produced at quarry locations and transported until needed for tool use or manufacture of new projectile points. The bifaces served as both a raw material source and functional artifacts. Clovis projectile points were not only used for weapon tips, but also for cutting tools (Kay 1996). Points were rejuvenated until their usefulness in that capacity was surpassed and then often modified for other functions.

In the Plains and Southwest, the majority of Clovis artifacts have been found at kill localities near springs, small playas, or ponded streams. In most cases, the primary activity appears to be mammoth butchering, although at Murray Springs, there was an associated bison kill (Haynes 1981). Johnson (1987) also reports smaller faunal species from a possible Clovis mammoth-processing area at Lubbock Lake.

The methods employed in killing proboscideans have not been determined. Impact-damaged Clovis weapon tips indicate that they were used as projectile points. Clovis hunters may have wounded or even poisoned the animals and waited until they died, or followed them until the mammoths became weakened and finally were dispatched. It would seem unlikely that additional hunting would have taken place following a successful mammoth kill or during processing. The bones of smaller animals found at kill sites may be the remains of food consumed by hunters as they waited for a wounded beast to die or may simply be the bones of unassociated animals that died of natural causes.

At several Clovis kill sites, more than one mammoth is represented in the faunal assemblage, although it is impossible to tell whether they represent synchronous or multiple kill events. Saunders (1977) hypothesized that entire family units may have been killed during

Table 2. Clovis radiocarbon dates.

Site	*Material*	*^{14}C Age Date B.P.*	*Lab. Number*	*Source*
Anzick	collagen	10,600 ± 300	AA——-	Taylor et al. 1985
	aspartic acid	10,240 ± 120	AA-2978	Haynes, 1991a
	glutamic acid	10,820 ± 100	AA-2979	
	hydroxyproline	10,710 ± 100	AA-2980	
	glycine	10,940 ± 90	AA-2981	
	alanine	10,370 ± 130	AA-2982	
Aubrey	unknown	10,946 ± 87	SMU-2194	Ferring 1990
	unknown	10,724 ± 90	SMU-2338	
	unknown	10,360 ± 150	Beta-32002	
	charcoal	11,540 ± 110	AA-5271	Humphrey & Ferrring 1994
	charcoal	11,590 ± 90	AA-5274	
Blackwater Draw	carbonized plant	11,630 ± 350	A-491	Haynes et al. 1984
Locality 1	carbonized plant	11,170 ± 110	A-481	
	carbonized plant	11,040 ± 240	A-490	
Colby	collagen	11,200 ± 200	RL-392	Frison 1976
	apatite	10,864 ± 141	SMU-254	Frison and Todd 1986
	collagen	8,719 ± 392	SMU-278	
Dent	bone organics	11,200 ± 500	I-622	Haynes et al. 1984
	XAD purified	10,980 ± 90	AA-2941	Haynes 1991a
	aspartic acid	10,660 ± 170	AA-2942	
	glutamic acid	10,800 ± 110	AA-2943	
	hydroxyproline	10,600 ± 90	AA-2945	
	glycine	10,710 ± 90	AA-2946	
	alanine	10,670 ± 120	AA-2947	Stafford et al. 1990
	XAD purified	10,590 ± 500	AAA-832	
	XAD purified	10,950 ± 480	AA-833	
Domebo	wood	11,045 ± 647	SM-695	Stafford et al. 1990
	wood	11,490 ± 450	AA-823	Haynes 1991a
	bone	11,220 ± 500	SI-172	
	bone	11,200 ± 600	SI-175	
	XAD purified	11,480 ± 450	AA-825	
	Pro-Hypro	10,860 ± 450	AA-811	
	XAD hydrate	10,810 ± 420	AA-805	
Lange/Ferguson	organics	10,730 ± 530	I-13104	Hannus 1989
	collagen	10,670 ± 300	I-11710	
	charcoal	11,140 ± 140	AA-905	Haynes 1991a
Lehner	charcoal	11,470 ± 110	SMU-308	Haynes et al. 1984
	charcoal	11,170 ± 200	SMU-264	
	charcoal	11,080 ± 230	SMU-196	
	charcoal	11,080 ± 200	SMU-181	
	charcoal	10,950 ± 110	SMU-194	
	charcoal	10,950 ± 90	SMU-290	
	charcoal	10,940 ± 100	A-378	
	charcoal	10,860 ± 280	SMU-164	
	charcoal	10,770 ± 140	SMU-168	
	charcoal	10,710 ± 90	SMU-340	
	charcoal	10,700 ± 150	SMU-297	
	charcoal	10,620 ± 300	SMU-347	

Site	Material	^{14}C Age Date B.P.	Lab. Number	Source
Lubbock Lake	clam	12,650 ± 250	I-2466	Holliday et al. 1983
Strat. I	clam	12,150 ± 90	SMU-295	
	wood	11,100 ± 100	SMU-548	
	wood	11,100± 80	SMU-263	
Murray Spring	charcoal	11,190 ± 180	SMU-18	Haynes et al. 1984
	charcoal	11,150 ± 450	A-805	
	charcoal	11,080 ± 180	Tx-1413	
	charcoal	10,930 ± 170	Tx-1462	
	charcoal	10,890 ± 180	SMU-27	
	charcoal	10,840 ± 70	SMU-41	
	charcoal	10,840 ± 140	SMU-42	
	charcoal	10,710 ± 160	Tx-1459	
12 Mile Creek	apatite	10,435 ± 260	GX-5812-A	Rogers and Martin 1984

one event. However, the amount of food gained from a single animal would be tremendous, and, unless storage systems were employed, it is likely that the remains of multiple animals accumulated from separate events that took place over a period of time.

At Escapule (Hemmings and Haynes 1969) and Naco (Haury 1953), taphonomic evidence, the number of complete projectile points, and the absence of butchering tools and resharpening flakes may indicate that the animals escaped their tormentors to die elsewhere (Haynes, personal communication 1984).

Murray Springs and possibly Lehner have small campsites associated with mammoth kills. These sites suggest that after a successful kill, a camp was set up nearby while processing the animals. Fisher's (1992) ethnoarchaeological studies of the Efe elephant hunters in Africa describe temporary campsites near elephant kills, which were occupied while butchering activities were conducted. Once the game was processed, the Efe returned to a base camp. Such a model might be applicable to Clovis kills and small associated campsites, although no Clovis base camps have been identified for western Clovis.

A hearth area at Lehner contained highly charred, immature mammoth bone, which may indicate bone grease processing and/or bone utilization for fuel, as well as food consumption. At Murray Springs are three localities: a mammoth kill site, a campsite, and another area where a small group of bison were killed. These localities can be linked with one another by refitted broken artifacts (Haynes 1981). It might be possible that the two kill events took place at different times by hunters operating from a base camp located elsewhere in the San Pedro Valley.

Mammoth hunting may have been a fall activity, providing a reliable winter food source that allowed the establishment of a winter base camp. Meat caches, such as those found at the Colby site, might support such a model (Frison and Todd 1986). Additional hunting during the occupation of the base camp could result in sites like Murray Springs and Lehner, which have multiple kill events.

As more sites are investigated, it appears that Clovis peoples had a broad-based economy and that proboscideans may not have been as important to their diet as once thought (Johnson 1991). At the Lewisville site in Texas, the occupational surface was eroded, leaving only the bottoms of the hearth features. Food remains found in these features included only small mammals, amphibians, reptiles, and reptile eggs, as well as baked mud-dauber larvae and hackberry seeds (Stanford et al. 1995). These food resources indicate that Lewisville was occupied during the summer. Alligators, turtles, armadillos, badgers, raccoons, and mice may have been among the animals used by Clovis peoples at Kincaid Rockshelter (Collins et al. 1989).

The Aubrey site, located near Denton, Texas, and currently under investigation by Reid Ferring (1990), is a Clovis campsite associated with a possible bison kill. Faunal remains found in the camp debris include sloth, small mammals, and turtles, along with the bison (Ferring 1995).

Paleoclimatic evidence indicates that the climate of the Southwest and Southern Plains had deteriorated during Clovis times from the lush conditions that existed during the glacial maxima (Haynes 1991b, 1993, 1995). Springs and lakes dried up, and animals and their predators concentrated around the remaining water sources. Water wells, such as those dug by

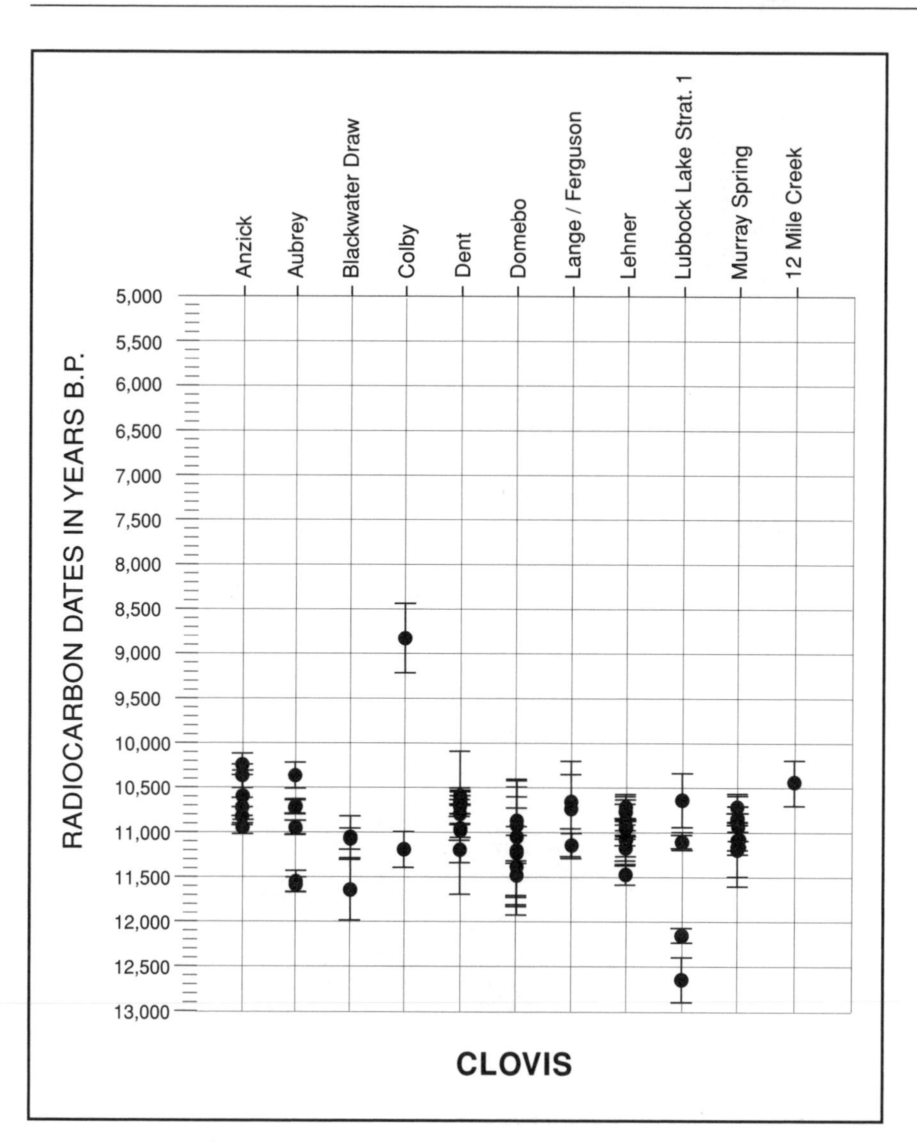

Figure 6. Clovis radiocarbon dates.

mammoths at Murray Springs (Haynes 1991b) and human excavated wells found at both Blackwater Draw (Haynes et al. n.d.) and Aubrey (Ferring 1995; Humphrey and Ferring 1994), suggest that drought conditions existed during the Clovis occupation. The wells probably were dug by Clovis peoples for human use, but also would have attracted animals to specific locations. It was during this period of climatic deterioration that many taxa became extinct.

The reduction of animal species at the end of the Pleistocene has been attributed to overkill by human predators by some scholars (Martin 1984) and to climatic change by others (Graham and Lundelius 1984; Grayson 1989). In fact, both events probably acted in concert, resulting in the extinction of many species. Drought conditions reduced the grassland's carrying capacity and increased competition for the available food and water resources, concentrating prey species at specific locations including, perhaps, artificial water sources created by humans. These circumstances allowed predators, among them humans, to maximize their hunting strategies, which no doubt seriously affected animal species that already were in jeopardy.

Paleoenvironmental studies suggest that by the end of the Clovis occupations on the Western Plains and in the Southwest, the environment was becoming wetter. This climatic shift can be seen at Backwater Draw, New Mexico, where stratigraphic evidence indicates that a rise in the water table was coincident with Folsom and resulted in the occurrence of shallow discontinuous ponds (Haynes 1975, 1993). At pluvial Lake Estancia, New Mexico, there was a renewed high-water phase marked by the appearance of freshwater gastropods (Bachhuber and McClellan 1977) by the end of Clovis times. San Augustin Lake, in west-central New Mexico, became less saline after 11,000 yr B.P., indicating that the climate was wetter than it had been from 16,000 to 11,000 yr B.P. (Markgraf et al. 1984).

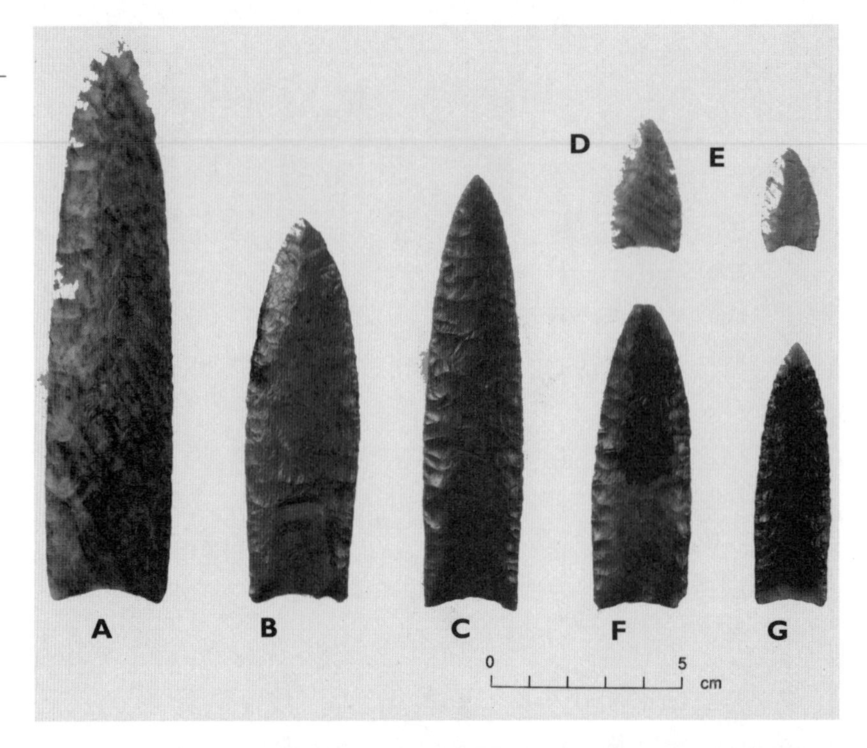

Figure 7. Clovis projectile points: A. Drake Cache, Colorado; B. Naco Site, Arizona; C.–E. Blackwater Draw, Locality 1; F–G. Dombo Site, Oklahoma.

Figure 8. Clovis blade core: surface find, Hamilton Co., Texas.

Evidence from pollen and plant macrofossils from the San Luis Valley in Colorado also suggests that the climate became much wetter following a dry climatic phase during Clovis times (Jodry and Stanford 1996; Jodry et al. 1989).

The net effect of an increase in moisture and a rising water table was that innumerable shallow basins found throughout the Western Plains and Southwest filled with fresh water. Correlated with this event would have been the stabilization and expansion of grasslands. These new environmental parameters opened up large expanses of territory, which may not have been attractive in earlier Clovis times.

Even though mammoths and other taxa hunted by Clovis peoples became extinct, bison remained. The bison essentially were released into a habitat for which they were ideally suited and, with the demise of many other large herbivores, for which there was little competition. Thus, the size of bison herds, which may have been regulated by species competition prior to the extinction, may have increased dramatically. Bison became the major big-game prey of most of the ensuing Plains hunters.

Figure 9. Clovis artifacts: A. Shaft straightener—Murry Spring Site, Arizona; B. Bone projectile point—Blackwater Draw, Locality 1, New Mexico; C.–D. Flake tool—Blackwater Draw Locality 1; E. End scraper made on Blade—Blackwater Draw Locality 1; F. flake/blade knife—Blackwater Draw Locality 1; flake knife—Blackwater Draw Locality 1.

Folsom

DURING THE BEGINNING of this wetter climatic phase, Clovis was replaced by Folsom technology. This technological transition may not signify a cultural replacement, but possibly represents a modification of weaponry as a response to increased specialization in bison as the major food resource.

A combination of Clovis and Folsom fluting and reduction techniques has been reported for the projectile points and preforms found at the Mockingbird Gap site, located in the northern end of the Tularosa Basin of south-central New Mexico (Webber and Agogino 1967). Consequently, they consider this assemblage transitional between Clovis and Folsom. Unfortunately, the investigation has not been completed, and, since no suitable organic remains were found for a radiocarbon assay, this site cannot be placed in chronological perspective.

Three broken Folsom point tips associated with extinct megafauna, including mammoth and camel, were found at the Wasden site located on the Snake River floodplain in Idaho (Miller and Dort 1978). Radiocarbon assays on the mammoth bone and obsidian hydration analyses suggest the bones accumulated between 12,850 and 9735 yr B.P. (Butler 1971; Plew and Pavesic 1982). Obsidian hydration studies suggest that the Folsom artifacts date between 12,000 and 11,200 yr B.P. (Green 1983). However, Miller (1982) suggests that the Folsom occupation at the Wasden site falls well within the Folsom time period. If the earlier dates and the association of Folsom points and mammoth bones are correct, it suggests that early Folsom and Clovis coexisted. Clearly, additional work needs to be conducted at this site.

Folsom sites have been radiocarbon assayed to as early as 10,900 yr B.P. at Hell Gap and as late as 10,200 yr B.P. at the Hanson site in Wyoming (Table 3, Figure 10). If these outside age estimates are correct, Folsom technology lasted nearly 700 years.

Figure 10. Folsom radiocarbon dates.

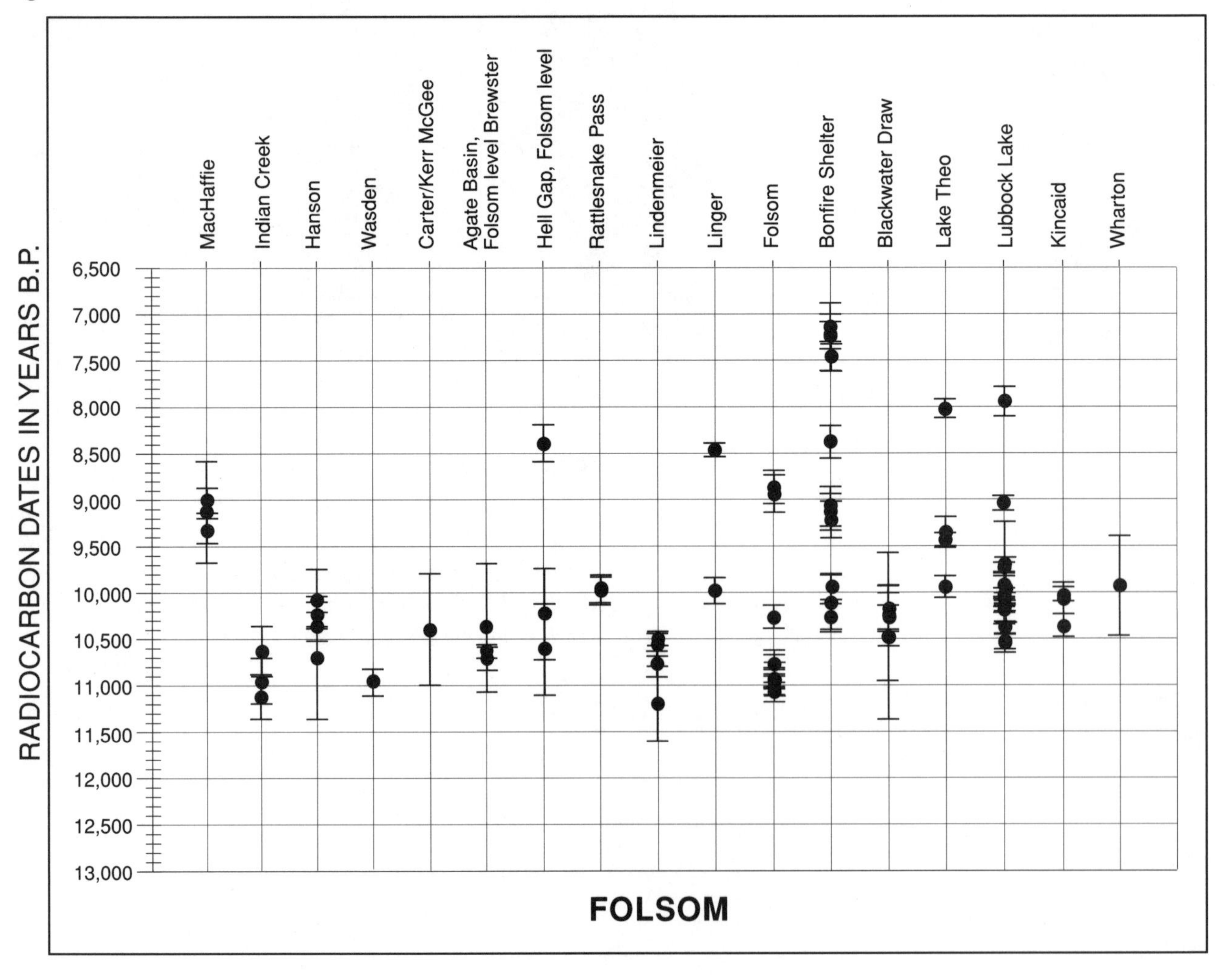

Table 3. Folsom radiocarbon dates.

Site	*Material*	*^{14}C Age Date B.P.*	*Lab. Number*	*Source*
Agate Basin,	charcoal	10,780 ± 120	SI-3733	Haynes et al. 1984
Folsom level	charcoal	10,665 ± 85	SI-3732	
Brewster	charcoal	10,375 ± 700	I-472	
Blackwater Draw	charcoal	10,250 ± 320	A-380-379	Haynes et al. 1992
	charcoal	10,490 ± 900	A-386	
	charcoal	10,170 ± 250	A-488	
	charcoal	10,490 ± 200	A-492	
	collagen	10,260 ± 110	SMU-179	
Bonfire Shelter	charcoal	10,230 ± 160	Tx-153	Haynes et al. 1984
	charcoal	10,100 ± 300	Tx-658	
	charcoal	9,920 ± 150	Tx-657	
	bone	8,380 ± 180	Tx-118	Tamers and Pearson 1965
	bone	7,470 ± 160	Tx-230-A	
	bone	7,110 ± 160	Tx-230-B	
	bone	9,120 ± 200	Tx-231-A	
	bone	7,230 ± 160	Tx-231-B	
	bone	9,210 ± 200	Tx-200-C	
	bone	9,080 ± 210	Tx-232-A	
	bone	7,230 ± 380	Tx-232-B	
Carter/Kerr-McGee	bone	10,400 ± 600	RL-917	Frison and Stanford 1982
Folsom	collagen	10,260 ± 110	SMU-179	Haynes et al. 1992
	charcoal	10,780 ± 100	AA-1213	
	charcoal	11,060 ± 100	AA-1708	
	charcoal	10,760 ± 140	AA-1709	
	charcoal	10,890 ± 150	AA-1710	
	charcoal	10,850 ± 190	AA-1711	
	charcoal	10,910 ± 100	AA-1712	
	bone	11.5 ± 1.4%M	SMU-153	
	bone	2,910 ± 190	SMU-161	
	bone	8,780 ± 180	SMU-162	
	bone	8,920 ± 200	SMU-163	
Hanson	charcoal	10,700 ± 670	RL-374	
	charcoal	10,080 ± 330	RL-558	
	charcoal	10,300 ± 150	Beta-22514-ETH-3229	
	charcoal	10,225 ± 125	Beta-31072	
Hell Gap, Folsom	charcoal	10,930 ± 200	A-503	
level	charcoal	10,690 ± 500	A-504	
	charcoal	10,290 ± 500	A-502	
Indian Creek	tephra	11,125 ± 130	Beta-4951	Davis 1984
	charcoal	10,980 ± 150	Beta-4619	Haynes et al. 1992
	charcoal	10,630 ± 280	Beta-13666	Haynes 1991a
	charcoal	10,980 ± 150	Beta-4619	
Kincaid	charcoal	10,025 ± 85	Tx-17	Haynes 1967
	charcoal	10,065 ± 185	Tx-19	
	charcoal	10,365 ± 110	Tx-20	
Lake Theo	humates	9,950 ± 110	SMU-866	Johnson et al. 1982
	humates	9,420 ± 85	SMU-856	
	bone	9,360 ± 170	Tx-2879	Harrison & Killen 1978
	bone	8,010 ± 100	Tx-2880	

Site	Material	^{14}C Age Date B.P.	Lab. Number	Source
Lindenmeier	charcoal	10,780 ± 135	I-141	Haynes et al. 1984
	charcoal	11,200 ± 400	GX-1282	
	charcoal	10,560 ± 110	TO-337	Haynes et al. 1992
	charcoal	10,500 ± 80	TO-342	
Linger	bone	8,480 ± 85	SI-3540	
	bone	9,885 ± 140	SI-3537	
Lubbock Lake	humates	10,015 ± 75	SI-3203	Haas et al. 1986
	humates	9,905 ± 140	SI-4975	
	humates	10,060 ± 70	SMU-251	
	humates	10,360 ± 80	SI-3200	
	humates	10,195 ± 165	SI-4976	
	charcoal	10,540 ± 100	SMU-547	
	humates	10,530 ± 90	SMU-285	
	bone	7,840 ± 170	SMU-247	Holliday et al. 1983
	bone	10,360 ± 80	SI-3200	Holliday et al. 1985
	humates	9,040 ± 90	SI-4592	
	humates	9,720 ± 80	SMU-975	
	humates	10,195 ± 195	SI-4976	
	humates	10,090 ± 100	SMU-1144	
	humates	10,160 ± 80	SMU-846	
	shell	9,700 ± 450	L-283G	Campbell 1961
	bone	9,883 ± 350	C-558	
MacHaffie	apatite	9,340 ± 120	Gx-15150-A-AMS	Davis et al. 1991
	apatite	9,130 ± 550	GX-15151-A	
	collagen	9,000 ± 130	GX-15151-G-AMS	
Owl Cave	collagen	10,920 ± 150	WSU-1786	Bryan 1980
		10,640 ± 85		Miller 1982
Rattlesnake Pass	charcoal	9770 ± 150	Tx-6305	Smith and McNees 1990
	charcoal	9950 ± 150	Tx-6304	
Wharton	charcoal	9,920 ± 530	AA-298	Patterson and Hudgins 1985

The Folsom core area covers a diverse topographic landscape encompassing the Rocky Mountains, the adjacent Plains and the eastern Basin and Range area west of the Rockies (Figure 11). The area approximates an elongated oval roughly 2,000 miles long on a northwest-southeast trending axis and about 800 miles wide. Although Folsom artifacts are found in Alberta and Saskatchewan (Forbis and Sperry 1952), the most northern excavated Folsom sites are in the Lake Ilo area of North Dakota (Root 1993; Root and Emerson 1994). To the west, Folsom artifacts have been excavated at Owl Cave in Idaho (Miller and Dort 1978) and occur as surface finds at the Montgomery site in eastern Utah (Davis 1985) and eastern Arizona (Huckel 1982). Folsom artifacts have been reported from as far east as western Iowa (Billeck n.d.; Morrow n.d.).

Within this area, Folsom weapon tips are extremely homogeneous and distinct from post-Clovis fluted projectile points found from the Midwest eastward—for example, the Parkhill complex (Deller and Ellis 1992; Roosa and Deller 1982) and Cumberland (Lewis 1954). Occasionally, Folsom points are reported from outside the core area; but usually these occur as single specimens, their context is unknown, they are associated with archaeological materials of different time periods, or they have been misidentified.

Because Folsom sites share a complex technology from the northern limit to the southern edge of their distribution, it is reasonable to assume that the humans who occupied this territory were interlocked by social networks. By ethnographic standards, the boundaries of such an area would be incredibly large (at the time of European contact, this area was the home of 38 distinct tribes). However, it must be kept in mind that during the early Holocene, the human population may have been extremely small, and social boundaries could have been much larger than in more populated times.

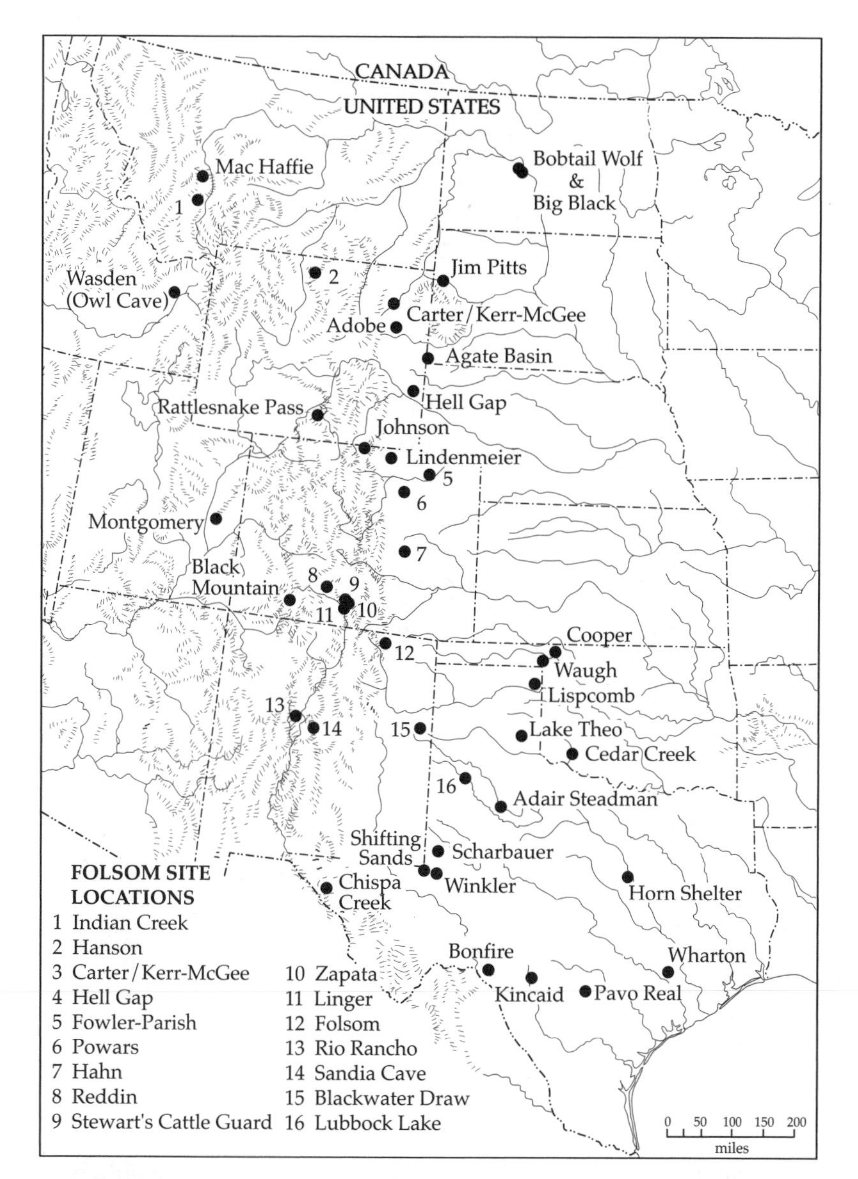

Figure 11. Folsom site locations.

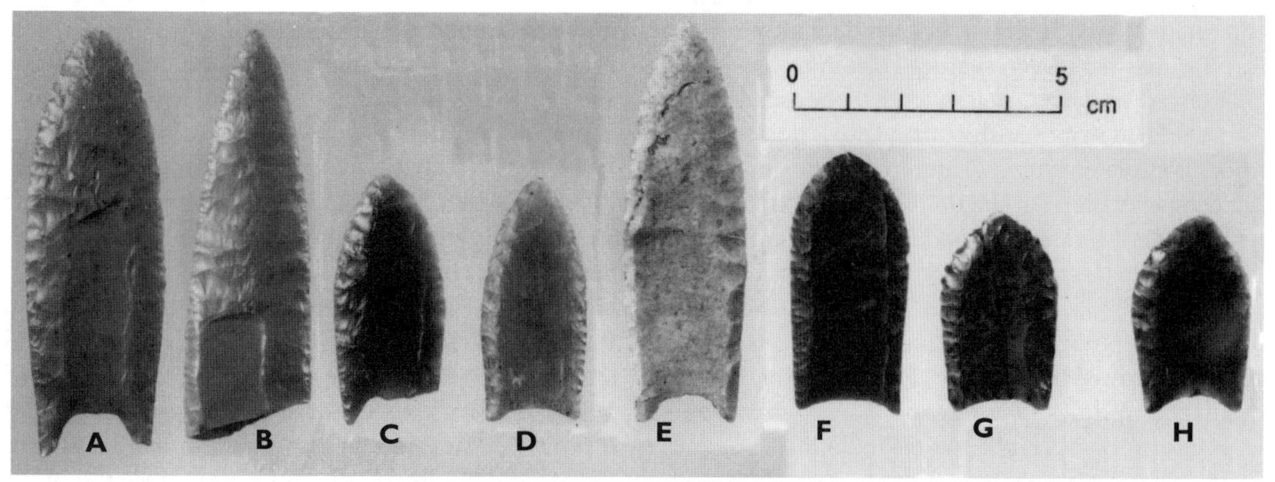

Figure 12. Folsom projectile points: A.–B. Blackwater Draw—Locality 1; C. Folsom Site, New Mexico; D.–E. & H. Lindenmeier Site, Colorado; F.–G. Stewart's Cattle Guard Site, Colorado.

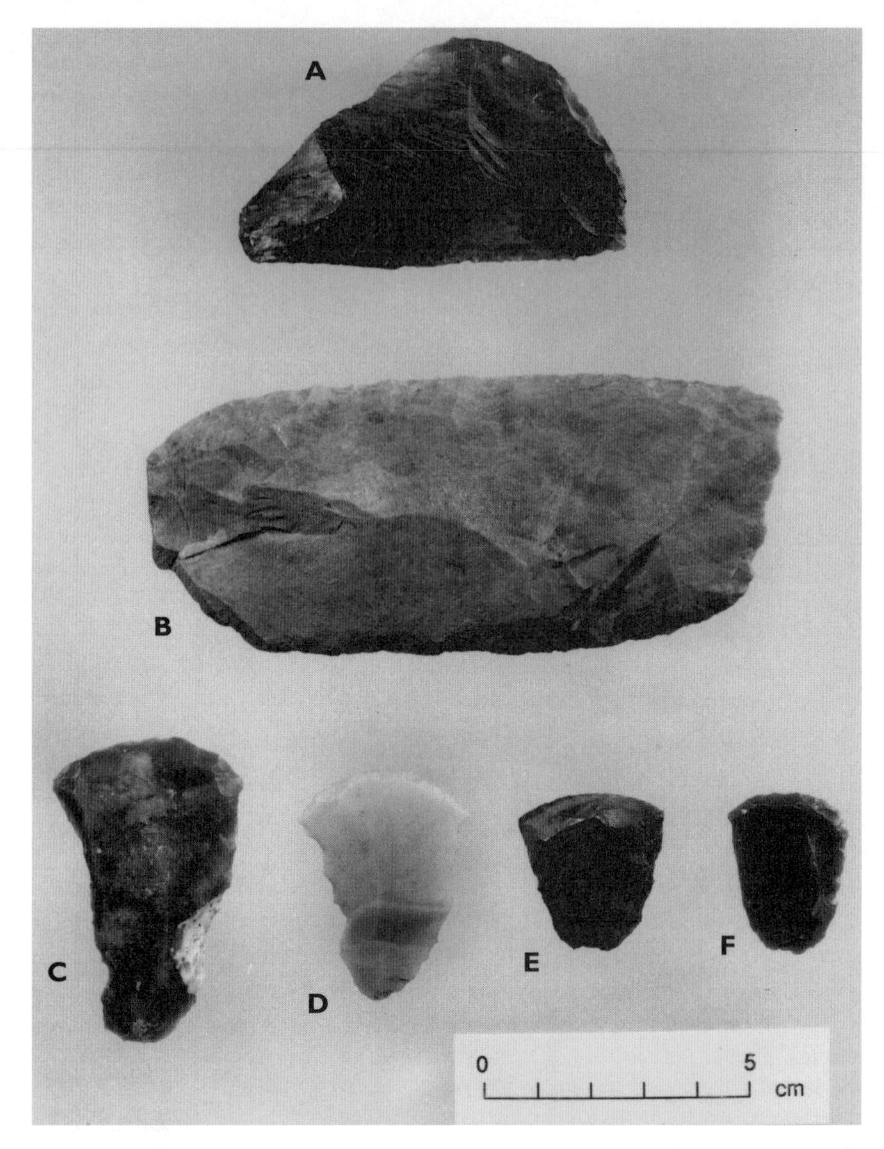

Figure 13. Folsom artifacts: A.–B. Unifacial flake knives—Stewart's Cattle Guard Site; end scrapers; C. Lindenmeier; D.–F. Stewart's Cattle Guard.

It also is possible that this entire area was not occupied simultaneously. On the other hand, multiple ethnic groups may have been sharing Folsom technology.

Folsom projectile points tend to be smaller, with more refined workmanship, than Clovis points and are more completely fluted (Figure 12). The Folsom tool kit contained unifacial (Figure 13a,b) and bifacial knives (Figure 14), a variety of end scrapers (Figure 13c-f), spoke shaves (Figure 15a-b), gravers (Figure 15c), drills or piercing tools (Figure 15d), burins made on biface fragments (Figure 15e), and wedges. Sandstone abraders stained by hematite (Figure 16c) and ground hematite nodules (Figure 16a, b) are common in collections. Blades and tools made on blades are rare, blade cores are absent, and ivory artifacts drop out of the assemblages.

Bone tools include incised bone discs (Figure 17a, b) and tiny eyed needles (Figure 17c); bone beads, including an extremely tiny bead found at the Shifting Sands site, Texas (Hofman 1996), and possible bone projectile points (see Frison and Craig 1982: Figures 2.107-2.110). A serrated bison bone flesher (Figure 17d) and a possible antler fluting tool have been found in the Folsom level at Agate Basin (see Frison and Craig 1982: Figure 2.106).

Folsom bison hunting techniques varied, but simple ambush kills around springs and playa lakes appear to have been a common hunting strategy. These would include sites such as Lubbock Lake (Johnson 1987), Blackwater Draw (Hester 1972), Linger (Dawson and Stanford 1975), and Zapata and Reddin (Stanford 1990). At Stewart's Cattle Guard (Jodry 1987) and Fowler-Parrish (Agogino and Parrish 1971) sites in Colorado the animals may have been trapped in a blow-out. Possibly, *ad hoc* ambush kills represent a Folsom hunting technique that may have been derived from Clovis hunting strategies. Hunters also may have begun to experiment with new, more efficient hunting and

Figure 14. Folsom bifacial knives: A. & D. Lindenmeier; B.–C. Stewart's Cattle Guard.

herd management techniques that were not known from Clovis times. These would include hunting methods such as cliff jumps at Bonfire shelter (Dibble and Lorrain 1968) and arroyo knickpoint traps at several sites, including Carter/Kerr-McGee (Frison 1984), Agate Basin (Frison and Stanford 1982), the Waugh and the Cooper sites (Bement 1994) in Oklahoma (Hofman and Carter 1991), and probably the Folsom type site.

The number of animals found in Folsom kill sites varies from five to more than 50. Two animals are reported from the Rattlesnake Pass site, in Wyoming (Smith and McNees 1990), but the site is incompletely excavated. The smaller figures are close to the number of bison found in Clovis kill sites (seven at Blackwater Draw [Hester 1972]; 10 at Twelve Mile Creek, Kansas [Rogers and Martin 1984, Williston 1902]; and 12 at Murray Springs [Hemmings 1970]). However, at Lipscomb, at least 55 animals were killed (Hofman et al. 1991b; Todd et al. 1992), which begins to approach the number of animals taken by later Paleoindian peoples. Forty-three animals were reported from the Frasier Agate Basin site (Cassells 1983), 150 animals per kill at Jones-Miller Hell Gap Site (Stanford 1978), and 100 bison were killed at the Casper Hell Gap site (Frison 1974).

The majority of Folsom bison kill sites appear to have been single events. Possible exceptions are Agate Basin (Frison and Stanford 1982) and the Cooper site (Bement 1994), thought to have had three kills, and Blackwater Draw, which may have had multiple kill locations (Hester 1972). The settlement pattern may have been one in which bands moved from kill to kill. In this regard, it should be noted that Folsom bison kills have been found for all annual seasons.

Non-bison faunal remains found at Folsom sites include duck, deer, pronghorn, rabbit, turtle, wolf, prairie dog, peccary, mountain sheep, marmot, and possibly camel (Davis and Greiser 1992; Wilmsen and Roberts 1978). This diverse array of faunal remains suggests that Folsom humans, like Clovis, had a broad-based economy that included a wide variety of animal resources.

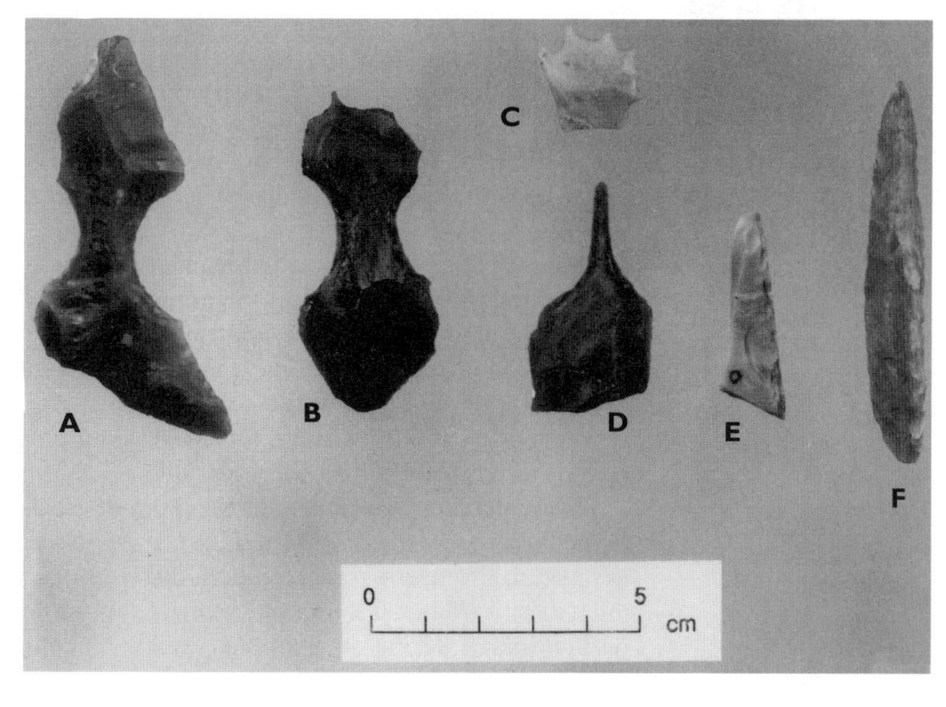

Figure 15. Folsom artifacts: (A.–D. & F. Lindenmeier) A. Combination tool with double spokeshave; B. Double spokeshave with graver tip; C. Multiple graver; D. Drill; F. Lamace; E. Radial fracture burin—Powar's I Site, Colorado.

Figure 16. A.–B. Folsom ground hematite nodules and C. Sandstone abraider with hematite staining from the Lindenmeier Site.

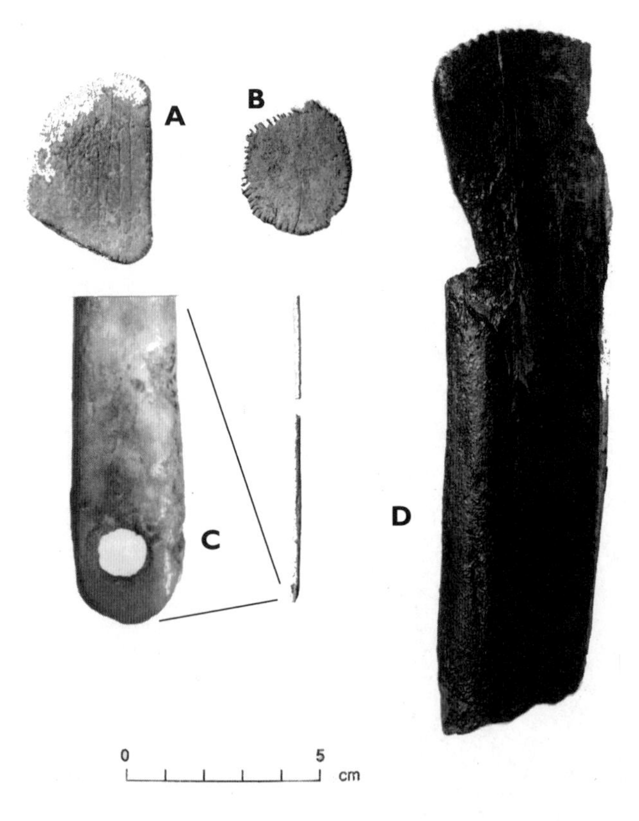

Figure 17. Folsom bone tools: A.–B. Incised bone discs—Lindenmeier; C. Eyed bone needle —Lindenmeier; D. Bison tibia flesher—Agate Basin Site, Wyoming.

Folsom settlement patterns were described by Judge (1973) for the central Rio Grande Valley, and Hester (1972, 1975) and Hester and Grady (1977) for the Llano Estacado in West Texas and eastern New Mexico. Amick (1994b) recently has described Folsom land use for the Tularosa Basin, New Mexico. The majority of sites usually are associated with playas, springs, or streams. The functional sites types reported include camps, kills, quarries, and lookouts. Recent investigations of the 10,200-foot-high Black Mountain site, Colorado (Jodry et al. 1996), provides evidence that Folsom bands were utilizing high-altitude resources during the summer season or early fall. Black Mountain, along with the Johnson site, Colorado (Galloway and Agogino 1961), and the Adobe site, Wyoming (Hofman and Ingbar 1988), are campsites situated adjacent to or on high topographic features that look out over large geographic areas where game movement could be monitored.

Folsom campsites tend to be small and usually are associated with a nearby bison kill. Evidence from Stewart's Cattle Guard (Jodry 1987), Agate Basin (Frison and Stanford 1982), and by inference, Shifting Sands (Hofman et al. 1990), suggests that once a successful hunt was completed, a nearby camp was occupied while the animals were butchered, where re-armament and tool maintenance as well as game-processing activities were conducted.

Ongoing excavations at the Stewart's Cattle Guard site in southern Colorado revealed at least five clusters of lithics and processed faunal remains associated with concentrations of burned lithics and charred bones (Jodry 1987, 1992; Jodry and Stanford 1992). These concentrations are interpreted as hearth-centered family residential areas. This evidence may suggest a band size of five or more families. If family size averaged five individuals, the band may have consisted of 25 or more people. These figures compare well to the average size of most hunter-gatherer bands (Steward 1969).

Unless quarry sites such as Lindenmeier (Wilmsen and Roberts 1978) and Adair-Steadman (Tunnell 1977) are base camps, there is little evidence that multiple bands congregated. The tremendous amount of campsite debris found at these sites may represent repeated occupations by single bands over long time periods to replace raw material stock.

Raw material acquisition was an important aspect of the Folsom settlement pattern. Like Clovis, Folsom raw materials were quarried at locations that were many miles distant. Material sources were selected not only on the basis of flaking qualities but possibly on color attributes as well. The author recently analyzed the use of Flattop chalcedony from three Folsom sites in Colorado—Lindenmeier, Powars, and Hahn. Flattop chalcedony occurs in two basic colors, white and lavender. Although the white variety can be worked as easily as the lavender and was employed by all other Paleoindian groups who used the quarry, only the lavender variety occurs in the studied Folsom assemblages. This seems to indicate that the white variety was rejected in favor of the lavender.

Niobrara chert (Republican River Jasper, Smokey Hills Jasper, etc.; see Banks 1990) is all but nonexistent in Folsom sites along the Front Range in Colorado, while it occurs in Clovis sites as well as all post-Folsom Paleoindian complexes in that area. Black Forest silicified wood, a very commonly used raw material in Folsom sites south of the South Platte River, is rare at the Lindenmeier site, which is located only a few miles north of sources for the wood. Raw material from the San Juan Basin in New Mexico is equally rare in Folsom assemblages east of the Rio Grande, and the percentage of Alibates found in Folsom sites south of the Red River in Texas is significantly less than to the north.

Most of these material-resource distribution anomalies can be equated with major river courses or topographic features. Material distributions may define boundaries of traditional areas of exploitation by independent Folsom bands.

Early-stage biface preforms were manufactured to replace tool stock at sites associated with quarries. Commonly, many bifaces were not reduced to the fluting stage at these sites, but, along with flake stock, were transported from the quarries as the band moved on to the next location. In this form, the raw material stock could be used to manufacture diverse types of tools. When projectile point manufacture was required, the bifaces were finished and fluted. In other cases, they were used for thin bifacial knives, acquiring beveled edges when resharpened (Figure 14c).

Although local raw materials were reduced into bifaces at Lindenmeier, the artifact assemblage contains many final-stage bifaces (Figure 18a,b), preforms broken in fluting (Figure 18d), and channel flakes (Figure 18c) made out of exotic cherts that were carried into the site from elsewhere.

A newly completed but intentionally broken projectile point from the Folsom level at Agate Basin, as well as the consideration that the process of fluting is wasteful of raw material, leads Frison and Bradley (1982) to suspect that fluting had a ritual component. Many hunting and gathering societies imbue supernatural powers to hunting weaponry, and great care is taken in manufacturing and the choice of materials. In the manufacture of Folsom points, the uniformity of the morphological variables and color preferences suggests that a high value was placed on

Figure 18. Examples of Folsom projectile point manufacturing debris: A. Stage 3 biface—Lindenmeier; B. Stage 4. Broken during first fluting attempt—Lindenmeier; C. Medial channel flake; D. Stage 5. Broken during the removal of seconbd flute —Lindenmeier; E. Final edge trimming—Stewart's Cattle Guard.

Figure 19. Midland projectile points—obverse side: A. Stewart's Cattle Guard Site, Colorado; B.–D. -Lindenmeier; E.–H. Midland Site, Texas. Midland projectile points—reverse side: I. Stewart's Cattle Guard Site, Colorado; J.–L.—Lindenmeier; M.–P. Midland Site, Texas.

these attributes. It is likely that this attention to detail reflects supernatural beliefs associated with weaponry and hunting success.

Among the activities identified around each hearth cluster at Stewart's Cattle Guard were projectile point manufacture and fluting. Analyses of channel flakes and preform fragments suggest that between four and six new projectile points were manufactured at each domestic hearth, and damaged points were discarded in these locations (Jodry 1987). Consequently, it appears that the manufacture and retooling of weapons were completed within the context of the family circle.

Unfluted Folsom points are found in almost every Folsom archaeological assemblage (Figure 19). In the Permian Basin of West Texas, unfluted Folsom points are so plentiful that Wendorf et al. (1955) considered them to be a new type—Midland points. However, only at the Winkler site (Blaine 1968), located in the Midland area, are Midland points found to the exclusion of fluted Folsom points. The common association of Midland and Folsom has led to speculation as to whether Midland points represent a separate complex or simply are Folsom points that were too thin to flute (Agogino 1969). Amick (1995) suggests that the high number of Midland points found on the Southern Plains results from tool stone conservation practices associated with logistical land use and high mobility (also see Hofman 1992).

Many weapon tips from Scharbauer, the type Midland site (Wendorf et al. 1955), and others in the region are unfluted on one side and fluted on the other (Figure 19c,k,f,n), while others retain remnants of former flute flake scars. Some Midland points were simply flakes that were retouched along the edges to create a projectile point shape (Figure 19b,j). These projectile point variations lead the author to speculate that the Folsom group that occupied this area of southwest Texas employed a hunting pattern in which their quarry sources were some distance away. Their raw material stock was nearly depleted by the time they reached that area and was at a premium. Raw material conservation techniques included not only rejuvenating existing points but using small remnant bifaces for tools that normally were made on flakes. New projectile points were made on thin bifaces and flakes, which were normally too thin for fluted point manufacture (Figure 19b, g, j, o).

Irwin (1967) noted a Midland level above Folsom at the Hell Gap site, which would argue for a temporal difference between the two point types. However, Haynes (personal communication 1989), the site geologist, suggests that Midland and Folsom were situated at the base of the same stratigraphic unit. Consequently, it may be that the Folsom and Midland components at Hell Gap were roughly contemporaneous, if not one and the same. For these reasons, I currently consider Midland to be a Folsom variant that resulted from projectile point rejuvenation and a material depletion/conservation strategy.

The fate of Folsom technology remains an unanswered question. Why Folsom fluting was discontinued is not known, but speculations suggest changing hafting systems, adapting to styles used by other groups, or population replacement. Flute-like basal thinning occurs on post-Folsom projectile points found on the Southern Plains and its eastern peripheries. These styles are found at the Rex Rodgers site (Willey et al. 1978) and in point types such as Brazos fishtail (Watt 1978) and San Patrice (Webb 1946). Radiocarbon dates establish these types as younger than Folsom, but it is not known how, or even if, they relate to Folsom.

Environmentally, the end of the Folsom period is marked by a decrease in moisture, which probably resulted in lakes, springs, and ponds reducing in size and number. This reduction in moisture likely decreased rangeland productivity, resulting in fewer bison on the Southern Plains and in the Southwest. Evidence for this drying trend can be seen at Blackwater Draw, where the pond deposits associated with Folsom ceased to form, and in the pollen records from the San Luis Valley, which indicate a shift to increased aridity after 10,500 yr B.P. (Jodry and Stanford 1996; Jodry et al. 1989).

Goshen/Plainview

THE PLAINVIEW TYPE originally was identified at a bison kill site, located near Plainview, Texas (Guffee 1979; Sellards 1945). The 18 projectile points and fragments found at Plainview were highly variable in form, but their general proportions were similar to Clovis and Folsom (Figure 20 e–h). The bases were primarily concave; and some specimens were thinned by a series of pressure flakes, including a central flute-like flake, while others were not as heavily basally thinned. Because of the absence of distinctive flutes and because several specimens were collaterally flaked, Kreiger (1947), who analyzed the Plainview artifacts, considered Plainview to be a transitional form between the Folsom and Yuma types. He cautioned, however, that the validity of that view depended upon the stratigraphic relationships between these forms, which were not known at the time of his writing. On the basis of fine collateral pressure flaking on some specimens, Knudson (1983) also suggested a strong correlation between Plainview technology and that of the Cody complex.

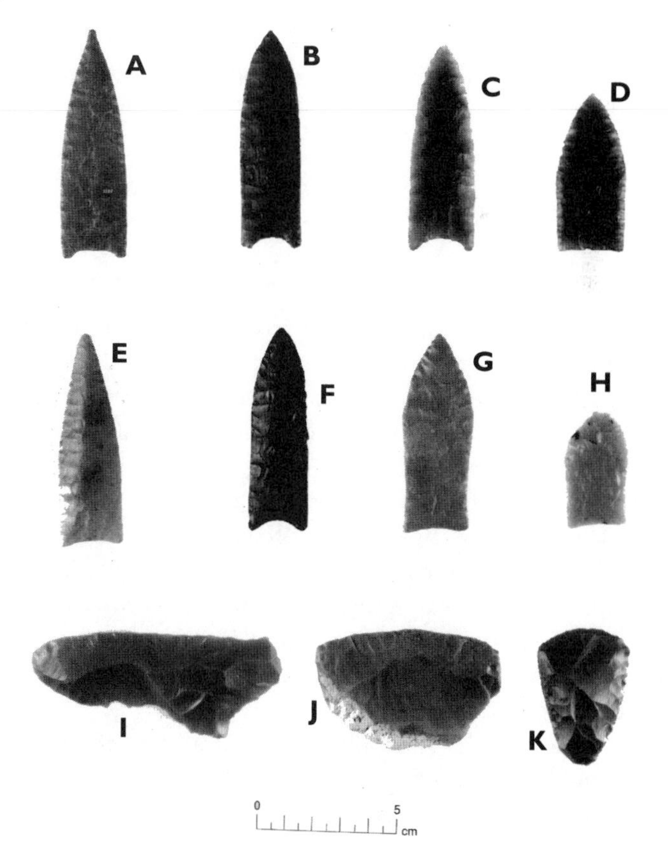

Figure 20. Goshen/Plainview projectile points. A-D Mill Iron site, Montana; E-K Plainview site, Texas.

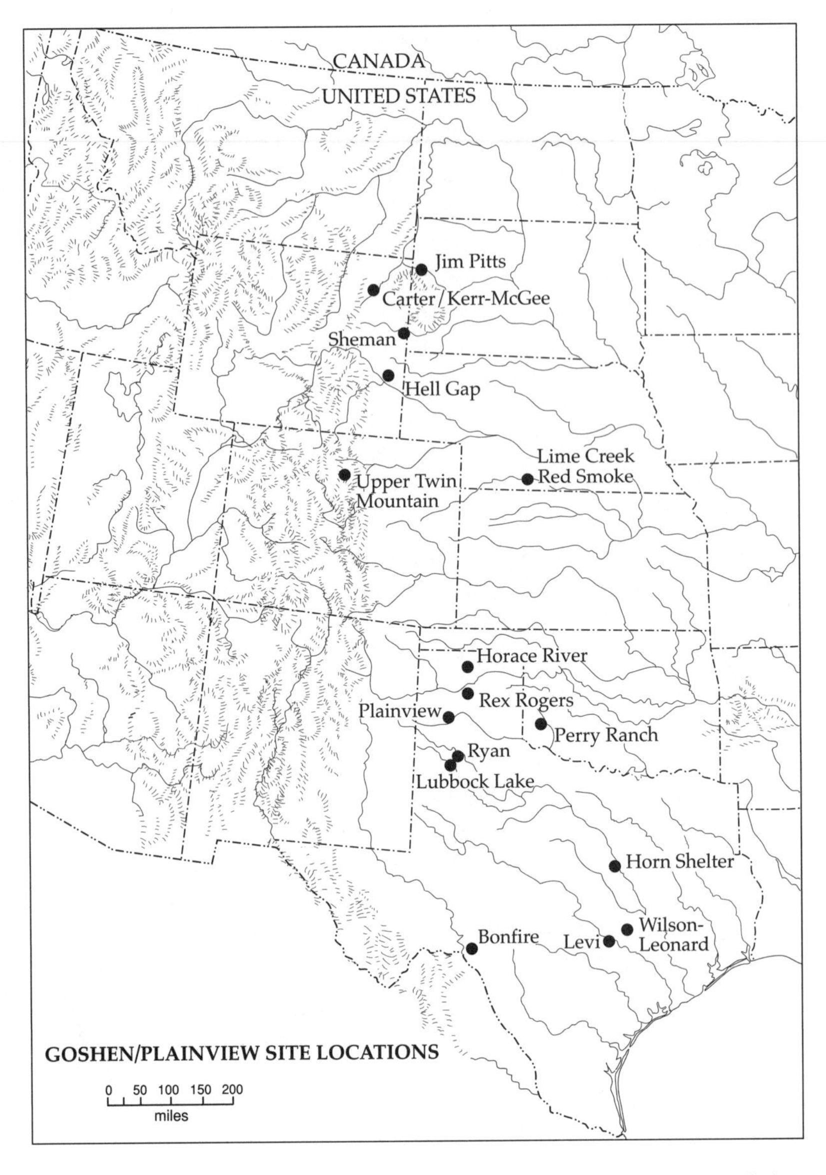

Figure 21 Goshen/Plainview site locations.

Plainview points have been reported from a number of sites throughout the Plains (Figure 21), but because of the remarkable degree of variation among the type specimens, there has been considerable confusion as to what constitutes a Plainview point. The type has become a catch-all category for unfluted, concave-based weapon tips, many of which probably are unrelated to Plainview. Adding to, or as a result of, the indiscriminate assignment of projectile points to the Plainview nomenclature, there is a large span of radiocarbon ages ascribed to Plainview on the Southern Plains (Table 4; Figure 22).

Much of the variability observed among the type Plainview specimens can be explained by projectile point rejuvenation. Consequently, the key attribute that identifies Plainview points is the basal-thinning technique (see Figure 20e). In order for an assemblage to be considered Plainview, it should contain specimens that exhibit well-developed, flute-like pressure flakes for basal thinning. On the basis of this thinning technique, Plainview is tentatively included here within the Fluted Point Pattern.

Sites containing projectile points that correspond to the Plainview type as considered in this paper are the Mill Iron site, Montana (Frison 1996); Jim Pitts, South Dakota (Donohue 1996; Frison 1996); Hell Gap (Irwin 1967); Upper Twin Mountain, Colorado (Frison and Kornfeld 1995; Kornfeld and Frison n.d.); the Plainview component of Bone Bed II at Bonfire Shelter, Texas (Dibble and Lorrain 1968); the Rex Rodgers site, Texas (Willey et al. 1978); Levi Rock Shelter Zone II (Alexander 1963); and the Perry Ranch site, Oklahoma (Saunders and Penman 1979). Other possible Plainview occupations are the Lubbock Lake site (Johnson and Holliday 1980) and the Ryan site, located near Lubbock Lake (Johnson et al. 1987). At

Table 4. Goshen/Plainview Radiocarbon Dates

Site	*Material*	*^{14}C Age Date B.P.*	*Lab. Number*	*Source*
Hell gap	charcoal	10,995 ± 135	AA-14434	Frison 1996
Horace Rivers	charcoal	9060 ± 90	Beta-55907	Mallouf, personal communication 1996
	charcoal	9040 ± 70	Beta-55908	
	charcoal	9000 ± 90	Beta-55909	
	charcoal	9290 ± 80	AA-9367	
Horn Rock Shelter #2	shell	8400 ± 110	Tx-1996	Watt 1978
	shell	9275 ± 360	SM-689	
	shell	9485 ± 300	SM-761	
Jim Pitts	charcoal	11,410 ± 250	AA-20290	Donohue 1996
	charcoal	10,280 ± 200	AA-20291	
	charcoal	11,790 ± 220	AA-20292	
	charcoal	11,720 ± 210	AA-20293	
	charcoal	10,115 ± 230	AA-20294	
	charcoal	9855 ± 645	AA-20295	
	charcoal	11,300 ± 260	AA-20296	
Levi Shelter Zone IV	charcoal	6750 ± 150	O-1105	Alexander 1963
	charcoal	9300 ± 160	O-1129	
	charcoal	7350 ± 150	O-1128	
Lime Creek	charcoal	9524 ± 450	C-451	Davis 1962
Lubbock Lake	bone	9960 ± 80	SMU-275	Holliday et al. 1985
	bone	9870 ± 140	SMU-828	
	bone	9605 ± 195	SI-4974	
	bone	9075 ± 100	SI-4179	
	bone	9170 ± 80	SMU-829f	
	bone	9959 ± 120	SMU-126	
	bone	9990 ± 100	SMU-728	Holliday et al. 1983
Mill Iron	charcoal	10,760 ± 130	Beta-20110	Haynes et al. 1992
	charcoal	10,770 ± 85	AA-3669	
	charcoal	11,010 ± 140	Beta-16178	
	charcoal	11,320 ± 130	Beta-16179	
	charcoal	11,360 ± 130	Beta-20111	
	charcoal	10,990 ± 170	NZA-623	Frison 1991b
	charcoal	11,560 ± 920	NZA-624	
	charcoal	11,570 ± 170	NZA-625	
Perry Ranch	bone	7,030 ± 190	Tx-2190	Saunders and Penman 1979
Plainview	apatite	10,200 ± 400	Tx-3907	Speer 1990
	apatite	9,860 ± 180	Tx-3908	
	bone	7,100 ± 600	O-171	Campbell 1961
	shell	9,800 ± 500	L-303	Broeker and Kulp 1957
Red Smoke	charcoal	8,862 ± 230	C-824	Davis 1962
Upper Twin Mountain	bone	8,090 ± 60	Beta 76593	Frison and Kornfield 1995
	bone	10,240 ± 70	CAMS-16081	

Site	Material	^{14}C Age Date B.P.	Lab. Number	Source
Wilson-Leonard	charcoal	8,090 ± 70	NSRL-1389	Collins n.d.
	charcoal	8,820 ± 120	Tx-4764a	
	charcoal	8,940 ± 100	Tx-4784b	
	charcoal	8,880 ± 150	Tx-4784c	
	charcoal	9,340 ± 60	Beta-79706	
	charcoal	9,850 ± 60	NRSL-1382	
	charcoal	9,520 ± 60	NRSL-1787	
	charcoal	9,530 ± 88	Tx-4828	
	charcoal	8,630 ± 90	NRSL-1558	
	charcoal	9,240 ± 70	Beta-80869	

Horn Shelter (Redder 1985), two Plainview levels were discovered above the main zone, which produced Brazos fishtail points. Plainview points also are reported from the Wilson-Leonard site, located north of Austin, Texas (Johnson 1989).

At Hell Gap, Wyoming, Irwin (1967) recovered a Plainview-like point, but he thought that it occurred stratigraphically below Folsom. Because of the post-Folsom radiocarbon dates for the Plainview site in Texas, Irwin coined a new type—Goshen—for the pre-Folsom manifestation. However, because of typological affinities, he later abandoned the Goshen terminology in favor of Plainview (Irwin 1971).

It was not until Frison's work at the Mill Iron site in Montana that the Goshen terminology achieved prominence in the literature (Frison 1988, 1990, 1991b, 1996). The Mill Iron site consisted of two localities. One was a location where at least 29 animals were killed during a spring hunt, and the other was possibly an associated campsite, containing projectile points similar to the Hell Gap "Goshen" specimen. Other artifacts found at Mill Iron included cutting and scraping tools made on blades or blade-like flakes, and an implement made of mammoth bone.

Radiocarbon assays from both localities fall into two distinct clusters, one averaging 11,360±70 yr B.P. and the other 10,840±60 yr B.P. It is unclear what caused this bimodality in the radiocarbon assays, but in either case the dates are older than those from Plainview sites found on the Southern Plains.

The shared traits between Goshen and Clovis chipped stone technologies, the pre-Folsom radiocarbon dates, and Irwin's opinion that Goshen occurred below Folsom at Hell Gap lead Frison to conclude that Goshen was intermediate between Clovis and Folsom on the Northern Plains (Frison 1991). The stratigraphic placement of Goshen below Folsom at Carter/Kerr-McGee, as well as at the recently discovered Jim Pitts site in South Dakota (Donohue 1996; Frison et al. 1996), support a Pre-Folsom, Goshen occupation of the Northern Plains.

Frison (1988) is now inclined to believe that the Sheaman locality at Agate Basin probably is Goshen, rather than Clovis as was first thought (Frison and Stanford 1982). Recovered at the Sheaman site along with an unfluted Clovis projectile point was an ivory foreshaft that is nearly identical to those found at the Anzick (Lahren and Bonnichsen 1974) and Blackwater Draw Clovis sites (Sellards 1952). Unfortunately, no charcoal was recovered at Sheaman to directly assess the age of the occupation.

If the earlier average date of 11,360 yr B.P. from Mill Iron is correct, Goshen would have existed at the time of early Clovis or even before Clovis on the Northern Plains. This early date, along with the co-occurrence of the ivory artifact and the unfluted Clovis point at Sheaman and the mammoth bone artifact from Mill Iron, might indicate that both Clovis and Goshen were co-traditions and may have developed from an even earlier lithic technology.

Leonhardy (1966) described a Plainview-like point from the Domebo mammoth kill site, Oklahoma, one of the earliest dated Clovis sites. In that case, the basal thinning noted on Goshen/Plainview points may represent an earlier stage in the development of fluting. There is a possibility that the unfluted projectile point found in the lowest level at Ventana Cave in Arizona (Haury 1950) falls into the Goshen/Plainview type. Two unfluted Clovis-like projectile points found below a Folsom occupation at Horn Rock Shelter (Redder 1985) support the existence of a pre-Folsom unfluted lanceolate point type, perhaps related to Clovis and/or Goshen/Plainview. The nature of the relationship between Clovis and the unfluted Clovis-like weapon tips awaits further research.

Clear similarities also exist between the Goshen and Folsom lithic technologies (Bradley and Frison 1996). These technological ties, along with stratigraphic

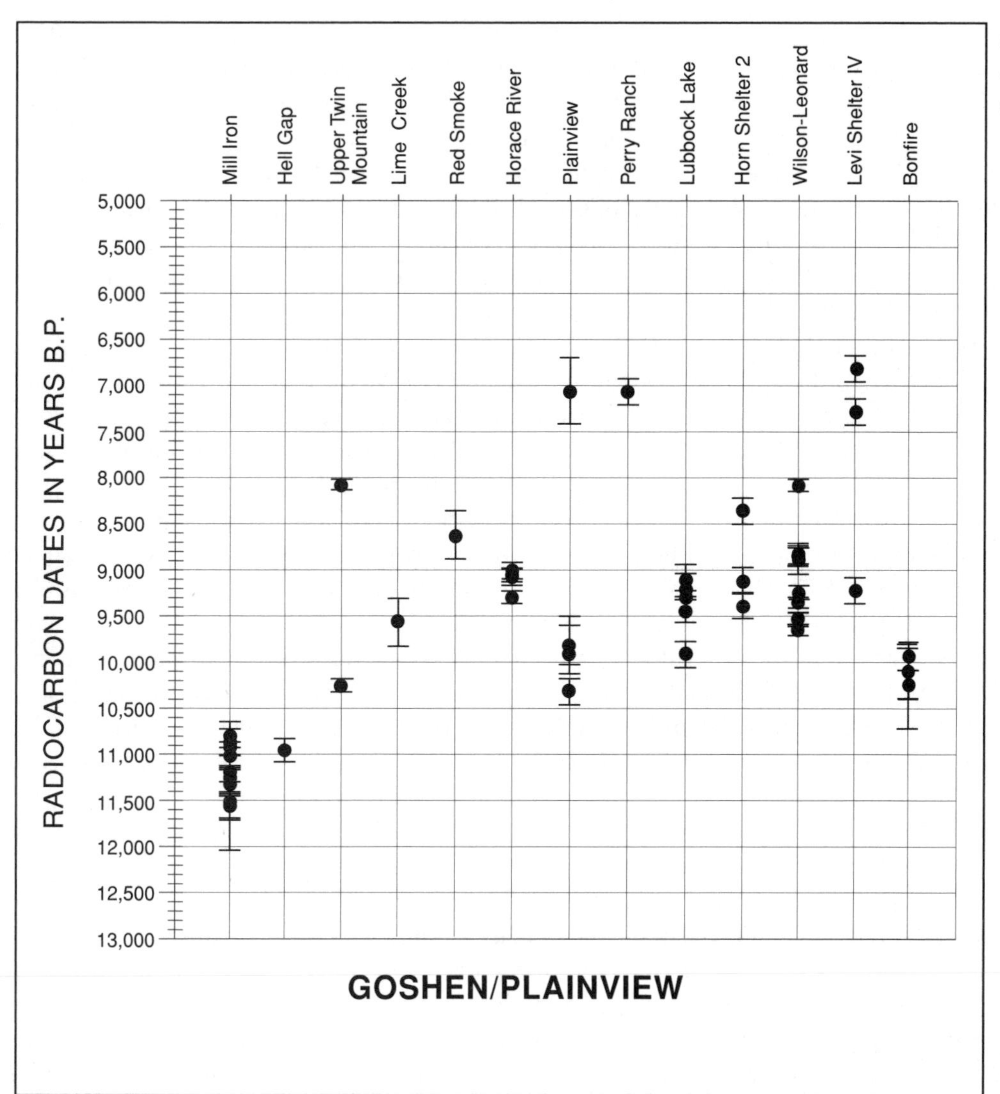

Figure 22. Goshen/Plainview radiocarbon dates.

placement, suggest that it is entirely possible that Folsom technology was derived from Goshen. Whatever the technological origins for either group, it is clear that Folsom was contemporaneous with Goshen. Both may have derived from Clovis technology, and Folsom flintknappers may have retained and enhanced their fluting technology to distinguish themselves from their Goshen/Plainview cousins.

An investigation of a Goshen/Plainview bison site known as Upper Twin Mountain is being conducted in Middle Park, Colorado (Frison and Kornfeld 1995; Kornfeld and Frison n.d.). At this site, the remains of approximately 15 animals killed during the fall or early winter were found associated with four projectile points identified as Goshen. However, a bone date of 10,240 yr. B.P. is considerably younger than the Goshen dates from the more northern Plains sites.

Rex Rodgers was a small kill site, which yielded the remains of six or more bison that were trapped in a gully (Willey et al. 1978). Two types of projectile points were found associated with the bison bone. The first variety has both Clovis and Plainview traits but is considered Plainview. The other variety is "side-hollowed" (slightly notched) and bears a considerable likeness to the fluted Brazos fishtail points found at Horn Shelter, Wilson-Leonard (Collins 1995), and Kincaid (Collins 1995). The Brazos fishtail type also might be considered early San Patrice, a common Archaic point type with basal thinning found in central and eastern Texas.

At Horn Shelter, located near Waco, Texas (Redder 1985; Watt 1978), both Plainview and Brazos fishtail points were found in stratigraphic context. The earliest occupation level at the site contained unfluted Clovis-like points, similar to Suwannee points found in the Southeast. Unfortunately this level has not been radiocarbon dated. Folsom artifacts were found above the unfluted points in the stratigraphic section.

Above the Folsom level are several strata that contained Brazos fishtail points associated with the remains of turtle, snake, rodents, rabbits, birds, deer, and fish scales. These levels, which also contained a Texas Scottsbluff point, have four radiocarbon assays (Watt 1978). Two charcoal assays are 9500 ± 200 yr B.P. (Tx 1830) and 9980 ± 370 yr B.P. (Tx 1722), and two additional assays of 10,310 ± 150 yr B.P. (Tx1997) and 10,030 ± 130 yr B.P. (Tx 1998) were run on snail shells. However, these latter dates may be too old because the cave is located in a limestone outcrop.

A burial of an adult and a juvenile was uncovered in the stratum that produced the Brazos fishtail projectile points (Redder 1985; Young et al. 1987). The burials were flexed, with the child facing the back of the adult; both were covered with limestone slabs. Burial goods were numerous and included antler billets, shell beads, red ocher, several bone tools, perforated canine pendants, large hawk or eagle claws, modified turtle shells, an eyed needle, and a non-diagnostic biface.

The projectile points identified as Plainview at Horn Shelter, occur in strata above the Brazos fishtail levels. These strata are dated to ca. 8400 yr B.P. (Redder 1985). No faunal remains are noted for the Plainview levels.

The Wilson-Leonard site, located north of Austin, Texas, contains a remarkable stratigraphic sequence, which enabled the investigators to assess the cultural chronology of central Texas (Collins 1995, n.d.). The stratigraphic sequence contains a point fragment, possibly Clovis, at the lowest level, followed by a bone bed dated between 10,800 and 11,200 yr B.P., with artifacts attributed to either Folsom or Goshen. Above the bone bed is a level with corner-notched dart points defined as Wilson. Although the Wilson type point usually is considered an Archaic form, it dates between 9500 and 10,000 yr B.P. at the Wilson-Leonard site. Plainview-like points along with Golondrina-Barber occur above the Wilson points and date between 8800 and 9500 yr B.P. The last projectile point type found at the site that is normally considered Paleoindian is Texas Angostura. However, this type apparently dates younger than 8,800 yr B.P. at Wilson-Leonard.

Of particular interest to this paper is a typological and statistical analysis of Texas lanceolate projectile points conducted during the Wilson-Leonard study (Collins n.d.). On the basis of their research, Plainview and Plainview-like projectile points cluster into two groups. The earliest cluster, dating between 11,000 yr B.P. and 10,100 yr B.P., is considered to be Plainview. This cluster includes the specimens from Bonfire, Ryan, and the Plainview type sites. The later cluster, identified as St. Mary's Hall, dates between 9990 yr. B.P. and 8700 yr B.P. The major difference is that the St. Mary's Hall projectile points are narrower and thicker in haft dimensions, have deeper basal concavities, and are not as basally ground as Plainview points.

St. Mary's Hall, Golondrina, and Texas Angostura occupation levels at Wilson-Leonard contain Archaic-like burned rock features. Collins (1995) considers these as late Paleoindian transitional forms between early Paleoindian and Archaic times.

Technologically it is difficult to separate the Goshen and Plainview projectile points. Goshen could be considered an earlier technological phase, perhaps with a more northern center, while Plainview is slightly later and occurs farther to the south. Although tentative, the Upper Twin Mountain site date may support a north-south time transgressive distribution for Goshen/Plainview occupation. With little evidence to the contrary, it appears to me that the St. Mary's Hall type simply may be a later phase of Goshen/Plainview. If this is true, then Goshen/Plainview technology occurs as a co-tradition with all of the classic Paleoindian technologies of the Plains.

Consequently, Krieger's (1947) admonition of caution relative to Plainview is still applicable. It is hoped that renewed investigations at the Hell Gap type site, as well as other future excavations, will resolve this long-standing and highly significant problem.

Lanceolate Point Pattern

THE LANCEOLATE PROJECTILE point pattern is a simple and probably ancient style of projectile point manufacture. Its roots likely are in northeastern Asia, where lanceolate bifaces date to at least 25,000 yr B.P. at sites such as Ust Ulm in Primoria (Derivinko 1989). Radiocarbon dates from the Northwest region of the United States suggest that lanceolate points are as old as Clovis, if not older, and may represent the technology from which Clovis derived (see Bryan 1980, 1988; Stanford 1991) or an unrelated cotradition.

The lanceolate pattern includes not only the classic Plano types found on the Plains, but also other non-fluted Paleoindian projectile points found throughout North and South America. Lanceolate-pattern projectile points have both stemmed and unstemmed haft elements with flat, convex, or concave bases. Agate Basin, Hell Gap, and Cody projectile points are considered representative of the lanceolate pattern. A number of later unfluted point types such as Lusk, James Allen, Fredericks, and others are thought to fall into this pattern. These later types have not been defined well enough to understand how or whether they fit into the sequence of this pattern, and therefore will not be discussed in this paper in great detail.

Agate Basin

AGATE BASIN POINTS first were described by Roberts (1943) from the Agate Basin type site in eastern Wyoming. Agate Basin points are rare in surface collections, and only a few sites with Agate Basin occupations have been found (Figure 23). These include the Agate Basin type site (Frison and Stanford 1982), the Hell Gap site (Irwin 1967), and a mixed Agate Basin-Hell Gap occupation at the Carter/Kerr-McGee site (Frison 1984) in Wyoming; the Frazier site (Wormington 1988) in Colorado; and Blackwater Draw Locality No. 1 (Sellards 1952) and the Kendall site (Haynes 1955) in New Mexico. Although there is morphological variation among the projectile points found at the Milnesand site in New Mexico (Sellards 1955), they also might fall into the Agate Basin type.

Unfortunately, of these sites, only Agate Basin has been published in detail (Frison and Stanford 1982);

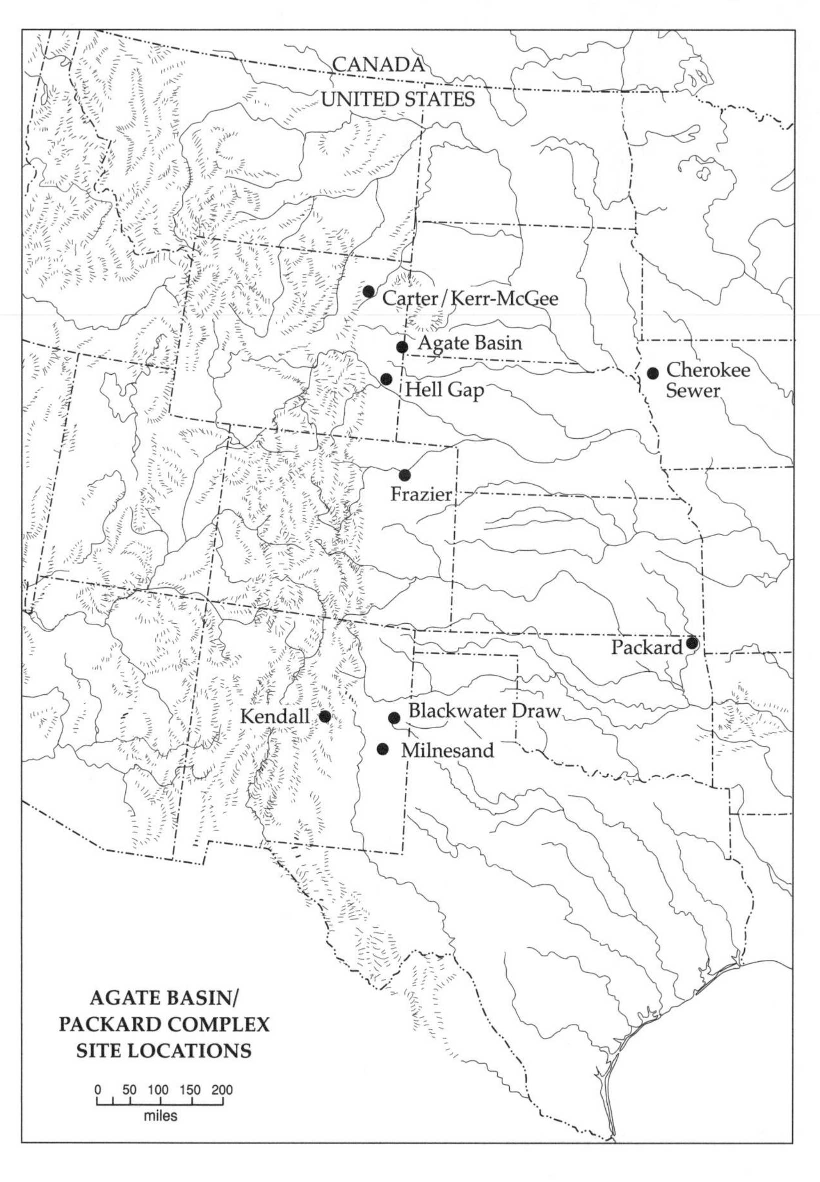

Figure 23. Agate Basin/Packard Complex site locations.

Figure 24. Projectile points from the Agate Basin Site, Wyoming.

thus, it is primarily from this type site that an assessment of Agate Basin culture must be derived.

Agate Basin points are unstemmed, lanceolate projectile points, with basal grinding extending as far as two-thirds of the lateral edges of the point blades (Figure 24). Bases are normally convex, but can be either concave or flat. The latter basal configurations usually occur after point rejuvenation. At the Agate Basin type site, a number of points occur that are nearly bipointed (Figure 24b, g, h) They are relatively narrow, with pressure-finishing flakes and tiny edge retouching. Although our sample is small, in most other respects, the remainder of the Agate Basin tool kit is similar to other Paleoindian tool assemblages (Figure 25).

Radiocarbon dates indicate that Agate Basin points were produced between ca. 10,500 and 10,250 yr B.P. (Table 5, Figure 26). Agate Basin occurs directly above Folsom at both the Agate Basin site and Hell Gap. At Blackwater Draw, the Agate Basin occupation is not well defined, but is thought to occur in the upper diatomite deposits, which would place its occurrence shortly after the Folsom occupation (Haynes and Agogino 1966). The stratigraphic evidence from these sites, along with overlapping radiocarbon dates, suggests that very little time elapsed between the two occupation periods and that early Agate Basin peoples may have been contemporaries of Folsom and Goshen.

The origin of Agate Basin technology is unknown, but it is likely to have derived from typologically similar early Northern Great Basin/Plateau lanceolate forms that may predate the occurrence of Agate Basin by nearly a millennium (Bryan 1988), and moved eastward around 10,500 years ago. This writer's opinion is that the technology involved in producing Agate Basin points is considerably different from that used in the manufacture of fluted points and may indicate that a different human population utilized Plains bison resources during the waning years of the Folsom period.

The Agate Basin occupation at the type site consisted of a bison kill and associated campsite (Frison and Stanford 1982). The animals apparently were driven into a knickpoint arroyo trap, where they were dispatched and dismembered. A butchering/

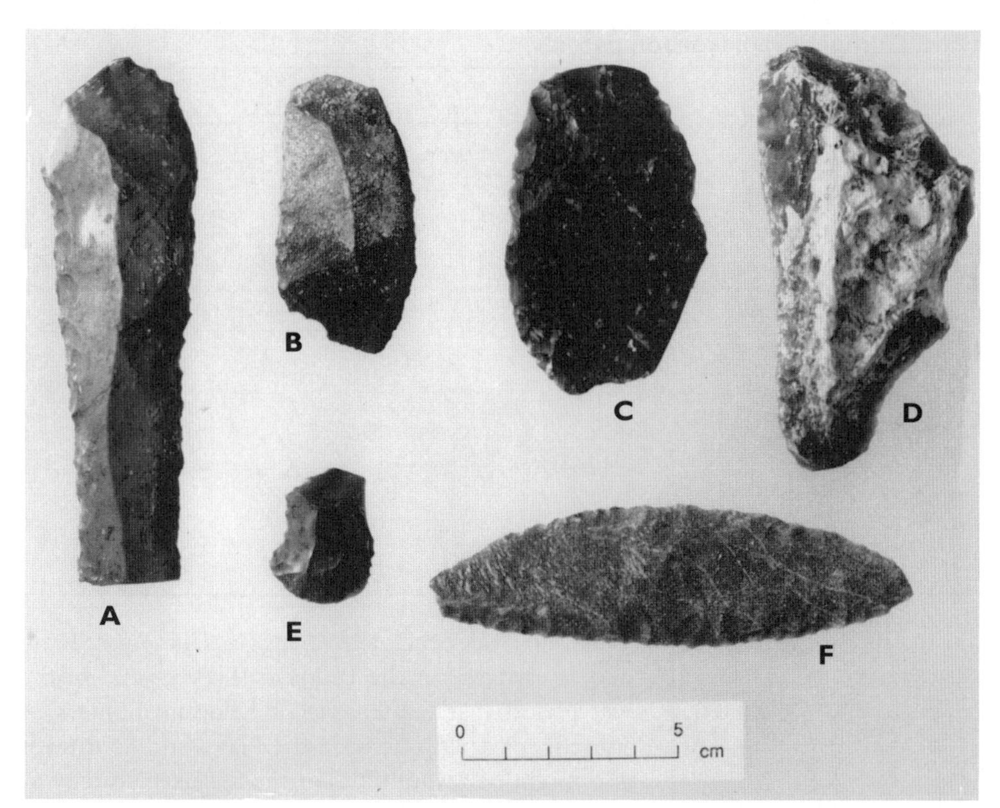

Figure 25. Flake tool from the Agate Basin Level, Agate Basin Site, Wyoming.

processing camp was established that may have been occupied throughout the winter, with the bison kill providing winter rations for the inhabitants. Two slight depositional levels separate additional thin scatters of Agate Basin artifacts from the majority of the cultural debris. These scatters are thought to have resulted from colluvial fill accumulating throughout the winter-long encampment.

At Hell Gap, Agate Basin artifacts were recovered from three excavation localities (Irwin 1967). The faunal remains found in these localities include deer, felid, and unspecified small mammals, as well as bison. Hell Gap is situated in a sheltered valley within the chert-rich Hartville uplift, and it is likely that the Agate Basin occupation, as well as the other occupations of the site, represent camps established during quarrying activities.

The Frazier site in Colorado is thought to be a butchering/processing site (Cassells 1983; Wormington 1988). Much of the Frazier site was eroded, but the remains of at least 43 bison were recovered. A minimal date of 9500 yr B.P. was obtained from a paleosol that overlay the occupation level.

Surface collections by amateurs throughout the Plains region contain relatively few Agate Basin projectile points, but there is a slight increase in their occurrence on the Northern Plains. The scarcity of sites and surface finds may suggest that the human population during Agate Basin times was relatively small compared to Folsom, that Agate Basin points were produced over a shorter time period, that their settlement pattern was such that the majority of sites are yet to be found, or that these people only occasionally were using the Plains for bison hunts.

Lithic material types found at Agate Basin sites are highly extralocal, perhaps indicative of movement from outside the area. Alibates dolomite from Texas constitutes a high percentage of the raw stone used at the Frazier site, while no tools made of Flattop chalcedony—one of the most common local materials used in northeastern Colorado—were found. The same is true of the Agate Basin type site, where Knife River flint from North Dakota constitutes the bulk of the raw material used.

Agate Basin kill sites are represented by somewhat more animals than those contained in the majority of Folsom kill sites. A minimum of 43 animals were found at Frazier (Cassells 1983) and more than 75 animals at Agate Basin (Walker 1982). These figures may indicate larger human groups and perhaps signal the beginnings of seasonal, cooperative, interband hunting strategies.

The occurrence of Agate Basin artifacts in the Upper Diatomite-carbonaceous silt deposits at Blackwater Draw (Haynes and Agogino 1966), along with plant microfossil evidence from the San Luis Valley in

Table 5. Agate Basin/Packard Complex radiocarbon dates.

Site	*Material*	*^{14}C Age Date B.P.*	*Lab. Number*	*Source*
Agate Basin	charcoal	10,430 ± 570	RL-557	Frison and Stanford 1982
Brewster	charcoal	9,990 ± 225	M-1131	Bryan 1980
	unknown	9,930 ± 450	O-1252	Frison 1978
Cherokee Sewer	charcoal	9,990 ± 225	M-1131	Anderson and Semken 1980
	charcoal	8,445 ± 250	UCR-490	
	charcoal	8,000 ± 270	UCR-604	
Frazier	unknown	9,000 ± 130	SMU-32	Cassells 1983
	unknown	9,550 ± 130	SMU-316	
Packard	charcoal	9,416 ± 193	NZ-478	Wyckoff 1985
	charcoal	9,880 ± 90	AA-3116	Wyckoff 1989
	charcoal	9,830 ± 70	AA-3117	
	charcoal	9,770 ± 80	AA-3118	
	charcoal	9,630 ± 100	AA-3119	

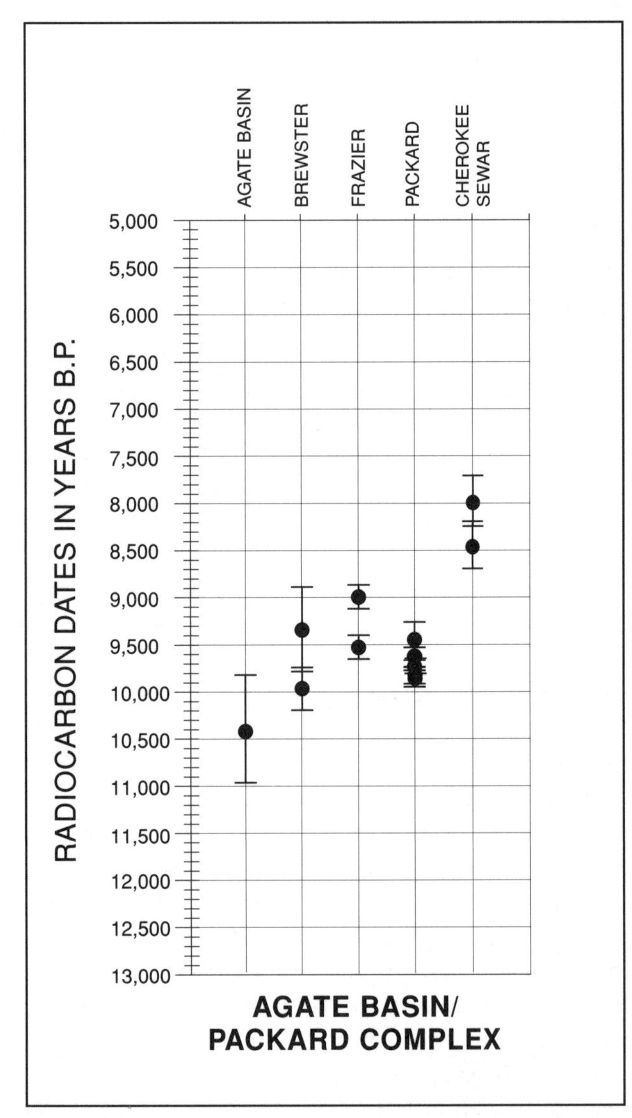

Figure 26. Agate Basin/Packard Complex radiocarbon dates.

Colorado (Jodry et al. 1989), suggests that Agate Basin peoples arrived on the Plains at the very end of the wet period that was enjoyed by Folsom hunters. A subsequent drying trend in the Plains and Southwest also might be responsible for the apparent scarcity or brevity of the Agate Basin occupation in those regions. Significantly more sites and surface finds are reported from the Northern Plains, which may, in fact, be the Agate Basin refugium.

The term "Agate Basin" has been applied to a number of projectile points from the Plains and adjacent geographic regions that are chronologically distinct from Agate Basin. These artifacts can be separated into three groups: Agate Basin-like points from the Rocky Mountains and foothill margins of the western Plains (see Frison 1978, 1992); artifacts identified as Packard complex (Wyckoff 1985) from the eastern margins of the Plains; and Northern Plano (Agate Basin phase) from northern Canada (see Clark 1987; Gordon 1981; Wright 1972a, 1972b, 1976). What the relationships between these complexes might be, if any, is highly conjectural.

The unstemmed Agate Basin-like lanceolate points (Figure 27a,b) found throughout the Rocky Mountains date to around 9000 yr B.P. and are thought to have been used by people adapted to mountain and high-altitude basin environments (Frison 1992). Whether these point styles represent local remnants of an Agate Basin population that settled into a montane lifestyle, or a reintroduction by an eastward extension of peoples from the Basin and Range inter-Mountain lanceolate complex is an important question to be resolved.

Figure 27. Packard Complex and Agate Basin-like projectile points: A.–E.—KhLn-2 Grant Lake, Kewatin, Canada; F.–J. -Packard Site, Oklahoma.

Wyckoff (1985) defines the Packard complex on the basis of Agate Basin-like artifacts recovered at the Packard site in northeastern Oklahoma, Horizon III of the Cherokee Sewer site in Iowa (Anderson and Semken 1980), and numerous surface finds along the Prairie-Woodlands border. At the Packard site, Agate Basin-like projectile points were found stratigraphically below a Dalton level and have been dated to around 9,400 yr B.P. Side-notched projectile points associated with lanceolate points were found at both the Packard site and Horizon III of the Cherokee Sewer site, which dates to ca. 8500 yr B.P.

Unlike the known High Plains Agate Basin points, some of the Packard specimens have been heavily reworked into artifacts that served functions other than that of projectile points (Figure 27h–j). Modification of expended projectile points into other tool types has been equated with Dalton and other early eastern Archaic lithic systems and suggests interaction between the makers of Agate Basin-like points and early Archaic peoples (see Johnson 1989; Wyckoff 1985).

North of the Plains, Agate Basin-like points (Figure 27c–e), have been found at a number of sites in the Canadian Arctic (Clark 1987). Radiocarbon assays, although few in number, indicate that these artifacts date to ca. 8500 to 7500 yr B.P. Clark (1987) suggests that these artifacts represent either a late Cordilleran complex or a northward expansion of the Plains Agate Basin type.

The possible relationship between Agate Basin and these later complexes leads to much speculation concerning the spread and development of an Agate Basin culture and will provide fertile ground for future research.

If the Agate Basin and Agate Basin-like projectile points were made by peoples who originated in the Basin and Range and Plateau environments of the West and Northwest, these artifacts may represent population expansions that encroached upon the eastern Rocky Mountains and Plains and eventually spread to the margin of the Prairie-Woodlands. Perhaps these people were generalized foragers, adapted to ecotonal environments surrounding the Plains, who ventured out onto the Plains only during periods of high bison populations or for occasional communal hunts.

The unshouldered lanceolate point was a dominant weapon tip style for several millennia in the Great Basin

(Bedwell 1970). However, regional stemmed variations eventually developed, including the Mojave type in the Basin and Range area (Amsden 1937), some of the Windust types found in the Plateau region (Rice 1972), and the Hell Gap type on the Plains (Agogino 1961).

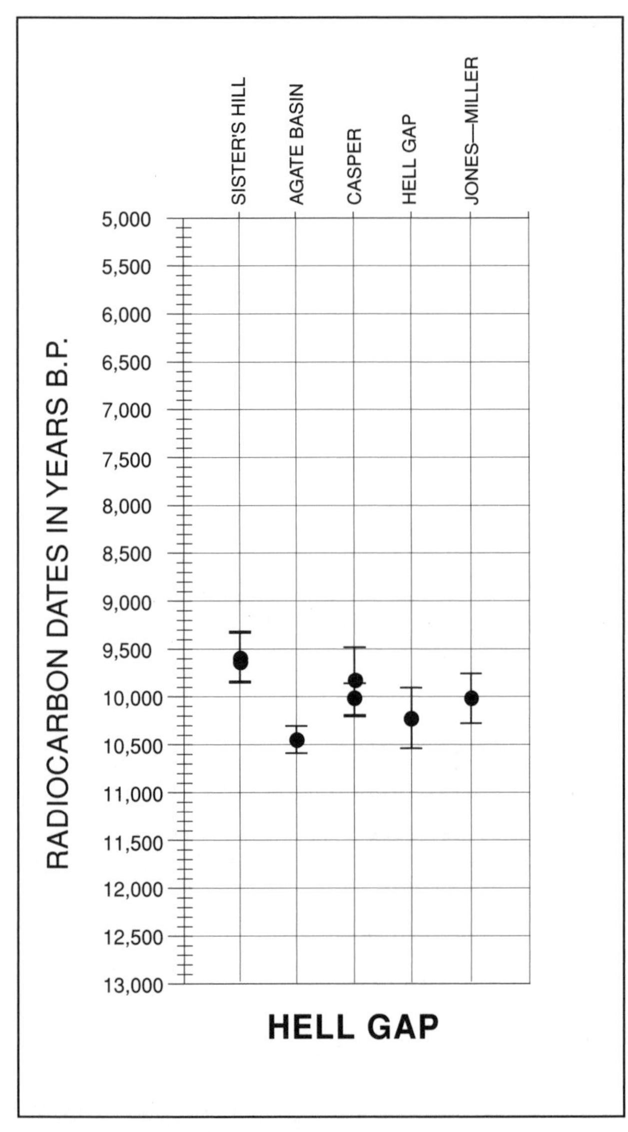

Figure 28. Hell Gap radiocarbon dates.

Hell Gap

ORIGINALLY DEFINED by Agogino (1961) at the Hell Gap site in Wyoming, Hell Gap points initially were thought to be older than Agate Basin. However, during subsequent excavations, the stratigraphic position of Hell Gap was found to be above the Agate Basin level. Radiocarbon assays from a number of Hell Gap sites now suggest this Paleoindian complex is slightly older than 10,000 yr B.P. (Table 6, Figure 28).

Hell Gap points are stemmed lanceolate points with rounded shoulders and relatively broad blades (Figure 29). Stems usually are ground to the shoulder and have flat bases. Rejuvenation of damaged stems frequently resulted in points with either convex or concave bases. Technologically, Hell Gap points are closely related to Agate Basin. Rejuvenated Hell Gap points that have their blade width narrowed (thereby removing the shoulders) are indistinguishable from Agate Basin points if they are not found in an excavated context.

Hell Gap projectile points are found throughout the Plains and Rocky Mountains, but the number of sites is significantly less than either Cody or Folsom-age occupations (Figure 30). Like Agate Basin, Hell Gap points are rare in surface collections from the Central Plains, but become more common in collections from both the Northern and Southern Plains. In Texas, projectile points resembling the Hell Gap type were found at the Lubbock Lake site, substratum 2sLBb (Johnson and Holliday 1985), yielding a date of ca. 10,000 yr B.P. Similar points are relatively common surface finds eastward in Texas and Oklahoma (Figure 29e). Hell Gap points were not found at Blackwater Draw and are relatively rare in surface collections in New Mexico.

Bison hunting during Hell Gap times appears to have been accomplished by large, organized communal hunts, which incorporated trapping techniques that have not yet been recognized during other Paleoindian time periods. At the Casper site, a late fall kill site, more than 100 animals were driven into a parabolic sand dune trap (Frison 1974). At Jones-Miller

Table 6. Hell Gap radiocarbon dates.

Site	*Material*	*^{14}C Age Date B.P.*	*Lab. Number*	*Source*
Agate Basin	charcoal	10,445 ± 110	SI-4430	Frison and Stanford 1982
Casper	charcoal	9,830 ± 350	RL-125	Frison 1974
	bone	10,060 ± 170	RL-208	
Hell Gap	charcoal	10,240 ± 300	A-500	Irwin 1967
Jones-Miller	charcoal	10,020 ± 320	SI-1989	Stanford 1984
Sister's Hill	charcoal	9,650 ± 250	I-221	Agogino and Galloway 1965
	charcoal	9,600 ± 230 A-372	A-372	Irwin 1967

Figure 29. Hell Gap artifacts: projectile points—A. Surface Find, Yuma Co., Colorado; B. Hell Gap Site, Wyoming; C. Agate Basin Site, Wyoming; D & F. Jones-Miller Site, Co.; E. Surface find, Denton Co., Texas; G. Sister's Hill site, Wyoming.

(Stanford 1978), an impound may have been constructed at the head of a small drainage system, where 150 animals were killed in each of at least two events—one in the late fall and another in the late winter or early spring. The animals were butchered almost completely, and presumably, meat products were removed to a nearby winter base camp. At the Agate Basin site (Frison and Stanford 1982), the remains of another Hell Gap bison kill suggest that knickpoint traps may have been used by Hell Gap hunters during the early winter season.

The Sister's Hill site in north-central Wyoming is a Hell Gap campsite (Agogino and Galloway 1965) which, while incompletely excavated, may provide information on Hell Gap camping activities that were not centered on big game hunting. Although few bones were recovered, the remains of rabbit, elk, deer, and porcupine were included in the faunal assemblage.

Hell Gap is known from three quarry-related sites: Seminole Beach (Miller 1986) and Hell Gap (Irwin 1967) in Wyoming; and the Tim Adrian site (O'Brien 1984) in Kansas. At Seminole Beach, Wyoming, finished projectile points were manufactured from tenacious quartzite cobbles found in the gravels of the North Platte River. The small amount of flaking debris recovered and the substandard quality of the quartzite suggest that Seminole Beach was used as an expedient source for raw material.

Raw materials used for artifacts recovered at the Jones-Miller site came from widely separated sources (Banks n.d.). Niobrara or Smokey Hills chert from Kansas, as well as Flattop chalcedony from Colorado and Wyoming cherts, were the most common materials used. Whether these cherts represent raw materials brought to the site by coalescing bands gathering for a communal kill, or sequential quarrying activities and re-use of the trap is yet to be determined. The spatial analysis of lithic artifacts suggests that the Niobrara chert, as well as a few pieces made of Alibates, were used during the fall event, while Flattop and Wyoming toolstones were used along with Niobrara during a later kill event.

Hell Gap reduction strategies usually produce a biface with broad, flat, soft-hammer flake scars covering both faces. Final shape is produced by pressure flaking the edges of the tool with short, steep flakes. During

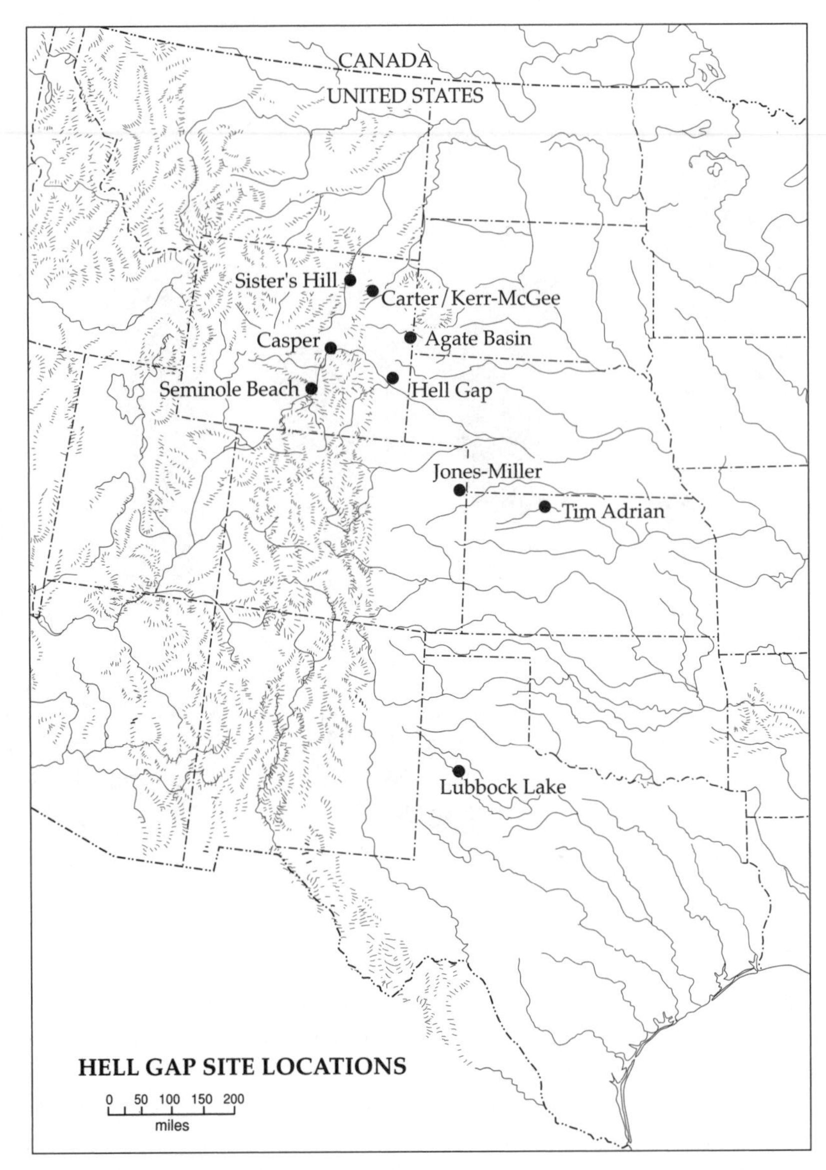

Figure 30. Hell Gap Site locations.

resharpening episodes, pressure flakes invade the biface surface until the last stage of biface manufacture is finally eliminated.

The remainder of the lithic tool kit is very similar to Agate Basin and other Paleoindian complexes. Irwin (1967; see also Irwin and Wormington 1970) described a bifacial knife from the Hell Gap site, which he speculated was a unique knife form that was ancestral to the Cody knife. At both the Casper and Jones-Miller sites, approximately 50 percent of the projectile points have wear and resharpening patterns that suggest they were used as knives (Kyriakidou 1993). A Hell Gap late-stage preform from Jones-Miller also was used as a cutting tool.

Bifacial reduction techniques of Hell Gap preforms are highly reminiscent of Alberta Cody reduction technology, and it is possible that Alberta is a derivative of the Hell Gap type. The basic difference is that the shoulders become more prominent on Alberta projectile points.

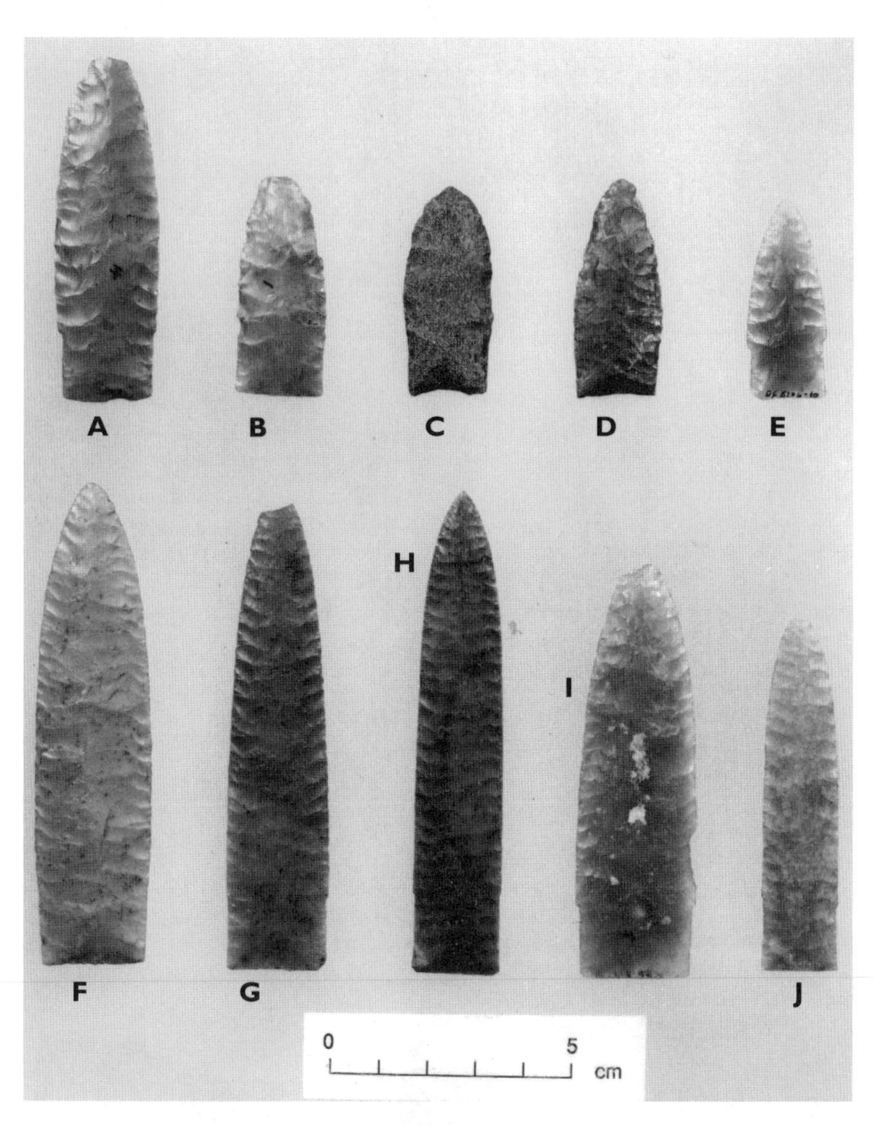

Figure 31. Cody projectile points: A.–B, San Jon Site, New Mexico; C.–D. R-6 Site, New Mexico; E. & H.–I. Frasca Site, Colorado; F. Olsen-Chubbock Site, Colorado; G. Jurgens Site, Colorado.

Cody Complex

THE CODY COMPLEX derives its name from Cody, Wyoming, located a few miles west of the Horner site (Frison and Todd 1987). Stemmed points, such as Scottsbluff from the bison quarry near Scottsbluff, Nebraska, Eden points from the Farson site in the Eden Valley of Wyoming, and Alberta points, were subsumed by Wormington (1957) under the term "Cody complex."

Points with square bases and slight shoulders, such as Portales points from Blackwater Draw, specimens from the San Jon site, New Mexico, and Frasier, Olsen-Chubbock, and Claypool weapon tips also are considered Cody types by most authors. However, Wheat (1972, 1979) distinguishes Firstview and Kersey points as belonging to two phases of a lanceolate, stemless projectile point style of the Central and Southern Plains (see Agenbroad 1978, Bradley and Stanford 1987, and Stanford 1981 for additional discussions).

For the purposes of this paper, I include all square-based and shouldered points, even if only slightly shouldered, as part of the Cody complex (Figures 31 and 32). Although these types have minor morphological and technological variations, they are all technologically linked and also may share a unique knife form, known as the Cody knife (see Figure 33).

Sites where Cody artifacts have been found (Figure 34) include Blackwater Draw (Sellards 1952), Lubbock Lake (Johnson 1987; Johnson and Holliday 1981), and Horn Shelter (Redder 1985; Watt 1978) on the Southern Plains, and R-6 (Stanford and Patten 1984) in the Southwest. Cody sites on the Central Plains include Claypool (Dick and Mountain 1960; Stanford and Albanese 1975); Frasca (Fulgham and Stanford 1982), Jurgens (Wheat 1979); Lamb Spring (Stanford et al. 1981); Lime Creek (Davis 1962); Nelson, Olsen-Chubbock (Wheat 1972); Scottsbluff (Barbour and Schultz 1932); and Wetzell. On the Northern Plains, Cody sites include Hudson-Meng (Agenbroad 1978),

Figure 32. Alberta artifacts from the Hudson-Meng Site, Nebraska: A. End Scraper; B. Gravers, C.–E. Utilized flaked; F.–K. Projectile points.

Carter/Kerr-McGee (Frison 1984), Hell Gap (Irwin-Williams et al. 1973), and the Fletcher site in Alberta (Forbis 1970).

Cody-related surface sites and scattered projectile points are more widespread than any other "classic" Plains Paleoindian point type. They are relatively common throughout the Plains and New Mexico, eastern Arizona, and southeastern Utah. Their distribution also extends westward across Wyoming (Frison and Todd 1987; Howard 1943; Moss et al. 1953), Montana (Bonnichsen et al. 1992; Forbis and Sperry 1952), Idaho, and into Nevada (Dansie et al. 1988). On the Plains and Prairie Provinces of Canada, Cody artifacts occur in many surface collections and are concentrated in the Little Gem area of Alberta. Cody artifacts are common in eastern Texas and Oklahoma, as well as Louisiana and Arkansas (Story 1990). East of the Plains, a burial containing Cody artifacts was recovered at the Renier site in Wisconsin (Mason and Irwin 1960). Cody-like projectile points with sharply expanded bases, known as Aqua Plano, are found from the plains of eastern Alberta southeastward into the Great Lakes region (Wormington and Forbis 1965), but these forms appear to occur later in time.

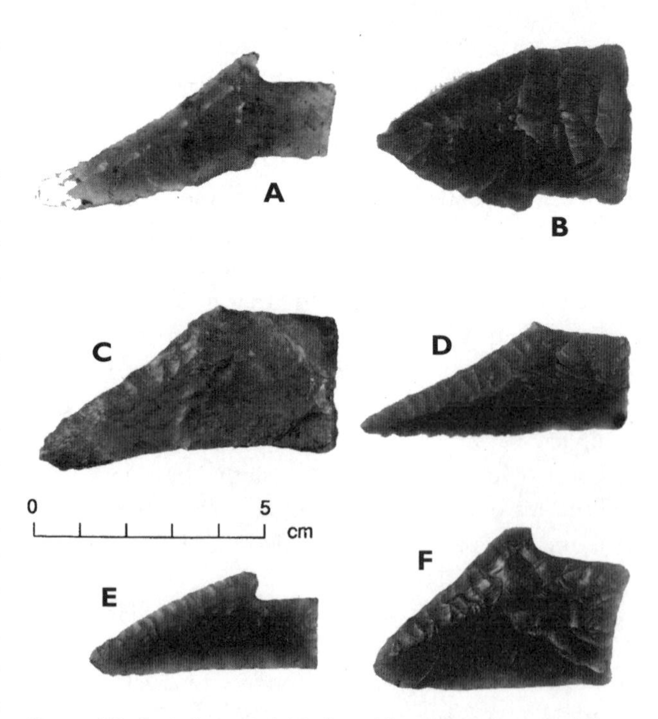

Figure 33. Cody knives: A. Hudson-Meng; B. Surface find from West Texas; C. R-6 Site, New Mexico; D.–E. Claypool Site, Co.; F. Sapello Site, New Mexico.

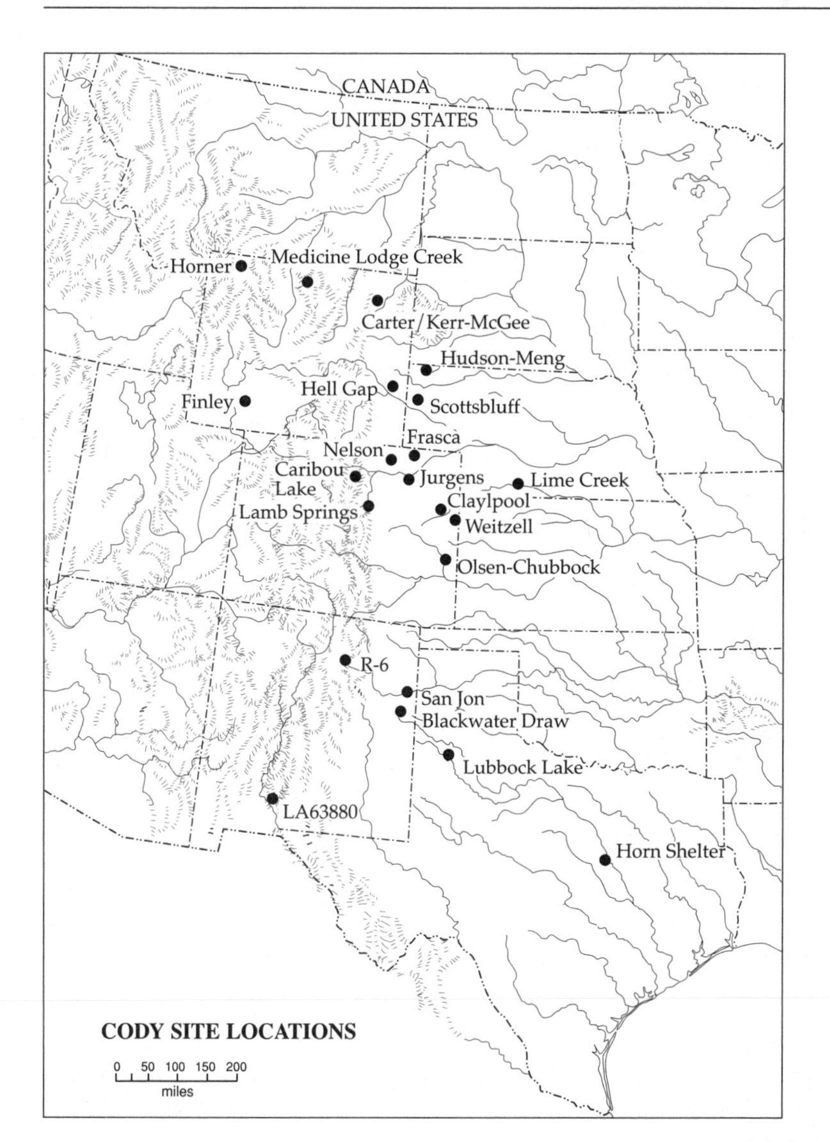

Figure 34. Cody Site locations.

Cody sites date between ca. 10,000 and 8,000 yr B.P. (Table 7, Figure 35). This wide range of dates may indicate that the earliest and latest dates are incorrect, or that stemmed points were used throughout this region for a long period. The large number of sites and extensive geographic distribution of Cody artifacts suggest both a lengthy duration of the tradition and higher population levels than the preceding Hell Gap and Agate Basin periods.

Cody hunters employed a number of methods to kill bison that required knowledge of herd behavior and the ability to manipulate animals into a diverse variety of traps, as well as hunting small groups of animals around springs and ponds. The high number of animals found in many Cody kill sites suggests that cooperative hunting efforts were seasonally employed. The Horner site contains several kill events (Frison and Todd 1987). Thus, it appears that these hunters utilized the same topographic features for kill sites on a reoccurring basis.

Driving bison into steep arroyos was the hunting strategy used at the Frasca (Fulgham and Stanford 1982), Nelson, and Olsen-Chubbock (Wheat 1972) sites. At Blackwater Draw (Hester 1972), Lubbock Lake (Johnson 1987), San Jon (Roberts 1942), Lamb Spring (Rancier et al. 1982), and Wetzel, the animals were killed at the margins of springs and ponds. Bison may have been driven over a cliff at the Hudson-Meng site in Nebraska (Agenbroad 1978) and up an arroyo to a knickpoint trap at Carter/Kerr-McGee in Wyoming (Frison 1984). The topographic setting at the Horner site in northwest Wyoming suggests that Cody hunters also constructed enclosures for trapping bison (Frison and Todd 1987).

It is likely that bison made up a large portion of the Cody diet and was acquired primarily through organized seasonal communal hunts. Individual hunters or small group efforts likely augmented the seasonal kills throughout the year. The available evidence for seasonality suggests that communal kills

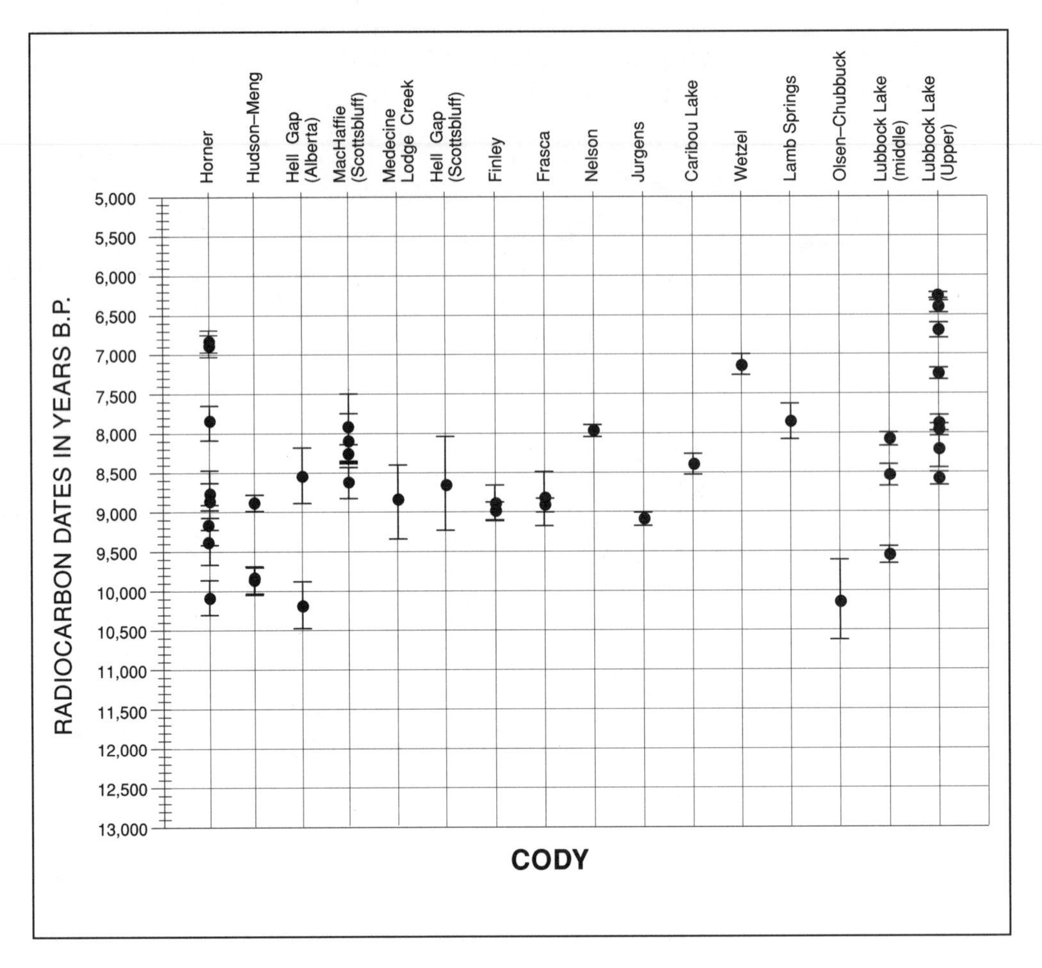

Figure 35. Cody radiocarbon dates.

occurred in the late fall, when the bison were in prime condition, and again in the spring, when food supplies may have reached a low level. Most kill sites contain the remains of cow-calf herds; however, the Lamb Spring Cody level consisted of a late winter or early spring kill of a herd of adult males (McCartney 1983).

In addition to bison, animals found in Cody assemblages include antelope, deer, elk, moose, jackrabbit, cottontail rabbit, turtle, mallard, cinnamon teal, gadwall, pintail, grouse, and fish. This wide variety of faunal remains, as well as the presence of grinding tools (Wheat 1979), and plant processing tools at Lubbock Lake (Bamforth 1985), suggests that Cody peoples took complete advantage of many food sources and cannot be considered simply big game hunters.

Cody-age campsites include Claypool (Dick and Mountain 1960), Lime Creek (Davis 1953), and Horn Shelter, Texas (Redder 1985). Campsites associated with bison butchering/processing areas include Jurgens (Wheat 1979) and Lubbock Lake (Johnson 1987). The large numbers of artifacts and the spatial distribution of activity areas found at most of these campsites represent extensive occupations, or, as Wheat (1979) suggests, that they were used repeatedly.

Artifacts found at the Cody campsites include a wide variety of cutting, drilling, and scraping implements, as well as grinding stones. Shaft abraders, which have small grooves indicating arrow-sized shafts, were recovered at both Jurgens and Claypool. Wheat (1979) reports two possible atlatl hooks from the Jurgens site.

Hell Gap (Irwin-Williams et al. 1973) and R-6 and the related Sapello sites (Stanford and Patten 1984) represent localities where processing of toolstone from nearby quarries was conducted.

R-6, located near Las Vegas, New Mexico, is one of several Cody-age sites found along the Mora River. Situated near a raw material source, known locally as Felcite, these sites probably were occupied in conjunction with the manufacture of tool stock. Testing was accomplished at two sites, Sapello 2 and 3, and more detailed work was completed at R-6 (Stanford and Patten 1984). Although much of the R-6 site had been destroyed by alluvial erosion, a wedge of intact sediment remained. A small feature was excavated consisting of a 2-m-wide semicircle of large cobbles around a slight depression. Within and directly in front of the feature were numerous flakes from primary biface-reduction activities, projectile points broken in

Table 7. Cody radiocarbon dates.

Site	*Material*	*^{14}C Age Date B.P.*	*Lab. Number*	*Source*
Caribou Lake	charcoal	8,460 ± 140	I-5449	Cassells 1983
Frasca	bone	8,870 ± 350	M-1463	
	bone	8,910 ± 90	SI-4846	
Finley	unknown	8,950 ± 220	RL-574	Frison 1978
	unknown	9,026 ± 118	SMU-250	
Hell Gap	unknown	10,240 ± 300	A-500	
(Scottsbluff)	unknown	8,600 ± 600	I-245	
Horner	bone	6,619 ± 350	C-302	Frison and Todd 1987
	charcoal	6,151 ± 500	C-795	
	bone	6,876 ± 120	UCLA-697A	
	bone	8,840 ± 140	UCLA-697B	
	charcoal	7,880 ± 1300	SI-74	
	charcoal	9,390 ± 75	SI-4851	
	charcoal	9,390 ± 85	SI-4851A	
	charcoal	10,060 ± 220	I-10900	
Hudson-Meng	apatite	8,990 ± 190	SMU-52	Agenbroad 1978
	collagen	9,380 ± 100	SMU-102	
	charcoal	9,820 ± 160	SMU-224	
Jurgens (Kersey)	charcoal	9,070 ± 90	SI-3726	Cassells 1983
Lamb Spring	bone	7,870 ± 240	SI-45	
Lubbock Lake	humates	6,240 ± 40	SMU-1094f	Haas et al. 1986
(upper)	humates	6,400 ± 80	SMU-544	
	humates	6,705 ± 95	SI-4178	
	humates	7,970 ± 80	SMU-262	
	humates	7,890 ± 100	SMU-302	
	humates	7,255 ± 75	SI-3204	
	humates	8,210 ± 240	SMU-830f	
	humates	8,655 ± 90	SI-4177	
(middle)	humates	8,130 ± 80	SMU-1089	
	humates	8,585 ± 145	SI-5499	
	humates	9,550 ± 90	SMU-1116	
	humates	9,550 ± 100	SMU-1118	
MacHaffie	wood	8,620 ± 200	GX-15152-AMS	Davis et al. 1991
(Scottsbluff)	collagen	8,280 ± 120	GX-15153-G-AMS	
	apatite	7,905 ± 435	GX-15153-A	
	wood	8,100 ± 3400	L-578A	
Medicine Lodge Creek	unknown	8,830 ± 470	RL-446	Frison 1978
Nelson	bone	7,995 ± 80	SI-4898	Cassells 1983
Olsen-Chubbuck	bone	10,150 ± 500	A-744	
Wetzel	bone	7,160 ± 135	SI-4849	

Figure 36. Cody artifacts from R-6 Site; A.–B. Projectile point preforms; C.–D. End scrapers; E.–F. Unifacial knives.

Figure 37. Texas Scottsbluff projectile points.

various stages of manufacture (Figure 36a,b), a Cody knife (also broken in manufacture), and flintknapping tools. Discarded, expended projectile points, scrapers (Figure 36c,d), and other flake tools (Figure 36e) also were found associated with the feature. The presence of these discarded tools suggests that rehafting activities were accomplished as part of the retooling process. A similar concentration of tools and debitage, associated with several large cobbles truncated by an erosional face, likely are the remains of another similar activity area. It is thought that these features are the remains of shelters used by flintknappers.

Bevelled triangular and quadrilateral bifaces were recovered from R-6, as well as at LA 63880 in the Tularosa Basin, New Mexico, which is thought to be Cody related (Elyea 1988). These tools are reminiscent of Dalton adzes and may support Johnson's (1989) notion of Cody and Dalton interaction. Scattered Dalton points have been found in the Southwest, but as yet, no Dalton sites are known from the area.

Stemmed lanceolate projectile points, known locally as Texas Scottsbluff, are common in surface collections from the Southern Plains, the Texas Gulf Coast, and eastward into Arkansas and Louisiana (Johnson 1989; Storey 1990). These projectile points are relatively large, broad, and thin (Figure 37). During resharpening episodes, their length is reduced, but they remain relatively wide (Figure 37d). The shoulders are well pronounced and haft elements are basally ground. Bases are usually square, with straight to slightly expanding stems. Because of their reduction attributes and overall dimensions, these points are technologically more similar to Alberta than Scottsbluff; thus, if a technological link is to be postulated, it likely would be with Alberta.

Bevelled bifaces, called Red River knives (see Figure 33b) are associated with Texas Scottsbluff points, but unlike Cody knives, they are almost invariably made out of projectile points (Johnson 1989). If Cody knives developed from using projectile points as cutting tools, it stands to reason that the Red River knife form may be indicative of the step between point use and the development of the formal knife type.

In central Texas, at Horn Shelter, Texas Scottsbluff points were found in strata 5F, 5G, and 6 (Redder 1985). Radiocarbon dates of stratum 5G range from ca. 9500 to 10,300 yr B.P., which falls into the early stages of Cody and is consistent with the Alberta dates from Hudson-Meng and the Horner sites.

Several models have been published that attempt to separate Cody into either geographic or temporal divisions (see Agenbroad 1978; Knudson 1983; Wheat 1972). The most common splits are made between Alberta and later Cody types, or northern and southern distributions. While these classifications reflect discrete, although slight, projectile point attribute differences, it is unclear whether these variations have cultural or temporal significance. This is especially true when considering Cody-like points found on the margins of the Plains, and those from the Great Basin. After more stratified sites have been excavated and published along with additional reliable radiocarbon dates, it may be possible to assess the significance of these regional variations.

The earliest manifestation of the Cody complex is Alberta or perhaps Texas Scottsbluff, which appears to have spread widely by 9,500 years ago. Concurrently with the rise of Cody technology, there appears to be a climatic shift that includes increased monsoonal rainfall, which likely produced cool-moist summer conditions for the Southwest (Thompson et al. 1993). These summer rainfalls along with melting winter snows produced reliable water sources from the seasonal ponds that dot the Southwest and western Plains. Along with the filling of these ponds and lakes, there probably was a significant increase in grassland productivity and bison populations.

During this same period, lake levels in northern Nevada and Idaho were elevated and the maximum effective moisture of the early Holocene was achieved (Thompson et al. 1993). These climatic conditions also may have produced excellent bison habitats and perhaps explain the expansion of Cody-like projectile points into those areas.

After the establishment of Cody technology, there was an onset of a more arid environment (Jodry et al. 1989; Thompson et al. 1993). However, as Graham and Mead (1987) point out, during this time period, climatic and environmental fluctuations were significantly greater than those of the late Pleistocene, or for that matter, the entire Holocene.

It is perhaps during this period of climatic instability that local variations in projectile point technology developed. The diversification of Cody technology may have resulted from an initial increase in human populations due to the excellent grassland productivity. However, as the environment became more arid and unstable, the available grasslands probably were reduced. This reduction of range size and the increased human population may have resulted in smaller territories for exploitation, as well as population pressure from other outside groups relocating into traditional Cody homelands.

Interactions with groups from outside the culture area have been noted throughout the Plains and Southwest. Collins (n.d.), has identified Archaic peoples such as Wilson moving into the Southern Plains. Dalton groups as well appear to expand out of the east along the river valleys (Johnson 1989). The same trend can be noted for the Central Rockies, where Basin and Range projectile points such as Elko Eared occurred with late Plains lanceolate types (Benedict 1992). At the same time in Montana, Bitterroot projectile points from the Plateau seem to be spreading eastward (Bonnichsen et al. 1992).

These events may well have isolated and effectively separated Cody cultural bands. The reduction of

Figure 38. Late Paleoindian projectile points.

interaction with other Cody groups may be inferred from the infrequent occurrence of extralocal raw materials at many late Cody sites. At Lamb Spring and R-6, for instance, although a few tools made of exotic cherts were found, the vast majority of toolstone used was from immediately local sources.

Late Paleoindian

THE LATE PALEOINDIAN phases of the Plains and Southwest are perhaps the most common, complex, and least understood of the Paleoindian cultures. I suspect this reflects the continuation of trends noted during the Cody period: increasing human populations caused further reduction in band territory sizes and resulted in a greater reliance on local resources, such as plants and other game animals. The general drying trend noted for the Cody period continued, and it is highly likely that most groups retreated to higher elevations or to river valleys where local environmental conditions provided better resources (Benedict 1992). Bison hunting no doubt continued, but on a smaller scale and perhaps only during periodic wetter periods.

Concave-base lanceolate projectile points of various types, such as Jimmy Allen (Mulloy 1959), Fredericks, and Lusk (Irwin 1967), which may have their origins with Meserve and Dalton to the east, are common (Figure 38). Other stemmed forms, such as the Pryor stemmed points, appear in the Big Horn Mountains of Wyoming (Frison 1992). Thus, it seems that, starting with the Cody complex, there was a period of transition and greater interaction among many different culture groups. However, this transition is a matter of degree, rather than a complete change of human exploitive patterns and life styles.

Summary and Conclusions

PALEOENVIRONMENTAL STUDIES in the Central Plains and southwestern United States suggest major shifts in the composition of biotic communities and hydrologic regimes at the late Pleistocene/early Holocene boundary. The late Pleistocene archaeological record of these areas consists primarily of Clovis assemblages. We now know that Clovis groups, once thought to be mammoth specialists, had a generalized foraging economy that utilized a wide variety of resources. This paper suggests that Clovis peoples were adapted, by virtue of their broad-based foraging economy, to exploit diverse ecological zones throughout North America. In the Rocky Mountains and Plains, Clovis economic and technological strategies were modified and probably evolved into Folsom as a response to changing environmental parameters.

Though many of the animals hunted by Clovis peoples became extinct throughout the Rocky Mountains and Plains regions, bison remained. Bison herd size may have been regulated by species competition prior to the early Holocene extinctions. Shortly thereafter, bison occupied a habitat for which they were ideally suited with no effective competitors. As a result, bison populations presumably increased. In the post-Clovis archaeological record, bison became the dominant, large-herbivore prey species, but aspects of the broad-based economic system were retained.

Overall, the evidence suggests a continuous population increase from Clovis to Folsom times, a possible decrease during the occurrence of Agate Basin, and slow increases throughout the remainder of the Paleoindian period. Extensive occupation and use of the Plains and Southwest took place only during relatively mesic times, which primarily coincided with the Folsom and Cody traditions. During the rest of the Paleoindian period, the evidence for occupation of the Plains and Southwest is relatively meager.

Although the situation is not clear cut, it is reasonable to postulate that at least two point patterns prevailed among early groups on the Plains and in the Southwest: Lanceolate (Plano), and Fluted (Llano), the definition of which is broadened to include Goshen/Plainview projectile point styles. Based on stratigraphic placement and overlapping radiocarbon assays (Figure 39), it is likely that early in the fluted point pattern there were two traditions, distinguished by fluted projectile points and unfluted points. These groups probably diverged during Clovis times or even earlier, with Clovis giving rise to Folsom, and the unfluted concave base Goshen points technology slowly evolving into Plainview and eventually, perhaps, St. Mary's Hall in Texas.

The lanceolate point pattern began on the Plains with Agate Basin/Hell Gap forms, but eventually was replaced by Cody technology. This pattern is manifest on the Plains near the end of Folsom and occurred as a co-tradition with the fluted point pattern until the end of the Paleoindian period.

During this period the environment became increasingly drier, and perhaps people lived along ecotone margins and riverine environments where water sources and woods were more plentiful.

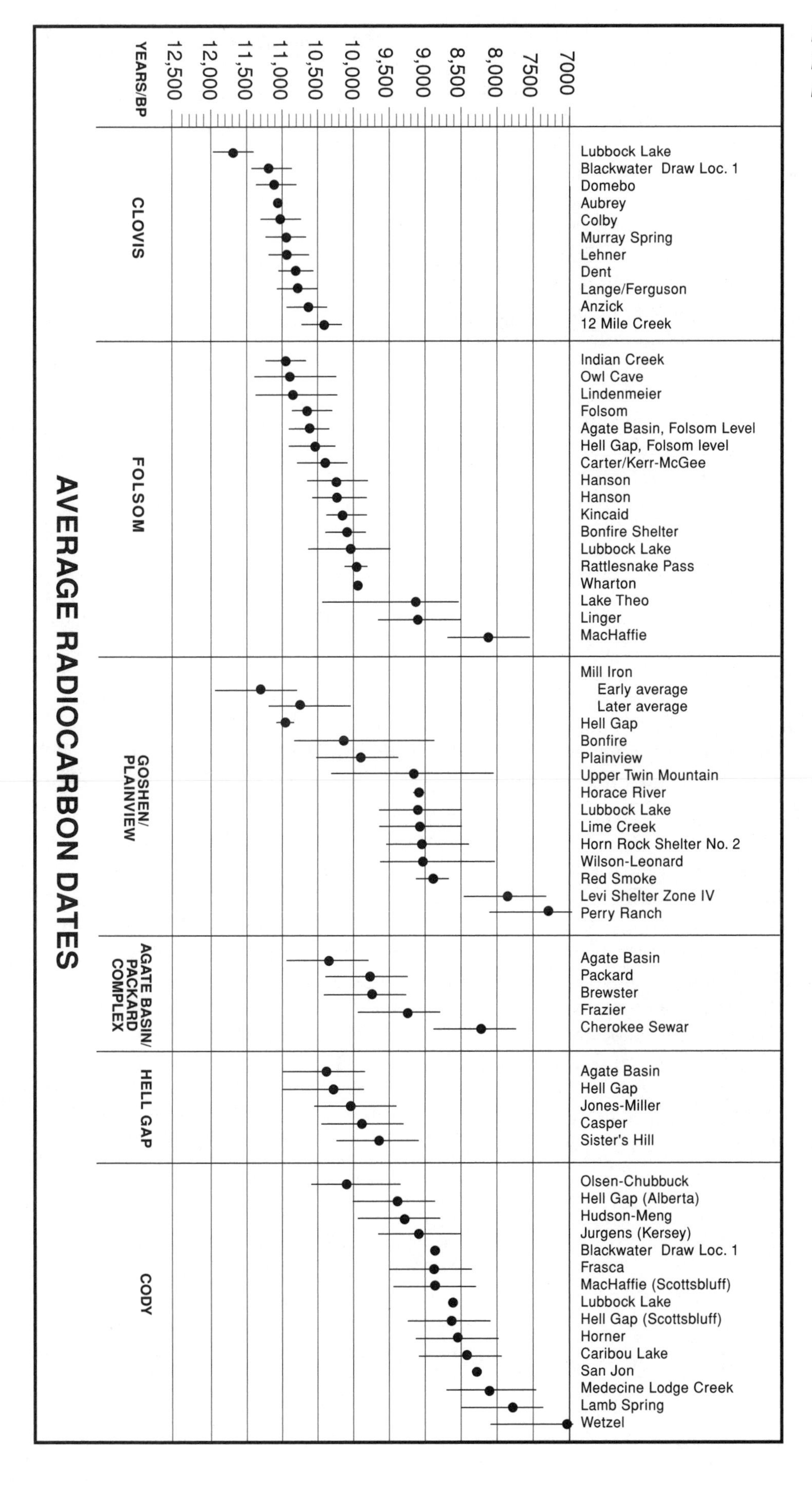

Figure 39. Summary of Plains/Southwest radiocarbon dates.

Communal hunts were only staged on a seasonal basis and perhaps depended on the numbers of animals available; only rarely did such a hunt occur. The overall subsistence strategies relied on smaller game animals.

Early in the Cody phase, a wetter climatic episode occurred, with an increase in the bison population. During the initial phase of Cody times, the square-based projectile point style spread over a wide area, including portions of the Midwest and Great Basin and Plateau. By late Cody times, when climatic conditions once again began to deteriorate, humans may have become more dependent on locally restricted resources, including plant processing. Also at this time, Archaic peoples began to move onto the Plains and into the Southwest from outside regions. Therefore, I would argue that the hunting and gathering of Paleoindian peoples became more geographically restricted at this time, and for all intents and purposes, the Archaic phase of the Plains and Southwest began.

Acknowledgments and Comments

The corpus of this paper originally was written before 1992. I have attempted to add recent references and adjust the manuscript accordingly. I no doubt omitted some papers and I apologize for those oversights. The radiocarbon assays are presented here in their original published form. I have not attempted to correct them; I leave that task to others.

I thank Margaret Jodry, Dee Ann Story, and Carolyn Rose for reading the manuscript and offering important suggestions. I thank Karen Turnmire and Rob Bonnichsen for their excellent editing and patience. Marcia Bakry produced the maps and radiocarbon figures, and Vic Krantz provided the photographs of the artifacts. Barbara Watanabe typed the radiocarbon charts and checked their references and the bibliography. I also thank my many colleagues, whose work I have drawn upon to produce this paper. I accept responsibility for any misinterpretations I may have made.

References Cited

Agenbroad, L. D.
1978 *The Hudson-Meng Site: An Alberta Bison Kill in the Nebraska High Plains.* University Press of America, Washington, D.C.

Agogino, G. A.
1961 A New Point Type from Hell Gap Valley, Eastern Wyoming. *American Antiquity* 26:558–560.

1969 The Midland Complex: Is it Valid? *American Anthropologist* 71:1117–1118.

Agogino, G. A., and E. Galloway
1965 The Sister's Hill Site: A Hell Gap Site in North-Central Wyoming. *Plains Anthropologist* 10:190-195.

Agogino, G. A., and A. Parrish
1971 The Fowler-Parrish Site: A Folsom Campsite in Eastern Colorado. *Plains Anthropologist* 16:111–114.

Albanese, J. P.
1978 Archaeology of the Northwestern Plains. In *Prehistoric Hunters of the High Plains,* edited by G. C. Frison, pp. 375–391. Academic Press, New York.

Alexander, H. L., Jr.
1963 The Levi Site: A Paleo-Indian Campsite in Central Texas. *American Antiquity* 24:510–528.

Amick, D. S.
1994a Technological Organization and the Structure of Inference in Lithic Analysis: An Examination of Folsom Hunting Behavior in the American Southwest. In *The Organization of North American Prehistoric Chipped Stone Tool Technologies,* edited by P. J. Carr, pp. 9–34. International Monographs in Prehistory, Archaeological Series 7, Ann Arbor.

1994b *Folsom Diet Breadth and Land Use in the American Southwest.* Unpublished Ph.D. Dissertation submitted to the Faculty of the Department of Anthropology, University of New Mexico. Albuquerque.

1995 Patterns of Technological Variation Among Folsom and Midland Projectile Points in the American Southwest. *Plains Anthropologist* 40:23–38.

Amsden, C. A.
1937 The Lake Mohave Artifacts. In E. W. C. Campbell, W. H. Campbell, E. Antevs, C. A. Amsden, J. A. Barbieri, and F. A. Bode, The Archaeology of Pleistocene Lake Mohave: A Symposium. *Southwest Museum Papers, No. 11,* pp. 51–98. Southwest Museum, Los Angeles.

Anderson, A. D.
1975 The Cooperton Mammoth: An Early Man Bone Quarry. *Great Plains Journal* 14:130–164.

Anderson, D. C., and H. A. Semken, Jr. (editors)
1980 *The Cherokee Excavations, Holocene Ecology and Human Adaptations in Northwestern Iowa.* Academic Press, New York.

Bachhuber, F. W., and W. A McClellan
1977 Paleoecology of Marine Foraminifera in the Pluvial Estancia Valley, Central New Mexico. *Quaternary Research* 7:254–267.

Bamforth, D. B.
1985 The Technological Organization of Paleo-Indian Small-Group Bison Hunting on the Llano Estacado. *Plains Anthropologist* 30:243–258.

1988 *Ecology and Human Organization on the Great Plains.* Plenum Press, New York.

Bamforth, D. B., and R. I. Dorn
1988 On the Nature and Antiquity of the Manix Lake Industry. *Journal of California and Great Basin Anthropology* 10:209–226.

Banks L. D.
1990 *From Mountain Peaks to Alligator Stomachs: A Review of Lithic Sources in the Trans-Mississippi South, the Southern Plains, and Adjacent Southwest.* Oklahoma Anthropological Society Memoir No.4., Norman.

n.d. *The Jones-Miller Site Chert Identification: A Study in the Central Great Plains.* Ms on file at the Smithsonian Institution.

Barbour, E. H., and C. B. Schultz
1932 *The Scottsbluff Bison Quarry and Its Artifacts.* Bulletin 34, vol. 1. Nebraska State Museum, Lincoln.

Bedwell, S. F.
1970 *Prehistory and Environment of the Pluvial Fort Rock Lake Area of Southcentral Oregon.* Unpublished Ph.D. dissertation, Department of Anthropology, University of Oregon, Eugene.

Bement, L. C.
1994 The Cooper Site: A Stratified Paleoindian Bison Kill in Northwest Oklahoma. *Current Research in the Pleistocene* 10:7–9.

Benedict, J.
1992 Along the Great Divide: High Colorado Front Range. In *Ice Age Hunters of the Rockies*, edited by D. J. Stanford and J. S. Day, pp. 343–359. Denver Museum of Natural History and University Press of Colorado, Niwot.

Billeck, W. T.
n.d. *Fluted Point Distribution in the Loess Hills of Southwestern Iowa.* Ms. on file at the Smithsonian Institution.

Binford, L. R.
1981 *Bones: Ancient Men and Modern Myths.* Academic Press.New York.

Blaine, J. C.
1968 A Preliminary Report on an Early Man Site in West Texas. In *Transactions of the Third Regional Archaeological Symposium for Southeastern New Mexico and Western Texas*, pp. 1–11. Southwestern Federation of Archaeological Societies, Lubbock.

Bonnichsen, R.
1991 Clovis Origins. In *Clovis Origins and Adaptations*, edited by R. Bonnichsen and K. Turnmire, pp. 309–329. Center for the Study of the First Americans, Oregon State University, Corvallis.

Bonnichsen, R., M. Beaty, M. D. Turner, J. C. Turner, and D. Douglas.
1992 Paleoindian Lithic Procurement at the South Fork of Everson Creek, Southwestern Montana: A Preliminary Statement. In *Ice Age Hunters of the Rockies*, edited by D. J. Stanford and J. S. Day, pp. 285–321. Denver Museum of Natural History and University Press of Colorado, Niwot.

Bonnichsen, R. and M. Sorg (editors)
1989 *Bone Modification.* Center for the Study of the First Americans, University of Maine, Orono.

Bonnichsen, R., D. Stanford, and J. L. Fastook
1987 Environmental Change and Developmental History of Human Adaptive Patterns; The Paleoindian Case. In *North America and Adjacent Oceans During the Last Deglaciation: The Geology of North America*, vol. K-3, edited by W. F. Ruddiman and H. E. Wright, Jr., pp. 403–424. Geological Society of America, Boulder.

Bonnichsen, R., and K. L. Turnmire (editors)
1991 *Clovis: Origins and Adaptations.* Center for the Study of the First Americans, Oregon State University, Corvallis.

Bradley, B. A.
1974 Comments on the Lithic Technology of the Casper Site Materials. In *The Casper Site: A Hell Gap Bison Kill on the High Plains*, edited by G. C. Frison, pp. 191–197. Academic Press, New York.

Bradley, B. A., and G. C. Frison
1996 Flaked-Stone and Worked-Bone Artifacts from the Mill Iron Site. In *The Mill Iron Site*, edited by G. C. Frison, pp. 43-71. University of New Mexico Press, Albuquerque.

Bradley, B. A., and D. J. Stanford
1987 Appendix 2, The Claypool Study. In *The Horner Site: The Type Site of the Cody Cultural Complex*, edited by G. C. Frison and L. C. Todd, pp. 405–434. Academic Press, New York.

Broecker, W. S., and J. L. Kulp
1957 Lamont Natural Radiocarbon Measurements IV. *Science* 126:1324–1334.

Bryan, A.
1980 The Stemmed Point Tradition: An Early Technological Tradition in Western North America. In *Anthropological Papers in Memory of Earl H. Swanson*, edited by L. B. Harten, C. N. Warren, and D. R. Tuohy, pp. 78–107. Special Publication of the Idaho State Museum of Natural History, Pocatello.

1988 The Relationship of the Stemmed Point and Fluted Point Traditions in the Great Basin. In *Early Human Occupation in Far Western North America: The Clovis-*

Archaic Interface, edited by J. A. Willig, C. M. Aikens, and J. L. Fagan, pp. 53–75. Nevada State Museum Anthropological Papers No. 21, Carson City.

Bryan, K.
1937 Geology of the Folsom deposits in New Mexico and Colorado. In *Early Man: As Depicted by Leading Authorities at the International Symposium, The Academy of Natural Science*, edited by G. G. MacCurdy, pp. 139–152. J. B. Lippincott Company, Philadelphia.

1941 Geologic Antiquity of Man in America. *Science* 93:505–524.

Butler, B. R.
1971 The Origin of the Upper Snake Country Buffalo. *Tebiwa* 14:1–20.

Campbell, T. N.
1961 A List of Radiocarbon Dates from Archaeological Sites in Texas. *Bulletin of the Texas Archaeological Society 30*: pp. 311–320.

Cassells, E. S.
1983 *The Archaeology of Colorado*. Johnson Press, Boulder.

Chrisman, D., R. S. MacNeish, J. Mavalwala, and H. Savage
1996 Late Pleistocene Human Friction Skin Prints from Pendejo Cave, New Mexico. *American Antiquity* 61:357–376.

Clark, D. W.
1987 *Archaeological Reconnaissance at Great Bear Lake.* Archaeological Survey of Canada Paper No. 136. Mercury Series. Canadian Museum of Civilization, Ottawa.

Collins, M. B.
1995 Forty Years of Archaeology in Central Texas. *Bulletin of the Texas Archaeological Society* 66:361–400.

Collins, M. B.
n.d. Wilson-Leonard, 11,500 years of Prehistory in Central Texas.

Collins, M. B., G. L. Evans, T. N. Campbell, M. C. Winans, and C. E. Mear
1989 Clovis Occupation at Kincaid Shelter, Texas. *Current Research in the Pleistocene* 6:3–5.

Collins, M. B., T. R. Hester, D. Olmstead, and P. J. Headrick
1991 Engraved Cobbles from Early Archaeological Contexts in Central Texas. *Current Research in the Pleistocene* 8:13–15.

Cotter, J. L.
1938a *The Occurrence of Flints and Extinct Animals in Pluvial Deposits near Clovis, New Mexico, pt. VI.* Report on the Excavations at the Gravel Pit in 1936. Proceedings of the Philadelphia Academy of Natural Science LXXXIX:2–16.

1938b *The Occurrence of Flints and Extinct Animals in Pluvial Deposits near Clovis, New Mexico, pt. VI.* Report on Field season of 1937. Proceedings of the Philadelphia Academy of Natural Sciences XC:2–16.

Crabtree, D.
1966 A Stoneworker's Approach to Analyzing and Replicating the Lindenmeier Folsom. *Tebiwa* 9:3-–39.

Dansie, A. J., J. O. Davis, and T. W. Stafford, Jr.
1988 The Wizards Beach Recession: Farmdalian (25,500 yr B.P.) Vertebrate Fossils Co-occur with Early Holocene Artifacts. In *Early Human Occupation in Far Western North America: The Clovis-Archaic Interface*, edited by J. A. Willig, C. M. Aikens, and J. L. Fagan, pp. 153–201. Nevada State Museum Anthropological Papers No. 21, Carson City.

Davis, E. M.
1953 Recent Data from Two Paleo-indian Sites on Medicine Creek, Nebraska. *American Antiquity* 18:380–386.

1962 *Archaeology of the Lime Creek Site in Southwestern Nebraska*. University of Nebraska State Museum, Special Publication No. 3.

Davis, L. B.
1984 Late Pleistocene to Mid-Holocene Adaptations at Indian Creek, West-central Montana Rockies. *Current Research* 1:9–10.

Davis, L. B., and S. T. Greiser
1992 Indian Creek Paleoindians: Early Occupation of the Elkhorn Mountains' Southeast Flank, West-Central Montana. In Ice *Age Hunters of the Rockies*, edited by D. J. Stanford and J. S. Day, pp. 225–283. Denver Museum of Natural History and University Press of Colorado, Niwot.

Davis, L. B., J. P. Albanese, L. S. Cummings, and J. W. Fisher, Jr.
1991 Reappraisal of the MacHaffie Site Paleoindian Occupational Sequence. *Current Research in the Pleistocene* 8:17–20.

Davis, W. E.
1985 The Montgomery Site. *Current Research in the Pleistocene* 2:11–12.

Dawson, J., and D. J. Stanford
1975 The Linger Site: A Re-investigation. *Southwestern Lore* 41:11–17.

Deller, D. B., and C. J. Ellis
1992 *Thedford II: A Paleo-Indian Site in the Ausable River Watershed of Southwestern Ontario.* Memoirs Museum of Anthropology University of Michigan No. 24. Ann Arbor.

Derevianko, A. P.
1989 The late Pleistocene Sites in the Slendia River Basin and Their Significance for Correlation with Upper Paleolithic Assemblages of the Pacific. In *Abstracts of the Circum-Pacific Prehistory Conference*, pp. 36. Seattle.

Dibble, D. S., and D. Lorrain
1968 *Bonfire Shelter: A Stratified Bison Kill Site, Val Verde County, Texas.* Miscellaneous Papers No. 1. Texas Memorial Museum, Austin.

Dick, H. W., and B. Mountain
1960 The Claypool Site: A Cody Complex Site in Northeastern Colorado. *American Antiquity* 26:223–235.

Dolzani, M.
1988 Rocking Around the Geomorphical Clock: Dating by the Rock Varnish Methods. *Mammoth Trumpet* 4(2):1.

Donohue, J.
1996 New Evidence for the Chronological Placement of the Goshen Complex in the Northwestern Plains. Paper Read at the 54th Annual Plains Anthropological Conference, Iowa City, Iowa.

Dorn, R. I.
1983 Cation-Ratio Dating: A New Rock Varnish Age-Determination Technique. *Quaternary Research* 20:49–73.

1989 Cation-Ratio Dating of Rock Varnish: A Geographic Assessment. *Progress in Physical Geography* 13:559–596.

Elyea, J.
1988 Analysis of Paleoindian Tools from LA 63880. In *The Border Star 85 Survey: Toward an Archaeology of Landscapes*, edited by T. J. Seaman, W. H. Doleman, and R. C. Chapman, pp. 231–237. Office of Contract Archaeology, University of New Mexico, Albuquerque.

Evans, G., and G. Meade
1945 *Quaternary of the Texas High Plains.* University of Texas, Austin, Bulletin 4401, pp. 485–507.

Ferring, C. R.
1990 The 1989 Investigations at the Aubrey Clovis Site, Texas. *Current Research in the Pleistocene* 7:10–12.

Ferring, C. R.
1995 Subsistence and Mobility Patterns at the Aubrey Clovis Site, Texas. Paper presented at the 60th annual meeting of the Society for American Archaeology. Minneapolis.

Figgins, J. D.
1927 The Antiquity of Man in America. *Natural History* 27:229–239.

1931 *An Additional Discovery of the Association of a "Folsom" Artifact and Fossil Mammal Remains.* Proceeding of the Colorado Museum of Natural History 10(2).

1933 *A Further Contribution to the Antiquity of Man in America.* Proceeding of the Colorado Museum of Natural History 12(2).

Fisher, J. W., Jr.
1992 Observations on the Late Pleistocene Bone Assemblage from the Lamb Spring Site, Colorado. In *Ice Age Hunters of the Rockies*, edited by D. J. Stanford and J. S. Day, pp. 51–83. Denver Museum of Natural History and University Press of Colorado, Niwot.

Forbis, R. G.
1970 *A Review of Alberta Archaeology to 1964.* National Museums of Canada, Publications in Archaeology No. 1. National Museum of Man, Ottawa.

Forbis, R. G., and J. D. Sperry
1952 An Early Man Site in Montana. *American Antiquity* 18:127–137.

Frison, G. C.
1974 *The Casper Site: A Hell gap Bison Kill on the High Plains.* Academic Press. New York.

1976 Cultural Activity Associated with Prehistoric Mammoth Butchering and Processing. *Science* 194:728–730.

1978 *Prehistoric Hunters of the High Plains.* Academic Press, New York.

1984 The Carter/Kerr-McGee Paleoindian Site: Cultural Resource Management and Archaeological Research. *American Antiquity* 49:288–314.

1988 Paleoindian Subsistence and Settlement During Post-Clovis Times on the Northwestern Plains, the Adjacent Mountain Ranges, and the Intermontane Basins. In *Americans Before Columbus: Ice Age Origins*, edited by R. C. Carlisle, pp. 83–106. Ethnology Monographs Number 12, Department of Anthropology, University of Pittsburgh.

1990 Clovis, Goshen, and Folsom: Lifeways and Cultural Relationships. In *Megafauna and Man: Discovery of America's Heartland*, edited by L. D. Agenbroad, J. I. Mead and L. W. Nelson, pp. 100–108. The Mammoth Site of Hot Springs, South Dakota, Inc. Scientific Papers, Volume 1. Hot Springs.

1991a *Prehistoric Hunters of the High Plains*, 2d ed. Academic Press, San Diego.

1991b The Goshen Paleoindian Complex; New Data for Paleoindian Research. In *Clovis: Origins and Adaptations*, edited by R. Bonnichsen and K. L. Turnmire, pp. 133–151. Center for the Study of the First Americans, Oregon State University, Corvallis.

1992 The Foothills-Mountains and Open Plains: The Dichotomy in Paleoindian Subsistence Strategies Between Two Ecosystems. In *Ice Age Hunters of the Rockies*, edited by D. J. Stanford and J. S. Day, pp. 323–342. Denver Museum of Natural History and University Press of Colorado, Niwot.

Frison, G. C. (editor)
1996 *The Mill Iron Site.* University of New Mexico Press, Albuquerque.

Frison, G. C., and B. A. Bradley
1980 *Folsom Tools and Technology at the Hanson Site, Wyoming.* University of New Mexico Press, Albuquerque.

1982 Fluting of Folsom Projectile Points. In *The Agate Basin Site: A Record of the Paleoindian Occupation of the Northwestern High Plains*, edited by G. C. Frison and D. J. Stanford pp. 209–213. Academic Press, New York.

Frison, G. C., and C. Craig
1982 Bone, Antler, and Ivory Artifacts and Manufacture Technology. In *The Agate Basin Site: A Record of the Paleoindian Occupation of the Northwestern High Plains*, edited by G. C. Frison and D. J. Stanford, pp. 157–173. Academic Press, New York.

Frison, G. C., C. V. Haynes, Jr., and M. L. Larson
1996 Summary and Conclusions. In *The Mill Iron Site*, edited by G. C. Frison, pp. 295-316. University of New Mexico Press, Albuquerque.

Frison, G. C., and M. Kornfeld
1995 *Interim Report on the 1994 Testing, Data Recovery, and Analysis at Three Paleoindian Sites in Grand County, Colorado, and Summary of Current Investigations.* Technical Report 6b. Department of Anthropology, University of Wyoming. Laramie.

Frison, G. C., and C. Reher
1970 *Age Determination of Buffalo Tooth Eruption and Wear.* In The Glenrock Buffalo Jump, 48SU304. By G. C. Frison. Plains Anthropologist Memoir 7, Appendix 1. Lawrence.

Frison, G. C., and D. J. Stanford (editors)
1982 *The Agate Basin Site: A Record of the Paleoindian Occupation of the Northwestern High Plains.* Academic Press, New York.

Frison, G. C., and L. C. Todd (editors)
1986 *The Colby Mammoth Site: Taphonomy and Archaeology of a Clovis Kill in Northern Wyoming.* University of New Mexico Press, Albuquerque.

1987 *The Horner Site: The Type Site of the Cody Cultural Complex*. Academic Press, Orlando.

Fulgham, T., and D. J. Stanford
1982 The Frasca Site: A Preliminary Report. *Southwestern Lore* 48:1–9.

Galloway, E., and G. A. Agogino
1961 The Johnson Site: A Folsom Campsite. *Plains Anthropologist* 6:205–208.

Gordon, B.
1981 Man-environment Relationships in Barrenland Prehistory. *Musk-Ox* 28:1–19

Graham, R. W., and E. Lundelius, Jr.
1984 Coevolutionary Disequilibrium and Pleistocene Extinctions. In *Quaternary Extinctions: A Prehistoric Revolution*, edited by P. S. Martin and R. G. Klein, pp. 223–249. University of Arizona Press, Tucson.

Graham, R. W., and J. I. Mead
1987 Environmental Fluctuations and Evolution of Mammalian Faunas During the Last Deglaciation in North America. In *North America and Adjacent Oceans During the Last Deglaciation: The Geology of North America*, vol. K-3, edited by W. F. Ruddiman and H. E. Wright, Jr., pp. 371–402. Geological Society of America, Boulder.

Graham, R. W., H. A. Semken, Jr., and M. A. Graham (editors)
1987 *Late Quaternary Mammalian Biogeography and Environments of the Great Plains and Prairies.* Illinois State Museum Scientific Papers No. 22. Springfield.

Grayson, D. K.
1989 The Chronology of North American Late Pleistocene Extinctions. *Journal of Archaeological Science* 16:153–165.

Green, F. E.
1963 The Clovis Blades: An Important Addition to the Llano Complex. *American Antiquity* 29:145–165.

Green, J. P.
1983 *Obsidian Hydration Chronology; The Early Owl Cave Remains.* Unpublished paper presented at the Eleventh Annual Conference of the Idaho Archaeological Society, Boise.

Greenberg, J. H., C. G. Turner II, and S. L. Zegura
1986 The Settlement of the Americas: A Comparison of Linguistic, Dental, and Genetic Evidence. *Current Anthropology* 27:477–497.

Guffee, E. J.
1979 *The Plainview Site: Relocation and Archaeological Investigation of a Late Paleo-Indian Kill Site in Hale County, Texas.* Archaeological Research Laboratory, Llano Estacado Museum, Plainview, TX.

Haas, H., V. T. Holliday, and R. Stuckenrath
1986 Dating of Holocene Stratigraphy with Soluble and Insoluble Organic Fractions at the Lubbock Lake Archaeological Site, Texas; An Ideal Case Study. *Radiocarbon* 28:473–85.

Hannus, L. A.
1989 Flaked Mammoth Bone from the Lange/Ferguson Site, White River Badland Area South Dakota. In *Bone Modification*, edited by R. Bonnichsen and M. H. Sorg, pp. 395–413. Center for the Study of the First Americans, University of Maine, Orono.

Harrison, B., and K. Killen
1978 *Lake Theo: A Stratified, Early Man Bison Butchering and Camp Site, Briscoe County, Texas: Archaeological Investigations Phase II.* Panhandle-Plains Historical Museum, Special Anthropological Report No. 1. Canyon.

Haury, E. W.
1950 *The Stratigraphy and Archaeology of Ventana Cave.* University of Arizona Press, Tucson.

1953 Artifacts with Mammoth Remains, Naco, Arizona, I: Discovery of the Naco Mammoth and Associated Projectile Points. *American Antiquity* 19:1–14.

Hayden, J. D.
1976 Pre-Altithermal Archaeology in the Sierra Pinacate, Sonora, Mexico. *American Antiquity* 41: 274–289.

Haynes, C. V., Jr.
1955 Evidence of Early Man in Torrence County, New Mexico. *Bulletin of the Texas Archaeological Society* 26:144–165.

1967 Carbon-14 Dates and Early Man in the New World. In *Pleistocene Extinctions: The Search for a Cause*, edited by P. S. Martin and H. E. Wright, Jr, pp. 267–286. Yale University Press, New Haven.

1975 Pleistocene and Recent Stratigraphy. In *Late Pleistocene Environments of the Southern High Plains*, edited by F. Wendorf and J. Hester, pp. 57–96. Fort Burgwin Research Center Publication No. 9. Southern Methodist University, Dallas.

1980 The Clovis Culture. In *The Ice-Free Corridor and Peopling of the New World*, edited by N. W. Rutter and C. E. Schweger, pp. 115–123. *Canadian Journal of Anthropology* 1(1).

1981 Geochronology and Paleoenvironments of the Murray Springs Clovis Site, Arizona. *National Geographic Society Research Reports* 13:243–251.

1984 Stratigraphy and Late Pleistocene Extinction in the United States. In *Quaternary Extinctions: A Prehistoric Revolution*, edited by P. S. Martin and R. G. Klein, pp. 345–353. University of Arizona Press, Tucson.

1990 The Antevs-Bryan Years and the Legacy for Paleoindian Geochronology. In *Establishment of a Geologic Framework for Paleoanthropology*, edited by L. R. Laporte, pp. 55–68. Geological Society of America, Special Paper 242, Boulder.

1991a Contributions of Radiocarbon Dating to the Geochronology of the Peopling of the New World. In *Radiocarbon After Four Decades: An Interdisciplinary Perspective*, edited by R. E. Taylor, A. Long, and R. Kra. University of Arizona Press, Tucson.

1991b Geoarchaeological and Peleohydrological Evidence for a Clovis-age Drought in North America and Its Bearing on Extinction. *Quaternary Research* 35:438–450.

1993 Clovis-Folsom Geochronology and Climatic Change. In *From Kostenki to Clovis, Upper Paleolithic-Paleo-Indian Adaptations*, edited by O. Soffer and N. D. Praslov, pp. 219–236, Plenum Press, New York.

1995 Geochronology of Paleoenvironmental Change, Clovis Type Site, Blackwater Draw, New Mexico. *Geoarchaeology: An International Journal* 10:317–388.

Haynes, C. V. Jr., and G. A. Agogino
1966 Prehistoric Springs and Geochronology of the Clovis Site, New Mexico. *American Antiquity* 31:812–821.

1986 *Geochronology of Sandia Cave*. Smithsonian Contributions to Anthropology No. 32. Washington, D.C.

Haynes, C. V., Jr., R. P. Beukens, A. J. T. Jull, and O. K. Davis
1992 New Radiocarbon Dates for Some Old Folsom Sites; Accelerator Technology. In *Ice Age Hunters of the Rockies*, edited by D. J. Stanford and J. S. Day, pp. 83–100. Denver Museum of Natural History and University of Colorado Press, Niwot.

Haynes, C. V., Jr., D. J. Donahue, A. J. T. Jull, and T. H. Zabel
1984 Application of Accelerator Dating to Fluted Point Paleoindian Sites. *Archaeology of Eastern North America* 12:184–191. Eastern States Archaeological Federation.

Haynes, C. V., Jr., and E. T. Hemmings
1968 Mammoth-bone Shaft Wrench from Murray Springs, Arizona. *Science* 159:186–187.

Haynes, C. V., Jr., D. J. Stanford, M. Jodry, J. Dickenson, J. L. Montgomery, P. H. Shelley, and G. A. Agogino
A Clovis Well at the Type Site 11,000 BC: The oldest Prehistoric Well in America. Ms, submitted to *Geoarchaeology*.

Haynes, G.
1991 *Mammoths, Mastodonts, and Elephants: Biology, Behavior, and the Fossil Record*. Cambridge University Press, Cambridge.

Hemmings, E. T.
1970 *Early Man in the San Pedro Valley, Arizona*. Unpublished Ph.D. Dissertation, Department of Anthropology, University of Arizona, Tucson.

Hemmings, E. T., and C. V. Haynes, Jr.
1969 The Escapule Mammoth and Associated Projectile Points San Pedro Valley, Arizona. *Journal of the Arizona Academy of Science* 5(3):184–188.

Henderson, J., and G. Goode
1991 Pavo Real: An Early Paleoindian Site in South Central Texas. *Current Research in the Pleistocene* 8:26–28.

Hester, J. J.
1972 *Blackwater Locality No. 1: A Stratified, Early Man Site in Eastern New Mexico*. Fort Burgwin Research Center No. 8, Southern Methodist University, Dallas.

1975 Paleoarchaeology of the Llano Estacado. In *Late Pleistocene Environments of the Southern High Plains*, edited by F. Wendorf and J. J. Hester, pp. 247–256. Fort Burgwin Research Center No. 9. Southern Methodist University, Dallas.

Hester, J. J., and J. Grady
1977 Paleoindian Social Patterns on the Llano Estacado. *The Museum Journal* 17:78–96.

Hibben, F. C.
1941 *Evidence of Early Occupation in Sandia Cave, New Mexico, and Other Sites in the Sandia-Manzano Region*. Smithsonian Miscellaneous Collection Vol. 99, No. 23. Washington, D.C.

1955 Specimens from Sandia Cave and Their Possible Significance. *Science* 122:688–689.

Hofman, J. L.
1992 Recognition and Interpretation of Folsom Technological Variability on the Southern Plains. In *Ice Age Hunters of the Rockies*, edited by D. J. Stanford and J. S. Day, pp. 193–225. Denver Museum of Natural History and University Press of Colorado, Niwot.

1996 Early Hunters-Gatherers of the Central Great Plains: Paleoindian and Mesoindian Cultures. In *Archaeology and Paleoecology of the Great Plains: A Volume in the Central and Northern Plains Archeological Overview*, edited by J. L. Hofman, pp. 41-100. Arkansas Archeological Survey Research Series No. 48, Fayetteville.

Hofman, J. L., and E. Ingbar
1988 A Folsom Hunting Overlook in Eastern, Wyoming. *Plains Anthropologist* 33: 337–350.

Hofman, J. L., D. S. Amick, and R. O. Rose
1990 Shifting Sands: A Folsom-Midland Assemblage From a Campsite in Western Texas. *Plains Anthropologist* 35:221–253.

Hofman, J. L., and B. J. Carter
1991 The Waugh Site: A Folsom-Bison Association in Northwestern Oklahoma. In *A Prehistory of the Plains Border Region: Guidebook 9th Annual Meeting, South-Central Friends of the Pleistocene*, edited by B. Carter and P. Ward, pp. 24–37. Oklahoma State University, Stillwater.

Hofman, J. L., L. C. Todd, and M. B. Collins
1991a Identification of Central Texas Edwards Chert at the Folsom and Lindenmeier Sites. *Plains Anthropologist* 36:297–-308.

Hofman, J. L., L. C. Todd, C. B. Schultz, and W. Hendy
1991b The Lipscomb Bison Quarry: Continuing Investigation at a Folsom Site on the Southern Plains. *Bulletin of the Texas Archaeological Society 50.*

Holliday, V. T.
1985 Archaeological Geology of the Lubbock Lake Site, Southern High Plains of Texas. *Geological Society of America Bulletin* 96:1483–1492.

Holliday, V. T., E. Johnson, H. Haas, and R. Stuckenrath.
1983 Radiocarbon Ages from the Lubbock Lake Site, 1950-1980: A Framework for Cultural and Ecological Change on the Southern High Plains. *Plains Anthropologist* 28:165–182.

1985 Radiocarbon Ages from the Lubbock Lake Site: 1981 -1984. *Plains Anthropologist* 30:277–291.

Howard, E. B.
1935a Evidence of Early Man in North America. *The Museum Journal* 24(2–3). University of Pennsylvania Museum, Philadelphia.

1935b Occurrence of Flints and Extinct Animals in Pluvial Deposits near Clovis, New Mexico, pt. 1, Introduction. *Proceedings Philadelphia Academy of Natural Sciences* 87:299–303.

1943 The Finley Site: Discovery of Yuma Points, in situ, near Eden, Wyoming. *American Antiquity* 8:224–234.

Howard, E. B., L. Satterthwaite, Jr., and C. Bache
1941 Preliminary Report on a Buried Yuma Site in Wyoming. *American Antiquity* 7:70–74.

Huckell, B. B.
1982 *The Distribution of Fluted Points in Arizona: A Review and an Update.* Archaeological Series No. 145, Cultural Resource Management Division, Arizona State Museum, University of Arizona, Tucson.

Hughes, J. T.
1949 Investigation in Western South Dakota and Northeastern Wyoming. *American Antiquity* 14:266–277.

Humphrey, J. D., and C. R. Ferring
1994 Stable Isotopic Evidence for Latest Pleistocene and Holocene Climatic Change in North-Central Texas. *Quaternary Research* 41:200–213.

Hurst, C. T.
1943 A Folsom Site in a Mountain Valley of Colorado. *American Antiquity* 8:250–253.

Irwin, H. T.
1967 *The Itama: Late Pleistocene Inhabitants of the Plains of the United States and Canada and the American Southwest.* Unpublished Ph.D. Dissertation, Department of Anthropology, Harvard University, Cambridge.

1971 Developments in Early Man Studies in Western North America, 1960-1970. *Arctic Anthropology* 8:42–67.

Irwin, H. T., and H. M. Wormington
1970 Paleo-Indian Tool Types in the Great Plains. *American Antiquity* 35:24–34.

Irwin-Williams, C., H. T. Irwin, G. Agogino, and C. V. Haynes Jr.
1973 Hell Gap: Paleo-Indian Occupation on the High Plains. *Plains Anthropologist* 18:40–53.

Jennings, J. D.
1955 *The Archaeology of the Plains: An Assessment.* Ms. prepared for the National Park Service. Salt Lake.

Jepsen, G. L.
1953 Ancient Buffalo Hunters of Northwestern Wyoming. *Southwestern Lore* 19:19–25.

Jodry, M. A.
1987 *Stewart's Cattle Guard Site: A Folsom Site in Southern Colorado; A Report on the 1981 and 1983 Field Seasons.* Unpublished Master's Thesis, Department of Anthropology, University of Texas at Austin.

1992 Fitting Together Folsom: Refitted Lithics and Site Formation Processes at Stewart's Cattle Guard Site. In *Piecing Together the Past: Applications of Refitting Studies in Archaeology,* edited by J. L. Hoffman and J. G. Enloe, pp. 179–209. BAR International Series 578.

Jodry, M. A., D. S. Shafer, D. J. Stanford, and O. K. Davis
1989 Late Quaternary Environments and Human Adaptation in the San Luis Valley, South-Central Colorado. In *Water in the Valley,* edited by E. J. Harmon, pp. 189–209. Colorado Ground-Water Association, Lakewood.

Jodry, M. A., and D. Stanford
1992 Stewart's Cattle Guard Site: An Analysis of Bison Remains in a Folsom Kill-Butchery Campsite. In *Ice Age Hunters of the Rockies,* edited by D. J. Stanford and J. S. Day, pp. 101–168. Denver Museum of Natural History and University Press of Colorado, Niwot.

1997 Changing Hydrologic Regimes and Prehistoric Landscape Use in the Northern San Luis Valley, Colorado. In Geologic Excursions to the Rocky Mountains and Beyond, Field Trip Guidebook for the 1996 Annual Meting, Geological Society of America. *Special Publication 44,* CD-Rom, edited by R. A. Thompson, M. R. Hudson, and C. L. Phillmore, Colorado Geological Survey, Denver.

Jodry, M. A., M. Turner, V. Spero, J. Turner, and D, Stanford
1996 Folsom in the Colorado High Country: The Black Mountain Site. *Current Research in the Pleistocene* 13:25-27.

Johnson, E.
1991 Late Pleistocene Cultural Occupation on the Southern Plains. In *Clovis: Origins and Adaptations,* edited by R. Bonnichsen and K. L. Turnmire, pp. 133–152. Center for the Study of the First Americans, Oregon State University, Corvallis.

Johnson, E. (editor)
1987 *Lubbock Lake: Late Quaternary Studies on the Southern High Plains.* Texas A&M Press, College Station.

Johnson E., and V. T. Holliday
1980 A Plainview Kill/Butchering Locale on the Llano Estcado—The Lubbock Lake Site. *Plains Anthropologist* 25:89–111.

1981 Late Paleo-indian Activity at the Lubbock Lake Site. *Plains Anthropologist* 26:173–193.

1985 Paleoindian Investigations at Lubbock Lake: The 1984 Season. *Current Research in the Pleistocene* 2:21–23.

Johnson, E., V. Holliday, and R. Neck
1982 Lake Theo: Late Quaternary Paleoenvironmental Data and a New Plainview (Paleo-indian) Date. *North American Archaeologist* 3:113–137.

Johnson, E., V. Holliday, R. Ralph, R. Knudson, and S. Lupton
1987 Ryan's Site: A Plainview Occupation on the Southern High Plains of Texas. *Current Research in the Pleistocene* 4:17–18.

Johnson, L.
1989 *Great Plains Interlopers in the Eastern Woodlands During Late Paleo-Indian Times: the Evidence from Oklahoma, Texas, and Areas Close By.* Office of the State Archaeologist Report 36, Texas Historical Commission. Austin.

Judge, W. J.
1973 *Paleoindian Occupation of the Central Rio Grande Valley in New Mexico.* University of New Mexico Press, Albuquerque.

Kay, M.
1996 Microwear Analysis of Some Clovis and Experimental Chipped Stone Tools. In *Stone Tools: Theoretical Insights into Human Prehistory,* edited by G. H. Odell, pp. 315–344. Plenum Press, New York.

Kearns, T. M., R. I. Dorn, and D. J. Stanford
1990 Flat Top Mountain and Initial Observations on Desert Varnish Cation Ratio Values from Southeastern Utah. *Current Research in the Pleistocene* 7:84–88.

Knudson, R.
1983 *Organizational Variability in Late Paleoindian Assemblages.* Washington State University, Laboratory of Anthropology, Reports of Investigations No. 60.

Kornfeld M. and G, C. Frison
n.d. Paleoindian Occupation of the High Country: The Case of Middle Park, Colorado. In *Recent Advances in Colorado Paleoindian Archaeology,* edited by R. H. Brunswig, Jr. University Press of Colorado, Niwot.

Krieger, A. D.
1947 Artifacts from the Plainview Bison Bed. Pages 932–952 in Fossil Bison and Associated Artifacts from Plainview, Texas. *Bulletin of the Geological Society of America* 8:927–954.

Kyriakidou, M.
1993 *Functional Analysis of the Hell Gap Projectile Point Complex: A Comparative Microwear Study.* Unpublished M.A. Thesis submitted to the Faculty of the Columbian College and Graduate Schools of George Washington University. Washington, D.C.

Lahren, L., and R. Bonnichsen
1974 Bone Foreshafts from a Clovis Burial in Southwestern Montana. **Science** 186:147–150.

Leonhardy, F. C.
1966 *Domebo: A Paleo-Indian Mammoth Kill in the Prairie-Plains.* Contributions of the Museum of the Great Plains No. 1. Lawton.

Lewis, T. M. N.
1954 The Cumberland Point. *Oklahoma Anthropological Society Bulletin* 2:7–8.

Lyman, R. L.
1994 *Vertebrate Taphonomy*. Cambridge Manuals in Archaeology, Cambridge University Press, Cambridge.

MacNeish, R. S.
1992 *The 1992 Excavations of Pendejo and Pintada Caves near Orogrande, New Mexico*. Andover Foundation for Archaeological Research, Andover.

Markgraf, V., J. P. Bradbury, R. M. Forester, G. Singh, and R. S. Sternberg.
1984 San Agustin Plains, New Mexico: Age and Paleoenvironmental Potential Reassessed. *Quaternary Research* 22:336–343.

Martin, P. S.
1984 Prehistoric Overkill: The Global Model. In *Quaternary Extinctions: A Prehistoric Revolution*, edited by P. S. Martin and R. G. Klein, pp. 354–404. University of Arizona Press, Tucson.

Mason, R.
1962 The Paleo-Indian Tradition in Eastern North America. *Current Anthropology* 3:227–278.

Mason, R. J., and C. Irwin
1960 An Eden-Scottsbluff Burial in Northeastern Wisconsin. *American Antiquity* 26:43–57.

McCartney, P. H.
1983 An Archaeological Analysis of Bison Remains from the Cody Paleo-Indian Site of Lamb Spring, Colorado. Unpublished M.A. Thesis submitted to the Faculty of the Department of Anthropology, The University of Arizona. Tucson.

Miller, M.
1986 Preliminary Investigations at the Seminoe Beach Site, Carbon County, Wyoming. *Wyoming Archaeologist* 29:83–96.

Miller, S.
1982 The Archaeology and Geology of an Extinct Megafauna/Fluted Point Association at Owl Cave, The Wasden Site, Idaho. In *Peopling of the New World*, edited by J. E. Ericson, J. E. Taylor, and R. Berger, pp. 81–95. Ballena Press, Los Altos.

Miller, S. J., and W. Dort Jr.
1978 Early Man at Owl Cave: Current Investigations at the Wasden Site, Eastern Snake River Plain, Idaho. In *Early Man in America from a Circum-Pacific Perspective*, edited by A. L. Bryan, pp.129–139. Occasional papers No. 1 of the Department of Anthropology, University of Alberta, Edmonton.

Morrow, T. A.
n.d. Folsom Points and Preforms in Iowa. Ms. on File at the Smithsonian Institution.

Moss, J. H., K. Bryan, G. W. Holmes, L. Satterthwaite Jr., H. P. Hansen, C. B. Schultz, and W. D. Frankforter
1953 *Early Man in the Eden Valley*. University of Pennsylvania, Museum Monographs No. 6, Philadelphia

Mulloy, W. T.
1959 The James Allen Site near Laramie, Wyoming. *American Antiquity* 25:112–116.

Nichols, J.
1990 Linguistic Diversity and the First Settlement of the New World. *Language* 66:475–521.

O'Brien, P. J.
1984 The Tim Adrian Site (14NT604): A Hell Gap Quarry Site in Norton County, Kansas. *Plains Anthropologist* 29:41–55

Patterson, L. W., and J. Hudgins
1985 Paleo-Indian Occupations in Wharton County, Texas. *Bulletin of the Texas Archaeological Society* 56:155–170.

Plew, M. G., and M. Pavesic
1982 A Compendium of Radiocarbon Dates for Southern Idaho Archaeological Sites. *Journal of California and Great Basin Anthropology* 4:113–122

Rancier J., D. J. Stanford, and G. Haynes
1982 1981 Investigations of Lamb Spring. *Southwestern Lore* 48:1–17.

Ray, C. N., and K. Bryan
1938 Folsomoid Point found in Alluvium Beside a Mammoth's Bones. *Science* (N.S.),88:257–258.

Redder, A. J.
1985 Horn Shelter Number 2, the South End: A Preliminary Report. *Central Texas Archaeologist* 10:37–66.

Reher, C.
1974 Population Study of Casper Site Bison. In *The Casper Site: A Hell Gap Bison Kill on the High Plains*, edited by G. C. Frison, pp. 113–124. Academic Press, New York.

Renaud, E. B.
1931 *Prehistoric Flaked Points from Colorado and Neighboring Districts*. Proceedings of the Colorado Museum of Natural History 10(2).

1932 *Yuma and Folsom Artifacts, New Material*. Proceedings of the Colorado Museum of Natural History 11(2).

Rice, D. G.
1972 *The Windust Phase in Lower Snake River Region Prehistory*. Washington State University Laboratory of Anthropology Report of Investigations No. 50. Pullman.

Roberts, F. H. H.
1935 *A Folsom Complex, Preliminary Report on the Lindenmeier Site in Northern Colorado*. Smithsonian Miscellaneous Collections 94(4).

1936 *Additional Information on the Folsom Complex: Report on the Second Season's Investigations at the Lindenmeier Site in Northern Colorado*. Smithsonian Miscellaneous Collections 95(4).

1940 Developments in the Problem of the North American Paleoindian. In *Essay of Historical Anthropology of North America*. Smithsonian Institution, Miscellaneous Collections 100:51–116.

1942 *Archaeological and Geological Investigations in the San Jon District, Eastern New Mexico*. Smithsonian Institution Miscellaneous Collections 103(4).

1943 A New Site. *American Antiquity* 8:300

Rogers, R., and L. Martin
1984 The 12 Mile Creek Site: A Reinvestigation. *American Antiquity* 49:757–764.

Roosa, W. B.
1956a Preliminary Report on the Lucy Site. *El Palacio* 63:36–49.

1956b The Lucy Site in Central New Mexico. *American Antiquity* 21:310.

Roosa, W. B., and D. B. Deller
1982 The Parkhill Complex and Eastern Great Lakes Paleo-indian. *Ontario Archaeology* 37:3–15

Root, M. J. (editor)
1993 *Site 32DU955A: Folsom Occupation of the Knife River Flint Primary Source Area*. Project Report Number 22, Center for Northwest Anthropology, Washington State University, Pullman.

Root, M. J., and A. M. Emerson
1994 *Archaeology of the Bobtail Wolf Site (32DU955A): 1993–1994 Progress Report*. Project Report Number 26 Center for Northwest Anthropology, Washington State University, Pullman.

Ruddiman, W. F., and H. E. Wright, Jr. (editors)
1987 *North American and Adjacent Oceans During the Last Deglaciation. The Geology of North America*, Vol. K-3, Geological Society of America, Boulder.

Saunders, J. J.
1977 Lehner Ranch Revisited. *The Museum Journal* 17:48–64. Lubbock.

Saunders, J. J., G. A. Agogino, A. T. Boldurian, and C. V. Haynes, Jr.
1991 A Mammoth-Ivory Burnisher-Billet from the Clovis Level, Blackwater Locality No. 1, New Mexico. *Plains Anthropologist* 36:359–363.

Saunders, J. J., C. V. Haynes, Jr., D. J. Stanford, and G. A. Agogino
1990 A Mammoth-Ivory Semifabricate from Blackwater Locality No. 1, New Mexico. *American Antiquity* 55:112–120.

Saunders, R. S., and J. T. Penman
1979 Perry Ranch: A Plainview Bison Kill on the Southern Plains. *Plains Anthropologist* 24:51–65.

Schultz, C. B.
1943 Some Artifact Sites of Early Man in the Great Plains and Adjacent Areas. *American Antiquity* 8:242–249.

Schultz, C. B., and W. D. Frankforter
1948 Preliminary Report on the Lime Creek Sites: New Evidence of Early Man in Southwestern Nebraska. *Bulletin of the University of Nebraska State Museum* 3(4):43–-62. Lincoln.

Sellards, E. H.
1938 Artifacts Associated with Fossil Elephant. *Bulletin Geological Society of America* 49:999–1010.

1945 Fossil Bison and Associated Artifacts from Texas (abstract). *Bulletin Geological Society of America* 56: 1196–1197.

1952 *Early Man in America: A Study in Prehistory*. University of Texas Press, Austin.

1955 Fossil Bison and Associated Artifacts from Milnesand, New Mexico. *American Antiquity* 20:336–345.

Sellards, E. H., G. L. Evans, and G. E. Meade
1947 Fossil Bison and Associated Artifacts from Plainview, Texas, with Description of Artifacts by Alex D. Krieger. *Bulletin Geological Society of America* 58:927–954.

Speer, R. D.
1990 History of the Plainview Site. In *Fifty Years of Discovery: The Lubbock Lake Landmark*, edited by V. T. Holliday and E. Johnson. Lubbock Lake Landmark Quaternary Research Center Series No. 2, Museum of Texas Tech University.

Smith, C. S., and L. M. McNees
1990 Rattlesnake Pass Site: A Folsom Occupation in South-Central Wyoming. *Plains Anthropologist* 35:273–289.

Stafford, T. Jr., P. E. Hare, L. Currie, A. J. T. Jull, and D. J. Donahue
1990 Accuracy of North American Human Skeleton Ages. *Quaternary Research* 34:11–121.

Stafford, T. Jr., P. E. Hare, L. Currie, A. J. T. Jull, and D. J. Donahue
1991 Accelerator Radiocarbon Dating at the Molecular Level. *Journal of Archaeological Sciences* 18:35–72.

Stanford, D. J.
1978 The Jones-Miller Site: An Example of Hell Gap Bison Procurement Strategy. In *Bison Procurement and Utilization: A Symposium*, edited by L. B. Davis and M. Wilson, pp. 89–97. Plains Anthropologist Memoir 14.

1981 Book Review: The Hudson-Meng Site: An Alberta Bison Kill in the Nebraska High Plains. *Plains Anthropologist* 26:339–341.

1984 *The Jones-Miller Site: A Study of Hell Gap Procurement and Processing*. National Geographic Research Projects, pp. 615–635.

1990 Archaeological Research in the San Luis Valley. *San Luis Valley Historian* 22:33–39.

1991 Clovis Origins and Adaptations: An Introductory Perspective. In *Clovis: Origins and Adaptations*, edited by R. Bonnichsen and K. Turnmire, pp. 1–13. Center for the Study of the First Americans, Oregon State University, Corvallis.

Stanford, D. J., and J. Albanese
1975 Preliminary Results of the Smithsonian Institution Excavation at the Claypool Site, Washington County, Colorado. *Southwestern Lore* 41:22–28.

Stanford, D. J., and R. Graham
1985 Archaeological Investigations of the Selby and Dutton Mammoth Kill Sites, Yuma County, Colorado. *National Geographic Society Research Reports* 19:519–541.

Stanford, D. J., and M. A. Jodry
1988 The Drake Clovis Cache. *Current Research in the Pleistocene* 5:21–22.

Stanford, D. J., M. A. Jodry, and L. Banks
1995 Early Paleoindian Diet Breadth as Seen from the Lewisville Site, Texas; Critter Buffet as an Alternative to Mammoth Barbeque. Paper read at the 60th Annual Meeting of the Society for American Archaeology, Minneapolis.

Stanford, D. J., and R. Patten
1984 R-6, a Preliminary Report of a Cody Site in North-Central New Mexico. In *Papers of the Philmont Conference on the Archaeology of Northeastern New Mexico*, edited by C. J. Condie. New Mexico Archaeological Council Proceedings, 6(1):187–201.

Stanford, D, J., W. R. Wedel, and G. Scott
1981 Archaeological Investigations of the Lamb Spring Site. *Southwestern Lore* 47:14–27.

Stevens, D. F., and G. A. Agogino
1975 Sandia Cave: A Study in Controversy. *Eastern New Mexico University Contribution to Anthropology* 7:52ps.

Steward. J. H.
1969 Postscripts to Bands: On Taxonomy, Processes, and Causes. In *Contributions to Anthropology: Band Societies*, edited by D. Damas, pp. 288–295. National Museums of Canada Bulletin 228. Ottawa.

Story, D. A.
1990 Culture History of the Native Americans. In *The Archaeology and Bioarchaeology of the Gulf Coastal Plain: Volume 1*, edited by D. A. Story, J. A. Guy, B. A. Burnett, M. D. Freeman, J. C. Rose, D. G. Steele, B. W. Olive, and K. J. Reinhard, pp. 163–367. Arkansas Archaeological Survey Research Series No. 38. Fayetteville.

Szathmary, E.
1985 Peopling of the Americas: Clues from Genetic Studies. In *Out of Asia: Peopling of the Americas and the Pacific*, edited by R. Kirk and E. Szathmary, pp. 79–112. Journal of Pacific History, Canberra.

Tamers, M. A., and F. J. Pearson, Jr.
1965 Validity of Radiocarbon Dates on Bone. *Nature* 205: 1054–1056.

Taylor, R. E., L. A. Payen, C. A. Prior, P. J. Slota, Jr., R. Gillespie, J. A. J. Gowlett, R. E. M. Hedges, A. J. T. Jull, T. H. Zabel, D. J. Donahue, and R. Berger
1985 Major Revisions in the Pleistocene Age Assignments for North America Human Skeletons by C-14 Accelerator Mass Spectrometry; None Older than 11,000 Years B.P.. *American Antiquity* 50:136–140.

Thompson, R. S., C. Whitlock, P. J. Bartlein, S. P. Harrison, and W. G. Spaulding
1993 Climatic Changes in the Western United States Since 18,000 yr B.P. In *Global Climates Since the Last Glacial Maximum*, edited by H. E. Wright, Jr., J. E. Kutzback, T. Webb III, W. F. Ruddiman, F. A. Street-Perrott, and P. J. Bartlein, pp. 468–513.

Todd, L. C., J. L. Hofman, and C. B. Schultz
1992 Faunal Analysis and Paleoindian Studies: A Reexamination of the Lipscomb Bison Bonebed. *Plains Anthropologist* 37:137–165.

Todd, L. C., and D. J. Stanford
1992 Application of Conjoined Bone Data to Site Structural Studies. In *Piecing Together the Past: Applications of Refitting Studies in Archaeology*, edited by J. L. Hofman and J. G. Enloe, pp. 21–35. BAR International Series 578.

Tunnell C.
1977 Fluted Projectile Point Production as Revealed by Lithic Specimens from the Adair-Steadman Site in Northwest Texas. *The Museum Journal* 17:140–169. Lubbock.

Turner, C. G., II
1985 The Dental Search for Native American Origins. In *Out of Asia: Peopling of the Americas and the Pacific*, edited by R. Kirk and E. Szathmary, pp. 31–78. Journal of Pacific History, Canberra.

Walker, D.
1982 Early Holocene Vertebrate Fauna. In *The Agate Basin Site: A Record of the Paleoindian Occupation of the Northwestern High Plains*, edited by G. C. Frison and D. J. Stanford, pp. 274–309. Academic Press, New York.

Watt, F. H.
1978 Radiocarbon Chronology of Sites in the Central Brazos Valley. *Bulletin of the Texas Archaeological Society* 49: 111–138.

Webb, C. H.
1946 Two Unusual Types of Chipped Stone Artifact from Northwest Louisiana. *Bulletin of the Texas Archaeological Society* 17:9–17.

Webber, R. H., and G. A. Agogino
1967 Mockingbird Gap Paleo-Indian Site: Excavations in 1967. Ms. on file at the Smithsonian Institution.

Wendorf, F., A. D. Krieger, C. C. Albritton, and T. D. Stewart
1955 *The Midland Discovery: A Report on the Pleistocene Human Remains from Midland, Texas.* University of Texas Press, Austin.

Wendorf, F., and J. J. Hester (editors)
1975 *Late Pleistocene Environments of the Southern High Plains.* Fort Burgwin Research Center No. 9. Southern Methodist University, Dallas.

Wheat, J. B.
1972 *The Olsen-Chubbuck Site: A Paleo-Indian Bison Kill.* Society for American Archaeology Memoir 26.

1979 *The Jurgens Site.* Plains Anthropologist Memoir No. 15.

Willey, P. S., B. R. Harrison, and J. T. Hughes
1978 The Rex Rodgers Site. In *Archaeology at Mackenzie Reservoir*, edited by J. T. Hughes and P. S. Willey, pp. 51–68. Texas Historical Commission, Office of the State Archaeological Survey Report 24.

Williams, R. C., A. G. Steinberg, H. Gershowitz, P. H. Bennet, H. C. Knowler, D. J. Pettitt, W. Butler, R. Baird, L. Dowd-Rea, T. A. Burch, H. G. Morse, and C. G. Smith
1985 Gm Allotypes in Native Americans: Evidence for Three Distinct Migrations Across the Bering Land Bridge. *American Journal of Physical Anthropology* 66:1–19.

Williston, S.
1902 An Arrow-head Found with the Bones of Bison occidentalis, Lucas, in Western Kansas. *American Geologist* 20:313–315.

Wilmsen, E. N., and F. H. H. Roberts
1978 *Lindenmeier, 1934-1974, Concluding Report on Investigations.* Smithsonian Contributions to Anthropology, Number 24.

Wormington, H. M.
1948 A Proposed Revision of Yuma Point Terminology. *Proceedings of the Colorado Museum of Natural History* 18(2):26–41

1957 *Ancient Man in North America.* Denver Museum of Natural History, Popular Series No. 4, Denver.

1988 The Frazier Site, Colorado. In *Guidebook to the Archaeological Geology of the Colorado Piedmont and High Plains of Southeastern Wyoming*, edited by V. T. Holliday, pp. 82–84. Department of Geography, University of Wisconsin-Madison.

Wormington, H. M., and R. G. Forbis
1965 *An Introduction to the Archaeology of Alberta, Canada.* Denver Museum of Natural History, Denver.

Wright, H. E., Jr. (editor)
1983 The Holocene. In *Late Quaternary Environments of the United States*, vol. 2, H. E. Wright, Jr., general editor. University of Minnesota Press, Minneapolis.

Wright, J. V.
1972a *The Aberdeen Site, Keewatin District, N.W.T.* Archaeological Survey of Canada Paper No. 2. National Museum of Man, Ottawa.

1972b *The Shield Archaic.* National Museums of Canada Publications in Archaeology No. 3, Ottawa.

1976 *The Grant Lake Site, Keewatin District, N.W.T.* Archaeological Survey of Canada paper No. 47. Mercury Series. National Museum of Man, Ottawa.

Wyckoff, D. G.
1985 The Packard Complex: Early Archaic Pre-Dalton Occupations on the Prairie-Woodlands Border. *Southeastern Archaeology* 4:1–26.

1989 Accelerator Dates and Chronology at the Packard Site, Oklahoma. *Current Research in the Pleistocene* 6:24–26.

Wyckoff, D. G., and B. J. Carter
1994 *Geoarchaeology at the Burnham Site: 1992 Investigations at a "Pre-Clovis Site" in Northwestern Oklahoma.* A Special Publication of the Oklahoma Archaeological Survey, University of Oklahoma. Norman.

Wyckoff, D. G., B. J. Carter, W. Dort, Jr., G. R. Brakenridge, L. D. Martin, J. L. Theler, and L. C. Todd.
1990 Northwestern Oklahoma's Burnham Site: Glimpses Beyond Clovis? *Current Research in the Pleistocene* 7:60–63.

Young, B., and M. B. Collins
1989 A Cache of Blades with Clovis Affinities from Northeastern Texas. *Current Research in the Pleistocene* 6:26–29.

Young, D., and R. Bonnichsen
1984 *Understanding Stone Tools: A Cognitive Approach.* Center for the Study of Early Man, University of Maine, Orono.

Young, D., S. Patrick, and D. G. Steele
1987 An Analysis of the Paleoindian Double Burial from Horn Shelter No. 2, In Central Texas. *Plains Anthropologist* 32:275–299.

The Burnham Site and Pleistocene Human Occupations of the Southern Plains of the United States

Don G. Wyckoff

Abstract

Interdisciplinary research on Paleoindians had its origin on the Southern Plains, and for 60 years archaeological sites there have yielded North America's longest and most detailed record of Pleistocene people. From 11,500 to 10,000 years ago, the Clovis–Folsom–Plainview cultural sequence attests to people who were frequenting the diverse Southern Plains settings and exploiting the animal and mineral resources of this area. As the region's unequivocal first residents, Clovis people display remarkable familiarity with the settings and resources. Such familiarity suggests they could have had precursors in the region, but only the Levi site in Texas seems to offer clues to someone here immediately before Clovis. More problematical are the flakes and implements from 26,000-year-old deposits at the Burnham site in northwestern Oklahoma. If their age and contextual relationships are verified, the Burnham findings will necessitate new models for the peopling of the Southern Plains and North America.

Introduction

For more than 60 years, Southern Plains archaeological sites have had key roles in documenting the human occupation of Pleistocene North America. In 1926, fluted spear points found with extinct bison remains at northeastern New Mexico's Folsom site provided the first unequivocal proof that humans were in North America during the last ice age (Figgins 1927; Meltzer 1983:34–38). By 1938, the combined efforts of archaeologists, geologists, and paleontologists at Blackwater Draw, New Mexico, and Miami, Texas, were further verifying the contemporaneity of humans with Pleistocene fauna while also providing hints that the Folsom artifacts were not the oldest (Antevs 1936; Bryan 1938; Cotter 1938; Howard 1935, 1936; Sellards 1938; Stock and Bode 1937). The participation of geologists in studying these Southern Plains locations is especially noteworthy. Not only did they help confirm the Pleistocene age of the artifact-bearing deposits, but they also fostered the interdisciplinary studies of Pleistocene settings and environments routinely expected in today's Paleoindian research. Consequently, by the mid-1960s, interdisciplinary studies at Southern High Plains sites like Blackwater Draw, Lubbock Lake, Scharbauer, Domebo, Plainview, and Milnesand had yielded a remarkable record of successive ancient hunting-oriented cultures, including their material assemblages, their prey, and the changing settings and environments to which they were adapting (Green 1962; Holden 1974; Leonhardy 1966; Sellards 1952, 1955; Sellards et al. 1947; Stevens 1973; Wendorf et al. 1955; Wheat 1974). The bison-hunting Folsom culture was now known to have been preceded by people who hunted mammoths with the fluted Clovis-style spear points. Moreover, with the increasing application of radiocarbon dating, a chronology for Plains Paleoindian cultures was developed (Stephenson 1965). Subsequent Southern Plains findings (Harrison and Killen 1978; Hester et al. 1972; Johnson 1987a; Leonhardy 1966) have elaborated this sequence and revised its chronology. Plainview bison hunters are known to have lived here by 10,000 years ago, whereas Folsom components date between 10,200 and 10,800 yr B.P. and those of Clovis are predominantly between 11,000 and 11,500 yr B.P. (Haynes 1987; Haynes et al. 1984, 1988; Johnson et al. 1982; Sellards et al. 1947).

Oklahoma Archeological Survey, University of Oklahoma, Norman, Oklahoma 73019

Throughout the 60 years that Paleoindian sites have been studied, a few Southern Plains locations have yielded clues interpreted to indicate someone was here before Clovis times (Alexander 1982; Anderson 1975; Cook 1927; Crook and Harris 1957, 1958; Evans 1930; Hay 1929). Despite such claims, Southern Plains archaeological findings repeatedly have supported the conclusions that Clovis artifacts are the region's oldest evidence of human habitation and that the Clovis–Folsom sequence is the principal manifestation of people residing here during the late Pleistocene. For these reasons, the region's Folsom and Clovis occupations are reviewed below and are contrasted with the evidence from purported pre-Clovis sites. Finally, preliminary findings are presented for northwestern Oklahoma's recently discovered Burnham site, a perplexing, ancient deposit located some 380 km downstream from the original Folsom site.

The Study Area

For this review, the Southern Plains consist of the High Plains and their eroded eastern and western borders that lie between the Cimarron watershed on the north and the Rio Grande on the south (Figure 1). Representing nearly 400,000 km^2 of eastern New Mexico, western Texas, western Oklahoma, and adjacent segments of Kansas and Colorado, the region has been described thoroughly by Fenneman (1931:1–60), Thornbury (1965:300–319), and Hunt (1974). Its climate is subhumid to semiarid continental, having 50 cm or less annual precipitation, notable departures from precipitation means, quick changes in temperature, and large daily and annual temperature ranges (Finley and Gustavson 1980:5–9). November through March are relatively arid due to dry, cold polar masses moving south and blocking moist air flow from the Gulf of Mexico (Haragan 1976). Most precipitation comes between April and September as either spring thunderstorms during the passing of fronts or as convectional storms from summertime heating and low-altitude moisture (Haragan 1970).

Central to the region is the Southern High Plains, a series of slightly (1.5–2.0 m/km) southeast-sloping, poorly drained, wind-swept, high plateaus (Figure 1) bordered by 100- to 350-m-high escarpments (Fenneman 1931; Walker 1978:10). On the plateaus, local relief often is only a few meters and is created by such wind erosion features as many shallow depressions (playas) and a few large dune fields (Evans and Meade 1945; Reeves 1966; Walker 1978). Although incised by the Cimarron, Canadian, and Pecos rivers, much of the Southern High Plains drains into either thousands of playas or the shallow (less than 15 m) headwaters of the North Canadian, Washita, Red, Brazos, and Colorado (Figure 1). Some stream courses and playas probably originated from salt dissolution in the underlying Permian bedrock (Gustavson and Finley 1985). Native vegetation is predominantly short grasses, bunch grasses, sage, yucca, and mesquite. Occasional cottonwoods and willows grow along streams, whereas juniper and scrub oak occur along canyon walls and the escarpments. Historically, bison was the most important game. The Southern High Plains are rich in knappable stone, which was highly favored by prehistoric people. Extensive aboriginal quarries for Alibates agatized dolomite occur along the Canadian River (Shaeffer 1958), and bedrock outcrops of cherts and jaspers are common elsewhere along southeast-draining canyons and eastern escarpments (Holliday and Welty 1981). Also, the Ogallala Formation, which caps much of the High Plains, contains Rocky Mountains outwash gravels with clasts of quartzite, chert, and jasper (Holliday and Welty 1981).

The study area's eastern border extends from the Arkansas River's "Great Bend" south to the eastern extent of the Edwards Plateau (Figure 1). Much of the northern half of this border is rolling plains (interrupted by the Wichita Mountains), but the southern half becomes more rugged where the Cretaceous limestone Edwards Plateau has eroded into east-dipping plateau remnants, mesas, deep valleys, and canyons (Fenneman 1931:54–59). This eastern border is the wettest part of the Southern Plains; lusher habitats occur as one moves south and east. In the northern half, mixed grasses flourish on rolling uplands, whereas cottonwood, elm, hackberry, and some walnut border southeast-flowing streams (Blair and Hubbell 1938:437–439). In the southern half, scrub oak, cedar, and chaparral occupy slopes, while mixed grasses grow luxuriously on the uplands (Fenneman 1931:54). As valleys widen and have deeper soils to the southeast, deciduous forest become more prevalent (Fenneman 1931:54). Bison, deer, turkey, and many small animals were important game to Native American residents of this eastern border. Highly knappable cherts and flints occur as residual and stream gravels throughout most of this eastern border (Banks 1984; Holliday and Welty 1981; Tunnell 1978).

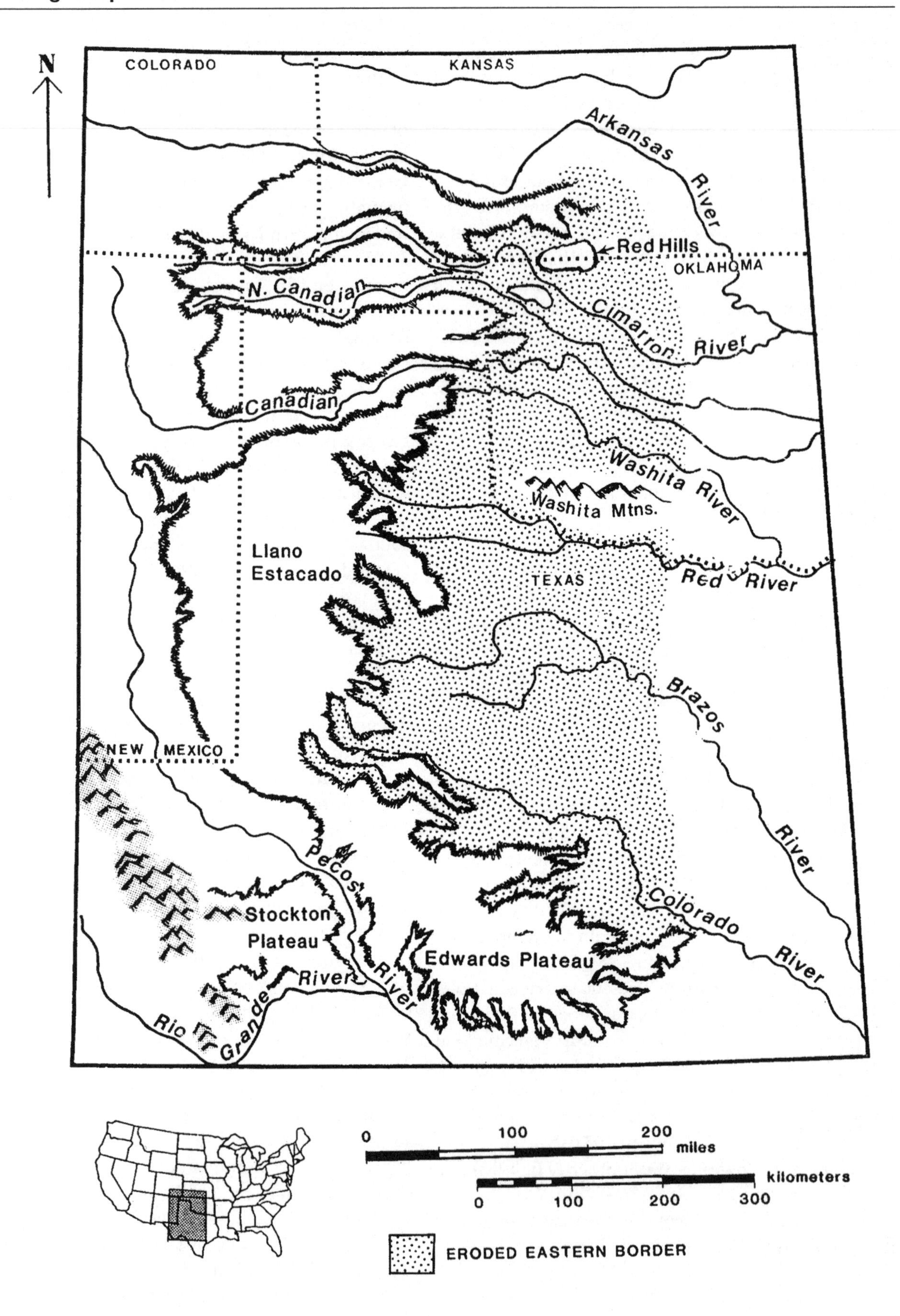

Figure 1. Location and geomorphic subdivisions of the Southern Plains study area.

The Southern Plains' western border varies from eroded Tertiary outwash occasionally broken by hogbacks (of Dakota sandstone and chert-bearing Niobrara limestone) in southern Colorado; to volcanic accumulations, mesas, and deeply cut plateaus in northern New Mexico; to the long, steeply sided trough of the Pecos valley in the south (Fenneman 1931:47–49). Between the Pecos and the Southern High Plains occur the valley bluffs, an east-sloping alluvium-mantled plain, and the Llano Estacado's escarpment (Fenneman 1931:47–49). Canyons become prevalent as the Pecos flows southeast and separates the Stockton and Edwards plateaus (Figure 1). This western border is the most desert-like part of the study area. Except after heavy rains, most streams are typically dry. Sparse cottonwoods and willows grow where seeps and underground water are not too saline. Bunch grass, sage, and mesquite are dominant in upland settings. Here, antelope and bison grazed when conditions were favorable. In more rugged settings, mule deer and turkey might be found. Outwash gravels are common and contain knappable cherts, jaspers, and quartzites; some bedrock outcrops of knappable stone may occur along the Southern High Plains western escarpment (Banks 1984:70–72; Jelinek 1967:16–17; Shelley 1984).

Without question, the Pleistocene Southern Plains looked different than they do today. Our knowledge of the lusher, cooler, and more moist settings and environments in which the earliest human inhabitants lived comes from the combined efforts of geologists, soils scientists, palynologists, and zoologists, most of whom were working in conjunction with archaeological projects.

Pleistocene Human Occupations of the Southern Plains

THE HUMAN OCCUPATION of the Pleistocene Southern Plains traditionally is perceived (Sellards 1952; Stephenson 1965; Wendel 1978:188–195; Wormington 1957) as a sequence of societies which mainly hunted large game and which are distinguished from one another by their principal prey and by stylistic changes in their bifacially flaked spear points. This sequence has Clovis as its earliest manifestation, followed by Folsom, Plainview or Agate Basin, and a series of other unfluted lanceolate projectiles. Given the increasing evidence for dramatic environmental change during the Pleistocene–Holocene transition (Holliday 1985a, 1985b, 1985c; Holliday et al. 1983; Johnson 1987a; Wendorf and Hester 1975), the changes in the cultural record seem too subtle. Bonnichsen et al. (1987:420) suggest that the proliferation of sophisticated projectile styles during this period represents different hunting–foraging societies responding to rapid environmental change and declining populations of large animals by intensifying their hunting of big game. In contrast, Bamforth (1988) believes the very modest material culture changes mask important shifts in the organizational complexity of these hunting societies. With these alternative explanatory models in mind, let us briefly review the Pleistocene record of human occupation.

Folsom Occupations and Adaptations

FOLSOM MATERIALS ARE well represented at 14 Southern Plains locations (Figure 2): Folsom, Blackwater Draw, Elida, Lubbock Lake, Lipscomb, Lake Theo, Adair-Steadman, Scharbauer, Shifting Sand, Horn Shelter, Bonfire Shelter, Beckner, Winters, and Cedar Creek (Cook 1927; Cotter 1938; Dibble and Lorrain 1968; Figgins 1927; Harrison and Killen 1978; Hester 1962; Hester et al. 1972; Hofman 1991; Hofman and Wyckoff 1987; Hofman et al. 1990; Howard 1935; Johnson 1987a; Redder 1985; Schultz 1943; Sellards 1952; Tunnell 1977; Warnica 1961; Wendorf et al. 1955). In addition, many Folsom points are reported as surface finds throughout the region (Broilo 1971; Hofman 1988; Polyak and Williams 1986). For this review, Folsom and Midland assemblages are viewed as one and the same. Folsom and the comparable but unfluted Midland points have overlapping distributions, similar flake tool assemblages, and often occur together in the same contexts (Hofman 1988; Hofman et al. 1990; Wendorf et al. 1955). Midland points probably are but one product of Folsom knappers who were at critical stages (needing to retool weapons but limited by a paucity of favored stone) in seasonal or annual cycles of movement (Hofman 1991).

At least 20 radiocarbon dates are reported for Folsom contexts at four Southern Plains sites: Folsom (11 dates: six on charcoal, five on bone), Blackwater Draw (three dates on charcoal), Bonfire Shelter (three on charcoal), and Lake Theo (two on bone) (Harrison and Killen 1978; Haynes et al. 1984, 1988; Holliday 1987). The less controversial charcoal dates cluster between 10,200 and 10,800 years ago. These 600 years

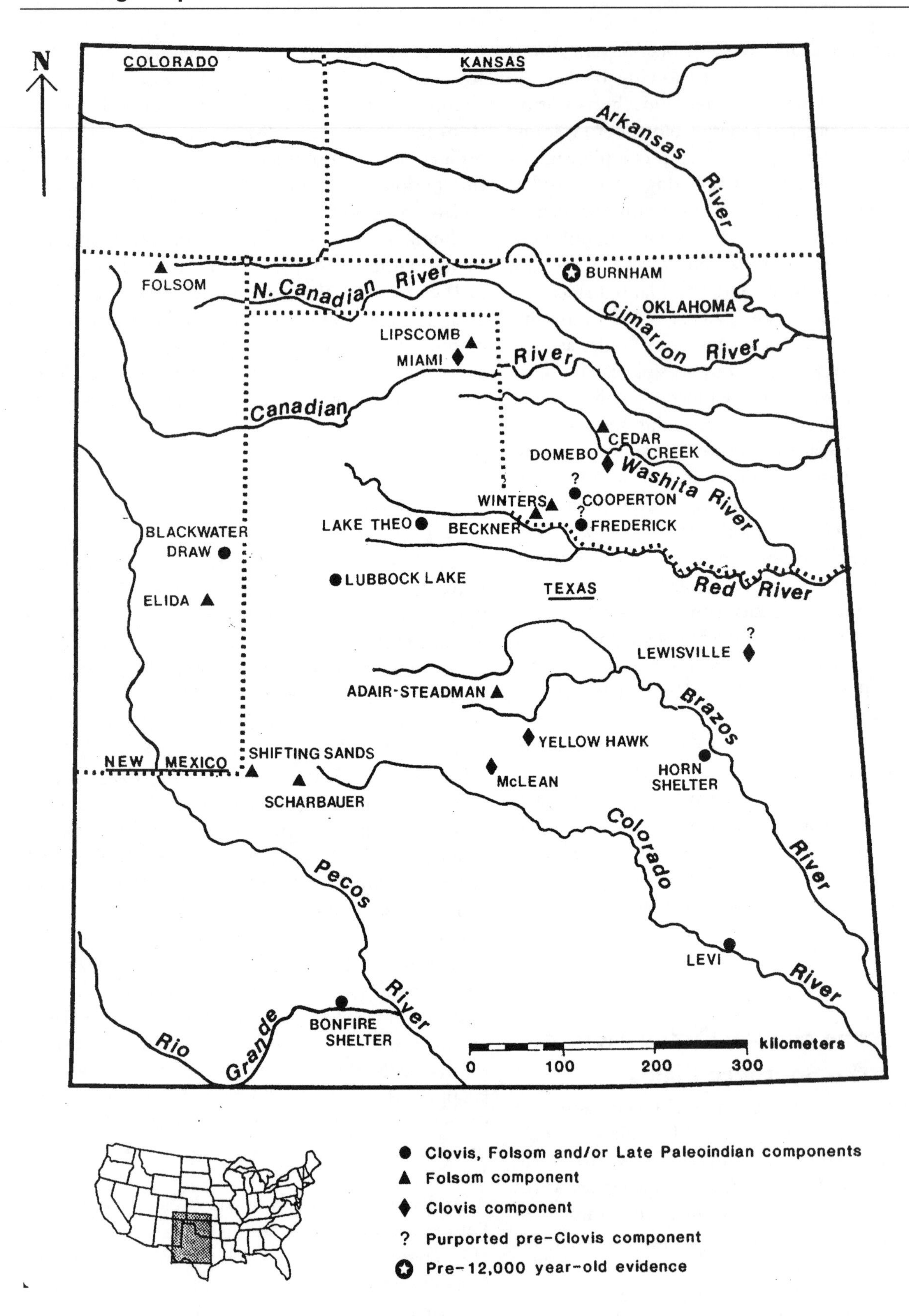

Figure 2. Locations of Paleoindian and potentially earlier sites discussed for the Southern Plains.

correspond with mild, somewhat moist conditions recognized from paleoenvironmental findings at Blackwater Draw and Lubbock Lake (Holliday et al. 1985; Johnson 1987c; Johnson and Holliday 1987a; Wendorf and Hester 1975). Winters apparently were mild but with some freezes, whereas summers were warmer than in Clovis times. At Blackwater Draw, springs stopped and then resumed flow, while at Yellowhouse Draw (Lubbock Lake) a shallow stream linked clear pools bordered with scattered hackberry trees. The former parkland setting around Yellowhouse Draw now was predominantly open grasslands (Johnson 1987c:92). Some 190 km to the south, however, Folsom materials were incorporated into dune deposits at the Scharbauer site (Wendorf and Hester 1975:267; Wendorf et al. 1955). These dunes attest to local aridity.

Two of the region's Folsom sites have yielded some of the few human remains known for Pleistocene North America. Portions of a long-headed skull and a few other fragmented bones of a female skeleton were recovered at the Scharbauer site and are thought (Wendorf et al. 1955) to be contemporaneous with the Folsom–Midland artifacts found there. Human teeth also are recently reported (Hofman et al. 1990) for the Shifting Sands site.

The region's reported Folsom sites comprise an array of activity situations. Folsom, Lipscomb, Bonfire Shelter, Blackwater Draw, and Lubbock Lake are bison kills, whereas Adair-Steadman, Elida, Scharbauer, Shifting Sands, Horn Shelter, Winters, and perhaps Beckner appear to be various kinds of encampments. Although not yet fully reported, Adair-Steadman may be a major (or often frequented) encampment where locally available, high-quality flint was collected and knapped into cores, preforms, and a variety of finished tools (Tunnell 1977). In contrast, sites such as Elida, Scharbauer, and Shifting Sands yielded high proportions of recycled hunting/butchering tools and very small unutilized flakes of Edwards chert (Hester 1962; Hofman et al. 1990; Warnica 1961; Wendorf et al. 1955). Their lack of initial knapping debris, their settings near small interdunal ponds, and their occasional traces of bison bones and hearths support the conclusion that these sites were temporary camps, perhaps near bison kills. Winters and Beckner may be similar situations, but sparse clues preclude much interpretation (Hofman and Wyckoff 1987). That Folsom people frequented natural overhangs is evidenced by the Strata 5A findings at the Horn Shelter (Redder 1985).

Unquestionably, Folsom people were proficient bison hunters. They killed 23 *Bison antiquus* at Folsom, more than 50 at Lipscomb, from 30 to 40 in six different episodes at Blackwater Draw, and some of the 120 animals represented in Bone Bed 2 at Bonfire Shelter (Dibble and Lorrain 1968:84; Hester et al. 1972:170; Hofman et al. 1988; Sellards 1952:49). At Lubbock Lake, at least three bison were killed and processed in that location's best-studied Folsom component (Johnson 1987b:124–126). Several strategies were employed when hunting bison. Folsom peoples drove animals over a cliff at Bonfire Shelter and probably were trapping herds at arroyo heads at Folsom, Lake Theo, and Lipscomb. At Blackwater Draw and Lubbock Lake, two or three animals were being killed at a time when they were at marshy settings along shallow ponds. The Lubbock Lake carcasses were processed incompletely with no special effort spent to derive marrow from appropriate elements or to fully use all bones suitable for tool manufacture (Johnson 1987b:124). The limited seasonality data from the Lubbock Lake site indicates the bison were killed in early spring or fall (Johnson 1987b:152). Limited butchering also seems evident at the Lipscomb bison kill, but that may be due to the event occurring when the fat, bone marrow, and hides were not in prime condition (Hofman et al. 1988). The large herd at Lipscomb probably was killed in late summer or early fall (Hofman et al. 1988). No season could be firmly established for the Bonfire Shelter bison bone accumulation; however, these remains were butchered thoroughly by cutting animals into large segments that were then sorted and processed further, resulting in concentrations of similar elements (Dibble and Lorrain 1968:80–108).

Differences in size and assemblage content are considered evidence that non-bison kill sites are either multiple-activity or limited-activity camps (Bamforth 1988). The latter tend to be near temporary sources of water, whereas the larger, multiple-activity camps are near permanent water (Bamforth 1988:168–182). Multiple-activity camps and large bison kills may have resulted from Folsom bands periodically joining forces for communal hunts. Such social aggregation appears more evident during Folsom times than during either the earlier Clovis or the succeeding late Paleoindian occupations (Bamforth 1988).

Clues to Folsom band movements would seem obtainable from studies of Folsom and Midland points from western Oklahoma (Hofman 1991). Despite the nearby availability of such knappable materials as

Tecovas jasper and Alibates agatized dolomite, more than 70 percent of the Oklahoma Folsom–Midland points are of West Texas Edwards chert; these specimens display a notable range of size, shape, and reuse (Hofman 1988). Using these findings in a model that couples projectile refurbishing with numbers of bison kill/butchering events and the seasons of these events, Hofman (1991) offers some initial perspectives on the direction, frequency, and magnitude of Folsom movements. Folsom hunters in western Oklahoma clearly were coming from the south or southwest.

Much is written about the manufacture of fluted Folsom points (e.g., Gryba 1988; Sollberger 1985; Tunnell 1977), but little is published on the technologies or strategies behind the production and use of the various other stone tools known from Southern Plains Folsom assemblages. Large bifacial cores are believed integral to the manufacture of most Folsom chipped stone tools (Hofman 1988; Stanford and Broilo 1981). These include diverse kinds of knives and scrapers made from flakes, as well as delicate multi-spurred gravers, possible wedges, and unshaped but utilized flakes (Hester 1962; Hester et al. 1972; Johnson and Holliday 1987b:104–107). Besides butchering tools made expediently from bison bone, eyed needles, disk ornaments, flakers, and possible fleshers were made from bone (Blaine and Wendorf 1972; Hester et al. 1972).

Although a hallmark of Paleoindian cultures, Folsom occupations on the Southern Plains still raise numerous questions. The full range of their hunting–foraging practices is unknown. Much remains to be learned about the pattern and seasonality of band movements and about their manufacture and use of tools other than projectiles. Perhaps most intriguing are questions of Folsom origins and their descendants. Are the occasional Folsom points that are found with Plainview points at Bonfire Shelter and Lake Theo hints of cultural ties rather than separate occupations? And where on the Southern Plains is there evidence for a culture transitional between Folsom and the earlier Clovis culture?

Clovis Occupations on the Southern Plains

CLOVIS COMPONENTS ARE reported for eight Southern Plains sites (Figure 2): Miami, McLean, Blackwater Draw, Lubbock Lake, Domebo, Yellow Hawk, Levi, and Lewisville (Alexander 1963, 1978, 1982; Bryan and Ray 1938; Crook and Harris 1957, 1962; Hester et al. 1972; Johnson 1987a; Leonhardy 1966; Mallouf 1989; Sellards 1938, 1952:17–46; Stanford 1983). In addition, numerous Clovis point surface finds are documented (Meltzer 1987) from the Texas portion of the study area.

Radiocarbon dates are reported for Clovis contexts at the Domebo site (29 dates: two on wood, one on lignite, one on soil, three on bone, and 22 accelerator dates on bone protein), Blackwater Draw (three on plant materials), Lubbock Lake (two on wood), Levi (one on shell and one on hackberry seeds), and Lewisville (three on lignite) (Alexander 1963, 1978; Crook and Harris 1962; Haynes et al. 1984:Table 2; Johnson and Holliday 1987c:Table 1.2; Leonhardy 1966:24–25; Stafford et al. 1987). The period of Clovis occupation of 11,000 to 11,500 yr B.P. is indicated by most results obtained from wood and plant material or reliable bone proteins (Haynes 1982:Figure 1, 1987:Figure 1; Stafford et al. 1987). These 500 years coincide with a period of moist, cool summers and mild, apparently frost-free winters ascertained from faunal, botanical, and sedimentological findings at the Lubbock Lake, Blackwater Draw, and Domebo sites (Hester et al. 1972; Johnson 1987a; Leonhardy 1966; Wendorf and Hester 1975). This equitable climate supported verdant grasslands in upland settings and parkland to closed galleria forests along streams over the Southern Plains.

Perhaps most striking in these lush late-Pleistocene settings is the menagerie of wildlife. Mammoths, camels, horses, bison, peccaries, llamas, bears, and giant armadillos are but a few of the animals identified in Clovis-age contexts at Lubbock Lake and Blackwater Draw. Given this array of game, did Clovis people really focus their hunting on mammoths? At the Miami, Domebo, Lubbock Lake, Blackwater Draw, and the McLean sites, mammoths were the principal large animals hunted by Clovis people. But a Clovis bison kill was uncovered at Blackwater Draw where seven *Bison antiquus* apparently were ambushed while they were at a pond (Hester et al. 1972:46–47, 178). At Lubbock Lake, bones of horse, bison, bear, armadillo, and turtle may be evidence of other Clovis prey (Johnson 1987b:121–123). Eighteen box turtle shells stacked near a hearth probably attest to an easily collected, favored food (Johnson 1987b). The Clovis hearth (#1) at Lewisville also yielded terrapin remains, along with the burned bones of deer, horse, bird, and wolf, burned mussel shell, and burned hackberry seeds (Crook and Harris 1957:24–28). At the Levi shelter, the Clovis zone (II) yielded bones of bison, and juvenile mammoths are represented, whereas Blackwater Draw has occurrences of one, two, and four animals in different kills (Hester et al. 1972:170; Johnson 1987b:121). Single mammoths are reported at the Domebo, Miami, and McLean sites (Bryan and Ray 1938; Leonhardy 1966; Sellards 1938). The Clovis hunting strategy at most locations was to attack the animals while they were at ponds, sloughs, or marshes. Perhaps mobility was slowed by mud and water. At Domebo, the enclosing walls of an arroyo also may have hindered the animal (Leonhardy 1966). Clovis points found *in situ* there were near articulated and disarticulated vertebrae. If they actually had been in the bones, the trajectories of these points might have indicated whether some hunters were on the arroyo bank above the victim. Mammoths were butchered where they fell by cutting the meat from the bones, taking it elsewhere, and leaving a partially disarticulated pile of bones (Hester et al. 1972:178). Evidence has yet to be found that Southern Plains Clovis hunters used mammoth bones to cache meat in wintertime (Frison 1982). At Lubbock Lake, some bones were smashed to obtain marrow or to make tools from thick-walled segments (Johnson 1987b:123).

Game processing and camping at Lubbock Lake occurred on fluvial bars along the stream bed (Johnson 1987b:121–123). At Blackwater Draw, open encampments were west and northwest (not the prevailing wind directions) of ponds where game was taken (Hester et al. 1972:178), but little was learned here about camp layout because sheetwash of thin soils eroded and mixed the setting. At Lewisville, apparent hearths are scattered and at different depths, suggesting repeated use of the location (Crook and Harris 1957:Figure 3). No habitation features or patterned distributions of tools and debris were observed for the Levi Clovis component (Alexander 1963). At the Yellow Hawk site, a workshop of a single Clovis knapper seems uniquely preserved; large Edwards chert flakes attest to debris discarded on the spot and not near other habitation features (Mallouf 1989).

Clovis residents of the Southern Plains most likely lived and moved in patterned ways. Bamforth (1988:166–183) believes the available evidence supports the conclusions that Clovis society was not complexly organized and that multiple-activity, large encampments are lacking. While most details to patterned mobility remain to be ascertained, the prevalence of central Texas chert at the Domebo mammoth kill (Leonhardy 1966) is a clue to movement or trade from the south. In contrast, Clovis materials at Blackwater Draw are largely Alibates agatized dolomite, but Edwards chert and Tecovas jasper are well represented. Given the different sources of these raw materials, a refurbishing model such as Hofman (1988) proposes for Folsom could be used to study lithic artifacts from diverse kinds of Clovis sites and delineate directions of movement. These findings in combination with any data on the seasonality of sites occupied should further our understanding of Clovis land use on the Southern Plains.

Much remains to be learned about the manufacture, use, and formal variation of Southern Plains Clovis tool kits. The Yellow Hawk site (Mallouf 1989) offers a first glimpse of preliminary knapping, core preparation, and discard. As with Folsom, large biface cores seem the principal initial product. Caches of unfinished or finished Clovis bifaces are not yet reported for the region, but a southwestern Oklahoma cache of large blade flakes of Edwards chert may be of Clovis origin (Hammett 1970). The best representative assemblage is described for Blackwater Draw (Hester et al. 1972:92–118) and includes small and large Clovis points, large blade scrapers and knives, end and side scrapers made from other flake forms, flake knives, burins, occasional gravers, choppers, grinding stones, bone foreshafts, bone expediency tools, and shell scrapers.

As manifest on the Southern Plains, the Clovis culture represents the material remains of people who confidently frequented the region's varied settings and were very knowledgeable of its mineral and animal resources. Though perhaps not numerous, these people are well represented by artifacts distributed throughout the region. If Clovis people were the Southern Plains' first human inhabitants, they needed little time to familiarize themselves with the region and to become a viable component in the region's late Pleistocene ecological system.

Pre-Clovis Occupations: Was Anybody Out There?

SINCE THE ORIGINAL Folsom discovery, a few Southern Plains locations have been cited sporadically as indicating the presence of people long before Clovis times. Once their stratigraphy, artifacts, and contextual integrity were scrutinized by trained scholars, most of these locations were discounted and dismissed. Yet some continue to recur in thinking about the antiquity of people in the New World. For this reason, the most noted cases are reviewed briefly below.

Lewisville, Texas

FOR NEARLY 30 YEARS, controversy raged and simmered regarding human artifacts, habitation features, Pleistocene fauna, and radiocarbon dates for the Lewisville site in north-central Texas (Figure 2). Here, 21 burned areas interpreted as hearths were found eroding from a second terrace of the Trinity River (Crook and Harris 1957, 1958). In and near Hearth #1 occurred a Clovis point, a flake scraper, and three flakes, whereas a cobble hammerstone and a cobble chopper were near other hearths and Pleistocene animals. These latter are represented by bones (often burned) of horse, bison, camel, land tortoise, terrapin, wolf, white-tailed deer, cottontail rabbit, and swamp rabbit. The kinds of animals seemed congruent with the terrace's geologic age and the presence of Clovis people, but everyone was astounded when charcoal samples from hearths were radiocarbon dated at more than 36,000 yr B.P. (Crook and Harris 1957, 1962).

Since these dates are three times older than the accepted age for Clovis, the site was argued to be badly disturbed, the recovered Clovis point a recent plant, and/or the "hearths" to be naturally burned Pleistocene trees or woodrat nests. These alternatives could not be resolved because the site was flooded by a reservoir.

In 1980, drought caused the lake level to lower, thus exposing more hearth-like features and affording a chance to reinvestigate. Limited excavations revealed that the burned areas are of human origin and probably of Clovis affiliation (Stanford 1983:70). An important discovery was that carbonized material from hearths was often truly ancient lignite. So the dates were accurate but obviously not relevant to people burning that material some 11,000 years ago (Stanford 1983).

Cooperton Mammoth Site, Oklahoma

IN 1961, WHILE THE Lewisville finds and dates were drawing attention, erosion exposed a *Mammuthus columbi* skull in southwest Oklahoma's Wichita Mountains. Called the Cooperton site (Figure 2), the location was investigated by archaeologists from the Museum of the Great Plains. They uncovered the disarticulated, partially piled bones of a single immature male mammoth buried in fluvial sands slightly more than a meter below the surface (Anderson 1975). Some bones displayed green fracture breaks and crushing, and a large granite cobble was found lying on smashed bones. These findings, plus the stacked appearance of some bones and the nearby occurrence of some cobbles possibly used as hammerstones, led to the conclusion the bones had been broken and arranged by humans (Anderson 1975:168–172). Samples of bone and teeth were submitted for radiocarbon dating; the three results range from 17,500 to 20,400 yr B.P. (Anderson 1975:156).

The Cooperton find is intriguing. Assuming the dated bones and tooth haven't undergone diagenesis, thus chemically affecting their reliability for dating (i.e., Stafford et al. 1987), the dates are substantially older than Clovis. While no chipped stone flakes or tools were found among the bones, the presence of fist-sized and larger cobbles and their close association with broken bones in a sandy stratum attests to processes other than the stream flow which deposited the stratum. If the dates do indicate the elephant's age, do they also indicate when people actually worked the bone? Even if the bone breakage was by humans rather than natural processes, perhaps the skeleton was exposed 9,000 to 10,000 years later and usable bone was then quarried by some Paleoindian hunter.

Levi Shelter, Texas

THE 1959–1960 EXCAVATIONS at this west-central Texas site (Figure 2) recovered a few artifacts from a stratum below those containing the already noted Plainview and Clovis components. Zone I (1–2 m below the surface) was briefly tested and yielded a chopper (or biface core), three tools made from percussion flakes, and a few bones of dire wolf, tapir, bison, deer, and several small mammals (Alexander 1963). Tested further in 1974 and 1977, Levi Zone I is a partially eroded, complex series of "carbonate consolidated cultural deposits capped in places by a vertical, laminated travertine flow" (Alexander 1982:144).

Hackberry seeds and collagen from bones in Zone I were radiocarbon dated respectively at around 12,800 and 10,800 yr B.P. (Alexander 1982). So far, workers have recovered two pointed bone tools, 13 chipped stone tools, and 81 flakes. The lithic items include a couple of biface cores or choppers and utilized flakes.

Depending on confirmation of its pre-12,000 yr B.P. age, Levi Zone I potentially comprises the best evidence we have for humans residing on the Southern Plains before Clovis. The significance attributable to this site awaits further dating and full publication of the internal stratigraphy of Zone I, the locations of its dated samples, and the distribution of thoroughly described artifacts and refuse.

Bonfire Shelter, Texas

THE 1963 AND 1964 excavations at this oldest and southernmost (Figure 2) bison jump included brief testing of a bone bed (#1) below the 10,200-year-old one where Folsom and Plainview points occurred (Dibble and Lorrain 1968). This lowest bed yielded remains of mammoth, horse, and camel, but no artifacts were found. Between 1982 and 1984, renewed testing was undertaken on Bone Bed #1 to recover more faunal remains, to see whether cultural materials were associated, and to recover material suitable for radiocarbon dating (Bement 1986). This recent work confirmed and refined the stratigraphy of Bone Bed #1; it actually consists of seven different bone deposits, one of which yielded charcoal flecks dated at 12,460 ± 490 yr B.P. (AA-344; Bement 1986:6–9). The animals identified (Bement 1986:11–18) for these deposits include fox, mammoth, bison (*B. antiquus*), horse (*Equus francisci*), camel (*Camelops hesternus*), and an extinct small antelope (*Capromeryx* sp.). No chipped stone tools or flakes were recovered, but broken bones clustered around large limestone spalls, several worn broken bones suggestive of expediency tools, and battering and cutting marks on some bones are cited (Bement 1986:61–64) as circumstantial evidence that these pre-Folsom bone deposits resulted at least partially from human activities.

The case for people being responsible for some of the Bone Bed #1 deposits leaves one with nagging doubt. The kinds of animals and the single radiocarbon date seem entirely reasonable for these deposits. Clearly, as Bement (1986:62) recognizes, carnivores actively worked bones in these deposits, but the lack of stone tools or resharpening flakes combined with the few marks attributable to human butchering don't seem to total enough evidence to interpret human processes as responsible. If the potentially contemporaneous Levi Zone I deposits are demonstrating anything, they are showing us that people were making, using, and discarding chipped stone materials by 12,500 years ago.

The Burnham Site, Oklahoma: A Preliminary Report

ABOUT 380 KM DOWN the Cimarron watershed from the Folsom site, the accidental uncovering of Pleistocene sediments has led to a puzzling find of artifacts seemingly associated with a long-extinct form of large-horned bison. Named after the landowner, the Burnham site was tested briefly in October 1986 and September 1988. Except for partial sorting of material recovered during waterscreening, preliminary examination of recovered bones and artifacts, and initial dating of deposits, detailed study of this site and its contents has yet to begin. Given the questions that have arisen already, much more fieldwork must be done.

The Burnham site is 2 km south of the Red Hills (Figure 1), eroded High Plains remnants consisting of east-trending ridges and mesas with south-facing escarpments capped with Tertiary outwash (the Ogallala Formation) from the Rocky Mountains (Fay 1965; Fenneman 1931:28–30). Six kms south of the site is a major salt deposit (the Big Salt Plain) along the Cimarron River. Permian sandstones and shales underlie the Red Hills and form an eroded, south-sloping surface on which Pleistocene lakes and streams have left deposits (Miller 1975; Myers 1959; Stephens 1960; Taylor and Hibbard 1955). The Burnham site consists of three Pleistocene fluvial deposits within 75 m of each other, uncovered during the 1986 construction of a farm pond.

Large bones observed in these sediments prompted a call to the Oklahoma Archeological Survey, and our initial visit resulted in the discovery of a partially damaged, large-horned bison skull. In October 1986, six days were spent recovering this skull and testing the immediately adjacent Pleistocene sediments for their potential to yield information on their age, origin, environments, and nearby settings. During subsequent sorting of waterscreened debris, chert flakes of undoubted human origin were found, particularly from sediments near the bison skull. In September 1988, 14 days were spent further testing the deposits to see if more bison bones were present, to learn if more flakes or tools were associated, and to document better the stratigraphy and context of this find.

All excavations were in meter squares of two grids (one of each side of the pond) which are mapped relative to a datum established on the undisturbed knoll east-southeast of the pond (Figure 3). All excavations were done in arbitrary 10-cm levels, the depths of which were recorded relative to the datum elevation. All excavated fill was washed through 2-mm mesh hardware cloth, and recovered debris was bagged according to grid, square, level, depth of level, date, and names of excavators. Every effort was made to uncover bones, flakes, and tools *in situ* so they could be piece-plotted and their depths (relative to datum) recorded. Stratigraphic profiles were recorded along north–south and east–west walls between squares.

The Western Exposures

TWO FLUVIAL DEPOSITS occur on the pond's west side. The northernmost deposit, called the Northwest Exposure, is on an east-projecting point (see NW Grid in Figure 3) where a northwest–southeast oriented remnant of an aggraded channel is completely uncovered. The channel fill is a gray loamy fine sand that is at least 80 cm in maximum thickness and contains thousands of aquatic snails and occasional bones. These latter include elements from as yet unspeciated turtle, bison, horse, and proboscidean (an exfoliated tusk segment initially was visible here). No gravel was exposed in this deposit.

The Northwest Exposure was tested by a 1-by-6-m trench (NW Grid in Figure 3) in September 1988. Nearly 2 cubic meters of channel fill were excavated and waterscreened. Only the southernmost three squares were taken to the channel's bottom: a relatively smooth contact with an underlying red, soft facies of the Marlow (Permian) sandstone. This bottom is at elevation 96.5 (relative to datum). A large, triangular boulder of waterworn dolomite caprock (from the Red Hills escarpment) was found resting on the channel bottom, and pieces of thick-walled bone and occasional turtle shell were found around it. Other bone and turtle shell fragments were recovered from levels of other squares. All bone is less than 15 cm in maximum dimension and displays faces and edges rounded and smoothed by water-borne sand. Several charcoal fragments were mapped and recovered, but none have been radiocarbon dated. No chipped stone tools or flakes were observed in the field, and the waterscreened debris has not been sorted.

The second fluvial deposit on the pond's west side is designated the Southwest Exposure and is 20 m south of the NW Grid. This second deposit is at least

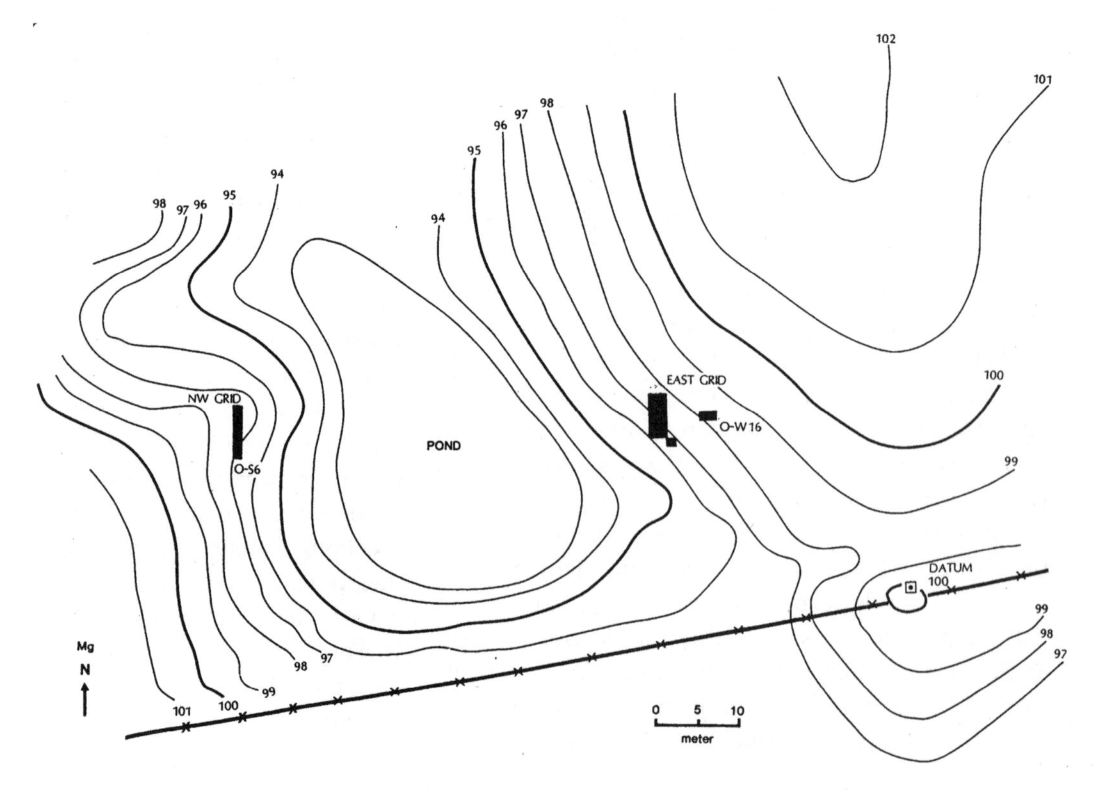

Figure 3. Contour and excavated grid map for the Burnham site (34Wo-73), Woods County, Oklahoma.

13 m in cross-section (north–south), is 40 to 60 cm thick, and has its base at elevation 97.4 (relative to datum). Five m of soil potentially overlie this exposure. The deposit consists of a gray-brown loamy fine sand that contains few aquatic snails and rare bison bones. These are either complete or only slightly broken and display little stream-induced damage or abrasion. Near its southern edge this deposit has a thin lens of pebbles and cobbles. No artifacts have been observed eroding from any of this deposit. Two charcoal fragments were collected within 10 cm of its bottom, but none have been radiocarbon dated.

With the limited data at hand, the origins and the contemporaneity of these two deposits are unknown. Given their different appearances and channel elevations, they may well be of different ages. Accelerator dating of the charcoal fragments from each undoubtedly would clarify their temporal relationships. Extensive backhoe trenching and stratigraphic profile study would help determine their origins.

The Eastern Exposure

MOST ATTENTION HAS centered on the pond's east side. Here, from 1 to 2.5 m of soil were removed and a once-vertical bank made into a 60-degree slope, exposing a gray loamy sand channel fill that contrasts starkly with the red Permian sandstone (Figure 4). This alluvial deposit is at least 10 m wide and 2 m thick. Its base is deeper than elevation 95.8 (relative to datum), but excavations have not clearly penetrated the deposit's floor or fully exposed a cross-section. A recently eroded gully (far right of Figure 4) shows the gray alluvium extends at least 5 m east of the graded slope. At elevation 98.8 (relative to datum), a 10- to 15-cm-thick layer of caliche is visible on the north side (Figure 4), and it appears to extend over the northern third of the aggraded deposit. One very friable bison bone was observed eroding from this caliche layer. Above the caliche the profile is unclear, but it seems to be 30 to 40 cm of gray fine sandy sediment that contains few aquatic snail shells. What was above this sediment is uncertain. The eroded graded surface now is cluttered with large angular blocks of carbonate. Gravel has not been observed eroding from the alluvium.

The alluvial deposit (designated the East Exposure) was striking not only for its color, but also because it contained thousands of gastropod shells and some bones. One of these latter was the skull of a large-horned bison found partially exposed (point b in Figure 4) at elevation 96.49 near the apparent base of the alluvium.

Recovering the skull entailed establishing the East Grid and excavating four squares (S1-W22, S2-W22, S1-W23, and S2-W23 in Figure 5) around the skull. This work revealed the bulldozer had mixed only 10

Figure 4. Looking east, the Burnham site's Eastern Exposure of Pleistocene alluvial deposits in Permian sandstone. Point a marks the massive caliche layer that appears to overlie the alluvial deposit. Point b is the location of the Bison alleni skull. Photo taken August 1986.

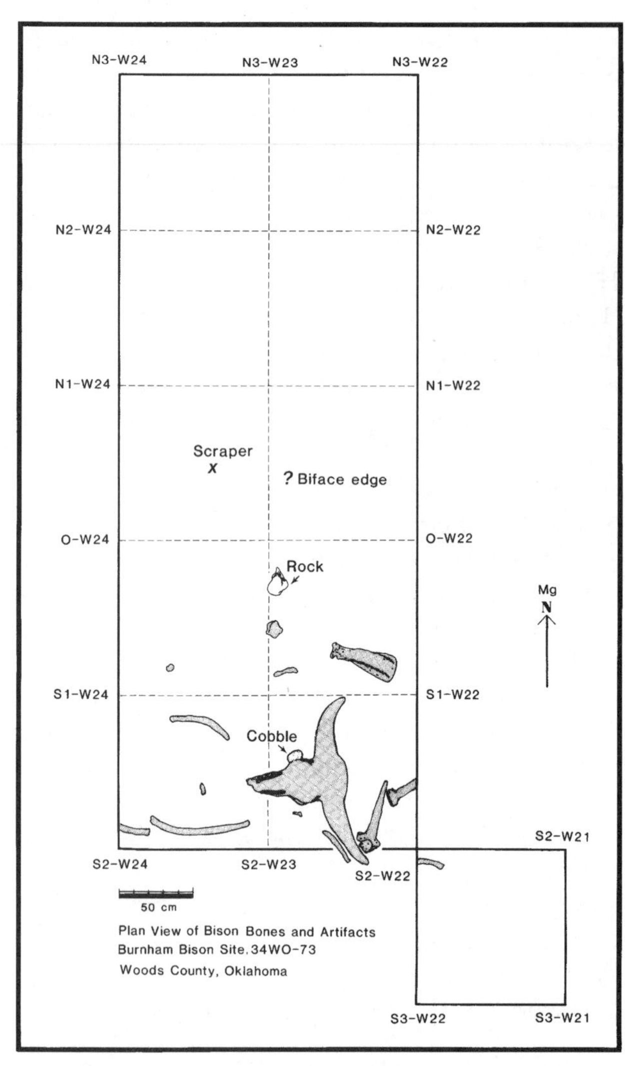

Figure 5. Plan view of Bison alleni remains and nearby artifacts in the East Grid of the Burnham site.

to 15 cm of the uppermost sediments in a few places, but its blade had sheared away part of the skull's lower right side. The skull was upside down in a gray loamy fine sand, but its left horn core projected down into an underlying red loamy sand that seems coarser than the overlying gray sediment. While uncovering the skull, other bison bones were found in both the gray and red sediments. A most surprising find was a large subangular cobble of local (Day Creek) chert 30 cm below the skull in the red loamy sand (Figures 5 and 6). As previously noted, gravel is noticeably absent in this alluvial deposit. Except for the southern 30 cm of square S1-W22, which was dug 15 cm deeper to extract the left horn core and a nearby scapula, the floors of the four squares were taken to elevation 96.56 (relative to datum), a depth near the boundary between the gray and red loamy sandy strata.

In the lab, sorting of residue waterscreened from sediments removed directly around the skull and from levels 6 and 7 (elevation 96.76 to 96.56) resulted in the discovery of 16 small, usually broken but not waterworn flakes of chert. Examination of the large cobble found under the skull revealed two flakes struck from one face.

These hints of the presence of humans stimulated further testing of the East Exposure during September of 1988. At this time, the four previously dug squares were excavated to elevation 96.1, and six new squares were established to the north and one to the south (Figures 3 and 5). These newly added seven squares were excavated to elevation 96.0 (0-W23), 96.1 (0-W22, N1-W22, N1-W23), 96.2 (S3-W21), and 96.6 (N2-W22 and N2-W23). In addition, squares 0-W16 and 0-W17 (Figure 3) were excavated to 97.9 (2.1 m below datum) to sample the uppermost channel fill and try to recover charcoal or sufficient snail shells for radiocarbon dating. All totaled, not quite 10 cubic meters of alluvium have been dug from the 13 squares worked in the East Grid.

East Exposure Stratigraphy and Dating

Perspectives and understanding of the East Exposure stratigraphy are very limited, as only an area 2 m wide (east–west) by 6 m long (north–south) has been excavated. Unfortunately, this trench isn't deep or long enough to show clearly the deposit's boundaries with the Permian sandstone. Until these boundaries are known and until a longitudinal profile eastward has been obtained, little can be said about the stratigraphic sequence, the origins of the strata, or the history of the formation of the deposit.

The exposed profiles create a first impression that there are but two strata: a gray loamy fine sand underlain by a red loamy sand. However, color and textural differences indicate the profile is more complex (Figure 7). The gray loamy sand actually has at least five expressions (Figure 7) based on subtle textural changes and the prevalence of variegated swirls of red, yellow, or green. Numerous gastropod shells occur in the gray loamy sand units, and preliminary analysis of these shells indicates 98 percent are species common to slow, sluggish moving water. A notable occurrence within the gray loamy sand is lumpy carbonate concretions, sometimes measuring up to 5 cm in maximum dimension. One series forms a discontinuous layer at roughly elevation 97.06; this series occurred

Figure 6. Bison alleni *skull with frontal in gray loamy sands while horn core extends into red loamy sands. The large angular flint cobble is in the red sediments under the skull. November 1, 1986, photo with view to the south-southeast.*

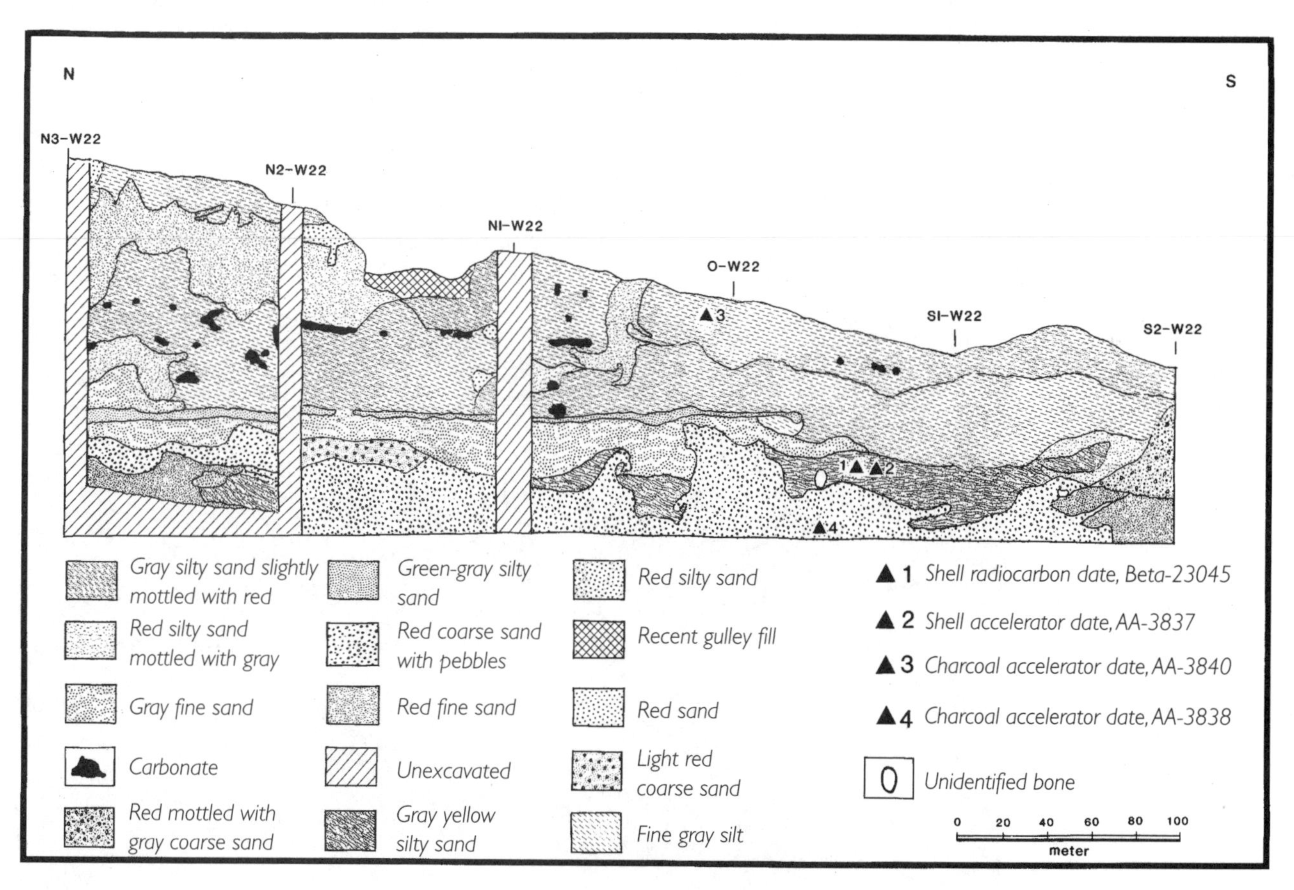

Figure 7. North-south profile along West 22 line of Burnham site's East Grid.

in situ above (3–4 cm) the bison skull. A charcoal fragment (at elevation 97.06) recovered near these carbonates in square 0-W22 (Figure 7) was accelerator-dated at 40,900 ± 1500 yr B.P. (AA-3840). Two samples of snail shells from the lowest expression of this gray loamy sand (between elevation 96.76 and 96.56 in square S1-W22; Figure 7) also were dated: 31,150 ± 700 yr B.P. (Beta-23045) and 35,890 ± 850 yr B.P.(AA-3837). The bison skull was in this lowest gray loamy sand.

An abrupt irregular boundary separates the gray loamy sand units and the underlying red loamy sand (Figures 7 and 8). This lowest stratum has far fewer, and usually broken, gastropod shells than the gray sediments, but bison bones definitely were present within the uppermost 15 cm. Occasional pea-sized pebbles were recovered from the red loamy sand, and one angular limestone cobble came from the northwest part of square S2-W22 (Figure 5). Several charcoal fragments were found in this stratum, and one from elevation 96.26 in square S1-W22 (Figure 7) yielded an accelerator date of 26,820 ± 350 yr B.P. (AA-3838).

The radiocarbon dates are in reverse order of their vertical occurrences in the deposit. Thus, the deposit can best be interpreted as being at least 26,000 years old. Because of its red color and sandy texture, its occasional small pebbles and rare cobbles, and its few (and usually broken) snail shells, the basal red loamy sand might be alluvium eroded from the soft Permian sandstone and deposited under different conditions than the overlying gray loamy sands. However, there is a very dramatic boundary (Figures 7 and 8) between these two strata. The sometimes flaring, sometimes undercut boundary attests to some kind of turbation that occurred after both strata were present. The vertical movement of sediments could result from the action of springs or perhaps even the churning of sediments by animals. The highly variegated colors and the presence of carbonate concretions might be clues to fluctuating ground water. Clearly, much is yet to be learned about the depositional environments responsible for the observable profiles.

East Exposure Fauna

EXCEPT FOR THE BISON skull, no formal analyses have been undertaken on any bones recovered from the East Exposure. Most bison bones are still in plaster jackets awaiting careful cleaning and examination for butchering marks or other clues to taphonomic processes.

A badly broken and weathered bison tooth, a few turtle shell fragments, and many gastropod shells were recovered from the gray loamy sand above the lumpy carbonates at elevation 97.06. Bones of the bison were clustered in the southernmost five squares (Figure 5) between elevations 96.2 and 96.0. Elsewhere at this

Figure 8. Dramatic boundary between gray loamy sands (top) and red loamy sands (bottom) along north wall of squares 0-W22 and 0-W23 of Burnham East Grid. Photo taken September 29, 1988.

depth were recovered an antler fragment, several pieces of deer-sized bones, turtle shell fragments, and occasional bones of small animals. As previously noted, gastropod shells are abundant in the gray loamy sands, much less so in the red loamy sand. Recently, horse (*Equus* sp.) bones have begun eroding from the gray loamy sands at least 1.5 m above the bison skull.

The bison is represented (Figure 5) by a nearly complete skull, a right mandible (under the skull), a right scapula (square S1-W22), a vertebra segment (S1-W22), a carpal bone (S1-W23), two thoracic vertebrae (S2-W22), and seven segments of ribs (S2-W23, S2-W22, and S3-W21). An unidentified bone of this animal is plotted in the square S1-W22 profile (Figure 7) and is evidence more elements lie to the east of what has been exposed. This bone, the skull, the mandible, the vertebra fragment, and three rib sections were in the gray loamy sand, whereas all other recovered elements (and the left horn core) were in the red loamy sand. In contrast to other bones found in the East Grid and the Northwest Grid, the bison bones show little smoothing or abrasion from stream flow, and they are not weathered, suggesting they were not exposed long before burial. The ribs and thoracic vertebra have angular breaks.

Based on horn-core dimensions (diameter, length, and curvature) and skull dimensions and attributes (narrow frontal and projecting orbital), the Burnham bison skull is most comparable to such extinct forms as *Bison alleni* and *Bison cheneyi*. Represented by a few scattered finds across the western United States, these forms are poorly known in terms of their ages and positions in bison evolution (Skinner and Kaisen 1947:183–186, 197–199). One would expect them to be transitional between *Bison latifrons* and *B. antiquus*, the species hunted by Clovis and Folsom Paleoindians.

Eastern Exposure Artifacts

Twenty-five chipped stone artifacts have been recorded thus far for the Eastern Exposure. None are believed flaked by natural processes. Gravel is virtually nonexistent in the sediments, and the artifacts display flake scars, bulbs of force, platforms, and terminations that are unmodified by water-induced abrasion or polish. Moreover, most of the artifacts are of cherts or flint that are lithologically different from the few small pebbles found in the sediments. Several artifacts are of material exotic to the Cimarron watershed.

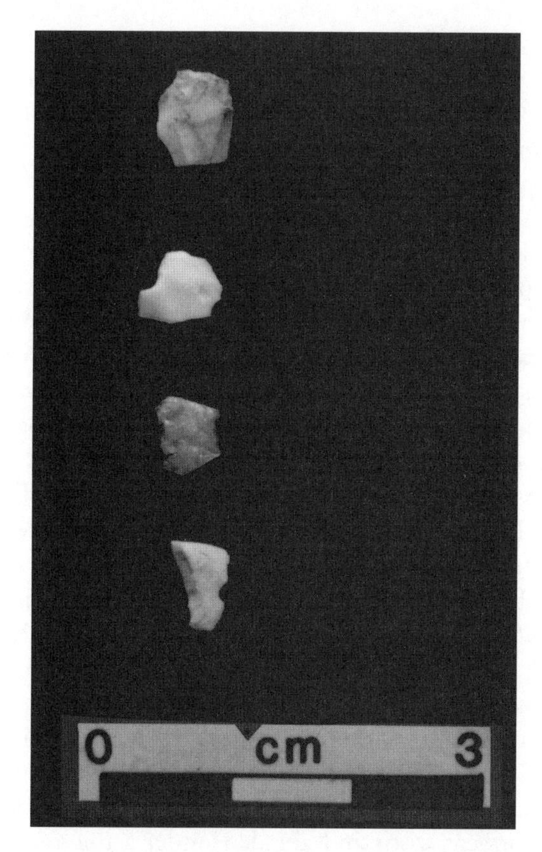

Figure 9. Four microflakes recovered in lowest gray loamy sand sediments around the bison bones, Burnham East Grid. View of dorsal faces with platforms on top. The top two specimens have overhanging lips on their ventral faces.

The artifacts include a flaked subangular cobble, a broken scraping-cutting implement, an edge fragment from an apparent biface, and 22 microflakes. These latter are all less than 12 mm in maximum dimension, and only five are complete. Four microflakes (Figure 9) have overhanging lips on the ventral sides of their platforms and represent flakes from resharpening bifaces. A fifth microflake also may be from a biface, whereas five others have platforms more like those on uniface implements. The other 12 microflakes are either midsections or terminations of probable resharpening flakes. Seven microflakes appear to be of local Day Creek chert, whereas another seven compare closely (color, grain, inclusions) with various cherts from the Edwards Plateau (Texas), one with Niobrara jasper of northwest Kansas, and seven of chalcedony or chert from unknown sources. All microflakes were found below the lumpy carbonate (elevation 97.06); their vertical distributions are: level 96.96 (n=1), level 96.86 (n=1), level 96.76 (n=1), level 96.56 (n=2), level 96.5 (n=2), level 96.3 (n=2), level 96.2 (n=2), and the gray sandy loam around the bison skull (n=11). All come from squares S1-W22, S1-W23, S2-W22, and S2-W23, the only squares whose residue has been sorted to date.

A large (12.4-by-10.8-by-9.7 cm; 262.1 g) subangular cobble of local (Day Creek) chert was uncovered in the red loamy sand 30 cm below the bison skull (Figure 6). This waterworn, patinated cobble derives from the Day Creek Formation, which is exposed in the Red Hills escarpments just 2 kms north of the site (Fay 1965:77–78). The cobble has several acute angles that could have served as chopping edges, but the only unpatinated flake scars are on opposite sides of a face with essentially right angles. One edge has a 1.8-by-2.0-cm flake scar, and the opposing edge has a single 3.2-by-2.7-cm hinge flake scar. These scars resemble efforts to test the cobble for its knapping suitability.

A broken scraping-cutting implement (Figure 10) came from square 0-W23 (Figure 5) at elevation 96.6, a depth at the boundary between the gray and red deposits. It has a diagonal bending-type break but measures 34 mm long, 23.5 mm in maximum width, and 7 mm in maximum thickness. Nearly continuous, bifacial, minute scalar scars occur along its margin; these scars appear worn and abraded under a microscope. For 13 mm along one edge, three overlapping scalar scars extend 7 mm on its convex (ventral) face (Figure 10). The patinated, flat, opposite face displays a prominent hinge-scar termination created before the tool was broken. The material's coloration and texture resemble Alibates agatized dolomite.

An apparent biface edge section (24.5 mm long, 21 mm wide, and 8 mm in maximum thickness) came from the red sandy loam near elevation 96.4. Although not found in situ, it came from the westernmost 25 cm of square 0-W22 (Figure 5). The material probably is Day Creek chert. Minute bifacial scalar scars occur along its edge. One face is mostly patinated cortex with segments of small flake scars. The opposite face has segments of three large flake scars.

Figure 10. Scraping-cutting implement from square 0-W23, elevation 96.6, East Grid of the Burnham site. Overlapping scalar scars of prepared edge visible on top of tool.

Burnham Site Discussion

The Burnham site has yielded bison bones, some broken hunting-butchering implements, and minute flakes like those resulting from resharpening such implements. All were found in ancient sediments near the bottom of a deep channel. These are familiar characteristics. They are the clues used to describe 10,000-year-old High Plains bison kills from Wyoming to Texas (Frison and Stanford 1982; Harrison and Killen 1978; Wheat 1972). But in light of what we know about the Burnham site, is such an interpretation valid there? Not now.

At this time, all that has been established is that the site has ancient deposits containing the bones of a bison much older than the species hunted by Clovis and Folsom humans. Surprisingly, these same deposits are yielding broken implements and flaking debris. The forms and material of these objects are comparable to those found at Southern Plains Paleoindian sites. If found with Clovis or Folsom points the human origin of the Burnham assemblage would never be questioned. So what are they doing in deposits that are at least 26,000 years old? Either they occur there because of stratigraphic mixing that can't yet be documented, or they are there because humans were present at that time and were involved with the death or dismemberment of that ancient bison. Resolution of these options must come from additional field work that exposes more perspectives of the aggraded deposit, that clarifies whether or not cultural materials are present only in the lowest sediments (those around the bison), and that permits more firmly establishing the ages of all the strata. It is hoped that such fieldwork can be undertaken soon.

Summary of Pleistocene People and the Southern Plains

FOR NEARLY 60 YEARS, interdisciplinary research on Southern Plains Paleoindian sites has developed an enviable archaeological record on the late Pleistocene and early Holocene residents of the region. Not only is the cultural sequence well established, but our knowledge of the ages, adaptive practices, and environmental conditions pertaining to specific cultures is increasing while being refined. The unequivocally best evidence for Pleistocene residents are the Clovis and Folsom cultures. By 10,500 years ago, people using Folsom points were following herds of *Bison antiquus* in patterned ways over the Southern High Plains and most of the eroded eastern and western margins. Band organization seemingly was well developed, and at least some hunting activities were undertaken that involved aggregations of bands. Some 800 years earlier, humans using Clovis spear points also were well represented throughout the region. Long renowned for their mammoth-hunting skills, Clovis bands actually were foragers in settings unlike any known in the region today. Considered the region's earliest human inhabitants, Clovis people manifest an awareness that bespeaks a long familiarity with the region. The archaeological problem is finding evidence that they had ancestors here before them. To date, only the Levi Shelter seems to hold tantalizing clues to pre-Clovis occupants, that is, someone residing in the region a millennium or so before the Clovis florescence.

More problematical are the recent findings at northwestern Oklahoma's Burnham site. Here, bones of a bison precursor to *B. antiquus* were found with artifacts in sediments dating at least 26,000 years ago. While much is yet to be learned to confirm the site's age and its clues to bison hunters in a time twice as old as Clovis, the site presently is our best opportunity to study the Pleistocene peopling of the region. To paraphrase a friend (Lowe 1987:9), it's pleasing to think that nobody knows how the past will turn out!

Addendum

SINCE THIS PAPER'S presentation, three extensive seasons of fieldwork have been completed at the Burnham site. In the fall of 1989, interdisciplinary studies were conducted with support from the National Geographic Society (Grant #4144-89), several state and local agencies, and numerous Oklahoma citizens. More fieldwork was conducted in 1990 and again in 1992, the latter supported by the National Science Foundation (Grant #DBS-9120314). All of this work clarified stratigraphic relationships and recovered a notable vertebrate and invertebrate faunal record dating from roughly 25,000 to 42,000 years ago. Nearly 60 artifacts (most being retouch flakes) were recovered from the third lowest of four stratified, ice-age pond deposits. Although not precisely dated, this artifact-bearing deposit is between 28,000 and 32,000 years old. Reports on these findings are being prepared for submission to *Quaternary Research* and *American Antiquity*. A monograph on all work and findings at the Burnham site will be published in 1999 by the Oklahoma Anthropological Society.

Acknowledgments

Drafts of this paper have benefited from the constructive criticisms of Jack Hofman, Bob Brooks, Peggy Flynn, and Kent Buehler. Kent merits special recognition for preliminarily analyzing the lithic materials from the Burnham site. The Keith, Gene, and Vic Burnham families are acknowledged gratefully for all their interest and cooperation. The Burnham site findings would not be available were it not for 27 select volunteers from the Oklahoma Anthropological Society. Encouragement, good advice, and insight on the Burnham study have been provided by Bob Brackenridge, Russell Graham, Larry Banks, and special colleagues Brian Carter, Wakefield Dort, Larry Martin, Jim Theler, Larry Todd, Jack Hofman, and Peggy Flynn. Dr. Michael Mares, Director of the Oklahoma Museum of Natural History, is gratefully acknowledged for funds to radiocarbon date the Burnham site. Doug Donahue and Austin Long of the University of Arizona NSF Accelerator Facility for Radioisotope Dating are acknowledged for their particular interest and contributions to dating the Burnham site. Finally, I thank Julie Rachel for her work on the graphics and Neva Grotts for running errands and interference while this paper was being written.

References Cited

Alexander, H. L., Jr.

1963 The Levi Site: A Late Paleo-Indian Campsite in Central Texas. *American Antiquity* 28:510–528.

1978 The Legalistic Approach to Early Man Studies. In *Early Man in America from a Circum-Pacific Perspective,* edited by A. L. Bryan, pp. 20–22. Occasional Paper No. 1. Department of Anthropology, University of Alberta, Edmonton.

1982 The Pre-Clovis and Clovis Occupations at the Levi Site. In *Peopling of the New World*, edited by J. E. Ericson, R. E. Taylor, and R. Berger, pp. 133–145. Anthropological Papers No. 23. Ballena Press, Los Altos.

Anderson, A. (editor)

1975 The Cooperton Mammoth, An Early Man Bone Quarry. *Great Plains Journal* 14:131–173.

Antevs, E.

1936 The Occurrence of Flints and Extinct Animals in Pluvial Deposits Near Clovis, New Mexico, Part II—Age of the Clovis Lake Clays. *Proceedings of the Academy of Natural Sciences of Philadelphia* 87:304–312.

Bamforth, D. B.

1988 *Ecology and Human Organization on the Great Plains.* Plenum Press, New York.

Banks, L. D.

1984 *Lithic Resources and Quarries. Prehistory of Oklahoma*, edited by R. E. Bell, pp. 65–95. Academic Press, Orlando.

Bement, L. C.

1986 *Excavation of the Late Pleistocene Deposits of Bonfire Shelter, Val Verde County.* Archeology Series No. 1. Texas Archaeological Survey, University of Texas, Austin.

Blaine, J. C., and F. Wendorf

1972 A Bone Needle from a Midland Site. *Plains Anthropologist* 17:50–51.

Blair, W. F. and T. H. Hubbell

1938 The Biotic Districts of Oklahoma. *American Midland Naturalist* 20:425–545.

Bonnichsen, R., D. Stanford, and J. L. Fastook

1987 Environmental Change and Developmental History of Human Adaptive Patterns; The Paleoindian Case. In *North America and Adjacent Oceans During the Last Deglaciation*, edited by W. F. Ruddiman and H. E. Wright, Jr., pp. 403–424. The Geology of North America, vol. K-3. Geological Society of America, Boulder.

Broilo, F. J.

1971 *An Investigation of Surface Collected Clovis, Folsom, and Midland Projectile Points from Blackwater Draw and Adjacent Localities.* Master's thesis, Department of Anthropology, Eastern New Mexico University, Portales.

Bryan, F.

1938 A Review of the Geology of the Clovis Finds Reported by Howard and Cotter. *American Antiquity* 4:113–130.

Bryan, K., and C. N. Ray

1938 Long Channelled Point Found in Alluvium Beside Bone of *Elephas columbi. Bulletin of the Texas Archeological Society* 10:263–268.

Cook, H. J.

1927 New Geological and Paleontological Evidence Bearing on the Antiquity of Mankind in America. *Natural History* 27:240–247.

Cotter, J. L.

1938 The Occurrences of Flints and Extinct Animals in Pluvial Deposits Near Clovis, New Mexico, Part 4—Report on Excavation at the Gravel Pit, 1936. *Proceedings of the Academy of Natural Sciences of Philadelphia* 89:1–16.

Crook, W. W., and R. K. Harris

1957 Hearths and Artifacts of Early Man Near Lewisville, Texas, and Associated Faunal Material. *Bulletin of the Texas Archeological Society* 28:7–97.

1958 A Pleistocene Campsite Near Lewisville, Texas. *American Antiquity* 23:233–246.

1962 Significance of a New Radiocarbon Date from the Lewisville Site. *Bulletin of the Texas Archeological Society* 32:327–330.

Dibble, D. S., and D. Lorrain

1968 *Bonfire Shelter: A Stratified Bison Kill Site, Val Verde County, Texas.* Miscellaneous Papers No. 1. Texas Memorial Museum, University of Texas, Austin.

Evans, G. L., and G. E. Meade

1945 *Quaternary of the Texas High Plains.* Contributions to Geology 1945, University of Texas Publication No. 4401. Austin.

Evans, O. F.

1930 The Antiquity of Man as Shown at Frederick, Oklahoma, A Criticism. *Journal of the Washington Academy of Sciences* 20:475–479.

Fay, R. O.

1965 *Geology of Woods County.* Bulletin No. 106. Oklahoma Geological Survey, Norman.

Fenneman, N. M.

1931 *Physiography of Western United States.* McGraw-Hill Book Company, New York.

Figgins, J. D.

1927 The Antiquity of Man in America. *Natural History* 27:229–239.

Finley, R. J. and T. C. Gustavson

1980 *Climatic Controls on Erosion in the Rolling Plains and Along the Caprock Escarpment of the Texas Panhandle.* Geological Circular No. 80-11. Bureau of Economic Geology, University of Texas, Austin.

Frison, G. C.
1982 Paleo-Indian Winter Subsistence Strategies on the High Plains. In *Plains Indian Studies*, edited by D. H. Ubelaker and H. J. Viola, pp. 193–201. Smithsonian Contributions to Anthropology No. 30. Washington, D.C.

Frison, G. C., and D. J. Stanford
1982 *The Agate Basin Site, A Record of the Paleoindian Occupation of the Northwestern High Plains.* Academic Press, New York.

Green, F. E.
1962 The Lubbock Reservoir Site. *The Museum Journal* 6:83–123.

Gryba, E. M.
1988 A Stone Age Pressure Method of Folsom Fluting. *Plains Anthropologist* 33:53–66.

Gustavson, T. C., and R. J. Finley
1985 *Late Cenozoic Geomorphic Evolution of the Texas Panhandle and Northeastern New Mexico.* Report of Investigation No. 148. Bureau of Economic Geology, University of Texas, Austin.

Hammett, H. H.
1970 A Paleo-Indian Butchering Kit. *American Antiquity* 35:141–152.

Haragan, D. R.
1970 *An Investigation of Clouds and Precipitation for the Texas High Plains.* Report No. 3. Texas Water Development Board.

1976 Spatial Variation of Precipitation on the Texas High Plains. *Water Resources Bulletin* 12:1191–1204.

Harrison, B. R., and K. L. Killen
1978 *Lake Theo: A Stratified, Early Man Bison Butchering and Camp Site, Briscoe County, Texas.* Special Archaeological Report No. 1. Panhandle-Plains Historical Museum.

Hay, O. P.
1929 On the Recent Discovery of Flint Arrowhead in Early Pleistocene Deposits at Frederick, Oklahoma. *Journal of the Washington Academy of Sciences* 19:93–98.

Haynes, C. V., Jr.
1982 Were Clovis Progenitors in Beringia? In *Paleoecology of Beringia*, edited by D. M. Hopkins, J. V. Matthews, Jr., C. E. Schweger, and S. B. Young, pp. 383–398. Academic Press, New York.

1987 Clovis Origin Update. *The Kiva* 52:83–93.

Haynes, C. V., Jr., R. P. Beukins, A. J. T. Jull, and O. K. Davis
1988 New Radiocarbon Dates for Some Old Folsom Sites Using Accelerator Technology. In *Guidebook to the Archaeological Geology of The Colorado Piedmont and High Plains of Southeastern Wyoming*, edited by V. T. Holliday, pp. 53–64. Department of Geography, University of Wisconsin, Madison.

Haynes, C. V., Jr., D. J. Donahue, A. J. T. Jull, and T. H. Zabel
1984 Application of Accelerator Dating to Fluted Point Paleoindian Sites. *Archaeology of Eastern North America* 12:184–191.

Hester, J. J.
1962 A Folsom Lithic Complex from the Elida Site, Roosevelt County, New Mexico. *El Palacio* 69:92–113.

Hester, J. J., E. L. Lundelius, Jr., and R. Fryxell
1972 *Blackwater Locality No. 1, A Stratified Early Man Site in Eastern New Mexico.* Publication No. 8. Fort Burgwin Research Center, Southern Methodist University, Dallas.

Hofman, J. L.
1988 *Folsom Research in Western Oklahoma: Rethinking the Folsom Occupation of the Southern Plains.* Transactions of the 23rd Regional Archeological Symposium for Southeastern New Mexico and Western Texas, pp. 6–30. Amarillo.

1991 Recognition and Interpretation of Folsom Technological Variability on the Southern Plains. In *Ice-Age Hunters of the Rockies*, edited by D. J. Stanford and J. S. Day, pp. 193–224. Denver Museum of Natural History, Denver.

Hofman, J. L., D. S. Amick, and R. O. Rose
1990 Shifting Sands: A Folsom–Midland Assemblage from a Campsite in Western Texas. *Plains Anthropologist* 35:221–253.

Hofman, J. L., L. C. Todd, and C. B. Schultz
1988 The Lipscomb Bison Quarry: Continuing Investigation at a Folsom Kill-Butchery Site on the Southern Plains. Paper presented at the 46th Annual Plains Anthropological Conference, Wichita.

Hofman, J. L., and D. G. Wyckoff
1987 Folsom Components at the Winters and Beckner Sites, Southwestern Oklahoma. *Current Research in the Pleistocene* 4:10–11.

Holden, W. C.
1974 Historical Background of the Lubbock Lake Site. *The Museum Journal* 15:11–14.

Holliday, V. T.
1985a Archaeological Geology of the Lubbock Lake Site, Southern High Plains of Texas. *Bulletin of the Geological Society of America* 96:1483–1492.

1985b New Data on the Stratigraphy and Pedology of the Clovis and Plainview Sites, Southern High Plains. *Quaternary Research* 23:388–402.

1985c Early and Middle Holocene Soils at the Lubbock Lake Archaeological Site, Texas. *Catena* 12:61–78.

1987 Cultural Chronology. In *Lubbock Lake: Late Quaternary Studies on the Southern High Plains*, edited by E. Johnson, pp. 22–25. Texas A&M University Press, College Station.

Holliday, V. T., E. Johnson, H. Haas, and R. Stuckenrath
1983 Radiocarbon Ages from the Lubbock Lake Site, 1950–1980: Framework for Cultural and Ecological Change on the Southern High Plains. *Plains Anthropologist* 28:165–182.

Holliday, V. T., E. Johnson, S. A. Hall, and V. M. Bryant
1985 Re-evaluation of the Lubbock Subpluvial. *Current Research in the Pleistocene* 2:119–121.

Holliday, V. T., and C. M. Welty
1981 Lithic Tool Resources of the Eastern Llano Estacado. *Bulletin of the Texas Archeological Society* 52:201–214.

Howard, E. B.
1935 Evidence of Early Man in North America. *Museum Journal* (2-3), University Museum, University of Pennsylvania, Philadelphia.

1936 The Occurrence of Flints and Extinct Animals in Pluvial Deposits Near Clovis, New Mexico, Part 1—Introduction. *Proceedings of the Academy of Natural Sciences of Philadelphia* 87:299–303.

Hunt, C. B.
1974 *Natural Regions of the United States and Canada.* W.H. Freeman and Company, San Francisco.

Jelinek, A. J.
1967 *A Prehistoric Sequence in the Middle Pecos Valley, New Mexico.* Anthropological Papers No. 31. Museum of Anthropology, University of Michigan, Ann Arbor.

Johnson, E. (editor)
1987a *Lubbock Lake: Late Quaternary Studies on the Southern High Plains.* Texas A&M University Press, College Station.

Johnson, E.
1987b Cultural Activities and Interactions. In *Lubbock Lake: Late Quaternary Studies on the Southern High Plains*, edited by E. Johnson, pp. 120–158. Texas A&M University Press, College Station.

1987c Paleoenvironmental Overview. In *Lubbock Lake: Late Quaternary Studies on the Southern High Plains*, edited by E. Johnson, pp. 90–99. Texas A&M University Press, College Station.

Johnson, E., and V. T. Holliday
1987a Summary. In *Lubbock Lake: Late Quaternary Studies on the Southern High Plains*, edited by E. Johnson, pp. 159–162. Texas A&M University Press, College Station.

1987b Lubbock Lake Artifact Assemblages. In *Lubbock Lake: Late Quaternary Studies on the Southern High Plains*, edited by E. Johnson, pp. 100–119. Texas A&M University Press, College Station.

1987c Introduction. In *Lubbock Lake: Late Quaternary Studies on the Southern High Plains*, edited by E. Johnson, pp. 3–13. Texas A&M University Press, College Station.

Johnson, E., V. T. Holliday, and R. W. Neck
1982 Lake Theo: Late Quaternary Paleoenvironmental Data and New Plainview (Paleoindian) Data. *North American Archaeologist* 3:113–137.

Leonhardy, F. C. (editor)
1966 *Domebo: A Paleo-Indian Mammoth Kill in the Prairie-Plains.* Contributions of the Museum of the Great Plains No. 1. Lawton, OK.

Lowe, K.
1987 Some Reflections on the Remarkable Fact of the Oklahoma Anthropological Society and Diverse Other Oddities. *Newsletter of the Oklahoma Anthropological Society* 35:8–9.

Mallouf, R. J.
1989 A Clovis Quarry Workshop in the Callahan Divide: The Yellow Hawk Site, Taylor County, Texas. *Plains Anthropologist* 34:81–103.

Meltzer, D. J.
1983 The Antiquity of Man and the Development of American Archaeology. In *Advances in Archaeological Method and Theory, vol. 6*, edited by M. B. Schiffer, pp. 1–51.

1987 The Clovis Paleoindian Occupation of Texas: Results of the Texas Clovis Fluted Point Survey. *Bulletin of the Texas Archeological Society* 57:27–68.

Miller, B. B.
1975 A Series of Radiocarbon-dated, Wisconsinan Nonmarine Molluscan Faunas from Southwestern Kansas–Northwestern Oklahoma. In *Studies in Cenozoic Paleontology and Stratigraphy*, edited by G. R. Smith and N. E. Friedland, pp. 9–18. Museum of Paleontology, University of Michigan, Ann Arbor.

Myers, A. J.
1959 *Geology of Harper County.* Bulletin No. 80. Oklahoma Geological Survey, Norman.

Polyak, V., and M. Williams
1986 Gaines County Paleo-Indian Projectile Point Inventory and Analysis. In *Transactions of the 21st Regional Archeological Symposium for Southeastern New Mexico and Western Texas*, edited by C. Hedrich, pp. 25–96. El Paso Archaeological Society, Texas.

Redder, A. J.
1985 Horn Shelter Number 2: The South End; A Preliminary Report. *Central Texas Archeologist* 10:37–65.

Reeves, C. C., Jr.
1966 Fluvial Lake Basins of West Texas. *Journal of Geology* 74:269–291.

Saunders, J. J.
1977 Lehner Ranch Revisited. *The Museum Journal* 17:48–64.

Schultz, C. B.
1943 Some Artifact Sites of Early Man in the Great Plains and Adjacent Areas. *American Antiquity* 8:242–249.

Sellards, E. H.
1938 Artifacts Associated with Fossil Elephant. *Bulletin of the Geological Society of America* 49:999–1010.

1952 *Early Man in America, A Study in Prehistory.* University of Texas Press, Austin.

1955 Fossil Bison and Associated Artifacts from Milnesand, New Mexico. *American Antiquity* 20:336–344.

Sellards, E. H., G. L. Evans, and G. E. Meade
1947 Fossil Bison and Associated Artifacts from Plainview, Texas. *Bulletin of the Geological Society of America* 58:927–954.

Shaeffer, J. B.
1958 The Alibates Flint Quarry, Texas. *American Antiquity* 24:189–191.

Shelley, P. H.
1984 Paleoindian Movement on the Southern High Plains: A Re-evaluation of Inferences Based on the Lithic Evidence from Blackwater Draw. *Current Research in the Pleistocene* 1:35–36.

Skinner, M. F., and O. C. Kaisen
1947 The Fossil Bison of Alaska and Preliminary Revision of the Genus. *Bulletin of the American Museum of Natural History* 89(3).

Sollberger, J. B.
1985 A Technique for Folsom Fluting. *Lithic Technology* 14:41–50.

Stafford, T. W., Jr., A. J. T. Jull, K. Brendel, R. C. Duhamel, and D. Donahue
1987 Study of Bone Radiocarbon Dating Accuracy at the University of Arizona NSF Accelerator Facility for Radioisotope Analysis. *Radiocarbon* 29:24–44.

Stanford, D.
1983 Pre-Clovis Occupation South of the Ice Sheets. *Early Man in the New World*, edited by R. Shutler, Jr., pp. 65–72. Sage Publications, Beverly Hills.

Stanford, D., and F. Broilo
1981 Frank's Folsom Campsite. *The Artifact* 19:1–13.

Stephens, J. J.
1960 Stratigraphy and Paleontology of a Late Pleistocene Basin, Harper County, Oklahoma. *Bulletin of the Geological Society of America* 71:1675–1702.

Stephenson, R. L.
1965 Quaternary Human Occupation of the Plains. In *The Quaternary of the United States*, edited by H. E. Wright, Jr. and D. G. Frey, pp. 685–696. Princeton University Press, Princeton.

Stevens, D. E. C.
1973 *Blackwater Draw Locality No. 1, 1963–1972, and Its Relevance to the Firstview Complex.* Master's thesis, Department of Anthropology, Eastern New Mexico University, Portales.

Stock, C., and F. D. Bode
1937 The Occurrence of Flints and Extinct Animals in Pluvial Deposits Near Clovis, New Mexico, Part 3—Geology and Vertebrate Paleontology of the Late Quaternary Near Clovis, New Mexico. *Proceedings of the Academy of Natural Sciences of Philadelphia* 88:219–240.

Taylor, D. W., and C. W. Hibbard
1955 *A New Pleistocene Fauna from Harper County, Oklahoma.* Circular No. 37. Oklahoma Geological Survey.

Thornbury, W. P.
1965 *Regional Geomorphology of the United States.* John Wiley and Sons, New York.

Tunnell, C. D.
1977 Fluted Point Production as Revealed by Lithic Specimens from the Adair-Steadman Site in Northwestern Texas. *The Museum Journal* 17:140–168.

1978 *The Gibson Lithic Cache from West Texas.* Report No. 30. Office of the State Archeologist, Texas Historical Commission, Austin.

Walker, J. R.
1978 *Geomorphic Evolution of the Southern High Plains.* Baylor Geological Studies No. 35. Department of Geology, Baylor University, Waco.

Warnica, J. M.
1961 The Elida Site, Evidence of a Folsom Occupation in Roosevelt County, Eastern New Mexico. *Bulletin of the Texas Archeological Society* 30:209–215.

Wedel, W. R.
1978 The Prehistoric Plains. In *Ancient Native Americans*, edited by J. D. Jennings, pp. 183–219. W.H. Freeman and Company, San Francisco.

Wendorf, F., and J. J. Hester (editors)
1975 *Late Pleistocene Environments of the Southern High Plains.* Publication No. 9. Fort Burgwin Research Center, Southern Methodist University, Dallas.

Wendorf, F., A. D. Krieger, and C. C. Albritton
1955 *The Midland Discovery, A Report on the Pleistocene Human Remains from Midland, Texas.* University of Texas Press, Austin.

Wheat, J. B.
1972 *The Olsen-Chubbuck Site: A Paleo-indian Bison Kill.* Memoir No. 26. Society for American Archaeology, Washington, D.C.

1974 First Excavation at the Lubbock Lake Site. *The Museum Journal* 15:15–42. West Texas Museum Association, Lubbock.

Wormington, H. M.
1957 *Ancient Man in North America.* Popular Series No. 4. Denver Museum of Natural History, Denver.

Pleistocene Peoples of Midcontinental North America

Bradley T. Lepper

Abstract

Midcontinental North America, as defined for the purposes of this paper, encompasses a vast area from the Allegheny Mountains westward to the upper Mississippi River basin and the eastern fringe of the Great Plains, and from the Ohio River basin northward to the Great Lakes. In the late Pleistocene, this region was a dynamic mosaic ranging from ephemeral tundra and spruce parkland in the wake of the waning Laurentide ice sheet to a complex deciduous and coniferous forest in the south.

This region has yielded the most compelling evidence for pre-Clovis occupations yet identified in North America. Meadowcroft Rockshelter in Pennsylvania and the Shriver site in Missouri are widely regarded as the best candidates for demonstrating the presence of humans in North America prior to 12,000 yr B.P.

Certainly this region has a rich record of the eastern Clovis occupation. Large numbers of fluted points have been recovered here, generally concentrated in discrete sites in the north and dispersed as isolated finds in the south. Such patterns of distribution likely are a reflection of paleoenvironmental variability and have important implications for understanding regional Clovis adaptations.

Future research in this region should be oriented toward the investigation of three basic themes: (1) the timing and nature of the Paleoindian radiation into the midcontinent; (2) settlement and subsistence patterns of eastern Clovis populations; and (3) the Paleoindian/early Archaic transition. The fruitful pursuit of these goals will require increased methodological and theoretical sophistication. Surveys will need to be designed explicitly to locate early sites. Such surveys must be sensitive to the potential importance of isolated finds and cognizant of the geological contexts in which early sites can occur.

Perhaps most importantly, the utility of a simplistic, unilineal model of cultural evolution for interpreting the Paleoindian archaeological record must be questioned. There is no evidence for a specialized big-game hunting adaptation in the eastern forests, and the oft-asserted claim for a pan-continental homogeneity in Clovis technology may well be an artifact of analytic and preservational biases.

Ohio Historical Society, 1982 Velma Avenue, Columbus, Ohio 43211-2497

Introduction

THE PURPOSE OF THIS PAPER is to review the evidence for Pleistocene peoples in midcontinental North America and to offer recommendations for future research. It may seem presumptuous to entitle the paper Pleistocene "peoples" when, in fact, what we are dealing with are scattered bits of chipped stone tools, but such are the limitations of the data. The title reflects not so much an intimate familiarity with any midwestern Pleistocene "people," but rather the goal we all are striving for of transforming the bare stones and bones into a vivid understanding of a dynamic people and their changing environment.

The region under consideration here, midcontinental North America, extends from the eastern fringe of the Great Plains to the western slopes of the Appalachian Mountains and from the Great Lakes southward to the Ohio River basin (Figure 1; Table 1). Gordon Willey (1966:248) divided this general region into three archaeological subareas: the Great Lakes Subarea, the Upper Mississippi Subarea, and the Ohio Valley Subarea. For the purposes of this review, the Mississippi and Ohio Valley subareas will be combined into a Midcontinent Riverine Subarea.

Willey's subareas, defined on the basis of regional variability in archaeological assemblages, reflect a degree of environmental variability within the eastern woodlands which influenced the cultural adaptations of Native American populations throughout prehistory except, some would argue, in the very beginning. One school of thought describes the progenitors of Native American peoples as bearers of a homogeneous Upper Paleolithic hunting culture (e.g., Haynes 1980b) and suggests that cultural evolution in the New World may be understood as a process of "settling-in" (e.g., Storck 1988a:248; cf. Binford 1983:197; Braidwood and Reed 1957), whereby these specialized hunters gradually attained what Caldwell (1958) described as "Primary Forest Efficiency": an increasing efficiency in exploiting the forest, manifested in the development of ambush hunting, seasonal cycles, and the discovery of new sources of natural foods (Caldwell 1958:vii; see also Kelly and Todd 1988:233 for an updated formulation of the same idea).

In other words, the first people imposed their essentially carnivorous way of life on the diverse environments of America and only later learned with "care and caution and endless experiment the virtues of local plants" (Eiseley 1955:10; see also Kelly and Todd 1988; Mason 1962; Stoltman and Baerreis 1983; West 1983).

This is a simplistic, unilineal model of human adaptation and cultural evolution with questionable underlying assumptions. It assumes, for example, that cultural evolution is a fundamentally gradual process. It assumes that the acquisition of knowledge is the

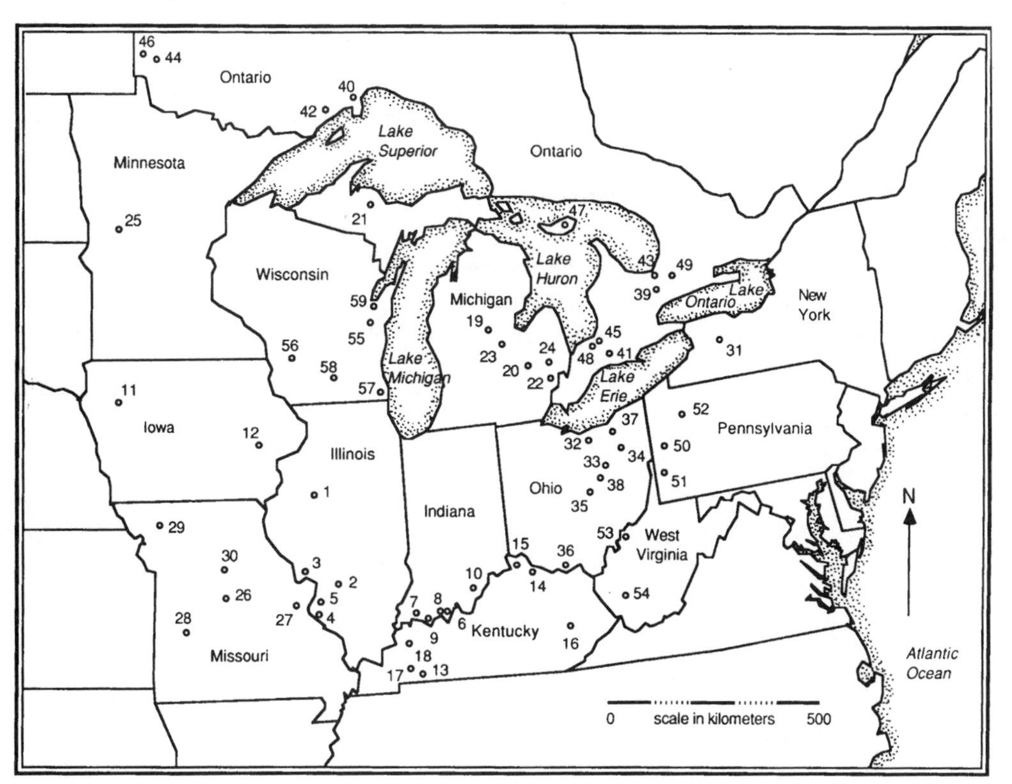

Figure 1. Map of principal late Pleistocene/early Holocene archaeological sites in midcontinental North America. (Refer to Table 1 for site information).

Table 1. Late Pleistocene/Early Holocene Archaeological Sites in Midcontinental North America. [a]

Illinois
1. Big Creek (Munson and Frye 1965)
2. Bostrom (Koldehoff 1983)
3. Lincoln Hills (Koldehoff 1983; Howard 1988)
4. Modoc Rockshelter (Fowler 1959; Styles et al. 1983)
5. Mueller (Koldehoff 1983)

Indiana
6. Magnet (Smith 1987)
7. Newburgh (Tankersley 1989)
8. Raaf (Tankersley 1989)
9. Rockport (Tankersley 1989)
10. Schafer (Tankersley 1989)

Iowa
11. Cherokee Sewer (Anderson and Semken 1980)
12. Rummels-Maske (Anderson and Tiffany 1972)

Kentucky
13. Adams (15Ch90) (Sanders 1988)
14. Adams mastodon (Walters 1988)
15. Big Bone Lick (Tankersley 1987)
16. Enoch Fork Rockshelter (Bush 1988)
17. Ledford (Tankersley 1989)
18. Parrish (Webb 1951)

Michigan
19. Barnes (Voss 1977)
20. Gainey (Simons et al. 1984)
21. Gorto (Buckmaster and Pacquette 1988)
22. Holcombe (Fitting et al. 1966)
23. Leavitt (Simons et al. 1987)
24. Rappuhn mastodon (Wittry 1965)

Minnesota
25. Pelican Rapids (Jenks 1936)

Missouri
26. Dalton (Chapman 1975)
27. Kimmswick (Graham et al. 1981; Graham and Kay 1988)
28. Rodgers Rockshelter (Wood and McMillan 1976)
29. Shriver (Reagan et al. 1978)
30. Walter (Biggs et al. 1970)

New York
31. Lamb (Gramly 1988)

Ohio
32. Cooper Hollow (Brose and Lee 1980)
33. Eppley Rockshelter (Brush, personal communication 1987)
34. Nobles Pond (Gramly and Summers 1986)
35. Munson Springs (Allison 1989)
36. Sandy Springs (Cunningham 1973)
37. Squaw Rockshelter (Brose 1988)
38. Welling/ Nellie Heights (Lepper 1986a; Prufer and Wright 1970)

Ontario
39. Banting/ Hussey (Storck 1979)
40. Brohm (MacNeish 1952; Julig 1988)
41. Crowfield (Deller and Ellis 1984)
42. Cummins (Dawson 1983; Julig 1988)
43. Fisher (Storck 1983)
44. Mud Portage (Steinbring et al. 1987)
45. Parkhill (Roosa 1977)
46. Rush Bay Road (Steinbring and Nielsen 1986)
47. Sheguiandah (Lee 1957)
48. Thedford II (Deller and Ellis 1986)
49. Udora (Storck 1988b)

Pennsylvania
50. Kellogg Farm (McConaughy et al. 1977)
51. Meadowcroft Rockshelter (Adovasio et al. 1983)
52. State Road Ripple (Konitzky 1988)

West Virginia
53. Blennerhassett Island (Hyde 1960)
54. Denison (Moxley 1982)

Wisconsin
55. Aebischer (Mason 1988)
56. Boaz mastodon (Palmer and Stoltman 1976)
57. Chesrow (Overstreet 1987; Mason 1988)
58. Kouba (Ritzenthaler 1966; Kouba 1985)
59. Renier (Mason and Irwin 1960)

[a] Refer to Figure 1 for site locations.

limiting factor in cultural evolution, and it implicitly suggests that fundamental principles of animal ecology do not apply to human hunter–gatherers. Specifically, the model implies that the diversifying selective forces driving an adaptive radiation could be abrogated by cultural conservatism. In other words, it is argued that Paleoindians would have maintained the highly specialized hunting way of life, presumably developed when they inhabited the arctic wastes of northeast Asia and Beringia, even after they had migrated into the resource-rich forests of the midcontinent.

Environment

The Ice Age

REGARDLESS OF PRECISELY WHEN humans first entered the North American midcontinent, the landscape into which they moved belonged to the Ice Age. The complex choreography of the waxing and waning Pleistocene ice sheets and the rise and fall of ocean levels shaped the geography of the Paleoindian world and ultimately determined the route and timing of human migrations into the Americas (e.g., Fladmark 1983).

It is impossible, in a review of this length, to characterize adequately the full spectrum of changing environments across a region as vast and varied as the midcontinent. Several overviews are available, and these should be consulted for a more comprehensive picture of the changing environments of the Pleistocene (e.g., Bernabo and Webb 1977; CLIMAP 1976; COHMAP 1988; Davis 1976; Delcourt et al. 1980; Fulton and Andrews 1987; Jacobson et al. 1987; Karrow and Warner 1988; Ogden 1977; Ruddiman and Wright 1987; Shane 1987; Watts 1983; Wright 1970, 1976, 1981). This review will attempt merely to sketch the outlines of late Pleistocene environments as a context for the consideration of contemporaneous human adaptive strategies.

The Wisconsin ice reached its maximum extent in the midcontinent at 21,000 yr B.P. in the east and 14,000 yr B.P. in the west (Mayewski et al. 1980:86). It extended as far south as 37° north latitude in Illinois. Fine-grained paleoenvironmental studies undertaken in the midcontinent reveal the strong presence of deciduous trees in the predominantly coniferous forests growing in close proximity to the glacial margin (e.g., Gillespie and Clendening 1968; Gruger 1972) and the co-occurrence of arctic and temperate animal species (e.g., Graham et al. 1983; Holman and Grady 1987). These observations indicate that modern zones of vegetation are recent phenomena and that plant and animal species respond individually to changing environmental parameters. The more equable climate of the Pleistocene allowed a more complex mix of plant and animal species to develop. In other words, milder winters and cooler summers resulted in an environmental mosaic that has no analogue in the world today (Brown and Cleland 1968; Graham 1976; Graham and Mead 1987; Guilday 1984; Lundelius et al. 1983; Morgan 1987).

By 14,000 years ago, the Laurentide ice sheet had begun a rapid, but spasmodic, retreat from the midcontinent (Andrews 1987; Mayewski et al. 1980). After 11,200 yr B.P., the ice margin had retreated so far north that its meltwater no longer drained southward through the Mississippi–Ohio system (Baker 1983:118). By 10,000 yr B.P., the ice sheet had retreated entirely beyond the midcontinent region, with the exception of a minor readvance into Lake Superior and northern Michigan at 9900 yr B.P. (Andrews 1987:29).

The freshly deglaciated landscape of the northern midcontinent would have appeared temporarily tundra-like. However, the "open bare areas" (Shane 1976:107) revealed in the wake of the receding midcontinental glacial margin were not true "tundra," but rather expanses of waterlogged, high-alkaline till with low levels of nitrogen and little organic content (e.g., Watts 1983). Such landscapes may develop dense coniferous forests within 35 to 40 years, even in cold subarctic latitudes (Crocker and Major 1955; see also Birks 1980). In the substantially lower latitudes of the midcontinent, the recovery time almost certainly would have been less, owing to the higher incidence of solar radiation and other factors (Ruddiman and Wright 1987). It is likely that only in the extreme northern portions of the midcontinent were tundra-like environments sustained for a prolonged period. Northern Minnesota, northern Wisconsin, and southern Ontario were areas in which tundra-like vegetation may have predominated for a time following deglaciation (Karrow and Warner 1988; Wright 1976, 1981).

Some deciduous elements are present universally in full-glacial pollen profiles across the midcontinent (e.g., Brown and Cleland 1968:118; Gruger 1972; Shane 1975; Taggart and Cross 1983). Frequently, these data are attributed to redeposition or other contamination. However, the recovery of deciduous macrofossils from late glacial deposits in Pennsylvania (Cushman 1982), West Virginia (Gillespie and Clendening 1968), and Iowa (Watts 1983:308) confirm that hardwood species constituted a significant percentage of the late-glacial forest mosaic. The distribution of animal species in the late Pleistocene midcontinent reflects the same complex mosaic (e.g., Graham 1976; Graham and Mead 1987; Guilday 1984; Lundelius et al. 1983; Morgan 1987).

In summary, a diverse array of independent and corroborating data indicate that the complex environmental mosaic of the late Pleistocene midcontinent included a substantial mesic, deciduous component. In the northern reaches of the Great Lakes Subarea, this component may have been restricted to isolated patches of hardwood trees within a predominantly coniferous forest/parkland. Such patches, even if infrequent, would have provided a diversity of floral and faunal resources for early Paleoindian groups and certainly would have been one focus of subsistence activities. Patches of tundra-like vegetation would have been localized and short-lived.

The End of an Age

BETWEEN 14,000 AND 7,000 years ago, the environment of the North American midcontinent was transformed from a complex and fluctuating ecological mosaic to a relatively stable and latitudinally stratified series of discrete forest types. One facet of this change was the extinction of numerous mammalian species, a disproportionate number of which were mammals of large body size (>20 kg). Extinction is a normal process in evolutionary history, particularly during periods of climatic change. However, the apparently "instantaneous" nature of the late Pleistocene extinctions (cf. Grayson 1989) and the simultaneous appearance of the Clovis complex throughout North America have suggested to some that human hunters drove these big game animals into extinction (Martin 1967, 1973). One of the most important problems in Paleoindian research centers on understanding the relationships between the dynamic environments of deglaciation, the extinction of the Pleistocene megafauna, and the appearance of the Clovis complex (e.g., Brown and Cleland 1968; Grayson 1987, 1989; Lundelius 1988; Martin and Klein 1984; Mead and Meltzer 1985; Storck 1988c).

Earliest Peopling of the Midcontinent

Introduction

WHO WERE THE EARLIEST peoples to occupy the North American midcontinent? For many scholars, the Clovis complex represents the material culture of the initial human occupation of North America (e.g., Haynes 1980b). However, a few sites in the midcontinent now are challenging this conservative position.

Meadowcroft Rockshelter

MEADOWCROFT ROCKSHELTER is a deeply stratified rockshelter site situated on the north bank of a small tributary of the Ohio River in the unglaciated Allegheny Plateau of southwestern Pennsylvania (e.g., Adovasio et al. 1982, this volume). An interdisciplinary team of scholars, directed by J. M. Adovasio, undertook the intensive excavation of this site as a long-term research project (Adovasio 1982). Between 1973 and 1978, impeccable excavation procedures uncovered a long sequence of human occupations.

The earliest cultural occupations at this site, from the middle and lower levels of Stratum IIa, were attributed to a pre-Clovis component predating 15,000 yr B.P. (Adovasio and Carlisle 1988:239) (see Table 2). Although particular aspects of the later Holocene occupations at Meadowcroft have aroused some controversy (e.g., claims for early Woodland maize [Lopinot 1988; Wymer 1987]), the claims of a late Pleistocene human presence prior to 12,000 yr B.P. resulted in considerable and heated debate (e.g., Adovasio et al. 1980, 1981; Dincauze 1981; Haynes 1977, 1980a; Kelly 1987; Mead 1980).

The cultural assemblage documented from lower Stratum IIa has been plausibly argued to represent a pre-Clovis Upper Paleolithic technology (Adovasio et al. 1988). The several radiocarbon dates for this stratum are entirely consistent with this interpretation. There are no "anomalous" later Paleoindian or Archaic artifacts associated with these dated early levels that might suggest substantial mixing or contamination.

It is unfortunate that a final report on the Meadowcroft excavations has not been published. Arguments on both sides of the debate occasionally have generated more heat than light. But personalities, dogma, and wishful thinking aside, the available data from Meadowcroft suggest that small groups of generalized foragers occupied midcontinental North

Table 2. Chronometric Dates for Putative Pre-Clovis Cultural Components in Midcontinental North America.

site/reference	*date*	*lab number*
Meadowcroft Rockshelter, PA (Adovasio et al. 1988)		
	19,600 ± 2400 yr B.P.	(SI-2060)
	19,100 ± 810 yr B.P.	(SI-2062)
	16,175 ± 975 yr B.P.	(SI-2354)
	15,120 ± 165 yr B.P.	(SI-1686)
	14,925 ± 620 yr B.P.	(SI-1872)
	13,270 ± 340 yr B.P.	(SI-2488)
	13,240 ± 1010 yr B.P.	(SI-2065)
	12,800 ± 870 yr B.P.	(SI-2489)
Shriver, MO (Rowlett and Garrison 1984)		
	14,850 ± 1500 yr B.P. TL dates[a]	
	13,250 ± 2400 yr B.P.	
Sheguiandah, Ontario (Lee 1956)		
	9130±250 yr B.P.	(W-345)
Rush Bay Road, Ontario (Steinbring 1986)		
	8450 ± 550 yr B.P.	(BGS 1103)

[a] Thermoluminescence dates, not strictly comparable with radiocarbon dates.

America prior to 14,000 years ago (Adovasio et al., this volume).

Shriver Site

The Shriver site is a multi-component open site overlooking the Grand River in Missouri (Reagan et al. 1978). Archaeological investigations undertaken here in 1975 by the University of Missouri uncovered stratified deposits that yielded evidence of at least two Paleoindian occupations. An upper Paleoindian component, which included a fluted point, was uncovered 25 cm above an earlier assemblage containing no associated diagnostic projectile points (Figures 2 and 3). The deep component represents a prepared core and flake industry. The lithic technology is described as being "reminiscent of the Old World Levalloisoid technique" (Reagan et al. 1978:1272), although the authors belatedly acknowledge that "it would be well to avoid attaching the 'Levalloisoid' label" to this assemblage (Reagan et al. 1978:1274).

Regardless of the label applied to the assemblage, the Shriver site yielded clear evidence for cultural material stratified beneath a fluted point occupation. Reagan et al. (1978:1274) suggest that the deep component represents a distinct pre-Clovis technology. However, in separate analyses, Reagan (1976) and Rowlett (1981) recognize that there are strong technological continuities. In fact, Reagan argues that in spite of slight differences in functional and "cultural" attributes, the "two assemblages are products of the same lithic tradition" (Reagan 1976:217). The question remains, however, just how old is the deepest occupation at Shriver? The single fluted point from the upper Paleoindian stratum is argued to be most similar to a Folsom point (Reagan et al. 1978:1273); therefore, the underlying component is not necessarily pre-Clovis in age.

Unfortunately, it has not been possible to resolve the question through radiocarbon dating (Reagan et al. 1978:1274; Rowlett 1981:14), so alternative dating techniques have been explored. Thermoluminescence (TL) dates were obtained for the fluted point component, which indicated an age of 10,650 ± 1100 yr B.P. (Rowlett and Garrison 1984:22). Although TL dates are less reliable than radiocarbon determinations, this is an acceptable estimate for a Folsom or eastern fluted point occupation (cf. Haynes et al. 1984). The deep component at Shriver yielded a TL date of 13,250 ± 2400 yr B.P. (Rowlett and Garrison 1984:22). In other words, it is most likely that the early occupation dates to between 15,650 and 10,850 yr B.P. Significantly, this range encompasses the duration of the Clovis complex (Haynes et al. 1984) (see also Table 3).

The Shriver site undoubtedly holds extremely important data for understanding the early Paleoindian occupation of the midcontinent. At present, the most parsimonious interpretation of the Shriver site Paleoindian components is that they both represent Clovis-era or later occupations. It is possible that the deep component is pre-Clovis in age; but even if it is not, the superposition of two or more early Paleoindian occupations offers an opportunity unique in the midcontinent to study changing adaptive strategies through this critical early period.

Rush Bay Road

The Rush Bay Road site complex is a series of occupations located on the flanks of outwash fans and kame terraces in northwestern Ontario (Steinbring 1986; Steinbring and Nielsen 1986). Steinbring describes the artifact assemblage recovered from these

Figure 2. A selection of stone tools from the Shriver site, Missouri. A–D) are from the upper Paleoindian component; E–M) are from the deep, possibly pre-Clovis component. Rowlett (1981) incorrectly includes C with the deep component. (Photograph courtesy of Ralph Rowlett, University of Missouri.)

sites as an "Unmodified Flake Tool Industry" (Steinbring 1986:10) similar to the early assemblage from Shriver (Steinbring and Nielsen 1986:10). The glacial landforms on which the sites are situated appear to have been deposited approximately 11,000 years ago (Steinbring 1986:10; Steinbring and Nielsen 1986:8). A radiocarbon date of 8450 ± 550 yr B.P. (BGS 1103) was obtained for one occupation level, thus the site does not appear to predate the Clovis complex. Nevertheless, Steinbring suggests that the site's occupants were a relict population of "pre-projectile point" peoples living in an isolated, unglaciated refugium (Steinbring 1986:14; Steinbring and Nielsen 1986:8, 12). These arguments are provocative, but for them to be plausible there must be more secure evidence of the alleged ancestral pre-Clovis occupation.

Summary

In summary, Meadowcroft Rockshelter is regarded as the only site yielding substantive evidence for a human presence in midcontinental North America prior to the eastern fluted point occupation. It is not possible, on the basis of current data, to indicate what relationship, if any, existed between the early inhabitants of Meadowcroft and the bearers of the Clovis industry. The Shriver and Rush Bay Road sites, and possibly the earliest components at the controversial Sheguiandah site on Manitoulin Island (Lee 1954, 1955, 1957; cf. Buckmaster 1988; Julig 1985), are interpreted here as probably related reflections of an as yet unappreciated variability in Clovis-era technology.

There are vague but tantalizing clues from localities such as the Big Creek site in Illinois (Munson and Frye 1965; cf. Griffin 1968:124), Eppley Rockshelter in Ohio (N. Brush, personal communication 1987), and Enoch Fork Rockshelter in Kentucky (C. Ison, personal communication 1988), which suggest that the record of early occupations at Meadowcroft may not be unique. Until such evidence from other sites replicates the Meadowcroft sequence, the conclusions offered

Figure 3. Additional artifacts from the deep component at Shriver. (Photograph courtesy of Ralph Rowlett, University of Missouri.)

by Adovasio et al. (Adovasio et al. 1983, this volume) may not be accepted by everyone.

Although Meltzer (1989:484) cogently has observed that one site should be enough to "prove" the case for a pre-Clovis occupation, the fact remains that this one site has not sufficed. The principal reasons for this appear to be unrelated to the quality of data from Meadowcroft. Instead, these objections involve a complex set of preconceptions about what a pre-Clovis industry should look like, which elements should characterize late Pleistocene environments in this region, and the demeanor that should be adopted when presenting controversial material.

Table 3. Chronometric Dates for Early Paleoindian Sites in Midcontinental North America.

site/reference	*date /lab. number*	*association*
Gainey, MI (Simons et al. 1987; Payne 1987)	12,360 ± 1224 yr B.P. TL dates[a]	Eastern Clovis
	11,420 ± 400 yr B.P.	
Durst Rockshelter, WI (Griffin 1965)	11,610 ± 300 yr B.P. (M-812)	Possible hearth; No definite cultural associations
State Road Ripple (36-Cl-52), PA (Herbstritt 1988)	11,385 ± 140 yr B.P. (UGa-878)	Paleoindian
Cloudsplitter Rockshelter, KY (Cowan et al. 1981)	11,278 ± 200 yr B.P. (UCLA-2340I)	Paleoindian
Shriver, MO (Rowlett and Garrison 1984)	10,650 ± 1100 yr B.P. TL date[a]	Eastern Clovis
Pleasant Lake mastodon, MI (Fisher 1984)	10,395 ± 100 yr B.P. (Beta-1388)	Possible butchering marks
Willard mastodon, OH (Falquet and Hanebert 1978)	9520 ± 205 yr B.P. (GX-4534)	Non-diagnostic stone tools in possible association
Kentucky mammoth, KY (Vesper and Tanner 1984)	8630 ± 310 yr B.P. (Beta-?)	Eastern Clovis points in possible association
Leavitt, MI (Simons et al. 1987)	7886 ± 115 yr B.P. (AA-1223)	Eastern Clovis
	1100 ± 600 yr B.P. (AA-1222)	[Parkhill Phase]

[a] Thermoluminescence dates, not strictly comparable with radiocarbon dates.

Fluted Point Occupation of the Midcontinent

Introduction

A NUMBER OF RECENT overviews of the Paleoindian occupation of eastern North America have included syntheses of the midcontinental record (e.g., Ellis 1989; Funk 1978; Lepper and Meltzer 1991; MacDonald 1983; Meltzer 1988; Meltzer and Smith 1986; Storck 1979, 1988c). This review will emphasize the most current research since the publication of these earlier summaries, but new interpretations also will be offered for old data. The subsequent discussion will follow the geographic divisions established previously in this paper and will be organized according to the following general subject headings: chronology, technology, settlement/subsistence patterns, and ritual and art.

Chronology

THE EARLIEST UNDISPUTED human presence in North America is represented by stone tool assemblages containing fluted projectile points. These artifacts first were identified as components of a late Pleistocene industry at Blackwater Draw in New Mexico (Howard 1935). Sites containing superficially similar projectile point forms have been documented from Alaska to Texas (and further south) and from Nova Scotia to California. The earliest reliable radiocarbon dates on Clovis sites were from the southwestern United States, where they range consistently from 11,500 to 11,000 yr B.P. (Haynes et al. 1984). The growing sample of radiocarbon-dated Paleoindian sites in northeastern North America suggests a somewhat later and longer range of 11,000 to 10,000 yr B.P. (Haynes et al. 1984).

The chronology of the early Paleoindian occupation of the midcontinent is problematic (see Table 3). Currently, there are no reliable radiocarbon dates for any fluted point site in the region. It is hoped that this situation will be remedied when samples from the Udora site in southern Ontario (Storck 1988b), the Nobles Pond site in northeastern Ohio (M. Seeman, personal communication 1989), and the Munson Springs site in central Ohio (Allison 1989; Frolking and Lepper 1990) are processed.

Great Lakes Subarea

A FLUTED POINT occupation at the Gainey site in central Michigan was dated by thermoluminescence. This technique is not directly comparable to radiocarbon dating, but the results obtained are suggestive and worthy of note. Two samples yielded dates of 12,360 ± 1224 yr B.P. (Simons et al. 1987:28) and 11,420 ± 400 yr B.P. (D. Simons, cited in Payne 1987:34).

The Pleasant Lake mastodon, in southern Michigan, was dated to 10,395 ± 100 yr B.P. (Beta-1388). Fisher (1984, 1987) has argued that the animal was butchered by Paleoindians; however, no stone tools or debitage were documented in association.

Midcontinent Riverine Subarea

THE FLUTED POINT component at the Shriver site in western Missouri was dated by thermoluminescence to 10,650 ± 1100 yr B.P. (Rowlett and Garrison 1984). As of this writing, the Gainey and Shriver TL dates are the only chronometric determinations for midcontinental fluted point sites that are reasonably consistent with dates for fluted point sites in other regions (cf. Haynes et al. 1984). It must be emphasized, however, that these dates are not considered equivalent to radiocarbon dates.

The deeply stratified State Road Ripple site in western Pennsylvania has produced a very small assemblage of nondiagnostic lithic artifacts in association with two features stratigraphically below an early Archaic component (G. Konitzky, personal communication 1989). Charcoal from one of these features was dated to 11,385 ± 140 yr B.P. (UGa-878) (Herbstritt 1988; Konitzky 1988). These data suggest that an in situ early Paleoindian component is present at this site.

Finally, test excavations at Enoch Fork Rockshelter in eastern Kentucky uncovered a series of cultural occupations including early Archaic and Paleoindian components (Bush 1988). A charcoal sample associated with chert debitage 11 cm below a small lanceolate projectile point yielded a date of 10,960 ± 240 yr B.P. (Beta-15424) (Bush 1988). Bush (1988) documented chert flakes at least 11 cm below this dated level, and even earlier dates recently have been obtained on these deeper occupations (C. Ison, personal communication 1989).

Technology

Introduction

IT HAS BEEN ARGUED that Paleoindian technology reflects a monolithic, homogeneous cultural tradition which emerged from the Asian Upper Paleolithic and exploded across the Americas (e.g., Mason 1962; West 1983). Certainly, the basic Paleoindian "tool kit," documented from sites across North America, is "surprisingly similar" (Ritchie 1983:30; see also Funk 1978:17; Haynes 1980b:119):

In addition to the fluted projectile point it comprises mainly: other uniface and biface knives; uniface end, side and spoke-shave scrapers; gravers; borers; drills; flint wedges ... and a few rough stone hammers and anvils (Ritchie 1983:30).

However, the "uniformity" in Paleoindian tool kits probably has been exaggerated by several factors (see, for example, Ellis and Deller 1988). Fluted points may resemble each other superficially while having been produced from different technological traditions (e.g., Young and Bonnichsen 1984). Moreover, similarities between fluted points in the midcontinent sometimes do not extend beyond the mere presence of large basal thinning flakes. Finally, Paleoindian sites in the midcontinent thus far have yielded evidence for only the lithic component of the material culture of these people. The perishable components of Paleoindian technology probably would reflect more interregional variability.

Great Lakes Subarea

RECENT ARCHAEOLOGICAL research in southern Ontario and southern Michigan has revolutionized our understanding of Paleoindian prehistory in the midcontinent (e.g., Deller 1979, 1988; Deller and Ellis 1988; Ellis 1984; Garrad 1971; Jackson 1983; Julig 1984, 1988; Roosa 1965, 1977; Shott 1989; Simons et al. 1984, 1987; Storck 1982, 1984a, 1984b, 1988a; Wright and Roosa 1966). Perhaps the most significant advance has been the definition of three distinct fluted point types which are argued to correspond with three Paleoindian cultural complexes (Deller and Ellis 1988; Ellis 1984; Storck 1984a). It is further argued that these complexes represent stages in Paleoindian technological development; however, the proposed sequence has not yet been corroborated stratigraphically.

Gainey points are similar to Clovis and are therefore considered to represent the earliest cultural complex in the Great Lakes (e.g., Deller and Ellis 1988) (see Figures 4 and 5). Barnes points, part of the Parkhill complex, are smaller, fully fluted, fishtailed points similar to Cumberland points (Roosa 1977) (Figure 5). Crowfield points are small, thin points similar to Holcombe, but with definite, often multiple, fluting (Figure 5).

These three types appear to encompass the fluted point variability in southern Ontario (Deller and Ellis 1988:255) and perhaps much of the Great Lakes Subarea. The majority of sites are single component,

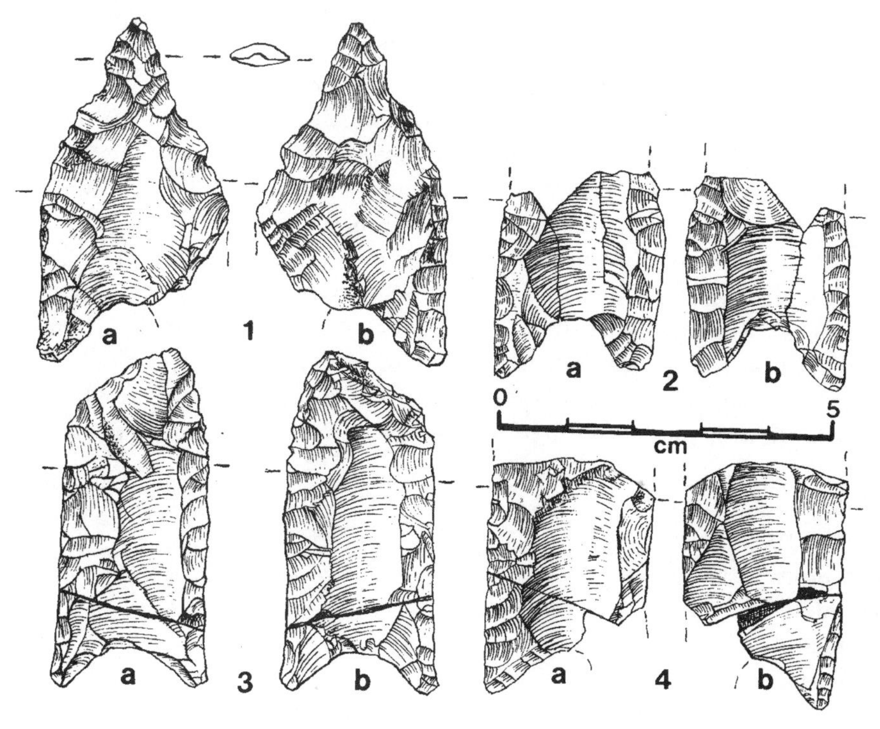

Figure 4. Fluted projectile points from the Udora site: 1) basal fragment reworked into bifacial drill; 2 and 4) basal fragments broken during use; 3) extensively resharpened point also broken during use. (Figure courtesy of Peter Storck, Royal Ontario Museum, Toronto, and the Center for the Study of the First Americans, Oregon State University, Corvallis.)

Figure 5. Selection of fluted projectile points from Ontario: 1) Gainey point, Upper Mercer chert, Fernhill; 2) Gainey point base, Onondaga chert, Thedford area; 3) Barnes point, Fossil Hill chert, Thedford II site; 4) Barnes point, Fossil Hill chert, Parkhill site; 5) Crowfield point, Onondaga chert, Crowfield site; 6) Crowfield point, Fossil Hill chert, Crowfield site. (Photograph courtesy of Christopher Ellis, University of Waterloo.)

and each complex favored different raw materials. These characteristics of the Great Lakes Paleoindian archaeological record facilitated the discovery and definition of the various complexes.

Midcontinent Riverine Subarea

FLUTED POINTS in the Midcontinent Riverine Subarea have not proven so amenable to typological analysis. The generalized Gainey/Clovis point is ubiquitous throughout the midcontinent (Figure 6), but only rare examples of the more specialized Barnes and Crowfield points have been documented south of the Great Lakes (e.g., Lepper 1986a). It is possible that a similar projectile point continuum eventually will be established for the Midcontinent Riverine Subarea, but large sites are rare here and localities are, almost without exception, multi-component. Moreover, although Paleoindian groups in this region had clear preferences for particular raw materials (e.g., Tankersley 1989:271), the same chert sources were used continuously by prehistoric peoples for more than 10,000 years. As a result, Paleoindian components generally cannot be identified unless a diagnostic projectile point is recovered. Significantly, although southern chert sources were used by Great Lakes Paleoindian groups (e.g., the Gainey site assemblage consists predominantly of Ohio Upper Mercer chert [Shott 1989; Simons et al. 1984]), no fluted points crafted from Great Lakes cherts have so far been documented in the Midcontinent Riverine Subarea.

Finally, although Wisconsin and Minnesota are included here in the Great Lakes Subarea, the fluted points documented from these states (e.g., Figure 7) appear to have more in common with the melange of fluted point forms from the Midcontinent Riverine Subarea than with the types defined for Michigan and Ontario (Mason 1986; Steinbring 1974; Stoltman and Workman 1969; O. C. Shane, III, personal communication 1989). This suggests that late Pleistocene cultural developments in the eastern Great Lakes may have been a spatially restricted response to unique conditions.

Figure 6. Selection of fluted projectile points from Coshocton County, Ohio: 1) basal fragment broken during manufacture; 2) complete point exhibiting extensive resharpening; 3) basal fragment broken during use. (Photograph courtesy of the Johnson-Humrickhouse Memorial Museum, Coshocton, Ohio.)

Settlement/Subsistence Patterns

Introduction

THE FIRST DOCUMENTED Clovis sites, located in the Plains and Southwest, were associated with the fossil remains of mammoth. Indeed, these sites often were discovered when passers-by noted the huge mammoth bones eroding from the bank of an arroyo. It is likely that deer or antelope bones found in similar situations would not have excited such interest. Because of this potential bias in the sample of Clovis kill sites, the importance of mammoths in the Clovis subsistence economy, even on the Plains, is not at all clear (Grayson 1988). Nevertheless, many archaeologists accept the interpretation that Clovis people were specialized mammoth hunters (e.g., Haynes 1966, 1980b; Martin 1973; West 1983).

The archaeological record of the fluted-point-using peoples in midcontinental North America long has been regarded as disappointing in terms of evidence for elephant hunting (e.g., Quimby 1960:27–33). Nevertheless, it has been argued that the uniformity in Paleoindian technology across such a wide area must reflect "a highly conservative way of life, attuned to the requirements of a specialized subsistence pattern dependent on the ubiquitous megafauna of the late Pleistocene" (Funk 1978:17).

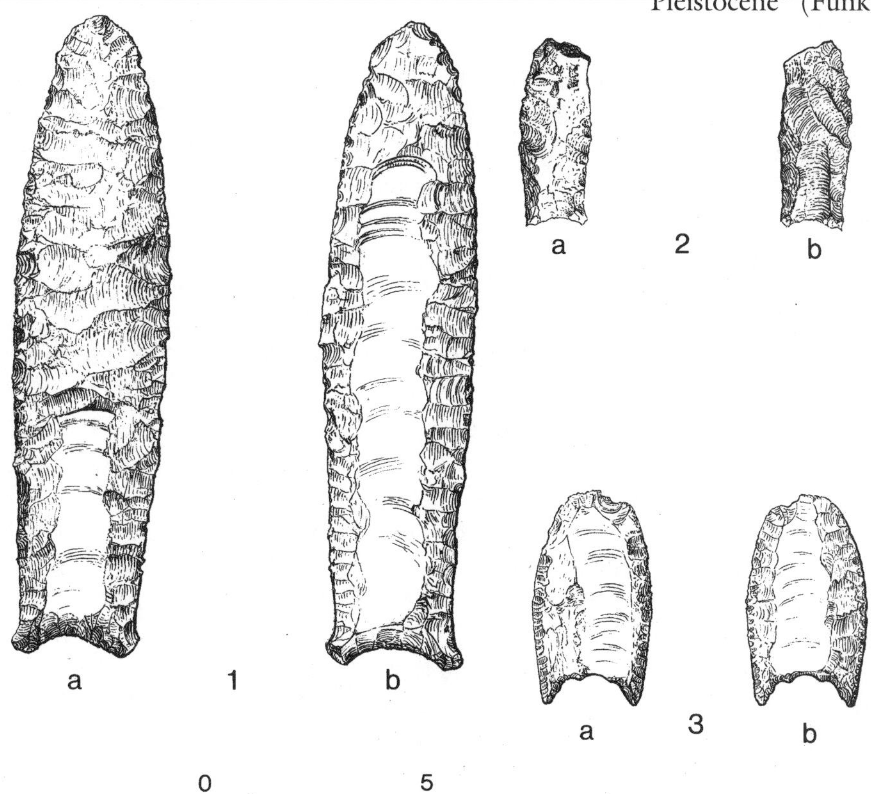

Figure 7. Selection of fluted projectile points from Minnesota: 1) large complete point; 2) small point with broken tip; 3) Folsom point. (Figure courtesy of O. C. Shane, III, The Science Museum of Minnesota, St. Paul.)

The general practice of using the often more complete record of the Paleoindian occupation of western North America to flesh out the relatively impoverished eastern Paleoindian archaeological record has a long history (e.g., Shetrone 1936). However, the assumption that what is "true" for one area will be true for another is an argument of last resort that is no longer necessary. The midcontinent has yielded a rich Paleoindian archaeological record that must be understood on its own terms. Forcing it to conform with interpretive models framed on the High Plains does justice neither to the eastern record nor to the western models.

Great Lakes Subarea

THE EVIDENCE FOR MAMMOTH or mastodon hunting in the Great Lakes Subarea is tenuous and unconvincing. Quimby (1960:27–33; see also Martin 1967:97–101; Mason 1986:191–192) noted that the distribution of fluted points in Michigan was correlated with the known distribution of mastodons and, in spite of the fact that no fluted point had ever been found in direct association with a mastodon, asserted that this relationship was a result of intensive Paleoindian predation on these animals. However, the samples of fluted points, as well as the samples of documented mastodon fossils, are affected by differential cultivation intensity and collector bias (Lepper 1983, 1986b; see also Dirst 1985:4; Hurley 1965:68).

The general arguments of Quimby (1960) find limited support in the specific claims of Palmer and Stoltman (1976) and Wittry (1965). Palmer and Stoltman (1976) discuss the Boaz mastodon, discovered in 1897 in southwestern Wisconsin, and present the claims of the original excavators that a fluted point was found in association.

Wittry (1965) presents a preliminary report on the excavation of the Rappuhn mastodon in southwestern Michigan. Wittry's argument that the animal had been butchered by humans is based on the disarticulation of the bones, alleged butchering marks on some of the bones, and the presence of an anomalous "layer of wood poles" (Wittry 1965:18).

Fisher (1984, 1987) recently has advanced similar arguments in support of the hypothesis that several mastodon sites in Michigan represent Paleoindian mastodon procurement and butchery. Patterns of disarticulation, cut marks across the bones, and sophisticated taphonomic analyses have provided the basis for Fisher's claim that male mastodons in their prime were being hunted (or scavenged) by Paleoindians in the late autumn (Fisher 1987). But, as with the Rappuhn mastodon, no lithic artifacts were recovered from any of Fisher's mastodon sites, in spite of the fact that "lithic tools must have been used to some extent" (Fisher 1984:272). Even if Paleoindians in the Great Lakes Subarea were religiously conserving lithic raw material (Fisher 1984:272), they would not have curated small resharpening flakes, such as are ubiquitous at the Kimmswick mastodon kill site in Missouri (Graham and Kay 1988:233).

Fisher's (1987) current argument is that the sites he has investigated represent unrecovered winter meat caches, and not mastodon procurement or processing loci. In his interpretation, a mastodon was butchered nearby and choice portions of the disarticulated carcass were transported to a pond and submerged in the icy waters for storage and later retrieval. In some cases, the meat was weighted down with cobbles or boulders and the location was marked with upright posts driven into the pond bottom (D. Fisher, personal communication 1989).

This scenario presents a compelling and parsimonious interpretation of the data. It is, however, not necessarily the correct interpretation. For example, G. Haynes (1988) has demonstrated that apparent cut marks may be produced on the bones of African elephants when they are "trampled against coarse substrates such as gravel or sand" (Haynes 1988:153). This does not mean that the "cut marks" observed on Michigan mastodon bones are natural. It does suggest that there are alternative natural explanations for the phenomena documented by Fisher. Until an actual mastodon kill or scavenging site is discovered in the Great Lakes Subarea, or until a Paleoindian artifact is recovered in direct association with one of these hypothetical meat caches (cf. Frison 1976), it must be concluded that there is no direct evidence for Paleoindian mastodon butchery in the Great Lakes.

In southern Ontario, Paleoindian sites belonging to the Parkhill complex consistently have been documented in association with the strandline of glacial Lake Algonquin (e.g., Storck 1982, 1984b). Some of these sites are extremely large (e.g., the Parkhill site [Roosa 1977]), and this large size, coupled with the strategic orientation of the sites, suggests that they represent base camps for the communal hunting of caribou (Deller and Ellis 1988:261; Peers 1985; Roosa 1977:353; Storck 1982). A similar association of Paleoindian sites with the strandlines of glacial lakes has been documented from other areas in the Great Lakes (e.g., Overstreet 1987; Peru 1967). Nevertheless, the importance of caribou hunting in this region probably has been exaggerated.

Storck (1982) acknowledges that archaeological survey strategies in southern Ontario had been focused on glacial lake strandlines and ". . . the resulting settlement pattern data probably represent only a limited aspect of the total settlement pattern" (Storck 1982:25; see also Deller and Ellis 1988:261–262). Recent surveys, conducted in the interior of south-central Ontario, confirm the presence of Paleoindians in interior settings not associated with strandlines (Jackson 1984). Such indications of a more generalized land use pattern suggest to Jackson that Paleoindian hunters exploited a broad range of species in the Great Lakes (Jackson 1988).

Exciting new discoveries at the Udora site in southern Ontario substantiate this argument (Figure 4). Recent excavations at this Gainey-complex site uncovered a feature containing abundant artifacts and debitage along with 293 g of calcined animal bone (Storck 1988b). Most of the bones could not be identified, but they include bones of caribou, hare, and Arctic fox (Speiss and Storck 1990).

Midcontinent Riverine Subarea

The Paleoindian archaeological record of the Midcontinent Riverine Subarea is quantitatively and qualitatively distinct from the record of the Great Lakes Subarea. Fluted point frequencies are higher by an order of magnitude in the Midcontinent Riverine Subarea (see, for example, Jackson 1978:86; Seeman and Prufer 1982:162). Moreover, these artifacts are recovered primarily as isolated finds in the Midcontinent Riverine Subarea (e.g., Holsten and Cochran 1986:17; Prufer and Baby 1963:2; Schwartz 1965:8), whereas in the Great Lakes Subarea, fluted points tend to occur in large, single-occupation habitation sites (Meltzer 1984, 1985).

Rare large sites in the Midcontinent Riverine Subarea generally are quarry-related sites reflecting multiple reoccupations. Examples include Lincoln Hills in Illinois (Howard 1988; Koldehoff 1983), Adams in Kentucky (Sanders 1988; Yahnig 1989), and Welling/Nellie Heights in Ohio (Lepper 1986a; Lepper and Wright 1989; Prufer and Wright 1970).

Aggregations of Paleoindian artifacts also occur in localities offering an especially favorable environmental situation. Sites such as Sandy Springs in Ohio (Cunningham 1973) and Big Bone Lick in Kentucky (Tankersley 1989) are located near saline springs, which are perennial attractions for a diversity of game animals. So it is not simply that sites do not occur in the Midcontinent Riverine Subarea, but that the nature of the occupations is different, producing a different archaeological signature—one that is dominated by widely scattered, isolated fluted points.

It has been typical of archaeologists to underestimate the significance of "isolated finds" and bemoan the fact that so few Paleoindian "sites" have been discovered in the Midcontinent Riverine Subarea (e.g., Moeller 1983; cf. Brooks 1979). Early attempts to use the record of isolated Paleoindian points to learn something about the Paleoindian occupation of the midcontinent generally were limited to gross counts of fluted points per county or per physiographic region. Distributional analyses of this sort have dominated Paleoindian archaeology in the midcontinent and their results have demonstrated overwhelmingly the abundance of isolated fluted points in this region (Broyles 1967; Chapman 1967; Dorwin 1966; Griffin 1968; Mason 1958; Prufer and Baby 1963; Quimby 1958; Ritchie 1957; Rolingson 1964; Seeman and Prufer 1982; Shetrone 1936).

Unfortunately, these data sets share a number of limitations. The broad, statewide distributions are biased by differential cultivation and collecting intensity (Lepper 1983). Also, lumping the isolated fluted point occurrences into modern counties or larger sampling units masks the microenvironmental variability of the individual find spots.

In order to study Paleoindian settlement and subsistence patterns in the Midcontinent Riverine Subarea it must be recognized explicitly that the isolated, fluted point is the primary manifestation of the Paleoindian archaeological record in this region (Meltzer 1984). Isolated finds must be analyzed as true sites, not merely as tallies on a state map. Recent studies of this nature have yielded important information on Paleoindian land use patterns.

The central Muskingum River basin in east-central Ohio is a region with a rich Paleoindian archaeological record, owing to the presence of extensive outcrops of Upper Mercer chert, the favored raw material of Ohio Paleoindians (Prufer and Baby 1963). Prufer (1971) intensively studied the distribution of Paleoindian artifacts in this area and concluded that fluted points tended to occur in concentrations at the "confluences of minor streams with the Walhonding and Tuscarawas rivers," but that "Stray finds occurred throughout the valleys" (Prufer 1971:309).

Lepper (1986a, 1988) developed a classification system that translated "stray finds" into "settlement" types and restudied the distribution of fluted point loci in the central Muskingum River basin. Large workshop/habitation sites, such as the Welling site (Prufer and Wright 1970), were situated on exposed floodplain terraces in close proximity to chert outcrops and intermediate workshop sites. Hunting sites, defined on the basis of isolated finds of complete fluted points or points broken in use, were widely distributed throughout the hills and valleys of the dissected Allegheny Plateau. This land use pattern suggests that Paleoindians in this region were exploiting dispersed faunal resources such as white-tailed deer or elk (Lepper 1986a, 1988; see also Lantz 1984; Lepper 1989; Lepper and Meltzer 1991).

Koldehoff's (1983) analysis of Paleoindian sites associated with the important outcrops of Burlington chert in southwestern Illinois produced broadly similar results. The distribution of sites between the Lincoln Hills workshop/habitation site and the Mueller site complex suggests a settlement/subsistence pattern "based primarily on elk hunting and other faunal and floral resources of the upland prairies and savannas" (H. Winters, cited in Koldehoff 1983:223). Comparable data were obtained across the Mississippi River in southeastern Iowa (Shutler and Charlton 1980).

As increasingly detailed studies of fluted point distributions are undertaken in the midcontinent, the picture of Paleoindian settlement patterns becomes more complex and complete. In Kentucky, Gatus and Maynard (1978) and Sanders and Maynard (1979) noted an apparent association of fluted points with sinkholes. However, Niquette's (1986) survey of Paleoindian points in south-central Kentucky yielded 39 fluted points, only one of which was recovered near a sinkhole. Holsten and Cochran (1986) conducted a survey of Paleoindian sites in the Upper Wabash drainage of northern Indiana to test a common model of Paleoindian site location, which predicted that most sites "would be located on high points overlooking the confluence of a stream with a larger stream" (Holsten and Cochran 1986:1; cf. Prufer 1971). The results obtained by this survey so far do not support the "overlook" model.

The western Lake Erie basin in northwestern Ohio is argued to have been avoided by Paleoindians (Prufer and Baby 1963; Seeman and Prufer 1982). However, recent surveys in this region have documented large numbers of surface finds "in diverse physiographic settings" (Stothers 1982; see also Payne 1982).

These results suggest that Paleoindian groups in the Midcontinent Riverine Subarea were not practicing a specialized big-game hunting subsistence strategy. The land use models indicating hunting patterns focused on white-tailed deer or elk are supported by paleoenvironmental reconstructions and applications of optimal foraging theory (Ford 1977; Leach and Conaty 1988; Rule 1983).

Perhaps the most important site for clarifying the nature of Paleoindian subsistence in the Midcontinent Riverine Subarea is the Kimmswick site in eastern Missouri (Graham et al. 1981). Clovis projectile points have been documented here in clear association with mastodon remains. But this site is more than a mastodon kill. In fact, a diverse fauna is represented, including 23 species of mammals in addition to fish, amphibians, reptiles, and birds (Graham and Kay 1988:232). There is good evidence that the extinct ground sloth Glossotherium was hunted, along with white-tailed deer and turtle (Graham and Kay 1988:233). Therefore, although the Kimmswick site has yielded evidence for the only confirmed mastodon kill in eastern North America, it also has demonstrated that Clovis foragers hunted white-tailed deer. Indeed, when the entire faunal assemblage is considered, the data "suggest a diverse economy for the Clovis hunters" (Graham et al. 1981:116).

Ritual and Art

Introduction

GIVEN THE LIMITED nature of the late Pleistocene archaeological record in the midcontinent, it would be surprising if there was much direct evidence for a ceremonial component of Paleoindian culture. Moreover, there is a lack of established archaeological method and theory for analyzing or even recognizing prehistoric ritual. In spite of these severe limitations, there are data that give us brief glimpses into the belief systems of the Paleoindian hunter–gatherers of the midcontinent.

Great Lakes Subarea

THE CLEAREST EXAMPLE of a Paleoindian site in midcontinental North America reflecting ceremonial activities of these early people is the Crowfield site in southern Ontario (Deller and Ellis 1984). Feature #1 at the site consisted of a shallow basin interpreted as a cremation-burial. This conclusion is based on the possible association of calcined bone with thousands of fragments of heat-fractured chert artifacts, as well as the unique character of the reconstructed lithic assemblage. More than 200 Paleoindian artifacts were reconstructed from this feature. The absence of "chert wastage," the lack of manufacturing failures and of artifacts broken-in-use, and the presence of several unusual artifact forms suggest that this assemblage represents a functioning tool kit, which terminated its uselife in a ceremonial context (Deller and Ellis 1984:49–50).

A possible cache of 13 fluted bifaces was discovered by Deller and Ellis (1992) at the Thedford II site, also in southern Ontario. This assemblage is quite similar to a collection of exquisite fluted projectile points and preforms documented from the Lamb site in western New York (Gramly 1988). Gramly interprets these artifacts as "burial furnishings," although no evidence of skeletal material or any subplowzone features were encountered (Gramly 1988:6). It is possible that these materials represent "insurance gear" (Binford 1979) cached for future use but never reclaimed. This interpretation is supported by the discovery of other apparent tool caches at Great Lakes Paleoindian sites. A cache of 80 gravers was recovered from the Kouba site in southern Wisconsin (Ritzenthaler 1967; but see Kouba 1985), and a pit feature containing "over sixty tools and large chert flakes" was identified at the Udora site in southern Ontario (Storck 1981).

Finally, although North America has yielded no evidence for Paleoindian art rivaling the spectacular cave paintings of Paleolithic Europe, there are hints in western Ontario that Native American artistic traditions may extend their roots into the early Holocene. The Mud Portage site consists of archaeological deposits partially overlying a bedrock surface upon which are inscribed numerous petroglyphs. Some naturalistic representations of animals, defined as Lake-of-the-Woods Style, were buried under Archaic materials, suggesting to Steinbring et al. (1987) that some of the petroglyphs may be pre-Archaic.

Midcontinent Riverine Subarea

IN CONTRAST TO the meager evidence documented for the Great Lakes Subarea, the archaeological record of Paleoindian ritual for the Midcontinent Riverine Subarea is virtually nonexistent. The Rummels-Maske site in eastern Iowa consists of an "isolated cache" of 20 fluted points and point fragments (Anderson and Tiffany 1972:58). Apart from a somewhat apocryphal account of a similar cache of fluted points from Lorain County, Ohio (Vietzen 1973:32) there is no other reported evidence for possible early Paleoindian ritual activities in the Midcontinent Riverine Subarea. And again, these caches may represent "insurance gear" rather than ceremonial features.

Late Paleoindian Transition

Introduction

STRATIFIED SITES on the Western Plains have documented a clear transition from fluted point industries associated with extinct megafauna to a series of unfluted lanceolate projectile point complexes associated with increasingly large numbers of bison remains (Judge 1974; Wormington 1957). The occurrence of both fluted points and a variety of unfluted lanceolate point forms in midcontinental North America has led many scholars to believe that this region participated in a similar transition. However, the Cherokee Sewer site, on the eastern margin of the Great Plains in western Iowa, is the only documented site in the midcontinent with lanceolate points in association with bison remains (Anderson and Semken

1980; but see also Newman and Julig 1989). Moreover, the radiocarbon dates for this site suggest that the eastward expansion of the Plains Plano complexes was relatively late (see Table 4).

A review of radiocarbon dates obtained for lanceolate point assemblages in midcontinental North America (Table 4) suggests that a generalized lanceolate shape has been a popular projectile point/knife form through at least the late Archaic. In view of this, it is probable that much material identified in the literature as "late Paleoindian" actually is late Archaic. Nevertheless, there are data indicating that a lanceolate point pattern (Bonnichsen et al. 1987:413–418) did follow the fluted point complexes in midcontinental North America.

Great Lakes Subarea

FLUTED POINT COMPLEXES appear to be absent from the Great Lakes Subarea by 10,400 yr B.P. (Deller and Ellis 1988:251). The continued importance of caribou procurement in the subsistence adaptation of Great Lakes populations is suggested by the single caribou bone recovered from the Holcombe site (Fitting et al. 1966:14) and the possible calcined caribou bone fragments from the Cummins site (Julig 1984:194). However, protein residues on Plano-tradition artifacts from Cummins indicate that a variety of game species were taken, including, perhaps, *Bison* (Newman and Julig 1989). Continuity in ritual is perhaps evidenced by the discovery of numerous cremation burials often associated with caches of broken lanceolate projectile points (e.g., Buckmaster and Paquette 1988; Julig 1984:192; Mason and Irwin 1960; Ritzenthaler 1972).

Midcontinent Riverine Subarea

UNFLUTED LANCEOLATE point forms are documented from the Midcontinent Riverine Subarea as early as 10,960 ± 240 yr B.P. (Bush 1988). The Dalton lanceolate point complex appears in the southern portions of the region by 10,500 yr B.P. (Goodyear 1982:389) (see Table 4). Notched projectile points appear in the same region as early as 10,000 yr B.P. (Goodyear 1982:389) (see Table 5).

There is increasing evidence that lanceolate point and notched point complexes were contemporaneous and sympatric in the Midcontinent Riverine Subarea (Brose 1988; Mason 1981:116; Mocas 1977). The limited evidence for faunal and floral remains in these late Paleoindian/early Archaic contexts reflects a continuous subsistence adaptation from the earliest Paleoindians in the midcontinent through the early Archaic. Elk remains and charred nut fragments were recovered from late Paleoindian/early Archaic contexts at the Cooper Hollow and Burrill Orchard sites in northern Ohio (Brose 1988).

Evidence for Dalton subsistence is more abundant and correspondingly diverse. McMillan (1976:214) identified deer, along with some turtle, turkey, fish, and a variety of small mammals from the Dalton levels of Rodgers Shelter in southwestern Missouri. Hickory nuts and black walnuts also were "a part of the Dalton subsistence base" (McMillan 1976:224).

Conclusions and Recommendations

MASON (1981:115) CONCLUDED that the fluted point tradition "underwent an adaptive bifurcation" in the midcontinent. Lanceolate point complexes developed first in the Great Lakes region, and early Archaic notched point complexes developed shortly thereafter in the Ohio Valley. The data discussed herein suggest that this conclusion is substantially correct, although the "adaptive bifurcation" appears to have occurred much earlier than previously supposed. Moreover, it is not correlated with the changes in projectile point morphology that characterize the Paleoindian/Archaic transition. The archaeological record of the earliest fluted point complexes in the midcontinent already reflects two distinct adaptive strategies corresponding to two diverse environments (Meltzer and Smith 1986).

The Midcontinent Riverine Subarea was largely unglaciated, and the portions of this area that were glaciated had been free of ice for a thousand years before fluted point-wielding foragers occupied the region. A complex mosaic environment developed here, including a substantial mesic deciduous component similar in composition, though not in structure, to the Holocene forests of this region (Leach and Conaty 1988).

The earliest Paleoindian peoples in this subarea were generalized foragers utilizing a broad spectrum of resources. Pleistocene megafauna were exploited infrequently as part of a rich smorgasbord of flora and fauna. As a result of the richness and stability of the environment, fluted points here are many and varied. This variability doubtless includes both regional variants

Table 4. Radiocarbon Dates for Late Paleoindian and Other Lanceolate Point Assemblages in Midcontinental North America.

site/reference	*date/lab. no.*	*association*
Meadowcroft Rockshelter, PA (Adovasio et al. 1988)	12,800 ± 870 yr B.P. (SI-2489) 11,300 ± 700 yr B.P. (SI-2491)	Bracketing dates for Miller lanceolate
Eppley Rockshelter, OH (Brush, personal communication 1987)	12,185 ± 130 yr B.P. (UCLA-2589C) 9890 ± 100 yr B.P. (UCLA-2589E)	lanceolate point
Cooper Hollow, OH (Brose, personal communication 1989)	12,590 ± 195 yr B.P. (DIC-446)	lanceolate points with LeCroy points
Enoch Fork Rockshelter, KY (Bush 1988)	10,960 ± 240 yr B.P.	Wheeler lanceolate
Modoc Rockshelter, IL (Fowler 1959)	10,651 ± 650 yr B.P.(C-907) 9101 ± 440 yr B.P.(C-908)	Dalton complex
Rodgers Shelter, MO (Chapman 1975:235)	10,480 ± 650 yr B.P. (ISGS-48) 10,200 ± 330 yr B.P. (M-2333)	Dalton complex
Squaw Rockshelter, OH (Brose 1988)	9480 ± 160 yr B.P. (DIC-586)	"Plano" with Kirk variant in burial
Sheguiandah, Ontario (Lee 1956)	9130 ± 250 yr B.P. (W-345)	Dated peat overlies Aqua Plano assemblage
Aurora Run Rockshelter, OH (Mason 1981:116)	9110 yr B.P.	"Plano" with Kirk
Cherokee Sewer, IA (Anderson and Semken 1980)	8570 ± 200 yr B.P. (UCLA 1877F) 8445 ± 250 yr B.P. (UCR 490)	Agate Basin component
Cummins, Ontario (Julig 1984)	8482 ± 390 yr B.P.	Cremation burial from "Plano" site
Lawrence site, KY (Mocas 1977)	7470 ± 85 yr B.P. 7325 ± 125 yr B.P. (UGa-436) 7265 ± 305 yr B.P. (UGa-240)	lanceolate point in burial
Burrell Orchard, OH (Brose and Lee 1980)	7120 ± 120 yr B.P. (DIC-734)	Stringtown stemmed with tanly and Morrow Mt. points
East Steubenville, WV (Crane and Griffin 1958; Dragoo 1959)	4220 ± 500 yr B.P. (M-229)	Steubenville complex
Late Archaic open site, OH (Morton and Carskadden 1975)	4130 ± 100 yr B.P. (I-7604)	"Plano" with Late Archaic
Globe Hill Shell Heap, WV (Murphy 1977)	4120 ± 220 yr B.P. (CWR-184)	Steubenville complex
Meadowcroft Rockshelter, PA (Adovasio et al. 1988; Boldurian 1985:144)	3970 ± 85 yr B.P. (SI-2058)	Steubenville complex
Davidson, Ontario (Kenyon 1980)	3780 ± 85 yr B.P.	Satchell complex
Nebo Hill type site, MO (Brown and Ziegler 1981)	3555 ± 65 yr B.P. (UGA-1332)	Nebo Hill complex
Pinegrove Cemetery, MI (Simons 1972)	3305 ± 135 yr B.P. 3010 ± 110 yr B.P. (N-110)	Satchell complex
Helmerick Shelter, MO (Chapman 1975)	3210 ± 90 yr B.P. (Gak-504)	Sedalia complex
Freeworth, OH (Stothers 1983)	3190 ± 65 yr B.P. (DIC-2589)	Satchell complex
Byler Mound, OH (Zakucia 1956, 1974)	3115 ± 80 yr B.P. (SI-1150)	Steubenville complex

Table 5. Radiocarbon Dates for Pre-Kirk Early Archaic Components in Midcontinental North America.

site/reference	*date/lab. no.*	*association*
Modoc Rockshelter, IL (Fowler 1959)	10,651 ± 650 yr B.P. (C-907)	Big Sandy with Dalton complex
	9101 ± 440 yr B.P. (C-908)	
St. Albans, WV (Broyles 1971)	9850 ± 500 yr B.P. (M-1827)	Kessell side-notched with Charleston corner-notched
Graham Cave, MO (Chapman 1957; Klippel 1971:22,27-28)	9700 ± 500 yr B.P. (M-130)	Thebes and St. Charles with Dalton complex
	9470 ± 400 yr B.P. (M-1928)	
	9290 ± 300 yr B.P. (M-1889)	

and change through time, but unless several of these forms are recovered in a stratified site, it is difficult to determine which processes were at work. Eventually, fluting was abandoned entirely, but the same lifeway continued for thousands of years unchanged in most other respects.

The Great Lakes Subarea, during the late Pleistocene, was an active environment still in the throes of deglaciation. Paleoindian peoples moving into the rapidly changing boreal/deciduous parkland were confronted with kaleidoscopic challenges and opportunities as the ice sheet waxed and waned and glacial lakes rose and fell, appeared and disappeared. The flora and fauna of this region were neither as rich nor as diverse as the resources of the more stable environments to the south. Paleoindian pioneers, moving north into the Great Lakes Subarea, would have been compelled eventually to focus their hunting efforts on the most abundant and predictable resource in an otherwise unpredictable environment (Meltzer and Smith 1986:12). But because of the relative instability of the environment, this region was inhabited later by Paleoindian groups and population density would not have been as great, at least initially. As a result, fluted points are much less common in the Great Lakes region and the variability is more limited in some areas. The series of fluted point complexes defined for Ontario and Michigan may represent some sort of cultural evolutionary "punctuated equilibrium," with the presumably early and generalized Gainey complex rapidly transforming into the specialized Parkhill complex. Aspects of this specialized way of life are perpetuated in the subsequent "Aqua-Plano" complexes (Quimby 1960:34), but this transition is not well understood.

It will have become clear by now that very little concerning the Pleistocene peoples of midcontinental North America is well understood. But much progress has been made in the last several years and, as analytical methods improve, knowledge of this early period will continue to grow.

Future research on the Pleistocene peoples of midcontinental North America should not be constrained by the pontifical pronouncements put forth by the authors of overviews. The essence of the scientific endeavor is the freedom of individual scholars to pursue whatever problems and issues are of interest. Nevertheless, with regard to the Paleoindian prehistory of this region, there is so much that is not known that it may be useful to organize our ignorance.

First, and most fundamental, are issues of chronology. When did humans first enter the midcontinent? When did Clovis foragers first launch their fluted projectiles in the valleys of the Mississippi and Ohio rivers? And when was this form abandoned in favor of lanceolate or notched points? Without a secure temporal framework we cannot begin to provide answers to more interesting processual questions. Answers to these "simple" questions of chronology will not come easily or cheaply. Meadowcroft Rockshelter may have yielded evidence for the earliest humans in midcontinental North America. But the data will not be accepted universally until and unless the Meadowcroft sequence is replicated at another site. In order to attempt to replicate these data it will be necessary to design and fund long-term research projects (see also Nicholas 1984). After all, Meadowcroft was not dug in a day.

Questions surrounding the origins of the Clovis complex aside, very little really is known about basic aspects of the peoples who made and used these characteristic artifacts. Much of what is written about early Paleoindian settlement and subsistence patterns in midcontinental North America is based not on data from this region but on extrapolations from sites excavated on the Great Plains. This overview has hinted at the variability in adaptive strategies that may be present within the midcontinent. Future research should be oriented towards exploiting the full richness and uniqueness of the Paleoindian archaeological record of the midcontinent so that empirically based comparisons can be made with other regions. It is no longer reasonable simply to assume that "the Clovis culture" is a single, homogeneous cultural entity (cf. Haynes 1980b).

Finally, having addressed problems of Paleoindian culture history and the reconstruction of past "lifeways," it is only fair to mention a few of the really interesting questions of culture process. What happened 10,000 years ago? How are the environmental changes that define the Pleistocene/Holocene transition related to the archaeologically observed changes, which demarcate Paleoindian and Archaic cultural patterns? This review has presented evidence suggesting that, for much of the midcontinent, the 10,000 yr B.P. rubicon is a red herring. In this region, early Paleoindian adaptive strategies appear to be essentially continuous through the early Archaic and the environmental changes at the close of the Pleistocene began much earlier and culminated earlier than 10,000 yr B.P. Therefore, the easy (if environmentally deterministic) explanation is denied us, and we are left with the disconcerting task of reexamining our basic units of investigation: What is "Paleoindian?" What is the "Archaic?" As currently applied in midcontinental North America, these labels may signify distinct projectile point configurations and nothing more. This is not necessarily bad, but it should be explicit. The "Paleoindian" label has carried too much unnecessary baggage for too long.

"That's a great deal to make one word mean," Alice said in a thoughtful tone.

"When I make a word do a lot of work like that," said Humpty Dumpty, "I always pay it extra."

Postscript

SINCE THIS PAPER was presented in May of 1989, a number of discoveries have been made that have added significantly to our knowledge of the Pleistocene peoples of the midcontinent and the environment in which they lived. In addition, several important syntheses have appeared that offer new theoretical approaches and alternative perspectives on the data and issues addressed in this review (Anderson 1990; Dincauze 1993; Gramly and Funk 1990; Julig 1991; Lepper and Meltzer 1991; see also the various papers in Dancey 1994; Dillehay and Meltzer 1991; Tankersley and Isaac 1990). In this postscript I refer to some of the new discoveries and briefly touch upon their implications. It has not been necessary to develop a totally new set of conclusions and recommendations. Indeed, I am both pleased and chagrined that so little emendation of my 1989 synthesis has been required—pleased at my foresight, but chagrined at how little, in some ways, we have advanced toward a clearer understanding of the Pleistocene peoples of the midcontinent.

Environment

A SURPRISING DEGREE of resolution in the paleoenvironmental record of the northern hemisphere is revealed in several recent papers. And, as our resolution improves, it becomes clear that climatic changes throughout the late Pleistocene could be extreme and remarkably abrupt (e.g., Alley et al. 1993; Dansgaard et al. 1989; Greenland Ice-core Project Members 1993; Jansen and Veum 1990). For example, the Younger Dryas climatic event[1], which occurred approximately 10,700 years ago, seems now to have ended with a bang over a period of scarcely 20 years (Alley et al. 1993; Dansgaard et al. 1989:533). Clearly the tempo of at least some of the climate changes during the late Pleistocene and early Holocene was much faster than many of us assumed (although others have appreciated this fact for some time; see, for example, Morgan [1973]). This discovery has important implications for our ideas about how Paleoindians adapted to the sometimes wildly shifting environments of the midcontinent.

Chronology

THERE STILL IS NO firm chronological framework on which to hang the shreds and patches that comprise the tapestry of Paleoindian archaeology in midcontinental North America. But the situation has improved since 1989.

Meadowcroft Rockshelter continues to arouse controversy and defy consensus (see Haynes [1991] and Tankersley and Munson [1992] versus Adovasio et al. [1992]). Matters are not helped by the fact that there *still* is no final report on this fundamentally important site.

There are now radiocarbon determinations for a fluted point occupation site in the midcontinent comparable to those from other regions. These dates are not from the Udora site or the Munson Springs site, both of which failed to fulfill the radiometric promise they appeared to have in 1989 (Lepper and Gill 1991; Storck 1990).

Early in 1992 (the much ballyhooed quincentennial of one rather belated "discovery" of America), Brose announced a series of radiocarbon dates for the so-called "Paleo Crossing" site located in northeastern Ohio (Brose and Barrish 1992). This site consists of numerous fluted projectile points, associated tools and debitage, and, miraculously preserved beneath the midcontinent's seemingly ubiquitous plow zone, subsurface features. Charcoal from a post mold, remains of a possible house, was dated to 12,250 ± 100 yr B.P. (AA-8250) and soil humates from a cylindrical pit yielded two disparate dates of 9230 ± 80 yr B.P. (AA-8252) and 13,100 ± 100 yr BP (AA-8251) (Brose and Barrish 1992:1). This less-than-perfectly resolved chronology has been refined, to some extent, by a series of new dates. Brose now claims that the Paleoindian occupation of "Paleo Crossing" dates to 10,990 ± 75 yr B.P. (average of three dates) (Brose 1992; Hall 1993a:3).

The Burning Tree mastodon site is located in central Ohio near the Munson Springs site (No. 35 on Figure 1). Fisher and I, after many and long animated discussions, interpret this site as a Paleoindian meat cache (Fisher et al. 1991, 1994). A series of radiocarbon dates on bone, gut contents, and associated peat and spruce wood provide a solid age assessment. One bone sample yielded a date of 10,860 ± 70 yr B.P. (Pitt-0832). A second sample of XAD-purified bone collagen, processed by Thomas Stafford, produced a more reliable date of 11,390 ± 80 yr B.P. (AA-6980). Dates on gut contents were 11,450 ± 70 (Pitt-0832) and 11,660 ± 120 yr B.P. (Beta-38241/ETH-6758). Spruce wood and peat associated with the skeleton yielded dates of 11,470 ± 90 (Pitt-0841), 11,720 ± 110 (Beta-35045), 12,230 ± 70 (Pitt-0833), and 12,620 ± 90 (Beta-35046) (Fisher et al. 1991, 1994; Lepper et al. 1991). These are relatively early dates for an eastern Paleoindian site, but since no lithic artifacts were recovered from the excavations, it is not possible to attribute this late Pleistocene abattoir to any particular cultural manifestation.

Settlement/Subsistence Patterns

IF THE INTERPRETATION of the Burning Tree mastodon as a butchered animal is correct (Fisher et al. 1991, 1994), then the question of the importance of proboscideans for the diet of midcontinental Paleoindians must be reconsidered. Furthermore, the interpretation of this less equivocal site has implications for the acceptance of the several other eastern sites which Fisher and others have argued also reflect Paleoindian butchery of mastodons and mammoths (e.g., Fisher 1987 and various other references cited in the 1989 portion of this review; Kirkpatrick and Fisher 1993; Overstreet et al. 1993).

Recent excavations at the Martin's Creek mastodon site in east-central Ohio offer even more definitive evidence of Paleoindian exploitation of mastodon (Hall 1993b). Here, Brush recovered a handful of lithic flakes in direct association with mastodon bones, and one of these flakes bears proboscidean blood residue (Brush et al. 1994).

In spite of this apparent stampede of butchered mastodons, there still is no evidence to support the once-popular notion of specialized elephant hunters in eastern North America (cf. Lepper 1993; Lepper and Meltzer 1991). Brush also recovered cervid bones at the Martin's Creek mastodon site, and cervid blood residue was identified on one of the other flakes (Brush et al. 1994).

Although it is not a new claim, an apocryphal reference to a fluted point lodged in an elk skeleton from Silver Lake, Ohio finally should be laid to rest. Mason (1981:99) reported the discovery in Great Lakes Archaeology, but, concerned that general readers would be intimidated by scholarly references, he gave no source for the claim. The report appears to have originated in a paper by Ogden (1977:19) who cites "R. S. Baby, pers. commun." as the authority. Baby, former curator of archaeology for the Ohio Historical Society, is now deceased. Martha Potter Otto, current curator of archaeology for OHS, is not aware of any discovery of a fluted point in association with an elk in Ohio (M. P. Otto, personal communication).

It is likely that the elk in question actually was recovered from Lake Mac-O-Chee in Logan County, Ohio (Goslin 1961). The right scapula and one rib bore evidence of a healed wound from a stone projectile, but only minute fragments of flint remained embedded in the bone. Goslin concluded that "the time at which the animal received the wound is not determined" (1961:85).

Finally, reports on two Paleoindian sites, one located in the Riverine Subarea and one in the Great Lakes Subarea, shed much light on regional (as well as temporal) variability in lithic technology. The Thedford II site, a Parkhill-complex site in southwestern Ontario, is treated ably by Deller and Ellis (1992). Sanders' (1990) report on the Adams site, a Clovis workshop-occupation in western Kentucky, is more limited in scope due to the nature of the artifact sample.

Late Paleoindian Transition

THERE HAVE BEEN few recent contributions to research on the transition from the Paleoindian to the early Archaic ways of life. The Manning site, along the Ohio River in southwestern Ohio, offers some potential in this regard (Lepper 1994; Lepper and Cummings 1993). A cultural resource management project uncovered a deeply buried series of three occupations. The earliest component dates to ca 9800 and the intermediate to 9720 ± 290 yr B.P. (Beta-27476). The most recent occupation is dated to the early Archaic by the presence of Kirk corner-notched projectile points. No diagnostic artifacts were recovered in the testing of the earliest strata, but the presence of *Picea* (spruce) charcoal associated with the two deepest occupations suggests that the cultural sequence at the Manning site "spans the transition from a mixed conifer-deciduous forest to a full deciduous forest" (Lepper and Cummings 1993:33).

Conclusion

OVER THE LAST five years, significant strides have been made in tracking the elusive first peoples of the midcontinent. I trust that the next five will see even more advances. I look forward to the next World Summit Conference on the Peopling of the Americas and hope that, by the time it convenes, some of the questions left unanswered in this review will be resolved. Perhaps by then the final report on Meadowcroft Rockshelter will be out.

Acknowledgments

My deepest appreciation is extended to Robson Bonnichsen for presenting me with the challenge and opportunity of synthesizing recent research on the Paleoindian occupation of the midcontinent. It would not have been possible to accomplish this overview without the gracious cooperation of the many scholars who supplied me with information on their current research. Special thanks are extended to the following: Jeffrey Behm, David Brose, David Bush, Gerald Conaty, Donald Cochran, Chris Ellis, Daniel Fisher, Russell Graham, William Green, Lawrence Jackson, Patrick Julig, Marvin Kay, Brad Koldehoff, Gustav Konitzky, Elizabeth Leach, Ronald J. Mason, David Meltzer, Patrick Munson, Charles Niquette, David Overstreet, Donna Roper, Ralph Rowlett, Mark Seeman, Jack Steinbring, Peter Storck, and Ken Tankersley.

Carl Albrecht of the Ohio Historical Society assisted with the drafting of Figure 1, and Kay Smith edited an early draft of the manuscript. Helpful comments on subsequent drafts were provided by Dena Dincauze, Chris Ellis, Pat Julig, Dave Meltzer, Donna Roper, and Dee Anne Wymer. Their contributions are gratefully acknowledged, but any errors of omission or commission that remain are solely the responsibility of the author.

Finally, my thanks to Karen A., Benjamin R., and Peter R. Lepper. Their sacrifices have made this work possible.

References Cited

Adovasio, J. M.
1982 Multidisciplinary Research in the Northeast: One View from Meadowcroft Rockshelter. *Pennsylvania Archaeologist* 52(3-4):57–68.

Adovasio, J. M., A. T. Boldurian, and R. C. Carlisle
1988 Who Are Those Guys?: Some Biased Thoughts on the Initial Peopling of the New World. In *Americans Before Columbus: Ice Age Origins*, edited by R. C. Carlisle, pp. 45–61. Ethnology Monographs No.12. Department of Anthropology, University of Pittsburgh, Pittsburgh.

Adovasio, J. M., and R. C. Carlisle
1988 The Meadowcroft Rockshelter. *Science* 239:713–714.

Adovasio, J. M., J. Donahue, K. Cushman, R. C. Carlisle, R. Stuckenrath, J. D. Gunn, and W. C. Johnson
1983 Evidence from Meadowcroft Rockshelter. In *Early Man in the New World*, edited by R. Shutler, Jr., pp. 163–189. Sage Publications, Beverly Hills.

Adovasio, J. M., J. Donahue, J. D. Gunn, and R. Stuckenrath
1981 The Meadowcroft Papers: A Response to Dincauze. *Quarterly Review of Archaeology* 2(3):14–15.

Adovasio, J. M., J. Donahue, and R. Stuckenrath
1992 Never Say Never Again: Some Thoughts on Could Haves and Might Have Beens. *American Antiquity* 57:327–331.

Adovasio, J. M., J. D. Gunn, J. Donahue, and R. Stuckenrath
1982 Meadowcroft Rockshelter, 1973–1977: A Synopsis. In *Peopling of the New World*, edited by J. E. Ericson, R. E. Taylor, and R. Berger, pp. 97–131. Ballena Press, Los Altos.

Adovasio, J. M., J. D. Gunn, J. Donahue, R. Stuckenrath, J. E. Guilday, and K. Volman
1980 Yes Virginia, It Really Is That Old: A Reply to Haynes and Mead. *American Antiquity* 45:588–595.

Alley, R. B., D. A. Meese, C. A. Shuman, A. J. Gow, K. C. Taylor, P. M. Grootes, J. W. C. White, M. Ram, E. D. Waddington, P. A. Mayewski, and G. A. Zielinski
1993 Abrupt Increase in Greenland Snow Accumulation at the End of the Younger Dryas Event. *Nature* 362:527–529.

Allison, N.
1989 The Munson Springs Site: 9,000 Years of Occupation in Central Ohio. *Mammoth Trumpet* 5(1):8.

Anderson, A. D., and J. A. Tiffany
1972 Rummels-Maske: A Clovis Find-Spot in Iowa. *Plains Anthropologist* 17:55–59.

Anderson, D. C., and H. A. Semken, Jr. (editors)
1980 *The Cherokee Excavations: Holocene Ecology and Human Adaptations in Northwestern Iowa.* Academic Press, New York.

Anderson, D. G.
1990 The Paleoindian Colonization of Eastern North America: A View from the Southeastern United States. *Research in Economic Anthropology*, Supplement 5:163–216.

Andrews, J. T.
1987 The Late Wisconsin Glaciation and Deglaciation of the Laurentide Ice Sheet. In *North America and Adjacent Areas During the Last Deglaciation: The Geology of North America*, vol. K-3, edited by W. F. Ruddiman and H. E. Wright, Jr., pp. 13–37. Geological Society of America, Boulder.

Baker, V.R.
1983 Late Pleistocene Fluvial Systems. In *The Late Pleistocene*, edited by S. C. Porter, pp. 115–129. *Late Quaternary Environments of the United States, vol. 1*, H. E. Wright, Jr., general editor. University of Minnesota Press, Minneapolis.

Bernabo, J. C., and T. Webb, III
1977 Changing Patterns in the Holocene Pollen Record of northeastern North America: A Mapped Summary. *Quaternary Research* 8:64–96.

Biggs, R. W., J. Stoutamire, and R. Vehik
1970 *The Walter Site: A Fluted Point Manifestation in North Central Missouri*, pp. 11–63. Missouri Archaeological Society Memoir No. 8.

Binford, L. R.
1979 Organization and Formation Processes: Looking at Curated Technologies. *Journal of Anthropological Research* 35:255–273.

1983 *In Pursuit of the Past.* Thames and Hudson, New York.

Birks, H. J. B.
1980 The Present Flora and Vegetation of the Moraines of the Klutan Glacier, Yukon Territory, Canada: A Study in Plant Succession. *Quaternary Research* 14:60–86.

Bonnichsen, R., D. Stanford and J. L. Fastook
1987 Environmental Change and Developmental History of Human Adaptive Patterns; The Paleoindian Case. In *North America and Adjacent Areas During the Last Deglaciation: The Geology of North America*, vol. K-3, edited by W. F. Ruddiman and H. E. Wright, Jr., pp. 13–37. Geological Society of America, Boulder.

Boldurin, A. T.
1985 *Variability in Flintworking Technology and the Krajacic Site: Possible Relationships to the Pre-Clovis Paleoindian Occupation of the Cross Creek Drainage in Southwestern Pennsylvania.* Ph.D. dissertation, University of Pittsburgh, Pittsburgh.

Braidwood, R. J., and C. A. Reed
1957 The Achievement and Early Consequences of Food Production: A Consideration of the Archaeological and Natural-Historical Evidence. *Cold Springs Harbor Symposia on Quantitative Biology* 22:19–31.

Brooks, R. L.
1979 Prehistoric Spot Finds, Localities, and Archaeological Context: A Cautionary Note from Kentucky. *Tennessee Anthropologist* 4(2):167–174.

Brose, D. S.
1988 The Squaw Rockshelter (33CU34): A Stratified Archaic Deposit in Cuyahoga County, Ohio. Ms. on file, Department of Archaeology, Cleveland Museum of Natural History, Cleveland.

1992 Archaeological Investigations at the 12,000 Year Old Paleo Crossing Site. Paper presented at the Ohio Archaeological Council's First Discovery of America Conference, 21 November 1992, Columbus.

Brose, D. S., and B. Barrish
1992 Investigations at Ohio Site Push Back Dates for Clovis. *Mammoth Trumpet* 7(4):1,3.

Brose, D. S., and A. M. Lee
1980 A Reinterpretation of the Late Paleoindian to Early Middle Archaic Period in Northern Ohio. Paper presented at the Ontario Archaeological Society Symposium on the Prehistory of Lake Erie, London, Ontario.

Brown, J., and C. Cleland
1968 The Late Glacial and Early Postglacial Faunal Resources in Midwestern Biomes Newly Opened to Human Adaptation. In *The Quaternary of Illinois*, edited by R. E. Bergstrom, pp. 114–122. Special Publication No. 14. College of Agriculture, University of Illinois, Urbana.

Brown, K. L., and R. J. Ziegler
1981 Nebo Hill Settlement Patterns in Northwestern Missouri. *Missouri Archaeologist* 42:43–55.

Broyles, B. J.
1967 Fluted Points in West Virginia. *West Virginia Archeologist* 20:46–57.

1971 *Second Preliminary Report: The St. Albans Site, Kanawa County, West Virginia, Report of Investigations No. 3.* West Virginia Geological and Economic Survey, Morgantown.

Brush, N., M. Newman, and F. Smith
1994 Immunological Analysis of Flint Flakes from the Martin's Creek Mastodon Site. *Current Research in the Pleistocene* 11:16-18.

Buckmaster, M. M.
1988 The Pacquette Site: A Possible Stratified Late Paleo-Indian Site. Paper presented at the 1988 Midwest Archaeological Conference, University of Illinois at Urbana-Champaign.

Buckmaster, M. M., and J. R. Pacquette
1988 The Gorto Site: Preliminary Report on a Late Paleo-Indian Site in Marquette County, Michigan. *Wisconsin Archaeologist* 69(3):101–124.

Bush, D. R.
1988 New evidence of Paleoindian and Archaic Occupations in Clay and Perry Counties, Kentucky. In *Paleoindian and Archaic Research in Kentucky*, edited by C. D. Hockensmith, D. Pollack and T. N. Sanders, pp. 47–65. Kentucky Heritage Council, Frankfort.

Caldwell, J. R.
1958 *Trend and Tradition in the Prehistory of the Eastern United States.* American Anthropological Association Memoir No. 88.

Chapman, C. H.
1957 *Graham Cave. A Report of Progress*, pp. 47–49. Missouri Archaeological Society, Columbia.

1967 Fluted Point Survey of Missouri: An Interim Report. *Newsletter of the Missouri Archaeological Society* 215:9–10.

1975 *The Archaeology of Missouri, I.* University of Missouri Press, Columbia.

CLIMAP Project Members
1976 The Surface of the Ice-Age Earth. *Science* 191:1131–1137.

COHMAP Members
1988 Climatic Changes of the Last 18,000 Years: Observations and Model Simulations. *Science* 241:1043–1052.

Cowan, C. W., H. E. Jackson, K. Moore, A. Nickelhoff, and T. L. Smart
1981 The Cloudsplitter Rockshelter, Menifee County, Kentucky: A Preliminary Report. *Southeastern Archaeological Conference Bulletin* 24:60–76.

Crane, H. R., and J. B. Griffin
1958 University of Michigan Radiocarbon Dates, III. *Science* 128:1117–1123.

Crocker, R. L. and J. Major
1955 Soil Development in Relation to Vegetation and Surface Age at Glacier Bay, Alaska. *Journal of Ecology* 43:427–448.

Cunningham, R. M.
1973 Paleo-Hunters Along the Ohio River. *Archaeology of Eastern North America* 1:118–126.

Cushman, K. A.
1982 Floral Remains from Meadowcroft Rockshelter, Southwestern Pennsylvania. In *Meadowcroft*, edited by R. C. Carlisle and J. M. Adovasio, pp. 207–220. Department of Anthropology, University of Pittsburgh, Pittsburgh.

Dancey, W. S. (editor)
1994 *First Discovery of America: Archaeological Evidence of the Early Inhabitants of the Ohio area.* Ohio Archaeological Council, Columbus.

Dansgaard, W., J. W. C. White, and S. J. Johnsen
1989 The Abrupt Termination of the Younger Dryas Climate Event. *Nature* 339:532–534.

Davis, M. B.
1976 Pleistocene Biogeography of Temperate Deciduous Forest. *Geoscience and Man* 13:13–26.

Dawson, K. C. A.
1983 Cummins Site: A Late Palaeo-Indian (Plano) Site at Thunder Bay, Ontario. *Ontario Archaeology* 39:3–31.

Delcourt, P. A., H. R. Delcourt, and L. E. Lackey
1980 Quaternary Vegetation History of the Mississippi Embayment. *Quaternary Research* 13:111–132.

Deller, D. B.
1979 Paleo-Indian Reconnaissance in the Counties of the Lambton and Middlesex, Ontario. *Ontario Archaeology* 32:3–20.

1988 *The Paleo-Indian Occupation of Southwestern Ontario: Distribution, Technology, and Social Organization.* Ph.D. dissertation, McGill University, Montreal.

Deller, D. B., and C. J. Ellis
1984 Crowfield: A Preliminary Report on a Probable Paleo-Indian Cremation in Southwestern Ontario. *Archaeology of Eastern North America* 12:41–71.

1988 Early Palaeo-Indian Complexes in Southwestern Ontario. In *Late Pleistocene and Early Holocene Paleoecology and Archeology of the Eastern Great Lakes Region*, edited by R. S. Laub, N. G. Miller, and D. W. Steadman, pp. 251–263. *Bulletin of the Buffalo Society of Natural Sciences* No. 33. Buffalo.

1992 *Thedford II: A Paleo-Indian Site in the Ausable River Watershed of Southwestern Ontario.* Memoirs, No. 24. Museum of Anthropology, University of Michigan, Ann Arbor.

Dillehay, T. D., and D. J. Meltzer (editors)
1991 *The First Americans: Search and Research.* CRC Press, Boca Raton, FL.

Dincauze, D. F.
1981 The Meadowcroft Papers. *Quarterly Review of Archaeology* 2:3–4.

1993 Fluted Points in the Eastern Forests. In *From Kostenki to Clovis: Upper Paleolithic-Paleo-Indian Adaptations*, edited by O. Soffer and N. D. Praslov, pp. 279–292. Plenum Press, New York.

Dirst, V.
1985 *The Paleo-Indians of East Central Wisconsin: A 1984 Survey and Testing Project.* Report on file, Historic Preservation Division, State Historical Society of Wisconsin, Madison.

Dorwin, J. T.
1966 *Fluted Points and Late Pleistocene Geochronology in Indiana.* Prehistory Research Series No. 4(3). Indiana Historical Society.

Dragoo, D. W.
1959 Archaic Hunters of the Upper Ohio Valley. *Annals of the Carnegie Museum* 35:139–245.

Eiseley, L. C.
1955 The Paleo-Indians: Their Survival and Diffusion. In *New Interpretations of Aboriginal American Culture History*, edited by B. J. Meggars and C. Evans, pp. 1–11. Anthropological Society of Washington, Washington, D.C.

Ellis, C. J.
1984 *Paleo-Indian Lithic Technological Structure and Organization in the Lower Great Lakes Area: A First Approximation.* Ph.D. dissertation, Simon Fraser University, Burnaby.

1989 Early Paleoindian Lithic Industries of Northeastern North America in Their Temporal, Spatial, Paleoenvironmental, Site and Cultural Contexts. Ms. submitted to *L'Anthropologie.*

Ellis, C. J., and D. B. Deller
1988 Some Distinctive Paleo-Indian Tool Types from the Lower Great Lakes Region. *Midcontinental Journal of Archaeology* 13:111–158.

Falquet, R. A., and W. C. Hanebert
1978 The Willard Mastodon: Evidence of Human Predation. *Ohio Archaeologist* 28(2):17.

Fisher, D. C.
1984 Mastodon Butchery by North American Paleo-Indians. *Nature* 308:271–272.

1987 Mastodont Procurement by Paleoindians of the Great Lakes Region: Hunting or Scavenging? In *The Evolution of Human Hunting*, edited by M. H. Nitecki and D. V. Nitecki, pp. 309–421. Plenum Press, New York.

Fisher, D. C., B. T. Lepper, and P. E. Hooge
1991 Taphonomic Analysis of the Burning Tree Mastodont. *Current Research in the Pleistocene* 8:88–91.

1994 Evidence for Butchery of the Burning Tree Mastodon. In *First Discovery of America: Archaeological Evidence of the Early Inhabitants of the Ohio Area*, edited by W. S. Dancey. Ohio Archaeological Council, Columbus.

Fitting, J. E., J. DeVisscher, and E. J. Wahla
1966 *The Paleo-Indian Occupation of the Holcombe Beach.* Anthropological Papers No. 27. Museum of Anthropology, University of Michigan, Ann Arbor.

Fladmark, K. R.
1983 Times and Places: Environmental Correlates of Mid-to-Late Wisconsinan Human Population Expansion in North America. In *Early Man in the New World*, edited by R. Shutler, Jr., pp. 13–41. Sage Publications, Beverly Hills.

Ford, R. I.
1977 Evolutionary Ecology and the Evolution of Human Ecosystems: A Case Study from the Midwestern U.S.A. In *Explanations of Prehistoric Change*, edited by J. N. Hill, pp. 153–184. University of New Mexico Press, Albuquerque.

Fowler, M. L.
1959 *Summary Report of Modoc Rock Shelter: 1952, 1953, 1955, 1956.* Reports of Investigations No. 8. Illinois State Museum, Springfield.

Frison, G. C.
1976 Cultural Activity Associated with Prehistoric Mammoth Butchering and Processing. *Science* 194:728–730.

Frolking, T. A., and B. T. Lepper
1990 The Late Pleistocene—Early Holocene Occupation of the Munson Springs Site (33-Li-251), Locus A, Licking County, Ohio. *Current Research in the Pleistocene* 7:12–14.

Fulton, R. J., and J. T. Andrews (editors)
1987 The Laurentide Ice Sheet. *Geographie physique et Quaternaire* 41(2).

Funk, R. E.
1978 Post-Pleistocene Adaptations. In *Northeast*, edited by B. G. Trigger, pp. 16–27. *Handbook of North American Indians, vol. 15,* W. G. Sturtevant, general editor. Smithsonian Institution, Washington, D.C.

Garrad, C.
1971 Ontario Fluted Point Survey. *Ontario Archaeology* 16:3–18.

Gatus, T. W., and D. R. Maynard
1978 Karst Topography: A Factor Associated with Paleo-Indian Settlement in Certain Areas of Kentucky. *Tennessee Anthropologist* 3(2):203–210.

Gillespie, W. H., and J. A. Clendening
1968 A Flora from Proglacial Lake Monongahela. *Castanea* 33:267–300.

Goodyear, A. C.
1982 The Chronological Position of the Dalton Horizon in the Southeastern United States. *American Antiquity* 47:382–395.

Goslin, R. M.
1961 Projectile Point in Elk Skeleton. *Ohio Archaeologist* 11(3):85.

Graham, R. W.
1976 Late Wisconsin Mammalian Faunas and Environmental Gradients of the Eastern United States. *Paleobiology* 2:343–350.

Graham, R. W., C. V. Haynes, D. L. Johnson, and M. Kay
1981 Kimmswick: A Clovis—Mastodon Association in Eastern Missouri. *Science* 213:1115–1117.

Graham, R. W., J. A. Holman, and P. W. Parmalee
1983 *Taphonomy and Paleoecology of the Christensen Bog Mastodon Bone Bed, Hancock County, Indiana.* Reports of Investigations No. 38. Illinois State Museum, Springfield.

Graham, R. W., and M. Kay
1988 Taphonomic Comparisons of Cultural and Noncultural Faunal Deposits at the Kimmswick and Barnhart Sites, Jefferson County, Missouri. In *Late Pleistocene and Early Holocene Paleoecology and Archeology of the Eastern Great Lakes Region,* edited by R. S. Laub, N. G. Miller, and D. W. Steadman, pp. 227–240. *Bulletin of the Buffalo Society of Natural Sciences* No. 33. Buffalo.

Graham, R. W., and J. I. Mead
1987 Environmental Fluctuations and Evolution of Mammalian Faunas During the Last Deglaciation in North America. In *North America and Adjacent Areas During the Last Deglaciation: The Geology of North America*, vol. K-3, edited by W. F. Ruddiman and H. E. Wright, Jr., pp. 13–37. Geological Society of America, Boulder.

Gramly, R. M.
1988 Discoveries at the Lamb Site, Genesee County, New York, 1986–7. *Ohio Archaeologist* 38(1):4–10.

Gramly, R. M., and F. E. Funk
1990 What Is Known and Not Known About the Human Occupation of the Northeastern United States Until 10,000 B.P. *Archaeology of Eastern North America* 18:5–31.

Gramly, R. M., and G. L. Summers
1986 Nobles Pond: A Fluted Point Site in Northeastern Ohio. *Midcontinental Journal of Archaeology* 11:97–123.

Grayson, D. K.
1987 An Analysis of Late Pleistocene Mammalian Extinctions in North America. *Quaternary Research* 25:281–289.

1988 Perspectives on the Archaeology of the First Americans. In *Americans Before Columbus: Ice Age Origins*, edited by R. C. Carlisle, pp.107–123. Ethnology Monographs No. 12. Department of Anthropology, University of Pittsburgh, Pittsburgh.

1989 The Chronology of North American Late Pleistocene Extinctions. *Journal of Archaeological Science* 16:153–165.

Greenland Ice-core Project Members
1993 Climate Instability During the Last Interglacial Period Recorded in the GRIP Ice Core. *Nature* 364:203–207.

Griffin, J. B.
1965 Late Quaternary Prehistory in the Northeastern Woodlands. In *The Quaternary of the United States*, edited by H. E. Wright, Jr. and D. G. Frey, pp. 655–667. Princeton University Press, Princeton.

1968 Observations on Illinois Prehistory in Late Pleistocene and Early Recent Times. In *The Quaternary of Illinois*, edited by R. E. Bergstrom, pp. 123–137. Special Publication No. 14. College of Agriculture, University of Illinois, Urbana.

Gruger, E.
1972 Pollen and Seed Studies of Wisconsinan Vegetation in Illinois, U.S.A. *Geological Society of America Bulletin* 83:2715–2734.

Guilday, J. E.
1984 Pleistocene Extinctions and Environmental Change: Case Study of the Appalachians. In *Quaternary Extinctions: A Prehistoric Revolution*, edited by P. S. Martin and R. G. Klein, pp. 250–258. University of Arizona Press, Tucson.

Hall, D. A.
1993a Ohio Focus Illuminates Wider Puzzle. *Mammoth Trumpet* 8(2):1, 3.

1993b Worked Flint Found with Mastodon Bones. *Mammoth Trumpet* 8(4):1, 8.

Haynes, C. V., Jr.
1966 Elephant-hunting in North America. *Scientific American* 214:104–112.

1977 When and From Where Did Man Arrive in Northeastern North America: A Discussion. In *Amerinds and Their Paleoenvironments in Northeastern North America*, edited by W. S. Newman and B. Salwen, pp. 165–166. *Annals of the New York Academy of Sciences* 288.

1980a Paleoindian Charcoal from Meadowcroft Rockshelter: Is Contamination a Problem? *American Antiquity* 45:582–587.

1980b The Clovis Culture. *Canadian Journal of Anthropology* 1:115–121.

1991 More on Meadowcroft Radiocarbon Chronology. *The Review of Archaeology* 12(1):8–14.

Haynes, C. V., Jr., D. J. Donahue, A. J. T. Jull, and T. H. Zabel
1984 Application of Accelerator Dating to Fluted Point Paleoindian Sites. *Archaeology of Eastern North America* 12:184–191.

Haynes, G.
1988 Longitudinal Studies of African Elephant Death and Bone Deposits. *Journal of Archaeological Science* 15:131–157.

Herbstritt, J. T.
1988 A Reference for Pennsylvania Radiocarbon Dates. *Pennsylvania Archaeologist* 58(2):1–29.

Holman, J. A., and F. Grady
1987 Herpetofauna of New Trout Cave. *National Geographic Research* 3(3):305–317.

Holsten, J. N., and D. R. Cochran
1986 *Paleo-Indian and Early Archaic in the Upper Wabash Drainage*. Reports of Investigations No. 19. Archaeological Resources Management Service, Ball State University, Muncie.

Howard, C. D.
1988 Fluting Technology at the Lincoln Hills Site. *Plains Anthropologist* 33:395–398.

Howard, E. B.
1935 Evidence of Early Man in America. *The Museum Journal* 24:2–3.

Hurley, W. M.
1965 Archaeological Research in the Projected Kickapoo Reservoir, Vernon County, Wisconsin. *Wisconsin Archeologist* 46(1):1–114.

Hyde, E. W.
1960 *Mid-Ohio Valley Paleo-Indian and Suggested Sequence of the Fluted Point Cultures*. Publication Series No. 5. West Virginia Archaeological Society.

Jackson, L. J.
1978 *Late Wisconsin Environments and Palaeo-Indian Occupation in the Northeastern United States and Southern Ontario*. Master's thesis, Trent University, Peterborough, ON.

1983 Geochronology and Settlement Disposition in the Early Palaeo-Indian Occupation of Southern Ontario. *Quaternary Research* 19:388–399.

1984 Early Palaeo-Indian Occupation in Interior South-central Ontario: The Plainville Complex. *Arch Notes* 84(6):9–13.

1988 Fossil Cervids and Fluted Point Hunters: A Review for Southern Ontario. *Ontario Archaeology* 48:27–41.

Jacobson, G. L., Jr., T. Webb, III, and E. C. Grimm
1987 Patterns and Rates of Vegetation Change During the Deglaciation of Eastern North America. In *North America and Adjacent Areas During the Last Deglaciation: The Geology of North America*, vol. K-3, edited by W. F. Ruddiman and H. E. Wright, Jr., pp. 13–37. Geological Society of America, Boulder.

Jansen, E., and T. Veum
1990 Evidence for Two-step Deglaciation and Its Impact on North Atlantic Deep-water Circulation. *Nature* 343:612–616.

Jenks, A.
1936 *Pleistocene Man in Minnesota: A Fossil Homo Sapiens*. University of Minnesota Press, Minneapolis.

Judge, W. J.
1974 An Interpretive Summary of the PaleoIndian Occupation of the Plains and Southwest. Ms. submitted to *Handbook of North American Indians*, W. C. Sturtevant, general editor. Smithsonian Institution, Washington, D.C.

Julig, P. J.
1984 Cummins Paleo-Indian Site and Its Paleoenvironment, Thunder Bay, Canada. *Archaeology of Eastern North America* 12:192–209.

1985 The Sheguiandah Site Stratigraphy: A Perspective from the Lake Superior Basin. *Ottawa Archaeologist* 12(8):3–13.

1988 *The Cummins Site Complex and Paleoindian Occupations in the Northwestern Lake Superior Region*. Ph.D. dissertation, University of Toronto, Toronto.

1991 Late Pleistocene Archaeology in the Great Lakes Region of North America: Current Problems and Prospects. *Journal of American Archaeology* 3:7–30.

Karrow, P. F., and B. G. Warner
1988 Ice, Lakes, and Plants, 13,000 to 10,000 Years B.P.: The Erie-Ontario Lobe in Ontario. In *Late Pleistocene and Early Holocene Paleoecology and Archeology of the Eastern Great Lakes Region,* edited by R. S. Laub, N. G. Miller, and D. W. Steadman, pp. 39–52. *Bulletin of the Buffalo Society of Natural Sciences* No. 33. Buffalo.

Kelly, R. L.
1987 A Comment on the Pre-Clovis Deposits at Meadowcroft Rockshelter. *Quaternary Research* 27:332–334.

Kelly, R. L., and L. C. Todd
1988 Coming into the Country: Early Paleoindian Hunting and Mobility. *American Antiquity* 53:231–244.

Kenyon, I. T.
1980 The George Davidson Site: An Archaic "Broadpoint" Component in Southwestern Ontario. *Archaeology of Eastern North America* 8:11–27.

Kirkpatrick, M. J., and D. C. Fisher
1993 Preliminary Research on the Moon Mammoth Site. *Current Research in the Pleistocene* 10:70–71.

Klippel, W. E.
1971 *Graham Cave Revisited: A Reevaluation of Its Cultural Position During the Archaic Period.* Memoir No. 9. Missouri Archaeological Society.

Koldehoff, B.
1983 Paleo-Indian Chert Utilization and Site Distribution in Southwestern Illinois. *Wisconsin Archaeologist* 64(3-4):201–238.

Konitzky, G. A.
1988 Deep, Stratified Sites in the Upper Allegheny Valley. Paper presented at 55th Annual meeting, Eastern States Archaeological Federation, Toronto.

Kouba, T. F.
1985 Letter. *Wisconsin Archeologist* 66(1):77.

Lantz, S. W.
1984 Distribution of Paleo-Indian Projectile Points and Tools from Western Pennsylvania: Implications for Regional Differences. *Archaeology of Eastern North America* 12:210–230.

Leach, E. K., and G. T. Conaty
1988 Subsistence Models for the Midcontinent and the Environmental Record. In *Diet and Subsistence: Current Archaeological Perspectives,* edited by B. V. Kennedy and G. M. LeMoine, pp. 32–42. Archaeological Association of the University of Calgary, Alberta.

Lee, T. E.
1954 The First Sheguiandah Expedition, Manitoulin Island, Ontario. *American Antiquity* 20:101–111.

1955 The Second Sheguianday Expedition, Manitoulin Island, Ontario. *American Antiquity* 21:63–71.

1956 Position and Meaning of a Radiocarbon Sample from the Sheguiandah Site, Ontario. *American Antiquity* 22:79.

1957 The Antiquity of the Sheguiandah Site. *Canadian Field Naturalist* 71:117–137.

Lepper, B. T.
1983 Fluted Point Distributional Patterns in the Eastern United States: A Contemporary Phenomenon. *Midcontinental Journal of Archaeology* 8(2):269–285.

1986a *Early Paleo-Indian Land Use Patterns in the Central Muskingum River Basin, Coshocton County, Ohio.* Ph.D. dissertation, Department of Anthropology, Ohio State University, Columbus.

1986b The "Mason-Quimby Line": Paleo-Indian Frontier, or Methodological Illusion? *The Chesopiean* 24(1):2–9.

1988 Early Paleo-Indian Foragers of Midcontinental North America. North *American Archaeologist* 9:31–51.

1989 Lithic Resource Procurement and Early Paleoindian Land Use Patterns in the Appalachian Plateau of Ohio. In *Eastern Paleoindian Lithic Resource Use,* edited by C. J. Ellis and J. C. Lothrop, pp. 239–257. Westview Press, Boulder.

1993 Ice Age Peoples of the Great Lakes. *Datum Points,* Newsletter of the Michigan Archaeological Society, 2(1):3–8.

1994 Locating Early Sites in the Central Ohio Valley: Lessons from the Manning Site. In *First Discovery of America: Archaeological Evidence of the Early Inhabitants of the Ohio Area,* edited by W. S. Dancey. Ohio Archaeological Council, Columbus.

Lepper, B. T. and L. S. Cummings
1993 Early Holocene Archaeology and Paleoecology of the Manning Site (33Ct476) in Southern Ohio. *Current Research in the Pleistocene* 10:32–34.

Lepper, B. T., T. A. Frolking, D. C. Fisher, G. Goldstein, D. A. Wymer, J. E. Sanger, J. G. Ogden, III, and P. E. Hooge
1991 Intestinal Contents of a Late Pleistocene Mastodont from Midcontinental North America. *Quaternary Research* 36:120–125.

Lepper, B. T., and J. B. Gill
1991 Recent Excavations at the Munson Springs Site, a Paleoindian Base Camp in Central Ohio. *Current Research in the Pleistocene* 8:39–41.

Lepper, B. T., and D. J. Meltzer
1991 Late Pleistocene Human Occupation of the Eastern United States. In *Clovis: Origins and Adaptations,* edited by R. Bonnichsen and K. L. Turnmire, pp.175–184. Center for the Study of the First Americans, Oregon State University, Corvallis.

Lepper, B. T., and N. L. Wright
1989 The Welling/Nellie Heights Site Complex: A Fluted Point Workshop and Habitation Locus in Coshocton County, Ohio. In *First World Summit Conference on*

the Peopling of the Americas, Abstracts, edited by J. Tomenchuk and R. Bonnichsen, p. 29. Center for the Study of the First Americans, University of Maine, Orono.

Lopinot, N. H.
1988 Hansen Site (15 Gp 14) Archaeobotany. In *Excavations at the Hansen Site in Northeastern Kentucky*, edited by S. R. Ahler, pp. 571–623. Program for Cultural Resource Assessment, Archaeological Report No. 173. University of Kentucky, Lexington.

Lundelius, E. L., Jr.
1988 What happened to the Mammoths? The Climate Model. In *Americans Before Columbus: Ice Age Origins*, edited by R. C. Carlisle, pp. 75–82. Ethnology Monographs No. 12. Department of Anthropology, University of Pittsburgh, Pittsburgh.

Lundelius, E. L., Jr., R. W. Graham, E. Anderson, J. Guilday, J. A. Holman, D. W. Steadman, and S. D. Webb
1983 Terrestrial Vertebrate Faunas. In *The Late Pleistocene*, edited by S. C. Porter, pp. 311–353. *Late Quaternary Environments of the United States, vol. 1*, H. E. Wright, Jr., general editor. University of Minnesota Press, Minneapolis.

MacDonald, G. F.
1983 Eastern North America. In *Early Man in the New World*, edited by R. Shutler, Jr., pp. 97–108. Sage Publications, Beverly Hills.

MacNeish, R. S.
1952 A Possible Early Site in the Thunder Bay District, Ontario. *National Museum of Canada Bulletin* 126:23–47.

Martin, P. S.
1967 Prehistoric Overkill. In *Pleistocene Extinctions*, edited by P. S. Martin and H. E. Wright, Jr., pp. 75–120. Yale University Press, New Haven.

1973 The Discovery of America. *Science* 179:969–974.

Martin, P. S., and R. G. Klein (editors)
1984 *Quaternary Extinctions: A Prehistoric Revolution*. University of Arizona Press, Tucson.

Mason, R. J.
1958 *Late Pleistocene Geochronology and the Paleo-Indian Penetration into the Lower Michigan Peninsula*. Anthropological Papers No. 11. Museum of Anthropology, University of Michigan, Ann Arbor.

1962 The Paleo-Indian Tradition in Eastern North America. *Current Anthropology* 3:227–246.

1981 *Great Lakes Archaeology*. Academic Press, New York.

1986 The Paleo-Indian Tradition. *Wisconsin Archaeologist* 67(3-4):181–206.

Mason, R. J., and C. Irwin
1960 An Eden–Scottsbluff Burial in Northeastern Wisconsin. *American Antiquity* 26:43–57.

Mason, R. P.
1988 Preliminary Report on the Fluted Point Component at the Aebischer Site (47Ct30) in Calumet County, Wisconsin. *Wisconsin Archaeologist* 69(4):211–226.

Mayewski, P. A., G. H. Denton, and T. J. Hughes
1980 Late Wisconsin Ice Sheets in North America. In *The Last Great Ice Sheets*, edited by G. H. Denton and T. J. Hughes, pp. 67–170. John Wiley and Sons, New York.

McConaughy, M. A., J. D. Applegarth, and D. J. Faingnaert
1977 Fluted Points from Slippery Rock, Pennsylvania. *Pennsylvania Archaeologist* 47(4):30–36.

McMillan, R. B.
1976 Man and Mastodon: A Review of Koch's 1840 Pomme de Terre Expeditions. In *Prehistoric Man and His Environments: A Case Study in the Ozark Highlands*, edited by W. R. Wood and R. B. McMillan, pp. 81–96. Academic Press, New York.

Mead, J. I.
1980 Is It Really That Old? A Comment About the Meadowcroft Rockshelter "Overview." *American Antiquity* 45:579–582.

Mead, J. I., and D. J. Meltzer (editors)
1985 *Environments and Extinctions: Man in Late Glacial North America*. Center for the Study of Early Man, University of Maine, Orono.

Meltzer, D. J.
1984 *Late Pleistocene Human Adaptations in Eastern North America*. Ph.D. dissertation, Department of Anthropology, University of Washington, Seattle.

1985 On Stone Procurement and Settlement Mobility in Eastern Fluted Point Groups. *North American Archaeologist* 6:1–24.

1988 Late Pleistocene Human Adaptations in Eastern North America. *Journal of World Prehistory* 2(1):1–52.

1989 Why Don't We Know When the First People Came to North America? *American Antiquity* 54:471–490.

Meltzer, D. J., and B. D. Smith
1986 Paleoindian and Early Archaic Subsistence Strategies in Eastern North America. In *Foraging, Collecting and Harvesting: Archaic Period Subsistence and Settlement in the Eastern Woodlands*, edited by S. W. Neusius, pp. 3–31. Occasional Paper No. 6. Center for Archaeological Investigations, Southern Illinois University at Carbondale.

Mocas, S. T.
1977 Excavations at the Lawrence site, 15 Tr 33, Trigg County, Kentucky. Ms. on file, University of Louisville Archaeological Survey, Louisville.

Moeller, R. W.
1983 There is a Fluted Baby in the Bath Water. *Archaeology of Eastern North America* 11:27–29.

Morgan, A. V.
1973 Late Pleistocene Environmental Changes Indicated by Fossil Insect Faunas of the English Midlands. *Boreas* 2:173–212.

1987 Late Wisconsin and Early Holocene Paleoenvironments of East-central North America Based on Assemblages of Fossil Coleoptera. In *North America and Adjacent Areas During the Last Deglaciation: The Geology of North America*, vol. K-3, edited by W. F. Ruddiman and H. E. Wright, Jr., pp. 13–37. Geological Society of America, Boulder.

Morton, J., and J. Carskadden
1975 Excavations at an Archaic Open Site. *Ohio Archaeologist* 25(2):16–19.

Moxley, R. W.
1982 The Denison Site (46 LG 16): A Mountaintop Site in Logan County. *West Virginia Archeologist* 34:34–42.

Munson, P. J., and J. C. Frye
1965 Artifact from Deposits of Mid-Wisconsin Age in Illinois. *Science* 150:1722–1723.

Murphy, J. L.
1977 Radiocarbon Date from the Globe Hill Shell Heap (46HK34-1), Hancock County, West Virginia. *Pennsylvania Archaeologist* 17(1):19–24.

Newman, M., and P. Julig
1989 The Identification of Protein Residues on Lithic Artifacts From a Stratified Boreal Forest Site. *Canadian Journal of Archaeology* 13:119-132.

Nicholas, G. P.
1984 Recommendations for the Management of Early Postglacial Archaeological Resources. Paper presented at the American Anthropological Association Annual Meeting, Denver.

Niquette, C. M.
1986 A Paleo-Indian Projectile Point Survey in South-central Kentucky. Ms. on file, Cultural Resource Analysts, Inc., Lexington.

Ogden, J. G., III
1977 The Late Quaternary Paleoenvironmental Record of Northeastern North America. In *Amerinds and Their Paleoenvironments in Northeastern North America*, edited by W. S. Newman and B. Salwen, pp. 16–34. *Annals of the New York Academy of Sciences* 288.

Overstreet, D. F.
1987 *Sub-surface Evaluation of 47 KN 40 and 47 KN 56/134, Kenosha County, Wisconsin.* Reports of Investigation No. 199. Great Lakes Archaeological Research Center, Inc.

Overstreet, D. F., D. J. Joyce, K. F. Hallin, and D. Wasion
1993 Cultural Contexts of Mammoth and Mastodont in the Southwestern Lake Michigan Basin. *Current Research in the Pleistocene* 10:75–77.

Palmer, H. A., and J. B. Stoltman
1976 The Boaz Mastodon: A Possible Association of Man and Mastodon in Wisconsin. *Midcontinental Journal of Archaeology* 1:163–177.

Payne, J.
1982 The Western Basin Paleo-Indian and Early Archaic Sequences. Unpublished B.A. honors thesis, Department of Sociology, Anthropology and Social Work, University of Toledo, Toledo.

1987 *Windy City (154-16): A Paleoindian Lithic Workshop in Northern Maine.* Unpublished master's thesis, Institute for Quaternary Studies, University of Maine, Orono.

Peers, L.
1985 Ontario Paleo-Indians and Caribou Predation. *Ontario Archaeology* 43:31–40.

Peru, D. V.
1967 The Distribution of Fluted Points in Cass County, Michigan. *Michigan Archaeologist* 13(3):137–146.

Prufer, O. H.
1971 Survey of Palaeo-Indian Remains in Walhonding and Tuscarawas Valleys, Ohio. *Ohio Archaeologist* 21:309–310.

Prufer, O. H., and R. S. Baby
1963 *Palaeo-Indians of Ohio.* Ohio Historical Society, Columbus.

Prufer, O. H., and N. L. Wright
1970 The Welling Site (33 Co 2): A Fluted Point Workshop in Coshocton County, Ohio. *Ohio Archaeologist* 20:259–268.

Quimby, G. I.
1958 Fluted Points and Geochronology of the Lake Michigan Basin. *American Antiquity* 23:247–254.

1960 *Indian Life in the Upper Great Lakes, 11,000 B.C. to A.D. 1900.* University of Chicago Press, Chicago.

Reagan, M. J.
1976 Lithic Analysis of Excavation Units A11 and A12. In *Archaeological Investigations at the Shriver Site, 23 DV 12 Davies County, Missouri 1975–1976,* edited by M. J. Reagan and D. R. Evans, pp. 183–217. Department of Anthropology, University of Missouri, Columbia.

Reagan, M. J., R. M. Rowlett, E. G. Garrison, W. Dort, Jr., V. M. Bryant, Jr., and C. J. Johannsen
1978 Flake Tools Stratified Below Paleo-Indian Artifacts. *Science* 200:1272–1275.

Ritchie, W. A.
1957 *Traces of Early Man in the Northeast.* New York State Museum and Science Service Bulletin 358.

1983 The Mystery of Things Paleo-Indian. *Archaeology of Eastern North America* 11:30–33.

Ritzenthaler, R.
1966 The Kouba Site: Paleo-Indians in Wisconsin. *Wisconsin Archeologist* 47(4):171–187.

1967 A Cache of Paleo-Indian Gravers from the Kouba Site. *Wisconsin Archeologist* 48(3):261–262.

1972 The Pope Site: A Scottsbluff Cremation? in Waupaca County. *Wisconsin Archeologist* 53(1):15–19.

Rolingson, M. A.
1964 *Paleo-Indian Culture in Kentucky: A Study Based on Projectile Points.* Studies in Anthropology No. 2. University of Kentucky Press, Lexington.

Roosa, W. B.
1965 Some Great Lakes Fluted Point Types. *Michigan Archaeologist* 11(3-4):89–102.

1977 Great Lakes Paleoindian: The Parkhill Site, Ontario. In *Amerinds and Their Paleoenvironments in Northeastern North America*, edited by W. S. Newman and B. Salwen, pp. 349–354. *Annals of the New York Academy of Sciences* 288.

Rowlett, R. M.
1981 A Lithic Assemblage Stratified Beneath a Fluted Point Horizon in Northwest Missouri. *Missouri Archaeologist* 42:7–16.

Rowlett, R. M., and E. G. Garrison
1984 Analysis of Shriver Site Artifacts by Thermoluminescence. *Missouri Archaeological Society Quarterly* 1(4):20–22.

Ruddiman, W. F., and H. E. Wright, Jr. (editors)
1987 *North America and Adjacent Areas During the Last Deglaciation: The Geology of North America*, vol. K-3. Geological Society of America, Boulder.

Rule, P. A.
1983 *The Development of Regional Subtraditions in Clovis Culture.* Ph.D. dissertation, Arizona State University, University Microfilms, Ann Arbor.

Sanders, T. N.
1988 The Adams Site: A Paleoindian Manufacturing and Habitation Site in Christian County, Kentucky. In *Paleoindian and Archaic Research in Kentucky*, edited by C. D. Hockensmith, D. Pollack, and T. N. Sanders, pp. 1–24. Kentucky Heritage Council, Frankfort.

1990 *Adams: The Manufacturing of Flakes Stone Tools at a Paleoindian Site in Western Kentucky.* Persimmon Press, Buffalo, New York.

Sanders, T. N., and D. R. Maynard
1979 *A Reconnaissance and Evaluation of Archaeological Sites in Christian County, Kentucky.* Archaeological Report No. 12. Kentucky Heritage Council, Frankfort.

Schwartz, D.
1965 The Paleo-Indian Era: Distribution of Finds. *Southeastern Archaeological Conference Bulletin* 2:6–9.

Seeman, M. F., and O. H. Prufer
1982 An Updated Distribution of Ohio Fluted Points. *Midcontinental Journal of Archaeology* 7:155–169.

Shane, L. C. K.
1975 Palynology and Radiocarbon Chronology of Battaglia Bog, Porage County, Ohio. *Ohio Journal of Science* 75(2):96–102.

1976 *Late-Glacial and Postglacial Palynology and Chronology of Darke County, West-central Ohio.* Ph.D. dissertation, Kent State University, Kent.

1987 Late-Glacial Vegetational and Climatic History of the Allegheny Plateau and the Till Plains of Ohio and Indiana. *Boreas* 16:1–20.

Shetrone, H. C.
1936 The Folsom Phenomena as Seen from Ohio. *Ohio State Archaeological and Historical Society Quarterly* 45:240–256.

Shott, M. J.
1989 *Technological Organization in Great Lakes Paleoindian Assemblages. In Eastern Paleoindian Lithic Resource Use,* edited by C. J. Ellis and J.C. Lothrop, pp. 221–237. Westview Press, Boulder.

Shutler, R., Jr., and T. H. Charlton
1980 Southeast Iowa Lake Calvin Area Paleo-Indian Survey, Final Report. Ms. on file, Iowa State Historical Department, Division of Historic Preservation.

Simons, D. B.
1972 Radiocarbon Date from a Michigan Satchell-Type Site. *Michigan Archaeologist* 18(4):209–213.

Simons, D. B., M. J. Schott, and H. T. Wright
1984 The Gainey Site: Variability in Great Lakes Paleo-Indian Assemblage. *Archaeology of Eastern North America* 12:266–279.

1987 Paleoindian Research in Michigan: Current Status of the Gainey and Leavitt Projects. *Current Research in the Pleistocene* 4:27–30.

Smith, E. E.
1987 The Magnet Site: A Late Paleoindian Site in Southcentral Indiana. *Current Research in the Pleistocene* 4:32–33.

Spiess, A. E., and P. L. Storck
1990 New Faunal Identifications from the Udora Site: A Gainey-Clovis Occupation Site in Southern Ontario. *Current Research in the Pleistocene* 7:127–129.

Steinbring, J.
1974 The Preceramic Archaeology of Northern Minnesota. In *Aspects of Upper Great Lakes Anthropology,* edited by E. Johnson, pp. 64–73. Minnesota Historical Society, St. Paul.

1986 Rush Bay Road Excavations, Northwest Ontario. *Arch Notes* 86-5:10–16.

Steinbring, J., E. Danziger, and R. Callaghan
1987 Middle Archaic Petroglyphs in Northern North America. *Rock Art Research* 4(1):3–9.

Steinbring, J., and E. Nielsen
1986 Reinterpretation of the Rush Bay Road Site in Northwestern Ontario. *Manitoba Archaeological Quarterly* 10(1):4–34.

Stoltman, J.B., and D. A. Baerreis
1983 The Evolution of Human Ecosystems in the Eastern United States. In *The Holocene*, edited by H. E. Wright, Jr., pp. 252–268. *Late-Quaternary Environments of the United States, vol. 2*, H. E. Wright, Jr., general editor. University of Minnesota Press, Minneapolis.

Stoltman, J.B., and K. Workman
1969 A Preliminary Study of Wisconsin Fluted Points. *Wisconsin Archeologist* 50:189–214.

Storck, P. L.
1979 Early Man Research in Northeastern North America: A Brief Review and New Developments. *Early Man News* 3/4:83–91.

1981 A "Behind the Scenes" View of Fieldwork, or the Coming of Age of a Research Programme. *Royal Ontario Museum Archaeological Newsletter* No. 188 (N.S.).

1982 Palaeo-Indian Settlement Patterns Associated with the Strandline of Glacial Lake Algonquin in Southcentral Ontario. *Canadian Journal of Archaeology* 6:1–31.

1983 The Fisher Site, Fluting Techniques, and Early Palaeo-Indian Cultural Relationships. *Archaeology of Eastern North America* 11:80–97.

1984a Research into the Paleo-Indian Occupations of Ontario: A Review. *Ontario Archaeology* 41:3–28.

1984b Glacial Lake Algonquin and Early Palaeo-Indian Settlement Patterns in Southcentral Ontario. *Archaeology of Eastern North America* 12:286–298.

1988a The Early Palaeo-Indian Occupation of Ontario: Colonization or Diffusion? In *Late Pleistocene and Early Holocene Paleoecology and Archeology of the Eastern Great Lakes Region*, edited by R. S. Laub, N. G. Miller, and D. W. Steadman, pp. 243–250. *Bulletin of the Buffalo Society of Natural Sciences*, No. 33. Buffalo.

1988b Recent Excavations at the Udora Site: A Gainey/Clovis Occupation Site in Southwestern Ontario. *Current Research in the Pleistocene* 5:23–24.

1988c The Late Wisconsinan Ice Margin and Early Paleo-Indian Occupation in the Mid-continent Region. *Midcontinental Journal of Archaeology* 13:259–272.

1990 The Other Face of Time. *Archaeological Newsletter*, Royal Ontario Museum, Series II, No. 38.

Stothers, D. M.
1982 Earliest Man in the Western Lake Erie Basin. *Man in the Northeast* 23:39–48.

1983 The Satchell Complex: Tool Kit or Culture? *Arch Notes* 83-3:25–27.

Styles, B. W., S. R. Ahler, and M. L. Fowler
1983 Modoc Rockshelter Revisited. In *Archaic Hunters and Gatherers in the American Midwest*, edited by J. L. Phillips and J. A. Brown, pp. 261–297. Academic Press, New York.

Taggart, R. E., and A. T. Cross
1983 Indications of Temperate Deciduous Forest Vegetation in Association with Mastodon Remains from Athens County, Ohio (abstract). *Ohio Journal of Science* 83(2):26.

Tankersley, K. B.
1987 Big Bone Lick: A Clovis Site in Northcentral Kentucky. *Current Research in the Pleistocene* 4:36–37.

1989 A Close Look at the Big Picture: Early Paleoindian Lithic Procurement in the Midwestern United States. In *Eastern Paleoindian Lithic Resource Use*, edited by C. J. Ellis and J. C. Lothrop, pp. 259–292. Westview Press, Boulder.

Tankersley, K. B., and B. L. Isaac (editors)
1990 *Early Paleoindian Economies of Eastern North America.* Research in Economic Anthropology, Supplement 5, JAI Press, Inc., Greenwich, Connecticut.

Tankersley, K. B., and C. A. Munson
1992 Comments on the Meadowcroft Rockshelter Chronology and the Recognition of Coal Contaminants. *American Antiquity* 57:321–326.

Vesper, D., and R. Tanner
1984 Man and Mammoth in Kentucky. *Ohio Archaeologist* 34(3):18–19.

Vietzen, R. C.
1973 *Yesterday's Ohioans.* Privately printed and circulated.

Voss, J. A.
1977 The Barnes Site: Functional and Stylistic Variability in a Small Paleo-Indian Assemblage. *Midcontinental Journal of Archaeology* 2:253–305.

Watts, W. A.
1983 Vegetational History of the Eastern United States 25,000 to 10,000 years ago. In *The Late Pleistocene*, edited by S. C. Porter, pp. 294–310. *Late Quaternary Environments of the United States, vol. 1*, H. E. Wright, Jr., general editor. University of Minnesota Press, Minneapolis.

Walters, M. M.
1988 The Adams Mastodon Site, Harrison County, Kentucky. In *Paleoindian and Archaic Research in Kentucky*, edited by C. D. Hockensmith, D. Pollack, and T. N. Sanders, pp. 43–46. Kentucky Heritage Council.

Webb, W. S.
1951 The Parish Village Site. *University of Kentucky Reports in Anthropology* 7(6):403–451.

West, F. H.
1983 The Antiquity of Man in America. In *The Late Pleistocene,* edited by S. C. Porter, pp. 364–382. *Late Quaternary Environments of the United States, vol. 1,* H. E. Wright, Jr., general editor. University of Minnesota Press, Minneapolis.

Willey, G. R.
1966 *An Introduction to American Archaeology, vol. 1: North and Middle America.* Prentice-Hall, Englewood Cliffs, NJ.

Wittry, W. L.
1965 The Institute Digs a Mastodon. *Cranbrook Institute of Science Newsletter* 35(2):14–25.

Wood, W. R., and R. B. McMillan
1976 *Prehistoric Man and His Environments: A Case Study in the Ozark Highland.* Academic Press, New York.

Wormington, H. M.
1957 *Ancient Man in North America.* 4th edition. Denver Museum of Natural History, Denver.

Wright, H. E., Jr.
1970 Vegetational History of the Central Plains. In *Pleistocene and Recent Environments of the Central Great Plains,* edited by W. Dort, Jr. and J. K. Jones, pp. 157– 172. University Press of Kansas, Lawrence.

1976 Ice Retreat and Revegetation in the Western Great Lakes Area. In *Quaternary Stratigraphy of North America,* edited by W. C. Mahaney, pp. 119–132. Dowden, Hutchinson, and Ross, Stroudsburg, PA.

1981 Vegetation East of the Rocky Mountains 18,000 years Ago. *Quaternary Research* 15:113–125.

Wright, H. T., and W. B. Roosa
1966 The Barnes Site: A Fluted Point Assemblage from the Great Lakes Region. *American Antiquity* 31:850–860.

Wymer, D. A.
1987 *The Paleoethnobotanical Record of Central Ohio—100 B.C. to A.D. 800: Subsistence Continuity Amid Cultural Change.* Ph.D. dissertation, Ohio State University, Columbus.

Yahnig, C. H.
1989 The Christian County Cluster: Paleoindian Artifacts from Four Clovis Sites in Amerindland near Hopkinsville, Kentucky. In *The First World Summit Conference on the Peopling of the Americas, Abstracts,* edited by J. Tomenchuk and R. Bonnichsen, pp. 72. Center for the Study of the First Americans, University of Maine, Orono.

Young, D. E., and R. Bonnichsen
1984 *Understanding Stone Tools: A Cognitive Approach.* Center for the Study of Early Man, University of Maine, Orono.

Zakucia, J.
1956 The Buyler Mound, A Middle Woodland Manifestation. *Eastern States Archaeological Federation Bulletin* 15:10–11.

1974 New Radiocarbon Dates from the Upper Ohio Valley, Appendix A. In *The Boarts Site: A Lithic Workshop in Lawrence County, Pennsylvania,* by J. M. Adovasio, G. F. Fry, J. Gunn, and J. Zakucia. Pennsylvania Archaeologist 44(1-2):100–102.

Notes

1. The so-called "Younger Dryas climate event" may (Shane 1987) or may not (Morgan 1987) be represented in the paleoenvironmental record of eastern North America. The point here is that the rate of climate change could be rapid, even when measured on the scale of an individual Paleoindian's lifespan.

Radiocarbon Chronology of Northeastern Paleoamerican Sites: Discriminating Natural and Human Burn Features

Robson Bonnichsen[1]
Richard F. Will[2]

Abstract

An assessment of the radiocarbon chronology of 13 Paleoamerican sites from northeastern North America indicates that 54 percent of these sites have yielded ^{14}C dates of Holocene age. These dates are regarded as too young by site investigators. Other sites produced ^{14}C dates of Holocene and late Pleistocene age, and in many cases the origin of dated charcoal is not clear. The authors emphasize the importance of using a site formation approach for understanding how charcoal is incorporated into archaeological deposits and in determining whether it is of natural or cultural origin.

Various processes are responsible for introducing and mixing carbonized plant remains into archaeological site deposits. Forest fires, alluvial transport, tree throws, and cooking hearths are but a few. Frequently, however, the discovery of charcoal in sites is interpreted as the unique product of human behavior, especially when ^{14}C dates corroborate expectations of archaeological age. But archaeological sites occur on the natural landscape and as such are subjected to the same non-human processes that affect the non-cultural environment. Unless natural and cultural features in archaeological deposits can be discriminated, then doubt remains whether a ^{14}C dated charcoal sample dates a human or a natural event. Using northeastern North America as an example, it is suggested that some ^{14}C dated features on Paleoamerican sites may date natural events, and not the cultural activity responsible for the creation of the archaeological remains.

In view of the ambiguity that exists in the chronology of northeastern Paleoamerican sites, it is impossible on the basis of the existing radiocarbon chronology alone to ascertain with certainty if Paleoamerican sites in the Northeast are as old as elsewhere in the country. The placement of sites on ancient landforms associated with deglaciation does suggest that human colonization likely was coincident with regional deglaciation.

1. Founder and Director, Center for the Study of the First Americans; deceased December 2004. Address inquiries to CSFA Director Michael R. Waters, Department of Anthropology, Texas A&M University, 4352 TAMU, College Station, TX 77843-4352.
2. Archaeological Research Consultants, Inc., 71 Oak Street, Ellsworth ME 04605.

Introduction

CURRENT KNOWLEDGE of the chronology of Paleoamerican prehistory in northeastern North America is based largely on a series of ^{14}C dates from a few sites obtained over a 40-year period. As new sites have been found and dated, a corpus of dates gradually has developed that now serves as the foundation for understanding when human colonization occurred in this region. These ^{14}C dates, and some assumptions regarding contemporaneity with dated Paleoamerican sites in other regions, based on similarities in artifact form, provide the temporal framework for relating human populations to late Pleistocene landscapes of this region.

Human colonization and adaptive patterns can be related most effectively to paleoenvironments by use of ^{14}C dates from archaeological sites. In fact, ^{14}C dating plays a pivotal role in reconstructing the history of the past by allowing the correlation of diverse paleoenvironmental and archaeological records from the same time period. Some researchers have even argued that ^{14}C dating is the most important postwar development in archaeology—a development that has revolutionized archaeology (Levine 1990:33). Despite its profound impact on prehistoric studies, however, there sometimes has been a lack of methodological rigor in assessing ^{14}C sample origin and accuracy of dating results. With the objective of enhancing our understanding of the early chronology of Northeast prehistory, we have approached the analysis of the northeastern radiocarbon record by drawing on principles presented by contemporary approaches to site formation and taphonomy. These approaches question the old assumption that only human behavior need be considered in decoding patterning found in the archaeological record. Recent innovative research emphasizes the need for developing criteria for discriminating between patterning created by nature versus human behavior. Some archaeologists have concentrated on site formation (Schiffer 1983, 1987, 1988; Will and Clark 1996; Wood and Johnson 1978); other researchers have focused on how various processes affect bone assemblages (Binford 1981, 1983; Bonnichsen and Sorg 1989). These conceptual frameworks for explaining site formation and assemblage composition have implications for approaches to reconstructing the past. A significant shift in perception has come with the recognition that geological and paleoecological processes yield outcomes that can be confused with those produced by humans.

One purpose of this study is to explore how charcoal becomes buried and distributed in archaeological sites. Rather than assuming that charcoal from archaeological sites always has a human origin, we explore the likelihood that both humans and nature introduce charcoal into archaeological deposits. For example, when trees are uprooted, they leave depressions. Available charcoal can be transported into tree-throw depressions by wind, sheet erosion, or other mechanisms. Tree-throw depressions serve as catchment basins, and after burial may resemble fire hearths to the untrained eye. The ^{14}C dates obtained on charcoal from such features can cause great frustration and more than a little retrospective analysis on how to interpret site context and age. But unless the ^{14}C dates are considered anomalous, then there is every likelihood that error in feature identification will go unnoticed. Taylor (1987:108) suggests "the cause of the majority of seriously anomalous ^{14}C values is a misidentification of sample context provenance." If two or more burial mechanisms yield similar characteristics, the risk of misinterpretation is significantly increased. Chamberlin's (1897) approach of multiple working hypotheses provides a vehicle for considering alternative explanations to account for charcoal provenance. To demonstrate that one competing hypothesis is more likely than another requires development of empirical criteria that can be used to discriminate among hypotheses.

We begin with a discussion of a few of the natural processes that can introduce charcoal into buried sediments. The presentation of modern forest-fire and tree-throw dynamics and their effects on the stratigraphic record sets the stage for consideration of the ^{14}C chronological record from the Northeast. Understanding these natural processes permits the development of signature characteristics for distinguishing between the residue of human hearths and the residue of tree throws and forest fires in the stratigraphic record. The utility of this approach for interpreting archaeological site contexts is explored by examining the record from ^{14}C dated Paleoamerican sites in northeastern North America.

Forest Fires, Tree Throws, and Hearths

MODERN ANALOGS provide a direct approach for understanding how cultural and natural processes produce, deposit, and preserve charcoal in shallow subsurface deposits. Here, we discuss differences between charcoal samples accumulated by forest fires and tree throws and hearths.

Forest Fires and Tree Throws

ONLY ABOUT 5 PERCENT of fires are catastrophic in nature but they account for 95 percent of the acreage burned (Connor et al. 1989:296). As such, wildfires produce the vast majority of charcoal that has the potential to intrude into subsurface deposits, including archaeological sites. Large wildfires often are a coalescence of several smaller fires within a region. Burning is not uniform and occurs in a mosaic pattern. The interaction of several factors, including availability of fuel, moisture level, slope, and wind velocity, determine direction and intensity of burns.

Some data show that burning is associated with climatic change. Barnosky (1987:29), for example, indicates that a climatic shift during the last millennium has led to drier conditions and an increased fire frequency in the Yellowstone area. In the northeastern United States, the extent of both pine and birch in forests during the early Holocene between 10,000 and 8,000 years ago, as indicated in pollen samples, "suggests that conditions were dry over much of this region, and that fire frequency may have been higher than in later times" (Jacobson et al. 1987:282). The frequency of natural fires and their role in restructuring ecosystems is poorly understood because of the lack of long-term evidence. Clark's (1988a, 1988b, 1989) northwestern Minnesota research into the effects of climate change on fire regimes provides an important model for understanding the linkage between fire and climatic change. By examining fire-burn scars scorched into the cambium layer of pine trees, tree-ring drought indices, and charcoal from varved lake sediments, Clark illuminates long-term trends governing intensity and periodicity of burning.

Both low-intensity and high-intensity fires occur naturally. Clark (1989) indicates that hardwood forests usually decompose rapidly. They leave behind a layer of lignen—a major constituent of plant cell walls that also is very combustible. Coarse woody debris constitutes another type of fuel. As early succession species, such as paper birch and aspen, die out, their branches and stems litter the ground and produce dangerous fire conditions. When fires occur frequently, these fuels remain sparse, do not accumulate, and prevent catastrophic burning. Without fire, a thick layer of organic humus and deadwood accumulates on the forest floor. If humus dries during drought conditions, the stage is set for intense burning. Under these conditions, fire will move rapidly through the forest understory, igniting fallen woody debris.

Under natural conditions, for at least the past 700 years, periods without major fires have been the exception in Minnesota (Clark 1989). The maximum abundance and frequency of low-intensity fires in northwestern Minnesota occurred during the warm and dry 15th and 16th centuries. Lower intensity fires burned on the average of every eight years, with higher intensity fires every 40 to 50 years. With the onset of the moister and cooler conditions of the "Little Ice Age" about 400 yr B.P., fire intensity decreased dramatically. Small fires burned every 14 years, with larger fires every 80 to 90 years.

The 1988 catastrophic wildfire in the Yellowstone region provides a natural laboratory for investigating the effects of natural wildfires on sediments, even if it is argued that the event was the product of fire-suppression practices (see Connor et al. 1989). In seeking to understand the effects of intense burning, Connor et al. (1989) excavated several locations in the Grand Teton National Park and Yellowstone National Park areas. In general they observed that the depth of the burn layer varied with soil type, moisture content of soil, and intensity and duration of the fire. Since 1988 was a dry year, soil moisture was very low. The fires burned the duff on the forest floor and left a thin layer of burned material, about 5–10 cm thick. Below this layer occurred an unaltered soil. At the John D. Rockefeller, Jr., Memorial Parkway (JDR Parkway section) south of Yellowstone National Park (Connor et al. 1989:295, Figure 2), fire burned through the duff and charred the upper surface of roots. Wettstead (1988), working in the Ashland District of the Custer National Forest, Montana, reports cases where the root system was totally burned out. Only holes were left in the soil.

Fire temperature also plays a role in influencing what remains after a burn. Connor et al. (1989) note that white ash occurs where fuel combustion is complete. White ash is an indicator of burns with high surface temperatures in the range of 500–700°C. These deposits rapidly disappear with post-fire precipitation. For example, Connor and her team found no evidence of white ash in their excavation at a 1979 Jackson Lake,

Wyoming, burn. Throughout much of the recent Yellowstone burn, orange-stained soil is noticeable where there was no protective duff. Oxidation occurs when temperatures reach 100–700° C. Soil colors change from light brown (Munsell 7.5 YR 6/4) to orange. These stains occur below deadfall and beneath trees that fell during the fire. Stains have half-moon shapes and occur under the center of deadwood.

Tree Throws

LARGE FIRES HAVE the capability to generate winds resulting from convection currents. These winds can spread fire and affect intensity of burning; they also have the ability to produce blow downs of trees. Figure 1 illustrates an area of Yellowstone Park impacted by tree falls during the 1988 fire. With the removal of surface vegetation, opportunities for erosion are enhanced. Charcoal from burning of surface timber, as well as the standing forest, will be carried by sheet erosion into topographically low areas of tree-throw pits and be buried.

Other natural activity, such as trees dying from lightning strikes, the attack of pathogenic organisms, or wind and ice storms and related catastrophic events, can cause trees to topple over. The latter process greatly affects soil stratigraphy and literally can result in the soil being entirely turned over through time. For example, Norton (1988) used soil turnover half-life (the period of time in which half the soil has been turned over) to determine the area of soil disturbed in a New Zealand forest. He amplified previous estimates by factoring into his equation the tendency of trees to become reestablished on mounds (Lyford and MacLean 1966), the period of time in which a forest reestablishes itself in an opening and grows to maturity, and the propensity of a forest to be blown over again. He arrived at a soil turnover half-life of 2,960 years by applying his method to a long-lived conifer forest. Using this estimate, 90 percent of the soil in a forest would be disturbed by uprooting trees after 10,000 years. When considered in the context of northeastern North America, where paleoecological reconstructions show the area was colonized by forest around 10,500 yr B.P. (Jacobson et al. 1987), then the possibility of extensive soil disturbance due to tree throwing is great.

Tree uprooting also produces features on the landscape that remain discernible for many years (Figure 2). Schaetzl et al. 1988c; Putz and co-workers (Putz 1983; Putz et al. 1983:1012) explain that a tree is uprooted when subjected to lateral forces on the crown and stem that exceed root-soil holding strength and that fail to break the stem. Soil adheres to the roots of uprooted trees and contributes to characteristic pit/mound microtopography and inverted soil horizons. Pits mark the former position of the roots and a mound forms where soil slumps off a deteriorating, displaced root plate (Schaetzl et al. 1988a, 1988b).

Figure 1. 1988 burn area in Yellowstone National Park. Note common occurrence of fire-induced tree falls provides opportunities for accelerated erosion.

Figure 2. Illustration of forest following 1979 Grand Teton, Wyoming burn. Die off following burning leads to tree falls and pit mound topography.

The initial size of the pit is a function of depth and horizontal spread of root systems. The amount of soil disturbed by uprooting is dependent on the depth and spread of the root system. Root-plate size is primarily a function of tree size. For many trees, rooting depths continue to increase as a function of tree diameters, up to the limit of 40 cm at breast height, beyond which root systems do not appear to expand. Maximum root-plate volumes reach values of 4 m^3. Healthy trees disturb more soil than do dead or dying trees.

The size of a pit/mound pair is conditioned by the amount of soil that returns to the pit through slump, wash, and splash processes that decrease pit and mound volume. Some of the factors that affect the slump process are soil texture, structure, gravel content, freeze/thaw activity, rate of decay of the binding roots, faunal activity within and on the surface of the root plate, and efficiency of rainwash in dislodging soil from the root plate (Schaetzl et al. 1988a, 1988b).

Pit/mound microsurfaces can be classified on the basis of shape characteristics. Simple tree falls usually result in ovoid pits. Slight backward displacement during tree fall may form crescentic pits. Partial backward displacement of the root mass may result in two small pits on either side of a mound. A complete backward displacement of the root plate during fall may form a pit on the lee side of the mound (Schaetzl et al. 1988a, 1988b).

The slump of soil particles and clasts from the root plate is an effective soil mixing (pedoturbation) mechanism, often creating irregular and discontinuous horizons within the tree-throw mound and pit. If root decay and/or deterioration occurs slowly, material slumps off the root plate in small structural units. In this case, most, if not all, of the original soil horizonation may be lost. On the other hand, rapid decay of the root plate, as is often the case with hardwoods, may cause soil to fall off the plate before other processes can break up large horizon clasts, and this soil may become buried in the mound or pit. During the slump process, large sections of horizons may fold over each other. Additionally, rocks, gravel, and large clasts may be brought to the surface by uprooting and redeposited in the mounds or pits.

Visible pit/mound longevity is a function of soil environment and dating accuracy. Several lines of evidence, including tree rings, buried wood, mound morphology, soil, and ^{14}C ages, have been used to estimate age of pit/mound features (Schaetzl et al. 1988a:Table 1). These data suggest age ranges from about 2,000 years ago to the present. Older mounds may be leveled and pits completely filled by sediments and organic materials transported by slopewash. Only through controlled excavations, such as those conducted on archaeological sites, will fossil evidence for pit/mound topography routinely be exposed. We safely may assume that evidence for stratigraphic disturbance by tree throws has great time depth.

To summarize, factors that distinguish pits created by tree throws and forest fires include: (1) pit depressions have mounds on only one side; (2) pit sizes vary substantially in diameter from less than 0.5 m to more than 4 m; (3) pit shape in planview varies from ovoid to irregular; (4) pit cross-sections usually are not symmetrical and profile bottoms vary considerably; (5) soil inversions and/or clasts of soil horizons may be present in pit fill; (6) pit-fill deposits may contain mixed assemblages of charcoal from more than one burning event; (7) rocks, artifacts, and charcoal may be scattered throughout the pit fill but seldom, if ever, are concentrated in discrete layers; and 8) no oxidation zone is present in pit bottoms from prolonged burning.

Hearths

ETHNOARCHAEOLOGICAL STUDIES document that hearths are locations where socializing, cooking, manufacturing, and other activities occur (Jodry and Stanford 1992:155). This probably is true in prehistory as well. Although hearth functions vary from area to area, everyone understood the importance of fire for warmth, cooking, and for processing activities. Hearths generally occur in two forms: as simple surface features where fires are built on the ground and as pits. Pit hearths protect fires from winds and conserve energy by retaining and radiating heat upward.

Probably the most common type of fireplace simply was a fire on the ground surface. Unfortunately, the residual charcoal scatter from this type of feature is difficult to recognize in archaeological contexts. Definite shaped hearths from the Paleoamerican period are described here to provide analogs for what to expect in hearth sizes and other characteristics in late Pleistocene and early Holocene archaeological sites. Lorenzo and Mirambell (1986) report one of the earliest published hearths. This undisturbed feature consisted of a circle of proboscidean tarsal bones surrounding a zone of charcoal about 30 cm in diameter and 2 cm thick. At the Agate Basin site, in the Folsom component, the actual limits of some hearths are difficult to determine. A hearth from the upper Folsom level, approximately 75 cm in diameter and 13.1 cm deep, is illustrated by Frison and Stanford (1982:74, Figure 2.43). The lower Folsom level hearth is semi-circular in planview and 75 cm in diameter. It was 6 cm deep and contained a small amount of charcoal (Frison and Stanford 1982:71, Figure 2.81). Associated with the Hell Gap component or the Agate Basin site, a semi-circular hearth occurred as a shallow oval basin about 7 cm in depth, with a maximum diameter of 75 cm. Charcoal ash, calcined bone, and fractured tools were associated with this hearth. A second hearth in the Hell Gap component had a semi-circular outline with a maximum diameter of 75 cm (Frison and Stanford 1982:141). Its shallow basin was about 8 cm in maximum depth and included fire-cracked rocks and part of the proximal end of a Hell Gap projectile point.

Bryan (1979, 1988) reports five hearths at Smith Creek Cave, near Baker, Nevada, in association with the Mount Moriah occupation. Eight dates from these hearths range in age from 9940 ± 160 yr B.P. (Tx-1420) to 11,140 ± 200 yr B.P. (Tx-1637). Although hearth depths are not provided, all have oval shapes under 1 m in maximum length, as illustrated in planview (Bryan 1988:Figure 6). Ash deposits associated with these hearths suggest to Bryan that they were reused by the same social group through time.

Table 1. Some Attributes that Differentiate Natural Pit Features from Hearth Features.

Attribute	*Natural Feature*	*Hearth Feature*
Pit size	From less than 0.5 m to more than 4 m in diameter	Usually less than 1 m in diameter
Planview	Varies from ovoid to irregular	Symmetrical
Cross-section	Not symmetrical and variable floor profile	Symmetrical with even floor profile
Charcoal location	Scattered throughout pit fill and seldom concentrated in discrete layers	Charcoal usually concentrated on the pit floor
Oxidation zone	None in pit floor	Often under charcoal layer from prolonged burning
Backdirt location	Usually on one side only	Usually on more than one side

In view of the above discussion, characteristics selected for identifying potential hearths include: (1) pit sizes usually are less than 1.0 m in diameter; (2) pits have a symmetrical planview; (3) charcoal usually is concentrated on the pit floor; (4) hearth pits intrude through soil development horizons; (5) backdirt from pit excavation usually occurs on more than one side of the pit; (6) pit bottoms may have a burned oxidation zone under a charcoal layer; and (7) hearth pits may be rock-lined to enhance the heating capabilities of the hearth.

The attributes that differentiate natural pit features from hearths are shown in Table 1. Although there is some overlap in size categories, the features are distinguished in the aggregate. In addition, soil inversions and/or clasts of soil horizons are not uncommon in tree-throw features but unexpected in hearth features. Hearths may be rock-lined, but this is never a characteristic of a natural pit feature.

Radiocarbon Dating Northeastern Paleoamerican Sites

DURING THE LAST DECADE, numerous Paleoamerican sites have been reported from northeastern North America (Bonnichsen et al. 1991; Deller 1988; Ellis 1984; Gramly 1982; Jackson 1983; Lepper 1983; MacDonald 1983; Meltzer 1984, 1987; Spiess and Wilson 1987). We begin with a discussion of ^{14}C dated features where the results clearly did not date to the Paleoamerican period. Closer examination of features reveals that they likely were the products of natural rather than cultural events. Next, we examine sites where late Pleistocene or early Holocene ^{14}C dates have been obtained, but where it is difficult to determine from reports whether natural or cultural events are being dated. The objective of the exercise is not to call into question the scholarship of individual researchers, but to make a plea for better reporting on cultural features and some reconsideration of when Paleoamericans may have colonized northeastern North America. The sites selected for discussion include: the Munsungun Lake site-complex in northern Maine; the Nicholas site in southwestern, Maine; the

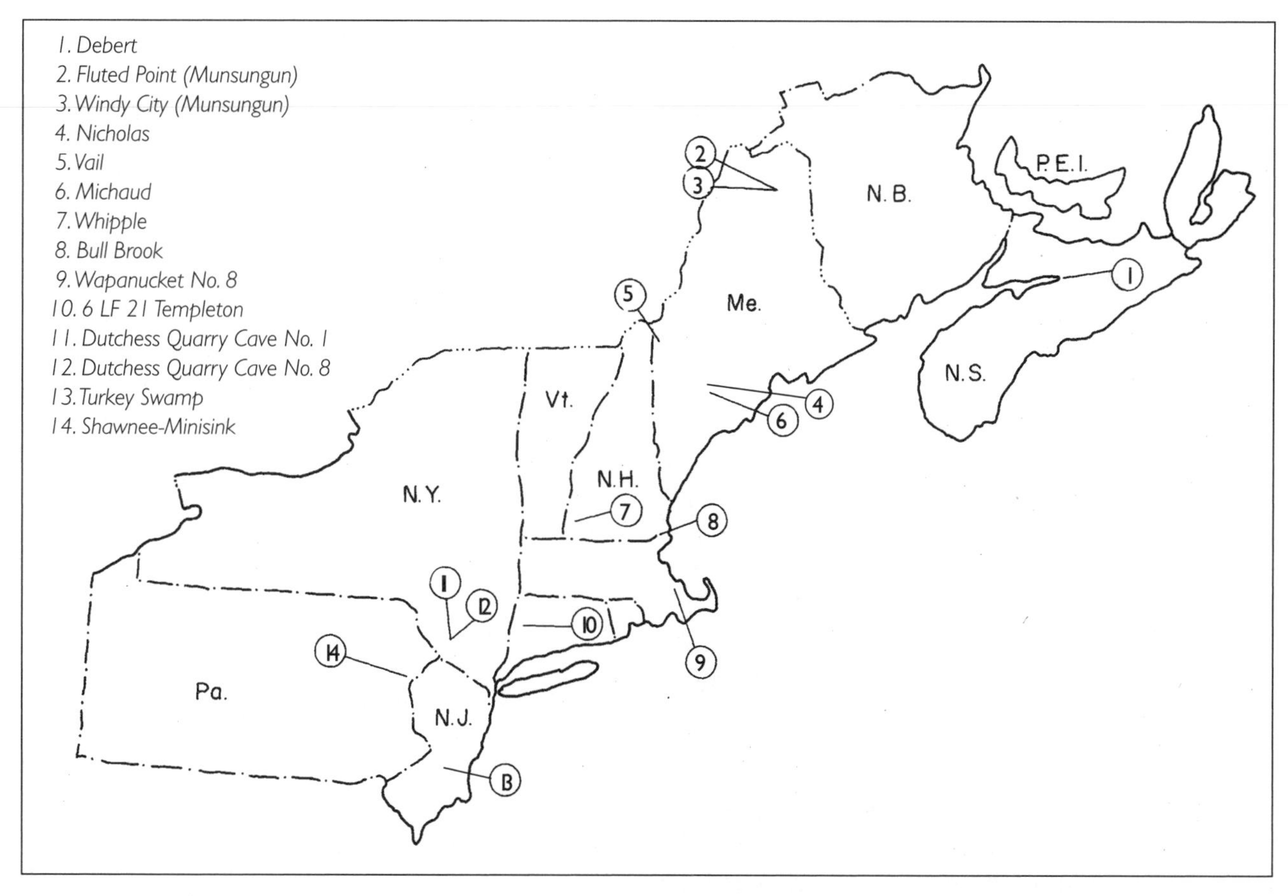

Figure 3. Locations of early sites in northeastern North America that are discussed in text.

Debert site, Nova Scotia; the Vail site in western Maine; the Michaud site in southern Maine; the Bull Brook site, Massachusetts; and the Dutchess Quarry Caves, No. 1 and No. 8, New York. A brief outline of site location, context, and stratigraphy is presented in conjunction with a discussion of the radiocarbon dates from each site. All cited ^{14}C dates are presented as uncorrected radiocarbon years before present. Rather than use the convention RCYRBP (radiocarbon years before present), we use yr B.P. to signify radiocarbon years before present.

Munsungun Lake Site-Complex

THE MUNSUNGUN LAKE site-complex is located in north-central Maine in the vicinity of Munsungun Lake, at the head of the Aroostook River drainage-system (Figure 3). During late glacial times, meltwater streams partially dissected the bedrock between the Chase and Munsungun lake basins, creating several glacial spillways. A series of kame terraces, marking former stream levels while ice was still in the basins, was deposited along the margins of the spillway channels (Bonnichsen 1984; Bonnichsen et al. 1981; Clay 1983). The Fluted Point and Windy City sites occur on the 14-m kame terrace and were the focus of excavations by University of Maine teams from 1980 to 1983.

The Fluted Point Site

THE FLUTED POINT SITE is located on the northwest end of Munsungun Lake and occurs between two glacial spillway channels on a section of the relatively flat north-south trending 14-m kame terrace. Shovel tests indicate human occupation covered the entire 3,000 m^2 ($^1/_3$ ha) of the terrace surface. Terrace sediments are composed of gravel and are overlain by about 0.5 m of colluvium. Till may underlay the gravel and is exposed at the base of a unit on the Fluted Point site (H. W. Borns, Jr. and D. Belknap, personal communication 1987). A thin spodosol, a podzolic soil, has developed in the colluvium. Post-glacial deposition has been minimal; most artifacts occur within 20 cm of the surface. See Bonnichsen et al. 1991 for a summary of the artifacts. Preliminary artifact analyses suggest this locality served as a workshop for manufacturing artifacts from nearby Munsungun Lake Formation cherts (Bonnichsen et al. 1981).

Charcoal samples from Munsungun were processed at the Smithsonian Institution Radiation Biology Laboratory, Washington, D.C. All samples received NaOH/Hcl pretreatment as well as nitration pretreatment for removal of all uncharred cellulose, including dissolved root material (Stuckenrath, personal communication 1981).

Feature 1, an intrusive pit, contained scattered charcoal, flakes, and burned rocks. It was interpreted as a hearth at the time of its discovery. Eight charcoal samples from the feature yielded radiocarbon determinations of 2810 + 60 yr B.P. (SI-4689), 3005 ± 40 yr B.P. (SI-4691), 3405 ± 45 yr B.P. (SI-4693), 3105 ± 80 yr B.P. (SI-4700), 3015 ± 70 yr B.P. (SI-4701), 3090 ± 75 yr B.P. (SI-4707), 3130 ± 65 yr B.P. (SI-4708), and 3265 ± 85 yr B.P. (SI-4713), with an average of 3103 yr B.P. (Table 2).

Four charcoal samples from a second "hearth" feature at the Fluted Point site yielded ^{14}C age determinations of 1150 ± 60 yr B.P. (SI-4715), 740 ± 64 yr B.P. (SI-4717), 830 ± 60 yr B.P. (SI-4718), and 905 ± 60 yr B.P. (SI-4719), with an average of 906 yr B.P. Soil dates run on the humic content of the local spodosol collected from several different locations at the site are 80 + 50 yr B.P. (SI-4684), 35 ± 50 yr B.P. (SI-4705), 185 ± 75 yr B.P. (SI-4705a) 410 ± 70 yr B.P. (SI-4706), and 945 ± 85 yr B.P. (SI-4703).

Upon receipt of these radiocarbon determinations of late Holocene age, and the acknowledgment that there were no contamination problems with the charcoal samples, the hypothesis that these features were Paleoamerican hearths had to be rejected. Re-examination of floor plans and stratigraphic contexts shows that the attributes of these features more closely resembled natural pits created when tree-throw cradles were filled with charcoal from natural burn events. Additional data support this conclusion. Orme (1982) suggests that plotting ^{14}C date errors to two standard deviations yields the most reliable results for interpreting radiocarbon ages. Figure 4 illustrates that the Munsungun radiocarbon ages cluster into three well-defined groups. The first cluster in the upper right-hand corner shows overlapping error bars between 3500 and 2800 yr B.P. The second cluster of radiocarbon determinations occurs between 1400 and 700 yr B.P. The third cluster of ages is based on humic soil samples, which cluster between 650 and 0 yr B.P.

The first two clusters suggest separate forest fires impacted the Munsungun Thoroughfare area. The last cluster of dates suggests that burning events may have destroyed the organic component of the upper soil

Table 2. Radiocarbon Dates from Northeastern Paleoamerican sites.

*Site/Material**	*14C Age*	*Lab No.*	*Reference*
Fluted Point Site154-14			
soil	80 ± 50	SI-4684	
cl	2810 ± 60	SI-4689	
cl	2455 ± 60	SI-4690	
cl	3005 ± 40	SI-4691	
cl	3405 ± 45	SI-4693	
cl	910 ± 100	SI-4695	
cl	340 ± 75	SI-4696	
cl	3105 ± 80	SI-4700	
cl	3015 ± 70	SI-4701	
cl	945 ± 85	SI-4703	
soil	35 ± 50	SI-4705	
soil	185 ± 75	SI-4705a	
soil	410 ± 70	SI-4706	
cl	3090 ± 75	SI-4707	
cl	3130 ± 65	SI-4708	
cl	3265 ± 85	SI-4713	
cl	1150 ± 60	SI-4715	
cl	740 ± 64	SI-4717	
cl	830 ± 60	SI-4718	
cl	905 ± 60	SI-4719	
Windy City			
(Feature 1) cl	3300	SI-N/A	Stuckenrath, pers. comm. 1986
Nicholas cl	6600 ± 90	Beta-81131	Wilson et. al. 1995
Debert			
pitch	5033 ± 70	P-744	MacDonald 1968
(Feature 3) cl	7685 ± 92	P-740	"
(Feature 4)	10,466 ± 128	P-743	"
(Feature 7) cl	10,656 ± 134	P-739	"
cl	10,545 ± 126	P-741	"
cl	10,572 ± 121	P-966	"
cl	10,641 ± 244	P-967	"
(Feature 11) cl	10,518 ± 120	P-970	"
(Feature 11) cl	10,467 ± 118	P-970A	"
(Feature 11) cl	10,773 ± 226	P-971	"
(Feature 12) cl	10,511 ± 120	P-972	"
(Feature 15) cl	10,652 ± 114	P-973	"
(Feature 16) cl	10,837 ± 119	P-974	"
(Feature 17) cl	11,026 ± 225	P-975	"
(Feature 19) cl	10,128 ± 275	P-977	"
(average of 13)	10,600 ± 47**	-	"
Vail Site			
(Feature 2) cl	10,500 ± 400	AA-117	Haynes et al. 1984
(Feature 1) cl	10,600 ± 400	AA-114	"
(Feature 2) cl	10,550 ± 800	AA-115	"
(average of 3)	10,500 ± 300		
(Feature 1) h	10,040 ± 400	AA-116	"
(Feature 1) cl	11,120 ± 180	Beta-1833	Gramly 1982
(Feature 1) cl	10,300 ± 90	SI-4617	"
Michaud			
cl	9010 ± 210	Beta-13833	Spiess and Brush 1987
cl	10,200 ± 620	Beta-15660	"
Whipple			
cl	9600 ± 500	AA-149a	Haynes et al. 1984
cl	9400 ± 500	AA-149a	"
cl	9700 ± 700	AA-149b	"
(average of 3)	9550 ± 320		"
cl	10,300 ± 500	AA-150a	Haynes et al. 1984
cl	11,400 ± 360	AA-150c	"
(average of 2)	11,050 ± 360		"
cl	8180 ± 360	GX-7496	Curran 1984
cl	8240 ± 340	GX-7497	Curran 1987
Bull Brook			
cl	6940 ± 800	M-809	Byers 1959
cl	9300 ± 400	M-807	"
cl	8940 ± 400	M-810	"
cl	8720 ± 400	M-808	"
cl	8560 ± 285	GX-6279	Grimes 1979
cl	7590 ± 255	GX-6278	"
cl	5440 ± 160	GX-6277	"
6LF-21/Templeton			
cl	10,190 ± 300	W-3931	Moeller 1980
Turkey Swamp			
cl	8739 ± 165	DIC-1059	Cavallo 1981
cl	7980 ± 150	DIC-1060	"
cl	7950 ± 110	DIC-1057	"
cl	7820 ± 215	DIC-1061	"
cl	7660 ± 325	DIC-1058	"
Dutchess Quarry Cave			
Cave No 1. b	12,530 ± 37	01-4317	Funk et al. 1970
Cave No 2. cl	5880 ± 340	DIC-14447	Kopper et al. 1980
Wapanucket No. 8			
cl	898 ± 100	Y-1168	Robbins and Agogino 1964
cl	4708 ± 140	M-1350	"

Code: cl=charcoal; h=humate; b=bone

**The average standard deviation of the 13 dates is 159, not 47.

horizon and that modern soil development did not begin until recent times. Corroborating evidence for local burning is found in the Chase Lake pollen diagram prepared by R. B. Davis (personal communication 1986). This unpublished pollen diagram indicates the presence of high charcoal counts in the Chase Lake pollen core at 3100 and 900 yr B.P. and again in historic times. Thus, it is reasonable to conclude that the shallowly buried Munsungun Lake sites have been seriously disturbed by tree throws and forest fires.

The Windy City Site

The Windy City site occurs within a thin mantle of loess on a point overlooking the outlet of Chase Lake (Figure 3). Its surface has a pit/mound topography and is partially covered by mature spruce (*Picea* sp.) and a forest mat. A shovel testing program revealed that flakes are distributed over about 200 m^2. See Payne (1987) and Bonnichsen et al. (1991) for discussion of the artifacts. During the 1983 field season, excavations exposed what initially was identified as a hearth (Figures 5 and 6). The fill deposits contained what appeared to be gray ash in association with fire-cracked rocks, and chert flakes. A charcoal lens exposed at the bottom of the feature yielded a radiocarbon age of 3300 yr B.P. (lab number was not assigned) (R. Stuckenrath, personal communication 1986). This unexpected date led to a reassessment of 135 mm colored slides of the feature. A more probable explanation is that a tree-throw pit, linked with a forest fire and sheet erosion, led to an association of charcoal, rock, and flakes within the pit. The orange color of the fill deposits likely is a disturbed B soil horizon. The gray ashy material from the bottom of the pit is not ash; rather it is an A2 soil horizon, part of a post-fire soil development. The 3300 yr B.P. determination from Windy City correlates well with the first cluster of dates from the Fluted Point site and it also correlates with the charcoal concentration from the Chase Lake pollen core.

The Nicholas Site

The Nicholas site is located on a former terrace of the Little Androscoggin River in Oxford, Maine (Wilson et al. 1995) (Figure 3). Four discrete loci covering approximately 25 m^2 each were discovered at this site and excavated in 1993 and 1994. They were deposited in sand near the terrace margin. The majority of artifacts were recovered between 10 and 50 cm below surface; the greatest density was found in a well-expressed B soil horizon. The site area had been previously plowed and disturbances caused by rodent activity were discernible. All of the loci contained

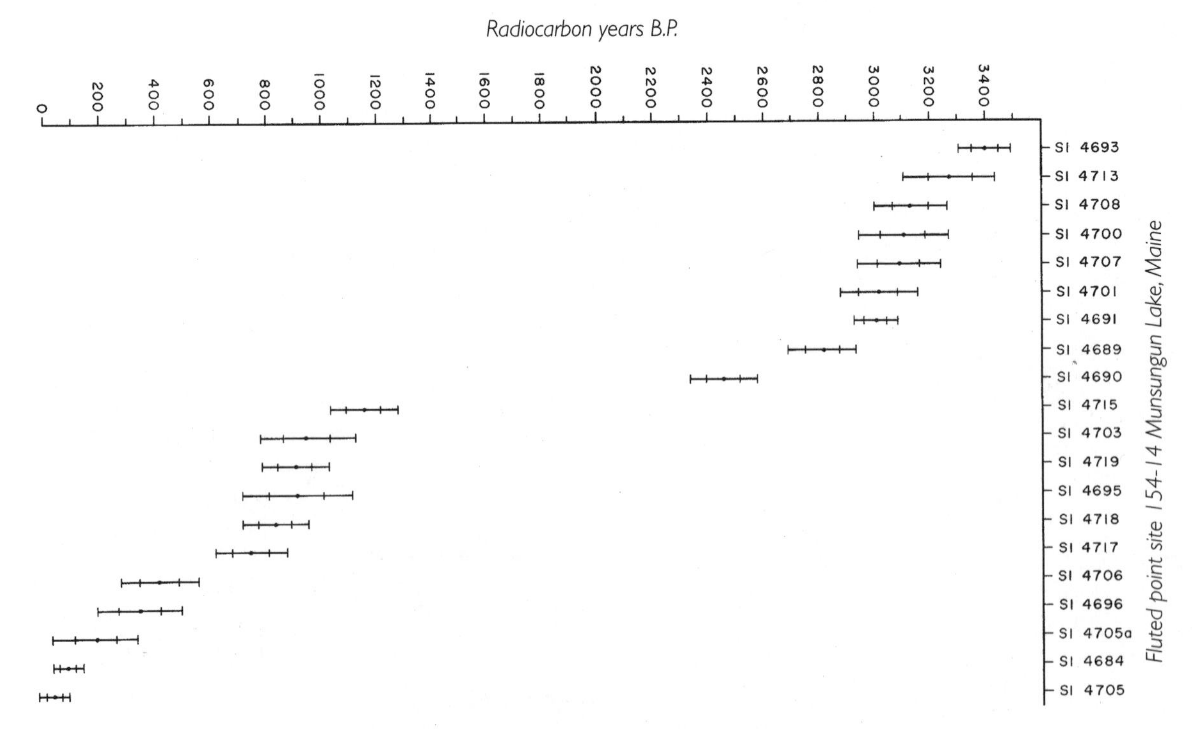

Figure 4. Radiocarbon dates from the Fluted Point site, Munsungun Lake Maine.

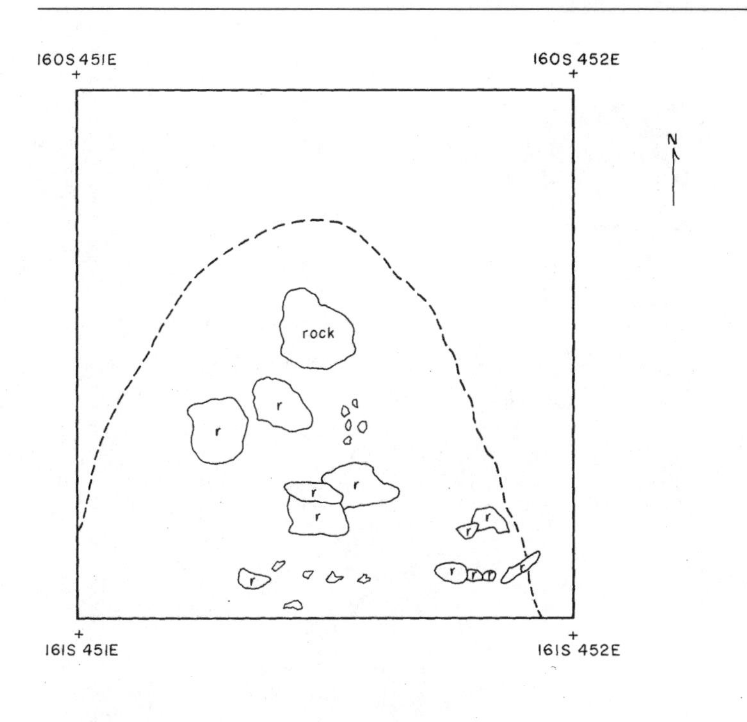

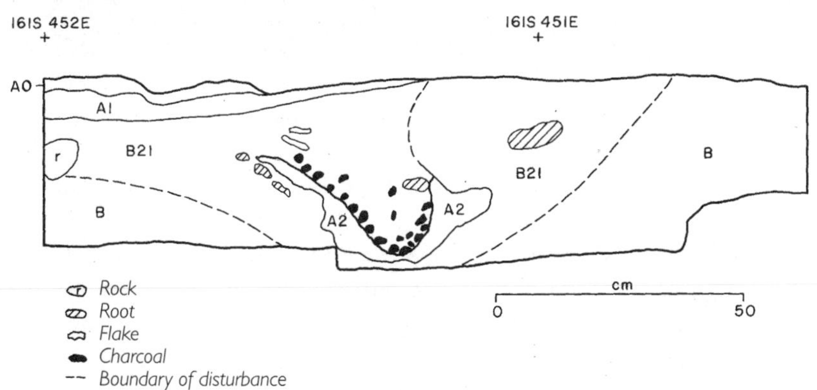

Figure 5. Planview (top) and profile (bottom) of tree-throw pit with charcoal lens and flakes, Windy City site, northern Maine (excavation unit 159S 450E, Feature 1).

cultural assemblages of lithic debitage, unifaces, and bifaces. Three loci contained small samples of tiny calcined bone fragments. The biface assemblage is composed of 39 specimens, including small lanceolate spearpoints with straight to slightly concave bases, some basal thinning, and pressure-flaked edges. The specimens most closely approximate in form and technology Holcombe points from the eastern Great Lakes region, which are thought to be about 10,000 years old.

Several probable tree-throw features were identified on site. One feature, however, which was located in locus 4, was more regularly shaped than the others. It was conical in cross-section and contained artifacts to a depth of almost 110 cm below surface. Pine (*Pinus* sp.) charcoal occurred in the feature between 40 and 50 cm below surface, and it produced a date of 6600 ± 90 yr B.P (Beta-81131). The investigators of the Nicholas site consider this ^{14}C date much too young for the archaeological assemblage. The characteristics of this feature are much more similar to those produced by a tree-throw event than those of a hearth feature (see Table 1).

The Debert site

The Debert site is located at the head of Cobeqid Bay, in the Bay of Fundy, Nova Scotia (Figure 3), on a sandy ridge approximately 4.2 km from the settlement of Debert (MacDonald 1968). Excavations occurred at Debert during the 1963 and 1964 field seasons. The site originally may have covered about 20 acres, but only 7 acres remained intact after bulldozer destruction.

Debert was the first large northeastern Paleoamerican site to be investigated systematically by an interdisciplinary team of professional specialists. More ^{14}C dates have been run on Debert charcoal than any other northeastern Paleoamerican site, other than

Figure 6. Close-up of tree-throw fill deposits Feature 1 from the Windy City site, Maine.

the Munsungun Lake Fluted Point site. Procedures for interpreting northeastern radiocarbon dates first were established at Debert and have since been followed elsewhere.

Archaeological materials from the Debert site occur in sandy deposits. The parent matrix for all stratigraphic horizons is the underlying red Wolfville Sandstone. Excavation of eight sections (A, B, C, F, G, H, I, and J) occurred within an area of 200 x 600 ft. Sections D, E, and One were scattered over another 20 acres (MacDonald 1968:21). Ten of the 11 features and more than 90 percent of the artifacts came from the concentrated central section. MacDonald (1968:23) is uncertain as to whether the shift of locations represents a temporal succession of occupations or simply different areas of occupational specialization (MacDonald 1968:23). For discussions of the stone-tool assemblage, refer to MacDonald (1968) and Bonnichsen et al. (1991).

Thirteen of the Debert ^{14}C dates average 10,600 ± 47 yr B.P. (MacDonald 1968). Differences with the interpretation of these dates by MacDonald can be found in Levine (1990:47-50). Feature 3 does not match the 10,000-year-old cluster of dates; it is associated with approximately 80 artifacts and produced a radiocarbon age of 7685 + 92 yr B.P. (P-740). On the one hand, the aberrant date of this feature is explained as the result of post-occupation contamination. An alternate hypothesis to explain Feature 3 is that it was created by a forest fire at 7600 yr B.P. And with this possibility in mind, it also is necessary to consider other site dates suspect even if they appear to date to the appropriate time period for Paleoamerican occupation. The combination of local forest fires and bioturbation of site deposits may have led to the intrusion of forest-fire charcoal into site deposits. Several lines of evidence suggest this indeed may be the case. For example, in Section F, Feature 17, traces of a burned tree were found to extend into the pit, blurring the pit outline. Additionally, MacDonald (1968) reports the widespread occurrence of thinly scattered charcoal around several features. In Section G, Feature 12, for instance, thin deposits of charcoal extend over an area covering approximately 6 m^2.

Planview maps of sections A–J in the Debert site report document feature outlines. Their forms range in shape from nearly circular, to elongated ovoids, to irregular. Sizes vary from under 0.5 m in diameter to almost 2 m across the longest axis. In addition, depth of features also varies considerably. Profiles of stratigraphic trenches are not presented for most sections of the site. Profiles from sections A, F, and J (MacDonald 1968:Figure 7) are adjacent to features 15 and 18, respectively (MacDonald 1968:Figure 7). These profile cross-sections display mounding on one side of the pit, different shapes, irregular bottom profiles, and scattered charcoal throughout the deposits. Taken together, many of these features conform more favorably in shape and cross-section with expectations for tree throws than for human hearths.

Stratigraphic inversions also occur at Debert. In Section D, Feature 7 consists of seven distinct pits that are intrusive into till deposits. The pits contained burned flakes and charcoal, and were partially covered by a capping of till. MacDonald believed that the till caps were produced by post-occupation tree throws, but later concluded that these features represented heat treatment ovens. Forest fires and tree throws also could account for the inclusion of flakes and charcoal and the inversion of underlying till deposits from tree uprooting into the fill deposits.

When shape and size data of "hearth" features are taken into account, along with inverted stratigraphy, considerable doubt is raised about the human origins of the features. By considering the regional environmental record, a case can be made that the climatic change that coincided with the Paleoamerican period may be responsible for the widespread burning and the production of charcoal that was incorporated into archaeological sites. Mott et al. (1986) and Mott (1988) report stratigraphic and palynologic evidence of a late glacial climatic oscillation in southern New Brunswick and Nova Scotia. They note a general warming trend during the late glacial that lasted until about 11,000 yr B.P., followed by a cooler and dryer interval that lasted until about 10,000 yr B.P. Preliminary evidence suggests this period of climatic change may correlate with the Younger Dryas of Europe. In his American Quaternary Association presentation, Mott (1988) noted that spruce (*Picea* sp.) advanced northward until about 11,000 yr B.P. and then retreated southward as cooling occurred.

Cooling and drying conditions, which prevailed between 11,000 and 10,000 B.P., may have fostered the occurrence of regional forest fires. Although Mott (personal communication 1988) has yet to analyze the charcoal content of his palynological cores, Green's (1981:Figure 2) pollen influx diagram from Everitt Lake, Nova Scotia, shows a high charcoal frequency during late Pleistocene and early Holocene times. Davis et al. (1986) and Jacobson (personal communication, 1990) also report that the preponderance of charcoal from Chase Lake, in northern Maine, Loon Lake, in eastern Maine, and Poland Spring and Sinkhole Pond, in southern Maine, bracket the Pleistocene/Holocene boundary (See Davis and Jacobson 1985:Figure 1 for locations of these coring sites). Collectively these data suggest widespread regional burning in northern New England during the Paleoamerican period.

If much of the charcoal from the Debert site is of natural rather than of human origin, then Debert may have been occupied prior to a major regional fire that occurred about 10,600 yr B.P. Exactly how much earlier the site was occupied remains to be determined, but a reasonable hypothesis is that occupation occurred during the warming interval about 11,000 years ago, as regional ice was retreating northward.

The Vail Site

The Vail site, located in western Maine, occurs in an intermontane valley along the margin of human-made Aziscohos Lake adjacent to an abandoned channel of the Magalloway River (Figure 3) (Gramly 1981a, 1981b, 1982; Gramly and Rutledge 1981). Artifactual remains occur in reworked silty-sandy-clayey sediments. The Vail site has been impacted by fluctuating lake levels and ice-scouring, processes that may have redistributed the large assemblage of flaked-stone artifacts. See Bonnichsen et al. (1991) and Gramly (1982) for discussion of the artifacts.

The complex history surrounding the interpretation of the radiocarbon record from Vail has been reviewed by Levine (1990:52–55) and will not be repeated here. Several ^{14}C dates were obtained on features; they are listed in Table 2. Unfortunately, the lack of stratigraphic profiles from the site does not permit the reader to form an independent evaluation of the degree of site disturbance. A personal visit to the site led one of the authors (Bonnichsen) to conclude that Vail has undergone serious disturbance, much in the same manner as the Munsungun Lake sites. The Vail site surface has been planed by ice ramparting and wave erosion. Consequently, the knob and kettle topography typical of extensive bioturbation is not readily apparent on the surface.

Gramly (1982:Figure 7) reports that Feature 2 was partially disturbed by a tree throw. Gramly believed this pit feature may have been a possible cache pit based on the discovery of debitage and a large end scraper in the pit. However, Feature 2, which consisted of a shallow elongated pit dated to 10,500 $\pm$ 400 yr B.P. (Haynes et al. 1984), also can be interpreted as an uprooted tree depression filled with redeposited archaeological material. Gramly does not indicate how he determined which part of Feature 2 was made by humans and which part was produced by a tree throw. As with the Debert site, the chronological affiliation of this feature seems reasonable for a Paleoamerican period affiliation. However, the attribution of the dated feature as cultural must remain suspect.

The Michaud Site

THE MICHAUD SITE is located in southern Maine near the Lewiston-Auburn Airport (Figure 3). The site is approximately 1 km south of the Little Androscoggin River and immediately north of Moose Brook, a tributary of the Royal River (Spiess 1985; Spiess and Brush 1987; Spiess and Wilson 1987).

The site occurs on an undulating surface formed by recently reactivated sand dunes. These deposits formed as the outwash delta of a late glacial marine transgression; an event which inundated much of coastal Maine between 12,800–11,800 yr B.P. Gray clay of the Presumpscot Formation underlies the dunes. Artifacts from Michaud were distributed over a 75 m^2 area and throughout eight loci. These loci, which average 6 m^2, range from immediately adjacent to one another to about 30 m apart. Excavation revealed a flaked stone-tool assemblage with fluted points (Bonnichsen et al. 1991; Spiess and Wilson 1987).

Feature 7, the best candidate for a Paleoamerican hearth, lay between two artifact concentrations. The undercut eastern wall of the bilobate pit (Spiess and Wilson 1987:Figure 4-2) is characterized as having ". . . two deep conical pit bases connected by a more shallow shelf" (Spiess and Wilson 1987:80). No calcined bone or lithic materials were associated with this feature.

The two charcoal samples from Feature 7 consisted of both hardwood and softwood species, a fragment of charred berry, and some frothy, non-charcoal substance—possibly pitch. The charcoal yielded ages of 9010 ± 210 yr B.P. (Beta-13833) and 10,200 ± 620 yr B.P. (Beta-15660), with an average age of 9605 yr B.P. Spiess and Wilson (1987:84) speculate that pitch in sample (Beta-13833) caused contamination and may be responsible for the younger date.

The excavators report that more than 40 soil-discoloration features were exposed and these are attributed to burned and/or rotten tree roots. The physical data from the site also can be used to support a non-human origin for the site features and charcoal. The discolored soil and burned tree roots are indicators that there is a history of forest fires at the site. Additionally, the bilobate form of Feature 7 may conform more readily to the expectations for a tree-throw event or burned-out slanted tree root.

Whipple

WHIPPLE OCCURS IN southwestern New Hampshire along the Ashuelot River, a tributary of the Connecticut River (Figure 3) (Curran 1984, 1987). The site is situated on the surface of a terrace or deltaic deposit. All archaeological remains occur within Stratum I of a complex sequence of sedimentary deposits of structured and unstructured fine to medium sands.

The site covers an area of about 875 m^2. Unfortunately, serious looting, which nearly destroyed Locus B, occurred between the time of discovery and the time of professional excavations. All Paleoamerican artifacts, charcoal, and bone occur as clusters within the B soil horizon in Loci A and C (Spiess et al. 1984).

Charcoal from Locus A is a mixture of either spruce or pine and hardwood from cherry (*Prunus* sp.) or another *Rosaceae* species. Using conventional dating procedures, pooled samples from six vertical levels (12 cm) from the Locus A feature yielded a date of 8180 ± 360 yr B.P. (GX-7496) (Table 2). The second sample of charcoal from Locus C is from softwood, hardwood, and willow or poplar. A pooled sample from Locus C, collected from 6 to 11 cm above a fluted point fragment, produced an age of 8240 ± 340 yr B.P. (GX-7497).

To clarify the age of Whipple, Haynes et al. (1984) used the TAMS method to produce five additional dates. Two samples were selected from Locus C. One sample (7060) consisted of two lumps of conifer charcoal and the other (7034) consisted of four lumps of hardwood charcoal. The conifer charcoal produced three values: 9600 ± 500 (AA-149a), 9400 ± 500 (AA-149a), and 9700 ± 700 (AA-149b) yr B.P., with an average of 9550 ± 320 yr B.P. The hardwood charcoal produced dates of 10,300 ± 500 (AA-150a) and 11,400 ± 360 (AA-150c) yr B.P., with an average of 11,050 ± 60 yr B.P.

Haynes et al. (1984) suggest there are at least two distinct populations of charcoal present at the Whipple site. With the objective of determing the time of occupation at Whipple, Curran (1984:13) averages all five ages to obtain a weighted mean of 10,680 ± 400 yr B.P. Averaging is particularly inappropriate because it is uncertain that all five age determinations provide values for the same event. On the basis of published information, it is not possible to determine whether the two populations of charcoal from Whipple are of human or natural origin, or a combination of the two.

Bull Brook

Bull Brook is located in northeastern Massachusetts in a seaboard lowland setting (Figure 3). The site consists of two sections: Bull Brook I and Bull Brook II (Curran 1987; Grimes 1979; Grimes et al. 1984). The site is located near Plum Island Sound and lies on delta-like sand and gravel deposits.

The site was collected by non-specialists over a 20-year period in response to a continuing earth removal operation. Artifacts and thousands of pieces of debitage were recovered from an area measuring 8 hectares. Bull Brook I consists of at least 12 loci and more than 1,000 tools. Bull Brook II, located about 300 m from Bull Brook I, has yielded at least six loci and 487 tools.

Byers' (1959) and Grimes' (1979) attempts to develop a radiocarbon chronology for this impressive site have resulted in a series of Holocene-age dates. These dates are difficult to evaluate because collection provenance is absent from the published literature. Byers (1959:428) notes the sample that produced the age of 8720±400 yr B.P. (M-808) apparently was in association with chips and artifacts and contained a few rootlets. Grimes' (1979) attempt to provide a more secure chronological framework for Bull Brook did not produce positive results. Age determinations of 8560 ± 285 (GX-6279) yr B.P. on wood charcoal from pine and oak, 7590 ± 255 (GX-6278) yr B.P. on mixed pine and oak charcoal, and 5440 ± 160 (GX-6277) yr B.P. on oak charcoal reflect problems similar to those encountered by Byers.

The scattered series of seven dates from Bull Brook range in age from 5440 to 9300 B.P. (Table 2). From the above, it is clear that the ^{14}C dates from Bull Brook do not meet expectations for a Paleoamerican site, which contains an undeniable fluted point assemblage. The absence of detailed provenance for the dated charcoal samples prevent a determination from being made as to whether the charcoal from this site was of human or natural origin.

Templeton (6LF21)

The Templeton site (6LF21) is located on the first terrace of the Shepaug River floodplain in Washington, Connecticut (Moeller 1980) (Figure 3). Early cultural-bearing deposits occur just above river gravels in a band of clay-coated sand. Excavation of 42.75 m^2, or approximately 90 percent of the site, led to the recovery of approximately 7,400 archaeological specimens.

Charcoal from red oak found in the Paleoamerican level produced a single date of 10,190 ± 300 (W-3931) yr B.P. (Table 2). The sample came from a small stained area, about 10 cm in diameter, within the clay-coated sand zone of square 9.0N 4.5W. The nearest diagnostic artifacts occurred within 75 cm of the charcoal. A cross-section exposure of the stain revealed a micro-feature with an erratic outline that circumscribed flakes and chunks of charcoal.

The charcoal stain apparently did not originate from a higher level and was sealed within the Paleoamerican component. Moeller proposes the charred wood occurred in a post mold, which burned as a result of a local fire. He reasoned that as the fire moved closer to the ground, the likelihood of charring increased because of the decrease in oxygen necessary for combustion. The sharp but erratic boundaries of the charcoal concentration have led Moeller to dismiss the natural-origin possibility that the charcoal is from burned root. However, charcoal from 6LF21could be of natural rather than human origin, because there are no accepted criteria for differentiating a root burn from that of a post mold.

Turkey Swamp

The Turkey Swamp site is located in the northeastern portion of New Jersey's coastal plain within the headwaters of the Manasquan River drainage system (Cavallo 1981) (Figure 3). The site occurs in floodplain deposits along a small river approximately 61.5 m from an unnamed tributary of the Manasquan.

Testing in 1974 suggests that undisturbed archaeological deposits cover an area of 185 by 231 m. These tests revealed late Archaic, early Woodland, and late Woodland components. By 1981, excavation by trowel had exposed 26 3.05 by 3.05 m (10 x 10 ft) squares to a depth of 139–152 cm below the surface.

A total of seven cultural components, including a Paleoamerican one, were discovered. Paleoamerican remains occur within a micropodsol soil in the bottom of the B3, and in the C1 and C soil horizons at a depth of 72–108 cm below the surface. These deposits relinquished a series of basally thinned, triangular projectile points as well as other artifacts.

Five charcoal samples (Table 2), apparently from a single feature, yielded ages of 8739 ± 165 (DIC-1059), 7980 ± 150 (DIC-1060), 7950 ± 110 (DIC-1057), 7820 ± 215 (DIC-1061), and 7660 ± 325 (DIC-1058) yr B.P. (Cavallo 1981:8). The feature from which these charcoal samples were collected is not described, nor is discussion offered in this preliminary report to explain the 1,100-year discrepancy between the 8739 and 7660 dates. Cavello has reservations about these dates and leaves open the possibility that the charcoal is intrusive. He suggests the Turkey Swamp assemblage represents a blend of late Paleoamerican and early Archaic stylistic elements and is of late Paleoamerican age. The lack of supporting documentation on sample provenance and composition precludes a detailed discussion of this series of dates, which appear to fall outside of the Paleoamerican period.

Dutchess Quarry Caves

DUTCHESS QUARRY CAVES occur in a karst area on the northwestern rim of Mount Lookout near Florida, Orange County, New York (Funk 1972; Funk et al. 1969; Funk et al. 1970; Kopper et al. 1980; Steadman and Funk 1987) (Figure 3). Attention first was drawn to the area with the discovery of a large cave, since named Dutchess Quarry Cave No. 1. Lesser caves and fissures occur in this face of Ordovician-age Halcyon Lake calcitic dolostone.

Dutchess Quarry Cave No. 1, a cylindrical, dolomite solution-cavity, is 20 m long and 5.2 m wide at the mouth. The cave occurs at an elevation of 177 m. Evidence for human occupation is from the three upper strata. Moving from top to bottom, Stratum 1A is a dark midden lens with late Woodland artifacts; Stratum 1B is a light brown zone with traces of Archaic occupation; Stratum 2 is a white cave earth. Associated with the artifacts were the bones of 44 species, including fish, amphibians, reptiles, birds, and mammals (Guilday 1969). Of these species, only woodland caribou (Rangifer *tarandus*) had not been recorded historically from New York. The caribou bones were found in apparent association with a fluted point of the Cumberland style at the base of Stratum 2 (Guilday 1969) and yielded a date of 12,530 ± 370 yr B.P. (I-4317) (Table 2).

Steadman and Funk (1987) suggest that the caribou bone and fluted point association do not provide a secure date for the earliest known occupation. They argue that: (1) the date is earlier than western fluted-point site dates summarized by Haynes (1982) by about 1,000 years; (2) although the caribou bone and fluted point were stratigraphically associated, they may have been deposited at different times; and (3) the bone date may be unreliable.

During 1978 and 1979, Kopper et al. (1980) used a resistivity meter to locate seven more cavities in the dolostone of Mount Lookout. The most significant of these is Dutchess Quarry Cave No. 8, which is much smaller than Dutchess Quarry Cave No.1 and is located about 15 m to the east.

Excavations to a depth of 3 m below the original surface at Dutchess Cave Quarry No. 8 encountered well-stratified deposits. The most significant artifacts are two fish-tailed fluted points from Stratum 3 and the upper part of Stratum 5. Steadman and Funk (1987) indicate that a rich faunal and plant macrofossil record also is present in Dutchess Quarry Cave No. 8.

Kopper et al. (1980:133) believed that the archaeological materials in the cave were largely of extraneous origin. During Paleoamerican times, there was not enough head room to stand comfortably in the cave. Large breakdown blocks were transported into the cave via a talus cone. Slopewash also played an important role in depositing the cave fill.

A small sample of charcoal from the vicinity of the fluted points produced a date of 5880 ± 340 yr B.P. (DIC-14447) (Table 2). Kopper et al. (1980) offer two explanations to account for this date. The deposits may have been transported into the cave during Archaic times from older deposits. Or, charcoal may have intruded into the Paleoamerican level from a higher Archaic level.

Conclusions

OUR OVERVIEW of Paleoamerican sites in northeastern North America sets the stage for considering how First Americans research in the Northeast contributes to our overall understanding of the peopling of the Americas. As previously noted, the radiocarbon record from the Northeast has developed in a piecemeal fashion as new sites were excavated, dated, and reported over a 40-year period. By focusing on the total population of dates, rather than on individual sites as has often been the case, some trends emerge that affect our understanding of the human chronology of this region. These trends include (1) sites with fluted points that have yielded radiocarbon ages of less than 10,000 yr B.P., (2) sites with fluted points that have yielded radiocarbon ages of Holocene and late Pleistocene age, and (3) sites with dates of late Pleistocene age. Each of these patterns will now be discussed.

The first pattern includes sites with Holocene radiocarbon ages. These sites include the Windy City,

Fluted Point, and Nicholas sites of Maine, Bull Brook I and Bull Brook II, Massachusetts, the Dutchess Quarry Cave No. 8, in New York, and the Turkey Swamp site of Delaware. To these can be added the Wapanucket No. 8 of Massachusetts, with dates that range from 3898 to 4708 yr B.P. (Robbins and Agogino 1964). These seven sites (including Wapanucket No. 8) constitute 54 percent of the dated sites that have yielded fluted points. These dates seem to reflect the age of intrusive charcoal.

The second pattern of sites with Holocene and Pleistocene dates includes three sites or 23 percent of the population of dated sites. In the case of Debert, MacDonald recognizes the Holocene-age charcoal as intrusive, but supports the view that the dates greater than 10,000 yr B.P. are from charcoal produced by site occupants. The investigators of the Whipple and Michaud sites also believe that site charcoal is of human origin and date the time of site occupation. As previously noted, however, these ^{14}C dates may date non-cultural events; actual human occupation may date earlier.

The third pattern of sites of late Pleistocene age includes three sites (23 percent of the population). Of these, the site investigators of Vail and Templeton propose that the dated charcoal is of human origin and thus provides a date of human occupation. Investigators of the excavations at Dutchess Quarry Cave No. 1 believe that the 12,000 yr B.P. date is too early for a fluted point occupation.

From the above discussion, it is clear that more than 50 percent of the fluted point sites have yielded charcoal too young to be accepted by their investigators and signals that there is considerable ambiguity in the way that the archaeological record is and has been interpreted at northeastern Paleoamerican sites. Alternative interpretations are possible for other sites whose charcoal has been attributed to humans by the site's original investigators.

In seeking to understand the ambiguity of the chronology patterns found in northeastern Paleoamerican sites, consideration needs to be given to site formation processes. Both natural and human behavioral processes can lead to the burial of charcoal in archaeological sites. A particularly troublesome issue has been the lack of criteria for discriminating between charcoal produced by humans and found in hearths and charcoal found in tree-throw pits that originated from natural burns. Modern analogs drawn from the 1988 Yellowstone burn and from forest fires in northwestern Minnesota, coupled with a review of the tree-throw and archaeological hearth literature, permit the development of criteria for discriminating between human hearths and natural charcoal intruded into subsurface deposits by tree throws and burning. Natural processes such as root burning, sheet erosion, alluvial transport, aeolian redeposition, along with geoturbation and bioturbation processes, can transport and deposit charcoal produced by forest fires to archaeological sites.

Some of the northeastern Paleoamerican period site reports with dated ^{14}C records have been examined using the criteria for discriminating between forest-fire/tree-throw pits and human hearths. Interestingly, ^{14}C dates that are considered anomalous are readily interpreted as intrusions and possibly caused by the introduction of forest-fire charcoal into the archaeological deposits. When pit features, whether or not they contain artifacts, yield charcoal with a ^{14}C date that meets chronological expectations, then the feature is usually accepted as cultural in origin. In some of the situations described, tree-throw pits containing forest-fire charcoal may more adequately explain some of these features.

Widespread burning during Paleoamerican times may be related to global climatic change. Changes in the seasonal and latitudinal distribution of solar radiation are produced by changes in earth-sun geometry. The 22,000-year precession cycle regulates the time of year when the earth-sun distance is at a maximum or minimum and thus affects seasonality (COHMAP 1988:1044). Between 12,000 and 9,000 years ago, summers would have been warmer and drier than at present and winters cooler and damper. These conditions led to accelerated ice retreat (Hughes 1987), rapid restructuring of vegetation (Jacobson et al. 1987; Webb 1988), and lowered lake levels (Webb 1990).

Drier summers set the stage for regional burning. Evidence from regional palynological cores with charcoal records indicates that the production of charcoal is not constant through time and that the preponderance of charcoal occurs at the late Pleistocene-early Holocene boundary in Maine and Nova Scotia coring sites (Davis et al. 1986; Green 1981; Jacobson, personal communication 1990). These environmental changes suggest that we should expect to find more intrusive charcoal in sites of Paleoamerican age than other time periods.

Radiocarbon dating is not sufficient in and of itself for determining the cultural attribution of pit features. An age estimate that meets expectations of site age does not provide proof that the charcoal is of human origin. Descriptive standards for documenting charcoal context need to include clear descriptive statements of charcoal context and be accompanied by plan-view and cross-section drawings of features.

New approaches can improve chances of identifying charcoal origin. When formulating site formation histories, all possible lines of evidence should be considered. For example, surface burning of artifacts is an often overlooked line of information (Payne 1987). Thermally spalled rocks are another potential source of information (Connor et al. 1989). Another important technique is the use of magnetometers to isolate burned areas and determine magnetic alignments of stones in suspected hearths. A useful approach to detect regional burning entails examining local pollen diagrams for charcoal peaks to see if these correlate with charcoal from the archaeological record, as has been documented for Maine. Clark (1988b) indicates that there is a good correlation between terrestrial burning and charcoal found in lake cores.

The above discussion clearly signals the need for interdisciplinary efforts involving archaeologists, geochemists, stratigraphers, soil scientists, and radiocarbon specialists to understand the site formation processes responsible for affecting archaeological sites. This is especially pertinent to the study of Paleoamerican period sites in northeastern North America where natural processes occurring in forested environments have had more than 10,000 years to affect the archaeological record.

In closing, we can not say with certainity that the Paleoamerican period of northeastern North America is as old as elsewhere in American or younger. The occurrence of sites on paleo-landforms associated with glacial spillway channels and meltwater streams tends to support the view that northeastern sites are as old as other fluted point sites in America and that these people advanced as glacial ice receeded. To more fully understand how humans participated in the paleoenvironments of late glacial times, emphasis must be placed on clarifying the ambiguity that characterizes the chronological record from this region.

Acknowledgments

We would like to thank Don Hall, Karen Turnmire, and several external referees for suggestions that led to improvements in the manuscript. Steve Bicknell, University of Maine, prepared the figures. We are particularly grateful to Melissa Connor of the Midwest Archaeological Center for generously sharing unpublished data on the Yellowstone burn.

References Cited

Barnosky, C. W.
1987 Late-Glacial and Postglacial Vegetation and Climate of Jackson Hole and the Pinyon Peak Highland, Wyoming. Report submitted to the University of Wyoming, National Park Service Research Center, Laramie.

Binford, L. R.
1981 *Bones: Ancient Men and Modern Myths.* Academic Press, New York.

1983 In *Pursuit of the Past.* Academic Press, New York.

Bonnichsen, R.
1984 Paleoindian Sites in the Munsungun Lake Region Northern Maine. Curr*ent Research in the Pleistocene* 1:3-4.

Bonnichsen, R., D. Keenlyside, and K. Turnmire
1991 Paleoindian Patterns in Maine and the Maritimes. In *Prehistoric Archaeology in the Maritime Provinces: Past and Present Research*, edited by M. Deal and S. Blair. pp. 1–26. The Council of Maritime Premiers, Maritime Committee on Archaeological Cooperation, Reports in Archaeology 8, Fredericton.

Bonnichsen, R., V. Konrad, V. Clay, T. Gibson, and D. Schnurrenberger
1981 Archaeological Research at Munsungun Lake: 1980 Preliminary Technical Report of Activities. Institute for Quaternary Studies, University of Maine, Orono, Maine.

Bonnichsen, R., and M. H. Sorg (editors)
1989 *Bone Modification.* Center for the Study of the First Americans, University of Maine, Orono.

Bryan, A. L.
1979 Smith Creek Cave. In *The Archaeology of Smith Creek Canyon, Eastern Nevada, edited* by D. R. Tuohy and D. L. Rendall, pp. 162–253. Nevada State Museum Anthropological Papers, Number 17. Carson City.

1988 The Relationship of the Stemmed Point and the Fluted Point Traditions in the Great Basin. In *Early Human Occupation in Far Western North America: The Clovis-Archaic Interface*, edited by J. A. Willig, C. M. Aikens, and J. L. Fagan, pp. 53–74. Nevada State Museum Anthropological Papers, Number 21. Carson City.

Byers, D. S.
1959 Radiocarbon Dates for the Bull Brook Site, Ipswich, Massachusetts. *American Antiquity* 24:427–429.

Cavallo, J.
1981 Turkey Swamp: A Late Paleo-Indian Site in New Jersey's Coastal Plain. *Archaeology of Eastern North America* 9:1–18.

Chamberlin, T. C.
1897 The Method of Multiple Working Hypotheses. *Journal of Geology* 5:837–848.

Clay, V.
1983 *Chemical Indicators of Human Activity in the Soils of Four Maine Archaeological Sites.* Master's thesis, Institute for Quaternary Studies, University of Maine, Orono.

Clark, A. S.
1988a Effect of Climate Change on Fire Regimes in Northwestern Minnesota. *Natural History* July:233–235.

1988b Stratigraphic Charcoal Analysis on Petrographic Thin Sections: Application to Fire History in Northwestern Minnesota. *Quaternary Research* 30: 81–91.

1989 The Forest is for Burning. Nat*ural History* January:50–53.

COHMAP
1988 Climatic Changes of the Last 18,000 Years: Observations and Model Simulations. *Science* 241:1043–1052.

Connor, M. A., K. P. Cannon, and D. C. Carlevato
1989 The Mountains Burnt: Forest Fires and Site Formation Processes. *North American Archaeologist* 10:293–310.

Curran, M. L.
1984 The Whipple Site Tool Assemblage Variation: A Comparison of Intrasite Structuring. *Archaeology of Eastern North America* 12:5–50.

1987 *The Spatial Organization of Paleoindian Populations in the Late Pleistocene of the Northeast.* Ph.D. dissertation, Department of Anthropology, University of Massachusetts, Amherst.

Davis, R. B., and G. L. Jacobson, Jr.
1985 Late Glacial and Early Holocene Landscapes in Northern New England and Adjacent Areas of Canada. *Quaternary Research* 23:341–368.

Davis, R. B., G. L. Jacobson, Jr., and R. S. Anderson
1986 *Macrofossils in Maine Lake Sediments Confirm and Extend Paleoecological Inferences Based on Pollen.* Program and Abstracts of the Ninth Biennial Meeting of the American Quaternary Association, June 2–4, 1986. University of Illinois, Champaign-Urbana.

Deller, B.
1988 *The Paleo-Indian Occupation of Southwestern Ontario: Distribution, Technology, and Social Organization.* Ph.D. dissertation, Department of Anthropology, McGill University, Montreal.

Ellis, C.
1984 *Paleo-Indian Lithic Technological Structure and Organization in the Lower Great Lakes Area: A First Approximation.* Ph.D. dissertation, Department of Archaeology, Simon Fraser University, Burnaby.

Frison, G. C., and D. J. Stanford
1982 *The Agate Basin Site: A Record of the Paleoindian Occupation of the Northwestern High Plains.* Academic Press, New York.

Funk, R. E.
1972 Early Man in the Northeast and the Late-Glacial Environment. *Man in the Northeast* 4:7–39.

Funk, R. E., G. R. Walters, and W. F. Ehlers, Jr.
1969 The Archaeology of Dutchess Quarry Cave, Orange County, New York. *Pennsylvania Archaeologist* 39:7–22.

Funk, R., D. W. Fisher, and E. M. Reilley, Jr.
1970 Caribou and Paleo-Indians in New York State: A Presumed Association. *American Journal of Sciences* 288:245–256.

Gramly, R. M.
1981a Eleven Thousand Years in Maine. *Archaeology* 34:32–39.

1981b Vail Archaeological Site Excavation. *Explorers Journal* 59:16–19.

1982 The Vail Site: A Paleoindian Encampment in Maine. *Bulletin of the Buffalo Society of Natural Sciences*, No. 30. Buffalo.

Gramly, R. M., and K. Rutledge
1981 A New Paleo-Indian Site in the State of Maine. *American Antiquity* 46:354–361.

Green, D. G.
1981 Time Series and Postglacial Forest Ecology. *Quaternary Research* 15:265–277.

Grimes, J. R.
1979 A New Look at Bull Brook. *Anthropology* 3:109–130.

Grimes, J. R., W. Eldridge, B. Grimes, A. Vaccaro, J. Vaccaro, N. Vaccaro, and N. Orsini
1984 Bull Brook II. *Archaeology of Eastern North America* 12:159–183.

Guilday, J. R.
1969 Faunal Remains from Dutchess Quarry Cave No. 1. In *The Archaeology of Dutchess Quarry Cave, Orange County, New York*, edited by R. E. Funk, G. Walters, and W. F. Ehlers, Jr., pp.17–19. P*ennsylvania Archaeologist* 39:7–22.

Haynes, C. V.
1982 Were Clovis Progenitors in Beringia? In *Paleoecology of Beringia*, edited by D. Hopkins, J. V. Matthews, C. E. Schweger, and S. B. Young, pp. 383–398. Academic Press, New York.

Haynes, C. V., D. J. Donahue, A. J. T. Jull, and T. H. Zabel
1984 Application of Accelerator Dating to Fluted Point Paleoindian Sites. *Archaeology of Eastern North America* 12:184–191.

Hughes, T.
1987 Ice Dynamics and Deglaciation Models When Ice Sheets Collapsed. In *North America and Adjacent Oceans During the Last Deglaciation*, DNAG volume k-3, edited by W. F. Ruddiman and H. E. Wright, Jr., pp. 183–220. Geological Society of America, Boulder.

Jackson, L. J.
1983 Geochronology and Settlement Deposition in the Early Palaeo-Indian Occupation of Southern Ontario, Canada. *Quaternary Research* 19:388–399.

Jacobson, G. L., Jr., T. Webb, III, and E. C. Grimm
1987 Patterns and Rates of Vegetation Change During the Deglaciation of Eastern North America. In *North America and Adjacent Oceans During the Last Deglaciation*, DNAG volume k-3, edited by W. F. Ruddiman and H. E. Wright, Jr., pp. 277–288. Geological Society of America, Boulder.

Jodry, M. A., and D. J. Stanford
1992 Stewart's Cattle Guard Site: An Analysis of Bison Remains in a Folsom Kill Butchery Campsite. In *Ice Age Hunters of the Rockies*, edited by J. Day and D. J. Stanford, pp. 101–168. Published by the Denver Museum of Natural History and University Press of Colorado, Niwot.

Kopper, J. S., R. E. Funk, and L. Dumont
1980 Additional Paleo-Indian and Archaic Materials from the Dutchess Quarry Cave Area, Orange County, New York. *Archaeology of Eastern North America* 8:125–137.

Lepper, B.
1983 Fluted Point Distributional Patterns in the Eastern United States. *Midcontinent Journal of Archaeology* 8(2):269–285.

Levine, M. A.
1990 Accommodating Age: Radiocarbon Results and Fluted Point Sites in Northeastern North America. *Archaeology of Eastern North America* 18:33–63.

Lorenzo, J. L., and L. Mirambell
1986 Preliminary Report on Archeological and Paleoenvironmental Studies in the Area of El Cedral, San Luis Potosi, Mexico 1977–1980. In *New Evidence for the Pleistocene Peopling of the Americas*, edited by A. L. Bryan, pp. 107–113. Center for the Study of Early Man, University of Maine, Orono.

Lyford, W. H., and D. W. MacLean
1966 *Mound and Pit Microrelief in Relation to Soil Disturbance and Tree Distribution in New Brunswick, Canada.* Harvard Forest Paper No. 15, Harvard University, Cambridge.

MacDonald, G. F.
1968 *Debert: A Palaeo-Indian Site in Central Nova Scotia.* Anthropology Papers of the National Museum of Canada, No. 16, Ottawa.

1983 Eastern North America. In *Early Man in the New World*, edited by R. Shutler, Jr., pp. 97–108. Sage Publications, Beverly Hills.

Meltzer, D.
1984 *Late Pleistocene Human Adaptation in Eastern North America.* Ph.D. dissertation, Department of Anthropology, University of Washington, Seattle.

1987 Late Pleistocene Human Adaptations in Eastern North America. *Journal of World Prehistory 2:1–52.*

Moeller, R. W.
1980 *6LF21: A Paleo Indian Site in Western Connecticut.* American Indian Archaeological Institute, Occasional Paper No. 2.

Mott, R. J.
1988 Late Glacial Climatic Oscillation in Atlantic Canada: An Equivalent to the Allerod/Younger Dryas of Europe. Paper presented at the 1988 AMQUA Conference, Amherst.

Mott, R. J., D. R. Grant, R. Stea, and S. Occhietti
1986 Late Glacial Climatic Oscillation in Atlantic Canada Equivalent to the Allerod/Younger Dryas Event. *Nature* 323:247–250.

Norton, D. A.
1988 Tree Windthrow and Forest Soil Turnover. *Canadian Journal of Forest Research 19:386–389.*

Orme, B.
1982 The Use of Radiocarbon Dates in the Somerset Levels. In *Problems and Case Studies in Archaeological Dating*, edited by B. Orme, pp. 5–34. Exeter Studies in History No. 4; Exeter Studies in Archaeology No.1. University of Exeter, Exeter.

Payne, J.
1987 *Windy City (154-16): A Paleoindian Lithic Workshop in Northern Maine.* Master's Thesis, Institute for Quaternary Studies, University of Maine, Orono.

Putz, F. E.
1983 Treefall Pits and Mounds, Buried Seeds, and the Importance of Soil Disturbance to Pioneer Trees on Barro Colorado Island, Panama. *Ecology* 64:1069–1074.

Putz, F. E., P. D. Coley, K. Lu, A. Montalvo, and A. Aiello
1983 Uprooting and Snapping of Trees: Structural Determinants and Ecological Consequences. *Canadian Journal of Forest Resources* 13:1011–1020.

Robbins, M., and G. A. Agogino
1964 The Wapanucket No. 8 Site: A Clovis-Archaic Site in Massachusetts. *American Antiquity* 29:509–513.

Schaetzl, R. J., S. F. Burns, T. W. Small, and D. L. Johnson
1988a The Uprooting of Trees as a Process in Physical Geography. *Vegetation* 79:165–176.

Schaetzl, R. J., S. F. Burns, D. L. Johnson, and T. W. Small
1988b Tree Uprooting: Review of Impacts on Forest Ecology Vegetation. *Vegetation* 79:165–176.

Schaetzl, R. J., D. L. Johnson, S. F. Burns, and T. W. Small
1988c Floralturbation of Soils by Tree Uprooting: Review of Terminology, Process, and Environmental Implications. *Canadian Journal of Forest Research* 19:1–11.

Schiffer, M. B.
1983 Toward the Identification of Formation Processes. *American Antiquity* 48:675–706.

1987 *Formation Processes of the Archaeological Record.* University of New Mexico Press, Albuquerque.

1988 The Structure of Archaeological Theory. *American Antiquity* 53:461–485.

Spiess, A.
1985 The Michaud site (23-12): A New Major Paleoindian Site in Auburn Maine. *The Maine Archaeological Society Bulletin* 25(2):38–42.

Spiess, A., and D. Brush
1987 Patterning in Paleoindian Behavior: The Michaud Site. *Current Research in the Pleistocene* 4:34–35.

Spiess, A. E., M. L. Curran, and J. R. Grimes
1984 Caribou (*Rangifer tarandus* L.) Bones from New England Paleoindian Sites. *North American Archaeologist* 6:145–159.

Spiess, A., and D. Wilson
1987 *Michaud: A Paleoindian Site in the New England Maritime Region.* The Maine Historical Commission and the Maine Archaeological Society, Inc. Occasional Publications in Maine Archaeology, No. 6.

Steadman, D. W., and R. E. Funk
1987 New Paleontological and Archaeological Investigations at Dutchess Quarry Cave no. 8, Orange County, New York. *Current Research in the Pleistocene* 4:118–120.

Taylor, R. E.
1987 *Radiocarbon Dating: An Archaeological Perspective.* Academic Press, Orlando.

Webb, T. III
1988 Eastern North America. In *Vegetation History*, edited by B. Huntley and T. Webb III, pp. 385–414. Kluwer Academic Publishers, Boston.

Webb, R. S.
1990 *Late Quaternary Water-Level Fluctuations in the Northeastern United States.* Ph.D.dissertation, Department of Geological Sciences, Brown University, Providence.

Wettstead, J. R.
1988 Forest Fires and Archaeology in the Ashland District, Custer National Forest, Montana. Paper presented at the 46th Annual Plains Conference, Wichita, Kansas.

Will, R., and J. Clark
1996 Stone Artifact Movement on Impoundment Shorelines: A Case Study from Maine. *American Antiquity* 61:499-519.

Wilson, D., R. Will, and J. Cormier
1995 The Nicholas Site: A Late Paleoindian Campsite in Southern Oxford County, Maine. Report on file with the Maine Historic Preservation Commission, Augusta

Wood, R., and D. L. Johnson
1978 A Survey of Disturbance Processes in Archaeological Site Formation. In *Advances in Archaeological Method and Theory*, Vol. 1, edited by M. Schiffer, pp. 315–381. Academic Press, New York.

No Vestige of a Beginning nor Prospect for an End: Two Decades of Debate on Meadowcroft Rockshelter

J. M. Adovasio[1]
D. Pedler[2]
J. Donahue[3]
R. Stuckenrath[4]

Abstract

Ever since the publication of the first of more than 50 internally consistent radiocarbon dates from Meadowcroft Rockshelter (36WH297), intense and sometimes acrimonious controversy has swirled around the timing of the initial human occupation of this deeply stratified site. Critics of a late Pleistocene presence at this locality have questioned its stratigraphy, floral and faunal associations, the "character" of its earliest artifact assemblage, and—with particular vigor—the radiocarbon dates from the site's basal deposits. While most conservative assessments concede a 12,000-year initial occupancy (cf. Fagan 1995), it nonetheless continues to be asserted that the site's earlier dates have suffered particulate or non-particulate contamination. Data bearing on myriad aspects of this controversy have been published since 1975, and in the continuing debate many once-vocal critics have become silent, bored, or perhaps both. To provide background for this debate, the Meadowcroft radiocarbon chronology and related issues are reviewed, and to continue it anew, assertions of particulate and non-particulate contamination are reassessed and evaluated in light of current information. The weight of all available data continues to suggest that this site still represents the best and earliest evidence for the presence of human beings south of the glacial front in North America. More specifically, the evidence further suggests that Native Americans possessing a technologically sophisticated core-and blade-based lithic technology not at typological or chronological variance with possible Siberian prototypes were present in southwestern Pennsylvania by 10,600–12,000 years ago at the very latest.

Introduction

Five generations of graduate students have passed through anthropology departments in American academic institutions since the publication of the initial Meadowcroft Rockshelter (36WH297) radiocarbon chronology in 1975 (Adovasio et al. 1975). These legions of students have been exposed to one or another view of the validity and reliability of the seemingly ever-growing Meadowcroft radiocarbon chronology, which not surprisingly, reflected the outlook (positive, neutral, or negative) of their teachers. As noted in Adovasio et al. (1990:348), some students accepted the antiquity of the site as soon as the first dates were published,

1. Anthropology/Archaeology and Geology, Mercyhurst College, Erie PA; Mercyhurst Archaeological Institute; Pennsylvania Historical and Museum Commission.
2. Mercyhurst Archaeological Institute, Mercyhurst College, Erie PA.
3. Department of Geology and Planetary Sciences, University of Pittsburgh, Pittsburgh PA.
4. University of Pittsburgh Radiocarbon Laboratory, Pittsburgh PA (deceased).

others rejected part of the chronology as too old, and still others posed a series of questions which in one form or another have been reiterated to this day.

Over the same span of time, and even since the presentation of the initial version of this contribution to the First World Summit on the Peopling of the Americas in 1989 (Adovasio et al. 1989), there have been not insignificant changes in the field of New World Paleoindian studies. Numerous sites in North and South America have been advanced as candidates for late Pleistocene human occupation of the New World, only to enjoy a Warholesque 15 minutes of fame (cf. Adovasio 1993) before disappearing into obscurity. (Interestingly, this phenomenon has occurred or is presently occurring in respect to many of the sites dramatically unveiled or presented with high hopes at Orono in 1989.) The majority of these sites were rescinded because they suffered one or another critical defect, reservations about which could not be countered with any convincing data. However, several of the putatively early sites—notably including Meadowcroft and Monte Verde in Chile—as noted by Meltzer (1993:75), have "cheated archaeology's actuarial tables" by systematically rebutting or at least addressing controversial issues, often in a long series of detailed publications.

The present form of this contribution represents an update and expansion of our original discussion in view of developments which have occurred since 1989, made possible through the generosity of volume editor R. Bonnichsen. As such, our explicitly synoptic approach draws from Adovasio et al. (1990:348) and other publications about Meadowcroft from the partisan camps, both pro (Adovasio 1993; Adovasio et al. 1988; Adovasio et al. 1990, 1992) and con (Haynes 1991; Tankersley and Munson 1992), as well as from more or less "neutral" observers (Dincauze 1989; Fagan 1990, 1991, 1995; Fiedel 1992; Meltzer 1993). It is hoped that this latest rendering of the continuing reservations about the antiquity of Meadowcroft Rockshelter and the validity of its early radiocarbon chronology will serve, if nothing else, to introduce yet another generation of students to the ongoing Meadowcroft controversy and provide a partially annotated guide to the literature on the site.

The Meadowcroft/Cross Creek Archaeological Project

MEADOWCROFT ROCKSHELTER is a deeply stratified multicomponent site located 48.3 km (30 mi) southwest of Pittsburgh, Pennsylvania, and 4 km (2.5 mi) northwest of Avella, Washington County, Pennsylvania. It is situated on the north bank of Cross Creek, a small tributary of the Ohio River, some 12.2 km (7.6 mi) east of the creek's confluence with that river. The site is a typical immature sandstone re-entrant oriented roughly east-west with a southern exposure (Donahue and Adovasio 1990). It is elevated 15.1 m (49.4 ft) above Cross Creek and ca. 259.9 m (852.5 ft) above mean sea level (msl). The rockshelter's extant overhang covers an area of ca. 65 m^2 (699.4 ft^2) and stands ca 13 m (42.6 ft) above the modern surface of the site.

Meadowcroft Rockshelter originally was discovered (and subsequently protected) by Albert Miller, whose family has owned the property continuously since 1795. The site was brought to the attention of J. M. Adovasio through the efforts of Miller and the late P. Jack, California State College, California, Pennsylvania. It quickly became the focal point of a long-term multidisciplinary project, the most intensive field phase of which began in the summer of 1973 and terminated in the fall of 1978. Additional field work was conducted in 1982, 1983, and 1987, with major re-excavation of the site's Holocene deposits occurring in 1994–1995. The analysis and publication phase is ongoing and to date has generated some 75 articles, book chapters, monographs, and papers. The final report is in preparation. Due to the unique multidisciplinary expertise brought to bear on every aspect of the research, facilitated in very large part by massive financial support, the Meadowcroft excavations are widely considered to represent the state-of-the-art in closed-site excavations (cf. Custer 1996; Fagan 1990, 1995; Feder 1996)

The 11 colluvially and attritionally emplaced strata identified at Meadowcroft, which include Stratum I (the culturally sterile shale "basement") and 10 overlying lithostratigraphic units (i.e., Strata II–XI) of widely varying thickness and composition, extend to a maximum depth of 4.6 m (15.08 ft) and have produced what is presently the longest intermittent occupational sequence in the New World. These sediments yielded some 20,000 artifacts (principally flaked stone), more than 150 fire pits (final tallies from the 1994–1995 excavation season are not yet available), 33 fire floors, 52 ash and charcoal lenses, 16 specialized activity areas, and 21 refuse/storage pits. The site's ecofactual yield is massive and includes nearly 1 million faunal remains and ca. 1.4 million plant remains.

The rockshelter excavations were complemented by archaeological reconnaissance of the Cross Creek drainage, which covered ca. 14,164.5 ha (35,000 acres) and identified 236 additional prehistoric sites. All of these sites were surface collected, 22 were tested, and two were extensively excavated. The resultant corpus of data is as detailed a prehistoric record as currently exists for any comparably sized study area anywhere in the Americas, if not the world.

The oldest archaeological manifestation identified at Meadowcroft and several other loci in the Cross Creek drainage is the Miller complex. Named after Albert Miller, this complex appears to represent the pioneer population in the upper Ohio Valley and, possibly, the Northeast. From a technological perspective, the Miller complex lithic debitage sample reflects secondary and tertiary core reduction and biface thinning from late-stage manufacture and the refurbishing of finished implements. The specimens create a clear impression that an essentially curated lithic tool kit was brought to Meadowcroft by its earliest inhabitants. Interestingly, the site's initial populations seem to have exploited, or at least utilized through exchange, raw materials from a fairly far-flung series of quarries. These include Flint Ridge in Ohio, several Kanawha chert sources in West Virginia, the Pennsylvania jasper quarries located well to the east of the site, and the local Monongahela chert outcrops in the Cross Creek drainage. This wide-ranging procurement pattern, in turn, suggests that the "serial quarry scenario" proposed by Custer (1984) might exhibit a truly venerable pedigree in eastern North America.

The flaked stone artifact inventory from lower and middle Stratum IIa at Meadowcroft Rockshelter contains small, prismatic blades that were detached from small, prepared cores. Although cores themselves were not recovered at Meadowcroft, the artifact assemblage from the nearby and apparently contemporaneous Krajacic site contains a great variety of the distinctive Meadowcroft-style blade implements and several small, cylindrical polyhedral cores. Recovered after the initial study of the Meadowcroft lithic assemblage had been undertaken in 1975, the Krajacic cores precisely parallel the core reduction strategy previously posited for the Meadowcroft blades.

In 1976, a small, lanceolate biface, subsequently called the Miller Lanceolate projectile point, was found *in situ* on the uppermost living floor of lower Stratum IIa at Meadowcroft Rockshelter. This floor is bracketed above and below by radiocarbon assays of 11,300 ± 700 yr B.P. and 12,800 ± 870 yr B.P., respectively. This unfluted biface is the only Miller Lanceolate point thus far recovered from a *directly dated stratigraphic context* (though others have been recovered elsewhere in the Cross Creek drainage), and particular care must be exercised in formulating even a provisional typological definition.

Many potentially diagnostic features of the Miller biface are difficult to identify because the type specimen had been resharpened in antiquity and therefore has undergone a considerable amount of change from its original or prototypic morphology. It is almost certain, however, that the prototype Miller Lanceolate was longer. The angles of articulation between its lateral margins and base suggest that the maximum width may have been achieved toward the distal end of the biface. One fragmentary artifact from the Krajacic site collection conforms exactly in most of its diagnostic characteristics to the Miller Lanceolate prototype. Together with the prismatic blades, the Miller type specimen is of special interest because of its great age and because it reflects its maker's sophisticated knowledge of flaked stone tool manufacture.

Collectively, these data suggest that the first inhabitants of eastern North America employed a technologically standardized and sophisticated, small, polyhedral core-and blade-based industry of decidedly Eurasiatic, Upper Paleolithic "flavor." Not surprisingly, although this assemblage is unique in eastern North America, it reflects precisely the sort of lithic reduction strategy that *should* be evidenced at this time. Moreover, this assemblage is not at variance technologically or chronologically with its possible Siberian prototypes.

It should be noted that despite unfounded observations to the contrary, nothing in the Miller complex lithic suite occurs in or is apparently related to any later cultural manifestations. Its unique blade-making technology in particular is unknown in later contexts. Additionally, though partially coeval at least in its later stages with Clovis, few connections between these two early cultures are presently apparent.

In the long view, it appears that the Miller complex populations can be tentatively characterized as generalized hunter-foragers rather than specialized hunters, and, further, that despite their geographically circumscribed distribution, they represent the baseline—as of 1998—for all subsequent cultural developments in the upper Ohio Valley and, perhaps, eastern North America.

History of the Debate

As noted in Adovasio et al. (1990:348–349), initial criticisms of the possible antiquity of Meadowcroft Rockshelter centered around quite basic and understandable issues. Following the appearance of the first date list (Adovasio et al. 1975), which included "only" 17 radiometric determinations, it was correctly pointed out that a large gap existed between the late Archaic dates and the earlier Paleoindian dates. It was further suggested that many more dates needed to be run, and this was done. It was also suggested that additional dates be obtained from laboratories other than the Smithsonian Institution, and this too was done.

By the later 1970s, almost 40 dates were available from two laboratories, but a new set of loosely interrelated issues was raised. These questions, eloquently articulated by Haynes (1980) and Mead (1980), among others, concerned the possibility of some sort of contamination of the earlier dates on the one hand, and the appropriateness of the associated flora and fauna on the other. Haynes (1980:583–584) suggested that while particulate contamination of the older Meadowcroft samples probably was unlikely, a soluble contaminant may have been introduced into the deepest samples via groundwater percolation or some similar mechanism. Regarding the fauna and flora, Mead (1980:579–587) concluded that the ecofactual materials associated with the oldest culture-bearing strata were discordant with then prevalent reconstructions of late Wisconsinan environments. Interestingly, as of 1980 not a single one of the hundreds of American and foreign archaeologists who visited the site between 1973 and 1978 or who wrote about it from afar questioned the rigor or precision of the excavation or data recovery methods, or the validity of the stratigraphy, context, or associations of the dates, artifacts, or ecofacts. With several notable exceptions, few criticisms were ever raised on these issues—unlike several other sites that have been advanced as pre-Clovis candidates.

The collective response to Haynes, Mead, and others (Adovasio et. al 1980) was among the earliest of the expositions of the dating issue and related matters prepared by the Meadowcroft/Cross Creek research group. By the early 1980s, a long series of publications had appeared, culminating in an edited volume (Carlisle and Adovasio 1982) that went through four printings and that presented the results of a well-attended, day-long SAA symposium in Minneapolis, Minnesota. This collection addressed and reassessed from a variety of angles the dating problem as well as the nature and degree of alleged discordance of the associated flora and fauna.

Later, major contributions to the debate include two lengthy treatments of paleoenvironmental reconstruction (Adovasio et al. 1984, 1985), which expanded considerably on the earlier assessments provided in Adovasio et al. (1977a, 1977b, 1979–1980a, 1979–1980b). The works stressed the generally nondiagnostic character and diminutive size of the oldest floral and faunal assemblages at Meadowcroft and underscored the unique topographic, geomorphologic, and micro-environmental circumstances of the site's general setting. In our view these points are worth reiterating, as they are still valid today.

The entire faunal and floral assemblage from the lower reaches of Stratum IIa at Meadowcroft consists of 278 bones and 11.9 grams of plant remains, respectively. Of this meager total, only 11 bones are identifiable, although a somewhat greater diversity of taxa are represented in the slightly larger floral assemblage. As noted in Adovasio et al. (1984:358–359), the identifiable vertebrates, white-tailed deer (*Odocoileus virginianus*), southern flying squirrel (*Glaucomys volans*), and passenger pigeon (*Ectopistes migratorius*), suggest—but do not dictate—a temperate setting, while the floral assemblage indicates a mixed conifer hardwood forest dominated by oak (*Quercus* sp.), hickory (*Carya* sp.), pine (*Pinus* sp.), and perhaps walnut (*Juglans* sp.), with hackberry (*Celtis* sp.) as an understory element. These two data sets, in turn, are taken to suggest that no radical ecological reorganization occurred at the site throughout its entire occupational sequence. Put another way, and paraphrasing Guilday et al. (1980), any environmental changes that occurred during the long span of time represented in the Meadowcroft occupational sequence took place within a predominantly mast forest context and were of such a low order that the biota were not seriously disturbed at the site. As noted above, this interpretation has caused no little distress to some critics and continues to be cited by several authorities (e.g., Curran 1996; Haynes 1991) as a problem area.

In this regard, we reiterate that the Cross Creek drainage at the time of its initial occupancy lay far south of the glacial front. The late Wisconsinan deglaciation commenced much earlier than previously estimated (cf. Adovasio et al. 1984), with the result that the ice margin already had retreated to the general vicinity of the present shoreline of Lake Erie (some 150 km [93 mi] to the north) when Meadowcroft was first visited (Adovasio et al. 1996). We also stress that Meadowcroft occurs in a topographical setting which in one recent year had 40–50 more frost-free days than did contiguous higher elevations and drainages. Indeed, modern Cross Creek has more "southerly" temperature regimes than any other drainage in the area. If this is now the situation, it may well have been the case prehistorically. The fact that the Cross Creek drainage trends generally east–west rather than north–south also may help to explain its enduring temperate ecology, as well as the southern exposure of the rockshelter.

Consistent with the greater number of frost-free days is Meadowcroft's lower elevation (259.9 m [852.5 ft] above msl) compared to other areas in the Cross Creek drainage, and especially in relation to other paleontologic sites to which the site is frequently compared (e.g., Hosterman's Pit [377 m above msl] and New Paris Sinkhole No. 4 [465 m above msl], Pennsylvania; Clark's Cave [448 m above msl], Virginia; or Baker Bluff Cave [450 m above msl], Tennessee). Taken as a whole, Meadowcroft's unique topographic setting, coupled with its considerable distance from the ice front, are—in our view—more than sufficient to account for the allegedly "ecologically anomalous" temperate character of the Meadowcroft micro-environment as reflected in the deepest deposits. Buttressed by similar data from other localities, which strongly support a mosaic rather than uniform conditions in glacial-front environments, these data were sufficient to answer the ecological objections of some of the most ardent critics of the site (e.g., Dincauze 1981), but the contamination issue was not stilled. Indeed, as a result of the papers and publications cited above, it was suggested that yet more assays be run, that still other labs be used, and that AMS be applied to small carbon samples to resolve the dating issue of this critically important site once and for all. As is detailed below, this and much more has been done.

Between 1985 and the First World Summit on the Peopling of the Americas in 1989, the issue of possible contamination was reiterated by Haynes (1987) and Tankersley et al. (1987) from two slightly different perspectives. A stratigraphic element was injected by Kelly (1987), and Dincauze (1984) continued to question (as she did in 1981) the non-Paleoindian character of the oldest lithic assemblages from the site as well as the alleged "hiatus" between the latest Paleoindian and middle Archaic deposits. All of the critics of the mid-1980s suggested yet more measures to clarify the dating issue, and these were undertaken—in some cases long before the critical suggestions appeared in print. Our original submission to the First World Summit on the Peopling of the Americas (Adovasio et al. 1989) addressed many of the questions raised by Haynes, Tankersley, and others and was followed by an article in *American Antiquity* (Adovasio et al. 1990), which represented a slightly modified version of that earlier paper.

In the early 1990s, Haynes (1991) and Tankersley and Munson (1992) again raised the specter of contamination, while Dincauze (personal communication 1995) persisted in questioning the Paleoindian ascription of the lower and middle Stratum IIa Meadowcroft lithic assemblage. A response to Tankersley and Munson was provided in 1992 (Adovasio et al. 1992), and a more general commentary on the broader issue of the overall antiquity of Meadowcroft and other putative pre-Clovis sites appeared in 1993 (Adovasio 1993).

The specific comments made by Haynes (1991), which actually appeared after the preparation (but not publication) of the responses noted above, have not heretofore been answered in print. The need for a response and the general direction taken by the most recent round of exchanges have convinced the present authors that the salient details of the Meadowcroft radiocarbon column and certain related facts are worth repeating yet again, although like Meltzer (personal communication 1994), we seriously doubt that the dating controversy will ever be settled to the satisfaction of all parties.

The Meadowcroft Radiocarbon Column

One hundred four charcoal samples from Meadowcroft have been submitted to four laboratories for radiometric dating. The Meadowcroft charcoal came from fire pits, fire floors, or charcoal features with the exception of two carbonized basketry fragments, one of which will be discussed further below. To date, 52 of these samples have produced dates (Figure 1). All but four dates are internally consistent and in absolute stratigraphic order, the four exceptions being low-magnitude reversals or "flip-flops" occurring in the middle Archaic, late Archaic, and late Woodland periods. The validity of the 39 dates younger than 12,800 yr B.P.—that is, the majority suite of dates that

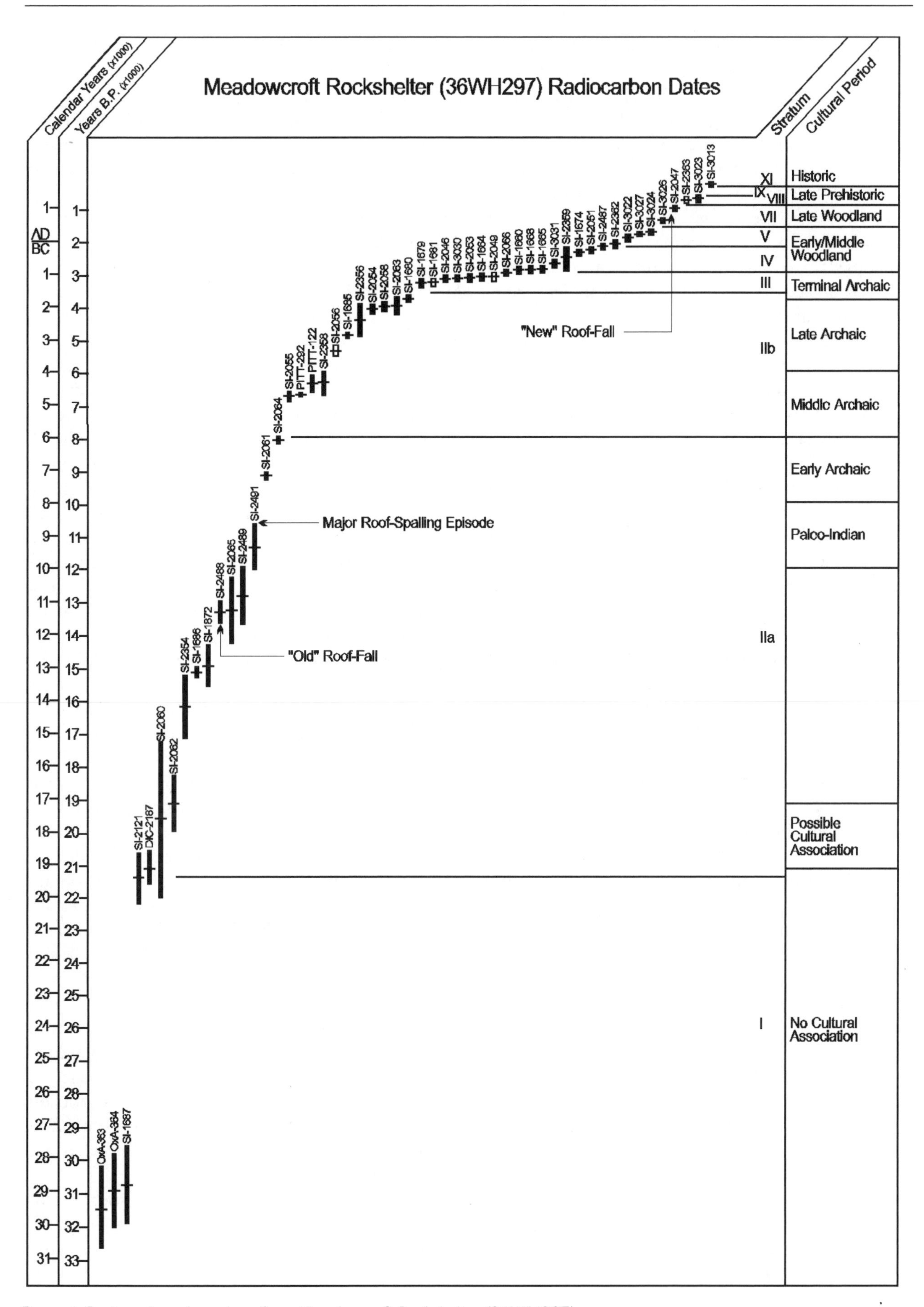

Figure 1. Radiocarbon chronology from Meadowcroft Rockshelter (36WH297).

includes the "later" Paleoindian component as well as the entire Archaic, Woodland, late Prehistoric, and early Historic periods in the site deposits—has never been seriously assailed, though Tankersley and Munson (1992:321–322) raised the possibility that some of these dates may be contaminated as well. In this regard, we can only restate that all of the post-Pleistocene dates from Meadowcroft are associated with temporally diagnostic projectile points and/or ceramics appropriate to and fully consistent with their radiocarbon ages as derived from comparative studies of other sites in eastern North America. This consistent series of artifacts specifically includes 21 named projectile point types ranging from Kirk Serrated and Kanawha Stemmed to Madison, three well-established ceramic wares (Half-Moon, Watson, and Monongahela), and several other chronologically sensitive diagnostic artifact types, none of which occur outside their known date range or position in the chronological sequence as established at scores of other sites. In light of this, we can only restate that if the upper levels at Meadowcroft are erroneously dated, so are all of the myriad sites that have produced diagnostics presumed to be of similar age (see Adovasio et al. 1992:329–330).

The persistent questions that have been raised, both recently and in the past, have been (again, with the exception of Tankersley and Munson [1992]) directed *solely* at the 13 remaining dates older than ca. 12,800 ± 870 yr B.P., of which only six have clear, undeniable, and extensive artifact associations. Critiques of the validity of the radiocarbon column as a whole, therefore, have been clearly selective and directed only at the strata that predate the apparently ever-younger Clovis efflorescence now placed at ca. 11,200–10,900 yr B.P.

As is well known, most of the questions articulated about the pre-12,800 yr B.P. dates have concerned the possibilities of either particulate or non-particulate contamination, though as noted above, even Haynes does not seriously entertain the possibility that particulates played a role in the possible contamination of the deepest Meadowcroft dates. Rather, in his most recent discussion of the dates, Haynes (1991) reasserts that dissolved or soluble contaminants probably are responsible for any postdepositional, artificial aging of the lower Stratum IIa samples.

Interestingly, Haynes (1991) reintroduces the notion that the associated ecofactual assemblage is "Holocene in character" and that there is no stratigraphic break or change at the Pleistocene–Holocene boundary (cf. Haynes 1980), which he places at ca. 11,000 yr B.P. We already have commented upon the floral and faunal associations but are somewhat surprised that Haynes continues to cite their "anomalous" character, particularly since similarly "mixed" floral assemblages have now been shown to be quite common in contemporary times and settings just west of the general study area (cf. Shane 1994:7–22).

The issue of the absence of a stratigraphic break at Meadowcroft has been thoroughly discussed previously (Adovasio et al. 1980), and we can only assume that it has been resurrected because Haynes, based on his experience in the American Southwest, is convinced that there is a continent-wide (if not a worldwide) stratigraphic signature for the Pleistocene–Holocene boundary (PHB) in the northern hemisphere. Although space precludes an extended discussion of this provocative idea, it may be stated that extensive evidence suggests that such a signature is absent from open-site contexts in much of western North America and is not evidenced at all in similar site settings in eastern North America. Even if there were a recognizable PHB signature in alluvial or fluvial settings, the extension of such a signature to closed depositional environments like caves and rockshelters is baseless, since deposition in most such cases is controlled by local structural factors and not by macro-climatic events (Donahue and Adovasio 1990). The absence of such a signature in both archaeological and paleontologic closed sites in eastern and western North America would seem to argue convincingly against its universality or the depositional hiatus it allegedly marks.

Haynes (1991) also suggests that the entire sediment package above basal Stratum I is of Holocene origin, despite the fact that the fluvial Cross Creek terrace *below* the site has been dated on the Ohio River to the 23rd millennium B.P. (Adovasio et al. 1980:592) and despite the utter absence of alluvial sedimentation or significantly higher stream levels after that date. Under these circumstances, it is simply not parsimonious to ascribe the >4 m (13.1 ft) column of Meadowcroft sediment to the last 11,000 years. The presence of precultural radiocarbon dates in the deepest portion of the depositional sequence would seem to confirm this observation, unless of course they also are contaminated.

Haynes (1991) devotes the bulk of his most recent Meadowcroft comments to a thoughtful and quite useful exposition of the nature of soluble contamination, and how to recognize and test for it.

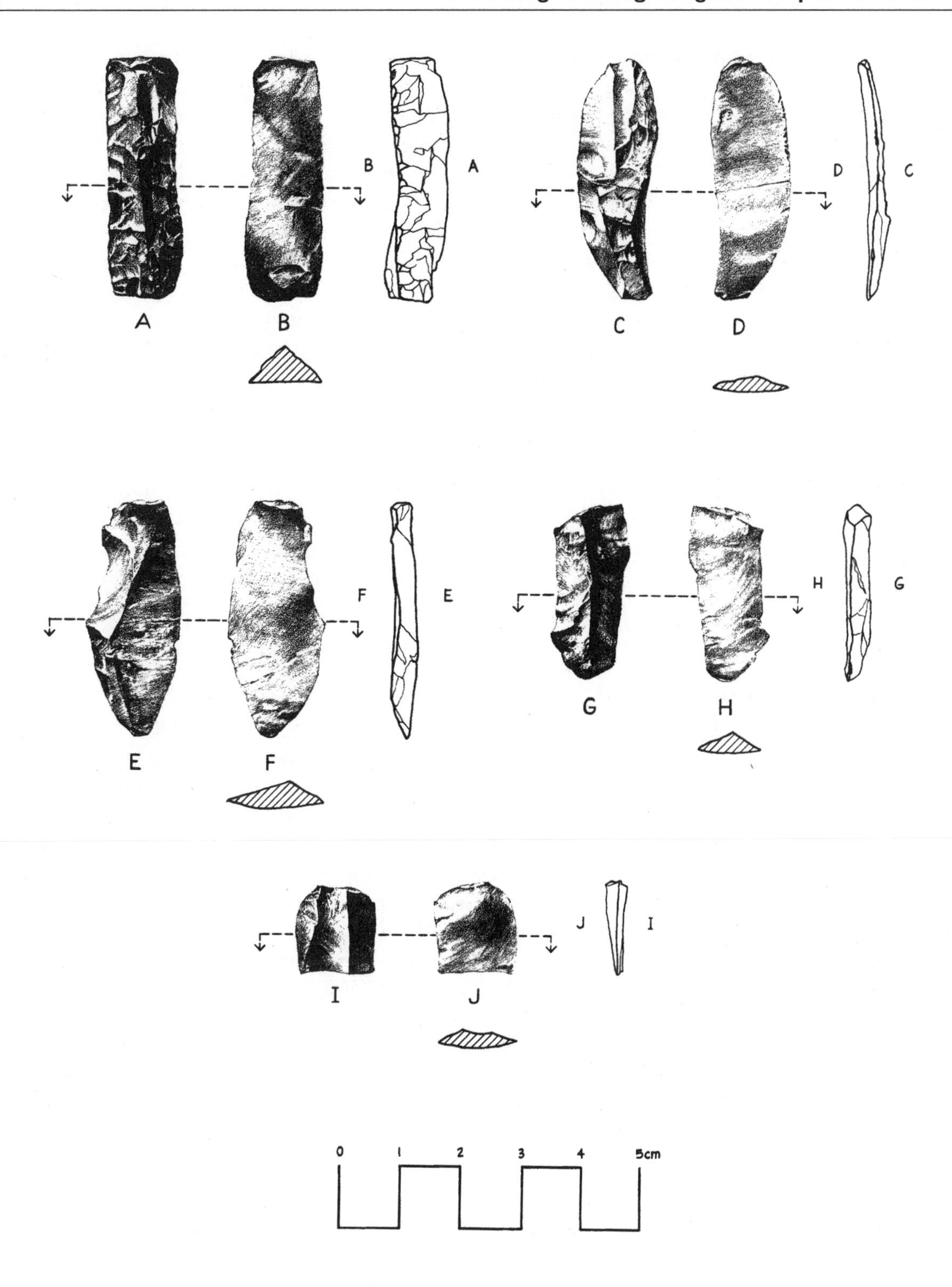

Figure 2. Representative sample of small prismatic blades from Paleoindian occupation levels at Meadowcroft Rockshelter (36WH297).

He reasserts, on the basis of at least two samples from lower Stratum IIa, that there is a serious possibility that all of the lower (and middle?) Stratum IIa samples are contaminated, either by older soluble carbon or that they may not be carbon at all (see below). He suggests several sources of possible contamination, including coal deposits up the hydropic gradient from the rockshelter and so-called "mung" from beneath the cultural layers of lower Stratum IIa. He then speculates on the possible origins of the carbonaceous "mung" and notes that observations about the preservation of a paleo-dripline signature in the deposits do not nullify the possibility that groundwater may have contaminated the deepest fire pits. Finally, Haynes suggests a number of ways to resolve the age of the oldest culture-bearing deposits at Meadowcroft. At the risk of being repetitive, the authors wish to address the following issues with rebuttals that are not in any sense "new."

Soluble Contamination

As noted in Adovasio et al. (1990:351–352), in only two of the 13 samples from lower and middle Stratum IIa were humic acid extractions arrested for fear that too little sample would be left to assay. Further, in only two of the remaining 11 samples was the dissolved fraction older than the solid fraction. The occasional occurrence of older carbon in radiocarbon samples is not as unusual as Haynes suggests. (In any case, such older material can be removed during pretreatment [cf. Adovasio et al. 1980:590].) It should be noted that during the course of AMS testing of one of the noncultural samples from lower Stratum IIa, the Oxford Laboratory conclusively indicated that the soluble fraction in that sample was *younger* than the residue and further that the residue was, in fact, charcoal. Similarly, when I. Stehli of Dicarb Radioisotope "blind-dated" a lower Stratum IIa sample—that is, examined it without any locational or stratigraphic data—she concluded that the sample was charcoal and was not contaminated. While neither the Oxford nor Dicarb assays conclusively prove the lack of soluble contamination of the lower and middle Stratum IIa samples, they certainly do not support such a possibility. The fact that both of these laboratories confirmed the charcoal origin and character of the dated material strongly corroborates the conclusions of the Smithsonian Institution and University of Pittsburgh radiocarbon labs that the material dated from the other Stratum IIa samples was also charcoal.

The notion that the "mung" may be a potential source of contamination presumes that somehow, either in particulate or dissolved form, precisely the right amount of this substance entered the deeper Paleoindian fire features and thereby contaminated them in such a way as to systematically render them artificially older in exact stratigraphic sequence. As noted above, it is no more likely that progressively smaller doses of particulate "mung" were introduced into the charcoal samples than were similar doses of particulate vitrite (i.e., vitrain) or fusain (cf. Adovasio et al. 1992). To posit the introduction of dissolved "mung" is to suggest yet another "could have or might have been" scenario similar to those raised by Tankersley and Munson (1992). We concur that this scenario or indeed many others are *theoretically* possible which is not to say—let alone prove—that they ever happened.

Mechanisms of Contamination

Critical to the issue of any of the soluble contamination scenarios is the mechanism of contamination. According to Haynes (1991), the likeliest choice is groundwater fluctuation. Haynes dismisses the lack of any evidence for a low water table at Meadowcroft by noting correctly that, in general, late Pleistocene water tables were higher than today and, further, that since Cross Creek is an effluent stream the effects of such a higher water table would be more pronounced. Haynes conjectures that, in fact, Pleistocene water tables were sufficiently high to not only repeatedly flood the deeper deposits but also to introduce the "mung" itself and the Stratum IIa samples, which may not be charcoal.

We find these conclusions insupportable for several reasons. First, as noted previously (Adovasio et al. 1980:592), the 3 to 9 m terrace below Meadowcroft is in excess of 20,000 years old and, in conjunction with the absence of any overbank deposits more than 10 m above the current stream level, strongly argues that Cross Creek was never substantially higher in the past than it is now. Currently, the surface of uppermost Stratum XI at Meadowcroft Rockshelter stands 15.1 m (49.4 ft) above the creek and 6 to 12 m (19.7 to 39.4 ft) above the 22,000 yr B.P. Pleistocene terrace. The deepest occupation surface within the colluvial pile is presently ca. 11 m (36.1 ft) above Cross Creek and 5 to 7 m (16.4 to 23 ft) above the late Pleistocene terrace. To propose a perched water table high enough to sequentially inundate the deeper Stratum IIa occupation surfaces under these circumstances stretches credulity to an extreme. Similarly, Haynes's suggestion that the Stratum I/IIa shale-sandstone contact is a likely place for groundwater sheet flow to be concentrated is belied by the fact that outside the rockshelter to the west where this contact is plainly visible, no such sheet flow is demonstrable.

The Paleo-Dripline Signature

HAYNES (1991) SUGGESTS that we may have misinterpreted the significance of the presence of a paleo-dripline signature in the deposits at Meadowcroft because the timing of the creation of such a signature is incorrect. This and a related issue are actually as critical to the whole groundwater percolation scenario as the topographic data offered above and merit extended comment.

Meadowcroft Rockshelter is a sandstone rockshelter. The deposits within the site are derived largely from three sources: grain-by-grain attrition of sand from the roof and walls of the shelter, detachment of roof spalls, and limited sheetwash from the eastern and western edges of the site after portions of the modern roof collapsed. The sandstone at Meadowcroft is cemented with $CaCo_3$—not $Si0_2$—and is relatively friable. Indeed, attrition occurs on a daily basis without interruption and produces a sediment rain on the site, which, among other things, precludes all pedogenesis within the deposits. This sediment rain also is the source for the $CaCo_3$ in the deposits. Haynes derives the $CaCo_3$ in the Meadowcroft sediment pile from illuviation and subsequent precipitation at capillary fringes with increasing depth. This happens in open-site settings, but it is not the process operating at Meadowcroft or, indeed, in most sandstone rockshelters with CaCo3 cement.

In such sites, $CaCo_3$ accumulates inside the dripline precisely because it cannot be carried away. It is not a secondary deposit; it is a primary deposit. Moreover,

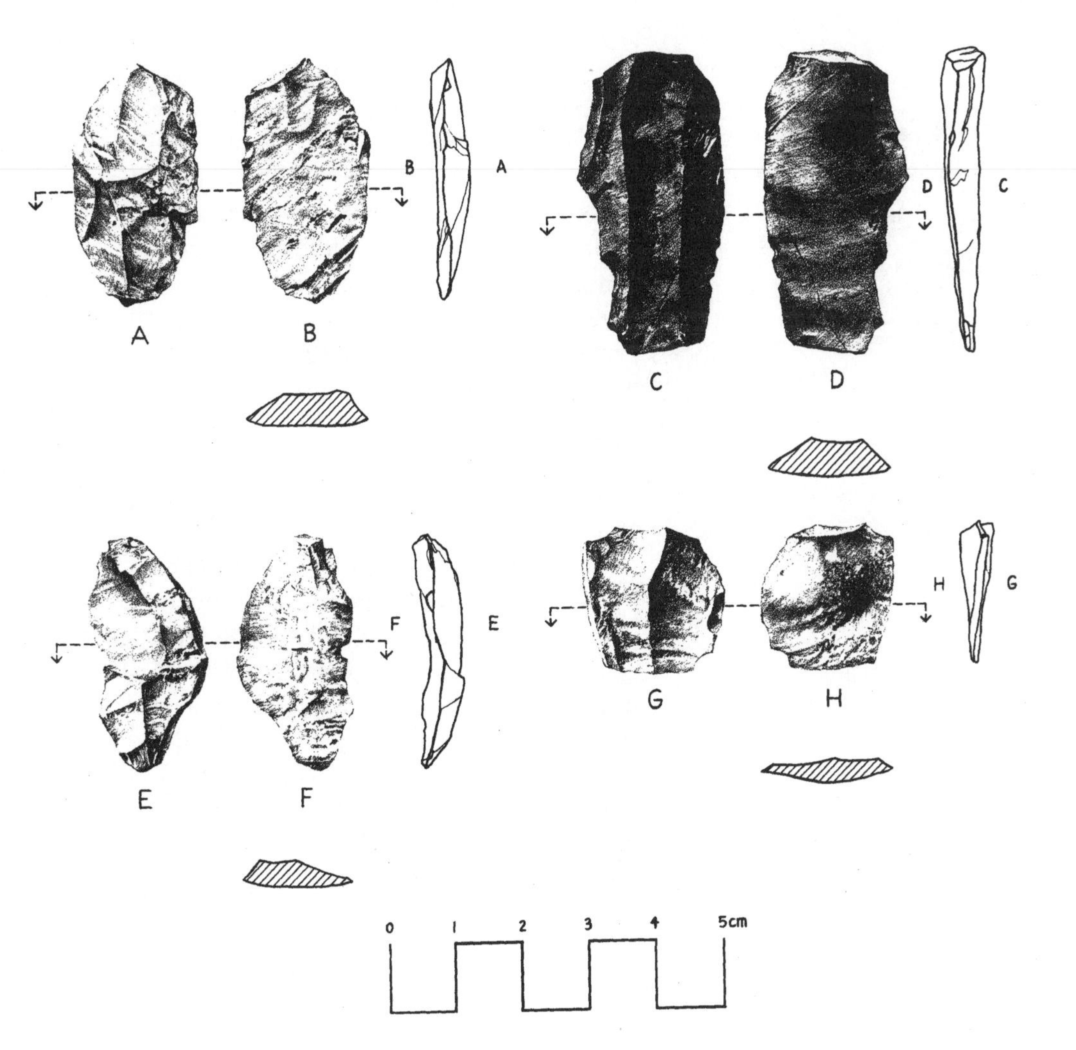

Figure 3. Representative sample of small prismatic blades from the Krajacic site (36WH351) in the Cross Creek drainage, southwestern Pennsylvania.

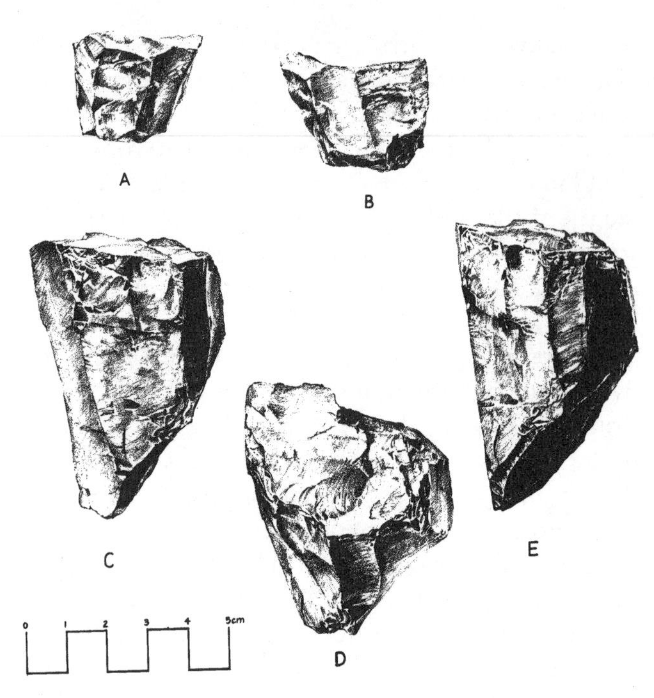

Figure 4. Cylindrical polyhedral cores from the Krajacic site (36WH351) in the Cross Creek drainage, southwestern Pennsylvania.

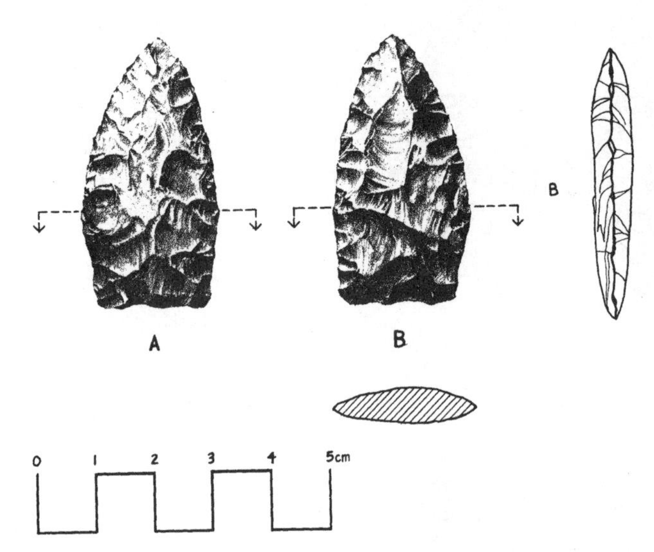

Figure 5. Type specimen Miller Lanceolate projectile point from Meadowcroft Rockshelter (36WH297).

it occurs in the deposits from top to bottom within the dripline. Outside the dripline, the $CaCo_3$ is illuviated, and the degree of illuviation normally is a function of depth below surface. As the roof retreats, a gradient is created, which, in the case of Meadowcroft, extends to the very base of the Stratum IIa deposits. This gradient directly reflects the retreat of the roof. Under these circumstances, if groundwater had fluctuated as much as Haynes' contamination scenario suggests, it would have to *obliterate* the primary $CaCo_3$ signature. The presence of the signature, coupled with no evidence whatsoever of subsurface flow structures or even postdepositional grain modification by moving water, suggests to us that there is no possibility—let alone probability—that groundwater fluctuations contaminated the stratified Paleoindian fire features in lower and middle Stratum IIa.

In this vein we reiterate that the anthropogenic origin of the fire features is incontrovertible and, contrary to the suggestions of Kelly (1987), there is absolutely no evidence of stratigraphic mixing via bioturbation or human activity in lower and middle Stratum IIa. Indeed, as noted by Adovasio et al. (1990:349), there is a definite and clear-cut separation of superimposed living floors, not only on both qualitative and quantitative geological, geochemical, and sedimentologic grounds, but also on the basis of lithic refitting and raw-material studies, which show no significant cross-horizon artifact movement whatsoever. Perhaps significantly, several of the Miller complex artifacts recovered from fire features are also thermally altered, further underscoring their penecontemporaneity with those thermal phenomena; in short, they are not intrusive.

Amino Acid Racemization

ALMOST AS AN AFTERTHOUGHT, Haynes (1991) concludes by noting that the amino acid racemization ages in two shell samples from the 14,000–15,000 yr B.P. occupation level at Meadowcroft may be 10–20 percent in error. We agree entirely, but note that even if this is the case and even if the error is toward the "younger" side, the samples are minimally 11,600–12,000 years old, which makes them substantially older than the mean age of 11,000 ± 200 yr B.P. currently attributed by Haynes (1993) to Clovis.

The Dating Issue in a Nutshell

Haynes (1991:8–14) suggests that the Meadowcroft/Cross Creek research group has never tested in a truly objective fashion the alternative suggestions or hypotheses proposed by himself and other site critics. He concludes his commentary by recommending the AMS dating of walnut (*Juglans* sp.) shells from lower Stratum IIa, a means whereby he might be convinced of the antiquity of the site (a suggestion echoed by Meltzer 1993). In light of the past two decades of research (and the time, effort, and expense entailed therein), we find this first observation curious since most of our work on the early occupations since 1978 has occurred to *satisfy* or *answer* the questions and recommendations of others. We have not, as Haynes (1991:8) asserts, "made the rules or defined the standards." Rather, they have been imposed on us by others and we have willingly complied.

As Haynes (1991) notes, the senior author is more than sympathetic with the idea of AMS dating the *Juglans* sp. shells, but for fairly simple reasons there is serious doubt (as we noted previously) that this will resolve anything. If the nutshells prove to be as old as the feature-derived charcoal, their ages may be just as easily attributed as the product of soluble contaminants. It is perhaps useful to remind the reader that one of the oldest radiocarbon dates from lower Stratum IIa at Meadowcroft is on a piece of carbonized *Betula*-like bark (the basketry fragment mentioned above), a substance whose chemical behavior as a dating medium is no different from that of carbonized nutshells. Haynes has already discounted the bark fragment, so our negative prognosis is not without foundation.

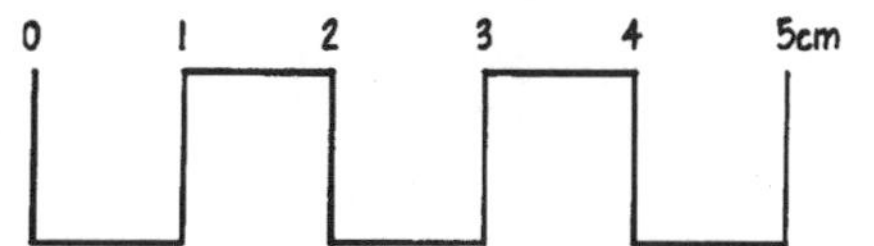

Figure 6. Postulated "prototype" Miller Lanceolate projectile point.

Overview and Prognosis

Despite the continued objections of the site's critics and considering the supporting data accumulated through two decades of research, the present authors (among others) are still convinced that Meadowcroft represents the earliest bona fide evidence of human occupation south of the glacial ice in North America. Applying the most conservative interpretation of the data, we conclude that even if only the youngest date from upper middle Stratum IIa is valid, the *minimum* age for the presence of human populations in this portion of Pennsylvania is on the order of 10,600–12,000 yr B.P. If the six deepest dates unequivocally associated with cultural material are averaged—a procedure with which we are uncomfortable in statistical terms—then humans were definitely present at this site (and by implication, throughout much and perhaps all of the Americas) sometime between 13,955 and 14,555 radiocarbon years ago.

As we stressed at the First World Summit on the Peopling of the Americas (Adovasio et al. 1989) and in Adovasio et al. (1990), it is important to note that the earliest Meadowcroft dates that have extensive artifact associations do not argue for any radical extension of 11,500-year Clovis "baseline." There is certainly no evidence at Meadowcroft, as has been posited for some other sites (e.g., Pedra Furada, Brazil, and Pendejo Cave, New Mexico) for an initial site occupation at 20,000, 30,000, 40,000, or more years ago. Although such an early time horizon in New World archaeology may ultimately be demonstrated by work at other sites, the Meadowcroft dates suggest, rather conservatively, that humans first occupied this locality perhaps as little as 500 radiocarbon years or at most 2,000–3,000 years before the well-established 11,500-year Clovis horizon marker. (Indeed, as noted by Dincauze [1989:137–138], our current estimates of the initial occupation of Meadowcroft Rockshelter have been reduced considerably over previous and probably overexuberant pronouncements.) The frequently cited twentieth millennium B.P. dates (SI-2060 and SI-2062) were both very small, diluted samples, one of which (SI-2060) has a very high standard deviation of 2,400 years. If the *younger* range of both of these dates is averaged, then, statistically,

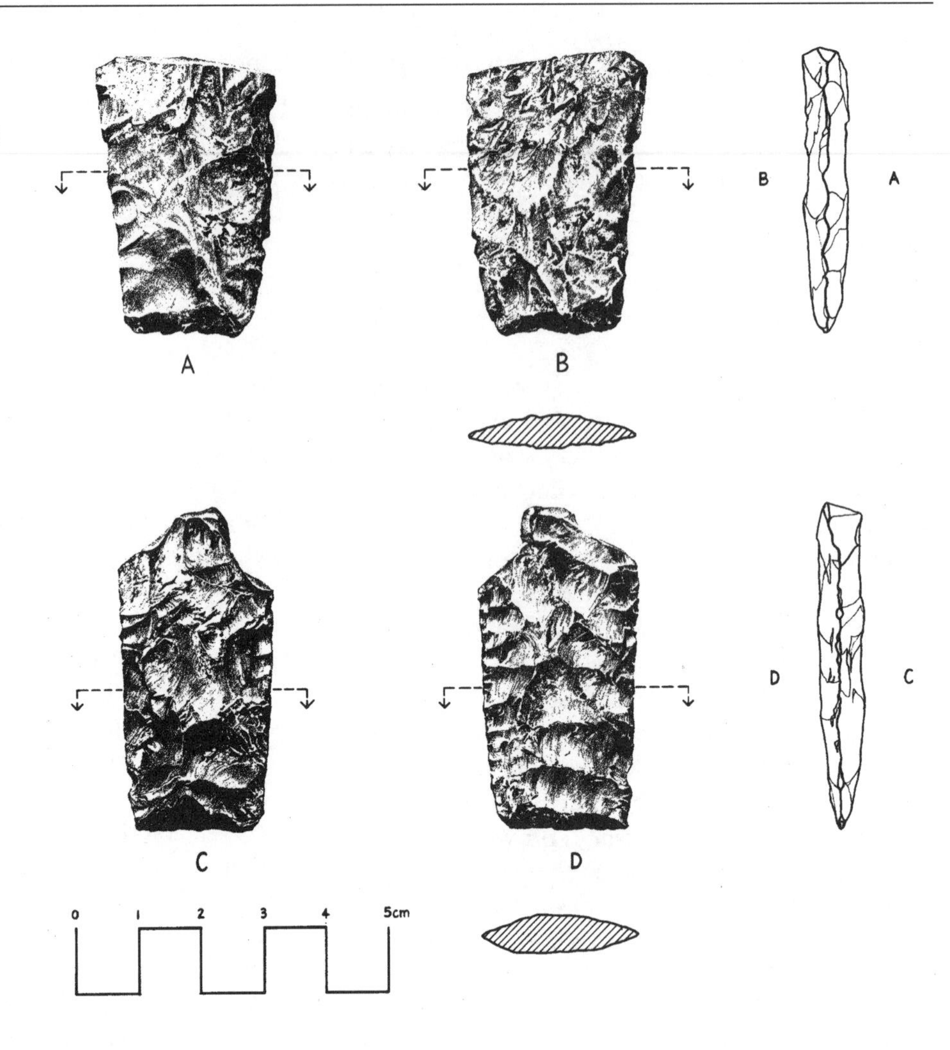

Figure 7. Miller Lanceolate projectile point fragment from the Krajacic site (36WH351) in the Cross Creek drainage, southwestern Pennsylvania.

the earliest possible occupation of the site *may* have occurred ca. 16,770 radiocarbon years ago.

Contrary to the assertions of Parry (1994), who never examined the Meadowcroft/Cross Creek collections, and Dincauze (personal communications 1995, 1996, 1997), who along with Haynes (personal communication 1996), persists in calling the earliest Meadowcroft material "Plano" or "Plano-like," the lower and middle Stratum IIa lithic assemblage is unique among deeply stratified radiocarbon-dated sites in eastern North America. This uniqueness is demonstrated by technologically sophisticated, small blades struck from polyhedral cores; lanceolate, unfluted projectile points; and other well-made bifaces and unifaces (Figures 2–7). Interestingly, materials of similar configuration—though made on coarser lithic raw materials—recently have been recovered from the Cactus Hill site in Virginia, where they were documented in sediments of broadly similar age (McAvoy and McAvoy 1997). Whatever the ultimate distribution of these artifacts, the Miller complex materials from Meadowcroft are technologically consistent with what several researchers (e.g., Boldurian 1985; Carr, personal communication 1997) suggest should exist at a genuine pre-Clovis site. Moreover, as has been stressed many times previously, in technological and chronological terms this assemblage is not dissimilar to its possible Siberian prototypes (Derevianko 1998; Yi and Clark 1985).

Rather than further belabor an already thoroughly belabored point, and to come full circle to our presentation at the First World Summit Conference on the Peopling of the Americas, we prefer instead to paraphrase our conclusions from Adovasio et al. (1989), reprinted in Adovasio et al. (1990:353). In the final analysis, however, the precise date of Meadowcroft's earliest occupation is of relatively little consequence. This unique site has produced a vast array of geological, archaeological, paleofloral, and paleofaunal data that collectively help one to understand more about the full temporal and cultural range of aboriginal human life in this part of the Ohio River system. Although the incipient occupation of the site has, understandably but perhaps unfortunately, captured the spotlight, the lion's share of the site's unquestioned deposits are an eloquent testimonial to thousands of years of subsequent human cultural adaptation. If the site accomplishes no more than to draw increased attention to this sometimes subtle, sometimes radically shifting relationship among humans, their technology, and the conditions of their natural environment, it will be enough.

Acknowledgments

The excavations and attendant analyses at Meadowcroft Rockshelter and the Cross Creek drainage were conducted under the auspices of the former Archaeological Research Program (subsequently the Cultural Resource Management Program) of the Department of Anthropology, University of Pittsburgh. Recent re-excavations in 1994 and 1995 were conducted under the aegis of the Mercyhurst Archaeological Institute, Mercyhurst College, Erie, Pennsylvania. The initial 1973 field project and the 1977–1978 field seasons were directed by J. M. Adovasio. The 1974–1976 field seasons were co-directed by J. M. Adovasio and J. D. Gunn. The 1994 and 1995 field projects were directed by J. M. Adovasio. Analysis of all materials recovered during the 1973–1995 field seasons is under the ultimate direction of J. M. Adovasio. Albert Miller, owner of the site, is acknowledged in particular for his long-standing support of the project and his warm humanitarianism.

Generous financial and logistic support for the 1973–1978 excavations and analyses was provided by the University of Pittsburgh, the Meadowcroft Foundation, the National Geographic Society, the National Science Foundation, the Alcoa Foundation, the Buhl Foundation, the Leon Falk Family Trust, and Messrs. John and Edward Boyle of Oil City, Pennsylvania. Support for the 1994 excavations was provided by the Western Pennsylvania Historical Society and the Pennsylvania Historic and Museum Commission. The 1995 excavations were partially underwritten by the National Geographic Society.

Figure 1 was redrafted and expanded by N. L. Yedlowski, Mercyhurst Archaeological Institute. Figures 2–7 were drafted by S. Patricia, Department of Anthropology, University of Pittsburgh. This paper was typed by D. Laush and edited by D. R. Pedler at Mercyhurst College.

This contribution to the Meadowcroft saga is dedicated to the fond memory of Robert Stuckenrath (1927–1994), who in response to critics of the site's radiocarbon chronology was known to have said, "F—'em if they can't read!"

References Cited

Adovasio, J. M.
1993 The Ones That Will Not Go Away: A Biased View of Pre-Clovis Populations in the New World. In *From Kostenki to Clovis: Upper Paleolithic–Paleo-Indian Adaptations*, edited by O. Soffer and N. D. Praslov, pp. 199–218. Plenum Press, New York.

Adovasio, J. M., A. T. Boldurian, and R. C. Carlisle
1988 Who Are Those Guys?: Some Biased Thoughts on the Initial Peopling of the New World. In *Americans Before Columbus: Ice Age Origins*, edited by R. C. Carlisle, pp. 45–61. Ethnology Monographs No. 12, Department of Anthropology, University of Pittsburgh, Pittsburgh.

Adovasio, J. M., R. C. Carlisle, K. A. Cushman, J. Donahue, J. E. Guilday, W. C. Johnson, K. Lord, P. W. Parmalee, R. Stuckenrath, and P. W. Wiegman
1985 Paleoenvironmental Reconstruction at Meadowcroft Rockshelter, Washington County, Pennsylvania. In *Environments and Extinctions: Man in Late Glacial North America*, edited by J. I. Mead and D. J. Meltzer, pp. 73–110. Peopling of the Americas Edited Volume Series, Center for the Study of Early Man, University of Maine, Orono.

Adovasio, J. M., J. Donahue, R. C. Carlisle, K. Cushman, R. Stuckenrath, and P. Wiegman
1984 Meadowcroft Rockshelter and the Pleistocene/Holocene Transition in Southwestern Pennsylvania. In *Contributions in Quaternary Vertebrate Paleontology: A Volume in Memorial to John E. Guilday*, edited by H. H. Genoways and M. R. Dawson, pp. 347–369. Special Publication No. 8, Carnegie Museum of Natural History, Pittsburgh.

Adovasio, J. M., J. Donahue, and R. Stuckenrath
1990 The Meadowcroft Rockshelter Radiocarbon Chronology 1975–1990. *American Antiquity* 55:348–354.

1992 Never Say Never Again: Some Thoughts on Could Haves and Might Have Beens. *American Antiquity* 57:327–331.

Adovasio, J. M., J. Donahue, R. Stuckenrath, and R. C. Carlisle
1989 The Meadowcroft Rockshelter Radiocarbon Chronology 1975–1989: Some Ruminations. Paper presented at the First World Summit Conference in the Peopling of the Americas, University of Maine, Orono, May 24–28.

Adovasio, J. M., R. Fryman, A. G. Quinn, D. C. Dirkmaat, and D. R. Pedler
1996 The Archaic West of the Allegheny Mountains: A View from the Cross Creek Drainage, Washington County, Pennsylvania. *Pennsylvania Archaeologist.*

Adovasio, J. M., J. D. Gunn, J. Donahue, and R. Stuckenrath
1975 Excavations at Meadowcroft Rockshelter, 1973–1974: A Progress Report. *Pennsylvania Archaeologist* 45(3):1–30.

1977a Meadowcroft Rockshelter: Retrospect 1976. *Pennsylvania Archaeologist* 47(2-3).

1977b Meadowcroft Rockshelter: A 16,000 Year Chronicle. In *Amerinds and Their Paleoenvironments in Northeastern North America*, edited by W. S. Newman and B. Salwen, pp. 137–159. *Annals of the New York Academy of Sciences 288.*

Adovasio, J. M., J. D. Gunn, J. Donahue, R. Stuckenrath, J. Guilday, and K. Volman
1980 Yes Virginia, It Really Is That Old: A Reply to Haynes and Mead. *American Antiquity* 45:588–595.

Adovasio, J. M., J. D. Gunn, J. Donahue, R. Stuckenrath, J. Guilday, and K. Lord
1979–1980a Meadowcroft Rockshelter—Retrospect 1977: Part 1. *North American Archaeologist* 1(1):3–44.

1979–1980b Meadowcroft Rockshelter—Retrospect 1977: Part 2. *North American Archaeologist* 1(2):99–137.

Boldurian, A. T.
1985 *Variability in Flintworking Technology at the Krajacic Site: Possible Relationships to the Pre-Clovis Paleo-Indian Occupation of the Cross Creek Drainage in Southwestern Pennsylvania.* Unpublished Ph.D. dissertation, University of Pittsburgh, Pittsburgh, Pennsylvania.

Carlisle, R. C., and J. M. Adovasio (editors)
1982 *Meadowcroft: Collected Papers on the Archaeology of Meadowcroft Rockshelter and the Cross Creek Drainage.* Department of Anthropology, University of Pittsburgh, Pittsburgh.

Curran, M. L.
1996 Paleoindians in the Northeast: The Problem of Dating Fluted Point Sites. *The Review of Archaeology* 17(1): 2–11.

Custer, J. F.
1984 *Delaware Prehistoric Archaeology: An Ecological Approach.* University of Delaware Press, Dover.

1996 *Prehistoric Cultures of Eastern Pennsylvania.* Anthropological Series Number 7. Commonwealth of Pennsylvania, Pennsylvania Historical and Museum Commission, Harrisburg.

Derevianko, A. P.
1998 *The Paleolithic of Siberia: New Discoveries and Interpretations.* Institute of Archaeology & Ethnography of the SB RAS, Novosibirsk, and the University of Illinois Press, Urbana and Chicago.

Dincauze, D. F.
1981 The Meadowcroft Papers. *Quarterly Review of Archaeology* 2:3–4.

1984 An Archaeo-Logical Evaluation of the Case for Pre-Clovis Occupations. *Advances in World Archaeology* 3:275–324.

1989 Introduction 1989. In The Meadowcroft Papers. Reprinted from 1981 with a new introduction. Originally published in *Quarterly Review of Archaeology* 2:3–4. *The Review of Archaeology* 10(1):137–141.

Donahue, J., and J. M. Adovasio
1990 The Evolution of Sandstone Rockshelters in Eastern North America; A Geoarchaeological Approach. In *Archaeological Geology of North America,* edited by N. P. Lasca and J. Donahue, pp. 231–251. Geological Society of America Centennial Special Volume 4. Geological Society of America, Boulder.

Fagan, B. M.
1990 Tracking the first Americans. *Archaeology*, Nov./ Dec.:14–20.

1991 *Ancient North Americans.* 1st ed. Thames and Hudson, Ltd., New York.

1995 *Ancient North Americans.* 2nd ed. Thames and Hudson, Ltd., New York.

Feder, K. L.
1996 *The Past in Perspective.* Mayfield Publishing Company, Mountain View, California.

Fiedel, S. J.
1992 *Prehistory of the Americas.* 2nd ed. Cambridge University Press, New York.

Guilday, J. E., P. W. Parmalee, and R. C. Wilson
1980 Vertebrate Faunal Remains from Meadowcroft Rockshelter (36WH297), Washington County, Pennsylvania. Ms. on file, Mercyhurst Archaeological Institute, Erie, Pennsylvania.

Haynes, C. V.
1980 Paleoindian Charcoal from Meadowcroft Rockshelter: Is Contamination a Problem? *American Antiquity* 45:582–587.

1987 Clovis Origin Update. *The Kiva* 52:83–93.

1991 More on Meadowcroft Rockshelter Radiocarbon Chronology. *The Review of Archaeology* 12(1):8–14.

1993 Clovis–Folsom Geochronology and Climatic Change. In *From Kostenki to Clovis: Upper Paleolithic–Paleo-Indian Adaptations*, edited by O. Soffer and N. D. Praslov, pp. 219–236. Plenum Press, New York.

Kelly, R. L.
1987 A Comment on the Pre-Clovis Deposits at Meadowcroft Rockshelter. *Quaternary Research* 27:332–334.

McAvoy, J., and L. McAvoy
1997 *Archaeological Investigations of Site 44SX202, Cactus Hill, Sussex County, Virginia*. Research Report Series No. 8, Virginia Department of Historic Resources, Nottoway River Survey Archaeological Research Report No. 2. Nottoway River Survey Archaeological Research, Sandston, Virginia.

Mead, J. I
1980 Is It Really That Old? A Comment About the Meadowcroft "Overview." *American Antiquity* 45:579–582.

Meltzer, D. J.
1993 *Search for the First Americans*. St. Remy Press, Montreal, and Smithsonian Books, Washington, D.C.

Parry, W. J.
1994 Prismatic Blade Technologies in North America. In *The Organization of American Prehistoric Chipped Stone Tool Technologies*, edited by P. J. Carr, pp. 87–98. International Monographs in Prehistory, Archaeological Series 7. Ann Arbor.

Shane, L. C. K.
1994 Intensity and Rate of Vegetation and Climatic Change in the Ohio Region Between 14,000 and 9000 14C YBP. In *The First Discovery of America*, edited by W. S. Dancey, pp. 7–21. The Ohio Archaeological Council, Inc., Columbus.

Tankersley, K. B., and C. A. Munson
1992 Comments on the Meadowcroft Rockshelter Radiocarbon Chronology and the Recognition of Coal Contaminants. *American Antiquity* 57:321–326.

Tankersley, K. B., C. A. Munson, and D. Smith
1987 Recognition of Bituminous Coal Contaminants in Radiocarbon Samples. *American Antiquity* 52:318–330.

Yi, S., and G. Clark
1985 The "Dyuktai Culture" and New World Origins. *Current Anthropology* 26:113, 19–20.

The Early Holocene Occupation of the Southeastern United States: A Geoarchaeological Summary

Albert C. Goodyear

Abstract

The southeastern United States has long been of interest to students of the North American Paleoindian period because of the abundant and diverse lithic remains found there. Several thousand fluted and unfluted lanceolate points have been found throughout the southern states. It has been estimated that the dense number of lanceolates found in the river valleys of the mid-South surpasses those of the western United States. Generally recognized point types have been formulated that are thought to have time and space significance. Among the fluted forms are Clovis—virtually identical with those from western Clovis sites—Redstone; Ross County; and Cumberland. The basally thinned or unfluted types include Quad, Suwannee, Simpson, and Dalton. Based on stratigraphic work and radiocarbon dating done outside the Southeast, as well as refinement of early Archaic sequences within the region, these types are thought to span a time from 11,500 to 10,000 yr B.P.

Despite the high archaeological potential of this region, few concentrations of Paleoindian artifacts have been found that would lend themselves to archaeological excavation. Most Paleoindian points have been found on the surface, often as isolated finds. Geological conditions during the late Pleistocene–early Holocene did not produce deeply buried sites over much of the Southeast, particularly on the interfluvial surfaces. The greatest success in locating and excavating dense Paleoindian sites has been associated with chert quarries such as Thunderbird, Carson-Conn-Short, Big Pine Tree, and Harney Flats.

The bulk of knowledge for the Paleoindian occupation of the South comes in the form of typologies and geographic distributional studies. Fluted point recording surveys have been established for most states. However, until sites are excavated that possess sufficient stratigraphic depth and/or integrity to allow chronological and paleoenvironmental studies, it will be difficult to interpret these remains in terms of cultural systems. Fieldwork needs to be concentrated on identifying late Pleistocene–early Holocene depositional environments in order to obtain badly needed archaeological contexts.

Toward that end, this chapter reviews in detail the geoarchaeological situations of a variety of sites throughout the Southeast in the hope of discerning patterns that might yield criteria for recognizing early Holocene deposits. Excavations in the floodplains of major drainages in the southern Appalachians have demonstrated a high potential for deep alluvial burial of early sites. A pedosedimentary pattern is recognized where Dalton period and earlier lithics are found in early Holocene fluvial sands, often pedogenically unmodified, overlying argillic Bt paleosols. The geologic contact of the two is suggested to represent the Pleistocene–Holocene transition. The recovery of faunal and other organic remains in the rivers and sinkholes of Florida provide another encouraging context that should allow radiocarbon dating and subsistence reconstruction. There is a high probability that intact early sites exist in the drowned river valleys of the west coast of Florida, inundated by Holocene sea-level rise.

South Carolina Institute of Archaeology and Anthropology,
University of South Carolina

> *A number of factors contribute to the paucity of knowledge about the cultures of the Paleoindian Era. First, the majority of fluted points occur as isolated surface finds, thus giving no information about the cultural matrix from which they were derived. Second, most Southeastern sites that have produced fluted points are shallow and multicomponent, so that stratigraphically defined or geographically isolated pure Paleoindian assemblages are very rare indeed* (Williams and Stoltman 1965:673).

THIS PAPER IS CONCERNED with the earliest known peoples of the southeastern United States. The Southeast is of fundamental interest to the study of Paleoindians in the Americas, owing to its environmental position, especially considering latitude, and the fact that a good portion of this area is and was subtropical in climate. In addition, there is an extensive coastline present, including both the Atlantic Ocean and the Gulf of Mexico, which must be taken into account when considering the Paleoindian landscape. This ecological situation, plus the rather dense and impressive Paleoindian technology that is known for the Southeast, combine to pique our intellectual curiosity about ancient human life in this region.

Although the above quote by Williams and Stoltman was published more than 30 years ago, in many ways it remains an apt description of Paleoindian archaeology in the Southeast. Generally speaking, until recently, archaeological studies in the southeastern United States have not been very successful in developing chrono-stratigraphic frameworks for the period from 11,500 to 10,000 yr B.P., compared to the Plains and Southwest and now even the Northeast. This is illustrated in a compilation of ^{14}C dates associated with fluted point sites in the East published a little over a decade ago (Haynes et al. 1984:Figure 2). All the ^{14}C dates are for the Northeast, with none from the Southeast (cf. Meltzer 1988:Table 3). As often noted, the Northeast dates are generally contemporaneous with Folsom dates and not Clovis (cf. Levine 1990). There has been some modest improvement in this situation for the Southeast, however, which will be discussed in this paper.

At the time of earlier generations of southeastern Paleoindian summaries (e.g., Mason 1962, Williams and Stoltman 1965), the preponderance of data came from surface finds from non-alluvial land surfaces. Specifically, these were projectile point finds from plowed and eroded interfluvial landforms, which often occurred as individual finds, or from sites with multi-component occupational histories. In the ensuing 30 years, a great deal more work has been done in paleoenvironmental studies of the Southeast, specifically palynology and geoarchaeology, which allows some explanation as to the contextual condition of the archaeological record. Mitigation-phase excavations in cultural resource management studies beginning in the 1970s produced a great deal of important data related to late Pleistocene and early Holocene geological contexts, particularly alluvial situations.

Productive research utilizing data derived from surface finds of Paleoindian lanceolate points has continued using statewide surveys (Anderson 1990; Anderson et al. 1990; Brennan 1982; Charles 1986; Dunbar and Waller 1983; McCary 1984; McGahey 1987). Mapping of surface finds and the spatial analysis of projectile point styles has allowed the evaluation of models related to colonization (e.g., Anderson 1990; McGahey 1987), land use and site function (O'Steen et al. 1986), landscape reconstruction (Dunbar 1991), and measures of the scale of regional mobility as well as directionality of movement (Anderson et al. 1990; Goodyear et al. 1989).

As noted by Williams and Stoltman (1965) and confirmed by more recent lanceolate point surveys, the majority of specimens have occurred as isolated finds with multiple cases from a single site being something of a rarity (see Anderson 1990:Table 2; Meltzer 1988:Table 2). This pattern of low density, along with the marked tendency for Paleoindian sites to be reoccupied by groups from subsequent early Archaic and other later time periods (cf. Anderson 1990:176), has resulted in a dearth of shallow, single-component Paleoindian sites that provide the assemblage clarity seen in northeastern sites, such as Debert and Vail. Shallow, virtually single-component sites like Brand and Sloan, Dalton sites in northeast Arkansas, have proven to be exceedingly rare. Sites with an artifact density warranting excavation, such as Thunderbird, Williamson, Carson-Conn-Short, Big Pine Tree, and Harney Flats, are nearly always associated with a high-quality chert source where much of the artifact record is related to stone tool manufacture.

It is likely that the natural presence of chert affected the density of points and other shaped tools on quarry-related sites in two ways. First, Paleoindian groups throughout the East were evidently dependent on high-quality lithic raw material for their tool kits (see Ellis and Lothrop 1989). This would have caused a high rate of reoccupation of quarry-associated sites, related to the need to continually reprovision portable tool kits (cf. Goodyear 1989). Second, in the presence of readily available chert supplies, some relaxation in the normally high degree of curation may have occurred. Because of the ease of replacement, artifact loss due to carelessness may have been more frequent, as well as the relatively premature discard of what would have been in other contexts normally useful tools. Even some complete tools at quarry-related sites may represent worn-out discarded implements imported from a previous locality (cf. Binford 1979; Gardner 1983).

Coupled with the lanceolate point surveys has been a strong interest in raw-material selection patterns represented in the various styles of lanceolate points. The pattern of cryptocrystalline utilization so frequently noted for North America has been well-documented for the Southeast, especially for fluted points (Gardner 1974a; Goodyear et al. 1989; McGahey 1987). Lithic raw-material identification studies of projectile points and searches for their geologic sources have been conducted sporadically (Daniel and Butler 1991; Daniel and Wisenbaker 1987; Goodyear and Charles 1984; Goodyear et al. 1983; Upchurch et al. 1981), but more are needed across the Southeast. The adaptive significance of cryptocrystalline utilization by Paleoindian groups has received differing interpretations, which include evidence of settlement restriction (Gardner 1974b) versus a technological strategy to facilitate mobility (Goodyear 1989).

At this point in southeastern United States Paleoindian archaeology, it would seem that little progress will be made in understanding these groups as functioning cultural systems until better stratigraphic contexts are obtained. Most of what is thought to be known is based on stylistic point typologies, themselves products of formal evolutionary assumptions, and comparisons with similar forms outside the Southeast. At issue is the identification of deposits that are likely to be of sufficient age (11,500–10,000 yr B.P.) to contain Paleoindian material and of adequate depth or integrity to preserve data critical to the isolation and dating of assemblages. Based on excavations conducted in recent years, it appears that floodplains and sinkholes offer the greatest potential for deposition in the Southeast. Caves and shelters, while containing substantial deposits in many cases, appear to have been occupied relatively late (ca. 10,500 yr B.P.) (Goodyear 1982) and often experienced disturbances from human and natural sources, complicating clear associations with ^{14}C dates. An interesting exception to this latter problem is Dust Cave, located in northern Alabama, a deep deposit which exhibits unusual stratigraphic integrity (Driskell 1994; Goldman-Finn and Driskell 1994).

A fundamental problem in the Southeast is the recognition and dating of the Pleistocene–Holocene boundary and an understanding of the climatic, environmental and cultural events that accompanied this transition. Archaeological and paleoenvironmental studies conducted within the past two decades, particularly in two major areas of the Southeast, have provided a body of field data that allow synthesis to begin, which, in turn, should enable the development of criteria for recognizing and dating this transition. These areas are the Southern Appalachians, especially the major floodplains along the Atlantic Slope, and the drowned sites located in sinks and rivers in the karstic regions of Florida. The primary purpose of this paper is to review these field studies in order to document depositional agencies and events and their associated archaeological records for the period from 11,500 to 10,000 yr B.P.

By convention, the end of the Pleistocene has been set at 10,000 yr B.P. (Griffin 1967; Whitehead 1965). This is an arbitrary designation for purposes of worldwide periodization (Harland et al. 1982). However, in the lower latitudes like that of the Southeast, the floristic responses to warmer climate can be seen as early as 16,500 yr B.P., with vegetation at 12,500 yr B.P. being much more similar to modern forests than previous late Wisconsin communities (Delcourt and Delcourt 1985:18–19). Of great import to the study of Paleoindians in the Southeast, as elsewhere in North America, is the timing of the onset of Holocene aggradation so necessary for deposition and burial of Paleoindian remains (Haynes 1984). Accordingly, in this paper the early Holocene will be referred to as the period from 11,000 to 8000 yr B.P.

Last, there is the important problem of correlating radiocarbon years with that of sidereal or calendrical time. Historically, there have been no tree ring correlations as old as Paleoindian radiocarbon dates so the issue has been moot. Dates have been reported as radiocarbon years before present. Lately, based on research with Greenland ice cores and corals in Barbados, there is considerable evidence to show that major ^{14}C plateaus existed during the critical period of 12,000 to 10,000 yr B.P. (Feidel 1997; Ellis et al. 1998). In addition to making certain Paleoindian complexes older than currently thought, they may also provide more temporal room for one phase to evolve into another, i.e., eliminating what may appear to be temporal compression of projectile point types (cf. Morse 1997a).

The Southeastern United States Paleoindian Sequence

To date, there exists no single documented stratigraphic deposit that can be said to empirically underwrite the following culture-historical sequence. Paleoindian projectile points occasionally have been excavated, but a pure assemblage has not been found. The main exception to this statement is the Thunderbird site (Gardner 1974a) in northern Virginia, located on the northern margin of the Southeast (Figure 1). At Thunderbird, however, the primary Paleoindian expression is Clovis, though it has not been ^{14}C dated. Post-Clovis Paleoindian occupations here are less definitely represented. In terms of stratigraphic integrity, the Dalton horizon is perhaps the best defined, based on stratigraphy and assemblage analysis. The following, therefore, is a sequence widely recognized by many archaeologists, but which, to some extent, exists largely as a convention constructed on typological grounds and partially complete stratigraphic sequences.

Pre-Clovis Period (11,500–? yr B.P.)

Until recently, the southeastern U.S. has not fared much better than the rest of North America in terms of generating convincing evidence of a pre-Clovis occupation. While occasional claims for pre-Clovis remains have been advanced (Lively 1965; Purdy 1983a), compelling proof for their antiquity has not been forthcoming. With the advent of the acceptance of the pre-12,000 yr B.P. age Monte Verde site in Chile (Meltzer et al. 1997), such developments will no doubt cause North Americanists to search more diligently for pre-Clovis remains. In the Southeast, the recently documented site of Cactus Hill in Virginia (Figure 1) appears to have a radiocarbon dated archaeological manifestation temporally and stratigraphically below Clovis.

The Cactus Hill site (44SX202) is a stratified multicomponent site situated in a sand dune overlooking the Nottoway River in the interior Coastal Plain of Virginia (McAvoy and McAvoy 1997). The report by the McAvoys summarizes excavations conducted in 1993, a small excavation of a Clovis component in 1995, and a final salvage of a threatened portion in 1996. Archaic and Paleoindian lithic artifacts were found lying in a stratified manner within a sand dune which is approximately 1.8 m in maximum thickness. Occupations from the 18th century back to Clovis are located within about the upper 1 m of windblown sand. A Clovis occupation has been identified by chert tools of the typical Paleoindian form along with fluted points found in floors at the bottom of the sequence. Clovis materials are found stratigraphically in zones of heavy lamellae formation in the lower part of the dune that are pedogenic in origin. One Clovis hearth was radiocarbon dated at 10,920 ±250 yr B.P., based on a sample of hard southern pine charcoal.

In the 1993 season in an area where a Clovis floor was found, which included flake tools and two fluted points, about 7 cm below this level a feature-like charcoal concentration appeared, which contained seven quartzite flakes and three quartzite "core blades," the latter also known as prismatic blades (McAvoy and McAvoy 1997:103). Wood charcoal from this feature consisting of white pine was radiocarbon dated at 15,070 ±70 yr B.P. In three other locations, prismatic blades made from local quartzite were found in excavations just below what are thought to be Clovis artifact surfaces. The pre-Clovis lithics are made from quartzite, the source for which was nearby river cobbles, while the Clovis levels have quarzite and significant numbers of chert artifacts imported to the site, much of the latter probably coming from the famous Williamson quarry site some 12 miles away.

The spring 1996 field season was conducted specifically to determine whether additional pre-Clovis deposits could be found. Six more clusters of quartzite prismatic blades were found. In one of these clusters, some evidence was found of two distinct layers of pre-Clovis lithics (Mc Avoy 1997). Clusters of quartzite prismatic blades were found superimposed over each other with the upper cluster containing smaller (<30 mm) blades with the lower cluster blades wider and thicker. A soil sample taken from a hearth-like concentration associated with one of the blade clusters yielded a radiocarbon date of 16,670 ±730 yr B.P. (Mc Avoy 1997).

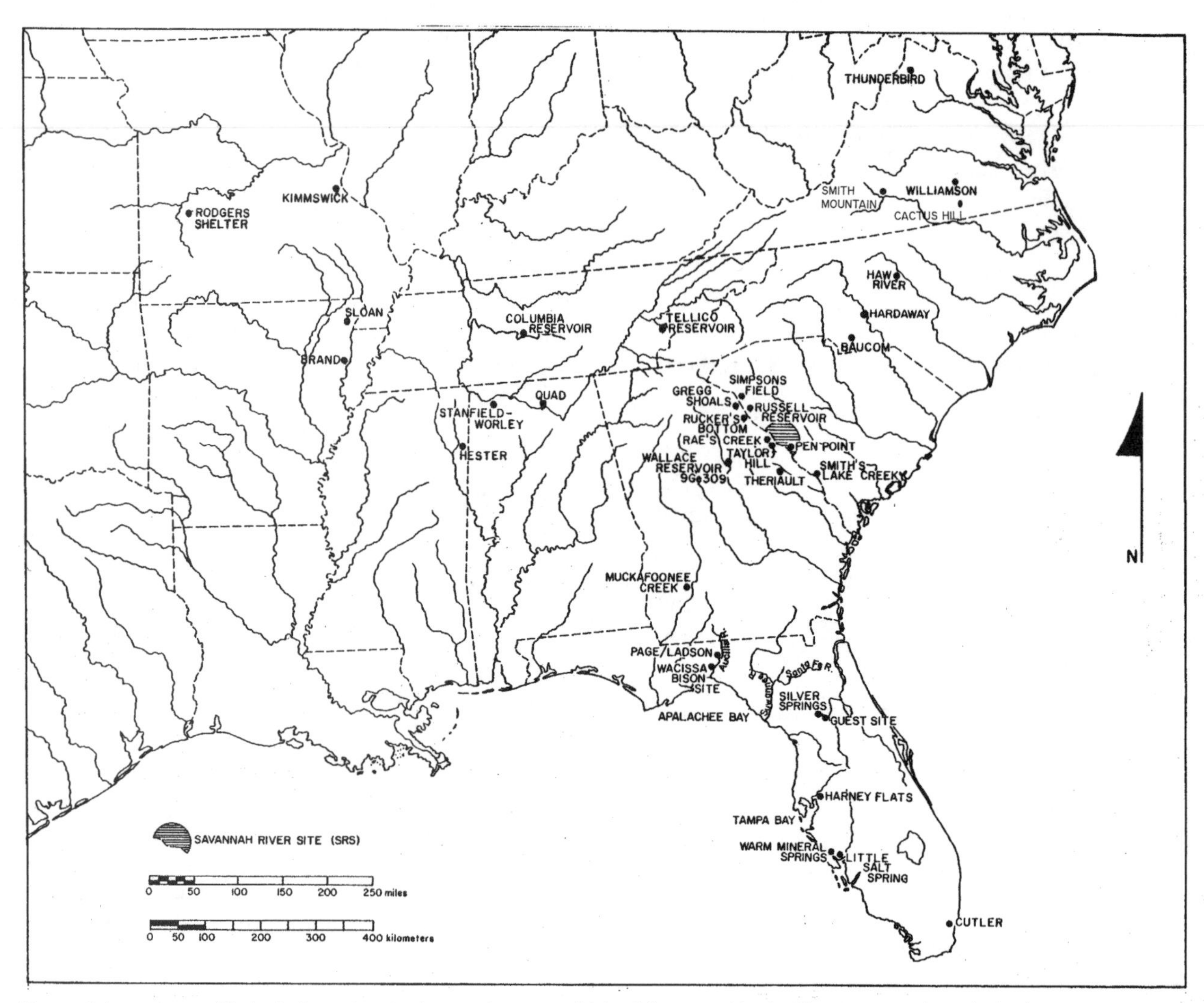

Figure 1. Locations of Paleoindian sites in the southeastern United States with significant geoarchaeological contexts.

The excavator of the site, Joseph Mc Avoy (1997), believes that the blade clusters found in the 1993 and 1996 seasons represent a pre-fluted point (pre-Clovis) occupation by groups making prismatic blades on prepared cores utilizing the local river cobble quartzite sources . He also believes there is a suggestion in the data that there is an earlier prismatic blade occupation followed by smaller blades. Two thin, basally thinned, trianguloid-to-lanceolate bifaces also were recovered in excavations that may be associated with the upper smaller blade clusters.

The finding of stratified, radiocarbon-dated Clovis remains at Cactus Hill is very significant for Paleoindian studies in the Southeast, and the radiocarbon date of 10,920 ±250 yr B.P. is concordant with traditional Clovis dates of the West. The discovery of one and possibly two blade industries coupled with an obvious raw material change immediately below Clovis surfaces is a major breakthrough in pre-Clovis archaeology. Both of the radiocarbon dates associated with these remains are substantially earlier than conventional ^{14}C dating of Clovis, a fact that reinforces the claim for pre-Clovis antiquity. However, like any archaeological complex, to gain validity and general acceptance it must be confirmed at more than one site. At a minimum, the findings at Cactus Hill have given some concrete clues as to what to look for.

Clovis Period (11,500–10,900 yr B.P.)

The Clovis culture, or at least the Clovis form of fluted point as documented in the Plains and Southwest, continues to provide the basis for recognizing the earliest widespread human inhabitants of the Southeast. The classic Clovis point, as found among mammoth remains in the Southwest and in the Richey–Roberts site in Washington, tends to be a large point, although not uniformly, and is characterized by convex or straight sides with a relatively minor basal concavity.

Points like the Western Clovis have been found throughout the southern states (Figure 2a–d), although their geographic distribution is not homogenous over the area. For some time, a great density of fluted points has been known from the Interior Low Plateau of northern Alabama, Tennessee, and Kentucky (Futato 1982:33; Williams and Stoltman 1965:675–676). This region is known for its high-quality cryptocrystalline lithic raw materials available in large pieces and the presence of salt licks. There also is a significant concentration of fluted points in the Virginia area related to jasper and Piedmont cryptocrystalline silicate sources (McCary 1975, 1984; Peck 1985) such as those from the Williamson site (Figure 1), and in the Piedmont of North Carolina related to the great availability of siliceous metalvolcanic rocks (Peck 1988; Perkinson 1971, 1973). As has been noted by William Gardner (1974b, 1983:55) and others, there is a strong geographic correlation between the availability of cryptocrystalline raw materials and the density of fluted points in the Southeast. This fact tends to complicate straightforward equations of fluted point densities and human demographic patterns.

Because of minimal ^{14}C dated fluted point assemblages in the Southeast, it is necessary to comment on the common practice of equating fluted points with Clovis or Clovis-contemporary cultures. First, there are several points from the Southeast that do meet the formal criteria of the Clovis point as defined in the Southwest (Figure 2a–d). However, perhaps just as many, if not more, do not meet these criteria. Many southeastern fluted points have a deep basal indentation not seen in the Southwest Clovis points (Figure 2e, f). Others have a waisted base with flaring ears also not typical of Western Clovis points (Figure 2j). Second, in fluted point surveys, such as that published in the *Archaeology of Eastern North America* (Brennan 1982:27–46), it is clear that some point types (Quad, Suwannee, and Simpson) that are not truly fluted were counted in the state tallies. Furthermore, many points that obviously are fluted, such as Cumberland, Redstone, and Ross County, were included that definitely are not Clovis-style points (Figure 2g, h, i, e).

These facts warrant caution in making inferences about the extent and age of Clovis occupations in the Southeast based on the sheer density of "fluted points." Radiocarbon dates in the Northeast from the Debert, Vail, and Whipple sites indicate that a non-Clovis style of fluted point existed between about 10,500 and 10,600 yr B.P., decidedly post-Clovis in age (Haynes et al. 1984). However, a Western Clovis-style fluted point has been recovered from the Shawnee-Minisink site that also has an average ^{14}C date of about 10,600 yr B.P. The fluted points from Thunderbird resemble the Western Clovis style, but these points are not dated by ^{14}C. Interestingly, though undated by ^{14}C, the fluted points found with the Kimmswick mastodon were of the Western style (Graham et al. 1981). As discussed above, the date of 10,920 yr B.P. from Cactus Hill is comparable to the western Clovis dates. One date of 11,980 ±110 yr B.P. from the Johnson site in Tennessee (Barker and Broster 1996:98) may be associated with Clovis fluted preforms. While the dates from Cactus Hill and Johnson are encouraging, there are not as yet enough ^{14}C dates from fluted point sites in the South to form any coherent pattern.

Following a strictly southwestern United States-derived typological definition of Clovis, an unknown number of Clovis-like fluted points have been recorded and mapped for the Southeast. There may, indeed, be more fluted points in the Southeast, but it is not at all certain how many are truly Clovis in origin based on a comparison with projectile point forms associated with elephants in the Southwest. Thus, the argument that because there are more fluted points in the Southeast than other areas of North America, fluted points may have originated here or are at least contemporaneous with those of the West, is not necessarily supported by the eastern states point tallies, given their unrefined typological condition. To provide an example of how seriously misleading such statements can be, Florida is reported to have well over 1,000 "Paleoindian" points recorded (Brennan 1982:29). However, the majority of these are not fluted, but are of the Suwannee type (cf. Purdy 1983b:29). In fact, James Dunbar, based on his extensive familiarity with the Florida points, estimates that only 10 percent of the Florida lanceolates are fluted (Dunbar et al. 1988:451; cf. Goodyear et al. 1983:51).

Another pattern concerning the distribution of Clovis points in the Southeast relates to their relative scarcity on the South Atlantic and Gulf coastal plains. At the time of his 1962 classic synthesis, Ronald Mason was able to state that the density of Clovis and other fluted points rapidly diminished from the central latitude of Mississippi and Alabama southward onto the Gulf coastal plain (Mason 1962:238–239). In the intervening years, this pattern has been verified

Figure 2. Types of fluted points found in the southeastern United States: a, Clovis, Bladen Co., N.C.; b, Clovis, Williamson site, Va.; c, Clovis, Rowan Co., N.C.; d, Clovis, Suwannee River, Fl.; e, Ross County fluted, Laurence Co., Al.; f, Clovis-like, Humphrey Co., Tn.; g, Cumberland, Taylor Co., Ky.; h, Cumberland (cast); i, Redstone, York Co., S.C.; j, waisted fluted, Dodge Co., Ga.

(Anderson 1990; Anderson et al. 1986; Futato 1982:31; McGahey 1987). The incidence of fluted points versus unfluted lanceolate points is substantially higher north of the 33rd parallel, from Louisiana eastward to South Carolina. South of this latitude, basally thinned lanceolates, variously called Suwannee, Simpson, Quad, and Coldwater, predominate. All are considered post-Clovis in age. As will be discussed below, the area south of 33° latitude had vegetation different from the flora to the north.

While Clovis-like fluted points are found in the lower Southeast coastal plains, they may have spotty distributions. For example, in Florida, where the overall ratio of fluted points to the unfluted Suwannee type is about one to nine, in the Aucilla River the ratio is about one to three, or 33 percent (Dunbar et al. 1988:451). This suggests that the Aucilla River locality could represent an initial colonization of Clovis populations in the lower Southeast. Other localities south of 33° latitude with anomalously high percentages of Clovis-like fluted points should be searched for and their environmental situation examined.

Middle Paleoindian Period (10,900–10,500 yr B.P.)

A POST-CLOVIS middle Paleoindian period is commonly recognized in the culture-historical taxonomies of the eastern United States (Gardner 1974b; MacDonald 1968; Williams and Stoltman 1965). The basis of this distinction is typological, with some supporting stratigraphic data (Walthall 1980). This period is essentially post-Clovis and pre-Dalton and should span the time from 10,900 to 10,500 yr B.P.

In the mid-South region of northern Alabama, Tennessee, and Kentucky, the Cumberland fluted point (Figure 2g, h) is found in relatively dense numbers. Its emphasis on full facial fluting is reminiscent of the Folsom point. The Cumberland point has a distinctive style and an equally distinctive regional distribution, providing strong evidence for regional stylistic patterning in the Southeast during Paleoindian times. It also appears to have been fluted using a "Folsom"-like nipple platform. The Beaver Lake point is similar to the Cumberland and is thought to be related, but lacks fluting. Another distinctive fluted point style is the Redstone (Figure 2i), which is characterized by a triangular, elongated outline with emphasis on long flutes. Redstones also are comparatively dense in the mid-South area but relatively rare outside this region. An exception may exist in the South Atlantic region, perhaps related to a connection with the Savannah River, which originates in the Blue Ridge Mountains and provides a travel corridor to Tennessee (e.g., Goodyear et al. 1989).

Another common projectile point type from the mid-South that is probably somewhat later in time is called the Quad (Figure 3d). These points have strongly incurvate basal margins, pronounced ears, and may or may not have fluting or strong basal thinning (Cambron and Hulse 1964). In technology and probably time, the Quad point is likely related to the Suwannee point (Figure 3a, c), a well-made lanceolate point with an incurvate base and slightly eared appearance (Bullen 1975). The Suwannee point and a related style, the Simpson, characterized by strongly incurvate basal margins with sharply projecting ears (Figure 3b), are abundant in the rivers, springs, and drowned coastal rivers of north and west-central Florida (Dunbar and Waller 1983). Most Suwannee and Simpson points are not fluted but are frequently finished on their bases by shallow basal thinning or through a technique of lateral thinning (Figure 4) (Goodyear et al. 1983:46). As a rule, Suwannee and Simpson points are made from Tertiary cherts, which are available in a belt of outcrops running from Tampa, Florida to Allendale County, South Carolina (Goodyear et al. 1985; Upchurch et al. 1981). Although specimens can be found in the lower Piedmont and Fall Line (Anderson et al. 1990:Figure 29; Goodyear et al. 1989), they are essentially coastal-plain artifacts.

The cultural significance of the diverse forms of fluted and unfluted lanceolate points assigned to the middle Paleoindian period would be related to the technological and stylistic variety represented in this group and the obvious regional patterns in their distributions. Much of the projectile point variety that is cited for the Paleoindian period in the Southeast can probably be ascribed to the forms just reviewed. The strong association of Cumberland, Beaver Lake, and Quad points with the mid-South region and the occurrence of Suwannee and Simpson points on the coastal plains indicate that demographic associations with certain regions were largely in place by at least 10,500 years ago, if not earlier. Occasional fragments of Cumberland fluted points, as well as Beaver Lake and Quad points, have been found in the highland rockshelters of Alabama (Driskell 1996; Futato 1980:115, 1982:32; Walthall 1980:31), but no Clovis-style fluted points have been recovered. The light occurrence of these point forms in rockshelters during

Figure 3. Middle and late period Paleoindian lanceolate points from the southeastern United States: a, Suwannee, Santa Fe River, Fl.; b, Simpson, Pinellas Co., Fl.; c, Suwannee, Pinellas Co., Fl.; d, Quad-like, Beaufort Co., S.C.; e, Dalton (cast), Sloan site, Ark.; f, Dalton (cast), Sloan site, Ark.; g, Dalton (cast), Hardaway site, N.C.; h, Dalton, 38AL135, Allendale Co., S.C.; i, San Patrice, St. Johns Var. (cast), probably Oklahoma.

the middle Paleoindian period presages the next period, characterized by Dalton points, which are found extensively in upland rockshelters throughout the South and Midwest (Futato 1980:117; Goodyear 1982; McMillan 1971).

Dalton Period (10,500–9900 yr B.P.)

THE END OF THE lanceolate Paleoindian point tradition comes with the occurrence of what is called the Dalton point or the Dalton horizon. Elsewhere it has been argued, based on stratigraphic studies and limited ^{14}C dating, that the Dalton period should date within a span of 10,500 to 9900 yr B.P. (Goodyear 1982). Recent ^{14}C dates from a zone bearing Dalton points at Dust Cave, Alabama would tend to support this interval (Driskell 1994, 1996). Other researchers would extend Dalton to 9500 years ago (Morse and Morse 1983:42; cf. Wyckoff 1985). The primary radiocarbon-dated exception to the 9900 yr B.P. upper limit of the Dalton horizon comes from the Packard site, located in northeast Oklahoma (Wyckoff 1985, 1989). The stratigraphic context of the Dalton assemblage there, however, and its deviation from the rest of the southeastern United States stratigraphic sequence, suggest that it was redeposited (cf. Jeter and Williams 1989:77).

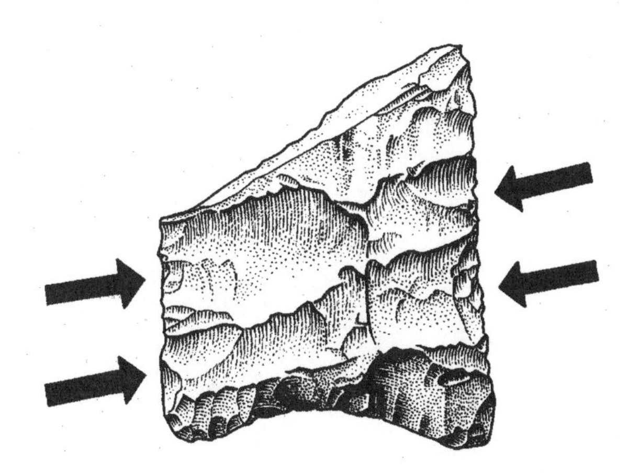

Figure 4. Illustration of lateral thinning technique on Suwannee point. From Goodyear et al. (1983:4).

The chipped stone technology of Dalton assemblages is clearly Paleoindian in character (Goodyear 1974; Morse 1973; Morse 1997b), although significant additions such as serrated, resharpened blade edges on hafted bifaces and adzes are present. It probably is not realistic to speak of a single Dalton culture in the Southeast at this time. Considerable regionalism already was manifest in the preceding middle Paleoindian period and continued during the next 500 years. A number of Dalton point varieties have been recognized: Hardaway from the North Carolina piedmont (Figure 3g); Nuckolls, Colbert, and Greenbriar from the Alabama–Tennessee area (DeJarnette et al. 1962); and Sloan (Figure 3e, f) from the Arkansas–Missouri area.

In the central and western Gulf coastal plain, the San Patrice (Figure 3i) series appears to represent a Dalton manifestation (Ensor 1986), perhaps a late one. Within the San Patrice series there are two major point varieties: Hope, which looks like a small Dalton point; and St. Johns, which has oblique, incipient side-notches (see Figure 3i). At the Hester site in Mississippi (Figure 1), Sam Brookes (personal communication 1991) has found lanceolate Daltons with straight lateral margins and Hope-variety San Patrice-like forms spatially associated in discrete clusters, implying contemporaneity. Story (1990:Figures 27 and 28) has plotted the distribution of Dalton and San Patrice points and has shown that the two types basically have different regional distributions. San Patrice occurs throughout Louisiana, exclusive of river floodplains and coastal zones, and in east Texas. These are all heavily wooded regions. The San Patrice points tend to be made on small, local chert gravels. Dalton points, on the other hand, are made on a variety of lithic raw materials concentrated more to the north of east Texas and Louisiana, and occur in a wider range of environments ". . . including the wooded edge of the Gulf Coastal Plain" (Story 1990:202). The dating and identification of San Patrice assemblages have been hindered by the lack of well-stratified or single-component sites (e.g., Webb et al. 1971).

Available faunal evidence indicates that modern plants and animals were the focus of subsistence by Dalton times. In a real sense, Dalton technology appears to be a somewhat modified Paleoindian tool kit applied to modern or Holocene biota. In this respect, Dalton can be considered the beginning of the early Archaic period in the Southeast. There also is evidence of a substantial population increase during Dalton times compared with previous periods. Sites and points increase by a factor of five to 10 from the Clovis and middle Paleoindian periods (Anderson 1990:Table 3).

Late Pleistocene–Early Holocene Environments

Based on palynological studies performed in the past 30 years by William Watts, Don Whitehead, and Hazel and Paul Delcourt (Delcourt and Delcourt 1985), a fairly detailed floral and climatic reconstruction is available for the late Pleistocene and early Holocene periods in the Southeast.

From the period of about 12,500 to 8500 yr B.P., there existed a unique forest described as a cool, mesic, broad-leaved forest (Figure 5) dominated by beech and hickory (Delcourt and Delcourt 1979, 1985; Watts 1980). This mixed-hardwood forest had cooler summers than today, with abundant moisture available during the growing season. This species-rich mesic forest had definable latitudinal boundaries between 37° and 33° north latitude (Delcourt et al. 1983:164). Referring to previous statements on the distribution of fluted points, more of the Clovis and Clovis-like material comes from this area of cool, mesic forest.

South of 33° latitude during the same period, vegetation was very similar to that of today (Figure 5). The coastal plains were warm and tended to be droughty. Vegetation consisted of modern species dominated by oak, hickory, sweetgum, and pine (Delcourt and Delcourt 1983). In Florida, surface water was severely restricted as a result of lowered sea level on the karst-controlled hydrology and by reduced rainfall.

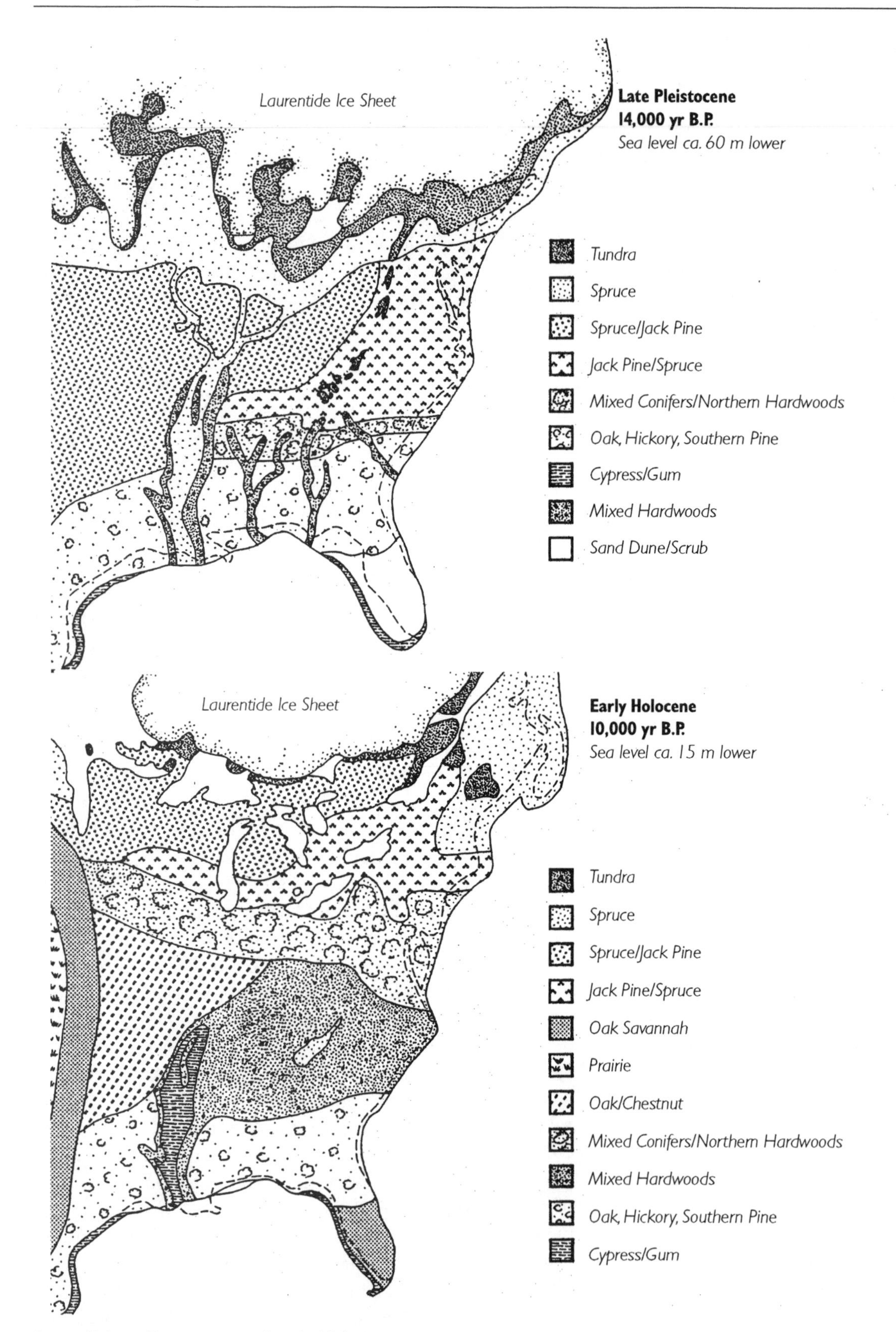

Figure 5. Late Pleistocene and early Holocene vegetation communities at 14,000 and 10,000 yr B.P. in the eastern United States. From Anderson et al. (1990: Figure 2) adapted from Delcourt and Delcourt (1981).

It should be noted that the Southeast was not in any sense glaciated or glacially influenced during this time period. These basic floristic differences above and below 33° latitude were controlled by the position of different weather systems. The Pacific air mass dominated the area of the mesic deciduous forest and the Maritime Tropical air mass controlled the coastal plains (Delcourt and Delcourt 1983). Thus, the first Clovis populations in the Southeast encountered a hardwood or mixed hardwood and pine forest (Figure 5).

According to paleontological reconstructions by S. David Webb, there was a similar faunal distribution by latitude. In his important synthesis, Webb (1981) identifies three distinct faunal regions (Figure 6): a northern Boreal zone covering the mid-Atlantic states; a Temperate zone positioned at about the latitude of South Carolina; and a Subtropical region situated from about 33° latitude southward into peninsular Florida. A great deal of biotic variation occurred within the Southeast, with the middle Temperate and Subtropical zones being very ecotonal and diverse. Some species from the Temperate zone ranged south into the Subtropical region, making the Subtropical region one of the richest and most diverse in terms of late Pleistocene vertebrate remains (Webb 1981:I–77). Webb, as well as Edwards and Merrill, agree that ". . . during the late Pleistocene the region from Florida to the Carolinas approached optimal conditions for the earliest Americans" (Edwards and Merrill 1977:35).

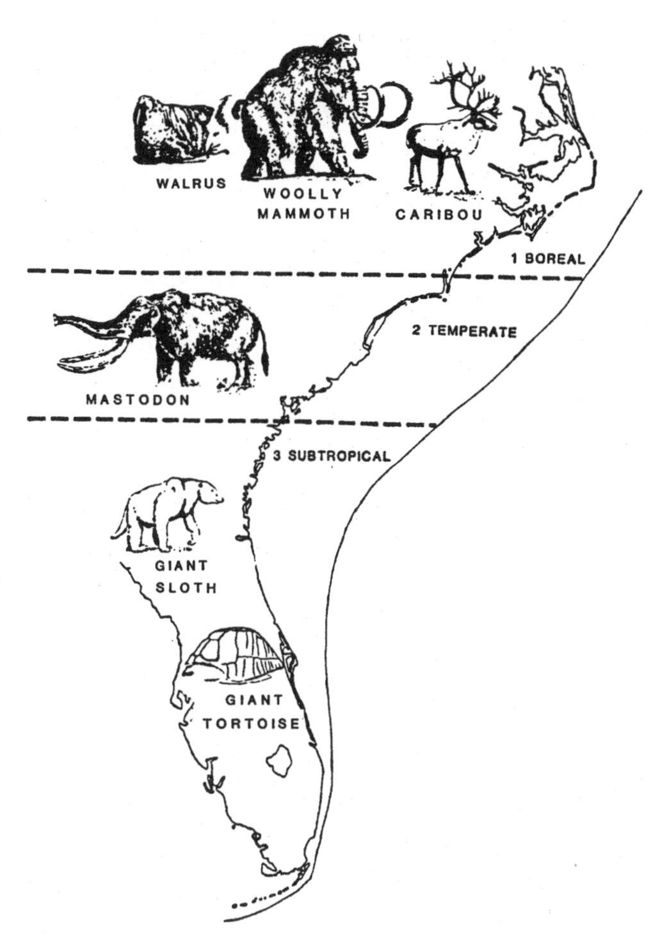

Figure 6. Late Pleistocene faunal regions of the southeastern United States coastal plains. From Webb (1981) as adapted by Carbone (1983).

The Pleistocene end dates for these zones are not well established and it is difficult at present to precisely relate them to human populations (Goodyear et al. 1989). It seems probable at this point that the megafauna of the Pleistocene did not survive as long as some radiocarbon dates have suggested.

The analysis of published radiocarbon dates by David Meltzer and Jim Mead (1985) is relevant here with regard to defining the end dates of Pleistocene megafauna. Their studies, based on strict criteria of date reliability, have indicated that these fauna were very likely extinct by 10,500 yr B.P., and there is a strong suggestion that they were gone by 10,800 yr B.P. This parallels the archaeological findings for Clovis versus Folsom in the West, where mammoth, horse, camel, and other economically useful megafauna were last used by Clovis peoples, and only now-extinct bison were associated with Folsom. Based on the stratigraphy of the Pleistocene–Holocene transition and the lack of extinct megafauna in post-Clovis sites, Haynes (1984) has argued that extinction took place during Clovis times and was complete no later than 10,500 yr B.P. To some extent this argument is supported by data from the Southeast, where the available faunal remains associated with Dalton indicate only modern animals were used (Goodyear 1982).

The dating of the extinction of proboscideans and other economically important North American megafauna is critical to the explanation of why so little archaeological evidence of megafaunal exploitation has been discovered in the East (cf. Meltzer 1988). If these species were essentially gone by 10,900 or 10,800 yr B.P., particularly if the Clovis occupation of the Southeast lags behind the West by a century or two, we are searching for a very narrow window in time within which such an association was possible. This scenario needs to be given more serious thought in modeling Clovis-age subsistence studies in the Southeast.

The final paleoenvironmental condition that must be mentioned is that of lowered sea levels. At the end of the Pleistocene, world sea levels began to rise. However, for the period from 12,000 to 9000 yr B.P. more subaerial landmass was available for human occupation than today and no doubt all coastal sites have been inundated. In Florida, lowered sea levels and an apparently drier climate had a pronounced effect on surface water availability (Brooks 1972), which is reflected in the utilization of famous early sites such as Warm Mineral Springs and Little Salt Spring. This was what Wilfred Neill (1964:20) called the "water-hole" effect on both animal and human populations, resulting in a geographic concentration of archaeological remains in springs and rivers. As can be seen based on the work of Dunbar and others (Dunbar and Waller 1983:Figures 1–2), most of the Paleoindian points in Florida have been recovered from the karst region, which provided more reliable freshwater resources.

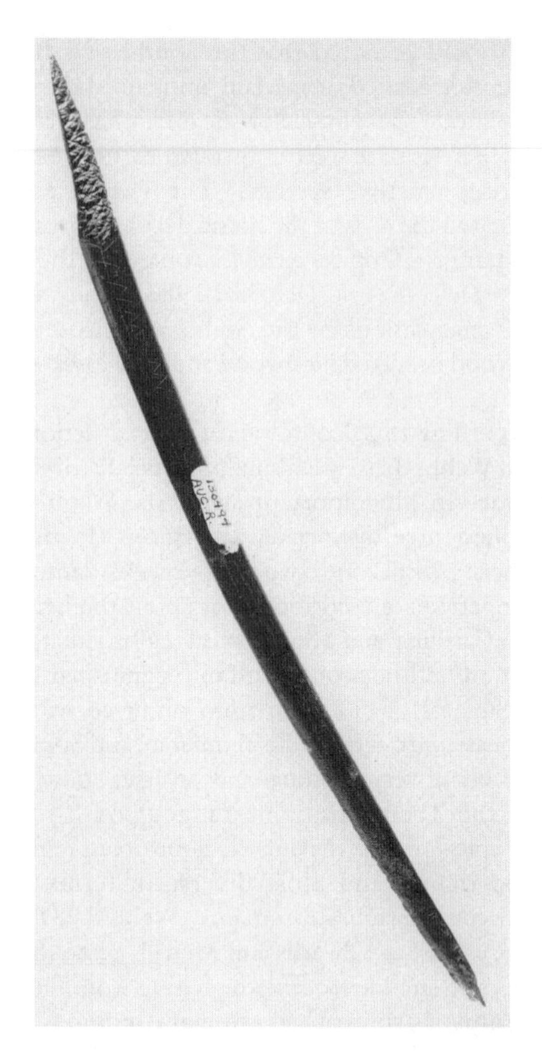

Figure 7. Complete ivory foreshaft, 307 mm long, from Sloth Hole, Aucilla River, Florida (UF 136494). Photograph and information courtesy of S. David Webb, Florida Museum of Natural History.

Evidence of Extinct Pleistocene Fauna Utilization

EVIDENCE OF HUMAN utilization of Pleistocene fauna is present in the Southeast, especially in Florida freshwater springs, sinkholes, and rivers. The best-known examples are the ivory "foreshafts" and points (Figure 7), which have been compared to similar pieces from Clovis sites (Cotter 1962; Jenks and Simpson 1941). Amateur divers have continued to find worked ivory artifacts in the Aucilla and Ichetucknee rivers of north Florida (Dunbar 1991:Table 1). The presumption here is that the ivory was worked while fresh. Neill (1964:23) states that "in Florida, fossil ivory is chalky, inclined to split into sheets, and unsuitable for manufacture into points." Haynes (1982:389–390) has offered evidence, based on the modification of proboscidean tusk structure, that ivory probably was worked while green.

In the early 1970s, underwater excavations were conducted at the Guest site, located east of Ocala, Florida (Figure 1), which has been interpreted as a mammoth kill site (Hoffman 1983; Rayl 1974). A bone deposit was found eroding out of the bank of Silver Springs Run about 3 m underwater, located several kilometers downstream from the main springs (Silver Springs). An apparently *in situ* mammoth was discovered during excavation (Hoffman 1983:Figure 1), which yielded "a small stemless point . . . in the vicinity of the proximal end of the right femur close to the ilium. Chert flakes were [also] found in the area of the ribs and vertebra" (Hoffman 1983:84). Hoffman (1983:Figure 2) provides a photograph of this point, which appears lanceolate and basally thinned or fluted, but with an excurvate rather than concave base. With the exception of Rayl's (1974) master's thesis, no published report is available to allow scientific evaluation of this excavation and geohydrological context. This is an unfortunate situation, as the Guest site appears to be a possible example of Paleoindian extinct megafauna utilization.

The famous underwater site of Little Salt Spring in southwest Florida (Figure 1) produced an association of a sharply pointed stake apparently driven into an extinct species of tortoise (*Geochelone crassiscutata*), found lying on its back. The tortoise was 26 m below the present water surface of a cenote on a formerly dry ledge. The investigators believe the animal was killed with the stake and cooked where it was found. A ^{14}C date on the stake was assayed at 12,030 ± 200 yr B.P. (Clausen et al. 1979:609). No other organic artifacts or diagnostic chipped stone tools were reported that date to this age. Other wooden artifacts were recovered in the spring that have been ^{14}C dated between about 9500 and 9000 yr B.P. (Clausen et al. 1979:Table 1). Assuming no contamination of the 12,030 date, this ^{14}C value could be pre-Clovis in age.

Based on their underwater excavations at nearby Warm Mineral Springs (Figure 1), Cockrell and Murphy (1978:1) report a combined ^{14}C date of 10,310 yr B.P. based on 16 assays taken from the general area of what they describe as a flexed human burial. The burial and dated material were collected from a ledge 13 m below water surface. Worked bone from the site is all from modern fauna. The earliest stone projectile points are side-notched in form following the Greenbriar and Bolen types (Cockrell and Murphy 1978:Figure 6), which should date about 10,000 yr B.P. The work of Clausen et al. (1975) at this same site produced similar results. Two human bones were found in stratified organic deposits that had accumulated on the 13-m ledge. A date of 10,260 ±190 yr B.P. was obtained on wood from the same level as one of the human bones. Four radiocarbon dates ranging from 9880 to 10,630 yr B.P. were obtained from four 10-cm levels. All fauna recovered were modern species.

This same situation applies at the Cutler Fossil site, a dry sinkhole located near Miami (Figure 1). Here the earliest firm archaeological evidence of occupation occurs at about 10,000 yr B.P., based on Dalton-like projectile points and ^{14}C dates (Carr 1987:62–63).

Although late Pleistocene fauna occur abundantly at Little Salt Spring, Warm Mineral Springs, and the Cutler site, with the exception of the extinct tortoise at Little Salt, a good association between people and extinct fauna has not yet been made. This could imply that the earliest penetration of humans into south Florida, as witnessed by these three sites, may be the Dalton time period (10,500–10,000 yr B.P.). The preservation of organic remains at the spring sites, including human brains, is nothing short of extraordinary (Clausen et al. 1979:203–204), suggesting that a Clovis or even pre-Clovis occupation, if present, could be easily dated and determined.

The most unequivocal evidence of human use and contemporaneity with extinct megafauna is that of a *Bison antiquus* skull with a broken chert projectile point embedded in its fronto-parietal bone (Webb et al. 1984). This specimen was found by a hobby diver in the Wacissa River in Jefferson County, Florida (Figure 1). The point base was missing, thus precluding any typological identification. Radiocarbon dates of bison bone indicate an age of about 11,000 yr B.P.

In riverbeds of the karst region of north and central Florida, including the Suwannee, Santa Fe, Ichetucknee, Wacissa, Aucilla, Withlacoochee, and Oklawaha, numerous finds of late Pleistocene mammal bones and Paleoindian-age artifacts are practically legendary (Mason 1962; Milanich and Fairbanks 1980:35–48; Neill 1964; Purdy 1981; Waller and Dunbar 1977; Webb 1974; Webb et al. 1984). With the exception of the well-described find of a butcher-marked vertebral mammoth spine (Bullen et al. 1970) and the recently published description of six obvious bone and ivory tools (Dunbar and Webb 1996), this modified faunal material has not been systematically described and published. Brief references in the literature to other worked or butcher-marked megafaunal specimens curated at the Florida Museum of Natural History and in private collections (Dunbar et al. 1989a:473–498; Webb et al. 1984:390) indicate that a substantial body of faunal data now exists which merits systematic study. Use of the scanning electron microscope is offering new avenues for distinguishing between human and natural agencies in the modification of archaeofaunal remains (Johnson and Shipman 1986; cf. Dunbar et al. 1989a).

At the very least, the Kimmswick mastodon site (Graham et al. 1981) in southeastern Missouri (Figure 1) and the Wacissa River bison kill (Webb et al. 1984) both show unmistakably that humans were present in the Southeast at a time early enough to be contemporary with late Pleistocene megafauna and in fact incorporated them into their subsistence base. It should be obvious that the underwater sites of Florida demonstrate enormous potential for elucidating this poorly known aspect of the earliest human inhabitants of the Southeast (cf. Dunbar and Webb 1996).

Late Pleistocene–Early Holocene Depositional Systems

BASED ON THE WORK of C. Vance Haynes and others, it is evident that over much of North America south of the Wisconsin ice, there was a marked period of erosion at the end of the Pleistocene dating between 12,500 and 11,500 yr B.P. (Haynes 1968). This was a broad geologic and probably climate-related event where stream regimens were dominated by net degradation and channel incision. Clovis sites, whether in the West, Midwest (Kimmswick), or East (Thunderbird, Shawnee-Minisink), exhibit initial human occupation at the contact of the previous erosional surface and the first episode of Holocene aggradation (Haynes 1984:350). Based on radiocarbon-dated geological stratigraphy of Clovis sites in the West and comparable stratigraphic contacts in the East, Haynes (1984:350) estimates that the first episode of fluvial aggradation began about 11,000 yr B.P.

Contemporary environmental scientists have focused on the role of floods and their capacity to move floodplains away from states of depositional equilibrium by erosion or aggradation (Knox 1976). Climate has emerged as the macro-determinant of floods mediated regionally by the effect of vegetation (Delcourt 1985; Knox 1984).

Based on historic flood records, J. C. Knox has shown that it is during periods of extreme climatic shifts rather than average climatic conditions that floodplains move from depositional regimes to those dominated by incision or degradation. He has speculated that severe storms, especially those occurring temporally in clusters, are most responsible for causing rivers to incise and erode their floodplains (Knox 1976, 1984). For the eastern United States, Knox hypothesizes that when weather patterns are dominated by zonal atmospheric movement across the Midwest, violent storms are less frequent and floodplains tend toward equilibrium and aggradation. Weather patterns dominated by meridional airflow, on the other hand, produce frequent, severe thunderstorms and concomitant major floods resulting in floodplain degradation. This occurs as a result of the Arctic air mass flowing southward in the winter and the movement of the Maritime Tropical air mass moving northward during the summer (Delcourt 1985:22; Knox 1984).

As previously mentioned, paleovegetation reconstructions based on radiocarbon-dated fossil pollen assemblages have demonstrated the prehistoric reality of the now-extinct mesic hardwood forest which existed from 33° to 37° north latitude (Figure 5). The climate represented by this forest is interpreted by Delcourt and Delcourt (1984:276) as "cool temperate" with abundant moisture during the growing season. The Delcourts (1984:280) attribute the presence of this forest to the interaction of the Pacific air mass dominating during the winter and the Maritime Tropical air mass in the summer. The climate during this time (12,500–8500 yr B.P.) is also regarded as exhibiting maximum seasonality compared to climates before this and afterward (Delcourt and Delcourt 1984:280). Sometime during the 12,000 to 11,000 year interval, the Arctic air mass must have made its presence felt in the southern latitudes, owing to the separation of the Cordilleran and Laurentide ice sheets (Bryson and Wendland 1967; Delcourt and Delcourt 1984:278). This would have caused strong meridional airflow, supporting Knox's (1984) storm hypothesis.

For the southeastern United States, Paul Delcourt, following Knox (1984), has shown the effects of climate and vegetation in determining the rate of overland surface runoff of precipitation and the resultant capacity for erosion of the landscape (Delcourt 1985). At Anderson Pond in Tennessee (36° latitude) and at Cupola Pond in Missouri (37° latitude), the onset of the mesic deciduous forest markedly reduced the amount of mineral sediment flowing into the basins compared to the previous full-glacial boreal forest (Delcourt 1985:20–21). In other words, closed canopied hardwood forests protected land surfaces from erosion, reducing the sediment available to river valleys.

To the south, palynological and sedimentological studies conducted on lakes in the southern Atlantic and Gulf coastal plains have revealed similar low rates of mineral sedimentation during the full-glacial to early Holocene periods (i.e., from ca. 20,000 to 8000 yr B.P.). Forests situated on the interfluves were dominated by oak, hickory, and southern pine, indicating a temperate climate with droughty summers. Mature forests, coupled with low precipitation during the summers, would be responsible for minimizing overland flow of sediment into ponds and lakes and into the watershed (Delcourt 1985:21). After 8000 yr B.P., summer precipitation increased, owing to the influence of the Maritime Tropical air mass, causing ponds to deepen, coniferous trees to increase, and mineral sedimentation rates to increase (Delcourt 1985:23).

Delcourt's (1985) sedimentological and palynological work with non-riverine, interfluvial pond sites helps explain the minimally stratified condition of many upland or inter-riverine Paleoindian sites throughout the Southeast. Vegetation cover was sufficient to prevent soil movement by both colluvial and eolian agencies. As discussed below, a different climatic and floristic situation existed in peninsular Florida, whereby sediment was moving and accumulating on Paleoindian sites.

Largely owing to federally funded mitigation projects of water reservoirs, geologists and archaeologists have worked together to study the paleohydrology and alluvial histories of southeastern United States river valleys. In general, alluvial features containing clear representations of archaeological assemblages began to consistently appear at about 9500 yr B.P. with what is called the Kirk phase or Kirk corner-notched cluster, so named for a corner-notched projectile point (Broyles 1966; Chapman 1976; Claggett and Cable 1982; Coe 1964). With the onset of Kirk-phase lithics, typically seen is an unbroken alluvial and archaeological series of depositions through the Holocene, indicating floodplain sedimentological regimes dominated by aggradation with minor episodes of erosion in the late Holocene.

Prior to the Kirk phase there is often recorded in the geological record an erosional hiatus like that discussed for the rest of the United States at the end of the Pleistocene. Recognizing and dating this erosional contact are critical for understanding the Holocene aggradation that was so necessary for burying and preserving Paleoindian remains. Geoarchaeology, or the application of geological techniques to aid in solving archaeological problems, has been conducted extensively in field studies throughout the Southeast in recent years, yielding an interesting database of case studies that can be examined profitably. The rest of this section will review and evaluate a number of these studies in an effort to summarize the state of knowledge regarding geological contexts and depositional environments of the Paleoindian time period (12,000–10,000 yr B.P.).

Owing to special geomorphic, and thus depositional, properties related to each, the review will be broken down by floodplain studies in the southern Appalachian Mountains and Piedmont, and floodplains and other depositional situations occurring on the coastal plains. As will be seen, the rivers of the southern Appalachians are rockbound with narrow floodplains, which tends to produce deep alluvial deposits conducive to archaeological stratigraphy and preservation. The non-rockbound rivers of the coastal plains, on the other hand, permit greater lateral channel migration and thus develop thinner deposits. Further south in peninsular Florida, the coastal plain is underlain by limestone, resulting in special depositional features such as springs and sinks, which have facilitated unique geological and archaeological deposits. Finally, when considering coastal-plain landforms, those that have been inundated by sea-level rise must also be considered, such as those that are known to exist in the Gulf of Mexico.

The Southern Appalachians

Little Tennessee River, Tellico Reservoir Project

EXTENSIVE DEEP-SITE excavations, directed by Jefferson Chapman during the 1970s, were conducted by the University of Tennessee in the Little Tennessee River valley (Figure 1) as mitigation measures for the Tellico Dam. Using a backhoe, deeply buried alluvial sites were systematically searched for as deep as 7.01 m below the floodplain surface.

No *in situ* alluvially buried Paleoindian remains were encountered, although surface finds of fluted points have been made on older adjacent terraces and hillsides (Chapman 1985:145). One obvious fluted point with a resharpened blade was found at the Bacon Farm site in an early Archaic Kirk-phase level, but was evidently redeposited (Chapman 1978:55). Two Dalton points in redeposited contexts also were found, one from Stratum H at Icehouse Bottom, which was a late early Archaic Kirk level, and another from Rose Island from a late early Archaic St. Albans horizon (Chapman 1977:49). The earliest *in situ* buried alluvial sites were dated to early Archaic Kirk corner-notched horizons beginning at 9500 yr B.P., based on several radiocarbon dates (Chapman 1985:146). Holocene-age sediments were present as much as 3 m deeper than the Kirk-horizon materials but produced no artifacts.

Geological and archaeological studies of the lower Little Tennessee River valley have provided the data for a model developed by Paul Delcourt (1980) of erosion and alluvial deposition, which can explain the lack of buried pre-10,000 yr B.P. sites. Chapman has summarized this model as follows:

From 1979 surveys and backhoe trench profiles, Delcourt has identified nine Quaternary alluvial terraces. These surfaces were created through valley incision by the Little Tennessee River in response to the progressive downcutting of the Tennessee River. Quaternary glacial/interstadial cycles modulated the mechanical production of rock debris under periglacial conditions on mid-to-high elevations in the Great Smoky Mountains, which resulted in reworking of sediment downslope and valley aggradation during late glacial and interglacial times. During the early Holocene, increased precipitation caused sediments derived from the exposed rock debris on mountain slopes to accumulate rapidly in the valleys, thus forming a thick series of first terraces (Delcourt 1980b) [Chapman 1985:144].

Chapman (1985) surmises that Paleoindian sites, if preserved, would be present in T1. Available radiocarbon dates from T2 range from 27,595 to 32,330 yr B.P., indicating that these terraces were formed prior to Paleoindian occupations. The possibility exists that fluted point sites might exist on remnant point bars within T1, although site discovery will be difficult. According to Chapman, the greater likelihood is that any 10,000 to 11,000 yr B.P. cultural occupations would have been eroded by the highly dynamic floods at the end of the late glacial period. The increased precipitation at the beginning of the Holocene evidently resulted in the extremely rapid formation of T1. To illustrate, radiocarbon dates of non-archaeological sediments located from 6.1 to 6.7 m below surface are contemporary with dates from in situ early Archaic Kirk horizons 3 m higher (i.e, 9000 to 9500 yr B.P.), indicating something of the speed with which T1 was formed (Chapman 1985:144–145).

Duck River, Tennessee, Columbia Reservoir Project

THE COLUMBIA RESERVOIR Project (Figure 1) combined archaeological and geological approaches in the study of the depositional history of the middle Duck River during the course of the Holocene. Extensive backhoe trenching allowed a reconstruction of the alluvial stratigraphy of the river valley beginning with the late Pleistocene and continuing to the present (Brakenridge 1984). "Severe bedrock and flood-plain erosion occurred near the end of the Pleistocene, and a major erosional unconformity was created" (Brakenridge 1984:9). The early Holocene aggradation was identified and dated to approximately 9000 yr B.P. based on diagnostic artifacts. Several pre-Dalton fluted points were found at or near the surface of the T2 Armour soils, which were the most stable land surfaces nearest the river (Turner and Klippel 1989:61). Deeply buried Archaic occupations were found in T1 sediments, with radiocarbon dates as old as 8885 yr B.P. Sediments of T1a1 (early Archaic) and T2b (Paleoindian) ages were penetrated but not well sampled by backhoe and bulldozer cuts, owing to their great depth and unstable trench conditions (Klippel, personal communication 1991).

Nashville Basin, Cumberland River, Tennessee

AS PART OF THEIR statewide Paleoindian projectile point and site survey, staff of the Tennessee Division of Archaeology discovered several alluvially buried and stratified Paleoindian and early Archaic sites along the Cumberland River within the Nashville Basin. The Johnson site (40DV400) (Figure 1), found eroding from the south bank of the Cumberland River, yielded diagnostic projectile points spanning Clovis through bifurcates (Broster et al. 1991). Total archaeological depth is on the order of 8 m, with culturally modified horizons of burned clay, charcoal, and organic matter evident in the cutbank profile. From the lowest cultural layer (Stratum IV), wood charcoal was obtained from a generally gathered sample yielding a date of 11,700± 980 yr B.P. A fluted preform base was found 30 cm away. A shallow basin feature, 33 cm deep and 62 cm wide, was recorded in the upper portion of the lowest cultural unit. The bottom of this basin contained "dark gray ash mixed with charcoal, burned bone, and numerous bifacial reduction flakes" (Broster et al. 1991:9). A radiocarbon date of 12,660 ± 970 yr B.P. was obtained on this feature (Broster et al. 1991:9). A second basin shaped feature in Stratum IV known as Feature 6, produced a date of 11,980 ±110 yr B.P. on unidentifiable charcoal (Barker and Broster 1996:103). Stratum IV is thought to be Clovis in age. Some 26 fluted preforms have been recovered from the site, 20 of which were in situ within Stratum IV (Barker and Broster 1996:112). Three Clovis points have been found washed out on the lower beach below the profile.

Another alluvial site found eroding into the Cumberland River was the Puckett site (40SW228). This site also has produced the full range of fluted, lanceolate, and early Archaic projectile point types. Test excavations revealed ". . . an intact level of Dalton projectile points overlain by a substantial Kirk corner-notched component. A radiocarbon sample from the Dalton component has produced a date of 9790 ± 160 yr B.P." (Broster and Norton 1996).

Published information in an expanded form is limited at this point for these sites, as well as for the important Kentucky Lake site of Carson-Conn-Short on the impounded Tennessee River, discussed below. However, the density of early diagnostic artifacts, including fluted points, the presence of visually apparent natural and cultural stratigraphy with charcoal and bone surviving, plus the great depth of burial, together provide an encouraging situation for establishing the geological context necessary for Paleoindian studies in the South. The three radiocarbon dates from the Johnson site seem comparatively old and in two cases their large standard deviations prevent precise cultural association. At two sigmas, both dates are within the North American Clovis range. The 11,980 date with the sigma of 110 yrs seems earlier than western Clovis dates even at three standard deviations. The radiocarbon date associated with the Dalton component at the Puckett site seems right for late Dalton.

Kentucky Lake, Tennessee River, Tennessee

Of several fluted point sites found in surveying the Kentucky Lake region of the Tennessee River by the State of Tennessee's Division of Archaeology, the site of Carson-Conn-Short (40BN190) (Figure 1) has received the most fieldwork. The site was recorded as part of the survey conducted by John Broster and Mark Norton (1993). It is comprised of seven distinct areas exposed at the surface on partially flooded terrace ridges located near the old Pleistocene channel of the Tennessee River.

One of the seven areas, A has received intensive mapping and testing with 1-m-square units. Area A is 50 by 300 m and has produced nearly exclusively Clovis fluted preforms, points, and related unifacial tools, along with a minor Cumberland occupation. Testing has indicated intact Paleoindian lithic material located from 30 to 55 cm below surface associated with two distinct soil strata. Several clusters of firecracked chert were found throughout the area of the Paleoindian artifacts, suggesting deflated hearths.

Subsequent radiocarbon dating of one cluster indicates late Archaic usage, although late Archaic artifacts are not found on the site (Broster and Norton 1996).

With approximately 1,700 tools recovered as of 1994, only a minor quantity are post-Paleoindian in age, indicating a rather dense fluted point site. Carson-Conn-Short is defined as a "quarry-workshop" by Broster and Norton (1996), as it is situated within a few hundred meters of high-quality chert. The site is dominated by fluted preforms and prismatic blades, which probably indicate the primary manufacturing activities. The site is significant because of its stratigraphic integrity and the domination of the lithic assemblage by what is apparently a Clovis-related technology. According to the authors, this may be one of the largest Clovis sites ever found in the Southeast (Broster and Norton 1996).

Carson-Conn-Short, like the sites discussed above for the Cumberland River in the Nashville Basin, has enormous potential for solving basic problems in southeastern Paleoindian studies, not the least of which is the age and origin of Clovis culture. Sophisticated field studies employing techniques of fluvial geology and soil morphology will be needed to fully document what appears to be excellent stratigraphic context.

Middle Tennessee River Valley, Alabama

Recent publications on the famous Quad site and geographically related sites, such as Pine Tree and Stone Pipe (Figure 1), allow some geoarchaeological interpretations to be made of these important Paleoindian sites.

Although these sites have enjoyed a certain prominence in eastern United States Paleoindian studies because of the exceptional quantities of Paleoindian and early Archaic artifacts they have yielded, full-scale intensive archaeological excavations by professional archaeologists never took place. The sites have remained largely inaccessible as they are covered by the waters of the Wheeler Reservoir and have sustained much damage due to water erosion from lowering and raising the reservoir level. Test excavations were conducted by amateur archaeologists who reported on the stratigraphic conditions (e.g., Cambron and Hulse 1960; Hulse and Wright 1989). These test excavations, conducted in the backwater areas of the floodplain away from the contemporary river channel, indicated that the early lithic material was not deeply buried nor clearly segregated stratigraphically from Archaic remains.

Based on recent visits to these sites by Charles Hubbert (1989), some clarification is available for the geological situation of the floodplain in the vicinity of the Quad site. Hubbert (1989:151) reports there are from three to four "levees" present on either side of the river. The first of these is along the present riverbank. Artifacts recovered from the bank indicate the levee is only 7,000 to 8,000 years old. Paleoindian and early Archaic bifaces are not found here. Up to 4 m of alluvial sediments have accumulated since 8000 yr B.P. Levee 2 is about 180 m back from the channel, is from 90 m to 180 m wide, and runs nearly continuously for several miles along the floodplain. Paleoindian and early Archaic artifacts are found that have eroded from Levee 2. Pea-gravel deposits often can be seen exposed on this levee. Levee 3 occurs from 90 m to 180 m away from the river and like Levee 2 produces numerous clusters of Paleoindian and early Archaic lithic materials. It exhibits no pea gravel. Hubbert (1989:154) reports that Levees 2 and 3 have yielded about equal quantities of Paleoindian and early Archaic artifacts, as well as sporadic occurrences of later Holocene cultural occupations. The fourth levee is above the lake level and is essentially uneroded (Hubbert 1989:155).

On Levee 2, Hubbert (1989:156) measured the distance from the highest lateral root scar of 11 tree stumps to the present ground surface to estimate the amount of modern soil loss due to erosion. Based on these measurements, he determined that about 48 cm of sediment have been lost. This sediment is described as silt that covered the artifacts after lowering of the lake level. "Beneath the dark silt, the surface upon which the artifacts rest is a yellow/orange-to-yellow/blue mottled clay which appears to be sterile" (Hubbert 1989:156).

It appears that during the Paleoindian time of occupation of the Quad site locality, the primary occupations were situated on Levees 2 and 3. Hubbert (1989:154) suggests that Levee 2 would have been the nearest riverbank for human occupation. In any event, little or no sediment was accumulating on these land surfaces to afford burial and stratigraphic separation of Paleoindian artifacts from subsequent Archaic occupations. In this regard, they are like the T2 terraces described for the Little Tennessee River and the middle Duck River, which produced Paleoindian artifacts at or near their surfaces.

Dust Cave, Alabama

DUST CAVE IS located in the karstic uplands north of the Tennessee River near Florence, Alabama (Figure 1). In 1988 it was tested by a team from the Alabama Museum of Natural History under the direction of Boyce Driskell and found to have deeply buried Archaic deposits. Subsequent excavations have revealed nearly 5 m of artifact-bearing sediments ranging in age from an estimated 10,500 to 5200 yr B.P. (Driskell 1996). The site is noteworthy for its deep stratigraphy, preservation of faunal and floral remains, and undisturbed deposits, indicated by a long string of radiocarbon dates in chronological order by depth (Driskell 1994:20; Goldman-Finn and Driskell 1994).

Two naturally defined archaeological horizons are of interest here. First is the early side-notched component corresponding to what is called "Big Sandy I" or Bolen side-notched elsewhere in the Southeast. Radiocarbon dates place this between 9000 and 10,000 yr B.P. Nearly a dozen side-notched points have come from an approximately 40-cm-thick layer, along with other typical early Archaic flake tools (Driskell 1994). The sediments associated are local colluvium in origin. Faunal remains from this side-notched horizon and the earlier one below are all Holocene and indicate a diverse biota (Grover 1994).

The lowest horizon is referred to as "late Paleoindian" (Driskell 1996). Radiocarbon dates indicate an age spread between 9990 ± 140 yr B.P. and 10,390 ± 80 yr B.P. Sediments in the lowest artifact-bearing layer possess muscovite (mica), indicating alluvium deposited by the Tennessee River (Goldberg and Sherwood 1994). Sediments above this zone are nearly free of mica, indicating local, colluvial sources. Diagnostic projectile points include one each of Cumberland, Quad, and Hardaway side-notched, two Dalton-like fragments, and three Beaver Lake points (Driskell 1996).

Compared to other cave and shelter sites of the Southeast, Dust Cave is exceptionally well preserved and exhibits great clarity in its stratigraphy. The early side-notched component is essentially typologically pure, with later Kirk corner-notched points lying above it and earlier Dalton and pre-Dalton projectile points below it. Clovis-type points and related artifacts are missing from the sequence, a fact Collins and his colleagues (Collins et al. 1994) attribute to a late Pleistocene, pre-10,500 yr B.P. flushing out of alluvial sediments deposited by the Tennessee River when it was flowing at a higher level. The quality of geoarchaeological and biological data preserved at Dust Cave and the interdisciplinary work being undertaken there (Goldman-Finn and Driskell 1994) guarantee that this site will form a benchmark in the study of the Pleistocene–Holocene transition from an archaeological perspective.

Smith Mountain, Virginia

SMITH MOUNTAIN is a deep, stratified, alluvially buried multicomponent prehistoric site within an ancient levee of the Piedmont portion of the upper Roanoke River (Figure 1). The levee is located in and adjacent to the flood pool of upper Leesville Lake, which is an artificial impoundment of the Roanoke. Due to heavy shoreline erosion from water level fluctuations, numerous early Archaic and some Paleoindian bifaces have been found along the beach (Childress 1993, 1996). Two loci have produced artifacts, an area designated 44PY7, located at the head of the levee, and 44PY152, which is located at the foot. The two loci are about 300 m apart and together are considered the Smith Mountain site (Childress 1993). Because of site loss due to erosion, investigations were undertaken to assess their stratigraphic integrity by the William and Mary Center for Archaeological Research, with the aid of the Roanoke Chapter of the Archeological Society of Virginia (Blanton et al. 1996). Owing to logistical problems of fluctuating water levels and extremely hard soil, 44PY152 received most of the field investigation.

Site 44PY152 was subsurface tested by the William and Mary team in 1994. Ten bucket auger tests were dug over a length of about 70 m along the levee crest with nine of 10 tests producing artifacts. Two 1x2 m test units were excavated to evaluate buried deposits. Auger testing indicated a relatively homogenous deposit with no distinct stratigraphic breaks, except a cobble layer encountered between 1.95 and 2.85 m below surface. A buried artifact deposit was found from 120 to 180 cm below surface consisting of quartz and chert flakes (Blanton et al. 1996:37). Test unit 1 was placed on the beach in an area of high artifact density and dug in six 10 cm levels. Only debitage and undiagnostic biface fragments were recovered, most of these in the first 0.5 m. Based on absolute elevation below the levee surface, the first level corresponded to Stratum V, a deeply buried artifact-producing horizon in the levee. Test unit 2 was placed on the levee top. A backhoe was used to remove soil down to 1.4 m below ground surface to Stratum V, at which point eight 10-cm levels were excavated (Blanton et al. 1996:45). Artifacts were recovered in the first seven levels consisting of debitage and projectile point fragments, one suggestive of a side notched point. Based on depth and lithic raw materials, Stratum V is thought to be Paleoindian-early Archaic.

Geoarchaeological studies were conducted in test unit 2 because of maximum profile depth. Schuldenrein (1996:99) identified three major alluvial cycles and their associated paleosols within 2.4 m of alluvium. Alluvial unit 3, the deepest and oldest horizon, began at about 1.4 m below surface and was observed in profile to about 2 m. The upper 0.5 m of unit 3 corresponded with Stratum V, the buried Paleoindian-early Archaic deposit. It was capped by a fragipan which is thought to have helped preserve its archaeological integrity. Schuldenrein (1996:102) classified the soil morphology of the upper portion of alluvial unit 3 (Stratum V) as a 3AB and attributed the high degree of humification to human inputs. This interpretation is bolstered by geochemical analysis that showed high values of potassium and phosphorous. Two radiocarbon dates were obtained from Stratum V, 8810 ±130 yr B.P. and 9863 ±130 yr B.P., confirming its early Holocene age. Subsequent to this fieldwork, Childress (Childress and Blanton 1996) obtained a ^{14}C date of 10,150 ±70 yr. B.P. on carbonized wood fragments excavated in an exposed layer of the erodig bank profile further west of the William and Mary excavations. This layer was about 0.8 m in thickness and is thought to correspond by depth and archaeological content to Stratum V. The date of 10,150 would further corroborate the early Holocene age of this stratum.

The lower portion of alluviul unit 3 (Stratum VI) was archaeologically sterile. Significantly, however, a 3Bt paleosol was present which Schuldenrein (1996:102) describes as "...the most deeply weathered and only argillic solum identified." Only the upper 0.2 to 0.3 m of this paleosol was observed. Auger testing below that for about 1.14 m encountered the cobble zone detected elsewhere in augering.

Although deep subsurface testing of this site was limited, there is a rather clear expression of an early stable Holocene surface with presumably Paleoindian and early Archaic artifacts associated. One fluted point and three other weakly fluted or basally thinned points have come from the adjacent beach surface implying some type of pre-Dalton occupation. Underneath the 3AB paleosol was a deeply weathered argillic soil (3Bt) that appears to be archaeologically sterile. Assuming the 3AB surface contains the Paleoindian material, this would appear to match the geoarchaeological stratigraphic sequence of the Thunderbird site where a Clovis occupation overlay the "Clovis clay" which Foss (1974) showed to be a buried argillic horizon.

The Haw River Project, North Carolina

Archaeological and geological investigations at two stratified sites (31Ch8 and 31Ch29) located on the Haw River floodplain in the Piedmont of North Carolina (Figure 1) provided an unusually clear stratigraphic picture of the Pleistocene–Holocene boundary and documented the presence of a late Paleoindian Dalton component. The fieldwork was conducted as part of cultural resource management mitigation studies in advance of the B. Everett Jordan Reservoir (Claggett and Cable 1982).

Within a 2-m-thick Holocene alluvial deposit, successive prehistoric occupations were recovered, beginning with Dalton and terminating in the Woodland period. The underlying geologic structure of the Haw River along this stretch is the Indian Creek fault zone, which causes the river to pond during floodstage, resulting in a depositional basin. During the early and middle Holocene, deposition dominated the floodplain primarily through overbank deposits, which effectively buried archaeological remains (Larsen and Schuldenrein 1990:178).

Artifact-bearing Holocene T1 sediments immediately overlie an eroded and weathered Pleistocene surface (T2) consisting of sandy silts. It is estimated that the late Pleistocene surface was exposed to erosion and weathering for as long as a millennium. "This is based on the occurrence of Paleoindian/early Archaic (Hardaway–Dalton and Clovis) projectile points within the buried stratum" (Larsen and Schuldenrein 1990:178). The contact between the lower T1 and the Pleistocene surface was very sharp, suggesting that any pre-Dalton occupation may have been scoured away. Selected excavations into this surface revealed sporadic finds of debitage thought to be fortuitous intrusions from Dalton and early Archaic occupations above (Cable 1982:317). No pre-Dalton diagnostic artifacts were encountered in the Haw River site excavations.

Immediately overlying the eroded late Pleistocene terrace were fine-to medium-grained sands from overbank deposition, which marked the onset of the Holocene aggradation of the Indian Creek fault zone. This is referred to as the Hardaway–Dalton occupation, as revealed at 31Ch29, Block A (Cable 1982:317). Within an approximately 18-cm-thick medium-sand layer, two Dalton points were found, referred to locally as Hardaway–Daltons, as described from the Hardaway type site (Coe 1964). Other associated lithic artifacts include a unifacial "adz"-like tool, end scrapers, and flake blanks. No organic remains were recovered, which eliminated radiocarbon dating. Early Archaic corner-notched Palmer and Kirk points were found above the Hardaway–Dalton layer. No organics were preserved in this layer either; thus radiocarbon dates are unavailable for the early Archaic levels.

The Haw River Project provides critical data toward the study of the Paleoindian period in the Southeast. First, the well-preserved occupational sequence revealed in the T1 terrace indicates that, at least in the remnant area represented by 31Ch29, Holocene sedimentation began at Dalton times (10,500–10,000 yr B.P.). The Holocene sediments formed a clear stratigraphic and textural break with earlier eroded Pleistocene sediments. These excavations also document, using the best geological contexts possible, the stratigraphic separation of Dalton points from later early Archaic notched points (cf. Goodyear 1982).

The Baucom Site, Union County, North Carolina

This alluvially stratified Archaic site was originally dug by artifact collectors from the Piedmont Archaeological Society. It is located on the south bank of the Rocky River in Union County, North Carolina (Figure 1). A published report described several Dalton points and early Archaic notched points, a reconstruction of excavation levels and features, and radiocarbon dates (Peck and Painter 1984). One date in particular, 11,100 ± 1530 yr B.P. (AA-351), based on charcoal, was exceptionally old but had a very large error (Peck and Painter 1984:37). The date was said to have come from the Hardaway side-notched level (Peck and Painter 1984:23). This date also was noted by Haynes (1987:Figure 1) but was not discussed. Sample AA-351 was subsequently rerun, yielding a new date of 8170 ± 110 yr B.P. (Vance Haynes letter to Rodney Peck, 1987). According to Haynes, the latter value is the more reliable, owing to its greater precision.

Given the existence of alluvially buried Dalton and other early Archaic diagnostic lithics, plus reports of hearths and the presence of early Holocene charcoal as witnessed by the ^{14}C dates (Peck and Painter 1984), Goodyear and Haynes (1987) tested the site using backhoe trenches to document the stratigraphy and to obtain new ^{14}C dates. Preliminary results indicate that the Dalton and early Archaic occupations have experienced some vertical mixing, an interpretation supported by small sample AMS ^{14}C dates that also do not appear to be temporally in order by depth. The ^{14}C dates from this work also indicate a possible depositional hiatus at the Pleistocene–Holocene transition. Although final interpretations have not been developed, fieldwork did indicate a Holocene deposit at least 2.7 m deep bearing evidence of continuous prehistoric occupation from Dalton to Woodland times.

Upper Savannah River, Richard B. Russell Reservoir, Georgia and South Carolina

Beginning in the late 1970s and continuing through the early 1980s, extensive cultural resource management mitigation research was conducted in the upper reaches of the Savannah River and its tributaries in the central Piedmont of Georgia and South Carolina related to the building of the Richard B. Russell Reservoir (Figure 1). A multidisciplinary program of environmental reconstruction was undertaken prior to much archaeological excavation in order to set an ecological perspective for archaeological studies (Anderson and Joseph 1988; Carbone et al. 1982). Geological and pedological fieldwork was oriented toward identifying and mapping late Pleistocene and Holocene sediments and landforms, in part, to discover buried Paleoindian and Archaic period remains (Foss et al. 1985; Segovia 1985).

Based on geological and archaeological fieldwork, Segovia (1985) reconstructed the evolution of the Savannah River valley in the project area. During the late Pleistocene (probably Sangamon age), a period of pronounced deposition occurred, resulting in a thin gravel deposit overlain by up to 6 m of reddish medium-to-fine sands. At the end of the Pleistocene this deposit was effectively removed from the valley by downcutting, leaving only a few terraces along valley walls or remnant islands protected on bedrock highs. Strong runoff of the Savannah River continued during the early Holocene, including scouring of the bedrock perhaps as late as 10,000 yr B.P. based on ^{14}C dates of organic matter lying on bedrock. Sometime between 10,000 and 9000 yr B.P., heavy channel-related aggradation began, resulting in the rapid accumulation of up to 4 m of relatively sandy sediments during the early to middle Holocene.

Because of their stratigraphic integrity and preservation, two alluvially buried sites, Gregg Shoals and Rucker's Bottom, received extensive geological and archaeological study, yielding data relevant to the Pleistocene–Holocene transition. These two sites form the primary empirical basis for the broader reconstruction of the late Quaternary evolution of the Savannah River valley.

Gregg Shoals (9Eb259) (Figure 1) was located on a high terrace/levee at the junction of Pickens Creek and the Savannah River on the Georgia side of the river. The site was unusual for the entire reservoir area in that ca. 6 m of Holocene alluvium were deposited over bedrock. The upper 3 m of alluvium contained an unbroken archaeological sequence beginning with the late Kirk phase (9000 yr B.P.?) and continuing on through the Mississippian (Tippitt and Marquardt 1984). No Dalton or pre-Dalton diagnostic artifacts were excavated from the site. Over a 30-year period, the site experienced considerable erosion from the raising and lowering of an upstream dam. Several private collections obtained from the beach contained diagnostic artifacts from all periods, beginning with the early Archaic Kirk phase. Three Dalton points were alleged to have been found on the beach but there were doubts by the principal investigators concerning the artifacts' provenience (Tippitt and Marquardt 1984:1–4). Because of its unusual depositional thickness and its exposure revealing the Pleistocene–Holocene contact, the site received considerable geoarchaeological study.

Two terrace segments at Gregg Shoals were preserved enough to provide data on the onset of Holocene aggradation. About 200 m north of the site proper, in an area of the terrace protected from late Pleistocene erosion by bedrock exposures, a potentially complete sedimentary section was observed. Upchurch (1984a:A-14) detected two basic depositional regimes, a "back levee swamp fill" followed by a "valley fill closely akin to levee and high-energy terrace deposits." The lowest bed (A16) consisted of coarse sand and cobbles, interpreted as thalweg material indicating lateral movement of the river over this spot. It is possible that these coarse sediments are Pleistocene (Upchurch 1984a:A-23). Above this layer was a bed of gray clay with lenses of organic matter (A14, A15), including what appears to have been large cedar logs. These peat lenses also were found in the immediate vicinity lying directly on bedrock (cf. Segovia 1985). Three radiocarbon dates, 10,370 ± 140 yr B.P., 10,170 ± 140 yr B.P., and 10,000 ± 140 yr B.P., were obtained for the peat material (Segovia 1985:5). Overlying the clay and peat bed was a clay-sand layer, indicating a "classic example of back levee swamp fill" (Upchurch 1984a:A-22). Above this began beds dominated by fine-and medium-sized sand, indicative of levee building characteristic of the modern river.

The second terrace segment was observed in the riverbank at the site itself. Here the section rested on bedrock with little evidence of back-levee fill and thalweg deposits. This is attributed to the fact that this portion of the terrace was not rock defended and was washed by Pickens Creek. The lowest bed above the water line, B18, was a sandy gray clay, which Upchurch correlates with the clay-peat layer upstream that produced the 10,000-year-old ^{14}C dates (Upchurch 1984a:A-24). Clay-rich sediments above this bed suggest crevasse splay deposition in a back-levee swamp. After this occurred, sand-dominated levee material reflecting regular Holocene terrace building was deposited.

Archaeological excavations adjacent to this exposure recovered artifacts as deep as 3.1 m below surface. Kirk corner-notched and other late early Archaic points (9000–8000 yr B.P.) were the earliest cultural manifestations encountered in excavations. Bedrock was contacted about 3.2 m below the early Archaic level (Tippitt and Marquardt 1984:6-2).

Gregg Shoals is significant for its lack of pre-Dalton and probably even Dalton remains. The geology indicates that prior to the Dalton period, Gregg Shoals was represented by a scoured bedrock surface, an active channel of the Savannah, and perhaps the beginning of a levee. The clays and organics from the bottom of the terrace are interpreted by Upchurch as related to the back swamp of a levee. The 10,370–10,000 yr B.P. ^{14}C dates obtained on peat should be contemporary with the Dalton horizon. The fact that some of this organic matter was resting on bedrock suggests that it dates the beginning of a levee, itself a product of the onset of Holocene aggradation. Thus, the transition from the Pleistocene to the Holocene as recorded at Gregg Shoals would indicate that alluviation necessary to bury and preserve archaeological remains did not begin until nearly 10,000 yr B.P., too late to provide sedimentation necessary for Paleoindian site occupation and burial.

The second major site studied that was related to the Pleistocene–Holocene transition was Rucker's Bottom (9Eb91) (Figure 1) (Anderson and Schuldenrein 1983, 1985). This was an extensive multicomponent site that contained a complete prehistoric cultural sequence beginning with the early Archaic (9500 yr B.P.) and probably Clovis period, and ending in the Mississippian, all within a 1.3-m-thick deposit. The site is located on a linear terrace-levee formation parallel to the Savannah River on the Georgia side immediately upstream from Van Creek. The 1.3-m Holocene deposit was lying on an eroded, weathered, relict Pleistocene terrace. The terminal Pleistocene terrace surface was marked by an argillic B horizon in coarse-medium sands (Anderson and Schuldenrein 1983:197). Excavations 0.8 m deep into this unit produced no artifacts. Within a 160-m^2 excavation unit, an extensive early Archaic deposit was encountered some 0.8 to 1 m below surface, characterized by ground side-notched and Palmer-like corner-notched points (Anderson and Hanson 1988). These are estimated to date between 10,000 and 9500 yr B.P. A single Clovis fluted point (Anderson and Schuldenrein 1983:Figure 2j, k) was recovered at the same depth as the notched point assemblage, in an area with a dense cluster of Palmer points. No definite association could be made between the Clovis point and any other tools or features. The fluted point was made of a fine black chert characteristic of cherts native to the Ridge and Valley province. Three of the early Archaic notched points recovered were made of a similar material.

It is not clear whether the fluted point was *in situ* or had been culturally redeposited (i.e., scavenged by early Archaic groups and left on the site). Several small black chert flakes also were found in the 160-m^2 excavation area, suggesting tool finishing or maintenance activities. It is not known whether this debitage relates to the Clovis point or the Palmer corner-notched points (Anderson and Schuldenrein 1985:296). If the fluted point was *in situ*, which it may well have been, it indicates a conflated stratigraphy (Anderson and Joseph 1988:107).

The presence of a Clovis point stratigraphically at the transition of the Pleistocene to the Holocene does fit the erosional situation so often cited for the Southeast. The first well-documented cultural assemblage buried by Holocene alluvium at Rucker's Bottom is the side-and corner-notched early Archaic material. Some 28 notched points were found within a 0.2-m-thick level of alluvium. (The single "Hardaway Dalton" point described for this site [Anderson and Schuldenrein 1985:Figures 10, 11B) appears to be a heavily resharpened side-notched point). If the onset of Holocene aggradation dates to 10,000 yr B.P. in the central Savannah River valley, as suggested at Gregg Shoals, Clovis-age occupations on the relict terrace, such as that found at Rucker's Bottom, would have little or no sediment to separate them from succeeding Archaic components.

Two other fluted points from two different sites also were excavated from the Russell Reservoir sites. A waterworn black chert fluted point was found in a culturally redeposited context in a Mississippian-period midden immediately south of Gregg Shoals at Clyde Gulley (9EB387) (Tippitt and Marquardt 1984:8-5, 8-10). A Clovis-like fluted point was excavated from Simpson's Field (38AN8) while searching for subplowzone Woodland features (Wood et al. 1986). The site was situated on the floodplain of the Savannah River on a long Pleistocene terrace bounded by two creeks and a low area. The excavation unit that produced the fluted point was located on a slight ridge of the floodplain, which is an eroded Pleistocene terrace. The fluted point was found just below the plowzone, embedded in light reddish-brown sandy clay (Wood et al. 1986:55–61). An early Archaic corner-notched point and two unifacial flake tools also were found within 20 m of the fluted point. Thus, like at Rucker's Bottom, Paleoindian and early Archaic artifacts were found lying at a common level on the surface of the eroded late Pleistocene surface.

In summary, the Richard B. Russell Reservoir archaeological field studies tend to confirm Segovia's (1985) reconstruction for the Savannah River valley floodplain at the end of the Pleistocene. Because of greater discharge during the terminal Pleistocene, the river moved laterally, removing Pleistocene deposits and scouring the channel bottoms to expose bedrock. The surviving Pleistocene terraces would have stood some 5 m above the river bottom, providing stark relief between the river and its banks. These elevated Pleistocene terrace remnants, according to Segovia, would have provided the best floodplain features for human habitation, although easy access to the river may have been limited. During the initial period of Holocene aggradation, these terrace remnants would have been too high to receive much flood sediment, a fact born out by the minimal sediment thicknesses at sites such as Rucker's Bottom and Simpson's Field. Very early Holocene deposits (11,000–10,000 yr B.P.), if preserved, would be on or near bedrock, as revealed at Gregg Shoals.

Rae's Creek (9Ri327), Richmond County, Georgia

Rae's Creek (Figure 1) was a multi-component, alluvially stratified site with early Archaic (9000 yr B.P.) through Colonoindian (300 yr B.P. [A.D. 1700]) occupations. Excavations were conducted as part of cultural resource mitigation measures related to the construction of a highway and the use of the site as a borrow pit (Crook 1990).

The site is located on the floodplain of the Savannah River at the fall line between the Piedmont and the coastal plain within the city of Augusta. A series of shoals lie immediately to the north of the site. Rae's Creek is located on a trianguloid landform, 400 m long and 175 m in greatest width, paralleling the Savannah River, which occurs some 200 m from the site. To the south, the broader end is bordered by Rae's Creek. Geological and archaeological analyses indicate that the landform is a Holocene point bar which rises some 4 m above the surrounding floodplain (Crook 1990:22, 23).

Grain-size analysis indicated that the 4.6-m-thick accumulation of alluvium are all sands formed by a migrating point bar (Mathews 1990). An early Archaic Kirk midden, defined by a Kirk corner-notched point, an unfinished point preform, and unifacial flake tools and debitage, was found from 3.9 to 4 m below surface. A single ^{14}C date of 9060 ± 110 yr B.P. was obtained from this midden. About 0.6 m below this layer was a "sterile dense sandy clay zone (Stratum R)" (Crook 1990:116). A bucket auger was used to test this zone for another 0.6 m, revealing that the clay content increased with depth (Crook 1990:116). The profile drawing indicates that Stratum R was a "Mottled Orange and Tan Sandy Clay" (Crook 1990:Figure 16).

Although no geological opinions are offered in the report (Crook 1990) as to the age of Stratum R, it seems likely that this zone represents the top of the late Pleistocene terrace. The high clay content of this zone relative to the known Holocene sand beds above, plus the increasingly clayish character of Stratum R with depth, suggest a weathered argillic horizon. The orange color indicates oxidization related to weathering. The contact between Stratum R and the immediately overlying bed is described as scoured (Mathews 1990:189). A total of 18 m^2 was excavated down to the R level, but no artifacts were found associated with that surface.

The contact of the overlying point-bar-related sands and the underlying sandy clay (Stratum R) provide a tantalizing situation for the discovery of in situ Paleoindian remains, if not scoured away. Because of the sands overlying an argillic horizon, the contact of T1 and probably T2 here is reminiscent of the Pleistocene–Holocene contacts as seen at the Haw River and Rucker's Bottom sites.

Oconee River, Wallace Reservoir, Georgia

SURVEYS AND EXCAVATIONS conducted by archaeologists from the University of Georgia in the late 1970s related to construction of the Wallace Dam on the Oconee River in the lower Georgia Piedmont resulted in the discovery of 91 Paleoindian sites. Of this number, 67 sites had Dalton components, with the remaining containing fluted points and other early lanceolate point forms, such as Suwannee. Three of these 91 sites, 9Ge309, 9Ge534, and 9Ge136, were found in alluvial contexts. The rest were found on the surface and not in alluvially active depositional situations (O'Steen et al. 1986).

The most impressive of the floodplain sites was 9Ge309. This site was located on a levee of Richland Creek near where it joins the Oconee River. A total of three fluted points was found—two in excavation levels (O'Steen et al. 1986:Figure 11a, b) and one in the backhoe spoil. Approximately 0.95 m of light-colored Holocene sands bearing a full Archaic through Woodland sequence of occupations overlay a sterile "compact reddish brown sand" (O'Steen et al. 1986:16). A 4-by-6-m unit was excavated in 0.1-m levels next to a backhoe trench that produced a fluted point in the initial site testing. The lowermost 0.6 m of sand contained early Archaic notched points and tools. Two fluted points also were found in the lower portion of the unit, one in the 0.75–0.85-m level and one in the upper portion of the 0.85–0.95-m level. There appears to be some mixing at the site, as a Dalton point, two side-notched early Archaic points, and two fluted points were all found between 0.75 and 0.95 m. A third fluted point, found in spoil from an initial backhoe trench, very likely came from this depth as well. No hearths or other features were reported for the lowest levels of the site.

This site would appear to be situated at the base of a shallow Holocene levee overlying an eroded, probably Pleistocene terrace. The contact between the artifact-bearing, light-colored sands and the reddish-brown compact sand is illustrated as sharp (O'Steen et al. 1986:Figure 9). The red, compacted condition of the basal sterile sands should indicate an oxidized, weathered B-horizon soil. Within the excavation unit, this terrace was described as sterile of artifacts, and the fluted points were said to be in the Holocene sands rather than lying on the surface of the terrace. O'Steen et al. (1986) classify the fluted points as Clovis and illustrate two basal portions of fluted points (O'Steen et al. 1986:Figure 11a, b).

Site 9Ge534 was discovered on the surface of a moderately elevated, alluvial feature within a back swamp of the Oconee River, after the ground had been disturbed by clear-cutting machinery. The base of a fluted point, made of unidentified chert, and some quartz flakes were recovered at the time of initial discovery (O'Steen et al. 1986:24–25). Two 10-m-long backhoe trenches dug to 1 m in depth were subsequently excavated. No hand excavations or screening were conducted. The trenches revealed a shallow alluvial deposit to a depth of 0.6 m, with artifacts apparently restricted to the upper 0.2 m. The sediments were said to be light brown sand (Ledbetter 1978; O'Steen et al. 1986:24). Although interpretations are limited, based on the nature of fieldwork and contextual descriptions, this site does not appear to have been deeply buried.

The third fluted point site, 9Ge136, was located on a levee of the Oconee River. It was found during reservoir construction when portions of the floodplain were bulldozed to bury tree stumps. A quartz fluted-point base and a reworked fluted point of unidentified chert were found to indicate a Paleoindian occupation. Woodland and late Archaic occupations also were evident (O'Steen et al. 1986:26–27). Apparently no other information is available for the site.

The Oconee Reservoir study seems significant for two reasons. First, an unusually large number of Paleoindian points were recovered both from alluvial sites and from adjacent uplands. "Ninety-one Paleo-Indian sites that produced nine early Paleo-Indian, 14 late Paleo-Indian, 67 Dalton, and three indeterminate Paleo-Indian components were identified in the surveyed areas" (O'Steen et al. 1986:2, 3). Compared to other reservoirs surveyed in the Southeast, this is an exceptionally high density (cf. Anderson and Joseph 1988). O'Steen (1983:73) points out that about 63 percent of the surface area of the Wallace Reservoir was exposed by clear-cutting, which certainly would enhance site detection compared to reservoirs where clear-cutting did not precede site survey (e.g., Taylor and Smith 1978). Nevertheless, a number of fluted points were discovered through subsurface testing and ground disturbance on the floodplain. The presence of quartz quarries and nearby Piedmont chert quarries also may have attracted Paleoindian groups to this locality (O'Steen et al. 1986:50, 52). The fact that three fluted points came from such a small area (4 by 6 m) from 9Ge309, along with probable associated tools, indicates a relatively dense Paleoindian site, one which would qualify as a "site" in the conventional sense of the word, as opposed to the more usual isolated fluted point find.

Second, based on the data available from 9Ge309, it would seem that fluted points were found in Holocene alluvium and above, rather than on what is suggested here to be a weathered Pleistocene surface (compact reddish-brown sand). The implication is that Holocene aggradation may have taken place in the Oconee River as early as 11,000 yr B.P. On the other hand, the fluted points lying in physical association with Dalton and early Archaic notched points may represent another example of conflated stratigraphy, as suggested at Rucker's Bottom (Anderson and Joseph 1988:107), complicated by bioturbation.

Coastal Plains

Savannah River Site, Aiken and Barnwell Counties, South Carolina

GEOARCHAEOLOGICAL RESEARCH has been conducted nearly continuously on the 485 km^2 Department of Energy's Savannah River site for the past decade. This research has focused specifically on the Holocene depositional history of the Savannah River (Brooks et al. 1986, 1989). The role of eustatic change in sea level and its effect on changing river gradients has been explicitly modeled to explain the evolutionary changes of the Savannah River in the Atlantic coastal plain during the last 10,000 years (Brooks et al. 1986; Colquhoun and Brooks 1986). Geoarchaeological field studies of the Savannah River site, which is located on the upper coastal plain (Figure 1), have concentrated on how and when alluvial terraces and point bars were formed, relying on chronologically diagnostic artifacts to date their formation (Brooks and Sassaman 1990; Brooks et al. 1989).

Three alluvial terraces have been recognized on the Savannah River site that are related to downcutting and lateral migration of the Savannah River. Adjacent to and elevationally above the active floodplain (To) is T1, which is divided into two subphases: T1a and T1b, based on an escarpment that separates them, which ranges from 36 m to 43 m amsl. A second-older terrace, T2, is located above T1, beginning at 43 m to 46 m amsl (Brooks et al. 1989:30–31).

As yet, no pre-Dalton Paleoindian points have been found *in situ* in a subsurface context on the Savannah River site. The few Dalton points that have been excavated were found about 1 m in depth in point-bar deposits within the T1a terrace. The Dalton period (10,500–10,000 yr B.P.) occupations are the earliest verified human presence on T1a landforms. Based on geological and archaeological data gathered to date, Brooks et al. (1989:58) believe that Dalton and pre-Dalton remains will be found on T1b or the toe of T2, since lower-elevation landforms were formed too late or were scoured by lateral migration of the Savannah. Alluvial deposition of point bars on T1a and T1b terraces is thought to be a result of lateral migration of the Savannah River during the early Holocene when the river flowed as a more braided-like stream or possibly in multiple channels during floodstage. Some T2 and T1b landforms may have been stranded, receiving no further point-bar deposition when the Savannah migrated toward the Georgia side of the valley. Paleoindian artifacts in these situations may be relatively shallow, less than 0.8 m (Brooks et al. 1989:30, 57–58).

The site of Pen Point (38Br383) has thus far received the most thorough geoarchaeological study on the SRS facility. It "is a point bar located at the toe of T1a at the confluence of Pen Branch and the Savannah River swamp" (Brooks et al. 1989:59). Archaeologically, the site is significant as it manifests an unbroken prehistoric cultural sequence beginning with Dalton and terminating with the late Woodland period, all contained within 1 m. The sediments are dominated by sands that are visually azonal with respect to depositional structure. Grain-size analysis verified four point-bar, sediment-fining-upward depositional sequences.

One Dalton-like preform or point was recovered from the 0.85–0.90-m level, which is the earliest archaeological diagnostic recovered from the site. Flake tools and debitage were found as deep as 1 m, including a side-notched Taylor point from 0.95 to 1 m (Brooks and Sassaman 1990:189; Sassaman 1985). Brooks and Sassaman (1990:189) relate the Dalton occupation to the top of the first point-bar depositional sequence, which ranges from 1 to 1.6 m below surface. Below a depth of 1.6 to 3.4 m, grain-size distributions are highly erratic from level to level, an indication of channel sands related to lateral migration of the Savannah. The pre-Dalton sediments are considered to be initial T1a subphase terrace development (Brooks and Sassaman 1990:191). No charcoal or other organics were recovered from the lower portions of the site suitable for ^{14}C dating.

Taylor Hill, 9Ri89, Richmond County, Georgia

THIS MULTI-COMPONENT site produced Paleoindian and Archaic artifacts during a testing project related to the proposed relocation of a railroad near Augusta, Georgia (Elliott and Doyon 1981). The site is in pure alluvium and is located about 0.5 km west of the present Savannah River channel. Two Dalton points were found in a controlled surface collection of 18,100 m^2, and three were excavated within multiple test units totaling 45 m^2. One complete fluted point and the base of a fluted preform were excavated in subplowzone soil. The total depth of the archaeological deposit is about 0.8 m.

Eleven 2-m^2 and one 1-m^2 excavation units (45 m^2) revealed a generally stratified preceramic deposit normally reaching maximum depths between 0.7 and 0.8 m below surface. Evidence of middle and early Archaic components, as well as Dalton and fluted point occupations, is well-documented based on recovered projectile points. It is clear from the distributions of diagnostic artifacts by levels (Elliott and Doyon 1981:Table 12) that considerable mixing of the various Paleoindian and Archaic components has taken place. A total of 565 stone tools was recovered from below the plowzone in the preceramic zone, most of which are probably Paleoindian and early Archaic in age. These include various end and side scrapers, retouched microblades, gravers, flake tools, and multifunctional uniface forms (Elliott and Doyon 1981:Table 15). Compared to other sites in the Southeast, the non-biface tool assemblage of Taylor Hill is remarkably dense (Meltzer 1984:212). Accordingly, it has been interpreted in various settlement models of the early Holocene as a habitation site (Elliott and Doyon 1981) or specialized logistical camp (Anderson and Hanson 1988; Anderson et al. 1990:29–30). Furthermore, the stone tool collection bears a strong resemblance to that of the Brand site in northeast Arkansas (Elliott and Doyon 1981:152; cf. Goodyear 1974).

Little data are available to assess the geological situation of the earliest occupations of Taylor Hill. The Dalton points, the fluted point, and the fluted preform, as well as side-and corner-notched early Archaic points, occur in a brown sand some 0.5 m in thickness overlying a "sterile light brown sand" (Elliott and Doyon 1981:Figure 53). Excavations did not extend deeper than 1 m. Sediments from the site were shown by granular analysis to be alluvial in origin, with more sand in the lower portion of the profile (Elliott and Doyon 1981:192). The sandy knoll-like condition of the field today suggests a series of point bars deposited during the late Pleistocene and early Holocene when the Savannah was flowing in a more braided-like channel configuration, as suggested by Brooks et al. (1989), based on the situation in the eastern side of the valley. Unfortunately, the total deposition over a several-thousand-year period is not very thick. Nevertheless, the existence of a site such as Taylor Hill is encouraging in that the Savannah or its floodstage channels were flowing in diverse places on the early Holocene floodplain and accordingly, if channels such as this were cut off rapidly and associated landforms stranded with no subsequent reoccupation, some spatially isolated Paleoindian sites could be present less than 1 m below surface (cf. Brooks et al. 1989:58–61).

Smith's Lake Creek, Allendale County, South Carolina

TWO EARLY LITHIC SITES located about 300 m apart have been studied in Allendale County, South Carolina. The sites are buried in the east bank of the floodplain along Smith's Lake Creek, a small tributary of the Savannah River as it flows through the middle coastal plain (Figure 1). It is known that the Savannah River flows through Smith's Lake Creek during times of flooding. The sites represent quarry/workshops related to chert processing of river cobbles found nearby in the bottom of the creek. Each site exhibits a basal Paleoindian lanceolate component sealed by river alluvium and bounded by a characteristic set of paleosols (Goodyear and Charles 1984; Goodyear and Foss 1993; Goodyear et al. 1985).

The Paleoindian occupation of the Charles site, 38AL135, is represented by an as yet undefined early lanceolate point assemblage characterized by basally thinned and fluted biface preforms (Figure 8). Typical Paleoindian unifacial flake tools are present, indicating other activities besides quarrying and biface manufacture. The Paleoindian component exists as a stratigraphically discrete unit (Figure 9) situated just above the Pleistocene terrace. Weathered coastal-plain chert artifacts occur from 1 to 1.25 m below surface, housed in pedogenically unmodified fluvial sands (C) or slightly weathered sandy loam (BC), and immediately overlie a similar but archaeologically sterile fluvial sand. These sands and sandy loams probably represent the first floods of the early Holocene. They overlie two argillic horizons (4Btl, SBt2), which,

Figure 8. Early lanceolate bifaces from the Charles site, 38AL135, Smith's Lake Creek, Allendale County, S.C.: a, Dalton point (rhyolite); b, Simpson point; c, fluted preform; d, fluted preform; e, bifacially thinned preform.

according to John Foss, based on heavy argillic development, are Pleistocene in age (Foss 1986; Goodyear 1992; Goodyear and Foss 1993).

Based on test excavations, bucket augering, and backhoe trenching, it is known that the Paleoindian horizon extends some 30 m back from the bank into the terrace (Goodyear 1992). Given the flood-sealed condition of the discrete buried layer as observed in the cutbank (Figure 9), it is possible that it represents a single Paleoindian occupation. The cultural identity of this material is yet to be determined. Surface collections taken from in front of the eroding bank profile have only yielded biface preforms in their early stage of reduction. A fluted preform came from the profile (Figure 8c), as well as other basally thinned and fluted lanceolate fragments (Figure 8d). Lithic material dredged from in front of the site has yielded other lanceolate preforms (Figure 8e). One rhyolite Dalton and a chert Simpson-like point (Figure 8a, b) were found some 50 m downstream where they had eroded from the terrace, indicating a later Paleoindian presence. No finished Paleoindian points have come from the bank profile or from test excavations behind it, nor have any been recovered from underwater dredging of the creek. The preform shown in Figure 8e, the closest to being finished of all the examples, came from the creek in front of the buried layer in the bank. It was found in two pieces and reconstructed. Its final intended state is ambiguous, although it appears to be post-Clovis in that it is a non-fluted, well-thinned bifacial lanceolate.

Extensive excavations of the remaining material in the terrace are planned for the Charles site. Hopefully, large block excavations will result in some diagnostic lanceolates associated with chert processing of the creek quarry. The apparently rapid burial of the Paleoindian layer offers the potential for feature preservation and charcoal for radiocarbon dating.

The Big Pine Tree site, 38AL143, is located some 300 m upstream from the Charles site and is very similar in terms of its occupational history and geoarchaeological context. Unlike the Charles site, it has recently received extensive excavations, as well as underwater data recovery, resulting in a sharper picture for the occupational history.

Backhoe testing in 1992 and 1993 to evaluate the geoarchaeological context has resulted in a good understanding of the pedosedimentary history of the site (Goodyear and Foss 1995). In 1994 and 1995, a total of nearly 50 m^2 was hand excavated, providing

Figure 9. Photograph of buried layer of weathered chert artifacts representing a Paleoindian biface occupation at the Charles site, 38AL135, Allendale County, S.C.

information on the archaeological sequence (Goodyear 1995).

The basic geoarchaeological sequence is as follows. Woodland period artifacts dating from ca. 550 yr B.P. to 3000 yr B.P. are found from 30 to 60 cm below surface in a sandy loam with a weakly developed B horizon (Bw). A preceramic middle Archaic midden exists from 60 to 90 cm, known locally as MALA (Sassaman 1985). In terms of soil morphology, this midden is classified by John Foss as a Bw/A. From 90 to 100 cm there exists a transitional zone of fine sand (BC) with diagnostic bifaces spanning 9500 to 6000 yr B.P. This is likely a time of minimal sedimentation by the Savannah River. From 100 to 115 cm there is an early Archaic occupation typified by Taylor side-notched points and numerous well-made unifacial flake tools. Dalton points have been found in this zone too. There is abundant evidence in the form of river smoothed cortical debris that a chert source in Smith's Lake Creek was being exploited. Easily recognized, spatially discrete lithic features are present, indicating core reduction, biface manufacture, and flake tool utilization. Soil morphology at this depth is a BC in a sandy loam.

From about 115 to 135 cm below surface exists a Paleoindian lanceolate complex dominated by bifacial preforms which exhibit strong basal fluting (Figure 10a, b, d, e). These preforms indicate that large flute flakes (ca. 50 mm) were removed prior to final pressure flaking and manufactured into projectile points. Several of these fluted preforms have been excavated (e.g., Figure 10 b, e) and many more recovered from underwater dredging in the adjacent creek. In all cases, fluting was accomplished from a beveled striking platform. No nipple-type preparations have been observed here or with the Charles site preforms. The soil morphology of the Paleoindian level is that of a BC or C in a loamy sand. The Paleoindian material exists in a clear horizontal floor, as can be seen in the photograph of Figure 11. Only lithic artifacts have been recovered; no bone is preserved. This basal lithic horizon is resting on a layer of sterile fine sands (Figure 11) immediately above a scoured Pleistocene terrace. Thin lamellae have formed in the sterile sands above the terrace or, as seen in Figure 11, rather thickly in sterile precultural alluvium. Foss has classified two Bt paleosols at the Pleistocene terrace surface: an upper 4Btlb over a 4Bt2b. The terrace is sterile of artifacts (Goodyear and Foss 1995).

The cultural identity of the lowermost artifact zone has not yet been established based on completed projectile points. There is a strong emphasis on percussion fluting of blanks in the early stage (Figure 10a, b, d, e), a trait that would seem linked to Clovis. The absence thus far of nipple-type fluting platforms would seem to reinforce this. That fluting or massive basal thinning would take place so early in biface reduction seems unusual, although it is not rare (cf. Goodyear et al. 1989; Morrow 1995; Painter 1974). However, it is possible that these flute scars were left on at least one face of the finished preform and incorporated unchanged into the final design. Percussion fluting that yields scars up to 50 mm in length would be less risky on thick blanks than thinner preforms more prone to shatter. A total of 10 Dalton points have been recovered from the site (Figure 10 c, f). The four that have been excavated in situ all came from the 100–115 cm level. Their recovery in the zone above that of the fluted blanks reinforces the antiquity of the latter.

Figure 10. Lanceolate points and preforms from the Big Pine Tree site, 38AL143, Smith's Lake Creek, Allendale County, S.C.: a, fluted preform; b, fluted preform; c, Dalton point; d, fluted preform; e, fluted preform; f, Dalton point.

Figure 11. Photograph of Pleistocene-Holocene transition stratigraphy exposed on south profile of BHT 1, E 94-E98, from the Big Pine Tree site, 38AL143, Allendale County, S.C.

Based on the numbers of tools recovered from both land excavations and underwater, it is clear that other activities were taking place at the site besides chert processing. Numerous unifacial flake tools such as side and end scrapers, flake knives, and gravers have been found, as well as prismatic blades and cores. Like the Taylor side-notched occupation above, the Paleoindians were exploiting chert from the creek, and several core-reduction features have been mapped. Feature-like concentrations of bifaces and unifaces have also been mapped, indicating some structured in-site use. The number of prismatic blades is remarkable. Many of the blades are microblades in that they are very thin and less than 20 mm long. Core fragments with multiple blade detachments also have been found.

AMS-sized charcoal samples have been taken from key locations within the terrace excavation for radiocarbon dating. Charcoal samples large enough for conventional dating have not been found. Two AMS dates from early contexts returned values of 7810 ±80 yr B.P. and 4720 ±70 yr B.P., dates which indicate bioturbation of small charcoal fragments down the profile.

In sum, the Big Pine Tree site, like that of the Charles site, holds great promise for resolving some of the substantive issues of southeastern U.S. Paleoindian archaeology which have remained intractable due to poor archaeological context. The hydrogeological conditions in Smith's Lake Creek at the end of the Pleistocene and onset of the Holocene were conducive to deposition and thus archaeological preservation. Various periods of landscape stability on the floodplain also were amenable to soil development, providing another factor which enhanced geoarchaeological context. Continued excavation, analysis, and radiocarbon dating should shed considerable light on the period from 11,500 to 10,000 yr B.P.

Finally, it is worth noting that the geoarchaeological situation at both sites on Smith's Lake Creek is like that of other alluvial sites reviewed for the Southeast. That is, there is a Paleoindian lithic assemblage associated with the first Holocene fluvial sands overlying a weathered terrace with argillic B-horizon paleosols.

Theriault Site, 9Bk2, Burke County, Georgia

THE THERIAULT SITE is located on the eastern bank of Brier Creek, a coastal-plain tributary of the Savannah River (Figure 1). It is a multi-component site that witnessed frequent flintknapping as well as other activities throughout the Holocene. This portion of the Brier Creek locality is known for its sources of high-quality chert (Goodyear and Charles 1984; Waring 1961) and a high incidence of Paleoindian points (Anderson et al. 1990; Waring 1968).

Because of its richness in lithic artifacts, the site received a great deal of uncontrolled digging by relic hunters. One professional report is available for the site by Brockington (1971), which is based on excavations done by William Edwards in 1966. The following is summarized from Brockington (1971).

Edwards excavated 62 1.5-m squares in three different areas using 15-cm levels. The quantity of lithic artifacts from these excavations was truly remarkable, as over 2,425 kg of debitage, 973 bifaces, and 120 identifiable projectile points and fragments were recovered, spanning 11,000 years of prehistory. The artifacts were found in "medium, well-sorted sand about 36 inches [92 cm] deep, overlying a sterile clay matrix. Ground water was encountered three to four inches [7 cm - 10 cm] into the clay" (Brockington 1971:25). There were no discernable natural stratigraphic units within this sand. One unusually large (120 mm) Clovis-like fluted point (Brockington 1971:Figure 10a) was found between 76 cm and 86 cm, immediately above the clay. Two Dalton points were found, one at 91 cm on top of the clay and one in the 46-cm–61-cm level. One lanceolate biface, which is compared to a "Hardaway Blade," was found in the 46-cm–61-cm level. The latter would appear to be some type of post-Clovis preform.

Although the Theriault site is generally stratified, the archaeological deposits appear to have undergone some mixing. Early Archaic notched points as well as middle Archaic stemmed points were all found in the lowest 30 cm of the site, along with the Paleoindian points (Brockington 1971:Figure 5). The origin of the sand overlying the clay is unknown; however, Brier Creek, a medium-sized stream over 125 km in length, is a likely source. No geologic analysis was conducted on the sediments. James Michie (personal communication 1991), who visited the site during Edwards' excavation, has described the basal clay as having an orange color. This should indicate that at some point the clay horizon was weathered or received oxidized sediments.

Muckafoonee Site, Dougherty County, Georgia

THE MUCKAFOONEE SITE is located on an alluvial terrace of Muckafoonee Creek, about 700 m upstream from its confluence with the Flint River near Albany, Georgia (Figure 1). The site was discovered during the testing phase of a cultural resource management project related to the use of the site for borrow material (Elliott 1982). Excavations were limited to two deep backhoe trenches, two 1-m squares, and a single 2-m square. Chert outcrops are present in the nearby vicinity and the site appears to have been a quarry-related workshop during Paleoindian and Archaic times. The site contained lithic material up to at least a depth of 0.9 m and a single fluted point was found between 0.7 and 0.8 m. Artifacts were dominated by biface manufacture and related flakes, with some Paleoindian-type unifaces found in the lower levels. Some mixing is evident, but the Paleoindian material is concentrated in the lower 0.3 m of the site.

Profile descriptions of the backhoe trenches and test squares give a good indication of natural stratigraphy up to a depth of 1.5 m (Elliott 1982). Archaic and Paleoindian-age artifacts in temporal order by depth were found consistently in a light brown sand of medium-coarse texture varying from 0.6 to 1 m in thickness. The upper 0.3 to 0.5 m of this unit possessed dark brown mottles over a light brown sand, which is probably the result of pedogenic influence from humic zones above (Elliott 1982:21). Underneath this artifact-bearing light brown sand, from about 1 to 1.5 m in depth, were three culturally sterile horizons. These were a "mottled light brown and reddish brown clayey sand," overlying a "compact reddish brown clayey sand," which overlay a "coarse light, almost white sand" (Elliott 1982:22, 23). The reddish-brown colors of the clayey sands and the compactness of the second horizon suggest these are Bt paleosols. The lowest coarse, nearly white sand layer may be unpedogenically modified sediment. No radiocarbon dates were reported from this testing phase of fieldwork.

Given that the site is situated on a terrace of Muckafoonee Creek near its juncture with the Flint River, alluvial burial seems most probable for these layers. Within the first meter, some significant portion of the deposit may be cultural in origin, given the density of debitage in the site.

The Hester Site, 22Mo569, Monroe County, Mississippi

THE HESTER SITE is located on the east bank of the Tombigbee River floodplain in northeast Mississippi (Figure 1). Standifer Creek runs into the Tombigbee just southeast of the site. The original proximity of the creek to the Hester site is undetermined due to modern rechannelization (Brookes 1979).

The Hester site was excavated by archaeologists from the Mississippi Department of Archives and History in 1973 and 1974, and again in 1978. Previous uncontrolled amateur excavations from one area of the site (Beachum-Harrison) yielded a number of Dalton points and early Archaic notched points and related unifacial tools, prompting subsequent professional investigations in 1973 and 1974. The available report for this site is based on the fieldwork of these two seasons (Brookes 1979). The site was excavated more extensively in 1978 by Samuel Brookes. Although the results of this third season are not yet available in a published format, Samuel Brookes (personal communication 1991) has provided me with relevant information concerning this latter excavation, which he has graciously allowed me to summarize here.

The original excavation was that of a trench ~1.5 m wide by 45.7 m long, excavated in 1.5-m squares in 6-cm arbitrary levels. The single published report for the site (Brookes 1979) is based primarily on data recovered from this trench (67.5 m^2). The 1978 excavations expanded both sides of this trench, resulting in a total excavation of 135 m^2.

The stratigraphy of the site can be described as five visually distinct zones:

Zone 1, from ground surface to ~0.4 m deep, is a plow-disturbed, black humus zone consisting of Historic to late Archaic fiber-tempered ceramics.

Zone 2 is a dark, red-brown sand extending to ~1 m below surface. It has a hard, cemented consistency. No visual stratigraphy is present within this zone. However, based on diagnostic projectile points, there are definable occupational horizons within the zone, occurring in temporal order by depth beginning with the middle Archaic and ending with early Archaic. Early Archaic Big Sandy side-notched points were found in the lower portion of the red-brown sand.

Zone 3 is a yellow sand occurring from ~1 m to 1.3 m below surface. The contact is very sharp between zone 2 and zone 3, as the former lies unconformably on the latter. The yellow sand is powdery when dry and very unstable, scarcely permitting artifacts to be pedestalled. Within the yellow sand layer, Brookes found evidence for what he believes are two separate Paleoindian occupations.

In the upper portion of the yellow sand, a Dalton occupation occurred that consisted of three different styles of Dalton points. These include 24 of the typical straight-sided lanceolate form, 10 side-notched points, and one square-based Dalton. Brookes likens the side-notched form to other examples of Dalton side-notching, namely San Patrice, St. Johns variety (Webb et al. 1971), and Hardaway side-notched (Coe 1964).

In the lower portion of the yellow sand zone about 5 cm below the Dalton occupation, Brookes found Quad points. Of the six Quad points recovered from the Hester site, four were recovered from the lower portion of the yellow sand zone and two from the upper portion. The designation of a lower Quad component is strengthened by the fact that two of the six Quad points were made from exotic cherts from the Tennessee Valley area, while the remaining four were from local gravel chert. (All but three of the Dalton points were made from local gravel chert; the exceptions being two of Ft. Payne chert and one of Tallahatta quartzite). A number of flakes and tools also were made from exotic cherts in the Quad zone.

Zone 4 begins at about 1.3 m and continues to about 1.7 m below surface. It is a white powdery sand of the same loose structure as the yellow sand above. The boundary between the white and yellow sands was not as sharp as between zones 2 and 3. Zone 4 contained no artifacts.

Zone 5 consists of a yellow-white mottled clay that was sterile of artifacts. Based on bore tests, this clay unit is at least 1.2 m thick in this portion of the site. Gravel was encountered from ~3.7 m to 4.6 m below surface.

There were originally three sandy "rises" on the Hester site floodplain: one destroyed by gravel mining; one destroyed by amateur digging and now designated 22Mo1011, Beachum-Harrison; and the third, designated 22Mo569 or the Hester site proper, excavated by Brookes and associates. Hard-packed dark gray clay with no cultural occupations associated occurs between the sand rises.

Evidence also exists for fluted point occupations of the Hester site. On the adjacent sandy rise dug by amateur excavators (22Mo1011, Beachum-Harrison), one complete Clovis point made of an exotic chert was said to have been found, as well as the base of another Clovis point, also made on exotic chert. No Quad points were discovered during the amateur excavation. In the rise destroyed by gravel mining, a collector found a fluted Cumberland point of exotic Ft. Payne chert on the surface. In the 1978 excavations, Brookes recovered a fragment of a Ft. Payne-chert Clovis point reworked by bipolar flaking from the Dalton zone, as well as a reworked Ft. Payne-chert fluted Cumberland point.

Although it is clear that fluted points, particularly those made of exotic chert, have been found at the Hester site, their stratigraphic position is not clear. The two examples found by Brookes "in situ" in the Dalton zone were reworked pieces that appear to be examples of points scavenged by Dalton people. The other examples were obtained by collectors who originally dug the site.

Although the final analysis and report of the Hester site are yet to be completed, these preliminary data do allow some tentative interpretations to be made.

First, there appears to be a good stratigraphic separation of the early Archaic notched points associated with the dark red-brown sand zone from the Dalton material in the yellow sand zone. The presence of "notched" varieties of Daltons may indicate a late Dalton (ca. 10,000 yr B.P.) time period. The positing of a Quad occupation immediately beneath the Dalton level in zone 3 is highly probable but requires published documentation.

Second, the presence of fluted points from the three different sandy rises on the site implies an earlier Paleoindian occupation of the Hester site. According to Brookes, the lower portion of the yellow sand zone manifests a higher proportion of exotic lithics, such as Ft. Payne chert from Alabama. When coupled with the fact that all fluted points known from the site are made from exotic cherts, the lower portion of the yellow sand zone is strongly implied as the stratigraphic location of one or more fluted point occupations. The fact that the white sand of zone 4 beneath the yellow sand thus far has been sterile of artifacts reinforces this possibility.

Additional studies of the site, including sedimentology and pedology, are needed to understand something of the origin and physical condition of these zones. The sharp boundary in structure and color between the dark red-brown sand and the yellow sand zones implies a depositional or erosional event or both. The yellow color of zone 3 may be simply iron leached from zone 2. The loose, powdery consistency of the white sand in zone 4 suggests that this was rapidly deposited, pedogenically unmodified flood alluvium. It would be useful to have a profile study of the contact between the sterile white sand (zone 4) and the basal clay unit (zone 5), as well as ^{14}C dates to determine the onset of aggradation indicated by what are probably channel-related sands.

Florida Silver Springs Site (8Mr92), Marion County, Florida

As ORIGINALLY DESCRIBED by Wilfred Neill (1958), the Silver Springs site (Figure 1) was a stratified multicomponent site situated within a windblown hill deposit. It is located on the south side of Silver Springs Run, on the edge of the uplands above the floodplain. The Silver Springs site (8Mr92) is not to be confused with the actual head springs of the river, also known as Silver Springs. This commercial attraction, which also was apparently an inundated subterranean cave, is referred to by Neill (1964) as the Cavern site. The head springs are about a half-mile upriver from 8Mr92. The Silver Springs site also is somewhat famous in North American archaeology according to Mason (1962:240), since it was at that time one of the few documented cases of fluted points found stratigraphically below Archaic occupations in the eastern United States.

The site, which was originally a wooded hill borrowed for its sand, was discovered to contain Paleoindian material when two fluted lanceolate points were discovered in the removed sand. Neill conducted excavations in the flattest portion of the remaining hill surface, recovering fluted points and Suwannee-like lanceolates and related tools in the lowest occupation level. Neill (1958:35–37) excavated 11 units totaling about 500 ft^2, using a trowel and measuring the depth of artifacts below ground surface. Artifacts were few in density but occurred lying flat in relatively undisturbed horizons that were interpreted as occupational surfaces.

Neill reported Woodland through Paleoindian (Suwannee) occupations in good stratigraphic order within approximately the first 2.4 m of sand. Neill (1958:46) believed the artifact-bearing sand was eolian in origin. This sand lay conformably over another sand unit, sterile of artifacts, which possessed roughly parallel bands of clay that he referred to as "laminated." These are now known to be lamellae, repeatedly found in sandy sediments of the early and middle Holocene in the Southeast and which are largely pedogenic in origin (cf. Foss et al. 1985; Larsen and Schuldenrein 1990).

Below the Archaic levels, between 1.9 m and 2.2 m below surface, was a nearly sterile zone possessing few flakes and very little charcoal or staining, unlike the site above this level. At the 2.2-m–2.4-m level and from 2.5 cm to 10 cm above the clay lamellae, Neill encountered obvious Paleoindian artifacts. These included two lanceolate bases (Neill 1958:Plate 3J, K), which are possibly preforms; two Suwannee point bases (Neill 1958:Plate 3D, G); and one fluted point missing its base (Neill 1958:Plate 3A). Recovered from the spread sand borrowed from the hill were one whole fluted point with lateral waisting and ears (Neill 1958:Plate 3B) and one point that resembles a Western Clovis (Neill 1958:Plate 3C). Other associated artifacts included nine utilized flakes, two sandstone abraders, a chopping tool, a crude uniface, and a possible worked piece of fossil shell. No bone, shell, or other organic remains were found, with the exception of scattered grains of charcoal, which Neill described as relatively plentiful throughout the site.

In 1973, Thomas Hemmings (1975) of the Florida State Museum partially excavated the Silver Springs site and described the geology. Hemmings placed two excavation units against the face of the borrow pit near Neill's A and F units. These excavations totalled 102 m^3. For the most part, Hemmings was able to replicate Neill's stratigraphy and post-Paleoindian archaeological deposits. However, very little was found in the lowermost level, aside from a few weathered flakes that were lying flat. One midsection of a fluted point was recovered 1.5 m below surface, well above the 2.1 m–2.4-m Paleoindian level (Hemmings 1975:148, Figure 6.1). Hemmings states that the differences between his results and those of Neill are attributable to sampling error. Neill (1958:44) reported that nine-tenths of the hill had been removed by workmen prior to his excavation, so it is possible that not much of the Paleoindian occupation was left.

Hemmings (1975) basically confirmed Neill's stratigraphic interpretation of the site. He describes the upper 2.4 m of stratified archaeological deposits (Unit A1, Upper Sand) as a "homogenous eolian sand without cross-bedding or other structure" (Hemmings 1975:144). A1 grades into Unit A2, the Lower Sand, which has both sand and clay (in the lamellae) and minor elements of limestone gravel. Hemmings believes Unit A2 was formed by both wind and slopewash from higher elevations to the south. In some places Unit A2 is 2.1 m thick. Based on the archaeology, Hemmings suggests that the Lower Sand is pre-10,000 years in age.

The Silver Springs site, now largely gone, is an important datum point in southeastern Paleoindian archaeology. As Mason (1962:240) pointed out, it was (and still is) one of the few examples in the East of Paleoindian lanceolates occurring stratigraphically beneath Archaic assemblages. Furthermore, the assemblage purity of the Paleoindian zone of Silver Springs is worthy of note. Only Suwannee and what may be Clovis points were found in the basal zone. This zone was separated from subsequent Archaic occupations by a relatively sterile zone about 0.3 m in thickness. The frequent situation of reoccupation by early Archaic peoples with chipped stone tools virtually identical to those of lanceolate point-making Paleoindian groups is fortunately absent, adding to the integrity of the Silver Springs Paleoindian assemblage.

Harney Flats, 8Hi507, Hillsborough County, Florida

THE HARNEY FLATS site, prior to its destruction by excavations and the construction of the Interstate 75 Bypass, was located about 10 km east of the city of Tampa (Figure 1). It originally was situated on a scarp overlooking a low swampy locality known as Harney Flats, for which the site was named. The multiphase testing and excavation projects were summarized by Daniel and Wisenbaker (1987). In all, 967 m^2 were excavated, making this one of the largest Paleoindian site excavations in the East. The total number of Paleoindian artifacts recovered from the excavations also is remarkable, as nearly 1,100 chipped stone artifacts were found, including 28 examples of Suwannee and Simpson points and their preforms. Some early Archaic notched material is included in the assemblage, as 13 Bolen side-notched points were recovered from the same matrix as the Suwannee points, along with an unspecifiable number of associated unifacial tools (Daniel and Wisenbaker 1987:42–62).

The geological and archaeological stratigraphy of Harney Flats is summarized as follows from Daniel and Wisenbaker (1987:Figure 12, 28–29). Zone 1, from ground surface to 0.15 m, was a humus-rich gray sand sterile of artifacts. Zone 2, from 0.15 to 0.75 m, consisted of a white sand. Occasional Woodland-period sherds were found at about the 0.4-m level. Beginning at 0.6 m and extending to 0.9 m, middle Archaic Newnan stemmed points were recovered. This point type is known to date from about 5,000 to 7,000 years ago. Zone 3 was a dark brown hardpan soil ranging from 0.75 to 0.85 m in depth. It is believed that this hardpan kept middle Archaic and later artifacts from intruding downward into the Suwannee–Bolen horizon. Newnan points were found in and above this hardpan. Zone 4 extended from 0.85 to 1.05 m and was a yellow-brown sand, probably stained by iron leached from the hardpan above. Two possible Kirk points were found in this zone from 0.9 to 1 m below surface. Zone 5 occurred from 1.05 m to its arbitrary termination at 2 m, where water appeared in the profile. It is characterized as a pale brown sand. The upper portion of this zone, from 1 to 1.6 m, produced the Suwannee–Bolen concentration, with most of the material found in the upper 0.3 m. Below 1.3 m, artifact density decreased significantly. Zone 6, located several meters below surface in most areas of the site, is a bluish-green clayish sand that overlies the Tertiary limestones and is presumed to have formed during the Miocene. The area from 1.6 m of Zone 5 to and including Zone 6 was sterile of human occupation.

Zones 1 to 5 were basically pedogenic manifestations of a homogenous soil type, that of Leon fine sand, rather than separate lithologic depositional units (Daniel and Wisenbaker 1987:28). Sedimentological studies of the sands were done by Upchurch (1984b) in an effort to reconstruct the stratigraphic formation of the Harney Flats site.

Upchurch (1984b) has noted the existence of sand-dune systems in this central west-coast Florida locality that ultimately originated from Pleistocene marine transgressions. Toward the end of the Pleistocene, sand was reworked into dunes from sands available in sediment-choked floodplains, marine terraces, and eolian sand sheets (Upchurch 1984b). Sands in the Harney Flats locality reflect two primary depositional regimes. First, there are marine-deposited sands that dominate the basal sections and have received little eolian reworking. Overlying these basal sands are surficial dune trains formed during the late Pleistocene and early Holocene. Phi analysis of grain-size distributions from excavation profiles at Harney Flats revealed unimodal, lognormal distributions typical of eolian transport. The grain size was unusually homogeneous regardless of vertical or horizontal location in the site, indicating bioturbation of an already homogenous dune source (Upchurch 1984b). Palynological studies for the Paleoindian time period in Florida indicate that climatic conditions still were dry (Watts and Hansen 1988:316–317), which would have allowed wind erosion and deposition on the landscape. Given the moderate slope of the Harney Flats site, it is likely that some of the eolian material migrated downslope as colluvium.

Like the Silver Springs site discussed above, there is evidence of burial of Paleoindian material from 11,000 to 10,000 yr B.P. in central Florida from windblown sediments. Because of the dry and permeable nature of the sediment matrix, other items of material culture made from bone and wood are not likely to be preserved. Nevertheless, sufficient eolian activity was present to bury Paleoindian sites, allowing excellent preservation of lithic assemblages. In the case of Harney Flats, however, sedimentation of the hillside during the Suwannee and Bolen occupation was not sufficient to separate these two phases stratigraphically. As discussed below, radiocarbon dates of Bolen side-notched assemblages elsewhere in Florida indicate they date from 10,000 to 9500 yr B.P.

Page/Ladson Site, 8Je591, Aucilla River, Jefferson County, Florida

PAGE/LADSON IS ONE of several inundated river sites in the Aucilla River basin and is located approximately 80 km southeast of Tallahassee (Figure 1). Multidisciplinary work featuring archaeology, geochronology, and paleontology has been ongoing in the Aucilla River since 1983, generating a variety of significant data relevant to the late Pleistocene-early Holocene transition (Dunbar et al. 1988, 1989a).

Dunbar et al. (1988:443) note that freshwater-inundated sites in Florida are of two types: stillwater sinkholes, such as Little Salt Spring and Warm Mineral Springs; and those sites located in the bottoms of slow-moving rivers common in the karst region of central and north Florida. River bottom sites have produced many of the Suwannee points and worked ivory artifacts for which Florida is famous (Mason 1962; Milanich and Fairbanks 1980; Purdy 1981). Since Paleoindian artifacts found in these rivers are in the same deposit or at the same surface as late prehistoric and even modern artifacts, little interpretive value has been accorded them because of poor context. However, the recent work of Dunbar, Faught, and Webb (Dunbar et al. 1988) at the Page/Ladson site has shown that there are in situ, stratified late Pleistocene and early Holocene artifact-bearing deposits in drowned sinkholes within formerly dry riverbeds.

The Aucilla River is unusual in that it runs both above and below ground through karstic limestone. Water originates in the massive Florida aquifer system, ultimately draining into the Gulf of Mexico. The longest aboveground stretch of the river is Half Mile Rise, nearly 1.5 km in length. Within this segment of the river are a number of sinks filled with alternating layers of peat and marl containing Paleoindian artifacts of stone and bone, and extinct Pleistocene fauna (Dunbar et al. 1988:443). It has been established that there was a general lowering of the water table in late Pleistocene in Florida due to a drastically lowered sea level and a drier climate (Brooks 1972). Under such conditions, what are now flowing riverbeds would have been subaerial arroyo-like features. It is thought that when the rivers were not flowing, some of the sinks still contained water in perched ponds. Radiocarbon dates ranging from 9540 to 13,130 yr B.P. (Dunbar et al. 1988:449) on peats, wood, and bone indicate enough water was present to allow organic preservation in the sinkholes. The general trend is "preserved wood and other organic remains in the sink bottoms (which) indicates a late Pleistocene sequence of generally shallow water sediments followed by a sequence of early Holocene generally deeper water sediments" (Dunbar et al. 1988:443). After 4000 yr B.P., increased water flow caused erosion of sink deposits, creating stratigraphic deflation whereby artifacts of all ages are found together in "blowout" features.

Page/Ladson consists of two contiguous inundated sinks that have undergone underwater excavation. Test pit B is a 4-m-deep unit located on the northern lip of the southernmost depression. Test pit C, located on the western edge of the same sink, began as a broadside but soon was confined to a small area and finally excavated to 7 m in depth. A series of common stratigraphic horizons, labeled zones A through E, have been observed in the test units (Dunbar et al. 1988:446).

Zones A and B represent redeposited late Archaic and Woodland-related sediments dating within the past 3,400 years. They overlie zones C and D, which are of interest here. Zones C and D are comprised of peats and calcareous clays with a very minor sand component. Preservation of wood and bone (even insects) in the calcium-rich layers is very good. Bone found in situ in these zones is colored light tan or off-white, which Dunbar et al. (1988:444) believe represents rapid burial. In contrast, bone and ivory artifacts customarily found in Florida river bottoms are dark brown from tannin staining (Figure 7), indicating to Dunbar and his colleagues that they have been eroded from their original sinkhole deposits.

Zone C has been radiocarbon dated at 9450 ± 100 yr B.P., 9730 ± 120 yr B.P., 10,000 ± 120 yr B.P., and 10,280 ± 110 yr B.P. (Dunbar et al. 1988:Table 1). In test pit B, side-notched Bolen beveled projectile points, unifaces, adzes, and other lithic tools were associated with the ^{14}C date of 9730 yr B.P. Preserved organic materials, such as desiccated bone, wood, and fern spores were found, but not pollen, indicating a dry land surface prior to inundation (Dunbar et al. 1988:444). Only modern fauna have been associated with zone C.

In zone C of test pit C, Dunbar and others exposed a 6-m^2 area of level A horizon soil development at a depth of 4 m in the pit and 6 m under the water. Limestone, lithic debitage, broken adze bits, and a Bolen Plain corner notched point were found with what appeared to be an activity surface [Dunbar et al. 1988:444].

This humic horizon has been referred to informally as "The Dirt," owing to its high organic content. Two radiocarbon dates were obtained from this horizon on charcoal (10,000 yr B.P.) and wood (10,280 yr B.P.). A date of 10,600 ± 70 yr B.P. was obtained just below this A horizon in unaltered zone D deposits (Dunbar et al. 1988:444).

Zone D is the oldest human-related horizon. This zone is the first to contain extinct fauna, including mastodon, camel, horse, and giant armadillo. The sediments of this zone are described as a lime-sand. Artifacts include a bolo stone and chert flakes. As yet, no Clovis or Suwannee points have been recovered *in situ* from any of the natural zones including zone D. Six ^{14}C dates for zone D range from 10,520 ± 90 to 13,130 ± 200 yr B.P. (Dunbar et al. 1988:Table 1).

Zone E is characterized as "Woody Peat" and identified by Lee Newsom as cypress. One ^{14}C date is available for this zone assayed at 18,430 ± 220 yr B.P. (Dunbar et al. 1988:Table 1). Compared to zones C and D, which were rich in calcium, zone E has less calcium carbonate, implying less breakdown in local limestone (Dunbar et al. 1988:444).

Dunbar et al. (1988:450) believe there are earlier in situ occupations of Page/Ladson than those indicated by early Archaic Bolen side-and corner-notched occupations. Paleoindian lanceolates, such as Clovis, Suwannee, and Simpson, as well as worked ivory are present at the site in river-eroded blowouts. Given the ^{14}C ages of the stratified sediments in zone D, there is good reason to think they will be *in situ.*

In sum, the work of Dunbar, Webb, Faught, and others at Page/Ladson has demonstrated the existence of stratified in situ late Pleistocene–early Holocene archaeological deposits in well-dated contexts. Contrary to previous results and opinions regarding the contextual integrity of Florida river sites, they have shown that, at least in some places, utilization of dry riverbeds was related to sinkholes with standing or quietly flowing waters, as evidenced by the presence of peat. These peat and marl-filled sinks evidently are stratified archaeologically and geologically and offer remarkable preservation of normally absent organic remains, including artifacts of bone, ivory, and wood. The presence of flowing water apparently was a later Holocene event, which caused the deflation of geological and archaeological deposits. Numerous chert outcrops in the Aucilla riverbed that show evidence of quarrying also are an indication that the river channels were dry at an earlier time (Dunbar et al. 1989b:27).

It also is clear that zone D is the provenience of Paleoindian remains dating 10,500 years ago and earlier. Based on the spread of the six ^{14}C dates (10,520–13,130 yr B.P.) and the abundance of preserved organics, including late Pleistocene megafauna, zone D is a prime candidate for further Paleoindian research at Page/Ladson. It also should be remembered that the lower Aucilla River has the highest density of Clovis points and ivory foreshafts known for all the rivers in Florida (Dunbar et al. 1988:451), heightening the possibility that such remains might be studied and dated in situ.

Drowned Sites in the Eastern Gulf of Mexico

Tampa Bay, Florida

Beginning in the early 1960s, Suwannee points, bone pins, Bolen points, and related unifacial flake tools, as well as later Archaic artifacts began to regularly appear in dredge spoil from private and federal dredging in Tampa Bay (Goodyear and Warren 1972; Warren 1964, 1970). The origin of these artifacts was two basic sources. The most common were shallow (<4 m) water-inundated late Pleistocene and early Holocene land surfaces now a few hundred meters from the present shore (Goodyear et al. 1983:42). On fills and spoil islands that produced early artifacts, there usually was a contemporary freshwater drainage nearby, suggesting that the artifacts were from sites associated with former creeks. The other source of artifacts was oyster shell deposits commercially mined for use as surface material for streets and parking lots (Goodyear and Warren 1972; Warren 1964). The latter deposits were estimated by private dredgers to be between 3 and 15 m thick and were substantial enough to allow commercial mining for several decades. The possibility that some of these shell deposits were related to human exploitation has been considered (Goodyear and Warren 1972; Warren 1964), although no demonstration that they were middens has been attempted. Dredge operators reported that the oyster shell deposits followed the old river channels in Tampa Bay, as well as modern ship channels, which are deepened natural channels (Goodyear and Warren 1972:52). The oyster shell deposits, located 2 and 3 km offshore and in the deepest portions of the bay, produced Paleoindian and Archaic stone tools but few examples of pottery. Evidence of occupation by humans appears to have ceased in the late Archaic period (ca. 4000 yr B.P.), which is also the approximate time of modern sea-level position. The fills, on the other hand, were comprised of sediments dredged from a few hundred meters offshore and often produced prehistoric artifacts from all time periods (Goodyear and Warren 1972:60).

At least 26 Suwannee points are known to have been recovered from inundated contexts either dredged from the periphery of Tampa Bay or recovered from relict oyster shell deposits (Goodyear et al. 1983). In all probability, these artifacts have been dredged from *in situ* inundated sites with little natural alterations from Holocene sea-level rise. Tampa Bay and the west coast of Florida in general is a zero- to low-energy marine environment with little sedimentation except in riverine settings (Sam Upchurch, personal communication 1991). The projectile points are sharp and unweathered, as are associated unifacial and bifacial tools and debitage. Suwannee points and later projectile point types were not found as isolated items but rather in dense concentrations with other lithic tools, forming meaningful assemblages. This indicates the dredge intercepted in situ sites and redeposited them on land nearby.

Tampa Bay and its upper reaches, Hillsborough Bay, is the Holocene-drowned portion of the Hillsborough River valley. The other major lobe of the bay is Old Tampa Bay, which is considered to have been formed by a large karst depression (Sam Upchurch, personal communication 1991). Given the known late Pleistocene–early Holocene reduction in surface water in Florida due to lowered sea level, it is likely that many prehistoric sites, particularly those of the Paleoindian period, are tightly associated with former river channels and tributaries. The waters of Tampa Bay, and indeed the entire Gulf of Mexico along the west coast of Florida, are relatively shallow, a situation that would facilitate underwater data recovery of what must be an extraordinarily rich early archaeological record in the former Hillsborough River valley. Serendipitously, the dredging activities of the 1960s in this region have given strong clues as to this underwater archaeological material.

Apalachee Bay Region, Florida

Based on the predictability of underwater sites in the Aucilla River on the land portion of the river, marine surveys are underway to project similar site locations in submerged river and karst-related features in Apalachee Bay (Dunbar 1988; Dunbar et al. 1989b; Faught 1988, 1990) The Apalachee Bay area is the northernmost reach of the Tertiary Karst Region, a Tertiary limestone shelf with little sediment accumulation, which runs continuously offshore southward to Tampa Bay (Dunbar et al. 1989b). Because of its karstic nature, this entire region is suspected to contain drowned Pleistocene and Holocene aboriginal sites on the Outer Continental Shelf in geologic situations similar to that observed onshore.

Michael Faught and his associates James Dunbar and Richard Anuskiewicz, in cooperation with both public agencies and private groups, have examined a number of potential underwater site targets in the Apalachee Bay region, including freshwater springs issuing from sinkholes in the Gulf, limestone and chert outcrops, and old river channels of the Aucilla and Econfina. To date, no definite Paleoindian or early Archaic artifacts have been encountered, but preceramic Archaic lithic sites and quarries appear to be common. These range in distance from 1 to 10 km offshore in a maximum water depth of 5.5 m (low tide) (Faught 1990:27). One particularly interesting geologic feature known as Ray Hole Spring was tested by Anuskiewicz of the Minerals Management Service and James Dunbar of the Florida Bureau of Archaeological Research. This spring is within a sinkhole located 38.6 km offshore and lying 11.6 m underwater (Anuskiewicz 1988:181). The sink measures 7.6 m in diameter and possesses a cave at the

18- to 30-m depth. At the time of the 1986 visit by Anuskiewicz and Dunbar, it was discovered that the sink had filled up with recent (since 1976) sand and shell, leaving only about 3 m of relief. The thick recent fill defied testing and coring; thus, the outer perimeter of the sink was test excavated. A crevice 0.15 m wide in the limestone was excavated with the hope that artifacts might be trapped in it. Excavation of the crevice from 0.15 to 0.2 m deep produced a number of chert flakes of probable human origin. At the 0.75-m level, a lens of oyster shell was encountered. At 1 m, waterlogged wood was found, below which the crevice ended on bedrock. A piece of wood recovered on the bedrock was identified as live oak and produced a ^{14}C date of 8220 ± 80 yr B.P. An oyster shell located above the wood dated 7390 ± 60 yr B.P. These organic remains imply a terrestrial environment subsequently inundated by brackish water (Anuskiewicz 1988:184).

The prospects for finding drowned, well-preserved Paleoindian and Archaic sites on the Tertiary karst shelf of the west coast of Florida are very good. Current research strategies by Dunbar, Faught, Webb, Anuskiewicz, and others include development of an absolute sea-level curve which can be used to stratify the shelf into probable late Pleistocene and early Holocene site locations by water depth. Based on a number of eustatic sea-level curves for the Gulf of Mexico, the earliest sites (12,000 to 8000 yr B.P.) would range from 56 to 177 km offshore and in water depths of 15 to 53 m (Faught 1990:30).

Conclusions

THE LATE PLEISTOCENE large-scale erosion described by Haynes (1968) for much of North America can be detected in the Southeast as well. The geological evidence for this erosion is most prevalent within the floodplains of the southern Appalachians (Brakenridge 1984; Larsen and Schuldenrein 1990; Segovia 1985). By examining palynological and sedimentological data from ponds and sinks in the interfluvial zones of the Southeast, Paul Delcourt (1985) has shown that little sediment movement was taking place outside the floodplains during the critical period of 20,000 to 8000 yr B.P. The erosion within the floodplains may have been the result of floods related to intense storm clusters rather than drought, according to the model of floodplain erosion developed by Knox (1984). The infrequent presence of fluted points at the contact of basal Holocene deposits and the eroded upper surfaces of Pleistocene terraces suggest that this period of erosion took place in the Southeast sometime prior to 11,000 yr B.P.

Critical to the preservation and dating of Clovis and other Paleoindian sites is the matter of site burial by sedimentary processes. The preceding review of buried Paleoindian sites has largely focused on alluvial contexts, since floodplains were the most geologically dynamic environments at the beginning of the Holocene. Particular sites were chosen that might illuminate the timing of burial related to the onset of Holocene aggradation. Some trends in the data are worth highlighting here.

In some watersheds, the onset of the Holocene aggradation was so energetic and rapid that it is likely Clovis and other Paleoindian sites were swept away. The Little Tennessee River, reported by Chapman (1985), qualifies here as a situation worsened by the proximity to intensive wasting of the Great Smoky Mountains, which provided huge quantities of sediment and a steep river gradient (cf. Schuldenrein and Anderson 1983). In some cases, the early Holocene deposits may be extraordinarily thick, rendering access even by backhoe difficult and dangerous. This was the case with the Duck River region, where the earliest Holocene sediments were very deeply buried and never completely reached (Klippel, personal communication 1991; cf. Broster et al. 1991).

On the Atlantic slope side of the southern Appalachians, there is some evidence, based on archaeology and limited ^{14}C dates, that the onset of Holocene aggradation took place after the Clovis period. At the Haw River site in North Carolina, a Hardaway Dalton assemblage was found in fine- to medium-grained sands, representing an initial pulse of Holocene alluvium. This zone overlay an archaeologically sterile, weathered, late Pleistocene terrace surface characterized by clayish silty sands. Based on the projectile points, this initial deposit of sand likely dates around 10,500 yr B.P. At Gregg Shoals on the Savannah River in Georgia, ^{14}C evidence indicates that the levee on which the site was occupied did not begin to build until sometime around 10,000 yr B.P. The radiocarbon dates were from lenses of peat lying on bedrock. These peat lenses indicate they formed in quiet water and subsequently were buried by flood-deposited sands. At nearby Rucker's Bottom, a Clovis point was excavated at the same level as a substantial early Archaic Kirk occupation, the deepest occupied zone of the site. In this case, it is likely that alluvial deposition did not effectively occur on the

Rucker's Bottom terrace until after 10,000 yr B.P. A similar situation was found at Simpson's Field, where a Clovis point and other early Archaic artifacts were found lying together in the same alluvium. The one exception to this trend where the earliest Paleoindian artifacts in Holocene alluvium are post-Clovis is 9Ge309, located on the Oconee River in Georgia. Here, two fluted points and a probable third were found in the lower portion of a shallow (1 m) sandy Holocene levee. However, the site was multi-component, not very deep, and evinced some mixing from bioturbation. The question here is, were the fluted points truly buried in the sands, or were they disturbed upward from the surface of what is suspected to be a weathered Pleistocene terrace surface?

Regarding the timing of the Holocene aggradation on the coastal plains of the Southeast, the picture differs from the Piedmont. There is some evidence that the Savannah River was flowing in a braided pattern at the beginning of the Holocene, as indicated by point-bar deposits at Pen Point and probably at Taylor Hill. Dalton period artifacts are clearly buried in each case, with probable pre-Dalton fluted bifaces at the latter site. In circumstances such as these, it does not appear that burial will be especially deep (ca. 1 m), creating problems of stratigraphic integrity where there is a strong pattern of reoccupation by later Archaic groups. However, in instances where a channel is cut off and buried by later overbank deposits, the chances are good that one might find a relatively pure expression of a Clovis-period occupation.

Smiths Lake Creek (38Al135) may represent such a situation, where changes in the hydrology of either Smiths Lake Creek or the Savannah River itself removed the chert source from use by subsequent aboriginal groups. In the case of the Big Pine Tree site, the initial human occupation may well be Clovis, situated as it is in the first surviving deposit of Holocene sands overlying an eroded and weathered Pleistocene terrace. A similar situation occurs downstream at the Charles site, although it is more difficult at this point to diagnose the earliest occupation there. It is not clear yet whether the two sites on Smith's Lake Creek were buried from sediments contributed primarily from the Savannah River, Smith's Lake Creek, or both. More work is needed to establish sediment sources. There may be differential sedimentation rates related to whether a stream originates on the coastal plain, usually possessing a small watershed, versus one that begins in the southern Appalachian Mountains, involving a much more extensive drainage basin.

At the Theriault site on Brier Creek, Georgia, a single Clovis-like fluted point was found at the base of probable fluvial sands just above what is described as a clay matrix. However, a Dalton point was found on the clay matrix. As previously pointed out, mixing of occupational zones has taken place at this locale, so the question of whether the fluted point was originally in the sand or resting on the clay surface is moot. Relatively shallow, sandy, heavily reoccupied sites do not tend to lend themselves to resolving such stratigraphically sensitive questions.

The Muckafoonee Creek site in Georgia and the Hester site in Mississippi share two common traits that bear on the timing of the Holocene aggradation. First, both are in alluvium from rivers that originate on the coastal plains. Second, both have Paleoindian artifacts, including possible Clovis components, which are obviously within sands as well as overlying sands. At Muckafoonee Creek, although the backhoe only penetrated to a depth of 1.5 m, the artifact-bearing level that produced a fluted point overlay at least three sterile horizons. These are a reddish-brown clayey sand, overlying a compact reddish brown clayey sand, which was underlain by a basal coarse, light, almost white sand. The first two probably are B-horizon paleosols. At the Hester site, Dalton, Quad, and probably Clovis points were buried in alluvial sands that lay atop a clean, alluvial sand unit that, in turn, overlay a sterile clay unit.

With only two sites to generalize from, strong conclusions cannot be drawn. However, the fact that at both sites coarse sediments underlay the fluted point zones indicates the potential for rapid deposition and burial of Paleoindian sites, including charcoal for ^{14}C dating. These data, like that from Smith's Lake Creek, suggest the possibility that Holocene aggradation on the coastal plains was contemporary with Clovis occupations and perhaps somewhat earlier. Where possible, archaeologists need to ^{14}C date the alluvium underlying early occupations. With the advent of AMS dating, even small particles of charcoal can be dated reliably from alluvial beds. As things stand now, fluted points and other diagnostic Paleoindian artifacts are being used to indirectly date geological horizons, and the artifacts, for the most part, have not been dated themselves by associated ^{14}C.

There is a clear stratigraphic pattern present at nearly all of the sites where Paleoindian and early Archaic bifaces have been recovered in alluvium that pertains to the recognition of the Pleistocene–Holocene boundary. At Haw River, probably Baucom, Rucker's

Bottom, Simpson's Field, Rae's Creek, Smith's Lake Creek, Theriault, and Muckafoonee, the Pleistocene–Holocene contact is indicated by basal Holocene sands overlying an alluvial terrace surface that has been modified by the formation of B-horizon paleosols. These B horizons are well developed (Bt) and more argillic than B horizons found in the Holocene alluvium. They invariably are sterile of artifacts in their primary position. The basal Holocene sands often are marked by lamellae if the grain size is not too coarse. The Bt horizons which have formed in the Holocene alluvium are not as argillic as those on the older Pleistocene terraces. Because of landscape instability accompanying the Holocene aggradation, which provided both erosion and the addition of new sediments, it is unlikely that pedogenesis could proceed to the point of mature argillic B horizons (cf. Foss and Segovia 1984; Foss et al. 1995).

Archaeologists and geologists should be aware of this contact and continue to excavate until conclusive evidence for archaeologically sterile Bt horizons, gravels, or bedrock is reached. In the case of the Bt horizon, it is on or just above this weathered surface that Clovis and other pre-Dalton materials should be located stratigraphically. A classic illustration of this is the "Clovis clay," a strongly pedogenically modified IIB2 horizon underlying the fluted point deposit at the Thunderbird site in Virginia (Foss 1974). The abrasive sand-bearing floods of the initial Holocene aggradation may, in many cases, have scoured away fluted point assemblages, such as seen in the sharp, undulating contact at Haw River and Rae's Creek. In any event, greater areas need to be excavated on these late Pleistocene terrace surfaces before it can be concluded that there are no buried fluted point sites present in the Southeast.

Further down the coastal plain and into Florida, climate and the karst topography were sufficiently different from higher latitudes that this region requires separate consideration. Because of relatively recent marine transgressions, sediments from dunes have been readily available for deposition. The Florida climate was arid at the end of the Pleistocene and, when coupled with reduced surface water from low rainfall and depressed ground water due to a lower sea level, conditions were prime for eolian deposition. Paleoindian sites may be buried at significant depths, judging from the Silver Springs and Harney Flats sites. Sites such as Page/Ladson in the riverine-drowned sinkholes are unique geologically and archaeologically, as are cenotes such as Warm Mineral Springs and Little Salt Spring. In addition to providing abundant, reliable organic materials for ^{14}C dating, excellent faunal preservation in the sinks should allow unassailable substantiation of human exploitation of extinct fauna in the Southeast.

Saltwater inundation of river valleys and the continental shelf itself no doubt has provided some form of burial and preservation of a substantial Paleoindian archaeological record. The artifactual evidence from Tampa Bay alone, the largest embayment on the west coast of Florida, is impressive, an occurrence that is likely repeated within the other bays along the Gulf coast. The existence of drowned river channels, sinks, and other karst features on the continental shelf, though logistically complicated by their distance offshore, also offer as yet unrealized potential for Paleoindian studies, including the possibility of preserved evidence for marine-resource exploitation.

While archaeologists always are wise to consult with scientists in other disciplines, given the geological conditions that prevailed in the southeastern United States at the time of the transition from the Pleistocene to the Holocene, research teams employing geologists and soil scientists are absolutely necessary. The work of William Gardner and his earth science colleagues at the Thunderbird site provided an early (and still admirable) model of such an approach. It is clear that the floodplains were the most geologically dynamic environments from about 11,000 yr B.P. onward, and thus the most amenable to deposition so needed for Paleoindian research. The fact that so many of these river valleys are now underwater reservoirs in the Southeast should cause the archaeological profession to regard the remaining undammed streams as a rare and endangered habitat. Floodplains need to be prioritized for both preservation and research before they are totally removed from scientific scrutiny.

Acknowledgments

A number of people aided me in the writing of this paper by supplying information and reading portions of the manuscript. Sam Brookes provided unpublished data on the Hester site. David Webb provided the photograph (Figure 7) of the ivory artifact from Florida. Rodney Peck allowed photography of many of his southeastern Paleoindian points, which are included here. Tommy Charles took most of the photographs illustrated in Figures 2 and 3. The following people read portions of the manuscript and gave valuable comments: David G. Anderson, Sam Brookes, Mark Brooks, Ray Crook, Randy Daniel, James Dunbar, John Foss, Vance Haynes, Sam Upchurch, David Webb, and Henry Wright. Dennis Blanton, John Broster, William Childress, Charles Hubbert, Michael Johnson, Joseph McAvoy, Mark Norton, and Joseph Schuldenrein provided additional information concerning their work. The staff of the South Carolina Institute of Archaeology and Anthropology are thanked for their support, especially Bruce Rippeteau, Director, Carole Shealy, and Nena Powell. I also would like to thank Rob Bonnichsen for inviting me to participate in the First World Summit Conference on the Peopling of the Americas (1989), where a preliminary version of the paper was read. His patience and that of the Center's staff while the final version was under construction are greatly appreciated.

References Cited

Anderson, D. G.
1990 The Paleoindian Colonization of Eastern North America: A View from the Southeastern United States. *Research in Economic Anthropology*, Supplement 5:163–216. JAI Press.

Anderson, D. G., and G. T. Hanson
1988 Early Archaic Settlement in the Southeastern United States: A Case Study from the Savannah River Valley. *American Antiquity* 53:262–286.

Anderson, D. G., and J. W. Joseph
1988 *Prehistory and History Along the Upper Savannah River: Technical Synthesis of Cultural Resource Investigations, Richard B. Russell Multiple Resource Area.* Interagency Archaeological Services Division, National Park Service, Russell Papers 1988. Atlanta.

Anderson D. G., R. J. Ledbetter, and L. O'Steen
1990 *Paleoindian Period Archaeology of Georgia.* University of Georgia Laboratory of Archaeology Series, Report No. 28. Athens.

Anderson, D. G., R. J. Ledbetter, L. O'Steen, D. T. Elliott, D. Blanton, G. T. Hanson, and F. Snow
1986 Paleoindian and Early Archaic in the Lower Southeast: A View from Georgia. Paper presented at the Ocmulgee National Monument 50th Anniversary Conference, Macon, GA.

Anderson, D. G., and J. Schuldenrein
1983 Early Archaic Settlement on the Southeastern Atlantic Slope: A View from the Rucker's Bottom Site, Elbert County, Georgia. *North American Archaeologist* 4:177–210.

1985 *Prehistoric Human Ecology Along the Upper Savannah River: Excavations at the Rucker's Bottom, Abbeville, and Bullard Site Groups.* Interagency Archaeological Services Division, National Park Service, Russell Papers 1985. Atlanta.

Anuskiewicz, R. J.
1988 Preliminary Archaeological Investigations at Ray Hole Spring in the Eastern Gulf of Mexico. *The Florida Anthropologist* 41:181–185.

Barker, G., and J. B. Broster
1996 The Johnson Site (40Dv400): A Dated Paleoindian and Early Archaic Occupation in Tennessee's Central Basin. *Journal of Alabama Archaeology* 42:97–153.

Blanton, D. B., W. Childress, J. Danz, L. Mitchell, J. Schuldenrein, and J. Zinn
1996 Archaeological Assessment of Sites 44PY7, 44PY43, and 44PY152 at Leesville Lake Pittsylvania County, Virginia. Virginia Department of Historic Resources, Research Report Series No. 7. Richmond.

Binford, L. R.
1979 Organization and Formation Processes: Looking at Curated Technologies. *Journal of Anthropological Research* 35:255–273.

Brakenridge, G. R.
1984 Alluvial Stratigraphy and Radiocarbon Dating Along the Duck River, Tennessee: Implications Regarding Floodplain Origin. *Geological Society of America Bulletin* 95(1):9–25.

Brennan, L.
1982 A Compilation of Fluted Points of Eastern North America by Count and Distribution: An AENA Project. *Archaeology of Eastern North America* 10:27–46.

Brockington, P. B.
1971 A Preliminary Investigation of an Early Knapping Site in Southeastern Georgia. *The Notebook* III:34–46. Institute of Archeology and Anthropology, University of South Carolina, Columbia.

Brookes, S. O.
1979 *The Hester Site: An Early Archaic Occupation in Monroe County, Mississippi.* Mississippi Department of Archives and History, Archaeological Report 5.

Brooks, H. K.
1972 Holocene Climatic Changes in Peninsular Florida. *Geological Society of America, 1973 Annual Meeting Abstracts* 5 (7):558–559.

Brooks, M. J., and K. E. Sassaman
1990 Point Bar Geoarchaeology in the Upper Coastal Plain of the Savannah River Valley, South Carolina; A Case Study. In *Archaeological Geology of North America*, edited by N. P. Lasca and J. Donahue, pp. 183–197. Geological Society of America, Centennial Special Volume 4. Boulder, Colorado.

Brooks, M. J., K. E. Sassaman, and G. T. Hanson
1989 Environmental Background and Models. In *Technical Synthesis of Prehistoric Archaeological Investigations on the Savannah River Site, Aiken and Barnwell Counties, South Carolina*, edited by K. E. Sassaman, M. J. Brooks, G. T. Hanson, and D. G. Anderson, pp. 19–66. Final report submitted to Savannah River Operations office, United States Department of Energy.

Brooks, M. J., P. A. Stone, D. J. Colquhoun, J. G. Brown, and K. B. Steele
1986 Geoarchaeological Research in the Coastal Plain Portion of the Savannah River Valley. *Geoarchaeology* 1:293–307.

Broster, J. B., D. P. Johnson, and M. R. Norton
1991 The Johnson Site: A Dated Clovis-Cumberland Occupation in Tennessee. *Current Research in the Pleistocene* 8:8–10.

Broster, J. B., and M. R. Norton
1993 The Carson-Conn-Short Site (40BN190): An Extensive Clovis Habitation in Benton County Tennessee. *Current Research in the Pleistocene* 10:3–5.

1996 Recent Paleoindian Research in Tennessee. In *The Paleoindian and Early Archaic Southeast*, edited by D. G. Anderson and K. E. Sassaman, pp. 288–297. The University of Alabama Press, Tuscaloosa.

Bullen, R. P.
1975 *A Guide to the Identification of Florida Projectile Points.* Kendall Books, Gainesville, Florida.

Bullen, R. P., S. D. Webb, and B. I. Waller
1970 A Worked Mammoth Bone from Florida. *American Antiquity* 35:203–205.

Broyles, B. J.
1966 Preliminary Report: The St. Albans Site (46Ka27), Kanawha County, West Virginia. *The West Virginia Archaeologist* 19.

Bryson, R. A., and W. M. Wendland
1967 Tentative Climatic Patterns for Some Late Glacial and Post-Glacial Episodes in Central North America. In *Life, Land and Water, Proceedings of the 1966 Conference of Environmental Studies of the Glacial Lake Agassiz Region*, edited by W. J. Mayer-Oaks, pp. 271–298. University of Manitoba Press, Winnipeg.

Cable, J. S.
1982 Description and Analysis of Lithic Assemblages. In *The Haw River Sites: Archaeological Investigations at Two Stratified Sites in the North Carolina Piedmont*, assembled by S. R. Claggett and J. S. Cable, pp. 291–598. Commonwealth Associates Inc. Report R-2386. Jackson, Michigan.

Cambron, J. W., and D. C. Hulse
1960 An Excavation on the Quad Site. *Tennessee Archaeologist* 16:14–26.

1964 *Handbook of Alabama Archaeology, Part 1: Point Types.* Archaeological Research Association of Alabama, Inc. Birmingham.

Carbone, V. A.
1983 Late Quaternary Environments in Florida and the Southeast. *The Florida Anthropologist* 36:3–17.

Carbone, V. A., A. Segovia, J. Foss, D. Whitehead, M. Sheehan, and S. Jackson
1982 The Paleoenvironmental Program of the Richard B. Russell Dam and Lake Project. Paper presented at the 39th Annual Meeting of the Southeastern Archaeology Conference, Memphis.

Carr, R. S.
1987 Early Man in South Florida. *Archaeology* 40 (6):62–63.

Chapman, J.
1976 The Archaic Period in the Lower Little Tennessee River Valley: The Radiocarbon Dates. *Tennessee Anthropologist I* (1):1–12.

1977 *Archaic Period Research in the Lower Little Tennessee River Valley—1975: Ice House Bottom, Harrison Branch, Thirty Acre Island, Calloway Island.* University of Tennessee, Department of Anthropology, Report of Investigations 18. Knoxville.

1978 *The Bacon Farm Site and a Buried Site Reconnaissance.* University of Tennessee, Department of Anthropology, Report of Investigations 23. Knoxville.

1985 Archaeology and the Archaic Period in the Southern Ridge-and-Valley Province. In *Structure and Process in Southeastern Archaeology*, edited by R. S. Dickens and H. T. Ward, pp. 137–153. University of Alabama Press, University.

Charles, T.
1986 The Fifth Phase of the Collectors Survey. *The Notebook* 18:1–27, South Carolina Institute of Archaeology and Anthropology, University of South Carolina, Columbia.

Childress, W. A.
1993 The Smith Mountain Site: A Buried Paleoindian Occupation in the Southwestern Piedmont of Virginia. *Current Research in the Pleistocene* 10:7--9.

1996 Description of Surface-Collected Artifacts from 44PY7 and 44PY152. In Archaeological Assessment of Sites 44PY7, 44PY43, and 44PY152 at Leesville Lake, Pittsylvania County, Virginia, by Blanton et al., pp. 51–86. Virginia Department of Historic Resources, Research Report Series No. 7. Richmond.

Childress, W. A., and D. B. Blanton
1996 A Radiocarbon Date on a Deeply Buried Stratum Yielding A Plano-like Projectile Point from the Smith Mountain Site in Virginia. *Current Research in the Pleistocene* 14:12-14.

Claggett, S. R., and J. S. Cable (assemblers)
1982 *The Haw River Sites: Archaeological Investigations at Two Stratified Sites in the North Carolina Piedmont.* Commonwealth Associates Inc. Report R-2386. Jackson, MI.

Clausen, C. J., H. K. Brooks, and A. B. Wesolowsky
1975 The Early Man Site at Warm Mineral Springs, Florida. *Journal of Field Archaeology* 2:191–213.

Clausen, C. J., A. D. Cohen, C. Emeliani, J. A. Holman, and J. J. Stipp
1979 Little Salt Spring, Florida: A Unique Underwater Site. *Science* 203:609–614.

Cockrell, W.A., and L. Murphy
1978 Pleistocene Man in Florida. *Archaeology of Eastern North America* 6:1–13.

Coe, J. L.
1964 The Formative Cultures of the Carolina Piedmont. *Transactions of the American Philosophical Society* 54(5). Philadelphia.

Collins, M. B., W. A. Gose, and S. Shaw
1994 Preliminary Geomorphological Findings at Dust and Nearby Caves. In *Preliminary Archaeological Papers on Dust Cave, Northwest Alabama*, edited by N. S. Goldman-Finn and B. N. Driskell, pp. 35–56. *Journal of Alabama Archaeology* 40 (1 & 2). The Alabama Archaeological Society.

Colquhoun, D. J., and M. J. Brooks
1986 New Evidence from the Southeastern U.S. for Eustatic Components in the late Holocene Sea Levels. *Geoarchaeology* 1:275–291.

Cotter, J. L.
1962 Comments. *Current Anthropology* 3:247–250.

Crook, M. R., Jr.
1990 Rae's Creek, A Multicomponent Archaeological Site at the Fall Line Along the Savannah River. Department of Anthropology, Georgia State University, Atlanta.

Daniel, I. R., and J. R. Butler
1991 Rhyolite Sources in the Carolina Slate Belt, Central North Carolina. *Current Research in the Pleistocene* 8:64–66.

Daniel, I. R., Jr., and M. Wisenbaker
1987 *Harney Flats: A Florida Paleoindian Site.* Baywood Publishing Company, Famingdale, New York.

Delcourt, H. R., and P. A. Delcourt
1985 Quaternary Palynology and Vegetational History of the Southeastern United States. In *Pollen Records of Late-Quaternary North American Sediments*, edited by V. M Bryant and R. G. Holloway, pp. 1–37. American Association of Stratigraphic Palynologists Foundation, Dallas.

Delcourt, P. A.
1980 Quaternary Alluvial Terraces of the Little Tennessee River Valley, East Tennessee. In *The 1979 Archaeological and Geological Investigations in the Tellico Reservoir*, edited by J. Chapman, pp. 110–121. The University of Tennessee, Department of Anthropology, Report of Investigations 29. Knoxville.

1985 The Influence of Late-Quaternary Climate and Vegetational Change on Paleohydrology in Unglaciated Eastern North America. *Ecologia Mediterranea Tome* XI (Fascicule 1):17–26.

Delcourt, P. A., and H. R. Delcourt
1979 Late Pleistocene and Holocene Distributional History of the Deciduous Forest in the Southeastern United States. *Veroffentlichungen des Geobotanischen Institutes der ETH, Stiftung Rubel (Zurich)* 68:79–107.

1981 Vegetation Maps for Eastern North America: 40,000 Yr. B.P. to the Present, in *Geobotany II*, edited by R. C. Romans, pp. 123-165. Plenum, New York.

1983 Late Quaternary Vegetational Dynamics and Community Stability Reconsidered. *Quaternary Research* 19:265–271.

1984 Late Quaternary Paleoclimates and Biotic Responses in Eastern North America and the Western North Atlantic Ocean. *Palaeogeography, Palaeoclimatology, Palaeoecology* 48:263–284.

Delcourt, H. R., P. A. Delcourt, and T. Webb III
1983 Dynamic Plant Ecology: The Spectrum of Vegetational Change in Space and Time. *Quaternary Science Reviews* 1:153–175.

DeJarnette, D. L., E. B. Kurjack, and J. W. Cambron
1962 Stanfield-Worley Bluff Shelter Excavations. *Journal of Alabama Archaeology* 8(1–2).

Dincauze, D. F.
1984 An Archaeo-Logical Evaluation of the Case for Pre-Clovis Occupations. *Advances in World Archaeology* 3:275–323. Academic Press.

Driskell, B. N.
1994 Stratigraphy and Chronology at Dust Cave. In *Preliminary Archaeological Papers on Dust Cave, Northwest Alabama*, edited by N.S. Goldman-Finn and B. N. Driskell, pp. 17–34. *Journal of Alabama Archaeology* 40 (1 & 2).

1996 Stratified Late Pleistocene and Early Holocene Deposits at Dust Cave, Northwest Alabama. In *The Paleoindian and Early Archaic Southeast,* edited by D. G. Anderson and K. E. Sassaman, pp. 315–330. The University of Alabama Press, Tuscaloosa.

Dunbar, J. S.
1988 Archaeological Sites in the Drowned Tertiary Karst Region of the Eastern Gulf of Mexico. *The Florida Anthropologist* 41:177–181.

1991 The Resource Orientation of Clovis and Suwannee Age Paleoindian Sites in Florida. In *Clovis:Origins and Adaptations*, edited by R. Bonnichsen and K. Turnmire, pp. 185–213. Center for the Study of the First Americans, Oregon State University, Corvallis.

Dunbar, J. S., M. K. Faught, and S. D. Webb
1988 Page/Ladson (8Je591): An Underwater Paleo-Indian Site in Northwestern Florida. *The Florida Anthropologist* 41:442–452.

Dunbar, J. S., and B. I. Waller
1983 A Distributional Analysis of Clovis/Suwannee Paleoindian Sites of Florida—A Geographic Approach. *The Florida Anthropologist* 36:18–30.

Dunbar, J. S., and S. D. Webb
1996 Bone and Ivory Tools from Submerged Paleoindian Sites in Florida. In The Paleoindian and Early Archaic Southeast, edited by D. G. Anderson and K. E. Sassaman, pp. 331–353. University of Alabama Press, Tuscaloosa.

Dunbar, J. S., S. D. Webb, and D. Cring
1989a Culturally and Naturally Modified Bones from a Paleoindian Site in the Aucilla River, North Florida. In *Bone Modification*, edited by R. Bonnichsen and M. Sorg, pp. 473–498. Center for the Study of the First Americans, University of Maine, Orono.

Dunbar, J. S., S. D. Webb, M. Faught, R. J. Anuskiewicz, and M. Stright
1989b Archaeological Sites in the Drowned Tertiary Karst Region of the Eastern Gulf of Mexico. In *Underwater Proceedings from the Society for Historic Archaeology Conference*, edited by J. Barto Arnold, III, pp. 25–31. Society for Historical Archaeology, Baltimore.

Edwards, R. L., and A. S. Merrill
1977 A Reconstruction of the Continental Shelf Areas of Eastern North America for the Times 9,500 B.P. and 12,500 B.P. *Archaeology of Eastern North America* 5:1–43.

Elliott, D.
1982 *Flint River Archaeological Survey and Testing, Albany, Georgia.* Soil Systems, Inc., Atlanta.

Elliott, D., and R. Doyon
1981 *Archaeology and Historical Geography of the Savannah River Floodplain Near Augusta, Georgia.* University of Georgia Laboratory of Archaeology Series, Report No. 22. Athens.

Ellis, C. J. , A. C. Goodyear, D. F. Morse, and K. B. Tankersley
1998 Archaeology of the Pleistocene-Holocene Transition in Eastern North America. *Quaternary International,* Journal of the International Quaternary Association, volumes 49/50, pp. 151-166. Elsevier Science Ltd.

Ellis, C. J., and J. C. Lothrop (editors)
1989 *Eastern Paleoindian Lithic Resource Use.* Westview Press, Boulder.

Ensor, H. B.
1986 San Patrice and Dalton Affinities on the Central and Western Gulf Coastal Plain. *Bulletin of the Texas Archaeological Society* 57:69–81.

Faught, M.
1988 Inundated Sites in the Apalachee Bay Area of the Eastern Gulf of Mexico. *The Florida Anthropologist* 41:185–190.

1990 *Report of the 1989 Offshore Field Session.* Report Submitted to The Bureau of Archaeological Research, Florida Department of State, Tallahassee.

Fiedel, S. J.
1997 Older Than We Thought: Implications of Corrected Dates for Paleoindians. Paper presented at the 62nd Annual Meeting of the Society for American Archaeology, Nashville.

Foss, J. E.
1974 Soils of the Thunderbird Site and Their Relationship to Cultural Occupation and Chronology. In *The Flint Run Paleo-Indian Complex: A Preliminary Report 1971–73 Seasons*, edited by W. M. Gardner, pp. 66–83. Occasional Paper No. 1, Archaeology Laboratory, Department of Anthropology, Catholic University of America, Washington, D.C.

1986 Notes on Pedological Investigations of 38AL23 and 38AL135. Ms. on file at the South Carolina Institute of Archaeology and Anthropology, University of South Carolina, Columbia.

Foss, J. E., and A. V. Segovia
1984 Rates of Soil Formation. In *Groundwater as a Geomorphic Agent*, edited by R. G. LaFleur, pp. 1–17. Allen and Unwin, Boston.

Foss, J. E., M. E. Timpson, and R. J. Lewis
1995 Soils in Alluvial Sequences: Some Archaeological Implications. In *Pedological Perspectives in Archaeological Research.*, Soil Science Society of America Special Publication Number 44, edited by M. E. Collins, B. J. Carter, B. G. Gladfelter, and R. J. Southard, pp. 1–14. Madison.

Foss, J. E., D. P. Wagner, and F. P. Miller
1985 *Soils of the Savannah River Valley.* Interagency Archaeological Services Division, National Park Service, Russell Papers 1985. Atlanta.

Futato, E.
1980 An Overview of Wheeler Basin Prehistory.*Journal of Alabama Archaeology* 26:110–135.

1982 Some Notes on the Distribution of Fluted Points in Alabama. *Archaeology of Eastern North America* 10:30–33.

Gardner, W. M. (editor)
1974a *The Flint Run Paleoindian Complex: A Preliminary Report 1971–73 Seasons.* Occasional Paper No. 1, Archaeology Laboratory, Catholic University of America, Washington, D.C.

1974b The Flint Run Complex: Pattern and Process During the Paleoindian to Early Archaic. In *The Flint Run Paleoindian Complex: A Preliminary Report 1971–73 Seasons*, edited by W. M. Gardner, pp. 5–47. Occasional Paper No. 1, Archaeology Laboratory, Catholic University of America, Washington, D.C.

1983 Stop Me if You've Heard This One Before: The Flint Run Paleoindian Complex Revisited. *Archaeology of Eastern North America* 11:49–59.

Goldberg, P., and S. C. Sherwood
1994 Micromorphology of Dust Cave Sediments: Some Preliminary Results. In *Preliminary Archaeological Papers on Dust Cave, Northwest Alabama*, edited by N. S. Goldman-Finn and B. N. Driskell, pp. 57–65. *Journal of Alabama Archaeology* 40 (1 & 2).

Goldman-Finn, N.S., and B. N. Driskell (editors)
1994 *Preliminary Archaeological Papers on Dust Cave, Northwest Alabama. Journal of Alabama Archaeology* 40 (1 & 2):1–255.

Goodyear, A. C.
1974 *The Brand Site: A Techno-Functional Study of a Dalton Site in Northeast Arkansas.* Arkansas Archaeological Survey, Research Series 7. Fayetteville.

1982 The Chronological Position of the Dalton Horizon in the Southeastern United States. *American Antiquity* 47:382–395.

1989 A Hypothesis for the Use of Cryptocrystalline Raw Materials Among Paleoindian Groups of North America. In *Eastern Paleoindian Lithic Resource Use*, pp. 1–9, edited by C. J. Ellis and J. C. Lothrop. Westview Press, Boulder.

1992 Archaeological and Pedological Investigations at Smith's Lake Creek (38AL135), Allendale County, South Carolina. *Current Research in the Pleistocene* 9:18–20.

1995 Archaeological Investigations at a Paleoindian and Archaic Site in Allendale County, S.C. Features and Profiles, July–August, pp. 1–6. Archaeological Society of South Carolina.

Goodyear, A. C., and T. Charles
1984 *An Archaeological Survey of Chert Quarries in Western Allendale County, South Carolina.* Research Manuscript Series 195. Institute of Archaeology and Anthropology, University of South Carolina, Columbia.

Goodyear, A. C., and C. V. Haynes
1987 Geoarchaeology of the Baucom Paleoindian Site, Union County, North Carolina. Proposal submitted to the National Geographic Society.

Goodyear, A. C., and J. E. Foss
1993 The Stratigraphic Significance of Paleosols at Smith's Lake Creek, 38AL135, for the Study of the Pleistocene–Holocene Transition in the Savannah River Valley. In *The Proceedings of the First International Conference on Pedo-Archaeology*, edited by J. E. Foss, M. E. Timpson, and M. W. Morris, pp. 27–40. The University of Tennessee, Knoxville.

1995 The Big Pine Tree Site: Early Holocene Quarry Production in the Savannah River Coastal Plain. Paper presented at the 52nd Annual Southeastern Archaeological Conference, Knoxville, Tennessee.

Goodyear, A. C., J. L. Michie, and T. Charles
1989 The Earliest South Carolinians. In *Studies in South Carolina Archaeology, Essays in Honor of Robert L. Stephenson*, edited by A. C. Goodyear and G. T. Hanson, pp. 19–52. Anthropological Studies 9, Occasional Papers of the South Carolina Institute of Archaeology and Anthropology, University of South Carolina, Columbia.

Goodyear, A. C., S. B. Upchurch, M. J. Brooks, and N. N. Goodyear
1983 Paleoindian Manifestations in the Tampa Bay Region, Florida. *The Florida Anthropologist* 36:40–66.

Goodyear, A. C., S. B. Upchurch, T. Charles, and A. B. Albright
1985 Chert Sources and Paleoindian Lithic Processing in Allendale County, South Carolina. *Current Research in the Pleistocene* 2:47–49.

Goodyear, A. C., and L. O. Warren
1972 Further Observations on the submarine Oyster Shell Deposits of Tampa Bay. *The Florida Anthropologist* 25:52–66.

Graham, R. W., C. V. Haynes, D. L. Johnson, and M. Kay
1981 Kimmswick: A Clovis–Mastodon Association in Eastern Missouri. *Science* 213:1115–1117.

Griffin, J. B.
1967 Eastern North American Archaeology: A Summary. *Science* 156:175–191.

Grover, J.
1994 Faunal Remains from Dust Cave. In *Preliminary Archaeological Papers on Dust Cave, Northwest Alabama*, edited by N. S. Goldman-Finn and B. N. Driskell, pp. 116–134. *Journal of Alabama Archaeology* 40 (1 & 2).

Harland, W. B., A. V. Cox, P. G. Llewellyn, C. A. G. Pickton, A. G. Smith, and R. Walters
1982 *A Geologic Time Scale*. Cambridge University Press, Cambridge.

Haynes, C. V.
1968 Geochronology of Late Quaternary Alluvium. In *Means of Correlation of Quaternary Successions*, edited by R. B. Morrison and H. E. Wright, Jr., pp. 591–631. Proceedings VIII INQUA Congress, University of Utah Press, Salt Lake.

1982 Were Clovis Progenitors in Beringia? In *Paleoecology of Beringia*, edited by D. M. Hopkins, J. V. Mathews, Jr., C. E. Schweger, and S. B. Young, pp. 383–398. Academic Press, New York.

1984 Stratigraphy and Late Pleistocene Extinction in the United States. In *Quaternary Extinctions: A Prehistoric Revolution*, edited by P. S. Martin and R. G. Klein, pp. 345–353. University of Arizona Press, Tucson.

1987 Clovis Origin Update. *The Kiva* 52:83–93.

Haynes, C. V., D. J. Donahue, A. J. T. Jull, and T. H. Zabel
1984 Application of Accelerator C-14 Dating to Fluted-Point Sites. *Archaeology of Eastern North America* 12:184–191.

Hemmings, E. T.
1975 The Silver Springs Site, Prehistory in the Silver Springs Valley, Florida. *The Florida Anthropologist* 28:141–158.

Hoffman, C. A.
1983 A Mammoth Kill Site in the Silver Springs Run. *The Florida Anthropologist* 36:83–87.

Hubbert, C. M.
1989 Paleoindian Settlement in the Middle Tennessee Valley: Ruminations from the Quad Paleoindian Locale. *Tennessee Anthropologist* 14:148–164.

Hulse, D. C., and J. L. Wright
1989 Pine Tree-Quad-Old Slough Complex. *Tennessee Anthropologist* 14:102–147.

Jenks, A. E. and Mrs. H. H. Simpson, Sr.
1941 Beveled Artifacts in Florida of the Same Type as Artifacts Found Near Clovis, New Mexico. *American Antiquity* 6:314–319.

Jeter, M. D., and G. I. Williams, Jr.
1989 Lithic Horizons and Early Cultures. In *Archaeology and Bioarchaeology of the Lower Mississippi Valley and Trans-Mississippi South in Arkansas and Louisiana*, pp.71–110, edited by M. D. Jeter, J. C. Rose, G. I. Williams, Jr., and A. M Harmon. Arkansas Archeological Survey, Research Series 37.

Johnson, E., and P. Shipman
1986 Scanning Electron Microscope Studies of Bone Modification. *Current Research in the Pleistocene* 3:47–48.

Kelly, A. R.
1938 A Preliminary Report on Archaeological Explorations at Macon, Georgia. *Bureau of American Ethnology Bulletin* 119:1–69.

Knox, J. C.
1976 Concept of the Graded Stream. In *Theories of Landform Development*, edited by W. N. Mehorn and R. C. Flemal, pp.169–198. Publications in Geomorphology, State University of New York, Binghamton.

1984 Responses of River Systems to Holocene Climates. In *The Holocene*, edited by H. E. Wright, Jr., pp. 26–41. *Late Quaternary Environments of the United States, vol. 2,* H. E. Wright, Jr., general editor. University of Minnesota Press, Minneapolis.

Larsen, C. E., and J. Schuldenrein
1990 Depositional History of An Archaeologically Dated Flood Plain, Haw River, North Carolina. In *Archaeological Geology of North America*, edited by N. P. Lasca and J. Donahue, pp. 161–181. Geological Society of America, Centennial Special Volume 4, Boulder.

Ledbetter, R. J.
1978 Wallace Project Backhoe Testing Program. Report on File, Department of Anthropology, University of Georgia, Athens.

Levine, M. A.
1990 Accommodating Age: Radiocarbon Results and Fluted Point Sites in Northeastern North America. *Archaeology of Eastern North America* 18:33–63.

Lively, M.
1965 The Lively Complex: Announcing a Pebble Tool Industry in Alabama. *Journal of Alabama Archaeology* 11:103–122.

MacDonald, G. F.
1968 *Debert: A Paleoindian Site in Central Nova Scotia.* Anthropology Papers 16. National Museum of Canada, Ottawa.

Mason, R. J.
1962 The Paleoindian Tradition in Eastern North America. *Current Anthropology* 3:227–246.

Mathews, J. M.
1990 Surficial Geology of the Rae's Creek Archaeological Site on the Savannah River, Augusta, GA. In *Rae's Creek, A Multicomponent Archaeological Site at the Fall Line Along the Savannah River*, by Morgan

Crook, pp. 176–186. Department of Anthropology, Georgia State University, Athens, Georgia.

McAvoy, J. M.
1997 Addendum: Excavation of the Cactus Hill Site, 44SX202, Areas A-B, Spring 1996: Summary Report of Activities and Findings. In *Archaeological Investigations of Site 44SX2202, Cactus Hill, Sussex County, Virginia*. Virginia Department of Historic Resources, Research Report Series No. 8. Richmond.

McAvoy, J. M., and L. D. McAvoy
1997 *Archaeological Investigations of Site 44SX202, Cactus Hill, Sussex County, Virginia*. Viriginia Department of Historic Resources, Research Report Series No. 8. Richmond.

McCary, B. C.
1975 The Williamson Paleoindian Site, Dinwiddie County, Virginia. *The Chesopiean* 13:47–131.

1984 *Survey of Virginia Fluted Points*. Archaeological Society of Virginia, Special Publication 12.

McGahey, S. O.
1987 Paleoindian Lithic Material: Implications of Distributions in Mississippi. *Mississippi Archaeology* 22:1–13.

McMillan, R. B.
1971 *Biophysical Change and Cultural Adaptation at Rodgers Shelter, Missouri*. Unpublished Ph.D. dissertation, Department of Anthropology, University of Colorado, Boulder.

Meltzer, D. J.
1984 Late Pleistocene Human Adaptations in Eastern North America. Ph.D. dissertation, University of Washington, Seattle.

1988 Late Pleistocene Human Adaptations in Eastern North America. *Journal of World Prehistory* 2:1–52

Meltzer, D. J., D. K. Grayson, G. Ardila, A. W. Barker, D. F. Dincauze, C. V. Haynes, F. Mena, L. Nunez, and D. J. Stanford
1997 On the Pleistocene Antiquity of Monte Verde, Southern Chile. *American Antiquity* 62: 659–663.

Meltzer, D. J., and J. I. Mead
1985 Dating Late Pleistocene Extinctions: Theoretical Issues, Analytical Bias, and Substantive Results. In *Environments and Extinctions: Man in Glacial North America*, edited by J. I. Mead and D. J. Meltzer, pp. 145–173. Center for the Study of Early Man, University of Maine, Orono.

Michie, J. L.
1977 Early Man in South Carolina. Senior thesis, Department of Anthropology, University of South Carolina, Columbia.

Milanich, J. T., and C. H. Fairbanks
1980 *Florida Archaeology*. Academic Press, New York.

Morrow, Juliet E.
1995 Clovis Projectile Point Manufacture: A Perspective from the Ready/Lincoln Hills Site, 11JY46, Jersey County, Illinois. *Midcontinental Journal of Archaeology* 20:167–191.

Morse, D. F.
1973 Dalton Culture in Northeast Arkansas. *The Florida Anthropologist* 26:23–38.

1997a An Overview of the Dalton Period in Northeastern Arkansas and in the Southeastern United States. In *Sloan, A Paleoindian Dalton Cemetery in Arkansas*, by Dan F. Morse, pp. 123–139. Smithsonian Institution.

1997b *Sloan, A Paleoindian Dalton Cemetery in Arkansas*. Smithsonian Institution.

Morse, D. F., and P. A. Morse
1983 *Archaeology of the Central Mississippi Valley*. Academic Press, New York.

Neill, W. T.
1958 A Stratified Early Site at Silver Springs, Florida. *The Florida Anthropologist* 11:33–52.

1964 The Association of Suwannee Points and Extinct Animals in Florida. *The Florida Anthropologist* 17:17–32.

O'Steen, L. D.
1983 *Early Archaic Settlement Patterns in the Wallace Reservoir: An Inner Piedmont Perspective*. Wallace Reservoir Project Contribution No. 25, Department of Anthropology, University of Georgia, Athens.

O'Steen, L. D., R. J. Ledbetter, D. T. Elliott, and W. W. Barker
1986 Paleo-Indian Sites of the Inner Piedmont of Georgia: Observations of Settlement in the Oconee Watershed. *Early Georgia* 14:1–63. Society for Georgia Archaeology.

Painter, F.
1974 The Cattail Creek Fluting Tradition and Its Complex—Determining Lithic Debris. *The American Archaeologist* 1 (1):20–32.

Peck, R. M. (editor)
1985 *The Williamson Site, Dinwiddie County, Virginia*. Privately Printed, Harrisburg, NC.

Peck, R. M.
1988 Clovis Points of Early Man in North Carolina. *The Piedmont Journal of Archaeology* 6:1–22.

Peck, R. M., and F. Painter
1984 The Baucom Hardaway Site: A Stratified Deposit in Union County, North Carolina. *The Chesopiean* 22:1–41.

Perkinson, P. H.
1971 North Carolina Fluted Projectile Points—Survey Report Number One. *Southern Indian Studies* 23:3–40.

1973 North Carolina Fluted Projectile Points—Survey Report Number Two. *Southern Indian Studies* 25:3–60.

Purdy, B. A.
1981 *Florida's Prehistoric Stone Technology.* A University of Florida Book, University Presses of Florida, Gainesville.

1983a Early Man Research in Southeastern North America: New Developments. *Early Man News* 7/8:19–29. Newsletter for Human Palecology, Commission for the Palecology of Early Man of INQUA. Tubingen.

1983b Comments on "A Compilation of Fluted Points of Eastern North America by Count and Distribution: An AENA Project." *Archaeology of Eastern North America* 11:29.

Rayle, S. L.
1974 *A Paleoindian Mammoth Kill Site Near Silver Springs, Florida.* Master's thesis on file, Department of Anthropology, Northern Arizona University, Flagstaff.

Sassaman, K. E.
1985 A Preliminary Typological Assessment of MALA Hafted Bifaces from the Pen Point Site, Barnwell County, South Carolina. *South Carolina Antiquities* 17:1–20.

Schuldenrein, J.
1996 Geoarchaeological Observations at 44PY152. In *Archaeological Assessment of Sites 44PY7, 44PY43, and 44PY152 at Leesville Lake, Pittsylvania County, Virginia* by Blanton et al. pp. 99–108. Virginia Department of Historic Resources, Research Report No. 7. Richmond.

Schuldenrein, J., and D. G. Anderson
1983 Human Ecology and Prehistory Along the Savannah River: A Geoarchaeological Perspective. Paper presented at the 48th Annual Meeting of the Society for American Archaeology, Pittsburgh.

Segovia, A. V.
1985 *Archaeological Geology of the Savannah River Valley and Main Tributaries in the Richard B. Russell Multiple Resource Area.* Interagency Archeological Services Division, National Park Service, Russell Papers 1985. Atlanta.

Story, D. A.
1990 Culture History of the Native Americans. In *The Archaeology and Bioarcheology of the Gulf Coastal Plain: Volume 1,* edited by D. A. Story, J. A. Guy, B. A. Burnett, M. D. Freeman, J. C. Rose, D. G. Steele, B. W. Olive, and K. J. Reinhard, pp. 163–366, Arkansas Archaeological Survey, Research Series 38.

Taylor, R. L., and M. F. Smith (editors)
1978 *The Report of the Intensive Survey of the Richard B. Russell Dam and Lake, Savannah River, Georgia and South Carolina.* Research Manuscript Series 142. Institute of Archaeology and Anthropology, University of South Carolina, Columbia.

Tippitt, V. A., and W. H. Marquardt
1984 *Archaeological Investigations at Gregg Shoals, A Deeply Stratified Site on the Savannah River.* Interagency Archaeological Services Division, National Park Service, Russell Papers, 1984. Atlanta.

Turner, W. B., and W. E. Klippel
1989 Hunter-Gatherers in the Nashville Basin: Archaeological and Geological Evidence for Variability in Prehistoric Land Use. *Geoarchaeology: An International Journal* 4:43–67. John Wiley and Sons, New York.

Upchurch, S. B.
1984a Geoarcheology of the Gregg Shoals–Clyde Gulley Group. In *Archeological Investigations at Gregg Shoals, A Deeply Stratified Site on the Savannah River*, by V. Ann Tippitt and W. H. Marquardt, Appendix A. Interagency Archeological Services Division, National Park Service, Russell Papers, 1984. Atlanta.

1984b Geology and Lithic Materials: Harney Flats Archaeological Site (8HI507), Hillsborough County, Florida. In *Salvage Excavations at Harney Flats: A Paleo-Indian Base Camp in Hillsborough County, Florida*, by R. Daniel and M. Wisenbaker, Appendix D. Report submitted to the Division of Archives, History and Records Management, Florida Department of State, Tallahassee.

Upchurch, S.B., R.N. Strom, and M.G. Nuckels
1981 *Methods of Provenance Determination of Florida Cherts.* Unpublished contract report submitted to the Florida Bureau of Historic Sites and Properties, Tallahassee.

Waller, B. I., and J. Dunbar
1977 Distribution of Paleo-Indian Projectiles in Florida. *The Florida Anthropologist* 30:79–80.

Walthall, J. A.
1980 *Prehistoric Indians of the Southeast, Archaeology of Alabama and the Middle South.* The University of Alabama Press, University.

Waring, A.J., Jr.
1961 Fluted Points on the South Carolina Coast. *American Antiquity* 26:550–552.

1968 Paleoindian Remains in South Carolina and Georgia. In T*he Waring Papers: The Collected Works of Antonio J. Waring, Jr.*, edited by S. Williams, pp. 236–240. Papers of the Peabody Museum of Archaeology and Ethnology, No. 58, Harvard University, Cambridge.

Warren, L. O.
1964 Possibly Submerged Oyster Shell Middens of Upper Tampa Bay. *The Florida Anthropologist* 17:227–230.

1970 The Kellogg Fill from Boca Ciega Bay, Pinellas County, Florida. *The Florida Anthropologist* 23:163–167.

Watts, W. A.
1980 Late-Quaternary Vegetation History at White Pond on the Inner Coastal Plain of South Carolina. *Quaternary Research* 13:187–199.

Watts, W. A., and B. C. S. Hansen
1988 Environments of Florida in the Late Wisconsin and Holocene. In *Wet Site Archaeology*, edited by B. A. Purdy, pp. 307–323. Telford Press, Caldwell, NJ.

Webb, C. H., J. L. Shiner, and E. W. Roberts
1971 The John Pearce Site (16CD56): A San Patrice Site in Caddo Parrish, Louisiana. *Bulletin of the Texas Archaeological Society* 42:1–49.

Webb, S. D.
1974 Chronology of Florida Pleistocene Mammals. In *Pleistocene Mammals of Florida*, edited by S. D. Webb, pp. 5–31. University Presses of Florida, Gainesville.

1981 *A Cultural Resources Survey of the Continental Shelf from Cape Hatteras to Key West. Volume I: Introduction and Physical Environment,* pp. I-73–I-112. Report submitted by Science Applications, Inc., to the Bureau of Land Management.

Webb, S. D., J. T. Milanich, R. Alexon, and J. S. Dunbar
1984 A *Bison Antiquus* Kill Site, Wacissa River, Jefferson County, Florida. *American Antiquity* 49:384–392.

Whitehead, D. R.
1965 Palynology and Pleistocene Phytogeography of Unglaciated Eastern North America. In *The Quaternary of the United States*, edited by H. E. Wright, Jr., and D. Frey, pp. 417–432. Princeton University Press, Princeton.

Williams, S., and J. B. Stoltman
1965 An Outline of Southeastern United States Prehistory with Particular Emphasis on the Paleo-Indian Era. In *The Quaternary of the United States*, edited by H. E. Wright, Jr. and D. Frey, pp. 669–683. Princeton University Press, Princeton.

Wood, W. Dean, D. T. Elliott, T. P. Rudolph, and D. B. Blanton
1986 *Prehistory in the Richard B. Russell Reservoir: The Archaic and Woodland Periods of the Upper Savannah River.* Interagency Archaeological Services Division, National Park Service, Russell Papers 1986. Atlanta.

Wyckoff, D. G.
1985 The Packard Complex: Early Archaic, Pre-Dalton Occupations on the Prairie–Woodlands Border. *Southeastern Archaeology* 4:1–26.

1989 Accelerator Dates and Chronology at the Packard Site, Oklahoma. *Current Research in the Pleistocene* 6:24–26.

The Inhabitants of Mexico During the Upper Pleistocene

Jose Luis Lorenzo[1]
Lorena Mirambell[2]

Abstract

Investigations of early human occupation in Mexico have been relatively limited. From 1952 until 1989, the Department of Prehistory studied nomadic and seminomadic hunter-gatherer groups. From 1952 to 1960, investigations focused on excavation of proboscidean skeletons, mostly in the Basin of Mexico. In 1961 systematic excavations and analysis using innovative methods and techniques began, interdisciplinary laboratories were organized, and research focused on four physiographic regions: endorreic basins, dry caves, coastal regions, and alpine areas.

The time of initial human occupation in Mexico has been named the Lithic stage and the cultural horizons defined have been termed Archaeolithic (40/35,000-14,000 yr B.P.), Cenolithic, Lower (14,000-9000 yr B.P.) and Upper (9000-7000 yr B.P.) and Protoneolithic (7000-4500 yr B.P.). Two research projects were developed: Tlapacoya in the Basin of Mexico and Rancho La Amapola, Cedral, San Luis Potosí, with occupation dates for the first between 24,000 and 22,000 yr B.P. and for the latter between 35/33,000 and 21,000 yr B.P.

Fluted projectile points—Clovis, Folsom, and "fish tails"—are also present in Mexico.

INVESTIGATIONS OF EARLY human occupation in Mexico, as in other countries with extensive prehistoric monumental architecture, have been relatively limited. Because archaeological interest has focused on architectural remains, the study of the first inhabitants, intimately related to the problem of the peopling of the Americas, has been relegated to the background.

Notwithstanding, for decades in Mexico, there has been an interest in the culture of the first Americans. In 1952, as a result of the controversial discovery of human remains in Tepexpan, the Department of Prehistory was founded for the purpose of studying nomadic or semi-nomadic hunter-gatherer groups of the past. These groups later were classified within a cultural tradition known as the Lithic stage.

In its first phase of work, between 1952 and 1960, the Department of Prehistory oriented its activities toward the excavation of proboscidean skeletons, mostly in the Basin of Mexico. With these remains, evidence of associated human activity appeared sporadically. During those years, prehistoric research, in a broad sense, was limited, as specific research projects were not conducted and attention was given to fortuitous finds. In fairness, it must be confessed that research-oriented investigations incorporating interdisciplinary studies were neglected as well.

It was not until 1961 that investigations based upon systematic excavation and analysis using innovative methods and techniques were utilized. For the implementation of this research, interdisciplinary laboratories were organized in the fields of paleobotany, paleozoology, Quaternary geology, petrography, chemistry, pedology, and sedimentology, followed years later by a chronometric dating laboratory (radiocarbon, thermoluminescence, and obsidian hydration). This battery of multidisciplinary sciences assisted efforts in an archaeological investigation of four physiographic regions: endorreic basins, dry caves, coastal regions, and alpine areas.

Endorreic basins

During the Pleistocene, these landforms remained closed or became closed, as was the case in the Basin of Mexico. These areas contained lakes, providing an environment favoring human settlement, due to the

1. Deceased.
2. Instituto Nacional de Anthropogíca e Historia, Mexico

availability of water, with opportunities for hunting, gathering, and fishing. These basins also yield abundant environmental information regarding lacustrine oscillations and accompanying climatic and paleoecological change.

Dry caves

Historically, caves were chosen by hunter-gatherer groups for temporary settlements. Because of their dry conditions, some caves contain preserved organic remains yielding both paleoecological records and evidence of human activity. These sites provide a rich source of information for the archaeologist that is difficult to obtain in other settings.

Coastal regions

Fluctuations in global marine levels provide a means for dating Quaternary deposits when other lines of evidence are lacking. These areas also yield information on human coastal adaptations and seasonal aspects of hunter-gatherer economies, as well as a fossil record of environmental change.

Alpine regions

These areas contain evidence of past climatic fluctuations indicative of glacial activity or periglacial environmental conditions.

With these four lines of study, the differing geographical, geomorphological, and ecological aspects of Mexico were opened to archaeological research in an investigation of early human activity.

Chronologic Stages of Human Occupation in Mexico

THE TIME PERIOD of the initial human occupation of Mexico is termed the Lithic stage. This stage begins sometime between 40,000 to 35,000 yr B.P., and extends to approximately 4500 yr B.P.; in certain regions, primarily in the northern zone, this period extends as late as the end of the 18th century A.D. The established cultural chronology is based upon the existence of lithic artifacts, although undoubtedly, artifacts manufactured from organic materials also were present. These lithic artifacts form the foundation of a technical criterion, as social and economic aspects are hardly perceptible at this time. Lorenzo (1967a), the author of this chronology, comments on the nature of prehistoric occupation during the Lithic stage, explaining that humans:

> *remained open to such processes as marginalization or fixation on a given cultural tradition, which, once determined, integrated its settlement in a given territory or situation and prevailed with very slight variations, since it was sufficient to permit subsistence without great difficulties. With this remains implicit the principle of multilinear evolution demonstrated by the coexistence of different modes of production in immediate proximity, which was what the first Europeans encountered [Editor's translation].*

The cultural horizons defined within the Lithic stage are termed the Archaeolithic, Cenolithic, and Protoneolithic. The Archaeolithic, as its name connotes, is the oldest period, followed by the Cenolithic. The Protoneolithic defines the most recent horizon within the Lithic stage.

The representative artifacts of the Archaeolithic (40,000–35,000 to 14,000 yr B.P.) are very crude and do not display great specialization. Artifact types include choppers and chopping tools, scrapers, denticulates, shaped flakes and blades, and utilized flakes. The artifacts are large, rarely less than 5 cm in length, depending on the size and quality of the raw material used; some are made by alternate percussion, demonstrating incipient bifacialism. The manufacturing technique involves the application of direct percussion, with a large angle of fracture, indicative of a Clactonian technique. This method of manufacture is the only technique used and commonly is associated with an absence of lithic projectile points.

The Cenolithic is more complex and better understood than the earlier horizon. It has been divided into lower and upper time periods. In the lower Cenolithic (14,000 to 9000 yr B.P.), lithic projectile points appear. Leaf-shaped and fluted forms are the most common, with flutes more or less marked on both the dorsal and ventral faces. Fluting facilitated fixing or attaching the point to the shaft and appears to be a typically American technique well characterized by Clovis and Folsom forms, and less so by "fishtail" points. Stemmed points also appear and are considered a possible product of edge abrasion on the lower third of the fluted pieces, precisely where the shaft would have been attached. This method results in projectile points without ears or tangs. Prismatic blades were manufactured in abundance and, logically, polyhedral cores appear.

The knapping technique during this time continues to be direct percussion, although the percussor is no longer always of stone and usage of bone, horn, and wood billets occurs. Thinner flakes and formal blades with sharper edges are obtained through direct percussion. Indirect percussion and incipient pressure flaking also are observed, although not abundant in the archaeological record. These innovations give rise to more functional lithic implements.

In the upper Cenolithic (9000 to 7000 yr B.P.), a great variety of lithic artifacts are present. Careful finishing of the pieces by both percussion and pressure flaking is noted. Lithic projectile points with stems and ears are abundant, although leaf-shaped points persist. In this phase, as in the earlier, choppers, chopping tools, side and end scrapers, perforators, and some denticulates and burins are present.

Artifacts made of ground and polished stone begin to appear as well, in the form of mortars and flat grindstones. Great technological complexity is observed, created through many different methods including percussion, pressure flaking, and abrasion with its variant of polishing.

This diverse assemblage is associated with an increase in production and, therefore, an improvement in the way of life, although the economic base continues to be hunting and gathering. Cenolithic peoples preferentially collected wild varieties of squash, avocado, chile, amaranth, corn, and perhaps beans. As differential gathering occurred during this phase, the first steps were taken toward domestication.

We have evidence that objects were manufactured using plant fibers. These included cordage, carrying nets, bags, and other items. Ornamental objects made of bone, shell, and stone were perforated and strung on cords.

The Protoneolithic period (7000 to 4500 yr B.P.) is designated by the introduction of agriculture. The cultivation of corn, squash, amaranth, and beans occurs at this time, though hunting and gathering continue to be basic activities. Nonetheless, incipient agriculture and the need to care for cultivated land requires sedentism during at least some of the year, although perhaps for only part of the social group.

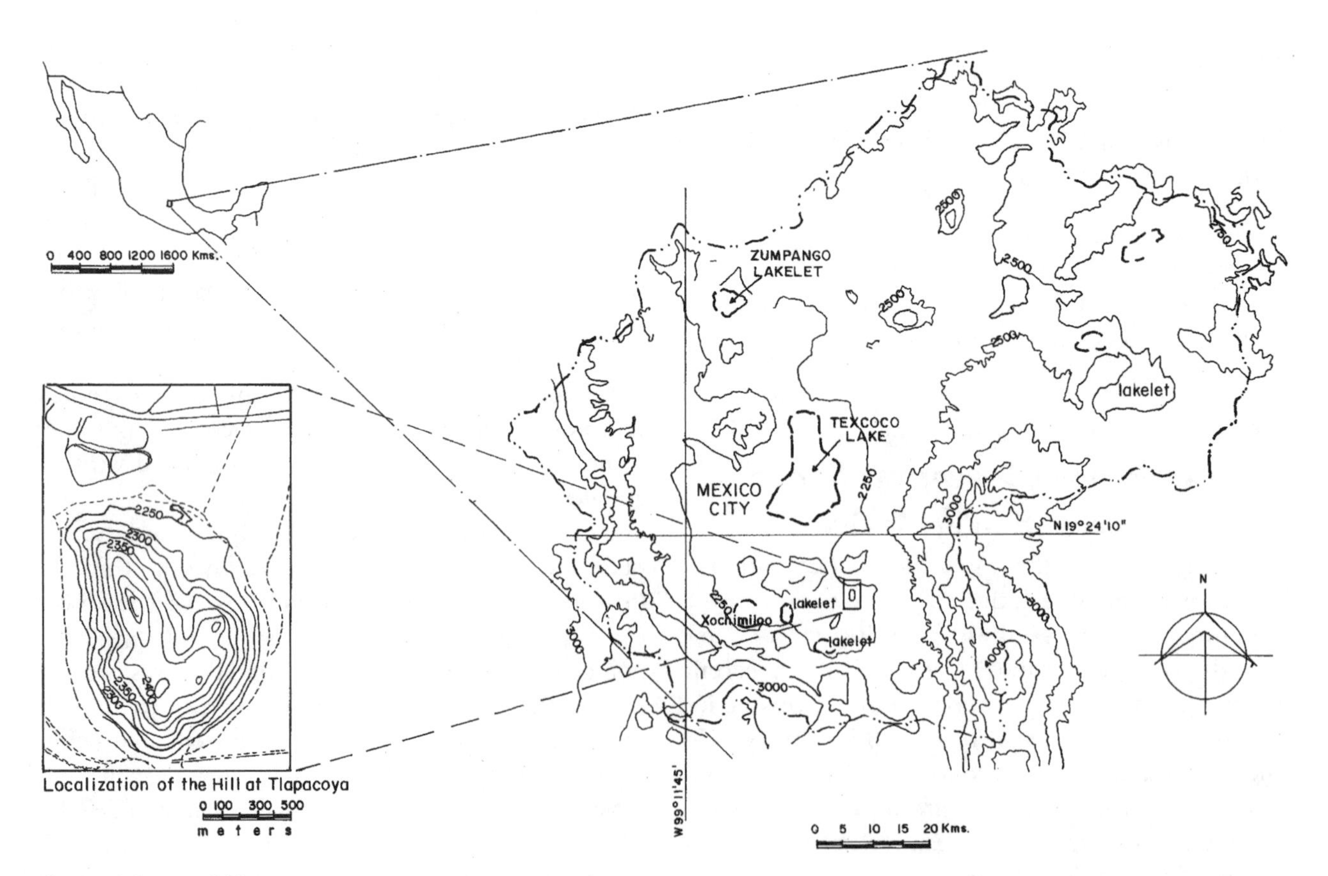

Figure 1. Basin of Mexico.

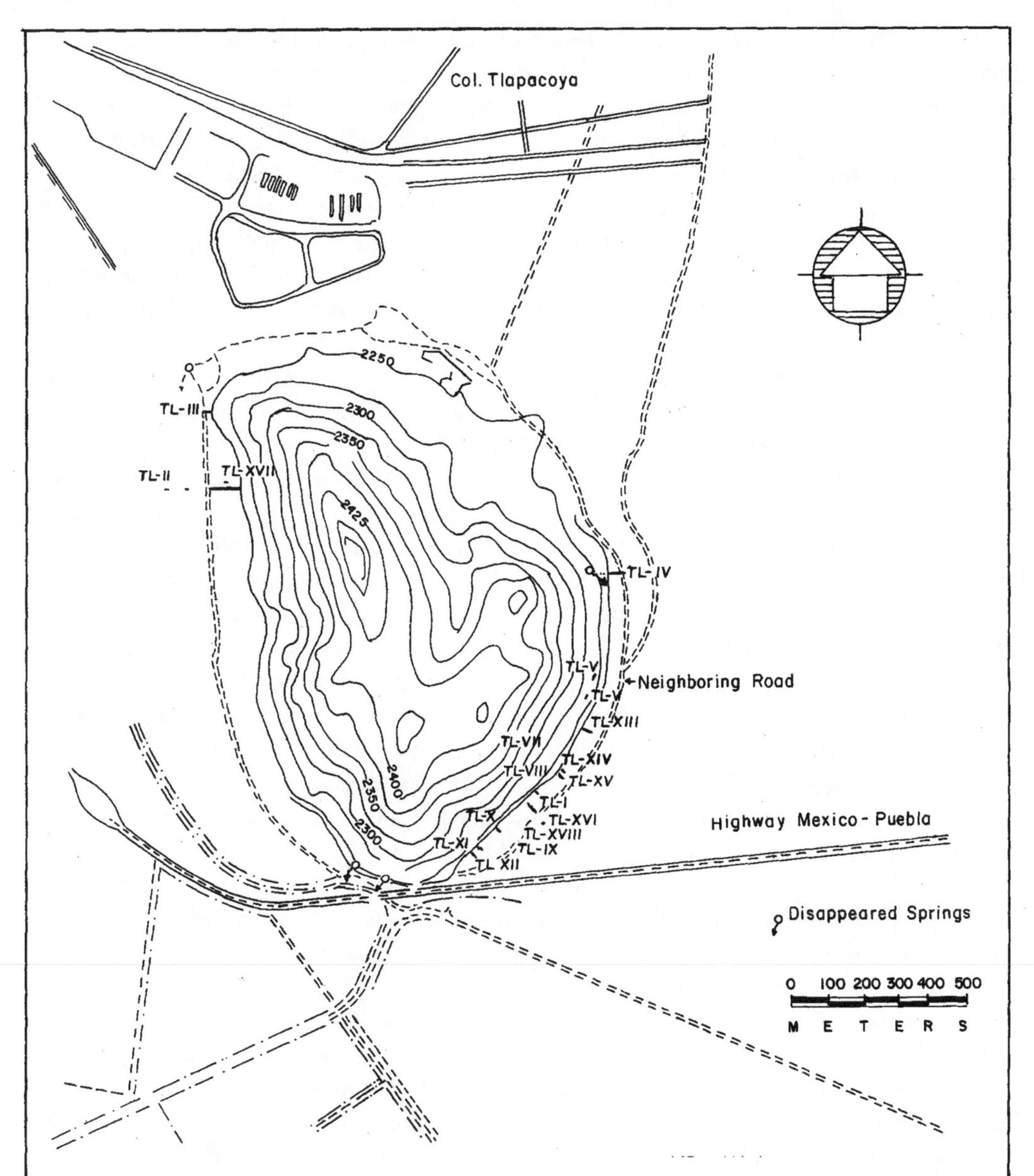

Figure 2. Excavated sites—the hill at Tlapacoya.

In terms of the lithic industry, a decrease in the size of artifacts is observed, while secondary working is perfected. Technological improvements are seen also in the manufacture of mortars and flat metates, with emphasis placed not only upon function, but also on regular forms. Polishing techniques are employed in the manufacture of axes, adzes, chisels, and beads; that is to say, for both functional and ornamental objects. At the end of this period, we find the presence of pottery and more consolidated agriculture (Lorenzo 1967b).

Tlapacoya

THE TERRITORY THAT Mexico presently occupies extends from 32°30' in the north to 14°30' in the south. Thus, a great portion of the country lies south of the Tropic of Cancer. Mexico's topography ranges from several tens of meters below sea level to peaks of almost 6,000 m in height, and includes glaciers, jungles, dunes, and lakes. In short, this area encompasses a very wide climatic variety resulting in numerous ecosystems.

To these observations must be added the variants that signified the great climatic alterations of the Pleistocene. This time was characterized by glacial advances and recessions in the more northern latitudes and on the highest mountains in the tropical zones. These glacial fluctuations coincided with marine regressions and transgressions. During periods of glacial advance, enormous tracts of land lay uncovered along the Gulf of Mexico and along the Pacific shores. In general terms, there was dry, cold weather in the tropical latitudes during the stadials and hot and humid conditions during the interstadials. A series of large lakes was present in Mexico until the terminal Pleistocene and perhaps into the initial part of the Holocene. These lakes, located in endorreic basins, supported a variety of plants and animals and would have favored human settlement and subsistence along their shorelines.

The Tlapacoya site complex retains a record of paleoclimatic alternations throughout the past 35,000 years (Lorenzo 1986). Tlapacoya is situated on an ancient volcanic promontory, which rises some 150 m above the plain of the now-dry ancient Lake Chalco to ca. 2,400 m a.s.l. The site is located in the southern part of the Basin of Mexico, at 19°10'N, 98°E55'W (see Figure 1). The geomorphology of the area comprises a landscape of hills and cinderous volcanic cones (Reyes-Cortes 1986). The site area is on one of the oldest hills in this zone—an Oligocene-Miocene volcanic structure formed by an outpouring of lamprobolite andesite, of which only a small part of its summit remains.

Between 1965 and 1973, excavations were carried out at a total of 18 sites on the perimeter of the hill. Best known among them are Tlapacoya I, Alpha and Beta; Tlapacoya II; and Tlapacoya VIII. These sites have produced evidence of the oldest human occupation (Figure 2) in the Basin of Mexico. Sedimentological and granulometric analyses, primarily conducted at Tlapacoya I, Alpha and Beta; Tlapacoya II; III; IV; XVI; and XVII, allowed for the construction of stratigraphic correlations. Twenty-three stratigraphic units were defined, originating from pyroclastic, colluvial, peat, and lacustrine depositional regimes. It was from these latter deposits that evidence of human activity was recovered, along with abundant faunal remains (Figure 3) (Limbrey 1986). There are 17 stratigraphic units that include pyroclastic material or tephras. These are further divided into 61 subunits (Lambert 1986:77–100), based upon depositional characteristics.

Significant changes are observed in the faunal material within the period between 33,000 to 9000 yr B.P. Three stages are noted, in which species disappear in a progressive pattern (Alvarez 1986). The first stage, from 33,000 to 22,000 yr B.P., comprises typically Pleistocene species, such as edentates, proboscideans, bovids, antilocaprids, equids, and camelids. Also within this stage are the remains of otter (*Lutra canadensis*) and capybara (*Hydrochoerus* sp.) This last animal still survives in South America, but is restricted to the Pleistocene in Mexico and the rest of North America.

The second stage, which extends from 24,000 to 15,000 yr B.P. (and thus is partially superimposed on the earlier one) is marked by the decline of Pleistocene fauna, with species present that are now found only in other latitudes. Faunal remains dating to this phase are associated with evidence of human activity. Several faunal species recovered at the Tlapacoya site locality represent animals now extinct or found in habitats beyond the Basin of Mexico. These include black bear (*Ursus americanus*), an extinct species of deer (*Odocoileus halli*), remains of an extinct or extirpated antilocaprid, and tuza (*Pappogeomys castanops*), which presently is found only in northern and central Mexico.

The third stage, from 15,000 to 9000 yr B.P., is characterized by extant species that have inhabited this region for 33,000 years. These include two species of rabbit (*Sylvilagus* sp.), rodents (*Liomys* sp., *Peromyscus* sp., *Neotoma* sp., *Microtus* sp.), coyote (*Canis latrans*), raccoon (*Procyon*), and deer (*Odocoileus virginianus*). Remains of the latter also are part of the collection of bones associated with hearth features. Other species of importance are the leaf-chinned bat (*Mormoops megalophylla*), which presently lives in dry subtropical to tropical regions, and Stock's vampire bat (*Desmodus stockii*), an extinct Pleistocene form. This leads us to infer a delay in the extinction of species at the end of the Pleistocene in the more southern latitudes (Alvarez 1986:174). Fish were abundant (e.g., *Algansea tincella* and *Chirostoma humboldtianum*) and undoubtedly served as a food source for humans, as well as supporting a nearby colony of aquatic birds.

For the most part, the identified species at Tlapacoya are from large mammals and, consequently, are not

Table 1. Phase 1 Vegetational Communities

Planiaciulifolic alpine forest	*Abies, Picea, Ribes, Salix, Saxifraga, and Compositae (large thorns)*
Aciculifolic temperate forest	*Pinus, Quercus, Alnus, and Fraxinus*
Subtropical latifolic meadow	*Opuntia and Agave*
Aquatic latifolic meadow	*Scirpus, Ceratophyllum, and Myriophyllum, as well as Lemma and Epilobium*
Pendulifolic temperate forest	*Taxodium and Salix*

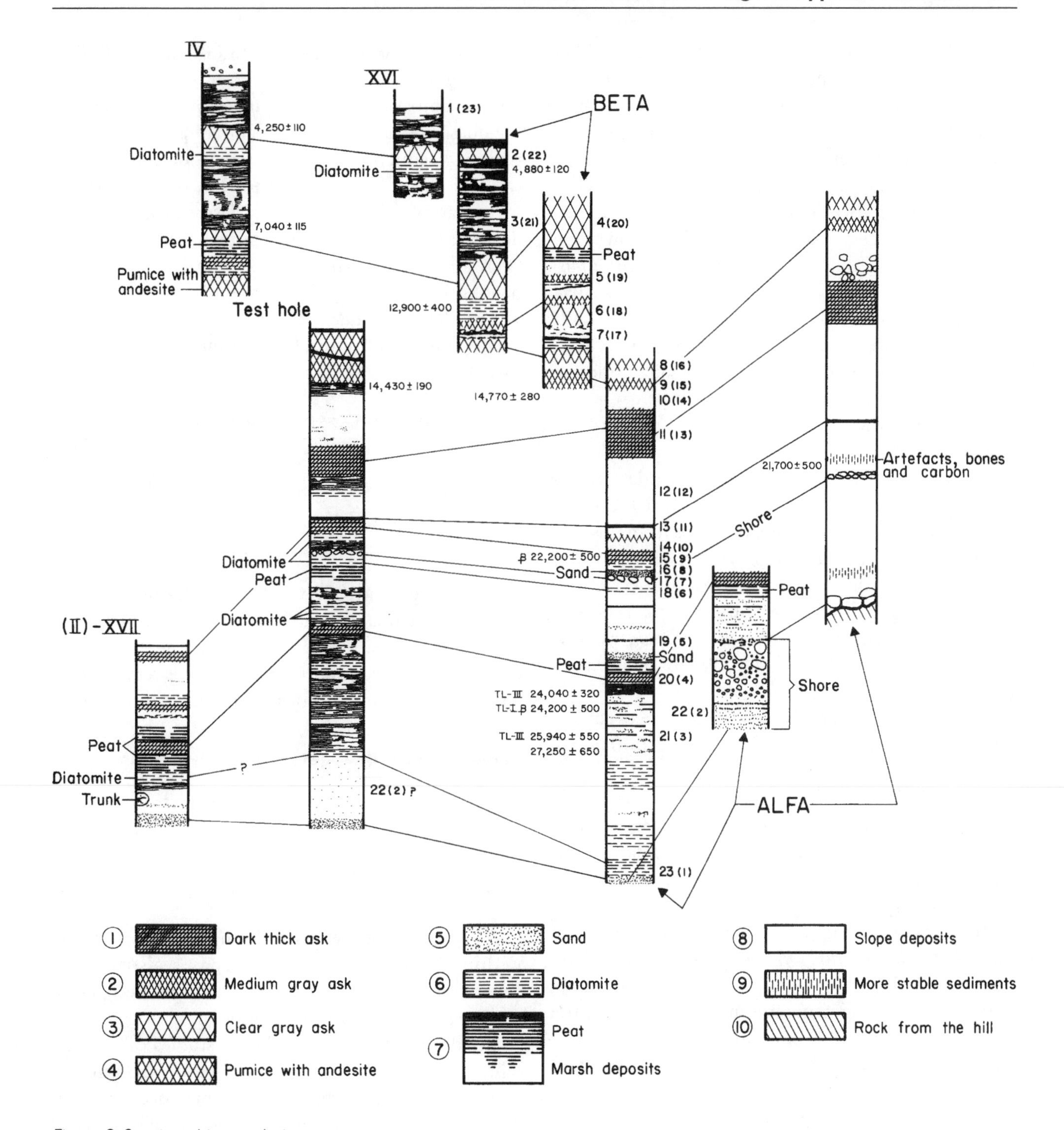

Figure 3. Stratigraphic correlations.

well linked to a specific type of climate because of their great mobility. Thus, the mammal remains provide little information with respect to environment, although the presence of capybara (*Hydrochoerus*) and otter (*Lutra*) indicates that greater moisture was evident during the first faunal stage. The occurrence of birds, such as double-crested cormorant (*Phalacrocorax auritus*), white pelican (*Pelecanus erythrorhynochos*), snowy egret (*Egretta thula*), common egret (*Casmorodius albus*), black-crowned nocturnal heron (*Nycticorax nycticorax*), five duck species, and common raven (*Corvus corax*), supports this finding. The avian assemblage represents a complete avifauna no longer present in the Basin of Mexico, appearing only occasionally as migratory residents (Brodkorp and Phillips 1986:205–206).

As we indicated, the third stage includes animals still present in the area. During the 1965–1973 excavations, extant fauna were collected from this area. These included bat (*Mormoops megalophylla*), which is still a sporadic visitor to the Basin of Mexico, coyote (*Canis latrans*), several rodents (*Liomys irroratus, Neotoma mexicana, Microtus mexicanus*), raccoon (*Procyon lotor*), and deer (*Odocoileus virginianus*) (Alvarez 1986).

Studies of vegetation indicate continued climatic fluctuations throughout the past 33,000 years, characterized by an increase in mesothermal affinities. Palynological records have established the occurrence of seven vegetational phases up to the present time. We will concern ourselves only with the first three, as they constitute our period of interest (Gonzalez-Quintero 1986).

In Phase I, from 33,000 to 23,000 yr B.P., ahueheutes (*Taxodium mucronatum*) populated the banks of the lake. Their presence is demonstrated by abundant wood fragments and an almost complete tree trunk, directly dated at 23,150 ± 950 yr B.P. (GX-0950). Within the 33,000 to 23,000 yr B.P. time span, palynological research has shown that the vegetational communities shown in Table I must have coexisted in the Basin of Mexico, in distinct altitudinous and edaphic positions.

Until 27,000 yr B.P., these communities generally did not change. Following this time, the planiacucifolic temperate forest began to reduce in size. Only the genus *Pinus*, because of its ecological plasticity, was able to withstand an apparent decrease in rain. Toward 23,000 yr B.P., climatic conditions became harsher, and *Pinus* appears as the sole arboreal constituent of the flora.

During Phase II, between 23,000 and 14,000 yr B.P., a gradual reduction of *Pinus* is observed. This species almost disappears entirely toward the end of the phase, as does *Abies*, which no longer exists in this region. A reduction in the lake level is detected during this period, and the exposed shoreline became covered with grasses. The climate was desert-like, as rainfall decreased and median annual temperatures must have been about 18°C; this is demonstrated by the large quantity of *Ambrosia* pollen. The sediment of this phase was moderately saline, as indicated by the increase in chenopods or amaranths. Floral communities comprise two clear groups.

Table 2. Phase II Vegetational Communities

Aciculifolic temperate meadow	*Increase in chenopods, amaranths,* and Ambrosia
Platicrasical desert bush	*Opuntia*

At the beginning of Phase III, from 14,000 to 8000 yr B.P., the climate became more mesic, as indicated by a rapid increase in *Pinus* and the appearance of cyperaceae. The vegetation in this phase is very uniform with only two communities clearly distinguishable.

Table 3. Phase III Vegetational Communities

Aciculifolic temperate forest	*Pinus and Quercus*
Latifolic aquatic meadow	*Scirpus*

As we previously explained, phases IV to VIII fall within the Holocene. These phases also exhibit vegetational change, but are not dealt with here, given the interest in earlier time periods.

In addition to interdisciplinary studies of the site, which provided a picture of paleoenvironmental conditions, an understanding of human occupation at Tlapacoya was revealed through archaeological investigations. Excavations yielded extensive evidence of prehistoric occupation at the site locality, which are divided here into three areas: material culture, human skeletal remains, and expressions of human cultural activity (e.g., hearths, midden deposits, and similar features).

At Tlapacoya I, Alpha, in the site area corresponding to the shore zone, three hearths with associated animal bone middens were found . Two of the hearth features were dated by radiocarbon assay: hearth 1 at 24,000

± 4000 yr B.P. (A-794 b); and hearth 3 at 21,700 ± 500 yr B.P. (I-4449). These dates provide clear evidence of human activity at the site about 22,000 years ago.

In the same area of the site, some 2,500 stone fragments were encountered in situ. Among these were artifacts that were not very discernable typologically, owing to their manufacture from a poor-quality local stone. When worked, this material—a gray or pink lamprobolite andesite with abundant phenocrysts, heterogenus matrix, and an irregular fracture pattern—results in very crude artifacts. The dimensions of these primary artifacts are variable, fluctuating between 25 and 150 mm in length, 15 and 75 mm in width, and 7 to 25 mm in thickness (Mirambell 1986a, 1986b).

Debitage and a knife made from a rounded pebble originate from raw material found in abundance on the ancient shores of Lake Chalco. The knife was formed by lateral flaking, providing a cutting edge, with portions of the cortex on the remainder of the piece. This is a coarse implement that would have been useful for heavy cutting tasks, possibly for dismembering animals during butchering activities.

From the study of these materials, we have concluded that this was a manufacturing area, associated with the hearth features, within the shoreline occupation stratum. The artifacts imply the sporadic presence of a human group, which manufactured expedient tools for such basic functions as cutting and scraping. This locus of human occupation lies on the northeast side of the shore, near a rock outcrop.

Artifacts manufactured from obsidian also were recovered from the site. The nearest obsidian source is found at the Otumba deposit, approximately 50 km away. Three obsidian flakes come from Tlapacoya I, Alpha. Two of the pieces came from screened material that lay above the shore area, adjacent to a concentration of animal bones, while the third was found in the center of one of the hearths (hearth No. 1).

A lanceolate point with subparallel bifacial flaking was found, fractured distally and proximally. Morphologically, it is reminiscent of a "Lerma" point. It was not possible to establish an exact age for this specimen because it was found within a very old rodent burrow, infilled with upper-level sediments. From its stratigraphic position, we consider the point to be around 15,000 years old.

Further excavations at Tlapacoya I, Beta, yielded a "discoidal" scraper manufactured from a quartz flake found in screened shore-horizon sediments. The specimen has a triangular striking platform with light work on almost the entire dorsal face and slight secondary work on its ventral surface. It exhibits evidence of water polishing. Given its geologic context, an age of 22,000 yr B.P. is estimated. Taxonomically unidentifiable bone fragments with clear modification marks also were recovered from this horizon.

Work at the Tlapacoya II site yielded a prismatic obsidian blade. Although we cannot provide a great deal of technological information, due to the lack of a striking platform, study of the piece suggests it originated from a core worked by bipolar percussion. This blade first was dated indirectly from its position beneath a tree trunk (*Taxodium mucronatum*) dated at 23,950 ± 950 yr B.P. (GX-0959); this does not necessarily mean that it has the same date as the wood. The blade was later subjected to dating by obsidian hydration, which provided a corroborating date between 21,250 and 25,000 yr B.P. On this basis, the blade is considered contemporaneous with Tlapacoya I (García-Bárcena 1986).

At the Tlapcoya XVIII site, an incomplete human cranium with adult, robust features, was found within a stratum dated at 9920 ± 250 yr B.P. (I-6897). Previously, in 1968, an incomplete human skull was found out of context at the site. Although both specimens show similar patterns of mineral accumulation on their surfaces, the general characteristics are different: the cranium first discovered in 1968 is elongated and narrow (a dolichocranium), while the second find is not. Nonetheless, we consider these specimens to be of similar age, as the mineral concretions on both consist of the same materials (Lorenzo and Mirambell 1986).

Similar finds assigned to the Archaeolithic phase also have been discovered at Laguna de Chapala, Baja California; Caulapan, Puebla; El Cedral, San Luis Potosi; Loltun, Yucatan; and Teopisca, Chiapas (Lorenzo 1967a; Mirambell 1994). The remains found to date of these first inhabitants of Mexico are rare and in poor condition.

The Distribution of Fluted Projectile Points in Mexico

THE MOST OUTSTANDING characteristic of the succeeding lower Cenolithic is the presence of fluted Clovis, Folsom, and "fishtail" projectile points. The approximate areas of fluted point distribution in Mexico are discussed below.

Three subgroups of projectile points characterize the Clovis group: typical, pentagonal, and concave-sided forms. The first category is the most widely distributed and is found from the Mexican-United States border to the highlands of Guatemala. The absence of typical Clovis in northeastern Mexico and in the zone between the Neovolcanic Axis and the Guatemalan highlands is significant. It is possible that these points will be found in the future in the states of Oaxaca and Guerrero, as the recovery of Clovis-type points from Guatemala, but not southern Mexico, is inexplicable. The absence of Clovis points in northeastern Mexico could be real, however, rather than attributable to archaeological ignorance (García-Bárcena 1979).

Pentagonal Clovis points have a more restricted distribution, extending from northwestern Mexico (state of Sonora) to approximately west-central Mexico (state of Jalisco). Concave-sided Clovis points occur from north-central Mexico (Durango) to as far south as Panama. The distribution of pentagonal and concave-sided Clovis points appears to be mutually exclusive, while the distribution of typical Clovis points, in part, coincides with the other two forms.

The regional chronology of Clovis points is not completely clear. The earliest appear to be represented by typical Clovis, with an age near 12,000 yr B.P. in Texas and neighboring areas, and 10,700 yr B.P. in Guatemala. In Mexico, about 26 locations with Clovis-type projectile points have been identified; but only one point, from Samalayuca, Chihuahua, has been classified as Folsom. Though Clovis points are distributed across a large part of Mexico, these finds, for the most part, have been recovered from surficial contexts (García-Bárcena 1979).

Interestingly enough, in the southern state of Chiapas, bordering Guatemala, two fishtail points were excavated in association with a fluted Clovis point at the Los Grifos site (Santamaría 1981). This association has been dated by radiocarbon and obsidian hydration between 9700 and 8000 yr B.P. (Santamaría 1981:64). Fluted points from earlier contexts have been found in North America, as have fishtail points from South America. Diffusion appears to have occurred from north to south in the first instance, and south to north in the second. Fell's Cave in Patagonia has yielded a date of 10,710 ±30 yr B.P. for fishtail points (García-Bárcena 1979).

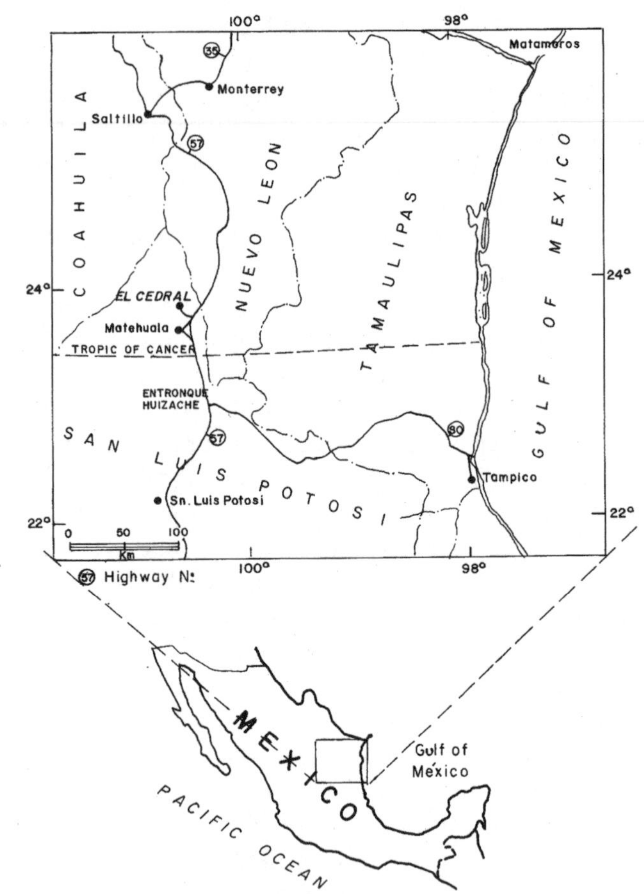

Figure 4. Locality of El Cedral site.

Rancho La Amapola Site, El Cedral

IN 1977, INTERDISCIPLINARY investigations began at the Rancho La Amapola site, El Cedral, San Luis Potosí, located in the north-central part of Mexico at 23°40'N, 100°43'W and at 1,700 m above sea level (Figure 4) (Lorenzo and Mirambell 1981). The site lies in an endorreic basin with abundant remains of Pleistocene animals attracted to this area by its numerous now-dry springs. Excavations were carried out from 1977 to 1984. The initial investigation was devoted exclusively to paleontological study, but an archaeologist was present in a monitoring capacity.

Work began with a topographic survey of the area and a geological study. Prior to the removal of a large quantity of debris, in which abundant fossilized bone and wood remains were found that had infilled the

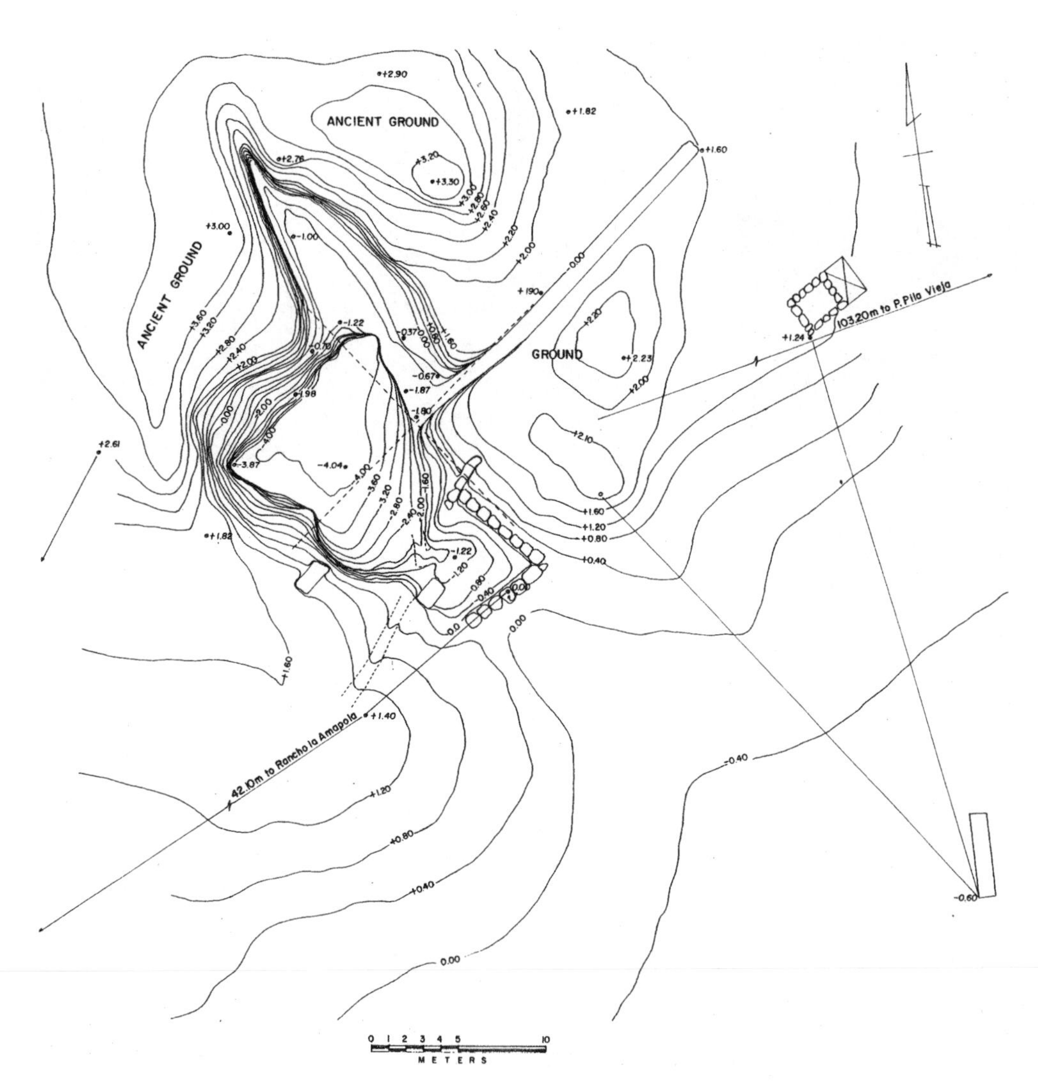

Figure 5. El Cedral project. Excavation process.

old spring, the site was divided into quadrants (NE, NW, SE, and SW). A grid was established with 1-by-1-m units for strict control of the excavation, and the resultant debris screened (Figures 5, 6, and 7).

Because the site was a spring in an arid or semiarid region, it is natural that fauna would have frequented the area. The abundance of faunal remains in a semidesert zone such as this is understandable, given that a watering hole is a dangerous place, particularly during drought when animals would have gathered in great number. For this reason, there is an abundance of faunal remains, including proboscideans, carnivora, equids, camelids, and many others. These animals may have arrived to quench their thirst or to obtain easy prey. Humans also frequented the site during droughts, although their presence must have been sporadic. Among the large quantity of bones found, some exhibit signs of use as tools.

Among the very few artifacts found in situ was a circular scraper, manufactured of microcrystalline quartz (chalcedony). The specimen was made from a primary flake, with some cortex remaining on the dorsal surface. The piece was shaped by direct percussion. The ventral surface is smooth except for two short flake scars, made to eliminate the bulb. The tool came from a stratum dated at 33,300 ± 2700 yr B.P. (GX-7684), an age that is surprising and requires verification. A limestone core also was found, which shows signs of having been used as a hammer. This artifact was recovered from a stratum dated at 15,000 yr B.P. It is important to note that the closest known limestone source lies 5 km east and lacks any natural drainage toward the site.

A Gary point, which dates between 7000 and 5000 yr B.P., was found at the site, as well as a distal point fragment. Also in the NE quandrant (sections K, L, sectors 101 and 1), a pit was discovered in undisturbed strata at approximately 2.30 m below the surface. This feature measures 90 cm in diameter by 85 cm in depth. It was clearly excavated and infilled with dark brown

Figure 6. Excavation process at El Cedral.

Figure 7. Excavation process at El Cedral.

argillaceous material with concretions, sediment completely different in texture and color from the surrounding strata. Chronostratigraphic correlation of this pit indicates it was dug into strata dated between 8000 and 6000 yr B.P. No cultural remains of any kind were found within it. We limit ourselves to verifying the presence of this feature, as it would be speculative to make inferences regarding its function, except to note that its location on the periphery of the spring may be indicative of efforts to obtain potable water.

During the initial investigation of the site, remains of a hearth ringed with proboscidean tarsi were found. A charcoal lens, some 30 cm in diameter and 2 cm thick, was located in the center of the hearth. The find was of great importance, as the position of the faunal remains and the charcoal leave no room for doubt that it is the product of human activity. The charcoal was dated at 31,850 ± 1600 yr B.P. (I-10438).

Seven additional hearths were found in 1983 and 1984. Charcoal from these features was dated in the Laboratorio de Radiocarbono of the present day Subdireción de Servicios Académicos of INAH (then the Department of Prehistory). The samples from Hearths 2 and 3 were insufficient for dating; however, these features lay between those from which dates were obtained.

A statistical comparison of the hearth dates was conducted. As a result, it has been determined that Hearths 6 and 7 (dated at 28,709 ± 827 [INAH-389] and 27,459 ± 812 yr B.P. [INAH-390]) can be considered contemporaneous (Ríos 1984). Four samples were processed from Hearth 4 (INAH-303, -302a, -302b, and -391). Two are statistically equal (INAH-303 and INAH-391), with an average date of 26,333 ± 827 yr B.P. The other two dates differ: INAH-302b has an age of 28,462 ± 507 yr B.P. and INAH-302a an age of 33,630 ± 2066 yr B.P.

Chronologically, Hearths 4, 6, and 7 can be grouped as being roughly contemporaneous, with ages between 26,000 and 28,000 yr B.P. The remaining features, Hearths 1 and 5, produced dates of 37,694 ± 1963 (INAH-305) and 21,468 ± 458 (INAH-388), respectively. These two dates provide lower and upper limiting ages for the El Cedral features.

Stratigraphically, Hearths 3 and 4 share the same context, and although no absolute dates have been obtained from Hearth 3, it may be correlated with Hearth 4, due to its spatial proximity. Hearths 1 (37,694 ± 1963 yr B.P. [INAH-305]) and 6 (28,709 ± 828 yr B.P. [INAH-389]) differ by 5 cm in depth (Hearth 1 above, and Hearth 6 below) and are not considered contemporaneous.

Hearth 2, the uppermost of these features in the stratigraphic sequence, lies at 2.46 m in depth and is undated. Its position is similar to that of Hearth 5 (at 2.50 m in depth), dated at 21,468 ± 458 yr B.P. For want of a more precise date, Hearth 2 can tentatively be assigned an age similar to that of Hearth 5 (Figure 8).

The span of time represented by the hearth-feature radiocarbon dates comprises a period of approximately 15,000–16,000 years. It is possible, as this locale would have presented favorable conditions for human activities, that the site was used sporadically by human

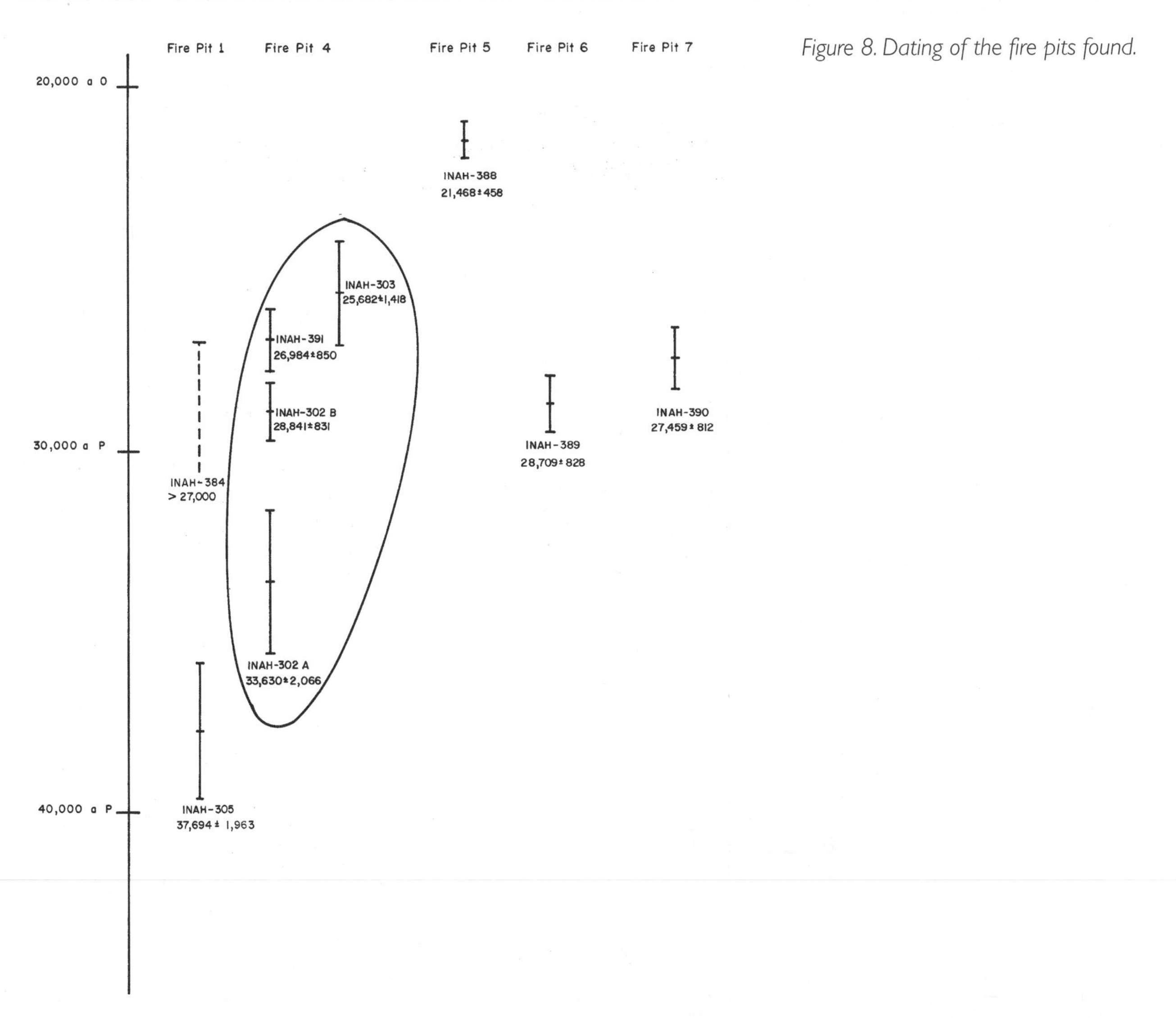

Figure 8. Dating of the fire pits found.

groups continuously during this time. On the other hand, it is feasible that two phases may be represented here, one older (Hearths 1 and 4) and the other later (Hearths 5, 6, and 7), but also of considerable age (Ríos 1984).

Doubts remain as to the accuracy of the El Cedral radiocarbon dates. To recover more datable material and evidence of human occupation, additional excavations are planned. Units near the locus of the hearth features will be extended, and new excavations will be placed at the opposite side of the channel. This latter area is of interest, as it also might have provided favorable conditions for human occupation.

Initially, the Hearth 1 date of 37,694 ± 1963 was viewed with much reservation. However, reports from Toca de Boqueirao da Pedra Furada in Brazil, a site dated at 31,500 yr B.P. (Niede Guidon, personal communication 1989), containing hearths, an associated lithic industry, and animal bone fragments, have provided a degree of optimism to the initial interpretation of El Cedral. It is not unexpected for signs of human presence on the American continents to be older in the north than in the south, since this is the route that the first Americans likely followed.

Those who question a significant time depth for human occupation in the Americas may allege that the hearths found and dated at Rancho la Amapola are the remains of natural fires. This evidence cannot be dismissed so easily. The features are superimposed, varying in size between 60 and 170 cm in diameter, and containing small fragments of burned bone. These features are concentrated between the spring and the adjacent lagoon—representing the portion of the site that would have been the most favorable for human settlement. The vertical banks of the spring would have made access to water difficult, while the lagoon would have contained stagnant, unpalatable water during periods of abundant moisture. Thus, the area where

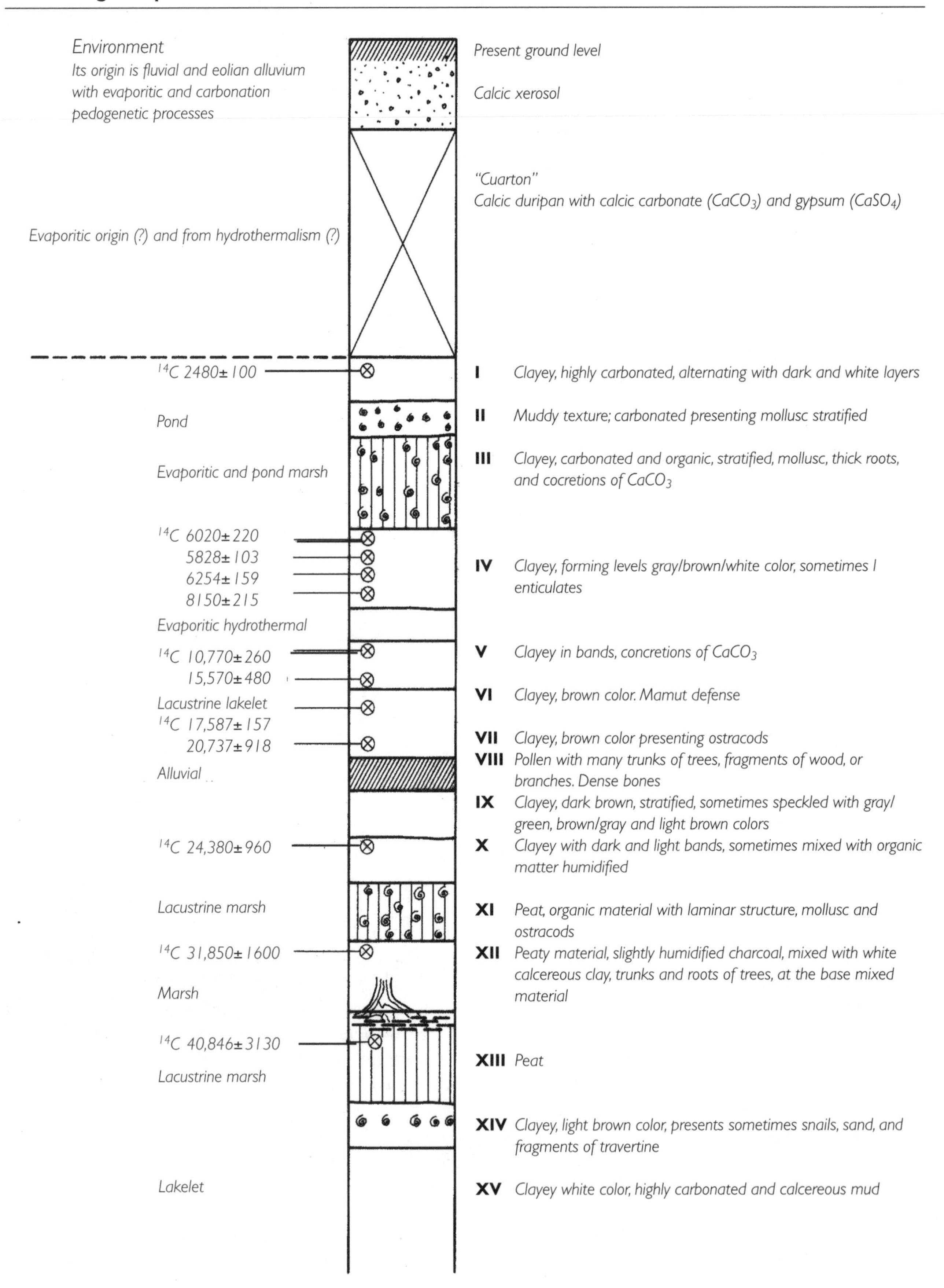

Figure 9. Tentative stratigraphic summary of El Cedral, S.L.P. (A. Flores-Diaz)

the hearths are situated, on the banks of the channel connecting the spring with the lagoon, would have been the best place for human settlement.

During the fifth field season (1982, units A and B 104–110; AA and BB 104–110; Quadrants NW and SW), lithic materials of limestone were found within strata dated at about 6000–7000 yr B.P. As previously noted, the nearest limestone deposit is 5 km east, thus these limestone pieces are considered to be manuports. The lithic materials were subjected to a preliminary classification, as follows:

(1) Whole stones—those that show no type of alteration by human activity, although their presence at the site indicates they were transported there by cultural processes.

(2) Stones that exhibit one or two fractures of unknown origin. It is not established whether this alteration is the product of human activity or derived from natural processes.

(3) Stones that display more than three fractures, caused by natural processes.

(4) Polyhedral flake cores.

(5) Artifacts created from a core—i.e., choppers and chopping tools.

(6) Flakes discarded as debitage during manufacture—primary and secondary reduction stages.

(7) Artifacts made from flakes—scrapers and flakes with worked edges.

(8) Blades—primary and secondary reduction stages.

(9) Smaller undiagnostic fragments—less than 20 mm at the largest axis.

(10) Primary mortar exhibiting usewear.

(11) Shapeless, unclassifiable lithic fragments.

These lithic objects were coated with a thick layer of argillaceous material mixed with calcium carbonate. The thickness of this material varies, to a maximum of 2 mm, occasionally obscuring evidence of cultural modification. It is possible that the excavated pit at the edge of the spring is associated with the human activity of this later phase.

Thus, archaeological investigations at Rancho La Amapola, El Cedral, and San Luis Potosí, have produced evidence of human occupation near a spring extending from about 37,000 to 21,000 yr B.P., followed by a later human presence between 7000 and 6000 yr B.P. This settlement covers a small area at the edge of a stream channel. During the period of occupation, this channel would have connected a spring and lagoon. The proof of an early human presence is small but assuring: seven superimposed hearths with burned, unidentifiable, small animal bone fragments. Unfortunately, there are no artifacts directly associated with these features. However, several artifacts have been recorded in different parts of the excavation in dated stratigraphic contexts, which correspond with the dates obtained from the hearths.

Finally, an interdisciplinary study also is being carried out at the site. Parallel investigations of vertebrate and molluscan paleofauna, palynological, paleobotanical, geomorphic, and sedimentological evidence, enhanced with a considerable quantity of radiocarbon dates, will serve to strenghthen the cultural evidence and provide insight into the paleoenvironmental condtions at the site (see Figure 9).

The El Cedral site has provided important information about the earliest human inhabitants of Mexico, and gives us a glimpse of what may have been the first Americans. Because of the importance of this site, ongoing investigations have been undertaken there, to corroborate evidence of an early human presence and to enrich our understanding of the occupation (Lorenzo and Mirambell 1978–1984).

References Cited

Alvarez, T.

1986 Fauna Pleistocénica. In *Tlapacoya: 35,000 Años de Historia del Lago de Chalco.* Coordinated by J. L. Lorenzo and L. Mirambell, pp. 173–203. Colección Científica 155. Instituto Nacional de Antropologia e Historia, Mexico City, Mexico.

Brodkorp, P., and A. R. Phillips

1986 Restos de Aves. In *Tlapacoya: 35,000 Años de Historia del Lago de Chalco.* Coordinated by J. L. Lorenzo and L. Mirambell, pp. 205–206. Colección Científica 155. Instituto Nacional de Antropologia e Historia, Mexico City, Mexico.

García-Bárcena, J.

1979 Una Punta Acanalada de la Cueva de los Grifos, Ocozocoautla, Chis. In *Cuadernos de Trabajo* 17. Departmento de Prehistoria, Mexico City, Mexico.

1986 Algunos Aspectos Cronológicos. In *Tlapacoya: 35,000 Años de Historia del Lago de Chalco.* Coordinated by J. L. Lorenzo and L. Mirambell, pp. 219–224. Colección Científica 155. Instituto Nacional de Antropologia e Historia, Mexico City, Mexico.

Genoves, S., C. M. Pijoan, and M. E. Salas

1982 El Hombre Temprano en México: Panorama General. In *Actas X Congreso Unión Internacional de Ceincias Prehistóricas y Protohistóricas*, pp. 370–399. Mexico City, Mexico.

Gonzales-Quintero, L.
1986 Análisis Polínico. In *Tlapacoya: 35,000 Años de Historia del Lago de Chalco.* Coordinated by J. L. Lorenzo and L. Mirambell, pp. 157–166. Colección Científica 155. Instituto Nacional de Antropologia e Historia, Mexico City, Mexico.

Lambert, W.
1986 Descripción Preliminar de los Estratos de Tefra de Tlapacoya I. In *Tlapacoya: 35,000 Años de Historia del Lago de Chalco.* Coordinated by J. L. Lorenzo and L. Mirambell, pp. 77–100. Colección Científica 155. Instituto Nacional de Antropologia e Historia, Mexico City, Mexico.

Limbrey, S.
1986 Análisis de Suelos y Sedimento. In T*lapacoya: 35,000 Años de Historia del Lago de Chalco.* Coordinated by J. L. Lorenzo and L. Mirambell, pp. 67–75. Colección Científica 155. Instituto Nacional de Antropologia e Historia, Mexico City, Mexico.

Lorenzo, J. L.
1967a *La Etapa Lítica en México.* Departmento de Prehistoria, 20 Instituto Nacional de Antropologia e Historia, Mexico City, Mexico.

1967b Mesoamerican Beginnings: Economies Based on Hunting, Gathering, and Incipient Agriculture. In *Indian Mexico: Past, Present,* edited by Betty Bell, pp. 24–45. Latin American Center, UCLA Los Angeles, California.

1986 Conclusiones. In *Tlapacoya: 35,000 Años de Historia del Lago de Chalco,* Coordinated by J. L. Lorenzo and L. Mirambell, pp. 225–287. Colección Científica 155. Instituto Nacional de Antropologia e Historia, Mexico City, Mexico.

Lorenzo, J. L., and L. Mirambell
1978–1984 Informes de la Temporadas de Excavaciones Realizadas en el Sitio Rancho La Amapola, El Cedral, San Luis Potosi. Departmento de Prehistoria. Instituto Nacional de Antropologia e Historia(Mecanoestritos), Mexico City, Mexico.

1981 El Cedral, S.L.P., México: Un Sitio con Presencia Humana de más de 30,000 aP. X Congreso Unión Internacinal de Ciencias Prehistóricas Protohistóricas. In *Comisión XII El Poblamiento de América.* Coloquio: Evidencia Arqueológica de Ocupación Humana en América, Anterior a 11,500 aP, pp. 112–125 Mexico.

Lorenzo, J. L., and L. Mirambell (coordinators)
1986 *Tlapacoya: 35,000 Años de Historia del Lago de Chalco.* Colección Científica 155. Instituto Nacional de Antropologia e Historia, Mexico City, Mexico.

Mirambell, L.
1986a Las Excavaciones. In *Tlapacoya: 35,000 Años de Historia del Lago de Chalco.* Coordinated by J. L. Lorenzo and L. Mirambell, pp. 13–56. Colección Científica 155. Instituto Nacional de Antropologia e Historia, Mexico City, Mexico.

1986b Restos Culturales en Horizontes Pleistocénicos. In *Tlapacoya: 35,000 Años de Historia del Lago de Chalco.* Coordinated by J. L. Lorenzo and L. Mirambell, pp. 207–217. Colección Científica 155. Instituto Nacional de Antropologia e Historia, Mexico City, Mexico.

1987 La Investigacion Prehistorica en el Instituto Nacional de Antropologia e Historia. In *Orígenes del Hombre Americano (Seminario),* pp. 307–318. Cien de Mexico, SEP Mexico City, Mexico.

In press Las Sociedades Cazadoras-Recolectoras. In *Historia Antiqua de México.* En Prensa. UNAM-Instituto Nacional de Antropologia e Historia, Mexico City, Mexico.

Reyes-Cortes, M.
1986 Geologia. In T*lapacoya: 35,000 Años de Historia del Lago de Chalco.* Coordinated by J. L. Lorenzo and L. Mirambell, pp. 57–65. Colección Científica 155. Instituto Nacional de Antropologia e Historia, Mexico City, Mexico.

Ríos, de los, M.
1984 *Informe Sobre los Trabajos de Comparación Estadística Realizado Sobre las Muestras.* INAH-302-A, INAH-302-B INAH-303, INAH-305, INAH-389, INAH-390, INAH-391. Departmento de Prehistoria, INAH (mecanoescrito), Mexico City, Mexico.

Santamaría, D.
1981 Precerámic Occupations at Los Grifos Rock Shelter, Ocozocoautla, Chiapas, México. In X Congreso Unión Internacional de Ciencias Prehistóricas y Protohistóricas. Miscelanea. Mexico City, Mexico.

Willey, G., and P. Phillips
1958 *Methods and Theory in American Archaeology.* The University of Chicago Press, Chicago, Illinois.

Breaking the Impasse on the Peopling of the Americas

Robson Bonnichsen[1]
Alan L. Schneider[2]

Abstract

Until quite recently, the controversy surrounding the initial peopling of the Americas has divided practitioners into two camps based upon their views about the timing of when the Americas were first peopled. In one camp were the proponents of the Clovis-First model, a variant of the Late-Entry model, who have advocated that the Americas were not peopled before 11,500 years ago. By contrast, proponents of the Early-Entry model have argued that the Americas were peopled well before 11,500 years ago. The publication of Dillehay's Monte Verde site report along with other evidence now indicate that the Clovis-First model is incorrect.

We propose that the debate that has occurred over the past 40 years is more complicated than simply a timing issue; it also is a debate about the validity of different models used to explain the peopling of the Americas. In the spirit of advancing this debate, we present a critical assessment of the low-, middle-, and high-range theoretical propositions on which the Clovis-First and Early-Entry models are based. We conclude that future research can focus profitably on pre-11,500-year old sites by drawing on the full range of specialties that modern science has to offer. First Americans specialists can enhance model validity and accuracy by integrating all possible lines of independent evidence. New paleobiological approaches, which emphasize skeletal and genetic studies, appear particularly promising for enhancing our understanding of who peopled the Americas.

Problem Statement

THE INITIAL PEOPLING of the Americas is one of the great unanswered research problems of modern science and one of the most contentious. Even a cursory review of First Americans literature quickly reveals differences on many issues. Much scientific discussion has focused on two contrasting models that seek to explain the initial peopling of the Americas. These can be loosely called the Late-Entry and the Early-Entry models.

Important recent developments in the field have advanced this traditional paradigm conflict. As noted by Bonnichsen and Turnmire (this volume), the recognition of multiple co-traditions as early as Clovis in North America and South America, the documentation of sites that are older than Clovis, and the publication of Dillehay's (1997) Monte Verde site report are all factors that suggest that the Clovis-First model is incorrect (Adovasio and Pedler 1997; Meltzer 1997).

The delegation of specialists, which included representatives from both camps, reviewed the Monte Verde collections and site context (geology, stratigraphy, and chronology). At the end of their January 1997 trip, they reached a consensus that Monte Verde is a bona fide site, and have claimed that the Clovis-First model" is dead (Meltzer 1997).

Our goal is to move beyond the site level of interpretation and offer a critical appraisal of model building procedures used to model the peopling of the Americas. Our discussion focuses on key premises that have been used in the Clovis-First versus Early-Entry debate and suggests some methods for creating more adequate models. Our approach will require a two-step process. The first step entails refining the procedures and logic used to assess data and to

1. Founder and Director, Center for the Study of the First Americans; deceased December 2004. Address inquiries to CSFA Director Michael R. Waters, Department of Anthropology, Texas A&M University, 4352 TAMU, College Station, TX 77843-4352.
2. Attorney, 1437 S.W. Columbia, Suite 200, Portland, OR 97201.

construct models. The second step entails using better and more intensive data recovery techniques to ensure the quantity and reliability of the data available for interpreting First Americans sites and for constructing explanatory models.

Before proceeding further, a term used in the following discussion needs definition. Many specialists use the term "pre-Clovis" to refer to pre-11,500-year-old populations in the Americas. We prefer not to use the term "pre-Clovis," as it implies that there are only two stages of cultural development in the Americas: Clovis and pre-Clovis. However, Clovis does not occur in every region of the New World and clearly is not appropriate as a descriptive term for all of North and South America. Bryan and Gruhn (1989) suggest the use of the term "Lower Paleolithic" in place of pre-Clovis. This term, however, implies that all "pre-11,500"-year-old populations in the Americas shared a common level of technological development. That proposition has yet to be proven. Accordingly, we prefer to use the term "pre-11,500" as a descriptive chronological term that has no technological or cultural implications and the term Early-Entry for models based upon pre-11,500 chronologies.

In the following discussion, we review both the Clovis-First and Early-Entry models using the same criteria to assess how well each currently explains available data on the peopling of the Americas. By necessity, we cannot cover all possible data in this limited presentation. Instead, we will focus on what we regard as some of the most important theoretical issues that have plagued the First Americans debate. Whether one subscribes to a Late-Entry or an Early-Entry position, the common denominator is that all practitioners must engage in scientific model building if they wish to explain the initial peopling of the Americas. Model building entails the use of theory, hypotheses, research designs, procedures, and systematics (definitions of terms, concepts, and procedures) to organize and interpret data. In developing our review of the Clovis-First and Early-Entry models, we ask a series of related questions that we propose each model must address in order to provide an adequate explanation of the peopling of the Americas:

- Is the model based on reliable site data that is clearly of cultural origin?
- Is the model based on reliable cultural affiliation and biological descent models?
- Does the model account for all available data from North America, South America, and Eurasia that is germane to understanding the peopling of the Americas?

Models that seek to explain the initial peopling of the Americas focus on origins—Where did the First Americans come from? Who were they? When did they arrive in the Americas? What routes did they take to get here? How did early peoples adapt to the natural environment? How many times were the Americas peopled?

Development of realistic answers to these questions involves the use of low-, middle-, and high-range theories. In First Americans studies, the development of low-range theory emphasizes finding linkages between processes and patterns, as well as discriminating between cultural and natural processes that sometimes can produce similar results. The next level, middle-range theory, builds from the patterns and behavioral correlates of low-range theory and uses these data to construct cultural models and to develop ideas of human adaptation that involve proposals about the linkages between cultural and the natural environment. High-range theory focuses on an even higher level of abstraction and moves beyond the local and regional scales and seeks to explain global-level patterns by focusing on problems such as the peopling of the Americas. The use of low-, middle-, and high-range theory in constructing models about the peopling of the Americas seldom is discussed in the literature. In the following discussion, we will use these different theoretical perspectives as the foundation for examining the two competing models presently used to explain the peopling of the Americas.

In addition to theoretical concerns, we also shall undertake a brief foray into the fascinating arena of how we construct, use, and sometimes misuse logical propositions in our effort to develop an objective knowledge of the past. Due to space limitations, we address only some of the most important concepts relevant to this topic. Many additional papers would be required to fully explore this area.

With respect to the second step involved in closing the First Americans "gulf" (i.e., use of better and more intensive data recovery techniques), we suggest that archaeology has much to learn from paleobiology and the molecular sciences. New scientific developments are beginning to occur that have the potential to significantly expand the range of evidence available for assessing the past and for developing models about the initial peopling of the Americas. These developments have created the foundation for a new interdisciplinary field of study that can be called molecular archaeology (Brown and Brown 1992). Application of the molecular archaeology approach will allow us to investigate new and previously uncharted aspects of the past.

Until now, excavators of Holocene-and Pleistocene-age sites generally have focused exclusively on the recovery of artifacts and other large-scale materials. This focus on the large-scale has caused excavators to overlook small-scale biological and cultural remains, which in many cases constitute a very significant component of the archaeological record. We submit that this untapped arena of evidence warrants closer attention from First Americans researchers. Very valuable information can be recovered from First Americans sites by use of a multidisciplinary approach that combines: (1) the use of fine-scale techniques to increase the recovery of ancient biological materials; (2) the use of sophisticated techniques of molecular biology to recover ancient DNA from naturally shed human and animal hair and other preserved organic remains; (3) the use of trace element techniques to address dietary and biogenic issues, and (4) the use of AMS ^{14}C radiocarbon techniques to place specimens in temporal perspective (Dillehay 1997).

In setting the stage for our discussion of how a molecular archaeology approach can advance First Americans studies, we begin by providing a general overview of the nature of the First Americans debate and the character and problems associated with each level of theory construction used in the two competing models. Following this background information, we will outline one approach to data recovery based on intensive research activities at the Mammoth Meadow site in southwestern Montana. We will then review the potential and significance of molecular archaeology for extracting new information from naturally shed human and animal hair. We submit that such information has the potential for answering important questions about the initial peopling of the America.

Competing Paradigms

The Clovis-First Model

For decades, the conventional position among most U.S. archaeologists has been that the earliest Americans were the Clovis peoples. They were named after the distinct style of point used to tip their spears that was first identified in 1933 near Clovis, New Mexico. Over time, a number of different versions of the Clovis-First model have been presented in the archaeological literature (Diamond 1987; Haynes 1964; Martin 1967, 1973, 1984, 1987; Mossiman and Martin 1975). According to the Clovis-First model, a small group of human hunters, possibly numbering under 100 individuals, entered the Americas from Siberia at the end of the last Ice Age approximately 11,500–12,500 years ago. Prior to that time, the Cordilleran ice sheet that was centered over the Rocky Mountains and the Laurentide ice sheet centered over Hudson Bay had together covered most of Canada. Their combined effect was to create a barrier to human movement during full glacial times.

At the end of the last Ice Age as glacial recession began to occur, an opening known as the Ice-Free Corridor is thought to have developed between the two great ice sheets. Martin and others postulate that the opening of this corridor led to the first migration into an unsettled continent from the Old World. According to the Clovis-First view, Clovis hunters, who were armed with a new, highly efficient weapon system and deadly hunting strategies, funneled out of the southern end of the Ice-Free Corridor and rapidly spread across what is now the United States and from there to the rest of North and South America.

In one of several alternative simulation scenarios, Mossiman and Martin (1975) propose that human population doubled every 20 years. After only 17 generations or 340 years, at this assumed rate of population increase Clovis people were able to saturate the previously unoccupied landscape of North America. The scenario further proposes that in their wake, the Clovis hunters exterminated up to 33 genera or 70 percent of the available megafauna in North America. The killing spree did not stop in the U.S. In approximately 800 years, these hunters are proposed to have expanded southward into South America and to have eliminated up to 80 percent of the large game in the southern hemisphere before arriving at the southern tip of the continent.

The Clovis-First model has several predictive implications that can be tested against the archaeological record. Some of these implications will be discussed in detail later in connection with middle- and high-range theory.

The Early-Entry Model

LIKE THE CLOVIS-FIRST model, there also is more than one version of the Early-Entry model. In seeking to explain the peopling of the Americas, Bryan (1969, 1973, 1977, 1978, 1980, 1986, 1987, 1988, 1990, 1993) and Gruhn (1988, 1990, 1994) propose an early migration from Northeast Asia in pre-Wisconsinan or Wisconsinan time. One scenario posits that these populations may have moved overland during a glacial period, when sea levels were much lower than today and Asia and America were one continuous landmass. Some investigators, on the other hand, favor the idea that the early colonists were boat-using peoples who moved along the rich coastal ecotones of the Pacific Rim in western North America and then on into South America.

Bryan and Gruhn argue that an initial population of modern humans may have arrived in the Americas 50,000 years ago and perhaps earlier. These people are thought to have adapted to a variety of environmental circumstances, using a simple core-flake tool technology. As population growth and geographical spread of the original group occurred, diversification took place. Adaptations to new environments gave rise to numerous social groups, different economic adaptive patterns, and linguistic groups. This set the stage for parallel cultural developments in North and South America.

It has been suggested that in most places evidence for the original ancestral populations in coastal regions has been drowned by rising sea levels. Indirect evidence in support of this model is suggested by the large number of language isolates and major subdivisions of language phyla along the Pacific Northwest Coast, in California, on the northern Gulf of Mexico Coast, in Central America, and South America. Following the conventional principles of historical linguistics, it is assumed that the development of language diversification is proportional to the time depth of human occupation of an area (Gruhn 1988).

Some of the principal predictive implications of the Early-Entry model are discussed under middle- and high-range theory. We will now consider how these competing models fare when assessed in terms of scientific model building principles.

Review of Models

AN IMPORTANT BASIC question in the task of explaining the peopling of the Americas is how to move from empirical observations of data collected in archaeological contexts to the next level of making statements about past biological populations and human cultures. Modelers who seek to explain the initial peopling of the Americas ultimately must develop and integrate three levels of theory: low-, middle-, and high-range theories. See Fiebleman (1954) for a detailed discussion of the theory of integrative levels.

At each level, the researcher is involved in a process of assessing various possibilities and searching for clues to separate probabilities from other possibilities. While we would like to search for absolutes, the fact is we must recognize that there is little, if anything, in archaeology that can be known with an absolute degree of certainty. Even such simple facts as the provenance of a discovery must be taken with some degree of faith, since the excavator's reports may be misleading or mistaken. The result is that when we are dealing with First American topics, we do not deal with absolutes, but with probabilities and possibilities.

As a result, the question that modelers must address is how to construct the most solid and reliable case that explains the available data. In most situations, this is accomplished by the use of independent lines of evidence. An independent line of evidence is data that stands on its own merits and can be assessed in respect to its own properties. For example, a series of multiple overlapping flake scars of approximately the same size on a stone object would signify that a series of repetitive events occurred to the specimen in question. This redundancy of patterning would be suggestive of purposeful human modification. By the same token, use wear analysis may reveal that the edge of an object exhibits microflaking, striae, and polish. Use wear data would, in this case, constitute a second independent line of evidence that would support the inference that the specimen is a human artifact. If blood residue also is found on the surface of the object, the blood would provide yet another independent line of evidence that would support the inference that the specimen is an artifact. Thus, the more independent lines of evidence that can be brought to bear in demonstrating a particular proposition, the greater the increase in the probability of the inferred conclusions.

When assessing the strength or reliability of an archaeological inference, it is important to keep in mind that probabilities are never refuted or disproved by a simple possibility. A probability is refuted or disproved only by a greater probability. For example, if the principal investigator of a site determines that an object probably is a human artifact based upon reliable objective criteria, the status of the artifact does not change because someone else raises the possibility that it may have been created by a natural event (e.g., tumbling down a hillside, trampling by animals, etc.). The possibilities of tumbling or trampling are nothing more than interesting conjectures. They "prove" nothing until something happens to elevate one of them to a probability. By the same token, simple possibilities do not refute or cancel one another. They merely pose different alternatives, any one of which may be true (Meltzer et al. 1994). The only way to determine which one is true (or whether either is true) is to obtain enough additional evidence to determine whether one of them (or some other explanation) is a probability.

The above considerations have an important bearing on how archaeological explanations are constructed and refuted. It is not the obligation of an explanation's proponent to refute all possibilities in advance. Such a task is impossible since all explanations, whether probabilities or simple possibilities, contain some possibility of being untrue. The obligation of the proponent is to account for those possibilities that have any reasonable chance of having played a role in the condition of an object being investigated. If that has been done, the burden of disproof falls on those who disagree with the explanation. Their burden is not carried or discharged by merely raising arguments based upon simple possibilities. Instead they must gather sufficient evidence to establish that either: (a) there is another explanation that is probably true; or (b) the original explanation is only a possibility and not a probability. Whether this can be done by citing published data or whether it will require new research depends upon the circumstances involved.

These principles apply regardless of the level of inference involved. Whether they are working at the low-, middle-, or high-range levels of model building, researchers must test each inference or explanation in terms of how possible or probable it is. As noted above, independent lines of evidence can be used to increase the probability of an inference. But each line of evidence must be assessed separately to determine its relative reliability. Likewise, when multiple lines of evidence are combined to support an inference, the resulting combination must be separately assessed to determine whether it is a probability or only a possibility. With these principals in mind, a detailed consideration will now be given to what is involved in low-, middle-, and high-range theory construction.

Low-Range Theory: Is the model based on reliable site data that is clearly of cultural origin?

At the lowest level, model builders must deal with site level information in constructing low-range theory. Low-range theory focuses on the linkage between pattern and process. It deals with defining various signature characteristics that can be used to distinguish cultural from natural processes. It also deals with defining signature characteristics that can be used to distinguish between different kinds of cultural processes. These first-order inferences are critical since they provide the structure from which middle- and high-range theory is constructed. For example, the patterns and processes defined by low-range theory are used to isolate human groups in time and space, infer mobility patterns, trace human dispersion, infer adaptive strategies, study the dynamics of cultural change, and trace phylogentic relationships among human groups through time.

Since they provide the foundation for all higher level inferences, the quality (i.e., accuracy and reliability) of first-order inferences is paramount. At the most basic level, researchers must be able to deal with the "ambiguity" of the archaeological record to determine what is relevant and what is not. Among other things, they must be able to demonstrate that the phenomenon that is being reported has a "cultural" and not a "natural" origin. At each "turn of the trowel," researchers must consider whether the observed phenomena (e.g., proposed artifacts, features, charcoal, etc.) were produced or caused by a cultural or natural process. Is the specimen an artifact or a geofact? Are the aligned rocks a product of human behavior or did they come to rest in their present position following a flash flood, a roof fall, or some other natural phenomena? Was the charcoal produced by a natural forest fire or is it from a human hearth that was scattered by subsequent events?

These are not easy issues. To make the determinations required for low-range inferences, First Americans specialists are compelled to become as conversant with "natural" phenomena as they are with "cultural" phenomena. This requires that they develop multidisciplinary expertise in the natural and social sciences that will allow them to develop objective research designs, methods, and criteria for discriminating between natural and cultural phenomena. They also must address the questions of what constitutes acceptable evidence for the presence of humans and what constitutes acceptable standards for assessing evidence.

So far, neither the Clovis-First nor the Early-Entry models have dealt all that well with low-range theoretical issues. Both have focused largely on dating questions (i.e., on the development of chronologies to place sites in temporal perspectives). As a result, there has been a tendency to overlook the development of other issues that require attention. With these considerations in mind, it is constructive to consider how low-range theory has been used to develop explanations for the peopling of the Americas. The question of whether or not data from Clovis sites are reliable is seldom considered. For example, researchers seldom question whether Clovis points, bifaces, bone rods, blades, and other implements commonly cited as the Clovis tool kit are of human origin rather than natural origin. In most cases, it is clear that they are cultural in origin. Likewise, the dates of most Clovis sites appear to be reasonably secure (within the limitations of current dating techniques).

The description of Clovis artifacts, however, has been uneven and usually focuses exclusively on artifact form. Other potential lines of investigation that would enhance interpretation of Clovis assemblages, such as materials, technology, and use wear analyses, are seldom conducted. As will be seen in the following sections, this has resulted in an inadequate database for the construction of middle- and high-range theories.

This has been particularly true for the Early-Entry model. Most proposed pre-11,500-year-old sites have failed to gain acceptance in the community due to questions relating to:

- whether the proposed artifacts are of human or natural origin; and
- whether the proposed dates are reliable.

In some cases, the objections raised against particular early sites are patently unfair and unscientific. A classic example is the practice of making attacks on the professional competence of a site investigator who is clearly well trained and highly qualified. Such attacks do nothing to advance scientific inquiry.

At the same time, however, Early-Entry proponents must bear some responsibility for the treatment they have received in the critical literature. It is an inescapable fact that very early sites and artifacts are likely to be more "ambiguous" than Clovis-aged sites and artifacts. Simple flake tools, for example, are not as clearly human in origin as finely crafted Clovis points. As a result, Early-Entry investigators are faced with the need to take extra measures to demonstrate that artifact identifications and dating associations are reliable and in order. When these efforts are not made, the investigator's conclusions are seen as speculative (i.e., as mere possibilities) and the site is discounted as another interesting but inconclusive incident. This need not be the result. Depending on the circumstances, there may be analytical techniques that can be used to dispel or at least reduce doubts.

The problems of dealing with "ambiguity" are not unique to First Americans studies. Over the past 20 years, taphonomists have made considerable progress in developing methodologies for sorting out "ambiguity problems" encountered in the fossil and archaeological records (Bonnichsen and Sorg 1989). To label a situation "ambiguous" implies only that two or more possibilities have the potential to explain the observed phenomena. In many cases, these possibilities can be sorted out by analyzing the patterns that survived through time. To explain patterning observed in the fossil and archaeological record, researchers use the characteristics of the patterns themselves to make inferences about the processes or casual mechanisms that produced the observed patterns. However, since the processes that produced the observed patterns no longer can be witnessed, the question arises as to how reliable inferences can be made for linking patterns and processes in the past.

Taphonomists (Bonnichsen and Sorg 1989, eds.; Lyman 1994) have made considerable progress in developing a robust methodology for resolving these low-range inference questions. They have responded to the ambiguity issue by developing modern analogs that serve as a comparative framework for interpreting the fossil or archaeological record. Two approaches commonly are used to create modern analogs. These are the actualistic and experimental approaches. For example, if we are attempting to determine whether flaked bones from the fossil record were modified by humans or carnivores, it is possible to develop modern analogs to assist with making our assessment. An "actualistic" study might seek to link modern-day processes to observed patterns by observing how carnivores gnaw bones and to link gnawing behavior to gnaw marks observed on the bone. By contrast, an experimental study might be used to simulate conditions that no longer can be observed. Since we no longer can observe how mammoth bones were flaked by living peoples, modern elephant bone might be substituted. A modern-day bone knapper, using elephant bone in place of mammoth bone, might produce bone flakes and cores in an effort to simulate patterns observed on Pleistocene-age specimens.

The results of actualistic and experimental studies can serve as a comparative framework for addressing ambiguity issues encountered in the analysis of remains from archaeological sites. By comparing the morphological patterns produced by carnivores and modern bone knappers, signature characteristics can be identified for discriminating between carnivore gnawing and human modification produced by bone knapping. These signature characteristics in turn can be used as criteria for interpreting ambiguous patterns found in the archaeological record. Through techniques of this kind, it is possible to decode many ambiguities found in the fossil and archaeological record. Use of modern analogs for defining signature characteristics also can be applied to the analysis of lithic tools. In this way, it is often possible to demonstrate with a high degree of reliability whether a given object (or assemblage of objects) was created by human or natural means.

In summary, fundamental epistemological problems exist in how we know what we know about the past. We propose that there are logical standards, such as provided in the examples above, that can be used to assess the possibilities and probabilities employed in the construction of models that seek to explain the peopling of the Americas. This is particularly important for low-range theory where the investigator provides a linkage between an empirical morphological pattern and an inferred process. However, the need for logical standards for linking process to pattern is not limited to low-range theory. It also occurs in middle- and high-range theory construction, as we shall see in the following discussions.

Middle-Range Theory: Is the model based on reliable cultural affiliation or biological descent models?

The second level often is called "middle-range" theory. Middle-range theory seeks to define the operational dynamics of cultural, biological, linguistic, and natural systems and the linkages among subsystems. It also seeks to explain the rise and demise of patterns observed in the archaeological record and to posit explanations of how observed changes have occurred through time.

Modelers who seek to develop middle-range theory are required to integrate multidisciplinary information including cultural and environmental data relating to individual sites and specific human populations into local and regional patterns. To be accepted, a middle-range model must be able to withstand the following kinds of questions: How did the investigator move from low-range theory based on artifacts, features, and human biological remains to making statements about human cultures and biological populations? Is the model based on a reliable low-range theory? Does the model accommodate all changes over time that are observed in the archaeological record? How reliable or probable is the model?

Among the many different areas of middle-range theory, three are particularly germane to First Americans studies. These are: (1) biological theories that seek to characterize human populations on the basis of biological data, i.e., blood groups, bones, and DNA; (2) cultural affiliation theories that seek to identify and track through time human cultures by the use of features, projectile points, and other artifactual remains; and (3) theories that posit a relationship between culture and environment, i.e., environmental forcing (Bonnichsen et al. 1987; Bonnichsen 1991). The following discussion is restricted to cultural and biological theories, as few efforts have been made to relate First Americans sites to local, regional, and global-scale environmental patterns.

In the following discussion, we use the term "cultural affiliation" to denote theoretical constructs that seek to link empirical archaeological data with socio-cultural concepts in an attempt to define "ethnic or cultural groups" and to define descent models. The construction of cultural affiliation models for Pleistocene and early Holocene peoples are troubled by numerous potential problems. The fact that cultural remains are far and away more numerous than biological evidence in archaeological sites does not automatically translate into ease of model building. Artifacts seldom supply unambiguous evidence to place specific prehistoric peoples in time and to link them to the artifacts they left in the archaeological record.

Unlike Europe, Asia, and the Middle East, prehistory in the New World is not blessed with early written records, an extensive pottery tradition, and distinctive permanent architectural structures. As a result, First Americans researchers have had to rely primarily upon stone tools (in most cases projectile points) and faunal remains in constructing cultural affiliation models. This is comparable to trying to reconstruct modern cultures from the sizes and shapes of the bullets used in hunting rifles and the steak bones left after a meal. Although models based on artifact forms are useful for characterizing artifact assemblages, they seldom provide a reliable method for identifying ethnic or cultural groups, for distinguishing one group from another, or for tracing groups across space and through time. It often is difficult to determine whether similarities and differences in artifact forms are due to ethnic and cultural factors or whether they are attributable to other factors such as differences in raw materials, functional constraints, or something else.

In addition, cultural affiliation models that are based on artifact forms without other lines of supporting data often are inadequate for explaining cultural change. Obviously, prehistoric people could and did change their tools as new situations arose. A focus exclusively on artifact forms does not provide an adequate framework for explaining why the artifacts found in one assemblage of specimens are different from those found in another level or at another site. Alternative competing hypotheses can be advanced to explain observed differences, e.g., migration, diffusion, or in situ development. It is difficult to discriminate between these hypotheses, and artifact form data alone cannot solve the dilemma. These problems can be overcome in part by using a holistic approach to artifact analyses that entails using multiple, independent lines of evidence, i.e., material, shape, technology, use wear, and blood-residue analyses. To date, however, few First Americans researchers, whether of the Clovis-First or the Early-Entry camps, have pursued such an approach on a long-term consistent basis. As a result, the cultural affiliation models that have been proposed have been unable to convincingly establish the cultural or ethnic composition of the populations that created the early archaeological record.

In recent years, some scientists have tried to address First Americans descent issues through the study of human skeletal remains. These approaches include the use of biometrics (Hall 1997; Jantz and Owsley 1997; Steele and Powell 1992, 1994) and discrete cranial and dental traits (Ossenberg 1994; Turner 1994). The combination of standardized measurement approaches, computer databases, and use of multivariant statistics has led to the development of robust scientific approaches for the study of ancient human remains. These new paleobiology methods hold great promise for defining racial and ethnic groups and for tracking colonizing groups across space and time. However, more work on these avenues of research is needed.

Other types of biological descent models have been advocated using mitochondrial DNA to look at genetic distances among American Native populations (Szathmary 1994a, 1994b; Torroni et al. 1993; Ward et al.1993). These models assume that genetic distances are strictly a function of time. In other words, populations with the greatest distance between them (i.e., the greatest DNA differences) are assumed to have separated earlier in time than did populations with smaller genetic distances. By assuming that human genetic change occurs at a standard rate among all human populations over all time periods, these modelers develop calculations of how many years have passed since two or more groups separated from one another. Although these models have provided some useful insights, they suffer from circular reasoning: rates of change are calculated from estimated times of divergence; these rates of change then are used to calculate divergence times between, for example, Asian and Native American populations.

Another important limitation on the present generation of biological descent models is what can be called the "modern analog issue." The raw data for these descent models are taken from modern populations. These are assumed to be representative of earlier populations. That assumption, however, may not be true. Its reliability can be determined only by examining ancient human DNA (Paabo 1993). So far, we are aware of only two published studies that have been done on human tissue from Paleoamerican remains. Paabo et al. (1988) from the University of Germany, Munich, has reported on 7,000-year-old brain tissues (6860 ± 110 [Beta 17208]) from the Little Salt Spring site in Florida. Ray Mathaney (personal communication 1994) and colleagues at Brigham Young University are working on mummified tissue from the 10,600-year-old Acha-2 site from Arica, northern Chile. In both cases, DNA extracted from these Paleoamerican remains does not match any of the modern analogues proposed by the Clovis-First three-wave colonization model. It thus appears that analyses of modern DNA alone cannot provide the full story of how the Americas were peopled—ancient DNA also is needed for constructing reliable biological descent models.

Some advocates of the Clovis-first position and the Early-Entry positions also have looked to linguistic data to support their models (see Gruhn 1997 for recent summary). For example, some Clovis-First proponents have argued that linguistic data demonstrate that the peoples of the Americas descended from three late Ice-Age immigrant populations: Eskimos, Na-Dene (Athabascans), and Amerindian (all groups south of the Wisconsin ice sheet) (Greenberg et al. 1986). However, even if one accepts the proposition that there were three late Ice-Age migrations, this does not rule out the possibility that human populations could have existed at earlier times in the Americas. Human groups generally do not have closed genetic systems—they maintain their viability through exogamous marriage (marrying outside of their own group). Such marriage practices could have led to the eventual disappearance of earlier New World populations. In addition, it is possible that some (or many) earlier populations may have become extinct due to environmental stress, diseases, conflict, or other factors. At present, the available data are insufficient to determine which, if any, of these alternatives is true.

Although Clovis-First and Early-Entry modelers have proposed that the great diversity among Native American cultures, languages, and biological populations is a function of time depth, there is no agreement on how to interpret the observed variability in temporal terms. We know very little about the actual rates of change in linguistic and genetic systems through time. Some modelers propose that rates of change are constant through time in all cultural and biological systems. While constant rates of change arguments might be true, this has not been demonstrated. Accordingly, propositions of this nature must be viewed as mere possibilities. At present, these possibilities have not been verified by use of independent lines of supporting evidence. Without the independent yardstick of time provided by the archaeological record, stratigraphy, or ^{14}C record, there is no way to correctly interpret diversity and rates of change propositions. Other possibilities exist, e.g., that rates of change are not constant through time and that rates of change may vary from group to group. It is possible that factors such as climate, environment, culture, and population growth rates may affect rates of change. Until rates of change have been independently calibrated, we suggest that descent models based on rates of change should be regarded as interesting but speculative.

In summary, the construction of middle-range theory has been hampered by limited data and the use of assumptions. Furthermore, cultural and biological descent models have been constructed by different groups of practitioners, and these two types of models remain poorly integrated. A desirable development would be an effort to integrate cultural and biological descent theories into unified local and regional models. As will be discussed later, achievement of this middle-range theory goal is potentially possible through the study of ancient hair found in archaeological contexts.

High-range Theory: Does the model account for all of the available data from North America, South America, and Eurasia that is germane to understanding the peopling of the Americas?

The third level is high-range theory. The patterns and proposed operational dynamics of middle-range research provide the data for developing multi-regional and global-scale models. These seek to explain large-scale questions such as the peopling of the Americas by defining large-scale patterns and processes. High-range theories integrate and link site, local, regional, and multi-regional patterns and their interpretations into global-scale models (Bryan 1978, 1986; Martin 1973). In evaluating high-range models that seek to explain the peopling of the Americas, we must ask whether the model accommodates "all relevant data" from North America, South America, and Eurasia. Ultimately, high-level theoretical abstractions about the peopling of the Americas rest on low- and middle-range theories. In other words, high-range theories about the peopling of the Americas are no better than the quality of information on which they are based. With these considerations in mind, we will now consider how high-range theory has been used in the construction of the Clovis-First and Early-Entry models.

The Clovis-First Model

PREDICTIVE IMPLICATIONS of the Clovis-First model are that:

(1) *Evidence of the Clovis founding populations should be found in Siberia.* To date, however, no evidence of fluted points or other elements of the "Clovis tool kit" has ever been found in Siberia. King and Slobodin (1996:634) report a possible 8500 yr B.P. fluted point from the Uptar site in the Magadan Basin. Upon close examination, the size, technology, and age of this specimen is a poor match with North American fluted points. The late Upper Paleolithic record from Northeast Asia is dominated by the Dyuktai tradition, which is typified by the use of microblades, microcores, use of composite tools, and bipointed bifaces (Goebel, this volume; Mochanov 1978a, 1978b; Mochanov and Fedoseeva 1996). The Dyuktai tradition appears to be closely related and ancestral to the Paleo-Arctic tradition of Alaska. If there is a relationship between Clovis and the Paleo-Arctic tradition, it remains elusive. As a result, one is forced to the conclusion that so far there is a total absence of convincing evidence that

can be used to support the proposition that Clovis originated in Siberia or with populations newly arrived from Siberia.

(2) *The overkill model hypothesis assumes that human population growth is linked to the use of a new and more efficient killing technology that rapidly spread throughout the Americas.* If this is true, the Clovis tool kit should occur as an archaeological horizon throughout North America and South America. In addition, fluted point sites should be older in northernmost North America and younger by as much as 800 to 1,000 years in southern South America.

The premise that there is a direct linkage between the introduction of the Clovis tool kit and the development of rapid population growth and expansion has never been tested. It is very difficult to demonstrate human population growth in the absence of human skeletal remains by using only archaeological data. Presumably Clovis hunters would have produced a variety of sites throughout the year. If these sites still exist, most will be buried and are no longer accessible for archaeological research. Until we devise definitive ways to link numbers of artifacts and settlement patterns to specific human-population growth patterns, little support for the rapid population growth possibility will be found through the analysis of archaeological data. Furthermore, even if a number of Clovis sites can be found in a given region, the resolution of radiocarbon dating is not fine enough to link sites to specific generations.

Likewise, the current radiocarbon record from North and South American fluted point sites do not support the predictions of the model. Since the formulation of the Clovis-First model more than 40 years ago, a great deal of additional archaeological research has been done on fluted point sites in North and South America (Bonnichsen and Turnmire 1991). There are no well-dated fluted point sites from eastern Beringia (Clark 1991) or from the Ice-Free Corridor (Carlson 1991). On the other hand, Politis (1991:Table 1) documents dates of greater than 11,000 yr B.P. for Fell's Cave and Cueva del Medio. This suggests that the emergence of fishtail points at the southern tip of the Southern Hemisphere overlaps the appearance of fluted points in North America. More dates are needed on fluted point assemblages from the Southern Hemisphere. Nonetheless, the pattern now emerging suggests that fluted points from the Southern Hemisphere are approximately the same age as fluted points in North America.

(3) *The Clovis cultural complex represents a single human culture with shared value systems.* If this is so, it would follow that tool assemblages, artifact forms, and manufacturing techniques should be homogenous and exhibit little variability from site to site and from region to region.

Clovis-First advocates argue that the sudden widespread appearance of Clovis represents the spread of a single human culture across North and South America. This position appears to rest in part on the assumption that human culture is normative. The normative approach views cultures as an integrated system in which all of the parts are functionally integrated. The normative conception of human culture envisions that each generation replicates the previous one. Thus, the normative approach has difficulty in accounting for culture change (Young and Bonnichsen 1984).

Furthermore, when we examine the archaeological correlate of the single-culture theory, it calls for a consistent set of archaeological traits that should be found across North and South America. Haynes (1987) has proposed the most succinct statement of the Clovis culture concept with its archaeological correlates (which he believes originated in America rather than Siberia). He posits a list of tool types that are said to form a tool kit that can be used to characterize the Clovis culture. Diagnostic artifacts include blades, end scrapers, burins, shaft wrenches, cylindrical bone points, knapped bone, unifacial flake tools, red ocher, and circumferentially chopped tusks (Haynes 1980). It should be noted, however, that no single site has produced all the artifact types included in the list. In fact, most Clovis cultural-affiliation models usually are constructed based on the occurrence of only one type of artifact—the fluted point.

As noted above, the normative approach on which the Clovis-First model is based does not easily accommodate change. Some specialists, nonetheless, feel that there is a "basal Clovis pattern," and from this pattern evolved regional variants (Willig 1991). A recent overview of the Clovis complex indicates there are a number of regional fluted point variants (Bonnichsen 1991:320). The principal variants are: (1) an Arctic style represented by the Putu variant; (2) the small Peace River variant from the Ice-Free Corridor region; (3) the Colby variant, known only from the Colby site, Wyoming; (4) the Gainey, Parkhill, and Crowfield variants from the Great Lake Regions; (5) the Debert variant from Nova Scotia; (6) small basally thinned points that are distributed from New Jersey to New Brunswick; (7) Cumberland points; (8) fishtail points from Panama and South America; and (9) the El Inga series of points from highland Ecuador that includes stemmed fluted points. There is no evidence to support the view that all these variants evolved from a basal Clovis pattern. Some workers favor the interpretation that Clovis actually represents the diffusion of a highly successful adaptive strategy across existing populations. (See Bonnichsen et al. 1987, 1991:23 for a discussion of the environmental-response model).

(4) *Clovis is the first culture in the Americas.* This is the key premise of the Clovis-First model and the cause of all the controversy that has characterized First Americans studies. It is the kind of proposition that can not be proven directly since it is based on a negative, i.e., that there are no contemporaneous or older New World cultures. It can, however, be tested by the archaeological record to see whether it can be disproved. This can be done in two ways: (1) by finding archaeological evidence of other human cultures that are as old as Clovis; and (2) by identifying archaeological sites that are older than Clovis.

Evidence is now accumulating that suggests there are several different bifacially flaked projectile-point patterns of Clovis age or older. The most important of these include lanceolate points of the Nenana complex (11,300 yr B.P.) in central Alaska (Goebel et al. 1991); the Goshen complex of the Northwestern Plains (with dates clustering at 11,300 and 10,800 yr B.P.) (Frison 1991); the Western Stemmed Point tradition (11,500–10,000 yr B.P.) of the Great Basin (Bryan 1988, 1990:53); the El Jobo point tradition (13,000 yr B.P.) in northern Venezuela (Gruhn and Bryan 1984; Ochsenius and Gruhn 1979); and the Magellaic "fishtail" point tradition (11,000–10,000 yr B.P.) in southern South America (Bird 1938; Bryan 1973; Politis 1991; Rouse 1976). The synchronous timing and sudden appearance of new lithic technologies and tool complexes across a number of different regions can be seen as support for the interpretation that a widespread reorganization in the adaptive systems of pre-existing New World populations occurred during an unprecedented period of rapid environmental change at the end of the last Ice Age. If this is true, then Clovis is not the earliest New World culture. At best, it is merely one of a number of early cultures, and may in fact be one of the later cultures.

Since the Clovis-First model was advanced in the 1960s, many potential pre-11,500-year-old sites have been investigated . Some of the most important sites include: Blue Fish Caves, Yukon Territory (24,000 yr B.P) (Cinq-Mars and Morlan, this volume; Morlan and Cinq-Mars 1989); Meadowcroft Rockshelter, Pennsylvania (14,000--15,000 yr B.P.) (Adovasio et al. 1990; Adovasio et al., this volume; Lepper, this volume); Burnham site, Oklahoma (25,000 yr B.P.) (Wyckoff, this volume; Wyckoff and Carter 1994;); Pendejo Cave, New Mexico (<55,000 yr B.P.) (MacNeish 1992, 1996); Tamia-tamia, Venezuela (13,000 yr B.P.) (Ochsenius and Gruhn 1979); Pedra Furada, Brazil (<45,000 yr B.P.) (Guidon and Arnaud 1991; Guidon and Delibras 1986; also, Pessis 1993); and Monte Verde, Chile (13,000 and 31,000 yr B.P.) (Dillehay 1989, 1997; Dillehay et al. 1992; Dillehay and Collins 1991). There are several other South American sites said to pre-date the pre-11,500-year-old watershed. See Lynch (1990), Gruhn and Bryan (1991), and Dillehay and Collins (1991) for discussions of the debate surrounding these sites. As noted earlier, these sites generally have failed to gain wide acceptance in the archaeological community due to artifact and/or dating questions. Now that Dillehay (1997) and his co-workers have demonstrated to critics that Monte Verde is earlier than 11,500 years old, perhaps a new and more friendly climate can be established for reviewing early New World sites (cf. Bonnichsen and Turnmire, this volume).

In summary, current archaeological data do not appear to support the key propositions of the Clovis-First model. No reliable evidence for the "Clovis culture" has been found in Northeast Asia, its putative homeland according to many proponents of the model. In addition, the radiocarbon ages of Clovis complex sites do not support the proposition that there was a north-to-south movement. Although radiocarbon-dated sites in South America are not numerous, the available dates do suggest that the appearance of fluted points in North and South America is synchronous in both hemispheres. The timing of dates from fluted point sites has led some researchers to conclude that the Clovis-style point actually developed in the United States, possibly in the Southeast. In addition, support for the notion that there was a basal Clovis culture is inconclusive as there is no clear consensus on the essential elements of such a basal culture. On the other hand, there is considerable evidence for numerous regional styles or variants of fluted points. However, the data for these regional variants are difficult to interpret, as many of the regional patterns are poorly dated. It is possible that they represent the diffusion of a new technology across existing populations during a period of rapid environmental change. Furthermore, there is considerable evidence that suggests the presence of multiple New World co-traditions as old as Clovis. Finally, not all of the "pre-11,500" sites that have been investigated over the past several decades can be dismissed as easily as their detractors would suggest. The completion of the Monte Verde site report that finally has been accepted by critics is a case in point. All of these considerations indicate that the Clovis-First model must be considered a possibility, but not a probability. It would seem that there is room for competing models that take into account available dates from fluted points sites and that explain the rise and demise of the Clovis complex and its many regional variants.

The Early-Entry Model

IN CONTRAST TO the Clovis-First position, other specialists propose that the Americas were occupied well before 11,500 years ago by peoples from Asia. The important predictive implications of this Early-Entry model are:

(1) *Early human sites should be found in Northeast Asia with simple core and flake tool industries.* Many students of prehistory have proposed that only modern humans (*Homo sapiens sapiens*) could have penetrated the far north, and this could not have happened until about 40,000 years ago. They reason that fire, shelter, and tailored skin clothing would be required to survive winters in the far north (Fagan 1987). In the past, these considerations have been seen as a major obstacle to acceptance of the Early-Entry model. However, recent research in Northeast Asia is beginning to indicate that the archaeological record is not quite as clear cut as it was assumed to be (see Bonnichsen and Turnmire, this volume).

Archaeological research is still at an embryonic stage of development in Northeast Asia. Simple flake and core industries are associated with late Pleistocene archaeological deposits (see Goebel, this volume) as well as Lower and Middle Paleolithic sites reviewed here.

Along the north Pacific Rim, a series of more than 40 Middle Paleolithic sites have been uncovered in the Babadan area, along the northeastern coast of Honshu Island, Japan. These sites are reported to range in age from 150,000 to more than 200,000 years and have yielded simple core and flake tools (Akazawa, this volume; Hiroshi et al. 1990; Masahito and Hiroyuki 1990; Yoshizaki and Iwasaki 1986). The Babadan archaeological record, as well as numerous Upper Paleolithic sites in Japan, suggest the presence of humans along the north Pacific Rim for at least the last 200,000 years. Thus, these data fit the predictive implication of the Early-Entry model and leave open the possibility that humans could have come from Asia to the Americas by middle Pleistocene times.

Also of interest is research occurring in north-central Siberia. Nikolay Drozdov and colleagues (Chlachula et al. 1994) have located a series of sites in the Krasnoyarsk Sea area in the vicinity of Kurtak, south of Krasnoyarsk on the Yenisei River. These sites, located at 55 degrees north latitude, span the last full-glacial cycle. Additionally, other sites have been reported along the Yenisei that are said to contain cobble tools that appear to be of middle Pleistocene age.

Mochanov's (1993) work at the Diring Yuriakh site, located at 61 degrees north latitude on the Lena River, potentially is of great importance (Ackerman and Carlson 1991). Mochanov's massive excavation of more than 26,000 square meters has exposed 30 clusters (or activity areas) of quartz and quartzite cobble cores, unifacial flake tools, hammerstones, and anvil stones over the past decade. Until recently, the age of this potentially significant site has been problematic and a source of some contention (Kuzmin and Krivonogov 1994). However, Michael Waters (personal communication 1994; Waters et al. 1997) and Steve Foreman at Ohio State University recently have used the thermoluminescence method to date level 5, which lies directly above the cultural-bearing strata. A series of 10 consistent dates indicate that the age of the Diring Yuriakh occupation is greater than 250,000 yr B.P. and less than 320,000 years old. Such dates would support the view that an archaic form of *Homo sapiens* or possibly *Homo erectus* had the ability to penetrate the subarctic (61° N latitude) much earlier than has been anticipated.

The above discoveries imply that by middle Pleistocene times, early *Homo sp.* had a cold-climate adaptive repertoire (i.e., fire, clothing, shelter, and ability to deal with frozen food) needed to allow viable populations to survive under the inhospitable conditions of Northeast Asia. These considerations suggest that cold adaptation to subarctic conditions no longer should be considered as a factor limiting human movement into the New World during middle and late Pleistocene time.

(2) *Early populations had a generalized economy and could easily adapt to a variety of local circumstances;*

they were not specialized big-game hunters. Evidence has yet to be advanced by Early-Entry modelers to support this proposition. Unfortunately, the tenuous nature of archaeological evidence reported from pre-11,500-year-old sites sheds little light on the economies and adaptive patterns of their inhabitants. The Monte Verde site in southern Chile is a rare exception. Unusual preservation circumstances have allowed house, plant, and animal remains to be recovered (Dillehay 1989, 1997). Other sites will be needed with well-preserved evidence before reliable generalizations can be developed about prehistoric economies. And those data have yet to be discovered.

Any attempt to build such generalizations should consider whether the use of a simple flake and core tool kit is unambiguous evidence that early populations had a general economy and were not big game hunters. In contrast to the hypothesis that pre-11,500-year-old populations had a generalized economy, an alternative possibility is that early populations had a generalized tool kit. This tool kit could have been used in the development of numerous specialized adaptive patterns in different environmental contexts, including big game hunting. It is possible that these early flaked stone-tool assemblages may have had a function similar to a carpenter's tool kit and may have been used for cutting, scraping, sawing, chopping, planing, and polishing of nonlithic materials such as wood, bone, and antler. Such materials in turn could have been converted into composite artifacts such as traps and spears for taking large game animals.

At present, too little is known about pre-11,500-year-old subsistence and economic patterns in most Pacific Rim areas to form any reliable generalized conclusions about this proposed stage of cultural development. Detailed analysis of artifacts from early sites using lithic technology, use wear, blood residue, and molecular archaeology methods could help determine how artifacts were used. In addition to the artifactual information, other lines of evidence such as fauna and plant remains would be helpful in developing an empirically based knowledge of the economic and subsistence patterns of the pre-11,500-year-old populations that are said to have inhabited the Americas.

(3) *Some of the earliest evidence of First Americans should be found along the coastal fringes of the Americas.* This postulate is based on the assumption that early colonizers coming to the Americas from Northeast Asia used boats. Possible support for this premise is provided by evidence from Japan that suggests boat use occurred in the North Pacific by at least 30,000 years ago. The presence of boats has been inferred from the occurrence of obsidian that has been found in a series of Upper Paleolithic sites from the Tokyo region (Oda 1990). Using trace element analysis, the original source for the obsidian has been traced to Kozushima Island, located about 170 km south of Tokyo. The island was always separated by open sea from the eastern shore of Honshu Island, even during the last glacial maximum when sea level was as much as 120 meters lower than today. Boats would have been necessary to move obsidian from the island to the mainland. These data suggest that Upper Paleolithic populations in Japan had the technology and ability to navigate in coastal environments. These data can be seen as indirect support for the hypothesis that the Americas could have been colonized by boat-using peoples.

Definitive archaeological data from the West Coast of North America to support the coastal-entry hypothesis has yet to be found. This, however, is not surprising, as much of the West Coast has been submerged by a rise in sea level that occurred at the end of the Pleistocene. Potential early sites have been reported from raised coastlines in southern California (Berger 1982; Reeves et al. 1986), although archaeological evidence from these localities has yet to win widespread acceptance from the archaeological community (Erlandson and Moss 1996). Other sites may be found in raised coastal environments that could provide support for the early coastal-entry hypothesis.

To summarize, some of the predictive implications of the Early-Entry model are beginning to find support in the archaeological record. An increasing amount of archaeological data from Northeast Asia supports the proposition that this region of the world was occupied by middle Pleistocene times or earlier. New evidence from Japan indicates that boat use was known in the North Pacific by about 30,000 years ago and perhaps earlier. However, archaeological data have yet to be reported from the West Coast of North America that can be used to support the proposition that early New World migrants used water craft in their movement from Northeast Asia. Likewise, the proposition that New World populations prior to 11,500 years ago followed a generalized hunting and foraging strategy has not yet been demonstrated convincingly by archaeological data. Most specialists believe these early hunters were highly mobile. Yet, the new data from Monte Verde suggest seasonal if not year-round communal village occupation.

Simple core and flake tools possibly representing a tool kit of Lower Paleolithic character have been reported from a number of potential pre-11,500-year-old sites in North and South America. It is difficult to make sound inference about social organization, mobility, and economic analysis only by working with stone tool data. The main obstacle, however, to general acceptance of the Early-Entry model continues to be questions over dating and whether the artifacts reported from many sites are human or natural in origin. These questions cannot be overcome without more careful descriptive and analytical studies of pre-11,500-year-old sites and materials.

A New Approach to Data Recovery

IT SHOULD BE APPARENT from the foregoing discussion that the debate between the Clovis-First and Early-Entry advocates cannot be fully resolved on the basis of current archaeological evidence. New archaeological data are needed. This means not only new sites to investigate, but also development of new techniques of data recovery. More data of the same nature already known from past archaeological projects is not likely to accomplish much except to create more disputes. What is needed are new lines of data that can place sites in a securely dated context.

The database for First Americans studies will never be as abundant as those periods of prehistory that were more settled and densely populated. Well-preserved early sites are not common in the archaeological record. In addition, those sites that are preserved tend to represent short-term, limited-use occupations that produce an extremely restricted range of artifactual materials. Well-developed residential sites with significant architectural features such as Monte Verde are a rarity. In most cases, the surviving artifacts that await the excavator's trowel are limited to a few projectile points (if one is lucky), flake tools, flakes, and a core remnant or two. With sites thought to be greater than 11,500 years old, the artifactual record is likely to be even more limited.

For these reasons, it is imperative that First Americans researchers develop new techniques of data recovery that fully exploit what is available. An example of one such technique is provided by the data recovery system developed by researchers at the Center for the Study of the First Americans, Oregon State University, Corvallis. The use of a fine-scale screen-washing recovery system, originally developed as part of an excavation program at the Mammoth Meadow site in the southwestern corner of Montana led to the recovery of an extensive record of organic materials, including fossilized insect parts, seeds, and plant detrital remains (Bonnichsen et al. 1992; Bonnichsen and Bolen 1985a, 1985b; Bonnichsen et al. 1986; Beatty and Bonnichsen 1994; Bonnichsen et al. 1996; Hall 1995a; Morell 1994). Based on the success of this system, its applicablity to other regions was tested by collecting and processing samples from a number of localities, e.g., Nobles Pond (Seeman et al. 1994), the 18,000-year-old La Sena Mammoth site in Nebraska (Hall 1995b; Steve Holen, personal communication 1994), the Cremer site (undated) in central Montana, Smith Creek Cave (10,500-11,500 yr B.P.) (Bryan 1979), Hand Print Cave (10,500 yr B.P.) (Alan L. Bryan, personal communication 1994), and other sites. These data clearly indicated that hair and other small-scale remains routinely can be found in dry caves, wet caves, permafrost localities, and open-air sites with buried anaerobic or non-acid sediments such as bogs and sediments derived from calcareous loess or limestone and sandstone bedrock.

Of greatest importance is naturally shed human and animal hair. Fortunately, it occurs at many sites, contains ancient DNA, and can be ^{14}C dated. It has the potential to yield much new information regarding human and animal paleoanthropology and paleobiology questions. Hair often is the only kind of biological remains that survives and can be used to address human evolutionary questions. As will be discussed below, the recovery of hair from ancient sites has important implications for modeling the peopling of the Americas.

Modern and Ancient DNA

IN RECENT YEARS, there have been numerous attempts to understand the peopling of the Americas and to develop evolutionary models by using one or more genetic markers, e.g., bloodgroup antigens, serum proteins, and red cell enzymes. See Szathmary (1993a, 1993b) for detailed overviews.

Mitochondrial DNA (mtDNA) has been the focus of much discussion. Modelers have been quick to take advantage of the unique proprieties of mtDNA because it is inherited only on the maternal line, and portions have a rapid rate of mutation that allow reliable estimation of the time since varieties of mtDNA diverged. The combination of these two factors would appear on the surface to make mtDNA ideally suited for modeling the peopling of the Americas.

Native American mtDNA contains four or possibly five mtDNA lineages (A, B, C, D, and X). These lineages originally were thought to represent the results of ancient founder effects attributable to different populations from Asia to North and South America. Modelers using genetic data have proposed a variety of contradictory DNA models to explain the peopling of the Americas in terms of four waves, three waves, two waves, and one wave (Greenburg et al. 1986; Merriwether et al. 1995; Powledge and Rose 1996; Torrini et al. 1992).

Szathamary (1993a) notes that it is dangerous to assume that the history of this single locus corresponds to the evolutionary history of the populations, as the random effects of mutation and drift at one locus do not necessarily reflect the phylogenetic history of the populations. She concludes that founder effects that reflect ancient migrations have yet to be demonstrated.

In addition to the phylogenetic issues mentioned above, there are other important reasons why specialists focusing on the peopling of the Americas have been slow to develop reliable genetic models to explain this process. Some of the important issues affecting the validity of genetic models include: (1) how time of divergence is calculated; (2) how modern analogs are used to interpret the past; and (3) the question of genetic admixture issue.

Meltzer (1995) has noted that although several of the DNA models support the pre-11,500 early-entry model, there are significant differences in these models as to the calculated timing of when the initial peopling of the Americas occurred. As noted earlier in this chapter, DNA modelers who seek to date the peopling of the Americas engage in circular reasoning: rates of change are calculated from estimated times of divergence, then these rates of change are used to calculate divergence times. These data are, in turn, then used to calculate the initial entry of founding populations into the New World. Until such dates have been verified by independent lines of archaeological evidence, they must be regarded as speculative.

Another potential problem is that present-day genetic systems may not be direct analogs to past genetic systems, especially genetic systems more than 10,000 years old. Lineages inferred from modern DNA may not represent all of the initial founding lineages that came to the New World. Szathmary (1993a) observes that all we are justified to conclude is that mtDNA radiation appears to have great antiquity and that the ancestral populations likely became distinct after divergence of DNA. This does not tell us who actually entered the Americas.

Admixture is another significant problem. If the present is any indication of the past, humans from different groups (if given the means and opportunity) will attempt to share their DNA. Thus, we should expect that the DNA of modern Native American populations represents an admixture of different lineages, instead of reflecting a precise copy of the original founding populations. For example, if the founding groups that entered the Americas had different mtDNA haplotypes, we should expect haplotype sharing or admixtures of lineages A, B, C, D, and X.

An additional concern in using only modern (or even DNA of early Holocene specimens) to model the peopling of the Americas is that such studies do not inform us of any lineages that may have gone extinct. The possibility must be considered that the Americas could have been populated by multiple groups over a long period of time. If this is true, any groups that failed to reproduce themselves into modern times would not be represented by lineages inferred from modern DNA studies.

Molecular Archaeology and Ancient Hair

The emerging field of molecular archaeology, which combines the interdisciplinary focus of environmental archaeology with the methods of molecular biology, focuses on the recovery and analysis of ancient DNA. The advantage of ancient DNA as compared to modern DNA is that by using archaeological methods, the age and context of ancient DNA can be determined by using an array of independent dating techniques without resorting to questionable "genetic clock" methods (based on inferred set rates that have not been calibrated with other dating methods). Work of this nature is essential for integrating genetic data within a reliable chronological framework so that it can be linked with other lines of data used to model the peopling of the Americas.

If preservation conditions are appropriate, DNA can be found in ancient bones, teeth, tissue, and hair. Bones, teeth, and tissue are rare finds in Paleoamerican sites. However, as discussed above, naturally shed human and animal hair appears to preserve well in many depositional environments.

Hair is of great interest, as it represents what has been up until now an untapped data source. Its value lies in its usefulness for identifying the presence of humans at early sites, thus providing an independent line of evidence to augment the identification of ambiguous artifacts and other materials thought to be of human origin. Recent advances in accelerator mass spectrometery (AMS) ^{14}C dating allows as little as 20 μg of hair to be dated (Taylor 1995; Taylor et al. 1995). By directly dating the same human hair that has been analyzed for ancient DNA, it will be possible to bypass many of the traditional difficulties often encountered in associating human presence with the material being radiocarbon dated.

Hair is relatively abundant in the archaeological record as compared to other data sets. Hair is the most common product that humans and animals produce. Although absolute figures are not presently available, it has been estimated that each person loses approximately 100 to 200 hairs and hair fragments per day, or up to 73,000 hairs per year. Over a 60-year life span, an individual would produce more than 4,000,000 hairs. As previously discussed, hair can be recovered from a wide variety of depositional environments, including dry and wet cave sites, bogs, stream terraces, loess deposits, and other open-air settings. The analysis of hair can help in the reconstruction of past environments by providing information on the distribution of extant and extinct species. When the morphological properties of hair (e.g., color, scale pattern, size, shape of medulla, etc.) are examined microscopically at 200x–400x, these properties may be used to make taxonomic identification (Appleyard 1978; Brunner and Coman 1974; Hicks 1977; Moore et al. 1974; Teerink 1991). Also, chemical element composition can provide insights about prehistoric diet (Minagawa 1992; Valkovic 1988). Hair also can provide information about health. For example, certain scalp diseases and the occurrence of some parasites can be inferred from the surface morphology characteristics of hair (Kobori and Montagna 1976). In addition, DNA analysis may be able to provide evidence for aging and certain genetic diseases (Wallace 1997)

Until now, research using ancient DNA has been severely limited by the relative scarcity of ancient organic remains. Thus, the discovery that replicable DNA is contained in ancient human and animal hair is highly significant. The ability to extract ancient DNA from human hairs opens the possibility, for the first time, of studying prehistoric populations in terms of their own genetic characteristics.

Such information can provide important data for the formulation of middle- and high-range theories. Among other things, ancient DNA has the potential to:

(1) Link specific populations to specific artifact assemblages and complexes from particular sites;

(2) Test whether changes in artifact assemblages are due to the entry of new populations to an area;

(3) Illuminate the biological relationships between adjacent and distant groups during any time period or across time periods;

(4) Determine how many episodes of migration occurred in an area; and

(5) Provide dates on rates of change for verification and/or calibration of biological descent models.

How well these objectives can be met will depend in part upon the quality of the DNA contained in ancient samples and on the ability of researchers to eliminate all potential sources of DNA contamination (Paabo 1993).

Conclusion

THE TIMING OF the initial peopling of the Americas has been debated for the past several decades. In the foregoing discussion, we have attempted to address issues in this debate through a two-pronged approach. We first analyzed the Clovis-First and Early-Entry models from a model-building perspective. Our analysis of low-, middle-, and high-range theoretical propositions of these two models indicates to us that fundamental unresolved problems exist in both models and that more thorough model-building procedures are needed. Second, we argue that new data recovery and analysis techniques will significantly augment First Americans studies.

It now appears that the single greatest impediment to widespread acceptance of the Early-Entry model can be attributed to inadequate low-range theory and a failure to distinguish carefully between mere possibilities and probabilities when evaluating whether potential artifacts, features, and charcoal are of human or natural origin. We anticipate that even if additional pre-11,500-year-old sites are found, they will become embroiled in debate unless clear and reliable criteria are set forth, probably on a case-by-case basis, for determining whether the patterning found in the archaeological record is of human or natural origin. Unless this basic issue can be overcome, it is unlikely that the intellectual focus of this field will move forward to other interesting and challenging questions about early New World peoples (e.g., how their economic and subsistence systems operated, how to construct more realistic cultural affiliation and biological descent models based on remains found in the archaeological record, etc.).

The Clovis-First model suffers severe weaknesses at the levels of middle- and high-range theory. Major predictive implications of the model are not supported by the archaeological record. Nonetheless, the widespread occurrence of fluted points in North America and South America begs for an explanation. To date, data to support the normative view of a unified Clovis culture have not been presented. Studies based solely on projectile point forms are not likely to advance our understanding of the cultural dynamics that led to the widespread distribution of Clovis.

The development of an adequate explanation for the initial peopling of the Americas cannot take place in the absence of a systematic body of well-verified knowledge. Ideally, the goal of this field is to integrate and interpret site, local, regional, and global-scale patterns by use of low-, middle, and high-range theory. Because of the overriding focus given to chronology in the First Americans debate, modelers have not given sufficient attention to issues of how data are used to support model propositions. For example, neither the Clovis-First nor the Early-Entry model draws on extensive comparative studies of artifacts at the regional, continental, or global scales. In-depth comparative studies have not been conducted among Clovis (and other fluted point assemblages) and pre-11,500-yr B.P. assemblages from North America, South America, and those found in Asia. Rather, sites often are grouped together simply on the basis of radiocarbon dates, and a search is then made for a common denominator. As a result, proposed similarities in artifacts used to support either model often are impressionistic judgments that are not supported by the use of scientific data analysis procedures. Now that the East/West "cold war" is over, the time is right for comparative studies between the most promising early Northeast Asian and American assemblages (Goebel, this volume; West 1996). In addition, there is a need to fully assess the similarities and differences of the alleged "core and flake tool" and "fluted point" assemblages to determine if these data actually support the "big-picture" models that have been proposed.

The primary building block in developing adequate models to explain the peopling of the Americas are individual site reports. Problems created by inadequate data collection and reporting methods generally cannot be rectified. Careful descriptive work is essential as it provides the basis of subsequent analysis. First Americans sites are a rare phenomenon and should be carefully scrutinized and evaluated using the most sophisticated techniques that modern science has to offer, including molecular archaeology. Site investigators, regardless of their theoretical persuasion, should develop as many independent lines of evidence as possible to determine whether the remains and patterns discovered at a site are of human or natural origin. The same is true when exploring the nature of cultural patterns and processes found at each individual site.

Since First Americans sites are so rare, it is imperative that researchers make every effort to "squeeze" as much data out of each site as possible. This can be done by refining existing recovery techniques and by developing new approaches to data recovery. Of particular interest to First Americans studies is the emerging field of molecular archaeology, which is well suited to addressing archaeological questions that have a genetic component. If the tests conducted to date are any indication of its ultimate potential, human hair may prove to be one of the most common "diagnostic" indicators that can be recovered from archaeological sites and one of the most reliable indictors of human presence at Clovis-age sites and potential pre-11,500-year-old sites. Its morphological and genetic characteristics provide unambiguous evidence for the presence of humans, and small samples of human hair can be directly dated by use of AMS ^{14}C method. In addition, researchers may be able to use DNA analysis of ancient hair to link specific populations with the archaeological record. If this can be done, it will provide a new and powerful approach for identifying specific populations, for tracing population movements, and for characterizing changes in human populations across space and through time. This approach could provide a vital missing link in First Americans studies and provide a common unifying element that would link low-, middle-, and high-range inferences, thereby allowing for the construction of more reliable models for explaining the peopling of the Americas.

In many ways, the debate about the peopling of the Americas is not merely a dispute about the peopling of the Americas. It is a debate about science, and a debate about how we develop an objective understanding of the past and the chain of events that lead to the present. By focusing on model building standards and data recovery techniques, First Americans specialists have an opportunity not only to enhance our understanding of the peopling of the Americas, but also to improve our understanding of the human species, its capabilities generally, and a tolerance for differences.

Acknowledgments

We would like to thank Mila Bonnichsen and Karen Turnmire for proofreading this manuscript. We also would like to thank Bradley Lepper for his thoughtful suggestions.

References Cited

Ackerman, R. E., and R. L. Carlson
1991 Diring Yuriak: An Early Paleolithic Site in Yakutia. *Current Research in the Pleistocene* 8: 1–2.

Adovasio, J. M., J. Donahue, and R. Stuckenrath
1990 The Meadowcroft Rockshelter Radiocarbon Chronology 1975–1990. *American Antiquity* 55: 348–354.

Adovasio, J. M., and D. R. Pedler
1997 Monte Verde and the Antiquity of Humankind in the Americas. *Antiquity* 71:573–580.

Appleyard, H. M.
1978 *Guide To the Identification of Animal Fibers.* Wira, Headingley Lane, Leeds.

Beatty, M. T., and R. Bonnichsen
1994 Dispersing Aggregated Soils and Other Fine Earth in the Field for Recovery of Organic Archaeological Materials. *Current Research in the Pleistocene* 11: 73–74.

Berger, R.
1982 The Wooley Mammoth Site, Santa Rosa Island, California. In *Peopling of the New World*, edited by J. E. Ericson, R. E. Taylor, and R. Berger, pp. 163–170. Ballena Press, Los Altos.

Bird, J. B.
1938 Antiquity and Migrations of the Early Inhabitants of Patagonia. *The Geographical Journal* 28: 250–75.

Bonnichsen, R.
1991 Clovis Origins. In *Clovis: Origins and Adaptations*, edited by R. Bonnichsen and K. L. Turnmire, pp. 309–330. Center for the Study of the First Americans, Oregon State University, Corvallis, OR.

Bonnichsen, R., M. T. Beatty, M. D. Turner, and M. Stoneking
1996 What Can be Learned from Hair? A Hair Record from the Mammoth Meadow Locus, Southwestern Montana. In *Prehistoric Mongoloid Dispersions*, edited by T. Akazawa and E. Szathmary, pp. 201–213. Oxford University Press, Cambridge.

Bonnichsen, R., M. T. Beatty, M. D. Turner, J. C. Turner, and D. Douglas.
1992 Paleoindian Lithic Procurement at the South Fork of Everson Creek, Southwestern Montana: A Preliminary Statement. In *Ice Age Hunters of the Rockies*, edited by D. J. Stanford and J. S. Day, pp. 285–321. University of Colorado Press, Niwot, CO.

Bonnichsen, R., and C. W. Bolen
1985a A Hair, Faunal and Flaked Stone Assemblage: A Holocene and Late Pleistocene Record from False Cougar Cave, Montana In *Woman, Poet, Scientists: Essays in New World Anthropology*, edited by the Great Basin Foundation, pp. 6–15. Ballena Press, Los Altos.

1985b On the Importance of Hair for Pleistocene Studies. *Current Research in the Pleistocene* 2: 63–66

Bonnichsen, R., C. W. Bolen, M. D. Turner, J.C. Turner, and M. T. Beatty
1992 Hair from Mammoth Meadow II, Southwestern Montana. *Current Research in the Pleistocene* 9: 75–78.

Bonnichsen, R., R. Graham, T. Geppert, G. Jacobson, V. Konrad, J. Mead, J. Oliver, S. Oliver, J. Purdue, D. Schnurrenberger, R. Stuckenrath, A. Tratebase, and D. Young
1986 Two High Altitude Caves, Pryor Mountains, Montana. *National Geographic Research* 2: 275–290.

Bonnichsen, R., D. Stanford, and J. L. Fastook
1987 Environmental Change and Developmental History of Human Adaptive Patterns; the Paleoindian Case. In *North America and Adjacent Oceans During the Last Deglaciation,* edited by W. F. Ruddiman and H. W. Wright, Jr., pp. 403–424. *The Geology of North America,* DNAG, *V. K-3.* Geological Society of America, Boulder, CO.

Bonnichsen, R., and M. Sorg (editors)
1989 *Bone Modification.* Center for the Study for the First Americans, University of Maine, Orono, ME.

Bonnichsen, R., and K. L Turnmire (editors)
1991 *Clovis: Origins and Adaptations.* Center for the Study of the First Americans, Oregon State University, Corvallis, OR

Brown, T. A., and K. A. Brown
1992 Ancient DNA and the Archaeologist. *Antiquity* 66: 10–23.

Brunner, H., and B. J. Coman
1974 *The Identification of Mammalian Hair.* Inkata Press, Melbourne.

Bryan, A. L.
1969 Early Man in America and the Late Pleistocene Chronology of Western Canada and Alaska. *Current Anthropology* 10: 339–365.

1973 Paleoenvironments and Cultural Diversity in Late Pleistocene South America. *Quaternary Research* 3:237–256.

1977 Developmental Stages and Technological Traditions. In *Amerinds and Their Paleoenvironments in Northeastern North America*, edited by W. S. Newman and B. Salwen, pp. 355–368. New York Academy of Sciences, Annals Volume 88.

1978 An Overview of Paleo-American Prehistory from a Circum-Pacific Perspective. In *Early Man in America from a Circum-Pacific Perspective*, edited by A. L. Bryan, pp. 306–327. Occasional Paper No. 1. Archaeological Researches International, Ltd. Department of Anthropology, University of Alberta, Edmonton.

1979 Smith Creek Cave. In *The Archaeology of Smith Creek Canyon, Eastern Nevada*, edited by D. R. Tuohy and D. L. Randall, pp. 162–253. Nevada State Museum Anthropology Papers, Number 17. Carson City.

1980 The Stemmed Point Tradition: An Early Technological Tradition in Western North America. In *Anthropological Papers in Memory of Earl H. Swanson*, Jr., edited by L. B. Harten, C. N. Warren, and D. R. Tuohy. pp. 77–107. Anthropological Papers in Memory of Earl H. Swanson, Jr., Pocatello.

1986 Paleoamerican Prehistory as Seen from South America. In *New Evidence for the Pleistocene Peopling of the Americas*, edited by A. L. Bryan, pp. 1–14. Center for the Study of Early Man, University of Maine at Orono, Orono.

1987 The First Americans: Points of Order. *Natural History* June 87: 6–11.

1988 The Relationship of the Stemmed Point and Fluted Point Traditions in the Great Basin. In *Early Human Occupation in Western North America, 11,500–7,000 B.P.*, edited by M. Aikens and J. Willig, pp. 53–74. Nevada State Museum, Carson City.

1990 The Pattern of Pleistocene Cultural Diversity in Eurasia and the Americas. In *Chronostratigraphy of the Paleolithic in North, Central, East Asia and America*, pp. 3–18. Academy of Sciences of the USSR Institute of History, Philology and Philosophy, Siberian Branch of the Academy of Sciences, Novosibirsk.

1993 Means to a Resolution of the Question of the Peopling of the Americas. *Actes du XII Congrès International des Sciences Prehistoricques et Protohistoriques*, tome 3: 478–482. Institus Archaeologique de L'Academie Slovaque des Scienc Bratislava.

Bryan, A. L., and R. Gruhn
1989 The Evolutionary Significance of the American Lower Paleolithic. *In Homenaje a Jose Luis Lorenzo*, edited by L.M. Mirambell, pp. 81–102. Instituto Nacional de Anthropologica e Historica, Serie Prehistorica, Mexico City.

Carlson, R. L.
1991 Clovis from the Perspective of the Ice-Free-Corridor. In *Clovis: Origins and Adaptations*, edited by R. Bonnichsen and K. L. Turnmire, pp. 81–90. Center for the Study of the First American, Oregon State University, Corvallis, OR.

Chlachula, J., N. I. Drozdov, and V. P. Chekha
1994 Early Paleolithic in the Minusinsk Basin, Upper Yenisei River Region, Southern Siberia. *Current Research in the Pleistocene* 11: 128–130.

Clark, D. W.
1991 The Northern (Alaska-Yukon) Fluted Points. In *Clovis: Origins and Adaptations*, edited by R. Bonnichsen and K. L. Turnmire, pp. 35–48. Center for the Study of the First Americans, Oregon State University, Corvallis, OR.

Diamond, J.
1987 The American Blitzkrieg: A Mammoth Undertaking. *Discover* June: 82–88.

Dillehay, T. D.
1989 *Monte Verde: Late Pleistocene Settlement in Chile*, Vol. I. Smithsonian Institution, Washington, D.C.

Dillehay, T. D. (editor)
1997 *The Archaeological Context, Vol II of Monte Verde: A Late Pleistocene Settlement in Chile.* Smithsonian Press, Washington, DC.

Dillehay, T. D., G. A. Calderon, G. Politis, and M.C. Beltrao
1992 Earliest Hunters and Gathers of South America. In *Journal of World Prehistory* 6 (2): 145–204.

Dillehay, T.D., and M .B. Collins
1991 A Comment on Lynch. *American Antiquity* 56: 333–341.

Erlandson, J. M., and M. L. Moss
1996 The Pleistocene-Holocene Transition Along the Pacific Coast of North America. In *Humans at the End of the Ice Age: The Archaeology of the Pleistocene-Holocene Transition*, edited by L. G. Straus, B. V. Erikson, J. M. Erlandson, and D. R. Yesner, pp. 278–302. Plenum Press, New York.

Fagan, B. M.
1987 *The Great Journey: The Peopling of Ancient America.* Thames and Hudson, New York.

Feibleman, J. K.
1954 Theory of Integrative Levels. *British Journal of the Philosophy of the Science* 5: 59–666.

Frison, G. C.
1991 The Goshen Paleoindian Complex: New Data for Paleoindian Research. In *Clovis: Origins and Adaptations*, edited by R. Bonnichsen and K. L. Turnmire, pp. 133–152. Center for the Study of the First Americans, Oregon State University, Corvallis, OR.

Goebel T., R. Powers, and N. Bigelow
1991 The Nenana Complex of Alaska and Clovis Origins. In *Clovis: Origins and Adaptations*, edited by R. Bonnichsen and K. L. Turnmire, pp. 49–80. Center for the Study of the First Americans, Oregon State University, Corvallis, OR.

Greenberg, J. H., C. R. Turner II, and S. L. Zegura
1986 The Settlement of the Americas: A Comparison of the Linguistic, Dental, and Genetic Evidence. *Current Anthropology* 27: 477–497.

Gruhn, R.
1988 Linguistic Evidence in Support of the Coastal Route of Earliest Entry Into the New World. *Man* 23 (1): 77–100.

Gruhn, R.
1990 Initial Settlement of the New World: The Coastal Settlement Model. *In Chronostratigraphy of the Paleolithic in North, Central, East Asia and America*, pp. 20–24. Academy of Sciences of the USSR Institute of History, Philology and Philosophy Siberian Branch of the Academy of Sciences, Novosibirsk.

1994 The Pacific Coast Route of Initial Entry: An Overview. In *Method and Theory for Investigating the Peopling of the Americas*, edited by R. Bonnichsen and D. G. Steele, pp. 249–256. Center for the Study of the First Americans, Oregon State University, Corvallis, OR.

1997 Language Classification and Models of the Peopling of the Americas. In *Archaeology and Linguistics: Aboriginal Australia in Global Perspective*, edited by P. McConvell and N. Evans, pp. 99–110. Oxford University Press, Melbourne.

Gruhn, R., and A. L. Bryan
1984 The Record of Pleistocene Megafaunal Extinctions at Tamia-tamia, Northern Venezuela. In *Quaternary Extinctions: A Prehistoric Revolution*, edited by P. S. Martin and R. G. Klein, pp. 128–137. University of Arizona Press, Tucson.

1991 A Review of Lynch's Descriptions of South American Pleistocene Sites. *American Antiquity* 56: 342–347.

Guidon, N., and B. Arnaud
1991 The Chronology of the New World: Two Faces of One Reality. *World Archaeology* 23: 167–178.

Guidon, N., and G. Delibrias
1986 Carbon-14 Dates Point to Man in the Americas 32,000 Years Ago. *Nature* 321: 769–771.

Hall, D. A.
1995a Clarification Is Sought Regarding State of Hair. *Mammoth Trumpet* 10: 3,7.

1995b Bones of Nebraska Mammoths Imply Early Human Presence. *Mammoth Trumpet* 10(1): 1,4–7.

Haynes, C. V., Jr.
1964 Fluted Projectile Points: Their Age and Dispersion. *Science* 145: 1408–1413.

1980 The Clovis Culture. *Canadian Journal of Anthropology* 1: 115–121.

1987 Clovis Origin Update. The *Kiva* 52: 83–93.

Hicks, J. W.
1977 *Microscopy of Hairs: A Practical Guide and Manual.* Federal Bureau of Investigation, FBI Laboratory, Washington, D.C.

Hiroshi, J., T. Kamata, and A. Yamada
1990 The Early-Middle Paleolithic Period in the Miyagi Prefecture. In *Chronostratigraphy of the Paleolithic in North Central, East Asia and America*, pp. 79–82. Academy of Sciences of the USSR Institute of History, Philology and Philosophy, Siberian Branch of the Academy of Sciences, Novosibirsk.

Jantz, R. L., and D. Owsley
1997 Pathology, Taphonomy, and Cranial Morphometrics of the Sprit Cave Mummy. *Nevada Historical Quarterly* 40: 62–84.

King, M. L., and S. B. Slobodin
1996 A Fluted Point from the Uptar Site, Northeastern Siberia. *Science* 273: 634–636.

Kobori, T. and W. Montagna (Consulting editors)
1976 *Biology and Disease of the Hair.* University Park Press, Tokyo.

Kuzmin, Y.V., and S. K. Krivonogov
1994 The Diring Paleolithic Site, Eastern Siberia: Review of Geoarchaeological Studies. *Geoarchaeology* 9(4): 287–300.

Lyman, R. L.
1994 *Vertebrate Taphonomy.* Cambridge Manuals in Archaeology. Cambridge University Press, Cambridge.

Lynch, T. F.
1990 Glacial-Age Man in South America? A Critical Review. *American Antiquity* 55: 12–36.

MacNeish, R. S.
1992 *The Fort Bliss Archaeological Project by Afar: Excavation of Pintada and Pendejo Caves Near Orogrande, New Mexico.* 1991 Annual Report and 1992 Briefing Booklet from February 3 through May 11. Andover Foundation for Archaeological Research, Andover.

1996 Pendejo Pre-Clovis Proofs and Their Implications. In *Fumdhamentos, Proceedings of the International Meeting on the Peopling of the Americas Sao Raimundo Nonato, Piaui, Brasil (1993),* pp.171–200. Funddacao Museum do Homenm Americano, Sao Raimundo Nonato.

Martin, P. S.
1967 Prehistoric Overkill. In *Pleistocene Extinctions: The Search for a Cause,* edited by P. S. Martin and H. E. Wright, Jr., pp. 75–80. Yale University Press, New Haven.

Martin, P. S.
1973 The Discovery of America. *Science* 179:969–974.

1984 Prehistoric Overkill: The Global Model. In *Quaternary Extinctions: A Prehistoric Revolution,* edited by P. S. Martin and R. G. Klein, pp. 354–403. University of Arizona Press, Tucson.

1987 Clovisia the Beautiful! *Natural History* 10: 10–13.

Masahito, A., and S. Hiroyuki
1990 Transition from Middle to Upper Paleolithic in Japan. In *Chronostratigraphy of the Paleolithic in North Central, East Asia and America.* pp. 97–105. Academy of Sciences of the USSR Institute of History, Philology and Philosophy, Siberian Branch of the Academy of Sciences, Novosibirsk.

Meltzer, D. J.
1995 Clocking the First Americans. *Annual Review of Anthropology* 24: 21–45.

1997 Monte Verde and the Pleistocene Peopling of the Americas. *Science* 276:754–755.

Meltzer, D. J., J. M. Advasio, and T. D. Dillehay.
1994 On a Pleistocene Human Occupation at Pedra Furada, Brazil. *Antiquity* 68: 695–714.

Merriwether, D. A., F. Rothhammer, F. Ferrell, and R. E. Ferrell.
1995 Distribution of the Four-founding Lineages Haplotypes in Native Americans Suggests a Single Wave of Migrations for the New World. *American Journal of Physical Anthropology* 98: 411–430.

Minagawa, M.
1992 Reconstruction of Human Diet from O^{13} and $O^{15}N$ in Contemporary Japanese Hair: A Stochastic Method for Estimating Multi-source Contribution by Double Isotopic Tracers. *Applied Geochemistry* 7: 145–158.

Mochanov, Y. A.
1978a Stratigraphy and Absolute Chronology of the Paleolithic of Northeast Asia. In *Early Man in America: From A Circum-Pacific Perspective,* edited by A. L. Bryan, p.67. Archaeological Researches International, Ltd., Department of Anthropology, University of Alberta, Edmonton.

1978b The Paleolithic of Northeast Asia and the Problem of the First Peopling of the America. In *Early Man in America: From A Circum-Pacific Perspective,* edited by A. L. Bryan, pp. 54–66. Archaeological Researches International, Ltd., Department of Anthropology, University of Alberta, Edmonton.

1993 The Most Ancient Paleolithic of the Diring and the Problem of a Nontropical Origin for Humanity. *Arctic Anthropology* 30(1): 22–53.

Mochanov, Y. A., and S. A. Fedoseeva
1996 Dyuktai Cave. In *American Beginnings: The Prehistory and Paleoecology of Beringia,* edited by F. H. West, pp.164–174. University of Chicago Press, Chicago.

Moore, T. D., L. E. Spense, and C. E. Dugholle
1974 *Identification of Dorsal Guard Hairs of Some Mammals of Wyoming.* Wyoming Game and Fish Department, Bulletin 14. Cheyenne.

Morlan, R. E., and J. Cinq-Mars
1989 *Abstracts: The First World Summit Conference on the Peopling of the Americas,* edited by J. Tomenchuk and R. Bonnichsen, pp. 11–12. Center for the Study of The First Americans, University of Maine, Orono.

Morell, V.
1994 Pulling Hair From the Ground. *Science* 265: 741.

Mossiman, J. E., and P. S. Martin
1975 Simulating Overkill by Paleo-indians. *American Scientists* 63: 304–313.

Ochsenius, C., and R. Gruhn (editors)
1979 *Tamia-Tamia: A Late Pleistocene Paleo-Indian Kill Site in Northernmost South America -Final Reports of 1976 Excavations.* South American Quaternary Documentation Program. Republished by the Center for the Study of the First Americans, Oregon State University, Corvallis, OR.

Oda, S.
1990 A Review of Archaeological Research in the Izu and Ogsawara Islands. In *Man and Culture in Oceania* 6:53–79.

Ossenberg, N. S.
1994 Origins and Affinities of the Native Peoples of Northwestern North America: The Evidence of Cranial Nonmetric Traits. In *Method and Theory for Investigating the Peopling of the Americas*, edited by R. Bonnichsen and D. G. Steele, pp. 79–116. Center for the Study of the First Americans, Oregon State University, Corvallis, OR.

Pessis, A. (editor)
1993 *Fundamentos.* Proceeding of the International Meeting on the Peopling of the Americas. Sao Raimundo Nonato, Piaui, Brasil.

Politis, G.
1991 Fishtail Projectile Points in the Southern Cone of South America: an Overview. *In Clovis: Origins and Adaptations*, edited by R. Bonnichsen and K. L. Turnmire, pp. 287–302. Center for the Study of the Study of the First Americans, Oregon State University, Corvallis, OR.

Powledge, T. M., and M. Rose.
1996 The Great DNA Hunt, Part II: Colonizing the Americas. *Archaeology* November/December, pp. 59–68.

Reeves, B., J. M. D. Pohl, and J. W. Smith
1986 The Mission Ridge Site and the Texas Street Question. In *New Evidence for the Pleistocene Peopling of the Americas*, edited by A. L. Bryan, pp. 65–80. Center for the Study of Early Man, University of Maine, Orono, ME.

Rouse, I.
1976 Peopling of the Americas. *Quaternary Research* 6: 567–612.

Paabo, S.
1993 Ancient DNA. *Scientific American* November 6: 86–92.

Paabo, S., J. A. Gifford, and C. C. Wilson.
1988 Mitochondrial DNA sequences from a 7000-year Old Brain. *Nucleic Acids Research* 16(2): 9775–9787.

Seeman, M. F., G. Summers, E. Dowd, and L. Morris.
1994 Fluted Point Characteristics at Three Large Sites: The Implications for Modelling Early Paleoindian Settlement Patterns in Ohio. In *The First Discovery of America: Archaeological Evidence of the Early Inhabitants of the Ohio Area*, edited by W. S. Dancey, pp. 77–94. The Ohio Archaeological Council, Columbus, OH.

Steele, D. G., and J. Powell
1992 Peopling of the Americas: Paleobiological Evidence. *Human Biology* 64:(3):303–316.

1994 Paleobiological Evidence of the Peopling of the Americas: A Morphometric Approach. In *Method and Theory for Investigating the Peopling of the Americas*, edited by R. Bonnichsen and D. G. Steele, pp. 141–164. Center for the Study of the First Americans, Oregon State University, Corvallis, OR.

Szathmary, E. J.
1993a Invited Editorial: mtDNA and the Peopling of the Americas. *American Journal of Human Genetics* 53: 793–799.

1993b Genetics of Aboriginal North America. *Evolutionary Anthropology* 1:(6) 202–217.

1994 Modelling Ancient Population Relationships from Modern Population Genetics. In *Method and Theory for Investigating the Peopling of the Americas*, edited by R. Bonnichsen and D. G. Steele, pp. 117–130. Center for the Study of the First Americans, Oregon State University, Corvallis, OR.

Taylor, R. E., P. E. Hare, C. A. Prior, D. L. Kirner, L. Wan, and R. B. Burky
1995 Radiocarbon Dating of Biochemically Characterized Hair. *Radiocarbon* 37: 1–11.

Teerink, B. J.
1991 *Hair of West-European Mammals.* Cambridge University Press, Cambridge.

Torroni, A., T. G. Schurr, C-C Yang, E. J. E. Szathmary, R. C. Williams, M. S. Chanfield, G. A. Troup, W. C. Knowler, D. N. Lawrence, K. M. Weiss, and D. C. Wallace.
1992 Native American Mitochondrial DNA Analysis Indicates that the Amerind and Nadene Populations Were Founded by Two Independent Migrations. *Genetics* 130: 153–162.

Torroni, A., J. V. Nell, R. Barrantes, T. G. Schurr, and D. C. Wallace
1993 Mitochondrial DNA "Clock" for the Amerinds and Its Implications for Timing Their Entry Into North America. *Proceedings of the National Academy of Sciences* 91: 1–6.

Turner, C .G., II
1985 The Dental Search for Native American Origins. *In Out of Asia: Peopling of the Americas and the Pacific*, edited by R. Kirk and E. Szathmary, pp. 31–78. The Journal of Pacific History, Canberra.

1994 Relating Eurasian and Native American Populations Through Dental Morphology. In *Method and Theory for Investigating the Peopling of the Americas*, edited by R. Bonnichsen and D. G. Steele, pp. 131–140. Center for the Study of the First Americans, Oregon State University, Corvallis, OR.

Valkovic, V.
1988 *Human Hair: Volume I, Fundamentals and Methods for Measurement of Elemental Composition.* CRC Press, Boca Raton, FL.

Wallace, D. C.
1997 Mitochondrial DNA in Aging and Disease. *Scientific American*, August, pp. 40–47.

Ward, R. H., A. Redd, D. Valencia, B. Frazier, and S. Paabo
1993 Genetic and Lingusitic Differentiation in the Americas. *Proceedings of the National Academy of Sciences* 90: 10663–10667.

Waters, M. R., S. L. Forman, and J. M. Pierson
1997 Diring Yuriakh: A Lower Paleolithic Site in Central Siberia. *Science* 275: 1281–1284.

West, F. H. (editor)
1996 *American Beginnings: The Prehistory and Paleoecology of Beringia*. The University of Chicago Press, Chicago.

Willig, J. A.
1991 Clovis Technology and Adaptation in Far Western North America: Regional Pattern and Environmental Context. In *Clovis: Origins and Adaptations*, edited by R. Bonnichsen and K. L. Turnmire, pp. 91–118. Center for the Study of the First Americans, Oregon State University, Corvallis, OR.

Wyckoff, D.G., and B. J. Carter
1994 Geoarchaeology at the Burnham Sites: 1992 Investigations at a "Pre-Clovis Sites" in Northeastern Oklahoma: A Report Prepared in Partial Fulfillment of the National Science Foundation Grant DBS-9120314. A Special Publication of the Oklahoma Archaeological Survey University of Oklahoma, Norman Oklahoma.

Yoshizaki, M., and M. Iwasaki
1986 Babadan Locality A: Recent Discovery of the Middle Pleistocene Occupation of Japan. *Canadian Journal of Anthropology* 5(1): 3–9.

Young, D. E., and R. Bonnichsen
1984 *Understanding Stone Tools*. Center for the Study of Early Man, University of Maine, Orono, ME.

Index